Tax Formula for Individuals

Income (broadly conceived)	$xx,xxx
Less: Exclusions	(x,xxx)
Gross income	$xx,xxx
Less: Deductions *for* adjusted gross income	(x,xxx)
Adjusted gross income	$xx,xxx
Less: The greater of—	
Total itemized deductions *or* standard deduction	(x,xxx)
Personal and dependency exemptions	(x,xxx)
Taxable income	$xx,xxx

Basic Standard Deduction Amounts

	Standard Deduction Amount	
Filing Status	**1991**	**1992**
Single	$3,400	$3,600
Married, filing jointly	5,700	6,000
Surviving spouse	5,700	6,000
Head of household	5,000	5,250
Married, filing separately	2,850	3,000

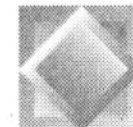

Amount of Each Additional Standard Deduction

Filing Status	**1991**	**1992**
Single	$850	$900
Married, filing jointly	650	700
Surviving spouse	650	700
Head of household	850	900
Married, filing separately	650	700

1993 Annual Edition

West's Federal Taxation:

Individual Income Taxes

1993 ANNUAL EDITION

WEST'S FEDERAL TAXATION:

INDIVIDUAL INCOME TAXES

GENERAL EDITORS

William H. Hoffman, Jr., J.D., Ph.D., C.P.A. **James E. Smith,** Ph.D., C.P.A.

Eugene Willis, Ph.D., C.P.A.

CONTRIBUTING AUTHORS

James H. Boyd, Ph.D., C.P.A.
Arizona State University

D. Larry Crumbley, Ph.D., C.P.A.
Texas A & M University

Steven C. Dilley, J.D., Ph.D., C.P.A.
Michigan State University

Patrica C. Elliott, D.B.A., C.P.A.
University of New Mexico

Mary Sue Gately, Ph.D., C.P.A.
Texas Tech University

William H. Hoffman, Jr., J.D., Ph.D., C.P.A.
University of Houston

Jerome S. Horvitz, J.D., LL.M. in Taxation
University of Houston

David M. Maloney, Ph.D., C.P.A.
University of Virginia

Marilyn Phelan, J.D., Ph.D., C.P.A.
Texas Tech University

William A. Raabe, Ph.D., C.P.A.
University of Wisconsin-Milwaukee

Boyd C. Randall, J.D., Ph.D.
Brigham Young University

W. Eugene Seago, J.D., Ph.D., C.P.A.
Virginia Polytechnic Institute and State University

James E. Smith, Ph.D., C.P.A.
College of William and Mary

Eugene Willis, Ph.D., C.P.A.
University of Illinois at Urbana

WEST PUBLISHING COMPANY

ST. PAUL NEW YORK LOS ANGELES SAN FRANCISCO

Copyediting: Patricia A. Lewis
Index: E. Virginia Hobbs
Composition: Carlisle Communications, Ltd.
Text and
Cover Design: John Rokusek

West's Commitment to the Environment

In 1906, West Publishing Company began recycling materials left over from the production of books. This began a tradition of efficient and responsible use of resources. Today, up to 95 percent of our legal books and 70 percent of our college texts are printed on recycled, acid-free stock. West also recycles nearly 22 million pounds of scrap paper annually—the equivalent of 181,717 trees. Since the 1960s, West has devised ways to capture and recycle waste inks, solvents, oils, and vapors created in the printing process. We also recycle plastics of all kinds, wood, glass, corrugated cardboard, and batteries, and have eliminated the use of styrofoam book packaging. We at West are proud of the longevity and the scope of our commitment to our environment.

Production, Prepress, Printing and Binding by West Publishing Company.

610 Opperman Drive
P.O. Box 64526
St. Paul, MN 55164–0526

Printed in the United States of America
99 98 97 96 95 94 93 92 8 7 6 5 4 3 2 1 0

Library of Congress
Cataloging in Publication Data

Main entry under title:
West's Federal Taxation.
Includes index.
1. Income tax—United States—Law
I. Hoffman, William H. III. Willis, Eugene

ISBN 0–314–00817–9
KF6369.W47 343'.73'052 77–20656

ISSN 0272–0329
1993 ANNUAL EDITION

PREFACE

This text is intended as a basis for a first course in Federal taxation for undergraduate or graduate accounting, business, and law students. With certain modifications in the coverage of the materials, the text may be used in a survey course on Federal taxation for undergraduate or graduate students. The materials may also be valuable as a tool for self-study, since they contain numerous clarifying examples adaptable to such an approach.

Tax policy considerations and historical developments are introduced in the text only to the extent that they shed light on the reason for a particular rule. The many simple and straightforward examples further clarify the materials by showing how a particular tax rule applies in an actual situation.

Since the original edition was issued in 1978, we have followed a policy of annually revising the text material to reflect statutory, judicial, and administrative changes in the Federal tax law and to correct any errors or other shortcomings. Not only do we encourage user input, we actively seek the advice of users as the basis for improving the text.

In the 1993 edition, we have retained the structural changes made several years ago that give more extensive coverage of the most important tax developments in recent years. Chapter 7 is devoted to coverage of the passive loss rules and at-risk limitations. Chapter 12 is concerned exclusively with expanded coverage of the alternative minimum tax. The market reaction to these changes has been very supportive.

While the primary emphasis of the text is on the income taxation of individuals, chapter 20 is an overview of the Federal taxation of other forms of business organization (corporations and partnerships). This chapter could be of particular significance to students who do not plan to take a second course in Federal taxation. For others, chapter 20 may serve as a lead-in to *West's Federal Taxation: Corporations, Partnerships, Estates, and Trusts.*

Special Features

A variety of pedagogical devices are used to assist the student in the learning process. Each chapter begins with a statement of the learning objectives for the chapter. The learning objectives are followed with a topical outline of the material in the chapter. Page references appear in the outline to provide the student access to each topic. The following items contribute to the readability of the material in the text.

- Three levels of headings which aid in organization and presentation.
- Italicizing key words to emphasize the importance to the student.
- Avoiding legal terminology except where such use is beneficial.
- Using Concept Summaries to synthesize important concepts in chart or tabular form.
- Organizing items in lists with bullets rather than presenting the material in lengthy sentences.
- Frequent use of examples to help the student to understand the tax concept being discussed.

Once knowledge of the tax law has been acquired, it needs to be used. The tax minimization process, however, normally requires careful planning. Because we recognize the importance of planning procedures, most chapters include a separate section (designated *Tax Planning Considerations*) illustrating the applications of such procedures to specific areas.

We believe that any basic course in Federal taxation should offer the reader the opportunity to learn and utilize the methodology of tax research. Such knowledge is requisite in today's environment with the increased emphasis on the concept of "learning to learn." Chapter 2 and Appendix E are devoted to this methodology. Also, most chapters contain *Research Problems* that require the use of research tools. Solutions to these Research Problems can be found in the Instructor's Guide. The effectiveness of the text does not, however, depend on the coverage of tax research procedures. Consequently, the treatment of this subject may be omitted without impairing the continuity of the remaining textual materials.

Although it is not our purpose to approach the presentation and discussion of taxation from the standpoint of preparation of tax returns, some orientation to forms is necessary. Because 1992 forms will not be available until later in the year, most tax return problems in this edition are written for tax year 1991. The 1991 problems may be solved manually, or many may be solved using the tax return preparation software (*TurboTax*) that may be purchased by students who use this text.

Appendix F contains two comprehensive tax return problems written for tax year 1991. Each of these problems lends itself for use as a term project because of the sophistication required for satisfactory completion. Solutions to the problems in Appendix F are contained in the Instructor's Guide.

For the reader's convenience, Appendix B contains a full reproduction of most of the 1991 tax forms frequently encountered in actual practice.

Most tax textbooks are published in the spring, long before tax forms for the year of publication are available from the government. We believe that students should be exposed to the most current tax forms. As a result, we develop some new problems and provide adopters with reproducible copies of these problems, along with blank tax forms and solutions on the new forms. Shortly after the beginning of 1993, adopters will receive selected tax return problems solved on 1992 forms.

Supplements

Other products in our 1993 instructional package include the following:

- The *Instructor's Guide with Lecture Notes* contains lecture notes for each chapter, and solutions to Research Problems and Comprehensive Tax Return problems found in the text. The lecture notes consist of a lecture outline which the professor can use as the basis for his or her classroom presentation. These lecture notes include not only material covered in the text, but also other relevant material and teaching aids. The lecture notes are also available on disk in ASCII files.

- *Test Bank* with questions and solutions referenced to pages in the text. The questions are arranged in accordance with the sequence of the material in the chapter. To assist the professor in selecting questions for an examination, all questions are labeled by topical coverage in a matrix which also includes which questions are new, modified, or unchanged in the new edition.
- A *Solutions Manual* that has been carefully checked to ensure that it is error-free. All problems are labeled by topical coverage in a matrix which also indicates which problems are new, modified, or unchanged in the new edition. The solutions are referenced to pages in the text.
- *Westest*, a microcomputer test generation program for IBM PC's and compatibles and the Macintosh family of computers.
- *West CD-ROM Federal Tax Library* (Compact Disk with Read-Only Memory) provides a complete tax research library on a desktop. The Federal Tax Library is a set of compact disks with a software package that reads the disks through a PC. Each of these disks has a remarkable storage capacity—roughly 1,000 times more than a single-sided floppy disk. A brief list of the library contents includes: complete IRS Code and Regulations, 1986 Tax Reform Act with Amendments and Legislative History, Federal Court Cases on Tax, Tax Court Cases, Revenue Rulings, and Revenue Procedures. This is available to qualified adopters.
- A *Student Study Guide* prepared by Gerald E. Whittenburg, San Diego State University, includes a chapter review of key concepts, and self-evaluation tests with solutions which are page referenced to the text.
- *Transparency Masters* for selected complex and cumulative problems, with a larger typeface for greater readability.
- *Transparency Acetates* contain charts and tables that can be used to enhance classroom lectures.
- *Instructor's Resource Notebook*—this three-ring binder can be used to house all or portions of the supplements.
- *WFT Individual Practice Sets*, 1992–93 Edition, prepared by John B. Barrack, University of Georgia, is designed to cover all the common forms that would be used by a tax practitioner for the average client.
- Limited free use to qualified adopters of WESTLAW, a computer-assisted tax and legal research service that provides access to hundreds of valuable information sources.
- *West's Internal Revenue Code of 1986 and Treasury Regulations: Annotated and Selected: 1993 Edition* by James E. Smith, College of William and Mary. This provides the opportunity for the student to be exposed to the Code and the Regulations in a single volume book, which also contains useful annotations that help the student in working with and understanding the Code.
- *West's Federal Taxation Newsletter Update* which is mailed to adopters twice a year. It focuses on new tax legislation and updated information.

Software

The trend toward increased use of the computer as an essential tool in tax practice has accelerated. To insure that the West's Federal Taxation instructional package continues to set the pace in this important area, the following products are available to be used with the 1993 edition:

- *TurboTax* © Personal/1040 for DOS version 9.01 by Chipsoft, Inc. is a commercial tax preparation package. It teaches students how to prepare over 80 forms, schedules, and worksheets, and automatically performs all mathematical calculations and data transfers. *TurboTax* also assists students with tax planning and helps them prepare "anticipated" tax returns. The *TurboTax* package, available for student purchase, includes disks bound with a 200-page workbook containing exercises and problems. The software runs on IBM PCs and compatibles with 512K memory. *MacInTax®* and *TurboTax© for Windows* are also available for the first time with the 1993 editions.

- WEST'S FEDERAL TAXATION: TAX PLANNING WITH ELECTRONIC SPREADSHEETS, prepared by Samuel A. Hicks, Jr., Virginia Polytechnic Institute and State University, contains Lotus-based tax computation and planning templates for individual taxpayers and is available free to adopters.

The outstanding features of these software products are that they are powerful, easy to learn, and easy to use. We believe that tax education can be raised to a higher level through the use of computers and well-designed software. These software packages take the drudgery out of performing the complex computations involved in solving difficult tax problems.

To enable students to take advantage of these new software products, the 1993 Edition contains numerous tax return and tax planning problems. Problems that lend themselves to solutions using the software packages described above are identified by a computer symbol. The instructions for each of these problems identify which software packages are appropriate for solving the problems.

Acknowledgements

We are most appreciative of the many suggestions that we have received for revising the text, many of which have been incorporated in past editions and in the 1993 edition. In particular, we would like to thank all those users who responded to our questionnaire and those who have called or written with suggestions for improving the book. We would also like to thank those people who have painstakingly worked through all the problems and test questions and generally acted as problem checkers to insure the accuracy of the book and ancillary package. They are Tracey A. Anderson, Indiana University at South Bend, Caroline K. Craig, Illinois State University, Mark B. Persellin, St. Mary's University, Debra L. Sanders, Washington State University, Thomas Sternburg, Arizona State University, and Raymond F. Wacker, Southern Illinois University at Carbondale.

Finally, this 1993 edition would not have been possible without the technical assistance of and manuscript review by Bonnie Hoffman, CPA, Freda Mulhall, CPA, and Nora Smith, M.Ed. We are indebted to them for their efforts.

William H. Hoffman, Jr.
James E. Smith
Eugene Willis

April 1, 1992

CONTENTS IN BRIEF

PART V PROPERTY TRANSACTIONS

PART VI ACCOUNTING PERIODS, ACCOUNTING METHODS, AND DEFERRED COMPENSATION

PART VII CORPORATIONS AND PARTNERSHIPS

TABLE OF CONTENTS

Part II Gross Income

Part III Deductions

PART V PROPERTY TRANSACTIONS

Appendixes

1993 Annual Edition

West's Federal Taxation:

Individual Income Taxes

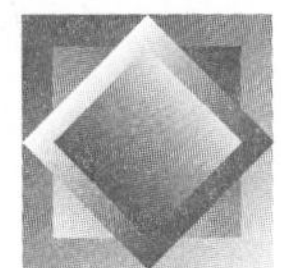

PART

INTRODUCTION AND BASIC TAX MODEL

Part I provides an introduction to taxation in the United States. Although the primary orientation of this text is income taxation, other types of taxes are also discussed briefly. The purposes of the Federal tax law are examined, and the legislative, administrative, and judicial sources of Federal tax law, including their application to the tax research process, are analyzed. Part I concludes with the introduction of the basic tax model for the individual taxpayer.

CHAPTER

CHAPTER

AN INTRODUCTION TO TAXATION AND UNDERSTANDING THE FEDERAL TAX LAW

OBJECTIVES

Provide a brief history, including trends, of the Federal income tax.

Describe some of the criteria for selecting a tax structure.

Explain the different types of taxes imposed in the United States at the Federal, state, and local levels.

Introduce the Federal income tax for individuals and corporations.

Describe the major employment taxes such as the Federal Insurance Contributions Act (FICA) and the Federal Unemployment Tax Act (FUTA).

Briefly review the role of the audit process in tax administration.

Discuss the statute of limitations applicable to assessments by the IRS and to refunds claimed by taxpayers.

Highlight the interest and penalty rules relating to taxpayer noncompliance.

Explain the economic, social, equity, and political considerations that justify various aspects of the tax law.

Review the role played by the IRS and the courts in the evolution of the Federal tax system.

OUTLINE

The primary objective of this chapter is to provide an overview of the Federal tax system. Some of the topics covered include the following:

- A brief history of the Federal income tax.
- A summary of the different types of taxes imposed at the Federal, state, and local levels.
- Some highlights of tax law administration.
- A discussion of tax concepts that help explain the reasons for various tax provisions.
- Illustrations of the influence that the Internal Revenue Service (IRS) and the courts have had in the evolution of current tax law.

Why does a text devoted primarily to the Federal individual income tax discuss state and local taxes? A simple illustration shows the importance of non-Federal taxes.

EXAMPLE 1

T is employed by X Corporation in State A. Y Corporation offers him a higher salary that, if accepted, will require relocating to State B. ◆

Although T must consider many nontax factors before he decides on a job change, he should also evaluate the tax climate. How do the state and local income taxes compare? State and local sales taxes could affect the cost of living differential. If T plans to remain (or become) a homeowner, how do state and local property taxes vary? After these questions are resolved, the higher salary that T was offered may no longer be attractive.

HISTORY OF U.S. TAXATION

◆

Early Periods

The concept of an income tax can hardly be regarded as a newcomer to the Western Hemisphere. Although an income tax was first enacted in 1634 by the English colonists in the Massachusetts Bay Colony, the Federal government did not adopt this form of taxation until 1861. In fact, both the Federal Union and the Confederate States of America used the income tax to provide funds to finance the Civil War. Although modest in its reach and characterized by broad exemptions and low rates, the income tax generated $376 million of revenue for the Federal government during the Civil War.

When the Civil War ended, the need for additional revenue disappeared, and the income tax was repealed. As was true before the war, the Federal government was able to finance its operations almost exclusively from customs duties (tariffs). It is interesting to note that the courts held that the Civil War income tax was not contrary to the Constitution.

When a new Federal income tax on individuals was enacted in 1894, its opponents were prepared to and did again challenge its constitutionality. The U.S. Constitution provided that " . . . No Capitation, or other direct, Tax shall be laid, unless in Proportion to the Census or Enumeration herein·before directed to be taken." In *Pollock v. Farmers' Loan and Trust Co.*,[1] the U.S. Supreme Court found that the income tax was a direct tax that was unconstitutional because it was not apportioned among the states in proportion to their populations.

1. 3 AFTR 2602, 15 S.Ct. 912 (USSC, 1895). See Chapter 2 for an explanation of the citations of judicial decisions.

A Federal corporate income tax, enacted by Congress in 1909, fared better in the judicial system. The U.S. Supreme Court found this tax to be constitutional because it was treated as an excise tax.[2] In essence, it was a tax on the right to do business in the corporate form. As such, it was likened to a form of the franchise tax.[3] Note that the corporate form of doing business was developed in the late nineteenth century and was an unfamiliar concept to the framers of the U.S. Constitution. Since a corporation is an entity created under law, jurisdictions possess the right to tax its creation and operation. Using this rationale, many states still impose franchise taxes on corporations.

The ratification of the Sixteenth Amendment to the U.S. Constitution in 1913 sanctioned both the Federal individual and corporate income taxes and, as a consequence, neutralized the continuing effect of the *Pollock* decision.

Revenue Acts

Following ratification of the Sixteenth Amendment, Congress enacted the Revenue Act of 1913. Under this Act, a flat 1 percent tax was levied upon the income of corporations. Individuals paid a normal tax rate of 1 percent on taxable income after deducting a personal exemption of $3,000 for a single individual and $4,000 for a married taxpayer. Surtax rates of 1 to 6 percent were applied to high-income taxpayers.

Various revenue acts were passed between 1913 and 1939. In 1939, all of these revenue laws were codified into the Internal Revenue Code of 1939. In 1954, a similar codification of the revenue law took place. The current law is entitled the Internal Revenue Code of 1986, which largely carries over the provisions of the 1954 Code. To date, the Code has been amended several times since 1986. This matter is discussed further in Chapter 2 under Origin of the Internal Revenue Code.

Historical Trends

The income tax has proved to be a major source of revenue for the Federal government. Figure 1–1 contains a breakdown of the major revenue sources.[4] The importance of the income tax is demonstrated by the fact that estimated income tax collections from individuals and corporations amount to 44 percent of the total receipts.

The need for revenues to finance the war effort during World War II converted the income tax into a *mass tax*. For example, in 1939, less than 6 percent of the U.S. population was subject to the Federal income tax. In 1945, over 74 percent of the population was subject to the Federal income tax.[5]

Certain changes in the income tax law are of particular significance in understanding the Federal income tax. In 1943, Congress passed the Current Tax Payment Act, which provided for the first pay-as-you-go tax system. A pay-as-you-go income tax system requires employers to withhold for taxes a specified portion of an employee's wages. Persons with income from other than wages must make periodic (e.g., quarterly) payments to the taxing authority (the Internal Revenue Service) for estimated taxes due for the year.

One trend that has caused considerable concern has been the increased complexity of the Federal income tax laws. Often, under the name of tax reform,

---

2. *Flint v. Stone Tracy Co.*, 3 AFTR 2834, 31 S.Ct. 342 (USSC, 1911).
3. See the discussion of state franchise taxes later in the chapter.
4. *Budget of the United States Government for Fiscal Year 1992*, Office of Management and Budget (Washington, D.C.: U.S. Government Printing Office, 1991).
5. Richard Goode, *The Individual Income Tax* (Washington, D.C.: The Brookings Institution, 1964), pp. 2–4.

Congress has added to this complexity through frequent changes in the tax laws. Increasingly, this has forced many taxpayers to seek the assistance of tax professionals. At this time, therefore, substantial support exists for tax law simplification.

CRITERIA USED IN THE SELECTION OF A TAX STRUCTURE

In the eighteenth century, Adam Smith identified certain *canons of taxation* that are still considered when evaluating a particular tax structure. These canons of taxation are as follows:[6]

- *Equality.* Each taxpayer enjoys fair or equitable treatment by paying taxes in proportion to his or her income level. Ability to pay a tax is the measure of how equitably a tax is distributed among taxpayers.
- *Convenience.* Administrative simplicity has long been valued in formulating tax policy. If a tax is easily assessed and collected and its administrative costs are low, it should be favored. An advantage of the withholding (pay-as-you-go) system is its convenience for taxpayers.
- *Certainty.* A tax structure is *good* if the taxpayer can readily predict when, where, and how a tax will be levied. Individuals and businesses need to know the likely tax consequences of a particular type of transaction.
- *Economy.* A *good* tax system involves only nominal collection costs by the government and minimal compliance costs on the part of the taxpayer. Although the government's cost of collecting Federal taxes amounts to less than one-half of 1 percent of the revenue collected, the complexity of our current tax structure imposes substantial taxpayer compliance costs.

By these canons, the Federal income tax is a contentious product. *Equality* is present as long as one accepts ability to pay as an ingredient of this component. *Convenience* exists due to a heavy reliance on pay-as-you-go procedures. *Certainty* probably generates the greatest controversy. In one sense, certainty is present since a mass of administrative and judicial guidelines exists to aid in interpreting the tax law. In another sense, however, certainty does not exist since many questions remain unanswered and frequent changes in the tax law by Congress lessen stability. *Economy* is present if only the collection procedure of the IRS is considered. Economy is not present, however, if one focuses instead on taxpayer compliance efforts.

THE TAX STRUCTURE

Tax Base

A tax base is the amount to which the tax rate is applied. In the case of the Federal income tax, the tax base is *taxable income.* As noted later in the chapter

FIGURE 1–1
Federal Budget Receipts—1992

Individual income taxes	37%
Corporation income taxes	7
Social insurance taxes and contributions	30
Excise taxes	3
Borrowing	19
Other	4
	100%

6. *The Wealth of Nations*, Book V, Chapter II, Part II (New York: Dutton, 1910).

(Figure 1–2), taxable income is gross income reduced by certain deductions (both business and personal).

Tax Rates

Tax rates are applied to the tax base to determine a taxpayer's liability. The tax rates may be proportional or progressive. A tax is *proportional* if the rate of tax remains constant for any given income level.

EXAMPLE 2

T has $10,000 of taxable income and pays a tax of $3,000, or 30%. Y's taxable income is $50,000, and the tax on this amount is $15,000, or 30%. If this constant rate is applied throughout the rate structure, the tax is proportional. ◆

A tax is *progressive* if a higher rate of tax applies as the tax base increases. The Federal income tax, Federal gift and estate taxes, and most state income tax rate structures are progressive.

EXAMPLE 3

If T, a married individual filing jointly, has taxable income of $10,000, the tax for 1992 is $1,500 for an average tax rate of 15%. If, however, T's taxable income is $50,000, the tax will be $9,346 for an average tax rate of 18.69%. The tax is progressive since higher rates are applied to greater amounts of taxable income. ◆

Incidence of Taxation

The degree to which various segments of society share the total tax burden is difficult to assess. Assumptions must be made concerning who absorbs the burden for paying the tax. For example, since dividend payments to shareholders are not deductible by a corporation and are generally taxable to shareholders, the same income is subject to a form of double taxation. Concern over double taxation is valid to the extent that corporations are *not* able to shift the corporate tax to the consumer through higher commodity prices. Many research studies have shown a high degree of shifting of the corporate income tax. When the corporate tax can be shifted, it becomes merely a consumption tax that is borne by the ultimate purchasers of goods.

The U.S. Federal income tax rate structure for individuals is becoming less progressive. For example, for 1986 there were 15 rates, ranging from 0 to 50 percent. Subsequently, these rates were reduced to 15 percent and 28 percent. Recently, a 31 percent rate was added. Because many deductions and other tax savings procedures have been eliminated, Congress expects the lower rates to reach a larger base of taxable income.

MAJOR TYPES OF TAXES

◆

Property Taxes

Normally referred to as *ad valorem* taxes because they are based on value, property taxes are a tax on wealth, or capital. In this regard, they have much in common with death taxes and gift taxes discussed later in the chapter. Although property taxes do not tax income, the income actually derived (or the potential for any income) may be relevant insofar as it affects the value of the property being taxed.

Property taxes fall into *two* categories: those imposed on realty and those imposed on personalty. Both have added importance since they usually generate a deduction for Federal income tax purposes (see Chapter 11).

Ad Valorem Taxes on Realty. Property taxes on realty are exclusively within the province of the states and their local political subdivisions (e.g., cities, counties, school districts). They represent a major source of revenue for local governments, but their importance at the state level has waned over the past few years.[7]

How realty is defined can have an important bearing on which assets are subject to tax. This is especially true in jurisdictions that do not impose ad valorem taxes on personalty. Primarily a question of state property law, *realty* generally includes real estate and any capital improvements that are classified as fixtures. Simply stated, a *fixture* is something so permanently attached to the real estate that its removal will cause irreparable damage. A built-in bookcase might well be a fixture, whereas a movable bookcase would not be a fixture. Certain items such as electrical wiring and plumbing cease to be personalty when installed in a building and become realty.

The following are some of the characteristics of ad valorem taxes on realty:

- Property owned by the Federal government is exempt from tax. Similar immunity usually is extended to property owned by state and local governments and by certain charitable organizations.
- Some states provide for lower valuations on property dedicated to agricultural use or other special uses (e.g., wildlife sanctuaries).
- Some states partially exempt the homestead portion of property from taxation. Modern homestead laws normally protect some or all of a personal residence (including a farm or ranch) from the actions of creditors pursuing claims against the owner.
- Lower taxes may apply to a residence owned by an elderly taxpayer (e.g., age 65 and older).
- When non-income-producing property (e.g., a personal residence) is converted to income-producing property (e.g., a rental house), typically the appraised value increases.
- Some jurisdictions extend immunity from tax for a specified period of time (a *tax holiday*) to new or relocated businesses.

Unlike the ad valorem tax on personalty (see below), the tax on realty is difficult to avoid. Since real estate is impossible to hide, a high degree of taxpayer compliance is not surprising. The only avoidance possibility that is generally available is associated with the assessed value of the property. For this reason, the assessed value of the property and, particularly, a value that is reassessed upward may be subject to controversy and litigation.

Four methods are currently in use for assessing the value of real estate:

1. Actual purchase or construction price.
2. Contemporaneous sales prices or construction costs of comparable properties.
3. Cost of reproducing a building, less allowance for depreciation and obsolescence from the time of actual construction.
4. Capitalization of income from rental property.

Because all of these methods suffer faults and lead to inequities, a combination of two or more is not uncommon. For example, when real estate values and

---

7. Some states have imposed freezes on upward revaluations of residential housing.

construction costs are rising, the use of actual purchase or construction price (method 1) places the purchaser of a new home at a definite disadvantage compared with an owner who acquired similar property years before. As another illustration, if the capitalization of income (method 4) deals with property subject to rent controls (e.g., Boston), the property may be undervalued.

The history of the ad valorem tax on realty has been marked by inconsistent application due to a lack of competent tax administration and definitive guidelines for assessment procedures. In recent years, however, significant steps toward improvement have occurred. Some jurisdictions, for example, have computerized their reassessment procedures so they will have an immediate effect on all property located within the jurisdiction.

Ad Valorem Taxes on Personalty. *Personalty* can be defined as all assets that are not realty. It may be helpful to distinguish between the *classification* of an asset (realty or personalty) and the *use* to which it is placed. Both realty and personalty can be either business use or personal use property. Examples include a residence (realty that is personal use), an office building (realty that is business use), surgical instruments (personalty that is business use), and regular wearing apparel (personalty that is personal use).[8]

Personalty can also be classified as tangible property or intangible property. For ad valorem tax purposes, intangible personalty includes stocks, bonds, and various other securities (e.g., bank shares).

The following generalizations may be made concerning the ad valorem taxes on personalty:

- Particularly with personalty devoted to personal use (e.g., jewelry, household furnishings), taxpayer compliance ranges from poor to zero. Some jurisdictions do not even attempt to enforce the tax on these items. For automobiles devoted to personal use, many jurisdictions have converted from value as the tax base to arbitrary license fees based on the weight of the vehicle. Some jurisdictions take into consideration the age factor (e.g., automobiles six years or older are not subject to the ad valorem tax because they are presumed to have little, if any, value).
- For personalty devoted to business use (e.g., inventories, trucks, machinery, equipment), taxpayer compliance and enforcement procedures are measurably better.
- Which jurisdiction possesses the authority to tax movable personalty (e.g., railroad rolling stock) always has been and continues to be a troublesome issue.
- Some jurisdictions impose an ad valorem tax on intangibles.

Transaction Taxes

Transaction taxes, which characteristically are imposed at the manufacturer's, wholesaler's, or retailer's level, cover a wide range of transfers. Like many other types of taxes (e.g., income taxes, death taxes, and gift taxes), transaction taxes usually are not within the exclusive province of any level of taxing authority (Federal, state, local government). As the description implies, these levies place

8. The distinction, important for ad valorem and for Federal income tax purposes, often becomes confused when personalty is referred to as "personal" property to distinguish it from "real" property. This designation does not give a complete picture of what is involved. The description "personal" residence, however, is clearer, since a residence can be identified as being realty. What is meant, in this case, is realty that is personal use property.

a tax on transfers of property and normally are determined by multiplying the value involved by a percentage rate.

Federal Excise Taxes. Long one of the mainstays of the Federal tax system, Federal excise taxes had declined in relative importance until recently.[9] In late 1982 and 1990, Congress substantially increased the Federal excise taxes on such items as tobacco products, fuel and gasoline sales, telephone usage, and air travel passenger tickets. Other Federal excise taxes include the following:

- Manufacturers' excise taxes on trucks, trailers, tires, firearms, sporting equipment, coal, and the gas guzzler tax on automobiles.[10]
- Alcohol taxes.
- Certain luxury items. These include passenger cars (on sales price in excess of $30,000); boats (on sales price in excess of $100,000); aircraft (on sales price in excess of $250,000); jewelry (on sales price in excess of $10,000); and furs (on sales price in excess of $10,000).
- Miscellaneous taxes (e.g., the tax on wagering).

The list of transactions covered, although seemingly impressive, has diminished over the years. At one time, for example, there was a Federal excise tax on admission to amusement facilities (e.g., theaters) and on the sale of such items as leather goods and cosmetics.

When reviewing the list of both Federal and state excise taxes, one should recognize the possibility that the tax laws may be trying to influence social behavior. For example, the gas guzzler tax is intended as an incentive for the automobile companies to build cars that are fuel efficient. Since many consider alcohol and tobacco to be harmful to a person's health, why not increase their cost with the imposition of excise taxes and thereby discourage their use? Unfortunately, the evidence as to the level of correlation between the imposition of an excise tax and consumer behavior is mixed.

State Excise Taxes. Many state and local excise taxes parallel the Federal version. Thus, all states tax the sale of gasoline, liquor, and tobacco products; however, the rates vary significantly. For gasoline products, for example, compare the 26 cents per gallon imposed by the state of Rhode Island with the 9 cents per gallon levied by the state of Wyoming. For tobacco sales, contrast the 2.5 cents per pack of cigarettes in effect in Virginia with the 43 cents per pack applicable in Minnesota. Given the latter situation, is it surprising that the smuggling of cigarettes for resale elsewhere is so widespread?

Other excise taxes found at some state and local levels include those on admission to amusement facilities; hotel occupancy and the rental of various other facilities; and the sale of playing cards, oleomargarine products, and prepared foods. Most states impose a transaction tax on the transfer of property that requires the recording of documents (e.g., real estate sales).[11] Some extend the tax to the transfer of stocks and other securities.

General Sales Taxes. The distinction between an excise tax and a general sales tax is easy to make. One is restricted to a particular transaction (e.g., the 14.1

9. For a definition of excise tax, see the Glossary of Tax Terms in Appendix C.
10. The gas guzzler tax is imposed on the manufacturers of automobiles and progresses in amount as the mileage ratings per gallon of gas decrease.
11. This type of tax has much in common with the stamp tax levied by Great Britain on the American colonies during thepre–revolutionary war period in U.S. history.

cents per gallon Federal excise tax on the sale of gasoline), while the other covers a multitude of transactions (e.g., a 5 percent tax on *all* retail sales). In actual practice, however, the distinction is not always that clear. Some state statutes exempt certain transactions from the application of the general sales taxes (e.g., sales of food to be consumed off the premises, sales of certain medicines and drugs). Also, it is not uncommon to find that rates vary depending on the commodity involved. Many states, for example, allow preferential rates for the sale of agricultural equipment or apply different rates (either higher or lower than the general rate) to the sale of automobiles. With many of these special exceptions and classifications of rates, a general sales tax can take on the appearance of a collection of individual excise taxes.

A *use tax* is an ad valorem tax, usually at the same rate as the sales tax, on the use, consumption, or storage of tangible property. The purpose of a use tax is to prevent the avoidance of a sales tax. Every state that imposes a general sales tax levied on the consumer also has a use tax. Alaska, Delaware, Montana, New Hampshire, and Oregon have neither tax.

EXAMPLE 4

T resides in a jurisdiction that imposes a 5% general sales tax but lives near a state that has no sales or use tax at all. T purchases an automobile for $10,000 from a dealer located in the neighboring state. Has T saved $500 in sales taxes? The state use tax is designed to pick up the difference between the tax paid in another jurisdiction and what would have been paid in the state where T resides. ◆

The use tax is difficult to enforce for many purchases and is therefore often avoided. In some cases, for example, it may be worthwhile to make purchases through an out-of-state mail-order business. In spite of shipping costs, the avoidance of the local sales tax that otherwise might be incurred could make the price of such products as computer components cheaper. Some states are taking steps to curtail this loss of revenue. For items such as automobiles (refer to Example 4), the use tax probably will be collected when the purchaser registers the item in his or her home state.

Local general sales taxes, over and above those levied by the state, are common. It is not unusual to find taxpayers living in the same state who pay different general sales taxes due to the location of their residence.

EXAMPLE 5

R and S, two individuals, both live in a state that has a general sales tax of 3%. S, however, resides in a city that imposes an additional general sales tax of 2%. In spite of the fact that R and S live in the same state, one is subject to a rate of 3%, while the other pays a tax of 5%. ◆

Severance Taxes. Severance taxes are an important source of revenue for many states. These transaction taxes are based on the notion that the state has an interest in its natural resources (e.g., oil, gas, iron ore, coal). Therefore, a tax is imposed when they are extracted.

Death Taxes

A *death tax* is a tax on the right to transfer property or to receive property upon the death of the owner. Consequently, a death tax falls into the category of an excise tax. If the death tax is imposed on the right to pass property at death, it is classified as an *estate tax*. If it taxes the right to receive property from a decedent, it is termed an *inheritance tax*. As is typical of other types of excise taxes, the value of the property transferred provides the base for determining the amount of the death tax.

The Federal government imposes only an estate tax. State governments, however, levy inheritance taxes, estate taxes, or both.

EXAMPLE 6

At the time of her death, D lived in a state that imposes an inheritance tax but not an estate tax. S, one of D's heirs, lives in the same state. D's estate is subject to the Federal estate tax, and S is subject to the state inheritance tax. ◆

The Federal Estate Tax. The Revenue Act of 1916 incorporated the estate tax into the tax law. Although never designed to generate a large amount of revenue, its original purpose was to prevent large concentrations of wealth from being kept within a family for many generations. Whether this objective has been accomplished is debatable. Like the income tax, estate taxes can be reduced through various planning procedures.

The gross estate includes property the decedent owned at the time of death. It also includes life insurance proceeds when paid to the estate or when paid to a beneficiary other than the estate if the deceased-insured had any ownership rights in the policy. Quite simply, the gross estate represents property interests subject to Federal estate taxation.[12] All property included in the gross estate is valued as of the date of death or, if the alternate valuation date is elected, six months later.[13]

Deductions from the gross estate in arriving at the taxable estate include funeral and administration expenses, certain taxes, debts of the decedent, casualty losses[14] incurred during the administration of the estate, transfers to charitable organizations, and, in some cases, the marital deduction. The marital deduction is available for amounts actually passing to a surviving spouse (a widow or widower).

Once the taxable estate has been determined and certain taxable gifts have been added to it, the estate tax can be computed. From the amount derived from the appropriate tax rate schedules, various credits should be subtracted to arrive at the tax, if any, that is due.[15] Although many other credits are also available, probably the most significant is the unified transfer tax credit. The main reason for this credit is to eliminate or reduce the estate tax liability for modest estates. For deaths after 1986, the amount of the credit is $192,800. Based on the estate tax rates, the credit covers a tax base of $600,000.

EXAMPLE 7

D had made no taxable gifts before his death in 1992. If D died with a taxable estate of $600,000 or less, no Federal estate tax will be due because of the application of the unified transfer tax credit. Under the tax law, the estate tax on a taxable estate of $600,000 is $192,800. ◆

State Death Taxes. As noted earlier, states usually levy an inheritance tax, an estate tax, or both. The two forms of death taxes differ according to whether the tax is imposed on the heir or on the estate.

12. For further information on these matters, see *West's Federal Taxation: Corporations, Partnerships, Estates, and Trusts.*

13. See the discussion of the alternate valuation date in Chapter 14.

14. For a definition of casualty losses, see the Glossary of Tax Terms in Appendix C.

15. For tax purposes it is always crucial to appreciate the difference between a deduction and a credit. A *credit* is a dollar-for-dollar reduction of tax liability. A *deduction*, however, only benefits the taxpayer to the extent of his or her tax bracket. An estate in a 50% tax bracket, for example, would need $2 of deductions to prevent $1 of tax liability from developing. In contrast, $1 of credit neutralizes $1 of tax liability.

Characteristically, an inheritance tax divides the heirs into classes based on their relationship to the decedent. The more closely related the heir, the lower the rates imposed and the greater the exemption allowed. Some states completely exempt from taxation amounts passing to a surviving spouse.

Gift Taxes

Like a death tax, a *gift tax* is an excise tax levied on the right to transfer property. In this case, however, the tax is imposed on transfers made during the owner's life and not at death. Also, a gift tax applies only to transfers that are not supported by full and adequate consideration.

EXAMPLE 8

D sells to his daughter property worth $20,000 for $1,000. Although property worth $20,000 has been transferred, only $19,000 represents a gift, since this is the portion not supported by full and adequate consideration. ◆

The Federal Gift Tax. First enacted in 1932, the Federal gift tax was intended to complement the estate tax. In the absence of a tax applicable to lifetime transfers by gift, it would be possible to avoid the estate tax and escape taxation entirely.

Only taxable gifts are subject to the gift tax. For this purpose, a taxable gift is measured by the fair market value of the property on the date of transfer less the annual exclusion of $10,000 per donee and, in some cases, less the marital deduction, which allows tax-free transfers between spouses. Each donor is allowed an annual exclusion of $10,000 for each donee.[16]

EXAMPLE 9

On December 31, 1991, D (a widow) gives $10,000 to each of her four married children, their spouses, and her eight grandchildren. On January 3, 1992, she repeats the same procedure. Although D transferred $160,000 [$10,000 × 16 (number of donees)] in 1991 and $160,000 [$10,000 × 16 (number of donees)] in 1992 for a total of $320,000 ($160,000 + $160,000), she has not made a taxable gift as a result of the annual exclusion. ◆

A special election applicable to married persons allows one-half of the gift made by the donor-spouse to be treated as being made by the nondonor-spouse. The effect of this election to split the gifts of property made to third persons is to increase the number of annual exclusions available. Also, it allows the use of the nondonor-spouse's unified transfer tax credit and may lower the tax brackets that will apply.

For taxable gifts made after 1976, the gift tax rate schedule is the same as that applicable to the estate tax. The schedule is commonly referred to as the *unified transfer tax schedule.*

The Federal gift tax is *cumulative* in effect. What this means is that the tax base for current taxable gifts includes past taxable gifts. Although a credit is allowed for prior gift taxes, the result of adding past taxable gifts to current taxable gifts is to force the donor into a higher tax bracket.[17] Like the Federal estate tax

16. The purpose of the annual exclusion is to avoid the need to report and pay a tax on *modest* gifts. Without the exclusion, the Internal Revenue Service could face a real problem of taxpayer noncompliance.

17. For further information on the Federal gift tax, see *West's Federal Taxation: Corporations, Partnerships, Estates, and Trusts.*

rates, the Federal gift tax rates are progressive (see Example 3 earlier in this chapter).

The unified transfer tax credit is available for all taxable gifts made after 1976. As with the Federal estate tax, the amount of this credit is $192,800. There is, however, only one unified transfer tax credit, and it applies both to taxable gifts and to the Federal estate tax. In a manner of speaking, therefore, once the unified transfer tax credit has been exhausted for Federal gift tax purposes, it is no longer available to insulate a decedent from the Federal estate tax.

In summary, transfers by gift and transfers by death made after 1976 will be subject to the unified transfer tax. The same rates and credits apply. Further, taxable gifts made after 1976 will have to be added to the taxable estate in arriving at the tax base for applying the unified transfer tax at death.

State Gift Taxes. The states currently imposing a state gift tax are Delaware, Louisiana, New York, North Carolina, and Tennessee. Most of the laws provide for lifetime exemptions and annual exclusions. Like the Federal gift tax, the state taxes are cumulative in effect. But unlike the Federal version, the amount of tax depends on the relationship between the donor and the donee. Like state inheritance taxes, larger exemptions and lower rates apply when the donor and donee are closely related to each other.

Income Taxes

Income taxes are levied by the Federal government, most states, and some local governments. The trend in recent years has been to place greater reliance on this method of taxation. This trend is not consistent with what is happening in other countries, and in this sense, our system of taxation is somewhat different.

Income taxes generally are imposed on individuals, corporations, and certain fiduciaries (estates and trusts). Most jurisdictions attempt to assure the collection of income taxes by requiring certain pay-as-you-go procedures (e.g., withholding requirements for employees and estimated tax prepayments for other taxpayers).

On occasion, Congress has seen fit to impose additional taxes on income. Such impositions were justified either by economic considerations or by special circumstances resulting from wartime conditions. During World War II, the Korean conflict, and the Vietnam conflict, excess-profits taxes were imposed in addition to the regular Federal income tax. The taxes were aimed at the profiteering that occurs when the economy is geared to the production of war materials.

Another additional income tax is the surcharge approach. During the period from April 1, 1968, to July 1, 1970, for example, taxpayers were subject to a surcharge of 10 percent of the amount of their regular income tax liability. This led to the strange result that taxpayers had to pay, so to speak, an income tax on their income tax. Justifications for the special tax included the need to place restraints on what was regarded as an overactive economy, to curtail inflation, and to reduce the Federal deficit.

In light of current budget deficits, the surcharge approach has its advocates in Congress and therefore may be of more than historical interest. The advantage of the surcharge approach is that it represents a temporary solution to the problem. Thus, the tax can be imposed on a one-shot basis without compelling Congress to modify the regular income tax rates or base.

Federal Income Taxes. Chapters 3 through 19 deal with the application of the Federal income tax to individuals. The procedure for determining the Federal income tax applicable to individuals is summarized in Figure 1–2.

The application of the Federal corporate income tax does not require the computation of adjusted gross income and does not provide for the standard deduction and personal and dependency exemptions. All allowable deductions of a corporation fall into the business-expense category. In effect, therefore, the taxable income of a corporation is the difference between gross income (net of exclusions) and deductions.

Chapter 20 summarizes the rules relating to corporations. For an in-depth treatment of the Federal income tax as it affects corporations, estates, and trusts, see *West's Federal Taxation: Corporations, Partnerships, Estates, and Trusts*, 1993 Edition, Chapters 2 through 9, 12, and 19.

State Income Taxes. All but the following states impose an income tax on individuals: Alaska, Florida, Nevada, South Dakota, Texas, Washington, and Wyoming. New Hampshire and Tennessee have an income tax, but it applies only to dividend and interest income.

Some of the characteristics of state income taxes are summarized as follows:

- With few exceptions, all states require some form of withholding procedures.
- Most states use as the tax base the income determination made for Federal income tax purposes.
- A minority of states go even further and impose a flat rate upon adjusted gross income (AGI) as computed for Federal income tax purposes. Several apply a rate to the Federal income tax liability. This is often referred to as the piggyback approach to state income taxation. Although the term *piggyback* does not lend itself to precise definition, in this context, it means making use, for state income tax purposes, of what was done for Federal income tax purposes.
- Because of the tie-in to the Federal return, the state may be notified of any changes made by the IRS upon audit of a Federal return.
- Most states allow a deduction for personal and dependency exemptions. Some states substitute a tax credit for a deduction.
- A diminishing minority of states allow a deduction for Federal income taxes.

Figure 1–2
Formula for Federal Income Tax on Individuals

Income (broadly conceived)	$xx,xxx
Less: Exclusions (income that is not subject to tax)	(x,xxx)
Gross income (income that is subject to tax)	$xx,xxx
Less: Certain business deductions (usually referred to as deductions *for* adjusted gross income)	(x,xxx)
Adjusted gross income	$xx,xxx
Less: The greater of certain personal and employee deductions (usually referred to as *itemized deductions*) *or* The standard deduction (including any additional standard deduction) *and*	(x,xxx)
Less: Personal and dependency exemptions	(x,xxx)
Taxable income	$xx,xxx
Tax on taxable income (see Tax Rate Schedules in Appendix A)	$ x,xxx
Less: Tax credits (including Federal income tax withheld and other prepayments of Federal income taxes)	(xxx)
Tax due (or refund)	$ xxx

- Most states allow their residents some form of tax credit for income taxes paid to other states.
- The due date for filing generally is the same as for the Federal income tax (the fifteenth day of the fourth month following the close of the tax year).

Nearly all states have an income tax applicable to corporations. It is difficult to determine those that do not because a state franchise tax sometimes is based in part on the income earned by the corporation.[18]

Local Income Taxes. Cities imposing an income tax include, but are not limited to, Baltimore, Cincinnati, Cleveland, Detroit, Kansas City (Mo.), New York, Philadelphia, and St. Louis.

Employment Taxes

Classification as an employee usually leads to the imposition of employment taxes and to the requirement that the employer withhold specified amounts for income taxes. The rules governing the withholding for income taxes are discussed in Chapter 13. The material that follows concentrates on the two major employment taxes: FICA (Federal Insurance Contributions Act—commonly referred to as the Social Security tax) and FUTA (Federal Unemployment Tax Act). Both taxes can be justified by social and public welfare considerations: FICA offers some measure of retirement security, and FUTA provides a modest source of income in the event of loss of employment.

Employment taxes come into play only if two conditions are satisfied. First, is the individual involved an *employee* (as opposed to *self-employed*)? The differences between an employee and a self-employed person are discussed in Chapter 10.[19] Second, if the individual involved is an employee, is he or she covered under FICA or FUTA or both? The coverage of both of these taxes is summarized in Figure 13–5 in Chapter 13.[20]

FICA Taxes. The FICA tax is comprised of two components: Social Security tax (old age, surviviors, and disability insurance) *and* Medicare tax (hospital insurance). The tax rates and wage base under FICA are not constant, and as Figure 1–3 indicates, the increases over the years have been quite substantial. There appears to be every reason to predict that the rate and base amount will continue to rise in the future. Until 1991, the maximum wage that was subject to the Medicare portion of FICA was the same as that applicable to the Social Security portion. Starting in 1991, however, the top base amount differs for the Medicare portion and for the Social Security portion. Also note that Figure 1–3 represents the employee's share of the tax. The employer must match the employee's portion.

In at least two situations it is possible for an employee to have paid excess FICA taxes.

EXAMPLE 10

During 1992, T changed employers in the middle of the year, and from each job he earned $30,000 (all of which was subject to FICA). As a result, each employer withheld $2,295 [(6.2% × $30,000) + (1.45% × $30,000)] for a total of $4,590. Although each

18. See the discussion of franchise taxes later in the chapter.
19. See also Circular E, Employer's Tax Guide, issued by the IRS as Publication 15.
20. Chapter 13 deals with the self-employment tax (the Social Security and Medicare taxes for self-employed persons).

employer acted properly, T's total FICA tax liability for the year is only $4,311 [(6.2% × $55,500) + (1.45% × $60,000)]. Thus, T has overpaid his share of FICA taxes by $279 [$4,590 (amount paid) − $4,311 (amount of correct liability)]. He should claim this amount as a tax credit when filing an income tax return for 1992. The tax credit will reduce any income tax T might owe or, possibly, generate a tax refund. ◆

EXAMPLE 11

During 1992, E earned $50,000 from her regular job and $10,000 from a part-time job (all of which was subject to FICA). As a result, one employer withheld $3,825 [(6.2% × $50,000) + (1.45% × $50,000)] while the other employer withheld $765 [(6.2% × $10,000) + (1.45% × $10,000)] for a total of $4,590. E's total FICA tax liability for the year is only $4,311 [(6.2% × $55,500) + (1.45% × $60,000)]. Thus, T has overpaid her share of FICA taxes by $279 [$4,590 (amount paid) − $4,311 (amount of correct liability)]. She should claim this amount as a tax credit when filing an income tax return for 1992. ◆

In both Examples 10 and 11, the employee was subject to overwithholding. In both cases, however, the employee was able to obtain a credit for the excess withheld. The same result does not materialize for the portion paid by the employer. Since this amount is not refundable, in some situations employers may pay more FICA taxes than the covered employees.

The mere fact that a husband and wife are both employed does not, by itself, result in overwithholding of FICA taxes.

EXAMPLE 12

During 1992, H and W (husband and wife) both are employed, and each earns wages subject to FICA of $30,000. Accordingly, each has FICA withheld of $2,295 [(6.2% × $30,000) + (1.45% × $30,000)] for a total of $4,590. Since neither spouse paid FICA tax on wages in excess of $55,500 (Social Security tax) and $130,200 (Medicare tax) [see Figure 1–3], there is no overwithholding. ◆

FIGURE 1–3
FICA Rates and Base

	Social Security Tax				**Medicare Tax**				
	Percent	×	**Base Amount**	+	**Percent**	×	**Base Amount**	=	**Maximum Tax**
1978	5.05%	×	$17,700	+	1.00%	×	$ 17,700	=	$1,070.85
1979	5.08%	×	22,900	+	1.05%	×	22,900	=	1,403.77
1980	5.08%	×	25,900	+	1.05%	×	25,900	=	1,587.67
1981	5.35%	×	29,700	+	1.30%	×	29,700	=	1,975.05
1982	5.40%	×	32,400	+	1.30%	×	32,400	=	2,170.80
1983	5.40%	×	35,700	+	1.30%	×	35,700	=	2,391.90
1984	5.40%	×	37,800	+	1.30%	×	37,800	=	2,532.60
1985	5.70%	×	39,600	+	1.35%	×	39,600	=	2,791.80
1986	5.70%	×	42,000	+	1.45%	×	42,000	=	3,003.00
1987	5.70%	×	43,800	+	1.45%	×	43,800	=	3,131.70
1988	6.06%	×	45,000	+	1.45%	×	45,000	=	3,379.50
1989	6.06%	×	48,000	+	1.45%	×	48,000	=	3,604.80
1990	6.20%	×	51,300	+	1.45%	×	51,300	=	3,924.45
1991	6.20%	×	53,400	+	1.45%	×	125,000	=	5,123.30
1992	6.20%	×	55,500	+	1.45%	×	130,200	=	5,328.90
1993 on	6.20%	×	*	+	1.45%	×	*	=	**

*Not yet determined by Congress.
**Cannot be computed until the wage base is set by Congress.

A spouse employed by another spouse is subject to FICA. However, children under the age of 18 who are employed in a parent's trade or business are exempted.

FUTA Taxes. The purpose of FUTA is to provide funds that the states can use to administer unemployment benefits. This leads to the somewhat unusual situation of one tax being handled by both Federal and state governments. The end result of such joint administration is to compel the employer to observe a double set of rules. Thus, state and Federal returns must be filed and payments made to both governmental units.

FUTA applies at a rate of 6.2 percent in 1992 on the first $7,000 of covered wages paid during the year to each employee. The Federal government allows a credit for FUTA paid (or allowed under a merit rating system) to the state. The credit cannot exceed 5.4 percent of the covered wages. Thus, the amount required to be paid to the IRS could be as low as 0.8 percent (6.2 % – 5.4 %).

States follow a policy of reducing the unemployment tax on employers who experience stable employment. Thus, an employer with little or no employee turnover might find that the state rate drops to as low as 0.1 percent or, in some states, even to zero. The reason for the merit rating credit is that the state has to pay fewer unemployment benefits when employment is steady.

FUTA is to be distinguished from FICA in the sense that the incidence of taxation falls entirely upon the employer. A few states, however, levy a special tax on employees either to provide disability benefits or supplemental unemployment compensation, or both.

Other Taxes

To complete the overview of the U.S. tax system, some missing links need to be covered that do not fit into the classifications discussed elsewhere in this chapter.

Federal Customs Duties. One tax that has not yet been mentioned is the tariff on certain imported goods.[21] Generally referred to as customs duties or levies, this tax, together with selective excise taxes, provided most of the revenues needed by the Federal government during the nineteenth century. In view of present times, it is remarkable to note that tariffs and excise taxes alone paid off the national debt in 1835 and enabled the U.S. Treasury to pay a surplus of $28 million to the states.

In recent years, tariffs have served the nation more as an instrument for carrying out protectionist policies than as a means of generating revenue. Thus, a particular U.S. industry might be saved from economic disaster, so the argument goes, by placing customs duties on the importation of foreign goods that can be sold at lower prices. Protectionists contend that the tariff therefore neutralizes the competitive edge held by the producer of the foreign goods.

Protectionist policies seem more appropriate for less-developed countries whose industrial capacity has not yet matured. In a world where a developed country should have everything to gain by encouraging international free trade, such policies may be of dubious value. History shows that tariffs often lead to retaliatory action on the part of the nation or nations affected.

---

21. Less-developed countries that rely principally on one or more major commodities (e.g., oil, coffee) are prone to favor *export* duties as well.

Miscellaneous State and Local Taxes. Most states impose a franchise tax on corporations. Basically, a *franchise tax* is levied on the right to do business in the state. The base used for the determination of the tax varies from state to state. Although corporate income considerations may come into play, this tax most often is based on the capitalization of the corporation (either with or without certain long-term indebtedness).

Closely akin to the franchise tax are *occupational taxes* applicable to various trades or businesses, such as a liquor store license, a taxicab permit, or a fee to practice a profession such as law, medicine, or accounting. Most of these are not significant revenue producers and fall more into the category of licenses than taxes. The revenue derived is used to defray the cost incurred by the jurisdiction in regulating the business or profession in the interest of the public good.

Value Added Taxes

At least in the Common Market countries of Western Europe, the *value added tax* (VAT) has gained acceptance as a major source of revenue. Although variously classified, a VAT resembles a national sales tax, since it taxes the increment in value as goods move through production and manufacturing stages to the marketplace. A VAT has its proponents in the United States as a partial solution to high Federal budget deficits and increases in employment taxes. Its incorporation as part of our tax system in the near future is problematical, however.

Tax Administration
◆

Internal Revenue Service

The responsibility for administering the Federal tax laws rests with the Treasury Department. Administratively, the IRS is part of the Department of the Treasury and is responsible for enforcing the tax laws.

The Commissioner of Internal Revenue is appointed by the President. His responsibilities are to establish policy and to supervise the activities of the entire IRS organization. The National Office organization of the IRS includes a Senior Deputy Commissioner and several Deputy Commissioners and Assistant Commissioners who have supervisory responsibility over field operations.

The field organization of the IRS consists of the following:

- Service Centers (10) that are primarily responsible for processing tax returns, including the selection of returns for audit.
- District Directors (63) who are responsible for audits and for the collection of delinquent taxes.
- Regional Commissioners (7) who are responsible for the settlement of administrative appeals of disputed tax deficiencies.

The Audit Process

Selection of Returns for Audit. Due to budgetary limitations, only a small minority of returns are audited. For calendar year 1988, for example, only 0.92 percent of *all* individual income tax returns were examined.

The IRS utilizes mathematical formulas and statistical sampling techniques to select tax returns that are most likely to contain errors and to yield substantial amounts of additional tax revenues upon audit.

Though the IRS does not openly disclose all of its audit selection techniques, the following observations may be made concerning the probability of selection for audit:

- Certain groups of taxpayers are subject to audit much more frequently than others. These groups include individuals with gross income in excess of $50,000, self-employed individuals with substantial business income and deductions, and taxpayers with prior tax deficiencies. Also vulnerable are cash businesses (e.g., cafes and small service businesses) where the potential for tax avoidance is high.

EXAMPLE 13

T owns and operates a liquor store on a cash-and-carry basis. Since all of T's sales are for cash, T might well be a prime candidate for an audit by the IRS. Cash transactions are easier to conceal than those made on credit. ◆

- If information returns (e.g., Form 1099, Form W–2) are not in substantial agreement with reported income, an audit can be anticipated.
- If an individual's itemized deductions are in excess of norms established for various income levels, the probability of an audit is increased.
- Filing of a refund claim by the taxpayer may prompt an audit of the return.
- Certain returns are selected on a random sampling basis under the Taxpayer Compliance Measurement Program (TCMP). The TCMP is used to develop, update, and improve the mathematical formulas and statistical sampling techniques used by the IRS.
- Information obtained from other sources (e.g., informants, news items) may lead to an audit. The tax law permits the IRS to pay rewards to persons who provide information that leads to the detection and punishment of those who violate the tax laws. Such rewards may not exceed 10 percent of the taxes, fines, and penalties recovered as a result of such information.

EXAMPLE 14

After 15 years of service, F is discharged by her employer, Dr. T. Shortly thereafter, the IRS receives an anonymous letter informing it that Dr. T keeps two separate sets of books, one of which substantially understates his cash receipts. ◆

EXAMPLE 15

During a divorce proceeding, it is revealed that T, a public official, kept large amounts of cash in a shoe box at home. Such information is widely disseminated by the news media and comes to the attention of the IRS. Needless to say, the IRS would be interested in knowing whether such amounts originated from a taxable source and, if so, whether they were reported on T's income tax returns. ◆

Types of Audits. Once a return is selected for audit, the taxpayer is notified accordingly. If the issue involved is minor, it may be that the matter can be resolved simply by correspondence between the IRS and the taxpayer.

EXAMPLE 16

During 1990, T received dividend income from Z Corporation. In early 1991, Z Corporation reflected the payment on Form 1099–DIV (an information return for the reporting of dividend payments), the original being sent to the IRS and a copy to T. When preparing his income tax return for 1990, T apparently overlooked this particular Form 1099–DIV and failed to include the dividend on Schedule B, Interest and Dividend Income, of Form 1040. In 1992, the IRS sends a notice to T calling his attention to the omission and requesting a remittance for additional tax, interest, and penalty. T promptly mails a check to the IRS for the requested amount, and the matter is closed. ◆

Other examinations generally fall into the classification of either office audits or field audits. An *office audit* usually is restricted in scope and is conducted in the facilities of the IRS. In contrast, a *field audit* involves an examination of numerous items reported on the return and is conducted on the premises of the taxpayer or the taxpayer's representative.

Upon the conclusion of the audit, the examining agent issues a Revenue Agent's Report (RAR) that summarizes the findings. The RAR will result in a refund (the tax was overpaid), a deficiency (the tax was underpaid), or a *no change* (the tax was correct) finding.

Settlement Procedures. If an audit results in an assessment of additional tax and no settlement is reached with the IRS agent, the taxpayer may attempt to negotiate a settlement with the IRS. If an appeal is desired, an appropriate request must be made to the Appeals Division of the IRS. In some cases, a taxpayer may be able to obtain a percentage settlement or a favorable settlement of one or more disputed issues. The Appeals Division is authorized to settle all disputes based on the *hazard of litigation* (the probability of favorable resolution of the disputed issue or issues if litigated).

If a satisfactory settlement is not reached within the administrative appeal process, the taxpayer may wish to litigate the case in the Tax Court, a Federal District Court, or the Claims Court. However, litigation is recommended only as a last resort because of the legal costs involved and the uncertainties relative to the final outcome. Tax litigation considerations are discussed more fully in Chapter 2.

Statute of Limitations

A *statute of limitations* is a provision in the law that offers a party a defense against a suit brought by another party after the expiration of a specified period of time. The purpose of a statute of limitations is to preclude parties from prosecuting stale claims. The passage of time makes the defense of such claims difficult since witnesses may no longer be available or evidence may have been lost or destroyed. Found at the state and Federal levels, such statutes cover a multitude of suits, both civil and criminal.

For our purposes, the relevant statutes deal with the Federal income tax. The two categories involved cover both the period of limitations applicable to the assessment of additional tax deficiencies by the IRS and the period that deals with claims for refunds by taxpayers.

Assessment by the IRS. Under the general rule, the IRS may assess (impose) an additional tax liability against a taxpayer within *three years* of the filing of the income tax return. If the return is filed early, the three-year period begins to run from the due date of the return (usually April 15 for a calendar year individual taxpayer).

There is *no* statute of limitations on assessments of tax if *no return* is filed or if a *fraudulent* return is filed.

Limitations on Refunds. If a taxpayer believes that an overpayment of Federal income tax was made, a claim for refund should be filed with the IRS. A *claim for refund,* therefore, is a request to the IRS that it return to the taxpayer the excessive income taxes paid.[22]

---

22. The forms to use in filing a claim for refund are discussed in Chapter 3.

A claim for refund generally must be filed within *three years* from the date the return was filed *or* within *two years* from the date the tax was paid, whichever is later. Income tax returns that are filed early are deemed to have been filed on the date the return was due.

Interest and Penalties

Interest rates are determined quarterly by the IRS based on the existing Federal short-term rate. The rates for tax refunds (overpayments) are 1 percent below those applicable to assessments (underpayments). For the first quarter (January 1–March 31) of 1992, the rates were 8 percent for refunds and 9 percent for assessments.[23]

For assessments of additional taxes, the interest begins running on the unextended due date of the return. With refunds, however, no interest is allowed if the overpayment is refunded to the taxpayer within 45 days of the date the return is filed. For this purpose, returns filed early are deemed to have been filed on the due date.

The tax law provides various penalties for lack of compliance by taxpayers. Some of these penalties are summarized as follows:

- For a *failure to file* a tax return by the due date (including extension—see Chapter 3), a penalty of 5 percent per month (up to a maximum of 25 percent) is imposed on the amount of tax shown as due on the return. Any fraction of a month counts as a full month.
- A penalty for a *failure to pay* the tax due (as shown on the return) is imposed in the amount of 0.5 percent per month (up to a maximum of 25 per cent). Again, any fraction of a month counts as a full month. During any month in which both the failure to file penalty and the failure to pay penalty apply, the failure to file penalty is reduced by the amount of the failure to pay penalty.

EXAMPLE 17

T files his tax return 18 days after the due date of the return. Along with the return, he remits a check for $1,000, which is the balance of the tax he owed. Disregarding the interest element, T's total penalties are as follows:

Failure to pay penalty (0.5% × $1,000)		$ 5
Plus:		
Failure to file penalty (5% × $1,000)	$50	
Less failure to pay penalty for the same period	(5)	
Failure to file penalty		45
Total penalties		$50

Note that the penalties for one full month are imposed even though T was delinquent by only 18 days. Unlike the method used to compute interest, any part of a month is treated as a whole month. ◆

- A *negligence* penalty of 20 percent is imposed if any of the underpayment was for intentional disregard of rules and regulations without intent to defraud. The penalty applies to just that portion attributable to the negligence.

23. The rates applicable after March 31, 1992, were not available when this text went to press.

EXAMPLE 18

T underpaid his taxes for 1991 in the amount of $20,000, of which $15,000 is attributable to negligence. T's negligence penalty is $3,000 (20% × $15,000). ◆

- Various fraud penalties may be imposed. *Fraud* is a deliberate action on the part of the taxpayer evidenced by deceit, misrepresentation, concealment, etc. For possible fraud situations, refer to Examples 14 and 15. The burden of proving fraud is on the IRS. This is in contrast to the usual deficiency assessment made by the IRS, in which case the burden is on the taxpayer to show that he or she does not owe any additional tax.

UNDERSTANDING THE FEDERAL TAX LAW

The Federal tax law is a mosaic of statutory provisions, administrative pronouncements, and court decisions. Anyone who has attempted to work with this body of knowledge would have to admit to its complexity. For the person who has to trudge through a mass of rules to find the solution to a tax problem, it may be of some consolation to know that the law's complexity can generally be explained. Whether sound or not, there is a reason for the formulation of every rule. Knowing these reasons, therefore, is a considerable step toward understanding the Federal tax law.

The Federal tax law has as its *major objective* the raising of revenue. But although the fiscal needs of the government are important, other considerations explain certain portions of the law. Economic, social, equity, and political factors also play a significant role. Added to these factors is the marked impact the IRS and the courts have had and will continue to have on the evolution of Federal tax law. These matters are treated in the remainder of the chapter, and, wherever appropriate, the discussion is referenced to subjects covered later in the text.

Revenue Needs

The foundation of any tax system has to be the raising of revenue to cover the cost of government operations. Ideally, annual outlays should not exceed anticipated revenues, thereby leading to a balanced budget with no resulting deficit. Many states have achieved this objective by passing laws or constitutional amendments precluding deficit spending. Unfortunately, the Federal government has no such conclusive prohibition, and mounting annual deficits have become an increasing concern for many.

When finalizing the Tax Reform Act (TRA) of 1986, a deficit-conscious Congress was guided by the concept of *revenue neutrality.* The concept means that the changes made will neither increase nor decrease the net result reached under the prior rules. Revenue neutrality does not mean that any one taxpayer's tax liability will remain the same, since this will depend upon the circumstances involved. Thus, one taxpayer's increased tax liability could be another's tax savings. Although revenue neutral tax reform does not reduce deficits, at least it does not aggravate the problem.

One can expect budget deficit considerations to play an ever-increasing role in shaping future tax policy. The most recent tax legislation, the Revenue Reconciliation Act of 1990, is intended to generate considerable revenue. Although it contains certain revenue loss provisions, these are more than made up by new taxes and increases in tax rates.

Economic Considerations

The use of the tax system in an effort to accomplish economic objectives has become increasingly popular in recent years. Generally, proponents of this goal use tax legislation to amend the Internal Revenue Code and promote measures designed to help control the economy or encourage certain activities and businesses.

Control of the Economy. Congress has used depreciation write-offs as a means of controlling the economy. Theoretically, shorter asset lives and accelerated methods should encourage additional investment in depreciable property acquired for business use. Conversely, longer asset lives and the required use of the straight-line method of depreciation dampen the tax incentive for capital outlays.

Compared with past law, TRA of 1986 generally cut back on faster write-offs for property acquired after 1986. Particularly hard hit was most depreciable real estate, where asset lives were extended from 19 years to as long as 31½ years and the straight-line method was made mandatory. These changes were made in the interest of revenue neutrality and in the belief that the current economy was stable.

A change in the tax rate structure has a more immediate impact on the economy. With lower tax rates, taxpayers are able to retain additional spendable funds. Although TRA of 1986 lowered tax rates for most taxpayers, it also reduced or eliminated many deductions and credits. Consequently, lower rates may not lead to lower tax liabilities.

Encouragement of Certain Activities. Without passing judgment on the wisdom of any such choices, it is quite clear that the tax law does encourage certain types of economic activity or segments of the economy. For example, the favorable treatment allowed research and development expenditures can be explained by the desire to foster technological progress. Under the tax law, such expenditures can be either deducted in the year incurred or capitalized and amortized over a period of 60 months or more. In terms of the timing of the tax savings, such options usually are preferable to a capitalization of the cost with a write-off over the estimated useful life of the asset created. If the asset developed has an indefinite useful life, no write-off would be available without the two options allowed by the tax law.

Other legislation has also attempted to stimulate technological progress through the tax laws. In addition to the favorable write-off treatment, certain research and development costs qualify for a 20 percent tax credit (see Chapter 13).

Is it desirable to encourage the conservation of energy resources? Considering the world energy situation and our own reliance on foreign oil, the answer to this question has to be yes. The concern over energy usage was a prime consideration in the enactment of legislation to make various tax savings for energy conservation expenditures available to taxpayers.

Is preserving the environment a desirable objective? Ecological considerations explain why the tax law permits a 60-month amortization period for costs incurred in the installation of pollution control facilities.

Is it wise to stimulate U.S. exports of goods and services? Considering the pressing and continuing problem of a deficit in the U.S. balance of payments, the answer should be clear. Along this line, Congress has created Foreign Sales Corporations (FSCs), which are designed to encourage domestic exports of goods. The FSC provisions exempt a percentage of profits from export sales from the Federal income tax. Also in an international setting, Congress has deemed it advisable to establish incentives for U.S. citizens who accept employment overseas. Such persons receive generous tax breaks through special treatment of their foreign-source income and certain housing costs.

Is saving desirable for the economy? Saving leads to capital formation and thereby makes funds available to finance home construction and industrial expansion. The tax law encourages saving by according preferential treatment to private retirement plans. Not only are contributions to Keogh (H.R. 10) plans and certain Individual Retirement Accounts (IRAs) deductible, but income from such contributions accumulates free of tax. As noted below, the encouragement of private-sector pension plans can also be justified under social considerations.

Encouragement of Certain Industries. No one can question the proposition that a sound agricultural base is necessary for a well-balanced national economy. Undoubtedly, this can explain why farmers are accorded special treatment under the Federal tax system. Among the benefits are the election to expense rather than capitalize certain soil and water conservation expenditures and fertilizers and the election to defer the recognition of gain on the receipt of crop insurance proceeds.

Encouragement of Small Business. At least in the United States, a consensus exists that what is good for small business is good for the economy as a whole. Whether valid or not, this assumption has led to a definite bias in the tax law favoring small business.

In the corporate tax area, several provisions can be explained by the desire to benefit small business. One provision permits the shareholders of a small business corporation to make a special election that generally will avoid the imposition of the corporate income tax.[24] Furthermore, such an election enables the corporation to pass through its operating losses to its shareholders.

Social Considerations

Some provisions of the Federal tax law can be explained by social considerations. This is particularly the case when dealing with the Federal income tax of individuals. Some notable examples and their rationales include the following:

- Certain benefits provided to employees through accident and health plans financed by employers are nontaxable to employees. Encouraging such plans is considered socially desirable since they provide medical benefits in the event of an employee's illness or injury.
- Most premiums paid by an employer for group term insurance covering the life of the employee are nontaxable to the employee. These arrangements can be justified on social grounds in that they provide funds for the family unit to help it adjust to the loss of wages caused by the employee's death.
- A contribution made by an employer to a qualified pension or profit sharing plan for an employee receives special treatment. The contribution and any income it generates will not be taxed to the employee until the funds are distributed. Such an arrangement also benefits the employer by allowing a tax deduction when the contribution is made to the qualified plan. Private retirement plans are encouraged to supplement the subsistence income level the employee otherwise would have under the Social Security system.[25]
- A deduction is allowed for contributions to qualified charitable organizations.[26] The deduction attempts to shift some of the financial and administrative burden of socially desirable programs from the public (the government) to the private (the citizens) sector.

24. Known as the S election, it is discussed in Chapter 20.

25. The same rationale explains the availability of similar arrangements for self-employed persons (the H.R. 10, or Keogh, plan). See Chapter 19.

26. The charitable contribution deduction is discussed in Chapter 11.

- A tax credit is allowed for amounts spent to furnish care for certain minor or disabled dependents to enable the taxpayer to seek or maintain gainful employment.[27] Who could deny the social desirability of encouraging taxpayers to provide care for their children while they work?
- A tax deduction is not allowed for certain expenditures deemed to be contrary to public policy. This disallowance extends to such items as fines, penalties, illegal kickbacks, bribes to government officials, and gambling losses in excess of gains. Social considerations dictate that the tax law should not encourage these activities by permitting a deduction.

Many other examples could be cited, but the conclusion would be unchanged. Social considerations do explain a significant part of the Federal tax law.

Equity Considerations

The concept of equity is relative. Reasonable persons can, and often do, disagree about what is fair or unfair. In the tax area, moreover, equity is most often tied to a particular taxpayer's personal situation. To illustrate, compare the tax positions of those who rent their personal residences with those who own their homes. Renters receive no Federal income tax benefit from the rent they pay. For homeowners, however, a large portion of the house payments they make may qualify for the Federal interest and property tax deductions. Although renters may have difficulty understanding this difference in tax treatment, the encouragement of home ownership can be justified on both economic and social grounds.

In the same vein, compare the tax treatment of a corporation with that of a partnership. Although the two businesses may be of equal size, similarly situated, and competitors in the production of goods or services, they are not treated comparably under the tax law. The corporation is subject to a separate Federal income tax; the partnership is not. Whether the differences in tax treatment can be justified logically in terms of equity is beside the point. The point is that the tax law can and does make a distinction between these business forms.

Equity, then, is not what appears fair or unfair to any one taxpayer or group of taxpayers. It is, instead, what the tax law recognizes. Some recognition of equity does exist, however, and explains part of the law. The concept of equity appears in tax provisions that alleviate the effect of multiple taxation and postpone the recognition of gain when the taxpayer lacks the ability or wherewithal to pay the tax. Equity considerations also mitigate the effect of the application of the annual accounting period concept and cope with the eroding results of inflation.

Alleviating the Effect of Multiple Taxation. The income earned by a taxpayer may be subject to taxes imposed by different taxing authorities. If, for example, the taxpayer is a resident of New York City, income might generate Federal, state of New York, and city of New York income taxes. To compensate for this apparent inequity, the Federal tax law allows a taxpayer to claim a deduction for state and local income taxes. The deduction does not, however, neutralize the effect of multiple taxation, since the benefit derived depends on the taxpayer's Federal income tax rate. Only a tax credit, rather than a deduction, would eliminate the effects of multiple taxation on the same income.

---

27. See Chapter 13.

Equity considerations can explain the Federal tax treatment of certain income from foreign sources. Since double taxation results when the same income is subject to both foreign and U.S. income taxes, the tax law permits the taxpayer to choose between a credit and a deduction for the foreign taxes paid.

The Wherewithal to Pay Concept. The *wherewithal to pay* concept recognizes the inequity of taxing a transaction when the taxpayer lacks the means with which to pay the tax. It is particularly suited to situations in which the taxpayer's economic position has not changed significantly as a result of the transaction.

An illustration of the wherewithal to pay concept is the provision of the tax law dealing with the treatment of gain resulting from the sale of a personal residence. If the proceeds are rolled over (reinvested) in another personal residence within a specified time period, the gain will not be taxed (see Chapter 15).

EXAMPLE 19

T sold his personal residence (cost of $60,000) for $100,000 and moved to another city. Shortly thereafter, T purchased a new personal residence for $100,000. ◆

In Example 19, T had a realized gain of $40,000 [$100,000 (selling price) − $60,000 (cost of residence)]. It would be inequitable to force T to pay a tax on this gain for two reasons. First, without disposing of the property acquired (the new residence), T would be hard-pressed to pay the tax. Second, T's economic position has not changed significantly.

A warning is in order concerning the application of the wherewithal to pay concept. It applies only in situations specified by the tax law. Otherwise, the absence of cash and no apparent change in economic position will not prevent a transaction from being taxed.

EXAMPLE 20

Assume the same facts as in Example 19 except that the sale and purchase involved rental houses and not personal residences. Now, the sale of the first rental house will result in a gain of $40,000 that will be subject to tax. The fact that T reinvested the $100,000 in another rental house is of no consequence. ◆

Reconciling the different results reached in Examples 19 and 20 may seem difficult. But simply stated, the tax law applies the wherewithal to pay concept to the rollover on the gain from the sale of a personal residence. It does not do so when a rental house is involved, as Example 20 illustrates.

Mitigating the Effect of the Annual Accounting Period Concept. For purposes of effective administration of the tax law, all taxpayers must report to and settle with the Federal government at periodic intervals. Otherwise, taxpayers would remain uncertain as to their tax liabilities, and the government would have difficulty judging revenues and budgeting expenditures. The period selected for final settlement of most tax liabilities, in any event an arbitrary determination, is one year. At the close of each year, therefore, a taxpayer's position becomes complete for that particular year. Referred to as the annual accounting period concept, its effect is to divide each taxpayer's life, for tax purposes, into equal annual intervals.

The finality of the annual accounting period concept could lead to dissimilar tax treatment for taxpayers who are, from a long-range standpoint, in the same economic position.

EXAMPLE 21

R and S are two sole proprietors and have experienced the following results during the past four years:

Year	Profit (or Loss) R	S
1989	$50,000	$150,000
1990	60,000	60,000
1991	70,000	70,000
1992	50,000	(50,000)

Although R and S have the same profit of $230,000 over the period from 1989 to 1992, the finality of the annual accounting period concept places S at a definite disadvantage for tax purposes. The net operating loss procedure offers S some relief by allowing him to apply some or all of his 1992 loss to the earlier profitable years (in this case, 1989). Thus, with a net operating loss carryback, he would be in a position to obtain a refund for some of the taxes he paid on the $150,000 profit reported for 1989. ◆

The same reasoning used to support the deduction of net operating losses can explain the special treatment the tax law accords to excess capital losses and excess charitable contributions.[28] Carryback and carryover procedures help mitigate the effect of limiting a loss or a deduction to the accounting period in which it was realized. With such procedures, a taxpayer may be able to salvage a loss or a deduction that might otherwise be wasted.

The installment method of recognizing gain on the sale of property allows a taxpayer to spread tax consequences over the payout period.[29] The harsh effect of taxing all the gain in the year of sale is thereby avoided. The installment method can also be explained by the wherewithal to pay concept since recognition of gain is tied to the collection of the installment notes received from the sale of the property. Tax consequences, then, tend to correspond to the seller's ability to pay the tax.

Coping with Inflation. Because of the progressive nature of the income tax, a wage adjustment to compensate for inflation can increase the income tax bracket of the recipient. Known as *bracket creep*, its overall impact is an erosion of purchasing power. Congress recognized this problem and began to adjust various income tax components, such as tax brackets, standard deduction amounts, and personal and dependency exemptions, through an indexation procedure. Indexation is based upon the rise in the consumer price index over the prior year.

Political Considerations

A large segment of the Federal tax law is made up of statutory provisions. Since these statutes are enacted by Congress, is it any surprise that political considerations influence tax law? For purposes of discussion, the effect of political considerations on the tax law is divided into the following topics: special interest legislation, political expediency situations, and state and local government influences.

28. The tax treatment of these items is discussed in Chapters 8, 11, and 16.

29. Under the installment method, each payment received by the seller represents both a recovery of capital (the nontaxable portion) and profit from the sale (the taxable portion). The tax rules governing the installment method are discussed in Chapter 18.

Special Interest Legislation. There is no doubt that certain provisions of the tax law can largely be explained by the political influence some pressure groups have had on Congress. Is there any other realistic reason that, for example, prepaid subscription and dues income are not taxed until earned while prepaid rents are taxed to the landlord in the year received?

A recent example of special interest legislation was a last minute amendment to TRA of 1986 made by former Senator Long (Louisiana) and Representative Pickle (Austin, Texas). Under the amendment, a charitable deduction was allowed for donations to certain institutions of higher education that enabled the donor to receive choice seating at athletic events. The definition of institutions of higher education was so limited, however, that only Louisiana State University and the University of Texas were qualified recipients. It was not until two years later that Congress modified the tax law to neutralize this apparent preferential treatment (see Chapter 11).

Special interest legislation is not necessarily to be condemned if it can be justified on economic, social, or some other utilitarian grounds. At any rate, it is an inevitable product of our political system.

Political Expediency Situations. Various tax reform proposals rise and fall in favor with the shifting moods of the American public. That Congress is sensitive to popular feeling is an accepted fact. Therefore, certain provisions of the tax law can be explained by the political climate at the time they were enacted.

Measures that deter more affluent taxpayers from obtaining so-called preferential tax treatment have always had popular appeal and, consequently, the support of Congress. Provisions such as the alternative minimum tax, the imputed interest rules, and the limitation on the deductibility of interest on investment indebtedness can be explained on this basis.[30]

Other changes explained at least partially by political expediency include the lowering of individual income tax rates, the increase in the personal and dependency exemptions, and the increase in the amount of the earned income credit.

State and Local Government Influences. Political considerations have played a major role in the nontaxability of interest received on state and local obligations. In view of the furor that has been raised by state and local political figures every time any modification of this tax provision has been proposed, one might well regard it as next to sacred.

Somewhat less apparent has been the influence state law has had in shaping our present Federal tax law. Of prime import in this regard has been the effect of the community property system employed in some states.[31] At one time, the tax position of the residents of these states was so advantageous that many common law states actually adopted community property systems. Needless to say, the political pressure placed on Congress to correct the disparity in tax treatment was considerable. To a large extent this was accomplished in the

30. See Chapters 4, 11, and 12.

31. The nine states with community property systems are Louisiana, Texas, New Mexico, Arizona, California, Washington, Idaho, Nevada, and Wisconsin. The rest of the states are classified as common law jurisdictions. The difference between common law and community property systems centers around the property rights possessed by married persons. In a common law system, each spouse owns whatever he or she earns. Under a community property system, one-half of the earnings of each spouse is considered owned by the other spouse. Assume, for example, H and W are husband and wife and their only income is the $40,000 annual salary H receives. If they live in New York (a common law state), the $40,000 salary belongs to H. If, however, they live in Texas (a community property state), the $40,000 salary is divided equally, in terms of ownership, between H and W. For further discussion, see Chapter 4.

Revenue Act of 1948, which extended many of the community property tax advantages to residents of common law jurisdictions.

The major advantage extended was the provision allowing married taxpayers to file joint returns and compute the tax liability as if the income had been earned one-half by each spouse. This result is automatic in a community property state, since half of the income earned by one spouse belongs to the other spouse. The income-splitting benefits of a joint return are now incorporated as part of the tax rates applicable to married taxpayers. See Chapter 3.

Influence of the Internal Revenue Service

The influence of the IRS is apparent in many areas beyond its role in issuing the administrative pronouncements that make up a considerable portion of our tax law. In its capacity as the protector of the national revenue, the IRS has been instrumental in securing the passage of much legislation designed to curtail the most flagrant tax avoidance practices (to close tax loopholes). In its capacity as the administrator of the tax law, the IRS has sought and obtained legislation to make its job easier (to attain administrative feasibility).

The IRS as Protector of the Revenue. Innumerable examples can be given of provisions in the tax law that stem from the direct influence of the IRS. Usually, such provisions are intended to prevent a loophole from being used to avoid the tax consequences intended by Congress. Working within the letter of existing law, ingenious taxpayers and their advisers devise techniques that accomplish indirectly what cannot be accomplished directly. As a consequence, legislation is enacted to close the loopholes that taxpayers have located and exploited. Some tax law can be explained in this fashion and is discussed in the chapters to follow.

In addition, the IRS has secured from Congress legislation of a more general nature that enables it to make adjustments based on the substance, rather than the formal construction, of what a taxpayer has done. One such provision permits the IRS to make adjustments to a taxpayer's method of accounting when the method used by the taxpayer does not clearly reflect income.[32]

EXAMPLE 22

T, an individual cash basis taxpayer, owns and operates a pharmacy. All drugs and other items acquired for resale (e.g., cosmetics) are charged to the purchases account and written off (expensed) for tax purposes in the year of acquisition. As this procedure does not clearly reflect income, it would be appropriate for the IRS to require that T establish and maintain an ending inventory account. ◆

Administrative Feasibility. Some of the tax law is justified on the grounds that it simplifies the task of the IRS in collecting the revenue and administering the law. With regard to collecting the revenue, the IRS long ago realized the importance of placing taxpayers on a pay-as-you-go basis. Elaborate withholding procedures apply to wages, while the tax on other types of income may be paid at periodic intervals throughout the year. The IRS has been instrumental in convincing the courts that accrual basis taxpayers should pay taxes on prepaid income in the year received and not when earned. The approach may be contrary to generally accepted accounting principles, but it is consistent with the wherewithal to pay concept.

32. See Chapter 18.

Of considerable aid to the IRS in collecting revenue are the numerous provisions that impose interest and penalties on taxpayers for noncompliance with the tax law. Provisions such as the penalties for failure to pay a tax or to file a return that is due, the negligence penalty for intentional disregard of rules and regulations, and various penalties for civil and criminal fraud serve as deterrents to taxpayer noncompliance.

One of the keys to an effective administration of our tax system is the audit process conducted by the IRS. To carry out this function, the IRS is aided by provisions that reduce the chance of taxpayer error or manipulation and therefore simplify the audit effort that is necessary. An increase in the amount of the standard deduction, for example, reduces the number of individual taxpayers who will choose the alternative of itemizing their personal deductions.[33] With fewer deductions to check, the audit function is simplified.[34]

The audit function of the IRS has also been simplified by provisions of the tax law dealing with the burden of proof. Suppose, for example, the IRS audits a taxpayer and questions a particular deduction. Who has the burden of proving the propriety of the deduction? The so-called presumption of correctness that attaches in favor of any deficiency assessed by the IRS can be explained by the nature of our tax system. The Federal income tax is a self-assessed tax, which means that each taxpayer is responsible for rendering an accounting to the IRS of all of his or her transactions during the year. A failure to do so means that any doubts will be resolved in favor of the IRS. Only in the case of fraud (which could involve fines and penal sanctions) does the IRS carry the burden of proof.

Influence of the Courts

In addition to interpreting statutory provisions and the administrative pronouncements issued by the IRS, the Federal courts have influenced tax law in two other respects.[35] First, the courts have formulated certain judicial concepts that serve as guides in the application of various tax provisions. Second, certain key decisions have led to changes in the Internal Revenue Code.

Judicial Concepts Relating to Tax. A leading tax concept developed by the courts deals with the interpretation of statutory tax provisions that operate to benefit taxpayers. The courts have established the rule that these relief provisions are to be narrowly construed against taxpayers if there is any doubt about their application.

EXAMPLE 23

When a taxpayer has a gain on the sale of a personal residence, the gain is not subject to Federal income tax if the proceeds from the sale are reinvested in another principal residence. The tax law specifies a period of time in which the reinvestment must take place. The courts have held that the nontaxability of gain is a relief provision to be narrowly construed. Thus, failure to meet the replacement period requirements, even if beyond the control of the taxpayer, will cause the gain to be taxed.[36] ◆

---

33. For a discussion of the standard deduction, see Chapter 3.
34. The same justification was given by the IRS when it proposed to Congress the $100 limitation on personal casualty and theft losses. Imposition of the limitation eliminated many casualty and theft loss deductions and, as a consequence, saved the IRS considerable audit time. Later legislation, in addition to retaining the $100 feature, limits deductible losses to those in excess of 10% of a taxpayer's adjusted gross income. See Chapter 8.
35. A great deal of case law is devoted to ascertaining congressional intent. The courts, in effect, ask: What did Congress have in mind when it enacted a particular tax provision?
36. These rules are discussed further in Chapter 15.

Important in this area is the *arm's length* concept. Particularly in dealings between related parties, transactions may be tested by looking to whether the taxpayers acted in an arm's length manner. The question to be asked is: Would unrelated parties have handled the transaction in the same way?

EXAMPLE 24

T, the sole shareholder of X Corporation, leases property to X Corporation for a yearly rent of $6,000. To test whether the corporation should be allowed a rent deduction for this amount, the IRS and the courts will apply the arm's length concept. Would X Corporation have paid $6,000 a year in rent if the same property had been leased from an unrelated party (rather than from the sole shareholder)? Suppose it is determined that an unrelated third party would have paid an annual rent for the property of only $5,000. Under these circumstances, X Corporation will be allowed a deduction of only $5,000. The other $1,000 it paid for the use of the property represents a nondeductible dividend. Accordingly, T will be treated as having received rent income of $5,000 and dividend income of $1,000. ◆

Judicial Influence on Statutory Provisions. Some court decisions have been of such consequence that Congress has incorporated them into statutory tax law. For example, many years ago the courts found that stock dividends distributed to the shareholders of a corporation were not taxable as income. This result was largely accepted by Congress, and a provision in the tax statutes now covers the issue.

On occasion, however, Congress has reacted negatively to judicial interpretations of the tax law.

EXAMPLE 25

L leases unimproved real estate to T for 40 years. At a cost of $200,000, T erects a building on the land. The building is worth $100,000 when the lease terminates and L takes possession of the property. Does L have any income either when the improvements are made or when the lease terminates? In a landmark decision, a court held that L must recognize income of $100,000 upon the termination of the lease. ◆

Congress felt that the result reached in Example 25 was inequitable in that it was not consistent with the wherewithal to pay concept. Consequently, the tax law was amended to provide that a landlord does not recognize any income either when the improvements are made (unless made in lieu of rent) or when the lease terminates.

Summary

In addition to its necessary revenue-raising objective, the Federal tax law has developed in response to several other factors:

- *Economic considerations.* The emphasis here is on tax provisions that help regulate the economy and encourage certain activities and types of businesses.
- *Social considerations.* Some tax provisions are designed to encourage (or discourage) certain socially desirable (or undesirable) practices.
- *Equity considerations.* Of principal concern in this area are tax provisions that alleviate the effect of multiple taxation, recognize the wherewithal to pay concept, mitigate the effect of the annual accounting period concept, and recognize the eroding effect of inflation.
- *Political considerations.* Of significance in this regard are tax provisions that represent special interest legislation, reflect political expediency, and exhibit the effect of state and local law.

- *Influence of the IRS.* Many tax provisions are intended to aid the IRS in the collection of revenue and the administration of the tax law.
- *Influence of the courts.* Court decisions have established a body of judicial concepts relating to tax law and have, on occasion, led Congress to enact statutory provisions to either clarify or negate their effect.

These factors explain various tax provisions and thereby help in understanding why the tax law developed to its present state. The next step involves learning to work with the tax law, which is the subject of Chapter 2.

PROBLEM MATERIALS

DISCUSSION QUESTIONS

1. T, a middle management employee, is offered a pay increase by her employer. As a condition of the offer, T must move to another state. What tax considerations should T weigh before making a decision on whether to accept the offer?
2. A tax protester refuses to pay the Federal income tax on the grounds that the tax is unconstitutional. Any comment?
3. Before the ratification of the Sixteenth Amendment to the U.S. Constitution, the Federal income tax on corporations was held to be constitutional, whereas the Federal income tax on individuals was not. Why?
4. A tax law that was enacted in 1953 would be part of which Internal Revenue Code (i.e., 1939, 1954, or 1986)? Explain.
5. How does the pay-as-you-go procedure apply to wage earners? To persons who have income from other than wages?
6. Analyze the Federal income tax in light of Adam Smith's canons of taxation.
7. Is FICA a proportional or progressive tax? Explain.
8. What difference does it make whether a capital improvement to real estate is classified as a *fixture*?
9. The use of computers by state and local taxing authorities usually has made the application of the ad valorem tax more equitable. Why is this the case?
10. T buys a new home for $150,000, its cost of construction plus the usual profit margin for the builder. The new home is located in a neighborhood largely developed 10 years ago when the homes sold for approximately $50,000 each. Assuming the homes of his neighbors are worth (in current values) in the vicinity of $150,000, could T be at a disadvantage with regard to the ad valorem tax on realty?
11. Recently, one of your friends successfully challenged a reappraisal of his personal residence by the county board of real estate tax assessors. He remarks to you that this should put him "in good shape for the next five years." What does he mean?
12. T's personal residence is appraised at the same amount as his next-door neighbor's residence. The neighbor is retired. T is somewhat surprised to learn that his neighbor pays less real estate property tax to the city than does T. Could there be a logical explanation for the apparent inequity?
13. Is there any particular tax reason that might explain, in part, why sales of high-priced luxury automobiles have declined? Explain.
14. While out of town on business, U stays at a motel with an advertised room rate of $30 per night. When checking out, U is charged $33. What would be a plausible reason for the extra $3 U had to pay?
15. On a recent trip to a nearby supermarket, T spent $42.00, of which $2.00 was for general sales tax. If T lives in a jurisdiction that imposes a 6% general sales tax on foodstuffs, why was the bill not $42.40?

16. T, a resident of Wyoming (which imposes a general sales tax), goes to Montana (which does not impose a general sales tax) to purchase her automobile. Will T successfully avoid the Wyoming sales tax? Explain.
17. "There is no national general sales tax." Explain this statement.
18. Why might a person who purchases a product from an establishment located in jurisdiction X wish to take delivery in jurisdiction Y? Would it matter whether or not the person resided in jurisdiction X? Explain.
19. When Alaska became a major oil producer, the state repealed its state income tax. Is there any correlation between these two events? Explain.
20. A death tax has been characterized as an excise tax. Do you agree? Why or why not?
21. Explain the difference between an inheritance tax and an estate tax.
22. What was the original objective of the Federal estate tax?
23. A decedent who leaves all of his property to his surviving spouse and to qualified charitable organizations will not be subject to a Federal estate tax. Explain.
24. The Federal gift tax is cumulative in nature. Explain.
25. How much property can D, a widow, give to her three married children, their spouses, and five grandchildren over a period of 12 years without making a taxable gift?
26. When married persons elect to split a gift, what tax advantages do they enjoy?
27. Contrast the major differences between the Federal income tax schemes applicable to individuals and to corporations.
28. When a state uses a "piggyback" approach for its state income tax, what is the state doing?
29. T lives in a state that imposes an income tax. His Federal income tax return for 1990 is audited in 1992, and, as a result of several adjustments made by the IRS, T has to pay additional Federal income tax. Several months later, T is notified that his 1990 state income tax return is to be audited. Are these two incidents a coincidence or does a reasonable explanation exist?
30. At a social function you attended in early July of 1992, you overhear a guest, the CEO of a corporation, remark, "Thank goodness this is the end of FICA for a while!" Interpret this remark.
31. An employee who has more than one job during the year will always have excess FICA withholdings. Do you agree? Why or why not?
32. H and W are husband and wife, and both are employed by X Corporation. Wages earned during 1992 are as follows: $65,000 by W and $46,000 by H. How much FICA must they pay for 1992?
33. T, a sole proprietor, owns and operates a grocery store. T's wife and his 17-year-old son work in the business and are paid wages. Will the wife and son be subject to FICA? Explain.
34. T, the owner and operator of a construction company that builds outdoor swimming pools, releases most of his construction personnel during the winter months. Should this hurt T's FUTA situation? Why or why not?
35. Compare FICA and FUTA in connection with each of the following:
    a. Incidence of taxation.
    b. Justification for taxation.
    c. Rates and base involved.
36. What is a value added tax (VAT) and how does it operate?
37. T, the owner and operator of a cash-and-carry military surplus retail outlet, has been audited many times by the IRS. When T mentions this fact to his next-door neighbor, an employee with Ford Motor Company, he is somewhat surprised to learn that the neighbor has never been audited by the IRS. Is there any explanation for this apparent disparity in treatment?
38. While Dr. T and his family are out of town on vacation, their home is burglarized. Among the items stolen and reported to the police are $35,000 in cash and gold coins

worth $80,000. Shortly after the incident, Dr. T is audited by the IRS. Could there be any causal connection between the burglary and the audit? Explain.

39. Distinguish between a field audit and an office audit by the IRS.
40. An IRS agent audits S's income tax return and, as a result, issues an RAR (Revenue Agent's Report). Does this mean that S owes additional taxes? Explain.
41. For tax year 1984, T failed to file a Federal income tax return. In 1992, the IRS notifies T that it wants an accounting of his tax-related transactions for tax year 1984. T is not concerned about the request because three years have passed since the due date (April 15, 1985) of the return. Is T's defense based on the statute of limitations valid? Why or why not?
42. T files her income tax return 45 days after the due date of the return without obtaining an extension from the IRS. Along with the return, she remits a check for $4,000, which is the balance of the tax she owes. Disregarding the interest element, what are T's penalties for failure to file and for failure to pay?
43. T overstated deductions on his Federal income tax return for 1991. Upon audit by the IRS, it is determined that the overstatement was partially the result of negligence. As a result, T owes additional income taxes of $10,000 ($8,000 attributable to the negligence). What is T's penalty?
44. Give an example of a possible fraud situation for Federal income tax purposes.
45. What is meant by revenue neutral tax reform?
46. Does the tax law provide any stimulus for the development of international trade? Explain.
47. Discuss the probable justification for the following provisions of the tax law:
    - **a.** The election permitted certain corporations to avoid the corporate income tax.
    - **b.** A provision that excludes from gross income certain benefits furnished to employees through accident and health plans financed by employers.
    - **c.** Nontaxable treatment for an employee for premiums paid by an employer for group term insurance covering the life of the employee.
    - **d.** The tax treatment to the employee of contributions made by an employer to qualified pension or profit sharing plans.
    - **e.** The deduction allowed for contributions to qualified charitable organizations.
48. What purpose is served by allowing a deduction for home mortgage interest and property taxes?
49. Give an example of how the community property system has affected the Federal tax law.
50. Forcing accrual basis taxpayers to recognize prepaid income when received (as opposed to when earned) accomplishes what objective?
51. On her income tax return for the year, T claims as a deduction certain charitable contributions that she did not make. When you question her about this, she responds:
    - **a.** "How is the IRS going to prove that I did not make these contributions?"
    - **b.** "Even if the IRS disallows the deductions, the worst that can happen is that I will owe the same amount of tax I would have paid anyway."

    Comment on T's misconceptions about the tax law.

Chapter

Working with the Tax Law

Objectives

Familiarize the reader with the statutory, administrative, and judicial sources of the tax law.

Develop the research skills needed to locate and work with appropriate tax law sources.

Determine the validity of the various tax law sources.

Discuss the importance of communicating tax research.

Apply research techniques and planning procedures.

Examine the influence of nontax factors.

Distinguish between tax avoidance and tax evasion.

Illustrate tax planning concepts through practical tax planning applications.

Introduce computer-assisted tax research concepts.

Outline

Tax Sources

◆

Understanding taxation requires a mastery of the sources of the *rules of tax law.* These sources include not only legislative provisions in the form of the Internal Revenue Code, but also Congressional Committee Reports, Treasury Department Regulations, other Treasury Department pronouncements, and court decisions. Thus, the *primary sources* of tax information include pronouncements from all three branches of government: legislative, executive, and judicial.

In addition to being able to locate and interpret the sources of the tax law, a tax professional must understand the relative weight of authority within these sources. The tax law is of little significance, however, until it is applied to a set of facts and circumstances. This chapter, therefore, both introduces the statutory, administrative, and judicial sources of tax law and explains how the law is applied to individual and business transactions. It also explains the application of research techniques and the effective use of planning procedures.

A large part of tax research focuses on determining the intent of Congress. Although Congress often claims simplicity as one of its goals, a cursory examination of the tax law indicates that it has not been very successful in achieving this objective. Commenting on his 48-page tax return, James Michener, the author, said "it is unimaginable in that I graduated from one of America's better colleges, yet I am totally incapable of understanding tax returns."

Frequently, uncertainty in the tax law causes disputes between the Internal Revenue Service (IRS) and taxpayers. Due to these *gray areas* and the complexity of the tax law, a taxpayer may have more than one alternative for structuring a business transaction. In structuring business transactions and engaging in other tax planning activities, the tax adviser must be cognizant that the objective of tax planning is not necessarily to minimize the tax liability. Instead a taxpayer should maximize his or her after-tax return, which may include maximizing nontax as well as noneconomic benefits.

Statutory Sources of the Tax Law

Origin of the Internal Revenue Code. Before 1939, the statutory provisions relating to Federal taxation were contained in the individual revenue acts enacted by Congress. Because of the inconvenience and confusion that resulted from dealing with many separate acts, in 1939 Congress codified all of the Federal tax laws. Known as the Internal Revenue Code of 1939, the codification arranged all Federal tax provisions in a logical sequence and placed them in a separate part of the Federal statutes. A further rearrangement took place in 1954 and resulted in the Internal Revenue Code of 1954, which continued in effect until 1986 when it was replaced by the Internal Revenue Code of 1986. Although Congress did not recodify the law in the Tax Reform Act (TRA) of 1986, the magnitude of the changes made by TRA of 1986 do provide some rationale for renaming the Federal tax law the Internal Revenue Code of 1986.

The following observations will help clarify the codification procedure:

- With some exceptions, neither the 1939 nor the 1954 Code substantially changed the tax law existing on the date of its enactment. Much of the 1939 Code, for example, was incorporated into the 1954 Code; the major change was the reorganization and renumbering of the tax provisions.

- Although the 1986 Code resulted in substantial changes, only a minority of the statutory provisions were affected.[1]
- Statutory amendments to the tax law are integrated into the Code. For example, the Technical and Miscellaneous Revenue Act of 1988, the Revenue Reconciliation Act of 1989, and the Revenue Reconciliation Act of 1990 all became part of the Internal Revenue Code of 1986. Based on the tax legislation enacted in the 1980s, it appears that the tax law will continue to be amended frequently.[2]

The Legislative Process. Federal tax legislation generally originates in the House of Representatives where it is first considered by the House Ways and Means Committee. Tax bills originate in the Senate when they are attached as riders to other legislative proposals.[3] If acceptable to the House Ways and Means Committee, the proposed bill is referred to the entire House of Representatives for approval or disapproval. Approved bills are sent to the Senate, where they are referred to the Senate Finance Committee for further consideration.[4] The next step involves referral from the Senate Finance Committee to the entire Senate. Assuming no disagreement between the House and Senate, passage by the Senate results in referral to the President for approval or veto. If the bill is approved or if the President's veto is overridden, the bill becomes law and part of the Internal Revenue Code of 1986.

When the Senate version of the bill differs from that passed by the House,[5] the Joint Conference Committee, which includes members of both the House Ways and Means Committee and the Senate Finance Committee, is called upon to resolve these differences. The result, usually a compromise between the two versions, is then voted on by both the House and the Senate. If both bodies accept the bill, it is referred to the President for approval or veto.

Referrals from the House Ways and Means Committee, the Senate Finance Committee, and the Joint Conference Committee are usually accompanied by Committee Reports. Because these Committee Reports often explain the provisions of the proposed legislation, they are a valuable source in ascertaining the intent of Congress. What Congress had in mind when it considered and enacted tax legislation is, of course, the key to interpreting such legislation by taxpayers, the IRS, and the courts. Since Regulations normally are not issued immediately

---

1. This point is important in assessing judicial decisions interpreting provisions of the Internal Revenue Code of 1939 and the Internal Revenue Code of 1954. If the same provision was included in the Internal Revenue Code of 1986 and has not been subsequently amended, the decision has continuing validity.
2. Some of the major law changes during this period include the Multi-Employer Plan Amendments Act of 1980, Economic Recovery Tax Act of 1981, Subchapter S Revision Act of 1982, Tax Equity and Fiscal Responsibility Act of 1982, Retirement Equity Act of 1984, Deficit Reduction Act of 1984, Tax Reform Act of 1986, Revenue Act of 1987, Technical and Miscellaneous Revenue Act of 1988, Revenue Reconciliation Act of 1989, and the Revenue Reconciliation Act of 1990.
3. The Tax Equity and Fiscal Responsibility Act of 1982 originated in the Senate, and its constitutionality was unsuccessfully challenged in the courts. The Senate version of the Deficit Reduction Act of 1984 was attached as an amendment to the Federal Boat Safety Act.
4. Some tax provisions are commonly referred to by the number the bill received in the House when first proposed or by the name of the member of Congress sponsoring the legislation. For example, the Self-Employed Individuals Tax Retirement Act of 1962 is popularly known as H.R. 10 (House of Representatives Bill No. 10) or as the Keogh Act (Keogh being one of the members of Congress sponsoring the bill).
5. This is frequently the case with major tax bills. One factor contributing to a different Senate version is the latitude each individual senator has to make amendments to a bill when the Senate as a whole is voting on a bill referred to it by the Senate Finance Committee. During the passage of the Tax Reform Act of 1986, Senate leaders tried to make the bill *amendment proof* to avoid the normal amendment process. Less latitude is allowed in the House of Representatives. Thus, the entire House either accepts or rejects what is proposed by the House Ways and Means Committee, and changes from the floor are not commonplace.

after a statute is enacted, taxpayers often look to legislative history materials to determine congressional intent.

The typical legislative process for dealing with tax bills is summarized as follows:

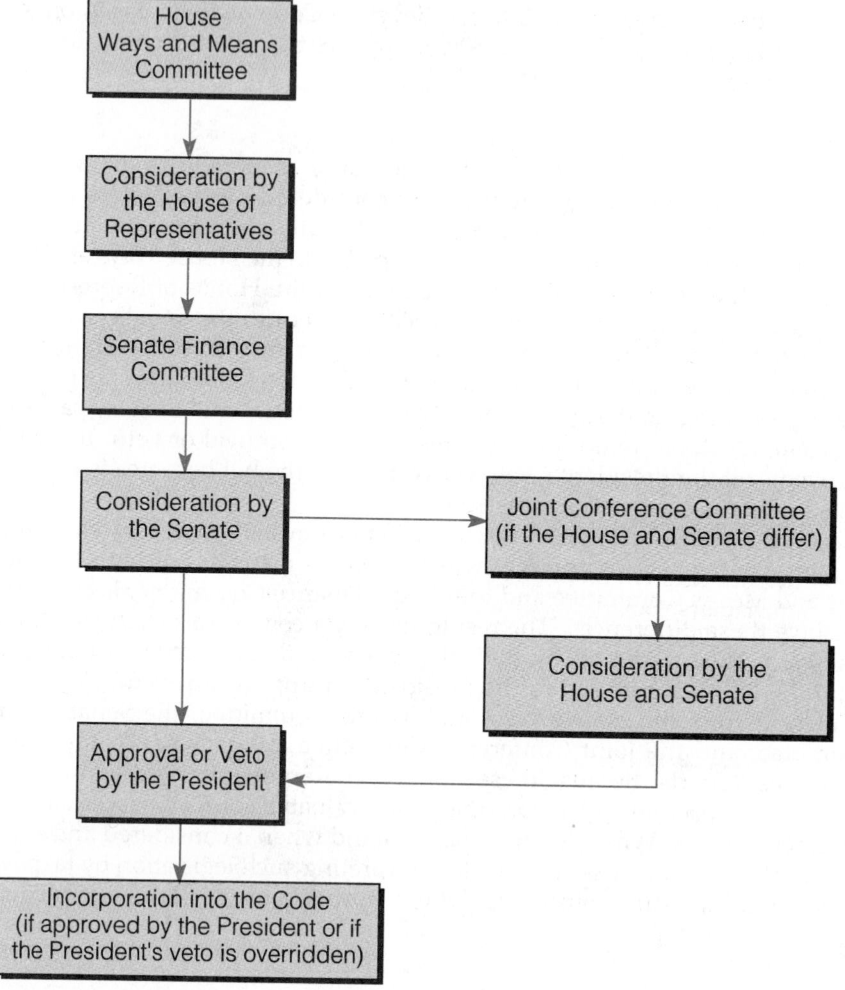

The role of the Joint Conference Committee indicates the importance of compromise in the legislative process. The practical effect of the compromise process can be illustrated by reviewing what happened to a new limitation on contributions by employees to their tax-sheltered annuities in the Tax Reform Act of 1986.

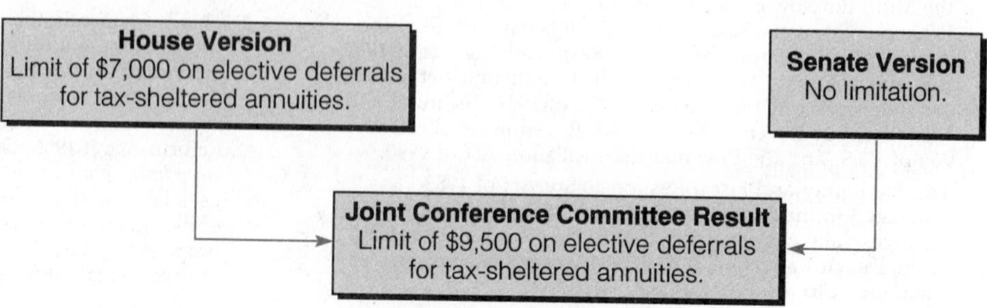

Arrangement of the Code. In working with the Code, it helps to understand the format. Note, for example, the following partial table of contents:

Subtitle A. Income Taxes

Chapter 1. Normal Taxes and Surtaxes

Subchapter A. Determination of Tax Liability

Part I. Tax on Individuals

Sections 1–5

Part II. Tax on Corporations

Sections 11–12

* * *

In referring to a provision of the Code, the *key* is usually the Section number involved. In citing Section 2(a) (dealing with the status of a surviving spouse), for example, it is unnecessary to include Subtitle A, Chapter 1, Subchapter A, Part I. Merely mentioning Section 2(a) will suffice, since the Section numbers run consecutively and do not begin again with each new Subtitle, Chapter, Subchapter, or Part. Not all Code Section numbers are used, however. Notice that Part I ends with Section 5 and Part II starts with Section 11 (at present there are no Sections 6, 7, 8, 9, and 10).[6]

Tax practitioners commonly refer to some specific areas of income taxation by their Subchapters. Some of the more common Subchapter designations include Subchapter C ("Corporate Distributions and Adjustments"), Subchapter K ("Partners and Partnerships"), and Subchapter S ("Tax Treatment of S Corporations and Their Shareholders"). In the last situation in particular, it is much more convenient to describe the subject of the applicable Code provisions (Sections 1361–1379) as S corporation status rather than as the "Tax Treatment of S Corporations and Their Shareholders."

Citing the Code. Code Sections often are broken down into subparts.[7] Section 2(a)(1)(A) serves as an example.

6. When the 1954 Code was drafted, some Section numbers were intentionally omitted so that later changes could be incorporated into the Code without disrupting its organization. When Congress does not leave enough space, subsequent Code Sections are given A, B, C, etc., designations. A good example is the treatment of §§ 280A through 280H.

7. Some Code Sections do not require subparts. See, for example, §§ 211 and 241.

8. Some Code Sections omit the subsection designation and use, instead, the paragraph designation as the first subpart. See, for example, §§ 212(1) and 1221(1).

Broken down by content, § 2(a)(1)(A) becomes:

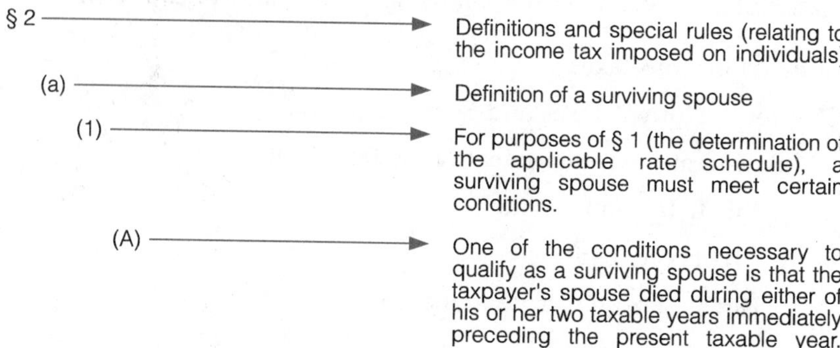
§ 2
Definitions and special rules (relating to the income tax imposed on individuals)
(a)
Definition of a surviving spouse
(1)
For purposes of § 1 (the determination of the applicable rate schedule), a surviving spouse must meet certain conditions.
(A)
One of the conditions necessary to qualify as a surviving spouse is that the taxpayer's spouse died during either of his or her two taxable years immediately preceding the present taxable year.

Throughout the remainder of the text, references to the Code Sections are in the form given above. The symbols "§" and "§§" are used in place of "Section" and "Sections." Unless otherwise stated, all Code references are to the Internal Revenue Code of 1986. The following table summarizes the format that will be used:

Complete Reference	Text Reference
Section 2(a)(1)(A) of the Internal Revenue Code of 1986	§ 2(a)(1)(A)
Sections 1 and 2 of the Internal Revenue Code of 1986	§§ 1 and 2
Section 2 of the Internal Revenue Code of 1954	§ 2 of the Internal Revenue Code of 1954
Section 12(d) of the Internal Revenue Code of 1939[9]	§ 12(d) of the Internal Revenue Code of 1939

Effect of Treaties. The United States signs certain tax treaties with foreign countries to render mutual assistance in tax enforcement and to avoid double taxation. The Technical and Miscellaneous Revenue Act of 1988 provided that neither a tax law nor a tax treaty takes general precedence. Thus, when there is a direct conflict, the most recent item will take precedence. A taxpayer must disclose on the tax return any position where a treaty overrides a tax law.[10] There is a $1,000 penalty per failure to disclose for individuals and a $10,000 per failure penalty for corporations.[11]

Administrative Sources of the Tax Law

The administrative sources of the Federal tax law can be grouped as follows: Treasury Department Regulations, Revenue Rulings and Revenue Procedures, and other administrative pronouncements (see Concept Summary 2–1). All are issued either by the U.S. Treasury Department or by one of its instrumentalities (e.g., the IRS or a District Director).

9. § 12(d) of the Internal Revenue Code of 1939 is the predecessor to § 2 of the Internal Revenue Code of 1954 and the Internal Revenue Code of 1986. Keep in mind that the 1954 Code superseded the 1939 Code and the 1986 Code has superseded the 1954 Code. Footnote 1 of this chapter explains why references to the 1939 or 1954 code are included.
10. § 7852(d).
11. Reg. §§ 301.6114–1 and 301.6712–1.

Treasury Department Regulations. Regulations are issued by the U.S. Treasury Department under authority granted by Congress.[12] Interpretative by nature, they provide taxpayers with considerable guidance on the meaning and application of the Code. Regulations may be issued in *proposed*, *temporary*, or *final* form. Regulations carry considerable weight and are an important factor to consider in complying with the tax law.

Since Regulations interpret the Code, they are arranged in the same sequence. A number is added at the beginning, however, to indicate the type of tax or administrative, procedural, or definitional matter to which they relate. For example, the prefix 1 designates the Regulations under the income tax law. Thus, the Regulations under Code § 2 are cited as Reg. § 1.2 with subparts added for further identification. The numbers of these subparts often do not correspond to the numbers of the Code subsections. The prefix 20 designates estate tax Regulations; 25 covers gift tax Regulations; 31 relates to employment taxes; and 301 refers to procedure and administration. This list is not all-inclusive.

New Regulations and changes to existing Regulations are usually issued in proposed form before they are finalized. The interval between the proposal of a Regulation and its finalization permits taxpayers and other interested parties to comment on the propriety of the proposal. Proposed Regulations under Code § 2, for example, are cited as Prop.Reg. § 1.2. The Tax Court indicates that proposed Regulations carry no more weight than a position advanced in a written brief prepared by a litigating party before the Tax Court. *Finalized* Regulations have the force and effect of law.[13]

CONCEPT SUMMARY 2–1
ADMINISTRATIVE SOURCES

Source	Location	Authority**
Regulations	*Federal Register**	Force and effect of law.
Proposed Regulations	*Federal Register** *Internal Revenue Bulletin* *Cumulative Bulletin*	Preview of final Regulations.
Temporary Regulations	*Federal Register** *Internal Revenue Bulletin* *Cumulative Bulletin*	May be cited as a precedent.
Revenue Rulings Revenue Procedures	*Internal Revenue Bulletin* *Cumulative Bulletin*	Do not have the force and effect of law.
General Counsel's Memoranda Technical Memoranda Action on Decisions Technical Advice Memoranda	*Tax Analysts' Tax Notes*; P-H's *Internal Memoranda of the IRS*; CCH's *IRS Position Reporter*	May not be cited as a precedent.
Letter Rulings	Prentice-Hall and Commerce Clearing House loose-leaf services	Applicable only to taxpayer addressed. No precedential force.

*Finalized, proposed, and temporary Regulations are published in soft-cover form by several publishers.
**Each of these sources may be substantial authority for purposes of the accuracy-related penalty in § 6662. A lower source has less weight than a higher source in this list. Notice 90–20, 1990–1 C.B. 328.

12. § 7805.

13. *F. W. Woolworth Co.*, 54 T.C. 1233 (1970); *Harris M. Miller*, 70 T.C. 448 (1978); and *James O. Tomerlin Trust*, 87 T.C. 876 (1986).

Sometimes the Treasury Department issues *temporary* Regulations relating to elections and other matters where speed is important. These Regulations are issued without the comment period required for proposed Regulations. Temporary Regulations have the same authoritative value as final Regulations and may be cited as precedents. Temporary Regulations must now also be issued as proposed Regulations and automatically expire within three years after the date of issuance.[14] Obviously, temporary Regulations and the simultaneously issued proposed Regulations carry more weight than traditional proposed Regulations. An example of a temporary Regulation is Temp.Reg. § 1.42–2T, which deals with the low-income housing credit for certain federally assisted buildings. In the past, the Treasury Department has been slow to finalize temporary Regulations.

Proposed, temporary, and final Regulations are published in the *Federal Register* and are reproduced in major tax services. Final Regulations are issued as Treasury Decisions.

Regulations may also be classified as *legislative, interpretative*, or *procedural*. This classification scheme is discussed under Assessing the Validity of a Treasury Regulation later in the chapter.

Revenue Rulings and Revenue Procedures. *Revenue Rulings* are official pronouncements of the National Office of the IRS.[15] Like Regulations, they are designed to provide interpretation of the tax law. However, they do not carry the same legal force and effect as Regulations and usually deal with more restricted problems. In addition, Regulations are approved by the Secretary of the Treasury, whereas Revenue Rulings are not. Both Revenue Rulings and Revenue Procedures serve an important function by providing *guidance* to IRS personnel and taxpayers in routine tax matters.

Although letter rulings (discussed below) are not the same as Revenue Rulings, a Revenue Ruling often results from a specific taxpayer's request for a letter ruling. If the IRS believes that a taxpayer's request for a letter ruling deserves official publication because of its widespread impact, the holding will be converted into a Revenue Ruling and issued for the information and guidance of taxpayers, practitioners, and IRS personnel. Names, identifying descriptions, and money amounts are changed to disguise the identity of the taxpayer. In addition to resulting from taxpayer requests, Revenue Rulings arise from technical advice to District Offices of the IRS, court decisions, suggestions from tax practitioner groups, and various tax publications.

Revenue Procedures are issued in the same manner as Revenue Rulings, but deal with the internal management practices and procedures of the IRS. Familiarity with these procedures can increase taxpayer compliance and help the IRS administer the tax laws efficiently. A taxpayer's failure to follow a Revenue Procedure can result in unnecessary delay or cause the IRS to decline to act in a discretionary situation on behalf of the taxpayer.

Revenue Rulings and Revenue Procedures are published weekly by the U.S. Government in the *Internal Revenue Bulletin* (I.R.B.). Semiannually, the bulletins for a six-month period are gathered together, reorganized by Code Section classification, and published in a bound volume called the *Cumulative Bulletin* (C.B.).[16] The proper form for citing Revenue Rulings and Revenue Procedures

---

14. § 7805(e).

15. § 7805(a).

16. Usually only two volumes of the *Cumulative Bulletin* are published each year. However, when Congress has enacted major tax legislation, other volumes may be published containing the Congressional Committee Reports supporting the Revenue Act. See, for example, the two extra volumes for 1984 dealing with the Deficit Reduction Act of 1984. The 1984–3 *Cumulative Bulletin*, Volume 1, contains the text of the law itself; 1984–3, Volume 2, contains the Committee Reports. This makes a total of four volumes of the *Cumulative Bulletin* for 1984: 1984–1; 1984–2; 1984–3, Volume 1; 1984–3, Volume 2.

depends on whether the item has been published in the *Cumulative Bulletin* or is only available in I.R.B. form. Consider, for example, the following transition:

Temporary Citation	Rev.Rul. 90–109, I.R.B. No. 52, 17. *Explanation:* Revenue Ruling Number 109, appearing on page 17 of the 52nd weekly issue of the *Internal Revenue Bulletin* for 1990.
Permanent Citation	Rev.Rul. 90–109, 1990–2 C.B. 191. *Explanation:* Revenue Ruling Number 109, appearing on page 191 of Volume 2 of the *Cumulative Bulletin* for 1990.

Since the second volume of the 1990 *Cumulative Bulletin* was not published until August of 1991, the I.R.B. citation had to be used until that time. After the publication of the *Cumulative Bulletin*, the C.B. citation is proper. The basic portion of both citations (Rev.Rul. 90–109) indicates that this document was the 109th Revenue Ruling issued by the IRS during 1990.

Revenue Procedures are cited in the same manner, except that "Rev.Proc." is substituted for "Rev.Rul." Some Revenue Procedures issued in 1991 had the following effects:

- Set out the qualification requirements of certain defined-contribution and defined-benefit plans.
- Provided the procedure by which a partnership can opt out of a previous election with respect to a cash or deferred arrangement plan.
- Increased the cost recovery ceilings for passenger automobiles for 1991.

Letter Rulings. Individual (*letter*) rulings are issued upon a taxpayer's request and describe how the IRS will treat a proposed transaction for tax purposes. They apply only to the taxpayer who asks for and obtains the ruling, but post-1984 letter rulings may be substantial authority for purposes of the accuracy-related penalty.[17] Though this procedure may sound like the only real way to carry out effective tax planning, the IRS limits the issuance of individual rulings to restricted, preannounced areas of taxation. The main reason the IRS will not rule in certain areas is that such areas involve fact-oriented situations. Thus, it is not possible to obtain a ruling on many of the problems that are particularly troublesome for taxpayers.[18]

Letter rulings may be either *mandatory* or *discretionary*. A taxpayer must obtain a favorable ruling for certain changes in accounting procedures (e.g., a change in accounting period under § 442 or a change in accounting method under § 446). Such rulings are mandatory rulings. Discretionary rulings are not required by law; taxpayers request them at their own discretion. Further, the IRS issues these rulings at its discretion. For example, a taxpayer might request a ruling as to the taxability of a corporate reorganization. In general, the IRS will rule on prospective transactions and on completed transactions where a return has not been filed for matters concerning income tax, gift tax, estate tax, generation-skipping transfer tax, and § 2032A ("Valuation of Certain Farm, Etc., Real Property").

---

17. Notice 90–20, 1990–1 C.B. 328. In this regard, letter rulings differ from Revenue Rulings, which are applicable to *all* taxpayers. Letter rulings may later lead to the issuance of a Revenue Ruling if the holding involved affects many taxpayers. In its Agents' Manual, the IRS indicates that letter rulings may be used as a guide with other research materials in formulating a District Office position on an issue. The IRS is required to charge a taxpayer a fee for letter rulings, determination letters, etc.

18. Rev.Proc. 92–3, I.R.B. No. 1, 55 contains a list of areas in which the IRS will not issue advance rulings. From time to time, subsequent Revenue Procedures are issued that modify or amplify Rev.Proc. 92–3.

The law now requires the IRS to make individual rulings available for public inspection after identifying details are deleted.[19] Published digests of private letter rulings can be found in *Private Letter Rulings* (published by Prentice-Hall), BNA *Daily Tax Reports*, and Tax Analysts & Advocates *Tax Notes*. *IRS Letter Rulings Reports* (published by Commerce Clearing House) contains both digests and full texts of all letter rulings. *Letter Ruling Review* (published by Tax Analysts) is a monthly publication that selects and discusses the more important of the over 300 letter rulings issued each month.

Letter rulings receive multidigit file numbers, which indicate the year and week of issuance as well as the number of the ruling during that week. Consider, for example, Ltt. Rul. 9111027 dealing with the deductibility of research and experimental expense:

91	11	027
Year 1991	11th week of issuance	Number of the ruling issued during the 11th week

Other Administrative Pronouncements. *Treasury Decisions* (TDs) are issued by the Treasury Department to promulgate new Regulations, amend or otherwise change existing Regulations, or announce the position of the Government on selected court decisions. Like Revenue Rulings and Revenue Procedures, TDs are published in the *Internal Revenue Bulletin* and subsequently transferred to the *Cumulative Bulletin.*

The IRS publishes other administrative communications in the *Internal Revenue Bulletin* such as Announcements, Notices, LRs (proposed Regulations), and Prohibited Transaction Exemptions.

Like letter rulings, *determination letters* are issued at the request of taxpayers and provide guidance on the application of the tax law. They differ from letter rulings in that the issuing source is the District Director rather than the National Office of the IRS. Also, determination letters usually involve completed (as opposed to proposed) transactions. Determination letters are not published and are made known only to the party making the request.

The following examples illustrate the distinction between letter rulings and determination letters:

EXAMPLE 1

The shareholders of X Corporation and Y Corporation want assurance that the consolidation of the corporations into Z Corporation will be a nontaxable reorganization. The proper approach would be to request the National Office of the IRS to issue a letter ruling concerning the income tax effect of the proposed transaction. ◆

EXAMPLE 2

T operates a barber shop in which he employs eight barbers. To comply with the rules governing income tax and payroll tax withholdings, T wants to know whether the barbers working for him are employees or independent contractors. The proper procedure would be to request a determination letter on their status from the appropriate District Director. ◆

19. § 6110.

The National Office of the IRS releases *Technical Advice Memoranda* (TAMs) weekly. Although TAMs and letter rulings both give the IRS's determination of an issue, they differ in several respects. Letter rulings deal with proposed transactions and are issued to taxpayers at their request. In contrast, TAMs deal with completed transactions and are often requested in relation to exempt organizations and employee plans. Futhermore, TAMs arise from questions raised by IRS personnel during audits and are issued by the National Office of the IRS to its field personnel, not to the taxpayers. TAMs are not officially published and may not be cited or used as precedent.[20] They are assigned file numbers according to the same procedure used for letter rulings. For example, TAM 9127008 refers to the 8th TAM issued during the 27th week of 1991.

Several internal memoranda that constitute the working law of the IRS now must be released. These General Counsel's Memoranda (GCMs), Technical Memoranda (TMs), and Actions on Decisions (AODs) are not officially published and the IRS indicates that they may not be cited as precedents by taxpayers.[21] However, these working documents do explain the IRS's position on various issues.

Judicial Sources of the Tax Law

The Judicial Process in General. After a taxpayer has exhausted some or all of the remedies available within the IRS (i.e., no satisfactory settlement has been reached at the agent or at the Appeals Division level), the dispute can be taken to the Federal courts. The dispute is first considered by a *court of original jurisdiction* (known as a trial court) with any appeal (either by the taxpayer or the IRS) taken to the appropriate appellate court. In most situations, the taxpayer has a choice of any of *four trial courts:* a Federal District Court, the U.S. Claims Court, the U.S. Tax Court, or the Small Claims Division of the U.S. Tax Court. The trial and appellate court scheme for Federal tax litigation is illustrated in Figure 2–1.

The broken line between the U.S. Tax Court and the *Small Claims Division* indicates that there is no appeal from the Small Claims Division. The jurisdiction of the Small Claims Division is limited to cases involving amounts of $10,000 or less. The proceedings of the Small Claims Division are informal (e.g., no necessity for the taxpayer to be represented by a lawyer or other tax adviser). Commissioners rather then Tax Court judges preside over these proceedings. The decisions of the Small Claims Division are not precedents for any other court decision and are not reviewable by any higher court. Proceedings can be more timely and less expensive in the Small Claims Division.

American law, following English law, is frequently *made* by judicial decisions. Under the doctrine of *stare decisis*, each case (except in the Small Claims Division) has precedential value for future cases with the same controlling set of facts. Most Federal and state appellate court decisions and some decisions of trial courts are published. Almost three and one-half million judicial opinions have been published in the United States; over 30,000 cases are published each year.[22] Published court decisions are organized by jurisdiction (Federal or state) and level of court (trial or appellate).

20. § 6110(j)(3). Post-1984 TAMs may be substantial authority for purposes of avoiding the accuracy-related penalty. Notice 90–20, 1990–1 C.B. 328.

21. These are unofficially published by the publishers listed in Concept Summary 2–1. Such internal memoranda for post-1984 may be substantial authority for purposes of the accuracy-related penalty. Notice 90–20, 1990–1 C.B. 328.

22. Jacobstein and Mersky, *Fundamentals of Legal Research*, 5th ed. (Mineola, N.Y.: The Foundation Press, 1990).

Trial Courts. The various trial courts (courts of original jurisdiction) differ in several respects:

- *Number of courts.* There is only one Claims Court and only one Tax Court, but there are many Federal District Courts. The taxpayer does not select the District Court that will hear the dispute but must sue in the one that has jurisdiction.
- *Number of judges.* Each District Court has only 1 judge, the Claims Court has 16 judges, and the Tax Court has 19 judges. In the case of the Tax Court, however, the entire court will decide a case (the court sits *en banc*) only when more important or novel tax issues are involved. Most cases will be heard and decided by one of the 19 judges.
- *Location.* The Claims Court meets most often in Washington, D.C., whereas a District Court meets at a prescribed seat for the particular district. Each state has at least one District Court, and many of the more populous states have more than one. Therefore, the inconvenience and expense of traveling for the taxpayer and his or her counsel (present with many suits in the Claims Court) are largely eliminated. Although the Tax Court is officially based in Washington, D.C., the various judges travel to different parts of the country and hear cases at predetermined locations and dates. Although this procedure eases the distance problem for the taxpayer, it may mean a delay before the case comes to trial and is decided.
- *Jurisdiction of the Claims Court.* The Claims Court has jurisdiction in judgment upon any claim against the United States that is based upon the Constitution, any Act of Congress, or any regulation of an executive department. Thus, the Claims Court hears nontax litigation as well as tax cases. This forum appears to be more favorable for issues having an equitable or pro-business orientation (as opposed to purely technical issues) and for those requiring extensive discovery.[23]

FIGURE 2–1
Federal Judicial System

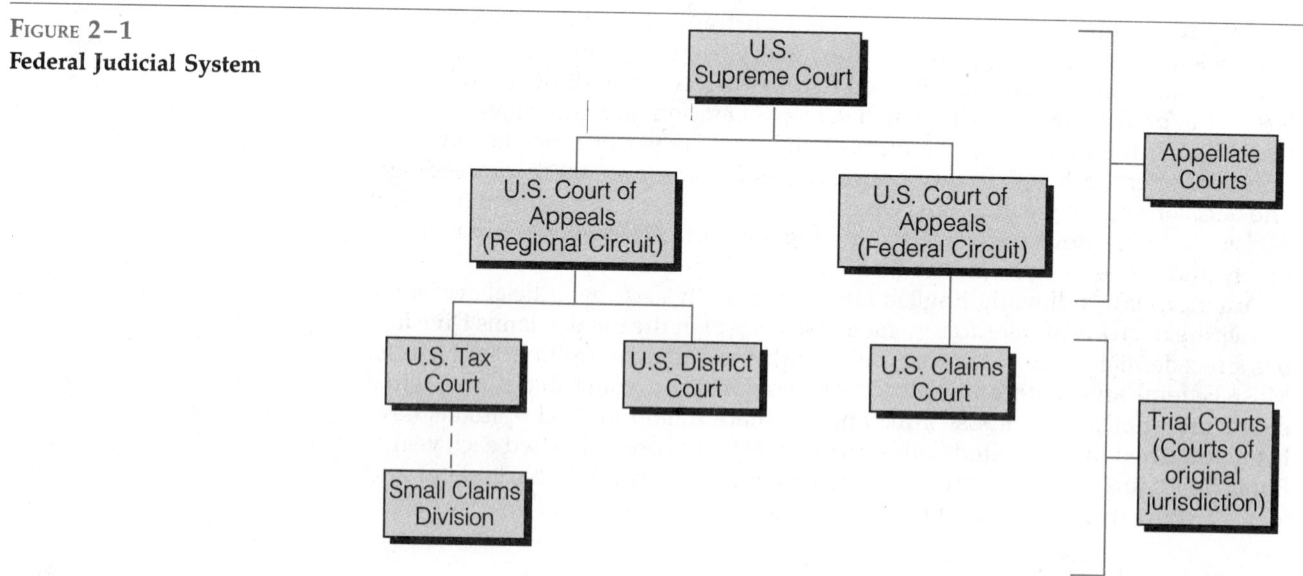

23. T. D. Peyser, "The Case for Selecting the Claims Court to Litigate a Federal Tax Liability," *The Tax Executive* (Winter 1988): 149.

- *Jurisdiction of the Tax Court and District Courts.* The Tax Court hears only tax cases and is the most popular forum. The District Courts hear nontax litigation as well as tax cases. Some Tax Court justices have been appointed from IRS or Treasury Department positions. For these reasons, some people suggest that the Tax Court has more expertise in tax matters.
- *Jury trial.* The only court in which a taxpayer can obtain a jury trial is a District Court. But since juries can only decide questions of fact and not questions of law, even taxpayers who choose the District Court route often do not request a jury trial. In that event, the judge will decide all issues. Note that a District Court decision is controlling only in the district in which the court has jurisdiction.
- *Payment of deficiency.* For the Claims Court or a District Court to have jurisdiction, the taxpayer must pay the tax deficiency assessed by the IRS and sue for a refund. A taxpayer who wins (assuming no successful appeal by the Government) recovers the tax paid plus appropriate interest. For the Tax Court, however, jurisdiction is usually obtained without first paying the assessed tax deficiency. In the event the taxpayer loses in the Tax Court (and does not appeal or an appeal is unsuccessful), the deficiency must be paid with appropriate interest. With the elimination of the deduction for personal (consumer) interest, the Tax Court route of delaying payment of the deficiency can become expensive. For example, to earn 11 percent after tax, a taxpayer with a 31 percent marginal tax rate would have to earn 15.94 percent. By paying the tax, a taxpayer limits underpayment interest and penalties on underpayment interest.
- *Termination of running of interest.* A taxpayer who selects the Tax Court may deposit a cash bond to stop the running of interest. The taxpayer must deposit both the amount of the tax and any accrued interest. If the taxpayer wins and the deposited amount is returned, the Government does not pay interest on the deposit.
- *Appeals.* Appeals from a District Court or a Tax Court decision are to the appropriate U.S. Court of Appeals. Appeals from the Claims Court go to the Court of Appeals for the Federal Circuit.

CONCEPT SUMMARY 2–2
FEDERAL JUDICIAL SYSTEM: TRIAL COURTS

Issue	U.S. Tax Court	U.S. District Court	U.S. Claims Court
Number of judges per court	19	1	16
Payment of deficiency before trial	No	Yes	Yes
Jury trial available	No	Yes	No
Types of disputes	Tax cases only	Most criminal and civil issues	Claims against the United States
Jurisdiction	Nationwide	Location of taxpayer	Nationwide
IRS acquiescence policy	Yes	No	No
Appeal route	U.S. Court of Appeals	U.S. Court of Appeals	U.S. Court of Appeals for the Federal Circuit

- *Decision for taxpayer versus IRS.* The won and loss record of the IRS and taxpayers in the trial courts and the appellate courts is summarized below. Although a taxpayer has little chance of a clear decision in the Tax Court, a split decision is more likely in that court.

	Decided in Favor of IRS	Decided in Favor of Taxpayer	Split Decision
U.S. Tax Court			
1989	46.4%	3.9%	49.7%
1988	45.8%	5.0%	49.2%
District Courts			
1989	78.8%	17.7%	3.5%
1988	81.5%	15.1%	3.4%
Claims Court			
1989	89.1%	8.2%	2.7%
1988	93.4%	2.4%	4.2%
Courts of Appeals			
1989	88.5%	9.5%	2.0%
1988	75.8%	17.4%	6.8%
Supreme Court			
1989	66.7%	33.3%	0%
1988	66.7%	33.3%	0%

Appellate Courts. The losing party can appeal a trial court decision to a Circuit Court of Appeals. The 11 geographical circuits, the circuit for the District of Columbia, and the Federal Circuit[24] are listed in Concept Summary 2–3. The appropriate circuit for an appeal depends upon where the litigation originated. For example, an appeal from New York goes to the Second Circuit.

If the Government loses at the trial court level (District Court, Tax Court, or Claims Court), it need not (frequently does not) appeal. The fact that an appeal is not made, however, does not indicate that the IRS agrees with the result and will not litigate similar issues in the future. The IRS may decide not to appeal for a number of reasons. First, the current litigation load may be heavy, and as a consequence, the IRS may decide that available personnel should be assigned to other, more important cases. Second, the IRS may determine that this is not a good case to appeal. Perhaps the taxpayer is in a sympathetic position or the facts are particularly strong in his or her favor. In that event, the IRS may wait to test the legal issues involved with a taxpayer who has a much weaker case. Third, if the appeal is from a District Court or the Tax Court, the Court of Appeals of jurisdiction could have some bearing on whether the IRS chooses to go forward with an appeal. Based on past experience and precedent, the IRS may conclude that the chance for success on a particular issue might be more promising in another Court of Appeals. If so, the IRS will wait for a similar case to arise in a different jurisdiction.

With the establishment of the Federal Circuit at the appellate level, a taxpayer has an alternative forum to the Court of Appeals of his or her home circuit for the appeal. Appeals from both the Tax Court and the District Court go to a taxpayer's home circuit. Now, when a particular circuit has issued an adverse

24. The Court of Appeals for the Federal Circuit was created, effective October 1, 1982, by P.L. 97–164(4/2/82) to hear decisions appealed from the Claims Court.

decision, the taxpayer may wish to select the Claims Court route, since any appeal will be to the Federal Circuit.

District Courts, the Tax Court, and the Claims Court must abide by the *precedents* set by the Court of Appeals of jurisdiction. A particular Court of Appeals need not follow the decisions of another Court of Appeals. All courts, however, must follow the decisions of the U.S. Supreme Court.

Because the Tax Court is a national court (it hears and decides cases from all parts of the country), the observation made in the previous paragraph has caused problems. For many years, the Tax Court followed a policy of deciding cases based on what it thought the result should be, even though its decision might be appealed to a Court of Appeals that had previously decided a similar case differently. A number of years ago this policy was changed in the *Golsen*[25] decision. Now the Tax Court will decide a case as it feels the law should be applied *only* if the Court of Appeals of appropriate jurisdiction has not yet passed on the issue or has previously decided a similar case in accord with the Tax Court's decision. If the Court of Appeals of appropriate jurisdiction has previously held otherwise, the Tax Court will conform under the *Golsen* rule even though it disagrees with the holding.

EXAMPLE 3

Taxpayer T lives in Texas and sues in the Tax Court on Issue A. The Fifth Court of Appeals is the appellate court of appropriate jurisdiction. The Fifth Court of Appeals has already decided, in a case based on similar facts and involving a different taxpayer, that Issue A should be resolved against the Government. Although the Tax Court feels that the Fifth Court of Appeals is wrong, under its *Golsen* policy it will render

CONCEPT SUMMARY 2–3
JURISDICTION OF THE COURTS OF APPEALS

First
Maine
Massachusetts
New Hampshire
Rhode Island
Puerto Rico

Second
Connecticut
New York
Vermont

Third
Delaware
New Jersey
Pennsylvania
Virgin Islands

District of Columbia
Washington, D.C.

Fourth
Maryland
North Carolina
South Carolina
Virginia
West Virginia

Fifth
Canal Zone
Louisiana
Mississippi
Texas

Sixth
Kentucky
Michigan
Ohio
Tennessee

Seventh
Illinois
Indiana
Wisconsin

Eighth
Arkansas
Iowa
Minnesota
Missouri
Nebraska
North Dakota
South Dakota

Ninth
Alaska
Arizona
California
Hawaii
Idaho
Montana
Nevada
Oregon
Washington
Guam

Tenth
Colorado
Kansas
New Mexico
Oklahoma
Utah
Wyoming

Eleventh
Alabama
Florida
Georgia

Federal
U.S. Claims Court

25. *Jack E. Golsen*, 54 T.C. 742 (1970).

judgment for T. Shortly thereafter, Taxpayer U, a resident of New York, in a comparable case, sues in the Tax Court on Issue A. Assume that the Second Court of Appeals, the appellate court of appropriate jurisdiction, has never expressed itself on Issue A. Presuming the Tax Court has not reconsidered its position on Issue A, it will decide against Taxpayer U. Thus, it is entirely possible for two taxpayers suing in the same court to end up with opposite results merely because they live in different parts of the country. ◆

Appeal to the U.S. Supreme Court is by Writ of Certiorari. If the Court accepts jurisdiction, it will grant the Writ (*Cert. Granted*). Most often, it will deny jurisdiction (*Cert. Denied*). For whatever reason or reasons, the Supreme Court rarely hears tax cases. The Court usually grants certiorari to resolve a conflict among the Courts of Appeals (e.g., two or more appellate courts have assumed opposing positions on a particular issue). The granting of a Writ of Certiorari indicates that at least four members of the Supreme Court believe that the issue is of sufficient importance to be heard by the full Court.

The *role* of appellate courts is limited to a review of the record of trial compiled by the trial courts. Thus, the appellate process usually involves a determination of whether or not the trial court applied the proper law in arriving at its decision. Rarely will an appellate court disturb a lower court's fact-finding determination.

Both the Code and the Supreme Court indicate that Federal appellate courts are bound by findings of facts unless they are clearly erroneous.[26] This aspect of the appellate process is illustrated by a decision of the Court of Appeals for the District of Columbia involving whether a taxpayer was engaged in an activity for profit under § 183.[27] This appeals court specifically held that the "Tax Court's findings of facts are binding on Federal courts of appeals unless clearly erroneous." The Court applauded the Tax Court for the thoroughness of its factual inquiry but could "not place the stamp of approval upon its eventual legal outcome." In reversing and remanding the decision to the Tax Court, the appellate court said that "the language of § 183, its legislative history and the applicable Treasury regulation combine to demonstrate that the court's [Tax Court's] standard is erroneous as a matter of law." The appeals court held that this taxpayer's claims of deductibility were to be evaluated by proper legal standards.

The result of an appeal could be any of a number of possibilities. The appellate court could approve (affirm) or disapprove (reverse) the lower court's finding, or it could send the case back for further consideration (remand). When many issues are involved, a mixed result is not unusual. Thus, the lower court could be affirmed (*aff'd*) on Issue A, reversed (*rev'd*) on Issue B, and Issue C could be remanded (*rem'd*) for additional fact finding.

When more than one judge is involved in the decision-making process, disagreements are not uncommon. In addition to the majority view, one or more judges may concur (agree with the result reached but not with some or all of the reasoning) or dissent (disagree with the result). In any one case, of course, the majority view controls. But concurring and dissenting views can have an influence on other courts or, at some subsequent date when the composition of the court has changed, even on the same court.

Judicial Citations—General. Having concluded a brief description of the judicial process, it is appropriate to consider the more practical problem of the relationship of case law to tax research. As previously noted, court decisions are

---

26. §§ 7482(a) and (c). *Comm. v. Duberstein*, 60–2 USTC ¶9515, 5 AFTR2d 1626, 80 S.Ct. 1190 (USSC, 1960).

27. *Dreicer v. Comm.*, 81–2 USTC ¶9683, 48 AFTR2d 5884, 665 F.2d 1292 (CA–DC, 1981).

an important source of tax law. The ability to cite a case and to locate it is, therefore, a must in working with the tax law. Judicial citations usually follow a standard pattern: case name, volume number, reporter series, page or paragraph number, and court (where necessary).

Judicial Citations—The U.S. Tax Court. A good starting point is with the Tax Court. The Court issues two types of decisions: Regular and Memorandum. The distinction between the two involves both substance and form. In terms of substance, *Memorandum* decisions deal with situations necessitating only the application of already established principles of law. *Regular* decisions involve novel issues not previously resolved by the Court. In actual practice, however, this distinction is not always preserved. Not infrequently, Memorandum decisions will be encountered that appear to warrant Regular status and vice versa. At any rate, do not conclude that Memorandum decisions possess no value as precedents. Both represent the position of the Tax Court and, as such, can be relied upon.

Another important distinction between the Regular and Memorandum decisions issued by the Tax Court involves their form. Memorandum decisions are officially published in mimeograph form only. Regular decisions are published by the U.S. Government in a series entitled *Tax Court of the United States Reports*. Each volume of these *Reports* covers a six-month period (January 1 through June 30 and July 1 through December 31) and is given a succeeding volume number. But, as was true of the *Cumulative Bulletin*, there is usually a time lag between the date a decision is rendered and the date it appears in bound form. A temporary citation might be necessary to aid the researcher in locating a recent Regular decision. Consider, for example, the temporary and permanent citations for *James A. Barrett*, a decision filed on May 20, 1991:

Temporary Citation	*James A. Barrett*, 96 T.C. ___, No. 31 (1991). *Explanation:* Page number left blank because not yet known.
Permanent Citation	*James A Barrett*, 96 T.C. 713 (1991). *Explanation:* Page number now available.

Both citations tell us that the case will ultimately appear in Volume 96 of the *Tax Court of the United States Reports*. But until this volume is bound and made available to the general public, the page number must be left blank. Instead, the temporary citation identifies the case as being the thirty-first Regular decision issued by the Tax Court since Volume 95 ended. With this information, the decision can easily be located in either of the special Tax Court services published by Commerce Clearing House or Prentice-Hall. Once Volume 96 is released, the permanent citation can be substituted and the number of the case dropped.

Before 1943, the Tax Court was called the Board of Tax Appeals, and its decisions were published as the *United States Board of Tax Appeals Reports* (B.T.A.). These 47 volumes cover the period from 1924 to 1942. For example, the citation *Karl Pauli*, 11 B.T.A. 784 (1928) refers to the eleventh volume of the *Board of Tax Appeals Reports*, page 784, issued in 1928.

One further distinction between Regular and Memorandum decisions of the Tax Court involves the IRS procedure of *acquiescence* ("A" or "Acq.") or *nonacquiescence* ("NA" or "Nonacq."). If the IRS loses in a Regular decision, it will usually indicate whether it agrees or disagrees with the result reached by the Court. The acquiescence or nonacquiescence will be published in the *Internal Revenue Bulletin* and the *Cumulative Bulletin*. The procedure is not followed for Memorandum decisions or for the decisions of other courts. The IRS can retroactively revoke an acquiescence. The IRS also sometimes announces that it will *or* will not follow a decision of another Federal court on similar facts. Such an announcement is not considered to be an acquiescence or nonacquiescence.

Most often the IRS issues nonacquiescences to Tax Court decisions that are not appealed. A nonacquiescence provides a warning to taxpayers that a similar case cannot be settled administratively. A taxpayer will incur fees and expenses even though the IRS may be unwilling to litigate a similar case.[28]

Although Memorandum decisions are not published by the U.S. Government, they are published by Commerce Clearing House (CCH) and Prentice-Hall (P-H). Consider, for example, the three different ways that *Jack D. Carr* can be cited:

> *Jack D. Carr,* T.C. Memo. 1985–19
> The 19th Memorandum decision issued by the Tax Court in 1985.
>
> *Jack D. Carr,* 49 TCM 507
> Page 507 of Vol. 49 of the CCH *Tax Court Memorandum Decisions.*
>
> *Jack D. Carr,* P-H T.C.Mem.Dec. ¶85, 019
> Paragraph 85,019 of the P-H *T.C. Memorandum Decisions.*

Note that the third citation contains the same information as the first. Thus, ¶85,019 indicates the following information about the case: year 1985, 19th T.C.Memo. decision.[29] Although the Prentice-Hall citation does not specifically include a volume number, the paragraph citation indicates that the decision can be found in the 1985 volume of the P-H Memorandum decision service.

Judicial Citations—The U.S. District Court, Claims Court, and Courts of Appeals. District Court, Claims Court, Court of Appeals, and Supreme Court decisions dealing with Federal tax matters are reported in both the CCH *U.S. Tax Cases* (USTC), and the P-H *American Federal Tax Reports* (AFTR) series.

Federal District Court decisions, dealing with *both* tax and nontax issues, also are published by West Publishing Company in its *Federal Supplement Series.* The following examples illustrate three different ways of citing a District Court case:

> *Simons-Eastern Co. v. U.S.,* 73–1 USTC ¶9279 (D.Ct.Ga., 1972).
>
> *Explanation:* Reported in the first volume of the *U.S. Tax Cases* (USTC) published by Commerce Clearing House for calendar year 1973 (73–1) and located at paragraph 9279 (¶9279).
>
> *Simons-Eastern Co. v. U.S.,* 31 AFTR2d 73–640 (D.Ct.Ga., 1972).
>
> *Explanation:* Reported in the 31st volume of the second series of the *American Federal Tax Reports* (AFTR2d) published by Prentice-Hall and beginning on page 640. The "73" preceding the page number indicates the year the case was published but is a designation used only in recent decisions.
>
> *Simons-Eastern Co. v. U.S.,* 354 F.Supp. 1003 (D.Ct.Ga., 1972).
>
> *Explanation:* Reported in the 354th volume of the *Federal Supplement Series* (F.Supp.) published by West Publishing Company and beginning on page 1003.

In all of the preceding citations, note that the name of the case is the same (Simons-Eastern Co. being the taxpayer), as is the reference to the Federal District Court of Georgia (D.Ct.Ga.) and the year the decision was rendered (1972).[30]

---

28. G. W. Carter, "Nonacquiescence: Winning by Losing," *Tax Notes* (September 19, 1988): 1301–1307.

29. In this text, the Prentice-Hall citation for Memorandum decisions of the U.S. Tax Court is omitted. Thus, *Jack D. Carr* would be cited as 49 TCM 507, T.C. Memo. 1985–19.

30. In this text, the case would be cited in the following form: *Simons-Eastern Co. v. U.S.,* 73–1 USTC ¶9279, 31 AFTR2d 73–640, 354 F.Supp. 1003 (D.Ct.Ga., 1972). Prentice-Hall Information Services has been acquired by Thomson Professional Publishing. While this edition continues to use the Prentice-Hall name in most instances, subsequent editions will reflect any name changes that Thomson chooses to make to the acquired Prentice-Hall publications.

Decisions of the Claims Court and the Courts of Appeals are published in the USTCs, AFTRs, and a West Publishing Company reporter called the *Federal Second Series* (F.2d). However, beginning October 1982, the Claims Court decisions are published in another West Publishing Company reporter entitled the *Claims Court Reporter*. The following examples illustrate the different forms:

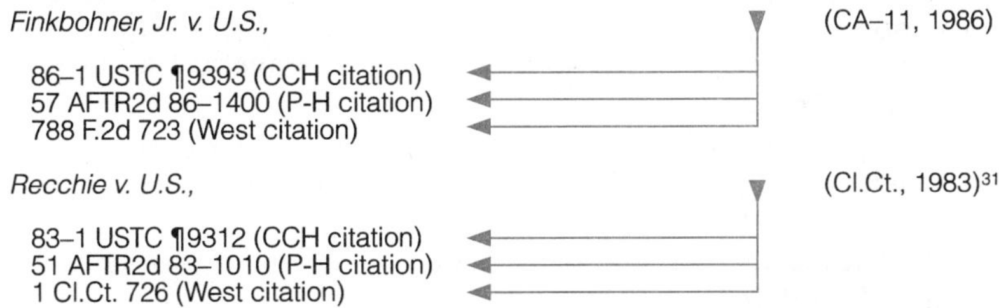

Note that *Finkbohner, Jr.* is a decision rendered by the Eleventh Court of Appeals in 1986 (CA–11, 1986), while *Recchie* was issued by the Claims Court in 1983 (Cl.Ct., 1983).

Judicial Citations—The U.S. Supreme Court. Like all other Federal tax cases (except those rendered by the Tax Court), Supreme Court decisions are published by Commerce Clearing House in the USTCs and by Prentice-Hall in the AFTRs. The U.S. Government Printing Office also publishes these decisions in the *United States Supreme Court Reports* (U.S.) as does West Publishing Company in its *Supreme Court Reporter* (S.Ct.) and the Lawyer's Co-operative Publishing Company in its *United States Reports, Lawyer's Edition* (L.Ed.). The following illustrates the different ways the same decision can be cited:

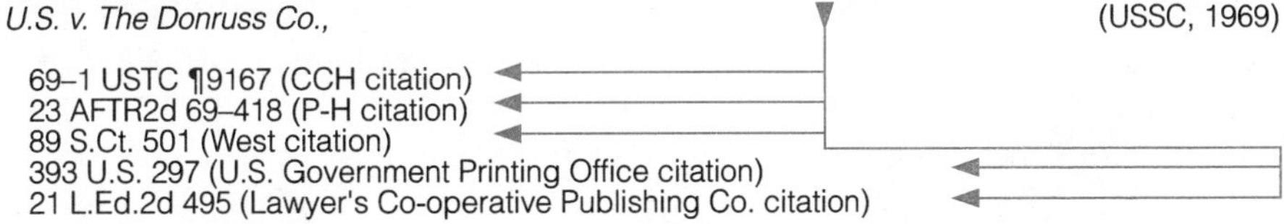

The parenthetical reference (USSC, 1969) identifies the decision as having been rendered by the U.S. Supreme Court in 1969. In this text, the citations of Supreme Court decisions will be limited to the CCH (USTC), P-H (AFTR), and West (S.Ct.) versions. For a summary, see Concept Summary 2–4.

Working with the Tax Law—Tax Research

◆

Tax research is the method by which a tax practitioner or professor determines the best available solution to a situation that possesses tax consequences. In other words, it is the process of finding a competent and professional conclusion to a tax problem. The problem may originate from completed or proposed transactions. In the case of a completed transaction, the objective of the research is to determine the tax result of what has already taken place. For example, was the expenditure incurred by the taxpayer deductible or not deductible for tax purposes? When dealing with proposed transactions, the tax research process is directed toward the determination of possible tax consequences. To the extent that tax research leads to a choice of alternatives or otherwise influences the future actions of the taxpayer, it becomes the key to effective tax planning.

31. Before October 1, 1982, the Claims Court was called the Court of Claims.

Tax research involves the following procedures:

- Identifying and refining the problem.
- Locating the appropriate tax law sources.
- Assessing the validity of the tax law sources.
- Arriving at the solution or at alternative solutions with due consideration given to nontax factors.
- Effectively communicating the solution to the taxpayer or the taxpayer's representative.
- Following up on the solution (where appropriate) in light of new developments.

These procedures are diagrammed in Figure 2–2. The broken lines reflect the steps of particular interest when tax research is directed toward proposed, rather than completed, transactions.

Identifying the Problem

Problem identification must start with a compilation of the relevant facts involved.[32] In this regard, *all* of the facts that may have a bearing on the problem must be gathered because any omission could modify the solution to be reached. To illustrate, consider what appears to be a very simple problem.

CONCEPT SUMMARY 2–4
JUDICIAL SOURCES

Court	Location	Authority
U.S. Supreme Court	S.Ct. Series (West) U.S. Series (U.S. Gov't.) L.Ed. (Lawyer's Co-op.) AFTR (P-H) USTC (CCH)	Highest authority
U.S. Courts of Appeal	Federal 2d (West) AFTR (P-H) USTC (CCH)	Next highest appellate court
Tax Court (Regular decisions)	U.S. Govt. Printing Office PH/CCH separate services	Highest trial court*
Tax Court (Memorandum decisions)	P-H T.C. Memo (P-H) TCM (CCH)	Less authority than regular T.C. decision
U.S. Claims Court	Claims Court Reporter (West) AFTR (P-H) USTC (CCH)	Similar authority as Tax Court
U.S. District Courts	F.Supp. Series (West) AFTR (P-H) USTC (CCH)	Lowest trial court
Small Claims Division of Tax Court	Not published	No precedent value

*Theoretically, the Tax Court, Claims Court, and District Courts are on the same level of authority. But some people believe that since the Tax Court hears and decides tax cases from all parts of the country (it is a national court), its decisions may be more authoritative than a Claims Court or District Court decision.

32. For an excellent discussion of the critical role of facts in carrying out tax research, see Ray M. Sommerfeld and G. Fred Streuling, *Tax Research Techniques*, Tax Study No. 5 (New York: The American Institute of Certified Public Accountants, 1981), Chapter 2.

EXAMPLE 4

Early in December, father, F, and mother, M, review their financial and tax situation with their son, S, and daughter-in-law, D. Both S and D are age 21. S, a student at a nearby university, owns some publicly traded stock that he inherited from his grandmother. S believes that the stock will decline significantly in value over the next several weeks and may never regain its current value. A current sale would result in approximately $7,000 of gross income. At this point, F and M provide about 55% of the support of S and D. Although neither is now employed, S has earned $960 and D has earned $900. The problem: Should the stock be sold, and would the sale prohibit F and M from claiming S and D as dependents? ◆

Refining the Problem

Initial reaction is that F and M in Example 4 could *not* claim S and D as dependents if the stock is sold, since S would then have earned more than the exemption amount under § 151(d).[33] However, S is a full-time student, and § 151(c)(1)(B) allows a son or daughter who is a full-time student and is under age 24 to earn more than the exemption amount without penalizing the parents with the loss of the dependency exemption. Thus, S could sell the stock without penalizing the parents with respect to the gross income test. However, the $7,000 income from the sale of the stock might lead to the failure of the greater than 50 percent support test, depending on how much S spends for his (or D's) support.

Assume, however, that further fact gathering reveals the following additional information:

- S does not really need to spend the proceeds from the sale of the stock.
- S receives a sizable portion of his own support from a scholarship.

With these new facts, additional research leads to § 152(d) and Reg. § 1.152–1(c), which indicate that a scholarship received by a student is not included for

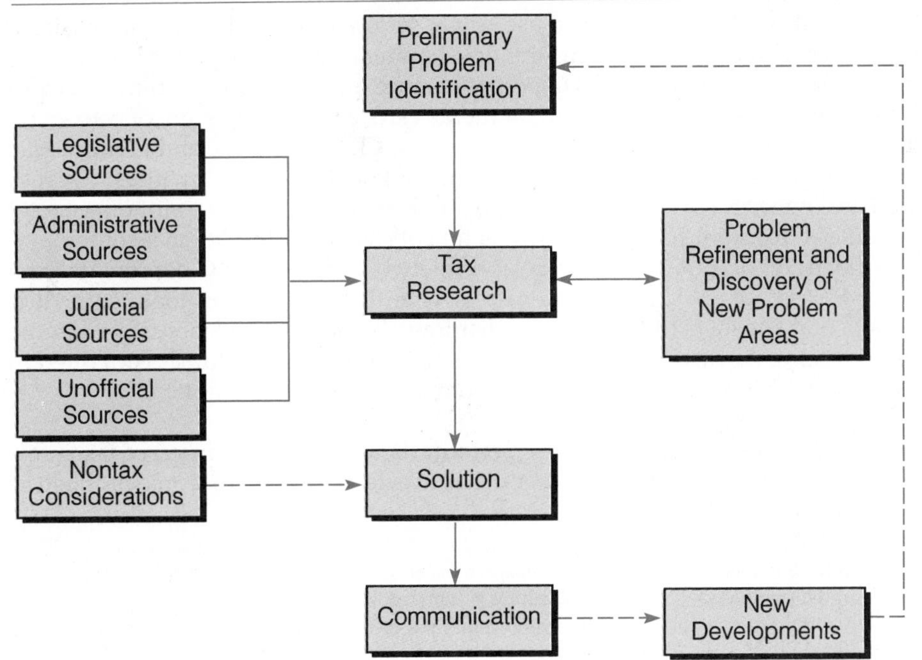

FIGURE 2–2
Tax Research Process

33. See the related discussion in Chapter 3.

purposes of computing whether the parents furnished more than one-half of the child's support. Further, if S does not spend the proceeds from the sale of stock, the unexpended amount is not counted for purposes of the support test. Thus, it appears that the parents would not be denied the dependency exemptions for S and D.

Locating the Appropriate Tax Law Sources

Once the problem is clearly defined, what is the next step? Although this is a matter of individual judgment, most tax research begins with the index volume of the tax service. If the problem is not complex, the researcher may bypass the tax service and turn directly to the Internal Revenue Code and the Treasury Regulations. For the beginner, the latter procedure saves time and will solve many of the more basic problems. If the researcher does not have a personal copy of the Code or Regulations, resorting to the appropriate volume(s) of a tax service will be necessary.[34] The major tax services available are as follows:

Standard Federal Tax Reporter, Commerce Clearing House.

Federal Taxes, Prentice-Hall (before acquisition mentioned in footnote 30).

United States Tax Reporter, Research Institute of America (entitled Federal Taxes prior to July, 1992).

Tax Coordinator, Research Institute of America.

Tax Management Portfolios, Bureau of National Affairs.

Rabkin and Johnson, *Federal Income, Gift and Estate Taxation*, Matthew Bender, Inc.

Bender's Federal Tax Service, Matthew Bender, Inc.

Mertens Law of Federal Income Taxation, Callaghan and Co.

Working with the Tax Services. In this text, it is not feasible to teach the use of any particular tax service; this can be learned only by practice.[35] However, several important observations about the use of tax services cannot be overemphasized. First, never forget to check for current developments. The main text of any service is not revised frequently enough to permit reliance on that portion as the *latest* word on any subject. Where current developments can be found depends, of course, on which service is being used. Both the Commerce Clearing House and Prentice-Hall (now RIA) services contain a special volume devoted to current matters. Second, when dealing with a tax service synopsis of a Treasury Department pronouncement or a judicial decision, remember there is no substitute for the original source.

To illustrate, do not base a conclusion solely on a tax service's commentary on *Simons-Eastern Co. v. U.S.*[36] If the case is vital to the research, look it up. It is possible that the facts of the case are distinguishable from those involved in the problem being researched. This is not to say that the case synopsis contained in the tax service is wrong; it might just be misleading or incomplete.

Tax Periodicals. The various tax periodicals are another source of tax information. The best way to locate a journal article pertinent to a tax problem is

---

34. Several of the major tax services publish paperback editions of the Code and Treasury Regulations that can be purchased at modest prices. These editions are usually revised twice each year. For an annotated and abridged version of the Code and Regulations that is published annually, see James E. Smith, *West's Internal Revenue Code of 1986 and Treasury Regulations: Annotated and Selected* (St. Paul, Minn.: West Publishing Company, 1992).

35. The representatives of the various tax services are prepared to provide the users of their services with printed booklets and individual instruction on the use of the materials.

36. Refer to Footnote 30.

through Commerce Clearing House's *Federal Tax Articles*. This three-volume service includes a subject index, a Code Section number index, and an author's index. The P-H (now RIA) tax service also has a topical "Index to Tax Articles" section that is organized using the P-H paragraph index system.

The following are some of the more useful tax periodicals:

The Journal of Taxation
Warren, Gorham and Lamont
210 South Street
Boston, MA 02111

Tax Law Review
Warren, Gorham and Lamont
210 South Street
Boston, MA 02111

Trusts and Estates
Communication Channels, Inc.
6255 Barfield Road
Atlanta, GA 30328

Oil and Gas Tax Quarterly
Matthew Bender & Co.
235 East 45th Street
New York, NY 10017

The International Tax Journal
Panel Publishers
14 Plaza Road
Greenvale, NY 11548

TAXES—The Tax Magazine
Commerce Clearing House, Inc.
4025 West Peterson Avenue
Chicago, IL 60646

National Tax Journal
21 East State Street
Columbus, OH 43215

The Tax Adviser
1211 Avenue of the Americas
New York, NY 10036

The Practical Accountant
1 Penn Plaza
New York, NY 10119

Estate Planning
Warren, Gorham and Lamont
210 South Street
Boston, MA 02111

Taxation for Accountants
Warren, Gorham and Lamont
210 South Street
Boston, MA 02111

The Tax Executive
1300 North 17th Street
Arlington, VA 22209

Journal of Corporate Taxation
Warren, Gorham and Lamont
210 South Street
Boston, MA 02111

Journal of Taxation for Individuals
Warren, Gorham and Lamont
210 South Street
Boston, MA 02111

The Tax Lawyer
American Bar Association
1800 M Street, N.W.
Washington, DC 20036

Journal of the American Taxation Association
American Accounting Association
5717 Bessie Drive
Sarasota, FL 34233

Tax Notes
6830 Fairfax Drive
Arlington, VA 22213

Assessing the Validity of the Tax Law Sources

Once a source has been located, the next step is to assess the source in light of the problem at hand. Proper assessment involves careful interpretation of the tax law with consideration given to its relevance and validity. In connection with validity, an important step is to check for recent changes in the tax law.

Interpreting the Internal Revenue Code. The language of the Code can be extremely difficult to comprehend fully. For example, a subsection [§ 341(e)] relating to collapsible corporations contains *one* sentence of more than 450 words (twice as many as in the Gettysburg Address). Within this same subsection is another sentence of 300 words. Research has shown that in one-third of the conflicts reaching the Tax Court, the Court could not discern the intent of Congress by simply reading the statute. Yet the overriding attitude of the Tax

Court judges is that the statute comes first. Even when the statute is unworkable, the Court will not rewrite the law.[37]

One author has noted 10 common pitfalls in interpreting the Code:[38]

1. Determine the limitations and exceptions to a provision. Do not permit the language of the Code Section to carry greater or lesser weight than was intended.
2. Just because a Section fails to mention an item does not necessarily mean that the item is excluded.
3. Read definitional clauses carefully.
4. Do not overlook small words such as *and* and *or*. There is a world of difference between these two words.
5. Read the Code Section completely; do not jump to conclusions.
6. Watch out for cross-referenced and related provisions, since many Sections of the Code are interrelated.
7. At times Congress is not careful when reconciling new Code provisions with existing Sections. Conflicts among Sections, therefore, do arise.
8. Be alert for hidden definitions; terms in a particular Code Section may be defined in the same Section *or in a separate Section*.
9. Some answers may not be found in the Code; therefore, a researcher may have to consult the Regulations and/or judicial decisions.[39]
10. Take careful note of measuring words such as *less than 50%*, *more than 50%*, and *at least 80%*.

Assessing the Validity of a Treasury Regulation. It is often stated that Treasury Regulations have the force and effect of law. This statement is certainly true for most Regulations, but some judicial decisions have held a Regulation or a portion thereof invalid. Usually, when a court holds a Regulation invalid, it does so on the ground that the Regulation is contrary to the intent of Congress when it enacted a particular Code Section. Most often the courts do not question the validity of Regulations because of the belief that "the first administrative interpretation of a provision as it appears in a new act often expresses the general understanding of the times or the actual understanding of those who played an important part when the statute was drafted."[40]

Keep the following observations in mind when assessing the validity of a Regulation:

- IRS agents must give the Code and the Regulations issued thereunder equal weight when dealing with taxpayers and their representatives.
- Proposed Regulations provide a preview of future final Regulations, but they are not binding on the IRS or taxpayers.
- In a challenge, the burden of proof is on the taxpayer to show that the Regulation is wrong. However, a court may invalidate a Regulation that

37. T. L. Kirkpatrick and W. B. Pollard, "Reliance by the Tax Court on the Legislative Intent of Congress," *The Tax Executive* (Summer 1986): 358–359.

38. H. G. Wong, "Ten Common Pitfalls in Reading the Internal Revenue Code," *The Practical Accountant* (July–August 1972): 30–33.

39. The Code is silent concerning the deductibility of education expenses. Such deductibility, however, falls under the general provision of § 162(a) (the allowance for "all the ordinary and necessary expenses paid or incurred during the taxable year in carrying on any trade or business . . . "). Guidelines for deductibility of education expenses can be found in Reg. § 1.162–5, and § 274(m)(2), which imposes a restriction on expenses for travel as a form of education. See Chapter 10 for a more complete discussion.

40. *Augustus v. Comm.*, 41–1 USTC ¶9255, 26 AFTR 612, 118 F.2d 38 (CA–6, 1941).

varies from the language of the statute and has no support in the Committee Reports.

- If the taxpayer loses the challenge, the imposition of a 20 percent negligence penalty can result.[41] This accuracy-related penalty applies to any failure to make a reasonable attempt to comply with the tax law and any disregard of rules and regulations.[42]
- Final Regulations tend to be legislative, interpretative, or procedural. *Procedural* Regulations neither establish tax laws nor attempt to explain tax laws. Procedural Regulations are *housekeeping-type instructions* indicating information that taxpayers should provide the IRS as well as information about the internal management and conduct of the IRS itself.
- Some *interpretative* Regulations merely reprint or rephrase what Congress stated in the Committee Reports that were issued when the tax legislation was enacted. Such Regulations are *hard and solid* and almost impossible to overturn because they clearly reflect the intent of Congress. An interpretative Regulation is given less deference than a legislative Regulation, however. The Supreme Court has told lower courts to analyze Treasury Regulations carefully before accepting the Treasury's interpretation.[43]
- In some Code Sections, Congress has given to the *Secretary or his delegate* the authority to prescribe Regulations to carry out the details of administration or to otherwise complete the operating rules. Under such circumstances, it could almost be said that Congress is delegating its legislative powers to the Treasury Department. Regulations issued pursuant to this type of authority truly possess the force and effect of law and are often called *legislative* Regulations (e.g., consolidated return Regulations).
- Courts tend to apply a legislative reenactment doctrine. A Regulation is assumed to have received congressional approval if a particular Regulation was finalized many years earlier and Congress has not amended the Code Section pertaining to the Regulation.

Assessing the Validity of Other Administrative Sources of the Tax Law. Revenue Rulings issued by the IRS carry less weight than Treasury Department Regulations. Revenue Rulings are important, however, in that they reflect the position of the IRS on tax matters. In any dispute with the IRS on the interpretation of tax law, therefore, taxpayers should expect agents to follow the results reached in any applicable Revenue Rulings. A 1986 Tax Court decision, however, indicated that Revenue Rulings "typically do not constitute substantive authority for a position."[44] Most Revenue Rulings apply retroactively unless a specific statement indicates the extent to which a Ruling is to be applied without retroactive effect.[45]

Revenue Rulings further tell the taxpayer the IRS's reaction to certain court decisions. Recall that the IRS follows a practice of either acquiescing (agreeing) or nonacquiescing (not agreeing) with the *Regular* decisions of the Tax Court. This does not mean that a particular decision of the Tax Court is of no value if, for example, the IRS has nonacquiesced in the result. It does, however, indicate that the IRS will continue to litigate the issue involved.

---

41. §§ 6662(a) and (b)(1).

42. § 6662(c).

43. *U.S. v. Vogel Fertilizer Co.*, 82–1 USTC ¶9134, 49 AFTR2d 82–491, 102, S.Ct. 821 (USSC, 1982); *National Muffler Dealers Assn., Inc.*, 79–1 USTC ¶9264, 43 AFTR2d 79–828, 99 S.Ct. 1304 (USSC, 1979).

44. *Nelda C. Stark*, 86 T.C. 243 (1986). See also *Ann R. Neuhoff*, 75 T.C. 36 (1980). For a different opinion, however, see *Industrial Valley Bank & Trust Co.*, 66 T.C. 272 (1976).

45. Rev.Proc. 87–1, 1987–1 C.B. 503.

Assessing the Validity of Judicial Sources of the Tax Law. The judicial process as it relates to the formulation of tax law has already been described. How much reliance can be placed on a particular decision depends upon the following variables:

- The level of the court. A decision rendered by a trial court (e.g., a Federal District Court) carries less weight than one issued by an appellate court (e.g., the Fifth Court of Appeals). Unless Congress changes the Code, decisions by the U.S. Supreme Court represent the last word on any tax issue.
- The legal residence of the taxpayer. If, for example, a taxpayer lives in Texas, a decision of the Fifth Court of Appeals means more than one rendered by the Second Court of Appeals. This result occurs because any appeal from a U.S. District Court or the Tax Court would be to the Fifth Court of Appeals and not to the Second Court of Appeals.[46]
- A Tax Court Regular decision carries more weight than a Memorandum decision since the Tax Court does not consider Memorandum decisions to be binding precedents.[47] Furthermore, a Tax Court *reviewed* decision carries even more weight. All of the Tax Court judges participate in a reviewed decision.
- A Circuit Court decision where certiorari has been requested and denied by the U.S. Supreme Court carries more weight than a Circuit Court decision that was not appealed. A Circuit Court decision heard *en banc* (all the judges participate) carries more weight than a normal Circuit Court case.
- Whether the decision represents the weight of authority on the issue. In other words, is it supported by the results reached by other courts?
- The outcome or status of the decision on appeal. For example, was the decision appealed and, if so, with what result?

In connection with the last two variables, the use of a citator is invaluable to tax research.[48] Citators and their use are discussed in Appendix E.

Assessing the Validity of Other Sources. *Primary sources* of tax law include the Constitution, legislative history materials, statutes, treaties, Treasury Regulations, IRS pronouncements, and judicial decisions. In general, the IRS considers only primary sources to constitute substantial authority. However, a researcher might wish to refer to *secondary materials* such as legal periodicals, treatises, legal opinions, general counsel memoranda, technical memoranda, and written determinations. In general, secondary sources are not authority.

Until 1990, the IRS considered only primary sources to constitute substantial authority. In Notice 90–20, [49] the IRS expanded the list of substantial authority *for purposes of* the accuracy-related penalty in § 6662 to include:

> . . . applicable provisions of the Internal Revenue Code and other statutory provisions; temporary and final regulations construing such statutes; court cases; administrative pronouncements (including revenue rulings and revenue procedures); tax treaties and regulations thereunder, and Treasury Department and other official explanations of such treaties; and congressional intent as reflected in

---

46. Before October 1, 1982, an appeal from the then-named U.S. Court of Claims (the other trial court) was directly to the U.S. Supreme Court.

47. *Severino R. Nico, Jr.*, 67 T.C. 647 (1977).

48. The major citators are published by Commerce Clearing House, Prentice-Hall (now RIA), and Shepard's Citations, Inc.

49. 1990–1 C.B. 328; see also Reg. § 1.6661–3(b)(2).

> committee reports, joint explanatory statements of managers included in conference committee reports, and floor statements made prior to enactment by one of the bill's managers.
>
> [T]he Service also will treat as authority General Explanations of tax legislation prepared by the Joint Committee on Taxation (the "Bluebook"), proposed regulations, information or press releases, notices, announcements, and any other similar documents published by the Service in the Internal Revenue Bulletin. In addition, . . . the Service will treat as authority private letter rulings, technical advice memoranda, actions on decisions, and general counsel memoranda after they have been released to the public and provided they are dated after December 31, 1984 (the date that is five years prior to the general effective date of the penalty provisions of the Act).

As under former § 6661, "authority" does not include conclusions reached in treatises, legal periodicals, and opinions rendered by tax professionals.

A letter ruling or determination letter is substantial authority only to the taxpayer to whom it is issued, except as noted above with respect to the accuracy-related penalty.

Upon the completion of major tax legislation, the staff of the Joint Committee on Taxation (in consultation with the staffs of the House Ways and Means and Senate Finance Committees) often will prepare a General Explanation of the Act, commonly known as the Bluebook because of the color of its cover. The IRS will not accept this detailed explanation as having legal effect, except as noted above with respect to the accuracy-related penalty. The Bluebook does, however, provide valuable guidance to tax advisers and taxpayers until Regulations are issued, and some letter rulings and General Counsel's Memoranda of the IRS cite its explanations.

Arriving at the Solution or at Alternative Solutions

Example 4 raised the question of whether dependency exemptions for a son and a daughter-in-law would be denied to a taxpayer if some stock were sold near the end of the year. A refinement of the problem supplies additional information:

- S was a full-time student during four calendar months of the year.
- S and D anticipate filing a joint return.

Additional research leads to Reg. § 1.151–3(b), which indicates that to qualify as a student, S must be a full-time student during each of five calendar months of the year at an educational institution. Thus, proceeds from the sale of the stock by S would cause the loss of at least one dependency exemption for the parents because S's gross income would exceed the exemption amount. The parents still might be able to claim D as an exemption if the support test is met.

Section 151(c)(2) indicates that a supporting taxpayer is not permitted a dependency exemption for a married dependent if the married individual files a joint return. Initial reaction is that a joint return by S and D would be disastrous to the parents. However, more research uncovers two Revenue Rulings that provide an exception if neither the dependent nor the dependent's spouse is required to file a return but does so solely to claim a refund of tax withheld. The IRS asserts that each spouse must have gross income of less than the exemption amount.[50] Therefore, a sale of stock by S combined with filing a joint return

50. Rev.Rul. 54–567, 1954–2 C.B. 108; Rev.Rul. 65–34, 1965–1 C.B. 86.

would cause the loss of a dependency exemption for both S and D. If the stock is not sold until January, both exemptions may still be available to the parents. However, under § 151(d)(2) a personal exemption is not available to a taxpayer who can be claimed as a dependent by another taxpayer (whether actually claimed or not). Thus, if the parents can claim S and D as dependents, S and D would lose their personal exemptions on their tax return.

Even if the stock is not sold until January, a refinement of the problem provides the additional information that D earned the $900 as a self-employed cosmetics salesperson. A self-employed individual with net earnings from a business of $400 or more must file a tax return regardless of his or her gross income. Not only is a return required, but D would be responsible for self-employment taxes. The IRS could argue that since D was required to file a tax return because her net earnings exceeded $400, the parents could not claim D as a dependent. D could no longer fall within the exception that she was merely filing a return to obtain a refund of tax withheld.

Communicating Tax Research

Once satisfied that the problem has been researched adequately, the researcher may need to prepare a memo setting forth the result. The form such a memo takes could depend on a number of considerations. For example, does an employer or professor recommend a particular procedure or format for tax research memos? Is the memo to be given directly to the client or will it first go to the researcher's employer? Whatever form it takes, a good research memo should contain the following elements:

- A clear statement of the issue.
- In more complex situations, a short review of the factual pattern that raises the issue.
- A review of the tax law sources (e.g., Code, Regulations, Revenue Rulings, judicial authority).
- Any assumptions made in arriving at the solution.
- The solution recommended and the logic or reasoning supporting it.
- The references consulted in the research process.

In short, a good tax memo should tell the reader what was researched, the results of that research, and the justification for the recommendation made.[51]

WORKING WITH THE TAX LAW—TAX PLANNING

◆

Tax research and tax planning are inseparable. The *primary* purpose of effective *tax planning* is to reduce the taxpayer's total tax bill. This does not mean that the course of action selected must produce the lowest possible tax under the circumstances. The minimization of tax liability must be considered in context with the legitimate business goals of the taxpayer.

A *secondary* objective of effective tax planning is to reduce or defer the tax in the current tax year. Specifically, this objective aims to accomplish one or more of the following: eradicating the tax entirely; eliminating the tax in the current year; deferring the receipt of income; converting ordinary income into capital gains; conversion of active to passive income; conversion of passive to active expense; proliferating taxpayers (i.e., forming partnerships and corporations or

51. See Chapter 6 of the publication cited in Footnote 32.

making lifetime gifts to family members); eluding double taxation; avoiding ordinary income; or creating, increasing, or accelerating deductions. However, this second objective should be approached with considerable reservation. Although the maxim "A bird in the hand is worth two in the bush" is generally valid, in a number of cases the rule breaks down. For example, a tax election in one year may reduce taxes currently, but saddle future years with a disadvantageous tax position.

Nontax Considerations

There is an honest danger that tax motivations may take on a significance that does not correspond to the true values involved. In other words, tax considerations may impair the exercise of sound business judgment by the taxpayer. Thus, the tax planning process can become a medium through which to accomplish ends that are socially and economically objectionable. All too often, planning seems to lean toward the opposing extremes of placing either too little or too much emphasis on tax considerations. The happy medium—a balance that recognizes the significance of taxes, but not beyond the point where planning detracts from the exercise of good business judgment—turns out to be the promised land that is seldom reached.

The remark is often made that a good rule is to refrain from pursuing any course of action that would not be followed were it not for certain tax considerations. This statement is not entirely correct, but it does illustrate the desirability of preventing business logic from being *sacrificed at the altar of tax planning*. In this connection, the following comment is significant:

> The lure of a quick tax dollar is often the only justification for a transaction that might have been accomplished with much sounder economic results and equivalent tax savings if more careful and deliberate consideration had been given to the problem. Certainly in this atmosphere of the tax-controlled economy a very heavy obligation is cast upon the tax adviser to give serious consideration as to whether a proposed action achieves a desirable economic result apart from tax savings or whether the immediate tax advantages may be more than offset by later economic or personal disadvantage. We cannot afford to develop successful cures that are killing our patients.[52]

Tax Avoidance and Tax Evasion

A fine line exists between legal tax planning and illegal tax planning—tax avoidance versus tax evasion. *Tax avoidance* is merely tax minimization through legal techniques. In this sense, tax avoidance is the proper objective of all tax planning. Tax evasion, while also aimed at the elimination or reduction of taxes, connotes the use of subterfuge and fraud as a means to an end. Popular usage—probably because of the common goals involved—has so linked these two concepts that many individuals are no longer aware of the true distinctions between them. Consequently, some taxpayers have been deterred from properly taking advantage of planning possibilities. The now classic words of Judge Learned Hand in *Commissioner v. Newman* reflect the true values the taxpayer should have:

---

52. Norris Darrell, "Some Responsibilities of the Tax Adviser in Regard to Tax Minimization Devices," *Proceedings of the New York University Eighth Annual Institute on Federal Taxation* (Albany, N.Y.: Matthew Bender & Co., 1950), pp. 988–989.

For a more detailed discussion of tax planning, see Norwood, *Federal Taxation: Research, Planning and Procedure* (Englewood Cliffs, N.J.: Prentice-Hall, 1990), Chapter 6.

> Over and over again courts have said that there is nothing sinister in so arranging one's affairs as to keep taxes as low as possible. Everybody does so, rich or poor; and all do right, for nobody owes any public duty to pay more than the law demands: taxes are enforced extractions, not voluntary contributions. To demand more in the name of morals is mere cant.[53]

Follow-up Procedures

Because tax planning usually involves a proposed (as opposed to a completed) transaction, it is predicated upon the continuing validity of the advice based upon the tax research. A change in the tax law (either legislative, administrative, or judicial) could alter the original conclusion. Additional research may be necessary to test the solution in light of current developments (refer to the broken lines at the right in Figure 2–2).

Tax Planning—A Practical Application

Returning to the facts of Example 4, what could be done to protect the dependency exemptions for the parents? If S and D were to refrain from filing a joint return, both could be claimed by the parents. This result assumes that the stock is not sold.

An obvious tax planning tool is the installment method. Could the securities be sold using the installment method under § 453 so that most of the gain is deferred into the next year? Under the installment method, certain gains may be postponed and recognized as the cash proceeds are received. The problem is that the installment method is not available for stock traded on an established securities market.[54]

A little more research, however, indicates that S can sell the stock and postpone the recognition of gain until the following year by selling short an equal number of substantially identical shares and covering the short sale in the subsequent year with the shares originally held. Selling short means that S sells borrowed stock (substantially identical) and repays the lender with the stock held on the date of the short sale. This *short against the box* technique would allow S to protect his $7,000 profit and defer the closing of the sale until the following year.[55] Further, if the original shares had been held for the required long-term holding period before the date of the short sale, S would be able to obtain long-term capital gain treatment.[56] Thus, some research and planning would reap tax savings for this family. Note the critical role of obtaining the correct facts in attempting to resolve the proper strategy for the taxpayers.

Throughout this text, most chapters include observations on Tax Planning Considerations. Such observations are not all-inclusive but are intended to illustrate some of the ways in which the material covered can be effectively utilized to minimize taxes.

Computer-Assisted Tax Research

The computer is being used more and more frequently in the day-to-day practice of tax professionals, students, and educators. Many software vendors offer tax

---

53. *Comm. v. Newman*, 47–1 USTC ¶9175, 35 AFTR 857, 159 F.2d 848 (CA–2, 1947).
54. See Chapter 18 for a discussion of installment sales.
55. §§ 1233(a) and 1233(b)(2). See Chapter 16 for a discussion of short sales.
56. Long-term capital gains may receive preferential tax rate treatment. In addition, if S had capital losses from other transactions, the capital gains and capital losses could be offset. See the discussion in Chapter 16.

return software programs for individual, corporate, partnership, and fiduciary returns. The use of computers, however, is not limited to batch-processed tax returns and computer timesharing for quantitative tax and problem-solving planning and calculations.

The microcomputer has become the revolutionary tool of the present—much as the electronic calculator did in the 1970s. Electronic spreadsheets are being used to replace the 14-column worksheet. The electronic spreadsheet approach can be used for retirement planning, 1040 projections, real estate projections, partnership allocations, consolidated tax return problems, compensation planning—wherever projections and calculations are needed. Many public accounting firms use internally prepared tax-related programs. Microcomputer software is available for estate planning calculations.

LEXIS, a computerized legal data bank from Mead Data Central, has been available since 1973 as a complement to the conventional research approach (available in many of the more than 100 graduate tax programs). WESTLAW, a competitive system from West Publishing Company, has been operational since 1975. Commerce Clearing House's legal data base is called ACCESS. Note, however, that WESTLAW, LEXIS, and ACCESS are actually document retrieval systems that cannot interpret the law.

Users have access to these computerized data banks through special terminals and long-distance telephone lines. A user selects key words, phrases, or numbers and types the search request on the keyboard of the terminal. A display screen then shows the full text or portions of the various documents containing the words, phrases, or numbers in the search request. A printer can be used to obtain hard copy of any documents or portions of a document. For example, a researcher can obtain the decisions of a particular judge or court over a specified time period. It is also possible to access judicial opinions containing specific words or phrases of statutory language. These computer-assisted tax systems can be used as a citator by collecting all judicial decisions that have cited a particular decision or statute as well as all decisions that have a specific combination of two or more earlier decisions or statutes.

Computer-assisted tax research is useful in searching for facts because human indexing centers on legal theories rather than fact patterns. Computer searching also is useful in finding new court decisions not yet in the printed indexes. Because computer searching probably does not find as many relevant cases as manual searching does, a combination of manual and computer searching can be quite effective.[57]

Problem Materials

Discussion Questions

1. Judicial decisions interpreting a provision of the Internal Revenue Code of 1939 or 1954 are no longer of any value in view of the enactment of the Internal Revenue Code of 1986. Assess the validity of this statement.

57. See p. 437 of the publication cited in Footnote 22; Thomas and Weinstein, *Computer-Assisted Legal and Tax Research* (Paramus, N.J.: Prentice-Hall, 1986); and Chapter 13 of W. A. Raabe, G. E. Whittenburg, and J. C. Bost, *West's Federal Tax Research*, 2d ed. (St. Paul, Minn.: West Publishing Co., 1990).

2. The Revenue Reconciliation Act of 1990 became part of the Internal Revenue Code of 1986. Explain this statement.
3. Where does tax legislation normally originate?
4. Why are Committee Reports of Congress important as a source of tax law?
5. Why are certain Code Section numbers missing from the Internal Revenue Code (e.g., §§ 6, 7, 8, 9, 10)?
6. If a treaty overrides a tax law and the taxpayer fails to disclose this position on the tax return, what is the penalty for failure to disclose?
7. Explain how Regulations are arranged. How would a proposed Regulation under § 66 be cited?
8. Distinguish between legislative, interpretative, and procedural Regulations.
9. Distinguish between:

   a. Treasury Regulations and Revenue Rulings.
   b. Revenue Rulings and Revenue Procedures.
   c. Revenue Rulings and letter rulings.
   d. Letter rulings and determination letters.

10. Rank the following items from the highest authority to the lowest in the Federal tax law system:

    a. Interpretative Regulation.
    b. Legislative Regulation.
    c. Letter ruling.
    d. Revenue Procedure.
    e. Internal Revenue Code.
    f. Proposed Regulation.

11. Interpret each of the following citations:

    a. Rev.Rul. 65–235, 1965–2 C.B. 88.
    b. Rev.Proc. 87–56, 1987–2 C.B. 674.
    c. Ltt.Rul. 9046036.

12. You find a 1992 letter ruling in which the factual situation is identical to the approach you wish to take. Can you rely on this letter ruling?
13. Discuss the two major types of letter rulings.
14. Does the government publish letter rulings?
15. **a.** What are Treasury Decisions (TDs)?
    b. What purpose do they serve?
    c. Where are they published?
16. What are the major differences between letter rulings and determination letters?
17. Summarize the trial and appellate court system for Federal tax litigation.
18. Which of the following statements would be considered advantages of the Small Claims Division of the Tax Court?

    a. Appeal to the Court of Appeals for the Federal Circuit is possible.
    b. A hearing of a deficiency of $11,200 is considered on a timely basis.
    c. Taxpayer can handle the litigation without using a lawyer or certified public accountant.
    d. Taxpayer can use other Small Claims Division decisions for precedential value.
    e. The actual hearing is held on an informal basis.
    f. Travel time will probably be reduced.

19. List an advantage and a disadvantage of using the U.S. Tax Court as the trial court for Federal tax litigation.
20. List an advantage and a disadvantage of using a U.S. District Court as the trial court for Federal tax litigation.
21. List an advantage and a disadvantage of using the U.S. Claims Court as the trial court for Federal tax litigation.

22. A taxpayer lives in Michigan. In a controversy with the IRS, the taxpayer loses at the trial court level. Describe the appeal procedure under the following different assumptions:

    a. The trial court was the Small Claims Division of the U.S. Tax Court.
    b. The trial court was the U.S. Tax Court.
    c. The trial court was a U.S. District Court.
    d. The trial court was the U.S. Claims Court.

23. Suppose the U.S. Government loses a tax case in the U.S. District Court of Idaho but does not appeal the result. What does the failure to appeal signify?
24. Because the U.S. Tax Court is a national court, it always decides the same issue in a consistent manner. Assess the validity of this statement.
25. For the U.S. Tax Court, U.S. District Court, and the U.S. Claims Court, determine the following:

    a. Number of judges per court.
    b. Availability of a jury trial.
    c. Whether the deficiency must be paid before the trial.

26. A taxpayer from a U.S. District Court in which of the following states could appeal the decision to the Fifth Court of Appeals?

    a. Arkansas.
    b. Arizona.
    c. Alabama.
    d. Maine.
    e. None of the above.

27. Explain the fact-finding determination of a Federal Court of Appeals.
28. What is the Supreme Court's policy on hearing tax cases?
29. In assessing the validity of a prior court decision, discuss the significance of the following on the taxpayer's issue:

    a. The decision was rendered by the U.S. District Court of Wyoming. Taxpayer lives in Wyoming.
    b. The decision was rendered by the U.S. Claims Court. Taxpayer lives in Wyoming.
    c. The decision was rendered by the Second Court of Appeals. Taxpayer lives in California.
    d. The decision was rendered by the U.S. Supreme Court.
    e. The decision was rendered by the U.S. Tax Court. The IRS has acquiesced in the result.
    f. Same as (e) except that the IRS has issued a nonacquiescence as to the result.

30. Where can a researcher locate a 1989 U.S. District Court decision?
31. What is the difference between a Regular and a Memorandum decision of the U.S. Tax Court?
32. The IRS may acquiesce or nonacquiesce to what court decisions? Can an acquiescence be withdrawn retroactively?
33. Interpret each of the following citations:

    a. 54 T.C. 1514 (1970).
    b. 408 F.2d 117 (CA–2, 1969).
    c. 69–1 USTC ¶9319 (CA–2, 1969).
    d. 23 AFTR2d 69–1090 (CA–2, 1969).
    e. 293 F.Supp. 1129 (D.Ct., Miss., 1967).
    f. 67–1 USTC ¶9253 (D.Ct., Miss., 1967).
    g. 19 AFTR2d 647 (D.Ct., Miss., 1967).
    h. 56 S.Ct. 289 (USSC, 1935).
    i. 36–1 USTC ¶9020 (USSC, 1935).
    j. 16 AFTR 1274 (USSC, 1935).
    k. 422 F.2d 1336 (Ct.Cls., 1970).

34. Explain the following abbreviations:

a. CA–2
b. Cls.Ct.
c. *aff'd.*
d. *rev'd.*
e. *rem'd.*
f. *Cert. Denied*
g. *acq.*
h. **B.T.A.**
i. USTC
j. AFTR
k. F.2d
l. F.Supp.
m. USSC
n. S.Ct.
o. D.Ct.

35. Give the Commerce Clearing House citation for the following courts:

a. Small Claims Division of the Tax Court.
b. Federal District Court.
c. Supreme Court.
d. Claims Court.
e. Tax Court Memorandum decision.

36. Where can you locate a published decision of the U.S. Claims Court?

37. Which of the following items can probably be found in the *Cumulative Bulletin*?

a. Revenue Ruling.
b. Small Claims Division of the U.S. Tax Court decision.
c. Letter ruling.
d. Revenue Procedure.
e. Proposed Regulation.
f. District Court decision.
g. Senate Finance Committee Report.
h. Acquiescences to Tax Court decisions.
i. Tax Court Memorandum decision.

38. What major tax services are available to a tax researcher?

39. In tax law, what has the highest tax authority or reliability?

40. Since a Regulation has the force and effect of tax law, can a Regulation be overturned by a court?

41. Which court has the higher level of authority: the Tax Court or a U.S. District Court?

42. When might a researcher need to refer to a citator?

43. List the elements that a good tax research memo should include.

44. A student/friend majoring in sociology says that tax advisers are immoral since they merely help people cheat the government. Defend tax planning by tax advisers.

45. Which of the following would be considered differences between the Prentice-Hall (now RIA) and Commerce Clearing House *Citators*?

a. Distinguishes between the various issues in a particular court decision.
b. Lists all court decisions that cite the court decision being researched.
c. Allows a researcher to determine the validity of a Revenue Ruling.
d. Indicates whether a court decision is explained, criticized, followed, or overruled by a subsequent decision.
e. Pinpoints the exact page on which a decision is cited by another case.

46. You inherit a tax problem that was researched five months ago. You believe the answer is correct, but you are unfamiliar with the general area. How would you find some recent articles dealing with the subject area? How do you evaluate the reliability of the authority cited in the research report? How do you determine the latest developments pertaining to the research problem?

47. When might a researcher wish to consult one of the three computerized legal data banks?

PROBLEMS

48. T, an individual taxpayer, has just been audited by the IRS, and as a result, has been assessed a substantial deficiency (which has not yet been paid) in additional income taxes. In preparing his defense, T advances the following possibilities:

  a. Although a resident of Kentucky, T plans to sue in a U.S. District Court in Oregon that appears to be more favorably inclined towards taxpayers.
  b. If (a) is not possible, T plans to take his case to a Kentucky state court where an uncle is the presiding judge.
  c. Since T has found a B.T.A. decision that seems to help his case, he plans to rely on it under alternative (a) or (b).
  d. If he loses at the trial court level, T plans to appeal either to the U.S. Claims Court or to the U.S. Second Court of Appeals. The reason for this choice is the presence of relatives in both Washington, D.C., and New York. Staying with these relatives could save T lodging expense while his appeal is being heard by the court selected.
  e. Whether or not T wins at the trial court or appeals court level, he feels certain of success on an appeal to the U.S. Supreme Court.

  Evaluate T's notions concerning the judicial process as it applies to Federal income tax controversies.

49. Using the legend provided, identify the governmental unit that produces the following tax sources:

Legend

T	=	U.S. Treasury Department
NO	=	National Office of the IRS
DD	=	District Director of the IRS
NA	=	Not applicable

  a. Proposed Regulations.
  b. Revenue Procedures.
  c. Letter rulings.
  d. Determination letters.
  e. Technical Advice Memoranda.
  f. Treasury Decisions.
  g. Revenue Rulings.

50. Using the legend provided, classify each of the following statements (more than one answer per statement may be appropriate):

Legend

D	=	Applies to the U.S. District Court
T	=	Applies to the U.S. Tax Court
C	=	Applies to the U.S. Claims Court
A	=	Applies to the U.S. Court of Appeals
U	=	Applies to the U.S. Supreme Court
N	=	Applies to none of the above

  a. Decides only Federal tax matters.
  b. Decisions are reported in the F.2d Series.
  c. Decisions are reported in the USTCs.
  d. Decisions are reported in the AFTRs.
  e. Appeal is by Writ of Certiorari.
  f. Court meets most often in Washington, D.C.
  g. A jury trial is available.
  h. Trial court.

i. Appellate court.
j. Appeal is to the Federal Circuit and bypasses the taxpayer's particular circuit court.
k. Has a Small Claims Division.
l. The only trial court where the taxpayer does not have to pay the tax assessed by the IRS first.

51. Using the legend provided, classify each of the following tax sources:

Legend

P = Primary tax source
S = Secondary tax source
B = Both
N = Neither

a. Sixteenth Amendment to the Constitution.
b. Tax treaty between the United States and the United Kingdom.
c. Proposed Regulations.
d. Revenue Rulings.
e. General Counsel Memoranda (1988).
f. Tax Court Memorandum decision.
g. *Harvard Law Review* article.
h. Temporary Regulations.
i. Letter ruling (before 1985).
j. District Court decision.
k. Small Claims Division of U.S. Tax Court decision.
l. Senate Finance Committee Report.
m. Technical Advise Memorandum (1990).

52. Using the legend provided, classify each of the following citations as to publisher:

Legend

P-H = Prentice-Hall
CCH = Commerce Clearing House
W = West Publishing Company
U.S. = U.S. Government
O = Others

a. 83–2 USTC ¶9600.
b. 52 AFTR2d 83–5954.
c. 49 T.C. 645 (1968).
d. 39 TCM 32 (1979).
e. 393 U.S. 297.
f. PH T.C. Memo ¶80,582.
g. 89 S.Ct. 501.
h. 2 Cl.Ct. 601.
i. 159 F.2d 848.
j. 592 F.Supp. 18.
k. Rev.Rul. 76–332, 1976–2 C.B. 81.
l. 21 L.Ed.2d 495.

53. Using the legend provided, classify each of the following statements:

Legend

A = Tax avoidance
E = Tax evasion
N = Neither

a. T writes a $250 check as a charitable contribution on December 28, 1992, but does not mail the check to the charitable organization until January 10. T takes a deduction in 1992.
b. W decided not to report interest income from a bank because it was only $11.75.
c. T pays property taxes on his home in December 1992 rather than waiting until February 1993.
d. W switches her investments from taxable corporate bonds to tax-exempt municipal bonds.
e. T encourages his mother to save most of her Social Security benefits so that he will be able to claim her as a dependent.

RESEARCH PROBLEMS

RESEARCH PROBLEM 1 Locate the following Internal Revenue Code citations and give a brief description of them:

a. § 118(a).
b. § 1231(c)(3).
c. § 4980A(c)(1).

RESEARCH PROBLEM 2 Locate the following Regulation citations and give a brief description of them:

a. Reg. § 1.151–3(a).
b. Prop.Reg. § 1.1031(a)–3(g)(2).
c. Reg. § 1.1502–75(c)(2)(i).

RESEARCH PROBLEM 3 What is the subject matter of the Revenue Procedure that begins on page 396 of the 1987–2 *Cumulative Bulletin*?

RESEARCH PROBLEM 4

a. Using Volume 7 of *Bender's Federal Tax Service* in I:24.44 [2], define an Alaska Native Corporation.
b. Using "S Corporation" Tax Management Portfolios (TMP) 60–7th, on page A–61, determine if royalties from a secret process are passive investment income.

RESEARCH PROBLEM 5

a. Find the *Forty-Second Annual USC Institute on Federal Taxation*, 1990, University of Southern California Law Center, and go to page 581, paragraph 401.2H. Can compensation paid to a shareholder be capitalized under the uniform capitalization rules of I.R.C. § 263A? Who is the author of this Chapter 4?
b. Locate the September 1990 issue of *The Tax Adviser*, page 581, footnote 16. What types of companies does Rev.Rul. 85–135 refer to? Who is the employer of the authors?

RESEARCH PROBLEM 6 Determine the acquiescence/nonacquiescence position of the IRS with respect to the following:

a. *Woods Investment Company*, 85 T.C. 274 (1985).
b. *Henry W. Schwartz Corp.*, 60 T.C. 728 (1973).
c. *Estate of Milton S. Lennard*, 61 T.C. 554 (1974).

RESEARCH PROBLEM 7 Locate the following tax services in your library and indicate the name of the publisher and whether the service is organized by topic or Code Section:

a. *Federal Taxes.*
b. *Standard Federal Tax Reporter.*
c. *Tax Coordinator 2d.*
d. *Mertens Law of Federal Income Taxation.*
e. *Tax Management Portfolios.*

f. Rabkin & Johnson, *Federal Income, Gift & Estate Taxation.*
g. Bender's Federal Tax Service.

Research Problem 8 In the Tax Publications Matrix below, place an X if a court decision can be found in the publication. There may be more than one X in a row for a particular court.

Court	U.S. Govt. Printing Office	West Publishing Company				Prentice-Hall			Commerce Clearing House	
		Federal Supp.	Federal 2d	Claims Court Reporter	S.Ct.	BTA Memo	TC Memo	AFTR	TC Memo	USTC
U.S. Supreme Court										
Court of Appeals										
Claims Court										
District Court										
Tax Court (regular decisions)										
Tax Court (memo decisions)										
Board of Tax Appeal										
BTA Memo										

Research Problem 9 Complete the following citations to the extent the research materials are available to you:

a. Rev.Proc. 90– ____ , I.R.B. No. 2, 10.
b. Rev.Rul. ____ , 1981–2 C.B. 243.
c. *Rutkin v. U.S.,* ____ S.Ct. ____ (____, 1952).
d. __________ , 40 B.T.A. 333 (1939).
e. *C. F. Kahler,* 18 T.C. ____ (____).
f. *Cowden v. Comm.,* 289 F.2d ____ (CA– ____ , 1961).
g. *Wolder v. Comm.,* 74–1 USTC ____ (CA–2, ____).
h. *Harry H. Goldberg,* 29 TCM ____ , T.C.Memo. 1970– ____ .
i. *Shopmaker v. U.S.* , 119 F. Supp. ____ (D.Ct. ____ , 1953).

Research Problem 10 Using the research materials available to you, answer the following questions:

a. Has Prop.Reg. § 1.482–2 been finalized?
b. What happened to *Golconda Mining Corp.,* 58 T.C. 736 (1972) on appeal?
c. Does Rev.Rul. 69–185 still represent the position of the IRS on the issue involved?

Research Problem 11 Determine the disposition of the following decisions at the Supreme Court level:

a. *International Business Machines Corp. v. U.S.,* 343 F.2d 914 (Ct.Cls., 1965).
b. *Knetsch v. U.S.,* 348 F.2d 932 (Ct.Cls., 1965).
c. *American Society of Travel Agents, Inc. v. Blumenthal,* 566 F.2d 145 (CA–D.C., 1977).
d. *Litchfield Securities v. U.S.,* 325 F.2d 667 (CA–2, 1963).
e. *Wilson Bros. & Co. v. Comm.,* 170 F.2d 423 (CA–9, 1948).

Research Problem 12 Determine the reliability of the following items:

a. *Simpson v. U.S.,* 261 F.2d 497 (CA–7, 1958).
b. Rev.Proc. 83–78, 1983–2 C.B. 595.
c. *Estate of Grace E. Lang,* 64 T.C. 404 (1975).

RESEARCH PROBLEM 13 Did the IRS agree or disagree with the following court decisions?

- **a.** *Longue Vue Foundation*, 90 T.C. 150 (1988).
- **b.** *Charles Crowther*, 28 T.C. 1293 (1957).
- **c.** *Sidney Merians*, 60 T.C. 187 (1973).
- **d.** *Ray Durden*, 3 T.C. 1 (1944).

RESEARCH PROBLEM 14 Determine the reliability of the following decisions:

- **a.** *Maid of The Mist Corp. v. Comm.*, T.C.Memo. 1977–263, 36 TCM 1068 (1977).
- **b.** *Lazisky v. Comm.*, 72 T.C. 495 (1979).
- **c.** *Farm Service Cooperative v. Comm.*, 70 T.C. 145 (1978).
- **d.** *Tufts v. Comm.*, 81–2 USTC ¶9754 (CA–5, 1981), *rev'g* 70 T.C. 756 (1978).

RESEARCH PROBLEM 15 Find the decision *Barbados #6 Ltd.*, 85 T.C. 900 (1985).

- **a.** Who was the presiding judge?
- **b.** Was the decision reviewed by the full court? If so, who dissented from the majority opinion?
- **c.** Who won?
- **d.** Was the decision entered under the Rule of 155?

RESEARCH PROBLEM 16 During 1992, T lived with and supported a 20-year-old woman who was not his wife. He resides in a state that has a statute that makes it a misdemeanor for a man and woman who are not married to each other to live together. May T claim his *friend* as a dependent assuming he satisfies the normal tax rules for the deduction? Should T consider moving to another state?

Partial list of research aids:

§ 152(b)(5).
John T. Untermann, 38 T.C. 93 (1962).
S.Rept. 1983, 85th Cong., 2d Sess., reprinted in the 1958 Code Cong. & Adm. News 4791, 4804.

RESEARCH PROBLEM 17 Locate *New York University's Forty-Third Annual Institute on Federal Taxation*.

- **a.** Turn to Chapter 35, page 35–35, Chart III, and determine the present cost of an employer's obligation to pay an employee $20,000 in 10 years. Assume a 12% employer rate of return.
- **b.** Turn to Chapter 56, page 56–19, and determine what IRA fees are deductible.

CHAPTER

TAX DETERMINATION; PERSONAL AND DEPENDENCY EXEMPTIONS; AN OVERVIEW OF PROPERTY TRANSACTIONS

OBJECTIVES

Explain how an individual's Federal income tax liability is determined.

Develop greater understanding of the components of the tax formula for individuals, including gross income, exclusions, the standard deduction, itemized deductions, and exemptions.

Apply the rules for determining dependency exemptions and filing status.

Introduce the basic concepts of property transactions and their effect on taxable income.

Discuss several basic tax planning ideas for individual taxpayers.

OUTLINE

Individuals are subject to Federal income tax based on taxable income. This chapter explains how taxable income and the income tax of an individual taxpayer are determined.

To compute taxable income, it is necessary to understand the tax formula in Figure 3–1. Although the tax formula is rather simple, determining an individual's taxable income can be quite complex. The complexity stems from the numerous provisions that govern the determination of gross income and allowable deductions.

After computing taxable income, the appropriate rates must be applied. This requires a determination of the individual's filing status, since different rates apply for single taxpayers, married taxpayers, and heads of household. The basic tax rate structure is progressive, with rates of 15 percent, 28 percent, and 31 percent.[1]

Once the individual's tax has been computed, prepayments and credits are subtracted to determine whether the taxpayer owes additional tax or is entitled to a refund.

When property is sold or otherwise disposed of, a gain or loss may result, which could affect the determination of taxable income. Although property transactions are covered in detail in Chapters 14–17, an understanding of certain basic concepts helps in working with some of the materials to follow. The concluding portion of this chapter furnishes an overview of property transactions, including the distinction between realized and recognized gain or loss, the classification of such gain or loss (ordinary or capital), and treatment for income tax purposes.

TAX FORMULA

Most individuals compute taxable income using the tax formula shown in Figure 3–1. Special provisions govern the computation of taxable income and the tax liability for certain minor children who have unearned income in excess of specified amounts. These provisions are discussed under Tax Determination—Unearned Income of Children under Age 14 Taxed at Parents' Rate later in the chapter.

Before illustrating the application of the tax formula, a brief discussion of the components of the formula is necessary.

FIGURE 3–1
Tax Formula

Income (broadly conceived)	$xx,xxx
Less: Exclusions	(x,xxx)
Gross income	$xx,xxx
Less: Deductions *for* adjusted gross income	(x,xxx)
Adjusted gross income	$xx,xxx
Less: The greater of—	
Total itemized deductions *or* the standard deduction	(x,xxx)
Personal and dependency exemptions	(x,xxx)
Taxable income	$xx,xxx

1. The 1992 Tax Table was not available from the IRS at the date of publication of this text. The Tax Table for 1991 and the Tax Rate Schedules for 1991 and 1992 are reproduced in Appendix A. For quick reference, the 1991 and 1992 Tax Rate Schedules are also reproduced inside the front cover of this text.

Components of the Tax Formula

Income (Broadly Conceived). This includes all the taxpayer's income, both taxable and nontaxable. Although it is essentially equivalent to gross receipts, it does not include a return of capital or receipt of borrowed funds.

EXAMPLE 1

T needed money to purchase a house. He sold 5,000 shares of stock for $100,000. He had paid $40,000 for the stock. In addition, he borrowed $75,000 from a bank. T has taxable income of $60,000 from the sale of the stock ($100,000 selling price − $40,000 return of capital). He has no income from the $75,000 borrowed from the bank because he has an obligation to repay that amount. ◆

Exclusions. For various reasons, Congress has chosen to exclude certain types of income from the income tax base. The principal income exclusions are discussed in Chapter 5. A partial list of these exclusions is shown in Figure 3–2 on the following page.

Gross Income. The Internal Revenue Code defines gross income broadly as "all income from whatever source derived."[2] It includes, but is not limited to, the items in the partial list in Figure 3–3 on the following page. It does not include unrealized gains. Gross income is discussed in Chapters 4 and 5.

EXAMPLE 2

L received the following amounts during the year:

Salary	$30,000
Interest on savings account	900
Gift from her aunt	10,000
Prize won in state lottery	1,000
Alimony from ex-husband	12,000
Child support from ex-husband	6,000
Damages for injury in auto accident	25,000
Increase in the value of stock held for investment	5,000

Review Figures 3–2 and 3–3 to determine the amount L must include in the computation of taxable income and the amount she may exclude. After you have determined these amounts, check your answer in footnote 3.[3] ◆

Deductions for Adjusted Gross Income. Individual taxpayers have two categories of deductions: (1) deductions *for* adjusted gross income (deductions to arrive at adjusted gross income) and (2) deductions *from* adjusted gross income.

Deductions *for* adjusted gross income include ordinary and necessary expenses incurred in a trade or business, one-half of self-employment tax paid, alimony paid, certain payments to an Individual Retirement Account, forfeited interest penalty for premature withdrawal of time deposits, the capital loss

2. § 61(a).

3. L must include $43,900 in computing taxable income ($30,000 salary + $900 interest + $1,000 lottery prize + $12,000 alimony). She can exclude $41,000 ($10,000 gift from aunt + $6,000 child support + $25,000 damages). The unrealized gain on the stock held for investment is not included in gross income. Such gain will be included in gross income only when it is realized upon disposition of the stock.

deduction, and others.[4] The principal deductions *for* adjusted gross income are discussed in Chapters 6, 7, 8, 9, and 10.

Adjusted Gross Income (AGI). AGI is an important subtotal that serves as the basis for computing percentage limitations on certain itemized deductions, such as medical expenses and charitable contributions. For example, medical expenses are deductible only to the extent they exceed 7.5 percent of AGI, and

FIGURE 3–2
Partial List of Exclusions from Gross Income

- Accident insurance proceeds
- Annuities (to a limited extent)
- Bequests
- Child support payments
- Cost-of-living allowance (for military)
- Damages for personal injury or sickness
- Death benefits (up to $5,000)
- Gifts received
- Group term life insurance, premium paid by employer (for coverage up to $50,000)
- Inheritances
- Life insurance paid on death
- Meals and lodging (if furnished for employer's convenience)
- Military allowances
- Minister's dwelling rental value allowance
- Railroad retirement benefits (to a limited extent)
- Scholarship grants (to a limited extent)
- Social Security benefits (to a limited extent)
- Veterans' benefits
- Welfare payments
- Workers' compensation benefits

FIGURE 3–3
Partial List of Gross Income Items

- Alimony
- Annuities
- Awards
- Back pay
- Bargain purchase from employer
- Bonuses
- Breach of contract damages
- Business income
- Clergy fees
- Commissions
- Compensation for services
- Death benefits in excess of $5,000
- Debts forgiven
- Director's fees
- Dividends
- Embezzled funds
- Employee awards (in certain cases)
- Employee benefits (except certain fringe benefits)
- Employee bonuses
- Estate and trust income
- Farm income
- Fees
- Gains from illegal activities
- Gains from sale of property
- Gambling winnings
- Group term life insurance, premium paid by employer (for coverage over $50,000)
- Hobby income
- Interest
- Jury duty fees
- Living quarters, meals (unless furnished for employer's convenience)
- Mileage allowance
- Military pay (unless combat pay)
- Notary fees
- Partnership income
- Pensions
- Prizes
- Professional fees
- Punitive damages (in certain cases)
- Reimbursement for moving expenses
- Rents
- Rewards
- Royalties
- Salaries
- Severance pay
- Strike and lockout benefits
- Supplemental unemployment benefits
- Tips and gratuities
- Travel allowance (in certain cases)
- Wages

4. § 62.

charitable contribution deductions may not exceed 50 percent of AGI. These limitations might be described as a 7.5 percent *floor* under the medical expense deduction and a 50 percent *ceiling* on the charitable contribution deduction.

Example 3

T earned a salary of $23,000 in the current tax year. He contributed $2,000 to his Individual Retirement Account (IRA) and sustained a $1,000 capital loss on the sale of XYZ Corporation stock. His AGI is computed as follows:

Gross income		
Salary		$23,000
Less: Deductions *for* AGI		
IRA contribution	$2,000	
Capital loss	1,000	3,000
AGI		$20,000

◆

Example 4

Assume the same facts as in Example 3, and that T also had medical expenses of $1,800. Medical expenses may be included in itemized deductions to the extent they exceed 7.5% of AGI. In computing his itemized deductions, T may include medical expenses of $300 [$1,800 medical expenses − $1,500 (7.5% × $20,000 AGI)]. ◆

Itemized Deductions. As a general rule, personal expenditures are disallowed as deductions in arriving at taxable income. However, Congress has chosen to allow specified personal expenses as itemized deductions. Such expenditures include medical expenses, certain taxes and interest, and charitable contributions.

In addition to these personal expenses, taxpayers are allowed itemized deductions for expenses related to (1) the production or collection of income and (2) the management of property held for the production of income.[5] These expenses, sometimes referred to as *nonbusiness expenses,* differ from trade or business expenses (discussed previously). Trade or business expenses, which are deductions *for* AGI, must be incurred in connection with a trade or business. Nonbusiness expenses, on the other hand, are expenses incurred in connection with an income-producing activity that does not qualify as a trade or business. Such expenses are itemized deductions.

Example 5

H is the owner and operator of a video game arcade. All allowable expenses he incurs in connection with the arcade business are deductions *for* AGI. In addition, H has an extensive portfolio of stocks and bonds. H's investment activity is not treated as a trade or business. All allowable expenses that H incurs in connection with these investments are itemized deductions. ◆

Itemized deductions include, but are not limited to, the expenses listed in Figure 3–4. See Chapter 11 for a detailed discussion of itemized deductions.

Standard Deduction. The standard deduction is a specified amount set by Congress, and the amount depends on the filing status of the taxpayer. The effect of the standard deduction is to exempt a taxpayer's income, up to the specified amount, from Federal income tax liability. In the past, Congress has

5. § 212.

attempted to set the tax-free amount represented by the standard deduction approximately equal to an estimated poverty level,[6] but it has not always been consistent in doing so.

The standard deduction is the sum of two components: the *basic* standard deduction and the *additional* standard deduction.[7] Figure 3–5 lists the basic standard deduction allowed for taxpayers in each filing status. All taxpayers allowed a *full* standard deduction are entitled to the applicable amount listed in Figure 3–5. The standard deduction amounts are subject to adjustment for inflation each year.

Certain taxpayers are not allowed to claim *any* standard deduction, and the standard deduction is *limited* for others. These provisions are discussed later in the chapter.

A taxpayer who is age 65 or over *or* blind qualifies for an *additional standard deduction* of $700 or $900, depending on filing status (see amounts in Figure 3–6). Two additional standard deductions are allowed for a taxpayer who is age 65 or over *and* blind. The additional standard deduction provisions also apply for a qualifying spouse who is age 65 or over or blind, but a taxpayer may not claim an additional standard deduction for a dependent.

To determine whether to itemize, the taxpayer compares the *total* standard deduction (the sum of the basic standard deduction and any additional standard

FIGURE 3–4
Partial List of Itemized Deductions

Medical expenses in excess of 7.5% of AGI
State and local income taxes
Real estate taxes
Personal property taxes
Interest on home mortgage
Investment interest (to a limited extent)
Charitable contributions
Casualty and theft losses in excess of 10% of AGI
Moving expenses
Miscellaneous expenses (to the extent such expenses exceed 2% of AGI)
- Union dues
- Professional dues and subscriptions
- Certain educational expenses
- Tax return preparation fee
- Investment counsel fees
- Unreimbursed employee business expenses (after 20% reduction for meals and entertainment)

FIGURE 3–5
Basic Standard Deduction Amounts

Filing Status	Standard Deduction Amount 1991	1992
Single	$3,400	$3,600
Married, filing jointly	5,700	6,000
Surviving spouse	5,700	6,000
Head of household	5,000	5,250
Married, filing separately	2,850	3,000

6. S.Rep. No. 92–437, 92nd Cong., 1st Sess., 1971, p. 54. Another purpose of the standard deduction was discussed in Chapter 1 under Influence of the Internal Revenue Service—Administrative Feasibility. The size of the standard deduction has a direct bearing on the number of taxpayers who are in a position to itemize deductions. Reducing the number of taxpayers who itemize also reduces the audit effort required from the IRS.

7. § 63(c)(1).

deductions) to total itemized deductions. Taxpayers are allowed to deduct the greater of itemized deductions or the standard deduction. Taxpayers whose itemized deductions are less than the standard deduction compute their taxable income using the standard deduction rather than itemizing.

EXAMPLE 6

T, who is single, is 66 years old. She had total itemized deductions of $4,400 during 1992. Her total standard deduction is $4,500 ($3,600 basic standard deduction plus $900 additional standard deduction). T will compute her taxable income for 1992 using the standard deduction ($4,500), since it exceeds her itemized deductions ($4,400). ◆

Exemptions. Exemptions are allowed for the taxpayer, the taxpayer's spouse, and for each dependent of the taxpayer. The exemption amount is $2,150 in 1991 and $2,300 in 1992.

Application of the Tax Formula

The tax formula shown in Figure 3–1 is illustrated in Example 7.

EXAMPLE 7

J, age 25, is single and has no dependents. She is a high school teacher and earned a $20,000 salary in 1992. Her other income consisted of a $1,000 prize won in a sweepstakes contest and $500 interest on municipal bonds received as a graduation gift in 1989. During 1992, she sustained a deductible capital loss of $1,000. Her itemized deductions are $3,800. J's taxable income for the year is computed as follows:

Income (broadly conceived)		
Salary		$20,000
Prize		1,000
Interest on municipal bonds		500
		$21,500
Less: Exclusion—		
Interest on municipal bonds		(500)
Gross income		$21,000
Less: Deduction *for* adjusted gross income—		
Capital loss		(1,000)
Adjusted gross income		$20,000
Less: The greater of—		
Total itemized deductions	$3,800	
or the standard deduction	$3,600	(3,800)
Personal and dependency exemptions (1 × $2,300)		(2,300)
Taxable income		$13,900

◆

FIGURE 3–6
Amount of Each Additional Standard Deduction

Filing Status	1991	1992
Single	$850	$900
Married, filing jointly	650	700
Surviving spouse	650	700
Head of household	850	900
Married, filing separately	650	700

The structure of the individual income tax return (Form 1040, 1040A, or 1040EZ) differs somewhat from the tax formula in Figure 3–1. On the tax return, gross income generally is the starting point in computing taxable income. With few exceptions, exclusions are not reported on the tax return.

Individuals Not Eligible for the Standard Deduction

The following individual taxpayers are ineligible to use the standard deduction and must therefore itemize:[8]

- A married individual filing a separate return where either spouse itemizes deductions.
- A nonresident alien.
- An individual filing a return for a period of less than 12 months because of a change in annual accounting period.

Special Limitations for Individuals Who Can Be Claimed as Dependents

Special rules apply to the standard deduction and personal exemption of an individual who can be claimed as a dependent on another person's tax return.

When filing his or her own tax return, a *dependent's* basic standard deduction is limited to the greater of $600 or the individual's earned income for the year.[9] However, if the individual's earned income exceeds the normal standard deduction, the standard deduction is limited to the appropriate standard deduction amount shown in Figure 3–5. These limitations apply only to the basic standard deduction. A dependent who is 65 or over or blind or both is also allowed the additional standard deduction amount on his or her own return (refer to Figure 3–6). These provisions are illustrated in Examples 8 through 11.

EXAMPLE 8

M, who is 17 years old and single, is claimed as a dependent on her parents' tax return. During 1992, she received $1,000 interest (unearned income) on a savings account. She also earned $400 from a part-time job. When M files her own tax return, her standard deduction is $600 (the greater of $600 or earned income of $400). ◆

EXAMPLE 9

Assume the same facts as in Example 8, except that M is 67 years old and is claimed as a dependent on her son's tax return. In this case when M files her own tax return, her standard deduction is $1,500 [$600 (the greater of $600 or earned income of $400) + $900 (the additional standard deduction allowed because M is 65 or over)]. ◆

EXAMPLE 10

P, who is 16 years old and single, earned $1,000 from a summer job and had no unearned income during 1992. She is claimed as a dependent on her parents' tax return. Her standard deduction for 1992 is $1,000 (the greater of $600 or earned income). ◆

EXAMPLE 11

J, who is a 20-year-old, single, full-time college student, is claimed as a dependent on his parents' tax return. He worked during the summer of 1992 as a musician, earning

8. § 63(c)(6).
9. § 63(c)(5). The $600 amount is subject to adjustment for inflation each year. The amount was $550 for 1991.

$3,800. J's standard deduction is $3,600 (the greater of $600 or $3,800 earned income, but limited to the $3,600 standard deduction for a single taxpayer). ◆

The taxpayer who claims an individual as a dependent is allowed to claim an exemption for the dependent. The dependent cannot claim a personal exemption on his or her own return.

PERSONAL AND DEPENDENCY EXEMPTIONS
◆

The use of exemptions in the tax system is based in part on the idea that a taxpayer with a small amount of income should be exempt from income taxation. An exemption frees a specified amount of income from tax ($2,150 in 1991 and $2,300 in 1992). The exemption amount is indexed (adjusted) annually for inflation. An individual who is not claimed as a dependent by another taxpayer is allowed to claim his or her own personal exemption. In addition, a taxpayer may claim an exemption for each dependent.

EXAMPLE 12

B, who is single, supports her mother and father, who have no income of their own, and claims them as dependents on her tax return. B may claim a personal exemption for herself plus an exemption for each dependent. On her 1992 tax return, B may deduct $6,900 for exemptions ($2,300 per exemption × 3 exemptions). ◆

Personal Exemptions

The Code provides a personal exemption for the taxpayer and an exemption for the spouse if a joint return is filed. However, when separate returns are filed, a married taxpayer cannot claim an exemption for his or her spouse unless the spouse has no gross income and is not claimed as the dependent of another taxpayer.

The determination of marital status generally is made at the end of the taxable year, except when a spouse dies during the year. Spouses who enter into a legal separation under a decree of divorce or separate maintenance before the end of the year are considered to be unmarried at the end of the taxable year. The following table illustrates the effect of death or divorce upon marital status:

	Marital Status for 1992
1. W is the widow of H who dies on January 3, 1992.	W and H are considered to be married for purposes of filing the 1992 return.
2. W and H entered into a divorce decree that is effective on December 31, 1992.	W and H are considered to be unmarried for purposes of filing the 1992 return.

Dependency Exemptions

As indicated in Example 12, the Code allows a taxpayer to claim a dependency exemption for each eligible individual. A dependency exemption may be claimed for each individual for whom the following five tests are met:

- Support.
- Relationship or member of the household.
- Gross income.
- Joint return.
- Citizenship or residency.

Support Test. Over one-half of the support of the individual must be furnished by the taxpayer. Support includes food, shelter, clothing, medical and dental care, education, etc. However, a scholarship received by a student is not included for purposes of computing whether the taxpayer furnished more than one-half of the child's support.[10]

EXAMPLE 13

H contributed $2,500 (consisting of food, clothing, and medical care) toward the support of his son, S, who earned $1,500 from a part-time job and received a $2,000 scholarship to attend a local university. Assuming that the other dependency tests are met, H may claim S as a dependent since he has contributed more than one-half of S's support. The $2,000 scholarship is not included as support for purposes of this test. ◆

If the individual does not spend funds that have been received from any source, the unexpended amounts are not counted for purposes of the support test.

EXAMPLE 14

S contributed $3,000 to her father's support during the year. In addition, her father received $2,400 in Social Security benefits, $200 of interest, and wages of $600. Her father deposited the Social Security benefits, interest, and wages in his own savings account and did not use any of the funds for his support. Thus, the Social Security benefits, interest, and wages are not considered as support provided by S's father. S may claim her father as a dependent if the other tests are met. ◆

Capital expenditures for items such as furniture, appliances, and automobiles are included in total support if the item does, in fact, constitute support.[11]

EXAMPLE 15

F purchased a television set costing $150 and gave it to his minor daughter. The television set was placed in the child's bedroom and was used exclusively by her. F should include the cost of the television set in determining the support of his daughter. ◆

EXAMPLE 16

F paid $6,000 for an automobile that was titled and registered in his name. F's minor son is permitted to use the automobile equally with F. Since F did not give the automobile to his son, the $6,000 cost is not includible as a support item. However, out-of-pocket operating expenses incurred by F for the benefit of his son are includible as support. ◆

One exception to the support test involves a *multiple support agreement*. A multiple support agreement permits one of a group of taxpayers who furnish more than half of the support of an individual to claim a dependency exemption for that individual even if no one person provides more than 50 percent of the support.[12] Any person who contributed more than 10 percent of the support is entitled to claim the exemption if each person in the group who contributed more than 10 percent files a written consent. This provision frequently enables one of the children of aged dependent parents to claim an exemption when none of the children meets the 50 percent support test. Each person who is a party to the multiple support agreement must meet all other requirements (except the

10. Reg. § 1.152–1(c).

11. Rev.Rul. 57–344, 1957–2 C.B. 112; Rev.Rul. 58–419, 1958–2 C.B. 57.

12. § 152(c).

support requirement) for claiming the exemption. A person who does not meet the relationship or member-of-household requirement, for instance, cannot claim the dependency exemption under a multiple support agreement. It does not matter if he or she contributes more than 10 percent of the individual's support.

EXAMPLE 17

M, who resides with her son, received $6,000 from various sources during 1992. This constituted her entire support for the year. She received support from the following:

	Amount	Percentage of Total
A, a son	$2,880	48
B, a son	600	10
C, a daughter	1,800	30
D, a friend	720	12
	$6,000	100

If A and C file a multiple support agreement, either may claim the dependency exemption for M. B may not claim M because he did not contribute more than 10% of her support. B's consent is not required in order for A and C to file a multiple support agreement. D does not meet the relationship or member-of-household test and cannot be a party to the agreement. The decision as to who claims M rests with A and C. It is possible for C to claim M, even though A furnished more of M's support. ◆

A second exception to the 50 percent support requirement can occur for a child of parents who are divorced or separated under a decree of separate maintenance. Under decrees executed after 1984, the custodial parent is allowed to claim the exemption unless that parent agrees in writing not to claim a dependency exemption for the child.[13] Thus, claiming the exemption is dependent on whether or not a written agreement exists, *not* on meeting the support test.

EXAMPLE 18

H and W obtain a divorce decree in 1989. In 1992, their two children are in the custody of W. H contributed over half of the support for each child. In the absence of a written agreement on the dependency exemptions, W (the custodial parent) is entitled to the exemptions in 1992. However, H may claim the exemptions if W agrees in writing. ◆

For the noncustodial parent to claim the exemption, the custodial parent must complete Form 8332 (Release of Claim to Exemption for Child of Divorced or Separated Parents). The release can apply to a single year, a number of specified years, or all future years. The noncustodial parent must attach a copy of Form 8332 to his or her return. Form 8332 is not required if there is a pre-1985 agreement that allows the noncustodial parent to claim the exemption and the noncustodial parent provides at least $600 of support for each child.

Relationship or Member-of-the-Household Test. To be claimed as a dependent, an individual must be either a relative of the taxpayer or a member of the taxpayer's household. The Code contains a detailed listing of the various blood and marriage relationships that qualify. Note, however, that the relationship test

13. § 152(e).

is met if the individual is a relative of either spouse. A relationship, once established by marriage, continues regardless of subsequent changes in marital status.

The following individuals may be claimed as dependents of the taxpayer if the other tests for dependency are met:[14]

- A son or daughter of the taxpayer, or a descendant of either (grandchild).
- A stepson or stepdaughter of the taxpayer.
- A brother, sister, stepbrother, or stepsister of the taxpayer.
- The father or mother of the taxpayer, or an ancestor of either (grandparent).
- A stepfather or stepmother of the taxpayer.
- A son or daughter of a brother or sister (nephew or niece) of the taxpayer.
- A brother or sister of the father or mother (uncle or aunt) of the taxpayer.
- A son-in-law, daughter-in-law, father-in-law, mother-in-law, brother-in-law, or sister-in-law of the taxpayer.
- An individual who, for the entire taxable year of the taxpayer, has as his or her principal place of abode the home of the taxpayer and is a member of the taxpayer's household. This does not include an individual who, at any time during the taxable year, was the spouse of the taxpayer.

The following rules are also prescribed in the Code:[15]

- A legally adopted child is treated as a natural child.
- A foster child qualifies if the child's principal place of abode is the taxpayer's household.

Gross Income Test. The dependent's gross income must be less than the exemption amount ($2,300 in 1992) unless the dependent is a child of the taxpayer and is under 19 or a full-time student under the age of 24.[16] A parent who provides over half of the support of his or her child who, at the end of the year, is under 19 or is a full-time student under 24 may claim a dependency exemption for the child, even if the child's gross income exceeds $2,300. However, if the parent claims a dependency exemption, the dependent child may not claim a personal exemption on his or her own income tax return.

A child is defined as a son, stepson, daughter, stepdaughter, adopted son, or adopted daughter and may include a foster child.[17] For the child to qualify as a student for purposes of the dependency exemption, he or she must be a full-time student at an educational institution during some part of five calendar months of the year.[18] This exception to the gross income test for dependent children who are under 19 or full-time students under 24 permits a child or college student to earn money from part-time or summer jobs without penalizing the parent with the loss of the dependency exemption.

Joint Return Test. If a dependent is married, the supporting taxpayer (e.g., the parent of a married child) generally is not permitted a dependency exemption if

---

14. § 152(a). However, under § 152(b)(5), a taxpayer may not claim someone who is a member of his or her household as a dependent if their relationship is in violation of local law. For example, the dependency exemption was denied because the taxpayer's relationship to the person claimed as a dependent constituted *cohabitation*, a crime under applicable state law. *Cassius L. Peacock, III*, 37 TCM 177, T.C.Memo. 1978–30.
15. § 152(b)(2).
16. § 151(c)(1).
17. Reg. § 1.151–3(a).
18. Reg. §§ 1.151–3(b) and (c).

the married individual files a joint return with his or her spouse.[19] However, if neither the dependent nor the dependent's spouse is *required* to file a return but they file a joint return solely to claim a refund of all tax withheld and no tax liability exists for either spouse on separate returns, the joint return rule does not apply. See Figure 3–8 later in the chapter and the related discussion concerning income level requirements for filing a return.

EXAMPLE 19

P provides over half of the support of his son J. He also provides over half of the support of M, who is J's wife. In 1992, J had wages of $1,500, and M earned $1,800. J and M file a joint return for the year. Neither J nor M was required to file a return because each had income below the $2,300 level for married taxpayers filing separate returns. P is allowed to claim both as dependents. ◆

Citizenship or Residency Test. To be a dependent, the individual must be either a U.S. citizen, resident, or national or a resident of Canada or Mexico for some part of the calendar year in which the tax year of the taxpayer claiming the exemption begins.

Phase-out of Exemptions. For tax years beginning after December 31, 1990 and before January 1, 1996, personal exemptions and exemptions for dependents are phased out as AGI exceeds specified threshold amounts. For 1992, phase-out begins at the following threshold amounts:

Joint returns/Surviving spouse	$157,900
Head of household	131,550
Single	105,250
Married, filing separately	78,950

These threshold amounts will be indexed for inflation in future years.

Exemptions are phased out by 2 percent for each $2,500 (or fraction thereof) by which the taxpayer's AGI exceeds the threshold amounts. For a married taxpayer filing separately, the phase-out is 2 percent for each $1,250 or fraction thereof.

The allowable exemption amount can be determined with the following steps:

1. AGI − threshold amount = excess amount
2. (Excess amount/$2,500) × 2 = phase-out percentage (rounded up to the next whole increment, e.g. 18.1 = 19, 19.7 = 20)
3. Phase-out percentage (from step 2) × exemption amount = amount of exemptions phased-out
4. Exemption amounts − phase-out amount = allowable exemption deduction

EXAMPLE 20

S is a single taxpayer with AGI of $191,250. He has only one exemption.

1. $191,250 − $105,250 = $86,000 excess amount
2. $86,000/$2,500 = 34.4 (rounded to 35) × 2 = 70% (phase-out percentage)

19. § 151(c)(2).

3. 70% × $2,300 = $1,610 amount of exemption phased out
4. $2,300 − $1,610 = $690 allowable exemption deduction ◆

EXAMPLE 21

H and W file a joint return claiming two personal exemptions and one dependency exemption for their child. Their AGI is $267,900.

1. $267,900 − $157,900 = $110,000 excess amount
2. $110,000/$2,500 = 44 × 2 = 88% (phase-out percentage)
3. 88% × $6,900 (3 × $2,300) = $6,072 amount of exemptions phased out
4. $6,900 − $6,072 = $828 allowable exemption deduction ◆

EXAMPLE 22

H is married but files a separate return. His AGI is $98,950. He is entitled to one personal exemption.

1. $98,950 − $78,950 = $20,000 excess amount
2. [($20,000/$1,250) × 2] = 32% (phase-out percentage)
3. 32% × $2,300 = $736 amount of exemption phased out
4. $2,300 − $736 = $1,564 allowable exemption deduction ◆

Note that the exemption amount is completely phased out when the taxpayer's adjusted gross income exceeds the threshold amount by more than $122,500 ($61,250 for a married taxpayer filing a separate return), calculated as follows:

$122,501/$2,500 = 49.0001, rounded to 50 and multiplying by 2 = 100% (phase-out percentage).

EXAMPLE 23

H and W file a joint return claiming two personal exemptions and one dependency exemption for their child. Their AGI equals $281,900.

$281,900 − $157,900 = $124,000 excess amount

Since the excess amount exceeds $122,500, the exemptions are completely phased out. ◆

Note also that it is possible for an additional $1 of income to cause an increase in tax liability that far exceeds the additional income.

EXAMPLE 24

H and W are a married couple with AGI of $157,900 and an exemption amount of $9,200 (4 × $2,300). An additional $1 of gross income would cause the exemptions to be reduced by $184 (2% × $9,200). Thus, the marginal tax on the additional $1 of income would be $57.35 [31% tax rate × ($1 additional income + $184 reduction of exemptions)]. ◆

TAX DETERMINATION

◆

Tax Table Method

Most taxpayers compute their tax using the Tax Table. Taxpayers who are eligible to use the Tax Table compute taxable income (as shown in Figure 3–1) and determine their tax by reference to the Tax Table. The following taxpayers, however, may not use the Tax Table method:

- An individual who files a short period return (see Chapter 18).
- Individuals whose taxable income exceeds the maximum (ceiling) amount in the Tax Table. The 1991 Tax Table applies to taxable income below $50,000.
- An estate or trust.

The 1992 Tax Table was not available at the date of publication of this text. Therefore, the 1991 Tax Table will be used to illustrate the tax computation using the Tax Table method.

EXAMPLE 25

B, a single taxpayer, is eligible to use the Tax Table. For 1991, B had taxable income of $25,025. To determine B's tax using the Tax Table (see Appendix A), find the $25,000 to $25,050 income line. The first column to the right of the taxable income column is for single taxpayers. B's tax for 1991 is $4,362. ◆

Tax Rate Schedule Method

The Tax Rate Schedules contain rates of 15, 28, and 31 percent. Separate schedules are provided for the following filing statuses: single, married filing jointly, married filing separately, and head of household. The rate schedules for 1991 and 1992 are reproduced inside the front cover of this text and also in Appendix A.

The rate schedules are adjusted for inflation each year. Comparison of the 1990 and 1991 schedules shows that the rates were 15, 28, and 31 percent in both years, but the amount of taxable income to which each rate applies changed in 1991.

The 1992 rate schedule for single taxpayers is reproduced in Figure 3–7. This schedule is used to illustrate the tax computations in Examples 26, 27, and 28.

EXAMPLE 26

T had $18,000 of taxable income in 1992. His tax is $2,700 ($18,000 × 15%). ◆

Several terms are used to describe tax rates. The rates in the Tax Rate Schedules are often referred to as *statutory* (or nominal) rates. The *marginal* rate is the highest rate that is applied in the tax computation for a particular taxpayer. In Example 26, the statutory rate and the marginal rate are both 15 percent.

EXAMPLE 27

K had taxable income of $41,450 in 1992. Her tax is $8,817.50 [$3,217.50 + 28%($41,450 − $21,450)]. ◆

The *average* rate is equal to the tax liability divided by taxable income. In Example 27, K had statutory rates of 15 percent and 28 percent, and a marginal rate of 28 percent. K's average rate was 21.3 percent ($8,817.50 tax liability ÷ $41,450 taxable income).

FIGURE 3–7
1992 Tax Rate Schedule for Single Taxpayers

If taxable income is Over	But not over	The tax is	of the amount over
$ -0-	$21,450	15%	$ -0-
21,450	$51,900	$ 3,217.50 + 28%	21,450
51,900		$11,743.50 + 31%	51,900

Note that $3,217.50, which is the starting point in the tax computation in Example 27, is 15 percent of the $21,450 taxable income in the first bracket. Income in excess of $21,450 is taxed at a 28 percent rate. This reflects the *progressive* (or graduated) rate structure on which the United States income tax system is based. A tax is progressive if a higher rate of tax applies as the tax base increases.

EXAMPLE 28

G had taxable income of $81,900 in 1992. His tax is $21,043.50 [$11,743.50 + 31%($81,900 − $51,900)]. Note that the effect of this computation is to tax part of G's income at 15%, part at 28%, and part at 31%. An alternative computational method provides a clearer illustration of the progressive rate structure:

Tax on $21,450 at 15%	$ 3,217.50
Tax on $51,900 − $21,450 at 28%	8,526.00
Tax on $81,900 − $51,900 at 31%	9,300.00
Total	$21,043.50

◆

A special computation limits the tax rate on long-term capital gain to 28 percent of the gain. The alternative tax on long-term capital gain is discussed in detail in Chapter 16.

Computation of Net Taxes Payable or Refund Due

The pay-as-you-go feature of the Federal income tax system requires payment of all or part of the taxpayer's income tax liability during the year. These payments take the form of Federal income tax withheld by employers or estimated tax paid by the taxpayer or both.[20] The payments are applied against the tax from the Tax Table or Tax Rate Schedules to determine whether the taxpayer will get a refund or pay additional tax.

Employers are required to withhold income tax on compensation paid to their employees and to pay this tax over to the government. The employer notifies the employee of the amount of income tax withheld on Form W–2 (Wage and Tax Statement). The employee should receive this form by January 31 after the year in which the income tax is withheld.

Estimated tax must be paid by taxpayers who receive income that is not subject to withholding or income from which not enough tax is withheld. These individuals must file Form 1040–ES (Estimated Tax for Individuals) and pay in quarterly installments the income tax and self-employment tax estimated to be due (see Chapter 13 for a thorough discussion).

The income tax from the Tax Table or the Tax Rate Schedules is reduced first by the individual's tax credits. There is an important distinction between tax credits and tax deductions. Tax credits reduce the tax liability dollar-for-dollar. Tax deductions reduce taxable income on which the tax liability is based.

EXAMPLE 29

L is a taxpayer in the 28% tax bracket. As a result of incurring $1,000 in child care expenses (see Chapter 13 for details), she is entitled to a $200 child care credit ($1,000 child care expenses × 20% credit rate). L also contributed $1,000 to the American Cancer Society and included this amount in her itemized deductions. The child care credit results in a $200 reduction of L's tax liability for the year. The contribution to the

20. § 3402 for withholding; § 6202 for estimated payments.

American Cancer Society reduces taxable income by $1,000 and results in a $280 reduction in L's tax liability ($1,000 reduction in taxable income × 28% tax rate). ◆

Tax credits are discussed in Chapter 13. The following are several of the more common credits:

- Earned income credit.
- Credit for child and dependent care expenses.
- Credit for the elderly.
- Foreign tax credit.

Computation of an individual's net tax payable or refund due is illustrated in Example 30.

EXAMPLE 30

Y, age 30, is a head of household with two dependents. During 1992, Y had the following: taxable income, $30,000; income tax withheld, $3,950; estimated tax payments, $600; and credit for child care expenses, $200. Y's net tax payable is computed as follows:

Income tax (from 1992 Tax Rate Schedule, Appendix A)		$ 4,662.50
Less: Tax credits and prepayments—		
Credit for child care expenses	$ 200	
Income tax withheld	3,950	
Estimated tax payments	600	(4,750.00)
Net taxes payable or (refund due if negative)		$ (87.50)

◆

Unearned Income of Children under Age 14 Taxed at Parents' Rate

Before the Tax Reform Act (TRA) of 1986, a dependent child could claim an exemption on his or her own return even if claimed as a dependent by the parents. This enabled a parent to shift investment income (such as interest and dividends) to a child by transferring ownership of the assets producing the income. The child would pay no tax on such income to the extent the income was sheltered by the child's exemption.

For pre-1987 years, an additional tax motivation existed for shifting income from parents to children. Although a child's unearned income in excess of the exemption amount was subject to tax, it was taxed at the child's rate, rather than the parents' rate.

To reduce the tax savings that result from shifting income from parents to children, the net unearned income (commonly called investment income) of certain minor children is taxed as if it were the parents' income.[21] Unearned income includes such income as taxable interest, dividends, capital gains, rents, royalties, pension and annuity income, and income (other than earned income) received as the beneficiary of a trust. This provision, commonly referred to as the *kiddie tax*, applies to any child for any taxable year if the child has not reached age 14 by the close of the taxable year, has at least one living parent, and has unearned income of more than $1,200. The *kiddie tax* provision does not apply to a child 14 or older. However, the limitation on the use of the standard deduction

21. § 1(i).

and the unavailability of the personal exemption do apply to such a child as long as he or she is eligible to be claimed as a dependent by a parent.

The term *parent* is defined in the Senate Finance Committee Report as a parent or stepparent of the child. No statutory definition exists for the term.

Net Unearned Income. Net unearned income of a dependent child is computed as follows:

Unearned income
Less: $600
Less: The greater of
- $600 of the standard deduction *or*
- The amount of allowable itemized deductions directly connected with the production of the unearned income

Equals: Net unearned income

If net unearned income is zero (or negative), the child's tax is computed without using the parent's rate. If the amount of net unearned income (regardless of source) is positive, the net unearned income will be taxed at the parent's rate. The $600 amounts in the preceding formula are subject to adjustment for inflation each year (refer to footnote 9).

Tax Determination. If a child under age 14 has net unearned income, there are two options for computing the tax on the income. A separate return may be filed for the child, or the parents may elect to report the child's income on their own return. If a separate return is filed for the child, the tax on net unearned income (referred to as the *allocable parental tax*) is computed as though the income had been included on the parents' return. Form 8615 (reproduced in Appendix B) is used to compute the tax. The steps required in this computation are illustrated below.

EXAMPLE 31

H and W have a child, S (age 10). In 1992, S received $2,600 of interest and dividend income and paid investment-related fees of $200. H and W had $69,450 of taxable income, not including their child's investment income. H and W do not make the parental election.

1. Determine S's net unearned income.	
Gross income	$ 2,600
Less: $600	(600)
Less: The greater of	
■ $600 or	
■ Investment expense	(600)
Equals: Net unearned income	$ 1,400
2. Determine allocable parental tax.	
Parents' taxable income	$ 69,450
Plus: S's net unearned income	1,400
Equals: Revised taxable income	$ 70,850
Tax on revised taxable income (rounded)	$ 15,184
Less: Tax on parents' taxable income	(14,792)
Allocable parental tax	$ 392

3. **Determine S's nonparental source tax.**

S's AGI	$ 2,600
Less: Standard deduction	(600)
Less: Personal exemption	(–0–)
Equals: Taxable income	$ 2,000
Less: Net unearned income	(1,400)
Nonparental source taxable income	$ 600
Equals: Tax ($600 × 15% rate)	$ 90

4. **Determine S's total tax liability.**

Nonparental source tax (step 3)	$ 90
Allocable parental tax (step 2)	392
Total tax	$ 482

◆

Election to Claim Certain Unearned Income on Parent's Return. If a child under 14 meets all of the following requirements, the parent may elect to report the child's unearned income that exceeds $1,000 on the parent's own tax return. The child, then, is treated as having no gross income and is not required to file a tax return.

- Gross income is from interest and dividends only.
- Gross income is more than $500 and less than $5,000.
- No estimated tax has been paid in the name and Social Security number of the child, and the child is not subject to backup withholding (see Chapter 13).

The parent(s) must also pay an additional tax equal to the smaller of $75 or 15 percent of the child's gross income over $500. If the child has any interest from certain private activity bonds, that amount is a tax preference to the parents for purposes of the parents' alternative minimum tax (see Chapter 12).

EXAMPLE 32

Assume the same facts as in Example 31, except that the parents elect to report S's unearned income on their own tax return. The gross income in excess of $1,000 for S amounts to $1,600 ($2,600 – $1,000). The parents include this amount in gross income. Their taxable income increases from $69,450 to $71,050, resulting in a tax liability of $448 more than would result on the parents' taxable income alone. To their tax liability, the parents must add for S the lesser of $75 or 15% of gross income over $500. Thus, they must include $75 [the smaller of $75 or 15% of $2,100 ($2,600 – $500)] for S. The following total tax for the family unit results:

	Without Election	With Election
H and W	$14,792	$15,315*
S	482	–0–
	$15,274	$15,315

*$15,240 + $75.

◆

Further, parents who have substantial itemized deductions based on AGI (see Chapter 11) may find that making the parental election also increases total taxes for the family unit. Calculations should be made both with the parental election and without the election to determine the appropriate choice.

Other Provisions. If parents have more than one child subject to the tax on net unearned income, the tax for the children is computed as shown in Example 31 and then allocated to the children based on their relative amounts of income. For children of divorced parents, the taxable income of the custodial parent is used to determine the allocable parental tax. This parent is the one who may elect to report the child's unearned income. For married individuals filing separate returns, the individual with the greater taxable income is the applicable parent.

FILING CONSIDERATIONS

Under the category of filing considerations, the following questions need to be resolved:

- Is the taxpayer required to file an income tax return?
- If so, which form should be used?
- When and how should the return be filed?
- In computing the tax liability, which column of the Tax Table or which Tax Rate Schedule should be used?

The first three of these questions are discussed under Filing Requirements, and the last is treated under Filing Status.

Filing Requirements

General Rules. An individual must file a tax return if certain minimum amounts of gross income have been received. The general rule is that a tax return is required for every individual who has gross income that equals or exceeds the sum of the exemption amount plus the applicable standard deduction.[22] For example, a single taxpayer under age 65 must file a tax return in 1992 if gross income equals or exceeds $5,900 ($2,300 exemption plus $3,600 standard deduction). Figure 3–8 lists the income levels[23] that require tax returns under the general rule, and also lists amounts that require tax returns under certain special rules.

The additional standard deduction for being 65 or older is considered in determining the gross income filing requirements. For example, note in Figure 3–8 that the 1992 filing requirement for a single taxpayer 65 or older is $6,800 ($3,600 basic standard deduction + $900 additional standard deduction + $2,300 exemption). However, the additional standard deduction for blindness is not taken into account. The 1992 filing requirement for a single taxpayer under 65 and blind is $5,900 ($3,600 basic standard deduction + $2,300 exemption).

Filing Requirements for Dependents. Computation of the gross income filing requirement for an individual who can be claimed as a dependent on another person's tax return is subject to more complex rules. Such an individual must file a return if he or she has either of the following:

- Earned income only and gross income that is more than the total standard deduction (including any additional standard deduction) that the individual is allowed for the year.

22. The gross income amounts for determining whether a tax return must be filed are adjusted for inflation each year.

23. § 6012(a)(1).

- Unearned income only and gross income of more than $600 plus any additional standard deduction that the individual is allowed for the year.
- Both earned and unearned income and gross income of more than the larger of earned income (but limited to the applicable basic standard deduction) or $600, plus any additional standard deduction that the individual is allowed for the year.

Thus, the filing requirement for a dependent who has no unearned income is the total of the *basic* standard deduction plus any *additional* standard deduction, which includes the additional deduction for blindness. For example, the 1992 filing requirement for a single dependent who is under 65 and not blind is $3,600, the amount of the basic standard deduction for 1992. The filing requirement for a single dependent under 65 and blind is $4,500 ($3,600 basic standard deduction + $900 additional standard deduction).

A self-employed individual with net earnings of $400 or more from a business or profession must file a tax return regardless of the amount of gross income.

Even though an individual's gross income is below the filing level amounts and he or she therefore does not owe any tax, the individual has to file a return to obtain a tax refund of amounts withheld. A return is also necessary to obtain the benefits of the earned income credit allowed to taxpayers with little or no tax liability. Chapter 13 discusses the earned income credit.

Selecting the Proper Form. The 1992 tax forms had not been released at the date of publication of this text. The following comments apply to 1991 forms. It is possible that some provisions will change for the 1992 forms.

Individual taxpayers file a return on either Form 1040 (the long form), Form 1040A (the short form), or Form 1040EZ (see Appendix B). Taxpayers who cannot use either Form 1040EZ or Form 1040A must use Form 1040.

FIGURE 3–8
Filing Levels

Filing Status	**1991 Gross Income**	**1992 Gross Income**
Single		
Under 65 and not blind	$ 5,550	$ 5,900
Under 65 and blind	5,550	5,900
65 or older	6,400	6,800
Married, filing joint return		
Both spouses under 65 and neither blind	$10,000	$10,600
Both spouses under 65 and one or both spouses blind	10,000	10,600
One spouse 65 or older	10,650	11,300
Both spouses 65 or older	11,300	12,000
Married, filing separate return		
All—whether 65 or older or blind	$ 2,150	$ 2,300
Head of household		
Under 65 and not blind	$ 7,150	$ 7,550
Under 65 and blind	7,150	7,550
65 or older	8,000	8,450
Qualifying widow(er)		
Under 65 and not blind	$ 7,850	$ 8,300
Under 65 and blind	7,850	8,300
65 or older	8,500	9,000

Form 1040EZ is a form for taxpayers with the least complicated tax situations. In 1991, this form could be used by single taxpayers with no dependents who satisfied all of the following requirements:

- Was not 65 or over or blind.
- Had taxable income of less than $50,000.
- Had only wages, salaries, tips, and taxable scholarships and had interest income of $400 or less.
- Did not itemize deductions, claim any adjustments to income, or claim any tax credits.

Form 1040A may also be used by many taxpayers with uncomplicated tax situations. In 1991, an individual with any of the following was required to use Form 1040 (the most complex form) rather than Form 1040A:

- Taxable income was $50,000 or more.
- The taxpayer had income other than wages, salaries, tips, unemployment compensation, dividends, or interest.
- The taxpayer claimed credits other than credits for child or dependent care or the earned income credit.
- The taxpayer was required to use the Tax Rate Schedules.
- The taxpayer claimed any deductions other than the deduction for payments to an IRA.

When and Where to File. Tax returns of individuals are due on or before the fifteenth day of the fourth month following the close of the tax year. For the calendar year taxpayer, the usual filing date is on or before April 15 of the following year.[24] When the due date falls on a Saturday, Sunday, or legal holiday, the last day for filing falls on the next business day. If the return is mailed to the proper address with sufficient postage and is postmarked on or before the due date, it is deemed timely filed.

If a taxpayer is unable to file his or her return by the specified due date, a four-month extension of time can be obtained by filing Form 4868 (Application for Automatic Extension of Time to File U.S. Individual Income Tax Return).[25] Further extensions may be granted by the IRS upon a showing by the taxpayer of good cause. For this purpose, Form 2688 (Application for Extension of Time to File U.S. Individual Income Tax Return) should be used. An extension of more than six months will not be granted if the taxpayer is in the United States.

Although obtaining an extension excuses a taxpayer from a penalty for failure to file, it does not insulate against the penalty for failure to pay.[26] If more tax is owed, the filing of Form 4868 should be accompanied by an additional remittance to cover the balance due.

The return should be sent or delivered to the Regional Service Center of the IRS for the area where the taxpayer lives.[27]

If it is necessary to file an amended return (e.g., because of a failure to report income or to claim a deduction or tax credit), Form 1040X is filed by individual taxpayers. The form generally must be filed within three years of the filing date of the original return or within two years from the time the tax was paid, whichever is later.

---

24. § 6072(a).

25. Reg. § 1.6081–4.

26. For an explanation of these penalties, refer to Chapter 1.

27. The Regional Service Centers and the geographical area each covers can be found on the back cover of *Your Federal Income Tax,* IRS Publication 17 for 1991.

Filing Status

The amount of tax will vary considerably depending on which Tax Rate Schedule is used. This is illustrated in the following example.

EXAMPLE 33

The following amounts of tax are computed using the 1992 Tax Rate Schedules for a taxpayer (or taxpayers in the case of a joint return) with $40,000 of taxable income (see Appendix A).

Filing Status	Amount of Tax (rounded)
Single	$8,412
Married, filing joint return	6,546
Married, filing separate return	8,873
Head of household	7,463

◆

Rates for Single Taxpayers. A taxpayer who is unmarried or separated from his or her spouse by a decree of divorce or separate maintenance and does not qualify for another filing status must use the rates for single taxpayers. Marital status is determined as of the last day of the tax year, except when a spouse dies during the year. In that case, marital status is determined as of the date of death. State law governs whether a taxpayer is considered married, divorced, or legally separated.

Under a special relief provision, however, married persons who live apart may be able to qualify as single. Married taxpayers who are considered single under the *abandoned spouse rules* are allowed to use the head of household rates. See the discussion of this filing status under Abandoned Spouse Rules later in the chapter.

Rates for Married Individuals. The joint return [Tax Rate Schedule Y, Code § 1(a)] was originally enacted in 1948 to establish equity between married taxpayers in common law states and those in community property states. Before the joint return rates were enacted, taxpayers in community property states were in an advantageous position relative to taxpayers in common law states because they could split their income. For instance, if one spouse earned $100,000 and the other spouse was not employed, each spouse could report $50,000 of income. Splitting the income in this manner caused the total income to be subject to lower marginal tax rates. Each spouse would start at the bottom of the rate structure.

Taxpayers in common law states did not have this income-splitting option, so their taxable income was subject to higher marginal rates. This inconsistency in treatment was remedied by the joint return provisions. Under the joint return Tax Rate Schedule, the progressive rates are constructed based on the assumption that income is earned equally by the two spouses.

If married individuals elect to file separate returns, each reports only his or her own income, exemptions, deductions, and credits, and each must use the Tax Rate Schedule applicable to married taxpayers filing separately. It is generally advantageous for married individuals to file a joint return, since the combined amount of tax is lower. However, special circumstances (e.g., significant medical expenses incurred by one spouse subject to the 7.5 percent limitation) may warrant the election to file separate returns. It may be necessary to compute the tax under both assumptions to determine the most advantageous filing status.

The Code places some limitations on deductions, credits, etc., when married individuals file separately. If either spouse itemizes deductions, the other spouse must also itemize. Married taxpayers who file separately cannot take either of the following:

- The credit for child and dependent care expenses (in most instances).
- The earned income credit.

The joint return rates also apply for two years following the death of one spouse, if the surviving spouse maintains a household for a dependent child.[28] This is referred to as surviving spouse status.

Example 34

H dies in 1991 leaving W with a dependent child. For the year of H's death (1991), W files a joint return with H (presuming the consent of H's executor is obtained). For the next two years (1992 and 1993), W, as a surviving spouse, may use the joint return rates. In subsequent years, W may use the head-of-household rates if she continues to maintain a household as her home that is the domicile of the child. ◆

Rates for Heads of Household. Unmarried individuals who maintain a household for a dependent (or dependents) are entitled to use the head-of-household rates.[29] The tax liability using the head-of-household rates falls between the liability using the joint return Tax Rate Schedule and the liability using the Tax Rate Schedule for single taxpayers.

To qualify for head-of-household rates, a taxpayer must pay more than half the cost of maintaining a household as his or her home. The household must also be the principal home of a dependent relative as defined in § 152(a).[30] As a general rule, the dependent must live in the taxpayer's household for over half the year.

The general rule has two exceptions. One exception is that an unmarried child (child also means grandchild, stepchild, or adopted child) need not be a dependent in order for the taxpayer to qualify as a head of household. This exception also applies to a married child if the child is claimed by the noncustodial parent as a result of a written agreement between the custodial parent and the noncustodial parent (refer to Example 18).

Example 35

M maintains a household where she and S, her nondependent unmarried son, reside. Since S is not married, M qualifies for the head-of-household rates. ◆

Another exception to the general rule is that head-of-household status may be claimed if the taxpayer maintains a separate home for his or her parent or parents if at least one parent qualifies as a dependent of the taxpayer.[31]

Example 36

S, an unmarried individual, lives in New York City and maintains a household in Detroit for his dependent parents. S may use the favorable head-of-household rates even though his parents do not reside in his New York home. ◆

Abandoned Spouse Rules. When married persons file separate returns, several unfavorable tax consequences result. For example, the taxpayer must use the Tax Rate Schedule for married taxpayers filing separately. To mitigate such

28. § 2(a).
29. § 2(b).
30. § 2(b)(1)(A)(i).
31. § 2(b)(1)(B).

harsh treatment, Congress enacted provisions commonly referred to as the abandoned spouse rules. These rules allow a married taxpayer to file as a head of household if all of the following conditions are satisfied:

- The taxpayer does not file a joint return.
- The taxpayer paid more than one-half the cost of maintaining his or her home for the tax year.
- The taxpayer's spouse did not live in the home during the last six months of the tax year.
- The home was the principal residence of the taxpayer's child, stepchild, or adopted child for more than half the year.
- The taxpayer could claim the child, stepchild, or adopted child as a dependent.[32]

Gains and Losses from Property Transactions—In General

Gains and losses from property transactions are discussed in detail in Chapters 14 through 17. Because of their importance in the tax system, however, they are introduced briefly at this point.

On the sale or other disposition of property, gain or loss may result. Such gain or loss has an effect on the income tax position of the party making the sale or other disposition when the *realized* gain or loss is *recognized* for tax purposes. Without realized gain or loss, generally, there can be no recognized gain or loss. The concept of realized gain or loss is expressed as follows:

$$\text{Amount realized from the sale} - \text{Adjusted basis of the property} = \text{Realized gain (or loss)}$$

The amount realized is the selling price of the property less any costs of disposition (e.g., brokerage commissions) incurred by the seller. Simply stated, adjusted basis of the property is determined as follows:

Cost (or other original basis) at date of acquisition[33]	
Add:	Capital additions
Subtract:	Depreciation (if appropriate) and other capital recoveries (see Chapter 9)
Equals:	Adjusted basis at date of sale or other disposition

All realized gains are recognizable (taxable) unless some specific part of the tax law provides otherwise (see Chapter 15 dealing with certain nontaxable exchanges). Realized losses may or may not be recognizable (deductible) for tax purposes, depending on the circumstances involved. Generally, losses realized from the disposition of personal use property (property neither held for investment nor used in a trade or business) are not recognizable.

Example 37

During the current year, T sells his sailboat (adjusted basis of $4,000) for $5,500. T also sells one of his personal automobiles (adjusted basis of $8,000) for $5,000. T's

32. The dependency requirement does not apply, however, if the taxpayer could have claimed a dependency exemption except for the fact that the exemption was claimed by the noncustodial parent under a written agreement. Refer to Example 18 and the related discussion.

33. Cost usually means purchase price plus expenses related to the acquisition of the property and incurred by the purchaser (e.g., brokerage commissions). For the basis of property acquired by gift or inheritance and other basis rules, see Chapter 14.

realized gain of $1,500 from the sale of the sailboat is recognizable. On the other hand, the $3,000 realized loss on the sale of the automobile is not recognized and will not provide T with any deductible tax benefit. ◆

Once it has been determined that the disposition of property results in a recognizable gain or loss, the next step is to classify the gain or loss as capital or ordinary. Although ordinary gain is fully taxable and ordinary loss is fully deductible, the same may not hold true for capital losses.

GAINS AND LOSSES FROM PROPERTY TRANSACTIONS—CAPITAL GAINS AND LOSSES

For tax years beginning after 1990, preferential tax treatment may apply to gains on capital assets that have been held for more than a year. The maximum rate on *net capital gain* (see Chapter 16 for details) is 28 percent. This provision could save 3 percent for taxpayers in the 31 percent bracket. Because of the potential tax savings on long-term capital gains, property transactions are important factors in effective tax planning.

Definition of a Capital Asset

Capital assets are defined in the Code as any property held by the taxpayer *other than* property listed in § 1221. The list in § 1221 includes inventory, accounts receivable, and depreciable property or real estate used in a business. Thus, the sale or exchange of assets in these categories usually results in ordinary income or loss treatment (see Chapter 17).

EXAMPLE 38

C owns a pizza parlor. During the current year, C sells two automobiles. The first automobile, which had been used as a pizza delivery car for three years, was sold at a loss of $1,000. Because this automobile is an asset used in his business, C has an ordinary loss deduction of $1,000, rather than a capital loss deduction. The second automobile, which C had owned for two years, was C's personal car. It was sold for a gain of $800. The personal car is a capital asset. Therefore, C has a capital gain of $800. ◆

The principal capital assets held by an individual taxpayer include assets held for personal (rather than business) use, such as a personal residence or an automobile, and assets held for investment purposes (e.g., corporate securities and land).

Computation of Net Capital Gains and Losses

Capital gains and losses must be classified as short term (those on assets held for one year or less) and long term (those on assets held for more than one year). Short-term capital losses (STCL) are offset against short-term capital gains (STCG). The result is either net short-term capital gain (NSTCG) or net short-term capital loss (NSTCL).

Long-term capital losses (LTCL) are offset against long-term capital gains (LTCG), and the result is either net long-term capital gain (NLTCG) or net long-term capital loss (NLTCL).

Several combinations are possible after this first round of offsetting. For example, if the taxpayer has NSTCL and NLTCG, these amounts are offset. Likewise, if the taxpayer has NLTCL and NSTCG, a similar offsetting is required. In general, the offsetting continues as long as there is gain in any category and loss in any other category.

EXAMPLE 39

In the current year, T has the following capital gains and losses: STCL of $4,000, STCG of $3,000, LTCG of $6,000, and LTCL of $2,000. This results in NSTCL of $1,000 ($4,000 STCL − $3,000 STCG) and NLTCG of $4,000 ($6,000 LTCG − $2,000 LTCL). The $1,000 NSTCL is used to offset the $4,000 NLTCG, resulting in an excess of NLTCG over NSTCL of $3,000. ◆

Capital Loss Limitation

Capital losses are first offset against capital gains (as illustrated in Example 39). If, after this offsetting, an individual taxpayer has net capital losses, such losses are deductible as a deduction *for* AGI to a maximum of $3,000 per year. Any unused amounts are carried over for an indefinite period.

EXAMPLE 40

During the year, T has $1,000 of NLTCL and $2,000 of NSTCL. T's other income is $100,000. T's capital loss deduction for the year is $3,000, which consists of $2,000 NSTCL and $1,000 NLTCL. ◆

When a taxpayer has both short-term and long-term capital losses, and the losses together exceed $3,000, the short-term losses must be used first in applying the $3,000 limitation.

EXAMPLE 41

R has NSTCL of $2,500 and NLTCL of $5,000 for the year. R's other income is $50,000. R uses the losses as follows:

NSTCL	$2,500
NLTCL	500
Maximum capital loss deduction	$3,000

The remaining NLTCL of $4,500 ($5,000 NLTCL minus $500 used) may be carried forward for an indefinite period until used. See Chapter 16 for a detailed discussion of capital loss carryovers. ◆

Corporate Capital Losses. Corporate taxpayers may offset capital losses only against capital gains. Capital losses in excess of capital gains may not be used to reduce ordinary income of a corporation. A corporation's unused capital losses are subject to a carryback and carryover. Capital losses are initially carried back three years and then carried forward five years to offset capital gains that arise in those years. See Chapter 16 for a discussion of capital losses of corporate taxpayers.

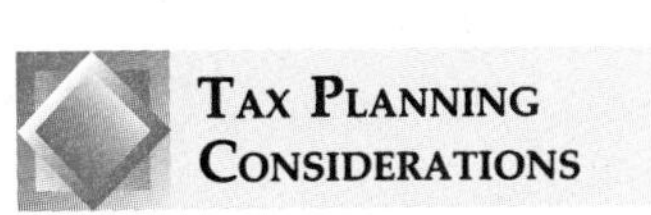

Taking Advantage of Tax Rate Differentials

It is natural for taxpayers to be concerned about the tax rates they are paying. How does a tax practitioner communicate information about rates to clients? There are several possibilities.

The marginal rate (refer to Examples 26 through 28) provides information that can help a taxpayer evaluate a particular course of action or structure a transaction in the most advantageous manner.

EXAMPLE 42

T, who is in the 28% marginal tax bracket for 1992, is considering the sale of corporate stock he has held as an investment for a $10,000 gain in December. If he sells the stock, his income tax increases by $2,800 ($10,000 gain × 28% marginal rate), and he has $7,200 of after-tax income ($10,000 − $2,800). ◆

EXAMPLE 43

Assume the same facts as in Example 42 and that T plans to retire early in 1993. Upon retirement, T's only source of income will be nontaxable Social Security benefits and municipal bond interest. If T waits until 1993 to sell the stock, his tax on the gain is $1,500, and his after-tax income is $8,500 ($10,000 gain −$1,500 tax). By being aware of the effect of marginal tax rates, T can save $1,300 in tax. ◆

The marginal rate analysis illustrated in Examples 42 and 43 for an income item can also help a taxpayer obtain the greatest tax benefit from a deductible expense. For example, a taxpayer who is in the 15 percent bracket this year and expects to be in the 31 percent bracket next year should, if possible, defer payment of deductible expenses until next year to maximize the tax benefit of the deduction.

A note of caution is in order with respect to shifting income and expenses between years. Congress has recognized the tax planning possibilities of such shifting and has enacted many provisions to limit a taxpayer's ability to do so. Some of these limitations on the shifting of income are discussed in Chapters 4, 5, and 18. Limitations that affect a taxpayer's ability to shift deductions are discussed in Chapters 6 through 11 and in Chapter 18.

A taxpayer's *effective rate* can be an informative measure of the effectiveness of tax planning. The effective rate is computed by dividing the taxpayer's tax liability by the total amount of income. A low effective rate can be considered an indication of effective tax planning.

One way of lowering the effective rate is to exclude income from the tax base. For example, a taxpayer might consider investing in tax-free municipal bonds rather than taxable corporate bonds. Although pre-tax income from corporate bonds is usually higher, after-tax income may be higher if the taxpayer invests in tax-free municipals.

Another way of lowering the effective rate is to make sure that the taxpayer's expenses and losses are deductible. For example, losses on investments in passive activities may not be deductible (see Chapter 7). Therefore, a taxpayer who plans to invest in an activity that will produce a loss in the early years should take steps to ensure that the business is treated as active rather than passive. Active losses are deductible while passive losses are not.

Income of Minor Children

Taxpayers can use several strategies to avoid or minimize the effect of the rules that tax the unearned income of certain minor children at the parents' rate. The kiddie tax rules do not apply once a child reaches age 14. Parents should consider giving a younger child assets that defer taxable income until the child reaches age 14. For example, U.S. government Series EE savings bonds can be used to defer income until the bonds are cashed in (see Chapter 4).

Growth stocks typically pay little in the way of dividends. However, the profit on an astute investment may more than offset the lack of dividends. The child can hold the stock until he or she reaches age 14. If the stock is sold then at a profit, the profit is taxed at the child's low rates.

Taxpayers in a position to do so can employ their children in their business and pay them a reasonable wage for the work they actually perform (e.g., light office help, such as filing). The child's earned income is sheltered by the standard deduction, and the parents' business is allowed a deduction for the wages. The kiddie tax rules have no effect on earned income, even if it is earned from the parents' business.

Alternating between Itemized Deductions and the Standard Deduction

When total itemized deductions are approximately equal to the standard deduction from year to year, it is possible for cash basis taxpayers to save taxes by proper timing of payments. To obtain a deduction for itemized deductions in one year and make use of the standard deduction in the next year, taxpayers should shift deductions from one year to the other. This results in a larger benefit over the two-year period than otherwise would be available.

EXAMPLE 44

T, who is single, is a cash basis and calendar year taxpayer. For tax years 1991 and 1992, T's itemized deductions are as follows:

	1991	1992
Charitable contribution	$1,800	$1,800
Other itemized deductions (e.g., interest, taxes)	1,300	1,300
Total itemized deductions	$3,100	$3,100

As presently structured, in neither year is T able to benefit from these itemized deductions, since they do not exceed the standard deduction applicable to a taxpayer claiming single status ($3,400 in 1991 and $3,600 in 1992). Thus, T's benefit for both years totals $7,000 ($3,400 + $3,600), all based on the standard deduction. ◆

EXAMPLE 45

Assume the same facts as in Example 44, except that in late 1991 T prepays the charitable contribution for 1992. With this change, T's position for both years becomes:

	1991	1992
Charitable contribution	$3,600	$ -0-
Other itemized deductions	1,300	1,300
Total itemized deductions	$4,900	$1,300

Under these circumstances, T claims itemized deductions of $4,900 for 1991 and the standard deduction of $3,600 for 1992. A comparison of the total benefit of $8,500 ($4,900 + $3,600) with the result reached in Example 44 of $7,000 ($3,400 + $3,600) clearly shows the advantage of this type of planning. ◆

Dependency Exemptions

The Joint Return Test. A married person can be claimed as a dependent only if that individual does not file a joint return with his or her spouse. If a joint return has been filed, the damage may be undone if separate returns are substituted on a timely basis (on or before the due date of the return).

EXAMPLE 46

While preparing a client's 1991 income tax return on April 10, 1992, the tax practitioner discovered that the client's daughter filed a joint return with her husband in late January of 1992. Presuming the daughter otherwise qualifies as the client's dependent, the exemption is not lost if she and her husband file separate returns on or before April 15, 1992. ◆

An initial election to file a joint return must be considered carefully in any situation in which the taxpayers might later decide to amend their return and file separately. As indicated above, separate returns may be substituted for a joint return only if the amended returns are filed on or before the normal due date of the return. If the taxpayers in Example 46 attempt to file separate returns after April 15, 1992, the returns will not be accepted, and the joint return election is binding.[34]

Keep in mind that the filing of a joint return will not be fatal to the dependency exemption if the parties are filing solely to recover all income tax withholdings, neither is required to file a return, and no tax liability would exist on separate returns. The filing requirement for married persons filing separate returns applies. The application of these rules can be interesting when contrasting common law and community property jurisdictions.

EXAMPLE 47

In 1992, T furnished 80% of the support of his son (S) and daughter-in-law (D). During the year, D earned $2,400 from a part-time job. As a result, D and S filed a joint return to obtain a refund of all the income tax withheld. All parties reside in New York (a common law state). Presuming the joint return stands (refer to Example 46), T cannot claim either S or D as his dependent. Although D and S filed a joint return to recover D's withholdings, D was required to file (she had gross income of $2,300 or more). ◆

EXAMPLE 48

Assume the same facts as in Example 47, except that all parties reside in Arizona (a community property state). Under these circumstances, T may claim both S and D as dependents. Not only have they filed a joint return to recover all of D's withholdings, but neither was required to file. Recall that in a community property state (unless otherwise altered by agreement between spouses, if permitted by state law), half of the wages of a spouse are attributable to the other spouse. S and D are treated as each having earned $1,200, which is less than the filing requirement for married persons filing separate returns. ◆

The Gross Income Test. The exception to the gross income test for a person under the age of 19 or a full-time student under the age of 24 applies only to a child of the taxpayer. The term *child* is limited to a son, stepson, daughter, stepdaughter, adopted son, or adopted daughter and may include a foster child.

EXAMPLE 49

Assume the same facts as in Example 47, except that S and D (the son and daughter-in-law) do not file a joint return. Further assume that D (the person who had gross income of $2,400) is a full-time student under age 24. Even though T may claim S as a dependent, D does not qualify since she has gross income of $2,300 or more. The student exception to the gross income test does not apply because D is not a *child* of T. ◆

As was true with Example 48, the residence of the parties in a common law or a community property state can produce different results.

EXAMPLE 50

In 1992, T furnishes 60% of the support of his son (S) and daughter-in-law (D), both over the age of 19. During the year, D earns $4,800 from a part-time job, while S is unemployed and not a full-time student. All parties reside in New Jersey (a common law state). T may claim S as a dependent, but D does not qualify because of the gross income test. ◆

34. Reg. § 1.6013–1(a)(1).

EXAMPLE 51

Assume the same facts as in Example 50, except that all parties reside in Washington (a community property state). T may not claim either S or D as dependents because of the application of the gross income test. Each spouse is treated as having gross income of $2,400 (one-half of $4,800), which is not below the $2,300 filing level. ◆

The Support Test. Adequate records of expenditures for support should be maintained in the event a dependency exemption is questioned on audit by the IRS. The maintenance of adequate records is particularly important for exemptions arising from multiple support agreements.

Relationship to the Deduction for Medical Expenses. Generally, medical expenses are deductible only if they are paid on behalf of the taxpayer, his or her spouse, and their dependents. Since deductibility may rest on dependency status, planning is important in arranging multiple support agreements.

EXAMPLE 52

During the year, M will be supported by her two sons (S_1 and S_2) and her daughter (D). Each will furnish approximately one-third of the required support. If the parties decide that the dependency exemption should be claimed by the daughter under a multiple support agreement, any medical expenses incurred by M should be paid by D. ◆

In planning a multiple support agreement, take into account which of the parties is most likely to exceed the 7.5 percent limitation (see Chapter 11). In Example 52, for instance, D might be a poor choice if she and her family do not expect to incur many medical and drug expenses of their own.

One exception permits the deduction of medical expenses paid on behalf of someone who is not a spouse or a dependent. If the person could be claimed as a dependent *except* for the gross income or joint return test, the medical expenses are, nevertheless, deductible.

EXAMPLE 53

During the year, T pays for all of the medical expenses of her uncle (U) and her married son (S). U otherwise qualifies as T's dependent, except that he had gross income of $2,500. Also, S otherwise qualifies as a dependent, except that he filed a joint return with his wife. Even though T may not claim dependency exemptions for U and S, she can claim the medical and drug expenses she paid on behalf of each. ◆

PROBLEM MATERIALS

DISCUSSION QUESTIONS

1. Rearrange the following components to show the formula for arriving at the amount of Federal taxable income:

   a. Deductions *for* adjusted gross income.
   b. The greater of the standard deduction or itemized deductions.
   c. Income (broadly conceived).
   d. Adjusted gross income.
   e. Exclusions.
   f. Personal and dependency exemptions.
   g. Gross income.

2. P earned a salary of $45,000 in the current year. To obtain money for a down payment on a house, she sold 100 shares of XYZ Corporation stock for $34,000. She had paid $22,000 for the stock five years ago. What is P's gross income?
3. J purchased 100 shares of X Corporation common stock in June 1992 for $100 per share. On December 15, he sold 50 shares for $120 per share. The remaining shares are worth $125 each on December 31, 1992. How much income must J report with respect to the stock in 1992?
4. H earned a salary of $43,000 and incurred a $3,500 capital loss in the current year. He incurred medical expenses of $4,500. He had other itemized deductions of $5,200. Compute H's total itemized deductions.
5. Contrast the treatment of expenses incurred in a trade or business with the treatment of expenses incurred in connection with the management of property held for the production of income.
6. Discuss the special limitations that apply to the personal exemption and standard deduction of an individual who can be claimed as a dependent of another taxpayer.
7. M is a student at Lakeland Community College. He earned $6,500 during 1992. Under what circumstances will M's parents be allowed to claim him as a dependent?
8. If an individual who may qualify as a dependent does not spend funds that he or she has received (e.g., wages or Social Security benefits), are these unexpended amounts considered in applying the support test? Are they included in applying the gross income test?
9. F contributed $2,100 toward the support of his son, S, who is 18 years old and a full-time college student. S earned $1,100 interest on a savings account and $900 working at a supermarket during the summer. S used all his earnings for his support. He also received a $1,000 scholarship from the college he attended. Can F claim S as a dependent? Explain.
10. M's only income was $2,200 in Social Security benefits she received during the year. She spent $1,700 of this amount toward her own support. M lives with her daughter D, who contributed $1,500 toward M's support. Can D claim M as a dependent? Explain.
11. M purchased a stereo system for her son G, age 16. The stereo was placed in G's room and used exclusively by G. M also purchased a new sports car, titled and registered in her own name, that was used 90% of the time by G. Should the cost of these items be considered as support in determining whether M may claim G as a dependent?
12. Z, who is a dependent of his parents, is a full-time student at Central City College. During the current year, Z, age 20, earned $1,500 from a part-time job. Because he is claimed as a dependent by his parents, Z will not be allowed to claim an exemption for himself when filing his own tax return. True or false? Explain.
13. F provided 75% of the support of N, her niece. N was a full-time student during the year and earned $3,800 from a part-time job. Can F claim N as a dependent?
14. T, age 20 and a full-time student at Midwestern State University, is claimed as a dependent on his parents' tax return. During the summer of 1992, T earned $3,500 from a part-time job. T's only other income consisted of $1,500 in interest on a savings account. Compute T's taxable income for 1992.
15. J's support is provided by her daughter (40%), her son (30%), and an unrelated friend (30%). Can J be claimed as a dependent by any of the individuals who contributed to her support? Explain.
16. B, who is married, must use either (a) the rates for married taxpayers filing jointly or (b) the rates for married taxpayers filing separately. True or false? Explain.
17. B is married to K, who left her and their six minor children in May of the current year. B does not know where K is and has not seen him since he left. She works two jobs to maintain a home for her children. What is the most advantageous filing status available to B?
18. A single individual age 65 or over and blind is required to file a Federal income tax return in 1992 if he or she has gross income of $6,800 or more (refer to Figure 3–8).

a. Explain how the $6,800 filing requirement was computed.
b. In general, explain the effect of the additional standard deduction on the determination of gross income requirements for filing.

19. T and S are engaged to be married. Each has gross income of $30,000 for 1992. Assume that they plan to make use of the standard deduction and have no dependency exemptions or tax credits. If they marry before the end of 1992, what is the overall effect on the total Federal income taxes that they will pay?
20. K, age 67 and blind, earned $6,500 of interest and received Social Security benefits of $7,200 in 1992. Is K required to file a tax return?
21. H, age 67, is married to W, who is age 62 and blind. H and W file a joint return. How much gross income can they earn before they are required to file an income tax return for 1992?
22. V, a high school student, earned $1,000 from a summer job during the current year. V is aware that this amount is below the income level that will require her to file a return and therefore does not plan to file. Do you have any advice for V?
23. K has been ill and will not be able to complete her Federal income tax return by April 15. Based on preliminary calculations, she estimates that she will owe $600 when she files her return. What procedure should K follow?
24. During the current year, T had a $6,000 long-term capital loss on the sale of common stock he had held as an investment. In addition, he had a $2,000 gain on the sale of his personal automobile, which he had owned for a year. How do these transactions affect T's taxable income?
25. Ten years ago, T purchased a personal residence for $140,000. In the current year, she sells the residence for $105,000. T's friend tells her she has a recognizable loss of $35,000 from the sale. Do you agree with the friend's comment? Elaborate.
26. List some assets that are not capital assets and some that are capital assets. Why is it important to determine whether an asset is an ordinary asset or a capital asset?
27. During the current year, P earned a salary of $50,000. She sold 20 shares of Y Corporation common stock at a loss of $2,000 and sold her personal automobile at a loss of $1,500. Compute P's AGI.
28. If T has a salary of $30,000 and net long-term capital losses of $4,500, what is his AGI?
29. If a corporation has net short-term capital losses of $20,000 and net long-term capital gains of $6,000, what amounts are deductible by the corporation? How are any unused losses treated?

PROBLEMS

30. Compute the taxpayer's taxable income for 1992 in each of the following cases:

    a. H is married and files a joint return with his wife W. H and W have two dependent children. They have AGI of $50,000 and $8,300 of itemized deductions.
    b. S is unmarried and has no dependents. He has AGI of $45,000 and itemized deductions of $3,200.
    c. G, age 22, is a full-time college student who is claimed as a dependent by her parents. She earned $3,600 from a part-time job and had interest income of $1,500.
    d. M, age 20, is a full-time college student who is claimed as a dependent by his parents. He earned $2,500 from a part-time job and had interest income of $4,100. His itemized deductions related to the investment income were $700.

31. Determine the standard deduction and exemption amount for 1992 for the following taxpayers:

    a. S, age 65, is a single taxpayer with no dependents.
    b. G, age 36, is a single taxpayer with no dependents.
    c. M is a full-time college student, age 22, who is claimed as a dependent on her parents' Federal income tax return in 1992. She earned interest of $900.
    d. Assume the same facts as in (c), except that M also earned $4,000 from a summer job.

Note: Problems 32 through 34 can be solved by referring to Figures 3–1 through 3–6 and the discussion under Deductions for Adjusted Gross Income in this chapter.

32. Compute taxable income for L on the basis of the following information:

Filing status	Head of household
Salary	$53,000
Inheritance	20,000
Capital loss	4,500
Charitable contributions	9,000
Medical expenses	7,000
State and local income taxes	2,800
Interest on home mortgage	6,000
Number of dependents	3
Age	66

33. Compute taxable income for M on the basis of the following information:

Filing status	Single
Salary	$52,000
Child support payments received	9,000
Gain from illegal activities	10,000
Contribution to Individual Retirement Account	2,000
Moving expenses	7,500
Theft loss (deductible portion)	5,500
State and local income taxes	900
Interest on home mortgage	3,500
Number of dependents	1
Age	34

34. Compute taxable income for C and N on the basis of the following information:

Filing status	Married, joint
C's salary	$38,000
Bonus from C's employer	7,000
Gift from N's uncle	9,000
Contribution to Individual Retirement Account	2,000
N's gambling winnings	1,000
Charitable contributions	400
State and local income taxes	2,100
Interest on home mortgage	2,900
Number of dependents	0
C's age	66
N's age	65

35. X, age 30, is single, and has no dependents. In 1992, X earned $62,000 and had itemized deductions of $9,100. Compute X's taxable income and tax before prepayments or credits for the year.

36. T, who is single, earned $80,000 in 1992. He incurred a short-term capital loss of $5,000 and had total itemized deductions of $12,500. Compute T's taxable income for 1992.

37. J, age 65, is single and has no dependents. His salary for 1992 was $45,000. He received interest of $600 from First National Bank and dividends of $750 from Acme Computer Corporation. J incurred a capital loss of $2,500 on the sale of Z Corporation common stock and had a capital gain of $1,200 on the sale of his personal automobile. He deposited $2,000 in his IRA, for which he is allowed a

deduction. He incurred medical expenses of $4,200, mortgage interest of $2,800, and real estate taxes on his home of $1,400. J contributed $1,200 to the United Fund. Compute J's taxable income for the year.

38. M, age 32, is single and has no dependents. She has custody of her 9-year-old son, who lives with her for 10 months during the year, but he is claimed as a dependent by his father. M's salary for 1992 was $51,000, and she earned interest of $1,300 on X Corporation bonds. She received alimony of $12,000 and child support of $6,000 from her former husband. Her itemized deductions were $5,200. Compute M's tax liability for the year.

39. H and W are married and file a joint return. H is 66 years of age, and W is 65. H's salary for 1992 was $33,000, and W earned $41,000. W won $10,000 in the state lottery and inherited $25,000 from her aunt. H incurred a $2,500 capital loss on stock he sold in December. H and W provided 90% of the support for D, their 23-year-old daughter, who is a full-time student. H and W also provided over half of the support of J, who is D's husband. J joined the army in March and earned $2,100. D and J filed a joint return. H and W also provide over half of the support of W's mother, M, who lives in a nursing home. M earned interest of $2,200 on a savings account and received Social Security benefits of $6,400. H and W had total itemized deductions of $7,800.

a. Compute taxable income for H and W for 1992.
b. Assume the same facts, except that J earned $6,100 in 1992. Compute taxable income for H and W for 1992.

40. B, age 13, is a full-time student supported by his parents who claim him on their tax return for 1992. B's parents present you with the following information and ask that you prepare B's 1992 Federal income tax return:

Wages from summer job	$1,400
Interest on savings account at First National Bank	1,200
Interest on XYZ Corporation bonds B received as a gift from his grandfather two years ago	600
Dividend from Z Corporation	200

a. What is B's taxable income for 1992?
b. B's parents file a joint return for 1992 on which they report taxable income of $66,000. Compute B's 1992 tax liability.

41. R is a wealthy executive who had taxable income of $200,000 in 1992. He is considering transferring title in a duplex he owns to his son S, age 16. S has no other income and is claimed as a dependent by R. Net rent income from the duplex is $4,000 a year, which S will be encouraged to place in a savings account. Will the family save income taxes in 1992 if R transfers title in the duplex to S? Explain.

42. H and J, both 40 years of age, are married and have no children. They file separate returns for 1992. H claims itemized deductions of $6,600, and J's itemized deductions total $1,700. Because her itemized deductions are less than the standard deduction, J intends to use the standard deduction for computing her taxable income. What is the amount of the standard deduction J may claim? Explain.

43. L, age 22, is single and lives with her parents, who provide 70% of her support. L, a full-time student at Parkland Community College, earned a salary of $9,200 in 1992 and had itemized deductions of $1,400. What is L's taxable income for the year?

44. Compute the 1992 tax liability for each of the following taxpayers:

a. H and M, both age 46, are married, have two dependent children, and file a joint return. Their combined salaries totaled $90,000. They had deductions *for* AGI of $4,000 and total itemized deductions of $6,000.
b. D, age 45, is single and has no dependents. He had a salary of $70,000, deductions *for* AGI of $3,000, and total itemized deductions of $12,000.
c. B and C, both age 65, are married, have no dependents, and file a joint return. Their combined salaries were $85,000. They had deductions *for* AGI of $6,000 and itemized deductions of $20,000.

45. Compute the 1992 tax liability for each of the following taxpayers:

   a. F, age 65, is single and has no dependents. He earned $94,260, had deductions *for* AGI of $4,000, and had itemized deductions of $3,700.
   b. J, who is single and has no dependents, has taxable income of $85,000.
   c. X, who is single and has no dependents, has taxable income of $95,000.
   d. N and P, both age 34, have one dependent child, L, age 10. N and P have taxable income of $96,000. L receives interest income of $3,000 during the year. Compute L's tax liability.

46. T, age 12, is claimed as a dependent on his parents' 1992 Federal income tax return, on which they reported taxable income of $95,000. During the summer, T earned $2,500 from a job as a model. His only other income consisted of $1,700 in interest on a savings account. Compute T's taxable income and tax liability.

47. L, who is 12 years old, is claimed as a dependent on her parents' tax return. During 1992, she received $12,200 in dividends and interest and incurred itemized deductions of $800 related to the management of her portfolio assets. She also earned $2,000 wages from a part-time job. Compute the amount of income that is taxed at her parents' rate.

48. M, who is 14 years old, is claimed as a dependent on her parents' tax return. During 1992, she received $9,000 in dividends and interest and incurred itemized deductions of $800 related to the management of her portfolio assets. She also earned $1,700 wages from a part-time job. Compute the amount of income that is taxed at her own rate.

49. W, age 67 and single, is claimed as a dependent by his daughter. He earned $900 interest and $1,050 wages from a part-time job. Compute W's taxable income for 1992.

50. G, age 67 and single, is claimed as a dependent by her son. She earned $300 interest and $1,650 wages from a part-time job. Compute G's income tax for 1992.

51. K, age 65 and single, had gross income of $63,000 in 1992. He had a capital loss of $5,000, medical expenses of $8,000, and other itemized deductions of $3,000. Compute his income tax.

52. C had the following gains and losses from the sale of capital assets during 1992: $7,000 STCG, $5,000 STCL, $1,000 LTCG, and $7,500 LTCL. What are the amount and character of C's capital loss carryover to 1993?

53. Determine the correct number of personal and dependency exemptions in each of the following independent situations:

   a. T, age 66 and disabled, is a widower who maintains a home for his unmarried daughter who is 24 years old. The daughter earned $3,000 and attends college on a part-time basis. T provides more than 50% of her support.
   b. T, a bachelor age 45, provides more than 50% of the support of his father, age 70. T's father had gross income of $3,500 from a part-time job.
   c. T, age 45, is married and has two dependent foster children who live with him and are totally supported by T. One of the foster children, age 14, had $2,200 of gross income. T and his spouse file a joint return.
   d. T, age 67, is married and has a married daughter, age 22. T's daughter attended college on a full-time basis and was supported by T. The daughter filed a joint return with her spouse. T filed a joint return with his spouse, age 62.

54. Compute the number of personal and dependency exemptions in the following independent situations:

   a. T, a single individual, provides 60% of the support of his mother, age 69. T's mother received dividend income of $1,000 and $1,500 in Social Security benefits.
   b. T, a married individual filing a joint return, provides 100% of the support of his son, age 21, who is a part-time student. T's son earned $2,500 during the year from part-time employment.
   c. T is divorced and provides $2,000 of child support for his child who is living with her mother, who provides support of $2,500. An agreement executed in

1986 between T and his former wife provides that the noncustodial parent is to receive the dependency exemption. T's former wife provides him with a completed Form 8332.

55. Has T provided more than 50% support in the following situations?

a. T paid $6,000 for an automobile that was titled in his name. His 19-year-old son, S, uses the automobile approximately 50% of the time while attending a local college on a full-time basis. S earned $4,000 from a part-time job that was used to pay his college and living expenses. The value of S's room and board provided by T amounted to $1,200.

b. T contributed $4,000 to his mother's support during the year. His mother received $5,000 in Social Security benefits that she placed in her savings account for future use.

c. Assume the same facts as in (b), except that T's mother used the funds for her support during the year.

56. F contributed the following items toward the support of his son, S:

Food, clothing, shelter	$2,300
Television set given to S as a Christmas present	300
Books for college	250

S, age 23, is a full-time student at the University of Georgia College of Law. In June, he married J, who is supported by her parents. S earned $3,500 during the summer and contributed the following items toward his own support:

Clothing	$ 600
Used car purchased for transportation to college	1,000
Insurance, maintenance, and operating expenses for car	800
Entertainment	420

S received a $2,000 scholarship from the University of Georgia. Which of the following statements is correct?

a. F provided over half of S's support but cannot claim S as a dependent because S's gross income exceeds the maximum amount allowable for a dependent.

b. S's income will not prevent F from claiming S as a dependent. However, F cannot claim S as a dependent because he provided less than half of S's support.

c. F cannot claim S as a dependent for two reasons: F did not provide over half of S's support, and S's income exceeds the maximum amount allowable for a dependent.

d. Based on the facts given, there is nothing that would prevent F from claiming S as a dependent. However, if S and J file a joint return, F will not be allowed to claim S as a dependent.

e. None of the above.

57. A, B, and C contribute to the support of their mother, M, age 67. M lives with each of the children for approximately four months during the year. Her total living costs amounted to $6,000 and were paid as follows:

From M's Social Security benefits	$1,700
By A	500
By B	1,300
By C	1,300
By T, M's unrelated friend	1,200
	$6,000

a. Which, if any, of these individuals may claim M as a dependent (assume no multiple support agreement is filed)?

b. If a multiple support agreement is filed, who must be a party to it, and who may claim the exemption for M under the agreement?

58. Calculate the allowable exemption amount for the following taxpayers for 1992:

 a. J is single and has no dependents for 1992. J's AGI for 1992 is $125,000.
 b. N and H are married and file a joint return for 1992. They have two qualifying dependents for the year. Their AGI for 1992 is $180,000.
 c. S files as head of household during 1992. He is entitled to claim one dependent. His AGI for 1992 is $160,000.
 d. K is married filing a separate return in 1992. She is entitled to claim two dependents for 1992. Her AGI for the year is $90,000.

59. Which of the following individuals are required to file a tax return for 1992? Should any of these individuals file a return even if filing is not required? Why?

 a. T is married and files a joint return with his spouse, B. Both T and B are 47 years old. Their combined gross income was $9,000.
 b. T is a dependent child under age 19 who received $1,000 in wages from a part-time job and $1,900 of dividend income.
 c. T is single and is 67 years old. His gross income from wages was $5,800.
 d. T is a self-employed single individual with gross income of $4,400 from an unincorporated business. Business expenses amounted to $3,900.

60. Can T use Tax Rate Schedule Z (head of household) in 1992?

 a. T's wife died in 1991. T maintained a household for his two dependent children during 1992 and provided over one-half of the cost of the household.
 b. T is unmarried and lives in an apartment. He supported his aged parents, who live in a separate home. T provides over one-half of the funds used to maintain his parents' home. T also claimed his parents as dependents since he provided more than one-half of their support during the year.
 c. T is unmarried and maintains a household (over one-half of the cost) for his 18-year-old married daughter and her husband. His daughter filed a joint return with her husband solely for the purpose of obtaining a refund of income taxes that were withheld. Neither T's daughter nor her husband was required to file a return.

61. Indicate in each of the following situations which of the Tax Rate Schedules T should use for calendar year 1992:

 a. T, the mother and sole support of her three minor children, was abandoned by her husband in late 1991.
 b. T is a widower whose wife died in 1991. T furnishes all of the support of his household, which includes two dependent children.
 c. T furnishes all of the support of his parents, who live in their own home in a different city. T's parents qualify as his dependents. T is not married.
 d. T's household includes an unmarried stepchild, age 18, who has gross income of $6,000 during the year. T furnishes all of the cost of maintaining the household. T is not married.

62. M, age 66, is a widow. Her husband died in 1990. M maintains a home in which she and her 28-year-old son reside. Her son G is a piano player at a local nightclub, where he earned $12,000 during 1992. G contributed $3,000 of his income toward household expenses and put the remainder in a savings account that he used to return to college full-time to pursue a master's degree in music starting in August 1992. M contributed $12,000 toward household expenses. What is the most favorable filing status available to M for 1992, and how many exemptions may M claim?

63. B, who is single and age 35, has AGI of $60,000 in 1991. He does not itemize deductions. N, his orphaned 10-year-old cousin, moved in with him in April, and B provided all of N's support during the remainder of 1991.

 a. Compute B's taxable income and tax liability for 1991.
 b. Assume that B has the same amount of AGI in 1992 and that N continues to reside with him through the end of the year. Compute B's taxable income and tax liability for 1992.

64. H, age 65 and single, earned a salary of $82,000 and made a deductible $2,000 contribution to his Individual Retirement Account in 1992. He incurred medical

expenses of $8,500 and had other itemized deductions of $2,000. Compute H's taxable income for 1992.

65. In the current year, D earned a salary of $50,000 and had a long-term loss of $6,000 on the sale of stock. She also had a $2,500 short-term gain on the sale of land held as an investment and a $2,000 gain on the sale of her personal automobile. She had owned the automobile for two years. Compute D's AGI.

66. K, age 39, is single. She maintains a household that is the residence of her two children, B, age 8, and G, age 11. The children are claimed as dependents by their father, who provides $2,000 child support for each of them. During 1992, K earned a salary of $100,000. Other items that affected her taxable income are as follows:

Total itemized deductions	$ 6,500
Capital gains	
Short-term	1,200
Long-term	3,500
Capital losses	
Short-term	(900)
Long-term	(7,600)
Interest income	2,100

K provides all the support for her mother, M, who lives in a nursing home. M qualifies as K's dependent.

a. Compute K's adjusted gross income and taxable income for 1992.
b. What is K's filing status for 1992?

67. P, age 61, earned a salary of $63,000 in 1992. She sold common stock that she had owned for 10 months at a loss of $1,500 and sold a fishing boat that she had bought in 1988 at a loss of $4,000. P also sold an antique desk for a gain of $10,000. She acquired the desk in 1953. Compute P's AGI for 1992.

68. T is a single, cash basis calendar year taxpayer. For the years 1991 and 1992, he expects AGI of $20,000 and the following itemized deductions:

Church pledge	$2,300
Interest on home mortgage	1,200
Property taxes	500

Discuss the tax consequences of the following alternatives:

a. In 1991, T pays his church pledge for 1991 and 1992 ($2,300 for each year).
b. T does nothing different.

CUMULATIVE PROBLEMS

69. John and Karen Sanders, both age 25, are married and file a joint return in 1991. They have one child, Linda, who was born on June 30, 1991. John's Social Security number is 266–77–2345, and Karen's is 467–33–1289. They live at 105 Bradley, Columbus, OH 43211.

John, a computer programmer, earned $48,000, and his employer withheld $8,900. Karen, a medical student at Ohio State University, received $25,000 of income from a trust her father had established to pay for her education. This amount must be included in computing taxable income. In addition, Karen was awarded a $10,000 nontaxable scholarship by the medical school in 1991.

In examining their records, you find that John and Karen are entitled to the following itemized deductions:

State and local income taxes	$1,200
Real estate taxes	2,500
Home mortgage interest	3,100
Charitable contributions	1,800

John and Karen made estimated Federal tax payments of $2,000 in 1991.

Part 1—Tax Computation

Compute (a) adjusted gross income, (b) taxable income, and (c) net tax payable or refund due for John and Karen. Suggested software (if available): *TurboTax* for tax return or WFT tax planning software.

Part 2—Tax Planning

Assume that all amounts from 1991 will be approximately the same in 1992 except for the following:

a. John's salary will increase by 10%.
b. John's employer will withhold $9,300 of Federal income tax.

How much estimated tax should the Sanders pay in 1992 so they will neither owe any tax nor receive any refund for 1992? Suggested software (if available): *TurboTax* for tax return or WFT tax planning software.

70. Henry and Wanda Black, 4030 Beachside Drive, Longboat Key, FL 33548, file a joint Federal income tax return for 1991. Henry, age 66, is a restaurant manager for Gourmet Tacos. His Social Security number is 344–99–7642. Wanda, who is 54, is a manager at Timothy's Beauty Salon. Her Social Security number is 354–33–7890. The Blacks come to you in early December 1991 seeking tax advice.
The Blacks have received or will receive the following amounts during 1991:

a. Henry's salary, $45,000.
b. Wanda's salary, $49,000.
c. Interest on bonds issued by the City of Sarasota, $900.
d. Life insurance proceeds received on the death of Henry's mother, $75,000.
e. Value of property inherited from Henry's mother, $130,000.

In examining the Blacks' records, you find the following items of possible tax consequence (all applicable to 1991):

f. The Blacks had other itemized deductions as follows:
   - Real estate taxes, $4,200.
   - Home mortgage interest, $5,500.
   - Charitable contributions (cash), $2,900.

g. Henry's employer withheld $6,800 of Federal income tax, and Wanda's employer withheld $7,400. In addition, they made estimated tax payments of $2,500.

Henry and Wanda's son Steven lived with the Blacks during 1991 except for nine months during which he was away at college. Steven, age 23, is a law student and plans to graduate in 1993. During the summer, Steven earned $2,500 and used the money he earned to pay for his college expenses. His parents contributed $3,000 toward his support.

Part 1—Tax Computation

Compute the following amounts for the Blacks if they file a joint return for 1991: gross income, adjusted gross income, taxable income, and net tax payable or refund due. Suggested software (if available): *TurboTax* for tax return or WFT tax planning software.

Part 2—Tax Planning

The Blacks are contemplating a divorce and would prefer not to file jointly. They have asked you to compute their tax liabilities if they file separately rather than jointly. If they file separately, they will split itemized deductions and estimated tax payments equally. Each spouse will report one-half of the bond interest since they owned the City of Sarasota bonds jointly (refer to item c). Wanda will claim an exemption for Steven (assume he qualifies as her dependent). Will the Blacks have to pay more tax if they file separately? Explain. Suggested software (if available): *TurboTax* for tax return or WFT tax planning software.

RESEARCH PROBLEMS

RESEARCH PROBLEM 1 Jerry, who is 13 years old, earned $1,200 from a paper route during 1991. In addition, he had two savings accounts. He earned interest of $1,200 on an account set up for him, in his name, by his grandparents. Jerry also earned $450 on a savings account he set up with earnings from his paper route over the last three years. How much of Jerry's interest income is treated as unearned income taxable at his parents' rate?

RESEARCH PROBLEM 2 Emily's daughter, Sarah, graduated from high school on May 15, 1992. Emily and Sarah's father were divorced in 1990, and Emily was awarded custody of Sarah. Under the custody agreement, Sarah spent the last half of May and the entire months of June, July, and August with her father. Sarah returned to Emily's home on September 1, stayed there the first week of September, and then went away to college and lived on campus for the rest of the year. Can Emily file as a head of household for 1992?

RESEARCH PROBLEM 3 Jerry maintained a home in which he, his daughter (Fran), and his son-in-law (Ed) lived. Ed died in June 1990, and Fran continued to reside with Jerry for the rest of the year. Fran filed a joint return with Ed for 1990. Jerry filed his 1990 tax return as a head of household. The IRS claims that Jerry was not entitled to head-of-household status because Fran was considered married as of the end of 1990. Should Jerry accept the IRS position and file as a single taxpayer, or should he challenge them for the right to file as a head of household?

Partial list of research aids:

Hilliard v. U.S., 63–1 USTC ¶9126, 10 AFTR2d 6135, 310 F.2d 631 (CA–6, 1962).
§ 2(b).

PART

GROSS INCOME

Part II presents the income component of the basic tax model. Included in this presentation are the determination of what is income and the statutory exclusions that are permitted in calculating gross income. Because the taxpayer's accounting method and accounting period affect when income is reported, an introductory discussion of these topics is also included.

CHAPTER

CHAPTER

GROSS INCOME: CONCEPTS AND INCLUSIONS

OBJECTIVES

Explain the all-inclusive concept of gross income and the underlying realization requirement.

Distinguish between the economic, accounting, and tax concepts of income.

Describe the cash and accrual methods of accounting for gross income.

Explain the principles applied to determine who is subject to tax on a particular item of income.

Analyze the sections of the Internal Revenue Code that describe the determination of gross income from the following specific sources: alimony, below-market interest rate loans, annuities, prizes and awards, group term life insurance, unemployment compensation, and Social Security benefits.

Identify tax planning strategies for minimizing gross income.

OUTLINE

Computation of the income tax liability of an individual or a corporation begins with the determination of gross income. Section 61 provides an all-inclusive definition of gross income and supplements it with a list of items (not all-inclusive) that are includible in gross income (e.g., compensation for services, rents, interest, dividends, alimony). Other Code sections contain specific rules for particular types of income. Still other sections provide guidance on acceptable accounting methods and for determining the tax period in which the income should be reported. Supreme Court decisions establish the framework for deciding who must pay the tax on the income.

Congress has provided that certain items are excluded from gross income (e.g., interest on certain state and municipal bonds). The exclusions appear in §§ 101–150 of the Code and are discussed in Chapter 5.

GROSS INCOME—WHAT IS IT?

◆

Definition

Section 61(a) of the Internal Revenue Code defines the term *gross income* as follows:

> Except as otherwise provided in this subtitle, gross income means all income from whatever source derived.

This definition is derived from the language of the Sixteenth Amendment to the Constitution.

Supreme Court decisions have made it clear that all sources of income are subject to tax unless Congress specifically excludes the type of income received:

> The starting point in all cases dealing with the question of the scope of what is included in "gross income" begins with the basic premise that the purpose of Congress was to use the full measure of its taxing power. [1]

Thus, the Court has held that any punitive damages (damages levied to punish a wrongdoer rather than to compensate the taxpayer for actual damages) the taxpayer receives must be included in gross income.[2] Also, proceeds from extortion[3] and the value of buried treasure found by the taxpayer[4] must be included in gross income. The types of income that are specifically excluded from gross income are discussed in Chapter 5.

Although at this point we know that *income* is to be broadly construed, we still do not have a satisfactory definition of the term *income*. Congress left it to the judicial and administrative branches to thrash out the meaning of income. Early in the development of the income tax law, a choice was made between two competing models: economic income and accounting income.

Economic and Accounting Concepts

The term *income* is used in the Code but is not separately defined. Thus, early in the history of our tax laws, the courts were required to interpret "the commonly understood meaning of the term which must have been in the minds of the

1. *James v. U.S.*, 61–1 USTC ¶9449, 7 AFTR2d 1361, 81 S.Ct. 1052 (USSC, 1961).
2. *Glenshaw Glass Co. v. Comm.*, 55–1 USTC ¶9308, 47 AFTR 162, 75 S.Ct. 473 (USSC, 1955).
3. *Rutkin v. U.S.*, 52–1 USTC ¶9260, 41 AFTR 596, 72 S.Ct. 571 (USSC, 1952).
4. Rev.Rul. 61, 1953–1 C.B. 17.

people when they adopted the Sixteenth Amendment to the Constitution."[5] In determining the definition of income, the Supreme Court rejected the economic concept of income.

Economists measure income by first determining the fair market value of the individual's net assets at the beginning and end of the year (change in net worth). Then, to arrive at economic income, this change in net worth is added to the goods and services that person actually consumed during the tax period. Economic income also includes imputed values for such items as the rental value of an owner-occupied home and the value of food a taxpayer might grow for personal consumption.[6]

EXAMPLE 1

T's economic income is calculated as follows:

Fair market value of T's assets on December 31, 1992	$220,000	
Less liabilities on December 31, 1992	(40,000)	
Net worth on December 31, 1992		$180,000
Fair market value of T's assets on January 1, 1992	$200,000	
Less liabilities on January 1, 1992	(80,000)	
Net worth on January 1, 1992		120,000
Increase in net worth		$ 60,000
Consumption		
Food, clothing, and other personal expenditures		25,000
Imputed rental value of T's home she owns and occupies		12,000
Economic income		$ 97,000

◆

The need to value assets annually would make compliance with the tax law burdensome and would cause numerous controversies between the taxpayer and the IRS over valuation. In addition, using market values to determine income for tax purposes could result in liquidity problems. That is, the taxpayer's assets may increase in value even though they are not readily convertible into the cash needed to pay the tax (e.g., commercial real estate). Thus, the IRS, Congress, and the courts have rejected the economic concept of income as impractical.

In contrast, the *accounting concept of income* is founded on the realization principle.[7] According to this principle, income is not recognized until it is realized. For realization to occur, (1) an exchange of goods or services must take place between the accounting entity and some independent, external group, and (2) the accounting entity must receive assets in the exchange that are capable of being objectively valued. Thus, the mere appreciation in the market value of assets before a sale or other disposition is not sufficient to warrant income recognition. In addition, the imputed savings that arise when an individual creates assets for his or her own use (e.g., feed grown for a farmer's own livestock) are not income because no exchange has occurred.

The Supreme Court expressed an inclination toward the accounting concept of income when it adopted the realization requirement in *Eisner v. Macomber*:[8]

5. *Merchants Loan and Trust Co. v. Smietanka*, 1 USTC ¶42, 3 AFTR 3102, 41 S.Ct. 386 (USSC, 1921).

6. See Henry C. Simons, *Personal Income Taxation* (Chicago: University of Chicago Press, 1933), Ch. 2–3.

7. See the American Accounting Association Committee Report on the "Realization Concept," *The Accounting Review* (April 1965): 312–322.

8. 1 USTC ¶32, 3 AFTR 3020, 40 S.Ct. 189 (USSC, 1920).

> Income may be defined as the gain derived from capital, from labor, or from both combined, provided it is understood to include profit gained through a sale or conversion of capital assets. . . . Here we have the essential matter: not a gain accruing to capital; not a *growth* or *increment* of value *in* investment; but a gain, a profit, something of exchangeable value, *proceeding from* the property, *severed from* the capital however invested or employed, and *coming in*, being *"derived"*—that is, *received* or *drawn by* the recipient for his separate use, benefit and disposal—*that* is, income derived from the property.

In summary, *income* represents an increase in wealth recognized for tax purposes only upon realization.

Comparison of the Accounting and Tax Concepts of Income

Although income tax rules frequently parallel financial accounting measurement concepts, differences do exist. Of major significance, for example, is the fact that unearned (prepaid) income received by an accrual basis taxpayer often is taxed in the year of receipt. For financial accounting purposes, such prepayments are not treated as income until earned.[9] Because of this and other differences, many corporations report financial accounting income that is substantially different from the amounts reported for tax purposes (see Chapter 20, Reconciliation of Taxable Income and Accounting Income).

The Supreme Court provided an explanation for some of the variations between accounting and taxable income in a decision involving inventory and bad debt adjustments:[10]

> The primary goal of financial accounting is to provide useful information to management, shareholders, creditors, and others properly interested; the major responsibility of the accountant is to protect these parties from being misled. The primary goal of the income tax system, in contrast, is the equitable collection of revenue. . . . Consistently with its goals and responsibilities, financial accounting has as its foundation the principle of conservatism, with its corollary that 'possible errors in measurement [should] be in the direction of understatement rather than overstatement of net income and net assets.' In view of the Treasury's markedly different goals and responsibilities, understatement of income is not destined to be its guiding light.
>
> . . . Financial accounting, in short, is hospitable to estimates, probabilities, and reasonable certainties; the tax law, with its mandate to preserve the revenue, can give no quarter to uncertainty.

In some instances, the tax law specifically permits rapid write-offs (e.g., limited expensing under § 179) and deferrals of income that are not available in financial accounting. In some of these cases, however, the tax law has a backup provision in the form of the alternative minimum tax to prevent abuse of the use of the tax benefits derived from exclusions, deductions, and credits.[11]

Form of Receipt

Gross income is not limited to cash received. "It includes income realized in any form, whether in money, property, or services. Income may be realized [and

9. Similar differences exist in the deduction area. Goodwill, for example, must be amortized for financial accounting purposes but cannot be deducted under the Federal income tax laws.

10. *Thor Power Tool Co. v. Comm.*, 79–1 USTC ¶9139, 43 AFTR2d 79–362, 99 S.Ct. 773 (USSC, 1979).

11. See Chapter 12 for a discussion of the alternative minimum tax.

recognized], therefore, in the form of services, meals, accommodations, stock or other property, as well as in cash."[12]

EXAMPLE 2

ABC Corporation allowed T, an employee, to use a company car for his vacation. T realized income equal to the rental value of the car for the time and mileage. ◆

EXAMPLE 3

M, an XYZ Corporation shareholder, bought real estate from the company for $10,000 when the property was worth $15,000. M realized income (a constructive dividend) of $5,000, the difference between the fair market value of the property and the price M paid. ◆

EXAMPLE 4

T owed $10,000 on a mortgage. The creditor accepted $8,000 in full satisfaction of the debt. T realized income of $2,000 from retiring the debt.[13] ◆

Recovery of Capital Doctrine

The Constitution grants Congress the power to tax income but does not define the term. Because the Constitution does not define income, it would seem that Congress could simply tax gross receipts. Although Congress does allow certain deductions, none are constitutionally required. However, the Supreme Court has held that there can be no income subject to tax until the taxpayer has recovered the capital invested.[14] This concept is known as the *recovery of capital doctrine*.

In its simplest application, this doctrine means that sellers can reduce their gross receipts (selling price) by the adjusted basis of the property sold.[15] This net amount, in the language of the Code, is gross income.

EXAMPLE 5

T sold common stock for $15,000. He had purchased the stock for $12,000. T's gross receipts are $15,000. This amount consists of a $12,000 recovery of capital and $3,000 of gross income. ◆

The recovery of capital doctrine has subtle implications.

EXAMPLE 6

B paid additional taxes of $5,000 because his accountant did not maintain proper documentation of expenses. B's loss was only temporary because he collected the $5,000 from the accountant after threatening a negligence suit. The $5,000 received from the accountant is not income because it merely replaces the capital taken by the tax collector as a result of the accountant's negligence.[16] B also lost one day's pay, $100, for time spent at the local office of the IRS protesting the additional taxes. The accountant reimbursed B for his loss of wages. The $100 is income rather than a recovery of capital because no capital was formed until either the income or its substitute (payment from the accountant) was received. ◆

12. Reg. § 1.61–1(a).
13. Reg. § 1.61–12. See *U.S. v. Kirby Lumber Co.*, 2 USTC ¶814, 10 AFTR 458, 52 S.Ct. 4 (USSC, 1931). Exceptions to this general rule are discussed in Chapter 5.
14. *Doyle v. Mitchell Bros. Co.*, 1 USTC ¶17, 3 AFTR 2979, 38 S.Ct. 467 (USSC, 1916).
15. For a definition of adjusted basis, see the Glossary of Tax Terms in Appendix C.
16. *Clark v. Comm.*, 40 B.T.A. 333 (1939).

EXAMPLE 7

Z Corporation recovered $150,000 as damages inflicted by a competitor on the goodwill of the corporation. The goodwill was the product of fast and efficient services to its customers, and no cost of the asset was reflected on the corporation's balance sheet. Because the company has no capital invested in its goodwill, the $150,000 is taxable.[17] ◆

EXAMPLE 8

C purchased an acre of land for $10,000. The following year X Electric Company paid C $1,000 for a permanent easement to run an underground cable across his property. The easement prevents C from making certain uses of his property (e.g., it affected where a house could be located and where trees could be planted), but C can still make some use of the property. The cost of the interest in the property C gave up for the $1,000 cannot be determined. Therefore, C may treat the $1,000 as a recovery of his original cost of the property and reduce his basis to $9,000. If C later sells the property for more than $9,000, he will recognize a gain. ◆

Collections on annuity contracts and installment payments received from sales of property must be allocated between recovery of capital and income. Annuities are discussed in this chapter, and installment sales are discussed in Chapter 18.

YEAR OF INCLUSION

Taxable Year

The annual accounting period or taxable year is a basic component of our tax system.[18] Generally, an entity must use the *calendar year* to report its income. However, a *fiscal year* (a period of 12 months ending on the last day of any month other than December) can be elected if the taxpayer maintains adequate books and records. This fiscal year option generally is not available to partnerships, S corporations, and personal service corporations, as discussed in Chapter 18.[19]

Determining the particular year in which the income will be taxed is important for determining when the tax must be paid. But the year each item of income is subject to tax can also affect the total tax liability over the entity's lifetime. This is true for the following reasons:

- With a progressive rate system, a taxpayer's marginal tax rate can change from year to year.
- Congress may change the tax rates.
- The relevant rates may change because of a change in the entity's status (e.g., a person may marry or a business may be incorporated).
- Several provisions in the Code are dependent on the taxpayer's gross income for the year (e.g., whether the person can be claimed as a dependent, as discussed in Chapter 3).

Accounting Methods

The year an item of income is subject to tax often depends upon which acceptable accounting method the taxpayer regularly employs.[20] The three

17. *Raytheon Production Corp. v. Comm.*, 44–2 USTC ¶9424, 32 AFTR 1155, 144 F.2d 110 (CA–1, 1944).
18. See Accounting Periods in Chapter 18.
19. §§ 441(a) and (d).
20. See Accounting Methods in Chapter 18.

primary methods of accounting are (1) the cash receipts and disbursements method, (2) the accrual method, and (3) the hybrid method. Most individuals use the cash receipts and disbursements method of accounting, whereas most corporations use the accrual method. The Regulations require the accrual method for determining purchases and sales when inventory is an income-producing factor.[21] Some businesses employ a hybrid method that is a combination of the cash and accrual methods of accounting.

In addition to these overall accounting methods, a taxpayer may choose to spread the gain from the sale of property over the collection periods by using the installment method of income recognition. Contractors may either spread profits from contracts over the periods in which the work is done (the percentage of completion method) or defer all profit until the year in which the project is completed (the completed contract method, which can be used only in limited circumstances).[22]

The IRS has the power to prescribe the accounting method to be used by the taxpayer. Section 446(b) grants the IRS broad powers to determine if the accounting method used *clearly reflects income*:

> Exceptions—If no method of accounting has been regularly used by the taxpayer, or *if the method used does not clearly reflect income, the computation of taxable income shall be made under such method as, in the opinion of the Secretary . . . does clearly reflect income.*

A change in the method of accounting requires the consent of the IRS.[23]

Cash Receipts Method. Under the *cash receipts method,* property or services received are included in the taxpayer's gross income in the year of actual or constructive receipt by the taxpayer or agent, regardless of whether the income was earned in that year.[24] The receipt of income need not be reduced to cash in the same year. All that is necessary for income recognition is that property or services received have a fair market value—a cash equivalent.[25] Thus, if a cash basis taxpayer receives a note in payment for services, he or she has income in the year of receipt equal to the fair market value of the note. However, a creditor's mere promise to pay (e.g., an account receivable), with no supporting note, is not usually considered to have a fair market value.[26] Thus, the cash basis taxpayer defers income recognition until the account receivable is collected.

EXAMPLE 9

D, an accountant, reports her income by the cash method. In 1992, she performed an audit for X and billed the client for $5,000, which was collected in 1993. In 1992, D also performed an audit for Y. Because of Y's precarious financial position, D required Y to issue an $8,000 secured negotiable note in payment of the fee. The note had a fair market value of $6,000. D collected $8,000 on the note in 1993. D's gross income for the two years is as follows:

---

21. Reg. § 1.446–1(c)(2)(i). See the Glossary of Tax Terms in Appendix C for a discussion of the terms "accrual method," "accounting method," and "accounting period." Other circumstances in which the accrual method must be used are presented in Chapter 18.
22. §§ 453(a) and (b), § 453A, and Reg. § 1.451–3. See Chapter 18 for limitations on the use of the installment method and the completed contract method.
23. § 446(e). See Chapter 18.
24. *Julia A. Strauss*, 2 B.T.A. 598 (1925). See the Glossary of Tax Terms in Appendix C for a discussion of the terms "cash equivalent doctrine" and "constructive receipt."
25. Reg. §§ 1.446–1(a)(3) and (c)(1)(i).
26. *Bedell v. Comm.*, 1 USTC ¶359, 7 AFTR 8469, 30 F.2d 622 (CA–2, 1929).

	1992	1993
Fair market value of note received from Y	$6,000	
Cash received		
From X on account receivable		$ 5,000
From Y on note receivable		8,000
Less: Recovery of capital		(6,000)
Total gross income	$6,000	$ 7,000

◆

Generally, a check received is considered a cash equivalent. Thus, a cash basis taxpayer must recognize the income when the check is received. This is true even though the taxpayer receives the check after banking hours.[27]

Accrual Method. Under *accrual accounting*, an item is generally included in the gross income for the year in which it is earned, regardless of when the income is collected. The income is earned when (1) all the events have occurred that fix the right to receive such income and (2) the amount to be received can be determined with reasonable accuracy.[28]

Generally, the taxpayer's rights to the income accrue when title to property passes to the buyer or the services are performed for the customer or client.[29] If the rights to the income have accrued but are subject to a potential refund claim (e.g., under a product warranty), the income is reported in the year of sale and a deduction is allowed in subsequent years when actual claims accrue.[30]

Where the taxpayer's rights to the income are being contested (e.g., when a contractor fails to meet specifications), the year in which the income is subject to tax depends upon whether payment has been received. If payment has not been received, no income is recognized until the claim has been settled. Only then is the right to the income established.[31] However, if the payment is received before the dispute is settled, the court-made *claim of right doctrine* requires the taxpayer to recognize the income in the year of receipt.[32]

EXAMPLE 10

A contractor completed a building in 1992 and presented a bill to the customer. The customer refused to pay the bill and claimed that the contractor had not met specifications. A settlement with the customer was not reached until 1993. No income would accrue to the contractor until 1993. If the customer paid for the work and then filed suit for damages, the contractor could not defer the income (the income would be taxable in 1992). ◆

The measure of accrual basis income is generally the amount the taxpayer has a right to receive. Unlike the cash basis, the fair market value of the customer's obligation is irrelevant in measuring accrual basis income.

EXAMPLE 11

Assume the same facts as in Example 9, except D is an accrual basis taxpayer. D must recognize $13,000 ($8,000 + $5,000) income in 1992, the year her rights to the income accrued. ◆

27. *Charles F. Kahler*, 18 T.C. 31 (1952).
28. Reg. § 1.451–1(a).
29. *Lucas v. North Texas Lumber Co.*, 2 USTC ¶484, 8 AFTR 10276, 50 S.Ct. 184 (USSC, 1930).
30. *Brown v. Helvering*, 4 USTC ¶1223, 13 AFTR 851, 54 S.Ct. 356 (USSC, 1933).
31. *Burnet v. Sanford and Brooks*, 2 USTC ¶636, 9 AFTR 603, 51 S.Ct. 150 (USSC, 1931).
32. *North American Oil Consolidated Co. v. Burnet*, 3 USTC ¶943, 11 AFTR 16, 52 S.Ct. 613 (USSC, 1932). See the Glossary of Tax Terms in Appendix C for a discussion of the term "claim of right doctrine."

Hybrid Method. The hybrid method is a combination of the accrual method and the cash method. Generally, when the hybrid method is used, inventory is an income-producing factor. Therefore, the regulations require that the accrual method be used for determining sales and cost of goods sold. In this circumstance, to simplify record keeping, the taxpayer accounts for inventory using the accrual method and uses the cash method for all other income and expense items (e.g., dividend and interest income). The hybrid method is primarily used by small businesses.

Exceptions Applicable to Cash Basis Taxpayers

Constructive Receipt. Income that has not actually been received by the taxpayer is taxed as though it had been received—the income is *constructively received*—under the following conditions:

- The amount is made readily available to the taxpayer.
- The taxpayer's actual receipt is not subject to substantial limitations or restrictions.[33]

The rationale for the constructive receipt doctrine is that if the income is available, the taxpayer should not be allowed to postpone the income recognition. For instance, a taxpayer is not permitted to defer income for December services by refusing to accept payment until January. However, determining whether the income is *readily available* and whether *substantial limitations or restrictions exist* necessitates a factual inquiry that leads to a judgment call.[34] The following are some examples of the application of the constructive receipt doctrine.

EXAMPLE 12

T is a member of a barter club. In 1992, T performed services for other club members and earned 1,000 points. Each point entitles him to $1 in goods and services sold by other members of the club; the points can be used at any time. In 1993, T exchanged his points for a new color TV. T must recognize $1,000 income in 1992 when the 1,000 points were credited to his account.[35] ◆

EXAMPLE 13

On December 31, an employer issued a bonus check to an employee but asked her to hold it for a few days until the company could make deposits to cover the check. The income was not constructively received on December 31 since the issuer did not have sufficient funds in its account to pay the debt.[36] ◆

EXAMPLE 14

R owned interest coupons that matured on December 31. The coupons could be converted to cash at any bank at maturity. Thus, the income is constructively received on December 31.[37] ◆

EXAMPLE 15

GM Company mails dividend checks on December 31, 1992. The checks will not be received by shareholders until January. The shareholders do not realize income until 1993.[38] ◆

33. Reg. § 1.451–2(a).

34. *Baxter v. Comm.*, 87–1 USTC ¶9315, 59 AFTR2d 87–1068, 816 F.2d 493 (CA–9, 1987).

35. Rev.Rul. 80–52, 1980–1 C.B. 100.

36. *L. M. Fischer*, 14 T.C. 792 (1950).

37. Reg. § 1.451–2(b).

38. Reg. § 1.451–2(b).

The constructive receipt doctrine does not reach income that the taxpayer is not yet entitled to receive even though he or she could have contracted to receive the income at an earlier date.

Example 16

X offered to pay Y $100,000 for land in December 1992. Y refused but offered to sell the land to X on January 1, 1993, when Y would be in a lower tax bracket. If X accepted Y's offer, the gain would be taxed in 1993 when the sale was completed.[39] ◆

Example 17

T is a professional athlete and reports his income by the cash method. In negotiating a contract, the club owner made two alternative offers to T:

1. $1,000,000 cash upon signing in 1992.
2. $100,000 per year plus 10% interest for 10 years.

T accepted the second offer. The income is taxed according to the amount he actually receives ($100,000 per year plus interest). The $1,000,000 T could have contracted to receive in 1992 is not constructively received in that year because he accepted the alternative offer.[40] If the final contract had provided that T could receive either the lump sum or installment payments, the $1,000,000 would have been constructively received in 1992. ◆

Income set apart or made available is not constructively received if its actual receipt is subject to *substantial restrictions.* The life insurance industry has used substantial restrictions as a cornerstone for designing life insurance contracts with favorable tax features. Ordinary life insurance policies provide (1) current protection—an amount payable in the event of death—and (2) a savings feature—a cash surrender value payable to the policyholder if he or she terminates the policy during his or her life. The annual increase in cash surrender value is not taxable because the policyholder must cancel the policy to actually receive the increase in value. Because the cancellation requirement is a substantial restriction, the policyholder does not constructively receive the annual increase in cash surrender value.[41] Employees often receive from their employers property subject to substantial restrictions. Generally, no income is recognized until the restrictions lapse.[42]

Example 18

C is a key employee of T, Inc. The corporation gave stock with a value of $10,000 to C. The stock could not be sold, however, for five years. C will not be required to recognize income until the restrictions lapse at the end of five years. ◆

Original Issue Discount. Lenders frequently make loans that require a payment at maturity of more than the amount of the original loan. The difference between the amount due at maturity and the amount of the original loan is actually interest but is referred to as *original issue discount.* Under the general rules of tax accounting, the cash basis lender would not report the original issue discount as interest income until the year the amount is collected, although an accrual basis borrower would deduct the interest as it is earned. However, the

39. *Cowden v. Comm.*, 61–1 USTC ¶9382, 7 AFTR2d 1160, 289 F.2d 20 (CA–5, 1961).

40. Rev.Rul. 60–31, 1960–1 C.B. 174, discussed further in Chapter 19.

41. *Theodore H. Cohen*, 39 T.C. 1055 (1963).

42. § 83(a). See also the discussion of Restricted Property Plans in Chapter 19.

Code puts the lender and borrower on parity by requiring that the original issue discount be reported when it is earned, regardless of the taxpayer's accounting method.[43]

EXAMPLE 19

On July 1, 1992, T, a cash basis taxpayer, paid $82,645 for a 24-month certificate of deposit with a maturity value of $100,000. The effective interest rate on the certificate was 10%. T must report $4,132 interest income for 1992:

(.10 × $82,645)(½ year) = $4,132 ◆

The original issue discount rules do not apply to U.S. savings bonds (discussed in the following paragraphs) or to obligations with a maturity date of one year or less from the date of issue.[44] See Chapter 16 for additional discussion of the tax treatment of original issue discount.

Series E and Series EE Bonds. Certain U.S. government savings bonds (Series E before 1980 and Series EE after 1979) are issued at a discount and are redeemable for fixed amounts that increase at stated intervals. No interest payments are actually made. The difference between the purchase price and the amount received on redemption is the bondholder's interest income from the investment.

The income from these savings bonds is generally deferred until the bonds are redeemed or mature. Furthermore, Series E bonds can be exchanged within one year of their maturity date for Series HH bonds, and the interest on the Series E bonds can be further deferred until maturity of the Series HH bonds.[45] Thus, U.S. savings bonds have attractive income deferral features not available with corporate bonds and certificates of deposit issued by financial institutions.

Of course, the deferral feature of government bonds issued at a discount is not an advantage if the investor has insufficient income to be subject to tax as the income accrues. In fact, the deferral may work to the investor's disadvantage if he or she has other income in the year the bonds mature or the bunching of the bond interest into one tax year creates a tax liability. Fortunately, U.S. government bonds have a provision for these investors. A cash basis taxpayer can elect to include in gross income the annual increment in redemption value.[46]

EXAMPLE 20

T purchases Series EE U.S. savings bonds for $500 (face value of $1,000) on January 2 of the current year. If the bonds are redeemed during the first six months, no interest is paid. At December 31, the redemption value is $519.60.

If T elects to report the interest income annually, she must report interest income of $19.60 for the current year. If she does not make the election, she will report no interest income for the current year. ◆

When a taxpayer elects to report the income from the bonds on an annual basis, the election applies to all such bonds the taxpayer owns at the time of the election and to all such securities acquired subsequent to the election. A change in the method of reporting the income from the bonds requires permission from the IRS.

---

43. §§ 1272(a)(3) and 1273(a).

44. § 1272(a)(2).

45. Treas. Dept. Circulars No. 1–80 and No. 2–80, 1980–1 C.B. 714, 715. Note that interest is paid at semiannual intervals on the Series HH bonds and must be included in income as received. Refer to Chapter 5 for a discussion of the savings bond interest exclusion.

46. § 454(a).

Amounts Received under an Obligation to Repay. The receipt of funds with an obligation to repay that amount in the future is the essence of borrowing. Because the taxpayer's assets and liabilities increase by the same amount, no income is realized when the borrowed funds are received. Because amounts paid to the taxpayer by mistake and customer deposits are often classified as borrowed funds, receipt of the funds is not a taxable event.

EXAMPLE 21

A customer erroneously paid a utility bill twice. The utility company does not recognize income from the second payment because it has a liability to the customer.[47] ◆

EXAMPLE 22

A lessor received a damage deposit from a tenant. No income is recognized by the lessor before forfeiture of the deposit because the lessor has an obligation to repay the deposit if no damage occurs.[48] However, if the deposit is in fact a prepayment of rent, it is taxed in the year of receipt. ◆

Exceptions Applicable to Accrual Basis Taxpayers

Prepaid Income. For financial reporting purposes, advance payments received from customers are reflected as prepaid income and as a liability of the seller. However, for tax purposes, the prepaid income often is taxed in the year of receipt.

EXAMPLE 23

In December 1992, a tenant paid his January 1993 rent of $1,000. The accrual basis landlord must include the $1,000 in his 1992 income for tax purposes, although the unearned rent income is reported as a liability on the landlord's December 31, 1992, balance sheet. ◆

Taxpayers have repeatedly argued that deferral of income until it is actually earned properly matches revenues and expenses. Moreover, a proper matching of income with the expenses of earning the income is necessary to clearly reflect income, as required by the Code. The IRS responds that § 446(b) grants it broad powers to determine whether an accounting method clearly reflects income. The IRS further argues that generally accepted financial accounting principles should not dictate tax accounting for prepaid income because of the practical problems of collecting Federal revenues. Collection of the tax is simplest in the year the taxpayer receives the cash from the customer or client.

Over 40 years of litigation, the IRS has been only partially successful in the courts. In cases involving prepaid income from services to be performed at the demand of customers (e.g., dance lessons to be taken at any time in a 24-month period), the IRS's position has been upheld.[49] In such cases, the taxpayer's argument that deferral of the income was necessary to match the income with expenses was not persuasive because the taxpayer did not know precisely when each customer would demand services and, thus, when the expenses would be

47. *Comm. v. Turney*, 36–1 USTC ¶9168, 17 AFTR 679, 82 F.2d 661 (CA–5, 1936).

48. *John Mantell*, 17 T.C. 1143 (1952).

49. *Automobile Club of Michigan v. U.S.*, 57–1 USTC ¶9593, 50 AFTR 1967, 77 S.Ct. 707 (USSC, 1957); *American Automobile Association v. U.S.*, 61–2 USTC ¶9517, 7 AFTR2d 1618, 81 S.Ct. 1727 (USSC, 1961); *Schlude v. Comm.*, 63–1 USTC ¶9284, 11 AFTR2d 751, 83 S.Ct. 601 (USSC, 1963).

incurred. However, taxpayers have had some success in the courts when the services were performed on a fixed schedule (e.g., a baseball team's season-ticket sales).[50] In some cases involving the sale of goods, taxpayers have successfully argued that the prepayments were mere deposits[51] or in the nature of loans.[52]

Against this background of mixed results in the courts, congressional intervention, and taxpayers' strong resentment of the IRS's position, in 1971 the IRS modified its prepaid income rules, as explained in the following paragraphs.

Deferral of Advance Payments for Goods. Generally, a taxpayer can elect to defer recognition of income from *advance payments for goods* if the method of accounting for the sale is the same for tax and financial reporting purposes.[53]

EXAMPLE 24

B Company will ship goods only after payment for the goods has been received. In December 1992, B received $10,000 for goods that were not shipped until January 1993. B can elect to report the income for tax purposes in 1993, assuming the company reports the income in 1993 for financial reporting purposes. ◆

Deferral of Advance Payments for Services. Revenue Procedure 71–21[54] permits an accrual basis taxpayer to defer recognition of income for *advance payments for services* to be performed by the end of the tax year following the year of receipt. No deferral is allowed if the taxpayer might be required to perform any services, under the agreement, after the tax year following the year of receipt of the advance payment.

EXAMPLE 25

X Corporation, an accrual basis taxpayer, sells its services under 12-month, 18-month, and 24-month contracts. The corporation provides services to each customer every month. In April of 1992, X Corporation sold the following customer contracts:

Length of Contract	Total Proceeds
12 months	$6,000
18 months	3,600
24 months	2,400

Fifteen hundred dollars of the $6,000 may be deferred (3/12 × $6,000), and $1,800 of the $3,600 may be deferred (9/18 × $3,600) because those amounts will not be earned until 1993. However, the entire $2,400 received on the 24-month contracts is taxable in the year of receipt (1992), since a part of the income will still be unearned by the end of the tax year following the year of receipt. ◆

Revenue Procedure 71–21 does *not apply* to prepaid rent or prepaid interest. Amounts received under guarantee or warranty contracts are not eligible for deferral unless the goods are also sold without such contracts. The reason these amounts cannot be deferred is to prevent the seller of goods from simply carving

---

50. *Artnell Company v. Comm.*, 68–2 USTC ¶9593, 22 AFTR2d 5590, 400 F.2d 981 (CA–7, 1968). See also *Boise Cascade Corp. v. U.S.*, 76–1 USTC ¶9203, 37 AFTR2d 76–696, 530 F.2d 1367 (Ct. Cls., 1976).

51. *Venstra & DeHavaan Coal Co.*, 11 T.C. 964 (1948).

52. *Consolidated-Hammer Dry Plate & Film Co. v. Comm.*, 63–1 USTC ¶9494, 11 AFTR2d 1518, 317 F.2d 829 (CA–7, 1963); *Comm. v. Indianapolis Power & Light Co.*, 90–1 USTC ¶50,007, 65 AFTR2d 90–394, 110 S.Ct. 589 (USSC, 1990).

53. Reg. § 1.451–5(b). See Reg. § 1.451–5(c) for exceptions to this deferral opportunity. The financial accounting conformity requirement is not applicable to contractors who use the completed contract method.

54. 1971–2 C.B. 549.

a service charge out of the selling price for the goods and attempting to defer the income from a service charge that may in reality be part of the price of the goods. Prepaid interest and rent are always taxed in the year of receipt. However, the term *rent* does not include payments for the use of space where the taxpayer also provides significant services (e.g., a hotel or motel).

In summary, Revenue Procedure 71–21 will result in conformity of tax and financial accounting in a very limited number of prepaid income cases. It is not apparent why prepaid rents and interest may not be deferred, why revenues under some service contracts may be spread over two years, and why revenues under longer service contracts must be reported in one year. Although Revenue Procedure 71–21 has reduced the number of controversies involving prepaid income, a consistent policy has not yet evolved.

INCOME SOURCES
◆

Personal Services

It is a well-established principle of taxation that income from personal services must be included in the gross income of the person who performs the services. This principle was first established in a Supreme Court decision, *Lucas v. Earl*.[55] Mr. Earl entered into a binding agreement with his wife under which Mrs. Earl was to receive one-half of Mr. Earl's salary. Justice Holmes used the celebrated *fruit* and *tree* metaphor to explain that the fruit (income) must be attributed to the tree from which it came (Mr. Earl's services). A mere assignment of income does not shift the liability for the tax.

However, services performed by an employee for the employer's customers are considered performed by the employer. Thus, the employer is taxed on the income from the services provided to the customer, and the employee is taxed on any compensation received from the employer.[56]

EXAMPLE 26

Dr. B. incorporated her medical practice and entered into a contract to work for the corporation for a salary. All patients contracted to receive their services from the corporation, and those services were provided through the corporation's employee, Dr. B. The corporation must include the patients' fees in its gross income. Dr. B must include her salary in her gross income. The corporation will be allowed a deduction for the reasonable salary paid to Dr. B (see the discussion of unreasonable compensation in Chapter 6). ◆

In the case of a child, the Code specifically provides that amounts earned from personal services must be included in the child's gross income. This result applies even though the income is paid to other persons (e.g., the parents).[57]

Income from Property

Income from property (interest, dividends, rent) must be included in the gross income of the *owner* of the property. If a father clips interest coupons from bonds shortly before the interest payment date and gives the coupons to his son, the interest will still be taxed to the father. A father who assigns rents from rental

55. 2 USTC ¶496, 8 AFTR 10287, 50 S.Ct. 241 (USSC, 1930).

56. *Sargent v. Comm.*, 91–1 USTC ¶50,168, 67 AFTR2d 91–718, 929 F.2d 1252, (CA–8, 1991).

57. § 73. For circumstances in which the child's unearned income is taxed at the parents' rate, see Unearned Income of Certain Minor Children Taxed at Parents' Rate in Chapter 3.

property to his daughter will be taxed on the rent since he retains ownership of the property.[58]

Often income-producing property is transferred after income from the property has accrued but before the income is recognized under the transferor's method of accounting. The IRS and the courts have developed rules to allocate the income between the transferor and the transferee.

Interest. According to the IRS, interest accrues daily. Therefore, the interest for the period that includes the date of the transfer is allocated between the transferor and transferee based on the number of days during the period that each owned the property.

EXAMPLE 27

F, a cash basis taxpayer, gave S bonds with a face amount of $10,000 and an 8% stated annual interest rate. The gift was made on January 31, 1992, and the interest was paid on December 31, 1992. F must recognize $68 in interest income (8% × $10,000 × 31/366). S will recognize $732 in interest income ($800 − $68). ◆

When the transferor must recognize the income from the property depends upon the method of accounting and the manner in which the property was transferred. In the case of a gift of income-producing property, the donor must recognize his or her share of the accrued income at the time it would have been recognized had the donor continued to own the property.[59] However, if the transfer is a sale, the transferor must recognize the accrued income at the time of the sale. This results because the accrued interest will be included in the sales proceeds.

EXAMPLE 28

Assume the same facts as in Example 27, except the interest that was payable as of December 31 was not actually or constructively received by the bondholders until January 3, 1993. As a cash basis taxpayer, F generally does not recognize interest income until it is received. If F had continued to own the bonds, the interest would have been included in his 1993 gross income, the year it would have been received. Therefore, F must include the $68 accrued income in his gross income as of January 3, 1993.

Further assume that F sold identical bonds on the date of the gift. The bonds sold for $9,900, including accrued interest. On January 31, 1992, F must recognize the accrued interest of $68 on the bonds sold. Thus, the selling price of the bonds is $9,832 ($9,900 − $68). ◆

Dividends. Unlike interest, dividends do not accrue on a daily basis because the declaration of a dividend is at the discretion of the corporation's board of directors. Generally, dividends are taxed to the person who is entitled to receive them—the shareholder of record as of the corporation's record date.[60] Thus, if a taxpayer sells stock after a dividend has been declared but before the record date, the dividend generally will be taxed to the purchaser.

If a donor makes a gift of stock to someone (e.g., a family member) after the declaration date but before the record date, the Tax Court has held that the

58. *Galt v. Comm.*, 54–2 USTC ¶9457, 46 AFTR 633, 216 F.2d 41 (CA–7, 1954); *Helvering v. Horst*, 40–2 USTC ¶9787, 24 AFTR 1058, 61 S.Ct. 144 (USSC, 1940).

59. Rev.Rul. 72–312, 1972–1 C.B. 22.

60. Reg. § 1.61–9(c). The record date is the cutoff for determining the shareholders who are entitled to receive the dividend.

donor does not shift the dividend income to the donee. The *fruit* has sufficiently ripened as of the declaration date to tax the dividend income to the donor of the stock.[61] In a similar set of facts, the Fifth Court of Appeals concluded that the dividend income should be included in the gross income of the donee (the owner at the record date). In this case, the taxpayer gave stock to a qualified charity (a charitable contribution) after the declaration date and before the record date.[62]

EXAMPLE 29

On June 20, the board of directors of Z Corporation declares a $10 per share dividend. The dividend is payable on June 30, to shareholders of record on June 25. As of June 20, M owned 200 shares of Z Corporation's stock. On June 21, M sold 100 of the shares to N for their fair market value and gave 100 of the shares to S (his son). Assume both N and S are shareholders of record as of June 25. N (the purchaser) will be taxed on $1,000 since he is entitled to receive the dividend. However, M (the donor) will be taxed on the $1,000 received by S (the donee) because the gift was made after the declaration date of the dividend. ◆

Income Received by an Agent

Income received by the taxpayer's agent is considered to be received by the taxpayer. A cash basis principal must recognize the income at the time it is received by the agent.[63]

EXAMPLE 30

F, a cash basis taxpayer, delivered cattle to the auction barn in late December. The auctioneer, acting as the farmer's agent, sold the cattle and collected the proceeds in December. The auctioneer did not pay F until the following January. F must include the sales proceeds in his gross income for the year the auctioneer received the funds. ◆

Income from Partnerships, S Corporations, Trusts, and Estates

A *partnership* is not a separate taxable entity. Rather, the partnership merely files an information return (Form 1065), which serves to provide the data necessary for determining the character and amount of each partner's distributive share of the partnership's income and deductions. Each partner must then report his or her distributive share of the partnership's income and deductions for the partnership's tax year ending within or with his or her tax year. The income must be reported by each partner in the year it is earned, even if such amounts are not actually distributed. Because a partner pays tax on income as the partnership earns it, a distribution by the partnership to the partner is treated under the recovery of capital rules.[64]

EXAMPLE 31

T owned a one-half interest in the capital and profits of T & S Company (a calendar year partnership). For tax year 1992, the partnership earned revenue of $150,000 and had operating expenses of $80,000. During the year, T withdrew from his capital account $2,500 per month (for a total of $30,000). For 1992, T must report $35,000 as his share of the partnership's profits [½ × ($150,000 − $80,000)] even though he received a distribution of only $30,000. ◆

61. *M. G. Anton*, 34 T.C. 842 (1960).
62. *Caruth Corporation v. U.S.*, 89–1 USTC ¶9172, 63 AFTR2d 89–716, 865 F.2d 644 (CA–5, 1989).
63. Rev.Rul. 79–379, 1979–2 C.B. 204.
64. § 706(a) and Reg. § 1.706–1(a)(1). For further discussion, see Chapter 20.

A *small business corporation* may elect to be taxed similarly to a partnership. Thus, the shareholders, rather than the corporation, pay the tax on the corporation's income.[65] The electing corporation is referred to as an *S corporation*. Generally, the shareholder reports his or her proportionate share of the corporation's income and deductions for the year, whether or not any distributions are actually made by the corporation.

EXAMPLE 32

Assume the same facts as in Example 31, except that T & S Company is an S corporation. T's income for the year is his share of the taxable income earned by the corporation ($35,000) rather than the amount actually distributed to him. ◆

The *beneficiaries of estates and trusts* generally are taxed on the income earned by the estates or trusts that is actually distributed or required to be distributed to them.[66] Any income not taxed to the beneficiaries is taxable to the estate or trust.

Income in Community Property States

General Rules. State law in Louisiana, Texas, New Mexico, Arizona, California, Washington, Idaho, Nevada, and Wisconsin is based upon a community property system. All other states have a common law property system. The basic difference between common law and community property systems centers around the property rights of married persons. Questions about community property income most frequently arise when the husband and wife file separate returns.

Under a *community property* system, all property is deemed either to be separately owned by the spouse or to belong to the marital community. Property may be held separately by a spouse if it was acquired before marriage or received by gift or inheritance following marriage. Otherwise, any property is deemed to be community property. For Federal tax purposes, each spouse is taxed on one-half of the income from property belonging to the community.

The laws of Texas, Louisiana, and Idaho distinguish between separate property and the income it produces. In these states, the income from separate property belongs to the community. Accordingly, for Federal income tax purposes, each spouse is taxed on one-half of the income. In the remaining community property states, separate property produces separate income that the owner-spouse must report on his or her Federal income tax return.

What appears to be income, however, may really represent a recovery of capital. A recovery of capital and gain realized on separate property retain their identity as separate property. Items such as nontaxable stock dividends, royalties from mineral interests, and gains and losses from the sale of property take on the same classification as the assets to which they relate.

EXAMPLE 33

H and W are husband and wife and reside in California. Among other transactions during the year, the following occurred:

- Nontaxable stock dividend received by W on stock that was given to her by her mother after her marriage.

65. §§ 1361(a) and 1366. For further discussion, see Chapter 20.

66. §§ 652(a) and 662(a). For further discussion of the taxation of income from partnerships, S corporations, trusts, and estates, see *West's Federal Taxation: Corporations, Partnerships, Estates, and Trusts*, Chapters 10, 11, 12, and 19.

- Gain of $10,000 on the sale of unimproved land purchased by H before his marriage.
- Oil royalties of $15,000 from a lease W acquired after marriage with her separate funds.

Since the stock dividend was distributed on stock held by W as separate property, it also is her separate property. The same result occurs for the oil royalties W receives. All of the proceeds from the sale of unimproved land (including the gain of $10,000) are H's separate property. ◆

In all community property states, income from personal services (e.g., salaries, wages, income from a professional partnership) is generally treated as if one-half is earned by each spouse.

EXAMPLE 34

H and W are married but file separate returns. H received $25,000 salary and $300 taxable interest on a savings account he established in his name. The deposits to the savings account were made from H's salary earned since the marriage. W collected $2,000 taxable dividends on stock she inherited from her father. W's gross income is computed as follows under three assumptions as to the state of residency of the couple:

	California	Texas	Common Law States
Dividends	$ 2,000	$ 1,000	$2,000
Salary	12,500	12,500	–0–
Interest	150	150	–0–
	$14,650	$13,650	$2,000

◆

Community Property Spouses Living Apart. The general rules for taxing the income from services performed by residents of community property states can create complications and even inequities for spouses who are living apart.

EXAMPLE 35

C and D were married but living apart for the first nine months of 1992 and were divorced as of October 1, 1992. In December 1992, C married E, who was married but living apart from F before their divorce in June 1992. C and F had no income from personal services in 1992.

C brought into the C–E marriage a tax liability on one-half of D's earnings for the first nine months of the year. However, E left with F a tax liability on one-half of E's earnings for the first six months of 1992. ◆

In circumstances such as those depicted in Example 35, the accrued tax liability could be factored into a property division being negotiated at a time when the parties do not need further complications. In other cases, an abandoned spouse could be saddled with a tax on income earned by a spouse whose whereabouts are unknown.

In 1980, Congress developed a simple solution to the many tax problems of community property spouses living apart. A spouse (or former spouse) will be taxed only on his or her actual earnings from personal services if the following conditions are met:[67]

- The individuals live apart for the entire year.
- They do not file a joint return with each other.
- No portion of the earned income is transferred between the individuals.

67. § 66.

EXAMPLE 36

H and W reside in a community property state, and both are gainfully employed. On July 1, 1992, they separated, and on June 30, 1993, they were divorced. Assuming their only source of income is wages, one-half of such income for each year is earned by June 30, and they did not file a joint return for 1992, each should report the following gross income:

	H's Separate Return	W's Separate Return
1992	One-half of H's wages	One-half of H's wages
	One-half of W's wages	One-half of W's wages
1993	All of H's wages	All of W's wages

The results would be the same if H or W married another person in 1993, except the newlyweds would probably file a joint return. ◆

It should be noted that the exception for community property spouses living apart does *not* apply to income from community property.

EXAMPLE 37

Assume the same facts as in Example 36, except that W had established a savings account with her earnings received while married to H. Because the savings account is community property, H and W must each report interest income from the account as follows:

	H's Separate Return	W's Separate Return
1992	One-half	One-half
Through June 30, 1993	One-half	One-half
After June 30, 1993	None	All

◆

The IRS may absolve from liability an *innocent spouse* who does not live apart for the entire year and files a separate return but omits his or her share of the community income received by the other spouse. To qualify for the innocent spouse relief, the taxpayer must not know or must have no reason to know of the omitted community income.

ITEMS SPECIFICALLY INCLUDED IN GROSS INCOME

◆

The general principles of gross income determination (discussed in the previous sections) as applied by the IRS and the courts have on occasion yielded results Congress found unacceptable. Consequently, Congress has provided more specific rules for determining the gross income from certain sources. Some of these special rules appear in §§ 71–90 of the Code.

Alimony and Separate Maintenance Payments

When a married couple divorce or become legally separated, state law generally requires a division of the property accumulated during the marriage. In addition, one spouse may have a legal obligation to support the other spouse. The Code distinguishes between the support payments (alimony or separate maintenance) and the property division in terms of the tax consequences.

Alimony and separate maintenance payments are *deductible* by the party making the payments and are *includible* in the gross income of the party receiving the payments.[68] Thus, income is shifted from the income earner to the income beneficiary, who is better able to pay the tax on the amount received.

68. §§ 71 and 215.

EXAMPLE 38

H and W were divorced, and H was required to pay W $15,000 of alimony each year. H earns $31,000 a year. The tax law presumes that because W received the $15,000, she is more able than H to pay the tax on that amount. Therefore, W must include the $15,000 in her gross income, and H is allowed to deduct $15,000 from his gross income. ◆

A transfer of property other than cash to a former spouse under a divorce decree or agreement is not a taxable event. The transferor is not entitled to a deduction and does not recognize gain or loss on the transfer. The transferee does not recognize income and has a cost basis equal to the transferor's basis. [69]

EXAMPLE 39

H transfers stock to W as part of a 1992 divorce settlement. The cost of the stock to H is $12,000, and the stock's value at the time of the transfer is $15,000. W later sells the stock for $16,000. H is not required to recognize gain from the transfer of the stock to W, and W has a realized and recognized gain of $4,000 ($16,000 − $12,000) when she sells the stock. ◆

In the case of cash payments, however, it is often difficult to distinguish payments under a support obligation (alimony) and payments for the other spouse's property (property settlement). In 1984 Congress developed objective rules to classify the payments.

Post-1984 Agreements and Decrees. Payments made under post-1984 agreements and decrees are *classified as alimony* only if the following conditions are satisfied:

1. The payments are in cash.
2. The agreement or decree does not specify that the payments are not alimony.
3. The payor and payee are not members of the same household at the time the payments are made.
4. There is no liability to make the payments for any period after the death of the payee.[70]

Requirement 1 simplifies the law by clearly distinguishing alimony from a property division; that is, if the payment is not in cash, it must be a property division. Requirement 2 allows the parties to determine by agreement whether or not the payments will be alimony. The prohibition on cohabitation—requirement 3—is aimed at assuring the alimony payments are associated with duplicative living expenses (maintaining two households).[71] Requirement 4 is an attempt to prevent alimony treatment from being applied to what is, in fact, a payment for property rather than a support obligation. That is, a seller's estate generally will receive payments for property due after the seller's death. Such payments after the death of the payee could not be for the payee's support.

Front-Loading. As a further safeguard against a property settlement being disguised as alimony, special rules apply to post-1986 agreements if payments in the first or second year exceed $15,000. If the change in the amount of the payments exceeds statutory limits, *alimony recapture* results to the extent of the

69. § 1041, added to the Code in 1984 to repeal the rule of *U.S. v. Davis*, 62–2 USTC ¶9509, 9 AFTR2d 1625, 82 S.Ct. 1190 (USSC, 1962). Under the Davis rule, which was applicable to pre-1985 divorces, a transfer incident to divorce was a taxable event.

70. § 71(b)(1).

71. *Alexander Washington*, 77 T.C. 601 (1981) at 604.

excess alimony payments. In the *third* year, the payor must include the excess alimony payments for the first and second years in gross income, and the payee is allowed a deduction for these excess alimony payments. The recaptured amount is computed as follows:[72]

$$R = D + E$$

$$D = B - (C + \$15{,}000)$$

$$E = A - \left(\frac{B - D + C}{2} + \$15{,}000\right)$$

R = amount recaptured in Year 3

D = recapture from Year 2

E = recapture from Year 1

A, B, C = payments in the first (A), second (B), and third (C) calendar years of the agreement or decree, where $D \geq 0$, $E \geq 0$

The recapture formula provides an objective technique for determining alimony recapture. Thus, at the time of the divorce, the taxpayers can ascertain the tax consequences. The general concept is that if the alimony payments decrease by over $15,000 between years in the first three years, there will be alimony recapture with respect to the decrease in excess of $15,000 each year. This rule is applied for the change between Year 2 and Year 3. However, rather than making the same calculation for Year 2 payments versus Year 1 payments, the Code requires that the *average* of the payments in Years 2 and 3 be compared with the Year 1 payments. For this purpose, revised alimony for Year 2 (alimony deducted for Year 2 minus the alimony recapture for Year 2) is used.

EXAMPLE 40

H and W were divorced in 1992. Under the agreement, W was to receive $50,000 in 1992, $20,000 in 1993, and nothing thereafter. The payments were to cease upon W's death or remarriage. In 1994, H must include an additional $32,500 in gross income for alimony recapture, and W is allowed a deduction for the same amount.

$$D = \$20{,}000 - (\$0 + \$15{,}000) = \$5{,}000$$

$$E = \$50{,}000 - \left(\frac{\$20{,}000 - \$5{,}000 + \$0}{2} + \$15{,}000\right) = \$27{,}500$$

$$R = \$5{,}000 + \$27{,}500 = \$32{,}500$$

If $50,000 were paid in 1992 and nothing is paid for the following years, $35,000 would be recaptured in 1994.

$$D = \$0 - (\$0 + \$15{,}000) = -\$15{,}000, \text{ but D must be} \geq \$0$$

$$E = \$50{,}000 - \left(\frac{\$0 - \$0 + \$0}{2} + \$15{,}000\right) = \$35{,}000$$

$$R = \$0 + \$35{,}000 = \$35{,}000$$

◆

For 1985 and 1986 agreements and decrees, alimony recapture is required during the second and third years if payments decrease by more than $10,000. A special formula is applied to compute the recapture amounts.[73]

---

72. § 71(f).

73. See § 421 of the Deficit Reduction Act of 1984 and § 1843(c)(2) of the Tax Reform Act of 1986.

Post-1984 agreements and decrees are not subject to alimony recapture if the decrease in payments is due to the death of either spouse or the remarriage of the payee. Recapture is not applicable because these events typically terminate alimony under state laws. In addition, the recapture rules do not apply to payments that are contingent in amount (e.g., a percentage of income from certain property or a percentage of the payor spouse's compensation), are to be made over a period of three years or longer (unless death, remarriage, or other contingency occurs), and in which the contingencies are beyond the payor's control.[74]

EXAMPLE 41

Under a 1992 divorce agreement, H was to receive an amount equal to one-half of W's income from certain rental properties for 1992–1995. Payments were to cease upon the death of H or W or upon the remarriage of H. H received $50,000 in 1992 and $50,000 in 1993; however in 1994, the property was vacant, and H received nothing. W, who deducted alimony in 1992 and 1993, is not required to recapture any alimony in 1994 because the payments were contingent. ◆

Pre-1985 Agreements and Decrees. Because payments will continue to be made under pre-1985 agreements for many years, these provisions are briefly reviewed here. The requirements for alimony treatment under pre-1985 agreements are as follows:

1. The payments must be made pursuant to either (a) a court order (a decree of divorce, separate maintenance decree, or decree of support) or (b) a written separation agreement (in short, the payments cannot be voluntary).
2. The payments must be either (a) for a period of more than 10 years or (b) subject to a contingency (e.g., the death of either spouse, remarriage of the recipient, or a change in the economic status of either spouse).
3. The payments must be in "discharge of a legal obligation arising from the marital or family obligations."[75]

The third requirement presents numerous problems because the *legal obligation* is determined under state law. Many states require that a spouse be paid for his or her *fair share* of the property that has been accumulated during the marriage but retained by the other spouse. Additionally, a state may impose a support obligation on the spouse. Only payments under the support obligation satisfy the third requirement (marital obligation). Thus, a cash payment may be (1) solely for support, (2) solely for property, or (3) in part for support and in part for property. Moreover, the labels the spouses attach to the payments (by pre-1985 agreement) do not control.

Child Support. A taxpayer does not realize income from the receipt of child support payments made by his or her former spouse. This result occurs because the money is received subject to the duty to use the money for the child's benefit. The payor is not allowed to deduct the child support payments because the payments are made to satisfy the payor's legal obligation to support the child.

In many cases, it is difficult to determine whether an amount received is alimony or child support. Under pre-1985 decrees and agreements, according to

74. §§ 71(f)(5)(A) and (C).

75. §§ 71(a) and (b) prior to amendment by § 422 of the Deficit Reduction Act of 1984.

the Supreme Court, if the decree or agreement does not specifically provide for child support, none of the payments will be treated as such.[76]

EXAMPLE 42

A pre-1985 divorce agreement provides that H is required to make periodic alimony payments of $500 per month to W. However, when H and W's child reaches age 21, marries, or dies (whichever occurs first), the payments will be reduced to $300 per month. W has custody of the child. Although it is reasonable to infer that $200 ($500 − $300) is for child support, the entire $500 is alimony because no payments are specified as child support. ◆

In 1984, Congress changed the results in Example 42 but only as to post-1984 agreements and decrees. Under the revision, if the amount of the payments would be reduced upon the happening of a contingency related to a child (e.g., the child attains age 21 or dies), the amount of the future reduction in the payment will be deemed child support.[77]

EXAMPLE 43

The facts are the same as in Example 42, except that the agreement is a post-1984 agreement. Child support payments are $200 each month and alimony is $300 each month. ◆

Imputed Interest on Below-Market Loans

As discussed earlier in the chapter, generally no income is recognized unless it is realized. Realization generally occurs when the taxpayer performs services or sells goods and thus becomes entitled to a payment from the other party. It follows that no income is realized if the goods or services are provided at no charge. Under this interpretation of the realization requirement, before 1984, interest-free loans were used to shift income between taxpayers.

EXAMPLE 44

D (daughter) is in the 20% tax bracket and has no investment income. F (father) is in the 50% tax bracket and has $200,000 in a money market account earning 10% interest. F would like D to receive and pay tax on the income earned on the $200,000. Because F would also like to have access to the $200,000 should he need the money, he does not want to make an outright gift of the money, nor does he want to commit the money to a trust.

Before 1984, F could achieve his goals as follows. F could transfer the money market account to D in exchange for D's $200,000 non-interest-bearing note, payable on F's demand. As a result, D would receive the income, and the family's taxes would be decreased by $6,000.

Decrease in F's tax— (.10 × $200,000) .50 =	($10,000)
Increase in D's tax— (.10 × $200,000) .20 =	4,000
Decrease in the family's taxes	($ 6,000)

◆

Under the 1984 amendments to the Code, F in Example 44 is required to recognize imputed interest income.[78] D is deemed to have incurred interest

76. *Comm. v. Lester*, 61–1 USTC 9463, 7 AFTR2d 1445, 81 S.Ct. 1343 (USSC, 1961).

77. § 71(c)(2). Pre-1985 agreements can be amended so that the revision will apply [§ 422(e) of the Deficit Reduction Act of 1984].

78. § 7872(a)(1).

expense equal to F's imputed interest income. D's interest may be deductible on her return as investment interest if she itemizes deductions (see Chapter 11). To complete the fictitious series of transactions, F is then deemed to have given D the amount of the imputed interest D did not pay. The gift received by D is not subject to income tax (see Chapter 5), although F may be subject to the gift tax (unified transfer tax) on the amount deemed given to D (refer to Chapter 1).

Imputed interest is calculated using the rate the Federal government pays on new borrowings and is compounded semiannually. This Federal rate is adjusted monthly and is published by the IRS.[79] Actually, there are three Federal rates: short-term (not over three years and including demand loans), mid-term (over three years but not over nine years), and long-term (over nine years).

EXAMPLE 45

Assume the Federal rate applicable to the loan in Example 44 is 12% through June 30 and 13% from July 1 through December 31. F made the loan on January 1, and the loan is still outstanding on December 31. F must recognize interest income of $25,780, and D has interest expense of $25,780. F is deemed to have made a gift of $25,780 to D.

Interest calculations	
January 1–June 30 —	
.12 ($200,000) (½ year)	$12,000
July 1–December 31 —	
.13 ($200,000 + $12,000) (½ year)	13,780
	$25,780

◆

If interest is charged on the loan but is less than the Federal rate, the imputed interest is the difference between the amount that would have been charged at the Federal rate and the amount actually charged.

EXAMPLE 46

Assume the same facts as in Example 45, except that F charged 6% interest, compounded annually.

Interest at the Federal rate	$ 25,780
Less interest charged (.06 × $200,000)	(12,000)
Imputed interest	$ 13,780

◆

CONCEPT SUMMARY 4–1 TAX TREATMENT OF PAYMENTS AND TRANSFERS PURSUANT TO POST-1984 DIVORCE AGREEMENTS AND DECREES

	Payor	Recipient
Alimony	Deduction from gross income.	Included in gross income.
Alimony recapture	Included in gross income of the third year.	Deducted from gross income of the third year.
Child support	Not deductible.	Not includible in income.
Property settlement	No income or deduction.	No income or deduction; basis for the property is the same as the transferor's basis.

79. §§ 7872(b)(2) and (f)(2).

The imputed interest rules apply to the following *types* of below-market loans:[80]

1. Gift loans (made out of love, affection, or generosity, as in Example 44).
2. Compensation-related loans (employer loans to employees).
3. Corporation-shareholder loans (a corporation's loans to its shareholders).
4. Tax avoidance loans and other loans that significantly affect the borrower's or lender's Federal tax liability (discussed in the following paragraphs).

The effects of the first three types of loans on the borrower and lender are summarized in Concept Summary 4–2.

Tax Avoidance and Other Below-Market Loans. In addition to the three specific types of loans that are subject to the imputed interest rules, the Code includes a catchall provision for *tax avoidance loans* and other arrangements that have a significant effect on the tax liability of the borrower or lender. The Conference Report provides the following example of an arrangement that might be subject to the imputed interest rules.[81]

EXAMPLE 47

Annual dues for the XY Health Club are $400. In lieu of paying dues, a member can make a $4,000 deposit, refundable at the end of one year. The club can earn $400 interest on the deposit.

If interest were not imputed, an individual with $4,000 could, in effect, earn tax-exempt income on the deposit. That is, rather than invest the $4,000, earn $400 in interest, pay tax on the interest, and then pay $400 in dues, the individual could avoid tax on the interest by making the deposit. Thus, income and expenses are imputed as follows: interest income and nondeductible health club fees for the club member; income from fees and interest expense for the club. ◆

Many commercially motivated transactions could be swept into this other below-market loans category. However, the temporary Regulations have carved out a frequently encountered exception for customer prepayments. If the prepayments are included in the recipient's income under the recipient's

CONCEPT SUMMARY 4–2
EFFECT OF CERTAIN BELOW-MARKET LOANS ON THE LENDER AND BORROWER

Type of Loan		Lender	Borrower
Gift	Step 1	Interest income	Interest expense
	Step 2	Gift made	Gift received
Compensation-related	Step 1	Interest income	Interest expense
	Step 2	Compensation expense	Compensation income
Corporation to shareholder	Step 1	Interest income	Interest expense
	Step 2	Dividend paid	Dividend income

80. § 7872(c).

81. H. Rep. No. 98–861, 98th Cong., 2d Sess., 1984, p. 1023.

method of accounting, the payments are not considered loans and, thus, are not subject to the imputed interest rules.[82]

EXAMPLE 48

Landlord, a cash basis taxpayer, charges tenants a damage deposit equal to one month's rent on residential apartments. When the tenant enters into the lease, the landlord also collects rent for the last month of the lease.

The prepaid rent for the last month of the lease is taxed in the year received and thus is not considered a loan. The security deposit is not taxed when received and is therefore a candidate for imputed interest. However, no apparent tax benefit is derived by the landlord or the tenant, and thus the security deposit should not be subject to the imputed interest provisions. But if making the deposit would reduce the rent paid by the tenant, the tenant could derive a tax benefit, much the same as the club member in Example 47. ◆

Exceptions and Limitations. No interest is imputed on total outstanding gift loans of $10,000 or less between individuals, unless the loan proceeds are used to purchase income-producing property.[83] This exemption eliminates from these complex provisions immaterial amounts that do not result in apparent shifts of income. However, if the proceeds of such a loan are used to purchase income-producing property, the limitations discussed in the following paragraphs apply.

On loans of $100,000 or less between individuals, the imputed interest cannot exceed the borrower's net investment income for the year (gross income from all investments less the related expenses).[84] As discussed above, one of the purposes of the imputed interest rules is to prevent high-income taxpayers from shifting income to relatives in a lower marginal bracket. This shifting of investment income is considered to occur only to the extent the borrower has investment income. Thus, the income imputed to the lender is limited to the borrower's net investment income. As a further limitation, or exemption, if the borrower's net investment income for the year does not exceed $1,000, no interest is imputed on loans of $100,000 or less. However, these limitations for loans of $100,000 or less do not apply if a principal purpose of a loan is tax avoidance. According to the Senate Report, if a principal purpose of a loan is to shift income to a taxpayer in a lower tax bracket (as illustrated in Example 44), the purpose is a proscribed one. Therefore, in such a case interest is imputed, and the imputed interest is not limited to the borrower's net investment income.[85]

EXAMPLE 49

F made interest-free gift loans as follows:

Borrower	Amount	Borrower's Net Investment Income	Purpose
S	$ 8,000	–0–	Education
D	9,000	500	Purchase of stock
B	25,000	–0–	Purchase of a business
M	90,000	15,000	Purchase of a residence
O	120,000	–0–	Purchase of a residence

Assume that tax avoidance is not a principal purpose of any of the loans. The S loan is not subject to the imputed interest rules because the $10,000 exception applies. The

82. Temp. Reg. § 1.7872–2(b)(1)(i).
83. § 7872(c)(2).
84. § 7872(d).
85. *Deficit Reduction Tax Bill of 1984: Explanation of the Senate Finance Committee* (April 2, 1984), p. 484.

$10,000 exception does not apply to the D loan because the proceeds were used to purchase income-producing assets. However, under the $100,000 exception, the imputed interest is limited to D's investment income ($500). Since the $1,000 exception also applies to this loan, no interest is imputed.

No interest is imputed on the B loan because the $100,000 exception applies. Interest is imputed on the M loan based on the lesser of (1) the borrower's $15,000 net investment income or (2) the interest as calculated by applying the Federal rate to the outstanding loan. None of the exceptions apply to the O loan because the loan was for more than $100,000.

Assume the relevant Federal rate is 10% and the loans were outstanding for the entire year. F would recognize interest income, compounded semiannually, as follows:

Loan to M:	
First 6 months (.10 × $90,000 × 1/2 year)	$ 4,500
Second 6 months (.10 × $94,500 × 1/2 year)	4,725
	$ 9,225
Loan to O:	
First 6 months (.10 × $120,000 × 1/2 year)	$ 6,000
Second 6 months (.10 × $126,000 × 1/2 year)	6,300
	$12,300
Total imputed interest ($9,225 + $12,300)	$21,525

◆

As with gift loans, there is a $10,000 exemption for compensation-related loans and corporation-shareholder loans. However, the $10,000 exception does not apply if tax avoidance is one of the principal purposes of a loan.[86] This vague tax avoidance standard makes practically all compensation-related and corporation-shareholder loans suspect. Nevertheless, the $10,000 exception should apply when an employee's borrowing was necessitated by personal needs (e.g., to meet unexpected expenses) rather than tax considerations.

Measuring Income. The measurement of the gift, compensation, or dividend resulting from a loan depends upon whether the loan is (1) a *demand loan* payable at the demand of the lender or (2) a *term loan* due as of a specific date. In the case of a demand loan, the interest is calculated using the short-term rate, and the forgone interest is the measure of the gift, compensation, or dividend. In the case of a term loan, the difference between the face amount of the loan and its present value at the date of the loan is the measure of the gift, compensation, or dividend.[87] The interest income is computed by applying the imputed interest rate to the balance of the loan. For both the demand loan and the term loan, semiannual compounding is required.

EXAMPLE 50

R, the employer, loaned $100,000 interest-free to E, an employee, on January 1 of the current tax year. The loan was due in five years, and the Federal *mid-term* rate was 10.7% compounded semiannually (the equivalent of 11% with annual compounding).

R's compensation expense and E's compensation income for the current tax year are computed as follows:

Face amount	$100,000
Less present value of $100,000 due in 5 years, i = 11%	(59,345)
Original issue discount	$ 40,655

86. § 7872(c)(3).

87. Joint Committee on Taxation, *Tax Reform Act of 1984: General Explanation of the Revenue Provisions*, p. 532.

R's interest income and E's interest expense are computed as follows:

Year	Beginning Balance	Applicable Interest @ 11%	Ending Balance
1992	$59,345*	$ 6,528	$ 65,873
1993	65,873	7,246	73,119
1994	73,119	8,043	81,162
1995	81,162	8,928	90,090
1996	90,090	9,910	100,000
		$40,655	

*Beginning loan balance equals $100,000 face amount minus $40,655 original issue discount. ◆

For income tax purposes (but not for gift tax purposes), term gift loans are treated as demand loans.

EXAMPLE 51

Assume the same facts as in Example 50, except that the $100,000 was received by E as a gift loan. Further assume that the Federal *short-term* rate was 9.76% compounded semiannually (the equivalent of 10% with annual compounding). The amount of the gift is $40,655 (calculated using the *mid-term* rate), but R's interest income and E's interest expense are equal to the Federal *short-term* rate times the amount of the loan (.10 × $100,000 = $10,000). ◆

The apparent rationale for treating all gift loans as demand loans is that as a practical matter, the lender could receive his or her principal at any time at his or her demand.

Income from Annuities

Annuity contracts generally require the purchaser (the annuitant) to pay a fixed amount for the right to receive a future stream of payments.[88] Typically, the issuer of the contract is an insurance company and will pay the annuitant a cash value if the annuitant cancels the contract. The insurance company invests the amounts received from the annuitant, and the income earned serves to increase the cash value of the policy. No income is recognized at the time the cash value of the annuity increases because the taxpayer has not actually received any income. The income is not constructively received because, generally, the taxpayer must cancel the policy to receive the increase in value (the increase in value is subject to substantial restrictions).

EXAMPLE 52

T, age 50, paid $30,000 for an annuity contract that is to pay him $500 per month beginning when he reaches age 65 and continuing until his death. If T should cancel the policy after one year, he would receive $30,200. The $200 increase in value is not includible in T's gross income as long as he does not actually receive the $200. ◆

The tax accounting problem associated with receiving payments under an annuity contract is one of apportioning the amounts received between recovery of capital and income.

88. See the Glossary of Tax Terms in Appendix C for a definition of the term "annuity."

EXAMPLE 53

In 1992, T purchased for $15,000 an annuity intended as a source of retirement income. In 1994, when the cash value of the annuity was $17,000, T collected $1,000 on the contract. Is the $1,000 gross income, recovery of capital, or a combination of recovery of capital and income? ◆

The statutory solution to this problem depends upon whether the payments began before or after the annuity starting date and upon when the policy was acquired.

Collections before the Annuity Starting Date. Generally, an annuity contract specifies a date on which monthly or annual payments will begin—the annuity starting date. Often the contract will also allow the annuitant to collect a limited amount before the starting date. The amount collected may be characterized as either an actual withdrawal of the increase in cash value or a loan on the policy. In 1982, Congress changed the rules applicable to these withdrawals and loans.

Collections (including loans) equal to or less than the post–August 13, 1982, increases in cash value must be included in gross income. Amounts received in excess of post–August 13, 1982, increases in cash value are treated as a recovery of capital until the taxpayer's cost has been entirely recovered. Additional amounts are included in gross income.[89] The taxpayer may also be subject to a penalty on early distributions of 10 percent of the income recognized. The penalty generally applies if the amount is received before the taxpayer reaches age 59½ or is disabled.[90]

EXAMPLE 54

T, age 50, purchased an annuity policy for $30,000 in 1991. In 1993, when the cash value of the policy has increased to $33,000, T withdraws $4,000. T must recognize $3,000 of income ($33,000 cash value − $30,000 cost) and must pay a penalty of $300 ($3,000 × 10%). The remaining $1,000 is a recovery of capital and reduces T's basis in the annuity policy. ◆

The 1982 rules were enacted because Congress perceived that the recovery of capital rule was being abused. Formerly, individuals could purchase annuity contracts that guaranteed an annual increase in cash value and withdraw the equivalent of interest on the contract but recognize no income. This is no longer possible. In addition, the individual must recognize income from borrowing on the contract (e.g., pledging the contract as security for a loan) as well as from an actual distribution.

Collections on and after the Annuity Starting Date. The annuitant can exclude from income (as a recovery of capital) the proportion of each payment that the investment in the contract bears to the expected return under the contract. The *exclusion amount* is calculated as follows:

$$\frac{\text{Investment}}{\text{Expected return}}$$  Annuity payment  Exclusion amount

89. § 72(c)(3); Reg. § 1.72–9.

90. § 72(q).

The *expected return* is the annual amount to be paid to the annuitant multiplied by the number of years the payments will be received. The payment period may be fixed (a *term certain*) or for the life of one or more individuals. When payments are for life, the taxpayer must use the annuity table published by the IRS to determine the expected return (see Figure 4–1). This is an actuarial table that contains life expectancies.[91] The expected return is calculated by multiplying the appropriate multiple (life expectancy) by the annual payment.

EXAMPLE 55

The taxpayer, age 54, purchased an annuity from an insurance company for $90,000. He was to receive $500 per month for life. His life expectancy (from Figure 4–1) is 29.5 years from the annuity starting date. Thus, his expected return is $500 × 12 × 29.5 = $177,000, and the exclusion amount is $3,051 [($90,000 investment/$177,000 expected return) × $6,000 annual payment]. The $3,051 is a nontaxable return of capital, and $2,949 is included in gross income. ◆

The exclusion ratio (investment ÷ expected return) applies until the annuitant has recovered his or her investment in the contract. Once the investment is recovered, the entire amount of subsequent payments is taxable. If the annuitant dies before recovering his or her investment, the unrecovered cost is deductible in the year the payments cease (usually the year of death).[92]

EXAMPLE 56

Assume the taxpayer in Example 55 received annuity payments for 30.5 years (366 months). For the last 12 months [366 − (12 × 29.5) = 12], the taxpayer would include $500 each month in gross income. If instead the taxpayer died after 36 months, he is eligible for a $80,847 deduction on his final tax return.

Cost of the contract	$90,000
Cost previously recovered $90,000/$177,000 × 36 ($500) =	(9,153)
Deduction	$80,847

◆

Prizes and Awards

Before 1954, the taxability of prizes and awards was not always clear. Taxpayers often sought to treat prizes and awards as nontaxable gifts. In many situations, it was difficult to determine whether the prize or award was in the nature of a gift. In 1954, Congress added § 74 to eliminate this uncertainty.

The fair market value of prizes and awards (other than scholarships exempted under § 117, to be discussed subsequently) must be included in income. Therefore, TV giveaway prizes, door prizes, and awards from an employer to an employee in recognition of performance are fully taxable to the recipient.

An exception permits a prize or award to be excluded from gross income if all of the following requirements are satisfied:

- The prize or award is received in recognition of religious, charitable, scientific, educational, artistic, literary, or civic achievement.

91. The life expectancies in Figure 4–1 apply for annuity investments made on or after July 1, 1986. See *Pension and Annuity Income,* IRS Publication 575 (Rev. Nov. 87), pp. 22–24 for the IRS table to use for investments made before July 1, 1986.

92. § 72(b).

- The recipient transfers the prize or award to a qualified governmental unit or nonprofit organization.
- The recipient was selected without any action on his or her part to enter the contest or proceeding.
- The recipient is not required to render substantial future services as a condition for receiving the prize or award.[93]

Because the transfer of the property to a qualified governmental unit or nonprofit organization ordinarily would be a charitable contribution (an item-

FIGURE 4–1
Ordinary Life Annuities: One Life–Expected Return Multiples

Age	Multiple	Age	Multiple	Age	Multiple
5	76.6	42	40.6	79	10.0
6	75.6	43	39.6	80	9.5
7	74.7	44	38.7	81	8.9
8	73.7	45	37.7	82	8.4
9	72.7	46	36.8	83	7.9
10	71.7	47	35.9	84	7.4
11	70.7	48	34.9	85	6.9
12	69.7	49	34.0	86	6.5
13	68.8	50	33.1	87	6.1
14	67.8	51	32.2	88	5.7
15	66.8	52	31.3	89	5.3
16	65.8	53	30.4	90	5.0
17	64.8	54	29.5	91	4.7
18	63.9	55	28.6	92	4.4
19	62.9	56	27.7	93	4.1
20	61.9	57	26.8	94	3.9
21	60.9	58	25.9	95	3.7
22	59.9	59	25.0	96	3.4
23	59.0	60	24.2	97	3.2
24	58.0	61	23.3	98	3.0
25	57.0	62	22.5	99	2.8
26	56.0	63	21.6	100	2.7
27	55.1	64	20.8	101	2.5
28	54.1	65	20.0	102	2.3
29	53.1	66	19.2	103	2.1
30	52.2	67	18.4	104	1.9
31	51.2	68	17.6	105	1.8
32	50.2	69	16.8	106	1.6
33	49.3	70	16.0	107	1.4
34	48.3	71	15.3	108	1.3
35	47.3	72	14.6	109	1.1
36	46.4	73	13.9	110	1.0
37	45.4	74	13.2	111	.9
38	44.4	75	12.5	112	.8
39	43.5	76	11.9	113	.7
40	42.5	77	11.2	114	.6
41	41.5	78	10.6	115	.5

93. § 74(b).

ized deduction as presented in Chapter 11), the exclusion produces beneficial tax consequences in the following situations:

- The taxpayer does not itemize deductions and thus would receive no tax benefit from the charitable contribution.
- The taxpayer's charitable contributions exceed the annual statutory ceiling on the deduction.
- Including the prize or award in gross income would reduce the amount of deductions the taxpayer otherwise would qualify for because of gross income limitations (e.g., the gross income test for a dependency exemption, the adjusted gross income limitation in calculating the medical expense deduction).

Another exception is provided for certain employee achievement awards in the form of tangible personal property (e.g., a gold watch). The awards must be made in recognition of length of service or safety achievement. Generally, the ceiling on the excludible amount is $400. However, if the award is a qualified plan award, the ceiling on the exclusion is $1,600.[94]

Group Term Life Insurance

Before 1964, the IRS did not attempt to tax the value of life insurance protection provided to an employee by the employer. Some companies took undue advantage of the exclusion by providing large amounts of insurance protection for executives. Therefore, Congress enacted § 79, which created a limited exclusion. Current law allows an exclusion for premiums on the first $50,000 of group term life insurance protection.

The benefits of this exclusion are available only to employees. Proprietors and partners are not considered employees. Moreover, the Regulations generally require broad-scale coverage of employees to satisfy the *group* requirement (e.g., shareholder-employees would not constitute a qualified group). The exclusion applies only to term insurance (protection for a period of time but with no cash surrender value) and not to ordinary life insurance (lifetime protection plus a cash surrender value that can be drawn upon before death).

As mentioned, the exclusion applies to the first $50,000 of group term life insurance protection. For each $1,000 coverage in excess of $50,000, the employee must include the amounts indicated in Figure 4–2 in gross income.[95]

EXAMPLE 57

XYZ Corporation has a group term life insurance policy with coverage equal to the employee's annual salary. T, age 52, is president of the corporation and receives an annual salary of $75,000. T must include $144 in gross income from the insurance protection for the year.

$$\frac{\$75{,}000 - \$50{,}000}{\$1{,}000} \times .48 \times 12 \text{ months} = \$144$$

◆

Generally, the amount that must be included in income, computed from Figure 4–2, is much less than the price an individual would pay for the same amount of protection. Thus, even the excess coverage provides some tax-favored income for employees when group term life insurance coverage in excess of $50,000 is

94. §§ 74(c) and 274(j).

95. Reg. § 1.79–3(d)(2) and Temp.Reg. § 1.79–3T.

desirable. However, if the plan discriminates in favor of certain key employees (e.g., officers), the key employees are not eligible for the exclusion. In such a case, the key employees must include in gross income the greater of actual premiums paid by the employer or the amount calculated from the Uniform Premiums table in Figure 4–2. The other employees are still eligible for the $50,000 exclusion and continue to use the Uniform Premiums table to compute the income from excess insurance protection.[96]

Unemployment Compensation

In a series of rulings over a period of 40 years, the IRS exempted unemployment benefits from tax. These payments were considered social benefit programs for the promotion of the general welfare. As previously discussed, the scope of § 61, gross income, is probably broad enough to include unemployment benefits (since an increase in wealth is realized when the payments are received). Nevertheless, the IRS had chosen to exclude such benefits.

In 1978, Congress addressed the unemployment compensation issue and provided that unemployment benefits are taxable only if the recipient's adjusted gross income exceeds certain levels. In 1986, Congress readdressed the issue by providing that all unemployment compensation benefits are includible in gross income.[97]

Social Security Benefits

If a taxpayer's income exceeds a specified base amount, as much as one-half of Social Security retirement benefits must be included in gross income. The taxable amount of Social Security benefits is the *lesser* of the following:[98]

- .50 (Social Security benefits)
- .50 [modified adjusted gross income + .50 (Social Security benefits) − base amount]

Modified adjusted gross income is, generally, the taxpayer's adjusted gross income from all sources (other than Social Security) plus the foreign earned income exclusion and any tax-exempt interest received. The *base amount* is as follows:

Attained Age on Last Day of Employee's Tax Year	Cost per $1,000 of Protection for One-Month Period
Under 30	8 cents
30–34	9 cents
35–39	11 cents
40–44	17 cents
45–49	29 cents
50–54	48 cents
55–59	75 cents
60–64	$1.17
65–69	$2.10
70 and over	$3.76

FIGURE 4–2
Uniform Premiums for $1,000 of Group Term Life Insurance Protection

96. § 79(d).
97. § 85.
98. § 86.

- $32,000 for married taxpayers who file a joint return.
- $0 for married taxpayers who do not live apart for the entire year but file separate returns.
- $25,000 for all other taxpayers.

EXAMPLE 58

A married couple with adjusted gross income of $40,000, no tax-exempt interest, and $11,000 of Social Security benefits who file jointly must include one-half of the benefits in gross income. This works out as the lesser of the following:

1. .50 ($11,000) = $5,500
2. .50 [$40,000 + .50 ($11,000) − $32,000] = .50 ($13,500) = $6,750

If the couple's adjusted gross income were $15,000 and their Social Security benefits totaled $5,000, none of the benefits would be taxable, since .50 [$15,000 + .50 ($5,000) − $32,000] is not a positive number. ◆

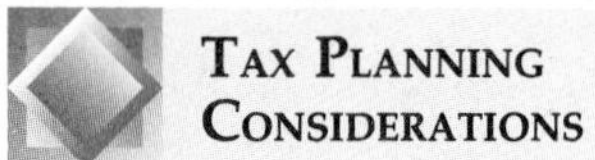

TAX PLANNING CONSIDERATIONS

The materials in this chapter have focused on the following questions:

- What is income?
- When is the income recognized?
- Who is the taxpayer?

Planning strategies suggested by these materials include the following:

- Maximize economic benefits that are not included in gross income.
- Defer the recognition of income.
- Shift income to taxpayers who are in a lower marginal tax bracket.

Some specific techniques for accomplishing these strategies are discussed in the following paragraphs.

Nontaxable Economic Benefits

Home ownership is the prime example of economic income from capital that is not subject to tax. If the taxpayer uses his or her capital to purchase investments, but pays rent on a personal residence, the taxpayer would pay the rent from after-tax income. However, if the taxpayer purchases a personal residence instead of the investments, the taxpayer would give up gross income from the forgone investments in exchange for the rent savings. The savings in rent enjoyed as a result of owning the home is not subject to tax. Thus, the homeowner will have substituted nontaxable for taxable income.

Tax Deferral

General. Since deferred taxes are tantamount to interest-free loans from the government, the deferral of taxes is a worthy goal of the tax planner. However, the tax planner must also consider the tax rates for the years the income is shifted from and to. For example, a one-year deferral of income from a year in which the taxpayer's tax rate was 15 percent to a year in which the tax rate will be 31 percent would not be advisable if the taxpayer expects to earn less than a 16 percent after-tax return on the deferred tax dollars.

The taxpayer can often defer the recognition of income from appreciated property by postponing the event triggering realization (the final closing on a sale or exchange of property). If the taxpayer needs cash, obtaining a loan by using the appreciated property as collateral may be the least costly alternative. When the taxpayer anticipates reinvesting the proceeds, a sale may be inadvisable.

Example 59

T owns 100 shares of XYZ Company common stock with a cost of $10,000 and a fair market value of $50,000. Although the stock's value has increased substantially in the past three years, T thinks the growth days are over. If he sells the XYZ stock, T will invest the proceeds from the sale in other common stock. Assuming T is in the 31% marginal tax bracket, he will have only $37,600 [$50,000 – .31 ($50,000 – $10,000)] to reinvest. The alternative investment must substantially outperform XYZ in the future in order for the sale to be beneficial. ◆

Selection of Investments. Because no tax is due until a gain has been recognized, the law favors investments that yield appreciation rather than annual income.

Example 60

S can buy a corporate bond or an acre of land for $10,000. The bond pays $1,000 of interest (10%) each year, and S expects the land to increase in value 10% each year for the next 10 years. She is in the 40% (combined Federal and state) tax bracket. Assuming the bond would mature or the land would be sold in 10 years and S would reinvest the interest at a 10% before-tax return, she would accumulate the following amount at the end of 10 years.

	Bond		Land
Original investment		$10,000	$10,000
Annual income	$1,000		
Less tax	(400)		
	$ 600		
Compound amount reinvested for 10 years at 6% after-tax	× 13.18	7,908	
		$17,908	
Compound amount, 10 years at 10%			× 2.59
			$25,900
Less tax on sale: 40% ($25,900 – $10,000)			(6,360)
			$19,540

Therefore, the value of the deferral that results from investing in the land rather than in the bond is $1,632 ($19,540 – $17,908). ◆

Series E and EE bonds can also be purchased for long-term deferrals of income. As discussed in the chapter, Series E bonds can be exchanged for new Series HH bonds to further postpone the tax. In situations where the taxpayer's goal is merely to shift income one year into the future, bank certificates of deposit are useful tools. If the maturity period is one year or less, all interest is reported in the year of maturity. Time certificates are especially useful for a taxpayer who realizes an unusually large gain from the sale of property in one year (and thus is in a high tax bracket) but expects his or her income to be less the following year.

Cash Basis. The timing of income from services can often be controlled through the use of the cash method of accounting. Although taxpayers are somewhat constrained by the constructive receipt doctrine (they cannot turn their backs on income), seldom will customers and clients offer to pay before they are asked. The usual lag between billings and collections (e.g., December's billings collected in January) will result in a continuous deferring of some income until the last year of operations. A salaried individual approaching retirement may contract with his or her employer before the services are rendered to receive a portion of compensation in the lower tax bracket retirement years.

Prepaid Income. For the accrual basis taxpayer who receives advance payments from customers, the transactions should be structured to avoid payment of tax on income before the time the income is actually earned. Revenue Procedure 71–21 provides the guidelines for deferring the tax on prepayments for services, and Reg. § 1.451–5 provides the guidelines for deferrals on sales of goods. In addition, both the cash and accrual basis taxpayer can sometimes defer income by stipulating that the payments are deposits rather than prepaid income. For example, a landlord should require an equivalent damage deposit rather than require prepayment of the last month's rent under the lease.

Shifting Income to Relatives

The tax liability of a family can be minimized by shifting income from higher- to lower-bracket family members. This can be accomplished through gifts of income-producing property. Furthermore, in many cases, the shifting of income can be accomplished with no negative effect on the family's investment plans.

EXAMPLE 61

B, who is in the 28% tax bracket, would like to save for her children's education. All of the children are under 14 years of age. B could transfer income-producing properties to the children, and the children could each receive income of up to $600 each year (refer to Chapter 3) with no tax liability. The next $600 would be taxed at the child's tax rate. After a child has more than $1,200 income, there is no tax advantage to shifting more income to the child (because the income will be taxed at the parents' rate) until the child is 14 years old (when all income will be taxed according to the child's tax rate). ◆

The Uniform Gifts to Minors Act, a model law adopted by all states (but with some variations among the states), facilitates income shifting. Under the Act, a gift of intangibles (e.g., bank accounts, stocks, bonds, life insurance contracts) can be made to a minor but with an adult serving as custodian. Usually, a parent who makes the gift is also named as custodian. The state laws allow the custodian to sell or redeem and reinvest the principal and to accumulate or distribute the income, practically at the custodian's discretion provided there is no commingling of the child's income with the parent's property. Thus, the parent can give appreciated securities to the child, and the donor custodian can then sell the securities and reinvest the proceeds, thereby shifting both the gain and annual income to the child. Such planning is limited by the tax liability calculation provision for a child under the age of 14 (refer to Chapter 3).

U.S. government bonds (Series E and EE) can be purchased by the parent for his or her children. When this is done, the children generally should file a return and elect to report the income on the accrual basis.

EXAMPLE 62

F (father) pays $7,500 for Series EE bonds in 1992 and immediately gives them to S (son), who will enter college the year of original maturity of the bonds. The bonds have a maturity value of $10,000. S elects to report the annual increment in redemption value as income for each year the bonds are held. The first year the increase is $250, and S includes that amount in his gross income. If S has no other income, no tax will be due on the $250 bond interest, since such an amount will be more than offset by S's available standard deduction. The following year, the increment is $260, and S includes this amount in income. Thus, over the life of the bonds, S will include $2,500 in income ($10,000 − $7,500), none of which will result in a tax liability, assuming S has no other income. However, if the election had not been made, S would be required to include $2,500 in income on the bonds in the year of original maturity, if they were redeemed as planned. This amount of income might result in a tax liability. ◆

In some cases, it may be advantageous for the child not to make the accrual election. For example, a child under age 14 with investment income of more than $1,200 each year and parents in the 28 or 31 percent tax bracket would probably benefit from deferring the tax on the savings bond interest. The child would also benefit from the use of the usually lower tax rate (rather than subjecting the income to his or her parents' tax rate) if the bonds mature after the child is age 14 or older.

Accounting for Community Property

The classification of income as community or separate property becomes important when either of two events occurs:

- Husband and wife, married taxpayers, file separate income tax returns for the year.
- Husband and wife obtain a divorce and therefore have to file separate returns for the year (refer to Chapter 3).

For planning purposes, it behooves married persons to keep track of the source of income (community or separate). To be in a position to do this effectively when income-producing assets are involved, it may be necessary to distinguish between separate and community property.[99]

Alimony

The person making the alimony payments favors a divorce settlement that includes a provision for deductible alimony payments. On the other hand, the recipient prefers that the payments do not qualify as alimony. If the payor is in a higher tax bracket than the recipient, both parties may benefit by increasing the payments and structuring them so that they qualify as alimony.

EXAMPLE 63

H and W are negotiating a divorce settlement. H has offered to pay W $10,000 each year for 10 years, but payments would cease upon W's death. W is willing to accept the offer, if the agreement will specify that the cash payments are not alimony. H is in the 31 percent tax bracket, and W's marginal rate is 15 percent.

---

99. Being able to distinguish between separate and community property is crucial to the determination of a property settlement incident to a divorce. It also is vital in the estate tax area (refer to Chapter 1) since the surviving wife's or husband's share of the community property is not included in the gross estate of the deceased spouse.

If H and W agree that H would pay W $12,000 of alimony each year, W as well as H would have improved after-tax cash flows.

	Annual Cash Flows	
	H	W
Nonalimony payments	$(10,000)	$10,000
Alimony payments	$(12,000)	$12,000
Tax effects		
.31 ($12,000)	3,720	
.15 ($12,000)		(1,800)
After-tax cash flows	$ (8,280)	$10,200
Benefit of alimony option	$ 1,720	$ 200

Both parties benefit at the government's expense if the $12,000 alimony option is used. ◆

PROBLEM MATERIALS

DISCUSSION QUESTIONS

1. The Internal Revenue Code contains a broad definition of gross income, but does not provide a listing of all possible types of income subject to tax. Would it improve the tax law if a complete listing of taxable sources of income were included in the Code?
2. Which of the following would be considered "income" for the current year by an economist but would not be gross income for tax purposes? Explain.
   - **a.** Securities acquired two years ago for $10,000 had a value of $12,000 at the beginning of the current year and a value of $13,000 at the end of the year.
   - **b.** An individual lives in the home he owns.
   - **c.** A corporation obtained a loan from a bank.
   - **d.** A shareholder paid a corporation $3,000 for property valued at $5,000.
   - **e.** An individual owned property that was stolen. The cost of the property three years ago was $2,000, and an insurance company paid the owner $6,000 (the value of the property on the date of theft).
   - **f.** An individual found a box of seventeenth-century Spanish coins while diving off the Virginia coast.
   - **g.** An individual received a $200 rebate from the manufacturer upon the purchase of a new car.
3. According to economists, because our tax system does not impute income to homeowners for the rental value of their homes, the nonhomeowner who invests in securities (rather than a home) is taxed more heavily than the homeowner. This leads to overinvesting in homes. Why do you suppose the laws are not changed to tax homeowners on the rental value of their homes?
4. Evaluate the following alternative proposals for taxing the income from property:
   - **a.** All assets would be valued at the end of the year, any increase in value that occurred during the year would be included in gross income, and any decrease in value would be deductible from gross income.
   - **b.** No gain or loss would be recognized until the taxpayer sold or exchanged the property.
   - **c.** Increases or decreases in the value of property traded on a national exchange (e.g., the New York Stock Exchange) would be reflected in gross income for the years the changes in value occurred. For all other assets, no gain or loss would be recognized until the property is sold or exchanged.

5. T had owned a tract of land for several years when the local government decided to build an airport near the property. The cost of the property to T was $50,000. The local government paid T $10,000 for invasion of his airspace. What is T's gross income from the receipt of the $10,000?
6. T is in the 28% tax bracket. He has the following alternative uses of his time: (1) he can work and earn $600 (before tax), or (2) he can stay at home and paint his house. If T selects (1), he must pay $500 to have his house painted. Which alternative would our tax laws encourage T to select?
7. Comment on the following: "Our tax laws encourage the taxpayer to hold appreciated assets and to sell assets that have declined in value."
8. A corporation pays all of its monthly salaried employees on the last Friday in each month. What would be the tax consequences to the employees if the date of payment were changed to the first Monday of the following month?
9. LMN, Inc., receives all of its income from repairing computers. The company reports its income by the cash method. On December 31, an employee went to a customer's office and repaired a computer. The customer gave LMN's employee a check for $300, but the employee did not remit the check to LMN until January of the following year. When is LMN required to recognize the income?
10. T is a cash basis surgeon who is usually paid through claims filed with insurance companies. Normally, it takes 60 days from the date of an operation until the charge is collected. What would be the consequences of T being required to change to the accrual method of accounting?
11. Is a cash basis taxpayer ever taxed on income before cash or its equivalent is actually or constructively received?
12. M, an accrual basis taxpayer, performed services for a client in 1992. The charge for the service was $450, but the customer paid only $200 in 1992 because he claimed that M did not perform the service adequately. M and the client negotiated a settlement in 1993, and the client paid an additional $150. What is M's 1992 income from the contract?
13. In 1992, T, an accrual basis taxpayer, rendered services for a customer with a poor credit rating. T's charge for the service was $1,000. T sent a bill to the customer for $1,000 but reported only $500 of income. He justified reporting only $500 as follows: "I'm being generous reporting $500. I'll be lucky if I collect anything." How much should T include as gross income from the contract in 1992?
14. In January 1992, T, a cash basis taxpayer, purchased for $2,000 a five-year Series EE U.S. government bond with a maturity value of $3,000. She also purchased for $2,000 a three-year bank certificate of deposit with a maturity value of $2,500. Is T required to recognize any interest income in 1992?
15. M is in the wholesale hardware business. His customers pay for the goods at the time they place the order. Often, M is out of stock on particular items and must back order the goods. When this occurs, he usually retains the customer's payment, orders the goods from the manufacturer, and ships the goods to the customer within a month. At the end of the year, there were several unfilled orders. Is it possible for M to defer the recognition of income from the receipt of advance payments on the unfilled orders?
16. F (father) paid $200 for an automobile that needed repairs. He worked nights and weekends to restore the car. Several individuals offered to purchase the car for $2,800. F gave the car and a list of potential buyers to S (son), whose college tuition was due in a few days. S sold the car for $2,800 and paid his tuition. Does F have any taxable income from the transaction?
17. F, a cash basis taxpayer, sold a bond with accrued interest of $750, for $10,250. F's basis in the bond was $9,000. Compute F's income from this transaction.
18. Father gave Son 100 shares of X Corporation stock on June 20. X Corporation had declared a $1 per share dividend on the stock on June 15, payable on June 30 to holders of record as of June 25. Who must report the dividend income, Father or Son?
19. P transferred rental properties to a corporation. P's objective was to minimize her liability for injuries that may occur on the property. The tenants continued to pay rents to P. Who must include the rents in gross income?

20. T is a bankruptcy consultant who has incorporated her practice. During the current year, the corporation received $225,000 in fees from clients. T received a salary of $100,000 in accordance with an employment contract between her and the corporation. The corporation has other operating expenses of $75,000. The remaining income was not distributed to T. Is T required to include the $50,000 ($225,000 – $100,000 – $75,000) in her gross income because she actually performed the services that generated the income?
21. Who pays the tax on (a) the income of an S corporation and on (b) the undistributed income of an estate?
22. H and W were residents of a community property state. In 1992, H left W for parts unknown. H and W were still married at year-end. How will H's absence complicate W's 1992 tax return?
23. What is the purpose of the front-loading rules related to alimony?
24. A post-1984 divorce agreement between H and W provides that H is to pay W $500 per month for 13 years. H and W have a child who is 8 years old. Termination of the monthly payments will coincide with the child's attaining age 21. Can the monthly payments qualify as alimony?
25. H and W were divorced. They jointly owned a home in the mountains with a basis of $50,000 and a fair market value of $80,000. According to the terms of the divorce, W gave H $40,000 for his one-half interest in the mountain home. W later sold the house for $85,000. What is W's gain from the sale?
26. In the case of a below-market loan between relatives, why is the lender required to recognize income although it is the borrower who appears to receive the economic benefit?
27. T is an employee and the sole shareholder of T Corporation. The corporation loaned T $50,000 and did not charge her interest. The IRS agent imputed interest on the loan, which the agent characterizes as a corporation-shareholder loan. T insists that the loan is an employer-employee loan. What difference does it make?
28. Suppose the annuity tables used by the IRS were outdated and that people lived longer than the tables indicated. How would this affect Federal revenues?
29. Discuss the difference in tax treatment, if any, between a taxpayer who wins the Nobel Prize and a taxpayer who is crowned Miss America.
30. T, Inc., pays $1,000 in premiums each year for a $250,000 insurance policy on the life of the company's president and controlling shareholder, C. The corporation owns the policy and is the beneficiary. Is the 52-year-old president of the corporation required to include any of the premiums in his gross income?
31. When a taxpayer is receiving Social Security benefits, could a $1,000 increase in income from services cause the taxpayer's adjusted gross income to increase by more than $1,000?
32. T paid $10,000 for a bond that yielded 10% interest each year. T reinvested the after-tax interest in certificates of deposits that also yielded 10% interest. Z bought land for $10,000. The land increased in value at the rate of 10% each year. T and Z were both in the 28% marginal tax bracket for all relevant years. At the end of 10 years, T received the principal amount of the bond, and Z sold the land. Explain why Z will have the greater after-tax proceeds.

PROBLEMS

33. Determine the effects of the following on T's gross income for the year:
    a. T bought a used sofa for $25. After T took the sofa home, she discovered $15,000 in a secret compartment. T was unable to determine who placed the money in the sofa. Therefore, T put the money in her bank account.
    b. T also discovered oil on her property during the year, and the value of the land increased from $10,000 to $3,000,000.

c. One year later, T found a diamond in the sofa she had purchased. Apparently, the diamond was in the sofa when T purchased it. The value of the diamond was $6,000, and T could not determine the former owner.
d. T's bank charges a $3 per month service charge. However, the fee is waived if the customer maintains an average balance for the month of at least $1,000. T's account exceeded the minimum deposit requirement, and as a result she was not required to pay any service charges for the year.

34. Compute the taxpayer's (1) economic income and (2) gross income for tax purposes from the following events:

a. The taxpayer sold securities for $10,000. The securities cost $6,000 in 1988. The fair market value of the securities at the beginning of the year was $12,000.
b. The taxpayer sold his business and received $15,000 under a covenant not to compete with the new owner.
c. The taxpayer used her controlled corporation's automobile for her vacation. The rental value of the automobile for the vacation period was $800.
d. The taxpayer raised vegetables in her garden. The fair market value of the vegetables was $900, and the cost of raising them was $100. She ate some of the vegetables and gave the remainder to neighbors.
e. The local government changed the zoning ordinances so that some of the taxpayer's residential property was reclassified as commercial. Because of the change, the fair market value of the taxpayer's property increased by $10,000.
f. During the year, the taxpayer borrowed $50,000 for two years at 9% interest. By the end of the year, interest rates had increased to 12%, and the lender accepted $49,000 in full satisfaction of the debt.

35. T received the following from his employer during the tax year:

- Salary of $60,000.
- Use of a company car for his vacation. Rental value for the period would have been $800.
- Inventory that cost the employer $2,000 and had a fair market value of $3,500.
- Loan of $5,000 for which T signed a promissory note.

Determine the effect of these items on T's gross income.

36. Determine the taxpayer's income for tax purposes in each of the following cases:

a. In the current year, RST Corporation purchased $1,000,000 par value of its own bonds and paid the bondholders $980,000 plus $50,000 of accrued interest. The bonds had been issued 10 years ago at par and were to mature 25 years from the date of issue. Does the corporation recognize income from the purchase of the bonds?
b. A shareholder of a corporation sold property to the corporation for $60,000 (the shareholder's cost). The value of the property on the date of sale was $50,000. Does the taxpayer have any gross income from the sale?
c. T was a football coach at a state university. Because of his disappointing record, he was asked to resign and accept one-half of his pay for the remaining three years of his contract. The coach resigned, accepting $75,000.

37. Which of the following investments will yield the greater after-tax value assuming the taxpayer is in the 40% tax bracket (combined Federal and state) in all years and the investments will be liquidated at the end of five years?

a. Land that will increase in value by 10% each year.
b. A taxable bond yielding 10% before tax, and the interest can be reinvested at 10% before tax.
c. Common stock that will increase in value at the rate of 5% (compounded) each year and pays dividends equal to 5% of the year-end value of the stock. The dividends can be reinvested at 10% before tax.
d. A tax-exempt state government bond yielding 8%. The interest can be reinvested at a before-tax rate of 10%, and the bond matures in 10 years.

Given: Compound amount of $1 at the end of five years:

Interest Rate	Factor
6%	1.33
8%	1.47
10%	1.61

Compound value of annuity payments at the end of five years:

Interest Rate	Factor
6%	5.64
8%	5.87
10%	6.11

38. Determine the taxpayer's income for tax purposes in each of the following cases:

   a. R borrowed $30,000 from the First National Bank. R was required to deliver to the bank stocks with a value of $30,000 and a cost of $10,000. The stocks were to serve as collateral for the loan.

   b. P owned a lot on Sycamore Street that measured 100 feet by 100 feet. The cost of the lot to P is $10,000. The city condemned a 10-foot strip of the land so that it could widen the street. P received a $2,000 condemnation award.

   c. M owned land zoned for residential use only. The land cost $5,000 and had a market value of $7,000. M spent $500 and several hundred hours petitioning the county supervisors to change the zoning to A–1 commercial. The value of the property immediately increased to $20,000 when the county approved the zoning change.

39. L is an attorney who conducts her practice as a sole proprietor. During the year, she received cash of $85,000 for legal services rendered. At the beginning of the year, she had fees receivable of $50,000. At the end of the year, she had fees receivable of $40,000. Compute L's gross income from her law practice:

   a. Using the cash basis of accounting.

   b. Using the accrual basis of accounting.

40. The taxpayer began operating a grocery store during the year. Her only books and records are based on cash receipts and disbursements, but she has asked you to compute her gross profit from the business for tax purposes.

Sales of merchandise	$150,000
Purchases of merchandise	130,000

You determine that as of the end of the year the taxpayer has accounts payable for merchandise of $9,000 and accounts receivable from customers totaling $1,500. The cost of merchandise on hand at the end of the year was $5,500. Compute the grocery store's accrual method gross profit for the year.

41. X, Inc., is a dance studio that sells dance lessons for cash, on open account, and for notes receivable. The company also collects interest on bonds held as an investment. The company's cash receipts for 1992 totaled $219,000:

Cash sales	$ 60,000
Collections on accounts receivable	120,000
Collections on notes receivable	30,000
Interest on bonds	9,000
	$219,000

The balances in accounts receivable, notes receivable, and accrued interest on bonds at the beginning and end of the year were as follows:

	1-1-92	12-31-92
Accounts receivable	$17,000	$22,000
Notes receivable	9,000	11,000
Accrued interest on bonds	2,500	4,000
	$28,500	$37,000

The fair market value of the notes is equal to 75% of their face amount. There were no bad debts for the year, and all notes were for services performed during the year. Compute the corporation's gross income:

a. Using the cash basis of accounting.
b. Using the accrual basis of accounting.
c. Using a hybrid method—accrual basis for lessons and cash basis for interest income.

42. Determine the effect of the following on the taxpayer's gross income for 1992:

a. Received his paycheck for $3,000 from his employer on December 31, 1992. He deposited the paycheck on January 2, 1993.
b. Received a bonus of $5,000 from his employer on January 10, 1993. The bonus was for the outstanding performance of his division during 1992.
c. Received a dividend check from IBM on November 28, 1992. He mailed the check back to IBM in December requesting that additional IBM stock be issued to him under IBM's dividend reinvestment plan.
d. Sold a building on December 1, 1992, for $75,000. His adjusted basis for the building was $60,000. He received a promissory note. The due date for the note is June 30, 1993.

43. M owns a life insurance policy. The cash surrender value of the policy increased $1,500 during the year. He purchased a certificate of deposit on June 30 of the current year for $41,322. The certificate matures in two years when its value will be $50,000 (interest rate of 10%). However, if M redeems the certificate before the end of the first year, he receives no interest. M also purchased a Series EE U.S. government savings bond for $6,000. The maturity value of the bond is $10,000 in six years (yield of 9%), and the redemption price of the bond increased by $400 during the year. M has owned no other savings bonds. What is M's current year gross income from the above items?

44. AC, Inc., an accrual basis taxpayer, sells and installs consumer appliances. Determine the effects of each of the following transactions on the company's 1992 gross income:

a. In December 1992, the company received a $1,200 advance payment from a customer. The payment was for an appliance that AC specially ordered from the manufacturer. The appliance had not arrived at the end of 1992..
b. At the end of 1992, the company installed an appliance and collected the full price of $750 for the item. However, the customer claimed the appliance was defective and asked the company for a refund. The company conceded that the appliance was defective, but claimed that the customer should collect from the manufacturer. The dispute had not been settled by the end of 1992. In early 1993, it was determined that AC did not install the appliance properly and the company was required to refund the full sales price.
c. At the end of 1992, a customer refused to pay for merchandise delivered in 1991. The customer claimed that the merchandise was defective. In 1992 the company replaced the merchandise at no charge to the customer.
d. The company sold an appliance for $1,200 (plus a market rate of interest) and received the customer's note for that amount. However, because of the customer's poor credit rating, the value of the note was only $700.

45. P is a cash basis taxpayer. Determine her 1992 gross income from the following transactions:

a. In 1990, P negotiated her 1991 salary. The employer offered to pay P $200,000 in 1991. P countered that she wanted $10,000 each month in 1991 and the remaining $80,000 in January 1992. P wanted the $80,000 income shifted to 1992 because she expected her 1992 tax rates to be lower. The employer agreed to P's terms.
b. In 1991, P was running short of cash and needed money for Christmas. Her employer loaned her $20,000 in November 1991. P signed a note for $20,000 plus 10% interest, the applicable Federal rate. In January 1992, the employer subtracted the $20,000 and $333 interest from the $80,000 due P and paid P $59,667.
c. On December 31, 1992, Z offered to buy land from P for $30,000 (P's basis was $8,000). P refused to sell in 1992, but at that time, P contracted to sell the land to Z in 1993 for $30,000.

46. Discuss the tax effects of the following transactions on an accrual basis taxpayer:

a. On December 15, 1991, B signed a contract to purchase land from T. Payment for the land was to be made on closing, January 15, 1992. During the interval between the contract and the closing dates, B's attorney was to verify that T had good title to the land. The closing was completed on January 15, 1992.
b. M collected $1,500 for services rendered the client in 1991. Late in 1991, the client complained that the work was not done in accordance with contract specifications. Also in 1991, the parties agreed to allow an arbitrator to settle the dispute. In January 1992, the arbitrator ordered M to refund $500 to the client.

47. The Z Apartments requires its new tenants to pay the rent for the first and last months of the annual lease and a $400 damage deposit, all at the time the lease is signed. In December 1992, a tenant paid $800 for January 1993 rent, $800 for December 1993 rent, and $400 for the damage deposit. In January 1994, Z refunded the tenant's damage deposit. What are the effects of these payments on Z's taxable income for 1992, 1993, and 1994?

a. Assume Z is a cash basis taxpayer.
b. Assume Z is an accrual basis taxpayer.

48. M has asked you to review portions of her tax return. She provides you with the following information.

Gain on redemption of a 2-year 10% certificate of deposit		
Proceeds received June 30, 1992	$10,000	
Purchase price July 1, 1990	(8,200)	
Gain		$1,800
Gain on redemption of a 6-month 9% certificate of deposit		
Proceeds received March 31, 1992	$ 5,000	
Purchase price October 1, 1991	(4,580)	
Gain		420
Gain from 8% Series E savings bond		
Proceeds received September 30, 1992	$ 2,500	
Purchase price June 30, 1979	(780)	
Gain		1,720
Distributions from a family partnership		1,500

M's share of the partnership's earnings were $1,400. Determine M's 1992 gross income from the above.

49. a. An automobile dealer has several new cars in inventory but often does not have the right combination of body style, color, and accessories. In some cases, the dealer makes an offer to sell a car at a certain price, accepts a deposit, and then orders the car from the manufacturer. When the car is received from the manufacturer, the sale is closed, and the dealer receives the balance of the sales price. At the end of the current year, the dealer has deposits totaling $8,200 for cars that have not been received from the manufacturer. When is the $8,200 subject to tax?

b. T Corporation, an exterminating company, is a calendar year taxpayer. It contracts to provide service to homeowners once a month under a one-year or a two-year contract. On April 1 of the current year, the company sold a customer a one-year contract for $60. How much of the $60 is taxable in the current year if the company is an accrual basis taxpayer? If the $60 is payment on a two-year contract, how much is taxed in the year the contract is sold?

c. X, an accrual basis taxpayer, owns an amusement park whose fiscal year ends September 30. To increase business during the fall and winter months, X sold passes that would allow the holder to ride free during the months of October through March. During the month of September, $6,000 was collected from the sale of passes for the upcoming fall and winter. When will the $6,000 be taxable to X?

d. The taxpayer is in the office equipment rental business and uses the accrual basis of accounting. In December, he collected $5,000 in rents for the following January. When is the $5,000 taxable?

50. T is employed by a CPA firm and receives an annual salary of $40,000. He works in the city during the day, but as part of his employment agreement, he maintains an office in his home during tax season to which clients of the CPA firm who live in his neighborhood in the suburbs can bring their tax return data. He prepares these tax returns in his home office during the evenings and on weekends. Such work generates total fees for the CPA firm of $20,000. For his overtime work, T receives additional compensation of $8,000 from his employer. Determine the effect of these transactions on T's gross income.

51. a. T is a cash basis taxpayer. On December 1, 1992, T gave a corporate bond to his son, S. The bond had a face amount of $10,000 and paid $900 of interest each January 31. Also on December 1, 1992, T gave common stocks to his daughter, D. Dividends totaling $720 had been declared on the stocks on November 30, 1992, and were payable on January 15, 1993. D became the shareholder of record in time to collect the dividends. What is T's 1993 gross income from the bond and stocks?

b. In 1992, T's mother was unable to pay her bills as they came due. T, his employer, and his mother's creditors entered into an arrangement whereby T's employer would withhold $500 per month from T's salary and the employer would pay the $500 to the creditors. In 1992, $3,000 was withheld from T's salary and paid to the creditors. Is T required to pay tax on the $3,000?

c. F is considering purchasing a zero coupon (no interest is paid until maturity) corporate bond for himself and for his minor son, S (age 4). The bonds have an issue price of $300 and pay $1,000 at the end of 10 years. F is in the 28% tax bracket, and S has no other taxable income. Would the zero coupon bond be an equally suitable investment for F and S?

52. T, a cash basis taxpayer, is employed by GA Corporation, also a cash basis taxpayer. T is a full-time employee of the corporation and receives a salary of $60,000 per year. He also receives a bonus equal to 10% of all collections from clients he serviced during the year. Determine the tax consequences of the following events to the corporation and to T:

a. On December 31, 1992, T was visiting a customer. The customer gave T a $3,000 check payable to the corporation for appraisal services T performed during 1992. T did not deliver the check to the corporation until January 1993.

b. The facts are the same as in (a), except that the corporation is an accrual basis taxpayer and T deposited the check on December 31, but the bank did not add the deposit to the corporation's account until January 1993.

c. The facts are the same as in (a), except the customer told T to hold the check until January when the customer could make a bank deposit that would cover the check.

53. X, Y, and Z each have a one-third interest in the capital and profits of the XYZ Partnership. At the beginning of the year, each partner had a $30,000 balance in his capital account. The partnership's gross income for the year was $180,000, and its

total expenses were $96,000. During the year, X contributed an additional $5,000 to the partnership and did not have any withdrawals from his capital account. Y withdrew $30,000, and Z withdrew $9,000. Compute each partner's taxable income from the partnership for the year.

54. H and W lived together for part of the year but were divorced on December 31, 1992. H earned $30,000 salary from his employer during the year. W's salary was $16,000. W also received $8,000 in taxable dividends from stock held as separate property.

  a. If H and W reside in Texas, how much income should be reported by each on their separate tax returns for 1992?
  b. If amounts are withheld from their salaries, how are these amounts reported on H and W's separate returns?
  c. If H and W reside in a common law state, how much income should be reported by each on their separate returns?

55. H and W were married on June 30, 1992, and resided in Dallas, Texas. On December 31, 1992, they separated, and on March 31, 1993, they were divorced. On July 1, 1993, H moved to Grundy, Virginia, and remarried in December 1993. W did not remarry. H's and W's incomes for the relevant periods were as follows:

Salary	H	W
January 1–June 30, 1992	$23,000	$15,000
July 1–December 31, 1992	24,000	16,000
January 1–March 31, 1993	25,000	18,000
April 1–December 31, 1993	40,000	20,000

In addition to the salaries listed, on January 31, 1993, H received $2,400 interest on savings certificates acquired on February 1, 1992. What is W's gross income for 1992 and 1993 as computed on separate returns?

56. H and W were divorced on July 1 of the current year after 10 years of marriage. Their current year's income received before the divorce was as follows:

H's salary	$20,000
W's salary	25,000
Rent on apartments purchased by W 15 years ago	6,000
Dividends on stock H inherited from his mother 4 years ago	1,200
Interest on a savings account in W's name funded with her salary	600

Allocate the income to H and W assuming they live in:

  a. California.
  b. Texas.

57. Mr. and Mrs. X are in the process of negotiating their divorce agreement. What would be the tax consequences to Mr. X and Mrs. X if the following, considered individually, become part of the agreement:

  a. Mrs. X is to receive $1,000 per month until she dies or remarries. She also is to receive $500 per month for 12 years for her one-half interest in their personal residence. She paid for her one-half interest out of her earnings.
  b. Mrs. X is to receive a principal sum of $100,000. Of this amount, $50,000 is to be paid in the year of the divorce, and $5,000 per year will be paid to her in each of the following 10 years or until Mrs. X's death.
  c. Mrs. X is to receive the family residence (value of $120,000 and basis of $75,000). The home was jointly owned by Mr. and Mrs. X. In exchange for the residence, Mrs. X relinquished all of her rights to property accumulated during the marriage. She also is to receive $1,000 per month until her death or remarriage, but for a period of not longer than 10 years.

58. Under the terms of a post-1986 divorce agreement, W is to receive payments from H as follows: $50,000 in Year 1, $40,000 in Year 2, and $20,000 each year for Years

3 through 10. W is also to receive custody of their minor son. The payments will decrease by $5,000 per year if the son dies or when he attains age 21 and will cease upon W's death.

a. What will be W's taxable alimony in Year 1?
b. What will be the effect of the Years 2 and 3 payments on W's taxable income?

59. Under the terms of their divorce agreement, H is to transfer common stocks (cost of $25,000, market value of $60,000) to W in satisfaction of W's property rights. W is also to receive $15,000 per year until her death or remarriage. W originally asked for $9,000 alimony and $5,000 child support. It was the understanding between H and W that W would use $5,000 of the amount received for the support of the children. How will the terms of the agreement affect H's taxable income?

60. a. M (mother) is in the 28% tax bracket, and S (son) is in the 15% tax bracket. M loans S $50,000, and S invests the money in a bond that yields an 8% return. If M had not made the loan, she would have purchased the bond. The relevant Federal rate is 9%. There are no other loans between the family members. What is the effect of the preceding transactions on M's and S's combined tax for the year?
b. T, an individual, had outstanding interest-free loans receivable as follows:

Borrower	Amount of Loan	Use of the Loan Proceeds
S, T's son	$ 15,000	Medical school tuition
D, T's daughter	25,000	Start of an unincorporated business
R, T's employee	2,000	Payment of medical bills
B, T's brother	110,000	Payment of attorney fees

S had $1,500 net investment income for the year. D's income was $5,000 earned by the business and $1,500 of dividends. R's only income was his $12,000 salary. B is in prison serving 145 years to life and has no income.

All loans were outstanding for the entire year, and the Federal rate is 9% compounded semiannually (9.21% effective annual rate).

Compute T's imputed interest income.

61. On June 30, 1992, T borrowed $52,000 from his employer. On July 1, 1992, T used the money as follows:

Interest-free loan to T's controlled corporation (operated by T on a part-time basis)	$21,000
Interest-free loan to S (T's son)	11,000
National Bank of Grundy 9% certificate of deposit ($15,260 due at maturity, June 30, 1993)	14,000
National Bank of Grundy 10% certificate of deposit ($7,260 due at maturity, June 30, 1994)	6,000
	$52,000

T's employer did not charge him interest. The applicable Federal rate was 12% throughout the relevant period. S had investment income of $800 for the year, and he used the loan proceeds to pay medical school tuition. There were no other outstanding loans between T and S. What are the effects of the preceding transactions on T's taxable income for 1992?

62. Indicate whether the imputed interest rules should apply in the following situations:

a. T is a cash basis attorney who charges his clients based on the number of hours it takes to do the job. The bill is due upon completion of the work. However, for clients who make an initial payment when the work begins, T grants a discount on the final bill. The discount is equal to 10% interest on the deposit.
b. L Telephone Company requires that customers make a security deposit. The deposit is refunded after the customer has established a good record for paying the telephone bill. The company pays 6% interest on the deposits.

c. D asked F for a $125,000 loan to purchase a new home. F made the loan and did not charge interest. F never intended to collect the loan, and at the end of the year F told D that the debt was forgiven.

63. Mr. Z is the sole shareholder of Z, Inc. He is also employed by the corporation. On June 30, 1992, Z borrowed $8,000 from Z, Inc., and on July 1, 1993, he borrowed an additional $3,000. Both loans were due on demand. No interest was charged on the loans, and the Federal rate was 10% for all relevant dates. Z used the money to purchase stock, and he had no investment income. Determine the tax consequences to Z and Z, Inc. in each of the following situations:

a. The loans are considered employer-employee loans.
b. The loans are considered corporation-shareholder loans.

64. T purchased an annuity from an insurance company for $12,000 on January 1, 1992. The annuity was to pay him $1,500 per year for life. At the time he purchased the contract, his life expectancy was 10 years.

a. Determine T's gross income from the annuity in the first year.
b. Assume T lives 20 years after purchasing the contract. What would be T's gross income in the nineteenth year?
c. Assume T died in 1995, after collecting a total of $6,000. What will be the effect of the annuity on his 1995 gross income?

65. In 1992, R purchased an annuity for $50,000. He was 59 at the time he purchased the contract. Payments were to begin when R attained age 62. In 1992, when the cash surrender value had increased to $51,000, R exercised a right to receive $1,500 and accept reduced payments after age 62. In 1994, when he had a life expectancy of 22.5 years, R received his first annual $3,000 payment under the contract.

a. What is R's income from the contract in 1992?
b. Compute R's taxable collections under the annuity contract in 1994.

66. For each of the following, determine the amount that should be included in gross income:

a. P was selected as the most valuable player in the Super Bowl. In recognition of this, he was awarded a sports car worth $60,000 and $50,000 in cash.
b. W won the Mrs. America beauty contest. She received various prizes valued at $75,000.
c. G was awarded the Nobel Peace Prize. He took the $345,000 check he received and donated it to State University, his alma mater.

67. The LMN Partnership has a group term life insurance plan. Each partner has $100,000 protection, and each employee has protection equal to twice his or her annual salary. Employee V (age 44) had $90,000 insurance under the plan, and partner N (age 46) had $100,000 coverage. The cost of V's coverage for the year was $180, and the cost of N's protection was $380.

a. Assuming the plan is nondiscriminatory, how much must V and N include in gross income from the insurance?
b. Assuming the plan is discriminatory, how much must N include in his gross income from the insurance?

68. T was employed during the first nine months of the year. For this period, he earned $60,000. He was unemployed during the last three months of the year and received unemployment compensation of $2,400. T was actively seeking employment during this period, but was unable to find another job because of the depressed nature of the industry in which he had been employed. He earned $1,000 of interest income on his savings account and withdrew $800 of the interest earned. Calculate T's gross income for the year.

69. M and W are married and file a joint return. In 1992, they received $9,000 in Social Security benefits and $28,000 taxable pension benefits, interest, and dividends.

a. Compute the couple's adjusted gross income on a joint return.
b. If M works part-time and earns $6,000, how much would M and W's adjusted gross income increase?
c. Assume W cashed certificates of deposit that had paid $8,000 in interest each year and purchases State of Virginia bonds that pay $6,000 in interest each year. How much would M and W's adjusted gross income decrease? (Assume W had no gain or loss from cashing the certificates.)

70. In the following problems, assume the unmarried taxpayer has no tax-exempt interest income and receives $7,000 per year in Social Security benefits:

a. Compute the maximum adjusted gross income from other sources the taxpayer can receive without including any of the Social Security benefits in adjusted gross income.
b. How much adjusted gross income from other sources must the taxpayer receive before $3,500 in Social Security benefits are included in adjusted gross income?

71. T does not think she has an income tax problem but would like to discuss her situation with you just to make sure she will not get hit with an unexpected tax liability. Base your suggestions on the following relevant financial information:

a. T's share of the SAT Partnership income is $40,000, but none of the income can be distributed because the partnership needs the cash for operations.
b. T's Social Security benefits totaled $8,400, but T loaned the cash received to her nephew.
c. T assigned to a creditor the right to collect $1,200 interest on some bonds she owned.
d. T and her husband lived together in California until September, when they separated. T has heard rumors that her husband had substantial gambling winnings since they separated.

CUMULATIVE PROBLEMS

72. Thomas R. Rucker, age 42, is single and is employed as a plumber for Ajax Plumbing Company. Tom's Social Security number is 262–06–3814. Tom lives at 252 Mason Place, Grand View, WV 22801. His salary was $40,250, and his employer withheld Federal income tax of $6,100.

Tom's mother, Sue Rucker, age 68, lives in a small house Tom bought for her in Florida. She has no income of her own and is totally dependent on Tom for her support. To provide his mother with some spending money, Tom assigned to her the income from some XYZ Corporation bonds he owns. The interest received by Tom's mother was $2,100. Tom retained ownership of the bonds but surrendered all rights to the interest on the bonds.

Over the years, Tom and his physician, Joe Zorn, have become good friends. During 1992, Tom incurred doctor bills of $350. Instead of paying Zorn in cash, Tom did the plumbing work for a new bar Zorn had installed in his basement in September 1992. Tom and Zorn agreed that the value of Tom's services was equal to the $350 in medical bills.

On September 5, 1992, Tom sold 100 shares of ABC Corporation stock for $1,800. He had acquired the stock on May 2, 1981, for $5,100.

Tom's itemized deductions for 1992 were as follows:

State income tax withheld	$ 910
Real estate taxes paid	750
Home mortgage interest (paid to Grand View Savings and Loan)	2,600
Cash contributions to First Church	900

Part 1—Tax Computation

Compute Tom's 1992 Federal income tax payable (or refund due). Suggested software (if available): *TurboTax* for tax return or WFT tax planning software.

Part 2—Tax Planning

For 1993, assume that all items of income and expense will be approximately the same as in 1992, except for the following:

- Tom expects a 10% increase in salary and taxes withheld beginning January 1, 1993.
- He does not expect to incur any medical expenses.
- His real estate taxes will increase to $800.
- He expects to contribute $1,200 to First Church.
- He does not expect to have any capital gains or losses in 1993.

Tom plans to marry in June 1993. His fiancée, Sarah, plans to quit her job in Pittsburgh and move to Grand View to be with Tom. She does not plan to seek employment after the move. Sarah will earn $18,000 through May 1993. Her employer will withhold Federal income tax of $3,600 and state income tax of $900.

Compute the estimated total tax liability for the Ruckers for 1993. Should Tom ask his employer to withhold more or less than the amount withheld last year? How much? Suggested software (if available): WFT tax planning software.

73. Dan and Freida Butler, husband and wife, file a joint return. The Butlers live at 625 Oak Street, Corbin, KY 27521. Dan's Social Security number is 482–61–1231, and Freida's is 162–79–1245.

During 1992, Dan and Freida furnished over half of the total support of each of the following individuals:

a. Gina, their daughter, age 22, who was married on December 21, 1991, has no income of her own, and for 1992 files a joint return with her husband, who earned $8,500 during 1992.
b. Sam, their son, age 17, who had gross income of $2,500 and who dropped out of high school in February 1992.
c. Ben Brow, Freida's brother, age 27, who is a full-time college student with gross income of $2,500.

Dan, a radio announcer for WJJJ, earned a salary of $36,000 in 1992. Freida was employed part-time as a real estate salesperson by Corbin Realty and was paid commissions of $18,000 in 1992. Freida sold a house on December 30, 1992, and will be paid a commission of $1,500 (not included in the $18,000) on the January 10, 1993, closing date.

Dan and Freida collected $15,000 on a certificate of deposit that matured on September 30, 1992. The certificate was purchased on October 1, 1990, for $12,397, and the yield to maturity was 10%.

Dan and Freida had itemized deductions as follows:

State income tax withheld	$1,900
Real estate taxes paid	900
Interest on home mortgage (paid to Corbin Savings and Loan)	5,600
Cash contributions to the Boy Scouts	420

Their employers withheld Federal income tax of $7,400 (Dan $4,400, Freida $3,000), and the Butlers paid estimated tax of $800.

Part 1—Tax Computation

Compute Dan and Freida's 1992 Federal income tax payable (or refund due). Suggested software (if available): *TurboTax* for tax return or WFT tax planning software.

Part 2—Tax Planning

Dan plans to reduce his work schedule and work only halftime for WJJJ in 1993. He has been writing songs for several years and wants to devote more time to developing a career as a songwriter. Because of the uncertainty in the music business, however, he would like you to make all computations assuming he will have no income from songwriting in 1993. To make up for the loss of income, Freida plans to increase the amount of time she spends selling real estate. She estimates she will be able to earn $33,000 in 1993. Assume all other income and expense items will be approximately the same as they were in 1992. Will the Butlers have more or less disposable income (after Federal income tax) in 1993? Suggested software (if available): WFT tax planning software.

74. Sam T. Seymour would like to forget 1991 (and almost did as a result of his drinking problem). Although he received a salary of $65,800 and $380 of interest income, a divorce nearly brought him to financial ruin. The divorce was final on February 28, 1991. Under the agreement, Sam was required to do the following:

- Pay his minor daughter Pam's private school tuition of $10,800.
- Pay his ex-wife, Patricia Ann Seymour, a $40,000 lump-sum payment on March 1, 1991, and $2,000 each month thereafter through February 1997. The payments are to cease upon Patricia's death.
- Transfer to Patricia stock acquired in 1984 for $40,000 that now has a market value of $82,000.

Patricia retained custody of Pam but spent only $4,000 for Pam's support in 1991. The divorce agreement was silent as to whether Sam could claim Pam as a dependent and as to whether the cash payments to Patricia would constitute alimony.

Sam paid the tuition and made the $40,000 lump-sum payment but, because he was dismissed from his job in August 1991, was able to make only seven of the monthly payments to Patricia.

On November 1, 1991, when the applicable Federal rate was 10%, Sam was compelled to borrow $35,000 from his mother (Mollie Seymour). He gave her a non-interest-bearing second mortgage on his residence. There were no other loans outstanding between Sam and his mother.

Other information relevant to Sam's 1991 return is as follows:

a. Sam's disabled brother, Fred Seymour, lived with Sam from April through December 1991. Fred's only income was $3,600 of Social Security disability payments, and Sam contributed $4,000 toward Fred's support. No one else contributed to Fred's support. Fred's Social Security number is 245–99–4444.
b. Sam's only deductible items were home mortgage interest, $2,080; state income tax, $2,380; county property taxes, $3,000; charitable contributions, $200.
c. Sam's employer withheld $12,337 of Federal income tax.
d. Sam is 47 years old, his Social Security number is 215–71–1041, and he lives at 170 Ford Street, Gretna, TN 37929.
e. Patricia Ann Seymour's Social Security number is 712–15–9701.

Compute Sam's 1991 Federal income tax payable (or refund due). If you use tax forms for your computations, you will need Form 1040 and Schedule A. Suggested software (if available): *TurboTax* for tax return or WFT tax planning software.

RESEARCH PROBLEMS

RESEARCH PROBLEM 1 T gave common stock to her daughter, D. The cost of the stock was $20,000, and its fair market value was $150,000. The uniform transfer tax on the gift was $30,000. T was liable for the transfer tax, but the gift was made on the condition that D would pay the gift tax (i.e., a "net gift"). D paid the $30,000 in accordance with the agreement.

The IRS agent contends that T must treat the transactions as part sale and part gift. That is, 20% of the stock ($30,000/$150,000 = .20) was sold, and the balance was given to D. According to the agent, T must recognize taxable gain of $26,000 [$30,000 − (.20)($20,000)]. T is having difficulty understanding why she would be required to recognize any income since she made a gift of property and did not receive anything. What is your opinion?

Research Problem 2 The First Bank exchanged a mortgage with the Second Bank. The mortgages were on identical condominium units in the same building. The interest rates and principal amounts on the mortgages were also identical. The interest rates on the mortgages were below the current market rate of interest. Thus, the exchange generated losses for both banks. The primary motivation for the exchange was to generate a tax loss. The IRS agent examining the First Bank's tax return contends that the loss is not deductible because there was no economic loss; that is, the bank now owns a mortgage identical to the one it previously owned. The bank argues that the exchange of mortgages is a transaction that constitutes realization. Therefore, a loss was realized during the year. What is your opinion?

Research Problem 3 Mr. A is a commissioned agent for a large insurance company. During the year, he purchased a policy on his life and the lives of his children and received a commission. Mr. A treated the commission on these policies as a reduction in cost rather than as income. However, during an audit the revenue agent indicates that Mr. A must include the commission in his gross income. The taxpayer seeks your assistance in resolving the matter with the agent.

Partial list of research aids:

Ostheimer v. U.S., 59–1 USTC ¶9300, 3 AFTR2d 886, 264 F.2d 789 (CA–3, 1959).
Rev.Rul. 55–273, 1955–1 C.B. 221.

Research Problem 4 The Great Electric Company requires new customers to make a $100 deposit to secure future payments for electricity. After the customer has established a good payment record (usually within two years), the company refunds the deposit to the customer. If the services are terminated before refund, the deposit is usually applied against the final bill. The IRS agent insists that the company must include the deposits in gross income for the year the deposits are received. Can you find authority for excluding the deposits from income?

Chapter

Gross Income: Exclusions

Objectives

Explain that statutory authority is required for the allowance of exclusions from income.

Analyze the Sections of the Internal Revenue Code that permit the following exclusions:

- Gifts and inheritances
- Life insurance proceeds
- Employee death benefits
- Scholarships
- Compensation for injuries and sickness
- Employer-sponsored accident and health plan coverage and benefits
- Meals and lodging
- Employee fringe benefits
- Foreign earned income
- Interest on government obligations
- Dividends
- Educational savings bonds interest

Discuss the extent to which receipts can be excluded under the tax benefit rule.

Describe the circumstances under which income must be reported from the discharge of indebtedness.

Suggest tax planning strategies for obtaining the maximum benefits from allowable exclusions.

Outline

Items Specifically Excluded from Gross Income

Chapter 4 discussed the concepts and judicial doctrines that affect the determination of gross income. If an income item is within the all-inclusive definition of gross income, the item can be excluded only if the taxpayer can locate specific authority for doing so. Chapter 5 focuses on the exclusions Congress has authorized.

Statutory Authority

Sections 101 through 150 provide the authority for excluding specific items from gross income. In addition, other exclusions are scattered throughout the Code. Each exclusion has its own legislative history and reason for enactment. Certain exclusions are intended as a form of indirect welfare payments. Other exclusions prevent double taxation of income or provide incentives for socially desirable activities (e.g., nontaxable interest on certain U.S. government bonds where the owner uses the funds for educational expenses).

In some cases, Congress has enacted exclusions to rectify the effects of judicial decisions. For example, the Supreme Court held that the fair market value of improvements (not made in lieu of rent) made by a tenant to the landlord's property should be included in the landlord's gross income upon termination of the lease.[1] The landlord was required to include the value of the improvements in gross income even though the landlord had not sold or otherwise disposed of the property. Congress provided relief in this situation by enacting § 109, which defers taxing the value of the improvements until the property is sold.[2]

Section 123 was enacted to counter a District Court's decision in *Arnold v. U.S.*[3] In *Arnold*, the court included in gross income the insurance proceeds paid to the taxpayer as reimbursement for temporary housing expenses incurred as a result of a fire in the taxpayer's home. Similar payments made by a government agency to families displaced by urban renewal projects had been held nontaxable in a previous Revenue Ruling. Dissatisfied with the results in *Arnold*, Congress exercised its authority by exempting from tax the insurance proceeds received in circumstances similar to that case.

Gifts and Inheritances

Beginning with the Income Tax Act of 1913 and continuing to the present, Congress has allowed the recipient of a gift to exclude the value of the property from gross income. The exclusion applies to gifts made during the life of the donor (*inter vivos* gifts) and transfers that take effect upon the death of the donor (bequests and inheritances).[4] However, as discussed in Chapter 4, the recipient of a gift of income-producing property is subject to tax on the income subsequently earned from the property. Also, as discussed in Chapter 1, the donor or the decedent's estate may be subject to gift or estate taxes on the transfer.

In numerous cases, gifts are made in a business setting. For example, a salesperson gives a purchasing agent free samples; an employee receives cash from his or her employer on retirement; a corporation makes payments to employees who were victims of a natural disaster; a corporation makes a cash payment to a former employee's widow. In these and similar instances, it is frequently unclear whether the payment was a gift or whether it represents compensation for past, present, or future services.

---

1. *Helvering v. Bruun*, 40–1 USTC ¶9337, 24 AFTR 652, 60 S.Ct. 631 (USSC, 1940).
2. If the tenant made the improvements in lieu of rent, the value of the improvements is not eligible for exclusion.
3. 68–2 USTC ¶9590, 22 AFTR2d 5661, 289 F.Supp. 206 (D.Ct.N.Y., 1968).
4. § 102.

Concept Summary 5–1
Summary of Principal Exclusions from Gross Income

1. Donative items
   Gifts, bequests, inheritances, and employee death benefits [§§ 102 and 101(b)]
   Life insurance proceeds paid by reason of death (§ 101)
   Scholarships (§ 117)

2. Personal and welfare items
   Injury or sickness payments (§ 104)
   Public assistance payments (Rev.Rul. 71–425, 1971–2 C.B. 76)
   Amounts received under insurance contracts for certain living expenses (§ 123)
   Reimbursement for the costs of caring for a foster child (§ 131)

3. Wage and salary supplements
   a. Fringe benefits
      Accident and health benefits (§§ 105 and 106)
      Lodging and meals furnished for the convenience of the employer (§ 119)
      Rental value of parsonages (§ 107)
      Employee achievement awards [§ 74(c)]
      Employer contributions to employee group term life insurance (§ 79)
      Group legal service plan benefits (§ 120)*
      Cafeteria plans (§ 125)
      Educational assistance payments (§ 127)*
      Child or dependent care (§ 129)
      Services provided to employees at no additional cost to the employer (§ 132)
      Employee discounts (§ 132)
      Working condition and *de minimis* fringes (§ 132)
      Athletic facilities provided to employees (§ 132)
      Tuition reductions granted to employees of educational institutions (§ 117)
   b. Military benefits
      Combat pay (§ 112)
      Housing, uniforms, and other benefits (§ 134)
   c. Foreign earned income (§ 911)

4. Investor items
   Interest on state and local government obligations (§ 103)
   Improvements by lessee to lessor's property (§ 109)

5. Benefits for the elderly
   Social Security benefits (except in the case of certain higher-income taxpayers) (§ 86)
   Gain from the sale of personal residence by elderly taxpayers (§ 121)

6. Other benefits
   Income from discharge of indebtedness (§ 108)
   Recovery of a prior year's deduction that yielded no tax benefit (§ 111)
   Educational savings bonds (§ 135)

*Exclusion treatment applies for tax years beginning before July 1, 1992 for amounts paid before July 1, 1992.

The courts have defined a *gift* as "a voluntary transfer of property by one to another without adequate [valuable] consideration or compensation therefrom."[5] If the payment is intended to be for services rendered, it is not a gift, even though the payment is made without legal or moral obligation and the payor receives no economic benefit from the transfer. To qualify as a gift, the payment must be made "out of affection, respect, admiration, charity or like impulses."[6] Thus, the cases on this issue have been decided on the basis of the donor's intent.

In a landmark case, *Comm. v. Duberstein*,[7] the taxpayer (Duberstein) received a Cadillac from a business acquaintance. Duberstein had supplied the businessman with the names of potential customers with no expectation of compensation. The Supreme Court concluded:

> . . . despite the characterization of the transfer of the Cadillac by the parties [as a gift] and the absence of any obligation, even of a moral nature, to make it, it was at the bottom a recompense for Duberstein's past service, or an inducement for him to be of further service in the future.

Duberstein was therefore required to include the fair market value of the automobile in gross income.

Similarly, a bequest may be taxable if it represents a disguised form of compensation for services.[8]

EXAMPLE 1

T agreed to perform services for D. In exchange for the services, D promised to bequeath specific securities to T. The value of the securities on the date of D's death must be included in T's gross income. ◆

In the case of cash or other property received by an employee from his or her employer, Congress has eliminated any ambiguity. Transfers from an employer to an employee cannot be excluded as a gift unless the transfer fits into one of the other statutory exclusion provisions.[9]

LIFE INSURANCE PROCEEDS

General Rule

Insurance proceeds paid to the beneficiary by reason of the death of the insured are exempt from income tax.[10]

EXAMPLE 2

M purchased an insurance policy on his life and named his wife L as the beneficiary. M paid $24,000 in premiums. When he died, L collected the insurance proceeds of $50,000. The $50,000 is exempt from Federal income tax. ◆

Congress chose to exempt life insurance proceeds for the following reasons:

- For family members, life insurance proceeds serve much the same purpose as a nontaxable inheritance.
- In a business context (as well as in a family situation), life insurance proceeds replace an economic loss suffered by the beneficiary.

5. *Estate of D. R. Daly*, 3 B.T.A. 1042 (1926).
6. *Robertson v. U.S.*, 52–1 USTC ¶9343, 41 AFTR 1053, 72 S.Ct. 994 (USSC, 1952).
7. 60–2 USTC ¶9515, 5 AFTR2d 1626, 80 S.Ct. 1190 (USSC, 1960).
8. *Wolder v. Comm.*, 74–1 USTC ¶9266, 33 AFTR2d 74–813, 493 F.2d 608 (CA–2, 1974).
9. § 102(c).
10. § 101(a).

EXAMPLE 3

X Corporation purchased a life insurance policy to cover its key employee. If the proceeds were taxable, the corporation would require more insurance coverage to pay the tax as well as to cover the economic loss of the employee. ◆

Thus, in general, Congress concluded that making life insurance proceeds exempt from income tax was a good policy. It should be noted, however, that life insurance proceeds may be subject to the Federal estate tax.

Exceptions to Exclusion Treatment

The income tax exclusion applies only when the insurance proceeds are received by reason of the death of the insured. If the owner cancels the policy and receives the cash surrender value, the owner of the policy must recognize gain to the extent of the excess of the amount received over the cost of the policy (a loss is not deductible). Also, if the beneficiary receives the insurance proceeds in payment of an amount due from the decedent, the amount is paid by reason of the liability rather than by reason of death. Thus, the insurance proceeds may be taxable.[11]

EXAMPLE 4

T sold property to D, who agreed to pay the purchase price in installments. T reported his gain by the installment method (gain is prorated on the basis of collections). D pledged his life insurance as security for the debt. T collected on the insurance policy when D died. The insurance proceeds are taxed to T the same as if D had paid his liability. ◆

Another exception to exclusion treatment applies if the insurance contract has been *transferred for valuable consideration*. The insurance proceeds are includible in the gross income of the transferee to the extent the proceeds received exceed the amount paid for the policy by the transferee plus any subsequent premiums paid.

EXAMPLE 5

A pays premiums of $500 for an insurance policy in the face amount of $1,000 upon the life of B and subsequently transfers the policy to C for $600. C receives the proceeds of $1,000 on the death of B. The amount that C can exclude from gross income is limited to $600 plus any premiums paid by C subsequent to the transfer. ◆

The Code, however, provides exceptions to the rule illustrated in the preceding example. The four exceptions that permit exclusion treatment include transfers to the following:

1. A partner of the insured.
2. A partnership in which the insured is a partner.
3. A corporation in which the insured is an officer or shareholder.
4. A transferee whose basis in the policy is determined by reference to the transferor's basis.

The first three exceptions facilitate the use of insurance contracts to fund buy-sell agreements.

EXAMPLE 6

R and S are equal partners who have an agreement that allows either partner to purchase the interest of a deceased partner for $50,000. Neither partner has sufficient

11. *Landfield Finance Co. v. U.S.*, 69–2 USTC ¶9680, 24 AFTR2d 69–5744, 418 F.2d 172 (CA–7, 1969).

cash to actually buy the other partner's interest, but each has a life insurance policy on his own life in the amount of $50,000. R and S could exchange their policies (usually at little or no taxable gain), and upon the death of either partner, the surviving partner could collect tax-free insurance proceeds. The proceeds could then be used to purchase the decedent's interest in the partnership. ◆

The fourth exception applies to policies that were transferred pursuant to a tax-free exchange or were received by gift. [12]

Interest on Life Insurance Proceeds

Investment earnings arising from the reinvestment of life insurance proceeds are generally subject to income tax. Often the beneficiary will elect to collect the insurance proceeds in installments. The annuity rules (discussed in Chapter 4) are used to apportion the installment payment between the principal element (excludible) and the interest element (includible).[13]

EXAMPLE 7

H is the beneficiary of a $100,000 life insurance policy on his wife. Under the terms of the policy, H elects to collect the proceeds as an annuity of $15,000 each year. His life expectancy is 10 years. Thus, H's investment in the contract is $100,000, his expected return is $150,000 (10 × $15,000), and his exclusion ratio is 100/150. Each payment received by H during the initial 10-year period is a recovery of capital of $10,000 [$15,000 × (100/150)] and interest income of $5,000. ◆

EMPLOYEE DEATH BENEFITS

Frequently, an employer makes payments to a deceased employee's surviving spouse, children, or other beneficiaries. If the decedent had a nonforfeitable right to the payments (e.g., the decedent's accrued salaries), the amounts are generally taxable to the recipient just the same as if the employee had lived and collected the payments. But where the employer makes voluntary payments, the gift issue arises. Generally, the IRS considers such payments to be compensation for prior services rendered by the deceased employee.[14] However, some courts have held that payments to an employee's surviving spouse or other beneficiaries are gifts if the following are true:[15]

- The payments were made to the surviving spouse and children rather than to the employee's estate.
- The employer derived no benefit from the payments.
- The surviving spouse and children performed no services for the employer.
- The decedent had been fully compensated for services rendered.
- Payments were made pursuant to a board of directors' resolution that followed a general company policy of providing payments for families of deceased employees (but not exclusively for families of shareholder-employees).

When all of the above conditions are true, the payment is presumed to have been made *as an act of affection or charity.* When one or more of these conditions

12. § 351. See the discussion of gifts in Chapter 14 and tax-free exchanges in Chapters 15 and 20.
13. Reg. §§ 1.72–7(c)(1) and 1.101–7T.
14. Rev.Rul. 62–102, 1962–2 C.B. 37.
15. *Estate of Sydney J. Carter v. Comm.*, 72–1 USTC ¶9129, 29 AFTR2d 332, 453 F.2d 61 (CA–2, 1972), and the cases cited there.

is not true, the surviving spouse and children may still be deemed the recipients of a gift if the payment is made in light of the survivors' financial needs.[16]

Section 101(b) attempts to eliminate or reduce controversy in this area by providing an *automatic exclusion* of the first $5,000 paid by the employer to the employee's beneficiaries by reason of the death of the employee. The $5,000 exclusion must be apportioned among the beneficiaries on the basis of each beneficiary's percentage of the total death benefits received. When the employer's payments exceed $5,000, the beneficiaries may still be able to exclude the entire amount received as a gift if they are able to show gratuitous intent on the part of the employer. Note that the § 101(b) exclusion does not apply to the decedent's accrued salary.

Example 8

When H died, his employer paid his accrued salary of $3,000 to W, H's widow. The employer's board of directors also authorized payments to W ($4,000), H's daughter ($2,000), and H's son ($2,000) "in recognition of H's many years of service to the company."

The $3,000 accrued salary is compensation for past services and was owed to H at the time of his death. Therefore, the $3,000 is includible in gross income. The additional payments to the widow and children were not owed to H. Because the payments were made in recognition of H's past service, under the *Duberstein* decision, the payments are not gifts. However, the employee death benefit exclusion enables the widow and children to exclude the following amounts:

Widow	$\frac{\$4,000}{\$8,000}$	× $5,000	=	$2,500
Daughter	$\frac{\$2,000}{\$8,000}$	× $5,000	=	1,250
Son	$\frac{\$2,000}{\$8,000}$	× $5,000	=	1,250
				$5,000

◆

Besides avoiding the gift issue in many cases, the employee death benefit exclusion is intended to allow a substitute for tax-exempt life insurance proceeds.

Scholarships
◆

General Information

Payments or benefits received by a student at an educational institution may be (1) compensation for services, (2) a gift, or (3) a scholarship. If the payments or benefits are received as compensation for services (past or present), the fact that the recipient is a student generally does not render the amounts received nontaxable.[17]

Example 9

State University waives tuition for all graduate teaching assistants. The tuition waived is intended as compensation for services and is therefore included in the graduate assistant's gross income. ◆

16. *Simpson v. U.S.*, 58–2 USTC ¶9923, 2 AFTR2d 6036, 261 F.2d 497 (CA–7, 1958), *cert. denied*, 79 S.Ct. 724 (USSC, 1958).

17. Reg. § 1.117–2(a). See *C. P. Bhalla*, 35 T.C. 13 (1960), for a discussion of the distinction between a scholarship and compensation. See also *Bingler v. Johnson*, 69–1 USTC ¶9348, 23 AFTR2d 1212, 89 S.Ct. 1439 (USSC, 1969). For potential exclusion treatment, see the subsequent discussion of qualified tuition reductions.

As discussed earlier, gifts are not includible in gross income.

The scholarship rules are intended to provide exclusion treatment for education-related benefits that cannot qualify as gifts but are not compensation for services. According to the Regulations, "a scholarship is an amount paid or allowed to, or for the benefit of, an individual to aid such individual in the pursuit of study or research."[18] The recipient must be a candidate for a degree (either undergraduate or graduate) at an educational institution.[19]

EXAMPLE 10

T enters a contest sponsored by a local newspaper. Each contestant is required to submit an essay on local environmental issues. The prize is one year's tuition at State University. T wins the contest. The newspaper has a legal obligation to T (as contest winner). Thus, the benefits are not a gift. However, since the tuition payment aids the individual in pursuing his studies, the payment is a scholarship. ◆

A scholarship recipient may exclude from gross income the amount used for tuition and related expenses (fees, books, supplies, and equipment required for courses), provided the conditions of the grant do not require that the funds be used for other purposes.[20] Amounts received for room and board are *not* excludible and are treated as earned income for purposes of calculating the standard deduction for a taxpayer who is another taxpayer's dependent.[21]

EXAMPLE 11

T received a scholarship from State University of $9,500 to be used to pursue a bachelor's degree. She spent $4,000 on tuition, $3,000 on books and supplies, and $2,500 for room and board. T may exclude $7,000 ($4,000 + $3,000) from gross income. The $2,500 spent for room and board is includible in T's gross income.

The scholarship was T's only source of income. Her parents provided more than 50% of T's support and claimed T as a dependent. T's standard deduction will equal her $2,500 gross income. Thus, she has no taxable income. ◆

Timing Issues

Frequently, the scholarship recipient is a cash basis taxpayer who receives the money in one tax year but pays the educational expenses in a subsequent year. The amount eligible for exclusion may not be known at the time the money is received. In that case, the transaction is held *open* until the educational expenses are paid.[22]

EXAMPLE 12

In August 1992, T received $10,000 as a scholarship for the academic year 1992–1993. T's expenditures for tuition, books, and supplies were as follows:

August–December 1992	$3,000
January–May 1993	4,500
	$7,500

T's gross income for 1993 includes $2,500 ($10,000 − $7,500) that is not excludible as a scholarship. ◆

---

18. Prop.Reg. § 1.117–6(a)(3)(i).
19. § 117(a).
20. § 117(b).
21. Prop.Reg. § 1.117–6(h).
22. Prop.Reg. § 1.117–6(b)(2).

Disguised Compensation

Some employers make scholarships available solely to the children of key employees. The tax objective of these plans is to provide a nontaxable fringe benefit to the executives by making the payment to the child in the form of an excludible scholarship. However, the IRS has ruled that the payments are generally includible in the gross income of the parent-employee.[23]

Qualified Tuition Reduction Plans

Employees (including retired and disabled former employees) of nonprofit educational institutions are allowed to exclude a tuition waiver from gross income, if the waiver is pursuant to a *qualified tuition reduction plan*.[24] The plan may not discriminate in favor of highly compensated employees. The exclusion applies to the employee, the employee's spouse, and the employee's dependent children. The exclusion also extends to undergraduate tuition reductions granted by any nonprofit educational institution to employees of any other nonprofit educational institution (reciprocal agreements).

EXAMPLE 13

University Y allows the dependent children of University X employees to attend University Y with no tuition charge. University X grants reciprocal benefits to the children of University Y employees. The dependent children can also attend tuition-free the university where their parents are employed. Employees who take advantage of these benefits are not required to recognize gross income. ◆

Generally, the exclusion is limited to undergraduate tuition waivers. However, in the case of teaching or research assistants, graduate tuition waivers may also qualify for exclusion treatment. According to the proposed Regulations, the exclusion is limited to the value of the benefit in excess of the employee's reasonable compensation.[25] Thus, a tuition reduction that is a substitute for cash compensation cannot be excluded.

EXAMPLE 14

T is a graduate research assistant. She receives a $5,000 salary for 500 hours of service over a nine-month period. This pay, $10 per hour, is reasonable compensation for T's services. In addition, T receives a waiver of $6,000 for tuition. T may exclude the tuition waiver from gross income. ◆

COMPENSATION FOR INJURIES AND SICKNESS

◆

Damages

A person who suffers harm caused by another is often entitled to compensatory damages. The tax consequences of the receipt of damages depend on the type of harm the taxpayer has experienced. The taxpayer may seek recovery for a loss of income, expenses incurred, property destroyed, or personal injury.

Generally, reimbursement for a loss of income is taxed the same as the income replaced. The recovery of an expense is not income, unless the expense was deducted.

EXAMPLE 15

T was required to pay a $75 penalty for failure to timely file her tax return. The return was late because T's accountant misplaced certain information. The accountant

23. Rev.Rul. 75–448, 1975–2 C.B. 55. *Richard T. Armantrout*, 67 T.C. 996 (1977).

24. § 117(d).

25. Prop.Reg. § 1.117–6(d).

reimbursed T for the penalty. Because the reimbursement exactly off-sets the nondeductible penalty, T is not required to recognize income. ◆

Damages that are a recovery of the taxpayer's previously deducted expenses are generally taxable under the tax benefit rule, discussed later in this chapter.

EXAMPLE 16

T's business automobile was damaged in 1992 when a mechanic left a bolt in the oil pan. T had to rent an automobile for the remainder of 1992. T deducted the rent as a business expense on his 1992 tax return. In 1993, the mechanic admits liability and reimburses T for the rent. T must include the recovery of the prior deduction in his 1993 gross income. ◆

A payment for damaged or destroyed property is treated as an amount received in a sale or exchange of the property. Thus, the taxpayer has a realized gain if the damage payments received exceed the property's basis. Damages for personal injuries receive special treatment under the Code.

Personal Injury. The legal theory of personal injury damages is that the amount received is intended "to make the plaintiff [the injured party] whole as before the injury."[26] It follows that if the damage payments received were subject to tax, the after-tax amount received would be less than the actual damages incurred and the injured party would not be "whole as before the injury."

Congress has specifically excluded from gross income the amount of any damage payments received (whether by suit or agreement) on account of personal injuries or sickness. The courts have applied the exclusion to any personal wrong committed against the taxpayer (e.g., breach of promise to marry, invasion of privacy, libel, slander, assault, battery). The exclusion also applies to compensation for loss of income (ordinarily taxable, as previously discussed) and recovery of expenses (except medical expenses deducted by the taxpayer) resulting from the personal injury.[27]

In libel and slander cases, a single event can cause both a personal injury and damage to a business reputation. Damage to a business reputation is measured on the basis of estimated loss of income. Taxpayers argue that the amount received for loss of income in these cases is no different from the payments in other personal injury cases and thus should be excluded. According to the IRS, however, the business reputation damages are separate from the personal injury and are taxable.[28]

EXAMPLE 17

P, a television announcer, was dissatisfied with the manner in which R, an attorney, was defending the television station in a libel case. P stated on the air that R was botching the case. R sued P for slander, claiming damages for loss of income from clients and potential clients who heard P's statement. R's claim is for damages to his business reputation, and the amounts received are taxable.

R collected on the suit against P and was on his way to a party to celebrate his victory when a negligent driver, N, drove his truck into R's automobile, injuring R. R

26. *C. A. Hawkins*, 6 B.T.A. 1023 (1928).

27. § 104(a)(2) and Rev.Rul. 85–97, 1985–2 C.B. 50.

28. Rev.Rul. 85–143, 1985–2 C.B. 55, in which the IRS announced it would not follow the Ninth Court of Appeals decision in *Roemer v. Comm.*, 83–2 USTC ¶9600, 52 AFTR2d 83–5954, 716 F.2d 693 (CA–9, 1983). See also *Wade E. Church*, 80 T.C. 1104 (1983).

filed suit for the personal injuries and claimed as damages the loss of income for the period he was unable to work as a result of the injury. All amounts received by R from N, including the reimbursement for lost income, are nontaxable because the claims are based on a personal injury. ◆

Punitive Damages. In addition to seeking *compensatory damages,* the injured party may seek *punitive* damages, which are often awarded to punish the defendant for gross negligence or the intentional infliction of harm. While some courts have held that punitive damages are taxable under the broad concept of gross income, other courts have permitted exclusion treatment.[29] The Revenue Reconciliation Act of 1989 clarified congressional intent on this issue by providing that punitive damages are includible in gross income *unless* the claim arises out of physical injury or physical sickness.[30] Thus, punitive damages received for loss of personal reputation are taxable, although the compensatory damages are excludible. Punitive damages arising out of a physical injury claim are excludible.

EXAMPLE 18

Assume R in Example 17 also received punitive damages in each suit. The punitive damages received by R from N may be excluded from gross income because the damages arose out of the physical injury claim. R's punitive damages received from P are taxable because the damages did not arise from a physical injury or sickness claim. ◆

Workers' Compensation

State workers' compensation laws require the employer to pay fixed amounts for specific job-related injuries. The state laws were enacted so that the employee will not have to go through the ordeal of a lawsuit (and possibly not collect damages because of some defense available to the employer) to recover the damages. Although the payments are intended, in part, to compensate for a loss of future income, Congress has specifically exempted workers' compensation benefits from inclusion in gross income.[31]

Accident and Health Insurance Benefits

The income tax treatment of accident and health insurance benefits depends on whether the policy providing the benefits was purchased by the taxpayer or the taxpayer's employer. Benefits collected under an accident and health insurance policy *purchased by the taxpayer* are excludible. In this case, benefits collected under the taxpayer's insurance policy are excluded even though the payments are a substitute for income.[32]

EXAMPLE 19

B purchased a medical and disability insurance policy. The insurance company paid B $200 per week to replace wages he lost while in the hospital. Although the payments serve as a substitute for income, the amounts received are tax-exempt benefits collected under B's insurance policy. ◆

---

29. Rev.Rul. 84–108, 1984–2 C.B. 32; *Glenshaw Glass v. Comm.*, 55–1 USTC ¶9308, 47 AFTR 162, 75 S.Ct. 473 (USSC, 1955); *Roemer v. Comm.*, 83–2 USTC ¶9600, 52 AFTR2d 83–5954, 716 F.2d 693 (CA–9, 1983).

30. § 104(a).

31. § 104(a)(1).

32. § 104(a)(3).

EXAMPLE 20

J's injury results in a partial paralysis of his left foot. He receives $5,000 from his accident insurance company, under a policy he had purchased, for the injury. The $5,000 accident insurance proceeds are tax-exempt. ◆

A different set of rules applies if the accident and health insurance protection was *purchased by the individual's employer*, as discussed in the following section.

EMPLOYER-SPONSORED ACCIDENT AND HEALTH PLANS

Congress encourages employers to provide employees, retired former employees, and their dependents with accident and health and disability insurance plans. The *premiums* are deductible by the employer and excluded from the employee's income.[33] Although § 105(a) provides the general rule that the employee has includible income when he or she collects the insurance *benefits*, two exceptions are provided.

Section 105(b) generally excludes payments received for medical care of the employee, spouse, and dependents. However, if the payments are for expenses that do not meet the Code's definition of medical care,[34] the amount received must be included in gross income. In addition, the taxpayer must include in gross income the amounts received for medical expenses that were deducted by the taxpayer on a prior return.

EXAMPLE 21

In 1993, D's employer-sponsored health insurance plan paid $4,000 for hair transplants that did not meet the Code's definition of medical care. D must include the $4,000 in his gross income for 1993.

Also in 1993, D was reimbursed for medical expenses he had paid in 1992. D was reimbursed $3,000, which was the amount of his actual expenses. The expenses met the definition of medical care, and D had claimed the $3,000 as an itemized deduction on his 1992 return. D's adjusted gross income for 1992 was $30,000, and he had no other medical expenses. Because only medical expenses in excess of 7.5% of adjusted gross income (refer to Chapter 11) may be claimed as a deduction, the expenses reduced taxable income by only $750 [$3,000 − .075($30,000)] on D's 1992 return. As a result of the reimbursement, D is required to include in gross income for 1993 only $750, the amount by which 1992 taxable income was reduced. ◆

Section 105(c) excludes payments for the permanent loss or the loss of the use of a member or function of the body or the permanent disfigurement of the employee, spouse, or a dependent. Payments that are a substitute for salary (e.g., related to the period of time absent) are includible.

EXAMPLE 22

E lost an eye in an automobile accident unrelated to his work. As a result of the accident, E incurred $2,000 of medical expenses, which he deducted on his return. He collected $10,000 from an accident insurance policy carried by his employer. The benefits were paid according to a schedule of amounts that varied with the part of the body injured (e.g., $10,000 for loss of an eye, $20,000 for loss of a hand). Because the payment was for loss of a *member or function of the body*, § 105(c) applies and the $10,000 is excluded from income. E was absent from work for a week as a result of the accident. His employer provided him with insurance for the loss of income due to illness or injury. E collected $500, which is includible in gross income. ◆

33. § 106, Reg. § 1.106–1, and Rev.Rul. 82–196, 1982–1 C.B. 106.

34. See the discussion of medical care in Chapter 11.

Medical Reimbursement Plans

In lieu of providing the employee with insurance coverage for hospital and medical expenses, the employer may agree to reimburse the employee for these expenses. The amounts received through the insurance coverage (insured plan benefits) are excluded from income under § 105 (as previously discussed). Unfortunately in terms of cost considerations, the insurance companies that issue this type of policy usually require a broad coverage of employees. An alternative is to have a plan that is not funded with insurance (a self-insured arrangement). The benefits received under a self-insured plan can be excluded from the employee's income, if the plan does not discriminate in favor of highly compensated employees.[35]

MEALS AND LODGING
◆

Furnished for the Convenience of the Employer

As discussed in Chapter 4, income can take any form, including meals and lodging. However, § 119 excludes from income the value of meals and lodging provided to the employee and the employee's spouse and dependents under the following conditions:[36]

- The meals and/or lodging are *furnished* by the employer, on the employer's *business premises*, for the *convenience of the employer*.
- In the case of lodging, the employee is *required* to accept the lodging as a condition of employment.

The courts have construed both of these requirements strictly.

At least two questions have been raised with regard to the *furnished by the employer* requirement:

- Who is considered an *employee*?
- What is meant by *furnished*?

The IRS and some courts have reasoned that because a partner is not an employee, the exclusion does not apply to a partner. However, the Tax Court and the Fifth Court of Appeals have ruled in favor of the taxpayer on this issue.[37]

The Supreme Court held that a cash meal allowance was ineligible for the exclusion because the employer did not actually furnish the meals.[38] Similarly, one court denied the exclusion where the employer paid for the food and supplied the cooking facilities but the employee prepared the meal.[39]

The *on the employer's business premises* requirement, applicable to both meals and lodging, has resulted in much litigation. The Regulations define business premises as simply "the place of employment of the employee."[40] Thus, the Sixth Court of Appeals held that a residence, owned by the employer and occupied by an employee, two blocks from the motel that the employee

35. § 105(h).

36. § 119(a). The meals and lodging are also excluded from FICA and FUTA tax. *Rowan Companies, Inc. v. U.S.*, 81–1 USTC ¶9749, 48 AFTR2d 81–5115, 101 S.Ct. 2288 (USSC, 1981).

37. Rev.Rul. 80, 1953–1 C.B. 62; *Comm. v. Doak*, 56–2 USTC ¶9708, 49 AFTR 1491, 234 F.2d 704 (CA–4, 1956); *Comm. v. Moran*, 56–2 USTC ¶9789, 50 AFTR 64, 236 F.2d 595 (CA–8, 1956); *Robinson v. U.S.*, 60–1 USTC ¶9152, 5 AFTR2d 315, 273 F.2d 503 (CA–3, 1959); *Briggs v. U.S.*, 56–2 USTC ¶10020, 50 AFTR 667, 238 F.2d 53 (CA–10, 1956), but see *G. A. Papineau*, 16 T.C. 130 (1951); *Armstrong v. Phinney*, 68–1 USTC ¶9355, 21 AFTR2d 1260, 394 F.2d 661 (CA–5, 1968).

38. *Comm. v. Kowalski*, 77–2 USTC ¶9748, 40 AFTR2d 6128, 98 S.Ct. 315 (USSC, 1977).

39. *Tougher v. Comm.*, 71–1 USTC ¶9398, 27 AFTR2d 1301, 441 F.2d 1148 (CA–9, 1971).

40. Reg. § 1.119–1(c)(1).

managed was not part of the business premises.[41] However, the Tax Court considered an employer-owned house across the street from the hotel that was managed by the taxpayer to be on the business premises of the employer.[42] Perhaps these two cases can be reconciled by comparing the distance from the lodging facilities to the place where the employer's business was conducted. The closer the lodging to the business operations, the more likely the convenience of the employer is served.

The *convenience of the employer* test is intended to focus on the employer's motivation for furnishing the meals and lodging rather than on the benefits received by the employee. If the employer furnishes the meals and lodging primarily to enable the employee to perform his or her duties properly, it does not matter that the employee considers these benefits to be a part of his or her compensation.

The Regulations give the following examples in which the tests for excluding meals are satisfied:[43]

- A waitress is required to eat her meals on the premises during the busy lunch and breakfast hours.
- A bank furnishes a teller meals on the premises to limit the time the employee is away from his or her booth during the busy hours.
- A worker is employed at a construction site in a remote part of Alaska. The employer must furnish meals and lodging due to the inaccessibility of other facilities.

The *employee required* test applies only to lodging. If the employee's use of the housing would serve the convenience of the employer, but the employee is not required to use the housing, the exclusion is not available.

EXAMPLE 23

U, a utilities company, has all of its service personnel on 24-hour call for emergencies. The company encourages its employees to live near the plant so that the employees can respond quickly to emergency calls. Company-owned housing is available rent-free. Only 10 of the employees live in the company housing because it is not suitable for families.

Although the company-provided housing serves the convenience of the employer, it is not required. Therefore, the employees who live in the company housing cannot exclude its value from gross income. ◆

In addition, if the employee has the *option* of cash or lodging, the *required* test is not satisfied.

EXAMPLE 24

T is the manager of a large apartment complex. The employer gives T the option of rent-free housing (value of $6,000 per year) or an additional $5,000 per year. T selects the housing option. Therefore, he must include $6,000 in gross income. ◆

Other Housing Exclusions

An *employee of an educational institution* may be able to exclude the value of campus housing provided by the employer. Generally, the employee does not

41. *Comm. v. Anderson*, 67–1 USTC ¶9136, 19 AFTR2d 318, 371 F.2d 59 (CA–6, 1966).

42. *J.B. Lindeman*, 60 T.C. 609 (1973).

43. Reg. § 1.119–1(f).

recognize income if he or she pays annual rents equal to or greater than 5 percent of the appraised value of the facility. If the rent payments are less than 5 percent of the value of the facility, the deficiency must be included in gross income.[44]

EXAMPLE 25

X University provides on-campus housing for its full-time faculty during the first three years of employment. The housing is not provided for the convenience of the employer. Professor B pays $3,000 annual rent for the use of a residence with an appraised value of $100,000 and an annual rental value of $12,000. Professor B must recognize $2,000 gross income [.05($100,000) – $3,000 = $2,000] for the value of the housing provided to him. ◆

Ministers of the gospel can exclude (1) the rental value of a home furnished as compensation or (2) a rental allowance paid to them as compensation, to the extent the allowance is used to rent or provide a home.[45] The housing or housing allowance must be provided as compensation for the conduct of religious worship, the administration and maintenance of religious organizations, or the performance of teaching and administrative duties at theological seminaries.

EXAMPLE 26

Pastor B is allowed to live rent-free in a house owned by the congregation. The annual rental value of the house is $6,000 and is provided as part of the pastor's compensation for ministerial services. Assistant Pastor C is paid a $4,500 cash housing allowance. He uses the $4,500 to pay rent and utilities on a home he and his family occupy. Neither Pastor B nor Assistant Pastor C is required to recognize gross income associated with the housing or housing allowance. ◆

Military personnel are allowed housing exclusions under various circumstances. Authority for these exclusions generally is found in Federal laws that are not part of the Internal Revenue Code.[46]

OTHER EMPLOYEE FRINGE BENEFITS

◆

Specific Benefits

In recent years, Congress has enacted exclusions to encourage employers to (1) finance and make available child care facilities, (2) provide the means for employees to obtain legal services, (3) provide athletic facilities for employees, and (4) finance certain employees' basic education. These provisions are summarized as follows:

- The employee does not have to include in gross income the value of child and dependent care services paid for by the employer and incurred to enable the employee to work. The exclusion cannot exceed $5,000 per year ($2,500 if married and filing separately). For a married couple, the annual exclusion cannot exceed the earned income of the spouse who has the lesser amount of earned income. For an unmarried taxpayer, the exclusion cannot exceed the taxpayer's earned income.[47]

44. § 119(d).
45. § 107 and Reg. § 1.107–1.
46. H. Rep. No. 99–841, 99th Cong., 2d Sess., p. 548 (1986). See also § 134.
47. § 129. The exclusion applies to the same types of expenses that, if they were paid by the employee (and not reimbursed by the employer), would be eligible for the Credit for Child and Dependent Care Expense discussed in Chapter 13.

- Any benefit received by employees from coverage under qualified group legal service plans provided by the employer is excluded.[48] The exclusion is limited to an annual premium value of $70 per employee.
- The value of the use of a gymnasium or other athletic facilities by employees, their spouses, and their dependent children may be excluded from an employee's gross income. The facilities must be on the employer's premises, and substantially all of the use of the facilities must be by employees and their family members.[49]
- Qualified employer-provided educational assistance (tuition, fees, books, and supplies) at the undergraduate and graduate levels is excludible from gross income. The exclusion is subject to an annual employee statutory ceiling of $5,250.[50]

Cafeteria Plans

Generally, if an employee is offered a choice between cash and some other form of compensation, the employee is deemed to have constructively received the cash even when the noncash option is elected. Thus, the employee has gross income regardless of the option chosen.

An exception to this constructive receipt treatment is provided under the cafeteria plan rules. Under such a plan, the employee is permitted to choose between cash and nontaxable benefits (e.g., group term life insurance, health and accident protection, and child care). If the employee chooses the otherwise nontaxable benefits, the cafeteria plan rules enable the benefits to remain nontaxable.[51] Cafeteria plans provide tremendous flexibility in tailoring the employee pay package to fit individual needs. Some employees (usually the younger group) prefer cash, while others (usually the older group) will opt for the fringe benefit program.

EXAMPLE 27

Y Corporation offers its employees (on a nondiscriminatory basis) a choice of any one or all of the following benefits:

	Cost
Group term life insurance	$ 200
Hospitalization insurance for family members	2,400
Child care payments	1,800
	$4,400

If a benefit is not selected, the employee receives cash equal to the cost of the benefit. T, an employee, has a spouse who works for another employer that provides hospitalization insurance but no child care payments. T elects to receive the group term life insurance, the child care payments, and $2,400 of cash. Only the $2,400 must be included in T's gross income. ◆

General Classes of Excluded Benefits

An employer can confer numerous forms and types of economic benefits on employees. Under the all-inclusive concept of income, the benefits are taxable

48. § 120(a). Exclusion treatment applies for tax years beginning before July 1, 1992 for amounts paid before that date by the employer for coverage before that date.
49. § 132(h)(5).
50. § 127. Exclusion treatment applies for tax years beginning before July 1, 1992 for amounts paid before that date.
51. § 125.

unless one of the provisions previously discussed specifically excludes the item from gross income. The amount of the income is the fair market value of the benefit. This reasoning can lead to results that Congress considers unacceptable, as illustrated in the following example.

EXAMPLE 28

T is employed in New York as a ticket clerk for Trans National Airlines. He has a sick mother in Miami, Florida, but has no money for plane tickets. Trans National has daily flights from New York to Miami that often leave with empty seats. The cost of a ticket is $400, and T is in the 28% tax bracket. If Trans National allows T to fly without charge to Miami, under the general gross income rules, T has income equal to the value of a ticket. Therefore, T must pay $112 tax (.28 × $400) on a trip to Miami. Because T does not have $112, he cannot visit his mother, and the airplane flies with another empty seat. ◆

If Trans National in Example 28 will allow employees to use resources that would otherwise be wasted, why should the tax laws interfere with the employee's decision to take advantage of the available benefit? Thus, to avoid the undesirable results that occur in Example 28 and in similar situations as well as to create uniform rules for fringe benefits, Congress established four broad classes of nontaxable employee benefits:[52]

- No-additional-cost services.
- Qualified employee discounts.
- Working condition fringes.
- *De minimis* fringes.

No-Additional-Cost Services. Example 28 illustrates this type of fringe benefit. The services will be nontaxable if all of the following conditions are satisfied:

- The employee receives services, as opposed to property.
- The employer does not incur substantial additional cost, including forgone revenue, in providing the services to the employee.
- The services are offered to customers in the ordinary course of the business in which the employee works.[53]

EXAMPLE 29

Assume that T in Example 28 can fly without charge only if the airline cannot fill the seats with paying customers. That is, T must fly on standby. Although the airplane may burn slightly more fuel because T is on the airplane and T may receive the same meal as paying customers, the additional costs would not be substantial. Thus, the trip could qualify as a no-additional-cost service.

On the other hand, assume that T is given a reserved seat on a flight that is frequently full. The employer would be forgoing revenue to allow T to fly. This forgone revenue would be a substantial additional cost, and thus the benefit would be taxable. ◆

Note that if T were employed in a hotel owned by Trans National, the receipt of the airline ticket would be taxable because T did not work in that line of business. However, the Code allows the exclusion for reciprocal benefits offered by employers in the same line of business.

52. See, generally, § 132.

53. Reg. § 1.132–2.

EXAMPLE 30

T is employed as a desk clerk for Plush Hotels, Inc. The company and Chain Hotels, Inc., have an agreement that allows any of their employees to stay without charge in either company's resort hotels during the off-season. T would not be required to recognize income from taking advantage of the plan by staying in a Chain Hotel. ◆

The no-additional-cost exclusion extends to the employee's spouse and dependent children and to retired and disabled former employees. In the Regulations, the IRS has conceded that partners who perform services for the partnership are employees for purposes of the exclusion.[54] (As discussed earlier in the chapter, the IRS's position is that partners are not employees for purposes of the § 119 meals and lodging exclusion.) However, the exclusion is not allowed to highly compensated employees unless the benefit is available on a nondiscriminatory basis.

Qualified Employee Discounts. When the employer sells goods or services (other than no-additional-cost benefits just discussed) to the employee for a price that is less than the price charged regular customers, the employee realizes income equal to the discount. However, the discount can be excluded from the gross income of the employee, subject to the following conditions and limitations:

- The exclusion is not available for real property (e.g., a house) or for personal property of the type commonly held for investment (e.g., common stocks).
- The property or services must be from the same line of business in which the employee works.
- In the case of *property,* the exclusion is limited to the *gross profit component* of the price to customers.
- In the case of *services,* the exclusion is limited to 20 percent of the customer price.[55]

EXAMPLE 31

X Corporation, which operates a department store, sells a television set to a store employee for $300. The regular customer price is $500, and the gross profit rate is 25%. The corporation also sells the employee a service contract for $120. The regular customer price for the contract is $150. The employee must recognize $75 income.

Customer price for property	$ 500
Less: Gross profit (25%)	(125)
	$ 375
Employee price	(300)
Income	$ 75
Customer price for service	$ 150
Less: 20 percent	(30)
	$ 120
Employee price	(120)
Income	$–0–

◆

54. Reg. § 1.132–1(b).

55. § 132(c).

EXAMPLE 32

Assume the same facts as in Example 31, except the employee is a clerk in a hotel operated by X Corporation. Because the line of business requirement is not met, the employee must recognize $200 income ($500 – $300) from the purchase of the television and $30 income ($150 – $120) from the service contract. ◆

As in the case of no-additional-cost benefits, the exclusion applies to employees (including service partners), employees' spouses and dependent children, and retired and disabled former employees. However, the exclusion does not apply to highly compensated individuals unless the discount is available on a nondiscriminatory basis.

Working Condition Fringes. Generally, an employee is not required to include in gross income the cost of property or services provided by the employer if the employee could deduct the cost of those items if he or she had actually paid for them.[56]

EXAMPLE 33

T is a certified public accountant employed by an accounting firm. The employer pays T's annual dues to professional organizations. T is not required to include the payment of the dues in gross income because if he had paid the dues, he would have been allowed to deduct the amount as an employee business expense (as discussed in Chapter 10). ◆

In many cases, this exclusion merely avoids reporting income and an offsetting deduction. However, in three specific situations, the working condition fringe benefit rules allow an exclusion where the expense would not be deductible if paid by the employee:

- The value of parking space provided to an employee may be excluded even though parking is ordinarily a nondeductible commuting expense (see Chapter 10).
- Automobile salespeople are allowed to exclude the value of certain personal use of company demonstrators (e.g., commuting to and from work).[57]
- The employee business expense would be eliminated by the 2 percent floor on miscellaneous deductions under § 67 (see Chapter 11).

Unlike the other fringe benefits discussed previously, working condition fringes can be made available on a discriminatory basis and still qualify for the exclusion.

EXAMPLE 34

R Corporation's offices are located in the center of a large city. The company pays for parking spaces to be used only by the company's officers. The parking space rental qualifies as a working condition fringe and may be excluded from the officers' gross income even though the plan is discriminatory. ◆

***De Minimis* Fringes.** As the term suggests, *de minimis* fringe benefits are so small that accounting for them is impractical. The House Report contains the following examples of *de minimis* fringes:

- The typing of a personal letter by a company secretary, occasional personal use of a company copying machine, monthly transit passes provided at a

56. § 132(d).

57. § 132(e)(2).

discount not exceeding $21, occasional company cocktail parties or picnics for employees, occasional supper money or taxi fare for employees because of overtime work, and certain holiday gifts of property with a low fair market value are excluded.

- Subsidized eating facilities (e.g., an employees' cafeteria) operated by the employer are excluded if located on or near the employer's business premises, if revenue equals or exceeds direct operating costs, and if nondiscrimination requirements are met.[58]

When taxpayers venture beyond the specific examples contained in the House Report and the Regulations, there is obviously much room for disagreement as to what is *de minimis.* However, note that except in the case of subsidized eating facilities, the *de minimis* fringe benefits can be granted in a manner that favors highly compensated employees.

EXAMPLE 35

R Corporation's officers are allowed to have personal letters typed by company secretaries. On the average, a secretary will spend one hour each month on the letters. The benefit is *de minimis,* which means accounting for the cost is impractical in view of the small amount of money involved. If the costs are too small to be of concern, whether the benefits are discriminatory is also immaterial. ◆

Nondiscrimination Provisions. For no-additional-cost services and qualified employee discounts, if the plan is discriminatory in favor of highly compensated employees, these key employees are denied exclusion treatment. However, the non-highly compensated employees who receive benefits from the plan can still enjoy exclusion treatment for the no-additional-cost services and qualifed employee discounts.[59]

EXAMPLE 36

T Company's officers are allowed to purchase goods from the company at a 25% discount. Other employees are allowed only a 15% discount. The company's gross profit margin on these goods is 30%.

R, an officer in the company, purchased goods from the company for $750 when the price charged to customers was $1,000. R must include $250 in gross income because the plan is discriminatory.

M, an employee of the company who is not an officer, purchased goods for $850 when the customer price was $1,000. M is not required to recognize income because he received a qualified employee discount. ◆

De minimis (except in the case of sudsidized eating facilities) and working condition fringe benefits can be provided on a discriminatory basis. The *de minimis* benefits are not subject to tax because the accounting problems that would be created are out of proportion to the amount of the additional tax that would result. A nondiscrimination test would simply add to the compliance problems. In the case of working condition fringes, the types of services required vary with the job. Therefore, a nondiscrimination test probably could not be satisfied, although usually there is no deliberate plan to benefit a chosen few.

Taxable Fringe Benefits

If the fringe benefits cannot qualify for any of the specific exclusions or do not fit into any of the general classes of excluded benefits, the taxpayer must

58. See also Reg. § 1.132–7(a).

59. § 132(h)(1).

recognize gross income equal to the fair market value of the benefits. Obviously, problems are frequently encountered in determining values. The IRS has issued extensive Regulations addressing the valuation of personal use of an employer's automobiles and meals provided at an employer-operated eating facility.[60]

If a fringe benefit plan discriminates in favor of highly compensated employees, generally, the highly compensated employees are not allowed to exclude the benefits they receive that other employees do not enjoy. However, the highly compensated employees, as well as the other employees, are generally allowed to exclude the nondiscriminatory benefits.[61]

EXAMPLE 37

T Company has a medical reimbursement plan that reimburses officers for 100% of their medical expenses, but reimburses all other employees for only 80% of their medical expenses. Mr. T, the president of the company, was reimbursed $1,000 during the year for medical expenses. Mr. T must include $200 in gross income [(1 − .80) × $1,000 = $200]. Mr. Z, an employee who is not an officer, received $800 (80% of his actual medical expenses) under the medical reimbursement plan. None of the $800 is includible in his gross income. ◆

FOREIGN EARNED INCOME

A U.S. citizen is generally subject to U.S. tax on his or her income regardless of the income's geographic origin. The income may also be subject to tax in the foreign country, and thus the taxpayer must carry a double tax burden. Out of a sense of fairness and to encourage U.S. citizens to work abroad (so that exports might be increased), Congress has provided alternative forms of relief from taxes on foreign earned income. The taxpayer can elect *either* (1) to include the foreign income in his or her taxable income and then claim a credit for foreign taxes paid or (2) to exclude the foreign earnings from his or her U.S. gross income.[62] The foreign tax credit option is discussed in Chapter 13, but as is apparent from the following discussion, most taxpayers will choose the exclusion.

Foreign earned income consists of the earnings from the individual's personal services rendered in a foreign country (other than as an employee of the U.S. government). To qualify for the exclusion, the taxpayer must be either of the following:

- A bona fide resident of the foreign country (or countries).
- Present in a foreign country (or countries) for at least 330 days during any 12 consecutive months.[63]

EXAMPLE 38

T's trips to and from a foreign country in connection with his work were as follows:

Arrived in Foreign Country	Arrived in United States
March 10, 1991	February 1, 1992
March 7, 1992	June 1, 1992

60. Reg. § 1.61–2 T(j). Generally, the income from the personal use of the employer's automobile is based on the lease value of the automobile (what it would have cost the employee to lease the automobile). Meals are valued at 150% of the employer's direct costs (e.g., food and labor) of preparing the meals.
61. §§ 79(d), 105(h), 127(b)(2), and 132(h)(1). See the discussion of the term "highly compensated employee" in Chapter 19.
62. § 911(a).
63. § 911(d). For the definition of resident, see Reg. § 1.871–2(b). Under the Regulations, a taxpayer is not a resident if he or she is there for a definite period (e.g., until completion of a construction contract).

During the 12 consecutive months ending on March 10, 1992, T was present in the foreign country for at least 330 days (366 days less 29 days in February and 7 days in March 1992). Therefore, all income earned in the foreign country through March 10, 1992, is eligible for the exclusion. The income earned from March 11, 1992, through May 31, 1992, is also eligible for the exclusion because T was present in the foreign country for 330 days during the 12 consecutive months ending on May 31, 1992.

The exclusion is *limited* to $70,000 per year. For married persons, both of whom have foreign earned income, the exclusion is computed separately for each spouse. Community property rules do not apply (the community property spouse is not deemed to have earned one-half of the other spouse's foreign earned income). A taxpayer who is present in the country for less than the entire year must compute the maximum exclusion on a daily basis ($70,000 divided by the number of days in the entire year and multiplied by the number of days present in the foreign country during the year).

EXAMPLE 39

T qualifies for the foreign earned income exclusion. He was present in France for all of 1992 except for 7 days in December. During this period, he was in the United States. T's salary for 1992 is $90,000. If T had been in France for all of the 366 days in 1992, he would have been able to exclude $70,000. However, since he was not present in the foreign country for 7 days, his exclusion is limited to $68,661 as follows:

$$\$70,000 \times \frac{\text{359 days in foreign country}}{\text{366 days in the year}} = \$68,661$$

◆

In addition to the exclusion for foreign earnings, the *reasonable housing costs* incurred by the taxpayer and the taxpayer's family in a foreign country in excess of a base amount may be excluded from gross income. The base amount is 16 percent of the U.S. government pay scale for a GS–14 (Step 1) employee, which varies from year to year.[64]

As previously mentioned, the taxpayer may elect to include the foreign earned income in gross income and claim a credit (an offset against U.S. tax) for the foreign tax paid. The credit alternative may be advantageous if the individual's foreign earned income far exceeds the excludible amount so that the foreign taxes paid exceed the U.S. tax on the amount excluded. However, once an election is made, it applies to all subsequent years unless affirmatively revoked. A revocation is effective for the year of the change and the four subsequent years.

INTEREST ON CERTAIN STATE AND LOCAL GOVERNMENT OBLIGATIONS

◆

At the time the Sixteenth Amendment was ratified by the states, there was some question as to whether the Federal government possessed the constitutional authority to tax interest on state and local government obligations. Taxing the interest on these obligations was thought to violate the doctrine of intergovernmental immunity in that the tax would impair the state and local governments' ability to finance their operations.[65] Thus, interest on state and local government obligations was specifically exempted from Federal income taxation.[66] However, the Supreme Court recently concluded that there is no constitutional prohibition against levying a nondiscriminatory Federal income tax on

64. § 911(c).
65. *Pollock v. Farmer's Loan & Trust Co.*, 3 AFTR 2557, 15 S.Ct. 912 (USSC, 1895).
66. § 103(a).

state and local government obligations.[67] Nevertheless, currently the statutory exclusion still exists.

Obviously, the exclusion of the interest reduces the cost of borrowing for state and local governments. A taxpayer in the 31 percent tax bracket requires only a 5.52 percent yield on a tax-exempt bond to obtain the same after-tax income as a taxable bond paying 8 percent interest [5.52% ÷ (1 − .31) = 8%].

The lower cost for the state and local governments is more than offset by the revenue loss of the Federal government. Also, tax-exempt interest is considered to be a substantial loophole for the very wealthy. For these reasons, bills have been proposed to Congress calling for Federal government subsidies to state and local governments that voluntarily choose to issue taxable bonds. Under the proposals, the tax-exempt status of existing bonds would not be eliminated.

The current exempt status applies solely to state and local government bonds. Thus, income received from the accrual of interest on a condemnation award or an overpayment of state income tax is fully taxable.[68] Nor does the exemption apply to gains on the sale of tax-exempt securities.

EXAMPLE 40

T purchases State of Virginia bonds for $10,000 on July 1, 1991. The bonds pay $400 interest each June 30th and December 31st. On March 31, 1992, T sells the bonds for $10,500 plus $200 accrued interest. T must recognize a $500 gain ($10,500 − $10,000), but the $200 accrued interest is exempt from taxation. ◆

During recent years, state and local governments have developed sophisticated financial schemes to attract new industry. For example, local municipalities have issued bonds to finance the construction of plants to be leased to private enterprise. Because the financing could be arranged with low-interest municipal obligations, the plants could be leased at a lower cost than the private business could otherwise obtain. However, Congress has placed limitations on the use of tax-exempt securities to finance private business.[69]

DIVIDENDS

General Information

A *dividend* is a payment to a shareholder with respect to his or her stock. Dividends to shareholders are taxable only to the extent the payments are made from *either* the corporation's *current earnings and profits* (in many cases the same as net income per books) or its *accumulated earnings and profits* (in many cases the same as retained earnings per books).[70] Distributions that exceed earnings and profits are treated as a nontaxable recovery of capital and reduce the shareholder's basis in the stock. Once the shareholder's basis is reduced to zero, any subsequent distributions are taxed as capital gains (see Chapter 14).[71]

Some payments are frequently referred to as dividends but are not considered dividends for tax purposes:

- Dividends received on deposits with savings and loan associations, credit unions, and banks are actually interest (a contractual rate paid for the use of money).

67. *South Carolina v. Baker III*, 88–1 USTC ¶9284, 61 AFTR2d 88–995, 108 S.Ct. 1355 (USSC, 1988).

68. *Kieselbach v. Comm.*, 43–1 USTC ¶9220, 30 AFTR 370, 63 S.Ct. 303 (USSC, 1943); *U.S. Trust Co. of New York v. Anderson*, 3 USTC ¶1125, 12 AFTR 836, 65 F.2d 575 (CA–2, 1933).

69. See § 103(b).

70. § 316(a).

71. § 301(c). See Chapter 4, *West's Federal Taxation: Corporations, Partnerships, Estates, and Trusts*, for a detailed discussion of corporate distributions.

- Patronage dividends paid by cooperatives (e.g., for farmers) are rebates made to the users and are considered reductions in the cost of items purchased from the association. The rebates are usually made after year-end (after the cooperative has determined whether it has met its expenses) and are apportioned among members on the basis of their purchases.
- Mutual insurance companies pay dividends on unmatured life insurance policies that are considered rebates of premiums.
- Shareholders in a mutual investment fund are allowed to report as capital gains their proportionate share of the fund's gains realized and distributed. The capital gain and ordinary income portions are reported on the Form 1099 that the fund supplies its shareholders each year.

Stock Dividends

When a corporation issues a simple stock dividend (e.g., common stock issued to common shareholders), the shareholder has merely received additional shares that represent the same total investment. Thus, the shareholder does not realize income.[72] However, if the shareholder has the *option* of receiving either cash or stock in the corporation, the individual realizes gross income whether he or she receives stock or cash.[73] A taxpayer who elects to receive the stock could be deemed to be in constructive receipt of the cash he or she has rejected.[74] However, the amount of the income in this case is the value of the stock received, rather than the cash the shareholder has rejected. See Chapter 14 for a detailed discussion of stock dividends.

EDUCATIONAL SAVINGS BONDS

The cost of a college education has risen dramatically during the past 10 years, increasing at a rate almost twice the change in the general price level. The U.S. Department of Education estimates that by the year 2007, the cost of attending a publicly supported university for four years will exceed $60,000. For a private university, the cost is expected to exceed $200,000.[75] Congress has attempted to assit low- to middle-income parents in saving for their children's college education.

The assistance is in the form of an interest income exclusion.[76] The interest on Series EE U.S. government savings bonds may be excluded from gross income if the bond proceeds are used to pay qualified higher education expenses. The exclusion applies only if both of the following requirements are satisfied:

- The savings bonds are issued after December 31, 1989.
- The savings bonds are issued to an individual who is at least 24 years old at the time of issuance.

The exclusion is not available for a married couple who file separate returns.

The redemption proceeds must be used to pay qualified higher education expenses. *Qualified higher education expenses* consist of tuition and fees paid to an eligible educational institution for the taxpayer, spouse, or dependent. In calculating qualified higher education expenses, the tuition and fees paid are reduced by excludible scholarships and veterans' benefits received. If the

72. *Eisner v. Macomber*, 1 USTC ¶32, 3 AFTR 3020, 40 S.Ct. 189 (USSC, 1920); § 305(a).
73. § 305(b).
74. Refer to the discussion of constructive receipt in Chapter 4.
75. See generally, Knight and Knight, "New Ways to Manage Soaring Tuition Costs," *Journal of Accountancy* (March 1989): 207.
76. § 135.

redemption proceeds (both principal and interest) exceed the qualified higher education expenses, only a pro rata portion of the interest will qualify for exclusion treatment.

EXAMPLE 41

T's redemption proceeds from qualified savings bonds during the taxable year were $6,000 (principal of $4,000 and interest of $2,000). T's qualified higher education expenses were $5,000. Since the redemption proceeds exceed the qualified higher education expenses, only $1,667 ($5,000/$6,000 × $2,000) of the interest is excludible. ◆

The exclusion is limited by the application of the wherewithal to pay concept. That is, once the modified adjusted gross income exceeds a threshold amount, the phase-out of the exclusion begins. *Modified adjusted gross income* is adjusted gross income prior to the § 911 foreign earned income exclusion and the educational savings bond exclusion. The threshold amounts are adjusted for inflation each year. For 1992, the phase-out begins at $44,150 ($66,200 on a joint return).[77] The phase-out is completed when modified adjusted gross income exceeds the threshold amount by more than $15,000 ($30,000 on a joint return). The otherwise excludible interest is reduced by the amount calculated as follows:

$$\frac{\text{Modified AGI} - \$44{,}150}{\$15{,}000} \times \begin{array}{c}\text{Excludible interest}\\ \text{before phase–out}\end{array} = \begin{array}{l}\text{Reduction in}\\ \text{excludible interest}\end{array}$$

On a joint return, $66,200 is substituted for $44,150 (in 1992), and $30,000 is substituted for $15,000.

EXAMPLE 42

Assume the same facts as in Example 41, except that T's modified adjusted gross income for 1992 is $50,000. The phase-out will result in T's interest exclusion being reduced by $650 [($50,000 − $44,150)/$15,000 × $1,667]. Therefore, T's exclusion is $1,017 ($1,667 − $650). ◆

TAX BENEFIT RULE

Generally, if a taxpayer obtains a deduction for an item in one year and in a later year recovers all or a portion of the prior deduction, the recovery is included in gross income in the year received.[78]

EXAMPLE 43

A taxpayer deducted as a loss a $1,000 receivable from a customer when it appeared the amount would never be collected. The following year, the customer paid $800 on the receivable. The taxpayer must report the $800 as income in the year it is received. ◆

However, § 111 provides that no income is recognized upon the recovery of a deduction, or the portion of a deduction, that did not yield a tax benefit in the year it was taken. If the taxpayer in Example 43 had no tax liability in the year of the deduction (e.g., itemized deductions and personal exemptions exceeded adjusted gross income), the recovery would be partially or totally excluded from income in the year of the recovery.[79]

77. The indexed amounts for 1991 are $41,950 and $62,900.

78. § 111(a). See the Glossary of Tax Terms in Appendix C for a discussion of the term "tax benefit rule."

79. Itemized deductions are discussed in Chapter 11.

EXAMPLE 44

Before deducting a $1,000 loss from an uncollectible business receivable, T had taxable income of $200, computed as follows:

Adjusted gross income	$ 13,300
Itemized deductions and personal exemptions	(13,100)
Taxable income	$ 200

The business bad debt deduction yields only a $200 tax benefit. That is, taxable income is reduced by only $200 (to zero) as a result of the bad debt deduction. Therefore, if the customer makes a payment on the previously deducted receivable in a subsequent year, only the first $200 will be a recovery of a prior deduction and thus will be taxable. Any additional amount collected will be nontaxable because only $200 of the loss yielded a reduction in taxable income. ◆

INCOME FROM DISCHARGE OF INDEBTEDNESS

A transfer of appreciated property (fair market value is greater than adjusted basis) in satisfaction of a debt is an event that triggers the realization of income. The transaction is treated as a sale of the appreciated property followed by payment of the debt.[80] Foreclosure by a creditor is also treated as a sale or exchange of the property.[81]

EXAMPLE 45

T owed the State Bank $100,000 on an unsecured note. T satisfied the note by transferring to the bank common stock with a basis of $60,000 and a fair market value of $100,000. T must recognize $40,000 gain on the transfer. T also owed the bank $50,000 on a note secured by land. When T's basis in the land was $20,000 and the land's fair market value was $50,000, the bank foreclosed on the loan and took title to the land. T must recognize a $30,000 gain on the foreclosure. ◆

In some cases, a creditor will not exercise his or her right of foreclosure and will even forgive a portion of the debt to assure the vitality of the debtor. In such cases, the debtor realizes income from discharge of indebtedness.

EXAMPLE 46

X Corporation is unable to meet the mortgage payments on its factory building. Both the corporation and the mortgage holder are aware of the depressed market for industrial property in the area. Foreclosure would only result in the creditor's obtaining unsalable property. To improve X Corporation's financial position and thus improve X's chances of obtaining the additional credit from other lenders necessary for survival, the creditor agrees to forgive all amounts past due and to reduce the principal amount of the mortgage. ◆

Generally, the income realized by the debtor from the forgiveness of a debt is taxable.[82] A similar debt discharge (produced by a different creditor motivation) associated with personal use property is illustrated in Example 47.

EXAMPLE 47

In 1987, T borrowed $60,000 from National Bank to purchase her personal residence. T agreed to make monthly principal and interest payments for 15 years. The interest rate on the note was 8%. In 1992, when the balance on the note had been reduced

80. Reg. § 1.1001–2(a).

81. *Estate of Delman v. Comm.*, 73 T.C. 15 (1979).

82. *U.S. v. Kirby Lumber Co.*, 2 USTC ¶814, 10 AFTR 458, 52 S.Ct. 4 (USSC, 1931), codified in § 61(a)(12).

through monthly payments to $48,000, the bank offered to accept $45,000 in full settlement of the note. The bank made the offer because interest rates had increased to 12%. T accepted the bank's offer. As a result, T must recognize $3,000 ($48,000 – $45,000) income.[83] ◆

The following discharge of indebtedness situations are subject to special treatment:[84]

1. Creditors' gifts.
2. Discharges under Federal bankruptcy law.
3. Discharges that occur when the debtor is insolvent.
4. Discharge of the farm debt of a solvent taxpayer.
5. A seller's cancellation of the buyer's indebtedness.
6. A shareholder's cancellation of the corporation's indebtedness.
7. Forgiveness of loans to students.

If the creditor reduces the debt as an act of *love, affection or generosity,* the debtor has simply received a nontaxable gift (situation 1). Rarely will a gift be found to have occurred in a business context. A businessperson may settle a debt for less than the amount due, but as a matter of business expediency (e.g., high collection costs or disputes as to contract terms) rather than generosity.[85]

In situations 2, 3, and 4, the Code allows the debtor to reduce his or her basis in the assets by the realized gain from the discharge.[86] Thus, the realized gain is merely deferred until the assets are sold (or depreciated). Similarly, in situation 5 (a price reduction), the debtor reduces the basis in the specific assets financed by the seller.[87]

A shareholder's cancellation of the corporation's indebtedness to him or her (situation 6) usually is considered a contribution of capital to the corporation. Thus, the corporation's paid-in capital is increased, and its liabilities are decreased by the same amount.[88]

Many states make loans to students on the condition that the loan will be forgiven if the student practices a profession in the state upon completing his or her studies. The amount of the loan that is forgiven (situation 7) is excluded from gross income.[89]

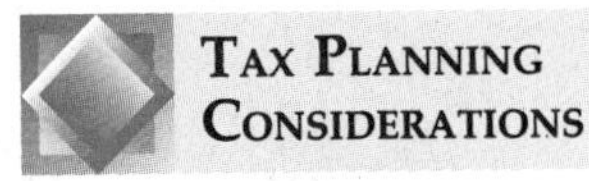

TAX PLANNING CONSIDERATIONS

The present law excludes certain types of economic gains from taxation. Therefore, taxpayers may find tax planning techniques helpful in obtaining the maximum benefits from the exclusion of such gains. Following are some of the tax planning opportunities made available by the exclusions described in this chapter.

Life Insurance

Life insurance offers several favorable tax attributes. As discussed in Chapter 4, the annual increase in the cash surrender value of the policy is not taxable (because no income has been actually or constructively received). By borrowing on the policy's cash surrender value, the owner can actually receive in cash the increase in value of the policy but without recognition of income.

83. Rev.Rul. 82–202, 1982–1 C.B. 35.
84. §§ 108 and 1017.
85. *Comm. v. Jacobson*, 49–1 USTC ¶9133, 37 AFTR 516, 69 S.Ct. 358 (USSC, 1949).
86. §§ 108(a), (e), and (g). Note that § 108(b) provides that other tax attributes (e.g., net operating loss) will be reduced by the realized gain from the debt discharge prior to the basis adjustment unless the taxpayer elects to apply the basis adjustment first.
87. § 108(e)(5).
88. § 108(e)(6).
89. § 108(f).

Employee Benefits

Generally, employees view accident and health insurance, as well as life insurance, as necessities. Employees can obtain group coverage at much lower rates than individuals would have to pay for the same protection. Premiums paid by the employer can be excluded from the employees' gross income. Because of the exclusion, employees will have a greater after-tax and after-insurance income if the employer pays a lower salary but also pays the insurance premiums.

EXAMPLE 48

Individual A receives a salary of $30,000. The company has group insurance benefits, but A was required to pay his own premiums as follows:

Hospitalization and medical insurance	$1,400
Term life insurance ($30,000 coverage)	200
Disability insurance	400
	$2,000

To simplify the analysis, assume A's tax rate on income is 28%. After paying taxes of $8,400 (.28 × $30,000) and $2,000 for insurance, A has $19,600 ($30,000 − $8,400 − $2,000) for his other living needs.

If A's employer reduced A's salary by $2,000 (to $28,000) but paid A's insurance premiums, A's tax liability would be only $7,840 ($28,000 × .28). Thus, A would have $20,160 ($28,000 − $7,840) to meet his other living needs. The change in the compensation plan would save $560 ($20,160 − $19,600). ◆

Similarly, employees must often incur expenses for child care and parking. The employee can have more income for other uses if the employer pays these costs for the employee but reduces the employee's salary by the cost of the benefits.

The use of cafeteria plans has increased dramatically in recent years. These plans allow the employees to tailor their benefits to meet their individual situations. Thus, where both spouses in a married couple are working, duplications of benefits can be avoided and other needed benefits can often be added. If less than all of the employee's allowance is spent, the employee can receive cash.

The meals and lodging exclusion enables employees to receive from their employer what they ordinarily must purchase with after-tax dollars. Although the requirements that the employee live and take his or her meals on the employer's premises limit the tax planning opportunities, in certain situations, the exclusion is an important factor in the employee's compensation (e.g., hotels, motels, restaurants, farms, and ranches).

The employees' discount provision is especially important for manufacturers and wholesalers. Employees of manufacturers can avoid tax on the manufacturer's, wholesaler's, and retailer's markups. The wholesaler's employees can avoid tax on an amount equal to the wholesale and retail markups.

It should be recognized that the exclusion of benefits is generally available only to employees. Proprietors and partners must pay tax on the same benefits their employees receive tax-free. By incorporating and becoming an employee of the corporation, the former proprietor or partner can also receive these tax-exempt benefits. Thus, the availability of employee benefits is a consideration in the decision to incorporate.

Investment Income

Tax-exempt state and local government bonds are almost irresistible investments for many high-income taxpayers. To realize the maximum benefit from the exemption, the investor can purchase zero coupon bonds. Like Series EE U.S. government savings bonds, these investments pay interest only at maturity. The advantage of the zero coupon feature is that the investor can earn tax-exempt interest on the accumulated principal and interest. If the investor purchases a bond that pays the interest each year, the interest received may be such a small amount that an additional tax-exempt investment cannot be made. In addition, reinvesting the interest may entail transaction costs (broker's fees). The zero coupon feature avoids these problems.

Series EE U. S. government savings bonds can earn tax-exempt interest if the bond proceeds are used for qualified higher education expenses. Many taxpayers can foresee these expenditures being made for their children's educations. In deciding whether to invest in the bonds, however, the investor must take into account the income limitations for excluding the interest from gross income.

PROBLEM MATERIALS

DISCUSSION QUESTIONS

1. T owned land that she leased to a corporation. The corporation constructed a building on the land. When the lease expired, the building would belong to T. The building had a fair market value of $40,000 when the lease expired. Why should T be allowed to exclude from gross income the fair market value of the building she received?
2. Who pays the income tax on a gift of the income from a certain piece of property—the donee or the donor?
3. C Company gave $500 to each household in the community that had suffered a flood loss. The purpose of the payments was to help the flood victims. If some of the recipients are employees of C Company, can the employees exclude the payments from gross income?
4. T's truck was stalled on the side of the road. Z stopped to help and called X, who agreed to repair the truck for $75. T paid X $75 and Z $25. The payment to X was made because of a contractual obligation and therefore is not a gift. The payment to Z was not made because of a contractual obligation. Does this mean that the payment Z received is a gift?
5. What are the two principal tax benefits of buying life insurance that has a cash surrender value?
6. M Corporation purchased a $1,000,000 insurance policy on the life of the company's president. The company paid $100,000 of premiums, the president died, and the company collected the face amount of the policy. How much must M Corporation include in gross income?
7. E died while employed by R Company. The company paid E's husband $2,000 in sales commissions that E had earned and $3,000 under the company's policy of making payments to the spouses of deceased employees. Is any of the $5,000 that E's husband received subject to income tax?
8. Company A provides its employees with $10,000 group term life insurance. Company B does not provide insurance but generally gives the family of a deceased employee $10,000. Compare the tax consequences of the insured and uninsured plans.
9. T received an academic scholarship to State University. Under the scholarship agreement, he received tuition ($1,500), books ($400), and room and board ($5,000). What is T's gross income from the scholarship?
10. T is a graduate assistant at State University. He receives $7,000 a year in salary. In addition, tuition of $4,000 is waived. The tuition waiver is available to all full- and

part-time employees. The fair market value of T's services is $11,000. How much is T required to include in his gross income?

11. R and T were traveling together in a defectively manufactured automobile. As a result of the defects, the automobile ran off the road and crashed into a tree. R and T each broke an arm in the accident. R was a baseball pitcher and was unable to pitch for one year as a result of the accident. He received a $400,000 damage award in a suit against the automobile manufacturer. T was a 65-year-old retiree and received $25,000 as an award for damages. The difference in the damage awards was largely due to R's greater loss of earnings. Is R taxed on any of the $400,000 received?

12. Under what conditions can the taxpayer exclude from gross income punitive damages received?

13. T purchases an accident and health insurance plan that was advertised in the Sunday newspaper. The annual premiums are $400. During the year, T received payments of $1,200 under the plan.

    a. How much of the $1,200 must T include in her gross income?

    b. Would the tax consequences differ if the $1,200 represented amounts paid by the insurance company to replace lost wages while T was hospitalized?

14. What nontaxable fringe benefits are available to employees that are not available to partners and proprietors?

15. How does one determine if the meals and lodging supplied by the employer are to serve a valid business purpose? Is the tax treatment of meals and lodging affected if the employer advertises that the meals and lodging provided are one of the employees' fringe benefits?

16. P, a full-time employee of State University, is allowed to use the university's tennis courts when they are not being used by the tennis team and physical education classes. Does P derive gross income from the use of the tennis courts?

17. The management of X Life Insurance Company believes it is good business to encourage employees to exercise and stay healthy. Therefore, the company built a gymnasium in the basement of the main office building and made the facility available to all of the company's 1,200 employees. Z Life Insurance Company has only 30 employees. It is not feasible for Z Company to maintain its own gymnasium, but the company would like to encourage employees to exercise. Therefore, Z Company has offered to pay membership fees for any employee who wishes to join the health club located in the adjoining building. Compare the tax treatment of the health facility benefits provided the employees of the two companies.

18. J works for a company that operates a cruise ship. All employees are allowed to take a one-week cruise each year at no cost to the employee. The employee is provided with a room, meals, and general recreation on the ship. Are the benefits received taxable to the employees?

19. T is employed by X, Inc., an automobile manufacturing company. X sells T a new automobile at company cost of $8,400. The price charged a dealer would have been $10,000, and the retail price of the automobile is $11,500. What is T's gross income from the purchase of the automobile?

20. R Company provides officers with a 30% discount on merchandise, but other employees are provided with only a 10% discount. The company's gross profit rate on the goods is 40%. If Z, an officer in the company, is allowed to buy goods for $70 when the regular price is $100, how much is Z required to include in gross income?

21. T is a U.S. citizen who worked in a foreign country for the period July 1, 1992, through May 31, 1993. Is T entitled to any foreign earned income exclusion for 1992?

22. Z Corporation is opening a branch in Kazonbi, an African country that does not levy an income tax on citizens of foreign countries. T, a U.S. citizen, is considering two offers from his employer, Z Corporation. He can work for 6 months in Kazonbi and 6 months in the United States and receive a salary of $4,000 per month, or he can work in Kazonbi for 12 months at the same monthly salary. T would prefer to spend as much time in the United States as possible and prefers the first alternative. However, he asks your advice as to how income taxes might affect his decision.

23. R received a $100,000 condemnation award when the state took his real estate for a new school. R used the money to purchase State of Virginia bonds, which paid him $7,500 interest in 1992. The state condemned other property owned by R. However, R contested the amount the state was willing to pay for this second piece of property. At the end of 1992, the court awarded R $100,000 for the land and $7,500 interest on the condemnation award. How much of the interest is R required to include in gross income?
24. H and W are married, file a joint return, and are in the 31% marginal tax bracket. They would like to save for their child's education. What would be the advantage of buying State of Virginia bonds as compared to buying Series EE U.S. government bonds?
25. T owns 100 shares of stock in XYZ Corporation. The corporation declares a dividend that gives T the option of receiving 10 additional shares of XYZ stock or $200 cash. T elects to receive 10 additional shares of stock. What are the tax consequences to T?
26. X, a cash basis taxpayer, was in a contract dispute with Y. In 1992, X performed services for Y, but Y would not pay. X had no gross income and $6,000 of itemized deductions and personal exemptions in 1992. In 1993, the dispute was settled, and X received $10,000. Can X exclude any of the $10,000 under the tax benefit rule?
27. In 1992, F received a $400 factory rebate on supplies purchased and deducted as a business expense in 1991. In 1992, S received a $400 factory rebate on a personal use automobile purchased in December 1991. Both F and S had over $10,000 of taxable income in 1991 and 1992. Is the receipt of $400 taxable to F or S?
28. How does the tax treatment of a corporation's income generated by the retirement of bonds for less than book value (issue price plus amortized discount or less amortized premium) differ from the income derived from a shareholder's forgiveness of the corporation's indebtedness?
29. In 1982, R purchased real estate for $50,000. By 1990, the property had appreciated to $150,000. In 1990, R borrowed $120,000 and gave a mortgage on the property as security for the debt. In 1992, when the value of the property equaled the balance on the mortgage ($120,000), R transferred the property to the mortgagee in satisfaction of the debt. Did R realize income from discharge of indebtedness?
30. While attending medical school, K received loans totaling $40,000 under a Commonwealth of Virginia student loan program. The loan program provides that the loan will be forgiven if K practices medicine for three years in specified rural areas in the western part of the state. If the loan is forgiven, what amount should K include in her gross income?

PROBLEMS

31. Determine whether the following may be excluded from gross income as gifts, bequests, scholarships, prizes, or life insurance proceeds:

    a. Uncle told Nephew, "Come live with me and take care of me in my old age and you can have all my property after my death." Nephew complied with Uncle's request. Uncle's will made Nephew sole beneficiary of the estate.

    b. Uncle told Nephew, "If you study hard and make the dean's list this year, I will pay your tuition for the following year." Nephew made the dean's list, and Uncle paid the tuition.

    c. Uncle told Nephew, "If you make the dean's list this year, I will pay you $500." Nephew made the dean's list, and Uncle paid the $500.

    d. D cashed in her life insurance contract and collected $10,000. She had paid premiums totaling $7,000.

    e. F received $500 from his employer to pay the medical expenses of F's child. The payment was not part of a medical reimbursement plan, and the employer made the payment out of compassion.

32. Determine the taxable life insurance proceeds in the following cases:

    a. B purchased a sports franchise and player contracts from S. As part of the transaction, B purchased a life insurance contract on a key player from S for

$50,000. One month later, the player was killed in an automobile accident, and B collected $500,000 on the life insurance contract.

b. P and R formed a partnership and agreed that upon the death of either partner, the surviving partner would purchase the decedent's partnership interest. P purchased a life insurance policy on R's life and paid $5,000 in premiums. Upon R's death, P collected $100,000 on the life insurance policy and used the proceeds to purchase R's interest in the partnership.

c. Same as (b), except the partnership was incorporated and P and R owned all the stock. Upon incorporation, P and R transferred their life insurance policies to the corporation in exchange for stock. When R died, the corporation redeemed (purchased) R's stock, using the $100,000 life insurance proceeds.

33. Determine the effect on Z's gross income of the following:

a. Z Company sells furniture to customers on credit. Customers are required to purchase credit life insurance, with the proceeds payable to Z. The company collected $6,000 when a customer died.

b. A, the controlling shareholder in Z Company, transferred his life insurance policy to the corporation in exchange for additional stock. A had paid $8,000 in premiums. When A died, the company collected the face amount of the policy of $25,000. During the time it held the policy, Z Company paid additional premiums of $1,000.

c. Z Company also purchased an insurance policy on the life of the company president, B. The company had paid $9,000 in premiums, and the cash surrender value of the policy was $6,000 when B died. The company collected $25,000, which was the face amount of the policy.

34. T died at age 35. He was married and had four minor children. His employer, XYZ Painting Company, made payments to Mrs. T as follows:

T's accrued salary at date of death	$4,000
Family death benefits under long-standing company policy ($2,000 is paid to the spouse and $1,000 is paid to each child of a deceased employee)	2,000
A payment authorized by the board of directors to help Mrs. T pay debts accumulated by T	7,000

In addition, Mrs. T was the beneficiary of her husband's life insurance policy of $50,000. XYZ Painting Company had paid for the policy. Mr. T had excluded all of the premiums paid by the employer from gross income as group term life insurance. Mrs. T left the insurance proceeds with the insurance company and elected to receive an annuity of $4,000 each year for life. Her life expectancy is 40 years. She collected one $4,000 payment at the end of the current year. Mr. and Mrs. T filed a joint return in the year of T's death. Which of the above amounts must be included in their gross income?

35. F was awarded an academic scholarship to State University. He received $5,000 in August and $6,000 in December 1992. F had enough personal savings to pay all expenses as they came due. F's expenditures for the relevant period were as follows:

Tuition, August 1992	$2,900
Tuition, December 1992	3,200
Room and board	
August–December 1992	3,000
January–May 1993	2,400
Books and educational supplies	
August–December 1992	800
January–May 1993	950

Determine the effect on F's gross income for 1992 and 1993.

36. R made the all-state football team during his junior and senior years in high school. He accepted an athletic scholarship from State University. The scholarship provided the following:

Tuition and fees	$4,000
Room and board	2,500
Books and supplies	500

Determine the effect of the scholarship on R's gross income.

37. Which of the following amounts received for damages would be taxable?

  a. A corporation collected $500,000 for damages to its business reputation. The amount received was the estimated decrease in value of the company's goodwill.
  b. An individual collected from his accountant for failure to timely file an amended state income tax return. Had the return been filed, the taxpayer would have collected a $600 refund of state income taxes that had been deducted as an itemized deduction on the Federal return.
  c. In settlement of a lawsuit, a taxpayer received $15,000 for actual damages to his reputation. The taxpayer also collected $25,000 of punitive damages.

38. R was injured in an accident that was not related to his employment. He incurred $12,000 in medical expenses and collected $4,000 on a medical insurance policy he purchased. He also collected $9,000 in medical benefits under his employer's group plan. Originally, the doctor diagnosed R's injury as requiring no more than 3 months of disability. Because of subsequent complications, R was unable to return to work until 14 months after the accident. While away from the job, R collected $200 per week on his employer's wage continuation plan. R also owned an insurance policy that paid him $100 per week while he was disabled. What are the tax consequences to R of the receipt of the following?

  a. $13,000 medical benefits.
  b. $300 per week to replace R's wages.

39. T, age 45, is an officer of XYZ Company, which provided T with the following nondiscriminatory fringe benefits in 1992:

  a. Hospitalization insurance for T and his dependents. The cost of coverage for T was $450, and the additional cost for T's dependents was $400.
  b. Reimbursement of $700 from an uninsured medical reimbursement plan available to all employees.
  c. Group term life insurance protection of $120,000. (Each employee received coverage equal to twice his or her annual salary.)
  d. Salary continuation payments of $2,600 while T was hospitalized for an illness.

While T was ill, he collected $1,600 on a salary continuation insurance policy he had purchased.

Determine the amounts T must include in gross income.

40. T served as the manager of an orphanage in 1992. In this connection, he had the following transactions:

  a. He received no salary from his job but was given room and board (valued at $9,600) on the premises. No other person was employed by the orphanage, which is a tax-exempt organization.
  b. The orphanage paid $500 in tuition for a night course T took at a local university. The course was in the field of philosophy and dealt with the meaning of life. The payment was authorized by the orphanage's trustees in a written resolution.
  c. The orphanage paid $900 of the premiums on T's life insurance policy and all of his medical expenses of $1,800. Again, the payment was made pursuant to a resolution approved by the trustees.

Determine the effect of these transactions on T's gross income.

41. The UW Union and T Corporation are negotiating contract terms. What would be the tax consequences of the following options? (Assume the union members are in the 28% marginal tax bracket and all benefits would be provided on a nondiscriminatory basis.)

   a. The company would eliminate the $100 deductible on health insurance benefits, and the employee would take a $100 reduction in pay. Most employees incur more than $100 each year in medical expenses.
   b. The employee would get an additional paid holiday with the same annual income (the same pay but less work) or an increase in pay equal to the holiday pay but no additional paid holiday (more pay and the same work).
   c. The employee who did not need health insurance (because the employee's spouse works and receives family coverage) would be allowed to receive the cash value of the coverage.

42. Determine the taxpayer's gross income for each of the following:

   a. T is the manager of a plant. The company owns a house one mile from the plant (rental value of $6,000) that T is allowed to occupy.
   b. M works for an insurance company that allows employees to eat in the cafeteria for $.50 a meal. Generally, the cost to the insurance company of producing a meal is $5.00, and a comparable meal could be purchased for $4.0[illegible] ate 150 meals in the cafeteria during the year.
   c. Z is a Methodist minister and receives a housing allowance of $600 per month from his church. Z is buying his home and uses the $600 to make house payments ($450) and to pay utilities ($150).
   d. P is a college professor and lives in campus housing. He is not charged rent. The value of the house is $100,000, and the annual rental value is $7,200.

43. Does the taxpayer recognize gross income in the following situations?

   a. A is a registered nurse working in a community hospital. She is not required to take her lunch on the hospital premises, but she can eat in the cafeteria at no charge. The hospital adopted this policy to encourage employees to stay on the premises and be available in case of emergencies. During the year, A ate most of her meals on the premises. The total value of those meals was $750.
   b. J is the manager of a hotel. His employer will allow him to live in one of the rooms rent free or to receive a $200 per month cash allowance for rent. J elected to live in the hotel.
   c. S is a forest ranger and lives in his employer's cabin in the forest. He is required to live there, and because there are no restaurants nearby, the employer supplies S with groceries that he cooks and eats on the premises.
   d. T is a partner in the ABC Ranch (a partnership). He is the full-time manager of the ranch. ABC has a business purpose for T's living on the ranch.

44. Under a company's former medical insurance plan, employees were responsible for the first $500 of their medical expenses. Under the new cafeteria plan, employees can choose between receiving $500 in cash or having the company provide coverage for all medical expenses. P elected the expanded medical benefits. In 1992, P incurred $1,500 of medical expenses that were paid for under the plan. How much is P required to include in gross income?

45. T is employed by F Bowling Lanes, Inc. Determine T's gross income in each of the following situations:

   a. T's children are allowed to use the lanes without charge. Each child can also bring a friend without charge. This benefit is available to all employees. During the year, the children bowled 200 games, and the usual charge was $1.50 per game. Friends of T's children bowled 150 games.
   b. The company has a lunch counter. T is allowed to take home the leftover donuts each night. The company's cost was $400, and the value of the donuts T took home was $150.
   c. The company pays T's subscription to *Bowling Lanes Management*, a monthly journal.

46. X Corporation would like you to review its employee fringe benefits program with regard to the effects of the plan on the company's president (P), who is also the majority shareholder:

   a. All employees receive free tickets to State University football games. P is seldom able to attend the games and usually gives his tickets to his nephew. The cost of P's tickets for the year was $75.
   b. The company pays all parking fees for its officers but not for other employees. The company paid $1,200 for P's parking for the year.
   c. Employees are allowed to use the copy machine for personal purposes as long as the privilege is not abused. P is president of a trade association and made extensive use of the copy machine to prepare mailings to members of the association. The cost of the copies was $900.
   d. The company is in the household moving business. Employees are allowed to ship goods without charge whenever there is excess space on a truck. P purchased a dining room suite for his daughter. Company trucks delivered the furniture to the daughter. Normal freight charges would have been $600.
   e. The company has a storage facility for household goods. Officers are allowed a 20% discount on charges for storing their goods. All other employees are allowed a 10% discount. P's discounts for the year totaled $400.

47. Z works for a company that operates a cruise ship. All employees are allowed to take a one-week cruise each year at no cost to the employee. The employee is provided with a room, meals, and general recreation on the ship. Determine the tax consequences of Z accepting a trip under the following assumptions:

   a. Z must travel on a standby basis; that is, Z can travel only if the ship is not completely booked. The room Z occupies has maid service, and the sheets and towels are changed each day.
   b. Z takes his meals with the other customers who pay a fixed amount for the cruise that includes meals and lodging.
   c. The recreation consists of the use of the pool, dancing, and bingo games.
   d. All guests must pay for their drinks and snacks between meals, but Z and the other employees are given a 20% discount.
   e. Employees at Z's level and above are provided with free parking at the pier. This group comprises about 25% of all employees of the company.

48. R is a U.S. citizen and a production manager for XYZ Company. On May 1, 1991, he was temporarily assigned to the Monterrey, Mexico, plant. On August 6, 1991, he returned to the United States for medical treatment. On September 1, 1991, he returned to his duties in Monterrey. Except for a two-week period in the United States (December 16–31, 1991), he worked in Monterrey until December 1, 1992, when he was transferred to Boston, Massachusetts. R's salary was $4,000 per month in 1991 and $5,000 per month in 1992. His housing expense did not exceed the base amount. Compute R's foreign earned income exclusion in 1991 and 1992.

49. Determine T's gross income from the following receipts for the year:

Interest on U.S. government savings bonds	$ 750
Interest on state income tax refund	100
Gain on sale of Augusta County bonds	700
Interest on Augusta County bonds	900
Patronage dividend from Potato Growers Cooperative	1,500

The patronage dividend was received in March of the current year for amounts paid and deducted in the previous year as expenses of T's profitable cash basis farming business.

50. Determine M's taxable income from the following items:

   a. M owns 100 shares of BE Company common stock. The company has a dividend reinvestment plan. Under the plan, M can receive an $18 cash dividend or an additional share of stock with a fair market of $18. M elected to take the stock.

b. M owns 100 shares of NB Corporation. The company declared a dividend, and M was to receive an additional share of the company's common stock with a fair market value of $18. M did not have the option to receive cash. However, a management group announced a plan to repurchase all available shares for $18 each. The offer was part of a takeover defense.
c. M also collected $125 on a corporate debenture. The corporation had been in bankruptcy for several years. M had correctly deducted the cost of the bond in a prior year because the bankruptcy judge had informed the bondholders they would not receive anything in the final liquidation. Later the company collected on an unanticipated claim and had the funds to make partial payment on the bonds.

51. L recently inherited $25,000. She is considering using the money to finance a college education for her 5-year-old child. L does not expect her gross income to ever exceed $40,000 a year. She is very concerned with the safety of the principal and has decided to invest the $25,000 in Series EE U.S. government savings bonds. The bonds earn 8% interest each year. At the end of 13 years, when L's child is 18 and ready to go to college, the bonds will be worth $68,000. This is the estimated cost of a 4-year college education at that time.

    a. What will be the amount of the after-tax proceeds from the bonds at maturity, assuming L purchases the bonds in her name but uses the proceeds for the child's college education?
    b. Should the bonds be purchased in the child's name (with L as custodian) or should L purchase the bonds in her own name?

52. How does the tax benefit rule apply in the following cases?

    a. In 1991, T paid X $5,000 for locating a potential client. The deal fell through, and in 1992, X refunded the $5,000 to T.
    b. In 1991, T paid an attorney $300 for services in connection with a title search. Because the attorney was negligent, T incurred some additional costs in acquiring the land. In 1992, the attorney refunded his $300 fee to T.
    c. In 1992, T received a $90 dividend with respect to 1992 premiums on her life insurance policy.
    d. In 1992, a cash basis farmer received a $400 patronage dividend with respect to 1991 purchases of cattle feed.

53. T, who is in the 31% tax bracket, recently collected $100,000 on a life insurance policy she carried on her father. She currently owes $120,000 on her personal residence and $120,000 on business property. National Bank holds the mortgage on both pieces of property and has agreed to accept $100,000 in complete satisfaction of either mortgage. The interest rate on the mortgages is 8%, and both mortgages are payable over 10 years. T can also purchase Montgomery County school bonds yielding 8%. What would be the tax consequences of each of the following alternatives, assuming T currently deducts the mortgage interest on her tax return?

    a. Retire the mortgage on the residence.
    b. Retire the mortgage on the business property.
    c. Purchase tax-exempt bonds but not pay off either mortgage.

    Which alternative should T select?

54. T had total assets of $100,000 and liabilities of $150,000; it was apparent that T could not meet his liabilities as they came due. Determine the consequences of the following agreements T reached with his creditors:

    a. The State Bank agreed to extend the due date for an additional year on a $30,000 note due in exchange for an increase in the interest rate.
    b. T's older brother, Z, forgave T's $10,000 debt. When asked about why he did it, Z responded, "T's my brother."
    c. An equipment supplier agreed to reduce the amount T owed for equipment by $5,000 "to help a good customer stay in business."

CUMULATIVE PROBLEMS

55. Oliver W. Hand was divorced from Sandra D. Hand on May 12, 1991. On September 6, 1992, Oliver married Beulah Crane. Oliver and Beulah will file a joint return for 1992. Oliver's Social Security number is 262–60–3814. Beulah's number is 259–68–4184, and she will adopt "Hand" as her married name. The Hands live at 210 Mason Drive, Atlanta, GA 30304. Sandra's Social Security number is 219–74–1361.

Oliver is 49 and is employed by Atom, Inc., as an electrical engineer. His salary for 1992 was $56,000. Beulah is 30 and earned $29,000 as a marriage counselor in 1992. She was employed by Family Counselors, Inc.

The divorce agreement required Oliver to make 132 monthly payments to Sandra. The payments are $1,200 per month for 84 months, at which time the payments decrease to $1,000 per month. Oliver and Sandra have a 14-year-old daughter, Daisy Hand. If Daisy should die before she attains age 21, Oliver's remaining payments to Sandra would be reduced to $1,000 per month. Sandra was granted custody of Daisy and can document that she provided $2,000 of support for Daisy. Oliver made 12 payments in 1992.

Oliver's employer provided him with group term life insurance coverage in the amount of $90,000 in 1992.

Beulah's employer provided Beulah with free parking in a parking garage adjacent to the office building where Beulah works. The monthly charge to the general public is $50.

Oliver received dividends of $40 on Z Corporation stock he owned before marriage, and Beulah received dividends of $50 on her separately owned M Corporation stock. They received dividends of $400 on jointly owned B Corporation stock, which they acquired after marriage. Oliver and Beulah live in a common law state.

Combined itemized deductions for Oliver and Beulah in 1992 were as follows:

State income taxes withheld		
Oliver	$2.600	
Beulah	800	$3,400
Real estate taxes on residence		1,120
Home mortgage interest		
(paid to Atlanta Federal Savings and Loan)		4,020
Cash contributions to church		900

In 1992, Beulah received a refund of 1991 state income taxes of $450. She had deducted state income taxes withheld as an itemized deduction on her 1991 return. Oliver received a $300 refund on his 1991 state income taxes. He had used the standard deduction in 1991.

Additional information:

- Oliver's employer withheld Federal income tax of $7,650 and $4,253 of FICA (Social Security) tax. Beulah's employer withheld $2,900 of Federal income tax and $2,219 of FICA tax.

Part 1—Tax Computation

Compute the Hands' net tax payable (or refund due) for 1992. Suggested software (*if available*): *TurboTax* for tax return or WFT tax planning software.

Part 2—Tax Planning

Assume the Hands came to you in early December of 1992 seeking tax planning advice for 1992 and 1993. They provide you with the following information:

a. All the facts previously presented will be essentially the same in 1993 except for the items described in (b), (c), (d), and (e).
b. Oliver inherited $100,000 from his mother on December 1. He will use part of his inheritance to pay off the mortgage on the Hands' residence on January 3, 1993. Consequently, there will be no mortgage interest expense in 1993.

c. Oliver expects a 6% salary increase in 1993, and Beulah expects a 10% increase.
d. The Hands have pledged to contribute $2,400 to their church in 1993 (as opposed to $900 contributed in 1992). However, they could use Oliver's inherited funds to pay the pledge before the end of 1992 if you advise them to do so to achieve an overall tax savings.
e. The Hands acquired 100 shares of ABC Corporation stock on July 5, 1992, at a total cost of $2,000. The value of the stock has increased rapidly, and it is now worth $5,000. The Hands plan to sell the stock and ask whether they should sell it in 1992 or wait until 1993.

Advise the Hands as to the appropriate tax planning strategy for 1992 and 1993. Support your recommendations by computing their tax liabilities for 1992 and 1993 considering the various available alternatives. Suggested software (*if available*): WFT tax planning software.

56. Archie S. Monroe (Social Security number 363-33-1411) is 35 years old and is married to Annie B. Monroe (Social Security number 259-68-4284). The Monroes live at 215 Adams Dr., Thor, VA 24317. They file a joint return and have two dependent children (Barry and Betty). In 1992, Archie and Annie had the following transactions:

a. Salary received by Archie from Allen Steel Company (Archie is vice president).	$69,000
b. Interest received on jointly owned State of Nebraska bonds.	8,000
c. Group term life insurance premiums paid by Archie's employer (coverage of $60,000).	220
d. Annual increment in the value of Series E government savings bonds (the Monroes have not previously included the accrued amounts in gross income).	400
e. Taxable dividends received from Allen Steel Company, a U.S. corporation (the stock was jointly owned). Of the $5,900 in dividends, $1,000 was mailed on December 31, 1992, and received by Archie and Annie on January 4, 1993.	5,900
f. Alimony payments to Archie's former wife (Rosa T. Monroe, Social Security number 800-60-2580) under a divorce decree.	9,000
g. Itemized deductions:	
State income tax	1,750
Real estate tax on residence	900
Interest on personal residence (paid to Thor Federal Savings)	3,200
Cash contribution to church	700
h. Federal income tax withheld.	9,634

Part 1—Tax Computation

Compute the Monroes' net tax payable (or refund due) for 1992. Suggested software (*if available*): *TurboTax* for tax return or WFT tax planning software.

Part 2—Tax Planning

The Monroes plan to sell 200 shares of stock they purchased on July 12, 1981, at a cost of $18,000. The stock is worth $10,000 in December 1992, and the Monroes' broker predicts a continued decline in value. Annie plans to resume her career as a model in 1993, and her earnings will move the Monroes into the 31% bracket. How much Federal income tax will the Monroes save for 1992 if they sell the stock in 1992? Should they sell the stock in 1992 or 1993? Suggested software (*if available*): WFT tax planning software.

RESEARCH PROBLEMS

RESEARCH PROBLEM 1 P is the minister at the First Baptist Church. As part of his compensation, P receives an $800 per month housing allowance. P is purchasing his residence, and he uses the $800 each month to make mortgage and property tax payments. The mortgage interest and property taxes are deducted (as itemized deductions) on P's tax return. The examining IRS agent thinks P would be enjoying a double benefit if the housing allowance is excluded and the itemized deductions are allowed. In addition, the agent contends that the housing allowance exclusion should apply only where the church provides the residence or the minister uses the funds to pay rent. Therefore, the agent maintains that P should include in gross income the $800 received each month. P has asked your assistance in this matter.

RESEARCH PROBLEM 2 E was recently hired as manager of Fertile Farm, Inc. E is required to live in the employer's house on the farm. E and the employer are trying to decide how to arrange terms with the electric company. The employer would like the utility account to be in E's name, but with the employer reimbursing E $200 each month. The $200 should be adequate to cover all charges. The employer requests this arrangement because the previous manager established the account in the company's name and left town without paying the bill. E has asked your tax advice on the matter.

Partial list of research aids:
Rev.Rul. 68–579, 1968–2 C.B. 61.

RESEARCH PROBLEM 3 T is a compulsive gambler. After losing $100,000 of his savings, he began to gamble on credit. That is, the casino would treat T's losses as an account receivable from T. Under state law, gambling debts are unenforceable. However, the casino has a very good collection rate. After T had accumulated an amount payable of $250,000, he refused to pay the casino. After threats on both sides, the casino finally accepted $50,000 in full payment of the debt. The IRS asserts that T has $200,000 income from discharge of indebtedness. What is the appropriate treatment of the $200,000?

RESEARCH PROBLEM 4 R was the sole surviving heir of H, his uncle. When H died, his will provided that all of his property would go to the Animal Benevolent Fund. R thought that his uncle had been unduly influenced by the director of the fund. Furthermore, R thought his uncle was incompetent to make a will. Therefore, R threatened to contest the will. The director of the fund paid R $100,000 to drop the will contest. R dropped the contest, but now the IRS wants him to pay tax on the $100,000. Is the amount R received to abandon his claim to the inheritance subject to tax?

Part

Deductions

Part III presents the deduction component of the basic tax model. Deductions are classified as business versus nonbusiness, "for" versus "from," employee versus employer, active versus passive, and reimbursed versus unreimbursed. The effect of each of these classifications is analyzed. The presentation includes not only the deductions that are permitted, but also limitations and disallowances associated with deductions. Because deductions can exceed gross income, the treatment of losses is also included.

Chapter

CHAPTER

DEDUCTIONS AND LOSSES: IN GENERAL

OBJECTIVES

Explain the importance of deductions *for* and *from* adjusted gross income.

Classify the deductions *for* and *from* adjusted gross income.

Define "ordinary," "necessary," and "reasonable" in relation to deductible business expenses.

Explain the differences between cash basis and accrual basis.

Discuss the following disallowance possibilities: public policy limitations, political activities, investigation of business opportunities, hobby losses, vacation home rentals, payment of others' expenses, personal expenditures, unrealized losses, capital expenditures, and transactions between related parties.

Explain the substantiation requirements that must be met to take a deduction.

Examine the nondeductibility of expenses and interest related to tax-exempt income.

Describe various tax planning techniques concerning the time value of deductions, unreasonable compensation, shifting deductions, hobby losses, and substantiation requirements.

OUTLINE

Classification of Deductible Expenses

◆

As discussed in Chapters 4 and 5, § 61 provides an all-inclusive definition of gross income. Deductions, however, must be specifically provided for by law. The courts have established the doctrine that an item is not deductible unless a specific provision in the tax law allows its deduction. Whether and to what extent deductions are allowed depends on legislative grace.[1]

It is important to classify deductible expenses as deductions *for* adjusted gross income (deductions subtracted from gross income in calculating adjusted gross income) or deductions *from* adjusted gross income (AGI). Deductions *for* AGI can be claimed whether or not the taxpayer itemizes. Deductions *from* AGI result in a tax benefit only if they exceed the taxpayer's standard deduction. If itemized deductions (*from* AGI) are less than the standard deduction, they have no tax benefit.

Deductions *for* AGI are also important in determining the *amount* of itemized deductions because many itemized deductions (e.g., medical expenses and personal casualty losses) are limited to amounts in excess of specified percentages of AGI. Itemized deductions that are deductible only to the extent that they exceed a specified percentage of AGI are increased when AGI is decreased. Likewise, when AGI is increased, these itemized deductions are decreased.

Example 1

T earns a salary of $20,000 and has no other income. He itemizes deductions during the current year. Medical expenses for the year are $1,800. Since medical expenses are deductible only to the extent they exceed 7.5% of AGI, T's medical expense deduction is $300 [$1,800 − (7.5% × $20,000)]. If T had a $2,000 deduction *for* AGI, his medical expense deduction would be $450 [$1,800 − (7.5% × $18,000)], or $150 more. If the $2,000 deduction was *from* AGI, his medical expense deduction would remain $300 since AGI is unchanged. ◆

Example 1 illustrates how deductions *for* AGI can affect AGI and thus can affect itemized deductions. Changes in income recognition (an increase or decrease) have a similar impact on itemized deductions.

A deduction *for* AGI is also more valuable to taxpayers who live in states that begin the tax computation with Federal AGI rather than with Federal taxable income. A lower base of Federal AGI results in lower state income taxes.

Deductions for Adjusted Gross Income

To understand how deductions of individual taxpayers are classified, it is necessary to examine the role of § 62. Section 62 merely classifies various deductions as deductions *for* AGI. It does not provide the authority for taking the deduction. For example, § 212 allows individuals to deduct expenses attributable to income-producing property. Section 62(a)(4) classifies § 212 expenses that are attributable to rents or royalties as deductions *for* AGI. Likewise, a deduction for trade or business expenses is allowed by § 162. The expenses are classified as deductions *for* AGI by § 62(a)(1).

If a deduction is not listed in § 62, it is an itemized deduction, *not* a deduction *for* AGI. Following is a *partial* list of the items classified as deductions *for* AGI by § 62:

1. Expenses attributable to a trade or business carried on by the taxpayer, if the trade or business does not consist of the performance of services by

---

1. *New Colonial Ice Co. v. Helvering*, 4 USTC ¶1292, 13 AFTR 1180, 54 S.Ct. 788 (USSC, 1934).

the taxpayer as an employee. These expenses include half of the self-employment tax paid (see Chapter 13).
2. Expenses incurred by a taxpayer in connection with the performance of services as an employee if the expenses are reimbursed and other conditions are satisfied.
3. Deductions that result from losses on the sale or exchange of property by the taxpayer.
4. Deductions attributable to property held for the production of rents and royalties.
5. The deduction for payment of alimony allowed by § 215.
6. Certain contributions to pension, profit sharing, and annuity plans of self-employed individuals.
7. The deduction for certain retirement savings allowed by § 219 (e.g., IRAs).
8. A certain portion of lump-sum distributions from pension plans taxed under § 402(e).
9. The penalty imposed on premature withdrawal of funds from time savings accounts or deposits.

These items are covered in detail in various chapters in the text.

Itemized Deductions

Section 63(d) defines itemized deductions as the deductions allowed other than "the deductions allowable in arriving at adjusted gross income"; that is, deductions that are not deductions *for* AGI are itemized deductions.

Section 212 allows deductions for ordinary and necessary expenses paid or incurred for the following:

- The production or collection of income.
- The management, conservation, or maintenance of property held for the production of income.
- Expenses paid in connection with the determination (including tax return preparation), collection, or refund of any tax.

Section 212 expenses related to rent and royalty income are deductions *for* AGI.[2] All other § 212 expenses are itemized deductions (deductions *from* AGI).

Investment-related expenses (e.g., safe deposit box rentals) are deductible[3] as itemized deductions attributable to the production of investment income.

Taxpayers are allowed to deduct certain expenses that are primarily personal in nature. These expenses, which generally are not related to the production of income, are deductions *from* AGI (itemized deductions). Some of the more frequently encountered deductions in this category include the following:

- Contributions to qualified charitable organizations (not to exceed a specified percentage of AGI).
- Medical expenses (in excess of 7.5 percent of AGI).
- State and local taxes (e.g., real estate taxes and state and local income taxes).
- Personal casualty losses (in excess of an aggregate floor of 10 percent of AGI and a $100 floor per casualty).
- Certain personal interest (e.g., mortgage interest on a personal residence).

---

2. § 62(a)(4).

3. Reg. § 1.212–1(g).

Some miscellaneous itemized deductions are deductible only to the extent that in the aggregate they exceed 2 percent of AGI. Other miscellaneous itemized deductions are fully deductible. Itemized deductions are discussed in detail in Chapter 11.

Trade or Business Expenses

Section 162(a) permits a deduction for all ordinary and necessary expenses paid or incurred in carrying on a trade or business. These include reasonable salaries paid for services, expenses for the use of business property, and one-half of self-employment taxes paid. Such expenses are deducted *for* AGI.

It is sometimes difficult to determine whether an expenditure is deductible as a trade or business expense. The term "trade or business" is not defined in the Code or Regulations, and the courts have not provided a satisfactory definition. Therefore, it is usually necessary to ask one or more of the following questions to determine whether an item qualifies as a trade or business expense:

- Was the use of the particular item related to a business activity? For example, if funds are borrowed for use in a business, the interest is deductible as a business expense (as a deduction *for* AGI).
- Was the expenditure incurred with the intent to realize a profit or to produce income? For example, expenses in excess of the income from raising horses are not deductible if the activity is classified as a personal hobby rather than a trade or business.
- Were the taxpayer's operation and management activities extensive enough to indicate the carrying on of a trade or business?

Section 162 excludes the following items from classification as trade or business expenses:

- Charitable contributions or gifts.
- Illegal bribes and kickbacks and certain treble damage payments.
- Fines and penalties.

A bribe paid to a domestic official is not deductible if it is illegal under the laws of the United States. Foreign bribes (sometimes referred to as grease payments) are deductible unless they are unlawful under the Foreign Corrupt Practices Act of 1977.[4]

Ordinary and Necessary Requirement. The terms "ordinary" and "necessary" are found in both §§ 162 and 212. Section 162 governs the deductibility of trade or business expenses, and § 62(a)(1) classifies trade or business expenses of individuals as deductions *for* AGI. To be deductible under § 162, any trade or business expense must be ordinary and necessary. In addition, compensation for services must be "reasonable" in amount.

Many expenses that are necessary are *not* ordinary. The words "ordinary and necessary" are not defined in the Code or Regulations. However, the courts have held that an expense is necessary if a prudent businessperson would incur the same expense and the expense is expected to be appropriate and helpful in the taxpayer's business.[5]

4. § 162(c)(1).

5. *Welch v. Helvering*, 3 USTC ¶1164, 12 AFTR 1456, 54 S.Ct. 8 (USSC, 1933).

EXAMPLE 2

T purchased a manufacturing concern that had just been adjudged bankrupt. Because the business had a poor financial rating, T satisfied some of the obligations to employees and outside salespeople incurred by the former owners. T had no legal obligation to pay these debts, but felt this was the only way to keep salespeople and employees. The Second Court of Appeals found that the payments were necessary in that they were both appropriate and helpful.[6] However, the Court held that the payments were *not* ordinary but were in the nature of capital expenditures to build a reputation. Therefore, no deduction was allowed. ◆

An expense is ordinary if it is normal, usual, or customary in the type of business conducted by the taxpayer and is not capital in nature.[7] However, an expense need not be recurring to be deductible as ordinary.

EXAMPLE 3

T engaged in a mail-order business. The post office judged that his advertisements were false and misleading. Under a fraud order, the post office stamped "fraudulent" on all letters addressed to T's business and returned them to the senders. T spent $30,000 on legal fees in an unsuccessful attempt to force the post office to stop. The legal fees (though not recurring) were ordinary business expenses because they were normal, usual, or customary in the circumstances.[8] ◆

The Regulations under § 212 require that expenses bear a reasonable and proximate relationship to the production or collection of income or to the management, conservation, or maintenance of property held for the production of income.[9]

EXAMPLE 4

W owns a small portfolio of investments, including 10 shares of T, Inc., common stock worth $1,000. W incurred $350 in travel expenses to attend the annual shareholders' meeting at which she voted her 10 shares against the current management group. No deduction is permitted because a 10-share investment is insignificant in value in relation to the travel expenses incurred.[10] ◆

Reasonableness Requirement. The Code refers to reasonableness solely with respect to salaries and other compensation for services.[11] The courts, however, have held that for any business expense to be ordinary and necessary it must also be reasonable in amount.[12]

What constitutes reasonableness is a question of fact. If an expense is unreasonable, the excess amount is not allowed as a deduction. The question of reasonableness generally arises with respect to closely held corporations where there is no separation of ownership and management. In such cases, transactions between the shareholders and the company may result in the disallowance of deductions for excessive salaries and rent expense paid by the corporation. However, the courts will view an unusually large salary in light of all relevant circumstances and may find that the salary is reasonable despite its size.[13] If

6. *Dunn and McCarthy, Inc. v. Comm.*, 43–2 USTC ¶9688, 31 AFTR 1043, 139 F.2d 242 (CA–2, 1943).
7. *Deputy v. DuPont*, 40–1 USTC ¶9161, 23 AFTR 808, 60 S.Ct. 363 (USSC, 1940).
8. *Comm. v. Heininger*, 44–1 USTC ¶9109, 31 AFTR 783, 64 S.Ct. 249 (USSC, 1943).
9. Reg. § 1.212–1(d).
10. *J. Raymond Dyer*, 36 T.C. 456 (1961).
11. § 162(a)(1).
12. *Comm. v. Lincoln Electric Co.*, 49–2 USTC ¶9388, 38 AFTR 411, 176 F.2d 815 (CA–6, 1949).
13. *Kennedy, Jr. v. Comm.*, 82–1 USTC ¶9186, 49 AFTR2d 82–628, 671 F.2d 167 (CA–6, 1982), *rev'g* 72 T.C. 793 (1979).

excessive payments for salaries and rents are closely related to the percentage of stock owned by the recipients, the payments are generally treated as dividends to the shareholders. Consequently, they are not deductible by the corporation.[14] However, deductions for reasonable salaries will not be disallowed solely because the corporation has paid insubstantial portions of its earnings as dividends to its shareholders.[15]

EXAMPLE 5

XYZ Corporation, a closely held corporation, is owned equally by X, Y, and Z. The company has been highly profitable for several years and has not paid dividends. X, Y, and Z are key officers of the company, and each receives a salary of $200,000. Salaries for similar positions in comparable companies average only $100,000. Amounts paid to X, Y, and Z in excess of $100,000 may be deemed unreasonable, and a total of $300,000 in salary deductions may be disallowed. The excess amounts may be treated as dividends rather than salary income to X, Y, and Z because the payments are proportional to stock ownership. Salaries are deductible by the corporation, but dividends are not. ◆

Business and Nonbusiness Losses

Section 165 provides for a deduction for losses not compensated for by insurance. As a general rule, deductible losses of individual taxpayers are limited to those incurred in a trade or business or in a transaction entered into for profit. However, individuals are also allowed to deduct losses that are the result of a casualty. Casualty losses include, but are not limited to, fire, storm, shipwreck, and theft (see Chapter 8 for a further discussion of this topic). Deductible personal casualty losses are reduced by $100 per casualty, and the aggregate of all casualty losses is reduced by 10 percent of AGI. A personal casualty loss is an itemized deduction. See Concept Summary 6–3 for the classification of expenses.

Reporting Procedures

All deductions *for* and *from* AGI wind up on pages 1 and 2 of Form 1040. All deductions *for* AGI are reported on page 1. The last line on page 1 is adjusted gross income.

The first item on page 2 is adjusted gross income. Itemized deductions (deductions *from*) AGI are entered next, followed by the deduction for dependency exemptions. The result is taxable income.

Most of the deductions *for* AGI on page 1 originate on supporting schedules. Examples include business expenses (Schedule C) and rent, royalty, partnership, and fiduciary deductions (Schedule E). Other deductions *for* AGI, such as IRAs, Keogh retirement plans, and alimony, are entered directly on page 1 of Form 1040. All deductions *from* AGI on page 2 are carried over from Schedule A. Some Schedule A deductions originate on other forms. Examples include home mortgage interest, investment interest, noncash charitable contributions in excess of $500, casualty losses, moving expenses, and unreimbursed employee expenses.

Form 1040 becomes a summary of other schedules and forms, pulling together the detailed information from the other forms and schedules. See Concept Summary 6–1.

14. Reg. § 1.162–8.

15. Rev.Rul. 79–8, 1979–1 C.B. 92.

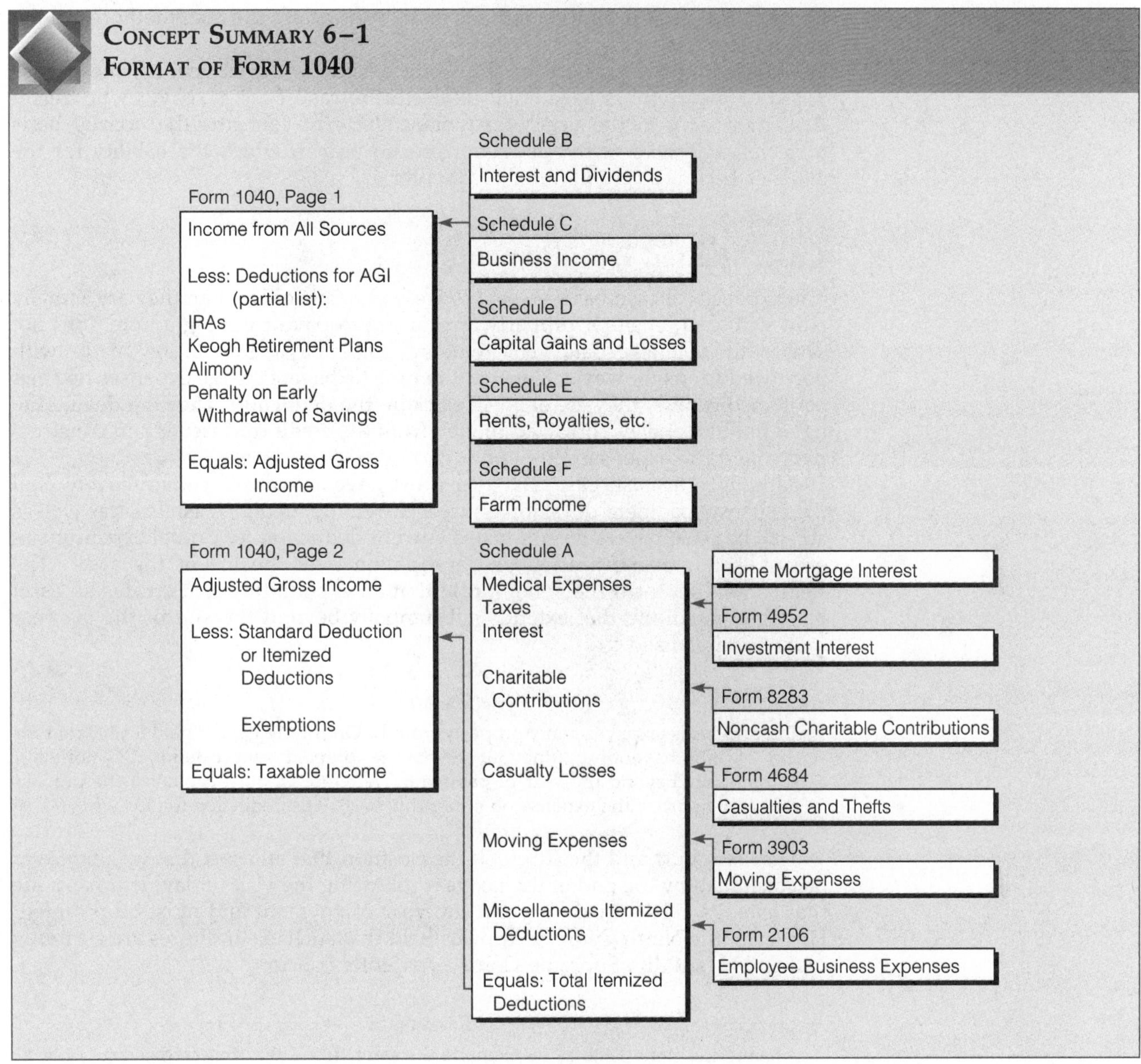

Importance of Taxpayer's Method of Accounting

Deductions and Losses—Timing of Expense Recognition

◆

A taxpayer's method of accounting is a major factor in determining taxable income. The method used determines when an item is includible in income and when an item is deductible on the tax return. Usually the taxpayer's regular method of recordkeeping is used for income tax purposes.[16] The taxing authorities do not require uniformity among all taxpayers, but they do require that the method used clearly reflect income and that items be handled consis-

16. § 446(a).

tently.[17] The most common methods of accounting are the cash method and the accrual method.

Throughout the portions of the Code dealing with deductions, the phrase "paid or incurred" is used. *Paid* refers to the cash basis taxpayer who gets a deduction only in the year of payment. *Incurred* concerns the accrual basis taxpayer who obtains the deduction in the year in which the liability for the expense becomes certain (refer to Chapter 4).

Cash Method Requirements

The expenses of cash basis taxpayers are deductible only when they are actually paid with cash or other property. Promising to pay or issuing a note does not satisfy the actually paid requirement.[18] The payment can be made with borrowed funds, however. Thus, at the time taxpayers charge expenses on their bank credit cards, they are allowed to claim the deduction. They are deemed to have simultaneously borrowed money from the credit card issuer and constructively paid the expenses.[19]

Although the cash basis taxpayer must have actually or constructively paid the expense, payment does not assure a current deduction. Cash basis as well as accrual basis taxpayers cannot take a current deduction for capital expenditures except through amortization or depreciation over the life of the asset. The Regulations set forth the general rule that an expenditure that creates an asset having a useful life that extends substantially beyond the end of the tax year must be capitalized.[20]

EXAMPLE 6

T, a cash basis taxpayer, rents property from L. On July 1, 1993, T paid $2,400 rent for the 24 months ending June 30, 1995. The prepaid rent extends 18 months—substantially beyond the year of payment. Therefore, T must capitalize the prepaid rent and amortize the expense on a monthly basis. His deduction for 1993 is $600. ◆

The Tax Court and the IRS took the position that an asset that will expire or be consumed by the end of the tax year following the year of payment has a life that extends substantially beyond the year of payment and must be prorated. However, the Ninth Court of Appeals held that such expenditures are currently deductible, and the Supreme Court apparently concurs.[21]

EXAMPLE 7

Assume the same facts as in Example 6 except that T was required to pay only 12 months rent in 1993. T paid $1,200 on July 1, 1993. The entire $1,200 would be deductible in 1993. ◆

The payment, however, must be required (not a voluntary prepayment) to obtain the current deduction under the one-year rule.[22]

---

17. §§ 446(b) and (e); Reg. § 1.446–1(a)(2).
18. *Page v. Rhode Island Trust Co., Exr.*, 37–1 USTC ¶9138, 19 AFTR 105, 88 F.2d 192 (CA–1, 1937).
19. Rev.Rul. 78–39, 1978–1 C.B. 73. See also Rev.Rul. 80–335, 1980–2 C.B. 170, which applies to pay-by-phone arrangements.
20. Reg. § 1.461–1(a).
21. *Zaninovich v. Comm.*, 80–1 USTC ¶9342, 45 AFTR2d 80–1442, 616 F.2d 429 (CA–9, 1980), *rev'g* 69 T.C. 605 (1978). Cited by the Supreme Court in *Hillsboro National Bank v. Comm.*, 83–1 USTC ¶9229, 51 AFTR2d 83–874, 103 S.Ct. 1134 (USSC, 1983).
22. *Bonaire Development Co. v. Comm.*, 82–2 USTC ¶9428, 50 AFTR2d 82–5167, 679 F.2d 159 (CA–9, 1982).

To obtain a current deduction for an asset, the taxpayer must also demonstrate that allowing the current deduction will not result in a material distortion of income. Generally, the deduction will be allowed if the item is recurring (e.g., rent) or was made for a business purpose (rather than to manipulate income).[23]

As Chapter 18 explains, not all taxpayers are allowed to use the cash method.[24]

Accrual Method Requirements

The period in which an accrual basis taxpayer can deduct an expense is determined by applying the economic performance test.[25] This test is met only when the service, property, or use of property giving rise to the liability is actually performed for, provided to, or used by the taxpayer.[26]

Example 8

On December 15, 1992, a rusted water main broke and flooded the business premises of T, an accrual basis calendar year taxpayer. An outside firm surveyed the damage and estimated the cleanup fee at $6,000. T signed a contract (paying 20% down) on December 20, 1992. Because of the holidays, the cleanup crew did not start work until January 2, 1993. T cannot deduct the $1,200 until 1993, when the services are performed. ◆

An exception to the economic performance requirements allows certain recurring items to be deducted if the following conditions are met:

- The items are treated consistently.
- Either they are not material in amount or accrual results in better matching of income and expenses.
- The all-events test is met. This test is met when all the events have occurred that determine the fact of the liability and the amount of the liability can be determined with reasonable accuracy.[27]
- Economic performance occurs within a reasonable period but not more than 8½ months after year-end.[28]

Example 9

T, an accrual basis calendar year taxpayer, entered into a monthly maintenance contract during the year. T makes a monthly accrual at the end of every month for this service and pays the fee sometime between the first and fifteenth of the following month when services are performed. The amount involved is immaterial, and all other tests are met. The December 1992 accrual is deductible even though the service is performed on January 12, 1993. ◆

Example 10

T, an accrual basis calendar year taxpayer, shipped merchandise sold on December 30, 1992, via Greyhound Van Lines on January 2, 1993, and paid the freight charges at that time. Since T reported the sale of the merchandise in 1992, the shipping charge should also be deductible in 1992. This procedure results in a better matching of income and expenses. ◆

---

23. *Keller v. Comm.*, 84–1 USTC ¶9194, 53 AFTR2d 84–663, 725 F.2d 1173 (CA–8, 1984), *aff'g* 79 T.C. 7 (1982).

24. § 448.

25. § 461(h)(1).

26. §§ 461(h)(2)(A) and (B).

27. Reg. § 1.461–1(a)(2).

28. § 461(h)(3)(A).

Reserves for estimated expenses (frequently employed for financial accounting purposes) generally are not allowed for tax purposes because the economic performance test cannot be satisfied.

EXAMPLE 11

T Airlines is required by Federal law to conduct tests of its engines after 3,000 flying hours. Aircraft cannot return to flight until the tests have been conducted. An unrelated aircraft maintenance company does all of the company's tests for $1,500 per engine. For financial reporting purposes, the company accrues an expense based upon $.50 per hour of flight and credits an allowance account. The actual amounts paid for maintenance are offset against the allowance account. However, for tax purposes, the economic performance test is not satisfied until the work has been done. ◆

DISALLOWANCE POSSIBILITIES

The tax law provides for the disallowance of certain types of expenses. Without specific restrictions in the tax law, taxpayers might attempt to deduct certain items that in reality are personal expenditures. For example, specific tax rules are provided to determine whether an expenditure is for trade or business purposes and therefore deductible, or related to a personal hobby and therefore nondeductible.

Certain disallowance provisions are a codification or extension of prior court decisions. For example, the courts had denied deductions for payments considered to be in violation of public policy. Thus, the tax law was changed to provide specific authority for the disallowance of these deductions. Detailed discussions of specific disallowance provisions in the tax law follow.

Public Policy Limitation

Justification for Denying Deductions. The courts developed the principle that a payment that is in violation of public policy is not a necessary expense and is not deductible.[29]

A bribe or fine, for example, may be appropriate, helpful, and even contribute to the profitability of an activity. The courts held, however, that to allow such expenses would frustrate clearly defined public policy. A deduction would dilute the effect of the penalty since the government would be indirectly subsidizing a taxpayer's wrongdoing.

The IRS was always free to restrict deductions if, in its view, the expenses were contrary to public policy. It was often necessary for taxpayers to go to court to determine if their expense violated public policy.

Recognizing that the public policy doctrine could be arbitrarily applied in cases where no clear definition had emerged, Congress enacted legislation that attempts to limit the use of the doctrine. Under the legislation, deductions are disallowed for certain specific types of expenditures that are considered contrary to public policy:

- Bribes and kickbacks (in the case of foreign bribes and kickbacks, only if the payments violate the U.S. Foreign Corrupt Practices Act of 1977).
- Fines and penalties paid to a government for violation of law.

29. *Tank Truck Rentals, Inc. v. Comm.*, 58–1 USTC ¶9366, 1 AFTR2d 1154, 78 S.Ct. 507 (USSC, 1958).

EXAMPLE 12

Y Corporation, a moving company, consistently loads its trucks with weights in excess of the limits allowed by state law because the additional revenue more than offsets the fines levied. The fines are for a violation of public policy and are not deductible. ◆

- Two-thirds of the treble damage payments made to claimants resulting from violation of the antitrust law.[30]

Under the Code, no deduction is permitted for a kickback that is illegal under state law (if the state law is generally enforced) and that subjects the payer to a criminal penalty or the loss of license or privilege to engage in a trade or business.

EXAMPLE 13

During the year T, an insurance salesman, paid $5,000 to U, a real estate broker. The payment represented 20% of the commissions earned by T from customers referred by U. Under state law, the splitting of commissions by an insurance salesperson is an act of misconduct that could warrant a revocation of the salesperson's license. The payments of $5,000 by T to U are not deductible provided the state law is generally enforced. ◆

Legal Expenses Incurred in Defense of Civil or Criminal Penalties. Generally, legal expenses are deductible *for* AGI as ordinary and necessary business expenses if incurred in connection with a trade or business. Legal expenses may also be deductible *for* AGI as expenses incurred in conjunction with rental property held for the production of income. Legal expenses are deductible *from* AGI if they are for fees for tax advice relative to the preparation of the taxpayer's income tax returns. These tax-related legal fees are itemized deductions (discussed more fully in Chapter 11) that are deductible only to the extent that they exceed 2 percent of AGI.

Personal legal expenses are not deductible. Legal fees incurred in connection with a criminal defense are deductible if the crime is associated with the taxpayer's trade or business.[31] To deduct legal expenses, the taxpayer must be able to show that the origin and character of the claim are directly related to a trade or business or an income-producing activity. Otherwise, the legal expenses are personal and nondeductible.

EXAMPLE 14

T, a financial officer of X Corporation, incurred legal expenses in connection with the defense in a criminal indictment for evasion of X Corporation's income taxes. T may deduct her legal expenses because she is deemed to be in the trade or business of being an executive. The legal action impairs her ability to conduct this business activity.[32] ◆

Expenses Relating to an Illegal Business. The usual expenses of operating an illegal business (e.g., a numbers racket) are deductible.[33] However, § 162 disallows a deduction for fines, bribes to public officials, illegal kickbacks, and other illegal payments.

---

30. §§ 162(c), (f), and (g).

31. *Comm. v. Tellier*, 66–1 USTC ¶9319, 17 AFTR2d 633, 86 S.Ct. 1118 (USSC, 1966).

32. Rev.Rul. 68–662, 1968–2 C.B. 69.

33. *Comm. v. Sullivan*, 58–1 USTC ¶9368, 1 AFTR2d 1158, 78 S.Ct. 512 (USSC, 1958).

EXAMPLE 15

S owns and operates an illegal gambling establishment. In connection with this activity, he had the following expenses during the year:

Rent	$ 60,000
Payoffs to the police	40,000
Depreciation on equipment	100,000
Wages	140,000
Interest	30,000
Criminal fines	50,000
Illegal kickbacks	10,000
Total	$430,000

All of the usual expenses (rent, depreciation, wages, and interest) are deductible; payoffs, fines, and kickbacks are not deductible. Of the $430,000 spent, therefore, $330,000 is deductible and $100,000 is not. ◆

An exception applies to expenses incurred in illegal trafficking in drugs.[34] Drug dealers are not allowed a deduction for ordinary and necessary business expenses incurred in their business. However, in arriving at gross income from the business, dealers may reduce total sales by the cost of goods sold.[35] In this regard, no distinction is made between legal and illegal businesses.

Political Contributions and Lobbying Activities

Political Contributions. Generally, no business deduction is permitted for direct or indirect payments for political purposes.[36] Historically, the government has been reluctant to accord favorable tax treatment to business expenditures for political purposes. Allowing deductions might encourage abuses and enable businesses to have undue influence upon the political process.

Lobbying Expenditures. A deduction is allowed for certain expenses incurred to influence legislation,[37] provided the proposed legislation is of direct interest to the taxpayer. A direct interest exists if the legislation will, or may reasonably be expected to, affect the trade or business of the taxpayer. Dues and expenses paid to an organization (e.g., labor union, trade association) that consists of individuals with a common direct interest in proposed legislation are deductible in proportion to the organization's allowable legislative activity. A common direct interest exists where an organization consists of persons with the same direct interests in legislation or proposed legislation. However, no deduction is allowed for expenses incurred to influence the public on legislative matters[38] or for any political campaign.

EXAMPLE 16

T, a contractor, drove to his state capitol to testify against proposed legislation that would affect building codes. T believes that the proposed legislation is unnecessary

34. § 280E.
35. Reg. § 1.61–3(a).
36. § 276.
37. § 162(e). Regulations relating to lobbying expenditures and other attempts to influence legislation are at Reg. § 1.162–20.
38. Reg. § 1.162–20(c)(4) establishes a three-factor test for determining when a *communication* (e.g., a news release, an advertisement) is an attempt to influence the general public.

and not in the best interest of his company. The expenses are deductible because the legislation is of direct interest to T's company. If T later travels to another city to speak at a Lion's Club meeting concerning the legislation, his travel expenses are not deductible. The expenses are incurred to influence the public on legislative matters. ◆

Investigation of a Business

Investigation expenses are expenses paid or incurred to determine the feasibility of entering a new business or expanding an existing business. They include such costs as travel, engineering and architectural surveys, marketing reports, and various legal and accounting services. How such expenses are treated for tax purposes depends on a number of variables, including the following:

- The current business, if any, of the taxpayer.
- The nature of the business being investigated.
- The extent to which the investigation has proceeded.
- Whether or not the acquisition actually takes place.

If the taxpayer is in a business the same as or similar to that being investigated, all expenses in this connection are deductible in the year paid or incurred. The tax result is the same whether or not the taxpayer acquires the business being investigated.[39]

EXAMPLE 17

T, an accrual basis sole proprietor, owns and operates three motels in Georgia. In 1993, T incurs expenses of $8,500 in investigating the possibility of acquiring several additional motels located in South Carolina. The $8,500 is deductible in 1993 whether or not T acquires the motels in South Carolina. ◆

When the taxpayer is not in a business that is the same as or similar to the one being investigated, the tax result usually depends on whether the new business is acquired. If the business is not acquired, all investigation expenses generally become nondeductible.[40]

EXAMPLE 18

R, a retired merchant, incurs expenses in traveling from Rochester, New York, to California to investigate the feasibility of acquiring several auto care centers. If no acquisition takes place (the project is abandoned), none of the expenses are deductible. ◆

If a taxpayer is in a business that is not the same as or similar to the business being investigated, and the investigation effort actually leads to the acquisition of a new business, the expenses must be capitalized. At the election of the taxpayer, the expenses may be amortized over a period of 60 months or more.[41]

Hobby Losses

Deductions for business or investment expenses are permitted only if the taxpayer can show that the business or investment activity was entered into for

39. *York v. Comm.*, 58–2 USTC ¶9952, 2 AFTR2d 6178, 261 F.2d 421 (CA–4, 1958).

40. Rev.Rul. 57–418, 1957–2 C.B. 143; *Morton Frank*, 20 T.C. 511 (1953); and *Dwight A. Ward*, 20 T.C. 332 (1953).

41. § 195.

the purpose of making a profit. Certain activities may have profit-seeking or personal attributes, depending upon individual circumstances (e.g., raising horses and operating a farm used as a weekend residence). Personal losses are not deductible, although losses attributable to profit-seeking activities may be deducted and used to offset a taxpayer's other income. For this reason, the tax law limits the deductibility of hobby losses.

General Rules. If a taxpayer (an individual or an S corporation) can show that an activity has been conducted with the intent to earn a profit, any losses from the activity are fully deductible. The hobby loss rules apply only if the activity is not engaged in for profit. Hobby expenses are deductible only to the extent of hobby income.[42]

The Regulations stipulate that the following nine factors should be considered in determining whether an activity is profit-seeking or a hobby:[43]

- Whether the activity is conducted in a businesslike manner.
- The expertise of the taxpayers or their advisers.
- The time and effort expended.
- The expectation that the assets of the activity will appreciate in value.
- The previous success of the taxpayer in the conduct of similar activities.
- The history of income or losses from the activity.
- The relationship of profits earned to losses incurred.
- The financial status of the taxpayer (e.g., if the taxpayer does not have substantial amounts of other income, this may indicate that the activity is engaged in for profit).
- Elements of personal pleasure or recreation in the activity.

Presumptive Rule of § 183. The Code provides a rebuttable presumption that an activity is profit-seeking if it shows a profit in at least three of any five consecutive years (two of seven years for activities involving horses) ending with the taxable year in question.[44] If these profitability tests are met, the activity is presumed to be a trade or business rather than a personal hobby. In effect, the IRS bears the burden of proving that the activity is personal rather than trade or business related.

EXAMPLE 19

N, an executive for a large corporation, is paid a salary of $200,000. His wife is a collector of antiques. Several years ago, she opened an antique shop in a local shopping center and spends most of her time buying and selling antiques. She occasionally earns a small profit from this activity but more frequently incurs substantial losses. If the losses are business related, they are fully deductible against N's salary income on a joint return. In resolving this issue, consider the following:

- Initially determine whether the antique activity has met the three-out-of-five years profit test.
- If the presumption is not met, the activity may nevertheless qualify as a business if the taxpayer can show that the intent is to engage in a profit-seeking activity. It is not necessary to show actual profits.
- Attempt to fit the operation within the nine criteria prescribed in the Regulations and listed above. These criteria are the factors considered in trying to rebut the § 183 presumption. ◆

42. § 183(b)(2).
43. Reg. §§ 1.183–2(b)(1) through (9).
44. § 183(d).

If an activity is deemed to be a hobby, the expenses are deductible only to the extent of the income from the hobby. These expenses must be deducted in the following order:

- Amounts deductible under other Code sections without regard to the nature of the activity, such as property taxes.
- Amounts deductible under other Code sections if the activity had been engaged in for profit, but only if those amounts do not affect adjusted basis (e.g., maintenance).
- Amounts deductible under other Code sections if the activity had been engaged in for profit, which affect adjusted basis (e.g., depreciation).[45]

These deductions are deductible *from* AGI (as itemized deductions to the extent they exceed 2 percent of AGI).[46]

EXAMPLE 20

T, the vice president of an oil company, has AGI of $80,000. He decides to pursue painting in his spare time. He uses a home studio, comprising 10% of the home's square footage. During the current year, T incurs the following expenses:

Frames	$ 350
Art supplies	300
Fees paid to models	1,000
Home studio expenses:	
Total property taxes	900
Total home mortgage interest	10,000
Depreciation on 10% of home	500
Total home maintenance and utilities	3,600

During the year, T sold paintings for a total of $3,200. If the activity is held to be a hobby, T is allowed deductions as follows:

Gross income		$3,200
Deduct: Taxes and interest (10% of $10,900)		1,090
Remainder		$2,110
Deduct: Frames	$ 350	
Art supplies	300	
Models' fees	1,000	
Maintenance and utilities (10%)	360	2,010
Remainder		$ 100
Depreciation ($500, but limited to $100)		100
Net income		$ -0-

T includes the $3,200 of income in AGI, making his AGI $83,200. The taxes and interest are itemized deductions, deductible in full. The remaining $2,110 of expenses are reduced by 2% of T's AGI ($1,664) so the net deduction is $446. Since the property taxes and home mortgage interest are deductible anyway, the net effect is a $2,754 ($3,200 less $446) increase in taxable income. ◆

EXAMPLE 21

If T's activity in Example 20 is held to be a business, he could deduct expenses totaling $2,510 ($2,010 plus $500 of depreciation) *for* AGI, in addition to the $1,090 of taxes and

45. § 183(b)(2) and Reg. § 1.183–1(b)(1).

46. § 183(b) and Rev. Rul. 75–14, 1975–1 C.B. 90.

interest. All expenses would be trade or business expenses deductible *for* AGI. His reduction in AGI would be as follows:

Gross income		$3,200
Less: Taxes and interest	$1,090	
Other business expenses	2,010	
Depreciation	500	3,600
Reduction in AGI		$ (400)

◆

Rental of Vacation Homes

Restrictions on the deductions allowed for part-year rentals of personal residences (including vacation homes) were written into the law to prevent taxpayers from deducting essentially personal expenses as rental losses. Before these restrictions were added, many taxpayers who had vacation homes tried to treat the homes as rental property and generate rental losses as deductions *for* AGI. For example, a summer cabin would be rented (or held out for rent) for 2 months per year, used for vacationing for 1 month, and left vacant the rest of the year. The taxpayer would then deduct 11 months' depreciation, maintenance, etc., as rental expenses, resulting in a rental loss. Section 280A eliminates this treatment by allowing deductions on residences used primarily for personal purposes only to the extent of income generated. Thus, only a break-even situation is allowed; no losses can be deducted.

There are three possible tax treatments for residences used for both personal and rental purposes. The treatment depends upon the relative time the residence is used for personal purposes versus rental use.

Primarily Personal Use. If the residence is rented for less than 15 days per year, it is treated as a personal residence. The rent income is excluded from income, and mortgage interest and real estate taxes are allowed as itemized deductions, as with any personal residence.[47] No other expenses (e.g., depreciation, utilities, maintenance) are deductible.

EXAMPLE 22

T owns a vacation cottage on the lake. During the current year, she rented it for $1,600 for two weeks, lived in it two months, and left it vacant the remainder of the year. The year's expenses amounted to $6,000 interest expense, $500 property taxes, $1,500 utilities and maintenance, and $2,400 depreciation. Since the property was not rented for at least 15 days, the income is excluded, the interest and property tax expenses are itemized deductions, and the remaining expenses are nondeductible personal expenses. ◆

Primarily Rental Use. If the residence is not used for personal purposes for more than the greater of (1) 14 days or (2) 10 percent of the total days rented, the residence is treated as rental property.[48] The expenses must be allocated between personal and rental days if there are any personal use days during the year. In that case, the deduction of the expenses allocated to rental days can exceed rent income and result in a rental loss. The loss may be deductible under the passive loss rules (discussed in Chapter 7).

EXAMPLE 23

Assume T in Example 22 had rented the cottage for 120 days. The cottage is primarily rental if she did not use it for personal purposes for more than 14 days. ◆

47. § 280A(g).

48. § 280A(d) and Prop.Reg. § 1.280A–3(c).

EXAMPLE 24

Assume T in Example 22 had rented the cottage for 200 days. She could use it for personal use for no more than 20 days (10% of the rental days) for it to be primarily rental. ◆

EXAMPLE 25

Assume that T in Example 22 used the cottage for 12 days and rented it for 48 days for $4,800. Since she did not use the cottage for more than 14 days, the expenses must be allocated between personal and rental days. The cottage is treated as rental property.

	Percentage of Use	
	Rental 80%	**Personal 20%**
Income	$4,800	$ -0-
Expenses		
Interest ($6,000)	$4,800	$1,200
Property taxes ($500)	400	100
Utilities and maintenance ($1,500)	1,200	300
Depreciation ($2,400)	1,920	480
Total expenses	$8,320	$2,080
Rental loss	($3,520)	$ -0-

T deducts the $3,520 rental loss *for* AGI (assuming she meets the passive loss rules, discussed in Chapter 7). She also has itemized interest of $1,200 and taxes of $100. The portion of utilities and maintenance and depreciation attributable to personal use is not deductible. ◆

Personal/Rental Use. If the residence is rented for 15 or more days *and* is used for personal purposes for more than the greater of (1) 14 days or (2) 10 percent of the total days rented, it is treated as a personal/rental residence, and expenses are allowed only to the extent of income.

EXAMPLE 26

Assume that T in Example 22 had rented the property for 30 days and lived in it for 30 days. The residence is classified as personal/rental property since T used it more than 14 days and rented it for more than 14 days. The expenses must be allocated, and the rental expenses are allowed only to the extent of rent income. ◆

If a residence is classified as personal/rental property, the expenses that are deductible anyway (e.g., real estate taxes) must be deducted first. If a positive net income results, otherwise nondeductible expenses (e.g., maintenance, utilities, insurance) are allowed next. Finally, depreciation is allowed if any positive balance remains.

Expenses must be allocated between personal and rental days before the limits are applied. The courts have held that taxes and interest, which accrue ratably over the year, are allocated on the basis of 365 days.[49] The IRS, however, disagrees and allocates taxes and interest on the basis of total days of use.[50] Other expenses (utilities, maintenance, depreciation, etc.) are allocated on the basis of total days used.

49. *Bolton v. Comm.*, 82–2 USTC ¶9699, 51 AFTR2d 83–305, 694 F.2d 556 (CA–9, 1982).

50. Prop.Reg. § 1.280A–3(d)(4).

Example 27

S rents her vacation home for 60 days and lives in the home for 30 days. The limitations on personal/rental residences apply. S's gross rent income is $10,000. For the entire year (not a leap year), the real estate taxes are $2,190; S's mortgage interest expense is $10,220; utilities and maintenance expense equals $2,400; and depreciation is $9,000. Using the IRS approach, these amounts are deductible in this specific order:

Gross income	$10,000
Deduct: Taxes and interest (60/90 × $12,410)	8,273
Remainder to apply to rental operating expenses and depreciation	$ 1,727
Deduct: Utilities and maintenance (60/90 × $2,400)	1,600
Balance	$ 127
Deduct: Depreciation (60/90 × $9,000 = $6,000 but limited to above balance)	127
Net income	$ -0-

The nonrental use portion of taxes and interest ($4,137 in this case) is deductible if the taxpayer elects to itemize (see Chapter 11). The personal use portion of utilities, maintenance, and depreciation is not deductible in any case. Also note that the basis of the property is not reduced by the $5,873 depreciation not allowed ($6,000 − $127) because of the above limitation. (See Chapter 14 for a discussion of the reduction in basis for depreciation allowed or allowable.) ◆

Example 28

Using the court's approach in allocating property taxes and interest, S, in Example 27, would have this result:

Gross income	$10,000
Deduct: Taxes and interest (60/365 × $12,410)	2,040
Remainder to apply to rental operating expenses and depreciation	$ 7,960
Deduct: Utilities and maintenance (60/90 × $2,400)	1,600
Balance	$ 6,360
Deduct: Depreciation (60/90 × $9,000, but limited to $6,360)	6,000
Net rent income	$ 360

S can deduct $10,370 ($12,410 paid − $2,040 deducted as expense in computing rent income) of personal use interest and taxes. ◆

Note the contrasting results in Examples 27 and 28. The IRS's approach (Example 27) results in no rental gain or loss and an itemized deduction for taxes and interest of $4,137. In Example 28, S has net rent income of $360 and $10,370 of itemized deductions. The court's approach decreases her taxable income by $10,010 ($10,370 itemized deductions less $360 net rent income). The IRS's approach reduces her taxable income by only $4,137.

Example 29

Assume that S in Example 27 had not lived in the home at all during the year. The house is rental property. The rental loss is calculated as follows:

Gross income	$10,000
Expenses	
Taxes and interest	$12,410
Utilities and maintenance	2,400
Depreciation	9,000
Total expenses	$23,810
Rental loss	($13,810)

Whether any of the rental loss would be deductible depends upon whether S actively participated in the rental activity and met the other requirements for passive losses (discussed in Chapter 7). ◆

Conversion to Rental Property. Section 280A(d) resolves the problem of whether or not a taxpayer's *primary residence* is subject to the preceding rules if it is converted to rental property. The deduction for expenses of the property incurred during a qualified rental period is not subject to the personal use test of the vacation home rules. A qualified rental period is a consecutive period of 12 or more months. The period begins or ends in the taxable year in which the *residence* is rented or held for rental at a fair price. The residence must not be rented to a related party [as defined in § 267(c)(4)]. If the property is sold before 12 months, the qualified rental period is the actual time rented.

See Concept Summary 6–2 for a summary of the vacation home rules.

Expenditures Incurred for Taxpayer's Benefit or Taxpayer's Obligation

An expense must be incurred for the taxpayer's benefit or arise from the taxpayer's obligation. An individual cannot claim a tax deduction for the payment of the expenses of another individual.

EXAMPLE 30

During the current year, F pays the interest on his son, T's, home mortgage. Neither F nor T can take a deduction for the interest paid. F is not entitled to a deduction because the mortgage is not his obligation. T cannot claim a deduction because he did not pay the interest. The tax result would have been more favorable had F made a cash gift to T and let him pay the interest. The interest then could have been deducted by the son, and (depending upon other gifts and the amount involved) F might not have been liable for any gift taxes. A deduction would have been created with no cash difference to the family. ◆

One exception to this rule is the payment of medical expenses for a dependent. Such expenses are deductible by the payer.[51]

Disallowance of Personal Expenditures

Section 262 states that "except as otherwise expressly provided in this chapter, no deduction shall be allowed for personal, living, or family expenses." Thus, to justify a deduction, an individual must be able to identify a particular Section of the Code that sanctions the deduction (e.g., charitable contributions, medical expenses). Sometimes the character of a particular expenditure is not easily determined.

EXAMPLE 31

During the current year, H pays $1,500 in legal fees and court costs to obtain a divorce from his wife, W. Involved in the divorce action is a property settlement that concerns the disposition of income-producing property owned by H. In a similar situation, the Tax Court[52] held that H could not deduct any of the $1,500 costs. "Although fees primarily related to property division concerning his income-producing property, they weren't ordinary and necessary expenses paid for conservation or maintenance of property held for production of income. Legal fees incurred in defending against claims that arise from a taxpayer's marital relationship aren't deductible expenses regardless of possible consequences on taxpayer's income-producing property." ◆

---

51. § 213(a).

52. *Harry H. Goldberg*, 29 TCM 74, T.C.Memo., 1970–27.

The IRS has clarified the issue of the deduction of legal fees incurred in connection with a divorce.[53] To be deductible, an expense must relate solely to tax advice in a divorce proceeding. For example, legal fees attributable to the determination of dependency exemptions of children are deductible if the fees

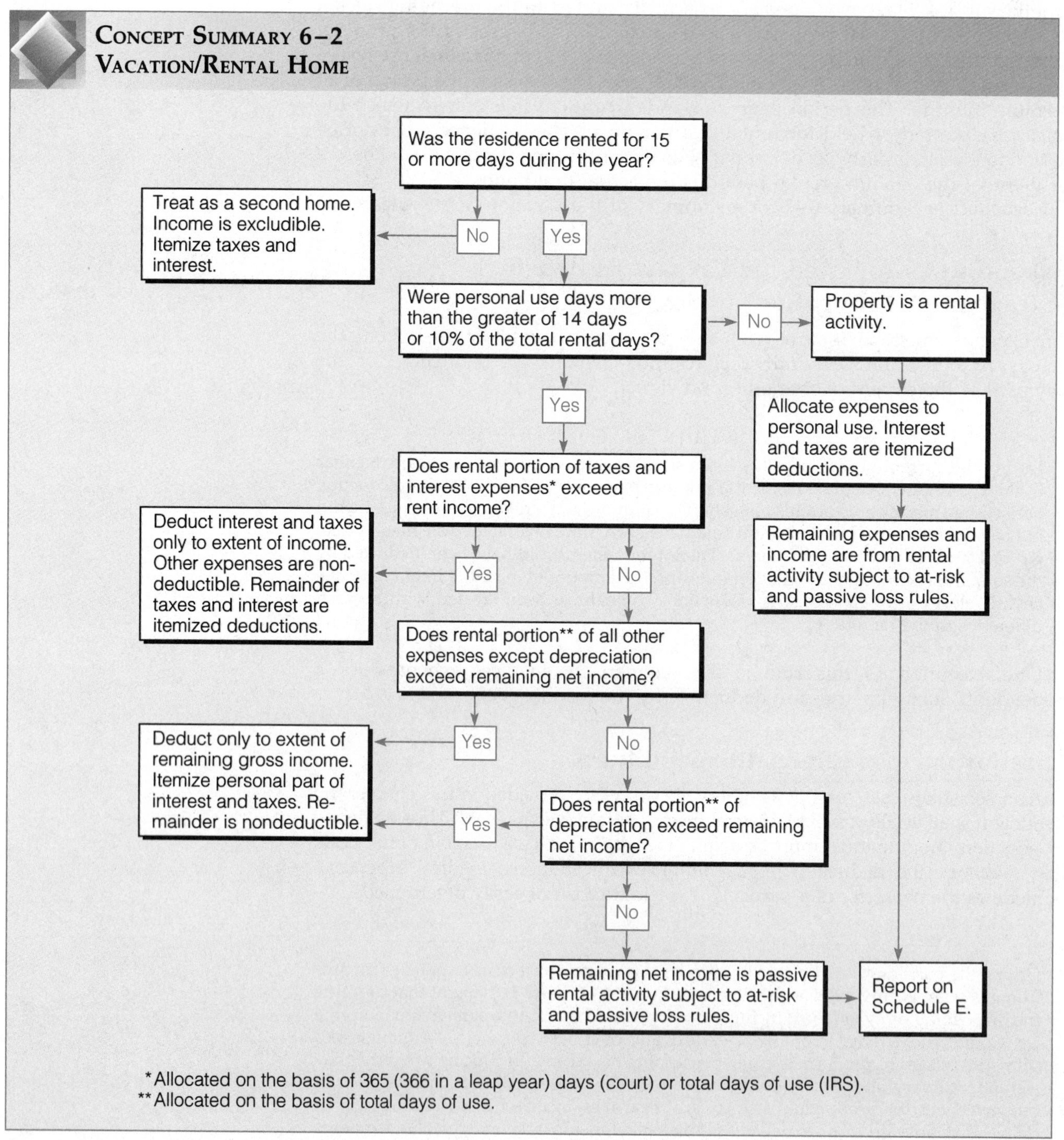

53. Rev.Rul. 72–545, 1972–2 C.B. 179.

are distinguishable from the general legal fees incurred in obtaining a divorce. Other examples are the costs of creating a trust to make periodic alimony payments and the determination of the tax consequences of a property settlement. Therefore, it is advisable to request an itemization of attorney's fees to substantiate a deduction for the tax-related amounts.

Disallowance of Deductions for Unrealized Losses

One of the basic concepts in the tax law is that a deduction can be taken only when a loss has actually been realized. For example, a drop in the market price of securities held by the taxpayer does not result in a loss until the securities are actually sold or exchanged at the lower price. Furthermore, any deductible loss is limited to the taxpayer's basis in the asset.

Disallowance of Deductions for Capital Expenditures

The Code specifically disallows a deduction for "any amount paid out for new buildings or for permanent improvements or betterments made to increase the value of any property or estate."[54] The Regulations further define capital expenditures to include those expenditures that add to the value or prolong the life of property or adapt the property to a new or different use.[55] Incidental repairs and maintenance of the property are not capital expenditures and can be deducted as ordinary and necessary business expenses. Repairing a roof is a deductible expense, but replacing a roof is a capital expenditure subject to depreciation deductions over its useful life. The tune-up of a delivery truck is an expense; a complete overhaul is probably a capital expenditure.

Exceptions. There are several exceptions to the general rule regarding capitalization of expenditures. Taxpayers can elect to expense certain mineral developmental costs and intangible drilling costs.[56] Certain farm capital expenditures (such as soil and water conservation) and certain research and experimental expenditures may be immediately expensed.[57]

In addition, § 179 permits an immediate write-off of certain amounts of depreciable property. These provisions are discussed more fully in Chapter 9.

Capitalization versus Expense. When an expenditure is capitalized rather than expensed, the deduction is at best deferred and at worst lost forever. Although an immediate tax benefit for a large cash expenditure is lost, the cost can be deducted in increments over a longer period of time. If the expenditure is for some improvement that has an ascertainable life, it can be capitalized and depreciated or amortized over that life. Costs that can be amortized include copyrights and patents. However, many other expenditures, such as land and payments made for goodwill, cannot be amortized or depreciated. Goodwill has an indeterminate life, and land is not a depreciable asset since its value generally does not decline.

EXAMPLE 32

T purchased a prime piece of land located in an apartment-zoned area. T paid $500,000 for the property, which had an old but usable apartment building on it. T immediately had the building demolished at a cost of $100,000. The $500,000 purchase price and the $100,000 demolition costs must be capitalized, and the basis of the land is $600,000.

54. § 263(a)(1).

55. Reg. § 1.263(a)–1(b).

56. §§ 263(c) and 616.

57. §§ 174, 175, and 180.

Since land is a nondepreciable asset, no deduction is allowed. More favorable tax treatment might result if T rented the apartments in the old building for a period of time to attempt to establish that there was no intent to demolish the building. If T's attempt is successful, it might be possible to allocate a substantial portion of the original purchase price of the property to the building (a depreciable asset). When the building is later demolished, any remaining adjusted basis can be deducted as an ordinary (§ 1231) loss. (See Chapter 17 for a discussion of the treatment of § 1231 assets.) ◆

Capitalization Elections. The treatment of most capital expenditures is not elective. However, in certain cases, a taxpayer may elect to capitalize a particular item *or* to expense it immediately. For example, § 266 allows some taxpayers (but not individuals, S corporations, or personal holding companies) an opportunity to capitalize certain "taxes and carrying charges." The election applies to carrying charges, interest on indebtedness, and certain taxes (such as property and employer-paid payroll taxes) paid during the construction period on realty or personalty. It does not matter whether the property is business or nonbusiness in nature.[58] A taxpayer may elect to capitalize some expenditures and not others. For example, one could elect to capitalize property taxes and expense interest on the construction indebtedness. A new election may be made for each project. One could elect to capitalize expenditures on a factory being constructed and expense the same type of items on a constructed machine. On unimproved and unproductive real estate (land held for later sale, for example), a new election must be made for each year.

Section 189 requires individuals, S corporations, and personal holding companies to capitalize construction period interest and taxes, subject to specific rules for amortizing such amounts (see Chapter 9). This Code Section was intended both to match expenses with income in accordance with the traditional accounting principle and to restrict tax shelter opportunities for individuals.

Transactions between Related Parties

The Code places restrictions on the recognition of gains and losses between related parties. Otherwise relationships created by birth, marriage, and business, would provide endless possibilities for engaging in financial transactions that would produce tax savings with no real economic substance or change. For example, to create an artificial loss, a wife could sell property to her husband at a loss and deduct the loss on their joint return, while her husband could hold the asset indefinitely. A complex set of laws has been designed to eliminate such possibilities.

Losses. The Code provides for the disallowance of any "losses from sales or exchanges of property . . . directly or indirectly" between related parties.[59] When the property is subsequently sold to a nonrelated party, any gain recognized is reduced by the loss previously disallowed.

EXAMPLE 33

F sells common stock with a basis of $1,000 to his son, T, for $800. T sells the stock several years later for $1,100. F's $200 loss is disallowed upon the sale to T, and only $100 of gain is taxable to T upon the subsequent sale. ◆

EXAMPLE 34

F sells common stock with a basis of $1,000 to his son, T, for $800. T sells the stock to an unrelated party for $900. T's gain of $100 is not recognized because of F's previously

58. Reg. § 1.266–1(b).

59. § 267(a)(1).

disallowed loss of $200. Note that the offset may result in only partial tax benefit upon the subsequent sale. If the property had not been transferred to T, F could have recognized a $100 loss upon the subsequent sale to the unrelated party ($1,000 basis − $900 selling price). ◆

EXAMPLE 35

F sells common stock with a basis of $1,000 to an unrelated third party for $800. F's son repurchased the same stock in the market on the same day for $800. The $200 loss is not allowed because the transaction is an indirect sale between related parties.[60] ◆

Unpaid Expenses and Interest. Section 267 also prevents related taxpayers from engaging in tax avoidance schemes in which one related taxpayer uses the accrual method of accounting and the other is on the cash basis. For example, an accrual basis closely held corporation could borrow funds from a cash basis individual shareholder. At the end of the year, the corporation would accrue and deduct the interest, but the cash basis lender would not recognize interest income since no interest had been paid. Section 267 specifically defers the deduction of the accruing taxpayer until the recipient taxpayer must include it in income (when actually paid to the cash basis taxpayer).[61] The rule applies to interest as well as other expenses, such as salaries and bonuses.

Relationships and Constructive Ownership. Section 267 operates to disallow losses and defer deductions only between related parties. Losses or deductions generated by similar transactions with an unrelated party are allowed. Related parties include the following:[62]

- Brothers and sisters (whether by the whole or half blood), spouse, ancestors (parents, grandparents), and lineal descendants (children, grandchildren) of the taxpayer.
- A corporation owned more than 50 percent (directly or indirectly) by the taxpayer.
- Two corporations that are members of a controlled group.
- A series of other complex relationships between trusts, corporations, and individual taxpayers.

The law provides that constructive ownership rules are applied to determine whether the taxpayers are related.[63] These rules state that stock owned by certain relatives or related entities is deemed to be owned by the taxpayer for purposes of applying the loss and expense deduction disallowance provisions. For example, a taxpayer is deemed to own not only his or her stock but the stock owned by his or her lineal descendants, ancestors, brothers and sisters or half-brothers and half-sisters, and spouse. The taxpayer is also deemed to own his or her proportionate share of stock owned by any partnership, corporation, estate, or trust of which he or she is a member. Additionally, an individual is deemed to own any stock owned, directly or indirectly, by his or her partner. However, constructive ownership by an individual of the partnership's and the other partner's shares does not extend to the individual's spouse or other relatives.

EXAMPLE 36

The stock of V Corporation is owned 20% by T, 30% by T's father, 30% by T's mother, and 20% by T's sister. On July 1 of the current year, T loaned $10,000 to V Corporation

60. *McWilliams v. Comm.*, 47–1 USTC ¶9289, 35 AFTR 1184, 67 S.Ct. 1477 (USSC, 1947).

61. § 267(a)(2).

62. § 267(b).

63. § 267(c).

at 11% annual interest, principal and interest payable on demand. For tax purposes, V Corporation uses the accrual basis, and T uses the cash basis. Both are on a calendar year. Since T is deemed to own the 80% owned by her parents and sister, she constructively owns 100% of V Corporation. If the corporation accrues the interest within the taxable year, no deduction can be taken until payment is made to T. ◆

Substantiation Requirements

The tax law is built on a voluntary system. Taxpayers file their tax returns, report income and take deductions to which they are entitled, and pay their taxes through withholding or estimated tax payments during the year. The taxpayer carries the burden of proof for substantiating expenses deducted on the returns and thus must retain adequate records. Upon audit, the IRS will disallow any undocumented or unsubstantiated deductions. These requirements have resulted in numerous conflicts between taxpayers and the IRS.

Some events throughout the year should be documented as they occur. For example, it is generally advisable to receive a pledge payment statement from one's church, in addition to a canceled check, for proper documentation of a charitable contribution. Other types of deductible expenditures may require receipts or some other type of support.

Specific and *more stringent* rules for deducting travel, entertainment, and gift expenses are discussed in Chapter 10. Certain mixed-use (both personal and business) and listed property is also subject to the adequate records requirement (discussed in Chapter 9).

Expenses and Interest Relating to Tax-Exempt Income

Certain income, such as interest on municipal bonds, is tax-exempt, but § 212 allows the taxpayer to deduct expenses incurred for the production of income. If it were not for the disallowance provisions of § 265, it might be possible to make money at the expense of the government by excluding interest income and deducting interest expense.

EXAMPLE 37

P, a taxpayer in the 28% bracket, purchased $100,000 of 6% municipal bonds. At the same time, she used the bonds as collateral on a bank loan of $100,000 at 8% interest. A positive cash flow would result from the tax benefit as follows:

Cash paid out on loan	($8,000)
Cash received from bonds	6,000
Tax savings from deducting interest expense (28% of $8,000 interest expense)	2,240
Net positive cash flow	$ 240

◆

To eliminate the possibility illustrated in Example 37, the Code specifically disallows as a deduction the expenses of producing tax-exempt income. Interest on any indebtedness incurred or continued to purchase or carry tax-exempt obligations also is disallowed. Special rules apply to nonbanking financial institutions.[64]

Judicial Interpretations. It is often difficult to show a direct relationship between borrowings and investment in tax-exempt securities. Suppose, for

64. § 265(b).

example, that a taxpayer borrows money, adds it to existing funds, buys inventory and stocks, then later sells the inventory and buys municipal bonds. A series of transactions such as these can completely obscure any connection between the loan and the tax-exempt investment. One solution would be to disallow interest on any debt to the extent that the taxpayer holds any tax-exempt securities. This approach would preclude individuals from deducting part of their home mortgage interest if they owned any municipal bonds. However, the law was not intended to go to such extremes. As a result, judicial interpretations have tried to be reasonable in disallowing interest deductions under § 265.

In one case,[65] a company used municipal bonds as collateral on short-term loans to meet seasonal liquidity needs. The Court disallowed the interest deduction on the grounds that the company could predict its seasonal liquidity needs. Thus, the company could anticipate the need to borrow the money to continue to carry the tax-exempt securities. The same company *was* allowed an interest deduction on a building mortgage, even though tax-exempt securities it owned could have been sold to pay off the mortgage. The Court reasoned that short-term liquidity needs would have been impaired if the tax-exempt securities were sold. Furthermore, the Court ruled that carrying the tax-exempt securities bore no relationship to the long-term financing of a construction project.

In another case,[66] the Court disallowed an interest deduction to a company that refused to sell tax-exempt securities it had received from the sale of a major asset. The company's refusal to sell the tax-exempt securities necessitated large borrowings to finance company operations. The Court found that the primary reason that the company would not sell its bonds to reduce its bank debt was the tax savings, even though other business reasons existed for holding the municipal bonds. Moreover, the bonds and the debt both arose from the same transaction and were therefore directly related.

EXAMPLE 38

In January of the current year, T borrowed $100,000 at 8% interest. She used the loan proceeds to purchase 5,000 shares of stock in P Corporation. In July, she sold the stock for $120,000 and reinvested the proceeds in City of Denver bonds, the income from which is tax-exempt. Assuming the $100,000 loan remained outstanding throughout the entire year, the interest attributable to the period in which the bonds were held cannot be deducted. ◆

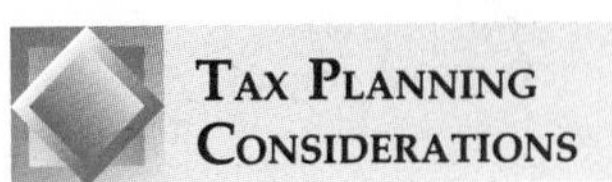

Time Value of Tax Deductions

Cash basis taxpayers often have the ability to make early payments for their expenses at the end of the tax year. This permits the payments to be deducted currently instead of in the following tax year. In view of the time value of money, a tax deduction this year may be worth more than the same deduction next year. Before employing this strategy, the taxpayer must consider next year's expected income and tax rates and whether a cash-flow problem may develop from early payments.

The time value of money as well as tax rate changes must be considered when an expense can be paid and deducted in either of two years.

65. *The Wisconsin Cheeseman, Inc. v. U.S.*, 68–1 USTC ¶9145, 21 AFTR2d 383, 388 F.2d 420 (CA–7, 1968).

66. *Illinois Terminal Railroad Co. v. U.S.*, 67–1 USTC ¶9374, 19 AFTR2d 1219, 375 F.2d 1016 (Ct.Cls., 1967).

EXAMPLE 39

T pledged $5,000 to her church's special building fund. She can make the contribution in December 1992 or January 1993. T is in the 31% tax bracket in 1992, and in the 28% bracket in 1993. She itemizes in both years. If she takes the deduction in 1992, she saves $254 ($1,550 – $1,296), due to the decrease in the tax rates and the time value of money.

CONCEPT SUMMARY 6–3
CLASSIFICATION OF EXPENSES

Expense Item	Deductible: For AGI	Deductible: From AGI	Not Deductible	Applicable Code §
Investment expenses				
Rent and royalty	X			§ 62(a)(4)
All other investments		X[4]		§ 212
Employee expenses				
Commuting expenses			X	§ 262
Travel and transportation[1]		X[4,5]		§ 162(a)(2)
Reimbursed expenses[1]	X			§ 62(a)(2)(A)
Moving expenses		X		§ 217
Entertainment[1]		X[4,5]		§ 162(a)
All other employee expenses[1]		X[4,5]		§ 162(a)
Certain expenses of performing artists	X			§ 62(a)(2)(B)
Trade or business expenses	X			§ 162
Casualty losses				
Business	X			§ 165(c)(1)
Personal		X[6]		§ 165(c)(3)
Tax determination				
Collection or refund expenses		X[4]		§ 212
Bad debts	X			§ 166
Medical expenses		X[7]		§ 213
Charitable contributions		X		§ 170
Taxes				
Trade or business	X			§ 162
Personal taxes				
Real property		X		§ 164(a)(1)
Personal property		X		§ 164(a)(2)
State and local income		X		§ 164(a)(3)
Investigation of a business[2]	X			§ 162
Interest				
Business	X			§ 162
Personal[3]		X		§ 163(a)
All other personal expenses			X	§ 262

1. Deduction *for* AGI if reimbursed, an adequate accounting is made, and employee is required to repay excess reimbursements.
2. Provided certain criteria are met.
3. Subject to the excess investment interest provisions and consumer interest phase-out.
4. Subject (in the aggregate) to a 2%-of-AGI floor imposed by § 67.
5. Only 80% of meals and entertainment are deductible.
6. Subject to a 10%-of-AGI floor and a $100 floor.
7. Subject to a 7.5%-of-AGI floor.

	1992	1993
Contribution	$5,000	$5,000
Tax bracket	.31	.28
Tax savings	$1,550	$1,400
Discounted @ 8%	1.0	.926
Savings in present value	$1,550	$1,296

◆

EXAMPLE 40

Assume the same facts as in Example 39, except that T is in the 28% bracket in both 1992 and 1993. T's savings by taking the deduction in 1992 is $104 ($1,400 – $1,296), due to the time value of money.

	1992	1993
Contribution	$5,000	$5,000
Tax bracket	.28	.28
Tax savings	$1,400	$1,400
Discounted @ 8%	1.0	.926
Savings in present value	$1,400	$1,296

◆

Unreasonable Compensation

In substantiating the reasonableness of a shareholder-employee's compensation, an internal comparison test is sometimes useful. If it can be shown that employees who are nonshareholders receive the same (or more) compensation as shareholder-employees in comparable positions, it is indicative that compensation is not unreasonable.

Another possibility is to demonstrate that the shareholder-employee has been underpaid in prior years. For example, the shareholder-employee may have agreed to take a less-than-adequate salary during the unprofitable formative years of the business, expecting the "postponed" compensation to be paid in later, more profitable years. The agreement should be documented, if possible, in the corporate minutes.

Keep in mind that in testing for reasonableness, the *total* pay package must be taken into account. Look at all fringe benefits or perquisites, such as contributions by the corporation to a qualified pension plan (even though those amounts are not immediately available to the covered employee-shareholder).

Shifting Deductions

Taxpayers should manage their obligations to avoid the loss of a deduction. Deductions can be shifted among family members, depending upon who makes the payment. For example, a father buys a condo for his daughter and puts the title in both names. The taxpayer who makes the payment gets the deduction for the property taxes. If the condo is owned by the daughter only and her father makes the payment, neither is entitled to a deduction.

Hobby Losses

To demonstrate that an activity has been entered into for the purpose of making a profit (it is not a hobby), a taxpayer should treat the activity as a business. The business should engage in advertising, use business letterhead stationery, and maintain a business phone.

If a taxpayer's activity earns a profit in three out of five consecutive years, the presumption is that the activity is engaged in for profit. It may be possible for a cash basis taxpayer to meet these requirements by timing the payment of expenses or the receipt of revenues. The payment of certain expenses incurred before the end of the year might be made in the following year, or the billing of year-end sales might be delayed so that collections are received in the following year.

Keep in mind that the three-out-of-five-years rule under § 183 is not absolute. All it does is shift the presumption. If a profit is not made in three out of five years, the losses may still be allowed if the taxpayer can show that they are due to the nature of the business. For example, success in artistic or literary endeavors can take a long time. Also, due to the present state of the economy, even full-time farmers and ranchers are often unable to show a profit. How can one expect a part-time farmer or rancher to do so?

Merely satisfying the three-out-of-five-years rule does not guarantee that a taxpayer is automatically home free. If the three years of profits are insignificant relative to the losses of other years, or if the profits are not from the ordinary operation of the business, the taxpayer is vulnerable. The IRS may still be able to establish that the taxpayer is not engaged in an activity for profit.

EXAMPLE 41

A taxpayer had the following gains and losses in an artistic endeavor:

1989	($50,000)
1990	(65,000)
1991	400
1992	200
1993	125

Under these circumstances, the IRS might try to overcome the presumption. ◆

If the taxpayer in Example 41 could show conformity with the factors enumerated in the Regulations[67] or could show evidence of business hardships (e.g., injury, death, or illness), the government cannot override the presumption.[68]

PROBLEM MATERIALS

DISCUSSION QUESTIONS

1. "All income must be reported and all deductions are allowed unless specifically disallowed in the Code." True or false? Discuss.
2. T, who had adjusted gross income of $30,000, had deductions of $5,000. Would it matter to T whether they were *for* or *from* AGI? Why or why not?
3. If a taxpayer is audited and $1,000 of income is added to his adjusted gross income, will his tax increase (ignoring penalties and interest) be equal to $1,000 multiplied by his tax marginal bracket? Discuss.

---

67. Reg. §§ 1.183–2(b)(1) through (9).
68. *Faulconer, Sr. v. Comm.*, 84–2 USTC ¶9955, 55 AFTR2d 85–302, 748 F.2d 890 (CA–4, 1984), *rev'g* 45 TCM 1084, T.C.Memo. 1983–165.

4. Are the following items deductible *for* AGI, deductible *from* AGI, or nondeductible personal items?

   a. Unreimbursed travel expenses of an employee.
   b. Alimony payments.
   c. Charitable contributions.
   d. Medical expenses.
   e. Safe deposit box rentals in which stocks and bonds are kept.
   f. Repairs made on a personal residence.
   g. Expenses related to tax-exempt municipal bonds.

5. Are the following expenditures deductible *for* AGI, deductible *from* AGI, nondeductible personal items, or capital expenditures?

   a. Repairs made to a rental property.
   b. State income taxes.
   c. Investment advice subscriptions.
   d. Child support payments.
   e. New roof on rental property.
   f. New roof on personal residence.
   g. Mortgage interest on personal residence.

6. Define and contrast the "ordinary" and "necessary" tests for business expenses.
7. T, a cash basis taxpayer, decides to reduce his taxable income for 1992 by buying $10,000 worth of supplies on December 28, 1992. The supplies will be used up in 1993. Can T deduct this expenditure in 1992? Would your answer differ if T bought the supplies because a supplier was going out of business and had given T a significant discount on the supplies?
8. What is the significance of the economic performance test?
9. What is the "actually paid" requirement for the deduction of an expense by a cash basis taxpayer? Does actual payment ensure a deduction?
10. T operates a drug-running operation. Which of the following expenses incurred by T are deductible?

    a. Bribes paid to border guards.
    b. Salaries to employees.
    c. Price paid for drugs purchased for resale.
    d. Kickbacks to police.
    e. Rent on an office.

11. When J died, he left equal shares of stock to his four children, although he made it clear that he wanted Jill and John (the two children who were interested in his business) to run the company. This was quite all right with the other two children, who were to receive $100,000 each per year from the company and were free to pursue their own interests. Jill and John each received reasonable salaries of $250,000 and $210,000, respectively. They paid the other two children salaries of $100,000 each. What were they trying to accomplish from a tax standpoint? Will it work? If not, what are the tax consequences to the corporation and to the other two children?
12. T is an executive in X Corporation. She used insider information to buy X Corporation stock just before public announcement of the discovery of huge oil reserves on company-owned property. She was caught and incurred legal expenses and treble damage payments. Can she deduct either expense?
13. How are expenses (e.g., travel, meals, and lodging) incurred in connection with the investigation of a new business opportunity treated if the new business is acquired? If the new business is *not* acquired?
14. If a taxpayer is unable to meet the requirements of § 183 relative to earning a profit in at least three of five consecutive years, is it possible to qualify the activity as a business? Why or why not?
15. If a taxpayer meets the requirements of § 183 relative to earning a profit in at least three of five consecutive years, is it still possible for the IRS to treat the activity as a hobby of the taxpayer? Why or why not?

16. T was transferred from Phoenix to North Dakota on March 1 of the current year. He immediately put his home in Phoenix up for rent. The home was rented May 1 to November 30 and was vacant during the month of December. It was rented again on January 1 for six months. What expenses, if any, can T deduct on his return? Which deductions are *for* AGI and which ones are *from* AGI?
17. Contrast the differing results obtained in a personal/rental situation by allocating property taxes and interest on the IRS's basis and the court's basis. Which method would the taxpayer prefer?
18. Discuss the tax treatment of the rental of a vacation home if it is:
    - **a.** Rented 10 days during the year.
    - **b.** Rented 130 days during the year; used personally for 12 days.
    - **c.** Rented for 250 days; used personally for 40 days.
19. Is it ever possible to deduct expenditures incurred for another individual's benefit? Explain.
20. T repaired the roof on his factory at a cost of $1,500 in the current year. During the same year, S replaced the roof on her small rental house for $1,500. Both taxpayers are on the cash basis. Are their expenditures treated the same on their tax returns? Why or why not?
21. T owns 20% of X Corporation; 20% of X's stock is owned by S, T's mother; 15% is owned by R, T's brother; the remaining 45% is owned by unrelated parties. T is on the cash basis, and X Corporation is on the accrual basis. On December 31, 1992, X accrued T's salary of $5,000 and paid it on April 4, 1993. Both are on a calendar year. What is the tax effect to T and X?
22. Discuss the reasons for the disallowance of losses between related parties. Would it make any difference if a parent sold stock to an unrelated third party and the child repurchased the same number of shares of the stock in the market the same day?
23. T sold 100 shares of XYZ Company stock to F, her brother, for $8,000. She had originally paid $7,100 for the stock. F later sold the stock for $6,000 on the open market. What are the tax consequences to T and F?
24. Would your answer to Question 23 differ if T had sold the stock to F for $6,500?
25. The Acme Corporation is owned as follows:

T	20%
P, T's wife	20%
S, T's mother	15%
R, T's father	25%
Q, an unrelated party	20%

T and P each loaned the Acme Corporation $10,000 out of their separate funds. On December 31, 1992, Acme accrued interest at 12% on both loans. The interest was paid on February 4, 1993. Acme is on the accrual basis, and T and P are on the cash basis. What is the tax treatment of this interest expense/income to T, P, and Acme?

26. Discuss the tracing problems encountered in the enforcement of the restrictions of § 265 that disallow a deduction for the expenses of producing tax-exempt income.

PROBLEMS

27. R filed his 1991 tax return, claiming two exemptions and itemizing his deductions as follows:

AGI (salary)			$20,000
Less: Itemized deductions:			
Medical expenses	$1,800		
Less: 7.5% of AGI	1,500	$ 300	
Charitable contributions		1,900	
Interest		5,300	

Taxes		900	
Miscellaneous	$ 600		
Less: 2% of AGI	400	200	
Total itemized deductions			8,600
			$11,400
Less: 2 exemptions			4,300
Taxable income			$ 7,100

In 1992, R realized that he had forgotten to deduct his $2,000 IRA contribution for 1991. On an amended return (Form 1040X), what is his new AGI? Taxable income?

28. P, who is single, has a sole proprietorship and keeps her books on the cash basis. Following is a summary of her receipts, disbursements, and other items related to her business account for 1992:

Receipts	
Sales	$28,000
Dividend received from AT&T	300
Interest on savings account	450
Long-term capital gain on sale of stock	1,200
Disbursements	
Rent on buildings used 75% for business and 25% for living quarters	6,000
Salary paid to part-time secretary	3,000
Taxes	
Gross receipts tax on sales	840
State income taxes	750
Charitable contributions	1,400
Insurance on business property (policy runs from October 1, 1992, to September 30, 1993)	1,200
Depreciation on business equipment	1,000
Business supplies	980

Calculate P's adjusted gross income for 1992.

29. T, a cash basis taxpayer, rented a building from J on October 1, 1992, paying $12,000 (one full year's rent) in advance. The lease is for 15 years with no option to renew. How much rent can T deduct in 1992?

30. D runs an illegal numbers racket. His gross income was $500,000. He incurred the following expenses:

Illegal kickbacks	$20,000
Salaries	80,000
Rent	24,000
Utilities and telephone	9,000
Bribes to police	25,000
Interest	6,000
Depreciation on equipment	12,000

What is his net income from this business that is includible in taxable income? If the business was an illegal drug operation, would your answer differ?

31. T traveled to a neighboring state to investigate the purchase of two restaurants. His expenses included travel, legal, accounting, and miscellaneous expenses. The total was $12,000. He incurred the expenses in March and April 1993.

   a. What can he deduct in 1993 if he was in the restaurant business and did not acquire the two restaurants?
   b. What can he deduct in 1993 if he was in the restaurant business and acquired the two restaurants and began operating them on July 1, 1993?

c. What can he deduct in 1993 if he did not acquire the two restaurants and was not in the restaurant business?
d. What can he deduct in 1993 if he acquired the two restaurants but was not in the restaurant business when he acquired them? Operations began on July 1, 1993.

32. L is a homemaker who makes pottery items at home for sale to others. She had the following income and expenses for the year:

Sales	$3,000
Expenses	
Materials	1,200
Advertising	500
Travel	700
Other related expenses	1,200
	$3,600
Net loss	$ (600)

How much must L include in income? What can she deduct, assuming AGI of $60,000?

33. T is an executive with an adjusted gross income of $100,000 before consideration of income or loss from his miniature horse business. His income comes from winning horse shows, stud fees, and sales of yearlings. His home is on 20 acres, 18 of which he uses to pasture the horses and upon which he has erected stables, paddocks, fences, tack houses, and so forth.
He uses an office in his home that is 10% of the square footage of the house. He uses the office exclusively for keeping records of breeding lines, histories, and show and veterinary records. His records show the following income and expenses for the current year:

Income from fees, prizes, and sales	$22,000
Expenses	
Entry fees	1,000
Feed and veterinary bills	4,000
Supplies	900
Publications and dues	500
Travel to horse shows (no meals)	2,300
Salaries and wages of employees	8,000
Depreciation on horse equipment	3,000
Depreciation on horse farm improvements	7,000
Depreciation on 10% of home	1,000
Total home mortgage interest	24,000
Total property taxes on home	2,200
Total property taxes on horse farm improvements	800

The mortgage interest is only on his home. The horse farm improvements are not mortgaged.

How must T treat the income and expenses of the operation if the miniature horse activity is held to be a hobby?

34. How would your answer in Problem 33 differ if the horse operation was held to be a business?

35. T makes macramé animals in her spare time. She sold $1,000 worth of animals during the year and incurred expenses as follows:

Supplies	$500
Depreciation on business property	800
Advertising	100

How are these items treated if the endeavor is a hobby? A business?

36. J is a promoter, real estate developer, and investor. Because he has inherited wealth, he can afford to be somewhat of a wheeler-dealer. He is single, age 41. During 1992, J incurred expenses in traveling to the state capitol to testify against proposed legislation for a green belt around the city because it interfered with some of his development plans. The expenses amounted to $900. He also spent $300 traveling to various locations to speak to civic groups against the proposed legislation.

J also incurred $1,600 of expense investigating the purchase of a computer franchising operation. He did not purchase the operation because he felt that his lack of expertise in that type of business was too big an obstacle to overcome.

J's other income and expenses for the year were as follows:

Income	
Interest	$ 80,000
Dividends	160,000
Short-term capital loss	(50,000)
Long-term capital gains	175,000
Fees for promotion and development	24,000
Expenses	
Office expenses	17,000
Expenses incurred on land held for resale	6,000
Tax advice	5,000
All other itemized deductions	34,000

Assume J's self-employment tax is $862. Calculate J's taxable income for 1992.

37. During the current year (not a leap year), P's vacation home was used as follows: 30 days of occupancy by P, 120 days of rental to unrelated parties, and 215 days of vacancy. Further information concerning the property is summarized as follows:

Rent income	$4,500
Expenses	
Real estate taxes	1,095
Interest on mortgage	2,555
Utilities and maintenance	1,200
Repairs	400
Landscaping	1,700
Depreciation	3,000

Compute P's net rent income or loss and the amounts that P can itemize on her income tax return.

38. Would your answer differ in Problem 37 if P had used the home for 5 days instead of 30? Explain, showing computations if needed.

39. Would your answer to Problem 37 differ if P had rented the home for 10 days instead of 120? Explain, showing computations if needed.

40. T, single, age 40, had the following income and expenses in 1992:

Income	
Salary	$43,000
Rental of vacation home (rented 60 days, used personally 60 days, vacant 246 days)	4,000
Municipal bond interest	2,000
Dividend from General Motors	400
Expenses	
Interest	
On home mortgage	$ 8,400
On vacation home	4,758
On loan used to buy municipal bonds	3,100

Taxes	
Property tax on home	2,200
Property tax on vacation home	1,098
State income tax	3,300
Charitable contributions	1,100
Tax return preparation fee	300
Utilities and maintenance on vacation home	2,600
Depreciation on rental 50% of vacation home	3,500

Calculate T's taxable income for 1992 before personal exemptions.

41. R incurred the following expenses in the the current tax year. Indicate, in the spaces provided, whether each expenditure is deductible *for* AGI, *from* AGI, or not deductible.

	Deductible		
Expense Item	**For AGI**	**From AGI**	**Not Deductible**
1. R's personal medical expenses	______	______	______
2. R's dependent daughter's medical expenses	______	______	______
3. Real estate taxes on rental property	______	______	______
4. Real estate taxes on R's personal residence	______	______	______
5. Real estate taxes on daughter's personal residence	______	______	______
6. R's state income taxes	______	______	______
7. Interest on rental property mortgage	______	______	______
8. Interest on R's personal residence mortgage	______	______	______
9. Interest on daughter's personal residence mortgage	______	______	______
10. Interest on business loans	______	______	______
11. Charitable contributions	______	______	______
12. Depreciation on rental property	______	______	______
13. Utilities & maintenance on:			
a. Rental property	______	______	______
b. R's home	______	______	______
c. Daughter's home	______	______	______
14. Depreciation on auto used in R's business	______	______	______
15. Depreciation on R's personal auto	______	______	______
16. Depreciation on daughter's personal auto	______	______	______

42. J sold stock (basis of $40,000) to her brother, B, for $32,000.

   a. What are the tax consequences to J?

   b. What are the tax consequences to B if he later sells the stock for $42,000? For $28,000? For $36,000?

43. What is R's constructive ownership of X Corporation, given the following information?

Shares owned by R	900
Shares owned by S, R's uncle	600
Shares owned by T, R's partner	30
Shares owned by U, a partnership owned by R and T equally	300
Shares owned by V, R's granddaughter	570
Shares owned by unrelated parties	600

44. J has a brokerage account and buys on the margin, which resulted in an interest expense during the year of $8,000. Income generated through the brokerage account was as follows:

Municipal interest	$30,000
Taxable dividends, interest, and capital gains	70,000

How much investment interest can he deduct?

CUMULATIVE PROBLEMS

45. T was divorced on November 1, 1992, after separating from her husband H, on June 1, 1992. Her 16-year-old daughter, D, who is a full-time student, lives with her. H provides over one-half of D's support. T has signed Form 8332 for 1992. T is 43 years of age. T, H, and D all live in Texas.

During the year, the following income items were noted by T:

T's salary	$24,000
H's salary	50,000
D's earnings	5,000
Municipal bond interest earned in December	300
General Motors dividend received during the marriage	180
Alimony received	4,000
FMV of land received in divorce settlement	18,000
Original cost of land received in divorce settlement	10,000

The following expenses were paid by T:

Cost of leveling the land received in the divorce settlement	$1,500
Interest paid	
On loan incurred to invest in municipal bonds	320
On T's share of home mortgage	6,000
On D's auto loan	1,600
Charitable contributions	2,500
Property taxes paid	600

a. Calculate T's taxable income for 1992. Suggested software (if available): *TurboTax* for tax return or WFT tax planning software.
b. What is T's filing status?

46. Thomas J. Smith, age 36, is single and lives at 1648 South Mill Road, Chicago, Illinois, 60609. His Social Security number is 523–33–9281. He does not want to designate $1 to the Presidential Election Campaign.

Thomas, who is employed as an executive, earned $60,000 during the year. His employer withheld $8,500 in Federal income tax, $1,100 in state income tax, and the appropriate amount of FICA (Social Security) tax.

Thomas was divorced in 1984 and is entitled to a dependency exemption under a pre-1985 agreement for Susan, his 8-year-old daughter who lives with her mother. Susan's Social Security number is 523–84–6144. Her mother, Joan, is 31, and her Social Security number is 466–44–8888. Thomas paid $5,000 for Susan's support and $6,000 in alimony to Joan. He sold 100 shares of General Co. stock on April 18, 1991, for $5,000. He had purchased them on September 4, 1989, for $3,000. He sold 300 shares of U.S. United Co. stock on July 8, 1991, for $6,000. He had acquired them on April 17, 1991, for $10,000. Thomas had the following interest and dividend items in 1991:

Interest credited to his savings account at State Street Savings	$400
Dividends from General Co. stock	300
Dividends from U.S. United Co. stock	200
Dividends from AT&T stock	400
Interest on City of Denver general obligation bonds	300

Other items that may have tax consequences are:

a. Thomas paid $600 for tax return preparation, $50 for a safe deposit box, and $320 for investment advice.
b. He made charitable contributions of $2,600 during the year, $500 of which was charged on his MasterCard.
c. Thomas paid the following expenses for Susan, in addition to child support:

Dental and medical bills	$1,400
Piano lessons	300
Private school fees	1,200

d. He incurred unreimbursed medical expenses (doctor and hospital) of $800, personal property taxes of $200, and $460 additional state income taxes paid in 1991 upon filing his 1990 state income tax return.
e. His home expenses included home mortgage interest of $8,400 (he bought the home in 1985 and the interest is on the original mortgage), real property taxes of $450, and utilities and maintenance of $2,400.

Calculate the net tax payable (or refund due) for 1991. If you use tax forms in your solution, you will need Form 1040 and Schedules A, B, and D. Suggested software (if available): *TurboTax* for tax return solutions, or WFT tax planning software.

47. John and Mary Jane are married, filing jointly. They are expecting their first child in early 1993. John's salary in 1992 was $50,000, from which $8,000 of Federal income tax and $3,000 of state income tax were withheld. Mary Jane made $25,000 and had $3,000 of Federal income tax withheld and $1,500 of state income tax withheld.

They had $400 of savings account interest and $800 of dividends during the year.

They made charitable contributions of $2,000 during the year and paid an additional $200 in state income taxes in 1992 upon filing their 1991 state income tax return. Their deductible home mortgage interest was $8,200, and their property taxes came to $1,600. They had no other deductible expenses.

a. Calculate their tax (or refund) due for 1992. Suggested software (if available): WFT tax planning software.
b. Assume that they come to you for advice in December 1992. John has learned that he will receive a $20,000 bonus. He wants to know if he should take it in December 1992 or in January 1993. Mary Jane will quit work in January to stay home with the baby. Their itemized deductions will decrease by $1,500 because Mary Jane will not have state income taxes withheld. Suggested software (if available): WFT tax planning software.

RESEARCH PROBLEMS

RESEARCH PROBLEM 1 Taxpayer sold his unmortgaged home for $150,000 cash. He made a down payment on a new home of $50,000 and acquired a mortgage of $135,000. He invested the remaining $100,000 of the sales proceeds in municipal bonds. Is he prohibited under § 265 from deducting the interest on $100,000 of the home mortgage?

RESEARCH PROBLEM 2 Taxpayer, an oil company, was assessed a civil penalty under the Federal Water Pollution Act as a result of a leak in one of its pipelines. The company took a deduction for an ordinary and necessary business expense.

The company also owned a gas processing plant that had become uneconomical to operate on its old site. The company dismantled the plant and moved it to a new location. During this process, the company repaired and overhauled the plant. The company deducted the cost related to moving and repairing the machinery in the plant.

Can the taxpayer deduct the civil penalty? Must the moving and repairs expense be capitalized under Code § 263(a)(1)?

RESEARCH PROBLEM 3 D is a graduate student working on her Ph.D. in microbiology. She attended the university under the G.I. bill, which pays her tuition and books in full. The G.I. benefits are not taxable. She was appointed to a research team, and the university paid her a monthly stipend of $450 for the year. She was required to register and pay tuition for the semesters she was on the research team. Her tuition was still paid for by the V.A. Can she deduct the tuition as a business expense?

Research aids:

§ 265
Rev.Rul. 83–3, 1983–1 C.B. 72

RESEARCH PROBLEM 4 S is a self-employed lawyer. One of his hobbies is songwriting. He had one song published in 1990. Over the next three years, S spent a considerable amount of time writing songs and meeting with producers. He has not shown a profit. He maintains a separate room in his house for the sole purpose of writing music, and he deducted a pro rata share of the utility bills and other home expenses. He incurred other expenses amounting to $4,000. Will his expenses for this endeavor be disallowed as a hobby loss?

RESEARCH PROBLEM 5 T was the director of labor relations for a trucking company and an unpaid (by law) trustee of his union's pension fund. Using funds from the pension fund, T conspired to bribe a congressman to influence trucking legislation. T was convicted and barred from working in labor relations for 15 years. He incurred legal fees of $80,000 in his unsuccessful defense. Can he deduct the $80,000 under § 162(a) as an expense that arose in connection with his business?

Research aid:

U.S. v. Gilmore, 63–1 USTC ¶9285, 11 AFTR2d 758, 83 S.Ct. 623 (USSC, 1963).

CHAPTER

PASSIVE ACTIVITY LOSSES

OBJECTIVES

Discuss tax shelters and the reasons for at-risk and passive loss limitations.
Explain the at-risk limitation.
Examine the rationale for the passive loss limitations.
Identify taxpayers who are subject to the passive loss limits.
Describe how the passive loss rules limit deductions for losses.
Examine the definition of passive activities.
Analyze and apply the tests for material participation.
Consider special rules related to rental activities.
Examine the rules for identifying passive activities.
Discuss the rental real estate exception.
Determine the proper tax treatment upon the disposition of a passive activity.
Suggest tax planning strategies to minimize the effect of the passive loss limitations.

OUTLINE

The Tax Shelter Problem

Before Congress enacted legislation to reduce or eliminate their effectiveness, tax shelters were popular investments for tax avoidance purposes. The typical tax shelter relied heavily on nonrecourse financing[1] and generated large losses in the early years of the activity. Investors would offset these tax shelter losses against other types of income. At the very least, the tax shelter deductions deferred income taxes for the investor until the activity was sold. In the best of situations, additional tax savings were realized because sale of the activity produced capital gain, which was taxed at much lower rates than ordinary income. The following example illustrates what was possible *before* Congress enacted legislation to curb tax shelter abuses.

Example 1

T, who earned a salary of $100,000, invested $20,000 for a 10% interest in a tax shelter. Through the use of $800,000 of nonrecourse financing, the partnership acquired assets worth $1,000,000. Depreciation, interest, and other deductions related to the activity resulted in a loss of $400,000, of which T's share was $40,000. T was allowed to deduct the $40,000 loss, even though he had invested and stood to lose only $20,000. ◆

In the heyday of tax shelters, promoters often promised multiple write-offs for the investor. A review of Example 1 shows that the taxpayer took a *two-for-one* write-off ($40,000 deduction, $20,000 investment).

The first major provision aimed at the tax shelter strategy was the at-risk limitation enacted in 1976. The objective of the at-risk rule is to limit a taxpayer's tax shelter deductions to the amount at risk, that is, the amount the taxpayer stands to lose if the investment turns out to be a financial disaster. Under the current at-risk rules, the investor in Example 1 would not be allowed to deduct more than $20,000.[2] The remaining $20,000 would be suspended under the at-risk rules and would be deductible in the future if the taxpayer's at-risk amount increased.

The second major attack on tax shelters came in the Tax Reform Act of 1986. The passive loss limits in that legislation have nearly made the term *tax shelter* obsolete. Now such investments are generally referred to as passive investments, or *passive activities*, rather than tax shelters.

The passive loss rules require the taxpayer to segregate income and losses into three categories: active, passive, and portfolio. In general, the passive loss limits disallow the deduction of passive losses against active or portfolio income, even if the taxpayer is at risk for the amount of the loss. Referring again to Example 1, if the activity in which the taxpayer invested is passive, the at-risk rules and passive loss limits would work together to disallow the entire $40,000 loss in the year it was incurred. However, the *suspended* loss may be carried forward and deducted in the future if the taxpayer has passive income or disposes of the activity.

At-Risk Limits

The at-risk provisions limit the deductibility of losses from business and income-producing activities. These provisions, which apply to individuals and closely held corporations, are designed to prevent a taxpayer from deducting losses in excess of the actual economic investment in an activity.

1. Nonrecourse debt is an obligation for which the endorser is not personally liable. An example of nonrecourse debt is a liability on real estate acquired by a partnership without the partnership or any of the partners assuming any liability for the mortgage. The acquired property generally is pledged as collateral for the loan.
2. If the investment is in a *passive activity*, the deduction is limited further under the passive loss rules.

Under the at-risk rules, a taxpayer's deductible losses from an activity for any taxable year are limited to the amount the taxpayer has at risk at the end of the taxable year (the amount the taxpayer could actually lose in the activity). The initial amount considered at risk is generally the sum of the following:[3]

- The amount of cash and the adjusted basis of property contributed to the activity.
- Amounts borrowed for use in the activity for which the taxpayer is personally liable or has pledged as security property not used in the activity.

This amount generally is increased each year by the taxpayer's share of income and is decreased by the taxpayer's share of losses and withdrawals from the activity.

A taxpayer generally is not considered at risk with respect to borrowed amounts if either of the following is true:

- The taxpayer is not personally liable for repayment of the debt (nonrecourse loans).
- The lender has an interest (other than as a creditor) in the activity (except to the extent provided in the Treasury Regulations).

Although taxpayers are generally not considered at risk for nonrecourse loans, there is an important exception. This exception provides that, in the case of an activity involving the holding of real property, a taxpayer is considered at risk for his or her share of any qualified nonrecourse financing that is secured by real property used in the activity.

The taxpayer also is not considered at risk for amounts for which he or she is protected against loss by guarantees, stop-loss arrangements, insurance (other than casualty insurance), or a similar arrangement.

Taxpayers can compute the deductible loss from an activity on Form 6198 (At Risk Limitations). Form 6198 is required if

- a taxpayer has a loss from an activity that is covered by the at-risk rules, and
- the taxpayer is not at risk for some of his or her investment in the activity.

Any losses disallowed for any given taxable year by the at-risk rules may be deducted in the first succeeding year in which the rules do not prevent the deduction. However, if the losses are incurred in a passive activity, they are subject to the passive loss limitations.

EXAMPLE 2

In 1992, T invests $40,000 in an oil partnership that, by the use of nonrecourse loans, spends $60,000 on intangible drilling costs applicable to T's interest. T's interest in the partnership is subject to the at-risk limits but is not subject to the passive loss limits. Since T has only $40,000 of capital at risk, he cannot deduct more than $40,000 against his other income and must reduce his at-risk amount to zero ($40,000 at-risk amount – $40,000 loss deducted). The nondeductible loss of $20,000 ($60,000 loss – $40,000 allowed) can be carried over to 1993. ◆

---

3. § 465(b)(1).

EXAMPLE 3

In 1993, T has taxable income from the oil partnership of $15,000 and invests an additional $5,000 in the venture. His at-risk amount is now $20,000 ($0 beginning balance + $15,000 taxable income + $5,000 additional investment). This enables T to deduct the carried-over loss, and again requires him to reduce his at-risk amount to zero ($20,000 at-risk amount − $20,000 carried-over loss). ◆

Recapture of previously allowed losses is required to the extent the at-risk amount is reduced below zero.[4] This rule applies if the amount at risk is reduced below zero by distributions to the taxpayer, by changes in the status of indebtedness from recourse to nonrecourse, or by the commencement of a guarantee or other similar arrangement that affects the taxpayer's risk of loss.

Generally, a taxpayer's amount at risk is separately determined for each activity. Nevertheless, activities are treated as one activity (aggregated) if the activities constitute a trade or business and either of the following is true:

- The taxpayer *actively participates* in the management of that trade or business.
- In the case of a trade or business carried on by a partnership or an S corporation, 65 percent or more of the entity's losses is allocable to persons who actively participate in the management of the trade or business.

All of the facts and circumstances must be examined to determine whether the taxpayer has met the *active participation* requirement. The following factors indicate active participation:

- Making decisions involving the operation or management of the activity.
- Performing services for the activity.
- Hiring and discharging employees.

These factors must be balanced against the factors that indicate lack of active participation:

- Lack of control in managing the operation of the activity.
- Having authority only to discharge the manager of the activity.
- Having a manager of the activity who is an independent contractor rather than an employee.

This active participation requirement differs from the active participation requirement that applies to real estate rental operations (discussed later under Real Estate Rental Activities).

PASSIVE LOSS LIMITS

Before the enactment of the passive loss rules, taxpayers were able, by investing in activities in which they did not participate (passive activities), to create tax losses that did not cause actual (or potential) economic losses.

A classic example of a tax shelter that created noneconomic tax losses was a limited partnership[5] owning rental property. Investors could write off losses in

4. § 465(e).

5. A *limited* partner is one whose liability to third-party creditors of the partnership is limited to the amount the partner has invested in the partnership. A partnership must have at least one *general* partner, who is fully liable in an individual capacity for the debts of the partnership to third parties.

excess of their investments because the at-risk limitation did not apply to real estate before 1987. An individual could buy an interest in a limited partnership, which in turn would buy rental property with a large nonrecourse mortgage. Since the entire cost attributable to the building could be depreciated and the interest paid on the mortgage could be expensed, tax losses were generated. There was no real *economic loss*, however, since the rent income generated was sufficient to make the mortgage payments and the real estate, in many cases, was appreciating on the open market. Furthermore, the individual limited partners were not personally liable for the mortgage.

EXAMPLE 4

T invested $20,000 for a 10% interest in a limited partnership. The partnership paid $200,000 down and negotiated a 10-year nonrecourse mortgage of $800,000 at 9% interest to acquire a $1,000,000 building to be used for rental purposes. The building was placed in service in January 1984, and the 15-year depreciation schedule applicable to 1984 was used (see Table 9–4 in Chapter 9). The depreciation deduction was 12% in 1984, 10% in 1985, and 9% in 1986. Total depreciation for the 3-year period was $310,000 ($1,000,000 × 31%). Interest was $72,000 in 1984 ($800,000 × 9%), $64,800 in 1985 [($800,000 − $80,000 payment on principal) × 9%], and $57,600 in 1986 [($800,000 − $80,000 − $80,000) × 9%]. Total interest was $194,400 ($72,000 + $64,800 + $57,600). The partnership's rent income was $390,000 during the 3-year period, and taxes, insurance, and other expenses totaled $120,000. The partnership had the following loss for the 3-year period:

Rent income		$390,000
Expenses		
Interest	$194,400	
Taxes, insurance, other	120,000	
Depreciation	310,000	624,400
Partnership's loss		$234,400
T's 10% share of loss		$ 23,440

At the end of three years, T would have deducted $23,440, or $3,440 more than he invested. From an economic perspective, however, T probably did not lose $23,440. The value of his partnership interest could have increased because of appreciation of the building (on which $310,000 of depreciation was taken), increased rents, or other factors. ◆

Classification of Income and Losses

The passive loss rules require classification of income and losses into three categories: active, passive, and portfolio. *Active income* includes, but is not limited to, the following:

- Wages, salary, commissions, bonuses, and other payments for services rendered by the taxpayer.
- Profit from a trade or business in which the taxpayer is a material participant.
- Gain on the sale or other disposition of assets used in an active trade or business.
- Income from intangible property if the taxpayer's personal efforts significantly contributed to the creation of the property.
- Income from a qualified low-income housing project that is not subject to the passive loss limitations under transitional rules.

Code § 469 provides that income or loss from the following activities is treated as *passive:*

- Any trade or business or income-producing activity in which the taxpayer does not materially participate.
- Any rental activity, whether the taxpayer materially participates or not.

Although the Code defines rental activities as passive activities, an exception allows losses from certain real estate rental activities to be offset against nonpassive (active or portfolio) income. The exception is discussed under Real Estate Rental Activities later in the chapter.

Portfolio income includes, but is not limited to, the following:

- Interest, dividends, annuities, and royalties not derived in the ordinary course of a trade or business.
- Gain or loss from the disposition of property that produces portfolio income or is held for investment purposes.

Taxpayers Subject to the Passive Loss Rules

The passive loss rules apply to individuals, estates, trusts, closely held C corporations, and personal service corporations.[6] Passive income or loss from investments in S corporations or partnerships flows through to the owners (see Chapter 20), and the passive loss rules are applied at the owner level.

Before enactment of the passive loss limits, taxpayers were able to defer or avoid taxes by investing in tax shelters that produced losses. These losses were used to offset income from other sources.

EXAMPLE 5

K, a physician, earned $150,000 from her practice in 1985 (before the passive loss rules were enacted). She also received $10,000 in dividends and interest on various portfolio investments. During the year, she acquired a 20% interest in a tax shelter that produced a $300,000 loss not subject to the at-risk limits. In 1985, K would have been allowed to deduct her $60,000 share of the tax shelter loss, resulting in AGI of $100,000 ($150,000 salary + $10,000 dividends and interest − $60,000 tax shelter loss). ◆

As a general rule, taxpayers who are subject to the passive loss limitations cannot offset passive losses against active income or portfolio income.

EXAMPLE 6

Assume the same facts as in Example 5, except that the year is 1992 and that K does not materially participate in the operations of the activity. K's $60,000 share of the loss is a *passive loss* and is not deductible in 1992. It is treated as a *suspended loss,* which is carried over to the future. If K has passive income from this investment, or from other passive investments, in the future, she can offset the suspended loss against that passive income. If K does not have passive income to offset the suspended loss in the future, she will be allowed to offset the loss against other types of income when she eventually disposes of the passive activity. K's AGI in 1992 is $160,000 ($150,000 salary + $10,000 portfolio income), compared to $100,000 based on the same set of facts for tax year 1985. ◆

An exception to the general rule illustrated in Example 6 allows closely held C corporations to offset passive losses against *active* income, but not against *portfolio* income.

---

6. § 469(a).

EXAMPLE 7

Y Corporation, a closely held C corporation, has $500,000 of passive losses from a rental activity, $400,000 of active income, and $100,000 of portfolio income. The corporation may offset $400,000 of the $500,000 passive loss against the $400,000 of active business income, but may not offset the remainder against the $100,000 of portfolio income. Thus, $100,000 of the passive loss is suspended ($500,000 passive loss − $400,000 offset against active income). ◆

Personal Service Corporations. Application of the passive loss limitation to personal service corporations is intended to prevent taxpayers from sheltering personal service income by creating personal service corporations and acquiring passive activities at the corporate level.

EXAMPLE 8

Five attorneys, who earn a total of $1,000,000 a year in their individual practices, form a personal service corporation. Shortly after its formation, the corporation invests in a passive activity that produces a $200,000 loss during the year. Because the passive loss rules apply to personal service corporations, the corporation may not deduct the $200,000 loss. ◆

Determination of whether a corporation is a *personal service corporation* is based on rather broad definitions. A personal service corporation is a corporation that meets *both* of the following conditions:

- The principal activity is the performance of personal services.
- Such services are substantially performed by owner-employees.

Personal service corporations include those in the fields of health, law, engineering, architecture, accounting, actuarial science, performing arts, and consulting.[7] A corporation is treated as a personal service corporation if more than 10 percent of the stock (by value) is held by owner-employees.[8] A shareholder is treated as an owner-employee if he or she is an employee or shareholder on *any day* during the testing period.[9] For these purposes, shareholder status and employee status do not even have to occur on the same day.

Closely Held Corporations. Application of the passive loss rules to closely held (non-personal service) corporations also is intended to prevent individuals from incorporating to avoid the passive loss limitation. A corporation is classified as a closely held corporation if, at any time during the taxable year, more than 50 percent of the value of its outstanding stock is owned, directly or indirectly, by or for not more than five individuals. Closely held corporations (other than personal service corporations) may offset passive losses against *active* income, but not against portfolio income.

Application of the passive loss limitation to closely held corporations (refer to Example 7) prevents taxpayers from transferring their portfolio investments to such corporations for the purpose of offsetting passive losses against portfolio income.

Individual taxpayers are not allowed to offset passive losses against *either* active or portfolio income.

---

7. § 448(d).
8. § 469(j)(2).
9. § 269A(b)(2).

Disallowed Passive Losses

The passive loss rules disallow 100 percent of losses on passive activities acquired after October 22, 1986. However, under transition rules the disallowance provisions for losses on passive activities acquired before October 23, 1986, were phased in over five years. If a taxpayer had a loss on a passive activity acquired before October 23, 1986 (the date TRA of 1986 was enacted), a percentage of the loss was deductible under the transition rules. Congress enacted the phase-in schedule to provide some relief to taxpayers who had committed their investment funds to passive activities prior to enactment of the passive loss limitations. The following table shows the percentages that applied during the five-year phase-in period.

Taxable Years Beginning in	Losses and Credits Allowed	Losses and Credits Disallowed
1987	65%	35%
1988	40%	60%
1989	20%	80%
1990	10%	90%
1991	0%	100%

Although the transition percentages do not allow the deduction of passive losses after 1990, it is necessary to understand how they affected taxpayers during the transition period (1987 through 1990). Losses suspended under the transition rules can be deducted in future years when the taxpayer has passive income, or upon a taxable disposition of the activity that produced the loss. Thus, the transition rules will continue to affect the computation of passive gains and losses as long as a taxpayer continues to own any pre-October 23, 1986 activity with suspended losses incurred during the transition period.

EXAMPLE 9

T acquired a passive activity in 1984. In 1990, she realized a loss of $10,000 on this activity. Under the transition rules, $1,000 (10% of $10,000) was deductible in 1990. The $9,000 disallowed loss is a suspended loss that can be carried forward and deducted against passive income in later years. If T has no passive income in later years, the suspended loss can be deducted when she disposes of the passive activity in a fully taxable transaction (see Example 62). If T had acquired the passive activity after October 22, 1986, no deduction would have been allowed in 1990, and the entire $10,000 would have been suspended. ◆

EXAMPLE 10

Assume that T in Example 9 has another loss of $20,000 on the pre-enactment passive activity in 1992. Pre-enactment passive activity losses are not deductible in 1992. The entire $20,000 loss is suspended. ◆

If a taxpayer had both pre-enactment and post-enactment activities prior to 1991, the transition percentage was applied to the lesser of (1) the pre-enactment passive activity loss, or (2) the net passive loss from pre-enactment and post-enactment activities.

EXAMPLE 11

T has two passive activity investments. Investment A was purchased in 1985, and Investment B was purchased in 1987. In 1990, Investment A generated a $10,000 loss, and Investment B generated an $8,000 gain. T's net passive loss was $2,000 ($10,000 loss − $8,000 gain). The allowable deduction was $200 (10% of $2,000). The remaining $1,800 would have been suspended and carried over. ◆

EXAMPLE 12

In Example 11, if Investment A had generated income of $10,000 and Investment B had generated an $8,000 loss, the net passive gain of $2,000 would have been included in income. ◆

EXAMPLE 13

In Example 11, assume Investment A (the pre-enactment activity) had generated a loss of $10,000 and Investment B had generated a loss of $8,000. The net passive loss was $18,000. Only $1,000 (10% of $10,000) could have been deducted in 1990. The remaining $17,000 ($8,000 post-enactment loss plus 90% of the $10,000 pre-enactment loss) would have been suspended and carried over to the future. ◆

Passive Activities Defined

Code § 469 specifies that the following types of activities are to be treated as passive:

- Any trade or business or income-producing activity in which the taxpayer does not materially participate.
- All rental activities, regardless of the level of the taxpayer's participation.

As originally enacted, § 469 required that a taxpayer participate on a *regular, continuous,* and *substantial* basis in order to be a material participant. In many situations, however, it was difficult or impossible to determine whether the taxpayer had met these vague material participation standards. The first set of Temporary Regulations under § 469,[10] issued in February 1988, helps taxpayers cope with these material participation issues.

The Temporary Regulations provide seven tests that can be applied to determine whether a taxpayer is a material participant in an activity. One of these tests specifies that a taxpayer who participates more than 500 hours a year in a nonrental trade or business activity is a material participant.

EXAMPLE 14

J spends 40 hours a week, 50 weeks a year, operating a restaurant that he owns. He also owns a men's clothing store in another state that is operated by an employee. Because J participates for more than 500 hours during the year, the restaurant is treated as an active business. However, because J does not participate in the operations of the clothing store, it is a passive activity. ◆

The seven tests for material participation provided by the Temporary Regulations, including the test reflected in Example 14, are discussed in detail under Material Participation later in the chapter.

Although the Code specifies that *rental activities* are to be treated as passive, identifying passive rental activities can be complicated. The general rule is that an activity is a rental activity if customers are charged rental fees for the use of tangible property (real or personal). However, the Temporary Regulations provide six exceptions that allow certain rental activities to escape *automatic* classification as passive activities.

10. The Temporary Regulations are also Proposed Regulations. Temporary Regulations have the same effect as Final Regulations. Refer to Chapter 2 for a discussion of the different categories of regulations.

EXAMPLE 15

K owns an apartment building and spends an average of 60 hours a week in its operation. The rental activity does not qualify under any of the six exceptions provided by the Temporary Regulations. Consequently, it is treated as a rental activity and is automatically classified as a passive activity, even though K spends more than 500 hours a year in its operation. ◆

Application of the passive loss limits to rental activities is complicated by the fact that some activites that involve rentals of real or personal property are not treated as rental activities for purposes of the passive loss provisions. As indicated above, the Temporary Regulations contain six exceptions that allow rental activities to escape automatic passive activity classification. The following example illustrates one of the exceptions.

EXAMPLE 16

T owns a videotape rental business. Because the average period of customer use is seven days or less, T's videotape business is not treated as a rental activity. ◆

The fact that T's videotape business in Example 16 is not treated as a rental activity does not necessarily mean that it is classified as a nonpassive activity. Instead, the videotape business is treated as a trade or business activity subject to the material participation standards. If T is a material participant, the business is treated as active. If T is not a material participant, it is treated as a passive activity.

The six rental exceptions provided in the Temporary Regulations, including the exception illustrated in Example 16, are discussed in detail under Rental Activities later in the chapter.

Material Participation

If an individual taxpayer materially participates in a nonrental trade or business activity, any loss from that activity is treated as an active loss that can be offset against active income. If a taxpayer does not materially participate, however, the loss is treated as a passive loss, which can only be offset against passive income. Therefore, controlling whether a particular activity is treated as active or passive is an important part of the tax strategy of a taxpayer who owns an interest in one or more businesses. Consider the following examples.

EXAMPLE 17

T, a corporate executive, earns a salary of $200,000 per year. In addition, T owns a separate business, acquired in 1988, in which he participates. The business produces a loss of $100,000 in 1992. If T materially participates in the business, the $100,000 loss is an active loss that may be offset against his active income from his corporate employer. If he does not materially participate, the loss is passive and is suspended. T may use the suspended loss in the future only if he has passive income or disposes of the activity. ◆

EXAMPLE 18

K, an attorney, earns $250,000 a year in her law practice. In 1988, she acquired interests in two activities, A and B, in which she participates in 1992. Activity A, in which she does *not* materially participate, produces a loss of $50,000. K has not yet met the material participation standard for Activity B, which produces income of $80,000. However, K can meet the material participation standard if she spends an additional 50 hours in Activity B during the year. Should K attempt to meet the material participation standard for Activity B? If she continues working in Activity B and becomes a material participant, the $80,000 income from the activity is *active,* and the

$50,000 passive loss from Activity A must be suspended. A more favorable tax strategy is for K to *not meet* the material participation standard for Activity B, thus making the income from that activity passive. This enables her to offset the $50,000 passive loss from Activity A against the passive income from Activity B. ◆

It is possible to devise numerous scenarios in which the taxpayer could control the tax outcome by increasing or decreasing his or her participation in different activities. Examples 17 and 18 demonstrate some of the possibilities. The conclusion reached in most analyses of this type is that taxpayers will benefit by having profitable activities classified as passive, so that any passive losses can be used to offset passive income. If the activity produces a loss, however, the taxpayer will benefit if it is classified as active so the loss is not subject to the passive loss limitations.

As discussed above, a nonrental trade or business in which a taxpayer owns an interest must be treated as a passive activity unless the taxpayer materially participates. The Staff of the Joint Committee on Taxation explained the importance of the material participation standard as follows:[11]

> Congress believed that there were several reasons why it was appropriate to examine the materiality of a taxpayer's participation in an activity in determining the extent to which such taxpayer should be permitted to use tax benefits from the activity. A taxpayer who materially participated in an activity was viewed as more likely than a passive investor to approach the activity with a significant nontax economic profit motive, and to form a sound judgment as to whether the activity had genuine economic significance and value. A material participation standard identified an important distinction between different types of taxpayer activities. It was thought that, in general, the more passive investor seeks a return on capital invested, including returns in the form of reductions in the taxes owed on unrelated income, rather than an ongoing source of livelihood. A material participation standard reduced the importance, for such investors, of the tax-reduction features of an investment, and thus increased the importance of the economic features in an investor's decision about where to invest his funds.

The Temporary Regulations provide specific tests for determining whether a taxpayer is a material participant.

Tests Based on Current Participation. Material participation is achieved by meeting any one of seven tests provided in the Regulations. The first four tests are quantitative tests that require measurement, in hours, of the taxpayer's participation in the activity during the year.

1. *Does the individual participate in the activity for more than 500 hours during the year?*

The purpose of the 500-hour requirement is to restrict deductions from the types of trade or business activities Congress intended to treat as passive activities. The 500-hour standard for material participation was adopted for the following reasons:[12]

- Few investors in traditional tax shelters devote more than 500 hours a year to such an investment.

11. *General Explanation of the Tax Reform Act of 1986 ("Blue Book")*, prepared by The Staff of the Joint Committee on Taxation, May 4, 1987, H.R. 3838, 99th Cong., p. 212.
12. T.D. 8175, 1988–1 C.B. 191.

- The IRS believes that income from an activity in which the taxpayer participates for more than 500 hours a year should not be treated as passive.

2. *Does the individual's participation in the activity for the taxable year constitute substantially all of the participation in the activity of all individuals (including nonowner employees) for the year?*

EXAMPLE 19

T, a physician, operates a separate business in which he participates for 80 hours during the year. He is the only participant and has no employees in the separate business. T meets the material participation standards of Test 2. If T had employees, it would be difficult to apply Test 2, because the Temporary Regulations do not define the term *substantially all.* ◆

3. *Does the individual participate in the activity for more than 100 hours during the year, and is the individual's participation in the activity for the year not less than the participation of any other individual (including nonowner employees) for the year?*

EXAMPLE 20

J, a college professor, owns a separate business in which she participates 110 hours during the year. She has an employee who works 90 hours during the year. J meets the material participation under Test 3, but probably does not meet it under Test 2 because her participation is only 55% of the total participation. It is unlikely that 55% would meet the *substantially all* requirement of Test 2. ◆

Tests 2 and 3 are included because the IRS recognizes that the operation of some activities does not require more than 500 hours of participation during the year.

4. *Is the activity a significant participation activity for the taxable year, and does the individual's aggregate participation in all significant participation activities during the year exceed 500 hours?*

A *significant participation* activity is one in which the individual's participation exceeds 100 hours during the year. The significant participation test treats taxpayers whose aggregate participation in several significant participation activities exceeds 500 hours as material participants. Test 4 thus accords the same treatment to an individual who devotes an aggregate of more than 500 hours to several significant participation activities as to an individual who devotes more than 500 hours to a single activity.

EXAMPLE 21

T owns five different businesses. He participated in each activity during the year as follows:

Activity	Hours of Participation
A	110
B	140
C	120
D	150
E	100

Activities A, B, C, and D are significant participation activities, and T's aggregate participation in those activities is 520 hours. Therefore, Activities A, B, C, and D are not treated as passive activities. Activity E is not a significant participation activity (not more than 100 hours), so it is not included in applying the 500-hour test. Activity E is treated as a passive activity, unless T meets one of the other material participation tests for that activity. ◆

EXAMPLE 22

Assume the same facts as in the previous example, except that Activity A does not exist. All of the activities are now treated as passive. Activity E is not counted in applying the more than 500-hour test, so T's aggregate participation in significant participation activities is 410 hours (140 in Activity B + 120 in Activity C + 150 in Activity D). T could meet the significant participation test for Activity E by participating for one more hour in the activity. This would cause Activities B, C, D, and E to be treated as nonpassive activities. Before deciding whether to participate for at least one more hour in Activity E, T should assess how the participation would affect his overall tax liability. ◆

Tests Based on Prior Participation. Tests 5 and 6 are based on material participation in prior years. Under these tests, a taxpayer who is no longer a participant in an activity can continue to be *classified* as a material participant. The IRS takes the position that material participation in a trade or business for a long period of time is likely to indicate that the activity represents the individual's principal livelihood, rather than a passive investment. Consequently, withdrawal from the activity, or reduction of participation to the point where it is not material, does not change the classification of the activity from active to passive.

5. *Did the individual materially participate in the activity for any 5 taxable years (whether consecutive or not) during the 10 taxable years that immediately precede the taxable year?*

Test 1 (the 500-hour test) is the only test that can be used in determining whether a taxpayer was a material participant in an activity for any taxable year beginning before 1987. Tests 2 through 7 are irrelevant for this purpose.[13]

EXAMPLE 23

D, who owns a 50% interest in a restaurant, was a material participant in the operations of the restaurant from 1986 through 1990. She retired at the end of 1990 and is no longer involved in the restaurant except as an investor. D will be treated as a material participant in the restaurant in 1991. Even if she does not become involved in the restaurant as a material participant again, she will continue to be treated as a material participant in 1992, 1993, 1994, and 1995. In 1996 and later years, D's share of income or loss from the restaurant will be classified as passive. ◆

6. *Is the activity a personal service activity, and did the individual materially participate in the activity for any three preceding taxable years (whether consecutive or not)?*

As indicated above, the material participation standards differ for personal service activities and other businesses. An individual who was a material

13. Temp. and Prop.Regs. § 1.469–5T(j).

participant in a personal service activity for *any three years* prior to the taxable year continues to be treated as a material participant after withdrawal from the activity.

EXAMPLE 24

E, a CPA, retires from the EFG Partnership after working full-time in the partnership for 30 years. As a retired partner, she will continue to receive a share of the profits of the firm for the next 10 years, even though she will not participate in the firm's operations. E also owns an interest in a passive activity that produces a loss for the year. E continues to be treated as a material participant in the EFG Partnership, and her income from the partnership is active income. She is not allowed to offset the loss from her passive investment against the income from the EFG Partnership. ◆

Facts and Circumstances Test. Test 7 is a facts and circumstances test to determine whether the taxpayer has materially participated.

7. *Based on all the facts and circumstances, did the individual participate in the activity on a regular, continuous, and substantial basis during the year?*

The Temporary Regulations do not define what constitutes regular, continuous, and substantial participation except to say that the taxpayer's activities will *not* be considered material participation under Test 7 in the following three circumstances:[14]

- The taxpayer satisfies the participation standards (whether or not a *material participant*) of any Code section other than § 469.
- The taxpayer manages the activity, unless
  - no other person receives compensation for management services, and
  - no individual spends more hours during the tax year managing the activity than does the taxpayer.
- The taxpayer participates in the activity for 100 hours or less during the tax year.

A part of the Temporary Regulations has been reserved for further development of this test. Presumably, additional guidelines will be issued in the future. For the time being, taxpayers should rely on Tests 1 through 6 in determing the nature of an activity.

Participation Defined. Participation generally includes any work done by an individual in an activity that he or she owns. Participation does not include work if it is of a type not customarily done by owners *and* if one of its principal purposes is to avoid the disallowance of passive losses or credits. Also, work done in an individual's capacity as an investor (e.g., reviewing financial reports in a nonmanagerial capacity) is not counted in applying the material participation tests. Participation by an owner's spouse counts as participation by the owner.[15]

EXAMPLE 25

T, who is a partner in a CPA firm, owns a computer store that has operated at a loss during the year. In order to offset this loss against the income from his CPA practice, T would like to avoid having the computer business classified as a passive activity.

14. Temp. and Prop.Regs. § 1.469–5T(b)(2).

15. Temp. and Prop.Regs. § 1.469–5T(f)(3).

Through December 15, he has worked 400 hours in the business in management and selling activities. During the last two weeks of December, he works 80 hours in management and selling activities and 30 hours doing janitorial chores. Also during the last two weeks in December, T's wife participates 40 hours as a salesperson. She has worked as a salesperson in the computer store in prior years, but has not done so during the current year. If any of T's work is of a type not customarily done by owners *and* if one of its principal purposes is to avoid the disallowance of passive losses or credits, it is not counted in applying the material participation tests. It is likely that T's 480 hours of participation in management and selling activities will count as participation, but the 30 hours spent doing janitorial chores will not. However, the 40 hours of participation by T's wife will count, and T will qualify as a material participant under the more-than-500-hour rule (480 + 40 = 520). ◆

Limited Partners. Generally, a *limited partner* is not considered a material participant unless he or she qualifies under Test 1, 5, or 6 in the above list. However, a *general partner* may qualify as a material participant by meeting any of the seven tests. If an unlimited, or general, partner also owns a limited interest in the same limited partnership, all interests are treated as a general interest.[16]

Rental Activities

As discussed previously (refer to Example 15), § 469 specifies that all rental activities are to be treated as passive activities.[17] A rental activity is defined as any activity where payments are received principally for the use of tangible property.[18] However, Temporary Regulations provide that in certain circumstances activities involving rentals of real and personal property are *not* to be treated as rental activities.[19]

Activities covered by any of the following six exceptions in the Temporary Regulations are not *automatically* treated as passive activities. Instead, the activities are subject to the material participation tests (refer to Example 16).

1. *The average period of customer use for the property is seven days or less.*

Under this exception, activities involving the short-term use of tangible property such as automobiles, videocassettes, tuxedos, tools, and other such property are not treated as rental activities. The provision also applies to short-term rentals of hotel or motel rooms.

This exception is based on the presumption that a person who rents property for seven days or less is generally required to provide *significant services* to the customer. Providing such services supports a conclusion that the person is engaged in a service business rather than a rental business.

2. *The average period of customer use for the property is 30 days or less, and the owner of the property provides significant personal services.*

For longer-term rentals, the presumption that significant services are provided is not automatic, as it is in the case of the seven-day exception. Instead, the taxpayer must be able to *prove* that significant personal services are rendered in connection with the activity. Therefore, an understanding of what constitutes significant personal services is necessary in order to apply the rule.

16. Temp. and Prop.Regs. § 1.469–5T(e)(3)(ii).
17. § 469(c)(2).
18. § 469(j)(8).
19. Temp. and Prop.Regs. § 1.469–1T(e)(3)(ii).

Significant personal services include only services provided by *individuals*. This provision excludes such items as telephone and cable television services. Four additional categories of *excluded services* are not considered significant personal services:[20]

- Services necessary to permit the lawful use of the property.
- Services performed in connection with the construction of improvements to property.
- Services performed in connection with the performance of repairs that extend the property's useful life for a period substantially longer than the average period for which the property is used by customers.
- Services similar to those commonly provided in connection with long-term rentals of high-grade commercial or residential real property (including cleaning and maintenance of common areas, routine repairs, trash collection, elevator service, and security at entrances or perimeters).

3. *The owner of the property provides extraordinary personal services. The average period of customer use is of no consequence in applying this test.*

Extraordinary personal services are services provided by individuals where the customers' use of the property is incidental to their receipt of the services. For example, a patient's use of a hospital bed is incidental to his or her use of medical services. Another example is the use of a boarding school's dormitory, which is incidental to the scholastic services received.

4. *The rental of the property is treated as incidental to a nonrental activity of the taxpayer.*

Rentals of real property incidental to a nonrental activity are not considered a passive activity. The Temporary Regulations provide that the following rentals are not passive activities:[21]

- *Property held primarily for investment.* This occurs where the principal purpose for holding the property is the expectation of gain from the appreciation of the property and the gross rent income is less than 2 percent of the lesser of (1) the unadjusted basis or (2) the fair market value of the property.

EXAMPLE 26

A taxpayer invests in vacant land for the purpose of realizing a profit on its appreciation. He leases the land during the period it is held. The unadjusted basis is $250,000, and the fair market value is $350,000. The lease payments are $4,000 per year. Because gross rent income is less than 2% of $250,000, the activity is not a rental activity. ◆

- *Property used in a trade or business.* This occurs where the property is owned by a taxpayer who is an owner of the trade or business using the rental property. The property must also have been used in the trade or business during the year or during at least two of the five preceding taxable years. The 2 percent test above also applies in this situation.

20. Temp. and Prop.Regs. § 1.469–1T(e)(3)(iv).

21. Temp. and Prop.Regs. §§ 1.469–1T(e)(3)(vi)(B) through (E).

EXAMPLE 27

A farmer owns land with an unadjusted basis of $250,000 and a fair market value of $350,000. He used it for farming purposes in 1990 and 1991. In 1992, he leased the land to another farmer for $4,000. The activity is not a rental activity. ◆

- *Property held for sale to customers.* If property is held for sale to customers and rented during the year, the rental of the property is not a rental activity.

EXAMPLE 28

An automobile dealer rents automobiles held for sale to customers to persons who are having their own cars repaired. The activity is not a rental activity. ◆

EXAMPLE 29

A taxpayer acquires land upon which to construct a shopping center. Before beginning construction, she rents it to a business for use as a parking lot. Since she did not acquire the land as an investment, nor use it in her trade or business, nor hold it for sale to customers, the rental is a rental activity. ◆

- *Lodging rented for the convenience of an employer.* If an employer provides lodging for an employee incidental to the employee's performance of services in the employer's trade or business, no rental activity exists.

EXAMPLE 30

J has a farming business. He rents houses on his property to migrant workers during the harvest season. J does not have a rental activity. ◆

- A partner who rents property to a partnership that is used in the partnership's trade or business does not have a rental activity.

EXAMPLE 31

B, the owner of a business, incorporates the business, retaining the land and building as her separate property. She then rents the property to the business. B does not have a rental activity. ◆

These rules were written to prevent taxpayers from converting active or portfolio income into a passive activity for the purpose of offsetting other passive losses.

In other cases, passive activity income is reclassified as nonpassive activity income. Such cases include significant participation activities, rentals of nondepreciable property, net investment income from passive equity-financed lending activities, net income from certain property rented incidental to development activities, and property rented to a nonpassive activity.[22]

5. *The taxpayer customarily makes the property available during defined business hours for nonexclusive use by various customers.*

EXAMPLE 32

P is the owner-operator of a public golf course. Some customers pay daily greens fees each time they use the course, while others purchase weekly, monthly, or annual passes. The golf course is open every day from sunrise to sunset, except on certain

22. Temp. and Prop.Regs. §§ 1.469–2T(f)(2) through (7).

holidays and on days when the course is closed due to weather conditions. P is not engaged in a rental activity, regardless of the average period customers use the course. ◆

6. *The property is provided for use in an activity conducted by a partnership, S corporation, or joint venture in which the taxpayer owns an interest.*

EXAMPLE 33

B, a partner in the ABC Partnership, contributes the use of a building to the partnership. The partnership has net income of $30,000 during the year, of which B's share is $10,000. Unless the partnership is engaged in a rental activity, none of B's income from the partnership is income from a rental activity. ◆

Calculation of Passive Losses

The Code defines passive activity loss as the amount (if any) by which aggregate losses from all passive activities exceed the aggregate income from all passive activities for the year.[23] The Temporary Regulations, on the other hand, define passive loss as the amount (if any) by which passive activity deductions for the taxable year exceed the passive activity gross income for the taxable year.[24]

While the passive loss definitions in the Code and Temporary Regulations appear very similar, there is an important difference. The Code definition implies that there are two steps in determining the amount of a passive loss:

- Compute the passive loss or passive income for each separate passive activity.
- Offset net passive income from profitable activities against net passive losses from unprofitable activities.

Under the approach specified in the Temporary Regulations, the *expenses* from all passive activities are subtracted from the *income* from all passive activities. If expenses exceed income, the net result is a passive loss.

Until the disparity between the Code and Temporary Regulations is resolved, taxpayers should follow the Code since it is a higher ranking source of authority. In addition, the Code requires any suspended passive losses to be allocated among different activities of the taxpayer (see Example 52). This cannot be done unless the Code approach to computing passive losses is followed. The following example illustrates the Code definition of passive loss.

EXAMPLE 34

In the current year, a taxpayer participates in two passive activities. Both activities were acquired in 1987. Activity A generates passive income of $5,500. Activity B generates a passive loss of $8,500. The $5,500 of passive income is sheltered by $5,500 of the passive loss. However, the net passive loss of $3,000 ($8,500 less $5,500) may not be applied against other nonpassive income. The loss may be carried forward to the succeeding year and applied against any passive income of that year. Such losses are called *suspended losses*. ◆

Identification of Passive Activity

Identifying what constitutes an *activity* is an important step in applying the passive loss limitations. Taxpayers who are involved in complex business

23. § 469(d)(1).

24. Temp. and Prop.Regs. § 1.469–2T(b).

operations need to be able to determine whether a given segment of their overall business operations constitutes a separate activity or is to be treated as part of a single activity. Proper treatment is necessary in order to determine whether income or loss from an activity is active or passive.

EXAMPLE 35

T owns a business with two separate departments. Department A generates $120,000 of income, and Department B produces a $95,000 loss. T participates for 700 hours in the operations of Department A. He participates for 100 hours in Department B. If T is allowed to treat both departments as a single activity, he is a material participant in the activity because his participation (700 + 100) exceeds 500 hours. Therefore, T can offset the $95,000 loss from Department B against the $120,000 of income from Department A. ◆

EXAMPLE 36

Assume the same facts as in Example 35. If T is required to treat each department as a separate activity, he is a material participant in Department A (700 hours), and the $120,000 profit is active income. However, he is not a material participant in Department B (100 hours), and the $95,000 loss is a passive loss. T cannot offset the $95,000 passive loss from Department B against the $120,000 of active income from Department A. ◆

Upon disposition of a passive activity, a taxpayer is allowed to offset suspended losses from the activity against other types of income. Therefore, identifying what constitutes an activity is of critical importance.

EXAMPLE 37

P owns a business with two departments. She participates for 200 hours in Department A, which had a loss of $125,000 in the current year. P participates for 250 hours in Department B, which had a $70,000 loss. P disposes of Department B during the year. She is allowed to treat the two departments as *separate activities.* P is allowed to offset the passive loss from Department B against other types of income in the following order: gain from disposition of the passive activity, other passive income, and nonpassive income. She has a suspended loss of $125,000 from Department A. ◆

EXAMPLE 38

Assume the same facts as in Example 37, except that P is required to treat the two departments as a *single activity.* Because she has not disposed of the entire activity (Departments A and B combined), P is not allowed to utilize the $70,000 loss from Department B. She has a suspended loss of $195,000 ($125,000 from Department A and $70,000 from Department B). ◆

In May 1989, the Treasury Department issued Temporary Regulations to provide guidance as to what constitutes an activity.[25] Because these Temporary Regulations are long (196 pages) and complex, only the general rules are discussed here. Refer to the Regulations for the numerous special rules and exceptions.

The Temporary Regulations specify that, as a general rule, each *undertaking* that a taxpayer owns is a separate activity. Therefore, the first step in determining what constitutes an activity is to identify a taxpayer's *undertakings.* An undertaking is the smallest unit that can constitute an activity. An undertaking may include diverse business and rental operations. The primary factors

25. Temp. and Prop.Regs. § 1.469–4T.

considered in identifying an undertaking are *location* and *ownership*. Generally, business and rental operations that are conducted at the same location and are owned by the same person are treated as part of the same undertaking. Operations conducted in the same physical structure or within close proximity of one another are treated as conducted in the same location. Business and rental operations that are conducted at different locations or are not owned by the same person constitute separate undertakings. Examples 39 through 41 illustrate these rules.[26]

EXAMPLE 39

J is the owner of a department store and a restaurant. He conducts both businesses in the same building. J participates 450 hours in the operations of the department store, which produces income of $100,000 during the year. He participates for 100 hours in the operations of the restaurant, which produces a $45,000 loss. The department store and the restaurant are treated as a single activity because they are owned by the same person and business is conducted at the same location. J is a material participant in the activity (450 hours + 100 hours exceeds 500 hours). Therefore, the $45,000 loss from the restaurant can be offset against the $100,000 of income from the department store. ◆

EXAMPLE 40

Assume the same facts as in Example 39 and that J also operates an automotive center in a mall near the department store/restaurant building. The department store, restaurant, and automotive center are all part of a single activity because all three undertakings are operated in close proximity. ◆

EXAMPLE 41

Assume the same facts as in Example 40, except that the automotive center is located several blocks from the department store/restaurant building. The department store/restaurant operations constitute an activity, and the automotive center constitutes a separate activity. ◆

The basic undertaking rule is modified if the undertaking includes both rental and nonrental operations. In these circumstances, the rental and nonrental operations generally must be treated as separate activities.[27] This rule is necessary because rental operations are always treated as passive, whereas nonrental operations are treated as passive only if the owner is not a material participant.

EXAMPLE 42

B owns a building in which she rents apartments to tenants and operates a restaurant. Sixty percent of B's gross income is attributable to the apartments, and 40% is attributable to the restaurant. The apartment undertaking and the restaurant operation are treated as two separate activities. The apartment undertaking is a passive activity. The classification of the restaurant undertaking depends on whether B is a material participant. ◆

Under a special exception, rental and nonrental operations may be treated as a single operation, rather than as separate operations, when either the rental or nonrental operations are a predominant part of the undertaking. This exception

---

26. Temp. and Prop.Regs. § 1.469–4T(c)(4), Examples 1, 2, and 3.

27. Temp. and Prop.Regs. § 1.469–4T(a)(3)(iv).

applies when less than 20 percent of the gross income from the undertaking is attributable to either rental or nonrental operations.[28]

EXAMPLE 43

Assume the same facts as in Example 42, except that 85% of B's gross income from the undertaking is attributable to apartment rentals and 15% is attributable to the restaurant. Because less than 20% of the gross income is attributable to nonrental operations (the restaurant), the rental operation and the restaurant operation are considered a single activity.[29] ◆

In Example 43, the rental operation is the predominant part of the undertaking (85 percent rental versus 15 percent nonrental). Therefore, the entire undertaking is treated as a single activity that is a rental activity. If, on the other hand, the restaurant produced 85 percent of the gross income and the apartment rentals produced 15 percent, the restaurant would be the predominant part of the undertaking. In this case, the entire undertaking is treated as a single activity that is a nonrental activity. The material participation tests are applied to determine whether the activity is active or passive.

The exception illustrated in Example 43 is intended to reduce the accounting burdens on taxpayers in circumstances where one part of the undertaking is predominant. When the exception applies, taxpayers are not required to separate their rental and nonrental operations into separate activities.

In addition to the basic rules discussed above, the activity regulations address many other complex issues. For example, taxpayers with rental real estate operations at different locations are covered by rather flexible rules. These rules permit taxpayers to treat their real estate operations at different locations as separate activities or to combine operations or portions of operations at different locations into larger activities.

Flexibility is also provided when a taxpayer sells part of an integrated, interrelated economic unit. Under certain circumstances, taxpayers may elect to treat the parts as separate activities in order to trigger the deduction of losses upon disposition.

Income Not Treated as Passive

Certain items of income and expense are not taken into account in computing passive activity losses.[30] Some of these income items are discussed in this section. Others are beyond the scope of this text. Deductions that are not treated as passive are covered in the following section.

Portfolio income of an activity is not included in computing the passive income or loss from the activity. This provision negates any tax benefit taxpayers would otherwise achieve by transferring assets that produce portfolio income to an activity that produces a passive loss. Thus, it is possible that an activity might produce a passive loss *and* portfolio income in the same year.

EXAMPLE 44

K owns an activity that produces a passive loss of $15,000 during the year. He transfers to the activity corporate stock that produces portfolio income of $15,000. The passive loss cannot be offset against the portfolio income. K must report a passive loss of $15,000 and portfolio income of $15,000 from the activity. ◆

---

28. Temp. and Prop.Regs. § 1.469–4T(d)(2).

29. Temp. and Prop.Regs. § 1.469–4T(d)(4), Example 2.

30. Temp. and Prop.Regs. § 1.469–2T(a)(2).

Portfolio income includes interest, annuities, royalties, dividends, and other items. However, such income is included in the passive loss computation if it is *derived* in the ordinary course of business.[31] For example, interest earned on loans made in the ordinary course of a trade or business of lending money is not treated as portfolio income. In addition, interest on accounts receivable arising from the performance of services or the sale of property is not treated as portfolio income if the business customarily offers credit to customers.

Gains on dispositions of portfolio assets are also treated as portfolio income. The rules for determining whether other gain is to be treated as portfolio income are very complex and are beyond the scope of this text. Refer to the Temporary and Proposed Regulations for additional information.[32]

Compensation paid to or on behalf of an individual for services performed or to be performed is not treated as passive activity gross income.[33]

EXAMPLE 45

T owns 50% of the stock of X, Inc., an S corporation that owns rental real estate. X pays T a $10,000 salary for services she performs for the corporation in connection with managing the rental real estate. The corporation has a $30,000 passive loss on the property during the year. T must report compensation income of $10,000 and a passive loss of $15,000 ($30,000 × 50%). ◆

The following are some of the other income items that are specifically excluded from the passive loss computation:[34]

- Gross income of an individual from intangible property (such as a patent, copyright, or literary, musical, or artistic composition) if the taxpayer's personal efforts significantly contributed to the creation of the property.
- Gross income attributable to a refund of any state, local, or foreign income, war profits, or excess profits tax.
- Gross income of an individual for a covenant not to compete.

Deductions Not Treated as Passive

The general rule is that a deduction is treated as a passive activity deduction if and only if the deduction arises in connection with the conduct of an activity that is a passive activity. The Temporary Regulations list several items that are not treated as passive activity deductions:[35]

- Any deduction for an expense that is clearly and directly allocable to portfolio income.
- Any deduction for a loss from the disposition of property of a type that produces portfolio income.
- Any deduction related to a dividend if the dividend is not included in passive activity gross income.
- Any deduction for qualified residence interest or interest that is capitalized under a capitalization provision.
- Any miscellaneous itemized deduction that is disallowed by operation of the 2 percent floor.

31. Temp. and Prop.Regs. § 1.469–2T(c)(3).
32. Temp. and Prop.Regs. § 1.469–2T(c)(2).
33. Temp. and Prop.Regs. § 1.469–2T(c)(4).
34. Temp. and Prop.Regs. § 1.469–2T(c)(7).
35. Temp. and Prop.Regs. § 1.469–2T(d).

- Any deduction allowed under § 170 for a charitable contribution.
- Any net operating loss carryforward allowed under § 172.
- Any capital loss carryforward allowed under § 1212(b).

EXAMPLE 46

P, who owns a sole proprietorship that is a passive activity, calculated a loss for the activity as follows:

Operating income	$ 50,000
Dividends on stock held for investment	15,000
Total income	$ 65,000
– Expenses:	
Operating expenses (wages, rent, supplies, etc.)	(60,000)
Investment interest	(8,000)
– Loss on sale of stock held for investment	(5,000)
= Net loss	$ (8,000)

◆

EXAMPLE 47

In computing P's passive loss, the net loss of $8,000 in Example 46 must be modified because the computation included gross income and deductions that are not to be considered in computing a passive loss. The passive loss is computed as follows:

Operating income	$ 50,000
– Operating expenses (wages, rent, supplies, etc.)	(60,000)
= Passive loss	$(10,000)

◆

A comparison of Examples 46 and 47 shows that the portfolio income is not included in computing the passive loss, and that no deduction is taken for the investment interest or the loss on the portfolio investment.

Suspended Losses

The determination of whether a loss is suspended under the passive loss rule is made after application of the at-risk rules, as well as other provisions relating to the measurement of taxable income. A loss that is not allowed for the year because the taxpayer is not at risk with respect to it is suspended under the at-risk provision and not under the passive loss rule.

A taxpayer's basis is reduced by deductions (e.g., depreciation) even if the deductions are not currently usable because of the passive loss rule.

EXAMPLE 48

T's adjusted basis in a passive activity is $10,000 at the beginning of 1991. His loss from the activity in 1991 is $4,000. Since T had no passive activity income, the $4,000 cannot be deducted. At year-end, T has an adjusted basis of $6,000 in the activity and a suspended loss of $4,000. ◆

EXAMPLE 49

T in Example 48 had a loss of $9,000 in the activity in 1992. Since the $9,000 exceeds T's at-risk amount ($6,000) by $3,000, that $3,000 loss is disallowed by the at-risk rules. If T has no passive activity income, the remaining $6,000 is suspended under the passive activity rules. At year-end, T has a $3,000 unused loss under the at-risk rules, $10,000 of suspended passive losses, and an adjusted basis in the activity of zero. ◆

EXAMPLE 50

T in Example 49 realized a $1,000 gain in 1993. Because the $1,000 increases his at-risk amount, $1,000 of the $3,000 unused loss can be reclassified as a passive loss. If T has no other passive income, the $1,000 income is offset against $1,000 of suspended passive losses. At the end of 1993, T has no taxable passive income, $2,000 ($3,000 − $1,000) of unused losses under the at-risk rules, $10,000 of (reclassified) suspended passive losses, ($10,000 + $1,000 of reclassified unused at-risk losses − $1,000 of passive losses offset against passive gains), and an adjusted basis in the activity of zero. ◆

EXAMPLE 51

In 1994, T had no gain or loss from the activity in Example 50. He contributed $5,000 more to the passive activity. Because the $5,000 increases his at-risk amount, the $2,000 of unused losses under the at-risk rules is reclassified as a passive loss. T gets no passive loss deduction in 1994. At year-end, he has no unused losses under the at-risk rules, $12,000 of suspended passive losses ($10,000 + $2,000 of reclassified unused at-risk losses), and an adjusted basis of $3,000 ($5,000 additional investment − $2,000 of reclassified losses). ◆

Interest deductions attributable to passive activities are treated as passive activity deductions but are not treated as investment interest. (See Chapter 11 for a detailed discussion of investment interest.) As a result, these interest deductions are subject to limitation under the passive loss rule and not under the investment interest limitation.

Carryovers of Suspended Losses. To determine the suspended loss for an activity, passive activity losses must be allocated among all activities in which the taxpayer has an interest. The allocation to the activity is made by multiplying the disallowed passive activity loss from all activities by a fraction. The numerator of the fraction is the loss from the activity, and the denominator is the sum of the losses for the taxable year from all activities having losses.

EXAMPLE 52

T has investments in three passive activities (acquired in 1992) with the following income and losses for that year:

Activity A	$(30,000)
Activity B	(20,000)
Activity C	25,000
Net passive loss	$(25,000)
Allocated to:	
A ($25,000 × $30,000/$50,000)	$ 15,000
B ($25,000 × $20,000/$50,000)	10,000
Total suspended losses	$(25,000)

◆

Suspended losses are carried over indefinitely and are offset against any passive income from the activities to which they relate in the future.[36]

EXAMPLE 53

Assume the same facts as in Example 52 and that Activity A produces $15,000 of income in 1993. The disallowed loss of $15,000 from 1992 for Activity A is offset against the income from Activity A. ◆

36. § 469(b).

Upon the taxable disposition of a passive activity, the suspended passive losses from that activity can be offset against the taxpayer's nonpassive and portfolio income. See Dispositions of Passive Interests later in the chapter.

Passive Credits

Credits arising from passive activities are limited much like passive losses. They can be utilized only against regular tax attributable to passive income,[37] which is calculated by comparing the tax on all income (including passive income) with the tax on income excluding passive income.

EXAMPLE 54

A taxpayer owes $50,000 of tax, disregarding net passive income, and $80,000 of tax, considering both net passive and other taxable income (disregarding the credits in both cases). The amount of tax attributable to the passive income is $30,000.

Tax due (before credits) including net passive income	$80,000
Less: Tax due (before credits) without including net passive income	(50,000)
Tax attributable to passive income	$30,000

◆

The taxpayer in the preceding example can claim a maximum of $30,000 of passive activity credits; the excess credits are carried over. These passive activity credits (such as the jobs credit, low-income housing credit, research activities credit, and rehabilitation credit) can be used against the *regular* tax attributable to passive income only. If a taxpayer has a net loss from passive activities during a given year, no credits can be used. Likewise, if a taxpayer has net passive income but the alternative minimum tax applies to that year, no passive activity credits can be used. (The alternative minimum tax is discussed in Chapter 12.) In addition, the unused passive losses are carried over.

When the passive activity that generates tax credits fits under the exception for real estate rental activities (discussed subsequently under Real Estate Rental Activities), the credits must be converted into *deduction equivalents*. The deduction equivalent is the deduction necessary to reduce one's tax liability by an amount equal to the credit. A taxpayer with $5,000 of credits and a tax bracket of 28 percent would have a deduction equivalent of $17,857 ($5,000 divided by 28 percent). See the subsequent discussion under Real Estate Rental Activities for examples calculating deduction equivalents.

Carryovers of Passive Credits. Tax credits attributable to passive activities can be carried forward indefinitely much like suspended passive losses. Unlike passive losses, however, passive credits can be lost forever when the activity is disposed of in a taxable transaction.

EXAMPLE 55

T sells a passive activity for a gain of $10,000. The activity had suspended losses of $40,000 and suspended credits of $15,000. The $10,000 gain is offset by $10,000 of the suspended losses, and the remaining $30,000 of suspended losses is deductible against T's active and portfolio income. The suspended credits are lost forever because the sale of the activity did not generate any tax. This is true even if T has positive taxable income or is subject to the alternative minimum tax. ◆

37. § 469(d)(2).

EXAMPLE 56

If T in Example 55 had realized a $100,000 gain on the sale of the passive activity, the $15,000 of suspended credits could have been used to the extent of regular tax attributable to the net passive income.

Gain on sale	$100,000
Less: Suspended losses	40,000
Net gain	$ 60,000

If the tax attributable to the net gain of $60,000 is $15,000 or more, the entire $15,000 of suspended credits can be used. If the tax attributable to the gain is less than $15,000, the excess of the suspended credit over the tax attributable to the gain is lost forever. ◆

When a taxpayer has adequate regular tax liability from passive activities to trigger the use of suspended credits, the credits lose their character as passive credits. They are reclassified as regular tax credits and made subject to the same limits as other credits (discussed in Chapter 13).

This reclassification of passive credits can occur when they cannot be used in the year of reclassification because the taxpayer is subject to the alternative minimum tax (discussed in Chapter 12). Tax credits cannot reduce the tax calculated under the alternative minimum tax rules; the credits are carried over under the general rules for tax credits. Form 8582–CR (Passive Activity Credit Limitations) is used to report passive activity credits.

EXAMPLE 57

During the year, T had the following regular tax, alternative minimum tax, and credits:

Activity	Regular Tax	Alternative Minimum Tax	Tax Credits	Carried Over as Passive	Carried Over as Regular
Passive	$ 50	$150	$150	$100	$ 50
Active	500	450	150	—	150
	$550	$600	$300	$100	$200

Even though T has to pay the alternative minimum tax of $600 since it exceeds the regular tax of $550, he can reclassify $50 of the suspended passive credits as regular credits because of the $50 of regular tax generated by passive income. He has suspended passive credits of $100 left over for use against future passive income tax. The $50 of reclassified credits can be used in a future year (together with the $150 of active credits) against tax attributable to active and portfolio income. The entire $200 of regular tax credit carryovers is subject to the general rules governing credits (see Chapter 13). ◆

Real Estate Rental Activities

The passive loss limits contain two exceptions related to real estate activities. These exceptions allow all or part of real estate rental losses to be offset against active or portfolio income, even though the activity is a passive activity.

The first exception provides favorable treatment for investors in low-income housing. Under a transition rule, losses from certain investments in low-income housing are not treated as passive losses for a period of up to seven years from the date of the original investment.

The second exception is more significant in that it is not restricted to low-income housing. This exception allows individuals to deduct up to $25,000 of losses on real estate rental activities against active and portfolio income.[38] The annual $25,000 deduction is reduced by 50 percent of the taxpayer's AGI in excess of $100,000. Thus, the entire deduction is phased out at $150,000. If married individuals file separately, the $25,000 deduction is reduced to zero unless they lived apart for the entire year. If they lived apart for the entire year, the loss amount is $12,500 each, and the phase-out begins at $50,000. AGI for purposes of the phase-out is calculated without regard to IRA deductions, Social Security benefits, and net losses from passive activities.

To qualify for the $25,000 exception, a taxpayer must meet the following requirements:[39]

- Actively participate in the real estate rental activity.
- Own 10 percent or more (in value) of all interests in the activity during the entire taxable year (or shorter period during which the taxpayer held an interest in the activity).

The difference between *active participation* and *material participation* is that the former can be satisfied without regular, continuous, and substantial involvement in operations as long as the taxpayer participates in the making of management decisions in a significant and bona fide sense. In this context, relevant management decisions include such decisions as approving new tenants, deciding on rental terms, and approving capital or repair expenditures.

The $25,000 allowance is available after all active participation rental losses and gains are netted and applied to other passive income. If a taxpayer has a real estate rental loss in excess of the amount that can be deducted under the real estate rental exception, that excess is treated as a passive loss.

EXAMPLE 58

K, who has $90,000 of AGI before considering rental activities, has $85,000 of losses from a real estate rental activity in which she actively participates. She also actively participates in another real estate rental activity from which she has $25,000 of income. She has other passive income of $36,000. The net rental loss of $60,000 is offset by the $36,000 of passive income, leaving $24,000 that can be deducted against other income. ◆

The $25,000 offset allowance is an aggregate of both deductions and credits in deduction equivalents. The deduction equivalent of a passive activity credit is the amount of deductions that reduces the tax liability for the taxable year by an amount equal to the credit.[40] If the total deduction and deduction equivalent exceed $25,000, the taxpayer must allocate on a pro rata basis, first among the losses (including real estate rental activity losses suspended in prior years) and then to credits in the following order: (1) credits other than rehabilitation credits, (2) rehabilitation credits, and (3) low-income housing credits.

EXAMPLE 59

T is an active participant in a real estate rental activity that produces $8,000 of income, $26,000 of deductions, and $1,500 of credits. T, who is in the 28% tax bracket, may deduct the net passive loss of $18,000 ($8,000 less $26,000). After deducting the loss,

38. § 469(i).

39. § 469(i)(6).

40. § 469(j)(5).

he has an available deduction equivalent of $7,000 ($25,000 less $18,000 passive loss). Therefore, the maximum amount of credits that T may claim is $1,960 ($7,000 × 28%). Since the actual credits are less than this amount, T may claim the entire $1,500 credit. ◆

EXAMPLE 60

B, who is in the 28% tax bracket, is an active participant in three separate real estate rental activities. She has $20,000 of losses from Activity A, $10,000 of losses from Activity B, and $4,200 of passive credits from Activity C. B's deduction equivalent from the credits is $15,000 ($4,200 ÷ .28). Total passive deductions and deduction equivalents are $45,000 ($20,000 + $10,000 + $15,000) and therefore exceed the maximum allowable amount of $25,000. B must allocate pro rata first from among losses and then from among credits. Deductions from Activity A are limited to $16,667 ($25,000 × [$20,000 ÷ ($20,000 + $10,000)], and deductions from Activity B are limited to $8,333 ($25,000 × [$10,000 ÷ ($20,000 + $10,000)]).

Since the amount of passive deductions exceeds the $25,000 maximum, the deduction balance of $5,000 and passive credit of $4,200 must be carried forward. B's suspended losses and credits by activity are as follows:

		Activity		
	Total	A	B	C
Allocated losses	$30,000	$20,000	$10,000	$ -0-
Allocated credits	4,200	-0-	-0-	4,200
Utilized losses	25,000	(16,667)	(8,333)	-0-
Suspended losses	5,000	3,333	1,667	-0-
Suspended credits	4,200	-0-	-0-	4,200 ◆

Further complications arise when passive rental activities generate both losses and credits. Recall that the phase-out of rental losses begins when the taxpayer's AGI reaches $100,000. For each two dollars by which AGI exceeds $100,000, one dollar of the $25,000 loss is disallowed. When the taxpayer's AGI reaches $150,000, no real estate rental loss is allowed.

Where real estate rental activities generate rehabilitation credits and low-income housing credits on property placed in service before 1990, the phase-out range is between $200,000 and $250,000 of AGI.

EXAMPLE 61

T has a net passive activity loss attributable to a low-income housing activity placed in service before 1990. If her AGI is $175,000, she cannot deduct a loss on the activity because her AGI exceeds the upper limit of the loss phase-out range of $150,000. She can use up to $25,000 of deduction equivalents ($7,000 of credits) of a low-income housing credit because that phase-out does not begin until AGI reaches $200,000. ◆

Low-income housing credits on property placed in service after 1989 are not subject to the $25,000 deduction equivalent phase-out rules.

Dispositions of Passive Interests

When a taxpayer disposes of his or her entire interest in a passive activity, the actual economic gain or loss on the investment finally can be determined. As a result, under the passive loss rules, upon a fully taxable disposition, any overall loss from the activity realized by the taxpayer is recognized and allowed against any income. Special rules apply to dispositions of certain property that disallow their classification as passive income. Included in these rules are dispositions of partnership interests and S corporation stock, partial interests in property,

property used in more than one activity, and substantially appreciated property formerly used in a nonpassive activity.[41]

Since the purpose of the disposition rule is to allow the taxpayer's real economic losses to be deducted, credits (which are not related to the measurement of such loss) are not allowable specially by reason of a disposition. Credits are allowed only when there is sufficient tax on passive income to absorb them.

A fully taxable disposition generally includes a sale of the property to a third party at arm's length and thus, presumably, for a price equal to the property's fair market value. Gain recognized upon a transfer of an interest in a passive activity generally is treated as passive and is first offset by the suspended losses from that activity.

EXAMPLE 62

T sold an apartment house with an adjusted basis of $100,000 for $180,000. In addition, T has suspended losses associated with that specific apartment house of $60,000. The total gain, $80,000, and the taxable gain, $20,000, are calculated as follows:

Net sales price	$ 180,000
Less: Adjusted basis	(100,000)
Total gain	$ 80,000
Less: Suspended losses	(60,000)
Taxable gain (passive)	$ 20,000

◆

If current and suspended losses of the passive activity exceed the gain realized or if the sale results in a realized loss, the sum of

- any loss from the activity for the tax year (including losses suspended in the activity disposed of), plus
- any loss realized on the disposition

in excess of

- net income or gain for the tax year from all passive activities (without regard to the activity disposed of)

is treated as a loss that is not from a passive activity.

EXAMPLE 63

T sold an apartment house with an adjusted basis of $100,000 for $150,000. In addition, T has current and suspended losses associated with that specific apartment house of $60,000 and has no other passive activities. The total gain, $50,000, and the deductible loss, $10,000, are calculated as follows:

Net sales price	$ 150,000
Less: Adjusted basis	(100,000)
Total gain	$ 50,000
Less: Suspended losses	(60,000)
Deductible loss	$ (10,000)

The $10,000 deductible loss is offset against T's ordinary income and portfolio income. ◆

41. Temp. and Prop.Regs. §§ 1.469–2T(c)(2)(i) through (iii).

Disposition of a Passive Activity at Death. A transfer of a taxpayer's interest in an activity by reason of the taxpayer's death results in suspended losses being allowed (to the decedent) to the extent they exceed the amount, if any, of the step-up in basis allowed.[42] Suspended losses are lost to the extent of the amount of the basis increase. The losses allowed generally are reported on the final return of the deceased taxpayer.

EXAMPLE 64

A taxpayer dies with passive activity property having an adjusted basis of $40,000, suspended losses of $10,000, and a fair market value at the date of the decedent's death of $75,000. The step-up in basis (see Chapter 14) is $35,000 (fair market value at date of death in excess of adjusted basis). None of the $10,000 suspended loss is deductible by either the decedent or the beneficiary. The suspended losses ($10,000) did not exceed the step-up in basis ($35,000). ◆

EXAMPLE 65

A taxpayer dies with passive activity property having an adjusted basis of $40,000, suspended losses of $10,000, and a fair market value at the date of the decedent's death of $47,000. Since the step-up in basis under § 1014 would be only $7,000 ($47,000 − $40,000), the suspended losses allowed are limited to $3,000 ($10,000 suspended loss at time of death − $7,000 increase in basis). The $3,000 loss available to the decedent is reported on the decedent's final income tax return. ◆

Disposition of a Passive Activity by Gift. In a disposition of a taxpayer's interest in a passive activity by a gift, the suspended losses are added to the basis of the property.[43]

EXAMPLE 66

A taxpayer makes a gift of passive activity property having an adjusted basis of $40,000, suspended losses of $10,000, and a fair market value at the date of the gift of $100,000. The taxpayer cannot deduct the suspended losses in the year of the disposition. The suspended losses transfer with the property and are added to the adjusted basis of the property. ◆

Installment Sale of a Passive Activity. An installment sale of a taxpayer's entire interest in a passive activity triggers the recognition of the suspended losses.[44] The losses are allowed in each year of the installment obligation in the ratio that the gain recognized in each year bears to the total gain on the sale.

EXAMPLE 67

T sold his entire interest in a passive activity for $100,000. His adjusted basis in the property was $60,000. If T uses the installment method, his gross profit ratio is 40% ($40,000/$100,000). If T received a $20,000 down payment, he would recognize a gain of $8,000 (40% of $20,000). If the activity had a suspended loss of $25,000, T would deduct $5,000 [($8,000 ÷ $40,000) × $25,000] of the suspended loss in the first year. ◆

Passive Activity Changes to Active. If a formerly passive activity becomes an active one, suspended losses are allowed to the extent of income from the now

42. § 469(g)(2).
43. § 469(j)(6).
44. § 469(g)(3).

active business.[45] If any of the suspended loss remains, it continues to be treated as a loss from a passive activity. The excess suspended loss can be deducted from passive income or carried over to the next tax year and deducted to the extent of income from the now active business in the succeeding year(s). The activity must continue to be the same activity.

Nontaxable Exchange of a Passive Activity. In a nontaxable exchange of a passive investment, the taxpayer keeps the suspended losses, which generally become deductible when the acquired property is sold. If the activity of the old and new property are the same, suspended losses can be used.

EXAMPLE 68

A taxpayer exchanged a duplex for a limited partnership interest in a § 721 nonrecognition transaction (see Chapter 20 for details). The suspended losses from the duplex are not deductible until the limited partnership interest is sold. Two separate activities exist: a real estate rental activity and a limited partnership activity. If the taxpayer had continued to own the duplex and the duplex had future taxable income, the suspended losses would have become deductible before the time of disposition. ◆

EXAMPLE 69

In a § 1031 nontaxable exchange (see Chapter 15 for details), a taxpayer exchanged a duplex for an apartment house. The suspended losses from the duplex are deductible against future taxable income of the apartment house. The same activity exists. ◆

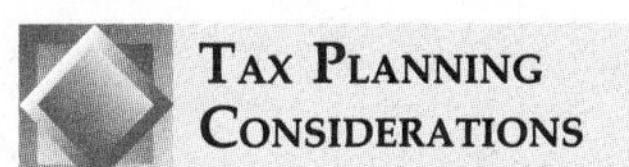

Utilizing Passive Losses

Taxpayers who have passive activity losses (PALs) should adopt a strategy of generating passive activity income that can be sheltered by existing passive losses. One approach is to buy an interest in any passive activity that is generating income (referred to as passive income generators, or PIGs). Then the PAL can be offset against income from the PIG. From a tax perspective, it would be foolish to buy a loss-generating passive activity (PAL) unless one has other passive income (PIG) to shelter or the activity is rental real estate that can qualify for the $25,000 exception.

A taxpayer with existing passive losses might consider buying rental property. If a large down payment is made and the straight-line method of ACRS (discussed in Chapter 9) is elected, a positive net income could be realized. The income would be sheltered by other passive losses, depreciation expense would be spread out evenly and preserved for future years, and depreciation recapture (discussed in Chapter 17) is avoided upon the sale of the property. Future gain realized upon the sale of the rental property could be sheltered by existing suspended passive losses.

Taxpayers with passive losses should consider all other trades or businesses in which they have an interest. If they show that they do not materially participate in the activity, the activity becomes a passive activity. Any income generated could be sheltered by existing passive losses and suspended losses. Family partnerships in which certain members do not materially participate would qualify. The silent partner in any general partnership engaged in a trade or business would also qualify.

45. § 469(f).

PROBLEM MATERIALS

DISCUSSION QUESTIONS

1. Discuss tax shelters and how taxpayers used such investments to reduce, defer, or eliminate income taxes.
2. What does "at risk" mean? What is its significance?
3. Explain how the at-risk limitation and the passive loss rules have reduced the effectiveness of tax shelter investments.
4. What is nonrecourse debt? How was it used to generate large tax shelter deductions?
5. What constitutes a taxpayer's initial at-risk amount, and what causes increases and decreases in the amount at risk?
6. T invested $10,000 in a cattle-feeding operation that used nonrecourse notes to purchase $100,000 in feed, which was fed to the cattle and expensed. T's share of the expense was $18,000. How much can he deduct?
7. What is a passive activity?
8. What are some examples of active income? Portfolio income? Passive income?
9. How do the passive loss limits for personal service corporations differ from those applicable to closely held corporations?
10. Describe the limitations that apply to passive activity losses and passive activity credits.
11. Passive losses and credits for any particular year may be suspended. When can suspended losses and credits be used?
12. What is the $25,000 real estate rental exception, and how does one qualify for it?
13. Why is it necessary to understand the transition rules that applied to passive losses from 1987 through 1990?
14. In 1990, T incurred a $100,000 loss on a passive activity that he acquired in 1985 and a $40,000 loss on a passive activity he acquired in 1988. How much was T allowed to deduct in 1990?
15. In 1990, T incurred a $100,000 loss on a passive activity that he acquired in 1985 and had $40,000 of income on a passive activity he acquired in 1988. How much was T allowed to deduct in 1990?
16. Discuss whether the passive loss rules apply to the following: individuals, closely held C corporations, S corporations, partnerships, and personal service corporations.
17. Define *passive activity,* and discuss the difficult questions raised by the Code definition of the term.
18. What is the significance of the term *material participation?* Why is the extent of a taxpayer's participation in an activity important in determining whether a loss from the activity is deductible or nondeductible?
19. T owns an interest in an activity that produces a $100,000 loss during the year. Would T generally prefer to have the activity classified as active or passive? Discuss.
20. T owns an interest in an activity that produces $100,000 of income during the year. Would T generally prefer to have the activity classified as active or passive? Discuss.
21. T owns an apartment building and a videotape rental business. She participates for more than 500 hours in the operations of each activity. Are the businesses active or passive?
22. Why did the IRS adopt the more-than-500-hour standard for material participation?
23. K, a physician, operates a separate business that he acquired in 1985. He participated for 90 hours in the business during the current year, and the business incurred a loss of $20,000. Under what circumstances will the loss be deductible as an ordinary loss?

24. J, an attorney, operates a separate business that he acquired in 1985. He has one part-time employee in the business. J participated for 130 hours in the business during the current year, and the business incurred a loss of $20,000. Under what circumstances will the loss be deductible as an ordinary loss?
25. Z, a professor, operates three separate businesses, all acquired in 1985. She participates for less than 500 hours in each business. Each business incurs a loss during the year. Are there any circumstances under which Z may treat the losses as active?
26. In 1991, P retired as a partner in a CPA firm he founded 30 years ago. He continues to share in the profits, although he no longer participates in the activities of the firm. P also owns an interest in a passive activity that he acquired in 1984. The passive activity produced a loss of $50,000 in 1992. Can P offset the passive loss against his income from the CPA firm?
27. Some types of work are counted in applying the material participation standards, and some types are not counted. Discuss and give examples of each type.
28. Some rental operations automatically are treated as passive activities, and others are treated as passive only if the owner does not meet the material participation standards. How can one differentiate between the two categories?
29. What are *significant personal services,* and what is their importance in determining whether a rental activity is treated as a passive activity?
30. What are *extraordinary personal services,* and what is their importance in determining whether a rental activity is treated as a passive activity?
31. Discuss which types of services are treated as significant personal services. Which types are not treated as significant personal services?
32. Discuss the following issues in connection with the calculation of passive losses:

    a. What constitutes a passive activity?
    b. What types of income are not treated as passive income?
    c. What types of deductions are not treated as passive deductions?

33. What is a suspended loss? Why is it important to allocate suspended losses in cases where a taxpayer has interests in more than one passive activity?
34. Upon a taxable disposition of a passive activity, the taxpayer can utilize any suspended losses and credits related to that activity. True or false? Explain.
35. In connection with passive activities, what is a *deduction equivalent?* How is a deduction equivalent computed?
36. What is the difference between material participation and active participation under the passive loss rules?
37. Upon the taxable disposition of a passive activity, what happens to the suspended losses? The suspended credits?
38. Is a hobby loss ever treated as a passive loss? Why or why not?

PROBLEMS

39. T, who earned a salary of $200,000, invested $40,000 for a 20% working interest in an oil and gas limited partnership (not a passive activity) in 1991. Through the use of $800,000 of nonrecourse financing, the partnership acquired assets worth $1,000,000. Depreciation, interest, and other deductions related to the activity resulted in a loss of $150,000, of which T's share was $30,000. T's share of loss from the partnership was $15,000 in 1992. How much of the loss from the partnership can T deduct?
40. In 1991, T invested $50,000 in a limited partnership that has a working interest in an oil well (not a passive activity). In 1991, his share of the partnership loss was $35,000. In 1992, his share of the partnership loss was $25,000. How much can T deduct in 1991 and 1992?
41. Taxpayer has an investment in a passive limited partnership purchased in 1985. He incurred losses from the investment of $100,000 in both 1991 and 1992. Assuming he has enough at risk to deduct the losses, how much can he deduct in 1991 and 1992?

42. D Corporation, a personal service corporation, earned active income of $500,000 in 1992. D received $60,000 in dividends during the year. In addition, D incurred a loss of $80,000 from an investment in a passive activity acquired in 1990. What is D's income for 1992 after considering the passive investment?
43. F Corporation, a closely held, non-personal service corporation, earned active income of $50,000 in 1992. F received $60,000 in dividends during the year. In addition, F incurred a loss of $80,000 from an investment in a passive activity acquired in 1991. What is F's net income for 1992 after considering the passive investment?
44. B, an attorney, earned $200,000 from his law practice in 1991. He received $45,000 in dividends and interest during the year. In addition, he incurred a loss of $50,000 from an investment in a passive activity acquired in 1990. What is B's net income for 1992 after considering the passive investment?
45. T acquired passive Activity A in January 1985 and Activity B in September 1986. Until 1991, Activity A was profitable. Activity A produced a loss of $100,000 in 1991, and a loss of $50,000 in 1992. T has passive income from Activity B of $10,000 in 1991 and $20,000 in 1992. After offsetting passive income, how much of the net losses may T deduct?
46. In 1985, C acquired an interest in a partnership in which she is not a material participant. The partnership was profitable until 1991. C's basis in her partnership interest at the beginning of 1991 was $40,000. In 1991, C's share of the partnership loss was $35,000. In 1992, her share of the partnership income was $15,000. How much can C deduct in 1991 and 1992?
47. F acquired a 20% interest in the ABC Partnership for $60,000 in 1985. The partnership was profitable until 1992, and F's basis in the partnership interest was $120,000 at the end of 1991. ABC incurred a loss of $400,000 in 1992 and reported income of $200,000 in 1993. Assuming F is not a material participant in ABC, how much of F's loss from ABC Partnership is deductible in 1992 and 1993, respectively?
48. H has two investments in nonrental passive activities. Activity A, which was acquired in 1985, was profitable until 1991. Activity B was acquired in 1991. H's share of the loss from Activity A was $10,000 in 1991, and his share of the loss from Activity B was $6,000. What was the total of H's suspended losses from these activities as of the end of 1991?
49. S acquired an activity in 1990. The loss from the activity was $50,000 in 1992. S had AGI of $140,000 before considering the loss from the activity. The activity is an apartment building, and S is an active participant. What is her AGI after the loss is considered?
50. B acquired an activity in 1990. The loss from the activity was $50,000 in 1992. B had AGI of $140,000 before considering the loss from the activity. The activity is an apartment building, and B is not an active participant. What is B's AGI after considering the activity?
51. N acquired an activity in 1990. The loss from the activity was $50,000 in 1992. N had AGI of $140,000 before considering the loss from the activity. The activity is a bakery, and N is not a material participant. What is N's AGI after considering this activity?
52. R acquired an activity in 1990. The loss from the activity was $50,000 in 1992. R had AGI of $140,000 before considering the loss from the activity. The activity is a service station, and R is a material participant. What is R's AGI after considering this activity?
53. K has a $40,000 loss from an investment in a partnership in which he does not participate. He paid $30,000 for his interest in the partnership. How much of the loss is disallowed by the at-risk rules? How much is disallowed by the passive loss rules?
54. In 1992, L invested $20,000 for an interest in a partnership in which she is a material participant. Her share of the partnership's loss for the year was $25,000. Discuss the tax treatment of L's share of the loss, and compute her at-risk amount.
55. Assume the same facts as in Problem 54 and that L's share of the partnership's income in 1993 is $15,000. What will be the net effect on L's taxable income for 1993?

56. K, a physician, earned $200,000 from his practice in 1992. He also received $18,000 in dividends and interest on various portfolio investments. During the year, he paid $45,000 to acquire a 20% interest in a partnership that produced a $300,000 loss.

a. Compute K's AGI assuming he does not participate in the operations of the partnership.
b. Compute K's AGI assuming he is a material participant in the operations of the partnership.

57. XYZ, Inc., earned $400,000 from operations in 1992. XYZ also received $36,000 in dividends and interest on various portfolio investments. During the year, XYZ paid $150,000 to acquire a 20% interest in a passive activity that produced a $200,000 loss.

a. How will this affect XYZ's taxable income, assuming the corporation is a personal service corporation?
b. How will this affect XYZ's taxable income, assuming the corporation is a closely held, non-personal service corporation?

58. K owns four activities. He participated for 120 hours in Activity A, 150 hours in Activity B, 140 hours in Activity C, and 100 hours in Activity D. Which of the following statements is correct?

a. Activities A, B, C, and D are all significant participation activities.
b. Activities A, B, and C are significant participation activities.
c. K is a material participant with respect to Activities A, B, and C.
d. K is a material participant with respect to Activities A, B, C, and D.
e. None of the above.

59. P owns interests in five businesses and has full-time employees in each business. He participates for 100 hours in Activity A, 120 hours in Activity B, 130 hours in Activity C, 140 hours in Activity D, and 125 hours in Activity E. Which of the following statements is correct?

a. All five of P's activities are significant participation activities.
b. P is a material participant with respect to all five activities.
c. P is not a material participant in any of the activities.
d. P is a material participant with respect to Activities B, C, D, and E.
e. None of the above.

60. Q, who owns a 50% interest in a restaurant, has been a material participant in the restaurant activity for the last 20 years. She retired from the restaurant at the end of 1991 and will not participate in the restaurant activity in the future. However, she continues to be a material participant in a retail store in which she is a 50% partner. The restaurant operations resulted in a loss for 1992, and Q's share of the loss is $80,000. Q's share of the income from the retail store is $150,000. She does not own interests in any other activities. Which of the following statements is correct?

a. Q cannot deduct the $80,000 loss from the restaurant because she is not a material participant.
b. Q can offset the $80,000 loss against the $150,000 of income from the retail store.
c. Q will not be able to deduct any losses from the restaurant until 1997.
d. None of the above.

61. S is a corporate executive who earns a salary of $500,000 during 1992. In addition, she owns a department store and a restaurant. She conducts both businesses in the same building and participates 430 hours in the department store's operations and 80 hours in the operations of the restaurant. S has full-time employees in both businesses. Which of the following statements is correct?

a. If the department store has $100,000 of income and the restaurant has a $95,000 loss, S cannot offset the loss against the income.
b. If the department store has a $100,000 loss and the restaurant has a $95,000 loss, S can offset the total loss of $195,000 against her salary income.
c. If the department store has a $100,000 loss and the restaurant has a $95,000 loss, S can offset only $100,000 against her salary income.

d. If the department store has a $100,000 loss and the restaurant has a $95,000 loss, S can offset only $95,000 against her salary income.
e. None of the above.

62. Taxpayer has investments in four passive activity partnerships purchased in 1984. In 1991, the income and losses were as follows:

Partnership	Income (Loss)
A	$ 60,000
B	(60,000)
C	(30,000)
D	(10,000)

In 1992, he sold all three interests as follows:

Partnership	Gain (Loss) on Sale*	1992 Income (Loss)
A	$ 80,000	$20,000
B	(20,000)	4,000
C	(17,000)	(9,000)
D	20,000	(3,000)

*Before suspended losses (none before 1991).

a. Calculate taxpayer's deductible loss, if any, in 1991.
b. Calculate taxpayer's gain or loss on the sale of each of the partnerships, and indicate how the gains or losses are treated.

63. H and W are married with no dependents and live together in Ohio, which is not a community property state. Since W has large medical expenses, H and W seek your advice about filing separately to save taxes. Their income and expenses for 1992 are as follows:

H's salary	$ 60,000
W's salary	20,000
Dividends and interest (joint)	1,500
Rental loss from actively managed units (joint)	(22,000)
W's medical expenses	5,800
All other itemized deductions:*	
H	8,000
W	2,000

*None subject to limitations.

Would H and W pay less in taxes if they filed jointly or separately for 1992?

64. T, who has AGI of $80,000 before considering rental activities, is active in three separate real estate rental activities and is in the 28% tax bracket. She had $12,000 of losses from Activity A, $18,000 of losses from Activity B, and income of $10,000 from Activity C. She also had $2,100 of tax credits from Activity A. Calculate her deductions and credits allowed and the suspended losses and credits.

65. Q, who owns a sole proprietorship that is a passive activity, calculated a loss for the activity as follows:

Operating income	$75,000
Dividends on stock held for investment	22,500
Total income	$97,500

Less expenses:	
Operating expenses (wages, rent, supplies, etc.)	(90,000)
Investment interest	(12,000)
Less: Loss on sale of stock held for investment	(7,500)
Net loss	$(12,000)

Compute Q's passive loss from the activity based on the above information.

66. K has $105,000 of losses from a real estate rental activity in which she actively participates. She has other rental income of $25,000 and other passive income of $32,000. How much rental loss can K deduct against active and portfolio income (ignoring at-risk rules and the phase-out rules)? Does she have any suspended losses to carry over?

67. T died owning an interest in a passive activity property with an adjusted basis of $80,000, suspended losses of $8,000, and a fair market value of $85,000. What can be deducted on her final income tax return?

68. In 1991, T gave her son a passive activity with an adjusted basis of $100,000. Fair market value of the activity was $180,000, and the activity had suspended losses of $25,000. In 1992, the son realized income from the passive activity of $12,000. What is the effect on T and T's son in 1991 and 1992?

69. K, who owns a sole proprietorship that is a passive activity, calculated a loss for the activity as follows:

Operating income	$ 70,000
Dividends on stock held for investment	25,000
Total income	$ 95,000
Less expenses:	
Operating expenses (wages, rent, supplies, etc.)	(90,000)
Investment interest	(6,000)
Less: Loss on sale of stock held for investment	(4,000)
Net loss	$ (5,000)

Compute K's passive loss for the year.

70. T invested $150,000 in a passive activity in 1982. On January 1, 1991, his adjusted basis in the activity was $30,000. His shares of the losses in the activity were as follows:

Year	**Gain (Loss)**
1991	$(40,000)
1992	(30,000)
1993	50,000

How much can T deduct in 1991 and 1992? What is T's taxable income from the activity in 1993? Keep in mind the at-risk rules as well as the passive loss rules.

71. T acquired a passive activity in 1991 that generated tax credits of $2,000 and income of $4,000. The regular tax attributable to the income was $1,120. However, T paid taxes of $80,000 under the alternative minimum tax provisions. In 1992, the activity generated $1,000 of income upon which $280 of regular tax was due. T paid regular taxes that year of $40,000. When and how can he use the $2,000 of credits?

72. T sold a passive activity in 1992 for $150,000. His adjusted basis was $50,000. T used the installment method of reporting the gain. The activity had suspended losses of $12,000. T received $60,000 in the year of sale. What is his gain? How much of the suspended losses can T deduct?

73. If T in Problem 72 had no suspended losses, was in the 28% tax bracket, and had $10,000 of tax credits attributable to the activity, how much of the credits could he use in 1992?

RESEARCH PROBLEMS

RESEARCH PROBLEM 1 H is a married individual who files a separate return for the taxable year. He is employed full-time as an attorney. H, who also owns an interest in a minor league baseball team, does no work in connection with the activity during the year. He anticipates that the activity will result in a loss for the taxable year. H pays his wife to work as an office receptionist in connection with the activity for an average of 20 hours a week during the year. Will H be allowed to deduct his share of the loss from the activity?

RESEARCH PROBLEM 2 J owns interests in three business activities, X, Y, and Z. J does not materially participate in any of the activities considered separately, but he does participate for 110 hours in Activity X, 160 hours in Activity Y, and 125 hours in Activity Z. J does not own interests in any other businesses. J's net passive income (loss) for the taxable year from Activities X, Y, and Z is as follows:

	X	Y	Z
Gross income	$ 600	$ 700	$ 900
Deductions	(200)	(1,000)	(300)
Net income (loss)	$ 400	$ (300)	$ 600

How much of the gross income from the three activities is treated as income that is not from a passive activity?

RESEARCH PROBLEM 3 T owns six grocery stores and a warehouse that receives and stores goods and delivers the goods to the different grocery stores as needed. How many separate activities does T have? How are the income and expenses of the warehouse treated?

CHAPTER

DEDUCTIONS AND LOSSES: CERTAIN BUSINESS EXPENSES AND LOSSES

OBJECTIVES

Determine the amount of the bad debt deduction.

Distinguish between business and nonbusiness bad debts and recognize the tax consequences of the distinction.

Examine the tax treatment for worthless securities and § 1244 stock.

Calculate the amount of loss for business use property.

Define the term "casualty" and compute the amount of casualty and theft losses.

Recognize the alternative tax treatments for research and experimental expenditures.

Determine the amount of the net operating loss.

Recognize the impact of the carryback and carryover of a net operating loss.

Suggest tax planning considerations in deducting certain business expenses and losses.

OUTLINE

Working with the tax formula for individuals requires the proper classification of items that are deductible *for* adjusted gross income (AGI) and items that are deductions *from* AGI (itemized deductions). Business expenses and losses, discussed in this chapter, are reductions of gross income to arrive at the taxpayer's adjusted gross income. Expenses and losses incurred in connection with a transaction entered into for profit and attributable to rents and royalties are deducted for AGI. All other expenses and losses incurred in connection with a transaction entered into for profit are deducted from AGI. Deductible losses on personal use property are deducted as an itemized deduction. Itemized deductions are deductions from AGI. While the general coverage of itemized deductions is in Chapter 11, casualty and theft losses on personal use property are discussed in this chapter.

BAD DEBTS

If a taxpayer sells goods or provides services on credit and the account receivable subsequently becomes worthless, a bad debt deduction is permitted only if income arising from the creation of the account receivable was previously included in income.[1] No deduction is allowed, for example, for a bad debt arising from the sale of a product or service when the taxpayer is on the cash basis because no income is reported until the cash has been collected. Permitting a bad debt deduction for a cash basis taxpayer would amount to a double deduction because the expenses of the product or service rendered are deducted when payments are made to suppliers and to employees, or at the time of the sale. A bad debt can also result from the nonrepayment of a loan made by the taxpayer or from purchased debt instruments.

EXAMPLE 1

T, an individual engaged in the practice of accounting, performed accounting services for X for which he charged $8,000. X never paid the bill, and his whereabouts are unknown.

If T is an accrual basis taxpayer, the $8,000 would be included in income when the services were performed. When it is determined that X's account will not be collected, the $8,000 will be expensed as a bad debt.

If T is a cash basis taxpayer, the $8,000 would not be included in income until payment is received. When it is determined that X's account will not be collected, the $8,000 will not be deducted as a bad debt expense since it was never recognized as income. ◆

Specific Charge-Off Method

For tax years beginning after 1986, taxpayers (other than certain financial institutions) may use only the *specific charge-off* method in accounting for bad debts. Certain financial institutions are allowed to use the *reserve* method for computing deductions for bad debts.[2]

A taxpayer using the specific charge-off method may claim a deduction when a specific business debt becomes either partially or wholly worthless or when a specific nonbusiness debt becomes wholly worthless.[3] The taxpayer must satisfy the IRS that a debt is partially worthless and must demonstrate the amount of worthlessness.

1. Reg. § 1.166–1(e).
2. See the Glossary of Tax Terms in Appendix C for a definition of the terms "specific charge-off method" and "reserve for bad debts."
3. § 166(a) and Reg. § 1.166.

If a business debt previously deducted as partially worthless becomes totally worthless in a future year, only the remainder not previously deducted can be deducted in the future year.

In the case of total worthlessness, a deduction is allowed for the entire amount in the year the debt becomes worthless. The amount of the deduction depends on the taxpayer's basis in the bad debt. If the debt arose from the sale of services or products and the face amount was previously included in income, that amount is deductible. If the taxpayer purchased the debt, the deduction is equal to the amount the taxpayer paid for the debt instrument.

One of the more difficult tasks is determining if and when a bad debt is worthless. The loss is deductible only in the year of partial or total worthlessness for business debts and only in the year of total worthlessness for nonbusiness debts. Legal proceedings need not be initiated against the debtor when the surrounding facts indicate that such action will not result in collection.

EXAMPLE 2

In 1990, J loaned $1,000 to K, who agreed to repay the loan in two years. In 1992, K disappeared after the note became delinquent. If a reasonable investigation by J indicates that he cannot find K or that a suit against K would not result in collection, J can deduct the $1,000 in 1992. ◆

Bankruptcy is generally an indication of at least partial worthlessness of a debt. Bankruptcy may create worthlessness before the settlement date. If this is the case, the deduction must be taken in the year of worthlessness, not in the later year upon settlement.

EXAMPLE 3

In Example 2, assume K filed for personal bankruptcy in 1991 and that the debt is a business debt. At that time, J learned that unsecured creditors (including J) were ultimately expected to receive 20¢ on the dollar. In 1992, settlement is made and J receives only $150. He should deduct $800 ($1,000 loan less $200 expected settlement) in 1991 and $50 in 1992 ($200 balance less $150 proceeds). J is not permitted to wait until 1992 to deduct the entire $850. ◆

If a receivable has been written off as uncollectible during the current tax year and is subsequently collected during the current tax year, the write-off entry is reversed. If a receivable has been written off as uncollectible, the collection of the receivable in a later tax year may result in income being recognized. Income will result if the deduction yielded a tax benefit in the year it was taken. See Examples 43 and 44 in Chapter 5.

Business versus Nonbusiness Bad Debts

A *nonbusiness* bad debt is a debt unrelated to the taxpayer's trade or business either when it was created or when it became worthless. The nature of a debt depends on whether the lender was engaged in the business of lending money or whether there is a proximate relationship between the creation of the debt and the lender's trade or business. The use to which the borrowed funds are put by the debtor is of no consequence. Loans to relatives or friends are the most common type of nonbusiness bad debt.

EXAMPLE 4

J loaned his friend, S, $1,500. S used the money to start a business, which subsequently failed. Even though proceeds of the loan were used in a business, the loan is a nonbusiness bad debt because the business was S's, not J's. ◆

The distinction between a business bad debt and a nonbusiness bad debt is important. A business bad debt is deductible as an ordinary loss in the year incurred, whereas a nonbusiness bad debt is always treated as a short-term capital loss. Thus, regardless of the age of a nonbusiness bad debt, the deduction may be of limited benefit due to the capital loss limitations on deductibility in any one year. The maximum amount of a net short-term capital loss that an individual can deduct against ordinary income in any one year is $3,000 (see Chapter 16 for a detailed discussion). Although no deduction is allowed when a nonbusiness bad debt is partially worthless, the taxpayer is entitled to deduct the net amount of the loss upon final settlement.

The following examples are illustrations of business bad debts adapted from the Regulations.[4]

EXAMPLE 5

In 1991, L sold his business but retained a claim (note or account receivable) against B. The claim became worthless in 1992. L's loss is treated as a business bad debt because the debt was created in the conduct of L's former trade or business. Business bad debt treatment is accorded to L despite the fact that he was holding the note as an investor and was no longer in a trade or business when the claim became worthless. ◆

EXAMPLE 6

In 1990, L died and left his business assets to his son, S. One of the business assets inherited by S was a claim against B that became worthless in S's hands in 1992. S's loss is a business bad debt since the loss is sustained as a proximate incident to the conduct of the trade or business in which S is engaged at the time the debt becomes worthless. ◆

The nonbusiness bad debt provisions are *not* applicable to corporations. It is assumed that any loans made by a corporation are related to its trade or business. Therefore, any bad debts of a corporation are business bad debts.

Loss of Deposits in Insolvent Financial Institutions

Qualified individuals can *elect* to deduct losses on deposits in qualified financial institutions as personal casualty losses in the year in which the amount of the loss can be reasonably estimated. If the election is made to treat a loss on a deposit as a personal casualty loss, no bad debt deduction for the loss will be

CONCEPT SUMMARY 8-1 SPECIFIC CHARGE-OFF METHOD

Expense deduction and account write-off	The expense arises and the write-off takes place when a specific business account becomes either partially or wholly worthless or when a specific nonbusiness account becomes wholly worthless.
Recovery of accounts previously written off	If the account recovered was written off during the current taxable year, the write-off entry is reversed. If the account recovered was written off during a previous taxable year, income is created subject to the tax benefit rule.

4. Reg. § 1.166–5(d).

allowed.[5] As a personal casualty loss, the loss is subject to the $100 per event floor and the 10 percent of AGI aggregate floor. Both floors limiting casualty losses are explained later in the chapter. The amount of loss to be recognized under the election is the difference between (1) the taxpayer's basis in the deposit and (2) a reasonable estimate of the amount to be received.

A *qualified individual* is any individual other than:

- An owner of 1 percent or more of the value of the stock of the institution in which the loss was sustained.
- An officer of the institution.
- Certain relatives and other persons who are tax-related to such owners and officers.

A *qualified financial institution* is a commercial bank, thrift institution, insured credit union, or any similar institution chartered and supervised under Federal or state law. A *deposit*, for purposes of this provision, is any deposit, withdrawal certificate, or withdrawable or repurchasable share of or in a qualified financial institution. The term *insolvent* generally denotes a situation where the liabilities exceed the fair market value of the assets.

If the individual does not elect to deduct the loss as a casualty loss, it will be treated as a nonbusiness bad debt and, hence, as a short-term capital loss. As a short-term capital loss, it will be subject to the capital loss limitation rules (see the discussion in Chapter 16).

Loans between Related Parties

Loans between related parties (especially family members) raise the issue of whether the loan was *bona fide* or was a gift. The Regulations state that a bona fide debt arises from a debtor-creditor relationship based on a valid and enforceable obligation to pay a fixed or determinable sum of money. Thus, individual circumstances must be examined to determine whether advances between related parties are gifts or loans. Some considerations are these:

- Was a note properly executed?
- Was there a reasonable rate of interest?
- Was collateral provided?
- What collection efforts were made?
- What was the intent of the parties?

Example 7

L loans $2,000 to his widowed mother for an operation. L's mother owns no property and is not employed, and her only income consists of Social Security benefits. No note is issued for the loan, no provision for interest is made, and no repayment date is mentioned. In the current year, L's mother dies leaving no estate. Assuming the loan is not repaid, L cannot take a deduction for a nonbusiness bad debt because the facts indicate that no debtor-creditor relationship existed. ◆

Worthless Securities

◆

A loss is allowed under § 165 for a security that becomes *completely* worthless during the year.[6] Such securities are shares of stock, bonds, notes, or other evidence of indebtedness issued by a corporation or government. The losses generated are treated as capital losses deemed to have occurred on the *last day*

5. § 165(l).

6. § 165(g).

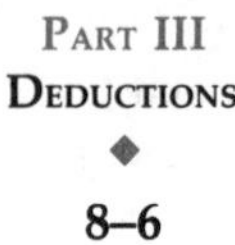

of the taxable year. By treating the loss as having occurred on the last day of the taxable year, a loss that would otherwise have been classified as short term (if the date of worthlessness was used) may be classified as a long-term capital loss. Capital losses may be of limited benefit due to the $3,000 capital loss limitation.

EXAMPLE 8

T, a calendar year taxpayer, owns stock in X Corporation (a publicly held company). The stock was acquired as an investment on November 30, 1991, at a cost of $5,000. On April 1, 1992, the stock became worthless. Since the stock is deemed to have become

CONCEPT SUMMARY 8–2
BAD DEBT DEDUCTIONS

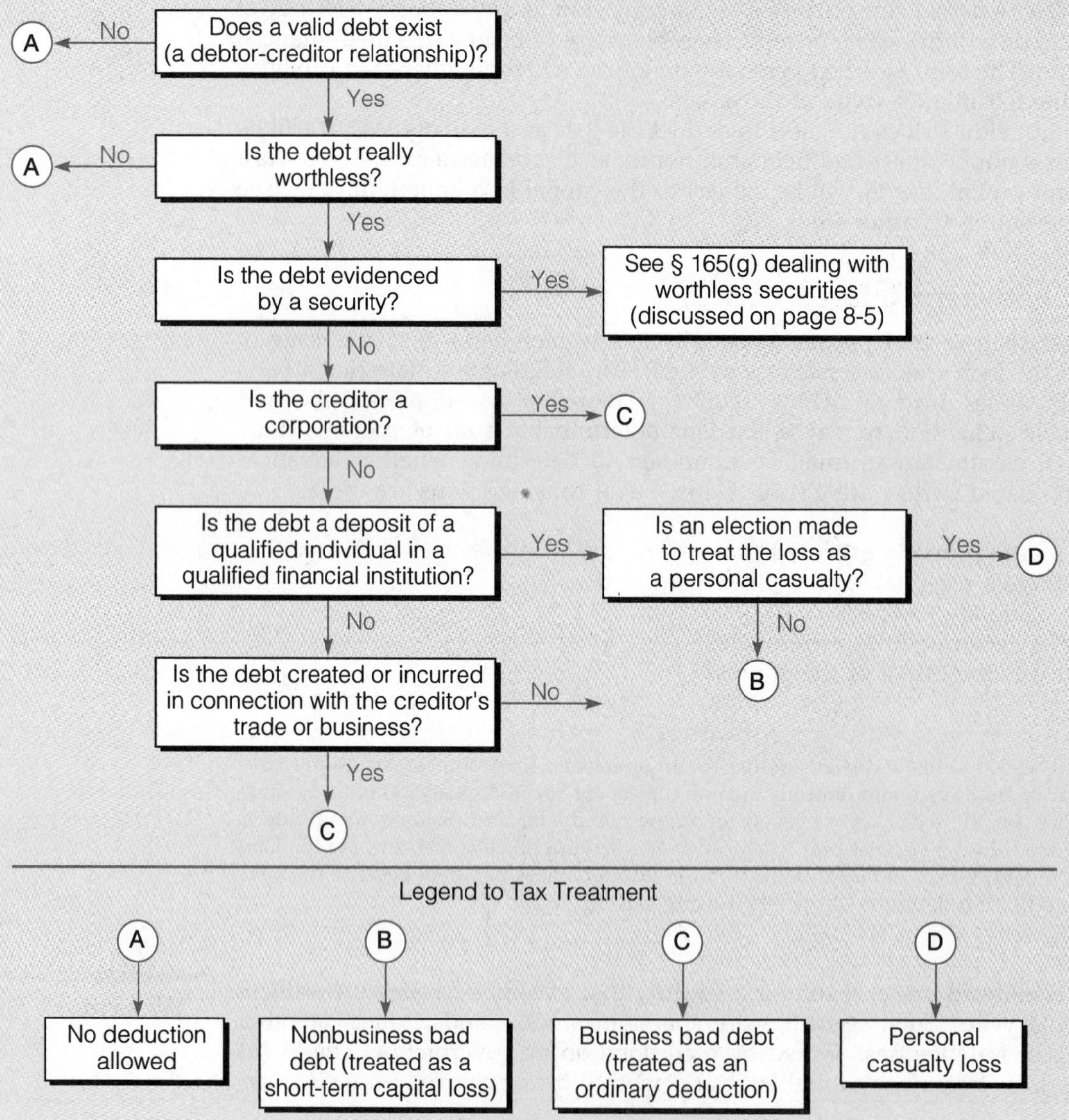

Does a valid debt exist (a debtor-creditor relationship)? — No → (A); Yes ↓

Is the debt really worthless? — No → (A); Yes ↓

Is the debt evidenced by a security? — Yes → See § 165(g) dealing with worthless securities (discussed on page 8-5); No ↓

Is the creditor a corporation? — Yes → (C); No ↓

Is the debt a deposit of a qualified individual in a qualified financial institution? — Yes → Is an election made to treat the loss as a personal casualty? — Yes → (D); No → (B). No ↓

Is the debt created or incurred in connection with the creditor's trade or business? — No → (B); Yes → (C)

Legend to Tax Treatment

(A) No deduction allowed

(B) Nonbusiness bad debt (treated as a short-term capital loss)

(C) Business bad debt (treated as an ordinary deduction)

(D) Personal casualty loss

worthless as of December 31 of 1992, T has a capital loss from an asset held for 13 months (a long-term capital loss). ◆

Securities in Affiliated Corporations

If securities of an affiliated corporation become worthless during the taxable year, the corporate taxpayer's loss will be treated as an *ordinary loss* rather than a capital loss. A corporation is treated as an affiliated corporation to the parent if two requirements are satisfied. First, the corporate shareholder must own at least 80 percent of the voting power of all classes of stock and at least 80 percent of each class of nonvoting stock of the affiliated company. Second, more than 90 percent of the gross receipts of the affiliate must be from sources other than royalties, rents, dividends, interest, annuities, and gains from sales or exchanges of stocks and securities.[7]

Small Business Stock

The general rule is that shareholders receive capital gain or loss treatment upon the sale or exchange of stock. However, it is possible to receive an ordinary loss deduction if the loss is sustained on small business stock—§ 1244 stock. This loss could arise from a sale of the stock or from the stock becoming worthless. Only *individuals*[8] who acquired the stock from the corporation are eligible to receive ordinary loss treatment under § 1244. The ordinary loss treatment is limited to $50,000 ($100,000 for married individuals filing jointly) per year. Losses on § 1244 stock in excess of the statutory limits receive capital loss treatment.

The corporation must meet certain requirements for the loss on § 1244 stock to be treated as an *ordinary*—rather than a capital—loss. The major requirement is that the total amount of money and other property received by the corporation for stock as a contribution to capital (or paid-in surplus) does not exceed $1,000,000. The $1,000,000 test is made at the time the stock is issued. Section 1244 stock can be common or preferred stock. Section 1244 applies only to losses. If § 1244 stock is sold at a gain, the Section has no application, and the gain will be capital gain.

Example 9

On July 1, 1990, T, a single individual, purchased 100 shares of X Corporation common stock for $100,000. The X stock qualified as § 1244 stock. On June 20, 1992, T sold all of the X stock for $20,000. Because the X stock is § 1244 stock, T would have $50,000 of ordinary loss and $30,000 of long-term capital loss. ◆

Losses of Individuals

An individual may deduct the following losses under § 165(c):

- Losses incurred in a trade or business.
- Losses incurred in a transaction entered into for profit.
- Losses caused by fire, storm, shipwreck, or other casualty or by theft.

An individual taxpayer may deduct losses to property used in the taxpayer's trade or business or losses to property used in a transaction entered into for profit. Examples include a loss on property used in a proprietorship, a loss on

7. § 165(g)(3).

8. The term "individuals" includes a partnership but not a trust or an estate.

property held for rent, or a loss on stolen bearer bonds. Note that an individual's losses on property used in a trade or business or on transactions entered into for profit are not limited to losses caused by fire, storm, shipwreck, or other casualty or by theft.

A taxpayer suffering losses from damage to nonbusiness property can deduct only those losses attributable to fire, storm, shipwreck, or other casualty or theft. Although the meaning of the terms *fire, storm, shipwreck, and theft* is relatively free from dispute, the term *other casualty* needs further clarification. It means casualties analogous to fire, storm, or shipwreck. The term also includes accidental loss of property provided the loss qualifies under the same rules as any other casualty. These rules are that the loss must result from an event that is (1) identifiable; (2) damaging to property; and (3) sudden, unexpected, and unusual in nature.

A *sudden event* is one that is swift and precipitous and not gradual or progressive. An *unexpected event* is an event that is ordinarily unanticipated and occurs without the intent of the individual who suffers the loss. An *unusual event* is one that is extraordinary and nonrecurring and does not commonly occur during the activity in which the taxpayer was engaged when the destruction occurred.[9] Examples include hurricanes, tornadoes, floods, storms, shipwrecks, fires, auto accidents, mine cave-ins, sonic booms, and vandalism. Weather that causes damages (drought, for example) must be unusual and severe for the particular region. Damage must be to the taxpayer's property to qualify as a casualty loss.

A taxpayer can take a deduction for a casualty loss from an automobile accident only if the damage was not caused by the taxpayer's willful act or willful negligence.

EXAMPLE 10

T parks her car on a hill and fails to set the brake properly and to curb the wheels. As a result of T's negligence, the car rolls down the hill and is damaged. The repairs to T's car should qualify for casualty loss treatment since T's act of negligence appears to be simple rather than willful. ◆

Events That Are Not Casualties

Not all acts of God are treated as casualty losses for income tax purposes. Because a casualty must be sudden, unexpected, and unusual, progressive deterioration (such as erosion due to wind or rain) is not a casualty because it does not meet the suddenness test.

Examples of nonsudden events that generally do not qualify as casualties include disease and insect damages. When the damage was caused by termites over a period of several years, some courts have disallowed a casualty loss deduction.[10] On the other hand, some courts have held that termite damage over periods of up to 15 months after infestation constituted a sudden event and was, therefore, deductible as a casualty loss.[11] Despite the existence of some judicial support for the deductibility of termite damage as a casualty loss, the current position of the IRS is that termite damage is not deductible.[12]

Other examples of events that are not casualties are losses resulting from a decline in value rather than an actual loss of the property. No loss was allowed

9. Rev.Rul. 72–592, 1972–2 C.B. 101.

10. *Fay v. Helvering*, 41–2 USTC ¶9494, 27 AFTR 432, 120 F.2d 253 (CA–2, 1941); *U.S. v. Rogers*, 41–1 USTC ¶9442, 27 AFTR 423, 120 F.2d 244 (CA–9, 1941).

11. *Rosenberg v. Comm.*, 52–2 USTC ¶9377, 42 AFTR 303, 198 F.2d 46 (CA–8, 1952); *Shopmaker v. U.S.*, 54–1 USTC ¶9195, 45 AFTR 758, 119 F.Supp. 705 (D.Ct.Mo., 1953).

12. Rev.Rul. 63–232, 1963–2 C.B. 97.

where the taxpayer's home declined in value as a result of a landslide that destroyed neighboring homes but did no actual damage to the taxpayer's home.[13] Similarly, a taxpayer was allowed a loss for the actual flood damage to his property but not for the decline in market value due to the property's being flood-prone.[14]

The Eleventh Court of Appeals has stated that loss of present value generated by a fear of future damage cannot be factored into the fair market value of the property. However, the Court has held that permanent buyer resistance, as evidenced by changes made to the neighborhood surrounding the taxpayer's home following a flood, does affect the fair market value and may be included in a determination as to what the fair market value is after the disaster.[15]

Theft Losses

Theft includes, but is not necessarily limited to, larceny, embezzlement, and robbery.[16] Theft does not include misplaced items.[17]

Theft losses are computed like other casualty losses (discussed in the following section), but the *timing* for recognition of the loss differs. A theft loss is deducted in the year of discovery, not the year of the theft (unless, of course, the discovery occurs in the same year as the theft). If, in the year of the discovery, a claim exists (e.g., against an insurance company) and there is a reasonable expectation of recovering the adjusted basis of the asset from the insurance company, no deduction is permitted.[18] If, in the year of settlement, the recovery is less than the asset's adjusted basis, a partial deduction may be available. If the recovery is greater than the asset's adjusted basis, gain may be recognized.

EXAMPLE 11

J's new sailboat, which he uses for personal purposes, was stolen from the storage marina in December 1990. He discovered the loss on June 3, 1991, and filed a claim with his insurance company that was settled on January 30, 1992. Assuming there is a reasonable expectation of full recovery, no deduction is allowed in 1991. A partial deduction may be available in 1992 if the actual insurance proceeds are less than the lower of the fair market value or the adjusted basis of the asset. (Loss measurement rules are discussed later in this chapter.) ◆

When to Deduct Casualty Losses

General Rule. Generally, a casualty loss is deducted in the year the loss occurs. However, no casualty loss is permitted if a reimbursement claim with a *reasonable prospect of full recovery* exists.[19] If the taxpayer has a partial claim, only part of the loss can be claimed in the year of the casualty, and the remainder is deducted in the year the claim is settled.

EXAMPLE 12

G's new sailboat was completely destroyed by fire in 1992. Its cost and fair market value were $10,000. G's only claim against the insurance company was on a $7,000

13. *H. Pulvers v. Comm.*, 69–1 USTC ¶9222, 23 AFTR2d 69–678, 407 F.2d 838 (CA–9, 1969).
14. *S. L. Solomon*, 39 TCM 1282, T.C.Memo 1980–87.
15. *Finkbohner, Jr. v. U.S.*, 86–1 USTC ¶9393, 57 AFTR2d 86–1400, 788 F.2d 723 (CA–11, 1986).
16. Reg. § 1.165–8(d).
17. *Mary Francis Allen*, 16 T.C. 163 (1951).
18. Reg. §§ 1.165–1(d)(2) and 1.165–8(a)(2).
19. Reg. § 1.165–1(d)(2)(i).

policy that was not settled by year-end. The following year, 1993, G settled with the insurance company for $6,000. G is entitled to a $3,000 deduction in 1992 and a $1,000 deduction in 1993. If G held the sailboat for personal use, the $3,000 deduction in 1992 would be reduced first by $100 and then by 10% of G's 1992 AGI. The $1,000 deduction in 1993 would be reduced by 10% of G's 1993 AGI (see the following discussion on the $100 and 10% floors). ◆

If a taxpayer receives reimbursement for a casualty loss sustained and deducted in a previous year, an amended return is not filed for that year. Instead, the taxpayer must include the reimbursement in gross income on the return for the year in which it is received to the extent that the previous deduction resulted in a tax benefit.

EXAMPLE 13

T had a deductible casualty loss of $5,000 on his 1991 tax return. T's taxable income for 1991 was $60,000. In June 1992, T was reimbursed $3,000 for the prior year's casualty loss. T would include the entire $3,000 in gross income for 1992 because the deduction in 1991 produced a tax benefit. ◆

Disaster Area Losses. An exception to the general rule for the time of deduction is allowed for casualties sustained in an area designated as a disaster area by the President of the United States.[20] In such cases, the taxpayer may *elect* to treat the loss as having occurred in the taxable year immediately preceding the taxable year in which the disaster actually occurred. The rationale for this exception is to provide immediate relief to disaster victims in the form of accelerated tax benefits.

If the due date, plus extensions, for the prior year's return has not passed, a taxpayer makes the election to claim the disaster area loss on the prior year's tax return. If the disaster occurs after the prior year's return has been filed, it is necessary to file either an amended return or a refund claim. In any case, the taxpayer must show clearly that such an election is being made.

Disaster loss treatment also applies in the case of a personal residence that has been rendered unsafe for use as a residence because of a disaster. This provision applies when, within 120 days after the President designates the area as a disaster area, the state or local government where the residence is located orders the taxpayer to demolish or relocate the residence.[21]

Measuring the Amount of Loss

Amount of Loss. The rules for determining the amount of a loss depend in part on whether business use, income-producing use, or personal use property was involved. Another factor that must be considered is whether the property was partially or completely destroyed.

If business property or property held for the production of income (e.g., rental property) is *completely destroyed*, the loss is equal to the adjusted basis of the property at the time of destruction.

EXAMPLE 14

T's automobile, which was used only for business purposes, was destroyed by fire. T had unintentionally allowed his insurance coverage to expire. The fair market value of the automobile was $9,000 at the time of the fire, and its adjusted basis was $10,000. T is allowed a loss deduction of $10,000 (the basis of the automobile). The $10,000 loss is a deduction *for* AGI. ◆

20. § 165(h).

21. § 165(k).

A different measurement rule applies for *partial destruction* of business property and income-producing property and for *partial* or *complete destruction* of personal use property. In these situations, the loss is the *lesser* of the following:

1. The adjusted basis of the property.
2. The difference between the fair market value of the property before the event and the fair market value immediately after the event.

EXAMPLE 15

K's uninsured automobile, which was used only for business purposes, was damaged in a wreck. At the date of the wreck, the fair market value of the automobile was $12,000, and its adjusted basis was $9,000. After the wreck, the automobile was appraised at $4,000. K's loss deduction is $8,000 (the lesser of the adjusted basis or the decrease in fair market value). The $8,000 loss is a deduction *for* AGI. ◆

The deduction for the loss of property that is part business and part personal must be computed separately for the business portion and the personal portion.

Any insurance recovery reduces the loss for business, production of income, and personal use losses. In fact, a taxpayer may realize a gain if the insurance proceeds exceed the amount of the loss. Chapter 17 discusses the treatment of net gains and losses on business property and income-producing property.

A taxpayer will not be permitted to deduct a casualty loss for damage to insured personal use property unless he or she files a timely insurance claim with respect to the damage to the property. This rule applies to the extent that any insurance policy provides for full or partial reimbursement for the loss.[22]

Generally, an appraisal before and after the casualty is needed to measure the amount of the loss. However, the *cost of repairs* to the damaged property is acceptable as a method of establishing the loss in value provided the following criteria are met:

- The repairs are necessary to restore the property to its condition immediately before the casualty.
- The amount spent for such repairs is not excessive.
- The repairs do not extend beyond the damage suffered.
- The value of the property after the repairs does not, as a result of the repairs, exceed the value of the property immediately before the casualty.[23]

Reduction for $100 and 10 Percent of AGI Floors. The amount of the loss for personal use property must be further reduced by a $100 *per event* floor and a 10 percent of AGI *aggregate* floor.[24] The $100 floor applies separately to each casualty and applies to the entire loss from each casualty (e.g., if a storm damages both a taxpayer's residence and automobile, only $100 is subtracted from the total amount of the loss). The losses are then added together, and the total is reduced by 10 percent of the taxpayer's AGI. The resulting loss is the taxpayer's itemized deduction for casualty and theft losses.

EXAMPLE 16

G, who had AGI of $30,000, was involved in a motorcycle accident. His motorcycle, which was used only for personal use and had a fair market value of $12,000 and an adjusted basis of $9,000, was completely destroyed. He received $5,000 from his

22. § 165(h)(4)(E).
23. Reg. § 1.165–7(a)(2)(ii).
24. § 165(c)(3).

insurance company. G's casualty loss deduction is $900 [$9,000 basis − $5,000 insurance − $100 floor − $3,000 (.10 × $30,000 AGI)]. The $900 casualty loss is an itemized deduction (*from* AGI). ◆

When a nonbusiness casualty loss is spread between two taxable years because of the *reasonable prospect of recovery* doctrine, the loss in the second year is not reduced by the $100 floor. This result occurs because this floor is imposed per event and has already reduced the amount of the loss in the first year. However, the loss in the second year is still subject to the 10 percent floor based on the taxpayer's second-year AGI (refer to Example 12).

Taxpayers who suffer qualified disaster area losses can elect to deduct the losses in the year preceding the year of occurrence. The disaster loss is treated as having occurred in the preceding taxable year. Hence, the 10 percent of AGI floor is determined by using the AGI of the year for which the deduction is claimed.[25]

Multiple Losses. The rules for computing loss deductions where multiple losses have occurred are explained in Examples 17 and 18.

EXAMPLE 17

During the year, T had the following casualty losses:

		Fair Market Value of Asset		
Asset	**Adjusted Basis**	**Before the Casualty**	**After the Casualty**	**Insurance Recovery**
A	$900	$600	$-0-	$400
B	300	800	250	100

Assets A and B were used in T's business at the time of the casualty. The following losses are allowed:

Asset A: $500. The complete destruction of a business asset results in a deduction of the adjusted basis of the property (reduced by any insurance recovery) regardless of the asset's fair market value.

Asset B: $200. The partial destruction of a business (or personal use) asset results in a deduction equal to the lesser of the adjusted basis ($300) or the decline in value ($550), reduced by any insurance recovery ($100).

Both Asset A and Asset B losses are deductions *for* AGI. The $100 floor and the 10% of AGI floor do not apply because the assets are business assets. ◆

EXAMPLE 18

During the year, T had AGI of $20,000 and the following casualty losses:

		Fair Market Value of Asset		
Asset	**Adjusted Basis**	**Before the Casualty**	**After the Casualty**	**Insurance Recovery**
A	$ 900	$ 600	$ -0-	$ 200
B	2,500	4,000	1,000	-0-
C	800	400	100	250

25. § 165(i).

Assets A, B, and C were held for personal use, and the losses to these three assets are from three different casualties. The loss for each asset is computed as follows:

Asset A: $300. The lesser of the adjusted basis of $900 or the $600 decline in value, reduced by the insurance recovery of $200, minus the $100 floor.
Asset B: $2,400. The lesser of the adjusted basis of $2,500 or the $3,000 decline in value, minus the $100 floor.
Asset C: $0. The lesser of the adjusted basis of $800 or the $300 decline in value, reduced by the insurance recovery of $250, minus the $100 floor.

T's itemized casualty loss deduction for the year is $700:

Asset A loss	$ 300
Asset B loss	2,400
Asset C loss	-0-
Total loss	$ 2,700
Less: 10% of AGI (10% × $20,000)	(2,000)
Itemized casualty loss deduction	$ 700

◆

Statutory Framework for Deducting Losses of Individuals

Casualty and theft losses incurred by an individual in connection with a trade or business are deductible *for* AGI.[26] These losses are not subject to the $100 per event and the 10 percent of AGI limitations.

Casualty and theft losses incurred by an individual in a transaction entered into for profit are not subject to the $100 per event and the 10 percent of AGI limitations. If these losses are attributable to rents or royalties, the deduction is *for* AGI.[27] However, if these losses are not connected with property held for the production of rents and royalties, they are deductions *from* AGI. More specifically, these losses are classified as other miscellaneous itemized deductions. An example of this type of loss would be the theft of a security. The aggregate of certain miscellaneous itemized deductions is subject to a 2 percent of AGI floor (explained in Chapter 10).

Casualty and theft losses attributable to personal use property are subject to the $100 per event and the 10 percent of AGI limitations. These losses are itemized deductions, but they are not subject to the 2 percent of AGI floor.[28]

Personal Casualty Gains and Losses

If a taxpayer has personal casualty and theft gains as well as losses, a special set of rules applies for determining the tax consequences. The term *personal casualty gain* means the recognized gain from a casualty or theft of personal use property. A *personal casualty loss* for this purpose is a casualty or theft loss of personal use property after the application of the $100 floor. A taxpayer who has both gains and losses for the taxable year must first net (offset) the personal casualty gains and personal casualty losses. If the gains exceed the losses, the gains and losses will be treated as gains and losses from the sale of capital assets. The capital gains and losses will be short term or long term, depending on the period the taxpayer held each of the assets. In the netting process, personal casualty and theft gains and losses are not netted with the gains and losses on business and income-producing property.

26. § 62(a)(1).
27. § 62(a)(4).
28. § 67(b)(3).

EXAMPLE 19

During the year, T had the following personal casualty gains and losses (after deducting the $100 floor):

Asset	Holding Period	Gain or (Loss)
A	Three months	($ 300)
B	Three years	(2,400)
C	Two years	3,200

T would compute the tax consequences as follows:

Personal casualty gain	$3,200
Personal casualty loss ($300 + $2,400)	(2,700)
Net personal casualty gain	$ 500

T would treat all of the gains and losses as capital gains and losses and would have the following:

Short-term capital loss (Asset A)	$ 300
Long-term capital loss (Asset B)	2,400
Long-term capital gain (Asset C)	3,200

◆

If personal casualty losses exceed personal casualty gains, all gains and losses are treated as ordinary items. The gains—and the losses to the extent of gains—will be treated as ordinary income and ordinary loss in computing AGI. Losses in excess of gains are deducted as itemized deductions to the extent the losses exceed 10 percent of AGI.[29]

EXAMPLE 20

During the year, T had AGI of $20,000 and the following personal casualty gain and loss (after deducting the $100 floor):

Asset	Holding Period	Gain or (Loss)
A	Three years	($2,700)
B	Four months	200

T would compute the tax consequences as follows:

Personal casualty loss	($2,700)
Personal casualty gain	200
Net personal casualty loss	($2,500)

T would treat the gain and the loss as ordinary items. The $200 gain and $200 of the loss would be included in computing AGI. T's itemized deduction for casualty losses would be computed as follows:

Casualty loss in excess of gain ($2,700 − $200)	$ 2,500
Less: 10% of AGI (10% × $20,000)	(2,000)
Itemized deduction	$ 500

◆

29. § 165(h).

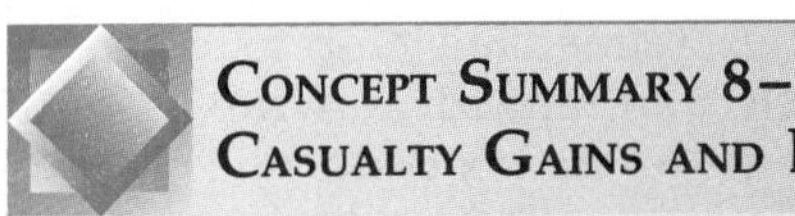

CONCEPT SUMMARY 8–3
CASUALTY GAINS AND LOSSES

	Business Use or Income-Producing Property	Personal Use Property
Event creating the loss	Any event.	Casualty or theft loss.
Amount	The lesser of the decline in fair market value or the adjusted basis, but always the adjusted basis if the property is totally destroyed.	The lesser of the decline in fair market value or the adjusted basis.
Insurance	Insurance proceeds received reduce the amount of the loss.	Insurance proceeds received (or for which there is an unfiled claim) reduce the amount of the loss.
$100 floor	Not applicable.	Applicable per event.
Gains and losses	Gains and losses are netted (see detailed discussion in Chapter 17).	Personal casualty and theft gains and losses are netted.
Gains exceeding losses		The gains and losses are treated as gains and losses from the sale of capital assets.
Losses exceeding gains		The gains—and the losses to the extent of gains—are treated as ordinary items in computing AGI. The losses in excess of gains, to the extent they exceed 10% of AGI, are itemized deductions.

RESEARCH AND EXPERIMENTAL EXPENDITURES

Section 174 covers the treatment of research and experimental expenditures. The Regulations define *research and experimental expenditures* as follows:

> . . . all such costs incident to the development of an experimental or pilot model, a plant process, a product, a formula, an invention, or similar property, and the improvement of already existing property of the type mentioned. The term does not include expenditures such as those for the ordinary testing or inspection of materials or products for quality control or those for efficiency surveys, management studies, consumer surveys, advertising, or promotions.[30]

Expenses in connection with the acquisition or improvement of land or depreciable property are not research and experimental expenditures. Rather, they increase the basis of the land or depreciable property. However, depreciation on a building used for research may be a research and experimental expense. Only the depreciation that is a research and experimental expense (not the cost of the asset) is subject to the three alternatives discussed below.

The law permits the following three alternatives for the handling of research and experimental expenditures:

- Expensed in the year paid or incurred.
- Deferred and amortized.
- Capitalized.

If the costs are capitalized, a deduction is not available until the research project is abandoned or is deemed worthless. Since many products resulting from research projects do not have a definite and limited useful life, a taxpayer should

30. Reg. § 1.174–2(a)(1).

ordinarily elect to write off the expenditures immediately or to defer and amortize them. It is generally preferable to elect an immediate write-off of the research expenditures because of the time value of the tax deduction.

The law also provides for a research activities credit. The credit amounts to 20 percent of certain research and experimental expenditures.[31] (The credit is discussed more fully in Chapter 13.)

Expense Method

A taxpayer can elect to expense all of the research and experimental expenditures incurred in the current year and all subsequent years. The consent of the IRS is not required if the method is adopted for the first taxable year in which such expenditures were paid or incurred. Once the election is made, the taxpayer must continue to expense all qualifying expenditures unless a request for a change is made to, and approved by, the IRS. In certain instances, a taxpayer may incur research and experimental expenditures before actually engaging in any trade or business activity. In such instances, the Supreme Court has applied a liberal standard of deductibility and permitted a deduction in the year of incurrence.[32]

Deferral and Amortization Method

The deferral and amortization method is allowed for the treatment of research and experimental expenditures if the taxpayer makes an election.[33] Under the election, research and experimental expenditures are amortized ratably over a period of not less than 60 months. A deduction is allowed beginning with the month in which the taxpayer first realizes benefits from the experimental expenditure. The election is binding, and a change requires permission from the IRS.

EXAMPLE 21

Y Corporation decided to develop a new line of adhesives. The project was begun in 1992. Y incurred the following expenses in 1992 in connection with the project:

Salaries	$25,000
Materials	8,000
Depreciation on machinery	6,500

Y incurred the following expenses in 1993 in connection with the project:

Salaries	$18,000
Materials	2,000
Depreciation on machinery	5,700

The benefits from the project will be realized starting in March 1994. If Y Corporation elects a 60-month deferral and amortization period, there will be no deduction prior to March 1994, the month benefits from the project begin to be realized. The deduction for 1994 would be $10,867, computed as follows:

31. § 41.
32. *Snow v. Comm.*, 74–1 USTC ¶9432, 33 AFTR2d 74–1251, 94 S.Ct. 1876 (USSC, 1974).
33. § 174(b)(2).

Salaries ($25,000 + $18,000)	$43,000
Materials ($8,000 + $2,000)	10,000
Depreciation ($6,500 + $5,700)	12,200
Total	$65,200
$65,200 × (10 months/60 months) =	$10,867

◆

The option to treat research and experimental expenditures as deferred expense is usually employed when a company does not have sufficient income to offset the research and experimental expenses. Rather than create net operating loss carryovers that might not be utilized because of the 15-year limitation on such carryovers, the deferral and amortization method may be used. The deferral of research and experimental expenditures should also be considered if the taxpayer expects higher tax rates in the future.

NET OPERATING LOSSES

The requirement that every taxpayer file an annual income tax return (whether on a calendar year or a fiscal year) may result in certain inequities for taxpayers who experience cyclical patterns of income or expense. Inequities result from the application of a progressive rate structure to taxable income determined on an annual basis. A net operating loss (NOL) in a particular tax year would produce no tax benefit if the Code did not provide for the carryback and carryforward of such losses to profitable years.

EXAMPLE 22

J has a business that realizes the following taxable income or loss over a five-year period: Year 1, $50,000; Year 2, ($30,000); Year 3, $100,000; Year 4, ($200,000); and Year 5, $380,000. She is married and files a joint return. P, on the other hand, has a taxable income pattern of $60,000 every year. He, too, is married and files a joint return. Note that both J and P have total taxable income of $300,000 over the five-year period. Assume there is no provision for carryback or carryover of NOLs. J and P would have the following five-year tax bills:

Year	J's Tax	P's Tax
1	$ 9,346	$12,146
2	-0-	12,146
3	23,751	12,146
4	-0-	12,146
5	110,551	12,146
	$143,648	$60,730

The computation of tax is made without regard to any NOL benefit. Rates applicable to 1992 are used to compute the tax.

Even though J and P realized the same total taxable income ($300,000) over the five-year period, J had to pay taxes of $143,648, while P paid taxes of only $60,730. ◆

To provide partial relief from this inequitable tax treatment, a deduction is allowed for NOLs.[34] This provision permits NOLs for any one year to be offset against taxable income of other years. The NOL provision is intended as a form of relief for business income and losses. Thus, only losses from the operation of a trade or business (or profession), casualty and theft losses, or losses from the

34. § 172.

confiscation of a business by a foreign government can create an NOL. In other words, a salaried individual with itemized deductions and personal exemptions in excess of gross income is not permitted to deduct the excess amounts as an NOL. On the other hand, a personal casualty loss is treated as a business loss and can therefore create (or increase) an NOL for an individual.

Carryback and Carryover Periods

General Rules. An NOL must be applied initially to the three taxable years preceding the year of the loss (unless an election is made not to carry the loss back at all). It is carried first to the third prior year, then to the second prior year, then to the immediately preceding tax year (or until used up). If the loss is not fully used in the carryback period, it must be carried forward to the first year after the loss year, and then forward to the second, third, etc., year after the loss year. The carryover period is 15 years. A loss sustained in 1992 is used in this order: 1989, 1990, 1991, 1993 through 2007.

If the loss is being carried to a preceding year, an amended return is filed on Form 1040X, or a quick refund claim is filed on Form 1045. In any case, a refund of taxes previously paid is requested. When the loss is carried forward, the current return shows an NOL deduction for the prior year's loss.

Sequence of Use of NOLs. Where there are NOLs in two or more years, the rule is always to use the earliest year's loss first until it is completely absorbed. The later years' losses can then be used until they also are absorbed or lost. Thus, one year's return could show NOL carryovers from two or more years. Each loss is computed and applied separately.

Election to Forgo Carryback. A taxpayer can *irrevocably elect* not to carry back an NOL to any of the three prior years. In that case, the loss is available as a carryover for 15 years. A taxpayer would make the election if it is to his or her tax advantage. For example, a taxpayer might be in a low marginal tax bracket in the carryback years but expect to be in a high marginal tax bracket in future years. Therefore, it would be to the taxpayer's advantage to use the NOL to offset income in years when the tax rate is high rather than use it when the tax rate is relatively low.

Computation of the Net Operating Loss

Since the NOL provisions apply solely to business-related losses, certain adjustments must be made so that the loss more closely resembles the taxpayer's *economic* loss. The required adjustments for corporate taxpayers are usually insignificant because a corporation's tax loss is generally similar to its economic loss. However, in computing taxable income, individual taxpayers are allowed deductions for such items as personal and dependency exemptions and itemized deductions that do not reflect actual business-related economic losses.

To arrive at the NOL (economic loss) for an individual, taxable income must be adjusted by adding back the following items:[35]

1. No deduction is allowed for personal and dependency exemptions. These amounts do not reflect economic, or business, outlays and hence must be added back.

35. § 172(d); Reg. § 1.172–3(a).

2. The NOL carryover or carryback from another year is not allowed in the computation of the current year's NOL.
3. Capital losses and nonbusiness deductions are limited in determining the current year's NOL. These limits are as follows:

   a. The excess of nonbusiness capital losses over nonbusiness capital gains must be added back.
   b. The excess of nonbusiness deductions over the sum of nonbusiness income and *net* nonbusiness capital gains must be added back. *Net nonbusiness capital gains* are the excess of nonbusiness capital gains over nonbusiness capital losses. *Nonbusiness income* includes such passive items as dividends and interest. It does not include such items as salaries, rents, and gains and losses on the sale or exchange of business assets. *Nonbusiness deductions* are total itemized deductions less personal casualty and theft losses.

      A taxpayer who does not itemize deductions computes the excess of nonbusiness deductions over nonbusiness income by substituting his or her standard deduction for total itemized deductions.
   c. The excess of business capital losses over the sum of business capital gains and the excess of nonbusiness income and net nonbusiness capital gains over nonbusiness deductions must be added back.
   d. The add-back for net nonbusiness capital losses and excess business capital losses does not include net capital losses not included in the current year computation of taxable income because of the capital loss limitation provisions (discussed in Chapter 16).

The capital loss and nonbusiness deduction limits are illustrated in Examples 23 through 26.

EXAMPLE 23

For 1992, taxpayer and spouse have $6,000 of nonbusiness capital losses and $4,000 of nonbusiness capital gains. They must add back $2,000 ($6,000 − $4,000) in determining the excess of nonbusiness capital losses over nonbusiness capital gains. ◆

EXAMPLE 24

For 1992, taxpayer and spouse have $2,000 of nonbusiness capital gains, $1,000 of nonbusiness capital losses, $2,000 of interest income, and no itemized deductions. They must add back $3,000 ($6,000 standard deduction − [$2,000 interest income + $1,000 ($2,000 − $1,000) net nonbusiness capital gains]). Note that, in this example, there is no excess of nonbusiness capital losses over nonbusiness capital gains. ◆

EXAMPLE 25

For 1992, taxpayer and spouse have $2,000 of nonbusiness capital gains, $1,000 of nonbusiness capital losses, $6,000 of interest income, $6,500 of itemized deductions (none of which are personal casualty and theft losses), $4,000 of business capital losses, and $1,000 of business capital gains. They must add back $2,500 {$4,000 business capital losses − [$1,000 business capital gains + ($6,000 nonbusiness income + $1,000 net nonbusiness capital gains − $6,500 nonbusiness deductions)]}. Note that, in this example there is no excess of nonbusiness capital losses over nonbusiness capital gains, nor is there an excess of nonbusiness deductions over the sum of nonbusiness income and net nonbusiness capital gains. ◆

EXAMPLE 26

For 1992, taxpayer and spouse have $2,000 of nonbusiness capital gains, $3,000 of nonbusiness capital losses, $6,000 of interest income, $7,000 of itemized deductions (none of which are personal casualty and theft losses), $8,000 of business capital losses, and $4,000 of business capital gains. They must add back $1,000 ($7,000 − $6,000), the excess of nonbusiness deductions over nonbusiness income, and $3,000, the excess of combined capital losses. Because of the capital loss limitations, only $3,000 of the loss would have been used in computing taxable income for the year. ◆

Example 27 illustrates the computation of a net operating loss.

EXAMPLE 27

T opened a retail store in 1991 and experienced an NOL of $185 for that year. T had no taxable income for 1988, 1989, or 1990. T is married, has no dependents, and files a joint return. For 1992, T and his wife had the following taxable income:

Gross income from the business	$ 67,000	
Less: Business expenses	(71,000)	($ 4,000)
Salary from a part-time job		875
Interest on savings account		525
Nonbusiness long-term capital gain		1,000
NOL carryover from 1991		(185)
Net loss on rental property		(100)
Adjusted gross income		($ 1,885)
Less: Itemized deductions		
Interest expense	$ 3,000	
Taxes	4,300	
Casualty loss	2,000	
Total itemized deductions		(9,300)
Exemptions (2 × $2,300)		(4,600)
Taxable income		($15,785)

T's NOL is computed as follows:

Taxable income				($15,785)
Add:				
Net operating loss from 1991			$ 185	
Personal exemptions (2)			4,600	
Excess of nonbusiness deductions over nonbusiness income				
Total itemized deductions		$ 9,300		
Less: Casualty loss		(2,000)		
		$ 7,300		
Less: Interest	$ 525			
Less: Long-term capital gain	1,000	(1,525)	5,775	10,560
Net operating loss				($ 5,225)

The net operating loss can be thought of as follows:

Business loss	($ 4,000)
Rental loss	(100)
Casualty loss	(2,000)
Salary income	875
Net operating loss	($ 5,225)

◆

Recomputation of Tax Liability for Year to Which Net Operating Loss Is Carried

When an NOL is carried back to a nonloss year, the taxable income and income tax for the carryback year must be recomputed by including the NOL as a deduction *for* AGI. Several deductions (such as medical expenses and charitable contributions) are based on the amount of AGI. When an NOL is carried back, all such deductions *except* the charitable contributions deduction must be recomputed on the basis of the new AGI after the NOL has been applied. The deduction for charitable contributions is determined without regard to any NOL carryback but with regard to any other modification affecting AGI. Furthermore, any tax credits limited by or based upon the tax must be recomputed, based on the recomputed tax.

EXAMPLE 28

J sustained an NOL of $11,000 in 1993. Because J had no taxable income in 1990 or 1991, the loss is carried back to 1992. For 1992, the joint income tax return of J and his wife was as follows:

Salary income		$10,000
Dividends		2,000
Net long-term capital gain		1,400
Adjusted gross income		$13,400
Itemized deductions		
Charitable contributions	$2,700	
Interest	2,800	
Taxes	1,420	(6,920)
Exemptions (2 × $2,300)		(4,600)
Taxable income		$ 1,880
Tax (married filing jointly)		$ 282

J's new tax liability for the carryback year is computed as follows:

Adjusted gross income	$ 13,400
Less: Net operating loss	(11,000)
Recomputed adjusted gross income	$ 2,400

CONCEPT SUMMARY 8–4
COMPUTATION OF NET OPERATING LOSS

Taxable income shown on the return

Add back:

1. Personal and dependency exemptions.
2. Net operating loss carryover or carryback from another year.
3. The excess of nonbusiness capital losses over nonbusiness capital gains.
4. The excess of nonbusiness deductions over the sum of nonbusiness income plus *net* nonbusiness capital gains.
5. The excess of business capital losses over the sum of business capital gains plus the excess of nonbusiness income and *net* nonbusiness capital gains over nonbusiness deductions. The add-back from the total of items 3 and 5 will not exceed $3,000 because of the capital loss limitation rules.

Equals the net operating loss.

Itemized deductions		
Charitable contributions	$2,700	
Interest	2,800	
Taxes	1,420	(6,920)
Exemptions (2 × $2,300)		(4,600)
Recomputed taxable income		$(9,120)
Tax		$ -0-
Tax originally paid and refund claim		$ 282

◆

Calculation of the Remaining Net Operating Loss

After computing the amount of refund claim for the initial carryback year, it is then necessary to determine the extent to which any NOL remains to carry over to future years. The amount of this carryover loss is the excess of the NOL over the taxable income of the year to which the loss is being applied. However, the taxable income of the year to which the loss is being applied must be determined with the following *modifications*:

- No deduction is allowed for excess capital losses over capital gains.
- No deduction is allowed for the NOL that is being carried back. However, deductions are allowed for NOLs occurring before the loss year.
- Any deductions claimed that are based on or limited by AGI must be determined after making the preceding adjustments. However, charitable contributions do not take into account any NOL carryback.
- No deduction is allowed for personal and dependency exemptions.

EXAMPLE 29

Referring to the facts in Example 28, the NOL carryover from 1992 available for future years would be ($4,520), computed as follows:

Salary income		$10,000
Dividends		2,000
Net long-term capital gain		1,400
Adjusted gross income		$13,400
Itemized deductions		
Charitable contributions	$2,700	
Interest	2,800	
Taxes	1,420	(6,920)
Exemptions (not allowed)		-0-
Modified taxable income		$ 6,480
Net operating loss		($11,000)
Modified taxable income		6,480
Net operating loss to carry forward		($ 4,520)

◆

Since the ending figure is negative, it represents the NOL remaining to carry over to 1994 or later years.

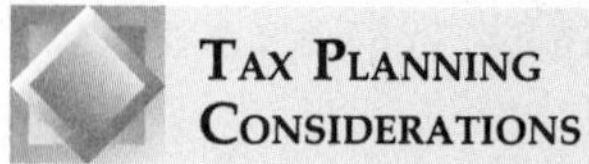

TAX PLANNING CONSIDERATIONS

Documentation of Related-Taxpayer Loans, Casualty Losses, and Theft Losses

Since non-bona fide loans between related taxpayers may be treated as gifts, adequate documentation is needed to substantiate a bad debt deduction if the loan subsequently becomes worthless. Documentation should include proper execution of the note (legal form) and the establishment of a bona fide purpose for the loan. In addition, it is desirable to stipulate a reasonable rate of interest and a fixed maturity date.

Since a theft loss is not permitted for misplaced items, a loss should be documented by a police report and evidence of the value of the property (e.g., appraisals, pictures of the property, newspaper clippings). Similar documentation of the value of property should be provided to support a casualty loss deduction because the amount of loss is measured by the decline in fair market value of the property.

Casualty loss deductions must be reported on Form 4684 (see Appendix B).

Small Business Stock

Because § 1244 limits the amount of loss classified as ordinary loss on a yearly basis, a taxpayer might maximize the benefits of § 1244 by selling the stock in more than one taxable year. The result could be that the losses in any one taxable year would not exceed the § 1244 limits on ordinary loss.

Example 30

T, a single individual, purchased small business stock in 1990 for $150,000 (150 shares at $1,000 per share). On December 20, 1992, the stock is worth $60,000 (150 shares at $400 per share). T wants to sell the stock at this time. T earns a salary of $80,000 a year, has no other capital transactions, and does not expect any in the future. If T sells all of the small business stock in 1992, his recognized loss will be $90,000 ($60,000 − $150,000). The loss will be characterized as a $50,000 ordinary loss and a $40,000 long-term capital loss. In computing taxable income for 1992, T could deduct the $50,000 ordinary loss but could deduct only $3,000 of the capital loss. The remainder of the capital loss could be carried over and used in future years subject to the $3,000 limitation if T has no capital gains. If T sells 82 shares in 1992, he will recognize an ordinary loss of $49,200 [82 × ($1,000 − $400)]. If T then sells the remainder of the shares in 1993, he will recognize an ordinary loss of $40,800 [68 × ($1,000 − $400)]. T could deduct the $49,200 ordinary loss in computing 1992 taxable income and the $40,800 ordinary loss in computing 1993 taxable income. ◆

Casualty Losses

A special election is available for taxpayers who sustain casualty losses in an area designated by the President as a disaster area. This election affects only the timing, not the calculation, of the deduction. The deduction can be taken in the year before the year in which the loss occurred. Thus, an individual can take the deduction on the 1991 return for a loss occurring between January 1 and December 31, 1992. The benefit, of course, is a faster refund (or reduction in tax). It will also be advantageous to carry the loss back if the taxpayer's tax rate in the carryback year is higher than the tax rate in the year of the loss.

To find out if an event qualifies as a disaster area loss, one can look in any of the major tax services or in the Weekly Compilation of Presidential Documents or the *Internal Revenue Bulletin*.

Net Operating Losses

In certain instances, it may be advisable for a taxpayer to elect not to carry back an NOL. For an individual, the benefits from the loss carryback could be scaled down or lost due to the economic adjustments that must be made to taxable income for the year to which the loss is carried. For example, a taxpayer should attempt to minimize the number of taxable years to which an NOL is carried. The more years to which the NOL is applied, the more benefits are lost from adjustments for items such as personal and dependency exemptions.

The election not to carry back the loss might also be advantageous if there is a disparity in marginal tax rates applicable to different tax years.

EXAMPLE 31

T sustained an NOL of $10,000 in Year 4. His marginal tax bracket in Year 1 was 15%. In Year 5, however, he expects his bracket to be 31% due to a large profit he will make on a business deal. If T carries his loss back, his refund will be $1,500 (15% × $10,000). If he elects not to carry it back to Year 1 but chooses, instead, to carry it forward, his savings will be $3,100 (31% × $10,000). Even considering the time value of an immediate tax refund, T appears to be better off using the carryover approach. ◆

PROBLEM MATERIALS

DISCUSSION QUESTIONS

1. Mr. X, an individual, cash basis taxpayer, is a CPA. X performed extensive tax work for Ms. B, for which he charged $10,000. Ms. B never paid for the work, and there is no possibility of X ever collecting any of the $10,000. X feels that he is entitled to a bad debt deduction of $10,000. Comment on Mr. X's tax position on this matter.
2. Distinguish between the specific charge-off method for bad debts and the reserve method for bad debts, and discuss the acceptability of each for Federal income tax purposes.
3. B made a loan to a friend three years ago to help the friend purchase an automobile. B's friend has notified him that the car has been sold and the most he will be able to repay is 50 percent of the loan. Discuss the possibility of B taking a bad debt deduction for half of the loan.
4. Discuss the difference between business and nonbusiness bad debts. How is the distinction determined? How is each treated on the return?
5. Discuss a taxpayer's options for the tax treatment of a loss incurred on a deposit in a qualified financial institution. Also note the consequences of each option.
6. What factors are to be considered in determining whether a bad debt arising from a loan between related parties is, in fact, a bad debt?
7. Discuss the tax treatment of a worthless security of an affiliated corporation.
8. Discuss the ordinary loss limitations on the sale of § 1244 stock and the advantages of such a characterization.
9. D, an individual and sole proprietor, discovers that her store has been extensively damaged by termites. Discuss whether D may take a deduction for the damage to her store.
10. How are thefts treated differently from acts of God for casualty loss purposes?
11. What is a disaster area loss? Why might a taxpayer benefit from making the disaster area loss election?
12. Discuss the tax consequences of property being completely destroyed in determining the amount of a casualty loss assuming no insurance proceeds are received.
13. How is a personal casualty loss computed? A business casualty loss? What effect do insurance proceeds have on both types of losses?
14. Discuss the tax consequences of not making an insurance claim when insured personal use property is subject to a casualty or theft loss.
15. M's 10-year-old automobile was extensively damaged in a collision in which he was not at fault. The original cost of the automobile was $10,000, and the cost of repairing it was $5,000. Discuss any problems with using the $5,000 as the measurement of the loss.
16. Discuss whether a loss in connection with a transaction entered into for profit is a deduction *for* AGI or *from* AGI.

17. When casualty losses exceed casualty gains, the amount of the casualty loss subject to the 10% of AGI floor is only the casualty loss in excess of casualty gains. Discuss the significance of netting losses against gains in this manner rather than having the entire casualty loss subject to the 10% of AGI floor.
18. If a taxpayer is required to spread a personal casualty loss between two years under the reasonable prospect of recovery doctrine, how will the $100 per event floor and the 10% of AGI limitation be treated?
19. Z, an individual, sustained a loss on an apartment building damaged by fire. Z owns the building and rents apartments to tenants. Discuss the tax treatment of the loss on Z's individual tax return.
20. If personal casualty losses exceed personal casualty gains, only the losses in excess of the gains are potential itemized deductions. Discuss why this is advantageous to the taxpayer.
21. Why do most taxpayers elect to write off research and experimental expenditures rather than capitalize and amortize such amounts? Are there some situations in which the capitalization and amortization approach would be preferable?
22. If a business does not elect to expense or amortize research expenditures, what is the possibility of writing off such expenditures?
23. Why can the sale of small business stock (§ 1244 stock) at a loss create or increase an NOL?
24. Discuss the periods to which NOLs may be carried. Can the taxpayer elect not to carry an NOL back to any one year? What possible benefit might result from not carrying a loss back to a particular year?
25. Why are such items as nonbusiness deductions and personal and dependency exemptions not allowed in computing the NOL?
26. If an individual has no nonbusiness capital transactions for the year, discuss the treatment of the excess of nonbusiness income over nonbusiness deductions with respect to the NOL.
27. Discuss the calculation of the NOL remaining after a carryback to a particular tax year.

PROBLEMS

28. M loaned T $20,000 on April 1, 1991. In 1992 T filed for bankruptcy. At that time, it was revealed that T's creditors could expect to receive 80¢ on the dollar. In February 1993, final settlement was made and M received $15,000. How much loss can M deduct and in which year? How is it treated on M's return?
29. In 1990, X loaned A $20,000. In 1992, X was notified that the most that could be expected from A would be 30¢ on the dollar. In 1993, X received $2,000 in final settlement of the debt. Compare the tax results if the debt is a business or a nonbusiness bad debt.
30. In 1991, W deposited $20,000 with a commercial bank. On July 1, 1992, W was notified that the bank was insolvent, and subsequently he received only 30% of the deposit. W also has a salary of $5,000, long-term capital gain of $9,000, and itemized deductions (other than casualty and theft) of $7,000. Determine W's possible deductions with respect to the deposit.
31. X, a married taxpayer filing a joint return, had the following items for 1992:

    - Salary of $150,000.
    - Gain of $10,000 on the sale of § 1244 stock X acquired three years ago.
    - Loss of $120,000 on the sale of § 1244 stock X acquired two years ago.
    - Stock acquired on December 15, 1991, for $5,000 became worthless on March 28, 1992.

    Determine X's adjusted gross income for 1992.
32. T, a single taxpayer, had the following items for the current year:

    - Worthless stock of $5,000. The stock was acquired two years earlier and became worthless in June of the current year.
    - A nonbusiness bad debt of $10,000.

- Gain of $27,000 on the sale of § 1244 stock acquired two years earlier.
- Loss of $58,000 on the sale of § 1244 stock acquired three months earlier.
- Salary of $70,000.

Determine T's adjusted gross income for the current year.

33. When J returned from a vacation in Hawaii on November 8, 1992, she discovered that a burglar had stolen her silver, stereo, and color television. In the process of removing these items, the burglar damaged some furniture that originally cost $1,400. J's silver cost $3,640 and was valued at $6,500; the stereo system cost $8,400 and was valued at $6,200; the television cost $840 and was worth $560. J filed a claim with her insurance company and was reimbursed in the following amounts on December 20, 1992.

Silver	$2,800
Stereo	5,600
Television	490

The insurance company disputed the reimbursement claimed by J for the damaged furniture, but she protested and was finally paid $280 on January 30, 1993. The repairs to the furniture totaled $448. J's adjusted gross income for 1992 was $12,000, and it was $15,000 for 1993. How much can J claim as a casualty and theft loss? In which year?

34. K owned three acres of land in Kansas upon which he had his home, two rental houses, an apartment building, and his construction company. A tornado hit the area and destroyed one of the rental houses, damaged the apartment building, and destroyed some of K's construction equipment. The tenant of K's other rental house moved out for fear of another tornado, and K lost $450 in rent. Other losses were as follows:

Item	Adjusted Basis	FMV Before	FMV After	Insurance Proceeds
Rental house #1	$ 34,500	$ 43,500	$ -0-	$30,000
Apartment building	100,000	225,000	180,000	31,500
Equipment	90,000	112,500	-0-	75,000

a. How much is K's casualty loss before applying any limitation?
b. Assuming the loss occurred on March 3, 1993, and that the area was designated by the President as a disaster area, what options are open to K with respect to the timing of the loss deduction?

35. On January 7 of the current year, T dropped off to sleep while driving home from a business trip. Luckily, she was only slightly injured in the resulting accident, but her car was completely destroyed.

T had purchased the car new two years ago and had driven it 64,000 miles at the time of the accident. Of these miles, 28,000 were business miles; the remaining miles were personal miles. The car cost $7,200 new. T has taken $1,985 of depreciation for the business use of the car. She carried $1,000 deductible collision insurance on the car. Her insurance company settled her claim by paying her $2,400 for the car (fair market value before the wreck was $3,400).

After T's release from the hospital the day after the accident, she could not find her purse (cost $65, fair replacement value $30) or its contents, which included $350 in cash and $500 in traveler's checks. The traveler's checks were replaced by the issuing company. She also was unable to locate the stone from her diamond engagement ring. The stone cost her husband $2,500 when purchased nine years ago and was worth $6,400 at the time of the loss.

a. Determine the amount of T's deductible loss *for* AGI.
b. Determine the amount of the loss deductible *from* AGI, assuming AGI for the year is $25,000.

36. On June 15, 1992, T was involved in an accident with his personal automobile. T had purchased the car new two years ago for $14,000. At the time of the accident, the car was worth $12,000. After the accident, the car was appraised at $4,000. T had an insurance

policy that had a 20% deductible clause. Because T was afraid that the policy would be canceled, he made no claim against the insurance policy for the damages to the car.

On September 17, 1992, T was involved in an accident with his business automobile. The automobile had a fair market value of $10,000 before the accident, and it was worthless after the accident. T had a basis in the car of $15,000 at the time of the accident. The car was covered by an insurance policy that insured the car for fair market value. T made a claim and collected against the policy.

T earned a salary of $60,000 and had other itemized deductions of $10,000 for the year. Determine taxable income for T and his wife, who file a joint return for 1992.

37. X Corporation, a manufacturing company, decided to develop a new line of fireworks. Because of the danger involved, X purchased an isolated parcel of land for $300,000 and constructed a building for $400,000. The building was to be used for research and experimentation in creating the new fireworks. The project was begun in 1992. X had the following expenses in 1992 in connection with the project:

Salaries	$60,000
Utilities	7,000
Materials	12,000
Insurance	20,000
Cost of market survey to determine profit potential for new fireworks line	8,000
Depreciation on the building	8,000

X had the following expenses in 1993 in connection with the project:

Salaries	$70,000
Utilities	10,000
Materials	15,000
Insurance	21,000
Depreciation on the building	11,000

The benefits from the project will be realized starting in June 1994.

a. If X Corporation elects to expense research and experimental expenditures, determine the amount of the deduction for 1992, 1993, and 1994.

b. If X Corporation elects a 60-month deferral and amortization period, determine the amount of the deduction for 1992, 1993, and 1994.

38. H and W, who file a joint return, had the following items for their 1992 tax return:

- H's salary—$40,000.
- W's salary—$42,000.
- Dividends from domestic corporations—$2,000.
- During the year, a fire completely destroyed an apartment building owned by H and W. The building was worth $400,000 at the time of the fire, and H and W had a basis for the building of $375,000. The building was insured for 60% of its fair market value.
- Other itemized deductions—$10,000.

a. What is H and W's taxable income for 1992?

b. What is H and W's NOL for 1992?

39. H, a single taxpayer, had the following items of income and expense during 1992:

Gross receipts from business	$120,000
Business expenses	150,000
H's salary	10,000
Interest from X Company bonds	12,000
Itemized deductions	8,000

a. Determine the amount of H's 1992 taxable income.

b. Determine the amount of H's 1992 NOL.

40. G, who is married and files a joint return, owns a grocery store. In 1992, his gross sales were $286,000 and operating expenses were $310,000. Other items on his 1992 return were as follows:

Nonbusiness capital gains (short-term)	$10,000
Nonbusiness capital losses (long-term)	9,000
Itemized deductions	10,000
Ordinary nonbusiness income	4,000
Salary from part-time job	10,000

During the years 1989 and 1990, G had no taxable income. In 1991, G had taxable income of $24,800 computed as follows:

Net business income		$ 60,000
Interest income		2,000
Adjusted gross income		$ 62,000
Less: Itemized deductions		
Charitable contributions of $40,000, limited to 50% of AGI	$31,000	
Medical expenses of $6,550, limited to the amount in excess of 7.5% of AGI ($6,550 − $4,650)	1,900	
Total itemized deductions		(32,900)
Exemptions (2 × 2,150)		(4,300)
Taxable income		$ 24,800

a. What is G's 1992 NOL?
b. Determine G's recomputed taxable income for 1991.

41. During 1992, T, married with one dependent child, had the following items of income, expense, and loss to report:

Gross receipts from business	$250,000
Business expenses	274,000
Interest received from State of Utah bonds	8,000
Interest received from bank savings account	2,000
Wife's salary from part-time work	6,000
Long-term capital gain on sale of stock held as an investment	9,000
Short-term capital loss on sale of State of Utah bonds	8,000
Itemized deductions	2,700

a. Assuming T files a joint return, what is T's taxable income for 1992?
b. What is the amount of T's NOL for 1992?

42. Assume that in addition to the information in Problem 41, T had no taxable income for the years 1989 and 1990 and $5,250 of taxable income for 1991 computed as follows:

Salary		$ 25,000
Capital loss		(1,000)
Adjusted gross income		$ 24,000
Less: Itemized deductions		
Charitable contributions of $20,000, limited to 50% of AGI	$12,000	
Medical expenses of $2,100, limited to the amount in excess of 7.5% of AGI ($2,100 − $1,800)	300	
Total itemized deductions		(12,300)
Exemptions (3 × $2,150)		(6,450)
Taxable income		$ 5,250

Determine the amount of T's 1992 NOL to be carried forward to 1993.

43. H is single and had the following income and deductions for 1992:

Business receipts	$ 90,000
Business expenses	130,000
Dividends from domestic corporations	20,000
Interest received from bank savings account	6,000
Itemized deductions	10,000
1991 NOL carried to 1992	25,000

a. What is H's taxable income for 1992?
b. What is H's NOL for 1992?

44. S, single and age 32, had the following items for the tax year 1992:

- Salary of $40,000.
- Interest income from U.S. government bonds of $2,000.
- Dividends from a foreign corporation of $500.
- Sale of small business § 1244 stock on October 20, 1992, for $10,000. The stock had been acquired two years earlier for $65,000.
- Business bad debt of $3,000.
- Nonbusiness bad debt of $5,000.
- Sale of small business § 1244 stock on November 12, 1992, for $4,000. The stock had been acquired on June 5, 1992, for $800.
- Sale of common stock on December 4, 1992, for $40,000. The stock was acquired four years ago for $18,000.
- Total itemized deductions of $8,000.

Determine S's NOL for 1992.

45. W, single and age 38, had the following income and expense items in 1992:

Nonbusiness bad debt	$ 6,000
Business bad debt	2,000
Nonbusiness long-term capital gain	4,000
Nonbusiness short-term capital loss	3,000
Salary	40,000
Interest income	1,000

Determine W's adjusted gross income for 1992.

46. Assume that in addition to the information in Problem 45, W had the following items in 1992:

Personal casualty gain on an asset held for four months	$10,000
Personal casualty loss on an asset held for two years	1,000

Determine W's adjusted gross income for 1992.

47. Assume that in addition to the information in Problems 45 and 46, W had the following items in 1992:

Personal casualty loss on an asset held for five years	$50,000
Interest expense on home mortgage	3,000

Determine W's taxable income and NOL for 1992.

CUMULATIVE PROBLEMS

48. Ned Wilson, age 60, single, and retired, has no dependents. Ned lives at 231 Wander Lane, Salt Lake City, UT 84201. Ned's Social Security number is 985–12–3774. During 1992, Ned had the following income and expense items:

a. On January 27, 1991, Ned deposited $8,000 in a savings account at the ABC Financial Company. The savings account bore interest at 15%, compounded semiannually. Ned received a $600 interest payment on July 27, 1991, but received no interest payments thereafter. The finance company filed for bankruptcy on January 12, 1992. Ned received a $710 check in final settlement of his account from the bankruptcy trustee on December 20, 1992.

b. On January 1, 1992, a fire severely damaged a two-story building owned by Ned, who occupied the second story of the building as a residence and had recently opened a hardware store on the ground level. The following information is available with respect to the incident:

	Adjusted Basis	Fair Market Value Before	Fair Market Value After
Building	$64,000	$130,000	$50,000
Inventory	35,000	55,000	None
Store equipment	3,000	1,800	None
Home furnishings	12,600	6,000	800
Personal auto	8,900	7,800	7,600

Ned's fire insurance policy paid the following amounts for damages covered by the policy:

Building	$50,000 (policy maximum)
Inventory	33,000
Store equipment	None
Home furnishings	1,000 (policy maximum)
Personal auto	None

Assume all of the destroyed property was acquired on December 15, 1991.

c. On March 1, 1987, Ned loaned a neighboring businessman $15,000. The debtor died of a heart attack on June 21, 1992. Ned had no security and was unable to collect anything from the man's estate.

d. Ned received $72,000 of interest income from Salt Lake City Bank.

e. On March 2, 1992, Ned sold a piece of real estate he had been holding for speculation for $90,000. Ned had bought the land July 18, 1977, for $52,800.

f. Ned made a charitable contribution of $3,000.

g. Ned made four quarterly estimated tax payments of $5,000 each.

Part 1—Tax Computation

Compute Ned's 1992 Federal income tax payable (or refund due), assuming he deducts the lost deposit as a bad debt. Suggested software (if available): *TurboTax* for tax return or WFT tax planning software.

Part 2—Tax Planning

Determine whether Ned should elect to treat the deposit in ABC Financial Company as a casualty loss rather than as a bad debt. Suggested software (if available): *TurboTax* for tax return or WFT tax planning software.

49. Sam Sampson, age 55, is single and has no dependents. He is employed by Acme Corporation as an internal auditor. Sam lives at 2135 Rosebud Avenue, Denver, CO 23106. Sam's Social Security number is 222–33–7077. During 1992, Sam had the following income and expense items:

a. Sam sold X Corporation stock on January 21, 1992, for $16,000. He had purchased the stock on July 6, 1985, for $4,000.

b. On September 1, 1992, Sam learned that Bart Smugg had been sentenced to jail in a foreign country for 20 years. Sam had loaned Bart $20,000 on June 1, 1991. The loan was due on June 1, 1992, and Sam has not been able to collect.

c. On August 15, 1992, Sam's broker informed him that the Y Corporation stock he owned was completely worthless. Sam had purchased the stock on December 23, 1991, for $3,000.

d. On April 15, 1992, Sam sold W Corporation stock to an unrelated party for $12,000. Sam's basis in the stock was $67,000. Sam had organized W Corporation on March 7, 1987, but the business never really got off the ground. The stock was § 1244 stock.

e. Sam sold D Corporation stock on May 11, 1992, for $11,000. He had purchased the stock on November 21, 1983, for $3,000.

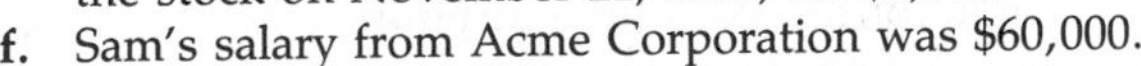

f. Sam's salary from Acme Corporation was $60,000.
g. Acme Corporation withheld Federal income tax of $2,000.

Compute Sam's 1992 Federal income tax payable (or refund due). Suggested software (if available): *TurboTax* for tax return or WFT tax planning software.

50. Jane Smith, age 40, is single and has no dependents. She is employed as a legal secretary by Legal Services, Inc. She owns and operates Typing Services located near the campus of San Jose State University at 1986 Campus Drive. She is a cash basis taxpayer. Jane lives at 2020 Oakcrest Road, San Jose, CA 95134. Jane's Social Security number is 123–89–6666. Jane indicates that she wishes to designate $1 to the Presidential Election Campaign Fund. During 1991, Jane had the following income and expense items:

a. $40,000 salary from Legal Services, Inc.
b. $15,000 gross receipts from her typing services business.
c. $300 cash dividend from Buffalo Mining Company, a Canadian corporation.
d. $1,000 Christmas bonus from Legal Services, Inc.
e. $10,000 life insurance proceeds on the death of her sister.
f. $5,000 check given to her by her wealthy aunt.
g. $100 won in a bingo game.
h. Expenses connected with the typing service:

Office rent	$5,000
Supplies	2,400
Utilities and telephone	3,680
Wages to part-time typists	4,000
Payroll taxes	600
Equipment rentals	3,000

i. $8,000 interest expense on a home mortgage (paid to San Jose Savings and Loan).
j. $5,000 fair market value of silverware stolen from her home by a burglar on October 12, 1991. Jane had paid $4,000 for the silverware on July 1, 1982. She was reimbursed $1,500 by her insurance company.
k. Jane had loaned $2,100 to a friend, Joan Jensen, on June 3, 1988. Joan declared bankruptcy on August 14, 1991, and was unable to repay the loan.
l. Legal Services, Inc., withheld Federal income tax of $7,000 and the required amount of FICA tax.

Part 1—Tax Computation

Compute Jane Smith's 1991 Federal income tax payable (or refund due). If you use tax forms for your computations, you will need Forms 1040 and 4684 and Schedules A, C, and D. Suggested software (if available): *TurboTax* for tax return or WFT tax planning software.

Part 2—Tax Planning

In 1992, Jane plans to continue her job with Legal Services, Inc. Therefore, items a, d, and l will recur in 1992. Jane plans to continue her typing services business (refer to item b) and expects gross receipts of $20,000. She projects that all business expenses (refer to item h) will increase by 10%, except for office rent, which, under the terms of her lease, will remain the same as in 1991. Items e, f, g, j, and k will not recur in 1992. Items c and i will be approximately the same as in 1991.

Jane would like you to compute the minimum amount of estimated tax she will have to pay for 1992 so that she will not have to pay any additional tax upon filing her 1992 Federal income tax return. Suggested software (if available): *TurboTax* for tax return or WFT tax planning software.

RESEARCH PROBLEMS

RESEARCH PROBLEM 1 While X was in the process of obtaining a divorce, his wife, without X's knowledge, had the furniture removed from X's apartment. Discuss whether X would be entitled to a tax deduction for the loss of the furniture.

Partial list of research aids:
Landis G. Brown, 30 TCM 257, T.C. Memo. 1971–60.
Goode v. Comm., 42 TCM 1209, T.C. Memo. 1981–548.

RESEARCH PROBLEM 2 John Morgan made deductible alimony payments of $60,000 for the year. The payments were deductible for AGI under §§ 62(a)(10) and 215. Because of the large deduction, John has a negative taxable income for the year. Discuss the possiblity of John having a net operating loss for the year as a result of the alimony payments.

RESEARCH PROBLEM 3 John Smith was engaged to be married to Nancy Brown. In contemplation of marriage, John deposited $10,000 in a bank account for Nancy, to be used after their marriage. Sometime thereafter, the engagement was broken off, and Nancy used the $10,000 for herself. John has attempted to collect the $10,000 from Nancy without success, and now Nancy has filed for bankruptcy. Discuss the possibility of John's claiming the $10,000 as a nonbusiness bad debt.

CHAPTER

DEPRECIATION, COST RECOVERY, AMORTIZATION, AND DEPLETION

OBJECTIVES

Determine the amount of depreciation under pre-ACRS rules.

Determine the amount of cost recovery under ACRS rules.

Determine the amount of cost recovery under modified ACRS rules.

Explain the operation of the rules governing listed property.

Determine the amount of amortization for intangible assets.

Explain the alternative tax treatments for intangible drilling and development costs.

Determine the amount of depletion expense.

Explain the reporting procedures for depreciation and cost recovery.

Develop tax planning ideas for depreciation, cost recovery, and depletion.

OUTLINE

The Internal Revenue Code provides for a deduction for the consumption of the cost of an asset through depreciation, cost recovery, amortization, or depletion. These deductions are applications of the recovery of capital doctrine (discussed in Chapter 4). Before discussing each cost consumption method, however, it is beneficial to review the difference between the classification of an asset (realty or personalty) and the use to which it is placed (business or personal). Personalty can be defined as all assets that are not realty.[1] Both realty and personalty can be either business use/income-producing property or personal use property. Examples of this distinction include a residence (realty that is personal use), an office building (realty that is business use), a dump truck (personalty that is business use), and regular wearing apparel (personalty that is personal use).

A further distinction is made between tangible and intangible property. Tangible property is any property with physical substance (e.g., equipment, buildings), while intangible property lacks such substance (e.g., goodwill, patents).

A write-off of the cost (or other adjusted basis) of an asset is known as depreciation, cost recovery, depletion, or amortization. Depreciation and cost recovery relate to tangible property, depletion involves certain natural resources (e.g., oil, coal, gravel), and amortization concerns intangible property. As noted later, a write-off for income tax purposes is not allowed when an asset lacks a determinable useful life (e.g., land, goodwill) or when it is not business use property.

The depreciation rules were completely overhauled by the Economic Recovery Tax Act of 1981 (ERTA). Hence, *most* property placed in service after December 31, 1980, is subject to the accelerated cost recovery system (ACRS). However, property placed in service before January 1, 1981, that is still in use, as well as *certain* property placed in service after December 31, 1980, is subject to the pre-ERTA depreciation rules. The Tax Reform Act (TRA) of 1986 completely revised the ACRS rules for property placed in service after December 31, 1986. Therefore, a knowledge of all of the depreciation and cost recovery rules may be needed as Example 1 illustrates.

EXAMPLE 1

ABC owns equipment purchased in 1980. The equipment has a 10-year useful life. The business also owns several trucks purchased in 1986. In 1989, the business purchased a computer. To compute the depreciation and cost recovery for 1992, ABC will use the pre-ERTA depreciation rules for the equipment, the pre-TRA of 1986 cost recovery rules for the trucks, and the post-TRA of 1986 cost recovery rules for the computer. ◆

This chapter first discusses the pre-ERTA depreciation rules and then examines the pre-TRA and post-TRA of 1986 ACRS rules.[2] The chapter concludes with a discussion of the amortization of intangible property and the depletion of natural resources.

DEPRECIATION

Section 167 permits a depreciation deduction in the form of a reasonable allowance for the exhaustion, wear and tear, and obsolescence of business property and property held for the production of income (e.g., rental property held by an investor).[3] Obsolescence refers to normal technological change due to reasonably foreseeable economic conditions. If rapid or abnormal obsolescence occurs, a taxpayer may change to a shorter estimated useful life if there is a

1. Refer to Chapter 1 for a further discussion.
2. Depreciation is covered in § 167, and ACRS appears in § 168.
3. § 167(a) and Reg. § 1.167(a)–1.

"clear and convincing basis for the redetermination." Depreciation deductions are not permitted for personal use property.

The taxpayer must adopt a reasonable and consistent plan for depreciating the cost or other basis of assets over the estimated useful life of the property (e.g., the taxpayer cannot arbitrarily defer or accelerate the amount of depreciation from one year to another). The basis of the depreciable property must be reduced by the depreciation allowed and by not less than the allowable amount.[4] The *allowed* depreciation is the depreciation actually taken, whereas the *allowable* depreciation is the amount that could have been taken under the applicable depreciation method. If the taxpayer does not claim any depreciation on property during a particular year, the basis of the property still must be reduced by the amount of depreciation that should have been deducted (the allowable depreciation).

EXAMPLE 2

On January 1, T paid $7,500 for a truck to be used in his business. He chose a five-year estimated useful life, no salvage value, and straight-line depreciation. Thus, the allowable depreciation deduction was $1,500 per year. However, depreciation actually taken (allowed) was as follows:

Year 1	$1,500
Year 2	–0–
Year 3	–0–
Year 4	1,500
Year 5	1,500

The adjusted basis of the truck must be reduced by the amount of allowable depreciation of $7,500 ($1,500 × 5 years) despite the fact that T claimed only $4,500 depreciation during the five-year period. Therefore, if T sold the truck at the end of Year 5 for $1,000, a $1,000 gain would be recognized, since the adjusted basis of the truck is zero. ◆

Qualifying Property

As mentioned earlier, the use rather than the character of property determines whether a depreciation deduction is permitted. Property must be used in a trade or business or held for the production of income to qualify as depreciable.

CONCEPT SUMMARY 9–1
DEPRECIATION AND COST RECOVERY: RELEVANT TIME PERIODS

System	Date Property Is Placed in Service
§ 167 depreciation	Before January 1, 1981, and *certain* property placed in service after December 31, 1980.
Pre-TRA of 1986 ACRS (original ACRS)	After December 31, 1980, and before January 1, 1987.
Post-TRA of 1986 ACRS (modified ACRS)	After December 31, 1986.

4. § 1016(a)(2) and Reg. § 1.167(a)–10(a).

EXAMPLE 3

T is a self-employed CPA who uses her automobile for both personal and business purposes. A depreciation deduction is permitted only for the business use part. Assume the automobile was acquired at a cost of $12,000 and T's mileage during the year was 10,000 miles, of which 3,000 miles were for business. Only 30% of the cost, or $3,600, will be subject to depreciation. ◆

The basis for depreciation generally is the adjusted cost basis used to determine gain if the property is sold or otherwise disposed of.[5] However, if personal use assets are converted to business or income-producing use, the basis for depreciation and for loss is the *lower* of the adjusted basis or fair market value at the time of the conversion of the property.[6] As a result of this lower of basis rule, losses that occurred while the property was personal use property will not be recognized for tax purposes through the depreciation of the property.

EXAMPLE 4

T acquires a personal residence for $30,000. Four years later, he converts the property to rental use when the fair market value is only $25,000. The basis for depreciation is $25,000, since the fair market value is less than the adjusted basis. The $5,000 decline in value is deemed to be personal (since it occurred while the property was held for personal use) and therefore nondeductible. ◆

The Regulations provide that tangible property is depreciable only to the extent that the property is subject to wear and tear, decay or decline from natural causes, exhaustion, and obsolescence.[7] Thus, land and inventory are not depreciable, but land improvements are depreciable (e.g., paved surfaces, fences, landscaping).

Other Depreciation Considerations

In determining the amount of the depreciation deduction, the following additional considerations need to be addressed:

- The salvage value of the asset.[8]
- The choice of depreciation methods.
- The useful life of the asset.

For property subject to depreciation under § 167, taxpayers generally must take into account the *salvage value* (assuming there is a salvage value) of an asset in calculating depreciation. An asset cannot be depreciated below its salvage value. However, the Code permits a taxpayer to disregard salvage value for amounts up to 10 percent of the basis in the property. This provision applies to tangible personal property (other than livestock) with an estimated useful life of three years or more.[9]

EXAMPLE 5

The XYZ Company acquired a machine for $10,000 in 1980 with an estimated salvage value of $3,000 after 15 years. The company may disregard salvage value to the extent of $1,000 and compute the machine's depreciation based upon a cost of $10,000 less $2,000 salvage value. The adjusted basis may be reduced to $2,000 (depreciation of $8,000 may be taken) despite the fact that the actual salvage value is $3,000. ◆

5. § 167(c).
6. Reg. § 1.167(g)–1.
7. Reg. § 1.167(a).
8. See the Glossary of Tax Terms in Appendix C for a definition of salvage value.
9. § 167(f) and Reg. § 1.167(a) –1(c).

This provision was incorporated into the law to reduce the number of IRS-taxpayer disputes over the amount of the salvage value that should be used.

Another consideration is the *choice of depreciation methods* from among the several allowed. The following alternative depreciation methods are permitted for property placed into service before January 1, 1981, and for *certain* property placed in service after December 31, 1980:

- The straight-line (SL) method (cost basis less salvage value ÷ estimated useful life).
- The declining-balance method (DB) using a rate not to exceed twice the straight-line rate. Common methods include 200 percent DB (double-declining balance), 150 percent DB, and 125 percent DB. Salvage value is not taken into account under any of the declining-balance methods. However, no further depreciation can be claimed once net book value (cost minus depreciation) and salvage value are the same.
- The sum-of-the-years' digits method (SYD).
- Any other consistent method that does not result in greater total depreciation being claimed during the first two-thirds of the useful life than would have been allowable under the double-declining balance method. Permissible methods include machine hours and the units-of-production method.

EXAMPLE 6

On January 1, 1980, T acquired a new automobile to be used in his business. The asset cost $10,000 with an estimated salvage value of $2,000 and a four-year estimated useful life. The following amounts of depreciation could be deducted, depending on the method of depreciation used (note that pre-ERTA rules [depreciation calculated under § 167] continue to apply for the entire useful life of assets acquired before 1981):

	1980	**1981**	**1982**	**1983**
1. Straight-line				
$10,000 cost less ($2,000 salvage value reduced by 10% of cost) ÷ 4 years	$2,250	$2,250	$2,250	$2,250
2. Double-declining balance				
a. $10,000 × 50% (twice the straight-line rate)	5,000			
b. ($10,000 − $5,000) × 50%		2,500		
c. ($10,000 − $5,000 − $2,500) × 50%			1,250	
d. ($10,000 − $5,000 − $2,500 − $1,250) × 50%				250[10]
3. Sum-of-the-years' digits*: $10,000 cost less ($2,000 salvage value reduced by 10% of cost) or $9,000				
a. $9,000 × 4/10	3,600			
b. $9,000 × 3/10		2,700		
c. $9,000 × 2/10			1,800	
d. $9,000 × 1/10				900

*The sum-of-the-years' digits (SYD) method formula is

$$\text{Cost} - \text{salvage value} \times \frac{\text{Remaining life at the beginning of the year}}{\text{Sum-of-the-years' digits of the estimated life}}$$

10. Total depreciation taken cannot exceed cost minus estimated salvage value ($1,000 in this example).

In this example, the denominator for SYD is 1 + 2 + 3 + 4, or 10. The numerator is 4 for Year 1 (the number of years left at the beginning of Year 1), 3 for Year 2, etc. The denominator can be calculated by the following formula:

$$S = \frac{Y(Y + 1)}{2} \quad \text{where } Y = \text{estimated useful life}$$

$$S = \frac{4(4 + 1)}{2} = 10$$

◆

EXAMPLE 7

Using the depreciation calculations in Example 6, the depreciation reserve (accumulated depreciation) and net book value at the end of 1983 are as follows:

	Cost	–	Depreciation	=	Net Book Value*
Straight-line	$10,000		$9,000		$1,000
Double-declining balance	10,000		9,000		1,000
Sum-of-the-years' digits	10,000		9,000		1,000

*Note that an asset may not be depreciated below its salvage value even when a declining-balance method is used.

◆

In 1969, Congress placed certain restrictions on the use of accelerated methods for new and used realty that are subject to the depreciation rules under § 167. These restrictions were imposed to reduce the opportunities for using real estate investments as tax shelters. The use of accelerated depreciation frequently resulted in the recognition of ordinary tax losses on economically profitable real estate ventures.

The following methods were permitted for residential and nonresidential real property:[11]

	Nonresidential Real Property (commercial and industrial buildings, etc.)	Residential Real Property (apartment buildings, etc.)
New property acquired after July 24, 1969, and generally before January 1, 1981	150% DB, SL	200% DB, SYD, 150% DB, or SL
Used property acquired after July 24, 1969, and generally before January 1, 1981	SL	125% DB (if estimated useful life is 20 years or greater) or SL

Congress chose to permit accelerated methods (200 percent declining-balance and sum-of-the-years' digits) for new residential rental property. Presumably, the desire to stimulate construction of new housing units justified the need for such accelerated methods.

Restrictions on the use of accelerated methods were not imposed on new tangible personalty (e.g., machinery, equipment, and automobiles). However,

11. See the Glossary of Tax Terms in Appendix C for a definition of residential rental property.

the 200 percent declining-balance and sum-of-the-years' digits methods were not permitted for used tangible personal property. The depreciation methods permitted for used tangible personal property were as follows:

	Useful Life of Three Years or More	Useful Life of Less Than Three Years
Used tangible personal property acquired after July 24, 1969, and generally before January 1, 1981	150% DB, SL	SL

Since the acquisition of used property does not result in any net addition to gross private investment in our economy, Congress chose not to provide as rapid accelerated depreciation for used property.

The determination of a *useful life* for a depreciable asset often led to disagreement between taxpayers and the IRS. One source of information was the company's previous experience and policy with respect to asset maintenance and utilization. Another source was the guideline lives issued by the IRS.[12] In 1971, the IRS guideline life system was modified and liberalized by the enactment of the Asset Depreciation Range (ADR) system.[13]

ACCELERATED COST RECOVERY SYSTEM (ACRS)

General Considerations

The depreciation rules before ERTA (before January 1, 1981) were designed to allocate depreciation deductions over the period the asset was used in business or held for the production of income so that the deductions for the cost of an asset were matched with the income produced by the asset (the so-called matching concept). Often this led to controversies between taxpayers and the IRS concerning the estimated useful life of an asset, and it delayed the tax benefit to be derived from the recoupment of a capital investment in the form of a deduction for depreciation.

One way to resolve the estimated useful life problem was to utilize the Asset Depreciation Range (ADR) system, which specified ranges for particular assets. Taxpayers could select a useful life for an asset within the specified range for that particular asset. However, many assets were not eligible for ADR, or taxpayers saw fit not to elect the system. In such cases, useful lives were determined according to the facts and circumstances pertaining to each asset or by agreement between the taxpayer and the IRS.

For property placed in service after December 31, 1980, the ADR system and depreciation calculated under § 167 have generally been replaced by the § 168 accelerated cost recovery system (ACRS). Under ACRS, the cost of an asset is recovered over a predetermined period that is generally shorter than the useful life of the asset or the period the asset is used to produce income. The change was designed to encourage investment, improve productivity, and simplify the law and its administration. However, the pre-ACRS depreciation rules will continue to apply in the following situations:

12. Rev.Proc. 72–10, 1972–1 C.B. 721, superseded by Rev.Proc. 83–35, 1983–1 C.B. 745.

13. Reg. § 1.167(a)–11. See the Glossary of Tax Terms in Appendix C for a definition of Asset Depreciation Range system.

- Property placed in service after 1980 whose life is not based on years (e.g., units-of-production method).
- The remaining depreciation on property placed in service by the taxpayer before 1981.
- Personal property acquired after 1980 if the property was owned or used during 1980 by the taxpayer or a related person (antichurning rule).[14]
- Property that is amortized (e.g., leasehold improvements).

ACRS does not distinguish between new and used property. However, the provisions discussed previously with respect to depreciation allowed and allowable and the basis for property converted from personal use continue to apply to ACRS property.

For property placed in service after December 31, 1986, ACRS has been revised by TRA of 1986. However, the pre-TRA of 1986 ACRS rules still apply to property placed in service after December 31, 1980, and before January 1, 1987.

Eligible Property under ACRS

Assets used in a trade or business or for the production of income are depreciable if they are subject to wear and tear, decay or decline from natural causes, or obsolescence. Assets that do not decline in value on a predictable basis or that do not have a determinable useful life (e.g., land, goodwill, stock, antiques) are not depreciable.

New or used tangible depreciable property (real or personal) placed in service after December 31, 1980 (except for the four exceptions noted above), is subject to the ACRS rules. Property placed in service before January 1, 1987, is subject to pre-TRA of 1986 ACRS (original ACRS) rules. Property placed in service after December 31, 1986, is subject to post-TRA of 1986 ACRS (modified ACRS [MACRS]) rules.

Personalty: Recovery Periods and Methods

Classification of Property: Pre-TRA of 1986. Pre-TRA of 1986 ACRS provides that the cost of eligible personalty (and certain realty) is recovered over 3, 5, 10, or 15 years. Property is classified by recovery period as follows:

3 years……	Autos, light-duty trucks, R & D equipment, racehorses over 2 years old and other horses over 12 years old, and personalty with an ADR midpoint life of 4 years or less.[15]
5 years……	Most other equipment except long-lived public utility property. Also includes single-purpose agricultural structures and petroleum storage facilities, which are designated as § 1245 property under the law.
10 years….	Public utility property with an ADR midpoint life greater than 18 but not greater than 25 years, burners and boilers using coal as a primary fuel if used in a public utility power plant and if replacing or converting oil- or gas-fired burners or boilers, railroad tank cars, mobile homes, and realty with an ADR midpoint life of 12.5 years or less (e.g., theme park structures).
15 years….	Public utility property with an ADR midpoint life exceeding 25 years (except certain burners and boilers using coal as a primary fuel).

14. § 168(f). The antichurning rules may also require the use of pre-TRA of 1986 ACRS rules on property placed in service after December 31, 1986.

15. Rev.Proc. 83–35, 1983–1 C.B. 745 is the source for the ADR midpoint lives.

Taxpayers have the choice of using (1) the straight-line method over the regular or optional (see below) recovery period or (2) a prescribed accelerated method over the regular recovery period. These two methods are both part of the ACRS system. However, a convenient name is not provided for either of the two methods. Hereafter, the straight-line method will be referred to as the *optional* (or *elective*) *straight-line method*. The method using percentages prescribed in the Code will be referred to as the *statutory percentage method*.

The rates to be used in computing the deduction under the statutory percentage method are shown in Table 9–1 (all tables are located at the end of the chapter prior to the Problem Materials) and are based on the 150 percent declining-balance method, using the half-year convention[16] and an assumption of zero salvage value.

EXAMPLE 8

In December 1982, T buys the following business assets: $34,000 of machinery, $6,000 of office furniture, and $16,000 of light-duty trucks. The machinery and office furniture are five-year properties, and the trucks are three-year properties. T's cost recovery deductions using the statutory percentage method are as follows:

1982	
25% of $16,000 (trucks)	$ 4,000
15% of $40,000 (machinery and furniture)	6,000
	$10,000
1983	
38% of $16,000	$ 6,080
22% of $40,000	8,800
	$14,880
1984	
37% of $16,000	$ 5,920
21% of $40,000	8,400
	$14,320
1985	
21% of $40,000	$ 8,400
1986	
21% of $40,000	$ 8,400

◆

Note that in 1982, T got a half-year's cost recovery deduction (since the half-year convention is reflected in the percentages in Table 9–1) although she held the property only one month.

In the year that personal property is disposed of, no cost recovery is allowed.

EXAMPLE 9

Assume the same facts as in Example 8. If T sold the trucks on December 1, 1983, T would only have cost recovery of $8,800 for the machinery and furniture. T would have no cost recovery for the trucks even though they were held for 11 months. ◆

Reduction of Basis for Investment Tax Credit. For personalty placed in service after 1982 and before January 1, 1986, the basis of the property for the ACRS

16. The half-year convention assumes all property is placed in service at mid-year and thus provides for a half-year's cost recovery.

write-off must be reduced by one-half the amount of the investment tax credit taken on the property.[17] Investment tax credit is not allowed on realty. (See Chapter 13 for details.)

EXAMPLE 10

On January 1, 1985, T purchases a machine, which is five-year ACRS property, for $10,000. T takes a $1,000 investment tax credit on the property (10% of $10,000). The basis of the property must be reduced by $500 (½ of the $1,000 investment tax credit). Thus, T's cost recovery allowance will be based on $9,500 [$10,000 (cost) − $500 (reduction for investment tax credit)]. T's cost recovery deduction for 1985 will be $1,425 (15% of $9,500). ◆

As an alternative to reducing the basis of the property, a taxpayer may elect to take a *reduced* investment tax credit. Under this election, the investment tax credit is 8 percent (rather than 10 percent) for recovery property that is not three-year property and 4 percent (instead of 6 percent) for three-year property. In Example 10, if the reduced investment tax credit election were made, T's cost recovery deduction for 1985 would be $1,500 (15 percent of $10,000).

TRA of 1986 generally repealed the investment tax credit for property placed in service after December 31, 1985. Therefore, the reduction of basis for the investment tax credit does not apply to such property.

Classification of Property: Post-TRA of 1986 (MACRS). The general effect of TRA of 1986 is to lengthen asset lives. Post-TRA of 1986 ACRS (MACRS) provides that the depreciation basis of eligible personalty (and certain realty) is recovered over 3, 5, 7, 10, 15, or 20 years. Property is classified by recovery period under MACRS as follows:[18]

3-year 200% class	ADR midpoints of 4 years and less.[19] Excludes automobiles and light trucks. Includes racehorses more than 2 years old and other horses more than 12 years old.
5-year 200% class	ADR midpoints of more than 4 years and less than 10 years, adding automobiles, light trucks, qualified technological equipment, renewable energy and biomass properties that are small power production facilities, research and experimentation property, semiconductor manufacturing equipment, and computer-based central office switching equipment.
7-year 200% class	ADR midpoints of 10 years and more and less than 16 years, adding single-purpose agricultural or horticultural structures and property with no ADR midpoint not classified elsewhere. Includes railroad track and office furniture, fixtures, and equipment.
10-year 200% class	ADR midpoints of 16 years and more and less than 20 years.
15-year 150% class	ADR midpoints of 20 years and more and less than 25 years, including sewage treatment plants, and telephone distribution plants and comparable equipment used for the two-way exchange of voice and data communications.
20-year 150% class	ADR midpoints of 25 years and more, other than real property with an ADR midpoint of 27.5 years and more, and including sewer pipes.

17. § 48(q).
18. § 168(e).
19. Rev.Proc. 87–56, 1987–2 C.B. 674 is the source for the ADR midpoint lives.

Accelerated depreciation is allowed for these six MACRS classes of property. Two hundred percent declining-balance is used for the 3-, 5-, 7-, and 10-year classes, with a switchover to straight-line depreciation when it yields a larger amount. One hundred and fifty percent declining-balance is allowed for the 15- and 20-year classes, with an appropriate straight-line switchover.[20]

The property in each of these classes may be depreciated using straight-line depreciation if an election is made. Certain property is not eligible for accelerated depreciation and must be depreciated under an alternative depreciation system (ADS). Both the straight-line election and ADS are discussed later in the chapter.

The original ACRS system gave the taxpayer a half-year of depreciation for the tax year an asset was placed in service but allowed the taxpayer to recover the balance of the depreciable basis over the years remaining in the property's recovery period. No cost recovery deduction was permitted for the year of disposition or retirement of the property. Thus, conceptually, the taxpayer was considered to have placed property in service at the beginning of the recovery period but was allowed only a half-year's worth of depreciation for the placed-in-service year. By contrast, MACRS views property as placed in service in the middle of the first year.[21] Thus, for example, the statutory recovery period for three-year property begins in the middle of the year an asset is placed in service and ends three years later. In practical terms, this means that taxpayers must wait an extra year to recover the cost of depreciable assets. That is, the actual write-off periods are 4, 6, 8, 11, 16, and 21 years. MACRS also allows for a half-year of cost recovery in the year of disposition or retirement.

The methodology for computing the cost recovery under MACRS is the same as under the original ACRS method. The cost recovery basis is multiplied by the percentages that reflect the applicable depreciation method and the applicable convention. The percentages are shown in Table 9–2.

EXAMPLE 11

T acquires a five-year class asset on April 10, 1992, for $30,000. T's cost recovery deduction for 1992 is $6,000 [$30,000 × .20 (Table 9–2)]. ◆

EXAMPLE 12

Assume the same facts as in Example 11, except that T disposes of the asset on March 5, 1994. T's cost recovery deduction for 1994 is $2,880 [$30,000 × ½ × .192 (Table 9–2)]. ◆

Under the original ACRS rules for personal property, the half-year convention was used no matter what the pattern of acquisitions was during the year. Thus, if a substantial dollar amount of assets was acquired late in the tax year, the half-year convention still applied. The law now contains a provision to curtail the benefits of such tax planning. If more than 40 percent of the value of property other than eligible real estate (see Realty: Recovery Periods and Methods: Post-TRA of 1986 [MACRS] for a discussion of eligible real estate) is placed in service during the last quarter of the year, a *mid-quarter convention* applies.[22] Property acquisitions are then grouped by the quarter they were acquired and depreciated accordingly. Acquisitions during the first quarter would receive 10.5 months of cost recovery; the second quarter, 7.5 months; the third quarter, 4.5 months; and the fourth quarter, 1.5 months. The percentages are shown in Table 9–3.

20. § 168(b).
21. § 168(d)(4)(A).
22. § 168(d)(3).

Concept Summary 9–2
Cost Recovery Periods: Post-TRA of 1986 (MACRS)

Class of Property	Examples
3-year	Tractor units for use over-the-road. Any horse that is not a racehorse and is more than 12 years old at the time it is placed in service. Any racehorse that is more than 2 years old at the time it is placed in service. Breeding hogs. Special tools used in the manufacturing of motor vehicles such as dies, fixtures, molds, and patterns.
5-year	Automobiles and taxis. Light and heavy general-purpose trucks. Buses. Trailers and trailer-mounted containers. Typewriters, calculators, and copiers. Computers and peripheral equipment. Breeding and dairy cattle.
7-year	Office furniture, fixtures, and equipment. Breeding and work horses. Agricultural machinery and equipment. Single-purpose agricultural or horticultural structures. Railroad track.
10-year	Vessels, barges, tugs, and similar water transportation equipment. Assets used for petroleum refining, manufacture of grain and grain mill products, manufacture of sugar and sugar products, and manufacture of vegetable oils and vegetable oil products.
15-year	Land improvements. Assets used for industrial steam and electric generation and/or distribution systems. Assets used in the manufacture of cement. Assets used in pipeline transportation. Electric utility nuclear production plant. Municipal wastewater treatment plant.
20-year	Farm buildings except single-purpose agricultural and horticultural structures. Gas utility distribution facilities. Water utilities. Municipal sewer.

Example 13

X Corporation acquires the following five-year class property:

Property Acquisition Dates	Cost
February 15	$ 200,000
July 10	400,000
December 5	600,000
Total	$1,200,000

If X Corporation uses the statutory percentage method, the cost recovery for the first two years would be computed as indicated below. Since 50% ($600,000/$1,200,000) of the acquisitions are in the last quarter, the mid-quarter convention applies.

Year 1		
February 15	[$200,000 × .35 (Table 9–3)]	$ 70,000
July 10	($400,000 × .15)	60,000
December 5	($600,000 × .05)	30,000
Total		$160,000

Year 2

February 15	[$200,000 × .26 (Table 9–3)]	$ 52,000
July 10	($400,000 × .34)	136,000
December 5	($600,000 × .38)	228,000
Total		$416,000

◆

EXAMPLE 14

Assume the same facts as in Example 13, except that X Corporation sells the $400,000 asset on November 30 of Year 2. The cost recovery for Year 2 would be as follows:

February 15	[$200,000 × .26 (Table 9–3)]	$ 52,000
July 10	[$400,000 × .34 × (3.5/4)]	119,000
December 5	($600,000 × .38)	228,000
Total		$399,000

◆

Realty: Recovery Periods and Methods

Pre-TRA of 1986. Under the original version of ACRS, realty is assigned a 15-year recovery period. Component depreciation generally is no longer allowed.[23]

Real property other than low-income housing can be depreciated using the 175 percent declining-balance method, with a switchover to straight-line depreciation when it yields a larger amount. Low-income housing is depreciated using the 200 percent declining-balance method, with an appropriate straight-line switchover. In either case, an assumption of zero salvage value is made. Statutory percentages for real property are shown in Table 9–4, which contains rates for low-income housing as well as for other 15-year real estate. As explained later in the chapter, the straight-line method may be elected for real property.

Since the half-year convention does not apply to 15-year real property, Table 9–4 is structured differently from Tables 9–1 and 9–2. The cost recovery deduction for 15-year real property is based on the month the asset is placed in service rather than on the half-year convention.

EXAMPLE 15

T purchased a warehouse for $100,000 on January 1, 1984. The cost recovery allowance for the years 1984 through 1992, using the statutory percentage method, is as follows (see Table 9–4 for percentages):

1984—$12,000 (12% × $100,000)
1985—$10,000 (10% × $100,000)
1986—$9,000 (9% × $100,000)
1987—$8,000 (8% × $100,000)
1988—$7,000 (7% × $100,000)
1989—$6,000 (6% × $100,000)
1990—$6,000 (6% × $100,000)
1991—$6,000 (6% × $100,000)
1992—$6,000 (6% × $100,000)

◆

23. See the Glossary of Tax Terms in Appendix C for a definition of component depreciation.

EXAMPLE 16

Assume the same facts as in Example 15, except the property is low-income housing. Cost recovery deductions using the statutory percentage method for 1984 through 1992 are as follows (see Table 9–4 for percentages):

1984—$13,000 (13% × $100,000)
1985—$12,000 (12% × $100,000)
1986—$10,000 (10% × $100,000)
1987—$9,000 (9% × $100,000)
1988—$8,000 (8% × $100,000)
1989—$7,000 (7% × $100,000)
1990—$6,000 (6% × $100,000)
1991—$5,000 (5% × $100,000)
1992—$5,000 (5% × $100,000) ◆

The Deficit Reduction Act of 1984 changed the recovery period for real property to 18 years. This applies generally to property placed in service after March 15, 1984. However, the 15-year recovery period is retained for low-income housing as well as for real property placed in service before March 16, 1984.

Eighteen-year real property placed in service after June 22, 1984, is subject to a mid-month convention.[24] This means that real property placed in service at any time during a particular month is treated as if it were placed in service in the middle of the month. This allows for one-half month's cost recovery for the month the property is placed in service. If the property is disposed of before the end of the recovery period, one-half month's cost recovery is permitted for the month of disposition regardless of the specific date of disposition. Statutory percentages for 18-year real property with a mid-month convention are shown in Table 9–5.

EXAMPLE 17

T purchased a building for $300,000 and placed it in service on August 21, 1984. The first year's cost recovery using the statutory percentage method is $12,000 (4% × $300,000). (See Table 9–5 for percentages.) ◆

EXAMPLE 18

Assume the same facts as in Example 17 and that T disposes of the building on May 3, 1992. The cost recovery in the year of disposition is $5,625 ($300,000 × 5% × 4.5/12). ◆

Public Law 99–121 extended the minimum recovery period for real property (except low-income housing) from 18 years to 19 years. This applies to property placed in service after May 8, 1985. Statutory percentages for 19-year real property are shown in Table 9–6. Because the percentages are determined using a mid-month convention, the computation of cost recovery is mechanically the same as for 18-year property with the mid-month convention.

Post-TRA of 1986 (MACRS). Residential rental real estate is given a recovery period of 27.5 years and is depreciated using the straight-line method. *Residential rental real estate* includes property where 80 percent or more of the gross rental revenues are from nontransient dwelling units (e.g., an apartment building). Hotels, motels, and similar establishments are not residential rental property.

24. A transitional rule, which provides for a full-month convention, is effective for property placed in service after March 15, 1984, and before June 23, 1984.

Concept Summary 9–3
Statutory Percentage Method under ACRS and MACRS

Pre-TRA of 1986 (ACRS)

	Personal Property	Real Property: 15-Year	Real Property: 18-Year	Real Property: 19-Year
Convention	Half-year	Full-month	Mid-month	Mid-month
Cost recovery deduction in the year of disposition	None	Full-month for month of disposition	Half-month for month of disposition	Half-month for month of disposition

Post-TRA of 1986 (MACRS)

	Personal Property	Real Property*
Convention	Half-year or mid-quarter	Mid-month
Cost recovery deduction in the year of disposition	Half-year for year of disposition or half-quarter for quarter of disposition	Half-month for month of disposition

*Straight-line method must be used.

Low-income housing is classified as residential rental real estate. Nonresidential real estate has a recovery period of 31.5 years and is depreciated using the straight-line method.[25]

Note that some items of real property are not real estate for purposes of MACRS. Single-purpose agricultural structures are in the 7-year MACRS class. Land improvements are in the 15-year MACRS class.

All eligible real estate is depreciated using the mid-month convention. Regardless of when during the month the property is placed in service, it is deemed to have been placed in service at the middle of the month. In the year of disposition, a mid-month convention is also used.

Cost recovery is computed by multiplying the applicable rate (Table 9–7) by the cost recovery basis.

Example 19

T acquired a building on April 1, 1992, for $800,000. If the building is classified as residential rental real estate, the cost recovery for 1992 is $20,608 (.02576 × $800,000). If the building is classified as nonresidential real estate, the 1992 cost recovery is $17,992 (.02249 × $800,000). (See Table 9–7 for percentages.) ◆

Straight-Line Election under ACRS and MACRS

Pre-TRA of 1986. Taxpayers may *elect* to write off an asset using the straight-line method rather than the statutory percentage method. The straight-line recovery period may be equal to the prescribed recovery period under the statutory percentage method, or it may be a longer period. Allowable straight-line recovery periods for each class of property are summarized as follows:

25. §§ 168(b), (c), and (e).

3-year property	3, 5, or 12 years
5-year property	5, 12, or 25 years
10-year property	10, 25, or 35 years
15-year property	15, 35, or 45 years
18-year real property and low-income housing (placed in service after March 15, 1984)	18, 35, or 45 years
19-year real property and low-income housing (placed in service after May 8, 1985)	19, 35, or 45 years

If the straight-line option is elected for personal property, the half-year convention is applied in computing the cost recovery deduction. The effect of electing the straight-line method for personal property is to extend the statutory recovery period by one year (e.g., three to four and five to six years). There is no cost recovery deduction in the year of the disposition of the property.

EXAMPLE 20

J acquired a light-duty truck (three-year property) on March 1, 1986, at a cost of $10,000. J elects to write off the cost of the truck using the optional straight-line method with a recovery period of five years. Because the half-year convention applies, J can deduct only $1,000 [($10,000 ÷ 5) × ½] in 1986. ◆

EXAMPLE 21

Assume the same facts as in Example 20. If J disposes of the truck at any time during 1987, no cost recovery deduction is allowed for 1987, the year of disposition. ◆

For each class of personal property, the straight-line election applies to *all* assets in a *particular class* that are placed in service during the year for which the election is made. The election applies for the entire recovery period of these assets. The election is not binding for personal property of the same class placed in service in another taxable year.

If the straight-line option is elected for 15-year real property, the first year's cost recovery deduction and the cost recovery deduction for the year of disposition are computed on the basis of the number of months the property was in service during the year.

EXAMPLE 22

K acquired a store building on October 1, 1983, at a cost of $150,000. K elects the straight-line method using a recovery period of 15 years. K's cost recovery deduction for 1983 is $2,500 [($150,000 ÷ 15) × 3⁄12]. ◆

EXAMPLE 23

Assume the same facts as in Example 22 and that K disposes of the asset on September 30, 1992. K's cost recovery deduction for 1992 would be $7,500 [($150,000 ÷ 15) × 9⁄12]. ◆

If the straight-line option is elected for 18-year or 19-year real property, the cost recovery allowances in the year the property is placed in service and in the year of disposition are computed in the same manner (except for the use of different rates) as under statutory percentage cost recovery. Note that 18-year and 19-year real property use a mid-month convention, whereas 15-year real property uses a full-month convention. Table 9–8 contains the applicable percentages to be used if the straight-line option is elected for 19-year real property. (The tables that contain the percentages for 18-year real property using the straight-line method over 18, 35, and 45 years and 19-year real property using the straight-line method over 35 and 45 years are not reproduced in this text.)

EXAMPLE 24

N acquired 19-year real property on October 1, 1986, at a cost of $150,000. N elects the straight-line method of cost recovery. N's cost recovery deduction for 1986 is $1,650 [$150,000 × 1.1% (Table 9–8)]. ◆

EXAMPLE 25

Assume the same facts as in Example 24 and that N disposes of the asset on September 20, 1992. N's cost recovery deduction for 1992 would be $5,631 [($150,000 × 5.3% × 8.5/12) (Table 9–8)]. ◆

The straight-line election for 15-year, 18-year, or 19-year real property may be made on a *property-by-property* basis within the same year.

Post-TRA of 1986 (MACRS). Although straight-line depreciation is required for all eligible real estate as previously discussed, the taxpayer may elect to use the straight-line method for personal property.[26] The property is depreciated using the class life (recovery period) of the asset with a half-year convention or a mid-quarter convention, whichever is applicable. The election is available on a

CONCEPT SUMMARY 9–4
STRAIGHT-LINE ELECTION UNDER ACRS AND MACRS

Pre-TRA of 1986 (ACRS)

	Personal Property	Real Property: 15-Year	Real Property: 18-Year	Real Property: 19-Year
Convention	Half-year	Full-month	Mid-month	Mid-month
Cost recovery deduction in the year of disposition	None	Full-month for month of disposition	Half-month for month of disposition	Half-month for month of disposition
Elective or mandatory	Elective	Elective	Elective	Elective
Breadth of election	Class by class	Property by property	Property by property	Property by property

Post-TRA of 1986 (MACRS)

	Personal Property	Real Property
Convention	Half-year or mid-quarter	Mid-month
Cost recovery deduction in the year of disposition	Half-year for year of dispositon or half-quarter for quarter of disposition	Half-month for month of disposition
Elective or mandatory	Elective	Mandatory
Breadth of election	Class by class	

26. § 168(b)(5).

class-by-class and year-by-year basis. The percentages for the straight-line election with a half-year convention appear in Table 9–9.

EXAMPLE 26

T acquired a 10-year class asset on August 4, 1992, for $100,000. T elects the straight-line method of cost recovery. T's cost recovery deduction for 1992 is $5,000 ($100,000 × .050). T's cost recovery deduction for 1993 is $10,000 ($100,000 × .100). (See Table 9–9 for percentages.) ◆

Election to Expense Assets

Section 179 (Election to Expense Certain Depreciable Business Assets) permits an election to write off up to $10,000 of the acquisition cost of tangible personal property used in a trade or business. Amounts that are expensed may not be capitalized and depreciated. The election is an annual election and applies to the acquisition cost of property placed in service that year. The immediate expense election is not available for real property or property used for the production of income.[27]

EXAMPLE 27

T acquires machinery (five-year class) on February 1, 1992, at a cost of $40,000 and elects to expense $10,000 under § 179. T's statutory percentage cost recovery deduction for 1992 is $6,000 [($40,000 cost − $10,000 expensed) × .200]. (See Table 9–2 for percentage.) T's total deduction for 1992 is $16,000 ($10,000 + $6,000). ◆

Section 179 has two additional limitations. First, the ceiling amount on the deduction is reduced dollar-for-dollar when property (other than eligible real estate) placed in service during the taxable year exceeds $200,000. Second, the amount expensed under § 179 cannot exceed the aggregate amount of taxable income derived from the conduct of any trade or business by the taxpayer. Taxable income of a trade or business is computed without regard to the amount expensed under § 179. Any expensed amount in excess of taxable income is carried forward to future taxable years and added to other amounts eligible for expensing (it is subject to the ceiling rules for the future years).

EXAMPLE 28

T owns a computer service and operates it as a sole proprietorship. In 1992, she will net $5,000 before considering any § 179 deduction. If T spends $204,000 on new equipment, her § 179 expense deduction is computed as follows:

§ 179 deduction before adjustment	$10,000
Less: Dollar limitation reduction ($204,000 − $200,000)	(4,000)
Remaining § 179 deduction	$ 6,000
Business income limitation	$ 5,000
§ 179 deduction allowed	$ 5,000
§ 179 deduction carryforward ($6,000 − $5,000)	$ 1,000

◆

The basis of the property for purposes of cost recovery is reduced by the § 179 amount after it is adjusted for property placed in service in excess of $200,000. This adjusted amount does not reflect any business income limitation. This is illustrated in Example 29.

27. §§ 179(b) and (d). The amount shown is per taxpayer, per year. On a joint return, the statutory amounts apply to the couple. If the taxpayers are married and file separate returns, each spouse is eligible for 50% of the statutory amount.

EXAMPLE 29

Assume the same facts as in Example 28 and that the new equipment is five-year class property. T's statutory percentage cost recovery deduction for 1992 is $39,600 [($204,000 − $6,000) × .200]. (See Table 9–2 for percentage.) ◆

Conversion of the expensed property to personal use at any time results in recapture income (see Chapter 17). A property is converted to personal use if it is not used predominantly in a trade or business. Regulations provide for the mechanics of the recapture.[28]

ACRS and MACRS Antichurning Rules

Pre-TRA of 1986. Generally, the ACRS deduction may be larger than the depreciation deduction under pre-1981 rules. Thus, there was concern that some taxpayers might engage in transactions that did not result in an actual ownership change in an attempt to change pre-1981 property into post-1980 recovery property. To prevent this, the original ACRS provisions contain antichurning rules that prevent the use of ACRS on personal property acquired after 1980 if the property was owned or used during 1980 by the taxpayer or a related person (it is *churned* property). Therefore, the taxpayer must use pre-1981 depreciation rules on churned property.

EXAMPLE 30

T began renting a tractor to use in his farming business in 1979. T used the tractor until 1982, at which time he purchased it. T is not entitled to use ACRS because he used the tractor in 1980. Instead, he must use the pre-1981 depreciation rules. ◆

In addition, ACRS does not apply to real property if *any* of the following is true:

- The property was owned by the taxpayer or a related person at any time during 1980.
- The taxpayer leases the property to a person who owned the property at any time during 1980 or to anyone related to such a person.
- The property is acquired in nonrecognition transactions, such as certain like-kind exchanges or involuntary conversions (see Chapter 15). However, this applies only to the extent that the basis of the property includes an amount representing the adjusted basis of other property owned by the taxpayer or a related person during 1980.

EXAMPLE 31

In 1986, J made a nontaxable like-kind exchange. He gave an apartment building, held since 1978, with an adjusted basis of $300,000 and a fair market value of $400,000. He also gave $200,000 in cash. In exchange, J received an apartment building worth $600,000. The basis of the new building is $500,000 [$300,000 (basis of old building) + $200,000 (cash paid)], but only $200,000 of the basis is subject to the ACRS rules. The $300,000 carryover basis is subject to the pre-ACRS rules. ◆

A person is considered related to a previous user or owner if a family or fiduciary relationship exists or if he or she owns 10 percent of a corporation or partnership that previously owned or used the property.

28. Reg. § 1.179–1(e).

Post-TRA of 1986 (MACRS). TRA of 1986 contains antichurning rules similar to those just discussed in connection with the original ACRS provisions. Hence, taxpayers are prevented from depreciating personal property placed in service by the taxpayer or a related person before 1987 under the MACRS provisions.[29]

Business and Personal Use of Automobiles and Other Listed Property

Limits exist on ACRS and MACRS deductions and investment tax credits with respect to business and personal use of automobiles and other listed property. These limits are generally effective for property placed in service after June 18, 1984. If the listed property is *predominantly used* for business, the taxpayer is allowed to take the investment tax credit and use the statutory percentage method to recover the cost. In cases where the property is *not predominantly used* for business, the cost is recovered using a straight-line recovery, and no investment tax credit can be taken.

TRA of 1986 generally repealed the investment tax credit for property placed in service after December 31, 1985. Therefore, the issue of whether investment tax credit can be taken is relevant only through 1985. (Because of the repeal of the investment tax credit, the credit is not discussed further in this section.)

Listed property includes the following:

- Any passenger automobile.
- Any other property used as a means of transportation.
- Any property of a type generally used for purposes of entertainment, recreation, or amusement.
- Any computer or peripheral equipment, with the exception of equipment used exclusively at a regular business establishment, including a qualifying home office.
- Any cellular telephone or other similar telecommunications equipment.
- Any other property specified in the Regulations.[30]

Automobiles and Other Listed Property Used Predominantly in Business. For listed property to be considered as predominantly used in business, the percentage of use for business must exceed 50 percent.[31] The use of listed property for production of income does not qualify as business use for purposes of the more-than-50 percent test. However, if the more-than-50 percent test is met, production of income and business use percentages are used to compute the cost recovery deduction.

EXAMPLE 32

On September 1, 1992, T places in service listed five-year recovery property. The property cost $10,000. If T uses the property 40% for business and 25% for the production of income, the property will not be considered as predominantly used for business. The cost would be recovered using straight-line cost recovery. If, however, T uses the property 60% for business and 25% for the production of income, the property will be considered as used predominantly for business. T's cost recovery for the year would be $1,700 ($10,000 × .200 × 85%). ◆

The method for determining the percentage of business usage for listed property is specified in the Regulations. The Regulations provide that for automobiles a mileage-based percentage is to be used. Other listed property is to

29. § 168(f)(5).
30. § 280F(d)(4).
31. § 280F(b)(4).

use the most appropriate unit of time (e.g., hours) the property is actually used (rather than available for use).[32]

The law places special limitations on the cost recovery deduction for passenger automobiles. These statutory dollar limits were imposed on passenger automobiles because of the belief that the tax system was being used to underwrite automobiles whose cost and luxury far exceeded what was needed for their business use.

A *passenger automobile* is any four-wheeled vehicle manufactured for use on public streets, roads, and highways with an unloaded gross vehicle weight rating of 6,000 pounds or less.[33] This definition specifically excludes vehicles used directly in the business of transporting people or property for compensation such as taxicabs, ambulances, hearses, and trucks and vans as prescribed by the Regulations.

The following limits are placed on the cost recovery deductions for passenger automobiles:[34]

Year	Recovery Limitation
1	$2,660
2	4,300
3	2,550
Succeeding years until the cost is recovered	1,575

However, these limits are imposed before any percentage reduction for personal use. In addition, the limitation in the first year includes any amount the taxpayer elects to expense under § 179.[35] If the passenger automobile is used partly for personal use, the personal use percentage is ignored for the purpose of determining the unrecovered cost available for deduction in later years.

EXAMPLE 33

On July 1, 1992, T places in service an automobile that cost $15,000. The car is always used 80% for business and 20% for personal use. The cost recovery for the automobile would be as follows:

1992—$2,128	[$15,000 × 20% (limited to $2,660) × 80%]
1993—$3,440	[$15,000 × 32% (limited to $4,300) × 80%]
1994—$2,040	[$15,000 × 19.2% (limited to $2,550) × 80%]
1995—$1,260	[$15,000 × 11.52% (limited to $1,575) × 80%]
1996—$1,260	[$15,000 × 11.52% (limited to $1,575) × 80%]
1997—$1,260	[$2,340 unrecovered cost ($15,000 − $12,660*) (limited to $1,575) × 80%]
1998—$ 612	[$765 unrecovered cost ($15,000 − $14,235) × 80%]

*($2,660 + $4,300 + $2,550 + $1,575 + $1,575). Although the statutory percentage method appears to restrict the deduction to $691 [$15,000 × 5.76% (limited to $1,575) × 80%], the unrecovered cost of $2,340 (limited to $1,575) multiplied by the business usage percentage is deductible. At the start of 1995 (Year 4), there is an automatic switch to the straight-line depreciation method. Under this method, the unrecovered cost up to the maximum allowable limit ($1,575) is deductible in the last year of the recovery period (1997 or Year 6). Because the limit restricts the deduction, the remaining unrecovered cost is deductible in the next or succeeding year(s), subject to the maximum allowable yearly limit ($1,575), multiplied by the business usage percentage.

The total cost recovery for the years 1992–1998 is $12,000 (80% business usage × $15,000). ◆

32. Reg. § 1.280F–6T(e).
33. § 280F(d)(5).
34. § 280F(a)(2). The 1991 amounts are used because the indexed amounts for 1992 were not available at the time of this writing.
35. § 280F(d)(1).

The cost recovery limitations are maximum amounts. If the regular calculation produces a lesser amount of cost recovery, the lesser amount is used.

EXAMPLE 34

On April 2, 1992, T places in service an automobile that cost $10,000. The car is always used 70% for business and 30% for personal use. The cost recovery for 1992 would be $1,400 ($10,000 × 20% × 70%), which is less than $1,862 ($2,660 × 70%). ◆

Note that the cost recovery limitations apply *only* to passenger automobiles and not to other listed property.

Automobiles and Other Listed Property Not Used Predominantly in Business. The cost of listed property that does not pass the more-than-50 percent business usage test in the year the property is placed in service must be recovered using the straight-line method.[36] The straight-line method to be used is that required under the alternative depreciation system (explained later in the chapter). This system requires a straight-line recovery period of five years for automobiles. However, even though the straight-line method is used, the cost recovery allowance for passenger automobiles cannot exceed the dollar limitations.

EXAMPLE 35

On July 27, 1992, T places in service an automobile that cost $20,000. The auto is used 40% for business and 60% for personal use. The cost recovery allowance for 1992 is $800 [$20,000 × 10% (Table 9–11) × 40%]. ◆

EXAMPLE 36

Assume the same facts as in Example 35, except that the auto cost $50,000. The cost recovery allowance for 1992 is $1,064 [$50,000 × 10% (Table 9–11) = $5,000 (limited to $2,660) × 40%]. ◆

If the listed property fails the more-than-50 percent business usage test, the straight-line method must be used for the remainder of the property's life. This applies even if at some later date the business usage of the property increases to more than 50 percent. However, even though the straight-line method must continue to be used, the amount of cost recovery will reflect the increase in business usage.

EXAMPLE 37

Assume the same facts as in Example 35, except that in 1993, T uses the auto 70% for business and 30% for personal use. T's cost recovery allowance for 1993 is $2,800 [$20,000 × 20% (Table 9–11) × 70%]. ◆

Change from Predominantly Business Use. If the business use percentage of listed property falls to 50 percent or lower after the year the property is placed in service, the property is subject to *cost recovery recapture*. The amount required to be recaptured and included in the taxpayer's return as ordinary income is the excess depreciation.

Excess depreciation is the excess of the cost recovery deduction taken in prior years using the statutory percentage method over the amount that would have been allowed if the straight-line method had been used since the property was placed in service.[37]

36. § 280F(b)(2).

37. § 280F(b)(3).

EXAMPLE 38

T purchased a car on January 22, 1992, at a cost of $20,000. Business usage was 80% in 1992, 70% in 1993, 40% in 1994, and 60% in 1995. Statutory percentage cost recovery deductions in 1992 and 1993 are $2,128 (80% × $2,660) and $3,010 (70% × $4,300), respectively. T's excess depreciation to be recaptured as ordinary income in 1994 is $738, calculated as follows:

1992	
Statutory percentage allowance	$ 2,128
Straight-line ($20,000 × 10% × 80%)	(1,600)
Excess	$ 528
1993	
Statutory percentage allowance	$ 3,010
Straight-line ($20,000 × 20% × 70%)	(2,800)
1993 excess	$ 210
1992 excess	528
Total excess	$ 738

◆

After the business usage of the listed property drops below the more-than-50 percent level, the straight-line method must be used for the remaining life of the property.

EXAMPLE 39

Assume the same facts as in Example 38. T's cost recovery allowance for the years 1994 and 1995 would be $1,020 and $945, computed as follows:

1994 — $1,020 [($20,000 × 20%) limited to $2,550 × 40%]
1995 — $ 945 [($20,000 × 20%) limited to $1,575 × 60%]

◆

Leased Automobiles. A taxpayer who leases a passenger automobile must include an *inclusion amount* in gross income. The inclusion amount is computed from a dollar amount provided in an IRS table for each taxable year for which the taxpayer leases the automobile. The purpose of this provision is to prevent taxpayers from circumventing the cost recovery dollar limitations by leasing, instead of purchasing, an automobile.

The dollar amount is based on the fair market value of the automobile and is prorated for the number of days the auto is used during the taxable year. The prorated dollar amount is then multiplied by the business and income-producing usage percentage to determine the amount to be included in gross income.[38] The taxpayer deducts the lease payments, multiplied by the business and income-producing usage percentage. The net effect is that the annual deduction for the lease payment is reduced by the inclusion amount.

EXAMPLE 40

On April 1, 1992, T leases and places in service a passenger automobile worth $40,000. The lease is to be for a period of five years. During the taxable years 1992 and 1993, T uses the automobile 70% for business and 30% for personal use. Assuming the dollar amounts from the IRS table for 1992 and 1993 are $267 and $584, T must include $140 in gross income for 1992 and $409 for 1993, computed as follows:

38. Reg. § 1.280F–7T(a).

1992 $267 × (275/366) × 70% = $140
1993 $584 × (365/365) × 70% = $409

In addition, T can deduct 70% of the lease payments each year because this is the business use percentage. ◆

Substantiation Requirements. Listed property is now subject to the substantiation requirements of § 274. This means that the taxpayer must prove the business usage as to the amount of expense or use, the time and place of use, the business purpose for the use, and the business relationship to the taxpayer of persons using the property. Substantiation will require adequate records or sufficient evidence corroborating the taxpayer's statement. However, these substantiation requirements do not apply to vehicles that, by reason of their nature, are not likely to be used more than a *de minimis* amount for personal purposes.[39]

CONCEPT SUMMARY 9–5
LISTED PROPERTY COST RECOVERY

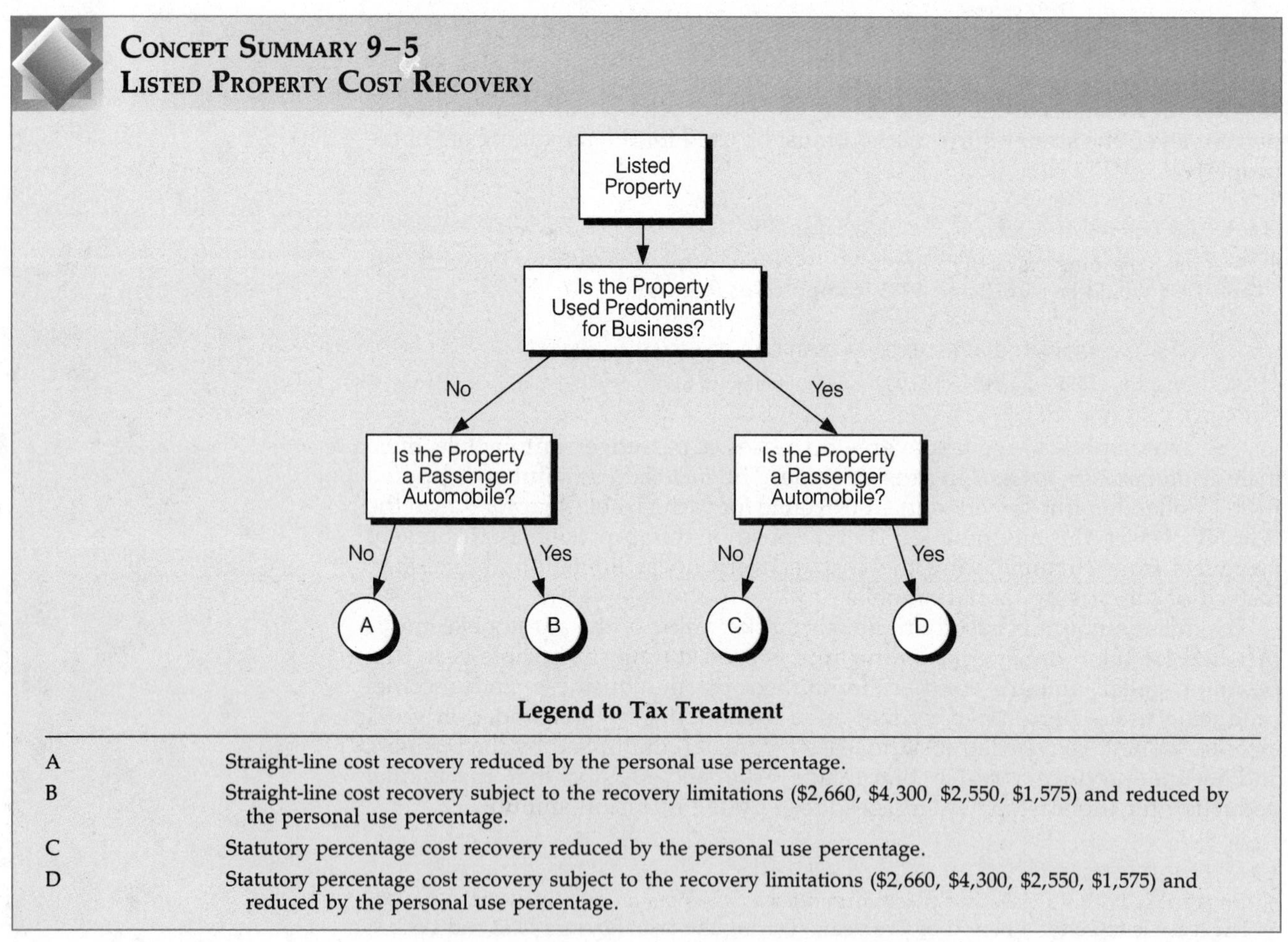

Legend to Tax Treatment

A	Straight-line cost recovery reduced by the personal use percentage.
B	Straight-line cost recovery subject to the recovery limitations ($2,660, $4,300, $2,550, $1,575) and reduced by the personal use percentage.
C	Statutory percentage cost recovery reduced by the personal use percentage.
D	Statutory percentage cost recovery subject to the recovery limitations ($2,660, $4,300, $2,550, $1,575) and reduced by the personal use percentage.

39. §§ 274(d) and (i).

Alternative Depreciation System (ADS)

The *alternative depreciation system (ADS)* must be used for the following:[40]

- To calculate the portion of depreciation treated as an alternative minimum tax (AMT) adjustment for purposes of the corporate and individual AMT (see Chapters 12 and 20).
- To compute depreciation allowances for property for which any of the following is true:
  - Used predominantly outside the United States.
  - Leased or otherwise used by a tax-exempt entity.
  - Financed with the proceeds of tax-exempt bonds.
  - Imported from foreign countries that maintain discriminatory trade practices or otherwise engage in discriminatory acts.
- To compute depreciation allowances for earnings and profits purposes (see Chapter 20).

In general, ADS depreciation is computed using straight-line recovery without regard to salvage value. However, for purposes of the AMT, depreciation of personal property is computed using the 150 percent declining-balance method with an appropriate switch to the straight-line method.

The taxpayer must use the half-year or the mid-quarter convention, whichever is applicable, for all property other than eligible real estate. The mid-month convention is used for eligible real estate. The applicable ADS rates are found in Tables 9–10, 9–11, and 9–12.

The recovery periods under ADS are as follows:[41]

- The ADR midpoint life for property that does not fall into any of the following listed categories.
- Five years for qualified technological equipment, automobiles, and light-duty trucks.
- Twelve years for personal property with no class life.
- Forty years for all residential rental property and all nonresidential real property.

Taxpayers may *elect* to use the 150 percent declining-balance method to compute the regular tax rather than the 200 percent declining-balance method that is available for personal property. Hence, if the election is made, there will be no difference between the cost recovery for computing the regular tax and the AMT. However, taxpayers who make this election must use the ADS recovery periods in computing the cost recovery for the regular tax, and the ADS recovery periods generally are longer than the regular recovery periods under MACRS.

The following are examples of the classification of property by class life for the ADS recovery periods:[42]

---

40. § 168(g).

41. The class life for certain properties described in § 168(e)(3) are specially determined under § 168(g)(3)(B).

42. Rev.Proc. 87–56, 1987–2 C.B. 674 is the source for the recovery periods.

3-year..........	Special tools used in the manufacture of motor vehicles, breeding hogs.
5-year..........	Automobiles, light general-purpose trucks.
7-year..........	Breeding and dairy cattle.
9.5-year	Computer-based telephone central office switching equipment.
10-year	Office furniture, fixtures, and equipment, railroad track.
12-year	Racehorses more than 2 years old at the time they are placed in service.

EXAMPLE 41

On March 1, 1992, T purchases computer-based telephone central office switching equipment for $80,000. If T uses statutory percentage cost recovery (assuming no § 179 election), the cost recovery for 1992 is $16,000 [$80,000 × 20% (Table 9–2, 5-year class property)]. If T elects to use ADS 150% declining-balance cost recovery (assuming no § 179 election), the cost recovery for 1992 is $6,312 [$80,000 × 7.89% (Table 9–10, 9.5-year class property)]. ◆

In lieu of depreciation under the regular MACRS method, taxpayers may *elect* straight-line under ADS for property that qualifies for the regular MACRS method. The election is available on a class-by-class and year-by-year basis for property other than eligible real estate. The election for eligible real estate is on a property-by-property basis. One reason for making this election is to avoid a difference between deductible depreciation and earnings and profits depreciation.

EXAMPLE 42

T acquires an apartment building on March 17, 1992, for $700,000. T takes the maximum cost recovery for determining taxable income. T's cost recovery for computing 1992 taxable income would be $20,153 [$700,000 × .02879 (Table 9–7)]. However, T's cost recovery for computing T's earnings and profits would be only $13,853 [$700,000 × .01979 (Table 9–12)]. ◆

AMORTIZATION

Intangible property used in a trade or business or in the production of income may be amortized if the property has a limited life that can be determined with a reasonable degree of accuracy.[43] Patents and copyrights are examples of intangible assets that have a definite limited life established by law and therefore can be amortized. Other examples of intangibles that have been found to have a useful life ascertainable with reasonable accuracy are covenants not to compete, customer lists, and sports player contracts.

Generally, intangible property is amortized using a straight-line method. The cost of the intangible property is divided by the useful life to determine the annual amortization deduction.

EXAMPLE 43

On January 2 of the current year, A Corporation was granted a 17-year patent. The costs associated with developing and acquiring the patent were $340,000. For the current year, A Corporation may amortize $20,000 ($340,000/17 years) of the cost of the patent. ◆

Intangibles that do not have a useful life ascertainable with reasonable accuracy, such as goodwill, may not be amortized. Case law further holds that to be amortizable, intangible property must have an ascertainable cost basis

43. Regs. § 1.167(a)–3.

separate and distinct from goodwill.[44] Goodwill has been defined as the expectation that "the old customers will resort to the old place."[45] An intangible asset is separate and distinct from goodwill if the asset has a measurable value for a specific use.[46] While covenants not to compete may be amortizable, a potential conflict exists due to the close relationship between a covenant not to compete with existing customers and the goodwill concept of old customers resorting to the old place. The argument is that the covenant not to compete is merely a transfer of goodwill.

For the purchaser of a covenant not to compete, the cost represents an intangible asset that is amortizable over the fixed life of the covenant. From the standpoint of the seller of a covenant not to compete, the proceeds from the sale are ordinary income, similar to compensation for forgone personal services. For the purchaser of goodwill, the cost represents an intangible asset that is not amortizable. The seller of goodwill, on the other hand, is selling an asset that will result in the recognition of capital gain.

Because of the different tax treatments accorded to a covenant not to compete and goodwill, the purchaser and the seller have conflicting goals with regard to taxes. The purchaser would prefer the increased amortization deductions associated with a covenant not to compete. The seller would prefer the potentially lower capital gain taxes (through the use of the alternative tax for net capital gains) associated with the sale of goodwill. The courts have often relied on this tax conflict between a purchaser and a seller to support the economic reality of a covenant not to compete.[47] However, to assure the creation of an amortizable asset, any agreement between a purchaser and seller should contain factors that weigh in favor of the independent economic significance or economic reality of the covenant not to compete. Examples of these factors are specific negotiations for the covenant, a specific allocation of the purchase price to the covenant, reasonable terms with respect to the covenant, and a reasonable price for the covenant.

DEPLETION

◆

Natural resources (e.g., oil, gas, coal, gravel, timber) are subject to depletion, which is simply a form of depreciation applicable to natural resources. Land generally cannot be depleted.

The owner of an interest in the natural resource is entitled to deduct depletion. An owner is one who has an economic interest in the property.[48] An economic interest requires the acquisition of an interest in the resource in place and the receipt of income from the extraction or severance of that resource. Like depreciation, depletion is a deduction *for* adjusted gross income.

Although all natural resources are subject to depletion, oil and gas wells are used as an example in the following paragraphs to illustrate the related costs and issues.

In developing an oil or gas well, the producer must make four types of expenditures. The first type is the payment for the natural resource (the oil under the ground). Because natural resources are physically limited, these costs are recovered through depletion. The second type occurs when the property is made ready for drilling: the cost of labor in clearing the property, erecting derricks, and drilling the hole. These costs, called *intangible drilling and develop-*

44. *Citizens and Southern Corp.* 91 T.C. 463 (1988), aff'd per curiam in an unpublished opinion (CA–2, March 22, 1990).

45. See the opinion cited in Footnote 44 at 480.

46. See the opinion cited in Footnote 44 at 516.

47. For example, see *Theophelis v. U.S.*, 751 F.2d 165 (CA–6, 1984) and *Better Beverages v. U.S.*, 619 F.2d 424 (CA–5, 1980).

48. Reg. § 1.611–1(b).

ment costs, generally have no salvage value and are a lost cost if the well is dry. The third type of cost is for tangible assets such as tools, pipes, and engines. Such costs are capital in nature and must be capitalized and recovered through depreciation. Finally, there are costs that are incurred after the well is producing, including such items as labor, fuel, and supplies. They are clearly operating expenses that are deductible currently when incurred (on the accrual basis) or when paid (on the cash basis).

The expenditures for depreciable assets and operating expenses pose no unusual problems for producers of natural resources. The tax treatment of depletable costs and intangible drilling and development costs is quite a different matter.

Intangible Drilling and Development Costs (IDC)

Intangible drilling and development costs (IDC) can be handled in one of two ways at the option of the taxpayer. They can be *either* charged off as an expense in the year in which they are incurred or capitalized and written off through depletion. The taxpayer makes the election in the first year such expenditures are incurred either by taking a deduction on the return or by adding them to the depletable basis. No formal statement of intent is required. Once made, the election is binding on both the taxpayer and the IRS for all such expenditures in the future. If the taxpayer fails to make the election to expense IDC on the original timely filed return the first year such expenditures are incurred, an automatic election to capitalize them has been made and is irrevocable.

As a general rule, it is more advantageous to expense IDC. The obvious benefit of an immediate write-off (as opposed to a deferred write-off through depletion) is not the only advantage. Since a taxpayer can use percentage depletion, which is calculated without reference to basis (see Example 47), the IDC may be completely lost as a deduction if they are capitalized.

Depletion Methods

There are two methods of calculating depletion: cost and percentage. Cost depletion can be used on any wasting asset (and is the only method allowed for timber). Percentage depletion is subject to a number of limitations, particularly for oil and gas deposits. Depletion should be calculated both ways, and generally the method that results in the *larger* deduction is used. The choice between cost and percentage depletion is an annual election.

Cost Depletion. *Cost depletion* is determined by using the adjusted basis of the asset.[49] The basis is divided by the estimated recoverable units of the asset (e.g., barrels, tons) to arrive at the depletion per unit. The depletion per unit then is multiplied by the number of units sold (*not* the units produced) during the year to arrive at the cost depletion allowed. Cost depletion, therefore, resembles the units-of-production method of calculating depreciation.

EXAMPLE 44

On January 1, 1992, T purchased the rights to a mineral interest for $1,000,000. At that time, the remaining recoverable units in the mineral interest were estimated to be 200,000. Under these circumstances, the depletion per unit becomes $5 [$1,000,000 (adjusted basis) ÷ 200,000 (estimated recoverable units)]. If during the year 60,000 units were mined and 25,000 were sold, the cost depletion would be $125,000 [$5 (depletion per unit) × 25,000 (units sold)]. ◆

49. § 612.

If the taxpayer later discovers that the original estimate was incorrect, the depletion per unit for future calculations must be redetermined based on the revised estimate.[50]

EXAMPLE 45

Assume the same facts as in Example 44. In 1993, T realizes that an incorrect estimate was made. The remaining recoverable units now are determined to be 400,000. Based on this new information, the revised depletion per unit becomes $2.1875 [$875,000 (adjusted basis) ÷ 400,000 (estimated recoverable units)]. Note that the adjusted basis is the original cost ($1,000,000) reduced by the depletion claimed in 1992 ($125,000). If 30,000 units are sold in 1993, the depletion for the year would be $65,625 [$2.1875 (depletion per unit) × 30,000 (units sold)]. ◆

Percentage Depletion. *Percentage depletion* (also referred to as statutory depletion) is a specified percentage provided for in the Code. The percentage varies according to the type of mineral interest involved. A sample of these percentages is shown in Figure 9–1. The rate is applied to the gross income from the property, but in no event may percentage depletion exceed 50 percent of the taxable income from the property before the allowance for depletion.[51]

EXAMPLE 46

Assuming gross income of $100,000, a depletion rate of 22%, and other expenses relating to the property of $60,000, the depletion allowance is determined as follows:

Gross income	$100,000
Less: Other expenses	(60,000)
Taxable income before depletion	$ 40,000
Depletion allowance [the lesser of $22,000 (22% × $100,000) or $20,000 (50% × $40,000)]	(20,000)
Taxable income after depletion	$ 20,000

The adjusted basis of the property would be reduced by $20,000, the depletion allowed. If the other expenses had been only $55,000, the full $22,000 could have been deducted, and the adjusted basis would have been reduced by $22,000. ◆

Note that percentage depletion is based on a percentage of the gross income from the property and makes no reference to cost. Thus, when percentage depletion is used, it is possible to deduct more than the original cost of the property. If percentage depletion is used, however, the adjusted basis of the property (for computing cost depletion) must be reduced by the amount of percentage depletion taken until the adjusted basis reaches zero.

Effect of Intangible Drilling Costs on Depletion. The treatment of IDC has an effect on the depletion deduction in two ways. If the costs are capitalized, the basis for cost depletion is increased. As a consequence, the cost depletion is increased. If IDC are expensed, they reduce the taxable income from the property. This reduction may result in application of the provision that limits depletion to 50 percent of taxable income before deducting depletion.

50. § 611(a).

51. § 613(a). Special rules apply for certain oil and gas wells under § 613A (e.g., the 50% ceiling is replaced with a 100% ceiling, and the percentage depletion may not exceed 65% of the taxpayer's taxable income from all sources before the allowance for depletion).

EXAMPLE 47

J purchased the rights to an oil interest for $1,000,000. The recoverable barrels were estimated to be 200,000. During the year, 50,000 barrels were sold for $2,000,000. Regular expenses amounted to $800,000, and IDC were $650,000. If the IDC are capitalized, the depletion per unit is $8.25 ($1,000,000 plus $650,000 divided by 200,000 barrels), and the following taxable income results:

Gross income	$2,000,000
Less: Expenses	(800,000)
Taxable income before depletion	$1,200,000
Cost depletion ($8.25 × 50,000) = $412,500	
Percentage depletion (15% × $2,000,000) = $300,000	
Greater of cost or percentage depletion	(412,500)
Taxable income	$ 787,500

If the IDC are expensed, the taxable income becomes $275,000, as follows:

Gross income	$ 2,000,000
Less: Expenses, including IDC	(1,450,000)
Taxable income before depletion	$ 550,000
Cost depletion [($1,000,000 ÷ 200,000 barrels) × 50,000 barrels] = $250,000	
Percentage depletion (15% of $2,000,000, limited to 50% of $550,000 taxable income before depletion) = $275,000	
Greater of cost or percentage depletion	(275,000)
Taxable income	$ 275,000

FIGURE 9–1
Sample of Percentage Depletion Rates

22% Depletion

Cobalt	Sulfur
Lead	Tin
Nickel	Uranium
Platinum	Zinc

15% Depletion

Copper	Oil and gas
Gold	Oil shale
Iron	Silver

14% Depletion

Borax	Magnesium carbonates
Calcium carbonates	Marble
Granite	Potash
Limestone	Slate

10% Depletion

Coal	Perlite
Lignite	Sodium chloride

5% Depletion

Gravel	Pumice
Peat	Sand

For further restrictions on the use or availability of the percentage depletion method, see § 613.

REPORTING PROCEDURES
◆

Sole proprietors engaged in a business should file a Schedule C, Profit or Loss from Business, to accompany Form 1040. Schedule C for 1991 is presented because the 1992 form was not yet available.

The top part of page 1 requests certain key information about the taxpayer (e.g., name, address, Social Security number) and the business methods involved (e.g., accounting method and inventory method used). Part I provides for the reporting of items of income. If the business requires the use of inventories and the computation of cost of goods sold (see Chapter 18 for when this is necessary), Part III must be completed and the cost of goods sold amount transferred to line 4 of Part 1.

Part II allows for the reporting of deductions. Some of the deductions discussed in Chapters 8 and 9 and their location on the form are bad debts (line 9), depletion (line 12), and depreciation (line 13). Other expenses (line 27) include those items not already covered (see lines 8–26). An example would be research and experimental expenditures.

If depreciation is claimed, it should be supported by completing Form 4562. Form 4562 for 1991 is presented because the 1992 form was not yet available. The amount listed on line 20 of Form 4562 is then transferred to line 13 of Part II of Schedule C.

EXAMPLE 48

Thomas Andrews, Social Security number 123–45–6789, was employed as an accountant until July 1990, when he opened his own practice. His address is 279 Mountain View, Ogden, UT 84201. Andrews keeps his books on the accrual basis and had the following revenue and business expenses in 1991:

- **a.** Revenue from accounting practice, $80,000.
- **b.** Bad debts, $2,000.
- **c.** Automobile expenses, $3,000.
- **d.** Insurance, $800.
- **e.** Office supplies, $4,000.
- **f.** Rent, $12,000.
- **g.** Furniture and fixtures acquired on July 15, 1990, for $8,000. Andrews used the statutory percentage cost recovery method.
- **h.** Business automobile acquired on May 20, 1990, for $10,000. Andrews used the statutory percentage cost recovery method. The automobile, which was driven 12,000 miles during 1991, was used only for business purposes.
- **i.** Microcomputer acquired on May 7, 1991, for $14,000. Andrews elects § 179 and uses the statutory percentage cost recovery method.

Andrews would report the above information on Schedule C and Form 4562 as illustrated on the following pages. ◆

Form **4562** | Department of the Treasury Internal Revenue Service (T)

Depreciation and Amortization
(Including Information on Listed Property)

▶ See separate instructions. ▶ Attach this form to your return.

OMB No. 1545-0172 | **1991** | Attachment Sequence No. 67

Name(s) shown on return: Thomas Andrews | Identifying number: 123-45-6789

Business or activity to which this form relates: Accounting Services

Part I Election To Expense Certain Tangible Property (Section 179) (Note: *If you have any "Listed Property," complete Part V.*)

1	Maximum dollar limitation (see instructions)	1	$10,000
2	Total cost of section 179 property placed in service during the tax year (see instructions)	2	14,000
3	Threshold cost of section 179 property before reduction in limitation	3	$200,000
4	Reduction in limitation—Subtract line 3 from line 2, but do not enter less than -0-	4	
5	Dollar limitation for tax year—Subtract line 4 from line 1, but do not enter less than -0-	5	10,000

	(a) Description of property	(b) Cost	(c) Elected cost
6	5-Year Class Prop.-Microcomputer	14,000	10,000
7	Listed property—Enter amount from line 26	7	

8	Total elected cost of section 179 property—Add amounts in column (c), lines 6 and 7	8	10,000
9	Tentative deduction—Enter the lesser of line 5 or line 8	9	10,000
10	Carryover of disallowed deduction from 1990 (see instructions)	10	
11	Taxable income limitation—Enter the lesser of taxable income or line 5 (see instructions)	11	10,000
12	Section 179 expense deduction—Add lines 9 and 10, but do not enter more than line 11	12	10,000
13	Carryover of disallowed deduction to 1992—Add lines 9 and 10, less line 12 ▶	13	

Note: *Do not use Part II or Part III below for automobiles, certain other vehicles, cellular telephones, computers, or property used for entertainment, recreation, or amusement (listed property). Instead, use Part V for listed property.*

Part II MACRS Depreciation For Assets Placed in Service ONLY During Your 1991 Tax Year (Do Not Include Listed Property)

(a) Classification of property	(b) Mo. and yr. placed in service	(c) Basis for depreciation (Business/investment use only—see instructions)	(d) Recovery period	(e) Convention	(f) Method	(g) Depreciation deduction
14 General Depreciation System (GDS) (see instructions):						
a 3-year property						
b 5-year property		4,000	5-YR	HY	200DB	800
c 7-year property						
d 10-year property						
e 15-year property						
f 20-year property						
g Residential rental property			27.5 yrs.	MM	S/L	
			27.5 yrs.	MM	S/L	
h Nonresidential real property			31.5 yrs.	MM	S/L	
			31.5 yrs.	MM	S/L	
15 Alternative Depreciation System (ADS) (see instructions):						
a Class life					S/L	
b 12-year			12 yrs.		S/L	
c 40-year			40 yrs.	MM	S/L	

Part III Other Depreciation (Do Not Include Listed Property)

16	GDS and ADS deductions for assets placed in service in tax years beginning before 1991 (see instructions)	16	1,959
17	Property subject to section 168(f)(1) election (see instructions)	17	
18	ACRS and other depreciation (see instructions)	18	

Part IV Summary

19	Listed property—Enter amount from line 25	19	3,200
20	Total—Add deductions on line 12, lines 14 and 15 in column (g), and lines 16 through 19. Enter here and on the appropriate lines of your return. (Partnerships and S corporations—see instructions)	20	15,959
21	For assets shown above and placed in service during the current year, enter the portion of the basis attributable to section 263A costs (see instructions)	21	

For Paperwork Reduction Act Notice, see page 1 of the separate instructions. Cat. No. 12906N Form **4562** (1991)

Form 4562 (1991) Page 2

Part V **Listed Property.—Automobiles, Certain Other Vehicles, Cellular Telephones, Computers, and Property Used for Entertainment, Recreation, or Amusement**

If you are using the standard mileage rate or deducting vehicle lease expense, complete columns (a) through (c) of Section A, all of Section B, and Section C if applicable.

Section A.—Depreciation (Caution: *See instructions for limitations for automobiles.)*

22a Do you have evidence to support the business/investment use claimed? ☒ Yes ☐ No **22b** If "Yes," is the evidence written? ☒ Yes ☐ No

(a) Type of property (list vehicles first)	(b) Date placed in service	(c) Business/ investment use percentage	(d) Cost or other basis	(e) Basis for depreciation (business/investment use only)	(f) Recovery period	(g) Method/ Convention	(h) Depreciation deduction	(i) Elected section 179 cost
23 *Property used more than 50% in a qualified business use (see instructions):*								
Automobile	5/20/90	100 %	10,000	10,000	5-YR	200DB-HY	3,200	
		%						
		%						
24 *Property used 50% or less in a qualified business use (see instructions):*								
		%				S/L –		
		%				S/L –		
		%				S/L –		

25 Add amounts in column (h). Enter the total here and on line 19, page 1 . . . . **25** 3,200

26 Add amounts in column (i). Enter the total here and on line 7, page 1 . . . . **26**

Section B.—Information Regarding Use of Vehicles—*If you deduct expenses for vehicles:*

- *Always complete this section for vehicles used by a sole proprietor, partner, or other "more than 5% owner," or related person.*
- *If you provided vehicles to your employees, first answer the questions in Section C to see if you meet an exception to completing this section for those vehicles.*

	(a) Vehicle 1		(b) Vehicle 2		(c) Vehicle 3		(d) Vehicle 4		(e) Vehicle 5		(f) Vehicle 6	
27 Total business/investment miles driven during the year (DO NOT include commuting miles).	12,000											
28 Total commuting miles driven during the year	-0-											
29 Total other personal (noncommuting) miles driven	-0-											
30 Total miles driven during the year—Add lines 27 through 29	12,000											
	Yes	No	Yes	No	Yes	No	Yes	No	Yes	No	Yes	No
31 Was the vehicle available for personal use during off-duty hours?		X										
32 Was the vehicle used primarily by a more than 5% owner or related person? . .	X											
33 Is another vehicle available for personal use?	X											

Section C.—Questions for Employers Who Provide Vehicles for Use by Their Employees
(Answer these questions to determine if you meet an exception to completing Section B. **Note:** *Section B must always be completed for vehicles used by sole proprietors, partners, or other more than 5% owners or related persons.)*

	Yes	No
34 Do you maintain a written policy statement that prohibits all personal use of vehicles, including commuting, by your employees?		
35 Do you maintain a written policy statement that prohibits personal use of vehicles, except commuting, by your employees? (See instructions for vehicles used by corporate officers, directors, or 1% or more owners.) .		
36 Do you treat all use of vehicles by employees as personal use?		
37 Do you provide more than five vehicles to your employees and retain the information received from your employees concerning the use of the vehicles?		
38 Do you meet the requirements concerning qualified automobile demonstration use (see instructions)? . .		

Note: *If your answer to 34, 35, 36, 37, or 38 is "Yes," you need not complete Section B for the covered vehicles.*

Part VI **Amortization**

(a) Description of costs	(b) Date amortization begins	(c) Amortizable amount	(d) Code section	(e) Amortization period or percentage	(f) Amortization for this year
39 Amortization of costs that begins during your 1991 tax year:					

40 Amortization of costs that began before 1991 . . . . **40**

41 Total. Enter here and on "Other Deductions" or "Other Expenses" line of your return. . . . **41**

SCHEDULE C (Form 1040)

Department of the Treasury Internal Revenue Service (T)

Profit or Loss From Business

(Sole Proprietorship)

▶ **Partnerships, joint ventures, etc., must file Form 1065.**

▶ **Attach to Form 1040 or Form 1041.** ▶ **See Instructions for Schedule C (Form 1040).**

OMB No. 1545-0074

1991

Attachment Sequence No. **09**

Name of proprietor: Thomas Andrews

Social security number (SSN): 123 : 45 : 6789

A Principal business or profession, including product or service (see instructions): Accounting Services

B Enter principal business code (from page 2) ▶ 7 | 6 | 5 | 8

C Business name: Andrews Accounting Services

D Employer ID number (Not SSN):

E Business address (including suite or room no.) ▶ 279 Mountain View
City, town or post office, state, and ZIP code: Ogden, UT 84201

F Accounting method: **(1)** ☐ Cash **(2)** ☒ Accrual **(3)** ☐ Other (specify) ▶

G Method(s) used to value closing inventory: **(1)** ☐ Cost **(2)** ☐ Lower of cost or market **(3)** ☐ Other (attach explanation) **(4)** ☒ Does not apply (if checked, skip line H)

		Yes	No
H	Was there any change in determining quantities, costs, or valuations between opening and closing inventory? (If "Yes," attach explanation.)		
I	Did you "materially participate" in the operation of this business during 1991? (If "No," see instructions for limitations on losses.)	X	
J	If this is the first Schedule C filed for this business, check here ▶ ☐		

Part I Income

1	Gross receipts or sales. **Caution:** *If this income was reported to you on Form W-2 and the "Statutory employee" box on that form was checked, see the instructions and check here* ▶ ☐	1	80,000
2	Returns and allowances	2	
3	Subtract line 2 from line 1	3	80,000
4	Cost of goods sold (from line 40 on page 2)	4	
5	Subtract line 4 from line 3 and enter the **gross profit** here	5	80,000
6	Other income, including Federal and state gasoline or fuel tax credit or refund (see instructions)	6	
7	Add lines 5 and 6. This is your **gross income** ▶	7	80,000

Part II Expenses (*Caution: Enter expenses for business use of your home on line 30.*)

8	Advertising	8	
9	Bad debts from sales or services (see instructions)	9	2,000
10	Car and truck expenses (see instructions—also attach **Form 4562**)	10	3,000
11	Commissions and fees	11	
12	Depletion	12	
13	Depreciation and section 179 expense deduction (not included in Part III) (see instructions)	13	15,959
14	Employee benefit programs (other than on line 19)	14	
15	Insurance (other than health)	15	800
16	Interest:		
a	Mortgage (paid to banks, etc.)	16a	
b	Other	16b	
17	Legal and professional services	17	
18	Office expense	18	4,000
19	Pension and profit-sharing plans	19	
20	Rent or lease (see instructions):		
a	Vehicles, machinery, and equipment	20a	
b	Other business property	20b	12,000
21	Repairs and maintenance	21	
22	Supplies (not included in Part III)	22	
23	Taxes and licenses	23	
24	Travel, meals, and entertainment:		
a	Travel	24a	
b	Meals and entertainment		
c	Enter 20% of line 24b subject to limitations (see instructions)		
d	Subtract line 24c from line 24b	24d	
25	Utilities	25	
26	Wages (less jobs credit)	26	
27a	Other expenses (**list type and amount**):		
27b	Total other expenses	27b	

28	Add amounts in columns for lines 8 through 27b. These are your **total expenses** before expenses for business use of your home ▶	28	37,759
29	Tentative profit (loss). Subtract line 28 from line 7	29	42.241
30	Expenses for business use of your home (attach **Form 8829**)	30	
31	**Net profit or (loss).** Subtract line 30 from line 29. If a profit, enter here and on Form 1040, line 12. Also enter the net profit on Schedule SE, line 2 (statutory employees, see instructions). If a loss, you MUST go on to line 32 (fiduciaries, see instructions)	31	42.241

32 If you have a loss, you MUST check the box that describes your investment in this activity (see instructions). If you checked 32a, enter the loss on Form 1040, line 12, and Schedule SE, line 2 (statutory employees, see instructions). If you checked 32b, you MUST attach **Form 6198.**

32a ☐ All investment is at risk.
32b ☐ Some investment is not at risk.

For Paperwork Reduction Act Notice, see Form 1040 instructions. Cat. No. 11334P **Schedule C (Form 1040) 1991**

Schedule C (Form 1040) 1991 Page 2

Part III Cost of Goods Sold *(See instructions.)*

33	Inventory at beginning of year. (If different from last year's closing inventory, attach explanation.)	33	
34	Purchases less cost of items withdrawn for personal use	34	
35	Cost of labor. (Do not include salary paid to yourself.)	35	
36	Materials and supplies	36	
37	Other costs	37	
38	Add lines 33 through 37	38	
39	Inventory at end of year	39	
40	**Cost of goods sold.** Subtract line 39 from line 38. Enter the result here and on page 1, line 4	40	

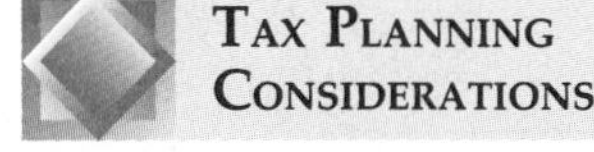
TAX PLANNING CONSIDERATIONS

Depreciation, ACRS, and MACRS

Depreciation schedules should be reviewed annually for possible retirements, abandonments, obsolescence, and changes in estimated useful lives.

EXAMPLE 49

An examination of the depreciation schedule of X Company reveals the following:

- Asset A was abandoned when it was discovered that the cost of repairs would be in excess of the cost of replacement. Asset A had an adjusted basis of $3,000.
- Asset D was being depreciated over a period of 20 years, but a revised estimate showed that its estimated remaining life is only 2 years. Its original cost was $60,000, and it had been depreciated under the straight-line method for 12 years.
- Asset J became obsolete this year, at which point, its adjusted basis was $8,000.

The depreciation expense on Asset D should be $12,000 [$60,000 (cost) − $36,000 (accumulated depreciation) = $24,000 ÷ 2 (remaining estimated useful life)]. Assets A and J should be written off for an additional expense of $11,000 ($3,000 + $8,000). ◆

Because of the deductions for depreciation, interest, and ad valorem property taxes, investments in real estate can be highly attractive. In figuring the economics of such investments, one should be sure to take into account any tax savings that result.

EXAMPLE 50

In early January 1992, T (an individual in the 31% tax bracket) purchased residential rental property for $170,000 (of which $20,000 was allocated to the land and $150,000 to the building). T made a down payment of $25,000 and assumed the seller's mortgage for the balance. Under the mortgage agreement, monthly payments of $1,000 are required and are applied toward interest, taxes, insurance, and principal. Since the property was already occupied, T continued to receive rent of $1,200 per month from the tenant. T actively participates in this activity and hence comes under the special rule for a rental real estate activity with respect to the limitation on passive activity losses (refer to Chapter 7).

During the first year of ownership, T's expenses were as follows:

Interest	$10,000
Taxes	800
Insurance	1,000
Repairs and maintenance	2,200
Depreciation ($150,000 × .03485)	5,228
Total	$19,228

The deductible loss from the rental property is computed as follows:

Rental income ($1,200 × 12 months)	$ 14,400
Less expenses (see above)	(19,228)
Net loss	$ (4,828)

But what is T's overall position for the year when the tax benefit of the loss is taken into account? Considering just the cash intake and outlay, it is summarized as follows:

Intake—		
Rental income	$14,400	
Tax savings [31% (income tax bracket) × $4,828 (loss from the property)]	1,497	$ 15,897
Outlay—		
Mortgage payments ($1,000 × 12 months)	$12,000	
Repairs and maintenance	2,200	(14,200)
Net cash benefit		$ 1,697

◆

It should be noted, however, that should T cease being an active participant in the rental activity, the passive activity loss rules would apply, and T could lose the current period benefit of the loss.

Depletion

Since the election to use the cost or percentage depletion method is an annual election, a taxpayer can use cost depletion (if higher) until the basis is exhausted and then switch to percentage depletion in the following years.

EXAMPLE 51

Assume the following facts for T:

Remaining depletable basis	$ 11,000
Gross income (10,000 units)	100,000
Expenses (other than depletion)	30,000

Since cost depletion is limited to the basis of $11,000 and if the percentage depletion is $22,000 (assume a 22% rate), T would choose the latter. His basis is then reduced to zero. In future years, however, he can continue to take percentage depletion since percentage depletion is taken without reference to the remaining basis. ◆

The election to expense intangible drilling and development costs is a one-time election. Once the election is made to either expense or capitalize the intangible drilling and development costs, it is binding on all future expenditures. The permanent nature of the election makes it extremely important for the taxpayer to determine which treatment will provide the greatest tax advantage. (Refer to Example 47 for an illustration of the effect of using the two different alternatives for a given set of facts.)

Tables

◆

Summary of Tables

Table 9–1	Original ACRS statutory percentage table for personality. Applicable depreciation method: 150 percent declining-balance switching to straight-line. Applicable recovery periods: 3, 5, 10, 15 years. Applicable convention: half-year.
Table 9–2	Modified ACRS statutory percentage table for personalty. Applicable depreciation methods: 200 or 150 percent declining-balance switching to straight-line. Applicable recovery periods: 3, 5, 7, 10, 15, 20 years. Applicable convention: half-year.
Table 9–3	Modified ACRS statutory percentage table for personalty. Applicable depreciation method: 200 percent declining-balance switching to straight-line. Applicable recovery periods: 3, 5, 7 years. Applicable convention: mid-quarter.
Table 9–4	Original ACRS statutory percentage table for realty. Applicable depreciation methods: 200 or 175 percent declining-balance switching to straight-line. Applicable recovery period: 15 years. Applicable convention: full-month.
Table 9–5	Original ACRS statutory percentage table for realty. Applicable depreciation method: 175 percent declining-balance switching to straight-line. Applicable recovery period: 18 years. Applicable convention: mid-month.
Table 9–6	Original ACRS statutory percentage table for realty. Applicable depreciation method: 175 percent declining-balance switching to straight-line. Applicable recovery period: 19 years. Applicable convention: mid-month.
Table 9–7	Modified ACRS straight-line table for realty. Applicable depreciation method: straight-line. Applicable recovery periods: 27.5, 31.5 years. Applicable convention: mid-month.
Table 9–8	Original ACRS optional straight-line table for realty. Applicable depreciation method: straight-line. Applicable recovery period: 19 years. Applicable convention: mid-month.
Table 9–9	Modified ACRS optional straight-line table for personalty. Applicable depreciation method: straight-line. Applicable recovery periods: 3, 5, 7, 10, 15, 20 years. Applicable convention: half-year.
Table 9–10	Alternative minimum tax declining-balance table for personalty. Applicable depreciation method: 150 percent declining-balance switching to straight-line. Applicable recovery periods: 3, 5, 9.5, 10 years. Applicable convention: half-year.
Table 9–11	Alternative depreciation system straight-line table for personalty. Applicable depreciation method: straight-line. Applicable recovery periods: 5, 9.5, 12 years. Applicable convention: half-year.
Table 9–12	Alternative depreciation system straight-line table for realty. Applicable depreciation method: straight-line. Applicable recovery period: 40 years. Applicable convention: mid-month.

TABLE 9–1 **ACRS Statutory Percentages for Property Other Than 15-Year Real Property, 18-Year Real Property, or 19-Year Real Property Assuming Half-Year Convention**

For Property Placed in Service after December 31, 1980, and before January 1, 1987

The applicable percentage for the class of property is:

Recovery Year	3-Year	5-Year	10-Year	15-Year Public Utility
1	25	15	8	5
2	38	22	14	10
3	37	21	12	9
4		21	10	8
5		21	10	7
6			10	7
7			9	6
8			9	6
9			9	6
10			9	6
11				6
12				6
13				6
14				6
15				6

TABLE 9–2 **MACRS Accelerated Depreciation for Personal Property Assuming Half-Year Convention**

For Property Placed in Service after December 31, 1986

Recovery Year	3-Year (200% DB)	5-Year (200% DB)	7-Year (200% DB)	10-Year (200% DB)	15-Year (150% DB)	20-Year (150% DB)
1	33.33	20.00	14.29	10.00	5.00	3.750
2	44.45	32.00	24.49	18.00	9.50	7.219
3	14.81*	19.20	17.49	14.40	8.55	6.677
4	7.41	11.52*	12.49	11.52	7.70	6.177
5		11.52	8.93*	9.22	6.93	5.713
6		5.76	8.92	7.37	6.23	5.285
7			8.93	6.55*	5.90*	4.888
8			4.46	6.55	5.90	4.522
9				6.56	5.91	4.462*
10				6.55	5.90	4.461
11				3.28	5.91	4.462
12					5.90	4.461
13					5.91	4.462
14					5.90	4.461
15					5.91	4.462
16					2.95	4.461
17						4.462
18						4.461
19						4.462
20						4.461
21						2.231

*Switchover to straight-line depreciation.

Table 9–3 **MACRS Accelerated Depreciation for Personal Property Assuming Mid-Quarter Convention**

For Property Placed in Service after December 31, 1986 (Partial Table*)

3-Year

Recovery Year	First Quarter	Second Quarter	Third Quarter	Fourth Quarter
1	58.33	41.67	25.00	8.33
2	27.78	38.89	50.00	61.11

5-Year

Recovery Year	First Quarter	Second Quarter	Third Quarter	Fourth Quarter
1	35.00	25.00	15.00	5.00
2	26.00	30.00	34.00	38.00

7-Year

Recovery Year	First Quarter	Second Quarter	Third Quarter	Fourth Quarter
1	25.00	17.85	10.71	3.57
2	21.43	23.47	25.51	27.55

*The figures in this table are taken from the official tables that appear in Rev.Proc. 87–57, 1987–2 C.B. 687. Because of their length, the complete tables are not presented.

TABLE 9–4 ACRS Statutory Percentages for 15-Year Real Property

For Property Placed in Service after December 31, 1980, and before January 1, 1987
15-Year Real Property: Low-Income Housing

If the recovery year is:	And the month in the first recovery year the property is placed in service is: 1	2	3	4	5	6	7	8	9	10	11	12
	The applicable percentage is (use the column for the month in the first year the property is placed in service):											
1	13	12	11	10	9	8	7	6	4	3	2	1
2	12	12	12	12	12	12	12	13	13	13	13	13
3	10	10	10	10	11	11	11	11	11	11	11	11
4	9	9	9	9	9	9	9	9	10	10	10	10
5	8	8	8	8	8	8	8	8	8	8	8	9
6	7	7	7	7	7	7	7	7	7	7	7	7
7	6	6	6	6	6	6	6	6	6	6	6	6
8	5	5	5	5	5	5	5	5	5	5	6	6
9	5	5	5	5	5	5	5	5	5	5	5	5
10	5	5	5	5	5	5	5	5	5	5	5	5
11	4	5	5	5	5	5	5	5	5	5	5	5
12	4	4	4	5	4	5	5	5	5	5	5	5
13	4	4	4	4	4	4	5	4	5	5	5	5
14	4	4	4	4	4	4	4	4	4	5	4	4
15	4	4	4	4	4	4	4	4	4	4	4	4
16	—	—	1	1	2	2	2	3	3	3	4	4

For Property Placed in Service after December 31, 1980, and before March 16, 1984
15-Year Real Property: Other Than Low-Income Housing

If the recovery year is:	1	2	3	4	5	6	7	8	9	10	11	12
1	12	11	10	9	8	7	6	5	4	3	2	1
2	10	10	11	11	11	11	11	11	11	11	11	12
3	9	9	9	9	10	10	10	10	10	10	10	10
4	8	8	8	8	8	8	9	9	9	9	9	9
5	7	7	7	7	7	7	8	8	8	8	8	8
6	6	6	6	6	7	7	7	7	7	7	7	7
7	6	6	6	6	6	6	6	6	6	6	6	6
8	6	6	6	6	6	6	5	6	6	6	6	6
9	6	6	6	6	5	6	5	5	5	6	6	6
10	5	6	5	6	5	5	5	5	5	5	6	5
11	5	5	5	5	5	5	5	5	5	5	5	5
12	5	5	5	5	5	5	5	5	5	5	5	5
13	5	5	5	5	5	5	5	5	5	5	5	5
14	5	5	5	5	5	5	5	5	5	5	5	5
15	5	5	5	5	5	5	5	5	5	5	5	5
16	—	—	1	1	2	2	3	3	4	4	4	5

Table 9–5 **ACRS Cost Recovery Table for 18-Year Real Property**

For Property Placed in Service after June 22, 1984, and before May 9, 1985
18-Year Real Property (18-Year 175% Declining Balance)
(Assuming Mid-Month Convention)

If the recovery year is:	And the month in the first recovery year the property is placed in service is: 1	2	3	4	5	6	7	8	9	10	11	12
	The applicable percentage is (use the column for the month in the first year the property is placed in service):											
1	9	9	8	7	6	5	4	4	3	2	1	0.4
2	9	9	9	9	9	9	9	9	9	10	10	10.0
3	8	8	8	8	8	8	8	8	9	9	9	9.0
4	7	7	7	7	7	8	8	8	8	8	8	8.0
5	7	7	7	7	7	7	7	7	7	7	7	7.0
6	6	6	6	6	6	6	6	6	6	6	6	6.0
7	5	5	5	5	6	6	6	6	6	6	6	6.0
8	5	5	5	5	5	5	5	5	5	5	5	5.0
9	5	5	5	5	5	5	5	5	5	5	5	5.0
10	5	5	5	5	5	5	5	5	5	5	5	5.0
11	5	5	5	5	5	5	5	5	5	5	5	5.0
12	5	5	5	5	5	5	5	5	5	5	5	5.0
13	4	4	4	5	4	4	5	4	4	4	5	5.0
14	4	4	4	4	4	4	4	4	4	4	4	4.0
15	4	4	4	4	4	4	4	4	4	4	4	4.0
16	4	4	4	4	4	4	4	4	4	4	4	4.0
17	4	4	4	4	4	4	4	4	4	4	4	4.0
18	4	3	4	4	4	4	4	4	4	4	4	4.0
19		1	1	1	2	2	2	3	3	3	3	3.6

TABLE 9–6 **ACRS Cost Recovery Table for 19-Year Real Property**

For Property Placed in Service after May 8, 1985, and before January 1, 1987
19-Year Real Property (19-Year 175% Declining Balance)
(Assuming Mid-Month Convention)

If the recovery year is:	And the month in the first recovery year the property is placed in service is:											
	1	2	3	4	5	6	7	8	9	10	11	12
	The applicable percentage is (use the column for the month in the first year the property is placed in service):											
1	8.8	8.1	7.3	6.5	5.8	5.0	4.2	3.5	2.7	1.9	1.1	0.4
2	8.4	8.5	8.5	8.6	8.7	8.8	8.8	8.9	9.0	9.0	9.1	9.2
3	7.6	7.7	7.7	7.8	7.9	7.9	8.0	8.1	8.1	8.2	8.3	8.3
4	6.9	7.0	7.0	7.1	7.1	7.2	7.3	7.3	7.4	7.4	7.5	7.6
5	6.3	6.3	6.4	6.4	6.5	6.5	6.6	6.6	6.7	6.8	6.8	6.9
6	5.7	5.7	5.8	5.9	5.9	5.9	6.0	6.0	6.1	6.1	6.2	6.2
7	5.2	5.2	5.3	5.3	5.3	5.4	5.4	5.5	5.5	5.6	5.6	5.6
8	4.7	4.7	4.8	4.8	4.8	4.9	4.9	5.0	5.0	5.1	5.1	5.1
9	4.2	4.3	4.3	4.4	4.4	4.5	4.5	4.5	4.5	4.6	4.6	4.7
10	4.2	4.2	4.2	4.2	4.2	4.2	4.2	4.2	4.2	4.2	4.2	4.2
11	4.2	4.2	4.2	4.2	4.2	4.2	4.2	4.2	4.2	4.2	4.2	4.2
12	4.2	4.2	4.2	4.2	4.2	4.2	4.2	4.2	4.2	4.2	4.2	4.2
13	4.2	4.2	4.2	4.2	4.2	4.2	4.2	4.2	4.2	4.2	4.2	4.2
14	4.2	4.2	4.2	4.2	4.2	4.2	4.2	4.2	4.2	4.2	4.2	4.2
15	4.2	4.2	4.2	4.2	4.2	4.2	4.2	4.2	4.2	4.2	4.2	4.2
16	4.2	4.2	4.2	4.2	4.2	4.2	4.2	4.2	4.2	4.2	4.2	4.2
17	4.2	4.2	4.2	4.2	4.2	4.2	4.2	4.2	4.2	4.2	4.2	4.2
18	4.2	4.2	4.2	4.2	4.2	4.2	4.2	4.2	4.2	4.2	4.2	4.2
19	4.2	4.2	4.2	4.2	4.2	4.2	4.2	4.2	4.2	4.2	4.2	4.2
20	0.2	0.5	0.9	1.2	1.6	1.9	2.3	2.6	3.0	3.3	3.7	4.0

TABLE 9–7 **MACRS Straight-Line Depreciation for Real Property Assuming Mid-Month Convention***

For Property Placed in Service after December 31, 1986
27.5-Year Residential Real Property

The applicable percentage is (use the column for the month in the first year the property is placed in service):

Recovery Year(s)	1	2	3	4	5	6	7	8	9	10	11	12
1	3.485	3.182	2.879	2.576	2.273	1.970	1.667	1.364	1.061	0.758	0.455	0.152
2–18	3.636	3.636	3.636	3.636	3.636	3.636	3.636	3.636	3.636	3.636	3.636	3.636
19–27	3.637	3.637	3.637	3.637	3.637	3.637	3.637	3.637	3.637	3.637	3.637	3.637
28	1.970	2.273	2.576	2.879	3.182	3.485	3.636	3.636	3.636	3.636	3.636	3.636
29	0.000	0.000	0.000	0.000	0.000	0.000	0.152	0.455	0.758	1.061	1.364	1.667

31.5-Year Nonresidential Real Property

The applicable percentage is (use the column for the month in the first year the property is placed in service):

Recovery Years(s)	1	2	3	4	5	6	7	8	9	10	11	12
1	3.042	2.778	2.513	2.249	1.984	1.720	1.455	1.190	0.926	0.661	0.397	0.132
2–19	3.175	3.175	3.175	3.175	3.175	3.175	3.175	3.175	3.175	3.175	3.175	3.175
20–31	3.174	3.174	3.174	3.174	3.174	3.174	3.174	3.174	3.174	3.174	3.174	3.174
32	1.720	1.984	2.249	2.513	2.778	3.042	3.175	3.175	3.175	3.175	3.175	3.175
33	0.000	0.000	0.000	0.000	0.000	0.000	0.132	0.397	0.661	0.926	1.190	1.455

*The official tables contain a separate row for each year. For ease of presentation, certain years are grouped in these two tables. In some instances, this will produce a difference of .001 for the last digit when compared with the official tables.

TABLE 9–8 **ACRS Cost Recovery Table for 19-Year Real Property: Optional Straight-Line**

For Property Placed in Service after May 8, 1985, and before January 1, 1987 19-Year Real Property for Which an Optional 19-Year Straight-Line Method Is Elected (Assuming Mid-Month Convention)

If the recovery year is:	And the month in the first recovery year the property is placed in service is:											
	1	2	3	4	5	6	7	8	9	10	11	12
	The applicable percentage is (use the column for the month in the first year the property is placed in service):											
1	5.0	4.6	4.2	3.7	3.3	2.9	2.4	2.0	1.5	1.1	.7	.2
2	5.3	5.3	5.3	5.3	5.3	5.3	5.3	5.3	5.3	5.3	5.3	5.3
3	5.3	5.3	5.3	5.3	5.3	5.3	5.3	5.3	5.3	5.3	5.3	5.3
4	5.3	5.3	5.3	5.3	5.3	5.3	5.3	5.3	5.3	5.3	5.3	5.3
5	5.3	5.3	5.3	5.3	5.3	5.3	5.3	5.3	5.3	5.3	5.3	5.3
6	5.3	5.3	5.3	5.3	5.3	5.3	5.3	5.3	5.3	5.3	5.3	5.3
7	5.3	5.3	5.3	5.3	5.3	5.3	5.3	5.3	5.3	5.3	5.3	5.3
8	5.3	5.3	5.3	5.3	5.3	5.3	5.3	5.3	5.3	5.3	5.3	5.3
9	5.3	5.3	5.3	5.3	5.3	5.3	5.3	5.3	5.3	5.3	5.3	5.3
10	5.3	5.3	5.3	5.3	5.3	5.3	5.3	5.3	5.3	5.3	5.3	5.3
11	5.3	5.3	5.3	5.3	5.3	5.3	5.3	5.3	5.3	5.3	5.3	5.3
12	5.3	5.3	5.3	5.3	5.3	5.3	5.3	5.3	5.3	5.3	5.3	5.3
13	5.3	5.3	5.3	5.3	5.3	5.3	5.3	5.3	5.3	5.3	5.3	5.3
14	5.2	5.2	5.2	5.2	5.2	5.2	5.2	5.2	5.2	5.2	5.2	5.2
15	5.2	5.2	5.2	5.2	5.2	5.2	5.2	5.2	5.2	5.2	5.2	5.2
16	5.2	5.2	5.2	5.2	5.2	5.2	5.2	5.2	5.2	5.2	5.2	5.2
17	5.2	5.2	5.2	5.2	5.2	5.2	5.2	5.2	5.2	5.2	5.2	5.2
18	5.2	5.2	5.2	5.2	5.2	5.2	5.2	5.2	5.2	5.2	5.2	5.2
19	5.2	5.2	5.2	5.2	5.2	5.2	5.2	5.2	5.2	5.2	5.2	5.2
20	.2	.6	1.0	1.5	1.9	2.3	2.8	3.2	3.7	4.1	4.5	5.0

TABLE 9–9 **MACRS Straight-Line Depreciation for Personal Property Assuming Half-Year Convention***

For Property Placed in Service after December 31, 1986

ACRS Class	% First Recovery Year	Other Recovery Years: Years	Other Recovery Years: %	Last Recovery Year: Year	Last Recovery Year: %
3-year	16.67	2–3	33.33	4	16.67
5-year	10.00	2–5	20.00	6	10.00
7-year	7.14	2–7	14.29	8	7.14
10-year	5.00	2–10	10.00	11	5.00
15-year	3.33	2–15	6.67	16	3.33
20-year	2.50	2–20	5.00	21	2.50

*The official table contains a separate row for each year. For ease of presentation, certain years are grouped in this table. In some instances, this will produce a difference of .01 for the last digit when compared with the official table.

TABLE 9–10 **Alternative Minimum Tax: 150% Declining-Balance Assuming Half-Year Convention**

For Property Placed in Service after December 31, 1986 (Partial Table*)

Recovery Year	3-Year 150%	5-Year 150%	9.5-Year 150%	10-Year 150%
1	25.00	15.00	7.89	7.50
2	37.50	25.50	14.54	13.88
3	25.00**	17.85	12.25	11.79
4	12.50	16.66**	10.31	10.02
5		16.66	9.17**	8.74**
6		8.33	9.17	8.74
7			9.17	8.74
8			9.17	8.74
9			9.17	8.74
10			9.16	8.74
11				4.37

*The figures in this table are taken from the official table that appears in Rev.Proc. 87–57, 1987–2 C.B. 687. Because of its length, the complete table is not presented.

**Switchover to straight-line depreciation.

TABLE 9–11 **ADS Straight-Line for Personal Property Assuming Half-Year Convention**

For Property Placed in Service after December 31, 1986 (Partial Table*)

Recovery Year	5-Year Class	9.5-Year Class	12-Year Class
1	10.00	5.26	4.17
2	20.00	10.53	8.33
3	20.00	10.53	8.33
4	20.00	10.53	8.33
5	20.00	10.52	8.33
6	10.00	10.53	8.33
7		10.52	8.34
8		10.53	8.33
9		10.52	8.34
10		10.53	8.33
11			8.34
12			8.33
13			4.17

*The figures in this table are taken from the official table that appears in Rev.Proc. 87–57, 1987–2 C.B. 687. Because of its length, the complete table is not presented. The tables for the mid-quarter convention also appear in Rev.Proc. 87–57.

TABLE 9–12 **ADS Straight-Line for Real Property Assuming Mid-Month Convention**

For Property Placed in Service after December 31, 1986

Recovery Year	Month Placed in Service											
	1	2	3	4	5	6	7	8	9	10	11	12
1	2.396	2.188	1.979	1.771	1.563	1.354	1.146	0.938	0.729	0.521	0.313	0.104
2–40	2.500	2.500	2.500	2.500	2.500	2.500	2.500	2.500	2.500	2.500	2.500	2.500
41	0.104	0.312	0.521	0.729	0.937	1.146	1.354	1.562	1.771	1.979	2.187	2.396

Problem Materials

Discussion Questions

1. Distinguish between depreciation, cost recovery, amortization, and depletion.
2. Discuss whether a taxpayer can depreciate personal property (personalty).
3. Distinguish between allowed and allowable depreciation.
4. If a personal use asset is converted to business use, why is it necessary to compute depreciation on the lower of fair market value or adjusted basis at the date of conversion?
5. Discuss whether a parking lot that is used in a business can be depreciated.
6. What depreciation methods can be used for the following assets that were acquired after 1969 and before January 1, 1981?

   a. Used machinery and equipment used in the business.
   b. New apartment building held for investment.
   c. Land held for business use.
   d. Used apartment building held for investment.
   e. New factory used for business.
   f. New automobile used in the business.

7. What information could a taxpayer use in determining an asset's useful life for an asset placed in service prior to January 1, 1981?
8. Distinguish between the treatment of salvage value on tangible personal property placed in service before January 1, 1981, and tangible personal property placed in service after December 31, 1980.
9. Discuss the half-year convention as it is used in the post-TRA of 1986 (MACRS) rules.
10. Discuss the mid-month convention as it is used in the post-TRA of 1986 (MACRS) rules.
11. Discuss the applicable conventions if a taxpayer elects to use straight-line cost recovery for property placed in service after December 31, 1986.
12. If a taxpayer makes a straight-line election under MACRS, discuss the possibility of taking a cost recovery deduction, for personal and real property, in the year of disposition.
13. Discuss the limitation on the § 179 amount that can be expensed and its impact on the basis of the property.
14. Discuss whether the statutory dollar limitations on cost recovery apply to the cost recovery of a computer that meets the more-than-50% business use test.
15. If a taxpayer does not pass the more-than-50% business use test on an automobile, discuss whether the statutory dollar limitations on cost recovery are applicable.
16. Discuss the tax consequences that result when a passenger automobile, which satisfied the more-than-50% business usage test during the first two years, fails the test for the third year.
17. Explain the reason for the inclusion amount with respect to leased passenger automobiles.
18. Explain how an inclusion amount is determined with respect to leased passenger automobiles.
19. Discuss the extent to which the 150% declining-balance method can be used under the alternative depreciation system.
20. What factors must exist for an intangible asset to be amortized?
21. Compare the tax treatment of the sale and purchase of a covenant not to compete with the tax treatment of the sale and purchase of goodwill.
22. Briefly discuss the differences between cost depletion and percentage depletion.

PROBLEMS

23. On January 1, 1988, X Company acquired an asset (three-year property) for use in its business for $10,000. In the years 1988 and 1989, X took $3,333 and $4,445 of cost recovery. The allowable cost recovery for the years 1990 and 1991 was $1,481 and $741, but X did not take the deductions. In those years, X had net operating losses, and the company wanted to "save" the deductions for later years. On January 1, 1992, the asset was sold for $2,000. Calculate the gain or loss on the sale of the asset in 1992.

24. X acquired a personal residence in 1978 for $70,000. In January 1980, when the fair market value was $80,000, he converted the residence to rental property.

    a. Calculate the amount of depreciation that can be taken in 1980, assuming that the straight-line rate is used, there is no salvage value, and the residence has a 30-year estimated useful life.
    b. What would your answer be if the property were worth only $50,000 in 1980?

25. T, who is single, acquired a new machine for $42,000 on January 1, 1979. Calculate the total depreciation deduction allowed in the first year if the estimated useful life is 20 years (salvage value of $5,200) under each of the following methods:

    a. 200% declining-balance.
    b. Sum-of-the-years' digits.
    c. 150% declining-balance.
    d. Straight-line.

26. T acquires a 10-year class asset on March 1, 1986, for $20,000. T does not elect immediate expensing under § 179. On October 5, 1992, T sells the asset.

    a. Determine T's cost recovery for 1986.
    b. Determine T's cost recovery for 1992.

27. H acquires a five-year class asset on February 17, 1992, for $12,000. H does not elect immediate expensing under § 179. On September 12, 1994, H sells the asset.

    a. Determine H's cost recovery for 1992.
    b. Determine H's cost recovery for 1994.

28. Y acquires a seven-year class asset on April 4, 1992, for $25,000. Y does not elect immediate expensing under § 179, but does elect the straight-line method. On June 2, 1996, Y sells the asset.

    a. Determine Y's cost recovery for 1992.
    b. Determine Y's cost recovery for 1996.

29. Taxpayer acquired a building for $300,000 (exclusive of land) on January 1, 1984. Calculate the cost recovery using the statutory percentage method for 1984 and 1992 if:

    a. The real property is low-income housing.
    b. The real property is a factory building.

30. On December 2, 1984, W purchased and placed in service a warehouse. The warehouse cost $800,000. W used the statutory percentage cost recovery method. On July 7, 1992, W sold the warehouse.

    a. Determine W's cost recovery for 1984.
    b. Determine W's cost recovery for 1992.

31. T, who is single, acquired a new copier (five-year class property) on March 2, 1992, for $28,000. What is the maximum amount that T can deduct in 1992 assuming the following:

    a. The taxable income derived from T's trade or business (without regard to the amount expensed under § 179) is $100,000.
    b. The taxable income derived from T's trade or business (without regard to the amount expensed under § 179) is $3,000.

32. H owns a small business that he operates as a sole proprietor. In 1992, H will net $9,000 of business income before consideration of any § 179 deduction. H spends $205,000 on new equipment in 1992. If H also has $3,000 of § 179 deduction carryforwards from 1991, determine his § 179 expense deduction for 1992 and the amount of any carryforward.

33. Q is the proprietor of a small business. In 1992, his business income, before consideration of any § 179 deduction, is $5,000. Q spends $203,000 on new equipment and furniture for 1992. If Q elects to take the § 179 deduction on a desk that cost $15,000 (included in the $203,000), determine Q's total cost recovery for 1992 with respect to the desk.

34. On March 10, 1992, T purchased three-year class property for $20,000. On December 15, 1992, T purchased five-year class property for $50,000.

    a. Calculate T's cost recovery for 1992, assuming T does not make the § 179 election or use straight-line depreciation.
    b. Calculate T's cost recovery for 1992, assuming T does elect to use § 179 and does not elect to use straight-line depreciation.

35. U acquires a warehouse on March 1, 1992, at a cost of $3,500,000. On September 30, 1999, U sells the warehouse. Calculate U's cost recovery for 1992. For 1999.

36. On July 1, 1992, A places in service a computer (five-year class property). The computer cost $20,000. A used the computer 65% for business. The remainder of the time, A used the computer for personal purposes. If A does not elect § 179, determine her cost recovery deduction for the computer for 1992.

37. On February 16, 1992, T purchased and placed into service a new car. The purchase price was $18,000. T drove the car 12,000 miles during the remainder of the year, 9,000 miles for business and 3,000 miles for personal use. T used the statutory percentage method of cost recovery. Calculate the total deduction T may take for 1992 with respect to the car.

38. On June 5, 1992, R purchased and placed in service a $19,000 car. The business use percentage for the car is always 100%. Compute R's cost recovery deduction in 1998.

39. On June 14, 1992, T purchased and placed in service a new car. The purchase price was $16,000. The car was used 75% for business and 25% for personal use in both 1992 and 1993. In 1994, the car was used 40% for business and 60% for personal use. Compute the cost recovery deduction for the car in 1994 and the cost recovery recapture.

40. In 1992 R purchased a computer (five-year property) for $120,000. The computer was used 60% for business, 20% for income production, and 20% for personal use. In 1993 the usage changed to 40% for business, 30% for income production, and 30% for personal use. Compute the cost recovery deduction for 1993 and any cost recovery recapture. Assume R did not make a § 179 election on the computer in 1992.

41. Midway through 1992, A leases and places in service a passenger automobile. The lease will run for five years, and the payments are $430 per month. During 1992, A uses the car 70% for business use and 30% for personal use. Assuming the dollar amount from the IRS table is $267, determine the tax consequences to A from the lease for the year 1992.

42. Use the information given in Problem 41, but assume the dollar amount is $584. A uses the car 60% for business use and 40% for personal use in 1993. Determine A's tax consequences from the lease in 1993.

43. On March 5, 1992, T purchased office furniture and fixtures for $40,000. The assets are seven-year class property and have an ADS midpoint of 9.5 years. Determine T's cost recovery deduction for computing 1992 taxable income using the alternative depreciation system and assuming T does not make a § 179 election.

44. In 1992 L purchased a light-duty truck for $12,000. The truck is used 100% for business. L did not make a § 179 election with respect to the truck. If L uses the statutory percentage method, determine L's cost recovery deduction for 1992 for computing taxable income and for computing L's alternative minimum tax.

45. In June 1992, T purchased and placed in service railroad track costing $600,000.

    a. Calculate T's cost recovery deduction for 1992 for computing taxable income, assuming T does not make the § 179 election or use straight-line cost recovery.
    b. Calculate T's cost recovery deduction for 1992 for computing taxable income, assuming T does not make the § 179 election but does elect to use ADS 150% declining-balance cost recovery.

46. On January 1, 1992, X Corporation acquired all of the assets of B's proprietorship. X paid B $1,000,000. In the agreement, B signed a covenant not to compete with X for five years. The agreement stipulated that $100,000 of the purchase price was for the covenant not to compete. X Corporation also allocates $50,000 of the purchase price to goodwill. Determine the tax consequences (with respect to the covenant not to compete and the goodwill) of the purchase to X for 1992.

47. T acquired a mineral interest during the year for $5,000,000. A geological survey estimated that 250,000 tons of the mineral remained in the deposit. During the year, 80,000 tons were mined and 45,000 tons were sold for $6,000,000. Other expenses amounted to $4,000,000. Assuming the mineral depletion rate is 22%, calculate T's lowest taxable income.

48. T purchased an oil interest for $2,000,000. Recoverable barrels were estimated to be 500,000. During the year, 120,000 barrels were sold for $3,840,000, regular expenses (including depreciation) were $1,240,000, and IDC were $1,000,000. Calculate the taxable income under the expensing and capitalization methods of handling IDC.

CUMULATIVE PROBLEMS

49. John Smith, age 31, is single and has no dependents. At the beginning of 1992, John started his own excavation business and named it Earth Movers. John lives at 1045 Center Street, Lindon, UT, and his business is located at 381 State Street, Lindon, UT. The zip code for both addresses is 84059. John's Social Security number is 321–09–6456, and the business identification number is 98–1234567. John is a cash basis taxpayer. During 1992, John had the following items in connection with his business:

Fees for services	$147,000
Building rental expense	12,000
Office furniture and equipment rental expense	2,400
Office supplies	500
Utilities	1,000
Salary for secretary	15,000
Salary for equipment operators	55,000
Payroll taxes	7,000
Fuel and oil for the equipment	10,000
Purchase of three front-end loaders on January 15, 1992, for $175,000. John made the election under § 179.	175,000
Purchase of a new dump truck on January 18, 1992	30,000
During 1992, John had the following additional items:	
Interest income from First National Bank	$ 8,000
Dividends from Exxon	500
Quarterly estimated tax payments	1,000

Assuming John does not itemize his deductions, compute his Federal income tax payable (or refund due). Suggested software (if available): *TurboTax* for tax return or WFT tax planning software.

50. Bob Brown, age 30, is single and has no dependents. He was employed as a barber until May 1991 by Hair Cuts, Inc. In June 1991, Bob opened his own styling salon, the Style Shop, located at 465 Willow Drive, St. Paul, MN 55455. Bob is a cash basis taxpayer. He lives at 1021 Snelling Avenue, St. Paul, MN 55455. His Social Security

number is 321–56–7102. Bob does not wish to designate $1 to the Presidential Election Campaign Fund. During 1991, Bob had the following income and expense items:

a. $20,800 salary from Hair Cuts, Inc.
b. $2,400 Federal income tax withheld by Hair Cuts, Inc.
c. $600 cash dividend from General Motors.
d. $7,000 gross receipts from his own hair styling business.
e. Expenses connected with Bob's hair styling business:

- $100 laundry and cleaning
- $4,400 rent
- $700 supplies
- $600 utilities and telephone

f. Bob purchased and installed a fancy barber chair on June 3, 1991. The chair cost $6,400. Bob did not make the § 179 election.
g. Bob purchased and installed furniture and fixtures on June 5, 1991. These items cost $7,000. Bob did not make the § 179 election.
h. Bob had no itemized deductions.

Compute Bob Brown's 1991 Federal income tax payable (or refund due). If you use tax forms for your computations, you will need Forms 1040 and 4562 and Schedules C and SE. Suggested software (if available): *TurboTax* for tax return or WFT tax planning software.

RESEARCH PROBLEMS

RESEARCH PROBLEM 1 H, who is one of your clients, is considering building a golf course in the resort area of Sun River, Oregon. Because the land is unimproved, all of the sand traps, greens, fairways, and tees will need to be constructed. Advise H as to whether any deductions can be taken on these landscaping improvements.

RESEARCH PROBLEM 2 KC operates a restaurant in a small town. In May of the current year, KC had a new septic tank installed for the restaurant. The town plans to construct a sewage system in five years. At that time, KC will be required to be connected to the town system, and his septic tank will be obsolete. KC believes that depreciation should represent wear, tear, and obsolescence, and, hence, he believes he should use a five-year life for the depreciation of the septic tank. Discuss the proper period and method for depreciating the septic tank.

Partial list of research aids:
J. O. Miller, 56 TCM 1242, T. C.Memo 1989–66.
Rev.Proc. 87–56, 1987–2 C.B. 674.

RESEARCH PROBLEM 3 B operates several garbage dumps throughout the Chicago area. In 1992, B purchased a tract of land for $150,000. This land contained a pit that could accommodate 2,500,000 cubic yards of garbage. In 1992, the land was reasonably estimated to be worth $55,000 without the pit. The sellers indicated that they had charged a premium for the land because they knew B needed land with a pit for dumping garbage in that area. At the end of 1992 and several times thereafter, B had the property surveyed to determine the amount of space filled and the amount remaining. In 1992, 2,300,000 cubic yards remained to be filled. Discuss whether B can depreciate the value of the air space that is now being reduced by the dumping of the garbage.

RESEARCH PROBLEM 4 T, a tenured professor at State University, purchased a personal computer. T uses the computer at home to store information and for word processing in his academic research. State University did not provide T with access to a computer. The university did not explicitly require T to purchase the computer as a condition of employment. Discuss the possibility of T deducting the cost of the computer on his income tax return.

CHAPTER

DEDUCTIONS: EMPLOYEE EXPENSES

OBJECTIVES

Discuss factors that determine whether an individual is self-employed or an employee.

Distinguish between self-employment and employee business expenses.

Determine which employee business expenses are deductions *for* adjusted gross income and which are deductions *from* adjusted gross income.

Identify miscellaneous itemized deductions subject to the 2 percent floor.

Distinguish between travel and transportation expenses.

Examine the requirements for deducting moving expenses and the limitations on the amount deductible.

Discuss when and how education expenses can be deducted.

Discuss the limitations on the deductibility of entertainment expenses.

Develop tax planning ideas related to employee business expenses.

OUTLINE

Employees frequently incur expenses in connection with employment activities. Some of these expenses are deductible and some are not. Certain deductible expenses are subject to specific reductions and limitations. After determining which expenses are deductible and applying any limitations, the expenses must be classified as deductions *for* or deductions *from* adjusted gross income (AGI).

The rules for computing and classifying expenses incurred by self-employed individuals sometimes differ from those applicable to employees. Therefore, it is important to determine whether an individual is an employee or is self-employed. Guidelines for making this determination are discussed in the following section. This discussion is followed by coverage of the rules for computing and classifying employee business expenses.

Classification of Employment-Related Expenses

◆

Self-Employed versus Employee Status

In many instances, it is difficult to distinguish between an individual who is self-employed and one who is performing services as an employee. Expenses of self-employed individuals are deductible as trade or business expenses (*for* AGI).

Example 1

N, a self-employed CPA, incurred transportation expenses of $1,000 in connection with his business. The transportation expenses are deductions *for* AGI because they are expenses incurred by a self-employed individual. ◆

Expenses incurred by an employee in an employment relationship are subject to limitations. Only reimbursed employee expenses are deductible *for* AGI. All other deductible employee expenses are deducted *from* AGI.

Example 2

K, a CPA employed by N, incurred unreimbursed transportation expenses of $1,000 in connection with his employment activities. Because K is an employee, the transportation expenses are deductions *from* AGI (subject to a 2% floor discussed in Example 7). ◆

Example 3

G, a CPA employed by N, incurred entertainment expenses of $1,000 in connection with his employment activities. N reimbursed G for these entertainment expenses under an accountable plan. The $1,000 of gross income is reduced by a $1,000 deduction *for* AGI. ◆

As the preceding examples illustrate, because of the differences in the treatment of expenses, it is important to determine when an employer-employee relationship exists.

Generally, an employer-employee relationship exists under common law rules when the employer has the right to specify the end result and the ways and means by which the end result is to be attained.[1] Thus, an employee is subject to the will and control of the employer with respect not only to what shall be done but also to how it shall be done. If the individual is subject to the direction or control of another only to the extent of the end result (e.g., the preparation of a taxpayer's return by an independent CPA) and not as to the means of accomplishment, an employer-employee relationship does not exist.

1. Reg. § 31.3401(c)–(1)(b).

Certain factors may indicate an employer-employee relationship. They include the right to discharge without legal liability the person performing the service, the furnishing of tools or a place to work, and payment based on time spent rather than the task performed. However, each case is tested on its own merits, and the right to control the means and methods of accomplishment is the definitive test. Generally, physicians, lawyers, dentists, contractors, subcontractors, and others who offer services to the public are not classified as employees.

EXAMPLE 4

D is a lawyer whose major client accounts for 60% of her billings. She does the routine legal work and income tax returns at the client's request. She is paid a monthly retainer in addition to amounts charged for extra work. D is a self-employed individual. Even though most of her income comes from one client, she still has the right to determine how the end result of her work is attained. ◆

EXAMPLE 5

E is a lawyer hired by D to assist D in the performance of services for the client mentioned in Example 4. E is under D's supervision; D reviews E's work and pays E an hourly fee. E is an employee of D. ◆

EXAMPLE 6

F is a licensed practical nurse who works as a private-duty nurse. She is under the supervision of the patient's doctor and is paid by the patient. F is not an employee of either the patient (who pays her) or the doctor (who supervises her). The ways and means of attaining the end result (care of the patient) are under her control. ◆

Real estate agents and direct sellers are classified as self-employed persons if two conditions are met. The first condition is that substantially all of their income for services must be directly related to sales or other output. The second condition is that their services must be performed under a written contract that specifies that they are not to be treated as employees for tax purposes.[2]

A self-employed individual is required to file Schedule C of Form 1040, and all related allowable expenses are deductions *for* AGI.[3]

A special category of employees is also allowed to file Schedule C to report income and deduct expenses for AGI. These employees are called statutory employees[4] because they are not common law employees under the rules explained above. The wages or commissions paid to statutory employees are not subject to Federal income tax withholding but are subject to Social Security tax.

Deductions for or from AGI

The Code specifies that employee expenses reimbursed under an accountable plan are deductible *for* AGI.[5] All unreimbursed employee expenses are deductions *from* AGI and can be deducted only if the employee-taxpayer itemizes deductions, with one exception. The employment-related expenses of a qualified performing artist[6] are deductible *for* AGI.

The distinction between deductions *for* and deductions *from* AGI is important. No benefit is received for an item that is deductible *from* AGI if a taxpayer's

2. § 3508(b).

3. §§ 62(a)(1) and 162(a). See Appendix B for a reproduction of Schedule C.

4. See Circular E, *Employers Tax Guide* (IRS Publication 15) for the dual nature of their employment.

5. § 62(a)(2).

6. Defined at § 62(b).

itemized deductions are less than the standard deduction. Refer to Chapter 6 for a detailed discussion of deductions *for* versus deductions *from* AGI.

Limitations on Itemized Deductions

Many itemized deductions, such as medical expenses and charitable contributions, are subject to limitations expressed as a percentage of AGI. These limitations may be expressed as floors or ceilings. For example, medical expenses are deductible only to the extent they exceed 7.5 percent of AGI (there is a 7.5 percent floor). Charitable contributions in excess of 50 percent of AGI are not deductible in the year of the contribution. In other words, there is a 50 percent ceiling on the deductibility of charitable contributions. These limitations are discussed more fully in Chapter 11.

Miscellaneous Itemized Deductions Subject to the 2 Percent Floor. Certain miscellaneous itemized deductions, including unreimbursed employee business expenses, must be aggregated and then reduced by 2 percent of AGI. Expenses subject to the 2 percent floor include the following:

- All § 212 expenses, except expenses of producing rent and royalty income (refer to Chapter 6).
- All unreimbursed employee expenses (after 20 percent reduction, if applicable).
- Professional dues and subscriptions.
- Union dues and work uniforms.
- Employment-related education expenses.
- Malpractice insurance premiums.
- Expenses of job hunting (including employment agency fees and resumé-writing expenses).
- Home office expenses of an employee or outside salesperson.
- Legal, accounting, and tax return preparation fees.
- Hobby expenses (up to hobby income).
- Investment expenses, including investment counsel fees, subscriptions, and safe deposit box rental.
- Custodial fees relating to income-producing property or an IRA or a Keogh plan.
- Any fees paid to collect interest or dividends.
- Appraisal fees establishing a casualty loss or charitable contribution.

Miscellaneous Itemized Deductions Not Subject to the 2 Percent Floor. Certain miscellaneous itemized deductions, including the following, are not subject to the 2 percent floor:

- Impairment-related work expenses of handicapped individuals.[7]
- Federal estate tax on income in respect of a decedent.[8]
- Certain adjustments when a taxpayer restores amounts held under a claim of right.[9]
- Amortizable bond premium.[10]
- Gambling losses to the extent of gambling winnings.[11]

7. § 67(d).
8. § 691(c).
9. § 1341.
10. § 171.
11. § 165(d).

- Deductions allowable in connection with personal property used in a short sale.
- Certain terminated annuity payments.[12]
- Certain costs of cooperative housing corporations.[13]

Example 7

T, who has AGI of $20,000, has the following miscellaneous itemized deductions:

Gambling losses (to extent of gains)	$1,200
Tax return preparation fees	300
Unreimbursed employee transportation	200
Professional dues and subscriptions	260
Safe deposit box rental	30

T's itemized deductions are as follows:

Deduction not subject to 2% floor (gambling losses)		$1,200
Deductions subject to 2% floor ($300 + $200 + $260 + $30)	$ 790	
Less 2% of AGI	(400)	390
Total miscellaneous itemized deductions		$1,590

If T's AGI were $40,000, the floor would be $800 (2% of $40,000), and T could not deduct any expenses subject to the 2% floor. ◆

Percentage Reduction for Meals and Entertainment Expenses

Deductions for meals and entertainment (including entertainment facilities) are limited to 80 percent of allowable expenditures.[14] The allowable expenditures are limited to reasonable amounts. In other words, "lavish or extravagant" expenses are excluded before application of the 80 percent rule.

Example 8

T spends $100 for deductible business entertainment. He is not reimbursed by his employer. Only $80 is allowed as a deduction. This $80 is combined with other miscellaneous itemized deductions subject to the 2% floor, and the total is reduced by 2% of AGI. ◆

Example 9

S, who is self-employed, purchased two tickets to an entertainment event from a scalper and used the tickets to entertain a client. She paid $220 and the face value of the tickets was $100. Since $120 is lavish or extravagant, S's deduction cannot exceed $80 (80% of $100). ◆

The 80 percent limit applies to the following:[15]

- Any expense for food or beverages.
- Any expense that constitutes entertainment, amusement, or recreation (or expense related to a facility used in connection with these activities).

---

12. § 72(b)(3).
13. § 216.
14. § 274(n).
15. § 274(n)(1).

Transportation expenses are not affected by this provision—only meals and entertainment. The 80 percent rule also applies to taxes and tips relating to meals and entertainment. Cover charges, parking fees at an entertainment location, and room rental fees for a meal or cocktail party are also subject to the 80 percent rule.

EXAMPLE 10

T pays a $20 cab fare to meet her client for dinner at The Ritz. The meal costs $90, and T leaves a $15 tip. T's deduction is $104 [($90 + $15) × 80% + $20 cab fare]. ◆

The 80 percent rule is applied before application of the 2 percent floor previously discussed.

EXAMPLE 11

T incurs unreimbursed meal and entertainment expenses of $1,000 in the course of his job as a salesman. His AGI is $20,000, and he has no other expenses subject to the 2% floor. If T itemizes, his deduction is limited to $400, as follows:

Expenses (80% of $1,000)	$800
Less 2% of AGI	(400)
Deductible	$400

◆

It does not matter where or how meal and entertainment expenses are incurred. Only 80 percent of meals incurred in the course of travel away from home, in connection with moving expenses, or in connection with education expenses are deductible. In addition, the cost of meals furnished by an employer to employees on the employer's premises is subject to the 80 percent rule in computing the employer's deduction.

Exceptions for Luxury Water Travel. If meals and entertainment incurred in the course of luxury water travel are not separately stated, the 80 percent rule does not apply. If meals and entertainment are separately stated or are clearly identifiable, the 80 percent rule is applied before the limitation on luxury water travel expenses (discussed later in the chapter).

Exceptions to the 80 Percent Rule. The 80 percent rule has a number of exceptions. Exceptions one and two apply where the full value of meals or entertainment is included in the compensation of employees[16] or the income of independent contractors.[17]

EXAMPLE 12

T won an all-expense-paid pleasure trip to Europe for selling the most insurance in her company during the year. X, T's employer, included the fair market value of the trip on T's W–2 (Wage and Tax Statement). X need not allocate any of the cost to meals or entertainment. X deducts the entire amount. ◆

The third exception applies to meals and entertainment in a subsidized eating facility or where the *de minimis* fringe benefit rule is met (refer to Chapter 5).[18]

16. § 274(e)(2).
17. § 274(e)(9).
18. § 274(n)(2)(B).

EXAMPLE 13

General Hospital has an employee cafeteria on the premises for doctors, nurses, and other employees. Such employees need to be available during meal breaks for emergencies. The cafeteria operates at cost. The 80% rule does not apply. ◆

EXAMPLE 14

Y Company gives a ham, a fruitcake, and a bottle of wine to each employee at year-end. Y's costs for these items are not subject to the percentage reduction rule. The *de minimis* fringe benefit exclusion applies to business gifts of packaged foods and beverages. ◆

Exception four applies to fully reimbursed employee business meals and entertainment expenses. The 80 percent rule applies to the person making the reimbursement.[19]

EXAMPLE 15

T is a salesman who paid for lunch with a customer. He made an adequate accounting to his employer, Y, who reimbursed T. T omits both the reimbursement and the expense on his return. Y (the employer) can deduct only 80% of the expenditure on his return. ◆

Exception five relates to traditional employer-paid recreation expenses for employees.[20]

EXAMPLE 16

X Company provides a yearly Christmas party and an annual spring picnic for its employees and their families. X's reasonable costs for these events are fully deductible. ◆

The remaining exceptions[21] are of limited applicability.

EMPLOYEE BUSINESS EXPENSES

◆

The tax treatment of employee business expenses depends on whether the expenses are reimbursed or unreimbursed and, if reimbursed, whether the expenses were reimbursed under an accountable plan or a nonaccountable plan.

Accountable Plans

In General. An accountable plan requires the employee to satisfy these two requirements:

- Adequately account for (substantiate) the expenses. An employee renders an *adequate accounting* by submitting a record, with receipts and other substantiation, to the employer.[22]
- Return any excess reimbursement or allowance. An "excess reimbursement or allowance" is any amount that the employee does not adequately account for as an ordinary and necessary business expense.

Substantiation. The law provides that no deduction will be allowed for any travel, entertainment, business gift, or listed property (automobiles, computers)

19. § 274(e)(3).
20. § 274(e)(4).
21. See §§ 274(e)(7) and (8) and § 274(n)(2)(C).
22. Reg. § 1.162–17(b)(4).

expenditure unless properly substantiated by adequate records. The records should contain the following information:[23]

- The amount of the expense.
- The time and place of travel or entertainment (or date of gift).
- The business purpose of the expense.
- The business relationship of the taxpayer to the person entertained (or receiving the gift).

This means the taxpayer must maintain an account book or diary in which the above information is recorded at the time of the expenditure. Documentary evidence, such as itemized receipts, is required to support any expenditure for lodging while traveling away from home and for any other expenditure of $25 or more.[24] If a taxpayer fails to keep adequate records, each expense must be established by a written or oral statement of the exact details of the expense and by other corroborating evidence.[25]

EXAMPLE 17

B has travel expenses substantiated only by canceled checks. The checks establish the date, place, and amount of the expenditure. Because neither the business relationship nor the business purpose is established, the deduction will be disallowed.[26] ◆

EXAMPLE 18

D has travel and entertainment expenses substantiated by a diary showing the time, place, and amount of the expenditure. His oral testimony provides the business relationship and business purpose; however, since he has no receipts, any expenditures of $25 or more will be disallowed.[27] ◆

Deemed Substantiation. In lieu of reimbursing actual expenses for travel away from home, many employers reduce their paperwork by adopting a policy of reimbursing employees a flat dollar amount per day of business travel (a *per diem* allowance). Of the substantiation requirements listed above, the *amount* of the expense is proved, or *deemed substantiated* (i.e., equivalent to substantiation), by using such a per diem allowance or reimbursement procedure. The amount of expenses that is deemed substantiated is equal to the lesser of the per diem allowance or the amount of the Federal per diem rate.

The regular Federal per diem rate is the highest amount that the Federal government will pay to its employees for lodging and meals[28] while in travel status (away from home) in a particular area. The rates are different for different locations.

To avoid the need to keep a current list of the per diem rate in effect for each city or locale, a simplified method, called the *high-low method,* can be used. The high-low method specifies a limited number of high travel cost locations where the per diem is considered to be the same for all cities on the list. All other cities are considered to have the same, but lower, Federal per diem rate in effect.[29]

---

23. § 274(d).
24. Reg. §§ 1.274–5T(c)(2)(iii)(A) and (B).
25. Reg. § 1.274–5T(c)(3).
26. *William T. Whitaker,* 56 TCM 47, T.C.Memo. 1988–418.
27. *W. David Tyler,* 43 TCM 927, T.C.Memo. 1982–160.
28. The meals per diem also covers incidental expenses, including laundry and cleaning of clothing and tips for waiters. Taxi fares and telephone calls are not included.
29. For 1992, Rev.Proc. 92–17, I.R.B. 8, 16 lists the high-cost localities and the high-low amounts. Each current edition of *Your Federal Income Tax* (IRS Publication 17) contains the list and amounts for that year.

The use of a standard meal allowance (at the Federal per diem for meals) constitutes an adequate accounting. Employees and self-employed persons can use the standard meal allowance instead of deducting the actual cost of daily meals, even if not reimbursed. There is no standard lodging allowance, however. With regard to automobile expenses, an employee who receives a reimbursement of not more than the Federal standard mileage rate (see subsequent discussion of automobile expenses) for the business miles substantiated will be treated as rendering an adequate accounting.

Only the amount of the expense is considered substantiated under the deemed substantiated method. The other substantiation requirements must be provided: place, date, and business purpose of the expense and the business relationship of the parties involved. Employees who are related to their employers under § 267(b) cannot use the per diem allowance (or standard meal allowance) as an adequate accounting. They must use the actual expense method. An employee who owns more than 10 percent of the employer corporation's stock is considered related to the corporation.

Timeliness. Both substantiation and the requirement that excess reimbursements be returned must be satisfied within a reasonable period of time. Although this timeliness requirement depends on the facts and circumstances, two safe harbor methods are set forth in the Regulations.[30] The first safe harbor is the *fixed date method*. In the following situations, the "reasonable period of time" requirement will be met:

- An advance is made within 30 days of when the expense is paid or incurred,
- an expense is substantiated within 60 days after it is paid or incurred, and
- the excess amount is returned within 120 days after the expense is paid or incurred.

The second safe harbor is the *periodic statement method*. Here, the employer provides the employee with a statement (no less frequently than quarterly) stating the amount paid in excess of the expenses that have been substantiated and requesting the employee to substantiate any additional business expenses and/or to return any remaining unsubstantiated amounts within 120 days of the statement. Any expenses substantiated or returned within that period will be treated as being substantiated or returned within a reasonable period of time.

Further, the requirement to return amounts of reimbursement in excess of expenses is fulfilled if the employee returns any portion of a per diem allowance that relates to days of travel not substantiated. The employee need not return the portion that exceeds the amount allowed for the substantiated days. Consider the following example.

EXAMPLE 19

E received from his employer an advance per diem allowance for meals of $200 based on an anticipated 5 days of business travel at $40 per day to a locality for which the Federal meals and incidental expenses rate is $34, and E substantiates 3 full days of business travel. E meets the requirement to return amounts in excess of expenses if he returns $80 ($40 × 2 days), the portion of the allowance attributable to the 2 unsubstantiated days of travel. The requirement is satisfied even though E does not

30. Reg § 1.62–2(g).

return the $18 portion of the allowance that exceeds the amount deemed substantiated for the 3 substantiated days of travel.

Actual per diem ($40 × 3 days)	$120
Deemed substantiated at Federal rate ($34 × 3 days)	102
Excess portion of per diem	$ 18

The $18 excess per diem is taxable to E and is reported as wages on E's Form W–2. ◆

Nonaccountable Plans

A nonaccountable plan is one in which an adequate accounting or return of excess amounts, or both, is not required. Any reimbursement of expenses is reported in its entirety as wages on the employee's Form W–2. Any allowable expenses are deductible in the same manner as are unreimbursed expenses.

Unreimbursed Employee Expenses. Unreimbursed employee expenses are treated in a straightforward manner. Meals and entertainment expenses are subject to the 80 percent limit. Total unreimbursed employee business expenses are reported as miscellaneous itemized deductions subject to the 2 percent of AGI floor. If the employee could have received, but did not seek, reimbursement for whatever reason, none of the employment-related expenses are deductible.

Failure to Comply with Accountable Plan Requirements. Even if an employer has an accountable plan and requires employees to return excess reimbursements or allowances, the failure of an employee to follow the rules of the accountable plan causes those expenses and reimbursements to be subject to nonaccountable plan treatment.

Reporting Procedures

The reporting requirements range from no reporting at all (accountable plans when all requirements are met) to the use of some or all of three forms, Form W–2 (Wage and Tax Statement), Form 2106 (Employee Expenses), and Schedule A (Itemized Deductions) for nonaccountable plans and unreimbursed employee expenses. These reporting procedures are set out in Concept Summary 10–1.

Reimbursed employee expenses that are adequately accounted for (including per diem or mileage allowances up to the Federal government rate) under an accountable plan are deductible *for* AGI on Form 2106. Allowed excess expenses, expenses reimbursed under a nonaccountable plan, and unreimbursed expenses are deductible *from* AGI on Schedule A, subject to the 2 percent of AGI floor.

When a reimbursement under an accountable plan is paid in separate amounts relating to a designated expense (specifically for meals and entertainment, for example, or for other employee expenses), no problem arises. The reimbursements and expenses are reported as such on the appropriate forms. However, if the reimbursement is made in a single amount and the employee wants to deduct excess expenses, an allocation must be made to determine the appropriate portion of the reimbursement that applies to meals and entertainment and to other employee expenses.

EXAMPLE 20

J, who is employed by T Company, had adjusted gross income of $40,000. During the year, she incurred $2,000 of transportation and lodging expense and $1,000 of meals and entertainment expense, all fully substantiated. J received $2,100 reimbursement under an accountable plan. The reimbursement rate that applies to meals and entertainment is 33.33% ($1,000 meals and entertainment expense/$3,000 total expenses). Thus, $700 ($2,100 × 33.33%) of the reimbursement applies to meals and entertainment and $1,400 ($2,100 − $700) applies to transportation and lodging. J's itemized deduction will consist of the $600 ($2,000 total − $1,400 reimbursement) of unreimbursed transportation and lodging expenses and $300 ($1,000 − $700) of unreimbursed meal and entertainment expenses as follows:

Transportation and lodging	$600
Meals and entertainment ($300 × 80%)	240
Total (reported on Form 2106)	$840
Less: 2% of $40,000 AGI	(800)
Deduction (reported on Schedule A)	$ 40

In summary, J must report $3,000 of expenses and the $2,100 reimbursement on Form 2106 and $40 as a miscellaneous itemized deduction on Schedule A. ◆

The reporting procedures for self-employed persons, statutory employees, performing artists, and handicapped individuals with impairment-related work expenses were discussed previously in the chapter.

TRANSPORTATION EXPENSES

◆

Qualified Expenditures

An employee may deduct unreimbursed employment-related transportation expenses as miscellaneous itemized deductions (*from* AGI, subject to the 2 percent floor). Transportation expense includes only the cost of transporting the employee from one place to another when the employee is not away from home *in travel status*. Such costs include taxi fares, automobile expenses, tolls, and parking.

Commuting between home and one's place of employment is a personal, nondeductible expense. The fact that one employee drives 30 miles to work and another employee walks six blocks is of no significance.[31]

EXAMPLE 21

G is employed by X Corporation. He drives 22 miles each way to work. One day G drove to a customer's office from his place of work. The drive was a 14-mile round trip to the customer's office. G can take a deduction for 14 miles of business transportation. The remaining 44 miles are a nondeductible commuting expense. ◆

Exceptions to Disallowance of Commuting Expenses. The general rule that disallows a deduction for commuting expenses has several exceptions. An employee who uses an automobile to transport heavy tools to work and who otherwise would not drive to work will be allowed a deduction. However, the deduction is allowed only for the additional costs incurred to transport work implements. Additional costs are those exceeding the cost of commuting by the same mode of transportation without the tools. For example, the rental of a trailer for transporting tools is deductible, but the expenses of operating the automobile are not deductible.[32] The Supreme Court has held that a deduction

31. *Tauferner v. U.S.*, 69–1 USTC ¶9241, 23 AFTR2d 69–1025, 407 F.2d 243 (CA–10, 1969).

32. Rev.Rul. 75–380, 1975–2 C.B. 59.

is permitted only if the taxpayer can show that he or she would not have used the automobile were it not necessary to transport tools or equipment.[33]

Another exception is provided for an employee who has a second job. The expenses of getting from one job to another are deductible. If the employee goes home between jobs, the deduction is based on the distance between jobs.

EXAMPLE 22

In the current year, T holds two jobs, a full-time job with B Corporation and a part-time job with C Corporation. During the 250 days that she works (adjusted for weekends,

CONCEPT SUMMARY 10–1 REPORTING EMPLOYEE TRAVEL, TRANSPORTATION, AND MEAL AND ENTERTAINMENT EXPENSES AND REIMBURSEMENTS[1]

Type of Reimbursement or Other Expense Allowance Arrangement	Employer Reports on Form W–2	Employee Shows on Form 2106	Employee Claims on Schedule A
Accountable			
Adequate accounting and excess returned.	No	No	No
Per diem or mileage allowance (up to government rate). Adequate accounting and excess returned.	No	All expenses and reimbursements only if excess expenses are claimed.[4] Otherwise, form is not filed.	Expenses the employee can prove and that exceed the reimbursements received.[4]
Per diem or mileage allowance (exceeds government rate). Adequate accounting up to the government rate only and excess not returned.	Excess reported as income.[2] Amount up to the government rate is reported as fringe benefit.[3]	All expenses, and reimbursements equal to the government rate only if expenses in excess of the government rate are claimed.[4] Otherwise, form is not filed.	Expenses the employee can prove and that exceed the government rate.[4]
Nonaccountable			
Adequate accounting or return of excess either not required or required but not met.	Entire amount is reported as wages.[2]	All expenses.[4,5]	Expenses the employee can prove.[4,5]
No reimbursement.	Normal reporting of wages.	All expenses.[4,5]	Expenses the employee can prove.[4,5]

1. Adapted from IRS chart on page 52 of *Tax Guide for Small Business* (Publication 334, 1991).
2. Subject to income tax withholding and all employment taxes.
3. Not subject to withholding.
4. Any allowable expense is carried to line 19 of Schedule A and deducted as a miscellaneous itemized deduction, subject to the 2 percent of AGI limitation.
5. Meals and entertainment are subject to the 80 percent limitation.

33. *Fausner v. Comm.*, 73–2 USTC ¶9515, 32 AFTR2d 73–5202, 93 S.Ct. 2820 (USSC, 1973).

vacation, and holidays), T customarily leaves home at 7:30 A.M. and drives 30 miles to the B Corporation plant, where she works until 5:00 P.M. After dinner at a nearby cafe, T drives 20 miles to C Corporation and works from 7:00 to 11:00 P.M. The distance from the second job to T's home is 40 miles. Her deduction is based on 20 miles (the distance between jobs). ◆

It is sometimes difficult to distinguish between a nondeductible commuting expense and a deductible transportation expense necessary to the taxpayer's business. If the taxpayer is required to incur a transportation expense to travel between work stations, that expense is deductible.

EXAMPLE 23

T, a general contractor, drove from his home to his office, then drove to three building sites to perform his required inspections, and finally drove home. The costs of driving to his office and driving home from the last inspection site are nondeductible commuting expenses. The other transportation costs are deductible. ◆

Likewise, the commuting costs from home to a temporary work station and from the temporary work station to home are deductible.[34]

EXAMPLE 24

V works for a firm in downtown Denver and commutes to work. V occasionally works in a customer's office. On one such occasion, he drove directly to the customer's office, a round-trip distance from his home of 40 miles. He did not go into his office, which is a 52-mile round-trip. His mileage is deductible. ◆

Also deductible is the reasonable travel cost between the general working area and a temporary work station outside that area. What constitutes the general working area depends on the facts and circumstances of each situation. Furthermore, if an employee customarily works on several temporary assignments in a localized area, that localized area becomes the regular place of employment. Transportation from home to these locations becomes a personal, nondeductible commuting expense.

EXAMPLE 25

S, a building inspector in Minneapolis, regularly inspects buildings for building code violations for his employer, a general contractor. During one busy season, the St. Paul inspector became ill, and S was required to inspect several buildings in St. Paul. The expenses for transportation for the trips to St. Paul are deductible. ◆

Computation of Automobile Expenses

A taxpayer has two choices in computing automobile expenses. The actual operating cost, which includes depreciation, gas, oil, repairs, licenses, and insurance, may be used. Records must be kept that detail the automobile's personal and business use. Only the percentage (based upon the ratio of business miles to total miles) allocable to business transportation and travel is allowed as a deduction. Complex rules for the computation of depreciation (discussed in Chapter 9) apply if the actual expense method is used.

Use of the automatic mileage method is the second alternative. For 1992, the deduction is based on 28 cents per mile for all business miles.[35] Parking fees

34. Rev.Rul. 90–23, 1990–1 C.B. 28.

35. Rev. Proc. 91–67, I.R.B. 52, 11.

and tolls are allowed in addition to expenses computed using the automatic mileage method.

Generally, a taxpayer may elect either method for any particular year. However, the following restrictions apply:

- The vehicle must be owned by the taxpayer.
- If two or more vehicles are in use (for business purposes) at the *same* time (not alternately), a taxpayer may not use the automatic mileage method.
- A basis adjustment is required if the taxpayer changes from the automatic mileage method to the actual operating cost method. Depreciation is considered allowed for the business miles in accordance with the following schedule for the most recent five years:

Year	Rate per Mile
1992	11.5 cents
1991	11 cents
1990	11 cents
1989	11 cents
1988	10.5 cents

EXAMPLE 26

T purchased his automobile in 1989 for $9,000. It is used 90% for business purposes. T drove the automobile for 10,000 business miles in 1991; 8,500 miles in 1990; and 6,000 miles in 1989. At the beginning of 1992, the basis of the business portion is $5,405.

Cost ($9,000 × 90%)	$8,100
Less depreciation:	
1991 (10,000 miles × 11 cents)	(1,100)
1990 (8,500 miles × 11 cents)	(935)
1989 (6,000 × 11 cents)	(660)
Adjusted business basis 1/1/92	$5,405

◆

- Use of the standard mileage rate in the first year the auto is placed in service is considered an election to exclude the auto from the ACRS method of depreciation (discussed in Chapter 9).
- A taxpayer may not switch to the automatic mileage method if the ACRS statutory percentage method or expensing under § 179 has been used.

TRAVEL EXPENSES

◆

Definition of Travel Expenses

An itemized deduction is allowed for unreimbursed travel expenses related to a taxpayer's employment, subject to the 2 percent floor. Travel expenses are more broadly defined in the Code than are transportation expenses. Travel expenses include transportation expenses and meals and lodging while away from home in the pursuit of a trade or business. Meals cannot be lavish or extravagant under the circumstances. Transportation expenses are deductible even though the taxpayer is not away from home. A deduction for travel expenses is available only if the taxpayer is away from his or her tax home. Travel expenses also include reasonable laundry and incidental expenses. To the extent that travel expenses are reimbursed, they are reported in the same manner discussed previously for employee expenses. The unreimbursed part is a miscellaneous itemized deduction subject to the 2 percent floor. Unreimbursed meals and entertainment expenses are subject to the 80 percent rule.

Away-from-Home Requirement

The crucial test for the deductibility of travel expenses is whether or not the employee is away from home overnight. "Overnight" need not be a 24-hour period, but it must be a period substantially longer than an ordinary day's work and must require rest, sleep, or a relief-from-work period.[36] A one-day or intracity business trip is not travel, and meals and lodging for such a trip are not deductible.

The employee must be away from home for a temporary period. If the taxpayer-employee is reassigned to a new post for an indefinite period of time, that new post becomes his or her tax home. *Temporary* indicates that the assignment's termination is expected within a reasonably short period of time. The position of the IRS is that the tax home is the business location, post, or station of the taxpayer. Thus, travel expenses are not deductible if a taxpayer is reassigned for an indefinite period and does not move his or her place of residence to the new location.

EXAMPLE 27

T's employer opened a branch office in San Diego. T was assigned to the new office for three months to train a new manager and to assist in setting up the new office. T tried commuting from his home in Los Angeles for a week and decided that he could not continue driving several hours a day. He rented an apartment in San Diego, where he lived during the week. He spent weekends with his wife and children at their home in Los Angeles. T's rent, meals, laundry, incidentals, and automobile expenses in San Diego are deductible. To the extent that T's transportation expense related to his weekend trips home exceed what his cost of meals and lodging would have been, the excess is personal and nondeductible. ◆

EXAMPLE 28

Assume that T in Example 27 was transferred to the new location to become the new manager permanently. T's wife and children continued to live in Los Angeles until the end of the school year. T is no longer "away from home" because the assignment is not temporary. T's travel expenses are not deductible. ◆

Determining the Tax Home. Under ordinary circumstances, there is no problem in determining the location of a taxpayer's tax home and whether or not the taxpayer is on a temporary work assignment away from that tax home. The tax home is the area in which the taxpayer derives his or her principal source of income or is based on the amount of time spent in each area when the taxpayer has more than one place of employment. Under other circumstances, however, this is a controversial problem that has found the IRS and various courts in conflict.[37] An example is the situation in which a construction worker cannot find work in the immediate area and takes work several hundred miles away, with the duration of that work uncertain.

---

36. *U.S. v. Correll*, 68–1 USTC ¶9101, 20 AFTR2d 5845, 88 S.Ct. 445 (USSC, 1967); Rev.Rul. 75–168, 1975–1 C.B. 58.

37. Rev.Rul. 73–529, 1973–2 C.B. 37.

The IRS has published criteria for determining whether a work assignment is temporary rather than permanent or indefinite.[38] In general, the IRS regards a work assignment of less than a year as temporary. A work assignment of more than two years is regarded as indefinite or permanent, regardless of the facts and circumstances. The nature of a work assignment expected to last between one and two years will be determined on the basis of the facts and circumstances of the specific case.

The following objective factors are to be used in determining whether the home that the taxpayer claims to be away from is the taxpayer's actual tax home:

- Whether the taxpayer has used the claimed home for lodging purposes while performing work in the vicinity immediately before the current job.
- Whether the taxpayer continues to maintain bona fide work contacts (such as job seeking, leave of absence, ongoing business) in the area during the alleged temporary employment.
- Whether the taxpayer's living expenses at the claimed home are duplicated because work requires the taxpayer to be away from home.
- Whether the taxpayer has a family member or members (marital or lineal only) currently residing at the claimed home or currently continues to use the claimed home frequently for the purposes of his or her own lodging.

Travel expenses are allowed if the taxpayer clearly demonstrates a realistic expectation as to the temporary nature of the job and satisfies all four of the above requirements. If the taxpayer clearly demonstrates the expectation that the job is of a temporary nature and satisfies two of the above requirements, the deductibility question will be decided on the basis of all the facts and circumstances of the case. If it is determined that the assignment is indefinite rather than temporary, no deduction will be allowed for the traveling expenses.

If an employee establishes a new home as the result of a work assignment or if there is no established tax home, living expenses are of a personal nature and are nondeductible.

EXAMPLE 29

H is employed as a long-haul truck driver. He stores his clothes and other belongings at his parents' home and stops there for periodic visits. The rest of the time, H is on the road, sleeping in his truck and in motels. His meals, lodging, laundry, and incidental expenses are not deductible because he has no tax home from which he can be absent.[39] ◆

Disallowed and Limited Travel Expenses

The possibility always exists that taxpayers will attempt to treat vacation or pleasure travel as deductible business travel. To prevent such practices, the law contains limitations for certain travel expenses.

Nonbusiness Conventions. One tactic taxpayers used in an attempt to deduct the cost of vacations was to attend a tax or financial seminar at a vacation resort. They then took the travel expenses as a deduction under § 212, which allows deductions related to the production of income or determination of taxes.

As a remedy, the law disallows all deductions related to attending a convention, seminar, or similar meeting unless the expenses are related to a

38. Rev.Rul. 83–82, 1983–1 C.B. 45.

39. *Moses Mitnick*, 13 T.C. 1 (1949).

trade or business of the taxpayer.[40] The restriction does not apply to trade or business conventions and seminars. For example, a CPA who is an employee of an accounting firm can deduct the expenses of attending a tax seminar. A stockbroker can deduct the cost of attending a convention concerning investments. A physician attending either the tax or the investment meeting can deduct nothing. If the lectures are videotaped, both the CPA and the stockbroker must attend convention sessions to view the videotaped materials along with other participants. This requirement does not disallow deductions for costs (other than travel, meals, and entertainment) of renting or using videotaped materials related to business.

EXAMPLE 30

A CPA is unable to attend a convention at which current developments in taxation are discussed. She paid $200 for videotapes of the lectures that she viewed at home later. The $200 is a miscellaneous itemized deduction (subject to the 2% floor) if the CPA is an employee. If she is self-employed, the $200 is a deduction *for* AGI. ◆

Luxury Water Travel. Limits are placed on the deductibility of travel by water.[41] The deduction is limited to twice the highest amount generally allowable for a day of travel for Federal employees serving in the United States.

EXAMPLE 31

During the taxable year, the highest Federal per diem rate is $136. T took a six-day trip from New York to London on the *Queen Mary II* to meet with customers. The maximum deduction related to the water travel is $1,632 [($136 × 2) × 6 days]. ◆

If the expenses of luxury water travel include separately stated amounts for meals or entertainment, those amounts must be reduced by 20 percent before the application of this per diem limitation. If the meals and entertainment are not separately stated (or otherwise clearly identifiable), the 20 percent reduction does not apply.

The per diem rule does not apply to any expense allocable to a convention, seminar, or other meeting held on any cruise ship. The deduction for such a meeting is limited to $2,000 per individual per year. This deduction is restricted to ships registered in the United States and sailing to ports of call located within the United States or its possessions (e.g., Puerto Rico).[42] Thus, a cruise on a ship of U.S. registry sailing to Bermuda would not qualify. A cruise on the same ship from Florida to Puerto Rico would qualify.

Educational Travel. No deduction is allowed for travel that by itself is deemed by the taxpayer to be educational.[43] This does not apply to a deduction claimed for travel that is necessary to engage in an activity that gives rise to a business deduction relating to education.

EXAMPLE 32

M, a German teacher, travels to Germany to maintain general familiarity with the language and culture. No travel expense deduction is allowed. ◆

---

40. § 274(h)(1).
41. § 274(m)(1).
42. §§ 274(h)(1) and (2). See § 274(h)(3)(B) for the definition of "cruise ship."
43. § 274(m)(2).

EXAMPLE 33

J, a scholar of French literature, travels to Paris to do specific library research that cannot be done elsewhere and to take courses that are offered only at the Sorbonne. The travel costs are deductible, assuming that the other requirements for deducting education expenses (discussed later in the chapter) are met. ◆

Combined Business and Pleasure Travel

To be deductible, travel expenses need not be incurred in the performance of specific job functions. Travel expenses incurred in attending a professional convention are deductible by an employee if attendance is connected with services as an employee. For example, an employee of a law firm could deduct travel expenses incurred in attending a meeting of the American Bar Association.

Travel deductions have been used in the past by persons who claimed a tax deduction for what was essentially a personal vacation. As a result, several provisions have been enacted to govern deductions associated with combined business and pleasure trips. If the business/pleasure trip is from one point in the United States to another point in the United States, the transportation expenses are deductible only if the trip is *primarily for business*.[44] If the trip is primarily for pleasure, no transportation expenses can be taken as a deduction.

EXAMPLE 34

J traveled from Seattle to New York primarily for business. She spent five days conducting business and three days sightseeing and attending shows. Her plane and taxi fare amounted to $560. Her meals amounted to $100 per day, and lodging and incidental expenses were $150 per day. She can deduct the transportation charges of $560, since the trip was primarily for business (five days of business versus three days of sightseeing). Meals are limited to $400 [5 days × ($100 × 80%)], and other expenses are limited to $750 (5 days × $150). All the travel expenses are miscellaneous itemized deductions subject to the 2% floor. ◆

EXAMPLE 35

Assume J goes to New York for a two-week vacation. While there, she spends several hours renewing acquaintances with people in her company's New York office. Her transportation expenses are not deductible. ◆

The incremental costs paid for travel of a taxpayer's relative cannot be deducted unless that person's presence has a bona fide business purpose. Incidental services performed by family members do not constitute a bona fide business purpose.

When the trip is *outside the United States,* special rules apply.[45] Transportation expenses must be allocated between business and personal unless the taxpayer is away from home for seven days or less or less than 25 percent of the time was for personal purposes. Also, no allocation is required if the taxpayer has no substantial control over arrangements for the trip or the desire for a vacation is not a major factor in taking the trip. If the trip is primarily for pleasure, no transportation charges are deductible. Days devoted to travel are considered as business days. Weekends, legal holidays, and intervening days are considered business days, provided that both preceding and succeeding days were business days.

EXAMPLE 36

K took a trip from New York to Japan primarily for business purposes. He was away from home from June 10 through June 19. He spent three days vacationing and seven

44. Reg. § 1.162–2(b)(1).

45. § 274(c) and Reg. § 1.274–4.

days conducting business (including two travel days). K's air fare was $2,500, his meals amounted to $100 per day, and lodging and incidental expenses were $160 per day. Since K was away from home for more than seven days and more than 25% of his time was devoted to personal purposes, only 70% (7 days business/10 days total) of the transportation is deductible. His deductions are as follows:

Transportation (70% × $2,500)		$1,750
Lodging ($160 × 7)		1,120
Meals ($100 × 7)	$700	
Less: 20%	(140)	560
Total		$3,430

◆

EXAMPLE 37

L, a fashion buyer for a large department store, travels to London primarily to view the spring collections. She is gone 10 days (including 2 days of travel). She spends 8 days (including travel time) engaged in business and 2 days sightseeing. Since less than 25% of the total time is spent vacationing, all her transportation expenses and all but 2 days of meals and lodging are deductible. ◆

Foreign Convention Expenses

Certain restrictions are imposed on the deductibility of expenses paid or incurred to attend conventions located outside the North American area. For this purpose, the North American area includes the United States, its possessions (including the Trust Territory of the Pacific Islands), Canada, and Mexico. The expenses will be disallowed unless it is established that the meeting is directly related to a trade or business of the taxpayer. Disallowance will also occur unless the taxpayer shows that it is as reasonable for the meeting to be held in a foreign location as within the North American area.

The foreign convention rules will not operate to bar a deduction to an employer if the expense is compensatory in nature. For example, a trip to Paris won by a top salesperson is included in the gross income of the employee and is fully deductible by the employer.

MOVING EXPENSES

Moving expenses are deductible for moves in connection with the commencement of work (either as an employee or as a self-employed individual) at a new principal place of work.[46] Reimbursement from employers must be included in gross income. Moving expenses are itemized deductions but *are not* subject to the 2 percent floor. Meals included as moving expenses *are* subject to the 80 percent rule. To be eligible for a moving expense deduction, a taxpayer must meet two basic tests: distance and time.

Distance Test

The distance test requires that the taxpayer's new job location must be at least 35 miles farther from the taxpayer's old residence than the old residence was from the former place of employment. In this regard, the location of the new residence is not relevant. This eliminates a moving deduction for taxpayers who purchase a new home in the same general area without changing their place of employment. Those who accept a new job in the same general area as the old job location are also eliminated.

46. § 217(a).

EXAMPLE 38

J is permanently transferred to a new job location. The distance from J's former home to his new job (80 miles) exceeds the distance from his former home to his old job (30 miles) by at least 35 miles. J has met the distance requirements for a moving expense deduction. (See the following diagram.)

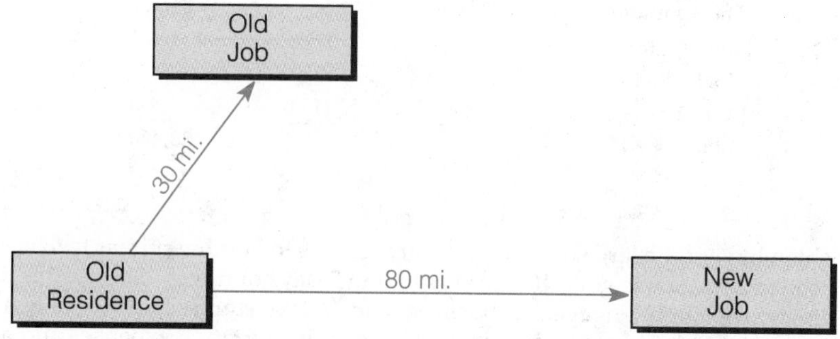

If J was not employed before the move, his new job must be at least 35 miles from his former residence. In this instance, the distance requirements would be met if J had not been previously employed. ◆

Time Requirements

To be eligible for a moving expense deduction, an employee must be employed on a full-time basis at the new location for 39 weeks in the 12-month period following the move. If the taxpayer is a self-employed individual, he or she must work in the new location for 78 weeks during the next two years. The first 39 weeks must be in the first 12 months. The taxpayer can work either as a self-employed individual or as an employee. The time requirement is suspended if the taxpayer dies, becomes disabled, or is discharged or transferred by the new employer through no fault of the employee.

A taxpayer might not be able to meet the 39-week requirement by the due date of the tax return (including extensions) for the year of the move. For this reason, two alternatives are allowed. The taxpayer can take the deduction in the year the expenses were incurred, even though the 39-week test has not been met. If the taxpayer later fails to meet the test, either the income of the following year must be increased by an amount equal to the deduction previously claimed for moving expenses, or an amended return must be filed for the year of the move. The second alternative is to wait until the test is met and then file an amended tax return for the year of the move.

When Deductible

The general rule is that expenses of a cash basis taxpayer are deductible only in the year of payment. However, a taxpayer who receives reimbursement from his or her employer may elect to deduct the moving expenses in the year of reimbursement in the following circumstances:

- The moving expenses are incurred and paid in 1992, and the reimbursement is received in 1993.
- The moving expenses are incurred in 1992 and are paid by the employee in 1993 (on or before the due date including extensions for filing the 1992 return), and the reimbursement from the employer is received in 1992.

The election to deduct moving expenses in the year of reimbursement is made by claiming the deduction on the return, or filing an amended return, for that year.

The moving expense deduction is allowed regardless of whether the employee is transferred by the existing employer or is employed by a new employer. Also, it is allowed if the employee moves to a new area and obtains employment or switches from self-employed status to employee status (and vice versa). In addition, the moving expense deduction is allowed if an individual is unemployed before obtaining employment in a new area.

Classification of Moving Expenses

There are five classes of moving expenses,[47] and different limitations and qualifications apply to each class.[48] Direct moving expenses include the following:

1. *The expense of moving household and personal belongings.* This class includes fees paid to a moving company for packing, storing, and moving possessions and the rental of a truck if the taxpayer moves his or her own belongings. Also included is the cost of moving household pets. Reasonableness is the only limit on these direct expenses. Such expenses as refitting rugs or draperies and losses on the disposal of club memberships are not deductible as moving expenses.
2. *Travel to the new residence.* This includes the cost of transportation, meals, and lodging of the taxpayer and the members of the taxpayer's household en route. It does not include the cost of moving servants or others who are not members of the household. The taxpayer can elect to take actual auto expenses (no depreciation is allowed) or the automatic mileage method. In this case, moving expense mileage is limited to nine cents per mile for each car. These expenses are also limited by the reasonableness standard. For example, if one moves from Texas to Florida via Maine and takes six weeks to do so, the transportation, meals, and lodging must be allocated between personal and moving expenses.

Indirect moving expenses include the following:

3. *House-hunting trips.* Expenses of traveling (including meals and lodging) to the new place of employment to look for a home are deductible only if the job has been secured in advance of the house-hunting trip. The dollar limitation is explained below.
4. *Temporary living expenses.* Meals and lodging expenses incurred while living in temporary quarters in the general area of the new job while waiting to move into a new residence are deductible. (The dollar limits are discussed below.) These living expenses are limited to any consecutive 30-day period beginning after employment is secured.
5. *Certain residential buying and selling expenses.* Buying and selling expenses include those that would normally be offset against the selling price of a home and those expenses incurred in buying a new home. Examples are commissions, escrow fees, legal expenses, points paid to secure a mortgage, transfer taxes, and advertising. Also deductible are costs involved in settling an old lease or acquiring a new lease or both. Fixing-up expenses, damage deposits, prepaid rent, and the like are not deductible.

---

47. § 217(b)(1)(A).

48. §§ 217(b)(1)(B), (C), (D), and (E).

Indirect moving expenses are limited to a total of $3,000. Furthermore, house-hunting and temporary living expenses may not exceed $1,500 in the aggregate. Direct moving expenses, as discussed previously, are unlimited.

Moving Expense Limits

Classes 1[49] + 2	=	No limit
Classes 3 + 4	=	$1,500 limit
Classes 3 + 4 + 5	=	$3,000 limit

Generally, the above dollar limitations apply regardless of filing status. If both spouses change jobs and file separate returns, the limitations are $750 (instead of $1,500) and $1,500 (instead of $3,000). If only one spouse makes a job change, the spouse who makes the change is allowed the full amount. If both change jobs, do not live together, and work at job sites at least 35 miles apart, each spouse applies the $1,500 and the $3,000 limits. It does not matter whether they file jointly or separately.

EXAMPLE 39

T, an employee of X Corporation, is hired by Y Corporation at a substantial increase in salary. T is hired in February 1992 and is to report for work in March 1992. The new job requires a move from Los Angeles to New York City. In connection with the move, T incurs the following expenses:

February 1992 house-hunting trip (no meals)	$ 650
Temporary living expenses in New York City incurred by T and family during March 10–30, 1992, while awaiting the renovation of their new apartment (including $400 of meals)	1,000
Penalty for breaking lease on Los Angeles apartment	2,400
Charge for packing and moving household goods	4,200
Transportation and lodging expenses during move (March 5–10)	700
Meal expense during move	300

T can deduct the following amount:

Moving household goods			$4,200
Transportation and lodging			700
Meals ($300 × 80%)			240
House-hunting trip	$ 650		
Temporary living expenses [$600 + ($400 cost of meals × 80%)]	920		
	$1,570		
Limited to		$1,500	
Lease penalty		2,400	
		$3,900	
Limited to			3,000
Total itemized moving expense deduction			$8,140

◆

49. The numbers refer to the types of moving expenses outlined on pages 10–21.

Form 3903 is used to report the detailed calculations of the ceiling limitations and change in job locations. If the employee is reimbursed for the move, the reimbursement is included in salary income.

EDUCATION EXPENSES
◆

General Requirements

An employee may deduct expenses incurred for education as ordinary and necessary business expenses provided the expenses were incurred for either of two reasons:

1. To maintain or improve existing skills required in the present job.
2. To meet the express requirements of the employer or the requirements imposed by law to retain his or her employment status.

Education expenses are not deductible if the education is for either of the following purposes:

1. To meet the minimum educational standards for qualification in the taxpayer's existing job.
2. To qualify the taxpayer for a new trade or business.[50]

Thus, fees incurred for professional qualification exams (the bar exam, for example) and fees for review courses (such as a CPA review course) are not deductible.[51] A deduction may be allowed for nonaccounting courses that also maintain and improve an accountant's existing skills in a present job.[52] If the education incidentally results in a promotion or raise, the deduction can still be taken as long as the education maintained and improved existing skills and did not qualify a person for a new trade or business. A change in duties is not always fatal to the deduction if the new duties involve the same general work. For example, the IRS has ruled that a practicing dentist's education expenses incurred to become an orthodontist are deductible.[53]

Requirements Imposed by Law or by the Employer for Retention of Employment

Teachers qualify under the provision that permits the deduction of education expenses if additional courses are required by the employer or are imposed by law. Many states require a minimum of a bachelor's degree and a specified number of additional courses to retain a teaching job. In addition, some public school systems have imposed a master's degree requirement and have required teachers to make satisfactory progress toward a master's degree in order to keep their positions. If the required education is the minimum degree required for the job, no deduction is allowed.

A taxpayer classified as an Accountant I who went back to school to obtain a bachelor's degree was not allowed to deduct the expenses. Although some courses tended to maintain and improve his existing skills in his entry-level position, the degree was the minimum requirement for his job.[54]

---

50. Reg. §§ 1.162–5(b)(2) and (3).
51. Reg. § 1.212–1(f) and Rev.Rul. 69–292, 1969–1 C.B. 84.
52. *Howard Sherman Cooper*, 38 TCM 955, T.C.Memo. 1979–241.
53. Rev.Rul. 74–78, 1974–1 C.B. 44.
54. Reg. § 1.162–5(b)(2)(iii) Example (2); *Collin J. Davidson*, 43 TCM 743, T.C.Memo. 1982–119.

Maintaining or Improving Existing Skills

The "maintaining or improving existing skills" requirement in the Code has been difficult for both taxpayers and the courts to interpret. For example, a business executive may be permitted to deduct the costs of obtaining an M.B.A. on the grounds that the advanced management education is undertaken to maintain and improve existing management skills. The executive would be eligible to deduct the costs of specialized, nondegree management courses that were taken for continuing education or to maintain or improve existing skills. If the business executive incurred the expenses to obtain a law degree, the expenses would not be deductible because they constitute training for a new trade or business. The Regulations deny the deduction by a self-employed accountant of expenses relating to law school.[55]

Classification of Specific Items

Education expenses include books, tuition, typing, and transportation (e.g., from the office to night school) and travel (e.g., meals and lodging while away from home at summer school).

EXAMPLE 40

T, who holds a bachelor of education degree, is a secondary education teacher in the Los Angeles, California, school system. The school board recently changed its minimum education requirement for new teachers by prescribing five years of college training instead of four. Under a grandfather clause, teachers who have only four years of college will continue to qualify if they show satisfactory progress toward a graduate degree. T enrolls at the University of California and takes three graduate courses. T's unreimbursed expenses for this purpose are as follows:

Books and tuition	$2,600
Lodging while in travel status (June–August)	1,150
Meals while in travel status	800
Laundry while in travel status	220
Transportation	600

T has a miscellaneous itemized deduction subject to the 2% floor as follows:

Books and tuition	$2,600
Lodging	1,150
Meals (80% of $800)	640
Laundry	220
Transportation	600
	$5,210

◆

ENTERTAINMENT EXPENSES

Many taxpayers attempt to deduct personal entertainment expenses as business expenses. For this reason, Code § 274 restricts the deductibility of entertainment expenses. The law contains strict recordkeeping requirements and provides restrictive tests for the deduction of certain types of entertainment expenses.

55. Reg. § 1.162–5(b)(3)(ii) Example (1).

Classification of Expenses

Entertainment expenses are categorized as follows: those *directly related* to business and those *associated with* business.[56] Directly related expenses are related to an actual business meeting or discussion. These expenses can be contrasted with entertainment expenses that are incurred to promote goodwill (e.g., to maintain existing customer relations). To obtain a deduction for directly related entertainment, it is not necessary to show that actual benefit resulted from the expenditure as long as there was a reasonable expectation of benefit. To qualify as directly related, the expense should be incurred in a clear business setting. If there is little possibility of engaging in the active conduct of a trade or business due to the nature of the social facility, it may be difficult to qualify the expenditure as directly related to business.

Expenses associated with, rather than directly related to, business entertainment must serve a specific business purpose, such as obtaining new business or continuing existing business. These expenditures qualify only if the expenses directly precede or follow a bona fide business discussion. Entertainment occurring on the same day as the business discussion meets the test.

Restrictions upon Deductibility

Business Meals. Any business meal is deductible only if the following are true:[57]

- The meal is directly related to or associated with the active conduct of a trade or business.
- The expense is not lavish or extravagant under the circumstances.
- The taxpayer (or an employee) is present at the meal.

A business meal with a business associate or customer is not deductible unless business is discussed before, during, or after the meal. This requirement is not intended to disallow the deduction for a meal consumed while away from home on business.

EXAMPLE 41

T travels to San Francisco for a business convention. She pays for dinner with three colleagues and is not reimbursed by her employer. They do not discuss business. She can deduct 80% of the cost of her meal. However, she cannot deduct the cost of her colleagues' meals. ◆

The *clear business purpose* test requires that meals be directly related to or associated with the active conduct of a business. A meal is not deductible if it serves no business purpose.

The taxpayer or an employee must be present at the business meal for the meal to be deductible.[58] An independent contractor who renders significant services to the taxpayer is treated as an employee.

EXAMPLE 42

T, a party to a contract negotiation, buys dinner for other parties to the negotiation but does not attend the dinner. No deduction is allowed. ◆

---

56. § 274(a)(1)(A).

57. § 274(k).

58. § 162(k)(3).

Entertainment Facilities. Deducting the cost of maintaining an entertainment facility (e.g., a hunting lodge, fishing camp, yacht, country club) lends itself to taxpayer manipulation, since such a facility could be used for personal vacations and entertainment. For this reason, the law allows a deduction only in limited situations and imposes stringent recordkeeping requirements.

To determine the deductibility of dues paid or incurred to maintain a club membership, a primary use test is imposed.[59] Unless the taxpayer can show that over 50 percent of the use of the facility was for business purposes, no deduction is permitted. In meeting the primary use test, the following rules govern:

- Consider only the days the facility is used. Thus, days of nonuse do not enter into the determination.
- A day of both business and personal use counts as a day of business use.
- Business use includes entertainment that is associated with or directly related to business.

Even if the primary use test is satisfied, only the portion of the dues attributable to the directly related entertainment qualifies for the deduction.

EXAMPLE 43

T, the sales manager of an insurance agency, is expected to incur entertainment expenses in connection with the sale of insurance. None of these expenses are reimbursed by his employer. During the year, T paid the following amounts to the Leesville Country Club:

Annual dues	$1,200
Meals relating to business use	900
Meals and other charges relating to personal use	400
Other charges relating to business use	200

T used the club 120 days for purposes directly related to business and 80 days for personal use. He did not use the club at all during the remaining days of the year. Since T used the facility for business more than 50% of the time (120 days out of 200 days), the primary use test is satisfied. The portion of the annual dues T can deduct is $720 (120/200 = 60% × $1,200). He is allowed a total deduction as follows:

Annual dues	$720
Business meals	900
Other business charges	200
Total	$1,820
Less 20%	(364)
Deductible	$1,456

Note that the $1,456 is a miscellaneous itemized deduction subject to the 2% floor. ◆

Ticket Purchases for Entertainment. A deduction for the cost of a ticket for an entertainment activity is limited to the face value of the ticket.[60] This limitation is applied before the 80 percent rule. The face value of a ticket includes any tax. Under this rule, the excess payment to a scalper for a ticket is not deductible. Similarly, the fee to a ticket agency for the purchase of a ticket is not deductible.

59. §§ 274(a)(2)(A) and (C).

60. § 274(i).

Expenditures for the rental or use of a luxury skybox at a sports arena in excess of the face value of regular tickets are disallowed as deductions. If a luxury skybox is used for entertainment that is directly related to or associated with business, the deduction is limited to the face value of nonluxury box seats. All seats in the luxury skybox are counted, even when some seats are unoccupied.

The taxpayer may also deduct stated charges for food and beverages under the general rules for business entertainment. The deduction for skybox seats, food, and beverages is limited to 80 percent of cost.

EXAMPLE 44

In the current year, AW, Inc., pays $6,000 to rent a 10-seat skybox at City Stadium for three football games. Nonluxury box seats at each event range in cost from $25 to $35 a seat. In March, an AW representative and five clients of AW use the skybox for the first game. The entertainment follows a bona fide business discussion, and AW spends $85 for food and beverages during the game. AW computes its deduction for the first sports event as follows:

Food and beverages	$ 85
Deduction for seats ($35 × 10 seats)	350
Total entertainment expense	$435
80% limitation	×.80
Deduction	$348

◆

Business Gifts. Business gifts are deductible to the extent of $25 per donee per year. An exception is made for gifts costing $4 or less (e.g., pens with the employee's or company's name on them) or promotional materials. Such items are not treated as business gifts subject to the $25 limitation. In addition, incidental costs such as engraving of jewelry and nominal charges for giftwrapping, mailing, and delivery are not included in the cost of the gift in applying the limitation. The $25 limitation applies to both direct and indirect gifts. A gift is indirect if it is made to a person's spouse or other family member or to a corporation or partnership on behalf of the individual. All such gifts must be aggregated in applying the $25 limit. Excluded from the $25 limit are gifts or awards to employees, such as for length of service, that are under $400.[61] Gifts to superiors and employers are not deductible.

It is necessary to maintain records substantiating the gifts.

OTHER EMPLOYEE EXPENSES

Office in the Home

Employees and self-employed individuals are not allowed a deduction for expenses of an office in the home unless a portion of the residence is used exclusively on a regular basis as either:

- The principal place of business for any trade or business of the taxpayer.
- A place of business used by clients, patients, or customers.

Employees must meet an additional test: The use must be for the convenience of the employer rather than merely being "appropriate and helpful."[62]

61. § 274(b)(1)(C). Section 274(b)(3)(C) allows a deduction for gifts to employees of up to $1,600 under a *qualified plan* as long as the average cost of all awards under the qualified plan does not exceed $400. Qualified plans are described in § 274(b)(3).

62. § 280A(c)(1).

The exclusive use requirement means that a specific part of the home must be used solely for business purposes. A deduction, if permitted, will require an allocation of total expenses of operating the home between business and personal use based on floor space or number of rooms.

Even if the taxpayer meets the above requirements, the allowable home office expenses may not exceed the gross income from the business less all other business expenses attributable to the activity. Furthermore, the home office expenses that must be deducted first are those that would be allowable as itemized deductions anyway (e.g., mortgage interest and real estate taxes). All home office expenses of an employee are miscellaneous itemized deductions subject to the 2 percent floor, except those (such as interest) that qualify as other personal itemized deductions. Home office expenses of a self-employed individual are trade or business expenses and are deductible *for* AGI.

Any disallowed home office expenses can be carried forward and used in future years subject to the same limitations.

EXAMPLE 45

T is a certified public accountant employed by a regional CPA firm as a tax manager. He operates a separate business in which he refinishes furniture in his home. For this business, he uses two rooms in the basement of his home exclusively and regularly. The floor space of the two rooms constitutes 10% of the floor space of his residence. Gross income from the business totals $8,000. Expenses of the business (other than home office expenses) are $6,500. T incurs the following home office expenses:

Real property taxes on residence	$4,000
Interest expense on residence	7,500
Operating expenses of residence	2,000
Depreciation on residence (based on 10% business use)	250

T's deductions are determined as follows:

Business income		$ 8,000
Less: Other business expenses		(6,500)
		$ 1,500
Less: Allocable taxes ($4,000 × 10%)	$400	
Allocable interest ($7,500 × 10%)	750	(1,150)
		$ 350
Allocable operating expenses of the residence ($2,000 × 10%)		(200)
		$ 150
Allocable depreciation ($250, limited to remaining income)		(150)
		$ -0-

T has a carryover of $100 (the unused excess depreciation). Because T is self-employed, the allocable taxes and interest ($1,150), the other deductible office expenses ($200 + $150), and $6,500 of other business expenses are deductible *for* AGI. ◆

Form 8829 (Expenses for Business Use of Your Home) is available from the IRS for computation of the office in the home deduction.

The home office limitation cannot be circumvented by leasing part of one's home to an employer, using it as a home office, and deducting the expenses as a rental expense under § 212.

Miscellaneous Employee Expenses

Some deductible miscellaneous employee expenses include special clothing and its upkeep, union dues, and professional expenses. Also deductible are professional dues, professional meetings, and employment agency fees for seeking employment in the same trade or business, whether or not a new job is secured. The employee reports these expenses in the same manner as other employee business expenses, discussed previously in the chapter.

To be deductible, special clothing must be both specifically required as a condition of employment and not generally adaptable for regular wear. For example, a police officer's uniform is not suitable for off-duty activities. An exception is clothing used to the extent that the clothing takes the place of regular clothing (e.g., military uniforms).

The current position of the IRS is that expenses incurred in seeking employment are deductible if the taxpayer is seeking employment in the same trade or business. The deduction is allowed whether or not the attempts to secure employment are successful. An unemployed taxpayer can take a deduction providing there has been no substantial lack of continuity between the last job and the search for a new one. No deduction is allowed for persons seeking their first job or seeking employment in a new trade or business (whether or not successful).

The basic cost of one telephone in the home is not deductible, even if used for business. Any long-distance or toll charges relating to business are deductible.

Contributions to Individual Retirement Accounts

An important and popular deduction *for* AGI is the amount contributed to an Individual Retirement Account (IRA). This amount may be as great as $2,000 per year for an individual (or $2,250 for spousal IRAs). IRAs are covered in detail in Chapter 19.

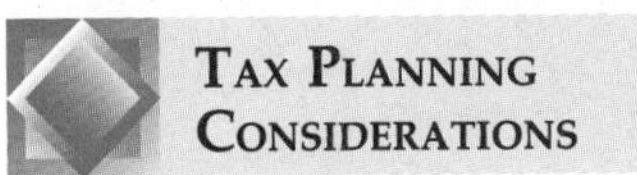

TAX PLANNING CONSIDERATIONS

Self-Employed Individuals

Some taxpayers have the flexibility to be classified as either employees or self-employed individuals (e.g., real estate agents or direct sellers). Such taxpayers should not automatically assume that the latter is better until all factors are considered.

It is advantageous to deduct one's business expenses *for* AGI and avoid the 2 percent floor. However, a self-employed individual may have higher expenses, such as local gross receipts taxes, license fees, franchise fees, personal property taxes, and occupation taxes. The recordkeeping and filing requirements can be quite burdensome.

One of the most expensive considerations is the Social Security tax versus the self-employment tax. For an employee in 1992, for example, the Social Security (old age, survivors, and disability insurance) tax applies at a rate of 6.2 percent on a base amount of wages of $55,500, and the Medicare (hospital insurance) tax applies at a rate of 1.45 percent on a base amount of $130,200. For self-employed persons, the rate, but not the base amount, for each tax doubles. Even though a deduction *for* AGI is allowed for one-half of the self-employment tax paid, an employee and a self-employed individual are not in the same tax position on equal amounts of earnings. The self-employment tax is explained in Chapter 13. For the applicability of these taxes to employees, see Chapter 1.

After analyzing all these factors, a taxpayer may decide that employee status is preferable to self-employed status.

Shifting Deductions between Employer and Employee

An employee can avoid the 2 percent floor for employee business expenses. Typically, an employee incurs travel and entertainment expenses in the course of employment. The corporation gets the deduction if it reimburses the employee, and the employee gets the deduction *for* AGI. An adequate accounting must be made, and excess reimbursements cannot be kept.

Transportation and Travel Expenses

Adequate detailed records should be kept of all transportation and travel expenses. Since the regular mileage allowance is 28 cents per mile, a new, expensive automobile used primarily for business may generate a higher expense based on actual cost. The election to expense part of the cost of the automobile under § 179, ACRS depreciation, insurance, repairs and maintenance, automobile club dues, and interest on the auto loan may result in automobile expenses greater than the automatic mileage allowance.

If a taxpayer wishes to sightsee or vacation on a business trip, it would be beneficial to schedule business on both a Friday and a Monday to turn the weekend into business days for allocation purposes. It is especially crucial to schedule appropriate business days when foreign travel is involved.

Unreimbursed Employee Business Expenses

The 2 percent floor for unreimbursed employee business expenses offers a tax planning opportunity for married couples. If one spouse has high miscellaneous expenses subject to the floor, it may be beneficial for the couple to file separate returns. If they file jointly, the 2 percent floor will be based on the incomes of both. Filing separately will lower the reduction to 2 percent of only one spouse's income.

Other provisions of the law should be considered, however. For example, filing separately could cost a couple losses of up to $25,000 from self-managed rental units under the passive activity loss rules (discussed in Chapter 7).

Another possibility is to negotiate a salary reduction with one's employer in exchange for the 100 percent reimbursement of employee expenses. The employee would be better off because the 2 percent floor would not apply. The employer would be better off because certain expense reimbursements are not subject to Social Security and other payroll taxes.

Moving Expenses

Reimbursements of moving expenses must be included in gross income, and certain moving expenses may not be deductible because of the ceiling limitations. As a result, an employee may be required to pay additional income tax because of an employment-related move. Some employers reimburse their employees for these additional taxes, which are estimated and included in the employee's reimbursement.

Persons who retire and move to a new location incur personal nondeductible moving expenses. However, if the retired person accepts a full-time job in the new location before moving, the moving expenses become deductible.

Education Expenses

Education expenses are treated as nondeductible personal items unless the individual is employed or is engaged in a trade or business. A temporary leave of absence for further education is one way to reasonably assure that the taxpayer is still qualified, even if a full-time student. It has been held that an individual could deduct education expenses even though he resigned from his job, returned to school full-time for two years, and accepted another job in the same field upon graduation. The Court held that the student had merely suspended active participation in his field.[63]

If the time period out of the field is too long, educational expense deductions will be disallowed. For example, a teacher who left the field for four years to raise her child and curtailed her employment searches and writing activities was denied a deduction. She was not actively engaged in the trade or business of being an educator.[64]

To secure the deduction, an individual should arrange his or her work situation to preserve employee or business status.

Entertainment Expenses

Proper documentation of expenditures is essential because of the strict record-keeping requirements and the restrictive tests that must be met. For example, credit card receipts and canceled checks as the sole source of documentation may be inadequate to substantiate the business purpose and business relationship.[65] Taxpayers should maintain detailed records of amounts, time, place, business purpose, and business relationships. A credit card receipt details the place, date, and amount of the expense. A notation made on the receipt of the names of the person(s) attending, the business relationship, and the topic of discussion should constitute proper documentation.

Associated with or goodwill entertainment is not deductible unless a business discussion is conducted immediately before or after the entertainment. Furthermore, a business purpose must exist for the entertainment. Taxpayers should arrange for a business discussion before or after such entertainment. They must provide documentation of the business purpose (e.g., to obtain new business from a prospective customer).

Since a 50 percent test is imposed for the deductibility of country club dues, it may be necessary to accelerate business use or reduce personal use of a club facility. The 50 percent test is made on a daily use basis, so the taxpayer should maintain detailed records to substantiate business versus personal use.

EXAMPLE 46

T confers with his CPA on December 5 and finds that he has used the country club 30 days for business and 33 days for personal use. On the advice of his CPA, T schedules four business lunches between December 5 and December 31 and refrains from using the club for personal purposes until January of the following year. Because of this action, T will meet the 50% test and will be permitted a deduction for a portion of the club dues. ◆

Unreimbursed meals and entertainment are subject to the 80 percent rule in addition to the 2 percent floor. Negotiating a salary reduction, as previously discussed under Unreimbursed Employee Business Expenses, is even more valuable to the taxpayer.

63. *Stephen G. Sherman*, 36 TCM 1191, T.C.Memo. 1977–301.

64. *Brian C. Mulherin*, 42 TCM 834, T.C.Memo. 1981–454; *George A. Baist*, 56 TCM 778, T.C.Memo. 1988–554.

65. *Kenneth W. Guenther*, 54 TCM 382, T.C.Memo. 1987–440.

PROBLEM MATERIALS

DISCUSSION QUESTIONS

1. What difference does it make if an individual's expenses are classified as employment-related expenses or as expenses from self-employment?
2. Discuss the factors that may indicate an employer-employee relationship. What is the definitive test?
3. What are the requirements for a real estate agent or a direct seller to be classified as a self-employed individual?
4. Why might a real estate agency prefer that its real estate agents be classified as self-employed persons rather than employees?
5. What is the advantage to being a "statutory employee" as opposed to a regular common law employee?
6. How does the tax treatment of meals and entertainment differ from the treatment of other employee business expenses? Does the treatment differ if the expenses are reimbursed?
7. What expenses are subject to the 80 percent rule? What are some exceptions?
8. What constitutes an adequate accounting to an employer?
9. What tax return reporting procedures must be followed by an employee under the following circumstances?
   - **a.** Expenses and reimbursements are equal under an accountable plan.
   - **b.** Reimbursements at the appropriate Federal per diem rate exceed expenses, and an adequate accounting is made to the employer.
   - **c.** Expenses exceed reimbursements under a nonaccountable plan.
10. What is a reasonable period of time for purposes of returning excess reimbursements?
11. Can an employee who receives a reimbursement of 15 cents per mile for job-related automobile expenses deduct any excess expense amounts on his or her tax return?
12. A taxpayer has two jobs. He drives 40 miles to his first job. The distance from the first job to the second is 32 miles. During the year, he worked 200 days at both jobs. On 150 days, he drove from his first job to the second job. On the remaining 50 days, he drove home (40 miles) and then to the second job (42 miles). How much can he deduct?
13. Distinguish between transportation expenses and travel expenses.
14. J incurred travel expenses while away from home on company business. These expenses were not reimbursed by his employer. Can J deduct the travel expenses? If so, where and how are they deducted?
15. T accepts a three-year work assignment in another city. Are the rental payments and meal expenses incurred because of that work assignment deductible as travel expenses?
16. Discuss the restrictions on nonbusiness conventions for tax purposes.
17. P took a cruise in the Hawaiian Islands on a ship of U.S. registry to attend a business-related seminar. The cost was $3,000. What, if anything, can she deduct?
18. Discuss the deductibility of travel related to educational activities.
19. J takes a combined business and pleasure trip to Hawaii. What portion of the expenses is deductible?
20. G took a combined business and pleasure trip to Europe. She traveled to London from New York on Friday, vacationed on Saturday and Sunday, conducted business on Monday, got snowed in at the airport on Tuesday, traveled to Paris on Wednesday, relaxed on Thursday (a legal holiday), conducted business on Friday,

went sightseeing on Saturday and Sunday, picked up business samples and papers on Monday, and flew back to New York on Tuesday. What portion of her air fare can she deduct?

21. What are the distance requirements for moving expenses?
22. What are a taxpayer's two alternatives if she moves in November and cannot meet the 39-week test by the due date for filing her tax return? Which alternative is financially preferable if she meets the test in the following year? If she does not meet the test?
23. Distinguish between direct moving expenses and indirect moving expenses. Why is it important to classify such items properly?
24. What difference does it make if a taxpayer is improving existing skills or acquiring new ones for the purpose of the education deduction? On what general tax principle is the justification for this rule based?
25. Discuss the difference between entertainment that is *directly related to* business and entertainment that is *associated with* business.
26. Discuss the requirements for the deductibility of business meals.
27. F asks your advice on December 1 regarding the tax deductibility of his country club dues. To date, F has used the club 40 days for purposes directly related to business use, 42 days for purposes associated with business use, and 84 days for personal use. During December, members of F's family have planned to use the facility 4 more days for personal parties. No business use is planned in December. What would you advise F to do?
28. What limits are imposed on the deduction of expenses for tickets purchased for business entertainment? How are such expenses treated on an employee's return if they are reimbursed? Not reimbursed?
29. To what extent may a taxpayer take a deduction for business gifts to a business associate? To an employee? To a superior?
30. How are deductible home office expenses treated for tax purposes? Is the deduction *for* or *from* AGI?

PROBLEMS

31. T incurred the following employee expenses:

Travel while away from home (including meals of $500)	$2,000
Transportation	1,000
Entertainment of customers	900
Professional dues	600
Telephone for business use	500

T's employer paid T $3,500 (not reported on Form W–2) to cover all of these expenses under an accountable plan. Calculate T's deductions *for* and *from* AGI. His AGI was $25,000.

32. P incurred the following expenses related to her employment as a chief executive officer:

Lodging while away from home	$2,800
Meals while away from home	1,200
Entertainment while away from home	2,000
Dues, subscriptions, and books	1,000
Transportation expenses	4,000

P's AGI was $100,000, and she received $6,600 under her employer's accountable plan. What are P's deductions *for* and *from* AGI?

33. K received $4,400 in reimbursements under an accountable plan after she had made an adequate accounting to her employer. Her expenses were as follows:

Transportation expenses	$3,200
Meals	1,400
Lodging and incidentals	2,300
Dues, phone, and subscriptions	100
Entertainment	1,000

How much can K deduct *for* and *from* AGI? Assume K had AGI of $50,000 and no other miscellaneous itemized deductions.

34. P, an executive with X Corporation, incurred the following employee business expenses:

Lodging	$2,000
Meals	1,600
Transportation	2,400
Entertainment	1,500
Phone	500

P received $5,600 under an accountable plan to cover the above expenses. He made an adequate accounting. In addition to incurring the above expenses, P incurred expenses in attending a seminar on communications for executives. He paid $500 for transportation, $100 for meals, and $300 for fees and books. He was not reimbursed.

P's salary was $50,000. He made a deductible contribution of $2,000 to his IRA. His only other income was interest of $800. He is 47 and single.

Calculate P's AGI and itemized employee expenses.

35. T, who is age 42 and single, earned a salary of $60,000. She had other income consisting of interest of $2,000, dividends of $1,600, and long-term capital gains of $4,000.

T loaned a friend $5,000 two years ago. In the current year, the friend died, leaving no assets. T will not receive any repayments on the loan. See Chapter 8 for treatment of nonbusiness bad debt. She incurred the following expenses during the year:

Transportation	$2,300
Meals	1,600
Dues and subscriptions	800
Entertainment of clients	300
Total	$5,000

T received reimbursements of $3,000 under an accountable plan. Calculate T's AGI and itemized employee business expenses.

36. In addition to air fare of $640 (first class), E incurred the following expenses on a recent trip. The trip was solely for business, and E was away from home overnight.

Room	$210
Meals	150
Taxis	60
Laundry	50
Entertainment	80

If the expenses are *not* reimbursed by E's employer, how much can E deduct? Is the deduction *for* or *from* AGI?

37. H, an investment counselor, attended a conference on the impact of the new tax law on investment choices. His unreimbursed expenses were as follows:

Air fare	$250
Lodging	500
Meals	300
Tuition and fees	400

a. How much can H deduct on his return? Are the expenses *for* or *from* AGI?
b. Would your answer differ if H were a self-employed physician?

38. J, an executive, traveled to England to confer with branch office officials of his company. Because an inner-ear birth defect prevents him from flying, he traveled to England on the *Queen Elizabeth II*. The journey, which took six days and cost $2,400, was sold as a package deal with no breakdown of costs. How much can J deduct in 1992, assuming the U.S. government per diem amount is $100? Would your answer differ if the cost were broken down between transportation ($1,000) and meals and entertainment ($1,400)?

39. D, a professor of French history, went to France during the year to research documents available only in France. His time on the trip was spent entirely on business. No vacation days were involved, and D kept adequate records. D received no reimbursements for the following carefully documented expenses:

Air fare and other transportation	$1,600
Hotels	1,200
Meals	900

a. What can D deduct in 1992 if he has AGI of $30,000 and no other miscellaneous itemized deductions? Are the deductions *for* or *from* AGI?
b. Would your answer differ if D had gone to France to soak up the culture and brush up on his French?

40. T is a single salesperson who earned $45,000 in 1992. Her employer gave her a $5,000 expense account intended to cover all her employee expenses. She incurred expenses of $3,000 for transportation; $2,000 for meals and entertainment; and $2,200 for dues, subscriptions, phone, and gifts (none of which exceeded $25).

She sold some stocks, realizing a $6,000 long-term capital gain. She had dividend income of $650 and earned interest of $900, of which $250 was on municipal bonds.

In November, she spent her vacation cruising the Hawaiian Islands on a ship of U.S. registry. Daily lectures and seminars on improving selling techniques were conducted. She can prove that the cruise, which cost her $3,500, was directly related to her job.

Calculate T's adjusted gross income and deductible itemized employee expenses.

41. M took a business trip from Chicago to Seattle. He spent two days in travel, conducted business for eight days, and visited friends for five days. He incurred the following expenses:

Air fare	$ 900
Lodging	2,100
Meals	1,500
Entertainment of clients	500

M received no reimbursements. What amount can M deduct?

42. N took a business trip of 10 days. Seven days were spent on business (including travel time) and 3 days were personal. His unreimbursed expenses were as follows:

Air fare	$3,000
Lodging (per day)	400
Meals (per day)	200
Entertainment of clients	600

a. How much can N deduct if the trip is within the United States?
b. How much can N deduct if the trip is outside the United States?

43. S traveled from New York to Helsinki primarily on business for his employer. He spent 16 days (including travel) on business and 4 days sightseeing. S's expenses were as follows:

Air fare	$3,600
Meals	2,250
Lodging	2,850
Incidental expenses	300

S was not reimbursed. How are these expenses reported assuming an AGI of $100,000?

44. T incurred the following expenses when she was transferred from San Francisco to Dallas:

Loss on the sale of old residence	$8,000
Moving company's charges	4,000
House-hunting trip	1,300
Temporary living expenses for 60 days (including meals of $1,000)	3,200
Broker's fees on residence sold	7,000
Charges for fitting drapes in new residence	1,500

a. How much can T deduct? Is the deduction *for* or *from* AGI?
b. What would be T's tax consequences if the employer reimbursed her for all of the expenses?

45. T was hired by a Los Angeles brokerage firm upon his graduation from college in Texas. His moving expenses were not reimbursed. How much can T deduct of the following expenses? Are the expenses *for* or *from* his AGI of $25,000?

Loss of apartment deposit because of damage done by cat	$ 200
Apartment-hunting trip to Los Angeles (including meals of $500)	1,600
Cost of shipping cat to Los Angeles	100
Payment to apartment-locating service	150
Expense of renting and driving a truck to Los Angeles to move household goods	2,600
Lodging in Los Angeles for two weeks after arrival (apartment was not ready)	750
Meals for two weeks after arrival	512

46. T belongs to a country club that he uses for both business and personal purposes. Assuming none of his expenses are reimbursed, how much can he deduct on his tax return in the following two cases?

Annual dues		$5,000
Meals *directly related to* business		400
Meals *associated with* business		300
Personal meals and charges		2,000
Case (a) Days directly related to business	110	
Days associated with business	30	
Days for personal use	150	
Case (b) Days directly related to business	70	
Days associated with business	80	
Days for personal use	75	

47. M is an executive with a large manufacturing firm. He is 54 and married and has two children. His compensation was $76,000. His wife is not employed.

M took a trip from New York to London primarily for business. He was away from home 12 days, spending 8 days conducting business and 4 days vacationing. He incurred transportation expenses of $3,000, lodging expenses of $200 per day, meals of $60 per day, and expenses while entertaining clients of $500.

M belongs to a country club that he uses for both personal and business entertainment. His records reveal that he used the facility 57 days for purposes directly related to business, 14 days for purposes associated with business, and 93 days for personal use during the year. Expenses are as follows:

Annual dues	$6,000
Business meals	1,800
Business entertainment	965
Personal meals and charges	3,100

M received $8,600 in dividends and $3,400 in interest during the year. He receives an annual allowance of $10,000 to cover all of his employment expenses.

Calculate M's adjusted gross income and his itemized employee business expenses.

48. D belongs to a country club that she uses for entertaining clients of her employer as well as for personal use. She incurred charges as follows:

Annual dues	$4,200
Business meals	3,000
Other business charges	700
Personal meals and charges	4,200

D kept careful records, which revealed the following use:

Days *associated with* business	60
Days *directly related to* business	50
Days for personal use	90

In addition, sixty of the personal use days occurred on the same days that the club was used for entertainment directly related to business.

a. How much can D deduct if she received no reimbursements?

b. Would your answer differ if she made an adequate accounting and received a $2,000 reimbursement under an accountable plan?

49. T is a single, 37-year-old executive who earned $60,000 in 1992. He also earned $2,000 in dividends and had interest of $1,800 credited to his savings account. An examination of T's records revealed the following:

- T incurred education expenses to maintain and improve his existing skills. Tuition and books cost $580, transportation expenses amounted to $960, and parking fines totaled $80.
- T paid $1,200 in country club dues and $920 for meals for clients. The club was used 200 days for business and 50 days for personal use.
- T took a business trip to London. He flew there on a Thursday, conducted business on Friday, went sightseeing on Saturday and Sunday, conducted business on Monday and Tuesday, and flew home on Wednesday. His unreimbursed expenses amounted to $2,100 for air fare, $500 for meals, and $1,400 for lodging.

Calculate T's adjusted gross income and his itemized employee deductions.

50. F, an executive of the ABC Corporation, owns 30% of the company's common stock. F incurred the following business expenses during the year:

Lodging	$2,100
Meals	1,200
Entertainment	980
Transportation	3,100

How should F treat these expenses on his 1992 income tax return, assuming that he was reimbursed in full under an accountable plan? How should he treat them if his firm did *not* have an accountable plan?

51. T is a professor who consults on the side. She uses one-fifth of her home exclusively for her consulting business, and clients regularly meet her there. T is single and under 65. Her AGI (before considering consulting income) is $40,000. Other relevant data follow:

Income from consulting business	$4,000
Consulting expenses other than home office	1,400
Total costs relating to home	
Interest and taxes	8,000
Utilities	1,400
Maintenance and repairs	900
Depreciation (business part only)	1,200

Calculate T's AGI for 1992.

52. J is an accountant with XYZ Company. He is also a self-employed tax consultant with several clients and earns $12,000 per year from his outside consulting. He has an office in his home that he uses exclusively for meeting with his consulting clients and for work he performs for his clients. Based on square footage, he estimates that total office expenses amount to $3,600, including $1,800 of taxes and interest on his home mortgage.

   a. Can J take a deduction for an office in the home? If so, how does he report it and how much can he deduct?
   b. If the office was also used for work J brought home from his regular job, how would your answer to (a) differ? Assume J used the office 80% for his consulting business and 20% for his regular job.

53. C is a self-employed wholesale jobber who had sales of $80,000 in 1992. He keeps meticulous business income and expense records.

   His business expenses included an office in his home, used exclusively for his business. Expenses allocated to the home office on the basis of square footage were as follows:

Taxes and interest	$1,300
Utilities and maintenance	620
Office depreciation	1,200
Office supplies	380
Office furniture depreciation	700

C incurred the following business expenses:

Transportation	$6,000
Business meals	1,400
Business entertainment	900
Telephone, dues, and books	1,500
Other business expenses	2,000

Assume that C's self-employment tax is $8,348. C received interest of $2,000 and dividends of $1,000 during the year. Calculate his AGI for 1992.

54. T and S are married and file a joint return. T is a manager and earned a salary and bonus of $51,000 in 1992. He incurred employee business expenses of $800 for transportation and $400 for meals and entertainment. He was fully reimbursed under an accountable plan. He took a combined business and pleasure trip to New York. He spent five days conducting business and three days sightseeing. His air fare and taxi expense amounted to $1,200, meals averaged $60 per day, and lodging was $80 per day. He was not reimbursed for this trip.

   S is a self-employed court reporter who works out of the home. One room is used regularly and exclusively for her business. She had receipts of $12,000 and incurred office expenses of $1,000 for depreciation, $300 for utilities, $150 for her business phone (a second line) and $500 for repairs and maintenance. She earned $200 in interest on her savings account and incurred other business expenses of $2,300. Assume that S's self-employment tax is $1,095. She made a payment of $2,000 to her IRA.

Calculate taxable income for T and S on a joint return, assuming all other itemized deductions totaled $5,100.

CUMULATIVE PROBLEMS

55. Sam Diamond is 38 and single with no dependents. His salary was $45,000, from which $4,900 was withheld for Federal income tax. The proper amount of FICA (Social Security) taxes and state income taxes of $1,600 were also withheld. Examination of his 1992 records revealed the following:

Sam had other receipts as follows:

Dividends on AT&T stock	$520
Interest credited to savings account	310
State income tax refund (he itemized in 1991)	220

Sam's other deductions were as follows:

Home mortgage interest	$8,600
Property taxes	890
Charitable contributions	720

Sam paid his former wife $2,400 for support of their child, Mary, who lives with her mother.

Sam received $5,000 in settlement of a damage claim resulting from a personal automobile accident.

He took a business trip during the year and was reimbursed $3,000 under a nonaccountable plan by his employer. His expenses were as follows:

Transportation	$1,700
Meals	320
Lodging and incidentals	680
	$2,700

He drove a total of 8,000 business miles and uses the standard mileage rate to compute his automobile expense.

Sam incurred the following unreimbursed employee business expenses:

Business meals	$500
Publications and dues	250
Phone and miscellaneous	60
Business entertainment	290
Tuition and books for course at local college to maintain existing skills	612

Compute Sam's Federal taxable income for 1992. Suggested software (if available): *TurboTax* for tax return or WFT tax planning software.

56. Robert T. Washington is 40 years old and divorced. He is a statutory employee for General Suppliers, Inc. His commissions and salary amounted to $104,000 in 1992. Robert lives in a state that has no state income tax. Examination of Robert's 1992 records revealed the following:

a. Robert paid his former wife Jean $12,000, of which $7,000 was alimony and $5,000 support for their daughter, Brenda, age 6. His ex-wife, who has custody of Brenda, can document that she spent $2,000 on her daughter's support. She has signed an agreement that Robert gets the exemption.

b. Robert received dividends from Acme Company of $1,000 and interest on his money market account at Citizen's Federal of $3,200. His favorite uncle gave him $10,000 as a Christmas gift, which he invested in municipal bonds that earned $75 interest in 1992.

c. Since General Suppliers, Inc., has no offices (only a warehouse), Robert works out of a home office that constitutes 20% of his home's floor space. His expenses in connection with his home were as follows:

Depreciation (on office space only)	$ 600
Property taxes	1,800
Interest on home mortgage	12,000
Cleaning, repairs, and maintenance	1,300
Utilities	2,600

His local business telephone service (second line in home) cost $300. His long-distance business calls totaled $800. His office furniture has been fully depreciated.

d. Robert belongs to a country club that he uses for business purposes. He used the club 80 days for purposes directly related to business and 120 days for personal use. His carefully kept records reveal that his dues amounted to $2,400, business-related meals were $1,560, and personal charges were $2,300.

e. Robert also had the following well-documented business expenses:

Magazines and dues	$160
Gifts to customers: (5 @ $50)	250
(10 @ $20)	200
Entertainment of customers	800
Cleaning and maintenance of business suits and silk ties	400

f. Business mileage on Robert's auto was 5,000 miles. Total mileage for the year on the car, which was placed in service on 1–1–87, was 30,000 miles.

g. Robert took a combined business and pleasure trip to San Francisco in June. He spent eight days conducting business and four days visiting museums. His air fare and taxi expense was $500; meals cost $50 per day; and lodging and incidentals amounted to $200 per day.

h. Other expenses included the following:

Contribution to United Negro College Fund	$1,000
Contribution to Methodist Church	1,200
Expenses of traveling to Olympia to speak to the Elks Club against proposed legislation regarding wholesalers	300
Personal doctor and dentist bills	2,600
Dentist bills for daughter	3,000
Tax preparation fee	350
Investment periodicals	50
Other itemized deductions	6,900

Compute Robert Washington's Federal taxable income for 1992. Suggested software (if available): *TurboTax* for tax return or WFT tax planning software.

57. George M. and Martha J. Jordan have no dependents and are both under age 65. George is a statutory employee of Consolidated Jobbers, and his Social Security number is 582–99–4444. Martha is an executive with General Corporation, and her Social Security number is 241–88–6642. The Jordans live at 321 Oak Street, Lincoln, NE 68024. They both want to contribute to the Presidential Election Campaign Fund.

In 1991, George earned $49,000 in commissions. His employer withholds FICA but not Federal income taxes. George paid $10,000 in estimated taxes. Martha earned $62,000, from which $10,508 was withheld for Federal income taxes. Neither George nor Martha received any expense reimbursements.

George uses his two-year-old car on sales calls and keeps a log of all miles driven. In 1991, he drove 36,000 miles, 25,000 of them for business. He made several out-of-state sales trips, incurring transportation costs of $1,600, meals of $800, and lodging costs of $750. He also spent $1,400 during the year taking customers to lunch.

Martha incurred the following expenses related to her work: taxi fares of $125, business lunches of $615, and a yearly commuter train ticket of $800. During the year, Martha received $1,200 in interest from the employees' credit union, $100,000 life insurance proceeds upon the death of her mother in December, and $500 in dividends from General Motors. She contributed $2,000 to her Individual Retirement Account. Neither George nor Martha is covered by an employee retirement plan. Martha gave a gift valued at $500 to the president of her firm upon his promotion to that position.

The Jordans had additional expenditures as follows:

Charitable contributions (cash)	$1,200
Medical and dental expenses	1,400
Real property taxes	1,200
Home mortgage interest	9,381
Charge account interest	193
Tax return preparation fee	150

Part 1—Tax Computation

Compute the Jordans' Federal income tax payable or refund due, assuming they file a joint income tax return for 1991. You will need Form 1040, Form 2106, and Schedules A, B, and C. Suggested software (if available): *TurboTax* for tax return or WFT tax planning software if tax return solutions are not desired.

Part 2—Tax Planning

Martha and George ask your help in deciding what to do with the $100,000 Martha inherited in 1991. They are considering three conservative investment alternatives:

- Invest in 8% long-term U.S. bonds.
- Invest in 7% Series EE bonds and elect to defer the interest earned.
- Invest in 6% municipal bonds.

a. Calculate the best alternative for next year. Assume that Martha and George will have the same income and deductions in 1992, except for the income from the investment they choose.

b. What other factors should the Jordans take into account?

Suggested software (if available): *TurboTax* for tax return or WFT tax planning software.

RESEARCH PROBLEMS

RESEARCH PROBLEM 1 T Corporation is in the business of supplying customers with temporary personnel, who work at customers' offices, receive their assignments by telephone, and rarely go into T Corporation's offices. Several times during the year, T rented a yacht for recreational cruises for its employees. No temporary employees were expressly excluded from taking the cruises. Very few of the temporary employees even learned of the cruises, however, because notices were posted in T's offices on a "first-come, first-served" basis. The IRS disallowed T's deduction for the cruises under § 274(e)(4), claiming that temporary employees were, in fact, excluded from the cruises. Is the IRS correct?

RESEARCH PROBLEM 2 T, a heart specialist, left his job in Texas to accept a position in a California medical center. In addition to seeing patients, he was required to work on the hospital's heart transplant project under the supervision of Dr. H. Dr. H was an impossible boss, who had already had two other doctors removed from the team. After 35 weeks of employment, Dr. H had T terminated from the project. Will T be able to deduct his moving expenses?

Research aid:
§ 217(c)(2).

RESEARCH PROBLEM 3 M and F are husband and wife. M owns a small company that manufactures business machines. Many of the machine parts are made in Japan. On average, M spends three months in Japan on business each year. In 1992, M and F took a 63-day trip to Japan to discuss a new contract. Fifteen days were spent vacationing. F did not participate in the business meetings. Can M deduct any of F's expenses? Must he allocate expenses between business and personal days?

Research aid:
§ 274(c)(2)(B).

RESEARCH PROBLEM 4 Taxpayer maintains a home office that he uses exclusively for business. He is an employee of the Ace Company, which provides him with an office, and has a consulting business on the side.

He used his home office 80% of the time in his consulting business and 20% of the time in connection with his job with Ace. Can he deduct his home office expenses?

Research aid:
§ 280A(c)(1).

CHAPTER

DEDUCTIONS AND LOSSES: CERTAIN ITEMIZED DEDUCTIONS

OBJECTIVES

Distinguish between deductible and nondeductible personal expenses.

Define medical expenses and compute the medical expense deduction.

Contrast deductible taxes and nondeductible fees, licenses, etc.

Discuss rules relating to the Federal tax treatment of state income taxes.

Determine whether various types of interest are deductible.

Define charitable contributions and discuss related measurement problems and percentage limitations.

Enumerate the business and personal expenditures that are deductible either as miscellaneous itemized deductions or as other itemized deductions.

Explain the new overall limitation on certain itemized deductions.

Identify tax planning procedures that can maximize the benefit of itemized deductions.

OUTLINE

General Classification of Expenses

Personal expenditures are specifically disallowed as deductions by § 262. In contrast, business expenses that are incurred in the production or expectation of profit are deductions from gross income in arriving at adjusted gross income (AGI) and are reported on Schedule C of Form 1040. Certain nonbusiness expenses are also deductible in arriving at AGI (e.g., expenses attributable to rents and royalties and forfeited interest on a time savings deposit).

This chapter is principally concerned with expenses that are essentially personal in nature but are deductible because of legislative grace (e.g., charitable contributions, medical expenses, and certain state and local taxes). If the Code does not specifically state that a personal type of expense is deductible, no deduction is permitted. Allowable personal expenses are deductible *from* AGI in arriving at taxable income if the taxpayer elects to itemize. The election is appropriate when the total of the itemized deductions exceeds the standard deduction[1] based on the taxpayer's filing status. At this point, it may be helpful to review the computation in the tax formula for individuals that appears in Chapters 1 and 3.

Medical Expenses

General Requirements

Medical expenses paid for the care of the taxpayer, spouse, and dependents are allowed as an itemized deduction to the extent the expenses are not reimbursed. The medical expense deduction is limited to the amount by which such expenses *exceed* 7.5 percent of the taxpayer's AGI.

Example 1

During 1992, T had medical expenses of $3,800. If T's AGI for the year is $40,000, the itemized deduction for medical expenses is limited to $800 [$3,800 − (7.5% × $40,000)]. ◆

Medical Expenses Defined

The term *medical care* includes expenditures incurred for the "diagnosis, cure, mitigation, treatment, or prevention of disease, or for the purpose of affecting any structure or function of the body."[2] A *partial* list of deductible and nondeductible medical items appears in Figure 11–1.

A medical expense does not have to relate to a particular ailment to be deductible. Since the definition of medical care is broad enough to cover preventive measures, the cost of periodic physical and dental exams qualifies even for a taxpayer in good health.

Under the Revenue Reconciliation Act of 1990, and effective for taxable years beginning after December 31, 1990, amounts paid for unnecessary *cosmetic surgery* are not deductible medical expenses.

Example 2

In 1992, T, a calendar year taxpayer, paid $11,000 to a plastic surgeon for a face lift. T, age 75, merely wanted to improve his appearance. The $11,000 does not qualify as a medical expense since the surgery was unnecessary. ◆

1. The total standard deduction is the sum of the basic standard deduction and the additional standard deduction (see Chapter 3). Chapter 3 also describes the situations in which a taxpayer is not eligible for the standard deduction.
2. § 213(d)(1)(A).

If cosmetic surgery is deemed necessary, it is deductible as a medical expense. Cosmetic surgery is necessary when it ameliorates (1) a deformity arising from a congenital abnormality, (2) a personal injury, or (3) a disfiguring disease.

EXAMPLE 3

As a result of a serious automobile accident, T's face is disfigured. The cost of restorative cosmetic surgery is deductible as a medical expense. ◆

The deductibility of *nursing home expenses* depends on the medical condition of the patient and the nature of the services rendered.[3] If an individual enters a home for the aged for personal or family considerations and not because he or she requires medical or nursing attention, deductions are allowed only for the costs attributable to the medical and nursing care.

EXAMPLE 4

T has a chronic heart ailment. His family decided to place T in a nursing home equipped to provide medical and nursing care facilities. Total nursing home expenses amount to $15,000 per year. Of this amount, $4,500 is directly attributable to medical and nursing care. Since T is in need of significant medical and nursing care and is placed in the facility primarily for this purpose, all $15,000 of the nursing home costs are deductible (subject to the 7.5% floor). ◆

EXAMPLE 5

Assume the same facts as in Example 4, except that T does not have a chronic heart ailment. T enters the nursing home because he and his family feel that all of them would be more comfortable with this arrangement. Under these circumstances, only $4,500 of the expenses is deductible because the move was primarily for personal considerations. ◆

Tuition expenses of a dependent at a special school may be deductible as a medical expense. The cost of medical care can include the expenses of a special school for a mentally or physically handicapped individual. The deduction is allowed if a principal reason for sending the individual to the school is the school's special resources for alleviating the infirmities. In this case, the

FIGURE 11–1
Illustration of Deductible and Nondeductible Medical Expenses

Deductible	Nondeductible
Medical (including dental, mental, and hospital) care	Funeral, burial, or cremation expenses
Prescription drugs	Nonprescription drugs (except insulin)
Special equipment	Bottled water
Wheelchairs	Toiletries, cosmetics
Crutches	Diaper service, maternity clothes
Artificial limbs	Programs for the *general* improvement of health
Eyeglasses (including contact lenses)	Weight reduction
Hearing aids	Health spas
Transportation for medical care	Stop-smoking clinics
Medical and hospital insurance premiums	Social activities (e.g., dancing and swimming lessons)
	Unnecessary cosmetic surgery

3. Reg. § 1.213–1(e)(1)(v).

cost of meals and lodging, in addition to the tuition, is a proper medical expense deduction.[4]

EXAMPLE 6

T's daughter D attended public school through the seventh grade. Because D was a poor student, she was examined by a psychiatrist who diagnosed an organic problem that created a learning disability. Upon the recommendation of the psychiatrist, D is enrolled in a private school so that she can receive individual attention. The school has no special program for students with learning disabilities and does not provide special medical treatment. The expense related to D's attendance is not deductible as a medical expense. The cost of any psychiatric care, however, qualifies as a medical expense. ◆

Example 6 shows that the recommendation of a physician does not make the expenditure automatically deductible.

Capital Expenditures for Medical Purposes

Some examples of capital expenditures for medical purposes are swimming pools if the taxpayer does not have access to a neighborhood pool and air conditioners if they do not become permanent improvements (e.g., window units).[5] Other examples include dust elimination systems,[6] elevators,[7] and a room built to house an iron lung. These expenditures are medical in nature if they are incurred as a medical necessity upon the advice of a physician, the facility is used primarily by the patient alone, and the expense is reasonable.

Capital expenditures normally are adjustments to basis and are not deductible. However, both a capital expenditure for a permanent improvement and expenditures made for the operation or maintenance of the improvement may qualify as medical expenses. If a capital expenditure qualifies as a medical expense, the allowable cost is deductible in the year incurred. The tax law makes no provision for depreciating medical expenses as it does for other capital expenditures.

A capital improvement that ordinarily would not have a medical purpose qualifies as a medical expense if it is directly related to prescribed medical care and is deductible to the extent that the expenditure *exceeds* the increase in value of the related property. Appraisal costs related to capital improvements are also deductible, but not as medical expenses. These costs are expenses incurred in the determination of the taxpayer's tax liability.[8]

EXAMPLE 7

T is advised by his physician to install an elevator in his residence so that T's wife, who is afflicted with heart disease, will not be required to climb the stairs. The cost of installing the elevator is $3,000, and the increase in the value of the residence is determined to be only $1,700. Therefore, $1,300 ($3,000 − $1,700) is deductible as a medical expense. Additional utility costs to operate the elevator and maintenance costs are deductible as medical expenses as long as the medical reason for the capital expenditure continues to exist. ◆

To enable a physically handicapped individual to live independently and productively, the full cost of certain home-related capital expenditures incurred

4. *Donald R. Pfeifer*, 37 TCM 816, T.C.Memo. 1978–189. Also see Rev.Rul. 78–340, 1978–2 C.B. 124.
5. Rev.Rul. 55–261, 1955–1 C.B. 307, modified by Rev.Rul. 68–212, 1968–1 C.B. 91.
6. *F. S. Delp*, 30 T.C. 1230 (1958).
7. *Riach v. Frank*, 62–1 USTC ¶9419, 9 AFTR2d 1263, 302 F.2d 374 (CA–9, 1962).
8. § 212(3).

qualifies as a medical expense. These expenditures are subject to the 7.5 percent floor only, and the increase in the home's value is deemed to be zero. Qualifying costs include expenditures for constructing entrance and exit ramps to the residence, widening hallways and doorways to accommodate wheelchairs, installing support bars and railings in bathrooms and other rooms, and adjusting electrical outlets and fixtures.[9]

Transportation and Lodging Expenses for Medical Treatment

Payments for transportation to and from a point of treatment for medical care are deductible as medical expenses (subject to the 7.5 percent floor). Transportation expenses for medical care include bus, taxi, train, or plane fare, charges for ambulance service, and out-of-pocket expenses for the use of an automobile. A mileage allowance of nine cents per mile[10] may be used instead of actual out-of-pocket automobile expenses. Whether the taxpayer chooses to claim out-of-pocket automobile expenses or the nine cents per mile automatic mileage option, related parking fees and tolls can also be deducted.

A deduction is also allowed for the transportation expenses of a parent who must accompany a child who is receiving medical care or for a nurse or other person giving medical assistance to a person who is traveling to get medical care and cannot travel alone.

A deduction is allowed for lodging while away from home for medical expenses if the following requirements are met:[11]

- The lodging is primarily for and essential to medical care.
- Medical care is provided by a doctor in a licensed hospital or a similar medical facility (e.g., a clinic).
- The lodging is not lavish or extravagant under the circumstances.
- There is no significant element of personal pleasure, recreation, or vacation in the travel away from home.

The deduction for lodging expenses included as medical expenses cannot exceed $50 *per* night for *each* person. The deduction is allowed not only for the patient but also for a person who must travel with the patient (e.g., a parent traveling with a child who is receiving medical care).

EXAMPLE 8

T, a resident of Winchester, Kentucky, is advised by his family physician that M, T's dependent and disabled mother, needs specialized treatment for her heart condition. Consequently, T and M fly to Cleveland, Ohio, where M receives the therapy at a heart clinic on an out-patient basis. Expenses in connection with the trip are as follows:

Round trip airfare ($250 each)	$500
Lodging in Cleveland for two nights ($60 each per night)	240

T's medical expense deduction for transportation is $500, and his medical expense deduction for lodging is $200 ($50 per night per person). Because M is disabled, it is assumed that T's accompaniment of her is justified. ◆

9. For a complete list of the items that qualify, see Rev.Rul. 87–106, 1987–2 C.B. 67.

10. Rev.Proc. 85–49, 1985–2 C.B. 716.

11. § 213(d)(2).

No deduction is allowed for the cost of meals unless they are part of the medical care and are furnished at a medical facility.

Amounts Paid for Medical Insurance Premiums

Medical insurance premiums are included with other medical expenses subject to the 7.5 percent floor. If amounts are paid under an insurance contract to cover loss of life, limb, sight, etc., no amount can be deducted unless the coverage for medical care is separately stated in the contract.

Medical insurance premiums paid by the taxpayer under a group plan or an individual plan are included as medical expenses. If an employer pays all or part of the taxpayer's medical insurance premiums, the amount paid by the employer is not included in gross income by the employee. Likewise, the premium is not included in the employee's medical expenses.

If a taxpayer is *self-employed,* special rules apply regarding medical insurance premiums. Up to 25 percent of the premiums paid for medical insurance coverage is deductible as a business expense (*for* AGI). Any excess can be claimed as a medical expense. For this special treatment to apply, the following conditions must be satisfied:

- The taxpayer must not be covered under a medical plan of an employer or of a spouse's employer.
- The plan must meet certain nondiscrimination rules.

The business deduction cannot exceed the net profit from the self-employment activity. [12]

EXAMPLE 9

For the calendar year 1992, T was a self-employed real estate broker with no employees. He had $45,000 net profit from real estate transactions and paid $4,000 in medical insurance premiums. T may deduct $1,000 (25% × $4,000) of the premiums as a business expense. The net profit limitation does not apply in this case because the business deduction for medical insurance premiums ($1,000) does not exceed T's net profit of $45,000 for the tax year. ◆

This provision applies through June 30, 1992.

Medical Expenses Incurred for Spouse and Dependents

In computing the medical expense deduction, a taxpayer may include medical expenses for a spouse and for a person who was a dependent at the time the expenses were paid or incurred. In determining dependency status for medical expense deduction purposes, neither the gross income nor the joint return tests (see Chapter 3) apply.

EXAMPLE 10

T (age 22) is married and a full-time student at a university. During 1992, T incurred medical expenses that were paid by M (T's mother). M provided more than half of T's support for the year. Even if T files a joint return with his wife, M may claim the medical expenses she paid for T. M would combine T's expenses with her own in applying the 7.5% floor. ◆

12. § 162(l).

Medical expenses paid on behalf of a former spouse are deductible if the parties were married when the expenditures were incurred. Also, medical expenses can be incorporated in the divorce decree and consequently may be deductible as alimony payments (*for* AGI).[13]

For divorced persons with children, a special rule applies to the noncustodial parent. The noncustodial parent may claim any medical expenses he or she pays even though the custodial parent claims the children as dependents. This rule applies if the dependency exemptions could have been shifted to the noncustodial parent by the custodial parent's waiver (refer to Chapter 3).

Example 11

F and M are divorced in 1991, and M is awarded custody of their child C. During 1992, F makes the following payments to M: $3,600 for child support and $2,500 for C's medical bills. Together, F and M provide more than one-half of C's support. Even though M claims C as a dependent, F can combine the medical expenses that he pays for C with his own. ◆

Year of Deduction

Regardless of a taxpayer's method of accounting, medical expenses are deductible only in the year *paid*. In effect, this places all individual taxpayers on a cash basis as far as the medical expense deduction is concerned. One exception, however, is allowed for deceased taxpayers. If the medical expenses are paid within one year from the day following the day of death, they can be treated as being paid at the time they were *incurred*.[14] Thus, such expenses may be reported on the final income tax return of the decedent or on earlier returns if incurred before the year of death.

No current deduction is allowed for payment of medical care to be rendered in the future unless the taxpayer is under an obligation to make the payment.[15] Whether an obligation to make the payment exists depends upon the policy of the physician or the institution furnishing the medical care.

Example 12

Upon the recommendation of his regular dentist, in late December 1992 T consults Dr. D, a prosthodontist, who specializes in crown and bridge work. Dr. D tells T that he can do the restorative work for $12,000. To cover his lab bill, however, Dr. D requires that 40% of this amount be prepaid. Accordingly, T pays Dr. D $4,800 in December 1992. The balance of $7,200 is paid when the work is completed in July 1993. Under these circumstances, the qualifying medical expenses are $4,800 for 1992 and $7,200 in 1993. The result would be the same even if T prepaid the full $12,000 in 1992. ◆

The IRS does allow a deduction for the portion of a lump-sum prepayment allocable to medical care made to a retirement home under a life care plan.[16]

Reimbursements

If medical expenses are reimbursed in the same year as paid, no problem arises. The reimbursement merely reduces the amount that would otherwise qualify for the medical expense deduction. But what happens if the reimbursement is received in a later year than the expenditure? Unlike casualty losses where

13. This assumes the requirements of § 215 are met.

14. § 213(c).

15. *Robert S. Basset*, 26 T.C. 619 (1956).

16. Rev.Rul. 75–302, 1975–2 C.B. 86.

reasonable prospect of recovery must be considered (refer to Chapter 8), the expected reimbursement is disregarded in measuring the amount of the deduction. Instead, the reimbursement is accounted for separately in the year in which it occurs.

As a general rule, when a taxpayer receives an insurance reimbursement for medical expenses deducted in a previous year, the reimbursement must be included in gross income in the year of receipt. However, taxpayers are not required to report more than the amount previously deducted as medical expenses. Thus, a taxpayer who did not itemize deductions in the year the expenses were incurred is not required to include a reimbursement in gross income.

The tax benefit rule applies to reimbursements if the taxpayer itemized deductions in the previous year. In this case, the taxpayer may be required to report some or all of the medical expense reimbursement in income in the year the reimbursement is received. Under the tax benefit rule, the taxpayer must include the reimbursement in income up to the amount of the deductions that decreased income tax in the earlier year.

EXAMPLE 13

T has AGI of $20,000 for 1991. He was injured in a car accident and paid $1,300 for hospital expenses and $700 for doctor bills. T also incurred medical expenses of $600 for his dependent child. In 1992, T was reimbursed $650 by his insurance company for his car accident. His deduction for medical expenses in 1991 is computed as follows:

Hospitalization	$1,300
Bills for doctor's services	700
Medical expenses for dependent	600
Total	$2,600
Less: 7.5% of $20,000	(1,500)
Medical expense deduction (assuming T itemizes his deductions)	$1,100

Assume that T would have elected to itemize his deductions even if he had no medical expenses in 1991. If the reimbursement for medical care had occurred in 1991, the medical expense deduction would have been only $450 [$2,600 (total medical expenses) − $650 (reimbursement) − $1,500 (floor)], and T would have paid more income tax.

Since the reimbursement was made in a subsequent year, T would include $650 in gross income for 1992. If T had not itemized in 1991, he would not include the $650 reimbursement in 1992 gross income because he would have received no tax benefit in 1991. ◆

TAXES

Section 164 permits the deduction of certain state and local taxes paid or accrued by a taxpayer. The deduction was created to relieve the burden of multiple taxes upon the same source of revenue.

Deductibility as a Tax

A distinction must be made between a tax and a fee, since fees are not deductible unless incurred as an ordinary and necessary business expense or as an expense in the production of income.

The IRS has defined a tax as follows:

> A tax is an enforced contribution exacted pursuant to legislative authority in the exercise of taxing power, and imposed and collected for the purpose of raising

> revenue to be used for public or governmental purposes, and not as payment for some special privilege granted or service rendered. Taxes are, therefore, distinguished from various other contributions and charges imposed for particular purposes under particular powers or functions of the government. In view of such distinctions, the question whether a particular contribution or charge is to be regarded as a tax depends upon its real nature.[17]

In accordance with this definition, fees for dog licenses, automobile inspection, automobile titles and registration, hunting and fishing licenses, bridge and highway tolls, drivers' licenses, parking meter deposits, postage, etc., are not deductible. These items, however, could be deductible if incurred as a business expense or for the production of income. Deductible and nondeductible taxes are summarized in Figure 11–2.[18]

Property Taxes, Assessments, and Apportionment of Taxes

Property Taxes. State, local, and foreign taxes on real property are generally deductible only by the person upon whom the tax is imposed. Cash basis taxpayers may deduct these taxes in the year of actual payment, and accrual basis taxpayers may deduct them in the year that fixes the right to deductibility.

Deductible personal property taxes must be *ad valorem* (assessed in relation to the value of the property). Therefore, a motor vehicle tax based on weight, model, year, and horsepower is not an ad valorem tax. However, a tax based on value and other criteria may qualify in part.

EXAMPLE 14

State X imposes a motor vehicle registration tax on 4% of the value of the vehicle plus 40 cents per hundredweight. B, a resident of the state, owns a car having a value of $4,000 and weighing 3,000 pounds. B pays an annual registration fee of $172. Of this amount, $160 (4% of $4,000) is deductible as a personal property tax. The remaining $12, based on the weight of the car, is not deductible. ◆

Assessments for Local Benefits. As a general rule, real property taxes do not include taxes assessed for local benefits since such assessments tend to increase

FIGURE 11–2
Deductible and Nondeductible Taxes

Deductible	Nondeductible
State, local, and foreign real property taxes	Federal income taxes
State and local personal property taxes	FICA taxes imposed on employees
State, local, and foreign income taxes	Employer FICA taxes paid on domestic household workers
The environmental tax	Estate, inheritance, and gift taxes
	General sales taxes
	Federal, state, and local excise taxes (e.g., gasoline, tobacco, spirits)
	Foreign income taxes if the taxpayer chooses the foreign tax credit option
	Taxes on real property to the extent such taxes are to be apportioned and treated as imposed on another taxpayer

17. Rev.Rul. 57–345, 1957–2 C.B. 132, and Rev.Rul. 70–622, 1970–2 C.B. 41.

18. Most deductible taxes are contained in § 164, while the nondeductible items are included in § 275.

the value of the property (e.g., special assessments for streets, sidewalks, curbing, and other similar improvements). A taxpayer cannot deduct the cost of a new sidewalk (relative to a personal residence), even though the construction was required by the city and the sidewalk may have provided an incidental benefit to the public welfare.[19] Such assessments are added to the adjusted basis of the taxpayer's property.

Assessments for local benefits are deductible as a tax if they are made for maintenance or repair or for meeting interest charges with respect to the benefits. In such cases, the burden is on the taxpayer to show the allocation of the amounts assessed for the different purposes. If the allocation cannot be made, none of the amount paid is deductible.

Apportionment of Real Property Taxes between Seller and Purchaser. Real estate taxes for the entire year are apportioned between the buyer and seller on the basis of the number of days the property was held by each during the real property tax year. This apportionment is required without regard to whether the tax is paid by the buyer or the seller or is prorated pursuant to the purchase agreement. The rationale for apportioning the taxes between the buyer and seller is based on the administrative convenience of the IRS in determining who is entitled to deduct the real estate taxes in the year of sale. In making the apportionment, the assessment date and the lien date are disregarded.

EXAMPLE 15

The real property tax year in County R is April 1 to March 31. S, the owner on April 1, 1992, of real property located in County R, sells the real property to B on June 30, 1992. B owns the real property from June 30, 1992, through March 31, 1993. The tax for the real property tax year April 1, 1992, through March 31, 1993, is $730. The portion of the real property tax treated as imposed upon S, the seller, is $180 (90/365 × $730, April 1 through June 29, 1992), and $550 (275/365 × $730, June 30, 1992 through March 31, 1993) of the tax is treated as imposed upon B, the purchaser. Note that the allocable part of the real estate tax year applicable to the seller ends on the day before the sale, and the date of sale is included in the part of the year applicable to the purchaser. ◆

If the actual real estate taxes are not prorated between the buyer and seller as part of the purchase agreement, adjustments are required. The adjustments are necessary to determine the amount realized by the seller and the adjusted basis of the property to the buyer. If the buyer pays the entire amount of the tax, he or she has, in effect, paid the seller's portion of the real estate tax and has therefore paid more for the property than the actual purchase price. Thus, the amount of real estate tax that is apportioned to the seller (for Federal income tax purposes) and paid by the buyer is added to the buyer's adjusted basis. The seller must increase the amount realized on the sale by the same amount.

EXAMPLE 16

S sells real estate on October 3, 1992, for $50,000. The buyer, B, pays the real estate taxes of $1,095 for the calendar year, which is the real estate property tax year. Of the real estate taxes, $826 is apportioned to and is deductible by the seller, S, and $269 of the taxes is deductible by B. The buyer has, in effect, paid S's real estate taxes of $826 and has therefore paid $50,826 for the property. B's basis is increased to $50,826, and the amount realized by S from the sale is increased to $50,826. ◆

19. *Erie H. Rose*, 31 TCM 142, T.C.Memo. 1972–39; Reg. § 1.164–4(a).

The opposite result occurs if the seller (rather than the buyer) pays the real estate taxes. In this case, the seller reduces the amount realized from the sale by the amount that has been apportioned to the buyer. The buyer is required to reduce his or her adjusted basis by a corresponding amount.

EXAMPLE 17

S sells real estate to B for $50,000 on October 3, 1992. While S held the property, he paid the real estate taxes of $1,095 for the calendar year, which is the real estate property tax year. Although S paid the entire $1,095 of real estate taxes, $269 of that amount is apportioned to B and is therefore deductible by B. The effect is that the buyer, B, has paid only $49,731 for the property. The amount realized by S, the seller, is reduced by $269, and B reduces his basis in the property to $49,731. ◆

Income Taxes

The position of the IRS is that state and local income taxes imposed upon an individual are deductible only as itemized deductions (deduction *from*) even if the taxpayer's sole source of income is from a business, rents, or royalties.

Cash basis taxpayers are entitled to deduct state income taxes withheld by the employer in the year such amounts are withheld. In addition, estimated state income tax payments are deductible in the year the payment is made by cash basis taxpayers even if the payments relate to a prior or subsequent year.[20] If the taxpayer overpays state income taxes because of excessive withholdings or estimated tax payments, the refund that is received is included in gross income of the following year to the extent that the deduction reduced the tax liability in the prior year.

EXAMPLE 18

T, a cash basis, unmarried taxpayer, had $800 of state income tax withheld during 1992. Additionally in 1992, T paid $100 that was due when she filed her 1991 state income tax return and made estimated payments of $300 on her 1992 state income tax. When T files her 1992 Federal income tax return in April 1993, she elects to itemize deductions, which amount to $5,500, including the $1,200 of state income tax payments and withholdings, all of which reduce her tax liability.

As a result of overpaying her 1992 state income tax, T receives a refund of $200 early in 1993. This amount will be included in T's 1993 gross income in computing her Federal income tax. It will not matter whether T received a check from the state for $200 or applied the $200 toward her 1993 state income tax. ◆

INTEREST

A deduction for interest has been allowed since the income tax law was enacted in 1913. Despite its long history of congressional acceptance, the interest deduction continues to be one of the most controversial areas in the tax law.

The controversy has centered around the propriety of allowing the deduction of interest charges for the purchase of consumer goods and services and interest on borrowings used to acquire investments (investment interest). TRA of 1986 effectively put an end to this controversy by phasing out the deduction for personal interest and further limiting the deduction for investment interest after 1990. Even when interest is allowed as a deduction, limits are imposed on the deductibility of prepaid interest. In addition, no deduction is permitted for interest on debt incurred to purchase or carry tax-exempt securities.

20. Rev.Rul. 71–190, 1971–1 C.B. 70. See also Rev.Rul. 82–208, 1982–2 C.B. 58, where a deduction is not allowed when the taxpayer cannot, in good faith, reasonably determine that there is additional state income tax liability.

Disallowed and Allowed Items

The Supreme Court has defined *interest* as compensation for the use or forbearance of money.[21] The general rule permits a deduction for all interest paid or accrued within the taxable year on indebtedness.[22] This rule is modified by other Code provisions that disallow or restrict certain interest deductions.

Personal (Consumer) Interest. *Personal interest* is any interest allowable as a deduction, with some exceptions as follows:

- Trade or business interest.
- Investment interest.
- Interest on passive activities.
- Home mortgage interest to a limited extent if it is qualified residence interest.

For this purpose, trade or business interest does not include interest on indebtedness to finance employee business expenses (e.g., interest on a loan to purchase an automobile used 80 percent for business). Such interest is personal interest. Personal, or consumer, interest also includes finance charges on department store and bank credit card purchases and on gasoline credit cards.[23] The term also includes late payment charges on utility bills[24] as well as interest on income tax deficiencies and assessments.

Beginning in 1991, personal interest is no longer deductible. The phase-out of the deduction took place over a five-year period.

Investment Interest. Taxpayers frequently borrow funds that they use to acquire investment assets. When the interest expense is large relative to the income from the investments, substantial tax benefits could result. Congress has therefore placed limitations on the deductibility of interest when funds are borrowed for the purpose of purchasing or continuing to hold investment property. Investment interest expense is *now* limited to net investment income for the year.[25]

Investment income is gross income from interest, dividends, annuities, and royalties not derived in the ordinary course of a trade or business. It also includes net gain attributable to the disposition of property producing the types of income just enumerated or held for investment. Income from a passive activity and income from a real estate activity in which the taxpayer actively participates are not included in investment income.

Net investment income is the excess of investment income over investment expenses. Investment expenses are those deductible expenses directly connected with the production of investment income. Investment expenses *do not* include interest expense. When investment expenses fall into the category of miscellaneous itemized deductions that are subject to the 2 percent of AGI floor, some may not enter into the calculation of net investment income because of the floor.

EXAMPLE 19

T has AGI of $80,000, which includes dividends and interest income of $18,000. Besides investment interest expense, she paid $3,000 of city ad valorem property tax on stocks and bonds and had the following miscellaneous itemized expenses:

21. *Old Colony Railroad Co. v. Comm.*, 3 USTC ¶880, 10 AFTR 786, 52 S.Ct. 211 (USSC, 1932).
22. § 163(a).
23. Rev.Rul. 73–136, 1973–1 C.B. 68.
24. Rev.Rul. 74–187, 1974–1 C.B. 48.
25. § 163(d).

Safe deposit box rental (to hold investment securities)	$ 120
Investment counsel fee	1,200
Unreimbursed business travel	850
Uniforms	600

Before T can determine her investment expenses for purposes of calculating net investment income, those miscellaneous expenses that are not investment expenses are disallowed before any investment expenses are disallowed under the 2% of AGI floor. This is accomplished by selecting the *lesser* of the following:

1. The amount of investment expenses included in the total of miscellaneous itemized deductions subject to the 2% of AGI floor.
2. The amount of miscellaneous expenses deductible after the 2% of AGI rule is applied.

The amount under item 1 is $1,320 [$120 (safe deposit box rental) + $1,200 (investment counsel fee)]. The item 2 amount is $1,170 [$2,770 (total of miscellaneous expenses) − $1,600 (2% of $80,000 AGI)].

Then, T's investment expenses are calculated as follows:

Deductible miscellaneous deductions investment expense (the lesser of item 1 or item 2)	$1,170
Plus: Ad valorem tax on investment property	3,000
Total investment expenses	$4,170

T's net investment income is $13,830 ($18,000 investment income − $4,170 investment expenses). ◆

After net investment income is determined, deductible investment interest expense can be calculated. Investment interest expense does not include the following:

- Qualified residence interest (see below).
- Interest taken into account in computing income or loss from a passive activity (see Chapter 7).
- Interest that is otherwise nondeductible (e.g., interest on amounts borrowed to purchase or carry tax-exempt securities).

EXAMPLE 20

For 1992, T is a single person employed by a law firm. His investment activities for the year are as follows:

Net investment income	$30,000
Investment interest expense	44,000

T's investment interest deduction for 1992 is $30,000. ◆

The amount of investment interest disallowed is carried over to future years. In Example 20, therefore, the amount that is carried over to 1993 is $14,000 ($44,000 investment interest expense − $30,000 allowed). No limit is placed on the carryover period.

The investment interest expense deduction is determined by completing Form 4952.

Qualified Residence Interest. As previously stated, personal interest does not include qualified residence interest (interest on a home mortgage). *Qualified* *residence interest* is interest paid or accrued during the taxable year on indebtedness (subject to limitations) *secured* by any property that is a qualified residence of the taxpayer. Qualified residence interest falls into two categories: interest on acquisition indebtedness and interest on home equity loans. Before discussing each of these categories, however, the term qualified residence must be defined.

A *qualified residence* means the taxpayer's principal residence and one other residence of the taxpayer or spouse. The *principal residence* is one that meets the requirement for nonrecognition of gain upon sale under § 1034 (see Chapter 15). The *one other residence*, or second residence, refers to one that is used as a residence if not rented or, if rented, meets the requirements for a personal residence under the rental of vacation home rules (refer to Chapter 6). A taxpayer who has more than one second residence can make the selection each year of which one is the qualified second residence. A residence includes, in addition to a house in the ordinary sense, cooperative apartments, condominiums, and mobile homes and boats that have living quarters (sleeping accommodations and toilet and cooking facilities).

Although in most cases interest paid on a home mortgage would be fully deductible, there are limitations.[26] If the indebtedness is acquisition indebtedness, interest paid or accrued during the tax year on aggregate indebtedness of $1,000,000 ($500,000 for married persons filing separate returns) or less is qualified residence interest. *Acquisition indebtedness* refers to amounts incurred in acquiring, constructing, or substantially improving a qualified residence of the taxpayer.

Any indebtedness incurred on or before October 13, 1987, and secured by a qualified residence at all times thereafter is treated as acquisition indebtedness and is not subject to the $1,000,000 limitation (but does reduce the $1,000,000 limitation).

Qualified residence interest also includes interest on *home equity* loans. These loans utilize the personal residence of the taxpayer as security. Since tracing rules do not apply to home equity loans, the funds from these loans can be used for personal purposes (e.g., auto purchases, medical expenses). By making use of home equity loans, therefore, what would have been nondeductible consumer interest becomes deductible qualified residence interest.

However, interest is deductible only on the portion of a home equity loan that does not exceed the *lesser of*:

- The fair market value of the residence, reduced by the acquisition indebtedness, *or*
- $100,000 ($50,000 for married persons filing separate returns).

EXAMPLE 21

T owns a personal residence with a fair market value of $150,000 and an outstanding first mortgage of $120,000. T issues a lien on the residence and in return borrows $15,000 to purchase a new family automobile. All interest on the $135,000 of debt is treated as qualified residence interest. ◆

EXAMPLE 22

H and W, married taxpayers, took out a mortgage on their home for $200,000 in 1982. In March 1992, when the home had a fair market value of $400,000 and they owed $195,000 on the mortgage, H and W took out a home equity loan for $120,000. They used the funds to purchase a boat to be used for recreational purposes. For 1992 on a joint return, H and W can deduct all of the interest on the first mortgage since it is

26. § 163(h)(3).

acquisition indebtedness. Of the $120,000 home equity loan, only the interest on the first $100,000 is deductible. The interest on the remaining $20,000 is not deductible because it exceeds the statutory ceiling of $100,000. ◆

Any interest paid on a mortgage secured by a third or more residences or paid on indebtedness that exceeds the allowable amounts is deductible according to the use of the proceeds. If the proceeds are used for personal purposes, the interest is nondeductible; if used for business, the interest is fully deductible. Interest on such proceeds used for investment purposes or in passive activities is subject to the limitations applicable to those activities.

Interest Paid for Services. It is common practice in the mortgage loan business to charge a fee for finding, placing, or processing a mortgage loan. Such fees are often called *points* and are expressed as a percentage of the loan amount. In periods of tight money, a borrower may have to pay points to obtain the necessary financing. To qualify as deductible interest, the points must be considered compensation to a lender solely for the use or forbearance of money. The points cannot be a form of service charge or payment for specific services if they are to qualify as deductible interest.[27]

Points are required to be capitalized and are amortized and deductible ratably over the life of the loan. A special exception permits the purchaser of a personal residence to deduct qualifying points in the year of payment.[28] The exception also covers points paid to obtain funds for home improvements. However, points paid to refinance an existing home mortgage cannot be immediately expensed but must be capitalized and amortized as interest expense over the life of the new loan.[29]

EXAMPLE 23

During 1992, T purchased a new residence for $130,000 and paid points of $2,600 to obtain mortgage financing. At T's election, the $2,600 can be claimed as an interest deduction for tax year 1992. ◆

EXAMPLE 24

R purchased her residence four years ago, obtaining a 30-year mortgage at an annual interest rate of 12%. In 1992, R refinances the mortgage in order to reduce the interest rate to 9%. To obtain the refinancing, she had to pay points of $2,600. The $2,600 paid comes under the usual rule applicable to points. The $2,600 must be capitalized and amortized over the life of the mortgage. ◆

Points paid by the seller are not deductible because the debt on which they are paid is not the debt of the seller. Points paid by the seller are treated as a reduction of the selling price of the property.

Prepayment Penalty. When a mortgage or loan is paid off in full in a lump sum before its term (early), the lending institution may require an additional payment of a certain percentage applied to the unpaid amount at the time of prepayment. This is known as a prepayment penalty and is considered to be interest (e.g., personal, qualified residence, investment) in the year paid.

Related Parties. Nothing prevents the deduction of interest paid to a related party as long as the payment actually took place and the interest meets the

27. Rev.Rul. 67–297, 1967–2 C.B. 87.

28. § 461(g)(2).

29. Rev.Rul. 87–22, 1987–1 C.B. 146.

requirements for deductibility. Recall from Chapter 6 that a special rule for related taxpayers applies when the debtor uses the accrual basis and the related creditor is on the cash basis. If this rule is applicable, interest that has been accrued but not paid at the end of the debtor's tax year is not deductible until payment is made and the income is reportable by the cash basis recipient.

Tax-Exempt Securities. The tax law provides that no deduction is allowed for interest on debt incurred to purchase or carry tax-exempt securities.[30] A major problem for the courts has been to determine what is meant by the words *to purchase or carry.* Refer to Chapter 6 for a detailed discussion of these issues.

Restrictions on Deductibility and Timing Considerations

Taxpayer's Obligation. Allowed interest is deductible if the related debt represents a bona fide obligation for which the taxpayer is liable.[31] Thus, a taxpayer may not deduct interest paid on behalf of another individual. For interest to be deductible, both the debtor and creditor must intend for the loan to be repaid. Intent of the parties can be especially crucial between related parties such as a shareholder and a closely held corporation. A shareholder may not deduct interest paid by the corporation on his or her behalf.[32] Likewise, a husband may not deduct interest paid on his wife's property if he files a separate return, except in the case of qualified residence interest. If both husband and wife consent in writing, either the husband or the wife may deduct the allowed interest on the principal residence and one other residence.

Time of Deduction. Generally, interest must be paid to secure a deduction unless the taxpayer uses the accrual method of accounting. Under the accrual method, interest is deductible ratably over the life of the loan.

EXAMPLE 25

On November 1, 1992, T borrows $1,000 to purchase appliances for a rental house. The loan is payable in 90 days at 12% interest. On the due date in January 1993, T pays the $1,000 note and interest amounting to $30. T can deduct the accrued portion (2/3 × $30 = $20) of the interest in 1992 only if he is an accrual basis taxpayer. Otherwise, the entire amount of interest ($30) is deductible in 1993. ◆

Prepaid Interest. Accrual method reporting is imposed on cash basis taxpayers for interest prepayments that extend beyond the end of the taxable year.[33] Such payments must be allocated to the tax years to which the interest payments relate. These provisions are intended to prevent cash basis taxpayers from *manufacturing* tax deductions before the end of the year by entering into prepayment of interest agreements. As previously noted, an exception allows immediate expensing of points paid to obtain funds to purchase or improve a personal residence.

Classification of Interest Expense

Whether interest is deductible *for* AGI or as an itemized deduction *(from)* depends on whether the indebtedness has a business, investment, or personal purpose. If the indebtedness is incurred in relation to a business (other than performing services as an employee) or for the production of rent or royalty

30. § 265(a)(2).

31. *Arcade Realty Co.*, 35 T.C. 256 (1960).

32. *Continental Trust Co.*, 7 B.T.A. 539 (1927).

33. § 461(g)(1).

income, the interest is deductible *for* AGI. However, if the indebtedness is incurred for personal use, such as consumer interest or qualified residence interest, any deduction allowed is reported on Schedule A of Form 1040 if the taxpayer elects to itemize. If the taxpayer is an employee who incurs debt in relation to his or her employment, the interest is considered to be personal, or consumer, interest. Business expenses appear on Schedule C of Form 1040, and expenses related to rents or royalties are reported on Schedule E.

If a taxpayer deposits money in a certificate of deposit (CD) that has a term of one year or less and the interest cannot be withdrawn without penalty, the full amount of the interest must still be included in income even though part of the interest is forfeited due to an early withdrawal. However, the taxpayer will be allowed a deduction *for* AGI for the forfeited amount.

For classification purposes, the IRS has issued complex tracing rules[34] to establish the use to which borrowed funds are put.

Interest on amounts borrowed in excess of $50,000 in total on life insurance policies covering the life of a self-employed taxpayer or an officer or employee of a corporation is nondeductible. This result occurs even though the borrowed funds are used in a trade or business.

CHARITABLE CONTRIBUTIONS

Section 170 permits individuals and corporations to deduct contributions made to qualified domestic organizations. Contributions to qualified charitable organizations serve certain social welfare needs and therefore relieve the government of the cost of providing these needed services to the community.

The charitable contribution provisions are among the most complex in the tax law. To determine the amount deductible as a charitable contribution, several important questions must be answered:

- What constitutes a charitable contribution?
- Was the contribution made to a qualified organization?
- When is the contribution deductible?
- What recordkeeping and reporting requirements apply to charitable contributions?
- How is the value of donated property determined?
- What special rules apply to contributions of property that has increased in value?
- What percentage limitations apply to the charitable contribution deduction?

These questions are addressed in the sections that follow.

Criteria for a Gift

Section 170(c) defines a *charitable contribution* as a gift made to a qualified organization. The major elements needed to qualify a contribution as a gift are a donative intent, the absence of consideration, and acceptance by the donee. Consequently, the taxpayer has the burden of establishing that the transfer was made from motives of *disinterested generosity* as established by the courts.[35] This test is quite subjective and has led to problems of interpretation.

Benefit Received Rule. When a donor derives a tangible benefit from a contribution, he or she cannot deduct the value of the benefit.

---

34. Reg. § 1.163–8T.

35. *Comm. v. Duberstein*, 60–2 USTC ¶9515, 5 AFTR2d 1626, 80 S.Ct. 1190 (USSC, 1960).

EXAMPLE 26

R purchases a ticket at $100 for a special performance of the local symphony (a qualified charity). If the price of a ticket to a symphony concert is normally $15, R is allowed only $85 as a charitable contribution. ◆

An exception to this benefit rule provides for the deduction of an automatic percentage of the amount paid for the right to purchase athletic tickets from colleges and universities.[36] Under this exception, 80 percent of the amount paid to or for the benefit of the institution qualifies as a charitable contribution deduction.

EXAMPLE 27

T donates $500 to State University's athletic department. The payment guarantees that T will have preferred seating on the 50-yard line. Subsequently, T buys four $35 game tickets. Under the exception to the benefit rule, however, T is allowed a $400 (80% of $500) charitable contribution deduction for the taxable year.

If, however, T's $500 donation includes four $35 tickets, that portion [$140 ($35 × 4)] and the remaining portion of $360 ($500 − $140) are treated as separate amounts. Thus, T is allowed a charitable contribution deduction of $288 (80% of $360). ◆

Contribution of Services. No deduction is allowed for a contribution of one's services to a qualified charitable organization. However, unreimbursed expenses related to the services rendered may be deductible. For example, the cost of a uniform (without general utility) that is required to be worn while performing services may be deductible, as are certain out-of-pocket transportation costs incurred for the benefit of the charity. In lieu of these out-of-pocket costs for an automobile, a standard mileage rate of 12 cents per mile is allowed.[37] Deductions are permitted for transportation, reasonable expenses for lodging, and 80 percent of the cost of meals while away from home incurred in performance of the donated services. The travel may not involve a significant element of personal pleasure, recreation, or vacation.[38]

EXAMPLE 28

M, a delegate representing her church in Miami, Florida, travels to a two-day national meeting in Denver, Colorado, in February. After the meeting, M spends two weeks at a nearby ski resort. Under these circumstances, none of the transportation, meals, or lodging is deductible since the travel involved a significant element of personal pleasure, recreation, or vacation. ◆

Nondeductible Items. In addition to the benefit received rule and the restrictions placed on contribution of services, the following items may not be deducted as charitable contributions:

- Dues, fees, or bills paid to country clubs, lodges, fraternal orders, or similar groups.
- Cost of raffle, bingo, or lottery tickets.
- Cost of tuition.
- Value of blood given to a blood bank.
- Donations to homeowners associations.

36. § 170(m).
37. § 170(j).
38. § 170(k).

- Gifts to individuals.
- Rental value of property used by a qualified charity.

Qualified Organizations

To be deductible, a contribution must be made to one of the following organizations:[39]

- A state or possession of the United States or any subdivisions thereof.
- A corporation, trust, or community chest, fund, or foundation that is situated in the United States and is organized and operated exclusively for religious, charitable, scientific, literary, or educational purposes or for the prevention of cruelty to children or animals.
- A veterans' organization.
- A fraternal organization operating under the lodge system.
- A cemetery company.

The IRS publishes a list of organizations that have applied for and received tax-exempt status under § 501 of the Code.[40] This publication is updated frequently and may be helpful in determining if a gift has been made to a qualifying charitable organization.

Because gifts made to needy individuals are not deductible, a deduction will not be permitted if a gift is received by a donee in an individual capacity rather than as a representative of a qualifying organization.

Time of Deduction

A charitable contribution generally is deducted in the year the payment is made. This rule applies to both cash and accrual basis individuals. An accrual basis corporation, however, is permitted a deduction in the year of accrual if the board of directors authorizes the payment during the taxable year and the contribution is made within two and one-half months after the close of the taxable year. The special exception for accrual basis corporations is illustrated in Example 6 in Chapter 20.

A contribution is ordinarily deemed to have been made on the delivery of the property to the donee. For example, if a gift of securities (properly endorsed) is made to a qualified charitable organization, the gift is considered complete on the day of delivery or mailing. However, if the donor delivers the certificate to his or her bank or broker or to the issuing corporation, the gift is considered complete on the date the stock is transferred on the books of the corporation.

A contribution made by check is considered delivered on the date of mailing. Thus, a check mailed on December 31, 1992, is deductible on the taxpayer's 1992 tax return. If the contribution is charged on a bank credit card, the date the charge is made determines the year of deduction. For a pay-by-phone account, the date shown on the statement issued by the financial institution is the date of payment.

---

39. § 170(c).

40. Although this *Cumulative List of Organizations,* IRS Publication 78 (available by purchase from the Superintendent of Documents, U.S. Government Printing Office, Washington, DC 20402), may be helpful, qualified organizations are not required to be listed. Not all organizations that qualify are listed in this publication (e.g., American Red Cross, University of Cleveland).

Recordkeeping and Valuation Requirements

Recordkeeping Requirements. Cash contributions must be substantiated by one of the following:[41]

- A canceled check.
- A receipt, letter, or other written communication from the charitable organization (showing the name of the organization, the date, and the amount of the contribution).
- Other reliable written records (contemporaneous records or other evidence, such as buttons and tokens, given to contributors by the donee organization).

The records required for noncash contributions vary depending on the amount of the contribution. If the value of the contribution is $500 or less, it must be evidenced by a receipt from the charitable organization. The receipt must show the following:

- The name of the charitable organization.
- The date and location of the charitable contribution.
- A reasonably detailed description of the contributed property.

Generally, charitable organizations do not attest to the fair market value of the donated property. Nevertheless, the taxpayer must maintain reliable written evidence of the following information concerning the donation:

- The fair market value of the property and how that value was determined.
- The amount of the reduction in the value of the property (if required) for certain appreciated property and how that reduction was determined.
- Terms of any agreement with the charitable organization dealing with the use of the property and potential sale or other disposition of the property by the organization.
- A signed copy of the appraisal if the value of the property was determined by appraisal. Only for a contribution of art with an aggregate value of $20,000 or more must the appraisal be attached to the taxpayer's return.

Additional information is required if the value of the donated property is over $500 but not over $5,000. Also, the taxpayer must file Section A of Form 8283 (Noncash Charitable Contributions) for such contributions.

For noncash contributions with a claimed value in excess of $5,000 ($10,000 in the case of nonpublicly traded stock), the taxpayer must obtain a qualified appraisal and must file Section B of Form 8283. This schedule must show a summary of the appraisal and must be attached to the taxpayer's return. Failure to comply with these reporting rules may result in disallowance of the charitable contribution deduction. Additionally, significant overvaluation exposes the taxpayer to rather stringent penalties.

Valuation Requirements. Property donated to a charity is generally valued at fair market value at the time the gift is made. The Code and Regulations give very little guidance on the measurement of the fair market value except to say, "The fair market value is the price at which the property would change hands between a willing buyer and a willing seller, neither being under any compulsion to buy or sell and both having reasonable knowledge of relevant facts."

---

41. *Your Federal Income Tax*, IRS Publication 17 (1991), p. 138.

Limitations on Charitable Contribution Deduction

In General. The potential charitable contribution deduction is the total of all donations, both money and property, that qualify for the deduction. After this determination is made, the actual amount of the charitable contribution deduction that is allowed for individuals for the tax year is limited as follows:

- If the qualifying contributions for the year total 20 percent or less of AGI, they are fully deductible.
- If the qualifying contributions are more than 20 percent of AGI, the deductible amount may be limited to either 20 percent, 30 percent, or 50 percent of AGI, depending on the type of property given and the type of organization to which the donation is made.
- In any case, the maximum charitable contribution deduction may not exceed 50 percent of AGI for the tax year.

To understand the complex rules for computing the amount of a charitable contribution, it is necessary to understand the distinction between capital gain property and ordinary income property. In addition, it is necessary to understand when the 50 percent, 30 percent, and 20 percent limitations apply. If a taxpayer's contributions for the year exceed the applicable percentage limitations, the excess contributions may be carried forward and deducted during a five-year carryover period. These topics are discussed in the sections that follow.

Corporations are subject to an overall limitation of 10 percent of taxable income computed without regard to the contributions made and certain other adjustments. The rules applicable to contributions by corporations are discussed in detail in Chapter 20.

Ordinary Income Property. *Ordinary income property* is any property that, if sold, will result in the recognition of ordinary income. The term includes inventory for sale in the taxpayer's trade or business, a work of art created by the donor, and a manuscript prepared by the donor. It also includes, for purposes of the charitable contribution calculation, a capital asset held by the donor for less than the required holding period for long-term capital gain treatment. Property that results in the recognition of ordinary income due to the recapture of depreciation is ordinary income property.[42]

If ordinary income property is contributed, the deduction is equal to the fair market value of the property less the amount of ordinary income that would have been reported if the property were sold. In most instances, the deduction is limited to the adjusted basis of the property to the donor.

EXAMPLE 29

T owned stock in EC Corporation that he donated to a local university on May 1, 1992. T had purchased the stock for $2,500 on March 3, 1992, and the stock had a value of $3,600 when he made the donation. Since the property had not been held for a sufficient period to meet the long-term capital gain requirement, T would have recognized a short-term capital gain of $1,100 if he had sold the property. Since short-term capital gain property is treated as ordinary income property for charitable contribution purposes, T's charitable contribution deduction is limited to the property's adjusted basis of $2,500 ($3,600 − $1,100 = $2,500). ◆

42. For a more complete discussion of the difference between ordinary income and capital gain property, see Chapter 16.

In Example 29, suppose the stock had a fair market value of $2,300 (rather than $3,600) when it was donated to charity. Because the fair market value now is less than the adjusted basis, the charitable contribution deduction is $2,300.

Capital Gain Property. *Capital gain property* is any property that would have resulted in the recognition of long-term capital gain or § 1231 gain if the property had been sold by the donor. As a general rule, the deduction for a contribution of capital gain property is equal to the fair market value of the property.

Two major exceptions preclude the deductibility of the appreciation on long-term capital gain property. One exception concerns certain private foundations. Private foundations are organizations that traditionally do not receive their funding from the general public (e.g., the Ford Foundation). Generally, foundations fall into two categories: operating and nonoperating. A private *operating* foundation is one that spends substantially all of its income in the active conduct of the charitable undertaking for which it was established.[43] Other private foundations are *nonoperating* foundations. However, if a private nonoperating foundation distributes the contributions it receives according to special rules within two and one-half months following the year of the contribution, the organization is treated the same as public charities and private operating foundations. Often, only the private foundation knows its status (operating or nonoperating) for sure, and the status can change from year to year.

If capital gain property is contributed to a private nonoperating foundation, the taxpayer must reduce the contribution by the long-term capital gain that would have been recognized if the property had been sold at its fair market value. The effect of this provision is to limit the deduction to the property's adjusted basis.

EXAMPLE 30

T purchases stock for $800 on January 1, 1975, and donates it to a private nonoperating foundation on June 21, 1992, when it is worth $2,000. T's charitable contribution is $800 ($2,000 − $1,200), the stock's basis. ◆

EXAMPLE 31

Assume the same facts as in Example 30, except that the donation is to either a private operating foundation or a public charity. Now, T's charitable contribution is $2,000. ◆

A second exception applying to capital gain property relates to *tangible personalty*.[44] If tangible personalty is contributed to a public charity such as a museum, church, or university, the charitable deduction may have to be reduced. The amount of the reduction is the long-term capital gain that would have been recognized if the property had been sold for its fair market value. The reduction occurs *if* the property is put to an unrelated use. The term *unrelated use* means a use that is unrelated to the exempt purpose or function of the charitable organization.

A taxpayer in this instance must establish that the property is not in fact being put to an unrelated use by the donee. The taxpayer must also establish that at the time of the contribution it was reasonable to anticipate that the property would not be put to an unrelated use. For a contribution of personalty to a museum, if the work of art is the kind of art normally retained by the museum, it is reasonable for a donor to anticipate that the work of art will not be put to an unrelated use. This will be the case even if the object is later sold or exchanged by the museum.[45]

---

43. § 4942.

44. Tangible personalty is all property that is not realty (land and buildings) and does not include intangible property such as stock or securities.

45. Reg. § 1.170A–4(b)(3)(ii)(b).

EXAMPLE 32

T contributes a Picasso painting, for which he paid $20,000, to a local museum. It had a value of $30,000 at the time of the donation. The museum displayed the painting for two years and subsequently sold it for $50,000. The charitable contribution is not reduced by the unrealized appreciation since the painting was put to a related use even though it was later sold by the museum. ◆

As noted in Chapter 12, for purposes of the alternative minimum tax, the net untaxed appreciation on charitable contributions usually is a tax preference item.

Fifty Percent Ceiling. Contributions made to public charities may not exceed 50 percent of an individual's AGI for the year. Excess contributions may be carried over to the next five years. The 50 percent ceiling on contributions applies to the following types of public charities:

- A church or a convention or association of churches.
- An educational organization that maintains a regular faculty and curriculum.
- A hospital or medical school.
- An organization supported by the government that holds property or investments for the benefit of a college or university.
- A governmental unit that is Federal, state, or local.
- An organization normally receiving a substantial part of its support from the public or a governmental unit.

The 50 percent ceiling also applies to contributions to the following organizations:

- All private operating foundations.
- Certain private nonoperating foundations that distribute the contributions they receive to public charities and private operating foundations within two and one-half months following the year they receive the contribution.
- Certain private nonoperating foundations in which the contributions are pooled in a common fund and the income and principal sum are paid to public charities.

Thirty Percent Ceiling. A 30 percent ceiling applies to contributions of cash and ordinary income property to private nonoperating foundations. The 30 percent ceiling also applies to contributions of appreciated capital gain property to 50 percent organizations unless the taxpayer makes a special election (see below).

In the event the contributions for any one tax year involve both 50 percent and 30 percent property, the allowable deduction comes first from the 50 percent property.

EXAMPLE 33

During 1992, T made the following donations to her church: cash of $2,000 and unimproved land worth $30,000. T had purchased the land four years ago for $22,000 and held it as an investment. T's AGI for 1992 is $50,000. Disregarding percentage limitations, T's potential deduction for 1992 is $32,000 [$2,000 (cash) + $30,000 (fair market value of land)]. Note that no reduction for the appreciation on the land is necessary since, if sold, it would have yielded a long-term capital gain.

In applying the percentage limitations, however, the *current* deduction for the land is limited to $15,000 [30% (limitation applicable to long-term capital gain property) × $50,000 (AGI)]. Thus, the total deduction for 1992 is $17,000 ($2,000 cash + $15,000 land). Note that the total deduction does not exceed $25,000, which is 50% of T's AGI. ◆

Under a special election, a taxpayer may choose to forgo a deduction of the appreciation on capital gain property. Referred to as the *reduced deduction election*, this enables the taxpayer to move from the 30 percent limitation to the 50 percent limitation.

EXAMPLE 34

Assume the same facts as in Example 33, except that T makes the reduced deduction election. Now the deduction for 1992 becomes $24,000 [$2,000 (cash) + $22,000 (basis in land)] because both donations fall under the 50% limitation. Thus, by making the election, T has increased her charitable contribution deduction for 1992 by $7,000 [$24,000 − $17,000 (Example 33)]. ◆

Although the reduced deduction election appears attractive, it should be considered carefully. The election sacrifices a deduction for the appreciation on long-term capital gain property that might eventually be allowed. Note that in Example 33, the potential deduction was $32,000, yet in Example 34 only $24,000 is allowed. The reason for the decrease of $8,000 ($32,000 − $24,000) of potential deduction is that no carryover is allowed for the amount sacrificed by the election.

Twenty Percent Ceiling. A 20 percent ceiling applies to contributions of appreciated long-term capital gain property to certain private nonoperating foundations.

Contribution Carryovers. Contributions that exceed the percentage limitations for the current year can be carried over for five years. In the carryover process, such contributions do not lose their identity for limitation purposes. Thus, if the contribution originally involved 30 percent property, the carryover will continue to be classified as 30 percent property in the carryover year.

EXAMPLE 35

Assume the same facts as in Example 33. Because only $15,000 of the $30,000 value of the land was deducted in 1992, the balance of $15,000 may be carried over to 1993. But the carryover will still be treated as long-term capital gain property and is subject to the 30 percent of AGI limitation. ◆

In applying the percentage limitations, current charitable contributions must be claimed first before any carryovers can be considered. If carryovers involve more than one year, they are utilized in a first-in, first-out order.

MISCELLANEOUS ITEMIZED DEDUCTIONS

According to § 262, no deduction is allowed for personal, living, or family expenses. However, a taxpayer may incur a number of expenditures related to employment. If an employee or outside salesperson incurs unreimbursed business expenses, including travel and transportation, the expenses are deductible as miscellaneous deductions.[46] Beyond unreimbursed employee expenses and those of an outside salesperson, certain other expenses fall into the special category of miscellaneous itemized deductions. Some are deductible only if, in total, they exceed 2 percent of the taxpayer's AGI. These miscellaneous itemized deductions include (but are not limited to) the following:

- Professional dues to membership organizations.
- Uniforms or other clothing that cannot be used for normal wear.
- Fees incurred for the preparation of one's tax return or fees incurred for tax litigation before the IRS or the courts.

46. Actors and performing artists who meet certain requirements are not subject to this rule.

- Job-hunting costs.
- Fee paid for a safe deposit box used to store papers and documents relating to taxable income-producing investments.
- Investment expenses that are deductible under § 212 as discussed in Chapter 6.
- Appraisal fees to determine the amount of a casualty loss or the fair market value of donated property.
- Hobby losses up to the amount of hobby income (see Chapter 6).

Certain employee business expenses that are reimbursed are not itemized deductions, but are deducted *for* AGI. Employee business expenses are discussed in depth in Chapter 10.

OTHER MISCELLANEOUS DEDUCTIONS

Certain expenses and losses do not fall into any category of itemized deductions already discussed but are nonetheless deductible.

- Moving expenses that meet the requirements for deductibility, discussed in Chapter 10.
- Casualty and theft losses, discussed in Chapter 8.
- Gambling losses up to the amount of gambling winnings.
- Impairment-related work expenses of a handicapped person.
- The unrecovered investment in an annuity contract when the annuity ceases by reason of death, discussed in Chapter 4.

The amount of each expense that is allowable as a deduction may be limited by the rules within a particular category (casualty and theft losses, moving expenses, gambling losses).

Moving expenses and casualty and theft losses are separate line items on Schedule A (Form 1040). The remaining expenses and losses are deductible as "Other Miscellaneous Deductions."

COMPREHENSIVE EXAMPLE OF SCHEDULE A

Harry and Jean Brown, married filing jointly, had the following transactions for the current year:

■ Medicines that required a prescription	$ 430
■ Doctor and dentist bills paid and not reimbursed	2,120
■ Medical insurance premium payments	1,200
■ Contact lenses	175
■ Transportation for medical purposes (425 miles × 9 cents/mile + $4.75 parking)	43
■ State income tax withheld	620
■ Real estate taxes	1,580
■ Interest paid on qualified residence mortgage	2,840
■ Charitable contributions in cash	860
■ Transportation in performing charitable services (860 miles × 12 cents/mile + $15.80 parking and tolls)	119
■ Unreimbursed employee expenses (from a Form 2106)	870
■ Tax return preparation	150
■ Professional expenses (dues and publications)	135
■ Safe deposit box (used for keeping investment documents and tax records)	35

SCHEDULES A&B (Form 1040) — Department of the Treasury, Internal Revenue Service (T)

Schedule A—Itemized Deductions

(Schedule B is on back)

▶ Attach to Form 1040. ▶ See Instructions for Schedules A and B (Form 1040).

OMB No. 1545-0074 — **1991** — Attachment Sequence No. **07**

Name(s) shown on Form 1040: Harry and Jean Brown — Your social security number: 371 : 30 : 3987

Medical and Dental Expenses		**Caution:** *Do not include expenses reimbursed or paid by others.*				
	1	Medical and dental expenses. (See page 38.)	1	3,968		
	2	Enter amount from Form 1040, line 32 [2: 40,000]				
	3	Multiply line 2 above by 7.5% (.075)	3	3,000		
	4	Subtract line 3 from line 1. Enter the result. If less than zero, enter -0- ▶			4	968
Taxes You Paid (See page 38.)	5	State and local income taxes	5	620		
	6	Real estate taxes	6	1,580		
	7	Other taxes. (List—include personal property taxes.) ▶	7			
	8	Add lines 5 through 7. Enter the total ▶			8	2,200
Interest You Paid (See page 39.)	9a	Home mortgage interest and points reported to you on Form 1098	9a	2,840		
	b	Home mortgage interest not reported to you on Form 1098. (If paid to an individual, show that person's name and address.) ▶	9b			
Note: Personal interest is no longer deductible.	10	Points not reported to you on Form 1098. (See instructions for special rules.)	10			
	11	Investment interest (attach Form 4952 if required). (See page 40.)	11			
	12	Add lines 9a through 11. Enter the total ▶			12	2,840
Gifts to Charity (See page 40.)		**Caution:** *If you made a charitable contribution and received a benefit in return, see page 40.*				
	13	Contributions by cash or check	13	979		
	14	Other than cash or check. (You **MUST** attach Form 8283 if over $500.)	14			
	15	Carryover from prior year	15			
	16	Add lines 13 through 15. Enter the total ▶			16	979
Casualty and Theft Losses	17	Casualty or theft loss(es) (attach Form 4684). (See page 40.) ▶			17	
Moving Expenses	18	Moving expenses (attach Form 3903 or 3903F). (See page 41.) ▶			18	
Job Expenses and Most Other Miscellaneous Deductions	19	Unreimbursed employee expenses—job travel, union dues, job education, etc. (You **MUST** attach Form 2106 if required. See instructions.) ▶	19	870		
(See page 41 for expenses to deduct here.)	20	Other expenses (investment, tax preparation, safe deposit box, etc.). List type and amount ▶ Tax preparation 150, professional expenses 135, safe deposit box 35	20	320		
	21	Add lines 19 and 20	21	1,190		
	22	Enter amount from Form 1040, line 32 [22: 40,000]				
	23	Multiply line 22 above by 2% (.02)	23	800		
	24	Subtract line 23 from line 21. Enter the result. If less than zero, enter -0- ▶			24	390
Other Miscellaneous Deductions	25	Other (from list on page 41 of instructions). List type and amount ▶			25	
Total Itemized Deductions	26	• If the amount on Form 1040, line 32, is $100,000 or less ($50,000 or less if married filing separately), add lines 4, 8, 12, 16, 17, 18, 24, and 25. Enter the total here. • If the amount on Form 1040, line 32, is more than $100,000 (more than $50,000 if married filing separately), see page 42 for the amount to enter. ▶			26	7,377
		Caution: *Be sure to enter on Form 1040, line 34, the* ***LARGER*** *of the amount on line 26 above or your standard deduction.*				

For Paperwork Reduction Act Notice, see Form 1040 Instructions. — Cat. No. 11330X — Schedule A (Form 1040) 1991

The Browns' adjusted gross income is $40,000. The completed Schedule A for 1991 reports itemized deductions totaling $7,377.

Overall Limitation on Certain Itemized Deductions

The Revenue Reconciliation Act of 1990 established a cutback of certain itemized deductions of high-income taxpayers. The threshold amount for 1992 is $105,250 ($52,625 for married persons filing a separate return). The threshold amount is the figure where the cutback begins to take effect. The threshold amounts are adjusted annually for inflation.[47] The cutback adjustment is reflected on line 26 of Schedule A of Form 1040. For computation purposes, the instructions for Form 1040 contain an "Itemized Deductions Worksheet." The worksheet is retained by the taxpayer for his or her records and is not filed with the tax return.

The cutback applies to all itemized deductions *except* the following:

- Medical expenses.
- Investment interest.
- Casualty and theft losses.
- Wagering losses to the extent of wagering gains.

The cutback adjustment is 3 percent of the excess of AGI over the threshold amount. In no case, however, may the cutback be more than 80 percent of the covered itemized deductions.

EXAMPLE 36

H and W are married, calendar year taxpayers and file a joint return. For 1992, they have AGI of $255,250. Their itemized deductions for the year amount to $20,000 and are entirely attributable to qualified residence interest, property taxes on their residence, charitable contributions, and state income taxes. The excess over the threshold amount is $150,000 [$255,250 (AGI) − $105,250 (threshold amount for 1992)]. Thus, the cutback adjustment under the 3% rule is $4,500 (3% of $150,000). As a result, only $15,500 [$20,000 (covered itemized deductions) − $4,500 (cutback adjustment)] of itemized deductions is allowed. The 80% limitation does not come into play because it would permit a larger cutback adjustment of $16,000 (80% × $20,000). ◆

EXAMPLE 37

Assume the same facts as in the preceding example, except that H and W have the following itemized deductions: medical expenses of $32,000 and state income taxes of $5,000. Of the medical expenses, only $12,856 [$32,000 − (7.5% × $255,250)] can be claimed. Note, however, that the cutback adjustment does not apply to medical expenses. For the state income taxes, the cutback rules yield the following results:

- Under the 3% rule—
  3% × $150,000 (excess amount) = $4,500
- Under the 80% rule—
  80% × $5,000 (covered itemized deductions) = $4,000

Thus, the 80% rule must be used since it provides a smaller cutback ($4,000 versus $4,500). Therefore, the total allowable itemized deductions are $13,856 [$12,856 (medical expenses) + $1,000 (state income taxes less cutback)]. ◆

The cutback adjustment is applied after taking into account other Code provisions that reduce the allowable deduction (e.g., the 2 percent of AGI floor that applies to miscellaneous itemized deductions).

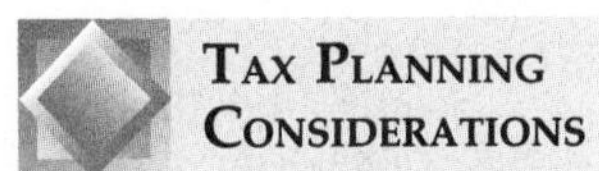
TAX PLANNING CONSIDERATIONS

Effective Utilization of Itemized Deductions

Since an individual may use the standard deduction in one year and itemize deductions in another year, it is frequently possible to obtain maximum benefit by shifting itemized deductions from one year to another. For example, if a

47. § 68. The threshold amount for 1991 was $100,000 ($50,000 for married persons filing a separate return).

taxpayer's itemized deductions and the standard deduction are approximately the same for each year of a two-year period, the taxpayer should use the standard deduction in one year and shift itemized deductions (to the extent permitted by law) to the other year. The individual could, for example, prepay a church pledge for a particular year or avoid paying end-of-the-year medical expenses to shift the deduction to the following year.

Utilization of Medical Deductions

When a taxpayer anticipates that medical expenses will approximate the percentage floor, much might be done to generate a deductible excess. Any of the following procedures can help build a deduction by the end of the year:

- Incur the obligation for needed dental work or have needed work carried out.[48] Orthodontic treatment, for example, may have been recommended for a member of the taxpayer's family.
- Have elective remedial surgery that may have been postponed from prior years (e.g., tonsillectomies, vasectomies, correction of hernias, hysterectomies).
- Incur the obligation for capital improvements to the taxpayer's personal residence recommended by a physician (e.g., an air filtration system to alleviate a respiratory disorder).

As an aid to taxpayers who may experience temporary cash-flow problems at the end of the year, the use of bank credit cards is deemed to be payment for purposes of timing the deductibility of charitable and medical expenses.

Example 38

On December 12, 1992, T (a calendar year taxpayer) purchases two pairs of prescription contact lenses and one pair of prescribed orthopedic shoes for a total of $305. These purchases are separately charged to T's credit card. On January 6, 1993, T receives his statement containing these charges and makes payment shortly thereafter. The purchases are deductible as medical expenses in the year charged (1992) and not in the year the account is settled (1993). ◆

Recognizing which expenditures qualify for the medical deduction also may be crucial to exceeding the percentage limitations.

Example 39

T employs E (an unrelated party) to care for her incapacitated and dependent mother. E is not a trained nurse but spends approximately one-half of the time performing nursing duties (e.g., administering injections and providing physical therapy) and the rest of the time doing household chores. An allocable portion of E's wages that T pays (including the employer's portion of FICA taxes) qualifies as a medical expense. ◆

To assure a deduction for the entire cost of nursing home care for an aged dependent, it is helpful if the transfer of the individual to the home is for medical reasons and is recommended by a doctor. In addition, the nursing home facilities should be adequate to provide the necessary medical and nursing care. To assure a deduction for all of the nursing home expenses, it is necessary to

48. Prepayment of medical expenses does not generate a current deduction unless the taxpayer is under an obligation to make the payment.

show that the individual was placed in the home for required medical care rather than for personal or family considerations.

Proper documentation is required to substantiate medical expenses. The taxpayer should keep all receipts for credit card or other charge purchases of medical services and deductible drugs as well as all cash register receipts. In addition, medical transportation mileage should be recorded.

If a taxpayer or a dependent of the taxpayer must be institutionalized in order to receive adequate medical care, it may be good tax planning to make a lump-sum payment that will cover medical treatment for future periods. It is advisable to negotiate a contract with the institution so that the expense is fixed and the payment is not a mere deposit.

Protecting the Interest Deduction

Although the deductibility of prepaid interest by a cash basis taxpayer has been severely restricted, a notable exception allows a deduction for points paid to obtain financing for the purchase or improvement of a principal residence in the year of payment. However, such points must actually be paid by the taxpayer obtaining the loan and must represent a charge for the use of money. It has been held that points paid from the mortgage proceeds do not satisfy the payment requirement.[49] Also, the portion of the points attributable to service charges does not represent deductible interest.[50] Taxpayers financing home purchases or improvements usually should direct their planning toward avoiding these two hurdles to immediate deductibility.

In rare instances, a taxpayer may find it desirable to forgo the immediate expensing of points in the year paid. Instead, it could prove beneficial to capitalize the points and write them off as interest expense over the life of the mortgage.

EXAMPLE 40

X purchases a home on December 15, 1992, for $95,000 with $30,000 cash and a 15-year mortgage of $65,000 financed by the Greater Metropolis National Bank. X pays two points in addition to interest allocated to the period from December 15 until December 31, 1992, at an annual rate of 10%. Since X does not have enough itemized deductions to exceed the standard deduction for 1992, she should elect to capitalize the interest expense by amortizing the points over 15 years. In this instance, X would deduct $86.67 for 1993, as part of her qualified residence interest expense [$1,300 (two points) divided by 15 years], if she elects to itemize that year. ◆

Because personal (consumer) interest is not deductible, taxpayers should consider making use of home equity loans. Recall that these loans utilize the personal residence of the taxpayer as security. Since the tracing rules do not apply to home equity loans, the funds from these loans can be used for personal purposes (e.g., auto loans, education). By making use of home equity loans, therefore, what would have been nondeductible consumer interest becomes deductible qualified residence interest.

Assuring the Charitable Contribution Deduction

For a charitable contribution deduction to be available, the recipient must be a qualified charitable organization. Sometimes the mechanics of how the contribution is carried out can determine whether or not a deduction results.

49. *Alan A. Rubnitz*, 67 T.C. 621 (1977).

50. *Donald L. Wilkerson*, 70 T.C. 240 (1978).

EXAMPLE 41

T wants to donate $5,000 to her church's mission in Seoul, Korea. In this regard, she considers three alternatives:

1. Send the money directly to the mission.
2. Give the money to her church with the understanding that it is to be passed on to the mission.
3. Give the money directly to the missionary in charge of the mission who is currently in the United States on a fund-raising trip.

If T wants to obtain a deduction for the contribution, she should choose alternative 2. A direct donation to the mission (alternative 1) is not deductible because the mission is a foreign charity. A direct gift to the missionary (alternative 3) does not comply since an individual cannot be a qualified charity for income tax purposes.[51] ◆

When making noncash donations, the type of property chosen can have decided implications in determining the amount, if any, of the deduction.

EXAMPLE 42

T wants to give $60,000 in value to her church in some form other than cash. In this connection, she considers four alternatives:

1. Stock held for two years as an investment with a basis of $100,000 and a fair market value of $60,000.
2. Stock held for five years as an investment with a basis of $10,000 and a fair market value of $60,000.
3. The rent-free use for a year of a building that normally leases for $5,000 a month.
4. A valuable stamp collection held as an investment and owned for ten years with a basis of $10,000 and a fair market value of $60,000. The church plans to sell the collection if and when it is donated.

Alternative 1 is ill-advised as the subject of the gift. Even though T would obtain a deduction of $60,000, she would forgo the potential loss of $40,000 that would be recognized if the property were sold.[52] Alternative 2 makes good sense since the deduction still is $60,000 and none of the $50,000 of appreciation that has occurred must be recognized as income. Alternative 3 yields no deduction at all and is not a wise choice. Alternative 4 involves tangible personalty that the recipient does not plan to use. As a result, the amount of the deduction is limited to $10,000, the stamp collection's basis.[53] ◆

For property transfers (particularly real estate), the ceiling limitations on the amount of the deduction allowed in any one year (50 percent, 30 percent, or 20 percent of AGI, as the case may be) could be a factor to take into account. With proper planning, donations can be controlled to stay within the limitations and therefore avoid the need for a carryover of unused charitable contributions.

EXAMPLE 43

T wants to donate a tract of unimproved land held as an investment to the University of Maryland (a qualified charitable organization). The land has been held for six years

51. *Thomas E. Lesslie*, 36 TCM 495, T.C.Memo. 1977–111.
52. *LaVar M. Withers*, 69 T.C. 900 (1978).
53. No reduction of appreciation is necessary in alternative 2 since stock is intangible property and not tangible personalty. As noted in Chapter 12, however, the untaxed appreciation usually is a tax preference item for purposes of the alternative minimum tax.

and has a current fair market value of $300,000 and a basis to T of $50,000. T's AGI for the current year is estimated to be $200,000, and he expects much the same for the next few years. In the current year, he deeds (transfers) an undivided one-fifth interest in the real estate to the university. ◆

What has T in Example 43 accomplished for income tax purposes? In the current year, he will be allowed a charitable contribution deduction of $60,000 (⅕ × $300,000), which will be within the applicable limitation of AGI (30% × $200,000). Presuming no other charitable contributions for the year, T has avoided the possibility of a carryover. In future years, T can arrange donations of undivided interests in the real estate to stay within the bounds of the percentage limitations. The only difficulty with this approach is the necessity of having to revalue the real estate each year before the donation, since the amount of the deduction is based on the fair market value of the interest contributed at the time of the contribution.

It may be wise to avoid a carryover of unused charitable contributions, if possible, because that approach may be dangerous in several respects. First, the carryover period is limited to five years. Depending on the taxpayer's projected AGI rather than actual AGI, some of the amount carried over may expire without tax benefit after the five-year period has ended. Second, unused charitable contribution carryovers do not survive the death of the party making the donation and as a consequence are lost.

EXAMPLE 44

D dies in October 1992. In completing her final income tax return for 1992, D's executor determines the following information: AGI of $104,000 and a donation by D to her church of stock worth $60,000. D had purchased the stock two years ago for $50,000 and held it as an investment. D's executor makes the reduced deduction election and, as a consequence, claims a charitable contribution deduction of $50,000. With the election, the potential charitable contribution deduction of $50,000 ($60,000 − $10,000) is less than the 50% ceiling of $52,000 ($104,000 × 50%). If the executor had not made the election, the potential charitable contribution deduction of $60,000 would have been reduced by the 30% ceiling to $31,200 ($104,000 × 30%). No carryover of the $28,800 ($60,000 − $31,200) would have been available. ◆

PROBLEM MATERIALS

DISCUSSION QUESTIONS

1. T, a self-employed individual taxpayer, prepared his own income tax return for the past year and asked you to check it over for accuracy. Your review indicates that T failed to claim certain business entertainment expenses.
   a. Will the correction of this omission affect the amount of medical expenses T can deduct? Explain.
   b. Would it matter if T were employed rather than self-employed?
2. Under what circumstances, if any, will the cost of cosmetic surgery qualify as a deductible medical expense?
3. T's son is performing poorly in public school. Not only is he failing most subjects but he responds negatively to constructive criticism from his teachers. Upon the recommendation of a child psychiatrist, T enrolls his son in X Academy, a private school that has a lower teacher-to-student ratio and more personalized instruction. Is the tuition T pays to X Academy deductible as a medical expense? Explain.

4. X has a history of heart disease. Upon the advice of his doctor, he installs an elevator in his residence so he does not have to climb stairs. Is this a valid medical expense? If it is, how much of the expense is deductible?
5. T is employed as an accountant in New Orleans, Louisiana. One of T's friends, Dr. D, practices general dentistry in Hot Springs, Arkansas. Once a year during the deer hunting season, T travels to Hot Springs for his annual dental checkup. While there, T makes use of Dr. D's deer lodge for hunting purposes. Do any of T's travel expenses for the trip to Arkansas qualify for the medical expense deduction? Why or why not?
6. Under what circumstances may a taxpayer claim as a deduction the medical expenses paid on behalf of another person who cannot be claimed as the taxpayer's dependent?
7. If T's medical expense deduction was $500 in 1992 and the amount reduced T's tax liability, how would a $300 insurance reimbursement be treated if received in 1993? Received in 1992? What if T had not itemized deductions in 1992 and received the $300 reimbursement in 1993?
8. Why would a taxpayer want to concentrate medical expenses in a particular tax year? Give *some* examples of how this can be accomplished.
9. T, a single individual, employs D as a housekeeper. T's household includes her infirm mother. Under what circumstances might some of D's wages qualify for the medical expense deduction claimed by T?
10. The city of Galveston, Texas, assessed beachfront property owners for the construction of jetties to protect shorelines from the destructive effects of the ocean. Is this assessment deductible?
11. T lives in a state that imposes a sizable sales tax but no income tax. U lives in a state that imposes an income tax but no sales tax. Are T and U similarly situated for Federal income tax purposes? Explain.
12. A buyer of property pays real estate taxes apportioned to the seller. What are the income tax consequences to each party?
13. If a taxpayer overpays his or her state income tax due to excessive withholdings or estimated tax payments, how is the refund check treated when received in the subsequent year? Are the excess amounts paid deductible in the current year?
14. Why has Congress imposed limitations on the deductibility of interest when funds are borrowed for the purpose of purchasing or continuing to hold investment property?
15. How can home equity loans be used to avoid the nondeductibility of interest on amounts borrowed to finance the purchase of consumer goods?
16. As to the deductibility of "points," comment on the following:
    - **a.** Those paid by the seller.
    - **b.** Those paid to finance the purchase of a rental house.
    - **c.** Those relating to the rendering of personal services.
    - **d.** When capitalization and amortization might be advisable.
    - **e.** Points paid from the mortgage proceeds.
17. Discuss the special problems that arise with respect to the deductibility of interest on a debt between related parties. How does § 267 of the Code relate to this problem?
18. If a taxpayer withdraws amounts from a certificate of deposit prematurely and a penalty applies, what are the income tax consequences?
19. An accountant normally charges $100 an hour when preparing financial statements for clients. If the accountant performs accounting services for a church without charge, can she deduct the value of the donated services on her tax return?
20. T makes a cash donation to an orphanage located in India. Does the donation qualify as a charitable contribution deduction? Explain.
21. What is ordinary income property? If inventory with an adjusted basis of $60 and fair market value of $100 is contributed to a public charity, how much is deductible?

22. What is capital gain property? What tax treatment is required if capital gain property is contributed to a private nonoperating foundation? To a public charity? What difference does it make if the contribution is tangible personalty and it is put to a use unrelated to the donee's business?
23. During 1992, T donated five dresses to the Salvation Army. She had purchased the dresses three years ago at a cost of $1,200 and worn them as personal attire. Because the dresses are long-term capital assets, T plans to deduct $1,200 on her 1992 income tax return. Comment on T's understanding of the tax law governing charitable contributions.
24. In the year of her death, T made significant charitable contributions of long-term capital gain property. In fact, the amount of the contributions exceeds 30% of her AGI. What might be a possible alternative for the executor of T's estate who prepares her final income tax return?
25. In 1991, V had an excess charitable contribution that he could not deduct because of the percentage limitations. In 1992, V made further charitable contributions. In applying the percentage limitations for 1992, how are these transactions handled?
26. Regarding the cutback adjustment for certain itemized deductions, comment on the following:

    a. The threshold amount.
    b. Itemized deductions not covered.
    c. The 3% and 80% rules.

PROBLEMS

27. H and W are married and together have AGI of $48,000. They have no dependents and filed a joint return in 1992. Each pays $700 for hospitalization insurance. During the year, they paid the following amounts for medical care: $3,100 in doctor and dentist bills and hospital expenses and $700 for prescribed medicine and drugs. They received an insurance reimbursement for hospitalization in December 1992 for $900. Determine the deduction allowable for medical expenses paid in 1992.
28. T is divorced and claims his father (F) and his son (S) as dependents. During the current year, he pays the following expenses:

Tuition (including room and board) to send S to XYZ Military Academy	$12,000
To Dr. P (a child psychiatrist) for consultations with S	2,500
Room and board at Happy Farms Assisted Living Home on behalf of F	18,000
Doctor and hospital charges to correct F's hernia	2,600

    Upon Dr. P's recommendation, S was sent to XYZ Military Academy to alleviate a truancy problem. The academy provides no medical care but does impose strict discipline. F moved to Happy Farms because he felt living with T was too dull. Disregarding percentage limitations, how much qualifies as a medical expense on T's tax return for:

    a. S?
    b. F?

29. Z lives in Arkansas and discovers that he has a rare disease that can be treated only with surgery by a surgeon in Germany. Z incurs $1,700 in airfare, $200 in meals taken at the medical facility, and $800 in lodging expenses for eight nights of lodging related to his medical care in Germany. What amount, if any, of these expenses is deductible?
30. During 1992, T paid the following medical expenses:

On behalf of S (T's son by a former marriage)	$9,000
On behalf of U (T's uncle)	5,000
Hospital bill for an operation performed on T in 1991	4,500

Of the $9,000 spent on S, $2,500 was for orthodontia services to be performed in 1993. The dentist required this amount as a deposit for the braces to be applied to S's teeth. T could claim S as a dependent, but S's mother refuses to sign the custodial parent's waiver. U could be claimed as T's dependent except for the gross income test. For these items, what amount qualifies as T's medical expenses for 1992?

31. Upon the advice of his physician, T, a heart patient, installs an elevator in his personal residence at a cost of $8,000. The elevator has a cost recovery period of five years. A neighbor who is in the real estate business charges T $60 for an appraisal that places the value of the residence at $60,000 before the improvement and $62,000 after. The value increases because T lives in a region where many older people retire and therefore would find the elevator an attractive feature in a home. As a result of the operation of the elevator, T noticed an increase of $75 in his utility bills for the current year. Disregarding percentage limitations, which of the above expenditures qualify as a medical expense deduction?

32. K, who had AGI of $21,000, incurred the following medical expenses during 1992: $3,000 for doctor and hospital bills, $1,100 for medical insurance premiums, and $400 for drugs and medicines that require a prescription. He was reimbursed for $1,600 of the doctor and hospital bills by his insurance company. Also, K is physically handicapped and spent $3,500 constructing entrance and exit ramps to his personal residence. The value of the home increased by $1,500 as a result of these expenditures. Compute K's medical expense deduction for 1992.

33. In County X, the real property tax year is the calendar year. The real property tax becomes a personal liability of the owner of real property on January 1 in the current real property tax year, 1992. The tax is payable on July 1, 1992. On May 1, 1992, S sells his house to B for $200,000. On July 1, 1992, B pays the entire real estate tax of $2,920 for the year ending December 31, 1992.

    a. How much of the property taxes may S deduct?
    b. How much of the property taxes may B deduct?

34. Assume the same facts as in Problem 33.

    a. What is B's basis for the residence?
    b. How much did S realize from the sale of the residence?

35. R uses the cash method of accounting and lives in a state that imposes an income tax (including withholding from wages). On April 14, 1992, he files his state return for 1991, paying an additional $900 in income taxes. During 1992, his withholdings for state income tax purposes amount to $3,100. On April 13, 1993, R files his state return for 1992 claiming a refund of $400. R receives the refund on August 3, 1993.

    a. If R itemizes deductions, how much may he claim as a deduction for state income taxes on his Federal return for calendar year 1992 (filed in April 1993)?
    b. How will the refund of $400 received in 1993 be treated for Federal income tax purposes?

36. In 1992, M has $8,000 of investment income and the following miscellaneous deductions:

Unreimbursed employee business expenses (meals included at 80%)	$1,000
Tax return preparation fee	150
Investment expenses	600

For purposes of the investment interest expense limitation, what is the total of M's net investment income in each of the following independent situations:

    a. AGI of $30,000.
    b. AGI of $70,000.
    c. AGI of $100,000.

37. X is married and files a joint tax return for 1992. X has investment interest expense of $95,000 for a loan made to him in 1992 to purchase a parcel of unimproved land. His income from investments (dividends and interest) totaled $15,000. After reducing his miscellaneous deductions by the applicable 2% floor, the deductible portion amounted to $2,500. In addition to $1,100 of investment expenses included in miscellaneous deductions, X paid $3,000 of real estate taxes on the unimproved land. X also has $3,000 as a net long-term capital gain from the sale of another parcel of unimproved land. Calculate X's investment interest deduction for 1992.

38. E borrowed $200,000 to acquire a parcel of land to be held for investment purposes. During 1992, she paid interest of $20,000 on the loan. She had AGI of $50,000 for the year. Other items related to E's investments include the following:

Investment income	$10,200
Long-term gain on sale of stock	4,000
Investment counsel fees	1,500

E is unmarried and elected to itemize her deductions. She had no miscellaneous deductions other than the investment counsel fees. Determine E's investment interest deduction for 1992.

39. In 1992, T borrows $120,000 to purchase an airplane (to be used for pleasure purposes) by placing a lien on his personal residence. At this time, the first mortgage on the residence has a balance of $300,000, and the residence has a fair market value of $600,000. How should T determine his interest deduction for 1992?

40. T and his wife W own a personal residence in the city. For many years, they have owned a beach house 50 miles away. They do not rent out the beach house because they spend every weekend there. Last year, they purchased a condominium in Boulder, Colorado, for their son to live in while he attends college. During 1992, they paid the following mortgage interest (each mortgage is secured by the respective property): $7,800 on their personal residence, $5,500 on the beach house, and $9,000 on the condominium. How much can T and W deduct for the year as qualified residence interest?

41. R and S are equal owners in Z Corporation. On July 1, 1992, each loans the corporation $30,000 at annual interest of 10%. R and S are brothers. Both shareholders are on the cash method of accounting, while Z Corporation is on the accrual method. All parties use the calendar year for tax purposes. On June 30, 1993, Z Corporation repays the loans of $60,000 together with the specified interest of $6,000.

   a. How much of the interest can Z Corporation deduct in 1992? In 1993?
   b. When is the interest taxed to R and S?

42. In 1992 T pays $500 to become a charter member of State University's Athletic Council. The membership ensures that T will receive choice seating at all of State's home football games. Also in 1992, T pays $120 (the regular retail price) for season tickets for himself and his wife. For these items, how much qualifies as a charitable contribution?

43. Taxpayer's child attends a parochial school operated by the church the family attends. Taxpayer made a donation of $300 to the church in lieu of the normal registration fee of $100 for children of nonmembers. In addition, the regular tuition of $75 per week is paid to the school. Based on this information, what is the taxpayer's charitable contribution?

44. Determine the amount of the charitable deduction allowed in each of the following situations:

   a. Donation of X Corporation stock (a publicly traded corporation) to taxpayer's church. The stock cost the taxpayer $2,000 four months ago and has a fair market value of $3,000 on the date of the donation.
   b. Donation of a painting to the Salvation Army. The painting cost the taxpayer $2,000 five years ago and has a fair market value of $3,500 on the date of the donation.

c. The local branch of the American Red Cross uses a building rent-free for half of the current year. The building normally rents for $500 a month.
d. Donation by a cash basis farmer to a church of a quantity of grain worth $900. The farmer raised the grain in the preceding year at a cost of $650, all of which was deducted for income tax purposes.

45. During 1992, T, an individual, made the following contributions to his church:

Cash	$20,000
Stock in Y Corporation (a publicly traded corporation)	30,000

The stock in Y Corporation was acquired as an investment three years ago at a cost of $10,000. T's AGI for 1992 is $70,000.

a. What is T's charitable contribution deduction for 1992?
b. How are excess amounts, if any, treated?

46. D died in 1992. Before she died, D made a gift of stock in Z Corporation (a publicly traded corporation) to her church. The stock was worth $35,000 and had been acquired as an investment two years ago at a cost of $30,000. In the year of her death, D had AGI of $60,000. In completing her final income tax return, how should D's executor handle the charitable contribution?

47. On December 30, 1992, R purchased four tickets to a charity ball sponsored by the city of San Diego for the benefit of underprivileged children. Each ticket cost $200 and had a fair market value of $35. On the same day as the purchase, R gave the tickets to the minister of her church for personal use by his family. At the time of the gift of the tickets, R pledged $4,000 to the building fund of her church. The pledge was satisfied by check dated December 31, 1992, but not mailed until January 3, 1993.

a. Presuming R is a cash basis and calendar year taxpayer, how much can she deduct as a charitable contribution for 1992?
b. Would the amount of the deduction be any different if R is an accrual basis taxpayer? Explain.

48. Classify each of the following independent expenditures as nondeductible *(ND)* items, business *(dfor)* deductions, or itemized *(dfrom)* deductions. (*Note:* In many cases, it may be necessary to refer to the materials in earlier chapters of the text.)

a. Interest allowed on home mortgage accrued by a cash basis taxpayer.
b. State income taxes paid by a sole proprietor of a business.
c. Subscription to the *Wall Street Journal* paid by a vice president of a bank and not reimbursed by her employer.
d. Automobile mileage for attendance at weekly church services.
e. Street-paving assessment paid to the county by a homeowner.
f. Speeding ticket paid by the owner-operator of a taxicab.
g. Interest and taxes paid by the owner of residential rental property.
h. Business entertainment expenses (properly substantiated) paid by a self-employed taxpayer.
i. State and Federal excise taxes on tobacco paid by a self-employed taxpayer who gave his clients cigars as Christmas presents. The business gifts were properly substantiated and under $25 each.
j. State and Federal excise taxes on cigarettes purchased by a heavy smoker for personal consumption.
k. Federal excise taxes (14.1 cents per gallon) on the purchase of gasoline for use in the taxpayer's personal automobile.
l. Theft loss of personal jewelry worth $300 but which originally cost $75.
m. Maternity clothing purchased by a taxpayer who is pregnant.
n. Medical expenses paid by an employer on behalf of an employee.

o. Qualified residence interest paid by a taxpayer on a loan obtained to build an artist studio in his personal residence. Assume that taxpayer's art activities are classified as a hobby.

p. Assume the same facts as in (o) except that the art activities are classified as a trade or business.

49. T had AGI of $50,000 in 1992. T's itemized deductions totaled $13,000, including $2,000 of miscellaneous itemized deductions (determined before considering the 2% floor). Determine T's allowable itemized deductions for 1992.

50. For calendar year 1992, H and W file a joint return reflecting AGI of $150,000. Their itemized deductions are as follows:

Medical expenses	$12,000
Casualty loss (not covered by insurance)	16,000
Interest on home mortgage	20,000
Property taxes on home	12,000
Charitable contributions	11,000
State income tax	8,000

After all necessary adjustments are made, what is the amount of itemized deductions H and W may claim?

Cumulative Problems

51. Jane and Bill Smith are married taxpayers, ages 44 and 42, who file a joint return. Their Social Security numbers are 451–19–6890 and 455–18–8354, respectively. In 1991, Bill was employed as an assistant manager for a Ramada Inn at a salary of $28,000. Jane is a high school teacher and earned $20,000. Jane has two children, Joe Harper (449–86–9756) and Sue Harper (461–31–4019), ages 13 and 15, from a previous marriage. The children reside with Jane and Bill throughout the school year and reside with Bob, Jane's former husband, during the summer. According to the divorce decree (which was executed in 1983), Bob pays $150 per month per child for each of the nine months during which Jane has custody of the children, but the decree is silent as to which parent may claim the exemptions. Bob claims that he spends $200 a month supporting each child during the three summer months when the children live with him. Jane can document that she and Bill provided support of $1,800 for each child in 1991.

In August, Bill and Jane decided to add a suite to their home to provide more comfortable accommodations for Mary Miller (263–75–1157), Jane's mother who had moved in with them the preceding February after the death of Jane's father. Not wanting to borrow the money for this addition, Bill and Jane sold 400 shares of Carson Corporation stock for $29 per share on May 9, 1991, and used the $11,600 to cover construction costs. They had purchased the stock on August 7, 1986, for $16 a share. They received dividends of $290 on the jointly owned stock before the sale.

Mary is 66 years old and received $3,600 in Social Security benefits during the year, of which she gave Bill and Jane $1,200 to use toward household expenses and deposited $2,400 in her personal savings account. Bill and Jane determine that they spent $1,500 of their own money for food, clothing, medical expenses, and other items for Mary, not counting the rental value of the portion of the house she occupies.

Bill and Jane received $1,600 interest on City of Akron bonds they had bought in 1991. Bill had heard from a friend that municipal bonds were paying good rates and that municipal bond interest was not taxable. To finance the purchase of the bonds, he borrowed $20,000 from the bank at 10% interest, figuring the deduction for interest would save him enough income tax to make the investment worthwhile. He paid the bank $2,000 interest during 1991. Other interest paid during the year included $4,560 on their home mortgage (paid to a Federal savings & loan).

Jane's favorite uncle died and willed Jane 50 shares of IBM stock worth $100 per share. Jane received dividends of $252 on the stock during the year.

In December 1991, Bill was riding a motorcycle he had just acquired for $8,200. In his eagerness to try it out, he neglected two things. First, he had forgotten to insure it. Second, he had not taken time to read the operating instructions. As a result of his lack of familiarity with the motorcycle, he lost control of it as he headed toward a large, concrete barn. Fortunately, Bill was able to jump off before the crash and escaped injury. The barn was not damaged. The motorcycle, however, was demolished. Bill sold it back to the dealer for parts for $600.

Bill and Jane paid doctor and hospital bills of $4,100 and were reimbursed by their insurance company for $1,400. Prescription medicines and drugs cost them $1,100, and premiums on their health insurance policy were $750. Included in the amounts paid for hospital bills was $700 for Mary, and of the $1,100 spent for medicines and drugs, $400 was for Mary.

Taxes paid during the year included $2,220 property taxes on their home and state income taxes (withheld) of $1,050. In March 1991, Bill and Jane received a refund on their 1990 state income taxes of $340. They had itemized deductions on their 1990 return and had received a tax benefit for the full amount of state income taxes reported.

Bill and Jane contribute $50 a week to the First United Church and have canceled checks for these contributions totaling $2,600. In addition, Bill's employer withheld $360 from his check, per his instructions, as a contribution to United Way. Bill and Jane also have a receipt from the Salvation Army for some used clothing the family had contributed. Bill and Jane estimated the value of the clothes at $300.

Bill and Jane had $4,779 ($2,160 for Bill, $2,619 for Jane) of Federal income tax withheld in 1991 and paid no estimated Federal income tax. Neither Bill nor Jane wishes to designate $1 to the Presidential Election Campaign Fund.

Compute net tax payable or refund due for Bill and Jane Smith for 1991. If they have overpaid, the amount is to be refunded. If you use tax forms for your computations, you will need Form 1040, Schedules A, B, and D, and Form 4684. Suggested software (if available): *TurboTax* for tax return or WFT tax planning software.

52. Sam Worthing, age 45, is married and has two dependent children. In 1992, he incurred the following:

Salary received from his employer, Geophysics, Inc.		$65,000
Cost of art supplies. Sam took up painting as a hobby and plans to sell the paintings to friends and art galleries but had no willing purchasers during 1992.		1,000
Contribution of shares of Xerox stock to his church (fair market value of $3,000, cost of $800, and acquired in 1976).		3,000
Sam's wife, Irene, had a diamond ring that was stolen in April 1992. A police report was filed, but her ring was not recovered. It is not covered by insurance. The ring had recently been appraised at $4,000, which was also its original cost.		4,000
Travel (meals included at 80%) and auto expenses incurred in connection with Sam's employment (none of which was reimbursed).		3,500
Sam and his family moved from Nashville to Boston during the year and incurred the following unreimbursed expenses:		
Moving van	$2,500	
House-hunting expenses (meals included at 80%)	2,000	
Sales commissions on the former house	3,500	8,000
Sam incurred and paid the following personal expenses:		
Medical and dental bills for the family		2,500
State and local income and property taxes		4,500

Determine the Worthings' AGI and taxable income for 1992, assuming that a joint return is filed and that there are no other items of income or expense. Suggested software (if available): *TurboTax* for tax return or WFT tax planning software.

Research Problems

Research Problem 1 T suffers from a degenerative spinal disorder. Her physician recommended the installation of a swimming pool at her residence for her use to prevent the onset of permanent paralysis. T's residence had a market value of approximately $500,000 before the swimming pool was installed. The swimming pool was built, and an appraiser estimated that the value of T's home increased by $98,000 because of the addition.

The pool cost $194,000, and T claimed a medical deduction on her tax return of $96,000. Upon audit of the return, the IRS determined that an adequate pool should have cost $70,000 and would increase the property value by only $31,000. Thus, the IRS claims that T should be entitled to a deduction of only $39,000.

- **a.** Is there any ceiling limitation on the amount deductible as a medical expense?
- **b.** Can capital expenditures be deducted as medical expenses?
- **c.** What is the significance of a "minimum adequate facility"? Should aesthetic or architectural qualities be considered in this determination?

Research Problem 2 Several years ago, R, a cash basis taxpayer, obtained a mortgage from State Bank to purchase a personal residence. In December 1992, $9,500 of interest was due on the mortgage, but R had only $75 in his checking account. On December 31, 1992, R borrowed $9,500 from State Bank, evidenced by a note, and the proceeds were deposited in R's checking account. On the same day, R issued a check in the identical amount of $9,500 to State Bank for the interest expense due. Is this interest expense deductible for the tax year 1992?

Partial list of research aids:
§ 163(h)(3).
William M. Roberts, 53 TCM 787, T.C.Memo. 1987–235.

Research Problem 3 T and his wife purchased a new residence. Because they were unable to obtain conventional mortgage financing, they borrowed the purchase price at City National Bank. Under the terms of the loan, they agreed to pay interest and make very modest repayments of the principal for three years. At the end of three years, the full amount of the loan would "balloon" and become due. During the three-year term of the loan, the taxpayers made the interest payments and only some of the repayments of principal.

By the end of the three-year loan, taxpayers managed to obtain long-term (30-year) mortgage financing with State Savings and Loan. Thus, the outstanding amounts due City National were rolled over into the new mortgage with State Savings and Loan.

As a cost of securing the refinancing, taxpayers had to pay points. These were paid from their own funds and not from the mortgage proceeds. Taxpayers concede that they did not possess the economic means to meet the balloon payment requirement under the City National Bank loan agreement.

Determine the income tax treatment of the points paid to State Savings and Loan.

Partial list of research aids:
§ 461(g)(2).

Research Problem 4 In 1992, T pledges $400,000 to her church, which is conducting a fund-raising campaign to construct a new sanctuary. To satisfy her pledge, she sells land (worth $500,000) to the church for $100,000. The land had been held by T for many years as an investment and had an adjusted basis of $100,000. T chose the sale approach in order to recoup her original investment in the property. Discuss the tax ramifications of this transaction.

Research Problem 5 The city of Sacramento wished to establish a scenic corridor along portions of Interstate 5, but did not have the funds to purchase all of the land involved and to make the necessary improvements (e.g., terracing and other landscaping). Likewise, the city was fearful of any personal liability that might result from the operation of the scenic corridor. If, however, state funding could be obtained to cover the improvements and liability costs, the project would be carried out. State funding was a possible but not a probable likelihood.

In 1990, all but one of the property owners affected by the project donated the necessary land to the city. The city purchased the land of the one owner who refused to make a donation. The city agreed to return the land to the donors in the event the project was not carried out. By 1992, it became certain that state funding would not be forthcoming. Therefore, the city returned the land to the donors, except for the parcel it had purchased.

T, one of the donors, claimed a charitable deduction for the fair market value of the land transferred in 1990. Upon audit of T's 1990 income tax return, the IRS disallowed the deduction and assessed the penalty for overvaluation. Is the IRS correct?

Partial list of research aids:
§ 6659 [now § 6662(b)(3)].
Reg. § 1.170A–1(e).
Ronald W. McCrary, 92 T.C. 827 (1989).

PART

SPECIAL TAX COMPUTATION METHODS, PAYMENT PROCEDURES, AND TAX CREDITS

Part IV presents several topics that relate to the theme of tax liability determination. The taxpayer must calculate the tax liability in accordance with the basic tax formula and also in accordance with the tax formula for the alternative minimum tax (AMT). The basic tax formula was presented in Part I, and the AMT formula is covered in Part IV. Tax credits reduce the amount of the calculated tax liability. The specific procedures for the timing of the payment of the tax liability are also discussed.

CHAPTER

CHAPTER

ALTERNATIVE MINIMUM TAX

OBJECTIVES

Examine the rationale for the individual alternative minimum tax.

Apply the formula for computing alternative minimum taxable income.

Discuss the role of adjustments in the computation of the alternative minimum tax and explain the adjustments required.

Differentiate tax preferences from alternative minimum tax adjustments and discuss specific tax preferences.

Explain the formula for computing alternative minimum taxable income to arrive at the alternative minimum tax.

Describe the role of the alternative minimum tax credit in the alternative minimum tax structure.

Introduce the corporate alternative minimum tax.

OUTLINE

Once gross income has been determined and various deductions accounted for, the income tax liability can be computed. Generally, the computation procedure requires only familiarity with use of the Tax Table or Tax Rate Schedules. Some taxpayers, however, may be subject to taxes in addition to the regular income tax. One such additional tax is the alternative minimum tax (AMT). Any taxpayer who is subject to the regular income tax may be subject to the AMT. This chapter explains the provisions of the AMT and the determination of tax liability under its terms.

The individual AMT is discussed in the first part of the chapter. The corporate AMT is similar to the individual AMT, but differs from it in several important ways. Details of the corporate AMT are covered in the last part of the chapter.

Individual Alternative Minimum Tax

◆

The tax law contains many incentives that are intended to influence the economic and social behavior of taxpayers (refer to Chapter 1). Some of the more prominent incentives designed to influence *economic* behavior permit rapid write-offs of certain costs, including the following:

- Accelerated depreciation write-offs for realty (buildings) and personalty (e.g., machinery and equipment).
- Immediate expensing of intangible drilling costs, circulation expenditures, mining exploration and development costs, and research and development expenditures.

Tax incentives designed to provide relief for taxpayers also include provisions that allow for deferral of income. For example, in limited circumstances taxpayers may use the completed contract method instead of the percentage of completion method for income tax purposes.

Other tax incentives that are intended to influence social or economic behavior include the following:

- Charitable contribution deductions based on the fair market value of appreciated long-term capital gain property.
- Deduction of certain personal expenditures, including personal interest and state and local taxes.
- Exclusion of interest received on debt obligations of state and local governmental units.

Statistical data compiled by the Department of the Treasury revealed that some taxpayers with large economic incomes were able to minimize or even avoid the payment of income tax by taking advantage of the incentive provisions that Congress had enacted. Although these taxpayers were reducing taxes legally through various investments that resulted in preferential treatment for income tax purposes, Congress was distressed by the resulting inequity. This point is made clear in the following extract from the Report by the Ways and Means Committee of the House of Representatives on the Tax Reform Act of 1969:

> This is obviously an unfair situation. In view of the tax burden on our citizens, at this time, it is particularly essential that our taxes be distributed in a fair manner. Your committee believes that no one should be permitted to avoid his fair share of the tax burden—to shift his tax load to the backs of other taxpayers.[1]

1. 1969–3 C.B. 249.

To ensure that taxpayers who benefit from such special provisions pay at least some amount of tax, Congress enacted a special tax, called the *alternative minimum tax,* that applies to corporations, individuals, trusts, and estates. Because it is referred to as a *minimum* tax, it is easy to misinterpret the nature of the tax. The AMT is *not* beneficial to taxpayers. Instead of saving (or minimizing) tax dollars through special computation procedures, it could result in additional tax liability.

Originally, the minimum tax was a special tax of 10 percent levied against specified items of tax preference in excess of $30,000 and was added on to the regular income tax; thus, it was commonly referred to as the add-on minimum tax. The present AMT, however, applies only if it exceeds the regular income tax.

In expanding the scope of the AMT in TRA of 1986, Congress reaffirmed the position taken in enacting the original minimum tax in 1969:

> [T]he minimum tax should serve one overriding objective: to ensure that no taxpayer with substantial economic income can avoid significant tax liability by using exclusions, deductions, and credits. Although these provisions may provide incentives for worthy goals, they become counterproductive when taxpayers are allowed to use them to avoid virtually all tax liability. The ability of high-income taxpayers to pay little or no tax undermines respect for the entire tax system and, thus, for the incentive provisions themselves. In addition, even aside from public perceptions . . . it is inherently unfair for high-income taxpayers to pay little or no tax due to their ability to utilize tax preferences.[2]

Overview of the Alternative Minimum Taxable Income (AMTI) Computation

The original minimum tax and previous versions of the AMT were based on tax preferences. For example, if a taxpayer deducted percentage depletion in excess of the basis of a mineral property, the excess depletion was treated as a tax preference and became a part of the minimum tax base. The *current* AMT is based on preferences *and* adjustments to regular taxable income.

AMT adjustments to taxable income arise because Congress has prescribed AMT treatment for certain income and deduction items that differs from the regular income tax treatment of these items. The alternative minimum taxable income (AMTI) computation starts with taxable income and makes adjustments to reflect these differences between income tax and AMT treatment of the specified items. Tax preferences are then added, and the total is labeled AMTI. The first step in the calculation of the AMT is the determination of AMTI, as shown in Figure 12–1.

In order to comprehend the structure of the AMT, it is important to understand the nature of adjustments and preferences.

Adjustments. As the AMTI formula in Figure 12–1 shows, taxable income is increased by *positive adjustments* and decreased by *negative adjustments.* Many of the positive adjustments arise as a result of timing differences related to deferral of income or acceleration of deductions. When these timing differences reverse, *negative adjustments* are made.

2. *General Explanation of the Tax Reform Act of 1986 ("Blue Book"),* prepared by The Staff of the Joint Committee on Taxation, May 4, 1987, H.R. 3838, 99th Cong., pp. 432–433.

Adjustments to taxable income that arise as a result of timing differences related to the acceleration of deductions for regular tax purposes include the following:

- Difference between modified ACRS depreciation deducted for income tax purposes and ADS (alternative depreciation system) depreciation deductible for AMT purposes.
- Difference between the amount allowed under *immediate expensing* provisions applicable for income tax purposes and the amount that would be allowed if the expenditures were *amortized* as prescribed for AMT purposes.

In addition, there are timing differences that relate to deferrals allowed for regular tax purposes but not for AMT purposes. Included in this category of adjustments is the difference between income reported under the completed contract method for income tax purposes and income that would be reported under the percentage of completion method prescribed for AMT purposes.

Several other adjustments do not relate to timing differences. These "adjustments" are more like preferences than adjustments in that they are always positive, never negative (they always increase and never decrease AMTI). Included in this category of adjustments are the following:

- Itemized deductions allowed for regular tax purposes but not for AMT purposes (e.g., state and local taxes).
- The standard deduction if the taxpayer does not itemize.
- The deduction for personal and dependency exemptions.

These adjustments, and their effect on AMTI, are discussed in detail under AMT Adjustments.

Refer to Figure 12–1 and note the subtotal "Taxable income after AMT adjustments." It is possible to compute this amount by direct application of the AMT provisions. Gross income, computed by applying the AMT rules applicable to income items, is reduced by deductions computed by applying the appropriate AMT rules. This method, however, requires much duplication of effort. Instead of computing "Taxable income after AMT adjustments" directly, it is less cumbersome to start with regular taxable income and adjust that figure to reflect differences in the income tax rules and the AMT rules. From a procedural perspective, this means that it is necessary to complete Form 1040 to the point of taxable income before computing AMTI on Form 6251.

Preferences. Some deductions allowed to taxpayers for regular income tax purposes provide extraordinary tax savings. Congress has chosen to single out these items, which are referred to as tax preferences. The AMT is designed to take back all or part of the tax benefits derived through the use of preferences in the computation of taxable income for regular income tax purposes. This is why taxable income, which is the starting point in computing AMTI, is increased by

FIGURE 12–1
Alternative Minimum Taxable Income (AMTI) Formula

Taxable income
Plus: Positive AMT adjustments
Minus: Negative AMT adjustments
Equals: Taxable income after AMT adjustments
Plus: Tax preferences
Equals: Alternative minimum taxable income

tax preference items. The effect of adding these preference items is to disallow for *AMT purposes* those preferences that were allowed in the regular income tax computation. Tax preferences include the following items:

- Percentage depletion in excess of the property's adjusted basis.
- Excess intangible drilling costs reduced by 65 percent of the net income from oil, gas, and geothermal properties.
- Certain net appreciation on contributed long-term capital gain property.
- Interest on certain private activity bonds.
- Excess of accelerated over straight-line depreciation on real property placed in service before 1987.
- Excess of accelerated over straight-line depreciation on *leased* personal property placed in service before 1987.
- Excess of amortization allowance over depreciation on pre-1987 certified pollution control facilities.

These preferences are discussed in detail under AMT Preferences.

AMT Adjustments

Circulation Expenditures. For income tax purposes, circulation expenditures, other than those the taxpayer elects to charge to a capital account, may be expensed in the year incurred.[3] These expenditures include expenses incurred to establish, maintain, or increase the circulation of a newspaper, magazine, or other periodical.

Circulation expenditures are not deductible in the year incurred for AMT purposes. In computing AMTI, these expenditures must be capitalized and amortized ratably over the three-year period beginning with the year in which the expenditures were made.[4]

The AMT adjustment for circulation expenditures is the amount expensed for income tax purposes minus the amount that can be amortized for AMT purposes. The adjustment can be either positive or negative, as shown in Example 1 below. The *nature* of AMT adjustments can be understood by examining the adjustments required for circulation expenditures.

Example 1

In 1992, T incurs $24,000 of deductible circulation expenditures. This amount is deducted for income tax purposes. For AMT purposes, the circulation expenditures must be deducted over a three-year period. This results in a deduction for AMT purposes of $8,000 ($24,000 ÷ 3). T's schedule of positive and negative adjustments follows:

Year	Income Tax Deduction	AMT Deduction	AMT Adjustment
1992	$24,000	$ 8,000	+$16,000
1993	–0–	8,000	– 8,000
1994	–0–	8,000	– 8,000
Total	$24,000	$24,000	$ –0–

◆

As mentioned previously, taxable income computed for income tax purposes is the starting point in the AMTI computation. Adjustments then are required to

3. § 173(a).

4. § 56(b)(2)(A)(i).

reconcile differences in the rules for computing taxable income and the rules for computing AMTI (refer to Figure 12–1).

EXAMPLE 2

Assume the same facts as in Example 1. In addition, assume that T's regular taxable income for 1992 was $100,000 and that he had no other AMT adjustments and had no tax preferences. In arriving at regular taxable income, T was allowed to deduct circulation expenditures of $24,000. However, for AMT purposes, T is allowed to deduct only $8,000. Therefore, T's taxable income after adjustment to reflect the AMT rules (rather than the income tax rules) is $116,000 ($100,000 + $16,000 positive adjustment for circulation expenditures). ◆

A taxpayer can avoid the AMT adjustments for circulation expenditures by electing to write off the expenditures over a three-year period for regular income tax purposes.[5]

Depreciation of Post-1986 Real Property. For real property placed in service after 1986, AMT depreciation is computed under the alternative depreciation system (ADS), which uses the straight-line method over a 40-year life. The depreciation lives for regular tax purposes are 27.5 years for residential rental property and 31.5 years for all other real property. The difference between AMT depreciation and regular tax depreciation is treated as an adjustment in computing the AMT. The differences will be positive during the regular tax life of the asset because the cost is written off over a shorter period for regular tax purposes. For example, during the 31.5-year income tax life of nonresidential real property, the regular tax depreciation will exceed the AMT depreciation because AMT depreciation is computed over a 40-year period.

Table 9–7 is used to compute regular income tax depreciation on real property placed in service after 1986. For AMT purposes, depreciation on real property placed in service after 1986 is computed under the ADS (refer to Table 9–12).

EXAMPLE 3

In January 1992, V placed in service a nonresidential building that cost $100,000. Depreciation for 1992 for income tax purposes is $3,042 ($100,000 cost × 3.042% from Table 9–7). For AMT purposes, depreciation is $2,396 ($100,000 cost × 2.396% from Table 9–12). In computing AMTI for 1992, V has a positive adjustment of $646 ($3,042 income tax depreciation − $2,396 AMT depreciation). ◆

After real property has been held for the entire depreciation period for income tax purposes, the asset will be fully depreciated. However, the depreciation period under the ADS is 40 years, so depreciation will continue for AMT purposes. This causes negative adjustments after the property has been fully depreciated for income tax purposes.

EXAMPLE 4

Assume the same facts as in the previous example, and compute the AMT adjustment for 2024 (the thirty-third year of the asset's life). Income tax depreciation is zero (refer to Table 9–7). AMT depreciation is $2,500 ($100,000 cost × 2.500% from Table 9–12). Therefore, V has a negative AMT adjustment of $2,500 ($0 income tax depreciation − $2,500 AMT depreciation). ◆

5. § 59(e)(2)(A).

After real property is fully depreciated for income tax and AMT purposes, the positive and negative adjustments that have been made for AMT purposes net to zero.

For real property and leased personal property placed in service before 1987, the difference between accelerated depreciation for regular income tax and straight-line depreciation for the AMT results in a tax preference rather than an AMT adjustment. These situations are explained later in the chapter under AMT Preferences.

Depreciation of Post-1986 Personal Property. For most personal property placed in service after 1986, the modified ACRS (MACRS) deduction for regular income tax purposes is based on the 200 percent declining-balance method with a switch to straight-line when that method produces a larger depreciation deduction for the asset. Refer to Table 9–2 for computing income tax depreciation.

For AMT purposes, the taxpayer must use the ADS. This method is based on the 150 percent declining-balance method with a similar switch to straight-line for all personal property. Refer to Table 9–10 for percentages to be used in computing AMT depreciation.

All personal property placed in service after 1986 may be taken into consideration in computing one net adjustment. Using this netting process, the AMT adjustment for a tax year is the difference between the total MACRS depreciation for all personal property computed for regular tax purposes and the total ADS depreciation computed for AMT purposes. When the total of MACRS deductions exceeds the total of ADS deductions, the amount of the adjustment is positive. When the total of ADS deductions exceeds the total of MACRS deductions, the adjustment for AMTI is negative.

The MACRS deduction for personal property is larger than the ADS deduction in the early years of an asset's life. However, the ADS deduction is larger in the later years. This is so because ADS lives (based on class life) are longer than MACRS lives (based on recovery period).[6] Over the ADS life of the asset, the same amount of depreciation is deducted for both regular tax and AMT purposes. In the same manner as other timing adjustments, the AMT adjustments for depreciation net to zero over the ADS life of the asset.

The taxpayer may elect to use the ADS for regular income tax purposes.[7] If this election is made, no AMT adjustment is required because the depreciation deduction is the same for regular tax and for the AMT.

Pollution Control Facilities. For regular tax purposes, the cost of certified pollution control facilities may be amortized over a period of 60 months. For AMT purposes, the cost of these facilities placed in service after 1986 must be depreciated under the ADS over the appropriate class life, determined as explained above for depreciation of post-1986 property. The required adjustment for AMTI is equal to the difference between the amortization deduction allowed for regular tax and the depreciation deduction computed under the ADS. The adjustment may be positive or negative.

In the case of pre-1987 facilities, a similar calculation results in an AMT preference, as discussed later in the chapter.

Mining Exploration and Development Costs. In computing taxable income, taxpayers are allowed to deduct certain mining exploration and development

6. Class lives and recovery periods are established for all assets in Rev.Proc. 87–56, 1987–2 C.B. 674.

7. § 168(g)(7).

expenditures. The deduction is allowed for expenditures paid or incurred during the taxable year for exploration[8] (ascertaining the existence, location, extent, or quality of a deposit or mineral) and for development of a mine or other natural deposit, other than an oil or gas well. Mining development expenditures are expenses paid or incurred after the existence of ores and minerals in commercially marketable quantities has been disclosed.[9]

For AMT purposes, however, mining exploration and development costs must be capitalized and amortized ratably over a 10-year period.[10] The AMT adjustment for mining exploration and development costs that are expensed is equal to the amount expensed minus the allowable expense if the costs had been capitalized and amortized ratably over a 10-year period. This provision does not apply to costs relating to an oil or gas well.

EXAMPLE 5

In 1992, M incurs $150,000 of mining exploration expenditures. This amount is deducted for income tax purposes. For AMT purposes, these mining exploration expenditures must be amortized over a 10-year period. M must make a positive adjustment for AMTI of $135,000 [$150,000 (allowed for income tax) − $15,000 (for AMT)] for 1992, the first year. In each of the next nine years for AMT purposes, M is required to make a negative adjustment of $15,000 [$0 (allowed for regular tax) − $15,000 (for AMT)]. ◆

To avoid the AMT adjustments for mining exploration and development costs, a taxpayer may elect to write off the expenditures over a 10-year period for income tax purposes.[11]

Research and Experimental Expenditures. For income tax purposes, a taxpayer may deduct research and experimental expenditures (see Chapter 8) in the year paid or incurred.[12] However, for AMT purposes, the expenditures must be capitalized and amortized ratably over a 10-year period.[13] For research and experimental expenditures that are expensed, the AMT adjustment is equal to the amount expensed minus the amount that would have been allowed if the expenditures had been capitalized and amortized ratably over a 10-year period. A taxpayer can avoid the AMT adjustment for research and experimental expenditures by electing to write the expenditures off over a 10-year period.

EXAMPLE 6

T incurs research and experimental expenditures of $100,000 in 1992 and elects to expense that amount for regular tax purposes. Since research and experimental expenditures must be amortized over a 10-year period for AMT purposes, T's AMT deduction is $10,000 each year ($100,000 ÷ 10 years) for 1992 and the succeeding nine years. T has a positive adjustment for 1992 of $90,000 ($100,000 allowed for regular tax − $10,000 allowed for AMT purposes). The adjustment reverses in each of the following nine years ($0 deduction for regular tax − $10,000 for AMT purposes = $10,000 negative adjustment). ◆

Assume that T in Example 6 elects to claim a tax credit amounting to $10,000 in regard to the research and experimental expenditures (see Chapter 13 for choices). The amount expensed currently must be reduced by 100 percent of the credit.[14] Thus, in this situation, T is allowed a current deduction of $90,000

8. § 617(a).
9. § 616(a).
10. § 56(a)(2).
11. §§ 59(e)(2)(D) and (E).
12. § 174(a).
13. § 56(b)(2)(A)(ii). For tax years beginning after 1990, a special rule applies to individuals who materially participate in an activity. They are not required to capitalize and amortize research and experimental expenditures generated by the activity.
14. § 280C(c).

[$100,000 (amount of expenditures) − $10,000 (100 percent of the $10,000 credit taken)] for regular tax purposes. For AMTI, T has a positive adjustment for 1992 of $81,000 [$90,000 allowed for regular tax − $9,000 ($90,000 ÷ 10 years) for AMT purposes]. In each of the next nine years, the AMT adjustment is a negative $9,000 [$0 (deduction for regular tax) − $9,000 (for AMT)].

Although the research and experimental expenditures tax credit cannot be used in the year of election if a taxpayer is liable for the AMT, the credit is subject to the general carryover rules applicable to unused business tax credits (see Chapter 13). Thus, the taxpayer will realize the benefit of the credit in a year when he or she is liable for the regular tax instead of the AMT.

Passive Activity Losses. Losses on passive activities acquired *after* October 22, 1986, are not deductible in computing either the income tax or the AMT.[15] However, for income tax purposes, losses incurred on passive activities acquired *before* October 23, 1986, were deductible as follows: 65 percent in 1987, 40 percent in 1988, 20 percent in 1989, 10 percent in 1990, and 0 percent thereafter.

The rules for computing taxable income differ from the rules for computing AMTI. It follows, then, that the rules for computing a loss for income tax purposes differ from the AMT rules for computing a loss. Therefore, any *passive loss* computed for income tax purposes may differ from the passive loss computed for AMT purposes.[16]

The Staff of the Joint Committee on Taxation provides this interpretation of the provisions related to AMT passive losses:

> . . . where a Code provision refers to a 'loss' of the taxpayer from an activity, for purposes of the alternative minimum tax the existence of a loss is determined with regard to the items that are includable and deductible for minimum tax, not regular tax, purposes. . . . With respect to the passive loss provision, for example, section 58 provides expressly that, in applying the limitation for minimum tax purposes, all minimum tax adjustments to income and expense *are made* and regular tax deductions that are items of tax preference *are disregarded*.[17]

This explanation by the Staff of the Joint Committee leads to the interpretations in Examples 7 and 8.

EXAMPLE 7

T acquired two passive activities in 1992. He received net passive income of $10,000 from Activity A and had no AMT adjustments or preferences in connection with the activity. Activity B had gross income of $28,000 and operating expenses (not affected by AMT adjustments or preferences) of $20,000. T claimed MACRS depreciation of $20,000 for Activity B; depreciation under the ADS would have been $15,000. In addition, T deducted $10,000 of percentage depletion in excess of basis. The following comparison illustrates the differences in the computation of the passive loss for income tax and AMT purposes.

	Income Tax	AMT
Gross income	$28,000	$28,000
Deductions:		
Operating expenses	$20,000	$20,000
Depreciation	20,000	15,000
Depletion	10,000	-0-
Total deductions	$50,000	$35,000
Passive loss	$22,000	$ 7,000

15. §§ 469(a) and 58(b)(2).
16. See Chapter 7.
17. *General Explanation of the Tax Reform Act of 1986 ("Blue Book")*, prepared by The Staff of the Joint Committee on Taxation, May 4, 1987, H.R. 3838, 99th Cong., pp 446–447.

Because the adjustment for depreciation ($5,000) applies and the preference for depletion ($10,000) is not taken into account in computing AMTI, the regular tax passive activity loss of $22,000 for Activity B is reduced by these amounts, resulting in a passive activity loss for AMT purposes of $7,000. ◆

For income tax purposes, T would offset the $10,000 of net passive income from Activity A with $10,000 of the passive loss from Activity B. For AMT purposes, T would offset the $10,000 of net passive income from Activity A with the $7,000 passive activity loss allowed from Activity B, resulting in passive activity income of $3,000. Thus, in computing AMTI, T makes a positive passive loss adjustment of $3,000 [$10,000 (passive activity loss allowed for regular tax) − $7,000 (passive activity loss allowed for the AMT)]. To avoid duplication, the AMT adjustment for depreciation and the preference for depletion are *not* reported separately. They are accounted for in determining the AMT passive loss adjustment. This reporting procedure also applies to tax shelter farm activities.

EXAMPLE 8

Assume the same facts as in the previous example. For regular tax purposes, T has a suspended passive loss of $12,000 [$22,000 (amount of loss) − $10,000 (used in 1992)]. This suspended passive loss can offset passive income in the future or can offset active or portfolio income when T disposes of the loss activity (see Chapter 7). For AMT purposes, T's suspended passive loss is $0 [$7,000 (amount of loss) − $7,000 (amount used in 1992)]. ◆

Passive Farm Losses. A passive farm loss is defined as any loss from a tax shelter farming activity (a farming syndicate or any other activity consisting of farming unless the taxpayer materially participates in the activity). For regular tax purposes, losses from passive farm activities were subject to the phase-in rules for passive losses (refer to Chapter 7).

The limitations for passive farm losses are more severe than the limitations for nonfarm passive losses. Each farming activity is treated separately for purposes of applying the limitation, and passive losses from one farming activity cannot be netted against passive income from a different farming activity. For AMT purposes, the passive farm loss limitations are applied before the general passive loss limitations. Thus, even though passive income from a farming activity cannot be offset by passive losses from other farming activities, the income can be offset by passive loss from nonfarm activities.

If a nonfarm passive activity results in a suspended loss, the suspended loss can offset passive income from other nonfarm activities. However, if a farm passive activity results in a suspended loss, the suspended loss can offset income only from the *same* activity in a subsequent year for AMTI. This rule does not apply, however, in the year of termination of the taxpayer's entire interest in the farm shelter activity. In this case, the amount of loss is allowed in determining AMTI and is not treated as a loss from a farm tax shelter activity.[18]

If a taxpayer is insolvent at the end of the taxable year, the amount of recomputed passive activity loss (both farm and nonfarm) for AMTI is reduced by the amount of insolvency. For this purpose, the taxpayer is insolvent to the extent that liabilities exceed the fair market value of assets.

Use of Completed Contract Method of Accounting. For any long-term contract entered into after March 1, 1986, taxpayers are required to use the percentage of

18. § 58(c)(2).

completion method for AMT purposes. However, in limited circumstances, taxpayers can use the completed contract method for income tax purposes.[19] Thus, a taxpayer recognizes a different amount of income for regular tax purposes than for AMT purposes. The resulting AMT adjustment is equal to the difference between income reported under the percentage of completion method and the amount reported using the completed contract method. The adjustment can be either positive or negative, depending on the amount of income recognized under the different methods.

A taxpayer can avoid an AMT adjustment on long-term contracts by using the percentage of completion method for regular income tax purposes rather than the completed contract method.

Incentive Stock Options. Incentive stock options (ISOs) are granted by employers to help attract new personnel and retain those already employed. At the time an ISO is granted, the employer corporation sets an option price for the corporate stock. If the value of the stock increases during the option period, the employee can obtain stock at a favorable price by exercising the option. Employees are generally restricted as to when they can dispose of stock acquired under an ISO (e.g., a certain length of employment may be required). Therefore, the stock may not be freely transferable until some specified period has passed. See Chapter 19 for details regarding ISOs.

The exercise of an ISO does not increase regular taxable income.[20] However, for AMT purposes, the excess of the fair market value of the stock over the exercise price is treated as an adjustment in the first taxable year in which the rights in the stock are freely transferable or are not subject to a substantial risk of forfeiture.

EXAMPLE 9

In 1990, M exercised an ISO that had been granted by his employer, X Corporation. M acquired 1,000 shares of X Corporation stock for the option price of $20 per share. The stock became freely transferable in 1992. The fair market value of the stock at the date of exercise was $50 per share. For AMT purposes, M has a positive gain or loss adjustment (see below) of $30,000 ($50,000 fair market value – $20,000 option price) for 1992. The transaction does not affect regular taxable income in 1990 or 1992. ◆

No adjustment is required if the taxpayer exercises the option and disposes of the stock in the same year. Nor is there an adjustment if the amount realized on the disposition is less than the value of the option at the time it was exercised.

The income tax basis of stock acquired through exercise of ISOs is different from the AMT basis. The income tax basis of the stock is equal to its cost, whereas the AMT basis is equal to the fair market value on the date the options are exercised. Consequently, the gain or loss upon disposition of the stock is different for income tax purposes and AMT purposes.

EXAMPLE 10

Assume the same facts as in the previous example and that M sells the stock for $60,000 in 1994. M's gain for income tax purposes is $40,000 ($60,000 amount realized – $20,000 income tax basis). For AMT purposes, the gain is $10,000 ($60,000 amount realized – $50,000 AMT basis). Therefore, M has a $30,000 negative adjustment in computing AMT in 1994 ($40,000 income tax gain – $10,000 AMT gain). Note that the $30,000 negative adjustment upon disposition in 1994 offsets the $30,000 positive adjustment upon exercise of the ISO in 1992. ◆

---

19. See Chapter 18 for a detailed discussion of the completed contract and percentage of completion methods of accounting.

20. § 421(a).

Adjusted Gain or Loss. When property is sold during the year or a casualty occurs to business or income-producing property, gain or loss reported for regular income tax may be different than gain or loss determined for the AMT. This difference occurs because the adjusted basis of the property for AMT purposes must reflect any current and prior AMT adjustments for the following:

- Depreciation
- Circulation expenditures
- Research and experimentation expenditures
- Mining exploration and development costs
- Amortization of certified pollution control facilities.

If the gain computed for AMT purposes is less than the gain computed for regular income tax *or* if the loss for AMT purposes is more than the loss for regular tax purposes *or* if a loss is computed for AMT purposes and a gain for regular tax, the difference is a negative gain or loss adjustment in determining AMTI. Otherwise, the AMT gain or loss adjustment is positive.

EXAMPLE 11

In January 1992, K paid $100,000 for a duplex acquired for rental purposes. Income tax depreciation in 1992 was $3,485 ($100,000 cost × 3.485% from Table 9–7). AMT depreciation was $2,396 ($100,000 cost × 2.396% from Table 9–12). For AMT purposes, K made a positive adjustment of $1,089 ($3,485 income tax depreciation − $2,396 AMT depreciation). ◆

EXAMPLE 12

K sold the duplex on December 20, 1993, for $105,000. Income tax depreciation for 1993 is $3,485 [($100,000 cost × 3.636% from Table 9–7) × 11.5/12]. AMT depreciation for 1993 is $2,396 [($100,000 cost × 2.500% from Table 9–12) × 11.5/12]. K's AMT adjustment for 1993 was $1,089 ($3,485 income tax depreciation − $2,396 AMT depreciation). ◆

Because depreciation on the duplex differs for income tax and AMT purposes, the adjusted basis is different for income tax and AMT purposes. Consequently, the gain or loss on disposition of the duplex is different for income tax and AMT purposes.

EXAMPLE 13

The adjusted basis of K's duplex for income tax purposes is $93,030 ($100,000 cost − $3,485 depreciation for 1992 − $3,485 depreciation for 1993). For AMT purposes, the adjusted basis is $95,208 ($100,000 cost − $2,396 depreciation for 1992 − $2,396 depreciation for 1993). The income tax gain is $11,970 ($105,000 amount realized − $93,030 income tax basis). The AMT gain is $9,792 ($105,000 amount realized − $95,208 AMT basis). Because the income tax and AMT gain on the sale of the duplex differ, K must make a negative AMT adjustment of $2,178 ($11,970 income tax gain − $9,792 AMT gain). Note that this negative adjustment offsets the $2,178 total of the two positive adjustments for depreciation ($1,089 in 1992 + $1,089 in 1993). ◆

Alternative Tax Net Operating Loss Deduction. In computing taxable income, taxpayers are allowed to deduct net operating loss (NOL) carryovers and carrybacks (refer to Chapter 8). The income tax NOL must be modified, however, in computing AMTI. The starting point in computing the alternative tax NOL (ATNOL) is the regular NOL computed for income tax purposes. The ATNOL, however, is determined by applying AMT adjustments and ignoring tax preferences. Thus, preferences that have been deducted in computing the income tax NOL are added back, thereby reducing or eliminating the ATNOL.

Example 14

In 1992, T incurred an NOL of $100,000. T had no AMT adjustments, but his deductions included tax preferences of $18,000. His ATNOL carryover to 1993 is $82,000 ($100,000 regular tax NOL − $18,000 tax preferences deducted in computing the NOL). ◆

In Example 14, if the adjustment was not made to the income tax NOL, the $18,000 in tax preference items deducted in 1992 would have the effect of reducing AMTI in the year the 1992 NOL is utilized. This would weaken the entire concept of the AMT.

A taxpayer who has an ATNOL that is carried back or over to another year must use the ATNOL against AMTI in the carryback or carryover year even if the regular tax, rather than the AMT, applies.

Example 15

K's ATNOL for 1993 (carried over from 1992) is $10,000. AMTI before considering the ATNOL is $25,000. If K's regular income tax exceeds the AMT, the AMT does not apply. Nevertheless, K's ATNOL of $10,000 is "used up" in 1993 and is not available for carryover to a later year. ◆

For income tax purposes, the NOL can be carried back 3 years and forward 15 years. However, the taxpayer may elect to forgo the 3-year carryback. These rules generally apply to the ATNOL as well, except that the election to forgo the 3-year carryback is not available for the ATNOL unless the taxpayer elected it for the income tax NOL.

Itemized Deductions. Taxes (state, local, foreign income, and property taxes) and miscellaneous itemized deductions that are subject to the 2 percent of AGI floor are not allowed in computing AMT. A positive AMT adjustment in the total amount of the income tax deduction for each is required. Moreover, if the taxpayer's gross income includes the recovery of any tax deducted as an itemized deduction for income tax purposes, a negative AMT adjustment in the amount of the recovery is allowed for AMTI purposes. For example, state, local, and foreign income taxes can be deducted for income tax purposes, but cannot be deducted in computing AMTI. Because of this, any refund of such taxes from a prior year is not included in AMTI. Therefore, the taxpayer must make a negative adjustment if an income tax refund has been included in computing regular taxable income. Under the tax benefit rule, a tax refund is included in taxable income to the extent that the taxpayer obtained a tax benefit by deducting the tax in a prior year.

Itemized deductions that are allowed for AMT purposes include the following:

- Casualty losses.
- Gambling losses.
- Charitable contributions.
- Medical expenses in excess of 10 percent of AGI.
- Estate tax on income in respect of a decedent.
- Qualified interest.

The 3 percent floor that applies to income tax itemized deductions of certain high-income taxpayers (refer to Chapter 11) does not apply in computing AMT.

Medical Expenses. The rules for determining the AMT deductions for medical expenses are sufficiently complex to require further explanation. For income tax purposes, medical expenses are deductible to the extent they exceed 7.5 percent of AGI. However, for AMT purposes, medical expenses are deductible only to the extent they exceed 10 percent of AGI.

EXAMPLE 16

K, who had AGI of $100,000 in 1992, incurred medical expenses of $12,000 during the year. For income tax purposes, K can deduct $4,500 ($12,000 medical expenses − 7.5% of $100,000 AGI). In computing the AMT, K can deduct only $2,000 ($12,000 medical expenses − 10% of $100,000 AGI). Because taxable income is the starting point in computing AMTI, K must make a positive adjustment of $2,500 ($4,500 income tax deduction − $2,000 AMT deduction). ◆

Interest in General. The AMT itemized deduction allowed for interest expense includes only qualified housing interest and investment interest to the extent of net investment income that is included in the determination of AMTI.

In computing regular taxable income, taxpayers who itemize can deduct the following types of interest (refer to Chapter 11):

- Qualified residence interest.
- Investment interest, subject to the investment interest limitations (discussed under Investment Interest below).

Housing Interest. Under current income tax rules, taxpayers who itemize can deduct qualified residence interest on up to two residences. The deduction is limited to interest on acquisition indebtedness up to $1,000,000 and home equity indebtedness up to $100,000. Acquisition indebtedness is debt that is incurred in acquiring, constructing, or substantially improving a qualified residence of the taxpayer and is secured by the residence. Home equity indebtedness is indebtedness secured by a qualified residence of the taxpayer, but does not include acquisition indebtedness.

EXAMPLE 17

G, who used the proceeds of a mortgage to acquire a personal residence, paid mortgage interest of $112,000 in 1992. Of this amount, $14,000 is attributable to acquisition indebtedness in excess of $1,000,000. For income tax purposes, G may deduct mortgage interest of $98,000 ($112,000 total − $14,000 disallowed). ◆

The mortgage interest deduction for AMT purposes is limited to *qualified housing interest,* rather than *qualified residence interest.* Qualified housing interest includes only interest incurred to acquire, construct, or substantially improve the taxpayer's principal residence. It also includes interest on one other dwelling used for personal purposes. When a loan is refinanced, interest paid is deductible as qualified housing interest for AMT purposes only if:

- The proceeds are used to acquire or substantially improve a qualified residence.
- Interest on the prior loan was qualified housing interest.
- The amount of the loan was not increased.

Further, a special rule applies to indebtedness incurred before July 1, 1982, and secured at that time by a qualified residence. Qualified housing interest includes interest on all such debt even if it does not fall under the definition of acquisition indebtedness.

A positive AMT adjustment is required in the amount of the difference between qualified *residence* interest allowed as an itemized deduction for regular tax purposes and qualified *housing* interest allowed in the determination of AMTI.

Investment Interest. Investment interest is deductible for income tax purposes and for AMT purposes to the extent of qualified net investment income.

EXAMPLE 18

For the year, J had net investment income of $16,000 before deducting investment interest. She incurred investment interest expense of $30,000 during the year. Her investment interest deduction is $16,000. ◆

Interest income on bonds issued by state and local governments is tax-exempt for income tax purposes. Therefore, any interest expense paid or incurred to purchase or carry such bonds is not deductible (refer to Chapter 6). As a result, the income tax base is not affected by either the income or the expense related to the state or local government bonds. For AMT purposes, however, the tax-exempt status that applies for income tax purposes does not apply to specified private activity bonds. Interest on these bonds is treated as a tax preference for AMT purposes. The treatment applies generally to private activity bonds issued on or after August 7, 1986.

If a taxpayer pays or incurs interest expense on an investment in certain private activity bonds, the interest expense is not deductible for income tax purposes because the income from the bonds is not included in taxable income. For AMT purposes, the interest expense on these private activity bonds is offset against the interest income that is treated as a tax preference item (as explained later in the chapter).

In applying the investment interest limitation for AMT purposes, the interest income on these private activity bonds is treated as investment income.

EXAMPLE 19

For income tax purposes, T had net investment income of $20,000 before deducting investment interest. He incurred investment interest expense of $35,000 during the year. In addition, T received interest income of $12,000 on private activity bonds. For income tax purposes, T may deduct $20,000 of interest expense. The income tax deduction is limited by the investment income reported for income tax purposes. In computing AMT, T must report investment income of $32,000 ($20,000 net investment income for income tax purposes + $12,000 interest on private activity bonds). His investment interest deduction for AMT purposes is $32,000. In computing AMT, T makes a negative adjustment of $12,000 ($32,000 AMT deduction − $20,000 income tax deduction). ◆

Qualified net investment income is the excess of qualified investment income over qualified investment expenses. Qualified investment income includes the following to the extent that such amounts are not derived from the conduct of a trade or business:

- Gross income from interest, dividends, rents, and royalties.
- Any net gain attributable to the disposition of property held for investment.

Qualified investment expenses include deductions directly connected with the production of qualified net investment income to the extent that the deductions are allowable in computing adjusted gross income and are not items of tax preference.

Other Adjustments. The standard deduction is not allowed as a deduction in computing AMTI. Although it would be rare for a person who does not itemize to be subject to the AMT, it is possible. In such a case, the taxpayer would be required to enter a positive adjustment for the standard deduction in computing the AMT.

The exemption amount deducted for income tax purposes is not allowed in computing AMT. Therefore, taxpayers must enter a positive AMT adjustment for the exemption amount claimed in computing the income tax. A separate exemption (discussed below) is allowed for AMT purposes. To allow both the income tax exemption amount and the AMT exemption amount would result in extra benefits for taxpayers.

EXAMPLE 20

T, who is single, has no dependents and does not itemize deductions. He earned a salary of $105,900 in 1992. Based on this information, T's taxable income for 1992 is $100,000 ($105,900 − $3,600 standard deduction − $2,300 exemption). ◆

EXAMPLE 21

Assume the same facts as in Example 20. In addition, assume T's tax preferences for the year totaled $150,000. T's AMTI is $255,900 ($100,000 taxable income + $3,600 adjustment for standard deduction + $2,300 adjustment for exemption + $150,000 tax preferences). ◆

AMT Preferences

Percentage Depletion. Congress originally enacted the percentage depletion rules to provide taxpayers with incentives to invest in the development of specified natural resources. Percentage depletion is computed by multiplying a rate specified in the Code times the gross income from the property (refer to Chapter 9). The percentage rate is based on the type of mineral involved. The basis of the property is reduced by the amount of percentage depletion taken until the basis reaches zero. However, once the basis of the property reaches zero, taxpayers are allowed to continue taking percentage depletion deductions. Thus, over the life of the property, depletion deductions may greatly exceed the cost of the property.

The percentage depletion preference is equal to the excess of the regular tax deduction for percentage depletion over the adjusted basis of the property at the end of the taxable year. Basis is determined without regard to the depletion deduction for the taxable year. This preference item is figured separately for each piece of property for which the taxpayer is claiming depletion.

EXAMPLE 22

T owns a mineral property that qualifies for a 22% depletion rate. The basis of the property at the beginning of the year was $10,000. Gross income from the property for the year was $100,000. For regular tax purposes, T's percentage depletion deduction (assume it is not limited by taxable income from the property) is $22,000. For AMT purposes, T has a tax preference of $12,000 ($22,000 − $10,000). ◆

Intangible Drilling Costs. In computing the income tax, taxpayers are allowed to deduct certain intangible drilling and development costs in the year incurred, although such costs are normally capital in nature. The deduction is allowed for costs incurred in connection with oil and gas wells and geothermal wells. A geothermal deposit is a geothermal reservoir consisting of natural heat that is stored in rock or in an aqueous liquid or vapor.[21]

21. § 613(e).

For AMT purposes, excess intangible drilling costs (IDC) for the year are treated as a preference.[22] The preference for excess IDC is computed as follows:

IDC expensed in the year incurred
Minus: Deduction if IDC were capitalized and amortized over 10 years
Equals: Excess of IDC expense over amortization
Minus: 65% of net oil and gas income
Equals: Tax preference item

EXAMPLE 23

J, who incurred IDC of $50,000 during the year, elected to expense that amount. J's net oil and gas income for the year was $60,000. J's tax preference for IDC is $6,000 [($50,000 IDC − $5,000 amortization) − (65% × $60,000 income)]. ◆

Charitable Contributions of Appreciated Property. For income tax purposes, taxpayers who contribute certain appreciated long-term capital gain property to a qualified charity are allowed to compute their itemized deduction based on the fair market value of the property (refer to Chapter 11). The result is a generous tax benefit if the property is greatly appreciated because the unrealized appreciation is not taxable.

EXAMPLE 24

T contributed X Corporation stock to the United Fund, a qualified charitable organization. T's basis in the stock was $5,000, and its fair market value at the date of contribution was $100,000. T's charitable contribution deduction is based on the $100,000 fair market value, even though the $95,000 of appreciation has never been included in income. ◆

For AMT purposes the contribution of appreciated long-term capital gain property to charity results in a tax preference item. Unrealized gain on the property is offset by unrealized loss on other long-term capital gain property contributed to charity. Thus, only the net amount of appreciation on all long-term capital gain properties contributed to charity becomes a preference.

EXAMPLE 25

H made two contributions of long-term assets to charity during the year. Asset A had a fair market value of $60,000 and an adjusted basis of $25,000. Asset B had a fair market value of $40,000 and an adjusted basis of $56,000. H's tax preference on the contributions is $19,000 ($35,000 appreciation on Asset A − $16,000 decline in value on Asset B). ◆

Recent legislation contained a provision that applies to charitable contributions of tangible personal property which is long-term capital gain property and meets the *related use* test (refer to Chapter 11). This provision, which initially applied only to tax years beginning in 1991 but has been extended through June 30, 1992, entitles the taxpayer to a deduction equal to the property's fair market value for AMT purposes as well as income tax purposes. As a result, untaxed

---

22. The Revenue Reconciliation Act of 1990 provides an AMT deduction for taxpayers who incur IDC attributable to qualified exploratory costs. Coverage of these rules is beyond the scope of this text.

appreciation on such property is not a preference item. Thus, for example, donations of appreciated art works to art museums do not result in an AMT preference, while donations of appreciated stocks to a university continue to generate an AMT preference.

It is interesting to note that Congress first considered including unrealized appreciation on contributed property (as well as tax-exempt interest discussed below) as tax preference items in 1969.[23] However, these items were not treated as preferences until TRA of 1986. Thus, a proposal is not necessarily dead if it is not enacted when originally considered by Congress. The Code contains numerous examples of proposals that were enacted many years after they no longer appeared to be a threat.

Interest on Private Activity Bonds. Income from private activity bonds is not included in taxable income, and expenses related to carrying such bonds are not deductible for income tax purposes. However, interest on private activity bonds is included in computing AMTI. Therefore, expenses incurred in carrying the bonds are allowed as an offset against the interest income in computing AMTI. Consequently, the preference is equal to the interest on the bonds minus any deduction that would have been allowed for income tax purposes if the interest had been included in gross income.

Depreciation. For real property and leased personal property placed in service before 1987, there is an AMT preference for the excess of accelerated depreciation over straight-line depreciation. The following discussion focuses on leased personal property, rather than real property, to illustrate the nature of this depreciation preference.

Accelerated depreciation on pre-1987 leased personal property was computed using specified ACRS percentages (refer to Table 9–1, Chapter 9). AMT depreciation was based on the straight-line method which was computed using the half-year convention, no salvage value, and a longer recovery period.[24] As a result, in the early years of the life of the asset, the cost recovery allowance used in computing income tax was greater than the straight-line depreciation deduction allowed in computing AMT. The excess depreciation was treated as a tax preference item.

EXAMPLE 26

P acquired personal property on January 1, 1986, at a cost of $30,000. The property, which was placed in service as leased personal property on January 1, was 10-year ACRS property. P's 1986 depreciation deduction for regular tax purposes was $2,400 ($30,000 cost × 8% rate from Table 9–1). For AMT purposes, the asset was depreciated over the AMT life of 15 years using the straight-line method with the half-year convention. Thus, AMT depreciation for 1986 was $1,000 [($30,000 ÷ 15) × ½ year convention]. P's tax preference for 1986 was $1,400 ($2,400 − $1,000). ACRS depreciation for 1992 is $2,700 ($30,000 × 9% ACRS rate), and straight-line depreciation is $2,000 ($30,000 ÷ 15). Therefore, the tax preference for 1992 is $700 ($2,700 − $2,000). P's tax preferences for excess depreciation are summarized below:

23. Treasury Tax Reform Studies and Proposals (Part 2), pp. 132 and 142 (1969).

24. The specified lives for AMT purposes are 5 years for 3-year property, 8 years for 5-year property, 15 years for 10-year property, and 22 years for 15-year property.

Year	ACRS Allowance	AMT Deduction	Preference
1986	$2,400	$1,000	$1,400
1987	4,200	2,000	2,200
1988	3,600	2,000	1,600
1989	3,000	2,000	1,000
1990	3,000	2,000	1,000
1991	3,000	2,000	1,000
1992	2,700	2,000	700

◆

The preference item for excess depreciation on leased personal property is figured separately for each piece of property. No preference is reported in the year the taxpayer disposes of the property.

Amortization of Certified Pollution Control Facilities. Under § 169 of the Code, for income tax purposes, taxpayers may elect to amortize the cost of certified pollution control facilities over a period of 60 months. For pre-1987 facilities, excess amortization is a tax preference item. Excess amortization equals the amortization deducted by the taxpayer minus the amount that would have been deducted if the asset had been depreciated over its longer useful life or cost recovery period. A similar calculation for certified pollution control facilities placed in service *after* 1986 results in an *adjustment*, discussed in a prior section of the chapter.

Other Components of the AMT Formula

Alternative minimum taxable income is a somewhat confusing term. For income tax purposes, once taxable income has been computed, it is possible to compute the income tax. But even after AMTI has been computed, the AMT cannot be computed until the *AMT base* has been determined. To arrive at the AMT base, the AMT exemption must be deducted. This procedure is shown in the AMT formula in Figure 12–2.

FIGURE 12–2
Alternative Minimum Tax Formula

Regular taxable income
Plus or minus: Adjustments
Equals: Taxable income after AMT adjustments
Plus: Tax preferences
Equals: Alternative minimum taxable income
Minus: Exemption
Equals: Alternative minimum tax base
Times: 24% rate
Equals: Tentative minimum tax before foreign tax credit
Minus: Alternative minimum tax foreign tax credit
Equals: Tentative minimum tax
Minus: Regular tax liability*
Equals: Alternative minimum tax (if amount is positive)

*This is the regular tax liability for the year reduced by any allowable foreign tax credit. It does not include any tax on lump-sum distributions from pension plans, any investment tax credit recapture, or any low-income credit recapture. See § 55(c).

Exemption Amount. The initial exemption amount is $40,000 for married taxpayers filing joint returns, $30,000 for single taxpayers, and $20,000 for married taxpayers filing separate returns. However, the exemption is phased out at a rate of 25 cents on the dollar when AMTI exceeds the levels listed below:

- $112,500 for single taxpayers.
- $150,000 for married taxpayers filing jointly.
- $75,000 for married taxpayers filing separately.

The following example explains the calculation of the phase-out of the AMT exemption.

EXAMPLE 27

G, who is single, has AMTI of $192,500 for the year. Her $30,000 initial exemption amount is reduced by $20,000 [($192,500 − $112,500) × 25% phase-out rate]. G's AMT exemption is $10,000 ($30,000 exemption − $20,000 reduction). ◆

The following table shows the beginning and end of the AMT exemption phase-out range for each filing status.

Status	Exemption	Phase-out Begins at	Phase-out Ends at
Married, joint	$40,000	$150,000	$310,000
Single or head of household	30,000	112,500	232,500
Married, separate	20,000	75,000	155,000

A special rule precludes the tax saving that might result when married taxpayers file separate returns. The AMTI of a married person filing a separate return is increased by the lesser of:

- 25 percent of the AMTI that exceeds $155,000 (the amount at which the exemption phases out on a separate return), or
- $20,000 (the maximum exemption amount of the taxpayer's spouse).

AMT Rate. The rate for the individual AMT is a flat 24 percent (21 percent before 1991).

Regular Tax Liability. The AMT is equal to the tentative minimum tax minus the *regular tax liability.* In most cases, the regular tax liability is equal to the amount of tax from the Tax Table or Tax Rate Schedules decreased by any foreign tax credit allowable for income tax purposes. Because only the foreign tax credit is allowed as a reduction of the tentative minimum tax, taxpayers who pay AMT lose the benefit of all other nonrefundable credits.

In an AMT year, the taxpayer's total tax liability is equal to the tentative minimum tax (refer to Figure 12–2). The tentative minimum tax consists of two components: the regular tax liability and the AMT. The disallowance of credits does not affect a taxpayer's total liability in an AMT year. However, it does decrease the amount of the AMT and, as a consequence, reduces the minimum tax credit available to be carried forward. Thus, for AMT purposes, the government denies all the credits (except the foreign tax credit) that apply in computing the income tax liability. Furthermore, the foreign tax credit cannot offset more than 90 percent of the tentative minimum tax.

It is also possible that taxpayers who have adjustments and preferences but *do not pay* AMT will lose the benefit of some or all of their nonrefundable credits. This result occurs because a taxpayer may claim nonrefundable credits only to the extent that his or her regular tax liability exceeds the tentative minimum tax.

EXAMPLE 28

T has total nonrefundable credits of $10,000, regular tax liability of $33,000, and tentative minimum tax of $25,000. T can claim only $8,000 of the nonrefundable credits in the current year. The disallowed $2,000 credit is lost unless a carryover provision applies.

Illustration of the AMT Computation

The computation of the AMT is illustrated in the following example.

EXAMPLE 29

T, who is single, had taxable income for 1992 as follows:

Salary		$ 92,000
Interest		8,000
Adjusted gross income		$100,000
Less itemized deductions:		
Medical expenses ($17,500 − 7.5% of $100,000 AGI)[a]	$10,000	
State income taxes	4,000	
Interest[b]		
Home mortgage (for qualified housing)	20,000*	
Investment interest	3,300*	
Contributions (cash)	5,000*	
Casualty losses ($14,000 − 10% of $100,000 AGI)	4,000*	(46,300)
		$ 53,700
Less exemption		(2,300)
Taxable income		$ 51,400

[a]Total medical expenses were $17,500, reduced by 7.5% of AGI, resulting in an itemized deduction of $10,000. However, for AMT purposes, the reduction is 10%, which leaves an AMT itemized deduction of $7,500 ($17,500 − 10% of $100,000 AGI). Therefore, an adjustment of $2,500 ($10,000 − $7,500) is required for medical expenses disallowed for AMT purposes.

[b]In this illustration, all interest is deductible in computing AMTI. Qualified housing interest is deductible. Investment interest ($3,300) is deductible to the extent of net investment income included in the minimum tax base. For this purpose, the $8,000 of interest income is treated as net investment income.

Deductions marked by an asterisk are allowed as *alternative tax itemized deductions.* Adjustments are required for state income taxes and for medical expenses to the extent the medical expenses deductible for income tax purposes are not deductible in computing AMT (see note a above). In addition to the items that affected taxable income, T had $35,000 interest on private activity bonds (an exclusion preference). AMTI is computed as follows:

Taxable income		$51,400
Plus:	Adjustments	
	State income taxes	4,000
	Medical expenses (see note a above)	2,500
	Personal exemption	2,300

Plus: Tax preference (interest on private activity bonds)	35,000
Equals: AMTI	$ 95,200
Minus: AMT exemption	30,000
Equals: Minimum tax base	$ 65,200
Times: AMT rate	×24%
	$ 15,648
Minus: Regular tax on taxable income	(11,604)
Equals: AMT	$ 4,044

◆

AMT Credit

As discussed previously, timing differences give rise to adjustments to the minimum tax base. In later years, the timing differences reverse, as was illustrated in several of the preceding examples. To provide equity for the taxpayer when timing differences reverse, the regular tax liability may be reduced by a tax credit for prior years' minimum tax liability attributable to timing differences. The minimum tax credit may be carried over indefinitely. Therefore, there is no need to keep track of when the minimum tax credit arose.

EXAMPLE 30

Assume the same facts as in Example 1. Also assume that in 1992, T paid AMT as a result of the $16,000 adjustment arising from the circulation expenditures. In 1993, $8,000 of the timing difference reverses, resulting in regular taxable income that is $8,000 greater than AMTI. Because T has already paid AMT as a result of the write-off of circulation expenditures, he is allowed an AMT credit in 1993. ◆

The AMT credit is applicable only for the AMT that results from timing differences. It is not available in connection with exclusions, which include the following:

- The standard deduction.
- Personal exemptions.
- Medical expenses, to the extent deductible for income tax purposes, but not deductible in computing AMT.
- Other itemized deductions not allowable for AMT purposes, including miscellaneous itemized deductions, taxes, and interest expense.
- Excess percentage depletion.
- Tax-exempt interest on specified private activity bonds.
- The charitable contribution preference.

EXAMPLE 31

D, who is single, has zero taxable income for 1992. He also has positive timing adjustments of $300,000 and exclusions of $100,000. His AMTI is $400,000 because his AMT exemption is phased out completely due to the level of AMTI. D's tentative AMT is $96,000 ($400,000 × 24% AMT rate). ◆

To determine the amount of AMT credit to carry over, the AMT must be recomputed reflecting only the exclusions and the AMT exemption amount.

EXAMPLE 32

Assume the same facts as in the previous example. If there had been no positive timing adjustments for the year, D's tentative AMT would have been $16,800 [($100,000 exclusions − $30,000 exemption) × 24% AMT rate]. D may carry over an AMT credit of $79,200 ($96,000 AMT − $16,800 related to exclusions). ◆

Concept Summary 12–1 presents an expanded version of the AMT formula, with brief descriptions of the components of the formula. Form 8801 should be used to calculate the credit for prior year minimum tax.

CONCEPT SUMMARY 12–1
EXPANDED ALTERNATIVE MINIMUM TAX FORMULA

Taxable income
Plus: Income tax NOL deduction.
Plus or minus: Adjustments to taxable income that are required to compute AMTI include, but are not limited to, the following:
- Standard deduction (if the taxpayer did not itemize).
- Personal and dependency exemption amounts.
- Itemized deductions allowed for income tax purposes but not for AMT:
  - Medical expenses deducted for income tax purposes minus amount deductible for AMT.
  - Miscellaneous itemized deductions in excess of 2% of AGI.
  - Taxes (includes state and local income taxes, real estate taxes, and personal property taxes).
  - Refund of taxes deducted in previous year if such taxes were not allowed for AMT (enter as negative amount).
  - Mortgage interest that is not qualified housing interest.
  - Difference between investment interest expense allowed for income tax purposes and investment interest expense allowed for AMT.
- Excess of ACRS over ADS depreciation on real property placed in service after 1986 (AMT alternative period is 40 years vs. regular tax periods of 27.5 years for residential rental property and 31.5 years for all other rental property).
- Excess of ACRS depreciation over alternative depreciation on all personal property placed in service after 1986 (AMT requires 150% declining-balance method, switching to straight-line, over the asset's ADR midpoint or class life).
- Circulation expenditures (AMT requires amortization over three years vs. immediate expensing allowed for income tax).
- Research and experimentation expenditures (AMT requires amortization over 10 years vs. immediate expensing allowed for income tax).
- Mining and exploration expenditures (AMT requires amortization over 10 years vs. immediate expensing allowed for income tax).
- Income on long-term contracts (AMT requires percentage of completion method; completed contract method is allowed in limited circumstances for income tax purposes).
- Pollution control facilities placed in service after 1986 (AMT requires ADS depreciation using the ADR class life and the straight-line method; 60-month amortization is allowed for income tax purposes).
- Adjusted gain or loss:
  - Incentive stock options (excess of fair market value over option price is a positive adjustment in the year the options are freely transferable or not subject to a substantial risk of forfeiture).
  - Dispositions of assets (if gain or loss for AMT purposes differs from gain or loss for income tax purposes—refer to Examples 11 through 13).
- Tax shelter farm loss if the farm activity is not a passive activity (difference between the amount reported for AMT purposes and income tax purposes).
- Passive activity loss (recompute gains and losses for AMT by taking into account all AMT adjustments and preferences; adjustment is for difference between AMT and income tax gains and losses).
- Beneficiary's share of AMTI from an estate or trust.

Plus: Preferences that must be added to compute AMTI include, but are not limited to, the following:
- Net appreciation on contribution of long-term capital assets (considering all contributions, whether the property has appreciated or declined in value; 1991–1992 exception for certain tangible personal property).
- Tax-exempt interest on private activity bonds issued on or after August 7, 1986.
- Percentage depletion in excess of the property's adjusted basis.
- Excess of accelerated over straight-line depreciation on real property placed in service before 1987.
- Excess of accelerated over straight-line depreciation on leased personal property placed in service before 1987.
- Excess intangible drilling costs (IDC) minus 65% of the net income from oil, gas, and geothermal properties (AMT requires amortization over 120 months vs. immediate expensing of IDC allowed for income tax purposes).

Equals: AMTI before deduction of alternative tax net operating loss (ATNOL).

Minus: Allowable ATNOL (which cannot exceed 90% of AMTI before deduction of ATNOL).
Equals: AMTI.
Minus: Exemption ($40,000 for married joint, $30,000 for single, $20,000 for married separate; exemption is subject to phase-out rules).
Equals: AMT base.
Times: 24% rate.
Equals: Tentative minimum tax before allowable AMT foreign tax credit.
Minus: Allowable AMT foreign tax credit (may not reduce tentative minimum tax before allowable AMT foreign tax credit by more than 90%).
Equals: Tentative minimum tax.
Minus: Regular income tax liability before credits (other than foreign tax credit allowed for income tax purposes).
Equals: AMT (if positive).

Corporate Alternative Minimum Tax

The AMT applicable to corporations is similar to that applicable to noncorporate taxpayers. However, there are several important differences:

- The corporate AMT rate is 20 percent versus 24 percent for noncorporate taxpayers.
- The AMT exemption for corporations is $40,000 reduced by 25 percent of the amount by which AMTI exceeds $150,000.
- Tax preferences applicable to noncorporate taxpayers are also applicable to corporate taxpayers, but some adjustments differ (see below).

Although there are computational differences, the objective of the corporate AMT is identical to the objective of the noncorporate AMT: to force taxpayers who are more profitable than their taxable income reflects to pay additional tax. The formula for determining the corporate AMT appears in Figure 12–3.

AMT Adjustments

Adjustments Applicable to Individuals and Corporations. The following adjustments that were discussed in connection with the individual AMT also apply to the corporate AMT:

FIGURE 12–3
AMT Formula for Corporations

Taxable income
Plus: Income tax NOL deduction
Plus or minus: AMT adjustments
Plus: Tax preferences
Equals: AMTI before ATNOL deduction
Minus: ATNOL deduction (limited to 90% of AMTI before ATNOL deduction)
Equals: AMTI
Minus: Exemption
Equals: AMT base
Times: 20% rate
Equals: AMT before AMT foreign tax credit
Minus: AMT foreign tax credit (possibly limited to 90% of AMT before AMT foreign tax credit)
Equals: Tentative AMT
Minus: Regular tax liability before credits minus regular foreign tax credit
Equals: AMT if positive

- Excess of ACRS over ADS depreciation on real and personal property placed in service after 1986.
- Mining and exploration expenditures (AMT requires amortization over 10 years versus immediate expensing allowed for income tax purposes).
- Income on long-term contracts (AMT requires percentage of completion method; completed contract method is allowed in limited circumstances for income tax purposes).
- Pollution control facilities placed in service after 1986 (AMT requires ADS depreciation over the asset's ADR life; 60-month amortization is allowed for income tax purposes).
- Dispositions of assets (if gain or loss for AMT purposes differs from gain or loss for income tax purposes).
- Allowable ATNOL (which cannot exceed 90 percent of AMTI before deduction for ATNOL).

Adjustments Applicable Only to Corporations. Three AMT adjustments are applicable only to corporations:

- The Merchant Marine capital construction fund adjustment.
- The adjustment for special deductions allowed to Blue Cross/Blue Shield organizations.
- The adjusted current earnings (ACE) adjustment.

The first two adjustments apply to specific types of corporations and are not discussed in detail in the chapter. On the other hand, the *ACE* adjustment generally applies to all corporations[25] and is expected to have a significant impact on both tax and financial accounting.

Capital Construction Funds of Shipping Companies. Amounts deposited in capital construction funds established under the Merchant Marine Act of 1936 are deductible for income tax purposes but not for AMT purposes. Also, earnings on such funds are excludible for income tax purposes, but are not excludible in computing the AMT.

Special Deduction for Blue Cross and Blue Shield Organizations. Section 833(b) allows Blue Cross, Blue Shield, and certain other organizations a special deduction for high-risk coverages. This deduction is allowed for income tax purposes but not for AMT purposes.

Ace Adjustment. For taxable years beginning after 1989, corporations are subject to an AMT adjustment equal to 75 percent of the excess of ACE over AMTI before the ACE adjustment. Historically, the government has not required conformity between tax accounting and financial accounting. For many years, the only *direct* conformity requirement was that a corporation that used the LIFO method for tax accounting also had to use LIFO for financial accounting.[26] Through the ACE adjustment, Congress is *indirectly* imposing a conformity requirement on corporations. While a corporation may still choose to use different methods for tax and financial accounting purposes, it may no longer be able to do so without incurring AMT as a result of the ACE adjustment. Thus, a corporation may incur AMT not only because of specifically targeted adjust-

---

25. The ACE adjustment does not apply to S corporations, regulated investment companies, real estate investment trusts, or REMICs. § 56(g)(6).

26. § 472(c).

ments and preferences, but also as a result of any methods that cause ACE to exceed AMTI before the ACE adjustment.

The ACE adjustment, which applies to taxable years beginning after 1989, is tax-based and can be either a positive or a negative amount. AMTI is increased by 75 percent of the excess of ACE over unadjusted AMTI. Or AMTI is reduced by 75 percent of the excess of unadjusted AMTI over ACE. The negative adjustment is limited to the aggregate of the positive adjustments under ACE for prior years reduced by the previously claimed negative adjustments. See Concept Summary 12–2. Thus, the ordering of the timing differences is crucial because any lost negative adjustment is permanent. Unadjusted AMTI is AMTI without the ACE adjustment or the ATNOL.[27]

EXAMPLE 33

A calendar year corporation has the following data:

	1991	1992	1993
Pre-adjusted AMTI	$3,000	$3,000	$3,100
Adjusted current earnings	4,000	3,000	2,000

In 1991, because ACE exceeds unadjusted AMTI by $1,000, $750 (75% × $1,000) is included as a positive adjustment to AMTI. No adjustment is necessary for 1992. As unadjusted AMTI exceeds ACE by $1,100 in 1993, there is a potential negative adjustment to AMTI of $825. Since the total increases to AMTI for prior years equal $750 and there are no negative adjustments, only $750 of the potential negative adjustment reduces AMTI for 1993. Further, $75 of the negative amount is lost forever. Prior book income adjustments are ignored for limitation purposes. ◆

ACE should not be confused with current earnings and profits. Although many items are treated in the same manner, certain variations exist. For example, Federal income taxes, deductible in computing earnings and profits, are not deductible in determining ACE.

The starting point for computing ACE is AMTI, which is defined as regular taxable income after AMT adjustments (other than the ATNOL and ACE adjustments) and tax preferences. The resulting figure is adjusted for the items listed below in order to arrive at ACE.

- *Exclusion items.* An exclusion item is an income item (net of related expenses) that is included in earnings and profits, but will never be included in regular taxable income or AMTI (except on liquidation disposal of a business). An example would be interest income from tax-exempt bonds. Exclusion expense items do not include fines and penalties, disallowed golden parachute payments, and the disallowed portion of meal and entertainment expense.
- *Depreciation.* The depreciation expense is calculated using the ADS. Thus, depreciation is computed using the straight-line method without regard to salvage value. The half-year or mid-quarter convention is used for all property other than eligible real estate. The mid-month convention is used for eligible real estate. The recovery periods are 5 years for automobiles, 12 years for property with no class life, and 40 years for all residential rental property and nonresidential real property. These methods are reflected in the appropriate depreciation tables in Chapter 9.

27. §§ 56(g)(1) and (2).

- *Disallowed items.* A deduction is not allowed in computing ACE if the same deduction is never deductible in computing earnings and profits. Thus, the dividends received deduction and the NOL deduction are not allowed. However, since the starting point for ACE is AMTI before the NOL, no adjustment is necessary for the NOL. One exception does allow the 100 percent dividends received deduction if the payor corporation and recipient corporations are not members of the same affiliated group. Another exception allows the 80 percent dividends received deduction when there is at least 20 percent ownership of the payor corporation. Note that these exceptions do not cover dividends received from corporations where the ownership percentage is less than 20 percent.
- *Other adjustments.* The following adjustments required for regular earnings and profits purposes are necessary: intangible drilling costs, construction period carrying charges, circulation expenditures, LIFO inventory adjustments, installment sales, and long-term contracts.[28]

Concept Summary 12–2
Determining the ACE Adjustment*

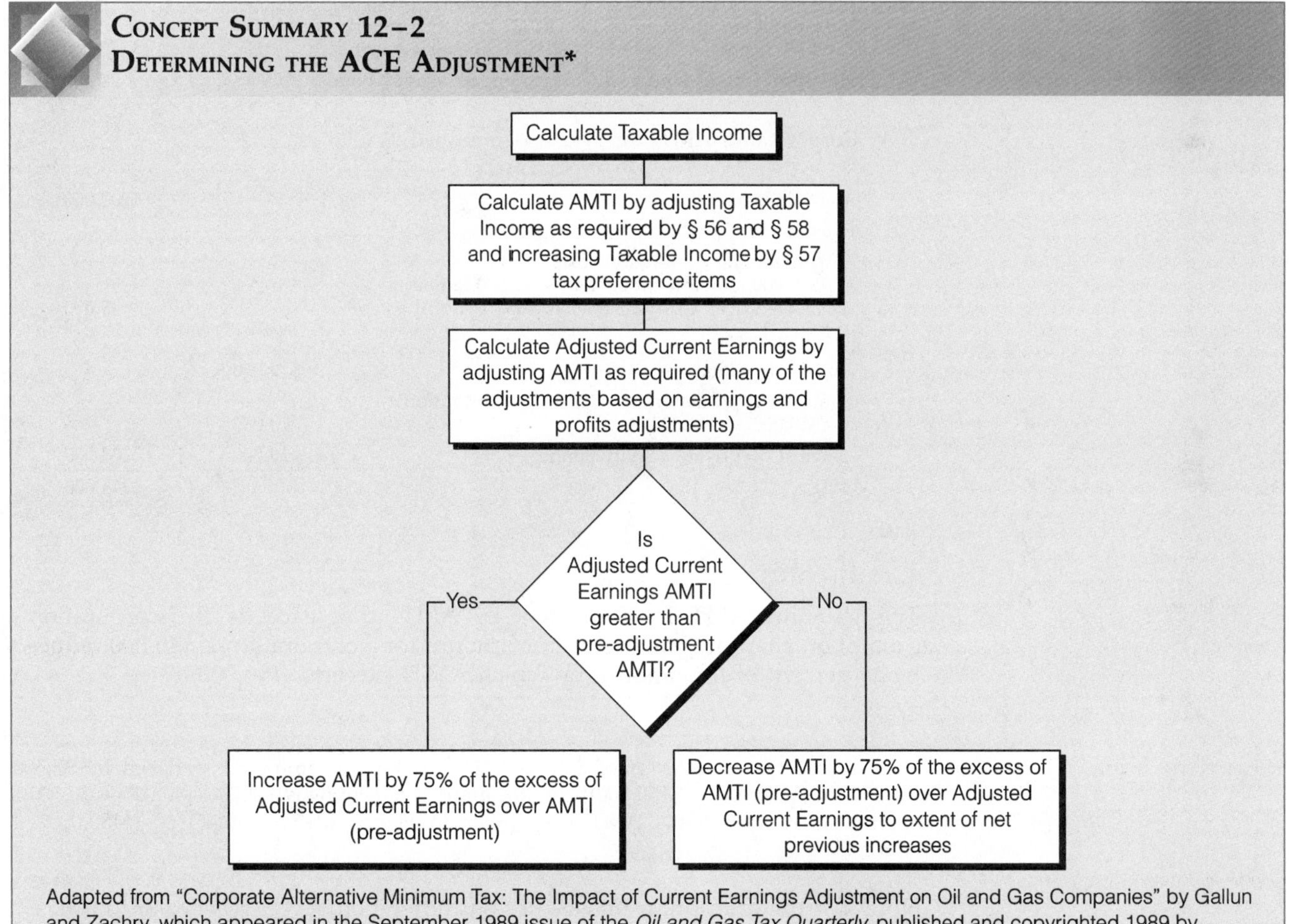
Calculate Taxable Income
Calculate AMTI by adjusting Taxable Income as required by § 56 and § 58 and increasing Taxable Income by § 57 tax preference items
Calculate Adjusted Current Earnings by adjusting AMTI as required (many of the adjustments based on earnings and profits adjustments)
Is Adjusted Current Earnings AMTI greater than pre-adjustment AMTI?
Yes
No
Increase AMTI by 75% of the excess of Adjusted Current Earnings over AMTI (pre-adjustment)
Decrease AMTI by 75% of the excess of AMTI (pre-adjustment) over Adjusted Current Earnings to extent of net previous increases

Adapted from "Corporate Alternative Minimum Tax: The Impact of Current Earnings Adjustment on Oil and Gas Companies" by Gallun and Zachry, which appeared in the September 1989 issue of the *Oil and Gas Tax Quarterly*, published and copyrighted 1989 by Matthew Bender & Co,. and apears here with their permission.

28. §§ 312(n)(1) through (6).

- *Special rules.* Other special rules apply to disallowed losses on the exchange of debt pools, acquisition expenses of life insurance companies, depletion, and certain ownership changes.

Tax Preferences

AMTI includes designated tax preference items. In some cases, this has the effect of subjecting nontaxable income to the AMT. Tax preference items that apply to individuals also apply to corporations.

EXAMPLE 34

The following information applies to W Corporation (a calendar year taxpayer) for 1992:

Taxable income	$200,000
Mining exploration costs	50,000
Percentage depletion claimed (the property has a zero adjusted basis)	70,000
Donation of land held since 1980 as an investment (basis of $40,000 and fair market value of $50,000) to a qualified charity	50,000
Interest on City of Elmira (Michigan) private activity bonds	20,000

W Corporation's AMTI for 1992 is determined as follows:

Taxable income		$200,000
Adjustments:		
Excess mining exploration costs [$50,000 (amount expensed) − $5,000 (amount allowed over a 10-year amortization period)]		45,000
Tax preferences:		
Excess depletion	$70,000	
Untaxed appreciation on charitable contribution ($50,000 − $40,000)	10,000	
Interest on private activity bonds	20,000	100,000
AMTI		$345,000

◆

Exemption

The tentative AMT is 20 percent of AMTI that exceeds the corporation's exemption amount. The exemption amount for a corporation is $40,000 reduced by 25 percent of the amount by which AMTI exceeds $150,000.

EXAMPLE 35

Y Corporation has AMTI of $180,000. The exemption amount is reduced by $7,500 [25% × ($180,000 − $150,000)], and the amount remaining is $32,500 ($40,000 − $7,500). Thus, Y Corporation's AMT base (refer to Figure 12–3) is $147,500 ($180,000 − $32,500). ◆

Note that the exemption phases out entirely when AMTI reaches $310,000.

Other Aspects of the AMT

Investment tax credit carryovers under the regular tax may offset up to 25 percent of AMT liability. Foreign tax credits can be applied against only 90 percent of tentative AMT liability for years before April 1, 1990. The 90 percent limit does not apply to certain corporations meeting specified requirements for tax years beginning after March 31, 1990.

For tax years before 1990, the AMT credit carryover was determined in a manner similar to that for individual taxpayers. For tax years beginning after 1989, *all* of a corporation's AMT is available for carryover as a minimum tax credit. This is so regardless of whether the adjustments and preferences originate from timing differences or exclusions.

EXAMPLE 36

In Example 34, the AMTI exceeds $310,000, so there is no exemption amount. The tentative minimum tax is $69,000 (20% of $345,000). Assuming the regular tax liability is $61,250, the AMT liability is $7,750 ($69,000 − $61,250). The amount of the minimum tax credit carryover is $7,750, which is all of the current year's AMT. ◆

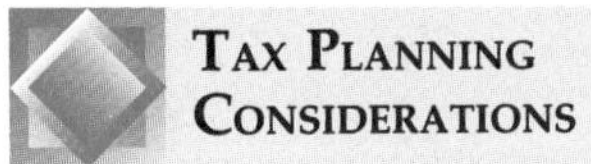

Avoiding Preferences and Adjustments

Several strategies and elections are available to help taxpayers avoid having preferences and adjustments.

- A taxpayer who is in danger of incurring AMT liability should not invest in tax-exempt private activity bonds unless doing so makes good investment sense. Any AMT triggered by interest on private activity bonds reduces the yield on an investment in the bonds. Other tax-exempt bonds or taxable corporate bonds might yield a better after-tax return.
- A taxpayer may elect to expense certain costs in the year incurred or to capitalize and amortize the costs over some specified period. The decision should be based on the present discounted value of after-tax cash flows under the available alternatives. Costs subject to elective treatment include circulation expenditures, mining exploration and development costs, and research and experimentation expenditures.

Controlling the Timing of Preferences and Adjustments

The AMT exemption often keeps items of tax preference from being subject to the AMT. To use the AMT exemption effectively, taxpayers should avoid bunching preferences and positive adjustments in any one year. To avoid this bunching, taxpayers should attempt to control the timing of such items when possible. For example, the contribution of appreciated long-term capital gain property results in a tax preference item, but the taxpayer usually can control the timing of the contribution. Therefore, before making a substantial contribution of appreciated long-term capital gain property, the taxpayer should assess his or her position relative to the AMT.

Taking Advantage of the AMT/Regular Tax Rate Differential

A taxpayer who cannot avoid triggering the AMT in a given year can usually save taxes by taking advantage of the rate differential between the AMT and the regular tax.

EXAMPLE 37

T, who expects to be in the 31% tax bracket in 1993, is subject to the AMT in 1992. He is considering the sale of a parcel of land at a gain of $100,000. If he sells the land in

1993, he will have to pay tax of $28,000 ($100,000 gain × 28% alternative capital gains rate). However, if he sells the land in 1992, he will pay tax of $24,000 ($100,000 gain × 24% AMT rate). Thus, accelerating the sale into 1992 will save T $4,000 in tax. ◆

EXAMPLE 38

B, who expects to be in the 31% tax bracket in 1993, is subject to the AMT in 1992. She is going to contribute $10,000 in cash to her alma mater, State University. If B makes the contribution in 1993, she will save tax of $3,100 ($10,000 contribution × 31% regular tax rate). However, if she makes the contribution in 1992, she will save tax of $2,400 ($10,000 contribution × 24% AMT rate). Thus, deferring the contribution until 1993 will save B $700 in tax. ◆

This deferral/acceleration strategy should be considered for any income or expenses where the taxpayer can control the timing. This strategy applies to corporations as well as to individuals.

PROBLEM MATERIALS

DISCUSSION QUESTIONS

1. Why did Congress enact the AMT?
2. Two elements in the AMT formula are tax preferences and AMT adjustments. Explain how these elements differ.
3. Adjustments considered in computing the AMT can be either positive or negative. Give an example of such an adjustment, including amounts. Explain the rationale behind the concept of positive and negative adjustments.
4. Why is it necessary for individual taxpayers to compute taxable income on Form 1040 before computing AMTI on Form 6251?
5. T incurred $30,000 of circulation expenditures in 1991 and expensed that amount. Compute T's AMT adjustments for 1991, 1992, and 1993 and indicate whether the adjustments are positive or negative.
6. During the year, F earned $10,000 interest on private activity bonds and incurred interest expense of $3,500 in connection with the bonds. How will this affect F's AMT for the year?
7. T, who owns and operates a sole proprietorship, acquired machinery and placed it in service in February 1992. If T has to pay AMT in 1992, he will be required to make an AMT adjustment for depreciation on the machinery. True or false? Explain.
8. How can an individual taxpayer avoid having an AMT adjustment for research and experimentation expenditures?
9. How does the AMT treatment of losses from passive farm activities differ from the treatment of losses from passive nonfarm activities?
10. Certain taxpayers have the option of using either the percentage of completion method or the completed contract method for reporting profit on long-term contracts. What impact could the AMT have on this decision?
11. M, a corporate executive, plans to exercise an incentive stock option granted by his employer to purchase 1,000 shares of the corporation's stock for an option price of $50 per share. The stock is currently selling for $125 per share. Explain the possible consequences of this action on M's regular tax and AMT.
12. K acquired stock under an incentive stock option plan in 1989. All conditions of employment were satisfied in 1991, and the stock became freely transferable. K sold the stock in 1992. Discuss the possible effects on taxable income and AMTI in each of the three years (1989, 1991, 1992).

13. Could computation of the AMT ever require an adjustment for the standard deduction?
14. H, who had adjusted gross income of $100,000, incurred medical expenses of $14,000 during the year. Compute H's medical expense deductions for income tax and AMT purposes. How much is H's AMT adjustment, and is it positive or negative?
15. Are all itemized deductions that are allowed in computing taxable income also allowed in computing AMTI? Explain any differences.
16. In computing the alternative tax itemized deduction for interest, it is possible that some interest allowed as an itemized deduction for income tax purposes will not be allowed. Explain.
17. Discuss why a taxpayer might have to make an AMT adjustment for investment interest expense for tax year 1992.
18. The NOL for computing taxable income differs from the ATNOL. Explain.
19. What is the purpose of the AMT credit? Briefly describe how the credit is computed.
20. Discuss tax planning strategies for minimizing the AMT.
21. T, an equipment dealer who will be subject to the AMT in 1992, has an opportunity to make a large sale of equipment in December 1992 or January 1993. Discuss tax planning strategies T should consider in connection with the sale.
22. Discuss the similarities and differences between the individual AMT and the corporate AMT.
23. Some observers believe the ACE adjustment will cause corporations to change some of the methods they use for financial accounting and tax accounting purposes. Comment.
24. In computing corporate AMTI, why is the ATNOL adjustment stated separately instead of being included with other adjustments?
25. Do situations arise when it would be advisable for a taxpayer to accelerate income into an AMT year? Explain and give an example of how this acceleration might be accomplished.
26. Do situations arise when it would be advisable for a taxpayer to defer deductions from an AMT year into a non-AMT year where the regular income tax applies? Explain and give an example of how such a deferral might be accomplished.

PROBLEMS

27. T owns and operates TC, a sole proprietorship. On January 3, TC acquired a warehouse for $200,000 and claimed MACRS depreciation of 3.042%. The alternative depreciation system (ADS) rate for the first recovery year is 2.396%. Compute T's AMT adjustment for depreciation with respect to the warehouse, and indicate whether the adjustment is positive or negative.
28. In January 1992, K acquired and placed in service a nonresidential building costing $120,000. For regular tax purposes, K depreciated the building over a 31.5-year period. Compute K's AMT adjustment for depreciation with respect to the building, and indicate whether the adjustment is positive or negative.
29. V sold an apartment building in October 1992 for $210,000. She had acquired the building in April 1989 for $200,000 and had deducted MACRS depreciation of $25,453 ($5,152 in 1989, $7,272 in 1990, $7,272 in 1991, and $5,757 in 1992). What adjustments must be made in computing V's AMTI in each year (1989, 1990, 1991, and 1992)?
30. T owns and operates T Auto Parts (TAP), a sole proprietorship. On January 3, TAP acquired a warehouse for $100,000 and claimed MACRS depreciation. Compute T's AMT adjustment for depreciation with respect to the warehouse. Refer to the appropriate depreciation tables in Chapter 9.
31. In 1992, M incurred $200,000 of mining and exploration expenditures. He elects to deduct the expenditures as quickly as the tax law allows for income tax purposes.
    - **a.** How will M's treatment of mining and exploration expenditures affect his income tax and AMT computations for 1992?
    - **b.** How can M avoid having AMT adjustments related to the mining and exploration expenditures?

32. F acquired a passive activity in 1992. Gross income from operations of the activity was $100,000. Operating expenses, not including depreciation, were $90,000. Income tax depreciation of $25,000 was computed under MACRS (post-1986 ACRS). AMT depreciation, computed under the ADS, was $16,000. Compute F's passive loss for income tax purposes and for AMT purposes.

33. In 1990, D exercised an incentive stock option, acquiring 1,000 shares of stock at an option price of $100 per share. The fair market value of the stock at the date of exercise was $150 per share. In 1992, the rights in the stock become freely transferable and are not subject to a substantial risk of forfeiture. How do these transactions affect D's AMTI in 1990 and 1992?

34. T is a vice-president of X Corporation. He acquired 1,000 shares of X Corporation stock in 1990 under the corporation's incentive stock option plan for an option price of $43 per share. At the date of exercise, the fair market value of the stock was $65 per share. The stock became freely transferable in 1991, and T sold the 1,000 shares for $69 per share in 1992. How do these transactions affect T's AMTI in 1990, 1991, and 1992?

35. In 1990, M exercised an incentive stock option that had been granted by her employer, Y Corporation. M acquired 100 shares of Y Corporation stock for the option price of $200 per share. The rights in the stock become freely transferable and not subject to a substantial risk of forfeiture in 1992. The fair market value of the stock at the date of exercise was $250 per share. M sells the stock for $275 per share in 1993. What is the amount of her AMT adjustment in 1993?

36. V owns and operates a news agency (as a sole proprietorship). During 1991, V incurred expenses of $24,000 to increase circulation of newspapers and magazines that her agency distributes. For income tax purposes, she elected to expense the $24,000 in 1991. In addition, V incurred $15,000 in circulation expenditures in 1992 and again elected expense treatment. What AMT adjustments will be required in 1991 and 1992 as a result of the circulation expenditures?

37. K, who is single and has no dependents, had adjusted gross income of $100,000 in 1992. K's potential itemized deductions were as follows:

Medical expenses (before percentage limitation)	$15,000
State income taxes	3,000
Real estate taxes	7,000
Mortgage (qualified housing and residence) interest	9,000
Cash contributions to various charities	4,000
Unreimbursed employee expenses (before percentage limitation)	4,300

What is the amount of K's AMT adjustment for itemized deductions for 1992?

38. During the current year, G earned $10,000 in dividends on corporate stock and incurred $13,000 of investment interest expense related to his stock holdings. G also earned $5,000 interest on private activity bonds during the year and incurred interest expense of $3,500 in connection with the bonds. How much investment interest expense can G deduct for income tax and AMT purposes for the year?

39. During 1992, M contributed $10,000 cash plus 50 shares of stock to his alma mater, State College. M had acquired the stock in 1985 at a cost of $5,000. Fair market value of the stock at the date of contribution was $12,000. M also contributed stock worth $3,500 to the United Church. He had acquired the stock for $8,000 in 1985. How much is M's tax preference for 1992 as a result of these contributions?

40. During the current year, D contributed $5,000 cash plus 100 shares of stock to his alma mater, Central College. D had acquired the stock in 1980 at a cost of $5,500. Fair market value of the stock at the date of contribution was $25,000. D also contributed stock worth $3,600 to the city's art museum. He had acquired the stock for $6,000 in 1985. How will D's AMTI for the current taxable year be affected by these contributions?

41. P, who is single and has no dependents, had taxable income of $150,000 and tax preferences of $50,000 in 1992. P did not itemize deductions for income tax purposes. Compute P's AMT exemption for 1992.

42. C, who is single, has no dependents and does not itemize deductions. He had taxable income of $79,900 in 1992. His tax preferences for 1992 totaled $100,000. What is C's AMTI for 1992?

43. T, who is single, has no dependents and does not itemize. She has the following items relative to her tax return for 1992:

Bargain element from the exercise of an incentive stock option (no restrictions apply to the stock)	$ 25,000
Accelerated depreciation on equipment acquired before 1987 (straight-line depreciation would have yielded $23,000)	45,000
Percentage depletion in excess of property's adjusted basis	75,000
Taxable income for regular tax purposes	120,000

a. Determine T's AMT adjustments and preferences for 1992.
b. Calculate the AMT (if any) for 1992.

44. B, who is single, has the following items for 1992:

Income	
Salary	$125,000
Interest from bank	5,000
Interest on corporate bonds	10,000
Dividends	4,000
Short-term capital gain	25,000
Expenses	
Unreimbursed employee business expenses (no meals or entertainment)	4,000
Total medical expenses	30,000
State income taxes	8,000
Real property taxes	7,000
Home mortgage (qualified housing) interest	5,000
Casualty loss on vacation home	
Decline in value	20,000
Adjusted basis	70,000
Insurance proceeds	12,000
Tax preferences	95,000

Compute B's tax liability for 1992 before credits or prepayments.

45. T, who does not itemize, incurred an NOL of $50,000 in 1991. T's deductions in 1991 included tax preference items of $20,000. What is T's ATNOL carryover to 1992?

46. During the course of your interview with Jim, who is one of your tax clients, you obtain the following information:

a. Jim, age 52, is single and has no dependents. He is independently wealthy and lives in Aspen, Colorado. In 1992, he earned $25,000 as a ski instructor.
b. Jim's savings account at First National Bank was credited with $20,000 of interest during the year. In addition, he received $32,000 of dividends from General Motors and $42,000 of interest on private activity bonds.
c. On March 15, 1992, Jim sold 1,000 shares of Widgets, Inc., stock for $60 per share. He had acquired 1,500 shares of Widgets stock on April 1, 1991, at a cost of $50 per share.
d. An examination of Jim's personal financial documents yields the following information:

- IRA contribution, $2,000 (Jim is not covered by his employer's pension plan).
- State income taxes withheld and estimated payments, $1,900.
- Real estate taxes on his residence, $10,800.
- Home mortgage interest, $25,500.

- Credit card interest, $900.
- Cash contributions to qualified (50% limit) charities, $10,000.
- Professional dues and subscriptions, $700.
- Tax return preparation fee, $2,100.

e. In 1985, Jim acquired an Aspen apartment complex, which he manages. Rent income in 1992 was $240,000. Expenses were $275,000.
f. In 1992, Jim invested in MNO Realty, a limited partnership. His share of the partnership's loss in 1992 was $200,000.
g. Jim's employer withheld $3,500 of Federal income tax in 1992. In addition, Jim made estimated payments of $4,500.

Analyze Jim's tax information and compute his tax liability for 1992. Suggested software (if available): WFT tax planning software.

47. The following itemized deductions were reported on M's Schedule A for 1992. On the basis of this information and the additional information in the notes below, determine the effect of M's itemized deductions on AMTI.

Medical expenses (before 7.5% floor)	$12,000
State income taxes	4,600
Real estate taxes	2,400
Mortgage (qualified housing) interest	5,400
Investment interest	2,100
Charitable contributions	8,600
Casualty loss	1,100
Moving expenses	3,600
Unreimbursed employee expenses (before 2% floor)	2,800
Gambling losses	1,500

Additional information:

a. M's AGI for 1992 was $100,000.
b. M reported $800 of interest income and $1,500 of dividends for the year.
c. M earned $1,300 interest on private activity bonds.
d. M contributed $2,100 cash to various charitable organizations. She also contributed 100 shares of stock to her church. She paid $40 per share for the stock in 1972, and it was worth $65 per share at the date of contribution.

48. K is single and has no dependents. Based on the financial information presented below, compute K's AMT for 1992.

Income:	
Salary	$30,000
Taxable interest on corporate bonds	1,500
Dividend income	2,500
Business income	60,000
Expenditures:	
Medical expenses	$10,000
State income taxes	7,000
Real estate taxes	9,000
Mortgage (qualified housing) interest	8,000
Investment interest	7,500
Cash contributions to various charities	2,400

Additional information:

a. The $60,000 business income is from Acme Office Supplies Company, a sole proprietorship K owns and operates. Acme claimed MACRS depreciation of $6,350 on real property used in the business. ADS depreciation on the property would have been $5,000.
b. T received interest of $25,200 on City of Columbus private activity bonds.

49. H and W filed a joint return in 1992. Details are shown below. They have no dependents. Based on the items listed below and other relevant financial information presented in the subsequent notes, compute H and W's AMT for the year.

Income:	
H's salary	$40,000
Dividend income (jointly owned stock)	5,500
W's business income	30,000
Expenditures:	
State income taxes	$ 1,500
Real estate taxes	4,800
Mortgage interest	8,600
Investment interest	7,000
Charitable contributions	28,000

Additional information:

a. W's business income was derived from a news agency (sole proprietorship) she owns and operates. During 1992, W incurred expenses of $30,000 to increase circulation of newspapers and magazines her agency distributes. She elected to expense these expenditures.

b. H and W earned $12,000 interest on State of New York bonds they acquired in 1988. These bonds are classified as private activity bonds.

c. H and W contributed corporate stock to W's alma mater, State University. They had acquired the stock in 1975 at a cost of $4,000. Fair market value of the stock at the date of contribution was $25,000.

50. For 1992, P Corporation (a calendar year taxpayer) had the following transactions:

Taxable income	$100,000
Accelerated depreciation on realty in excess of straight-line (placed in service in 1988)	150,000
Excess amortization of certified pollution control facilities	10,000
Tax-exempt interest on municipal bonds (funds were used for nongovernmental purposes)	30,000
Untaxed appreciation on property donated to charity	8,000
Percentage depletion in excess of the property's basis	60,000

a. Determine P Corporation's AMTI for 1992.
b. Determine the AMT base (refer to Figure 12–3).
c. Determine the tentative minimum tax.
d. What is the amount of the AMT?

51. T owns mineral property that qualifies for a 22% depletion rate. The basis of the property at the beginning of 1992 was $12,000. Gross income from the property in 1992 was $100,000. Based on this information, what is T's tax preference for 1992?

52. F, who is single with no dependents and does not itemize, provides you with the following information for 1992:

Short-term capital loss	$ 5,000
Long-term capital gain	25,000
Municipal bond interest received on private activity bonds acquired in 1989	9,000
Dividends from General Motors	1,500
Excess of FMV over cost of incentive stock options (the rights became freely transferable and not subject to a substantial risk of forfeiture in 1992)	35,000
Fair market value of corporate stock contributed to charity (basis of $5,000)	30,000

What is the total amount of F's tax preference items and AMT adjustments for 1992?

53. M, who is single, had taxable income of $0 in 1992. She has positive timing adjustments of $200,000 and exclusion items of $100,000 for the year. What is the amount of M's AMT credit for carryover to 1993?

54. B, who is single, had taxable income of $100,000 for 1992. She had positive AMT adjustments of $50,000, negative AMT adjustments of $15,000, and tax preference items of $57,500.

    a. Compute her AMTI.
    b. Compute B's tentative minimum tax.

55. W Corporation, a calendar year taxpayer, has AMTI of $300,000 for 1992. What is W Corporation's tentative minimum tax for 1992?

56. X Corporation, a calendar year taxpayer, has AMTI (before the ACE adjustment) of $600,000 for 1992. X Corporation's ACE is $1,500,000. What is X's tentative minimum tax for 1992?

57. In each of the following independent situations, determine the tentative AMT:

	AMTI (before the exemption amount)
Q Corporation	$150,000
R Corporation	160,000
T Corporation	320,000

58. Q Corporation (a calendar year corporation) reports the following information for the years listed below:

	1991	**1992**	**1993**
Unadjusted AMTI	$3,000	$2,000	$5,000
Adjusted current earnings	4,000	3,000	2,000

Compute the ACE adjustment for each year.

CUMULATIVE PROBLEMS

59. X, who is single and age 46, has no dependents. In 1992, he earned a salary of $65,000 as vice president of ABC Manufacturing Corporation. Over the years, he has invested wisely and owns several thousand shares of stock and an apartment complex.

In January 1992, X sold 500 shares of stock for a gain of $12,000. He had owned the stock for 11 months. X received dividends of $800 on the stock he retained.

On May 20, 1989, X exercised his rights under ABC's incentive stock option plan. For an option price of $26,000, he acquired stock worth $53,000. The stock became freely transferable in 1992.

On September 15, X contributed 100 shares of JKL stock to the American Red Cross. The basis of the stock was $32 per share, and its fair market value was $70 per share.

Gross rent income from the apartment complex, which was acquired in 1982, was $150,000. Deductible expenses for the complex were $180,000. X actively participates in the management of the complex.

X received $24,000 interest on private activity bonds in 1992. His itemized deductions were as follows: state and local income taxes, $4,100; property taxes on residence, $3,900; mortgage interest on home (qualified housing), $16,500.

Compute X's lowest legal tax liability, before prepayments or credits, for 1992. Suggested software (if available): *TurboTax* for tax return or WFT tax planning software.

60. R, age 38, is single and has no dependents. He is independently wealthy as a result of having inherited sizable holdings in real estate and corporate stocks and bonds. R is a minister at First Methodist Church, but he accepts no salary from the church. However, he does reside in the church's parsonage free of charge. The rental value

of the parsonage is $400 a month. The church also provides R a cash grocery allowance of $100 a week. Examination of R's financial records provides the following information for 1992:

a. On January 16, 1992, R sold 2,000 shares of stock for a gain of $10,000. The stock was acquired four months ago.
b. R received $85,000 of interest on private activity bonds in 1992.
c. R received gross rent income of $145,000 from an apartment complex he owns and manages.
d. Expenses related to the apartment complex, which he acquired in 1983, were $230,000.
e. R's dividend and interest income (on a savings account) totaled $26,000.
f. R had the following itemized deductions *from* adjusted gross income:

- $3,000 fair market value of stock contributed to Methodist church (basis of stock was $1,000)
- $3,000 interest on consumer purchases.
- $1,600 state and local taxes.
- $7,000 medical expenses (before 7.5% floor).
- $1,000 casualty loss (in excess of the $100 floor and the 10% limitation).

Compute R's tax, including AMT if applicable, before prepayments or credits, for 1992. Suggested software (if available): *TurboTax* for tax return or WFT tax planning software.

61. Michael Young, a 36-year-old architect, is single and has no dependents. He lives at 8685 Midway Road, Kent, OH 44240. His Social Security number is 357–97–2873.

Michael reported adjusted gross income of $100,000 and taxable income before exemptions (amount from line 35, Form 1040) of $88,250 for 1991. His itemized deductions reported on Schedule A included the following:

- Total medical expenses, $11,500.
- State and local income taxes, $3,800.
- Real property taxes on personal residence, $2,900.
- Miscellaneous itemized deductions in excess of 2% floor, $1,050.

In February 1988, Michael exercised an incentive stock option and acquired 1,000 shares of his employer's stock for the option price of $20 per share. The fair market value of the stock at the date of exercise was $85 per share. The stock became freely transferable in 1991.

Michael acquired private activity bonds on January 2, 1991. He earned interest of $5,600 on the bonds during the year.

Determine whether Michael is subject to the AMT. Use Form 6251, Alternative Minimum Tax—Individuals, for your computations. Suggested software (if available): *TurboTax* for tax return or WFT tax planning software.

RESEARCH PROBLEMS

RESEARCH PROBLEM 1 T is a full-time gambler whose only source of income is money that he wins from his gambling activities. The IRS contends that T's gambling losses should be treated as itemized deductions for purposes of computing the AMT. T argues that the gambling losses should be treated as trade or business expenses. Who is correct, T or the IRS?

RESEARCH PROBLEM 2 B owns two warehouses that were placed in service before 1987. Accelerated depreciation for 1990 on Warehouse A was $12,000, and straight-line depreciation would have been $8,000. On Warehouse B, accelerated depreciation was $6,000, and straight-line depreciation would have been $7,500. What is the amount of B's tax preference for excess depreciation in 1990?

Chapter

Tax Credits and Payment Procedures

Objectives

Discuss the use of tax credits as a tool of Federal tax policy.

Distinguish between refundable and nonrefundable credits.

Discuss carryover provisions and the priority system for determining the order in which credits are utilized.

Explain the various tax credits that apply to businesses and to individuals.

Describe the pay-as-you-go system of withholding and estimated tax payments.

Apply the wage-bracket and percentage methods for computing withholding.

Discuss the requirements for making estimated tax payments and the penalties on underpayments.

Identify tax planning opportunities related to tax credits and payment procedures.

Outline

Tax credits are important factors in determining the final amount of tax that must be paid or the amount of refund a taxpayer receives. Tax credits have the general effect of directly reducing a taxpayer's tax liability. This chapter begins by discussing important tax policy considerations relevant to tax credits. Tax credits are categorized as being either refundable or nonrefundable. The distinction between refundable and nonrefundable credits is important because it may affect the taxpayer's ability to enjoy a tax benefit from a particular credit.

Next an overview of the priority of tax credits is presented. The credit portion of the chapter continues with a discussion of the credits available to businesses and to individual taxpayers and the ways in which credits enter into the calculation of the tax liability.

The Federal tax system has long been based on the pay-as-you-go concept. That is, taxpayers or their employers, are required to make regular deposits with the Federal government during the year as payment toward the tax liability that will be determined at the end of the tax year. These deposits are in effect refundable credits. In addition to presenting the procedures used in calculating these payments and the special problems self-employed persons encounter in estimating their payments, the penalties on underpayment are discussed.

TAX POLICY CONSIDERATIONS

Congress has generally used tax credits to achieve social or economic objectives or to provide equity for different types of taxpayers. For example, the investment tax credit was introduced in 1962. It was expected to encourage economic growth, improve the competitive position of American industry at home and abroad, and help alleviate the nation's balance of payments problem.[1] Since 1962, however, the investment tax credit has had a *checkered* history. It has been suspended, reinstated, repealed, reenacted, and finally repealed again in response to changing economic and political conditions. More specifically, under current law, the investment tax credit has been repealed for property placed in service after December 31, 1985. This repeal is in line with Congress's goal of removing or reducing the effect of taxes as a factor in business decisions. It will be interesting to see if Congress maintains this objective in light of changing economic conditions (e.g., sluggish economic growth).

A tax credit should not be confused with an income tax deduction. Certain expenditures of individuals are permitted as deductions from gross income in arriving at adjusted gross income (e.g., business expenses). Additionally, individuals are allowed to deduct certain nonbusiness personal and investment-related expenses *from* adjusted gross income (AGI). Whereas the tax benefit received from a tax deduction depends on the tax rate, a tax credit is not affected by the tax rate of the taxpayer.

EXAMPLE 1

Assume Congress wishes to encourage a certain type of expenditure. One way to accomplish this objective is to allow a tax credit of 25% for such expenditures. Another way to accomplish this objective is to allow an itemized deduction for the expenditures. Assume taxpayer A's tax rate is 15%, while taxpayer B's tax rate is 31%. In addition, assume that taxpayer C does not incur enough qualifying expenditures to itemize deductions. The following tax benefits are available to each taxpayer for a $1,000 expenditure:

1. Summary of remarks of the Secretary of the Treasury, quoted in S.Rept. 1881, 87th Cong., 2nd Sess., reported in 1962–3 C.B. 707.

	Taxpayer A	Taxpayer B	Taxpayer C
Tax benefit if a 25% credit is allowed	$250	$250	$ 250
Tax benefit if an itemized deduction is allowed	150	310	-0-

As these results indicate, tax credits provide benefits on a more equitable basis than do tax deductions. Equally apparent is the fact in this case that the deduction approach benefits only taxpayers who itemize deductions, while the credit approach benefits all taxpayers who make the specified expenditure. ◆

For many years, Congress used the tax credit provisions of the Code liberally in implementing tax policy. Although existing tax credits still carry out this objective, budget constraints and economic considerations have dictated the repeal of some credits (e.g., investment tax credit, political contributions credit). Nevertheless, such credits as those applicable to jobs for certain disadvantaged persons, child and dependent care, and expenses related to qualified low-income housing still reflect social policy considerations. Other credits, such as those applicable to research activities, have been retained based on economic considerations. Finally, note that the use of tax credits as a tax policy tool continues to evolve as economic and political circumstances change as illustrated by the recent enactment of several other credits (e.g., the disabled access credit).

OVERVIEW AND PRIORITY OF CREDITS

◆

Refundable versus Nonrefundable Credits

As illustrated in Figure 13–1, certain credits are refundable while others are nonrefundable. *Refundable credits* are paid to the taxpayer even if the amount of the credit (or credits) exceeds the taxpayer's tax liability.

EXAMPLE 2

T, who is single, had taxable income of $27,000 in 1992. His income tax from the 1992 Tax Rate Schedule is $4,772. During 1992, T's employer withheld income tax of $5,349. T is entitled to a refund of $577 because the credit for tax withheld on wages is a refundable credit. ◆

Nonrefundable credits are not paid if they exceed the taxpayer's tax liability.

EXAMPLE 3

T is single, age 67, and retired. T's taxable income for 1992 is $1,320, and the tax on this amount is $198. T's tax credit for the elderly is $225. This credit can be used to reduce T's net tax liability to zero, but it will not result in a refund, even though the credit ($225) exceeds T's tax liability ($198). This result occurs because the tax credit for the elderly is a nonrefundable credit. ◆

Some nonrefundable credits, such as the foreign tax credit, are subject to carryover provisions if they exceed the amount allowable as a credit in a given year. Other nonrefundable credits, such as the tax credit for the elderly (refer to Example 3), are not subject to carryover provisions and are lost if they exceed the limitations. Because some credits are subject to carryover provisions while others are not, the order in which credits are offset against the tax liability is important. The Code provides that nonrefundable credits are to be offset against a taxpayer's income tax liability in the order shown in Figure 13–1.

General Business Credit

Two special rules apply to the general business credit. First, any unused credit must first be carried back 3 years, then forward 15 years. Second, for any tax year, the general business credit is limited to the taxpayer's *net income tax* reduced by the greater of:[2]

- The *tentative minimum tax.*
- 25 percent of *net regular tax liability* that exceeds $25,000.[3]

Before discussing the general business credit limitation, several terms need defining:

- *Net income tax* is the sum of the regular tax liability and the alternative minimum tax reduced by certain nonrefundable tax credits.
- *Tentative minimum tax* for this purpose is reduced by the foreign tax credit allowed.

FIGURE 13–1
Refundable and Nonrefundable Credits

Section	Credit
	Refundable Credits
31	Taxes withheld on wages
32	Earned income credit
33	Tax withheld at the source on nonresident aliens and foreign corporations*
34	Credit for certain uses of gasoline and special fuels*
	Nonrefundable Credits
21	Child and dependent care expense credit
22	Credit for the elderly and disabled
25	Credit for mortgage interest paid*
27	Foreign tax credit
28	Orphan drugs testing credit*
29	Nonconventional source fuel credit*
38	General business credit, which is the sum of the following:
46	■ Investment tax credit, which includes
	■ Regular investment tax credit
	■ Tax credit for rehabilitation expenditures
	■ Business energy credit
	■ Reforestation credit*
51	■ Jobs credit
40	■ Alcohol fuels credit*
41	■ Research activities credit
42	■ Low-income housing credit
44	■ Disabled access credit

*A discussion of this credit is beyond the scope of this text.

2. § 38(c).
3. This amount is $12,500 for married taxpayers filing separately unless one of the spouses is not entitled to the general business credit.

- *Regular tax liability* is determined from the appropriate tax table or tax rate schedule, based on taxable income. However, the regular tax liability does not include certain taxes (e.g., alternative minimum tax).
- *Net regular tax liability* is the regular tax liability reduced by certain nonrefundable credits (e.g., child and dependent care credit, foreign tax credit).

EXAMPLE 4

T's general business credit for 1992 is $70,000. His net income tax is $150,000, tentative minimum tax is $130,000, and net regular tax liability is $150,000. He has no other tax credits. T's general business credit allowed for the tax year is computed as follows:

Net income tax	$ 150,000
Less: The greater of	
■ $130,000 (tentative minimum tax)	
■ $31,250 [25% × ($150,000 − $25,000)]	(130,000)
Amount of general business credit allowed for tax year	$ 20,000

T then has $50,000 ($70,000 − $20,000) of unused general business credits that may be carried back or forward as discussed below. ◆

Treatment of Unused General Business Credits

Unused general business credits are initially carried back three years (to the earliest year in the sequence) and are applied to reduce tax during these years. Thus, the taxpayer may receive a tax refund as a result of the carryback. Any remaining unused credits are then carried forward 15 years.[4]

A FIFO method is applied to the carryovers, carrybacks, and utilization of credits earned during a particular year. The oldest credits are used first in determining the amount of the general business credit. The FIFO method minimizes the potential for loss of a general business credit benefit due to the expiration of credit carryovers, since the earliest years are used before the current credit for the taxable year.

EXAMPLE 5

This example illustrates the use of general business credit carryovers.

General business credit carryovers		
1989	$ 4,000	
1990	6,000	
1991	2,000	
Total carryovers	$12,000	
1992 general business credit		$ 40,000
Total credit allowed in 1992 (based on tax liability)	$50,000	
Less: Utilization of carryovers		
1989	(4,000)	
1990	(6,000)	
1991	(2,000)	
Remaining credit allowed	$38,000	
Applied against		
1992 general business credit		(38,000)
1992 unused amount carried forward to 1993		$ 2,000

◆

4. § 39(a)(1).

Specific Business-Related Tax Credit Provisions

The business-related tax credits that form a single general business credit include the investment tax credit, jobs credit, research activities credit, low-income housing credit, and disabled access credit. Each is determined separately under its own set of rules and is explained here in the order listed.

Investment Tax Credit: Introduction

Since its original enactment in 1962, the investment tax credit (ITC) has been suspended, reinstated, repealed, and reenacted in response to varying economic conditions and political pressures. These changes in the tax laws have created a nightmare for tax practitioners. This phenomenon continued with the TRA of 1986 provisions related to the ITC. Although this act repealed the *regular* credit for most property placed in service after 1985, other components of the ITC (*rehabilitation expenditures credit* and *business energy credit*) are still allowed in certain situations. In addition, practitioners will have to deal with carryover and recapture provisions related to the ITC for many years in the future. Because of all of these factors, a basic understanding of the pre-1986 ITC is necessary.

The ITC has three components: the regular ITC, the credit for rehabilitation expenditures, and the business energy credit. The regular ITC was allowed before 1986 for most tangible personal property and up until 1991 for transition property. The rehabilitation credit is allowed for exenditures to rehabilitate (1) industrial and commercial buildings originally placed in service before 1936 and (2) certified historic structures. The third component of the ITC, the business energy credit, is allowed to a limited extent for certain energy conservation expenditures by businesses. Each of the ITC components is discussed below.

Regular Investment Tax Credit

Qualifying Property. Prior to its repeal by TRA of 1986, the ITC was allowed for most business tangible personal property (e.g., automobiles, machinery, furniture) and was not allowed for most real property (e.g., land, buildings). Both categories had exceptions. It was sometimes difficult to determine whether an item was tangible personal property that was eligible for the ITC or a structural component of a building that was not eligible for the ITC. However, an item is generally considered to be tangible personal property if it can be removed without causing structural damage to the building.

In addition, up until 1991, qualifying property also included *transition property.* Transition property was certain property placed in service after 1985 that satisfied certain restrictive requirements.

Upon premature disposition of property on which the ITC was taken, all or part of the credit is subject to recapture. Therefore, upon the disposition of property, it will continue to be necessary to determine whether the ITC was taken on the property if the recapture provisions apply.

Computation of Qualified Investment. Because of the recapture provisions and the carryover provisions applicable to the ITC, it is necessary to understand how the credit was computed. The ITC was based on the aggregate amount, without limit, of qualifying new property that was placed in service during the year. In addition, although used ITC property was included in the calculation of the ITC, the maximum includible cost for *used* property was $125,000 per year. For transition property in tax years after 1987, the maximum includible cost for used property was $150,000.

Example 6

In 1990, T acquired used transition property for use in his business. The cost of the property was $200,000. Only $150,000 of the machinery qualified for the ITC because of the limitation on used property. ◆

That portion of the cost of property that was deducted under the § 179 election to expense certain depreciable business assets could not be used for the credit computation.

Amount of the Credit. The credit was based on the recovery period under ACRS (refer to Chapter 9 for details). To avoid a basis reduction, the taxpayer could have elected a reduced ITC rate. Rates for the full credit and the reduced credit were as follows:

Recovery Period (in years)	Full Credit Rate	Reduced Credit Rate
3	6%	4%
5, 10, or 15	10%	8%

EXAMPLE 7

In 1985, T acquired and placed in service the following new assets: automobile, $9,000; light-duty truck, $12,000; office furniture, $2,500; airplane, $120,000; building, $500,000; and land, $100,000. T's tentative ITC (using the full credit rates) was computed as follows:

Qualifying Property	Cost	Recovery Period	Rate of Credit	Investment Tax Credit
Automobile	$ 9,000	3 years	6%	$ 540
Light-duty truck	12,000	3 years	6%	720
Office furniture	2,500	5 years	10%	250
Airplane	120,000	5 years	10%	12,000
Building	500,000	19 years	0%	–0–
Land	100,000	NA	0%	–0–
Tentative investment tax credit				$13,510

◆

The amount computed in Example 7 is described as the tentative investment tax credit because the allowable credit for any year was subject to a ceiling limitation based on the tax liability before deducting credits. Any ITC unused under this rule could first be carried back, then carried forward, as explained earlier in the chapter under Overview and Priority of Credits.

Taxpayers could compute the ITC using the full credit rate or a reduced credit rate. Taxpayers who used the full ITC rate generally were required to reduce the basis of the property by one-half of the ITC taken. No basis reduction was required if the ITC was computed using the reduced rate. The basis of transition property was reduced by the full amount of any credit taken on the property, and the reduced ITC rate election was not available.[5]

EXAMPLE 8

In 1985, T purchased a machine, which was five-year ACRS property, for $10,000. T took a $1,000 ITC on the property (10% of $10,000). The basis of the property had to be reduced by $500 [½ of $1,000 (ITC)]. Thus, T's cost recovery allowance was based on $9,500 [$10,000 (cost) – $500 (reduction for one-half of ITC)]. ◆

5. § 49(d), prior to amendment by the Revenue Reconciliation Act of 1990.

EXAMPLE 9

Assume the same facts as in the previous example, except that the property was qualifying transition property that was placed in service prior to January 1, 1991. The ITC available to T would have been $1,000 (10% of $10,000). However, T's cost recovery allowance would be based on only $9,000 [$10,000 (cost) − $1,000 (reduction for the full amount of the ITC]. ◆

Recapture of Investment Tax Credit. The amount of the ITC is based on the recovery period of the qualifying property (refer to Example 7). However, if property is disposed of (or ceases to be qualified ITC property) before the end of the recovery period, the taxpayer must recapture all or a portion of the ITC originally taken.[6] The amount of the ITC that is recaptured in the year of premature disposition (or disqualification as ITC property) is added to the taxpayer's regular tax liability for the recapture year (except for purposes of computing the alternative minimum tax). In addition, one-half of the recapture amount (100 percent for transition property) is *added* to the asset's adjusted basis for purposes of determining the amount of gain or loss realized on the asset's disposition. Note that if the ITC was computed using the reduced rate, no positive basis adjustment is available.

The portion of the credit recaptured is a specified percentage of the credit that was taken by the taxpayer. This percentage is based on the period the ITC property was held by the taxpayer, as shown in Figure 13–2.

EXAMPLE 10

T acquired office furniture (five-year recovery property) on October 3, 1985, at a cost of $5,000. T's ITC on the office furniture was $500 (10% of $5,000). T sold the furniture in June 1990. Since T held the furniture more than four years but less than five, he is required to recapture ITC of $100 (20% of $500). The effect of the recapture is to increase T's 1990 tax liability by the $100 of ITC recaptured.

T could have avoided the ITC recapture by postponing the disposition of the furniture until after October 3, 1990. In addition, if T had delayed selling the furniture until early 1991, he could not only have avoided the $100 of ITC recapture, but could also have postponed any recognized gain until 1991. ◆

Subject to certain exceptions, recapture of the ITC generally is triggered by the following:[7]

- Disposition of property through sale, exchange, or sale-and-leaseback transactions.
- Retirement or abandonment of property or conversion to personal use.
- Gifts of ITC property.
- Transfers to partnerships and corporations.
- Like-kind exchanges.

FIGURE 13–2
ITC Recapture

	The Recapture Percentage Is	
If the Property Is Held for	**For 15-Year, 10-Year, and 5-Year Property**	**For 3-Year Property**
Less than 1 year	100	100
One year or more but less than 2 years	80	66
Two years or more but less than 3 years	60	33
Three years or more but less than 4 years	40	0
Four years or more but less than 5 years	20	0
Five years or more	0	0

6. § 50(a).

7. Reg. § 1.47–2.

Reduction of Investment Tax Credit. In general, a 35 percent reduction of the ITC is required for ITC related to transition property *and* for carryovers of the ITC from pre-1986 years.[8]

Example 11

In 1990, T placed in service qualified transition property that cost $54,000. The ITC of $5,400 (10% of $54,000) must be reduced by 35%. This reduction amount of $1,890 (35% of $5,400) is *not* allowed as a credit for any other year. The 35% reduction results in an effective rate of 6½% [10% − (35% of 10%)]. Thus, T is allowed a reduced regular ITC of $3,510 [$5,400 − $1,890 (reduction amount)] or 6½% × $54,000. ◆

The 35 percent reduction also applies to *carryforwards* of the regular ITC, regardless of when the property was placed in service.

Example 12

In 1985, T placed property into service that qualified for the ITC. The property, five-year recovery property, cost $10,000 and generated a tentative ITC of $1,000 ($10,000 × 10%). However, T was not able to actually use the ITC generated in his tax computation until 1992. The $1,000 ITC carried forward to 1992 produces a credit of $650 [$1,000 − $350 (reduction amount)]. ◆

Tax Credit for Rehabilitation Expenditures

Taxpayers are allowed a tax credit for expenditures to rehabilitate industrial and commercial buildings and certified historic structures. This credit was introduced in 1978, as an extension of the regular ITC, to discourage businesses from moving from older, economically distressed areas (e.g., inner city) to newer locations and to preserve historic structures. Thus, no credit is allowed for the rehabilitation of personal use property.

Congress has changed the rates of credit and the structures to which the credit applies from time to time to ensure that the credit accomplishes its intended purpose. The current operating features of this credit are as follows:[9]

Rate of the Credit for Rehabilitation Expenses	Nature of the Property
10%	Nonresidential buildings, other than certified historic structures, originally placed in service before 1936
20%	Residential and nonresidential certified historic structures

To qualify for the credit, a taxpayer is required to depreciate the costs of the rehabilitation using the straight-line method (refer to Chapter 9 for details on depreciation provisions). The basis of a rehabilitated building must be reduced by the full rehabilitation credit allowed.[10]

Example 13

T spent $60,000 to rehabilitate a building (adjusted basis of $40,000) that had originally been placed in service in 1932. T is allowed a credit of $6,000 (10% of $60,000) for rehabilitation expenditures. T then increases the basis of the building by $54,000 [$60,000 (rehabilitation expenditures) − $6,000 (credit allowed)] and must depreciate

8. The reduction does not apply to qualified timber property. § 49(c)(5)(B)(ii), prior to amendment by the Revenue Reconciliation Act of 1990.

9. § 47.

10. § 50(c).

these capitalized expenditures using the straight-line method. If the building were a historic structure, the credit allowed would be $12,000 (20% of $60,000), and the building's depreciable basis would increase by $48,000 [$60,000 rehabilitation expenditures) − $12,000 (credit allowed)]. ◆

To qualify for the credit, buildings must be substantially rehabilitated. A building has been *substantially rehabilitated* if qualified rehabilitation expenditures exceed the greater of (1) the adjusted basis of the property before the rehabilitation or (2) $5,000. Qualified rehabilitation expenditures do not include the cost of acquiring a building, the cost of facilities related to a building (such as a parking lot), and the cost of enlarging an existing building. Stringent rules apply concerning the retention of internal and external walls.

The rehabilitation credit must be recaptured if the rehabilitated property is disposed of prematurely or if it ceases to be qualifying property. The amount recaptured is based on a holding period requirement of five years. In addition, the recapture amount is *added* to the adjusted basis of the rehabilitation expenditures for purposes of determining the amount of gain or loss realized on the property's disposition.

Example 14

On March 15, 1989, M placed in service $30,000 of rehabilitation expenditures on a building qualifying for the 10% credit. A credit of $3,000 ($30,000 × 10%) was allowed, and the basis of the building was increased by $27,000 ($30,000 − $3,000). The building was sold on December 15, 1992. M must recapture a portion of the rehabilitation credit based on the schedule in Figure 13–2. Because M held the rehabilitated property for more than three years but less than four, 40% of the credit, or $1,200, must be added to M's 1992 tax liability. Also, the adjusted basis of the rehabilitation expenditures is increased by the $1,200 recaptured amount. ◆

For tax years after 1989, the passive activity rules applicable to the rehabilitation credit claimed on rental activities are more liberal than for the rehabilitation credit on nonrental activities.[11] Refer to Chapter 7.

Business Energy Credits

Since 1978, a business energy credit has been allowed to encourage the conservation of natural resources and the development of alternative energy sources (to oil and natural gas). Most of these credits have now expired. While the two remaining business energy credits are scheduled to expire after June 30, 1992, Congress is expected to extend this expiration date. The remaining credits are for solar energy property (10 percent rate) and geothermal property (10 percent rate). Except that only new property is eligible for the credit, the rules regarding the regular ITC apply to these credits as well. In the case of recapture, however, if the property ceases to be energy property but still qualifies for the regular ITC, only the energy credit portion is affected. This is so because the business energy credit was allowed in addition to the regular ITC.

Reporting the Investment Tax Credit

Reporting the ITC involves one or all of several forms:

- Form 3468, Investment Credit, is used for determining the amount of current year credit. Schedule B of the form is used for calculating the business energy credit.

11. § 469(i)(3)(B).

- Form 4255, Recapture of Investment Credit, is used to determine the increase in tax from recapture.
- If the taxpayer also has any of the other business credits (e.g., disabled access credit), Form 3800, General Business Credit, consolidates them for purposes of determining the current year amount allowed. This form is also used when the taxpayer has carrybacks or carryforwards of general business credits from other years.

Jobs Credit

The jobs credit (also referred to as the targeted jobs credit) was enacted to encourage employers to hire individuals from one or more of the following target groups traditionally subject to high rates of unemployment:[12]

- Vocational rehabilitation referrals.
- Economically disadvantaged youths (age 18 to 22).
- Economically disadvantaged Vietnam-era veterans.
- Recipients of certain Social Security supplemental security income benefits.
- General assistance recipients.
- Youths (age 16 to 19) participating in cooperative education programs.
- Economically disadvantaged ex-convicts.
- Eligible work incentive employees.
- Qualified summer youth employees (age 16 and 17).

The credit is available for wages paid to employees in their first year of service. This provision is scheduled to expire for employees who started work after June 30, 1992, but Congress is expected to extend this expiration date.

Computation of the Regular Jobs Credit. The regular jobs credit is equal to 40 percent of the first $6,000 of wages (per eligible employee) for the *first year* of employment. Thus, the credit is not available for any wages paid to an employee after his or her first year of employment. However, if the employee's first year of employment overlaps two of the employer's tax years, the employer may take the credit over two tax years. If the jobs credit is elected, the employer's tax deduction for wages is reduced by the amount of the credit. For an employer to qualify for the credit, an unemployed individual must be certified by a local jobs service office of a state employment security agency. The jobs credit is not available for wages paid to certain related parties.

Wages will be taken into account in computing the regular jobs credit only if paid to an individual who is employed for at least 90 days or has completed 120 hours of work. The equivalent thresholds for qualified summer youth employees (discussed below) are 14 days or 20 hours.

Example 15

In January 1992, T Company hires four handicapped individuals (certified to be eligible employees for the jobs credit). Each of these employees is paid wages of $7,000 during the year. T Company's jobs credit is $9,600 [($6,000 × 40%) × 4 employees]. If the tax credit is taken, T Company must reduce its deduction for wages paid by $9,600. No credit is available for wages paid to these employees after their first year of employment. ◆

Example 16

On June 2, 1992, M, a calendar year taxpayer, hired a member of a targeted group and obtained the required certification. During the last seven months of 1992, this employee

12. § 51.

is paid $3,500. M is allowed a jobs credit of $1,400 ($3,500 × 40%). The employee continues to work for M in 1993 and is paid $7,000 through May 31. Because up to $6,000 of first-year wages are eligible for the credit, M is also allowed a 40% credit on $2,500 [$6,000 − $3,500 (wages paid in 1992)] of wages paid in 1993, or $1,000 ($2,500 × 40%). None of this employee's wages paid after May 31, the end of the first year of employment, are eligible for the jobs credit. Likewise, no credit is allowed for wages paid to persons newly hired after June 30, 1992. ◆

Computation of the Jobs Credit for Qualified Summer Youth Employees. The credit for qualified summer youth employees is allowed on wages for services during any 90-day period between May 1 and September 15 if the employee is hired by June 30, 1992. A qualified summer youth employee generally must be age 16 or 17 on the hiring date. The maximum wages eligible for the credit are $3,000 per summer youth employee. Thus, the maximum credit per employee for 1992 is $1,200 ($3,000 × 40%). If the employee continues employment after the 90-day period as a member of another targeted group, the amount of wages subject to the regular jobs credit must be reduced by the wages paid to the employee as a qualified summer youth employee.

EXAMPLE 17

X Corporation employs T as a qualified summer youth employee beginning May 1, 1992. After 90 days, T continues his employment as a member of a second targeted group. T was paid $2,000 as a qualified summer youth employee. As a member of the second targeted group, T is paid another $5,000 during the year. Of the $7,000 total paid to T, only $6,000 qualifies for the jobs credit. This amount consists of the $2,000 wages paid under the qualified summer youth employee program plus $4,000 ($6,000 − $2,000) paid to T as a member of the other targeted group. X Corporation's jobs credit will be 40% of $6,000 ($2,000 + $4,000), or $2,400. ◆

Research Activities Credit

To encourage research and experimentation, usually described as research and development (R & D), a credit is allowed for certain qualifying expenditures paid or incurred through June 30, 1992.[13] The research activities credit is the *sum* of two components: an incremental research activities credit and a basic research credit.[14]

Incremental Research Activities Credit. The incremental research activities credit applies at a 20 percent rate to the *excess* of qualified research expenses for the current taxable year (the credit year) over the base amount. These components of the credit are explained below.

For expenses to be treated as *qualified research expenditures,* the research must meet the following tests:

- The expenditures must qualify for treatment as expenses under § 174 of the Code.
- The research must be for the purpose of discovering information technological in nature.
- Application of the research must be intended to be useful in the development of a new or improved business component of the taxpayer.

A business component is any product, process, computer software, technique, formula, or invention that is to be held for sale, lease, or license or used by the

13. The research activities credit is scheduled to expire for qualifying expenditures after June 30, 1992, but Congress is expected to extend this expiration date.

14. § 41.

taxpayer in an *existing* trade or business of the taxpayer. For a start-up company (defined later), the trade or business requirement is satisfied if the results of the research are used in the active conduct of a *future* trade or business.

In general, research expenditures qualify if the research relates to a new or improved function, performance, reliability, or quality. The expenses qualify fully if the research is performed in-house (by the taxpayer or employees). If the research is conducted by persons outside the taxpayer's business (under contract), only 65 percent of the amount paid qualifies for the credit.[15]

EXAMPLE 18

M incurs the following research expenditures for the tax year.

In-house wages, supplies, computer time	$50,000
Paid to XY Scientific Foundation for research	30,000

M's qualified research expenditures are $69,500 [$50,000 + ($30,000 × 65%)]. ◆

Beyond the general guidelines discussed above, the Code does not give specific examples of qualifying research. However, the credit is *not* allowed for research that falls into any of the following categories:[16]

- Research conducted after the beginning of commercial production of the business component.
- Research related to the adaptation of an existing business component to a particular customer's requirement or need.
- Research related to the reproduction of an existing business component (in whole or in part) from a physical examination of the business component itself or from plans, blueprints, detailed specifications, or publicly available information about that business component.
- Surveys and studies such as market research, testing, and routine data collection.
- Research on computer software developed by or for the benefit of the taxpayer primarily for internal use (unless the software relates to a research activity that is qualified).
- Research conducted *outside* the United States.
- Research in the social sciences, arts, or humanities.
- Research to the extent funded by any grant or contract or otherwise by another person or government entity.

The *base amount* for the credit year is determined by multiplying the taxpayer's fixed base percentage by the average gross receipts for the four preceding taxable years. The fixed base percentage depends on whether the taxpayer is an existing firm or a start-up company. For purposes of the incremental research activities credit, an *existing firm* is one that both incurred qualified research expenditures *and* had gross receipts during each of at least three years from 1984 to 1988. A *start-up company* is one that did not have both of the above during each of at least three years in the same 1984–1988 period.

For existing firms, the fixed base percentage is the ratio of total qualified research expenses for the 1984–1988 period to total gross receipts for this same period. Gross receipts are net of sales returns and allowances. The fixed base percentage cannot exceed a maximum ratio of .16, or 16 percent. Start-up companies are *assigned* a fixed base percentage ratio of .03, or 3 percent.

15. § 41(b)(3)(A).

16. § 41(d).

In working with the tax credit, the following steps should be followed:

1. Calculate the fixed base percentage.
2. Determine the base amount.
3. Multiply the excess of qualified research expenses over the base amount by 20 percent.

This step procedure is applied in the following example.

EXAMPLE 19

Y, a calendar year taxpayer, has both gross receipts (net of sales returns and allowances) and qualified research expenses as follows:

	Gross Receipts	Qualified Research Expenses
1984	$150,000	$25,000
1985	300,000	45,000
1986	400,000	30,000
1987	350,000	35,000
1988	450,000	50,000
1989	450,000	50,000
1990	500,000	55,000
1991	650,000	73,000
1992	700,000	80,000

Step 1. Aggregate qualified research expenses for the period 1984–1988 equal $185,000 ($25,000 +$45,000 + $30,000 + $35,000 + $50,000). Aggregate gross receipts for the same period total $1,650,000. Y's fixed base percentage is

$$\frac{\$185{,}000}{\$1{,}650{,}000} = .1121, \text{ or } 11.21\%$$ [17]

Step 2. Average gross receipts for the four preceding tax years are $512,500 [($450,000 for 1988 + $450,000 for 1989 + $500,000 for 1990 + $650,000 for 1991) ÷ 4]. Thus, Y's base amount is $57,451 ($512,500 × 11.21%).

Step 3. Calculation of the credit.

Qualified research expenses for 1992	$80,000
Less: Base amount	57,451
Excess	$22,549
Rate	× 20%
Incremental research activities credit	$ 4,510

Y's incremental research activities credit is $4,510. ◆

A special rule limits the credit available for taxpayers who have incurred small amounts of research and experimentation costs during the base period. The rule provides that in no event shall the base amount be less than 50 percent of qualified research expenses for the credit year.

17. Calculations are rounded to 1/100th of 1%. § 41(c)(3)(D).

EXAMPLE 20

Assume the same facts as in Example 19, except that qualified research and experimentation expenses in 1992 were $200,000. Incremental research and experimentation expenditures eligible for the credit are computed as follows:

Qualified research expenses in 1992	$200,000
Minus: Base amount (50% of $200,000, because actual base amount of $57,451 is less than 50% of the 1992 expenses)	100,000
Incremental expenses	$100,000

◆

Qualified research and experimentation expenditures not only are eligible for the 20 percent credit but also can be *expensed* in the year incurred.[18] In this regard, the taxpayer has two choices:[19]

1. Use the full credit and reduce the expense deduction for research expenses by 100 percent of the credit.
2. Retain the full expense deduction and reduce the credit by the product of 50 percent of the credit times the maximum corporate tax rate.

As an alternative to the expense deduction, the taxpayer may *capitalize* the research expenses and *amortize* them over 60 months or more. In this case, the amount capitalized and subject to amortization is reduced by the full amount of the credit *only* if the credit exceeds the amount allowable as a deduction.

EXAMPLE 21

Assume the same facts as in Example 20. The potential incremental research activities credit is $20,000 ($100,000 × 20%). The expense that the taxpayer can deduct currently and the credit are as follows:

	Credit Amount	Deduction Amount
■ Full credit and reduced deduction		
$20,000 − $0	$20,000	
$200,000 − $20,000		$180,000
■ Reduced credit and full deduction		
$20,000 − [(.50 × $20,000) × .34]	16,600	
$200,000 − $0		200,000
■ Full credit and capitalize and elect to amortize costs over 60 months		
$20,000 − $0	20,000	
$200,000/60 × 12		40,000

◆

Basic Research Credit. Corporations (but not S corporations or personal service corporations) are allowed an additional 20 percent credit for basic research payments through June 30, 1992, in *excess* of a base amount. This credit is not available to individual taxpayers. *Basic research payments* are defined as amounts paid in cash (property transfers do not qualify) to a qualified basic research organization. However, two requirements must be met for the payments to qualify. First, the payments must be made under a written agreement

18. § 174. Also refer to the discussion of rules for deduction of research and experimental expenditures in Chapter 8.

19. § 280C(c), effective for tax years after 1989.

between the corporation and the qualified organization. Second, the qualified organization must perform basic research.

Basic research is defined generally as any original investigation for the advancement of scientific knowledge not having a specific commercial objective. The definition excludes basic research conducted outside the United States and basic research in the social sciences, arts, or humanities. This reflects the intent of Congress to encourage high-tech research in the United States.

The calculation of this additional credit for basic research expenditures is complex and is based on expenditures in excess of a specially defined base amount.[20] This amount in turn may be subject to cost of living adjustments.

The portion of the basic research expenditures that does not exceed the base amount is not eligible for the basic research credit, but the amount does become a component of the regular credit for incremental research activities.

EXAMPLE 22

Y Corporation, a qualifying corporation, pays $75,000 to a university for basic research. Assume that Y Corporation's specially calculated base amount is $50,000. The basic research activities credit allowed is $5,000 [($75,000 − $50,000) × 20%]. The $50,000 of current year basic research expenditures that are not eligible for the credit because they do not exceed the base amount are treated as contract research expenses for purposes of the regular incremental research activities credit. ◆

Low-Income Housing Credit

A credit is available to owners of qualified low-income housing projects.[21] This credit is scheduled to expire after June 30, 1992, but Congress is expected to extend the expiration date. The purpose of this low-income housing credit is to encourage building owners to make affordable housing available for low-income individuals. Generally, the credit applies only if the qualifying expenses within a 24-month period *exceed* (1) not less than 10 percent of the building's adjusted basis or (2) $3,000 or more per low-income unit, but special exceptions abound.

This credit, more than any other, is influenced by nontax factors. For example, certification of the property by the appropriate state or local agency authorized to provide low-income housing credits is required. These credits are issued based on a nationwide allocation. Once issued, however, they remain in effect for the entire credit period. Additional units require new certification based on allocations in effect at that later time.

The amount of credit is based on the qualified basis of the property. The qualified basis depends on the number of units rented to low-income tenants. Tenants are low-income tenants if their income does not exceed a specified percentage of the area median gross income. Area median gross income is determined under the United States Housing Act of 1937. These special rules are seemingly endless.

Once declared eligible, the property must meet the required conditions continuously throughout a 30-year compliance period, although the credit itself is allowed over a 10-year period. After an initial 15-year compliance period, a 15-year *extended low-income commitment period* can be terminated in certain cases.

The credit rate is set monthly by the IRS so that the annualized credit amounts have a present value of either 70 percent or 30 percent[22] of the basis attributable to qualifying low-income units. Once determined, though, the percentage remains constant for that property.

---

20. § 41(e).
21. § 42.

22. The credit rate for 30% present value property applies to property that is Federally subsidized through various means.

The *qualified basis* is that portion of the basis of the entire property (eligible basis) that is rented to qualifying low-income tenants. The amount of credit is determined by multiplying the qualified basis by the applicable percentage.

EXAMPLE 23

C spends $100,000 to build a qualified low-income housing project completed January 1, 1992. The entire project is rented to low-income families. The credit rate for this 70% present credit value property for January 1992 is 8.70%.[23] C may claim a credit of $8,700 ($100,000 × 8.70%) in 1992 and in each of the following nine years. Generally, first-year credits are prorated based on the date the project is placed in service. A full year's credit is taken in each of the next nine years, and any remaining first-year credit is claimed in the eleventh year. ◆

Recapture of a portion of the credit may be required if the number of units set aside for low-income tenants falls below a minimum threshold, if the taxpayer disposes of the property or the interest in it, or if the taxpayer's amount at risk decreases.

Finally, the passive activity rules (see Chapter 7) as applied to low-income housing are more generous than for rental property in general.[24]

Disabled Access Credit

The disabled access credit is designed to encourage small businesses to make their businesses more accessible to disabled individuals. The credit is available for any eligible access expenditures paid or incurred by an eligible small business after the date of enactment (after November 5, 1990). The credit is calculated at the rate of 50 percent of the eligible expenditures that exceed $250 but do not exceed $10,250. Thus, the maximum amount for the credit is $5,000 ($10,000 × 50 percent). This nonrefundable credit is part of the general business credit.[25]

An *eligible small business* is one that satisfies either of the following:

- Had gross receipts for the previous year of $1 million or less.
- Had no more than 30 full-time employees during the previous year.

An eligible business can include a sole proprietorship, partnership, regular corporation, or S corporation. However, in the case of a partnership or S corporation, the limitation on the eligible expenditures is determined at both the entity and the owner level.

Eligible access expenditures are generally any reasonable and necessary amount that will satisfy any of the following:

- Lead to the removal of architectural, communication, physical, or transportation barriers that prevent a business from being accessible to, or usable by, disabled individuals.
- Provide qualified interpreters or other effective methods of making aurally delivered materials available to hearing-impaired individuals.
- Provide qualified readers, taped texts, and other effective methods of making visually delivered materials available to visually impaired individuals.

---

23. Rev.Rul. 92–1, I.R.B. No. 1.

24. § 469(i)(3)(C).

25. §§ 38(b)(7) and 44.

- Acquire or modify equipment or devices for disabled individuals.
- Provide other similar services, modifications, materials, or equipment.

However, eligible expenditures do *not* include amounts that are paid or incurred in connection with any facility that is placed into service after the enactment of the provision.

To the extent a disabled access credit is available, no deduction or credit is allowed under any other provision of the tax law. The adjusted basis for depreciation is reduced by the amount of the credit.

EXAMPLE 24

In 1992, T, an eligible business, made $11,000 of capital improvements to business realty that had been placed in service in June 1990. The expenditures were intended to make T's business more accessible to the disabled and were considered eligible expenditures for purposes of the disabled access credit. The amount of the credit is $5,000 [($10,250 − $250) × 50%]. Although $11,000 of eligible expenditures were incurred, only the excess of $10,250 over $250 qualifies for the credit. Further, the depreciable basis of the capital improvement is $6,000 because the basis must be reduced by the amount of the credit [$11,000 (cost) − $5,000 (amount of the credit)]. ◆

OTHER TAX CREDITS
◆

Earned Income Credit

Taxpayers whose income is below a specified level may be eligible for an earned income credit.[26] The credit has three components:

- Basic earned income credit.
- Supplemental young child credit.
- Supplemental health insurance credit.

Each component is discussed below.

Basic Earned Income Credit. In 1992, the basic earned income credit is determined by multiplying a maximum amount of earned income ($7,520 in 1992) by the appropriate credit percentage (refer to Figure 13–3). The credit percentage used in the calculation is based on the number of the taxpayer's qualifying children. Thus, in 1992, the maximum basic earned income credit for a taxpayer with one qualifying child is $1,324 ($7,520 × 17.6%) and $1,384 for a taxpayer with two or more qualifying children ($7,520 × 18.4%). However, the maximum basic earned income credit is phased out completely if the taxpayer's earned income or AGI exceeds $22,373. To the extent that the greater of earned income or AGI exceeds $11,840, the difference, multiplied by the appropriate phase-out percentage, is subtracted from the maximum basic earned income credit.

EXAMPLE 25

In 1992, T, who otherwise qualifies for the earned income credit, receives wages of $12,000 and has no other income. T has one qualifying child. T's earned income credit is $1,324 ($7,520 × 17.6%) reduced by $20 [($12,000 − $11,840) × 12.57%]. Thus, T's earned income credit is $1,304. If T has two or more qualifying children, the calculation would produce a credit of $1,384 ($7,520 × 18.4%) reduced by $21 [($12,000 − $11,840) × 13.14%]. Thus, T's earned income credit would be $1,363. ◆

26. § 32.

Supplemental Young Child Credit. A taxpayer with a qualifying child who has not attained the age of one at the end of the taxpayer's tax year is allowed an additional earned income credit. The supplemental young child credit is calculated by simply increasing the credit percentage by 5 percentage points and increasing the phase-out percentage by 3.57 percentage points (see Figure 13–3). Thus, in 1992, the applicable credit percentages and phase-out rates are:

Number of Qualifying Children	Credit Percentage	Phase-out Percentage
One child	22.6	16.14
Two or more children	23.4	16.71

However, if the taxpayer *elects* to supplement the basic earned income credit with the supplemental young child credit, the taxpayer cannot also claim the child as a qualifying individual for purposes of the child and dependent care expenses credit (see the discussion later in the chapter).

EXAMPLE 26

Assume the same facts as in the previous example, except the taxpayer has one child below the age of one at the end of 1992 and one additional qualifying child. Then the credit would be $1,760 ($7,520 × 23.4%) reduced by $27 [($12,000 − $11,840) × 16.71%]. Thus, T's total earned income credit, including the supplemental young child credit, would be $1,733. ◆

Supplement Health Insurance Credit. In addition to the basic earned income credit, a credit may be claimed up to the amount of the cost of health insurance coverage on one or more qualifying children. To determine the supplemental credit, the same rules that apply in calculating the basic earned income credit are used except the credit percentage is 6 percent and the phase-out percentage is 4.285 percent of the excess of the taxpayer's AGI (or earned income, if greater) over $11,840. However, the credit claimed cannot exceed the actual amount of the qualified health insurance expenses incurred. These percentages apply regardless of the size of the taxpayer's family.

EXAMPLE 27

In 1992, T, who otherwise qualifies for the earned income credit, receives wages of $11,000 and has no other income. However, T has paid qualifying health insurance premiums of $750 during the year on behalf of her qualifying child. T's supplemental health insurance credit is $451 ($7,520 × 6%) reduced by $0 [($11,000 − $11,840) × 4.285%]. Thus, T's supplemental health insurance credit is $451. In this case, the credit is not limited by the amount of the health insurance premiums paid because they exceed the amount of the credit. If T has two or more qualifying children, the credit would be the same amount. ◆

FIGURE 13–3
Basic Earned Income Credit: Credit and Phase-out Percentages

Tax Year	Number of Qualifying Children	Credit Percentage	Phase-out Percentage
1992	One child	17.6	12.57
	Two or more children	18.4	13.14
1993	One child	18.5	13.21
	Two or more children	19.5	13.93
1994	One child	23.0	16.43
	Two or more children	25.0	17.86

To the extent a supplemental health insurance credit is claimed, qualifying medical care expenses must be reduced for purposes of the medical expense itemized deduction and the deduction available to self-employed individuals in computing AGI (see Chapter 11).

It is not necessary to compute the credit as was done in Examples 25 through 27. As part of the tax simplification process, the IRS issues an Earned Income Credit Table for the determination of the appropriate amount of the earned income credit. This table and a worksheet are included in the instructions to both Form 1040 and Form 1040A.

To be *eligible* for the credit, the taxpayer must not only meet the earned income and AGI thresholds, but must also have a qualifying child. A *qualifying child* must meet the following tests:

- *Relationship test.* The individual must be a son, daughter, descendant of the taxpayer's son or daughter, stepson, stepdaughter, or an eligible foster child of the taxpayer. A legally adopted child of the taxpayer is considered the same as a child by blood.
- *Residency test.* The qualifying child must share the same principal place of abode, which must be located within the United States, with the taxpayer for more than one-half of the tax year of the taxpayer. Temporary absences (e.g., due to illness or education) are disregarded for purposes of this test. For foster children, however, the child must share the same home as the taxpayer for the entire year.
- *Age test.* The child must not have reached the age of 19 (24 in the case of a full-time student) as of the end of the tax year. In addition, the child is considered to meet the age test if the child is permanently and totally disabled at any time during the year.

In addition to these eligibility requirements, several restrictions limit the credit for some taxpayers. For example, if a child qualifies more than one taxpayer for the credit (e.g., divorced parents), the taxpayer with the highest AGI can claim the credit for the child. Secondly, a qualifying child may not also claim the earned income credit. Lastly, the credit is available to a married couple only if they file a joint return.

The earned income credit is a form of negative income tax (a refundable credit for taxpayers who do not have a tax liability). An eligible individual may elect to receive advance payments of the earned income credit from his or her employer (rather than receiving the credit from the IRS upon filing the tax return). The amount that can be received in advance is limited to the credit that is available to a taxpayer with only one qualifying child. If this election is made, the taxpayer must file a certificate of eligibility (Form W–5) with his or her employer and *must* file a tax return for the year the income is earned.

Tax Credit for Elderly or Disabled Taxpayers

The credit for the elderly was originally enacted in 1954 as the retirement income credit to provide tax relief for those who were not receiving substantial benefits from tax-free Social Security payments.[27]

EXAMPLE 28

X is a retired taxpayer who received $8,000 of Social Security benefits as his only income in 1992. X's Social Security benefits are excluded from gross income. There-

27. § 22. This credit is not subject to indexation.

fore, his income tax is $0. In 1992, Y, a single taxpayer 66 years of age, has $8,000 of income from a pension plan funded by his former employer. Assuming Y has no itemized deductions or deductions *for* AGI, his income tax for 1992 (before credits) is $180. The retirement income credit was enacted to mitigate this inequity. ◆

The credit for the elderly and disabled applies to the following:

- Taxpayers age 65 or older.
- Taxpayers under age 65 who are retired with a permanent and total disability and who have disability income from a public or private employer on account of the disability.

The *maximum* allowable credit is $1,125 (15% × $7,500 of qualifying income), but the credit will be less for a taxpayer who receives Social Security benefits or has AGI exceeding specified amounts. Under these circumstances, the base used in the credit computation is reduced. Many taxpayers receive Social Security benefits or have AGI high enough to reduce the base for the credit to zero.

The eligibility requirements and the tax computation are somewhat complicated. Consequently, an individual may elect to have the IRS compute his or her tax and the amount of the tax credit.

The credit is based on an initial amount (referred to as the *base amount*) and the filing status of the taxpayer in accordance with Figure 13–4. To qualify for the credit, married taxpayers who live together must file a joint return. For taxpayers under age 65 who are retired on permanent and total disability, the base amounts could be less than those shown in Figure 13–4 because these amounts are limited to taxable disability income.

This initial base amount is *reduced* by (1) Social Security, Railroad Retirement, and certain excluded pension benefits and (2) one-half of the taxpayer's AGI in excess of $7,500 for a single taxpayer, a head of household, or a surviving spouse. The AGI factor is $10,000 for married taxpayers filing jointly. It is generally $5,000 for married taxpayers filing separately. The credit is equal to 15 percent of the base amount after subtracting the adjustments just described.

EXAMPLE 29

H and his wife W are both over age 65 and received Social Security benefits of $2,400 in 1992. On a joint return, H and W reported AGI of $14,000.

Base amount		$ 7,500
Less: Social Security benefits	$2,400	
One-half of the excess of AGI of $14,000 over $10,000	2,000	(4,400)
Balance subject to credit		$ 3,100
Tax credit allowed ($3,100 × 15%)		$ 465

◆

The credit for the elderly is reduced by any alternative minimum tax. Schedule R of Form 1040 is used to calculate and report the credit.

FIGURE 13–4
Base Amounts for Tax Credit for Elderly or Disabled

Status	Base Amount
Single, head of household, or surviving spouse	$5,000
Married, joint return, only one spouse qualified	5,000
Married, joint return, both spouses qualified	7,500
Married, separate returns, spouses live apart the entire year	3,750 each

Foreign Tax Credit

Both individual taxpayers and corporations may claim a tax credit for foreign income tax paid on income earned and subject to tax in another country or a U.S. possession.[28] As an alternative, a taxpayer may claim a deduction instead of a credit.[29] In most instances the tax credit is advantageous since it is a direct offset against the tax liability.

The purpose of the foreign tax credit (FTC) is to mitigate double taxation since income earned in a foreign country is subject to both U.S. and foreign taxes. However, the ceiling limitation formula may result in some form of double taxation or taxation at rates in excess of U.S. rates when the foreign tax rates are higher than the U.S. rates. This is a distinct possibility because U.S. tax rates are lower than those of many foreign countries.

Other special tax treatments applicable to taxpayers working outside the United States include the foreign earned income exclusion (refer to Chapter 5) and limitations on deducting expenses of employees working outside the United States (refer to Chapter 10). Recall from the earlier discussion that a taxpayer may not take advantage of *both* the FTC and the foreign earned income exclusion.

Computation. Taxpayers are required to compute the FTC based upon an overall limitation.[30] The FTC allowed is the *lesser* of the foreign taxes imposed or the *overall limitation* determined according to the following formula:

$$\frac{\text{Foreign-source taxable income}}{\text{Worldwide taxable income}} \times \begin{array}{c}\text{U.S. tax}\\ \text{before FTC}\end{array}$$

For individual taxpayers, worldwide taxable income in the overall limitation formula is determined *before* personal and dependency exemptions are deducted.

EXAMPLE 30

In 1992, T, a calendar year taxpayer, has $10,000 of income from Country Y, which imposes a 15% tax, and $20,000 from Country Z, which imposes a 50% tax. T has taxable income of $60,800 from within the United States, is married filing a joint return, and claims two dependency exemptions. Thus, although T's taxable income for purposes of determining U.S. tax is $90,800, taxable income amounts used in the limitation formula are not reduced by personal and dependency exemptions. Thus, for this purpose, taxable income is $100,000 [$90,800 + (4 × $2,300)]. Assume that T's U.S. tax before the credit is $20,899. Overall limitation:

$$\frac{\text{Foreign-source taxable income}}{\text{Worldwide taxable income}} = \frac{\$30{,}000}{\$100{,}000} \times \$20{,}899 = \$6{,}270$$

In this case, $6,270 is allowed as the FTC because this amount is less than the $11,500 of foreign taxes imposed [$1,500 (Country Y) + $10,000 (Country Z)]. ◆

Thus, the overall limitation may result in some of the foreign income being subjected to double taxation. Unused FTCs can be carried back two years and forward five years. Form 1116, Computation of Foreign Tax Credit, is used to compute the limitation on the amount of FTC.

---

28. Section 27 provides for the credit, but the qualifications and calculation procedure for the credit are contained in §§ 901–908.

29. § 164.

30. § 904.

Only foreign income taxes, war profits taxes, and excess profits taxes (or taxes paid in lieu of such taxes) qualify for the credit. In determining whether or not a tax is an income tax, U.S. criteria are applied. Thus, value added taxes (VAT), severance taxes, property taxes, and sales taxes do not qualify because they are not regarded as taxes on income. Such taxes may be deductible, however.

Credit for Child and Dependent Care Expenses

A credit is allowed to taxpayers who incur employment-related expenses for child or dependent care.[31] The credit is a specified percentage of expenses incurred to enable the taxpayer to work or to seek employment. Expenses on which the credit is based are subject to limitations.

Eligibility. To be eligible for the credit, an individual must maintain a household for either of the following:

- A dependent under age 13.
- A dependent or spouse who is physically or mentally incapacitated.

Generally, married taxpayers must file a joint return to obtain the credit. The credit may also be claimed by the custodial parent for a nondependent child under age 13 if the noncustodial parent is allowed to claim the child as a dependent under a pre-1985 divorce agreement or under a waiver in the case of a post-1984 agreement.

Eligible Employment-Related Expenses. Eligible expenses include amounts paid for household services and care of a qualifying individual that are incurred to enable the taxpayer to be employed. Child and dependent care expenses include expenses incurred in the home, such as payments for a housekeeper. Out-of-the-home expenses incurred for the care of a dependent under the age of 13 also qualify for the credit. In addition, out-of-the-home expenses incurred for an older dependent or spouse who is physically or mentally incapacitated qualify for the credit if that person regularly spends at least eight hours each day in the taxpayer's household. This makes the credit available to taxpayers who keep handicapped older children and elderly relatives in the home instead of institutionalizing them. Out-of-the-home expenses incurred for services provided by a dependent care center will qualify only if the center complies with all applicable laws and regulations of a state or unit of local government.

Child care payments to a relative are eligible for the credit unless the relative is a dependent of the taxpayer or the taxpayer's spouse or is a child (under age 19) of the taxpayer.

EXAMPLE 31

M is an employed mother of an eight-year-old child. M pays her mother, G, $1,500 per year to care for the child after school. M does not claim G as a dependent. M pays her daughter D, age 17, $900 for the child's care during the summer. Of these amounts, only the $1,500 paid to G qualifies as employment-related child care expenses. ◆

Earned Income Ceiling. The total for qualifying employment-related expenses is limited to an individual's earned income. For married taxpayers, this limitation applies to the spouse with the *lesser* amount of earned income. Special rules are provided for taxpayers with nonworking spouses who are disabled or are

31. § 21.

full-time students. If a nonworking spouse is physically or mentally disabled or is a full-time student, he or she is *deemed* to have earned income. The deemed amount is $200 per month if there is one qualifying individual in the household or $400 per month if there are two or more qualifying individuals in the household. In the case of a student-spouse, the student's income is *deemed* to be earned only for the months that the student is enrolled on a full-time basis at an educational institution.

Calculation of the Credit. In general, the credit is equal to a percentage of *unreimbursed* employment-related expenses up to $2,400 for one qualifying individual and $4,800 for two or more individuals. The credit rate varies between 20 percent and 30 percent, depending on the taxpayer's AGI. The following chart shows the applicable percentage for taxpayers as AGI increases:

Adjusted Gross Income		
Over	But Not Over	Applicable Rate of Credit
$ 0	$10,000	30%
10,000	12,000	29%
12,000	14,000	28%
14,000	16,000	27%
16,000	18,000	26%
18,000	20,000	25%
20,000	22,000	24%
22,000	24,000	23%
24,000	26,000	22%
26,000	28,000	21%
28,000	No limit	20%

EXAMPLE 32

W, who has two children under age 13, worked full-time while her spouse, H, was attending college for 10 months during the year. W earned $21,000 and incurred $5,000 of child care expenses. H is *deemed* to be fully employed and to have earned $400 for each of the 10 months (or a total of $4,000). Since H and W have AGI of $21,000, they are allowed a credit rate of 24%. H and W are limited to $4,000 in qualified child care expenses (the lesser of $4,800 or $4,000). They are entitled to a tax credit of $960 (24% × $4,000) for the year. ◆

Dependent Care Assistance Program. Recall from Chapter 5 that a taxpayer is allowed an exclusion from gross income for a limited amount reimbursed for child or dependent care expenses. However, the taxpayer is not allowed both an exclusion from income and a child and dependent care credit on the same amount. The allowable child and dependent care expenses are reduced dollar for dollar by the amount of reimbursement.[32]

EXAMPLE 33

Assume the same facts as in Example 32, except that of the $5,000 paid for child care, W was reimbursed $2,500 by her employer under a qualified dependent care assistance program. Under the employer's plan, the reimbursement reduces W's taxable wages. Thus, H and W have AGI of $18,500 ($21,000 − $2,500). The maximum amount of child care expenses for two or more dependents of $4,800 is reduced by the $2,500 reimbursement, resulting in a tax credit of $575 [25% × ($4,800 − $2,500)]. ◆

32. § 21(c).

Concept Summary 13–1
Tax Credits

Credit	Computation	Comments
Tax withheld on wages (§ 31)	Amount is reported to employee on W–2 form.	Refundable credit.
Earned income (§ 32)	Amount is determined by reference to Earned Income Credit Table published by IRS. Computations of underlying amounts in Earned Income Credit Table are illustrated in Examples 25–27.	Refundable credit. A form of negative income tax to assist low-income taxpayers. Earned income and AGI must be less than certain threshold amounts. Child must satisfy relationship, residency, and age requirements.
Child and dependent care (§ 21)	Rate ranges from 20% to 30% depending on AGI. Maximum base for credit is $2,400 for one qualifying individual, $4,800 for two or more.	Nonrefundable personal credit. No carryback or carryforward. Benefits taxpayers who incur employment-related child or dependent care expenses in order to work or seek employment. Eligible dependents include children under age 13 or dependent (any age) or spouse who is physically or mentally incapacitated.
Elderly and disabled (§ 22)	15% of sum of base amount minus reductions for (a) Social Security and other nontaxable benefits and (b) excess AGI. Base amount is fixed by law (e.g., $5,000 for a single taxpayer).	Nonrefundable personal credit. No carryback or carryforward. Provides relief for taxpayers not receiving substantial tax-free retirement benefits.
Foreign tax (§ 27)	Foreign income/total worldwide taxable income × U.S. tax = overall limitation. Lesser of foreign taxes imposed or overall limitation.	Nonrefundable credit. Unused credits may be carried back two years and forward five years. Purpose is to prevent double taxation on foreign income.
General business (§ 38)	May not exceed net income tax minus the greater of tentative minimum tax or 25% of net regular tax liability that exceeds $25,000.	Nonrefundable credit. Components include investment tax credit, jobs credit, alcohol fuels credit, research activities credit, low-income housing credit, and disabled access credit. Unused credit may be carried back 3 years and forward 15 years. FIFO method applies to carryovers, carrybacks, and credits earned during current year.
Investment (§ 46)	Qualifying investment times regular percentage, energy percentage, or rehabilitation percentage, depending on type of property. Part of general business credit and subject to its limitations.	Nonrefundable credit. Part of general business credit and therefore subject to same carryback, carryover, and FIFO rules. Regular percentage applies to transition property. Energy percentage is 10%. Regular rehabilitation rate is 10%; rate for certified historic structures is 20%.
Jobs (§ 51)	Regular credit is 40% of first $6,000 of wages paid to each eligible employee. Qualified summer youth employee (QSYE) credit is 40% of first $3,000 of wages paid to QSYE. Eligible employees must begin work by June 30, 1992.	Nonrefundable credit. Part of general business credit and therefore subject to same carryback, carryover, and FIFO rules. Purpose is to encourage employment of specified groups. QSYE generally must be age 16 or 17 on hiring date.
Research activities (§ 41)	Incremental credit is 20% of excess of computation year expenditures minus the base amount. Basic research credit is allowed to certain corporations for 20% of cash payments to qualified organizations that exceed a specially calculated base amount.	Nonrefundable credit. Part of general business credit and therefore subject to same carryback, carryover, and FIFO rules. Purpose is to encourage high-tech research in the United States.

Credit	Computation	Comments
Low-income housing (§ 42)	Appropriate rate times eligible basis (portion of project attributable to low-income units).	Nonrefundable credit. Part of general business credit and therefore subject to same carryback, carryover, and FIFO rules. Credit is available each year for 10 years. Recapture may apply.
Disabled access (§ 44)	Credit is 50% of eligible access expenditures that exceed $250, but do not exceed $10,250. Maximum credit is $5,000.	Nonrefundable credit. Part of general business credit and therefore subject to same carryback, carryover, and FIFO rules. Available only to eligible small businesses.

Reporting Requirements. The credit is claimed by completing and filing Form 2441, Credit for Child and Dependent Care Expenses (see Appendix B). However, the child and dependent care credit will not be allowed unless, at the time the credit is claimed, the taxpayer reports the correct name, address, and tax identification number (either Social Security number or Employer Identification number) of the care provider on the form. If the care provider is a tax-exempt organization, the name and address but not the tax identification number are required.

Payment Procedures

The tax law contains elaborate rules that require the prepayment of various Federal taxes. Consistent with the pay-as-you-go approach to the collection of taxes, these rules carry penalties for lack of compliance.[33] Prepayment procedures fall into two major categories: those applicable to employers and those applicable to self-employed persons. For employers, both payroll taxes (FICA and FUTA) and income taxes may be involved. With self-employed taxpayers, the focus is on the income tax and the self-employment tax.

Procedures Applicable to Employers

As noted in Chapter 1, *employment taxes* include FICA (Federal Insurance Contributions Act) and FUTA (Federal Unemployment Tax Act). The employer usually is responsible for withholding the employee's share of FICA (commonly referred to as Social Security tax) and appropriate amounts for income taxes. In addition, the employer must match the FICA portion withheld and fully absorb the cost of FUTA. The sum of the employment taxes and the income tax withholdings must be paid to the IRS at specified intervals.

The key to employer compliance in this area involves the resolution of the following points:

- Ascertaining which employees and wages are covered by employment taxes and are subject to withholding for income taxes.
- Arriving at the amount to be withheld.
- Reporting and paying employment taxes and income taxes withheld to the IRS on a timely basis through the use of proper forms.

33. See, for example, § 3403 (employer liable for any taxes withheld and not paid over to the IRS), § 6656 (up to 15% penalty on amounts withheld and not paid over), and § 6654 (penalty for failure by an individual to pay estimated income taxes).

Coverage Requirements. Circular E (Employer's Tax Guide), Publication 15, issued by the IRS contains a complete list of which employees and which wages require withholdings for income taxes and employment taxes. Figure 13–5 extracts a portion of this list and is reproduced on page 13–28. In working with Figure 13–5, consider the following observations:

- The designation "Exempt" in the income tax withholding column does not mean that the amount paid is nontaxable to the employee. It merely relieves the employer from having to withhold.

EXAMPLE 34

T works for X Corporation and has the type of job where tips are not common but do occur. If the total tips T receives are less than $20 per month, X Corporation need not withhold Federal income taxes on these amounts. Nevertheless, T must include the tips in his gross income. ◆

- In some cases, income tax withholding is not required but is voluntary. This is designated "Exempt (taxable if both employer and employee voluntarily agree)."

EXAMPLE 35

T is employed as a gardener by a wealthy family. In the past, he has encountered difficulty in managing his finances so as to be in a position to pay the income tax due every April 15. To ease the cash-flow problem that develops in April, T requests that the employer withhold income taxes from his wages. ◆

- The FICA (Social Security) column refers to the employer's share. The same is true of the Federal Unemployment (FUTA) column since the employee does not contribute to this tax.

Amount of Withholding. In the case of FICA, withholdings from employees must continue until the base amounts are reached (refer to Figure 1–3 in Chapter 1). In tax year 1992, for example, FICA withholding ceases for the Social Security portion (6.2%) once the employee has earned wages subject to FICA in the amount of $55,500 and for the Medicare portion (1.45%) once the employee has earned subject wages of $130,200.

Arriving at the amount to be withheld for income tax purposes is not so simple. It involves three basic steps:[34]

- Have the employee complete Form W–4, Employee's Withholding Allowance Certificate.
- Determine the employee's payroll period.
- Compute the amount to be withheld, usually using either the wage-bracket tables or the percentage method.

Form W–4 reflects the employee's marital status and withholding allowances. Generally, it need not be filed with the IRS and is retained by the employer as part of the payroll records. A copy of the Form W–4 must be filed with the IRS, though, if the employee claims more than 10 exemptions or, in certain cases, claims exempt status. The IRS is aware that some employees deliberately avoid income tax withholding through the use of either of these procedures.

34. The withholding provisions are contained in §§ 3401 and 3402. These Sections will not be referenced specifically in the discussion that follows.

FIGURE 13–5
Withholding Classifications

Special Classes of Employment and Special Types of Payment	Treatment under Different Employment Taxes		
	Income Tax Withholding	**Social Security and Medicare**	**Federal Unemployment**
Dismissal or severance pay	Taxable	Taxable	Taxable
Family employees			
a. Son or daughter employed by parent (or by partnership consisting only of parents).	Taxable	Exempt until age 18	Exempt until age 21
b. Spouse employed by spouse.	Taxable	Taxable if in course of spouse's business.	Exempt
c. Parent employed by a son or daughter.	Taxable	Taxable if in course of the son's or daughter's business. For household work in private home of employer, see Household Employees on page 12 of Circular E.	Exempt
Household workers (domestic service in private homes; farmers, see Circular A).	Exempt (taxable if both employer and employee voluntarily agree).	Taxable if paid $50 or more in cash in quarter.	Taxable if employer paid cash wages of $1,000 or more in any calendar quarter in the current or preceding year.
Interns working in hospitals	Taxable	Taxable	Exempt
Meals and lodging including those furnished at a bargain charge to the employee.	**a.** Meals—taxable unless furnished for employer's convenience and on the employer's premises. **b.** Lodging—taxable unless furnished on employer's premises, for the employer's convenience, and as a condition of employment.		
Ministers of churches performing duties as such.	Exempt (taxable if both employer and employee voluntarily agree).	Exempt	Exempt
Moving expenses, reimbursement for.	Exempt if it is reasonable to believe expenses may be deductible by the employee; otherwise taxable.		
Newspaper carrier under age 18 delivering to customers.	Exempt (taxable if both employer and employee voluntarily agree).	Exempt	Exempt
Tips, if less than $20 in a month.	Exempt from withholding. Taxable to employee.	Exempt	Exempt
Workers' compensation.	Exempt	Exempt	Exempt

The employer need not verify the number of exemptions claimed. Any misinformation in the form will be attributed to the employee. However, if the employer has reason to believe that the employee made a false statement, the IRS District Director should be notified. In the meantime, the Form W–4 should be honored. Employees are subject to both civil and criminal penalties for filing false withholding statements.

On Form W–4 an employee may claim *withholding allowances* for the following: personal exemptions for self and spouse (unless either is claimed as a dependent of another person) and dependency exemptions. One *special withholding allowance* may be claimed if the employee is single and has only one job, if the employee is married and has only one job and the spouse is not employed, or if wages from a second job or a spouse's wages (or both) are $1,000 or less. An employee who plans to itemize deductions or claim adjustments to income (e.g., alimony, deductible IRA contributions) should use the worksheet provided on Form W–4 to determine the correct number of additional allowances.

To avoid having too little tax withheld, some employees may find it necessary to reduce their withholding allowances. This might be the case for an employee who is single and has more than one job. Likewise, a married employee who has a working spouse or more than one job might wish to claim fewer allowances.

If both spouses of a married couple are employed, they may allocate their total allowances between themselves as they see fit. The same allocation procedure is required if a taxpayer has more than one job. In no event should the same allowance be claimed more than once at the same time. It is permissible to declare *fewer* allowances than the taxpayer is entitled to in order to increase the amount of withholding. Doing so, however, does not affect the number of exemptions allowable on the employee's income tax return. An employee is also permitted to have the employer withhold a certain dollar amount in addition to the required amount. This additional dollar amount can be arbitrary or calculated in accordance with a worksheet and tables on Form W–4.

EXAMPLE 36

H, who earns $15,000, is married to W, who earns $25,000. They have three dependent children and will claim the standard deduction. Together they should be entitled to five allowances [2 (for personal exemptions) + 3 (for dependency exemptions)]. The special withholding allowance is not available since both spouses earn more than $1,000. If H were the spouse first employed and his Form W–4 reflects five allowances, W's Form W–4 should claim none. They could, however, reallocate their allowances between them as long as the total claimed does not exceed five. ◆

The period of service for which an employee is paid is known as the *payroll period*. Daily, weekly, biweekly, semimonthly, and monthly periods are the most common arrangements. If an employee has no regular payroll period, he or she is considered to be paid on a daily basis.

Once the allowances are known (as reflected on Form W–4) and the payroll period determined, the amount to be withheld for Federal income taxes can be computed. The computation usually is made through the use of the wage-bracket tables or by the percentage method.

Wage-bracket tables are available for daily, weekly, biweekly, semimonthly, and monthly payroll periods for single (including heads of household) and married taxpayers. An extract of the tables dealing with married persons on a monthly payroll period is reproduced in Figure 13–6.

The table in Figure 13–6 is for the period after February 1992. Example 37 illustrates the use of withholding tables.

EXAMPLE 37

T is married and has three dependent children and no additional allowances for itemized deductions, adjustments to income, or child care credit. In his job with X Corporation, T earns $2,770 in May 1992. Assuming T's wife is not employed and all available allowances are claimed on Form W-4, X Corporation should withhold $170 a month from T's wages. This amount is taken from the six allowances column in the wage bracket of $2,760–$2,800. The six allowances result from personal exemptions (two) plus the special withholding allowance (one) plus dependency exemptions (three). ◆

FIGURE 13–6
Withholding Table*

MARRIED Persons—**MONTHLY** Payroll Period
(For Wages Paid After February 1992)

And the wages are—		And the number of withholding allowances claimed is—										
At least	But less than	0	1	2	3	4	5	6	7	8	9	10
		The amount of income tax to be withheld shall be—										
$0	$500	$0	$0	$0	$0	$0	$0	$0	$0	$0	$0	$0
500	520	2	0	0	0	0	0	0	0	0	0	0
520	540	5	0	0	0	0	0	0	0	0	0	0
540	560	8	0	0	0	0	0	0	0	0	0	0
560	580	11	0	0	0	0	0	0	0	0	0	0
580	600	14	0	0	0	0	0	0	0	0	0	0
600	640	18	0	0	0	0	0	0	0	0	0	0
640	680	24	0	0	0	0	0	0	0	0	0	0
680	720	30	1	0	0	0	0	0	0	0	0	0
720	760	36	7	0	0	0	0	0	0	0	0	0
760	800	42	13	0	0	0	0	0	0	0	0	0
800	840	48	19	0	0	0	0	0	0	0	0	0
840	880	54	25	0	0	0	0	0	0	0	0	0
880	920	60	31	3	0	0	0	0	0	0	0	0
920	960	66	37	9	0	0	0	0	0	0	0	0
960	1,000	72	43	15	0	0	0	0	0	0	0	0
1,000	1,040	78	49	21	0	0	0	0	0	0	0	0
1,040	1,080	84	55	27	0	0	0	0	0	0	0	0
1,080	1,120	90	61	33	4	0	0	0	0	0	0	0
1,120	1,160	96	67	39	10	0	0	0	0	0	0	0
1,160	1,200	102	73	45	16	0	0	0	0	0	0	0
1,200	1,240	108	79	51	22	0	0	0	0	0	0	0
1,240	1,280	114	85	57	28	0	0	0	0	0	0	0
1,280	1,320	120	91	63	34	5	0	0	0	0	0	0
1,320	1,360	126	97	69	40	11	0	0	0	0	0	0
1,360	1,400	132	103	75	46	17	0	0	0	0	0	0
1,400	1,440	138	109	81	52	23	0	0	0	0	0	0
1,440	1,480	144	115	87	58	29	0	0	0	0	0	0
1,480	1,520	150	121	93	64	35	6	0	0	0	0	0
1,520	1,560	156	127	99	70	41	12	0	0	0	0	0
1,560	1,600	162	133	105	76	47	18	0	0	0	0	0
1,600	1,640	168	139	111	82	53	24	0	0	0	0	0
1,640	1,680	174	145	117	88	59	30	2	0	0	0	0
1,680	1,720	180	151	123	94	65	36	8	0	0	0	0
1,720	1,760	186	157	129	100	71	42	14	0	0	0	0
1,760	1,800	192	163	135	106	77	48	20	0	0	0	0
1,800	1,840	198	169	141	112	83	54	26	0	0	0	0
1,840	1,880	204	175	147	118	89	60	32	3	0	0	0
1,880	1,920	210	181	153	124	95	66	38	9	0	0	0
1,920	1,960	216	187	159	130	101	72	44	15	0	0	0
1,960	2,000	222	193	165	136	107	78	50	21	0	0	0
2,000	2,040	228	199	171	142	113	84	56	27	0	0	0
2,040	2,080	234	205	177	148	119	90	62	33	4	0	0
2,080	2,120	240	211	183	154	125	96	68	39	10	0	0
2,120	2,160	246	217	189	160	131	102	74	45	16	0	0
2,160	2,200	252	223	195	166	137	108	80	51	22	0	0
2,200	2,240	258	229	201	172	143	114	86	57	28	0	0
2,240	2,280	264	235	207	178	149	120	92	63	34	5	0
2,280	2,320	270	241	213	184	155	126	98	69	40	11	0
2,320	2,360	276	247	219	190	161	132	104	75	46	17	0
2,360	2,400	282	253	225	196	167	138	110	81	52	23	0
2,400	2,440	288	259	231	202	173	144	116	87	58	29	1
2,440	2,480	294	265	237	208	179	150	122	93	64	35	7
2,480	2,520	300	271	243	214	185	156	128	99	70	41	13
2,520	2,560	306	277	249	220	191	162	134	105	76	47	19
2,560	2,600	312	283	255	226	197	168	140	111	82	53	25
2,600	2,640	318	289	261	232	203	174	146	117	88	59	31
2,640	2,680	324	295	267	238	209	180	152	123	94	65	37
2,680	2,720	330	301	273	244	215	186	158	129	100	71	43
2,720	2,760	336	307	279	250	221	192	164	135	106	77	49
2,760	2,800	342	313	285	256	227	198	170	141	112	83	55
2,800	2,840	348	319	291	262	233	204	176	147	118	89	61
2,840	2,880	354	325	297	268	239	210	182	153	124	95	67
2,880	2,920	360	331	303	274	245	216	188	159	130	101	73
2,920	2,960	366	337	309	280	251	222	194	165	136	107	79
2,960	3,000	372	343	315	286	257	228	200	171	142	113	85
3,000	3,040	378	349	321	292	263	234	206	177	148	119	91
3,040	3,080	384	355	327	298	269	240	212	183	154	125	97
3,080	3,120	390	361	333	304	275	246	218	189	160	131	103
3,120	3,160	396	367	339	310	281	252	224	195	166	137	109

*This table replaces the withholding table that was originally issued for 1992. The revised table requires smaller amounts to be withheld from an employee's salary than that required by the original table. The original table is not illustrated in this text because of space limitations.

Although the wage-bracket table requires few, if any, calculations, the percentage method is equally acceptable and sometimes is used by employers. Its use may be necessary for payroll periods where no wage-bracket tables are available (quarterly, semiannual, and annual payroll periods) and where wages paid exceed the amount allowed for use of the wage-bracket tables. The percentage method is particularly useful when payroll computations are computerized. This method, however, requires the use of a conversion chart based on one withholding allowance. That is, the amount of one allowance is equal to the exemption amount divided by the number of payroll periods in a year. For example, the amount of one allowance for a taxpayer who is paid weekly is $44.23 ($2,300/52 payroll periods).

Payroll Period	Amount of One Allowance
Daily	$ 8.85
Weekly	44.23
Biweekly	88.46
Semimonthly	95.83
Monthly	191.67
Quarterly	575.00
Semiannual	1,150.00
Annual	2,300.00

To use the percentage method, proceed as follows:

Step 1. Multiply the amount of one allowance (as specified in the conversion chart) by the employee's total allowances (taken from Form W–4).
Step 2. Subtract the product reached in step 1 from the employee's wages. The remainder is called "amount of wages."
Step 3. Using the result derived in step 2, compute the income tax withholding under the proper percentage-method table.

The table used in applying the percentage method for those with monthly payroll periods is reproduced in Figure 13–7.

An illustration of the percentage method follows.

FIGURE 13–7
Table for Percentage Method of Withholding[35]

TABLE 4—If the Payroll Period With Respect to an Employee is Monthly

(a) SINGLE person—including head of household:

If the amount of wages (after subtracting withholding allowances) is: / The amount of income tax to be withheld shall be:

Over—	But not over —		of excess over—
Not over $204		0	
$204	—$1,896	15%	—$204
$1,896	—$3,954	$253.80 plus 28%	—$1,896
$3,954		$830.04 plus 31%	—$3,954

(b) MARRIED person—

If the amount of wages (after subtracting withholding allowances) is: / The amount of income tax to be withheld shall be:

Over—	But not over—		of excess over—
Not over $500		0	
$500	—$3,292	15%	—$500
$3,292	—$6,558	$418.80 plus 28%	—$3,292
$6,558		$1,333.28 plus 31%	—$6,558

35. This table is for wages paid after February 1992.

EXAMPLE 38

Assume the same facts as in Example 37, except that T's income tax withholding is determined using the percentage method.

Step 1. $191.67 (amount of one allowance for a monthly payroll period) × 6 (total allowances) = $1,150.02.
Step 2. $2,770 (monthly salary) − $1,150.02 (step 1) = $1,619.98 (amount of wages).
Step 3. Referring to Figure 13–7: 15% × $1,119.98 (excess of step 2 amount over $500) = $168. ◆

Note that the wage-bracket tables yield an amount for income tax withholding of $170 (refer to Example 37) while the percentage method results in $168 (refer to Example 38). The difference is explained by the fact that the wage-bracket table amounts are derived by computing the withholding on the median wage within each bracket.

Reporting and Payment Procedures. Proper handling of employment taxes and income tax withholdings requires considerable compliance effort on the part of the employer. Among the Federal forms that have to be filed are the following:

Form Designation	Title
SS–4	Application for Employer Identification Number
W–2	Wage and Tax Statement
W–3	Transmittal of Income and Tax Statements
940 or 940 EZ	Employer's Annual Federal Unemployment Tax Return
941	Employer's Quarterly Federal Tax Return

Form SS–4 is the starting point since it provides the employer with an identification number that must be used on all of the other forms filed with the IRS and the Social Security Administration. The number issued consists of nine digits and is hyphenated between the second and third digits (e.g., 72–1987316).

Form W–2 furnishes essential information to employees concerning wages paid, FICA, and income tax withholdings. The multiple copies of Form W–2 are distributed as follows:

- Copy A is sent by the employer to the Social Security Administration office that services the area.
- Copy B goes to the employee and is to be attached to his or her income tax return.
- Copy C also goes to the employee for retention in personal records.
- Copy D is kept by the employer as part of the usual payroll records.

Extra copies of Form W–2 may have to be prepared for state and local use. An employee who lives in New York City, for example, would require additional copies of Form W–2 for state and city income tax purposes. Form W–2 must be furnished to an employee not later than January 31 of the following year. If an employee leaves a place of employment before the end of the year, Form W–2 can be given to him or her at any time after employment ends. However, if the terminated employee asks for Form W–2, it must be given to him or her within 30 days after the request or the final wage payment, whichever is later.

Form W–3 must accompany the Copies A of Forms W–2 filed by the employer. Its basic purpose is to summarize and reconcile the amounts withheld for FICA and income taxes from *all* employees.

Form 940 (or Form 940 EZ) constitutes the employer's annual accounting for FUTA purposes. It must be filed on or before January 31 of the following year and must be accompanied by the payment of any undeposited FUTA due the Federal government.

Regardless of whether or not deposits[36] are required, most employers must settle its employment taxes every quarter. To do this, Form 941 must be filed on or before the last day of the month following the end of each calendar quarter.

Withholding on Pensions. Withholding is required for pension payments unless the taxpayer affirmatively *elects* to have *no* tax withheld. Part of the reason for this provision is to ease the burden on retirees of filing and paying quarterly estimated tax payments.

Backup Withholding. Some types of payments made to individuals by banks or businesses are subject to backup withholding under certain conditions. Backup withholding is designed to ensure that income tax is collected on interest and other payments reported on a Form 1099. If backup withholding applies, the payer must withhold 20 percent of the amount paid. Backup withholding applies when the taxpayer does not give the business or bank his or her identification number in the required manner and in other situations.[37]

Procedures Applicable to Self-Employed Persons

Although the discussion to follow largely centers on self-employed taxpayers, some of the procedures may be applicable to employed persons. In many cases, for example, employed persons may be required to pay estimated tax if they have income other than wages that is not subject to withholding. An employee may have a second trade or business conducted in a self-employment capacity. Depending on the circumstances, the second job may require the payment of a self-employment tax. In addition, taxpayers whose income consists primarily of rentals, dividends, or interest (this list is not all-inclusive) may be required to pay estimated tax.

Estimated Tax for Individuals. *Estimated tax* is the amount of tax (including alternative minimum tax and self-employment tax) an individual expects to owe for the year after subtracting tax credits and income tax withheld. Any individual who has estimated tax for the year of $500 or more *and* whose withholding does not equal or exceed the required annual payment (discussed below) must make quarterly payments.[38] Otherwise, a penalty may be assessed. No quarterly payments are required (no penalty will apply on an underpayment) if the taxpayer's estimated tax is under $500. No penalty will apply if the taxpayer had no tax liability for the preceding tax year *and* the preceding tax year was a taxable year of 12 months *and* the taxpayer was a citizen or resident for the entire preceding tax year. In this regard, having no tax liability is not the same as having no additional tax to pay.

---

36. Deposit requirements are specified in each current issue of Circular E, *Employer's Tax Guide*, IRS Publication 15.

37. § 3406(a).

38. § 6654(c)(1).

The required annual payment must first be computed. This is the *smallest* of the following amounts:

- Ninety percent of the tax shown on the current year's return.
- One hundred percent of the tax shown on the preceding year's return (the return must cover the full 12 months of the preceding year). In certain circumstances, however, this option is not available.
- Ninety percent of the tax determined by placing taxable income, alternative minimum taxable income, and adjusted self-employment income on an annualized basis.

One-fourth of this required annual payment is due on April 15, June 15, and September 15 of the tax year and January 15 of the following year. If no estimated tax was due on April 15 of the tax year but, because of a change in income, estimated tax was due after April 15, one-half of the estimated tax is due on June 15, one-fourth on September 15, and one-fourth on January 15. Likewise, if estimated tax becomes due after June 15, three-fourths must be paid on September 15 and one-fourth on January 15. If estimated tax first becomes due after September 15, 100 percent of the estimated tax is due on January 15. If the taxpayer files his or her return on or before January 31 following the tax year and pays the full amount shown as payable, no penalty applies for any underpaid fourth-quarter required installment.

An equal part of withholding is deemed paid on each due date. Thus, the quarterly installment of the required annual payment reduced by the applicable withholding is the estimated tax to be paid. Payments are to be accompanied by the payment voucher for the appropriate date from Form 1040–ES.

Married taxpayers may make joint estimated tax payments even though a joint income tax return is not subsequently filed. In such event, the estimated tax payments may be applied against the separate return liability of the spouses as they see fit. If a husband and wife cannot agree on a division of the estimated tax payments, the Regulations provide that the payments are to be allocated in proportion to the tax liability on the separate returns.

Penalty on Underpayments. A nondeductible penalty is imposed on the amount of underpayment of estimated tax. The rate for this penalty is the same as the rate for underpayments of tax and is adjusted quarterly to reflect changes in the average prime rate.

An *underpayment* occurs when any installment (the sum of estimated tax paid and income tax withheld) is less than 25 percent of the required annual payment. The penalty is applied to the amount of the underpayment for the period of the underpayment.[39]

Example 39

T made the following payments of estimated tax for 1992 and had no income tax withheld:

April 15, 1992	$1,400
June 15, 1992	2,300
September 15, 1992	1,500
January 15, 1993	1,800

T's actual tax for 1992 is $8,000 and tax in 1991 was $10,000. Therefore, each installment should have been at least $1,800 [($8,000 × 90%) × 25%]. Of the payment

39. § 6654(b)(2).

on June 15, $400 will be credited to the unpaid balance of the first quarterly installment due on April 15,[40] thereby effectively stopping the underpayment penalty for the first quarterly period. Of the remaining $1,900 payment on June 15, $100 is credited to the September 15 payment, resulting in this third quarterly payment being $200 short. Then $200 of the January 15 payment is credited to the September 15 shortfall, ending the period of underpayment for that portion due. The January 15, 1993, installment is now underpaid by $200, and a penalty will apply from January 15, 1993, to April 15, 1993 (unless paid sooner). T's underpayments for the periods of underpayment are as follows:

1st installment due:	$400 from April 15–June 15
2nd installment due:	Paid in full
3rd installment due:	$200 from September 15, 1992–January 15, 1993
4th installment due:	$200 from January 15–April 15, 1993

◆

If a possible underpayment of estimated tax is indicated, Form 2210 should be filed to compute the penalty due or to justify that no penalty applies.

Self-Employment Tax. The tax on self-employment income is levied to provide Social Security benefits (old age, survivors, and disability insurance and hospital insurance) for self-employed individuals. Individuals with net earnings from self-employment of $400 or more are subject to the self-employment tax.[41] For 1992, the self-employment tax is 15.3 percent on self-employment income up to $55,500 and 2.9 percent on self-employment income in excess of $55,500 up to $130,200. In other words, for 1992 the self-employment tax is 12.4 percent of self-employment earnings up to $55,500 (for the Social Security portion) *plus* 2.9 percent of self-employment earnings up to $130,200 (for the Medicare portion). See Figure 13–8.

Currently, self-employed taxpayers are allowed a deduction from net earnings from self-employment, at one-half of the self-employment rate, for purposes of determining self-employment tax[42] *and* an income tax deduction for one-half the amount of self-employment tax paid.[43]

Determining the amount of self-employment tax to be paid for 1992 involves the following steps, which entail computations for both the Social Security portion and the Medicare portion of the self-employment tax.

Step 1. Determine 92.35 percent of net earnings from self-employment. This is the percentage that results after 100 percent of net earnings from self-employment is reduced by one-half (7.65 percent) of the total self-employment tax rate (15.3 percent). Thus, 100 percent − 7.65 percent = 92.35 percent.

FIGURE 13–8
Self-Employment Tax: Social Security and Medicare Portions

Year		Tax Rate	Ceiling Amount
1991	Social Security portion	12.4%	$ 53,400
	Medicare portion	2.9%	125,000
	Aggregate rate	15.3%	
1992	Social Security portion	12.4%	$ 55,500
	Medicare portion	2.9%	130,200
	Aggregate rate	15.3%	

40. Payments are credited to unpaid installments in the order in which the installments are required to be paid. § 6654(b)(3).

41. § 6017.

42. § 1402(a)(12).

43. § 164(f).

Step 2. Compare the result in step 1 with $55,500 and select the smaller amount. This amount is self-employment income for this portion of the self-employment tax.
Step 3. Multiply the amount in step 2 by 12.4 percent.
Step 4. Determine 92.35 percent of net earnings from self-employment. This is the same percentage that was calculated in step 1 above.
Step 5. Compare the result in step 4 with $130,200 and select the smaller amount. This amount is self-employment income for the Medicare portion of the self-employment tax.
Step 6. Multiply the amount in step 5 by 2.9 percent.
Step 7. Add the amounts from steps 3 and 6.

The result of step 7 is the amount of self-employment tax to be paid. For *income tax purposes,* the amount to be reported is net earnings from self-employment before the deduction for one-half of the self-employment tax. Then the taxpayer is allowed a deduction *for* AGI of one-half of the self-employment tax.

EXAMPLE 40

Using the step procedure just described, the self-employment tax is determined for four taxpayers with net earnings from self-employment for 1992 as follows: M, $30,000; N, $55,000; O, $80,000; P, $150,000.

	M	N	O	P
Step 1. Determine 92.35% of net earnings from self-employment				
M ($30,000 × 92.35%)	$ 27,705			
N ($55,000 × 92.35%)		$ 50,793		
O ($80,000 × 92.35%)			$ 73,880	
P ($150,000 × 92.35%)				$ 138,525
Step 2. Select the smaller of the step 1 amount or $55,500	$ 27,705	$ 50,793	$ 55,500	$ 55,500
Step 3. Multiply the step 2 amount by 12.4%	×12.4%	×12.4%	×12.4%	×12.4%
Social Security portion of self-employment tax	$3,435.42	$6,298.33	$6,882.00	$ 6,882.00
Step 4. Determine 92.35% of net earnings from self-employment				
M ($30,000 × 92.35%)	$ 27,705			
N ($55,000 × 92.35%)		$ 50,793		
O ($80,000 × 92.35%)			$ 73,880	
P ($150,000 × 92.35%)				$ 138,525
Step 5. Select the smaller of the step 4 amount or $130,200	$ 27,705	$ 50,793	$ 73,880	$ 130,200
Step 6. Multiply the step 5 amount by 2.9%	×2.9%	×2.9%	×2.9%	×2.9%
Medicare portion of self-employment tax	$ 803.45	$1,473.00	$2,142.52	$ 3,775.80
Step 7. Add the amounts from steps 3 and 6 Total self-employment tax	$4,238.87	$7,771.33	$9,024.52	$10,657.80

◆

For income tax purposes, M has net earnings from self-employment of $30,000 and a deduction *for* AGI of $2,119.44 (one-half of $4,238.87 self-employment tax paid). N has net earnings from self-employment of $55,000 and a deduction *for* AGI of $3,885.67 (one-half of $7,771.33). O has net earnings from self-employment of $80,000 and a deduction *for* AGI of $4,512.26 (one-half of $9,024.52). P has net earnings from self-employment of $150,000 and a deduction *for* AGI of $5,328.90 (one-half of $10,657.80). All four benefit from the deduction for one-half of the self-employment tax paid.

For 1991, the self-employment tax computations are similar to those for 1992. The only difference is that the tax bases were lower for 1991 than they are for 1992 (see Figure 13–8).

If an individual also receives wages subject to FICA tax in 1992, the ceiling amounts on which the self-employment tax is computed are reduced. Thus, no self-employment tax is due if a self-employed individual also receives FICA wages in excess of the ceiling amounts.

EXAMPLE 41

In 1992, T had $32,000 of net earnings from the conduct of a bookkeeping service (trade or business activity). He also received wages as an employee amounting to $25,000 during the year. The amount of T's self-employment income subject to the Social Security portion (12.4%) is $29,552 and the amount subject to the Medicare portion (2.9%) is $29,552.

	Social Security Portion	**Medicare Portion**
Ceiling amount	$55,500	$130,200
Less: FICA wages	25,000	25,000
Net ceiling	$30,500	$105,200
Net self-employment income ($32,000 × 92.35%)	$29,552	$ 29,552
Lesser of net ceiling or net self-employment income	$29,552	$ 29,552

◆

Net earnings from self-employment include gross income from a trade or business less allowable trade or business deductions, the distributive share of any partnership income or loss derived from a trade or business activity, and net income from the rendering of personal services as an independent contractor. Gain or loss from the disposition of property (including involuntary conversions) is excluded from the computation of self-employment income unless the property involved is inventory.

Director's fees, which are paid to a nonemployee, are also considered self-employment income because a director is considered to be engaged in a trade or business activity. However, director's fees received on a deferred basis are not subject to the self-employment tax until the fees are paid or constructively received and thus are subject to the income tax.

EXAMPLE 42

P, a former treasurer, is retired from X Company but is retained as a corporate director. She performs these duties in 1992 under a deferred arrangement whereby she will be paid $12,000 in 1994, at which time she will be 70 years old. In 1992, the year earned, none of the director's fees will be subject to self-employment tax. For income tax purposes and for self-employment tax purposes, the $12,000 of director's fees will be subject to tax in 1994, the year received. ◆

EXAMPLE 43

Assume the same facts as in Example 42, except that P is not retired. In addition to the director's fees, she is paid a salary of $150,000 in her capacity as treasurer of the company. Because her salary exceeds both wage bases ($55,500 and $130,200) for FICA tax purposes, the director's fees are not subject to self-employment tax if the director's fees were paid in 1992. If not paid until 1994, the director's fees will be subject to self-employment tax in 1994 unless P's salary in 1994 exceeds both wage bases. Thus, P will need to consider both the income tax deferral consequences and the self-employment tax consequences for the year the director's fees are to be paid. ◆

An employee who performs services on a part-time basis as an independent contractor or an employee who is engaged in a separate trade or business activity may be subject to the self-employment tax.

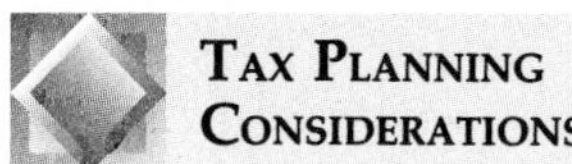

TAX PLANNING CONSIDERATIONS

Foreign Tax Credit

A U.S. citizen or resident working abroad (commonly referred to as an *expatriate*) may elect to take either a foreign tax credit or the foreign earned income exclusion. In cases where the income tax of a foreign country is higher than the U.S. income tax, the credit choice usually is preferable. If the reverse is true, electing the foreign earned income exclusion probably reduces the overall tax burden.

Unfortunately, the choice between the credit and the earned income exclusion is not without some limitations. The election of the foreign earned income exclusion, once made, can be revoked for a later year. However, once revoked, the earned income exclusion will not be available for a period of five years unless the IRS consents to an earlier date. This will create a dilemma for expatriates whose job assignments over several years shift between low- and high-bracket countries.

EXAMPLE 44

In 1991, T, a calendar year taxpayer, is sent by his employer to Saudi Arabia (a low-tax country). For 1991, therefore, T elects the foreign earned income exclusion. In 1992, T's employer transfers him to France (a high-tax country). Accordingly, T revokes the foreign earned income exclusion election for 1992 and chooses instead to use the foreign tax credit. If T is transferred back to Saudi Arabia (or any other low-tax country) within five years, he no longer may utilize the foreign earned income exclusion. ◆

Credit for Child and Dependent Care Expenses

A taxpayer may incur employment-related expenses that also qualify as medical expenses (e.g., a nurse is hired to provide in-the-home care for an ill and incapacitated dependent parent). Such expenses may be either deducted as medical expenses (subject to the 7.5 percent limitation) or utilized in determining the child and dependent care expenses credit. If the dependent care credit is chosen and the employment-related expenses exceed the limitation ($2,400, $4,800, or earned income, as the case may be), the excess may be considered a medical expense. If, however, the taxpayer chooses to deduct qualified employment-related expenses as medical expenses, any portion that is not deductible because of the 7.5 percent limitation may not be used in computing the child and dependent care expenses credit.

EXAMPLE 45

T, a single individual, has the following tax position for tax year 1992.

Adjusted gross income		$30,000
Itemized deductions *from* AGI—		
Other than medical expenses	$2,500	
Medical expenses	6,000	$ 8,500

All of T's medical expenses were incurred to provide nursing care for her disabled father while she was working. The father lives with T and qualifies as T's dependent. ◆

What should T do in this situation? One approach would be to use $2,400 of the nursing care expenses to obtain the maximum dependent care credit allowed of $480 (20% × $2,400). The balance of these expenses should be claimed as medical expenses. After a reduction of 7.5 percent of AGI, this would produce a medical expense deduction of $1,350 [$3,600 (remaining medical expenses) − (7.5% × $30,000)].

Another approach would be to claim the full $6,000 as a medical expense and forgo the dependent care credit. After the 7.5 percent adjustment of $2,250 (7.5% × $30,000), a deduction of $3,750 remains.

The choice, then, is between a credit of $480 plus a deduction of $1,350 or a credit of $0 plus a deduction of $3,750. Which is better, of course, depends on the relative tax savings involved.

One of the traditional goals of *family tax planning* is to minimize the total tax burden within the family unit. With proper planning and implementation, the child and dependent care expenses credit can be used to help achieve this goal. For example, payments to certain relatives for the care of qualifying dependents and children qualify for the credit if the care provider is *not* a dependent of the taxpayer or the taxpayer's spouse or is *not* a child (under age 19) of the taxpayer. Thus, if the care provider is in a lower tax bracket than the taxpayer, the following benefits result:

- Income is shifted to a lower-bracket family member.
- The taxpayer qualifies for the child and dependent care expenses credit.

In addition, the goal of minimizing the family income tax liability can be enhanced in some other situations, but only if the credit's limitations are recognized and avoided. For example, tax savings may still be enjoyed even if the qualifying expenditures incurred by a cash basis taxpayer have already reached the annual ceiling ($2,400 or $4,800). To the extent that any additional payments can be shifted into future tax years, the benefit from the credit may be preserved on these excess expenditures.

EXAMPLE 46

T, a calendar year and cash basis taxpayer, has spent $2,400 by December 1 on qualifying child care expenditures for his dependent 11-year-old son. The $200 that is due the care provider for child care services rendered in December does not generate a tax credit benefit if the amount is paid in the current year because the $2,400 ceiling has been reached. However, if the payment can be delayed until the next year, the total credit over the two-year period for which T is eligible may be increased. ◆

A similar shifting of expenditures to a subsequent year may be wise if the potential credit otherwise generated would exceed the tax liability available to absorb the credit.

Adjustments to Increase Withholding

The penalty for underpayment of estimated tax by individuals is computed for each quarter of the tax year. A taxpayer can play *catch-up* to a certain extent. Each quarterly payment is credited to the unpaid portion of any previous required installment. Thus, the penalty stops on that portion of the underpayment for the previous quarter. Since income tax withheld is assumed to have been paid evenly throughout the year and is allocated equally among the four installments in computing any penalty, a taxpayer who would otherwise be subject to a penalty for underpayment should increase withholdings late in the year. This can be done by changing the number of allowances claimed on Form W–4 or by special arrangement with the employer to increase the amount withheld.

A similar way to avoid (or reduce) a penalty for underpayment is to have the employer continue Social Security withholding beyond the base amount.

EXAMPLE 47

T, a calendar year taxpayer, earns $72,000 from her job. In late August of 1992, T realizes that she will be subject to a penalty for underpayment of estimated tax due to income from outside sources. Consequently, she instructs her employer to continue FICA withholdings for the rest of 1992. If this is done, an extra $16,500 [$72,000 (annual salary) – $55,500 (base amount of the Social Security portion for 1992)] will be subject to the 6.2% Social Security portion of the FICA tax [7.65% (total FICA rate) – 1.45% (Medicare portion of the FICA rate)]. Thus, T generates an additional $1,023 (6.2% × $16,500) that will be deemed withheld ratably during 1992. ◆

Adjustments to Avoid Overwithholding

Publication 505, Tax Withholding and Estimated Tax, contains worksheets that taxpayers may use to take advantage of special provisions for avoiding overwithholding. Extra exemptions for withholding purposes are allowed if the taxpayer has unusually large itemized deductions, deductions *for* AGI, or tax credits. Net losses from Schedules C, D, E, and F may be considered in computing the number of extra withholding exemptions. Net operating loss carryovers may also be considered in the computation. A taxpayer who is entitled to extra withholding exemptions for any of these reasons should file a new Form W–4, Employee's Withholding Allowance Certificate, with his or her employer.

PROBLEM MATERIALS

DISCUSSION QUESTIONS

1. Would an individual taxpayer receive greater benefit from deducting an expenditure or from taking a credit equal to 25% of the expenditure?
2. What is a refundable credit? Give examples. What is a nonrefundable credit? Give examples.
3. What are the components of the general business credit?
4. Discuss the order in which credits are offset against the tax liability. Why is the order in which credits are utilized important?
5. In determining the maximum amount of general business credit allowed an individual taxpayer for a tax year, net income tax, tentative minimum tax, and net regular tax liability are important concepts.

a. Define each term.
b. Using these terms, state the general business credit limitation for an individual taxpayer for 1992.

6. Discuss the treatment of unused general business credits.
7. The investment tax credit is comprised of three components. Identify these components, and indicate whether the credit is available for qualifying expenditures made in 1992.
8. If investment tax credit property is prematurely disposed of or ceases to be qualified property, how is the tax liability affected in the year of the disposition?
9. The regular investment tax credit was repealed for property placed in service after December 31, 1985. Is there any way a taxpayer can benefit from unused ITC related to investment tax credit property placed in service on or before that date? Explain.
10. V is considering the purchase and renovation of an old building. He has heard about the tax credit for rehabilitation expenditures but does not know the specific rules applicable to the credit. He has asked you to explain the most important details to him. What will you tell V?
11. The jobs credit was enacted to encourage employers to hire individuals from one or more target groups. Identify the groups of individuals who have been targeted by this provision.
12. Explain the alternatives a taxpayer has in claiming the deduction and credit for research and experimentation expenditures incurred.
13. Explain the purpose of the disabled access credit and describe the general characteristics of its computation.
14. Which of the following taxpayers are eligible for the earned income credit for the tax year 1992?
    a. H and W are married and have a 15-year-old dependent child living with them. H earned $7,600 and W earned $7,000.
    b. A, a single parent, supports her 20-year-old daughter who is a full-time college student. A earns $14,000 and has no other income.
    c. P, an unmarried taxpayer, earns $12,000 and has no other income. He claims a dependency exemption for his aunt under a multiple support agreement.
15. What three tests must be met for a child to be considered a qualifying child for purposes of the earned income credit? Describe.
16. Is the earned income credit a form of negative income tax? Why?
17. Individuals who receive substantial Social Security benefits are usually not eligible for the tax credit for the elderly because these benefits effectively eliminate the base upon which the credit is computed. Explain.
18. What purpose is served by the overall limitation to the foreign tax credit?
19. Do all foreign taxes qualify for the U.S. foreign tax credit? Explain.
20. In general, when would an individual taxpayer find it more beneficial to take advantage of the foreign earned income exclusion rather than the foreign tax credit in the computation of his or her income tax liability?
21. Do child care payments to relatives qualify for the child care expenses credit?
22. T is not concerned with the child and dependent care expenses credit because his AGI is considerably in excess of $20,000. Is T under a misconception regarding the tax law? Explain.
23. J and K are married and have a dependent child eight years of age. J earned $15,000 during 1992. K, a full-time student for the entire year, was not employed. J and K believe they are not entitled to the credit for child and dependent care expenses because K was not employed. Is this correct? Explain your answer.
24. W and her spouse, H, file a joint return and expect to report AGI of $95,000 in 1992. W's employer offers a child and dependent care reimbursement plan that allows up to $2,500 of qualifying expenses to be reimbursed in exchange for a $2,500 reduction in the employee's salary. Because W and H have one minor child requiring child care

that costs $2,500 each year, she is wondering if she should sign up for the program instead of taking advantage of the child and dependent care credit. What is your response?

25. Discuss the underlying rationale for the enactment of the following tax credits:

    a. Foreign tax credit.
    b. Tax credit for the elderly or disabled.
    c. Earned income credit.
    d. Credit for child and dependent care expenses.
    e. Jobs credit.

26. Although T is entitled to four allowances, she claimed just one on her Form W–4.

    a. Why would T claim fewer allowances than she is entitled to?
    b. Is this procedure permissible?
    c. Will this affect the number of exemptions T can claim on her Federal income tax return?

27. If the employer is not required to withhold income taxes on an item of income paid to an employee, does this mean that the item is nontaxable? Explain.

28. Under what circumstances will the special withholding allowance be allowed for purposes of determining income tax withholding?

29. Describe the exposure (i.e., wage base and tax rate) that a self-employed individual has to the self-employment tax for 1992.

30. You read that self-employed taxpayers get a double deduction for one-half of the self-employment tax, not only as a deduction in computing the self-employment tax but also as a deduction *for* AGI. Is this true? Explain.

PROBLEMS

31. B has a tentative general business credit of $110,000 for 1992. B's net regular tax liability before the general business credit is $125,000; tentative minimum tax is $100,000. Compute B's allowable general business credit for 1992.

32. XYZ Corporation has the following general business credit carryovers:

1988	$50,000
1989	15,000
1990	5,000
1991	20,000
Total carryovers	$90,000

If the general business credit generated by activities during 1992 equals $45,000 and the total credit allowed during the current year is $80,000 (based on tax liability), what amounts of the current general business credit and carryovers are utilized against the 1992 income tax liability? What is the amount of unused credit carried forward to 1993?

33. B claimed the investment tax credit on the following property acquired in December 1985:

Asset	Recovery Period	Cost
Truck	3 years	$20,000
Machinery	5 years	80,000

    a. Compute B's maximum tentative investment tax credit for 1985.
    b. Assume B sells both assets in 1991 after holding them for five full years. What is the amount of investment tax credit B must recapture in 1991?

34. On August 1, 1985, R acquired and placed in service a pre-1936 office building. The cost was $250,000, of which $50,000 applied to the land. The building is 19-year real

property. In order to keep tenants, R spent $150,000 renovating the building in 1992. The expenses were of the type that qualify for the rehabilitation credit. These improvements were placed in service on May 1.

a. Compute R's rehabilitation tax credit for 1992.
b. Determine cost recovery for the year.
c. What is R's basis in the property at the end of 1992?

35. T acquires a qualifying historic structure for $250,000 (excluding the cost of land) in 1992 with full intentions of substantially rehabilitating the building. Compute the rehabilitation tax credit that is available to T and the impact on the depreciable basis if the following amounts are incurred for the rehabilitation project:

a. $200,000.
b. $400,000.

36. X Company hired six handicapped individuals (qualifying X Company for the jobs credit) in March 1992. Three of these individuals received wages of $7,000 each during 1992 while the other three received wages of $5,000 each.

a. Calculate the amount of the jobs credit for 1992.
b. Assume X Company paid total wages of $120,000 to its employees during the year. How much of this amount is deductible in 1992 if the jobs credit is elected?

37. On May 15, 1992, Y Corporation hired four individuals (A, B, C, and D), all of whom qualified Y Corporation for the jobs credit. A and B also were certified as qualified summer youth employees. D moved out of state in September, quitting his job after earning $4,000 in wages. A, B, and C all continued as employees of Y Corporation. During 1992, C earned $6,500. A and B each earned $3,500 during their first 90 days of employment. Beginning on August 15, A and B were certified for participation in the company's cooperative education program. In this capacity, A earned $2,000 to December 31 and $2,500 to the end of school on May 15, 1993. B also earned an additional $2,000 to December 31, at which time he quit school and left the program. Compute Y Corporation's jobs credit, without regard to the tax liability ceiling limitation, for 1992. Also compute Y's deduction for wages paid to A, B, C, and D during 1992. Will Y receive any benefit in 1993?

38. M, a calendar year taxpayer, furnishes the following information. Gross receipts are net of returns and allowances.

	Gross Receipts	Qualified Research Expenses
1992	$180,000	$60,000
1991	170,000	50,000
1990	160,000	35,000
1989	120,000	45,000
1988	120,000	45,000
1987	135,000	40,000
1986	110,000	20,000
1985	95,000	–0–
1984	80,000	30,000

a. Determine M's incremental research activities credit for 1992.
b. M is in the 28% tax bracket. M decides to deduct, not capitalize, the 1992 research expenses. Assuming M does not wish to capitalize and then amortize the qualifying research expenditures, should M elect the full expense deduction and reduced credit or the full credit and reduced expense deduction?

39. T Corporation is an eligible small business for purposes of the disabled access credit. During the year, T Corporation makes the following expenditures on a structure originally placed in service in 1984:

Removal of architectural barriers	$4,250
Acquired equipment for disabled persons	3,000
	$7,250

In addition, on a building placed in service in the current year, an additional $3,500 was expended to ensure easy accessibility by disabled individuals. Calculate the amount of the disabled access credit available to T Corporation.

40. Which of the following individuals qualify for the earned income credit for 1992?
    - **a.** T is single and has no dependents. His income consisted of $7,000 wages and taxable interest of $1,000.
    - **b.** T maintains a household for a dependent 12-year-old son and is eligible for head-of-household tax rates. Her income consisted of $10,000 salary and $800 taxable interest.
    - **c.** T is married and files a joint return with his wife. T and his wife have no dependents. Their combined income consisted of $8,000 salary and $600 taxable interest. Adjusted gross income is $8,600.

41. T, who qualifies for the earned income credit, has three qualifying children who live with her. T's earns a salary of $13,500 during 1992.
    - **a.** Calculate T's basic earned income credit for the year.
    - **b.** If you learn that one of T's children is 6 months of age at the end of 1992, what is the maximum earned income credit available?

42. T, a widower, lives in an apartment with his three minor children (ages 3, 4, and 5) whom he supports. T earned $17,100 during 1992. He contributed $1,000 to an IRA and uses the standard deduction. Calculate the amount, if any, of T's earned income credit.

43. H, age 67, and W, age 66, are married retirees who received the following income and retirement benefits during 1992:

Fully taxable pension from H's former employer	$ 8,000
Dividends and interest	2,500
Social Security benefits	4,000
	$14,500

Assume H and W file a joint return, have no deductions *for* AGI, and do not itemize. Are they eligible for the tax credit for the elderly? If so, calculate the amount of the credit, assuming the credit is not limited by their tax liability.

44. H, age 67, and W, age 66, are married retirees who received the following income and retirement benefits during 1992:

Fully taxable pension from H's former employer	$ 5,000
Dividends and interest	8,000
Social Security benefits	1,750
	$14,750

Assume H and W file a joint return, have no deductions *for* AGI, and do not itemize. Are they eligible for the tax credit for the elderly? If so, calculate the amount of the credit assuming their actual tax liability (before credits) is $150.

45. T, a U.S. citizen and resident, owns and operates a novelty goods business. During 1992, T has taxable income of $100,000, made up as follows: $50,000 from foreign sources and $50,000 from U.S. sources. In calculating taxable income, the standard deduction is used. The income from foreign sources is subject to foreign income taxes of $26,000. For 1992, T files a joint return claiming his three children as dependents. Assuming T chooses to claim the foreign taxes as an income tax credit, what is his income tax liability for 1992?

46. Q Corporation, a U.S. corporation, is a manufacturing concern that sells most of its products in the United States. It does, however, do some business in Europe through various branches. During 1992, Q Corporation had taxable income of

$500,000, of which $350,000 was U.S.-sourced and $150,000 was foreign-sourced. Foreign income taxes paid are $45,000. Q Corporation's U.S. income tax liability before any foreign tax credit is $170,000. What is Q Corporation's U.S. income tax net of the allowable foreign tax credit?

47. H and W are husband and wife, and both are gainfully employed. They have three children under the age of 13. During 1992, H earned $25,000, while W earned $30,000. In order for them to work, they paid $5,800 to various unrelated parties to care for their children. Assuming H and W file a joint return, what, if any, is their child and dependent care expenses credit for 1992?

48. R and T are husband and wife and have two dependent children under the age of 13. Both R and T are gainfully employed and during 1992 earned salaries as follows: $12,000 (R) and $3,000 (T). To care for their children while they work, R and T pay M (R's mother) $3,600. M does not qualify as the dependent of R and T. Assuming R and T file a joint return, what, if any, is their child and dependent care expenses credit?

49. K and J are husband and wife and have one dependent child, age 9. K is a full-time student for all of 1992, while J earns $18,000 as a nurse's aid. In order to provide care for their child while K attends classes and J is working, they pay S (J's 17-year-old sister) $2,300. S is not the dependent of K and J. Assuming K and J file a joint return, what, if any, is their child and dependent care expenses credit?

50. In each of the following independent situations, determine the amount of FICA that should be withheld from the employee's salary by the employer:

   a. H earns a $50,000 salary, files a joint return, and claims four withholding allowances.
   b. H earns a $70,000 salary, files a joint return, and claims four withholding allowances.
   c. H earns a $150,000 salary, files a joint return, and claims four withholding allowances.
   d. T's 17-year-old son, S, earns a $10,000 salary at the family business.

51. In each of the following independent situations, determine the maximum withholding allowances permitted T (an employee) on Form W–4:

   a. T is single with no dependents.
   b. T is married to a nonemployed spouse, and they have no dependents.
   c. T is married to S, an employed spouse, and they have three dependent children. On the Form W–4 that she filed with the employer, S claimed zero allowances.
   d. Assume the same facts as in (c), except that T and S fully support T's mother, who lives with them. The mother (age 70 and blind) qualifies as their dependent. (Refer to Chapter 3.)
   e. T is single with no dependents but works for two employers, one on a full-time basis and the other on a part-time basis. The Form W–4 filed with the first employer (the full-time job) reflects two withholding exemptions. The wages from each job exceed $1,000.
   f. Assume the same facts as in (e), except that T is married to a nonemployed spouse.

52. T is married to a nonemployed spouse and has four dependents. T is employed by Z Corporation and is paid a monthly salary of $2,620 ($31,440 per year). Using these facts, determine the amount to be withheld by Z Corporation for Federal income tax purposes under the wage-bracket tables and under the percentage method for 1992.

53. During 1992, T, the owner of a store, had the following income and expenses:

Gross profit on sales	$36,000
Income from part-time job (subject to FICA)	14,000
Business expenses (related to store)	15,000
Fire loss on store building	1,200
Dividend income	200
Long-term capital gain on the sale of a stock investment	2,000

Compute T's self-employment tax.

54. In 1992, S has self-employed earnings of $150,000. Compute S's self-employment tax liability and the allowable income tax deduction for the self-employment tax paid.

CUMULATIVE PROBLEMS

55. H and W, ages 38 and 36, are married and file a joint return. Their household includes S, their 10-year-old son, and F, who is H's 76-year-old father. F is very ill and has been confined to bed for most of the year. He has no income of his own and is fully supported by H and W. H and W had the following income and expenses during 1992:

H's wages	$19,800
W's salary	27,200
Interest from First National Bank	50
Unemployment compensation received by H, who was laid off for five months during the year	4,500
Dividends received on January 3, 1993; the corporation mailed the check on December 31, 1992	250
Amounts paid to N, H's niece, for household help and caring for S and F while H and W were working	3,000
Unreimbursed travel expenses (including meals of $200) incurred by W in connection with her job	1,250
Total itemized deductions (not including any potential deductions mentioned elsewhere in the problem)	4,700
Federal income taxes withheld by their employers	5,000

Compute net tax payable or refund due for H and W for 1992. Suggested software (if available): *TurboTax* for tax return or WFT tax planning software.

56. H and W are married and file a joint return. They have two dependent children, S and D, ages 12 and 16, respectively. H is a self-employed businessman (sole proprietor of an unincorporated business), and W is a corporate executive. H has the following income and expenses from his business:

Gross income	$280,000
Business expenses (including accelerated depreciation in excess of straight-line on real property of $26,000)	166,000

Records related to W's employment provide the following information:

Salary	$130,000
Unreimbursed travel expenses (including $200 of meals)	1,000
Unreimbursed entertainment expenses	600

Other pertinent information relating to 1992 is as follows:

Proceeds from sale of stock acquired on July 15, 1992 (cost of $10,000), sold on August 1	$ 8,000
Proceeds from sale of stock acquired in 1977 (cost of $6,000)	4,800
Wages paid to full-time domestic worker for housekeeping and child supervision	10,000
Dividends ($6,000) and interest ($2,000) received	8,000
Total itemized deductions (not including any potential deductions above)	26,900
Federal income tax withheld	27,000
Estimated payments on Federal income tax	43,000

Compute the lowest net tax payable or highest refund due for H and W for 1992. Suggested software (if available): *TurboTax* for tax return or WFT tax planning software.

57. Ray Jones (Social Security number 265–33–1982) lives at 960 Elm Street, Franklin, KY 40601. He is the sole proprietor of Ray's Plumbing Repair, located at 1420 Main Street. Since Ray's business is confined to plumbing repairs, he maintains only a nominal amount of plumbing supplies.

Ray generally works alone. On occasion, however, his brother handles some calls. For this help, the brother is paid an agreed-upon rate per hour, and Ray withholds and matches FICA taxes.

Ray's widowed mother is disabled and lives with him. Ray provides all of her support and maintains the household in which they live. The mother qualifies as Ray's dependent. Because of the mother's disability, Ray pays various housekeepers $2,800 during the year to care for her while he works.

Ray's business records for 1992 reflect the following information:

Gross income from business	$93,900
Plumbing supplies	2,100
Rent paid on shop	5,100
Interest expense paid on trade payables	600
Utilities paid on shop	2,200
Advertising	870
Depreciation	1,100
Salaries	10,100
Employer's share of FICA	773

Other transactions occurring during 1992 are summarized below:

- Medical expenses of Ray ($8,200) and his mother ($400). All of these expenses were paid by Ray, and none were covered by insurance.
- Real estate taxes on personal residence of $2,100.
- Interest on home mortgage of $3,700.
- Concerned about rising energy costs and the need to conserve limited resources, Ray had storm windows installed on his home ($3,500) and converted his home heating system from oil to natural gas ($4,000).
- Charitable contributions of $500.
- Dividends received from a Canadian corporation of $2,000. The checks Ray received total $1,700 after $300 of Canadian income tax was withheld at the source. The Canadian tax liability was $300.
- Interest of $800 on his credit cards used for personal purchases.

Based on his tax liability (including self-employment tax) for 1991, Ray made estimated tax payments of $19,500 during 1992.

Determine the amount of tax due (or refund) for 1992. Suggested software (if available): *TurboTax* for tax return or WFT tax planning software.

58. James R. Jordan lives at 2322 Branch Road, Mesa, AZ 85202. He is a tax accountant with Mesa Manufacturing Company. He also writes computer software programs for tax practitioners and has a part-time tax practice. James, age 35, is single and has no dependents. His Social Security number is 111–35–2222. He wants to contribute one dollar to the Presidential Election Campaign Fund.

During 1991, James earned a salary of $45,680 from his employer. He received interest of $890 from Home Federal Savings and Loan and $435 from Home State Bank. He received dividends of $620 from Acme Corporation, $470 from Jason Corporation, and $360 from General Corporation.

James received a $1,600 income tax refund from the state of Arizona on May 12, 1991. On his 1990 Federal income tax return, he reported total itemized deductions of $6,700, which included $2,000 of state income tax withheld by his employer.

Fees earned from his part-time tax practice in 1991 totaled $4,200. He paid $500 to have the tax returns processed by a computerized tax return service.

On February 1, 1991, James bought 500 shares of Acme Corporation common stock for $17.60 a share. On July 16, James sold the stock for $15 a share.

James bought a used pickup truck for $3,000 on June 5, 1991. He purchased the truck from his brother-in-law, who was unemployed and was in need of cash. On November 2, 1991, he sold the truck to a friend for $3,400.

On January 2, 1981, James acquired 100 shares of Jason Corporation common stock for $30 a share. He sold the stock on December 19, 1991, for $75 a share.

During 1991, James received royalties of $15,000 on a software program he had written. James incurred the following expenditures in connection with his software writing activities:

Cost of microcomputer (100% business use)	$8,000
Cost of printer (100% business use)	2,000
Supplies	650
Fee paid to computer consultant	3,500

James elected to expense the maximum portion of the cost of the microcomputer and printer allowed under the provisions of § 179.

Although his employer suggested that James attend a convention on current developments in corporate taxation, James was not reimbursed for the travel expenses of $1,360 he incurred in attending the convention. The $1,360 included $200 for the cost of meals.

During 1991, James paid $300 for prescription medicines and $2,875 in doctor bills, hospital bills, and medical insurance premiums. His employer withheld state income tax of $1,954. James paid real property taxes of $1,766 on his home. Interest on his home mortgage was $3,845, and interest to credit card companies was $320. James contributed $20 each week to his church and $10 each week to the United Way. Professional dues and subscriptions totaled $350.

James's employer withheld Federal income taxes of $9,500 during 1991. James paid estimated taxes of $1,600. What is the amount of James Jordan's net tax payable or refund due for 1991? If James has a tax refund due, he wants to have it credited toward his 1992 income tax. If you use tax forms for your solution, you will need Forms 1040, 2106, and 4562 and Schedules A, B, C, D, and SE. Suggested software (if available): *TurboTax* for tax return or WFT tax planning software.

RESEARCH PROBLEMS

RESEARCH PROBLEM 1 T is a CPA employed by an international accounting firm. In 1986, the accounting firm asked T to transfer to its Paris office. As part of the inducement to get T to accept the transfer, the accounting firm agreed to reimburse him for all expenses incurred in the move. The firm also agreed to pay all of T's moving expenses on his eventual return to the United States. Reimbursement of moving expenses for the return move was not contingent on T's continued employment by the firm. In 1992, T returned to the United States and was assigned to the firm's New York office. T properly included the reimbursement in gross income in 1992. In computing his foreign tax credit, T treated the reimbursement as income earned from personal services performed outside the United States. The IRS treated the income as earned from services performed within the United States and reduced T's foreign tax credit. Should T contest the IRS treatment of the moving expense reimbursement?

RESEARCH PROBLEM 2 T has been participating in a carpool arrangement from her home to her work with others in her office for a number of years. Carpooling has worked out well from her perspective because the physical and financial burdens of driving to and from work are reduced by being shared equally among several people. However, her family situation has changed recently, and she is now required to delay her departure for work until her 8-year-old child's school bus arrives each morning. Although she looked for help with this problem, she was unable to find anyone to care for her child during the early morning hours. Unfortunately, the others in the carpool were not willing to leave for work any later than they previously had. Therefore, the only recourse for T was to give up her carpool and to begin driving to and from work by herself. T figures that the cost of individually driving to and from work for the year was $1,000, while the cost of the carpool arrangement was $200. Because the incremental $800 costs relate to and are necessary for the care of her dependent child, she feels that they should be considered qualifying expenditures for purposes of the child and dependent care expenses credit. T approaches you and asks your advice. How do you respond?

RESEARCH PROBLEM 3 T, a gainfully employed attorney, has custody of two children by a former marriage. During the school year in 1992, T hires Mrs. B to care for the children from the time school ends until T gets home from work. Mrs. B also cares for the children on the few occasions T must go to the office on weekends. As part of their arrangement, T pays Mrs. B a set rate per hour of care. T also covers Mrs. B under FICA and pays for *both* the employer's and employee's share of these taxes.

Mrs. B is unavailable for employment during the Christmas break, so T sends the children to her mother's home out-of-state. In connection with the trip, T pays for two round-trip airline tickets. The airline tickets cost T more than she would have paid Mrs. B had she been free to work.

Comment on which of the above expenditures qualify for the child and dependent care expenses credit.

RESEARCH PROBLEM 4 X Corporation is in the business of creating, manufacturing, and distributing board games based on science fiction themes. The research underlying the creation of the games is extensive and is absolutely necessary to make the games as intriguing and alluring as possible. In the current year alone, X Corporation has spent over $100,000 on research activities where employees assigned to the project consulted libraries, government documents, museums, and various other sources. The controller at X Corporation is under the impression the research expenditures incurred qualify for the research activities credit under § 41. What is your reaction to his impression?

PART

PROPERTY TRANSACTIONS

Part V presents the tax treatment of sales, exchanges and other dispositions of property. Included are the determination of the realized gain or loss, recognized gain or loss, and the classification of the recognized gain or loss as capital or ordinary. The topic of basis is evaluated both in terms of its effect on the calculation of the gain or loss and in terms of the determination of the basis of any contemporaneous or related subsequent acquisitions of property.

CHAPTER

PROPERTY TRANSACTIONS: DETERMINATION OF GAIN OR LOSS AND BASIS CONSIDERATIONS

OBJECTIVES

Explain the computation of realized gain or loss on property dispositions.

Define the terms "amount realized" and "adjusted basis."

Distinguish between realized and recognized gain or loss.

Discuss the recovery of capital doctrine.

Explain how basis is determined for various methods of asset acquisition.

Present various loss disallowance provisions.

Identify tax planning opportunities related to selected property transactions.

OUTLINE

This chapter and the following three chapters are concerned with the income tax consequences of property transactions (the sale or other disposition of property). The following questions are considered with respect to the sale or other disposition of property:

- Is there a realized gain or loss?
- If so, is the gain or loss recognized?
- If the gain or loss is recognized, is it ordinary or capital?
- What is the basis of replacement property, if any, that is acquired?

Chapters 14 and 15 discuss the determination of realized and recognized gain or loss and the basis of property. Chapters 16 and 17 cover the classification of the recognized gain or loss as ordinary or capital.

DETERMINATION OF GAIN OR LOSS

◆

Realized Gain or Loss

Realized gain or loss is measured by the difference between the amount realized from the sale or other disposition of property and the property's adjusted basis on the date of disposition. If the amount realized exceeds the property's adjusted basis, the result is a *realized gain*. Conversely, if the property's adjusted basis exceeds the amount realized, the result is a *realized loss*.[1]

EXAMPLE 1

T sells X Corporation stock with an adjusted basis of $3,000 for $5,000. T's realized gain is $2,000. If T had sold the stock for $2,000, he would have had a $1,000 realized loss. ◆

Sale or Other Disposition. The term *sale or other disposition* is defined broadly in the tax law and includes virtually any disposition of property. Thus, transactions such as trade-ins, casualties, condemnations, thefts, and bond retirements are treated as dispositions of property. The most common disposition of property is through a sale or exchange. The key factor in determining whether a disposition has taken place usually is whether an identifiable event has occurred[2] as opposed to a mere fluctuation in the value of the property.[3]

EXAMPLE 2

T owns X Corporation stock that cost $3,000. The stock has appreciated in value by $2,000 since T purchased it. T has no realized gain since mere fluctuation in value is not a disposition or identifiable event for tax purposes. Nor would T have a realized loss had the stock declined in value by $2,000. ◆

Amount Realized. The *amount realized* from a sale or other disposition of property is the sum of any money received plus the fair market value of other property received. The amount realized also includes any real property taxes treated as imposed on the seller that are actually paid by the buyer.[4] The reason for including these taxes in the amount realized is that by paying the taxes, the purchaser is, in effect, paying an additional amount to the seller of the property.

1. § 1001(a) and Reg. § 1.1001–1(a).
2. Reg. § 1.1001–1(c)(1).
3. *Lynch v. Turrish*, 1 USTC ¶18, 3 AFTR 2986, 38 S.Ct. 537 (USSC, 1918).
4. § 1001(b) and Reg. § 1.1001–1(b). Refer to Chapter 11 for a discussion of this subject.

The amount realized also includes any liability on the property disposed of, such as a mortgage debt, if the buyer assumes the mortgage or the property is sold subject to the mortgage.[5] The amount of the liability is included in the amount realized even if the debt is nonrecourse and the amount of the debt is greater than the fair market value of the mortgaged property.[6]

Example 3

T sells property on which there is a mortgage of $20,000 to U for $50,000 cash. T's amount realized from the sale is $70,000 if the mortgage is assumed by U or if U takes the property subject to the mortgage. ◆

The *fair market value* of property received in a sale or other disposition has been defined by the courts as the price at which property will change hands between a willing seller and a willing buyer when neither is compelled to sell or buy.[7] Fair market value is determined by considering the relevant factors in each case.[8] An expert appraiser is often required to evaluate these factors in arriving at fair market value. When the fair market value of the property received cannot be determined, the value of the property surrendered may be used.[9]

In calculating the amount realized, selling expenses such as advertising, commissions, and legal fees relating to the disposition are deducted. The amount realized is the net amount received directly or indirectly by the taxpayer from the disposition of property regardless of whether it is in the form of cash.

Adjusted Basis. The *adjusted basis* of property disposed of is the property's original basis adjusted to the date of disposition.[10] Original basis is the cost or other basis of the property on the date the property is acquired by the taxpayer. *Capital additions* increase and *recoveries of capital* decrease the original basis so that on the date of disposition the adjusted basis reflects the unrecovered cost or other basis of the property.[11] Adjusted basis is determined as follows:

Cost (or other adjusted basis) on date of acquisition
\+ Capital additions
− Capital recoveries
= Adjusted basis on date of disposition

Capital Additions. Capital additions include the cost of capital improvements and betterments made to the property by the taxpayer. These expenditures are distinguishable from expenditures for the ordinary repair and maintenance of the property that are neither capitalized nor added to the original basis (refer to Chapter 6). The latter expenditures are deductible in the current taxable year if they are related to business or income-producing property. Amounts representing real property taxes treated as imposed on the seller but paid or assumed by the buyer are part of the cost of the property.[12] Any liability on property that is

---

5. *Crane v. Comm.*, 47–1 USTC ¶9217, 35 AFTR 776, 67 S.Ct. 1047 (USSC, 1947). Although a legal distinction exists between the direct assumption of a mortgage and taking property subject to a mortgage, the tax consequences in calculating the amount realized are the same.
6. *Comm. v. Tufts*, 83–1 USTC ¶9328, 51 AFTR 2d 83–1132, 103 S.Ct. 1826 (USSC, 1983).
7. *Comm. v. Marshman*, 60–2 USTC ¶9484, 5 AFTR 2d 1528, 279 F.2d 27 (CA–6, 1960).
8. *O'Malley v. Ames*, 52–1 USTC ¶9361, 42 AFTR 19, 197 F.2d 256 (CA–8, 1952).
9. *U.S. v. Davis*, 62–2 USTC ¶9509, 9 AFTR2d 1625, 82 S.Ct. 1190 (USSC, 1962).
10. § 1011(a) and Reg. § 1.1011–1.
11. § 1016(a) and Reg. § 1.1016–1.
12. Reg. §§ 1.1001–1(b)(2) and 1.1012–1(b). Refer to Chapter 11 for a discussion of this subject.

assumed by the buyer is also included in the buyer's original basis of the property. The same rule applies if property is acquired subject to a liability. Amortization of the discount on bonds increases the adjusted basis of the bonds.[13]

Capital Recoveries. The following are examples of capital recoveries:

1. *Depreciation and cost recovery allowances.* The original basis of depreciable property is reduced by the annual depreciation charges (or cost recovery allowances) while the property is held by the taxpayer. The amount of depreciation that is subtracted from the original basis is the greater of the *allowed* or *allowable* depreciation on an annual basis.[14] In most circumstances, the allowed and allowable depreciation amounts are the same (refer to Chapter 9).
2. *Investment tax credit.* For property placed in service after 1982 and before 1986, the taxpayer may be required to reduce the adjusted basis of the property by 50 percent of the available investment tax credit. This reduction in the adjusted basis of the property is required unless the taxpayer has elected to take a reduced investment tax credit (refer to Chapters 9 and 13).[15]
3. *Casualties and thefts.* A casualty or theft may result in the reduction of the adjusted basis of property.[16] The adjusted basis is reduced by the amount of the deductible loss. In addition, the adjusted basis is reduced by the amount of insurance proceeds received. However, the receipt of insurance proceeds may result in a recognized gain rather than a deductible loss. The gain increases the adjusted basis of the property.[17]

EXAMPLE 4

An insured truck used in a trade or business is destroyed in an accident. The adjusted basis is $8,000, and the fair market value is $6,500. Insurance proceeds of $6,500 are received. The amount of the casualty loss is $1,500 ($6,500 insurance proceeds − $8,000 adjusted basis). The adjusted basis is reduced by the $1,500 casualty loss and the $6,500 of insurance proceeds received. ◆

EXAMPLE 5

An insured truck used in a trade or business is destroyed in an accident. The adjusted basis is $6,500, and the fair market value is $8,000. Insurance proceeds of $8,000 are received. The amount of the casualty gain is $1,500 ($8,000 insurance proceeds − $6,500 adjusted basis). The adjusted basis is increased by the $1,500 casualty gain and is reduced by the $8,000 of insurance proceeds received ($6,500 basis before casualty + $1,500 casualty gain − $8,000 insurance proceeds = $0 basis). ◆

4. *Certain corporate distributions.* A corporate distribution to a shareholder that is not taxable is treated as a return of capital, and it reduces the basis of the shareholder's stock in the corporation.[18] For example, if a corporation makes a cash distribution to its shareholders and has no earnings and profits, the distributions are treated as a return of capital. If the corporation does have earnings and profits but makes a distribution in

13. §§ 1232(a)(2)(A) and 1232A(a) and (c)(5). See Chapter 16 for a discussion of bond discount and the related amortization.
14. § 1016(a)(2) and Reg. § 1.1016–3(a)(1)(i).
15. §§ 48(q)(1) and (4) and 1016(a)(22).
16. Refer to Chapter 8 for the discussion of casualties and thefts.
17. Reg. § 1.1016–6(a).
18. § 1016(a)(4) and Reg. § 1.1016–5(a). See Chapter 20 for further discussion of corporate distributions.

excess of the earnings and profits, the excess distribution is treated as a return of capital. Once the basis of the stock is reduced to zero, the amount of any subsequent distributions is a capital gain if the stock is a capital asset.

EXAMPLE 6

U Corporation has accumulated earnings and profits of $140,000 at the beginning of 1992. For 1992, U Corporation generates current earnings and profits of $30,000. During 1992, U Corporation makes cash distributions to its only shareholder, T, in the amount of $200,000. T's basis for his U Corporation stock is $20,000. Of the $200,000 cash distributed to T, $170,000 is classified as dividend income (to the extent of current earnings and profits of $30,000 and beginning accumulated earnings and profits of $140,000). The next $20,000 is treated as a return of capital and reduces T's basis for his U Corporation stock to zero. The remaining $10,000 is a capital gain. ◆

5. *Amortizable bond premium.* The basis in a bond purchased at a premium is reduced by the amortizable portion of the bond premium.[19] Investors in taxable bonds may *elect* to amortize the bond premium, but the premium on tax-exempt bonds *must be* amortized.[20] The amount of the amortized premium on taxable bonds is permitted as an interest deduction. Therefore, the election produces the opportunity for an annual interest deduction to offset ordinary income in exchange for a larger capital gain or smaller capital loss on the disposition of the bond. No such interest deduction is permitted for tax-exempt bonds.

The amortization deduction is allowed for taxable bonds because the premium is viewed as a cost of earning the taxable interest from the bonds. The reason the basis of taxable bonds is reduced is that the amortization deduction is a recovery of the cost or basis of the bonds. The basis of tax-exempt bonds is reduced even though the amortization is not allowed as a deduction. No amortization deduction is permitted on tax-exempt bonds since the interest income is exempt from tax and the amortization of the bond premium merely represents an adjustment of the effective amount of such income.

EXAMPLE 7

T purchases J Corporation taxable bonds with a face value of $100,000 for $110,000, thus paying a premium of $10,000. The annual interest rate is 7%, and the bonds mature 10 years from the date of purchase. The annual interest income is $7,000 (7% × $100,000). If T elects to amortize the bond premium, the $10,000 premium is deducted over the 10-year period. T's basis for the bonds is reduced each year by the amount of the amortization deduction. Note that if the bonds were tax-exempt, amortization of the bond premium and the basis adjustment would be mandatory. However, no deduction would be allowed for the amortization. ◆

Recognized Gain or Loss

Recognized gain is the amount of the realized gain included in the taxpayer's gross income.[21] A *recognized loss,* on the other hand, is the amount of a realized loss

19. § 1016(a)(5) and Reg. § 1.1016–5(b). The accounting treatment of bond premium amortization is the same as for tax purposes. The amortization results in a decrease in the bond investment account.

20. § 171(c).

21. § 61(a)(3) and Reg. § 1.61–6(a).

that is deductible for tax purposes.[22] As a general rule, the entire amount of a realized gain or loss is recognized.[23]

Concept Summary 14–1 summarizes the realized gain or loss and recognized gain or loss concepts.

Nonrecognition of Gain or Loss

In certain cases, a realized gain or loss is not recognized upon the sale or other disposition of property. One of the exceptions to the recognition of gain or loss involves nontaxable exchanges, which are covered in Chapter 15. Additional exceptions include losses realized upon the sale, exchange, or condemnation of personal use assets (as opposed to business or income-producing property) and gains realized upon the sale of a residence by taxpayers 55 years of age or older (see Chapter 15). In addition, realized losses from the sale or exchange of business or income-producing property between certain related parties are not recognized.[24]

Sale, Exchange, or Condemnation of Personal Use Assets. A realized loss from the sale, exchange, or condemnation of personal use assets (e.g., a personal residence or an automobile not used at all for business or income-producing purposes) is not recognized for tax purposes. An exception exists for casualty or theft losses from personal use assets (see Chapter 8). In contrast, any gain realized from the sale or other disposition of personal use assets is, generally, fully taxable. The following examples illustrate the tax consequences of the sale of personal use assets.

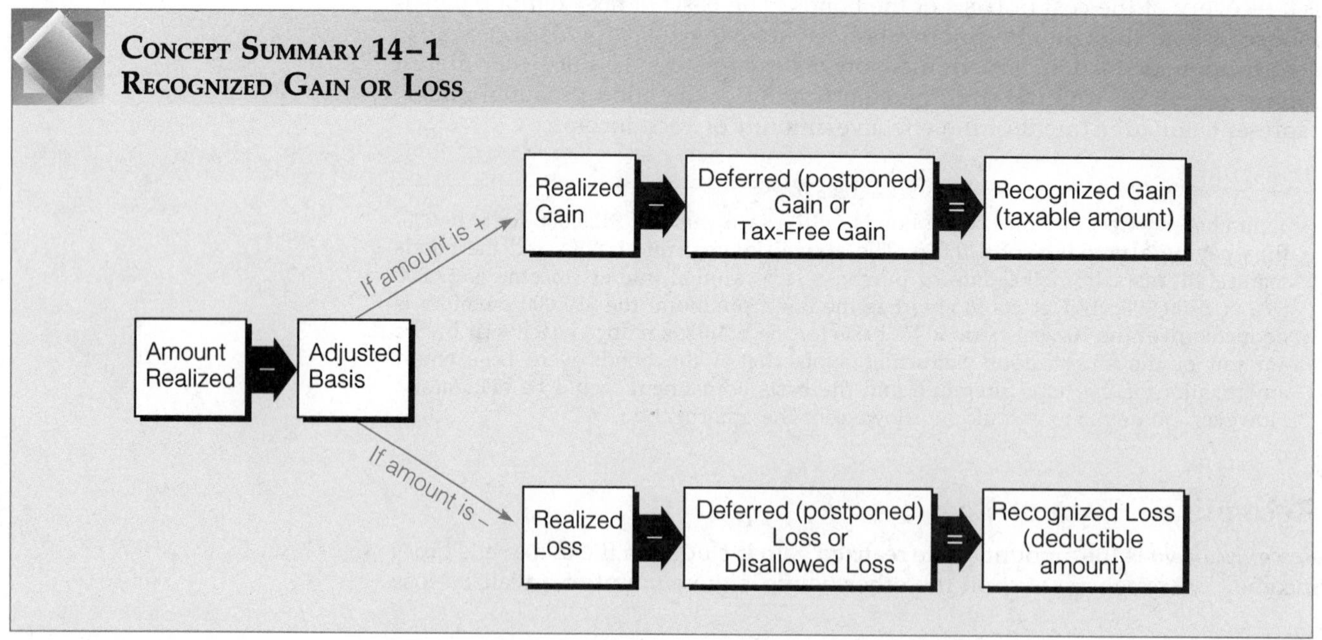

22. § 165(a) and Reg. § 1.165–1(a).
23. § 1001(c) and Reg. § 1.1002–1(a).
24. § 267(a)(1).

EXAMPLE 8

T sells an automobile, which is held exclusively for personal use, for $6,000. The adjusted basis of the automobile is $5,000. T has a realized and recognized gain of $1,000. ◆

EXAMPLE 9

T sells the automobile in Example 8 for $4,000. T has a realized loss of $1,000, but the loss is not recognized. ◆

Recovery of Capital Doctrine

Doctrine Defined. The *recovery of capital doctrine* pervades all the tax rules relating to property transactions and is very significant with respect to these transactions. The doctrine derives its roots from the very essence of the income tax—a tax on income. Therefore, as a general rule, a taxpayer is entitled to recover the cost or other original basis of property acquired and is not taxed on that amount.

The cost or other original basis of depreciable property is recovered through annual depreciation deductions. The basis is reduced as the cost is recovered over the period the property is held. Therefore, when property is sold or otherwise disposed of, it is the adjusted basis (unrecovered cost or other basis) that is compared to the amount realized from the disposition to determine realized gain or loss.

Relationship of the Recovery of Capital Doctrine to the Concepts of Realization and Recognition. If a sale or other disposition results in a realized gain, the taxpayer has recovered more than the adjusted basis of the property. Conversely, if a sale or other disposition results in a realized loss, the taxpayer has recovered less than the adjusted basis.

The general rules for the relationship between the recovery of capital doctrine and the realized and recognized gain and loss concepts are summarized as follows:

Rule 1. A realized gain that is *never recognized* results in the *permanent recovery* of more than the taxpayer's cost or other basis for tax purposes. For example, all or a portion of the realized gain on the sale of a personal residence by taxpayers 55 years of age or older can be excluded from gross income under § 121.

Rule 2. A realized gain on which *recognition is postponed* results in the *temporary recovery* of more than the taxpayer's cost or other basis for tax purposes. For example, an exchange of like-kind property under § 1031, an involuntary conversion under § 1033, and a replacement of a personal residence under § 1034 are all eligible for postponement treatment.

Rule 3. A realized loss that is *never recognized* results in the *permanent recovery* of less than the taxpayer's cost or other basis for tax purposes. For example, a loss on the sale of an automobile held for personal use is not deductible.

Rule 4. A realized loss on which *recognition is postponed* results in the *temporary recovery* of less than the taxpayer's cost or other basis for tax purposes. For example, the realized loss on the exchange of like-kind property under § 1031 is postponed.

These rules are illustrated in discussions to follow in this and the next chapter.

BASIS CONSIDERATIONS

◆

Determination of Cost Basis

The basis of property is generally the property's cost. Cost is the amount paid for the property in cash or other property.[25] This general rule follows logically from the recovery of capital doctrine; that is, the cost or other basis of property is to be recovered tax-free by the taxpayer.

A *bargain purchase* of property is an exception to the general rule for determining basis. A bargain purchase may result when an employer transfers property to an employee at less than the property's fair market value (as compensation for services) or when a corporation transfers property to a shareholder at less than the property's fair market value (a dividend). The basis of property acquired in a bargain purchase is the property's fair market value.[26] If the basis of the property were not increased by the bargain amount, the taxpayer would be taxed on this amount again at disposition.

EXAMPLE 10

T buys a machine from her employer for $10,000 on December 30, 1992. The fair market value of the machine is $15,000. T must include the $5,000 difference between cost and the fair market value of the machine in gross income for the taxable year 1992. The bargain element represents additional compensation to T. T's basis for the machine is $15,000, the machine's fair market value. ◆

Identification Problems. Cost identification problems are frequently encountered in securities transactions. For example, the Regulations require that the taxpayer adequately identify the particular stock that has been sold.[27] A problem arises when the taxpayer has purchased separate lots of stock on different dates or at different prices and cannot adequately identify the lot from which a particular sale takes place. In this case, the stock is presumed to come from the first lot or lots purchased (a FIFO presumption).[28] When securities are left in the custody of a broker, it may be necessary to provide specific instructions and receive written confirmation as to which securities are being sold.

EXAMPLE 11

T purchases 100 shares of Q Corporation stock on July 1, 1990, for $5,000 ($50 a share) and another 100 shares of the same stock on July 1, 1991, for $6,000 ($60 a share). She sells 50 shares of the stock on January 2, 1992. The cost of the stock sold, assuming T cannot adequately identify the shares, is $50 a share, or $2,500. This is the cost T will compare to the amount realized in determining the gain or loss from the sale. ◆

Allocation Problems. When a taxpayer acquires *multiple assets in a lump-sum purchase,* it is necessary to allocate the total cost among the individual assets.[29] Allocation is necessary because some of the assets acquired may be depreciable (e.g., buildings) and others not (e.g., land). In addition, only a portion of the assets acquired may be sold, or some of the assets may be capital or § 1231 assets that receive special tax treatment upon subsequent sale or other disposition. The lump-sum cost is allocated on the basis of the fair market values of the individual assets acquired.

EXAMPLE 12

T purchases a building and land for $800,000. Because of the depressed nature of the industry in which the seller was operating, T was able to negotiate a very favorable

25. § 1012 and Reg. § 1.1012–1(a).
26. Reg. §§ 1.61–2(d)(2)(i) and 1.301–1(j).
27. Reg. § 1.1012–1(c)(1).
28. *Kluger Associates, Inc.,* 69 T.C. 925 (1978).
29. Reg. § 1.61–6(a).

purchase price. Appraisals of the individual assets indicate that the fair market value of the building is $600,000 and that of the land is $400,000. T's basis for the building is $480,000 ($600,000/$1,000,000 × $800,000), and the basis for the land is $320,000 ($400,000/$1,000,000 × $800,000). ◆

If a business is purchased and *goodwill* is involved, a special allocation rule applies. Initially, the purchase price is assigned to the assets, excluding goodwill, to the extent of the total fair market value of the assets. This assigned amount is allocated among the assets on the basis of the fair market value of the individual assets acquired. Goodwill is then assigned the residual amount of the purchase price. The resultant allocation is applicable to both the buyer and the seller.[30]

EXAMPLE 13

T sells his business to P. T and P agree that the values of the individual assets are as follows:

Inventory	$ 50,000
Building	500,000
Land	200,000
Goodwill	150,000

Negotiations conducted by T and P result in a sales price of $1 million. The application of the residual method with respect to goodwill results in the following allocation of the $1 million purchase price:

Inventory	$ 50,000
Building	500,000
Land	200,000
Goodwill	250,000

The residual method requires that all of the excess of the purchase price over the fair market value of the assets ($1,000,000 − $900,000 = $100,000) be allocated to goodwill. Without this requirement, the purchaser could allocate the excess pro rata to all of the assets, including goodwill, based on their respective fair market values. This would have resulted in only $166,667 [$150,000 + ($150,000 ÷ $900,000 × $100,000)] being assigned to goodwill. ◆

In the case of *nontaxable stock dividends*, the allocation depends upon whether the dividend is a common stock dividend on common stock or a preferred stock dividend on common stock. If the dividend is common on common, the cost of the original common shares is allocated to the total shares owned after the dividend.[31]

EXAMPLE 14

T owns 100 shares of R Corporation common stock for which he paid $1,100. He receives a 10% common stock dividend, giving him a new total of 110 shares. Before the stock dividend, T's basis was $11 per share ($1,100 divided by 100 shares). The basis of each share after the stock dividend is $10 ($1,100 divided by 110 shares). ◆

30. § 1060.

31. §§ 305(a) and 307(a). The holding period of the new shares includes the holding period of the old shares. § 1223(5) and Reg. § 1.1223–1(e). See Chapter 16 for a discussion of the importance of the holding period.

If the dividend is preferred stock on common, the cost of the original common shares is allocated between the common and preferred shares on the basis of their relative fair market values on the date of distribution.[32]

EXAMPLE 15

S owns 100 shares of X Corporation common stock for which she paid $1,000. She receives a stock dividend of 50 shares of preferred stock on her common stock. The fair market values on the date of distribution of the preferred stock dividend are $30 a share for common stock and $40 a share for preferred stock. Thus, the total fair market value is $3,000 ($30 × 100) for common stock and $2,000 ($40 × 50) for preferred stock. The basis of S's common stock after the dividend is $600, or $6 a share ($3,000/$5,000 × $1,000), and the basis of the preferred stock is $400, or $8 a share ($2,000/$5,000 × $1,000). ◆

In the case of *nontaxable stock rights,* the basis of the rights is zero unless the taxpayer elects or is required to allocate a portion of the cost of the stock to the rights. If the fair market value of the rights is 15 percent or more of the fair market value of the stock, the taxpayer is required to allocate. If the value of the rights is less than 15 percent of the fair market value of the stock, the taxpayer may elect to allocate.[33] The result is that either the rights will have no basis or the cost of the stock on which the rights are received will be allocated between the stock and rights on the basis of their relative fair market values.

EXAMPLE 16

T receives nontaxable stock rights with a fair market value of $1,000. The fair market value of the stock on which the rights were received is $8,000 (cost $10,000). T does not elect to allocate. The basis of the rights is zero. If the rights are exercised, the basis of the new stock will be the exercise (subscription) price. ◆

EXAMPLE 17

Assume the same facts as in Example 16, except the fair market value of the rights is $3,000. T must allocate because the value of the rights is 15% or more of the value of the stock ($3,000/$8,000 = 37.5%). The basis of the rights is $2,727 ($3,000/$11,000 × $10,000), and the basis of the stock is $7,273 ($8,000/$11,000 × $10,000). If the rights are exercised, the basis of the new stock will be the exercise (subscription) price plus the basis of the rights. If the rights are sold, gain or loss is recognized. This allocation rule applies only when the rights are exercised or sold. Therefore, if the rights are allowed to lapse (expire), the rights have no basis, and the basis of the original stock is the stock's cost, $10,000. ◆

The holding period of nontaxable stock rights includes the holding period of the stock on which the rights were distributed. However, if the rights are exercised, the holding period of the newly acquired stock begins with the date the rights are exercised.[34] The significance of the holding period for capital assets is discussed in Chapter 16.

Gift Basis

When a taxpayer receives property as a gift, there is no cost to the recipient. Thus, under the cost basis provision, the donee's basis would be zero. However, this would violate the statutory intent that gifts are not subject to the income tax.

32. Reg. § 1.307–1(a).
33. § 307(b).
34. § 1223(5) and Reg. §§ 1.1223–1(e) and (f).

With a zero basis, a sale by the donee would result in all of the amount realized being treated as realized gain. Therefore, a basis is assigned to the property received depending on the following:[35]

- The date of the gift.
- The basis of the property to the donor.
- The amount of the gift tax paid.
- The fair market value of the property.

Gifts Prior to 1921. If property was acquired by gift before 1921, its basis for income tax purposes is its fair market value on the date of the gift.[36]

Gift Basis Rules if No Gift Tax Is Paid. Property received by gift can be referred to as *dual basis* property; that is, the basis for gain and the basis for loss might not be the same amount. The present basis rules for gifts of property are as follows:

- If the donee subsequently disposes of gift property in a transaction that results in a gain, the basis to the donee is the same as the donor's adjusted basis.[37] The donee's basis in this case is referred to as the *gain basis*. Therefore, a *realized gain* results if the amount realized from the disposition exceeds the donee's gain basis.

Example 18

T purchased stock in 1991 for $10,000. He gave the stock to his son, S, in 1992, when the fair market value was $15,000. Assume no gift tax is paid on the transfer and the property is subsequently sold by S for $15,000. S's basis is $10,000, and S has a realized gain of $5,000. ◆

- If the donee subsequently disposes of gift property in a transaction that results in a loss, the basis to the donee is the *lower* of the donor's adjusted basis or fair market value on the date of the gift. The donee's basis in this case is referred to as the *loss basis*. Therefore, a *realized loss results* if the amount realized from the disposition is less than the donee's loss basis.

Example 19

T purchased stock in 1991 for $10,000. He gave the stock to his son, S, in 1992, when the fair market value was $7,000. Assume no gift tax is paid on the transfer. S later sells the stock for $6,000. S's basis is $7,000 (fair market value is less than donor's adjusted basis of $10,000), and the loss from the sale is $1,000 ($6,000 amount realized − $7,000 basis). ◆

The amount of the loss basis will differ from the amount of the gain basis only if at the date of the gift the adjusted basis of the property exceeds the property's fair market value. Note that the loss basis rule prevents the donee from receiving a tax benefit from the decline in value while the donor held the property. Therefore, in Example 19, S has a loss of only $1,000 rather than a loss of $4,000. The $3,000 difference represents the decline in value while T held the property.

35. § 102(a). See the Glossary of Tax Terms in Appendix C for a definition of the term "gift."

36. § 1015(c) and Reg. § 1.1015–3(a).

37. § 1015(a) and Reg. § 1.1015–1(a)(1). See Reg. § 1.1015–1(a)(3) for cases in which the facts necessary to determine the donor's adjusted basis are unknown. Refer to Example 24 for the effect of depreciation deductions by the donee.

It is perhaps ironic, however, that the gain basis rule may eventually result in the donee's being subject to income tax on the appreciation that occurs while the donor held the property, as illustrated in Example 18.

If the amount realized from sale or other disposition is *between* the basis for loss and the basis for gain, no gain or loss is realized.

EXAMPLE 20

Assume the same facts as in Example 19, except that S sold the stock for $8,000. The application of the gain basis rule produces a loss of $2,000 ($8,000 – $10,000). The application of the loss basis rule produces a gain of $1,000 ($8,000 – $7,000). Therefore, neither a gain nor a loss is recognized because the amount realized is between the gain basis and the loss basis. ◆

Adjustment for Gift Tax. If gift taxes are paid by the donor, the donee's gain basis may exceed the adjusted basis of the property to the donor. This occurs only if the fair market value of the property at the date of the gift is greater than the donor's adjusted basis (the property has appreciated in value). The portion of the gift tax paid that is related to the appreciation is added to the donor's basis in calculating the donee's gain basis for the property. In this circumstance, the following formula is used for calculating the donee's gain basis:[38]

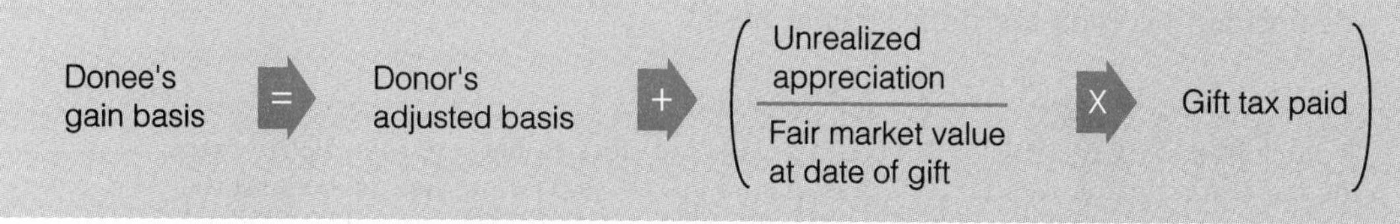

EXAMPLE 21

F made a gift of stock to S in 1992, when the fair market value of the stock was $40,000. F had purchased the stock in 1981 for $10,000. Because the unrealized appreciation is $30,000 ($40,000 fair market value less $10,000 adjusted basis) and the fair market value is $40,000, three-fourths ($30,000/$40,000) of the gift tax paid is added to the basis of the property. If the gift tax paid is $4,000, S's basis in the property is $13,000 [$10,000 + $3,000 (¾ of the $4,000 gift tax)]. ◆

EXAMPLE 22

F made a gift of stock to S in 1992, when the fair market value of the stock was $40,000. Gift tax of $4,000 was paid by F, who had purchased the stock in 1981 for $45,000. Because there is no unrealized appreciation at the date of the gift, none of the gift tax paid is added to the donor's basis in calculating the donee's gain basis. Therefore, the donee's gain basis is $45,000. ◆

For *gifts made before 1977*, the full amount of the gift tax paid is added to the donor's basis. However, the ceiling on this total is the fair market value of the property at the date of the gift. Thus, in Example 21, if the gift had been made before 1977, the basis of the property would be $14,000 ($10,000 + $4,000). In Example 22, the gain basis would still be $45,000 ($45,000 + $0).

Holding Period. The *holding period* for property acquired by gift begins on the date the property was acquired by the donor if the gain basis rule applies.[39] The

38. § 1015(d)(6).

39. § 1223(2) and Reg. § 1.1223–1(b).

holding period starts on the date of the gift if the loss basis rule applies.[40] The significance of the holding period for capital assets is discussed in Chapter 16.

The following example summarizes the basis and holding period rules for gift property:

EXAMPLE 23

T acquires 100 shares of X Corporation stock on December 30, 1981, for $40,000. On January 3, 1992, when the stock has a fair market value of $38,000, T gives it to S and pays gift tax of $4,000. There is no increase in basis for a portion of the gift tax paid because the property has not appreciated in value at the time of the gift. Therefore, S's gain basis is $40,000. S's basis for determining loss is $38,000 (fair market value) because the fair market value on the date of the gift is less than the donor's adjusted basis.

- If S sells the stock for $45,000, he has a recognized gain of $5,000. The holding period for determining whether the capital gain is short term or long term begins on December 30, 1981, the date the property was acquired by the donor.
- If S sells the stock for $36,000, he has a recognized loss of $2,000. The holding period for determining whether the capital loss is short term or long term begins on January 3, 1992, the date of the gift.
- If S sells the property for $39,000, there is no gain or loss since the amount realized is less than the gain basis of $40,000 and more than the loss basis of $38,000. ◆

Basis for Depreciation. The basis for depreciation on depreciable gift property is the donee's gain basis.[41] This rule is applicable even if the donee later sells the property at a loss and uses the loss basis rule in calculating the amount of the realized loss.

EXAMPLE 24

F gave a machine to D in 1992, when the adjusted basis was $32,000 (cost of $40,000 − accumulated depreciation of $8,000) and the fair market value was $26,000. No gift tax was paid. D's gain basis at the date of the gift is $32,000, and D's loss basis is $26,000. During 1992, D deducts depreciation (cost recovery) of $10,240 ($32,000 × 32%). Therefore, at the end of 1992, D's gain basis is $21,760 ($32,000 − $10,240), and D's loss basis is $15,760 ($26,000 − $10,240). ◆

Property Acquired from a Decedent

General Rules. The basis of property acquired from a decedent is generally the property's fair market value at the date of death (referred to as the *primary valuation amount*).[42] The property's basis is the fair market value six months after the date of death if the executor or administrator of the estate *elects* the alternate valuation date for estate tax purposes. This amount is referred to as the *alternate valuation amount*. If an estate tax return does not have to be filed because the estate is below the threshold amount for being subject to the estate tax, the alternate valuation date and amount are not available. Even if an estate tax return is filed and the executor elects the alternate valuation date, the six months after death date is available only for property that the executor has not distributed before this date. Any property distributed or otherwise disposed of

40. Rev.Rul. 59–86, 1959–1 C.B. 209.

41. § 1011 and Reg. §§ 1.1011–1 and 1.167(g)–1.

42. § 1014(a).

by the executor during this six-month period will have an adjusted basis to the beneficiary equal to the fair market value on the date of distribution or other disposition.[43]

For inherited property, both unrealized appreciation and decline in value are taken into consideration in determining the basis of the property for income tax purposes. Contrast this with the carryover basis rules for property received by gift.

The alternate valuation date can be elected only if the election results in the reduction of both the value of the gross estate and the estate tax liability below the amounts they would have been if the primary valuation date had been used. This provision prevents the alternate valuation election from being used to increase the basis of the property to the beneficiary for income tax purposes without simultaneously increasing the estate tax liability (because of estate tax deductions or credits).[44]

EXAMPLE 25

D and various other family members inherited property from D's father, who died in 1992. At the date of death, her father's adjusted basis for the property D inherited was $35,000. The property's fair market value at date of death was $50,000. The alternate valuation date was not elected. D's basis for income tax purposes is $50,000. This is commonly referred to as a *stepped-up basis.* ◆

EXAMPLE 26

Assume the same facts as in Example 25, except the property's fair market value at date of death was $20,000. D's basis for income tax purposes is $20,000. This is commonly referred to as a *stepped-down basis.* ◆

EXAMPLE 27

D inherited all the property of her father, who died in 1992. Her father's adjusted basis for the property at date of death was $35,000. The property's fair market value was $750,000 at date of death and $760,000 six months after death. The alternate valuation date cannot be elected because the value of the gross estate has increased during the six-month period. D's basis for income tax purposes is $750,000. ◆

EXAMPLE 28

Assume the same facts as in Example 27, except the property's fair market value six months after death was $745,000. If the executor elects the alternate valuation date, D's basis for income tax purposes is $745,000. ◆

EXAMPLE 29

Assume the same facts as in the previous example, except the property is distributed four months after the date of the decedent's death. At the distribution date, the property's fair market value is $747,500. Since the executor elected the alternate valuation date, D's basis for income tax purposes is $747,500. ◆

The Code contains a provision designed to eliminate a tax avoidance technique referred to as *deathbed gifts.* If the time period between the date of the gift of appreciated property and the date of the donee's death is not greater than one year, the usual basis rule (stepped-up basis) for inherited property may not apply. The adjusted basis of such property inherited by the donor or his or her

43. § 2032(a)(1) and Rev.Rul. 56–60, 1956–1 C.B. 443.

44. § 2032(c).

spouse from the donee shall be the same as the decedent's adjusted basis for the property rather than the fair market value at the date of death or the alternate valuation date.[45]

EXAMPLE 30

N gives stock to his uncle, U, in 1992. N's basis for the stock is $1,000, and the fair market value is $9,000. No gift tax is paid. Eight months later, N inherits the stock from U. At the date of U's death, the fair market value of the stock is $12,000. N's adjusted basis for the stock is $1,000. ◆

Survivor's Share of Property. Both the decedent's share and the survivor's share of *community property* have a basis equal to fair market value on the date of the decedent's death.[46] This result applies to the decedent's share of the community property because the property flows to the surviving spouse from the estate (fair market value basis for inherited property). Likewise, the surviving spouse's share of the community property is deemed to be acquired by bequest, devise, or inheritance from the decedent. Therefore, it will also have a basis equal to fair market value.

EXAMPLE 31

H and W reside in a community property state. H and W own community property (200 shares of XYZ stock) that was acquired in 1974 for $100,000. Assume that H dies in 1992, when the securities are valued at $300,000. One-half of the XYZ stock is included in H's estate. If W inherits H's share of the community property, the basis for determining gain or loss is:

> $300,000 [$150,000 (W's share of one-half of the community property) plus $150,000 (½ × $300,000, the value of XYZ stock at the date of H's death)] for the 200 shares of XYZ stock. ◆

In a *common law* state, only one-half of jointly held property of spouses (tenants by the entirety or joint tenants with rights of survivorship) is includible in the estate.[47] In such a case, no adjustment of the basis is permitted for the excluded property interest (the surviving spouse's share).

EXAMPLE 32

Assume the same facts as in the previous example, except that the property is jointly held by H and W who reside in a common law state. Also assume that H purchased the property and made a gift of one-half of the property when the stock was acquired, with no gift tax being paid. Only one-half of the XYZ stock is included in H's estate. W's basis for determining gain or loss in the excluded half is not adjusted upward for the increase in value to date of death. Therefore, W's basis is $200,000 ($50,000 + $150,000). ◆

Holding Period of Property Acquired from a Decedent. The holding period of property acquired from a decedent is *deemed to be long term* (held for the required long-term holding period). This provision is applicable regardless of whether the property is disposed of at a gain or a loss.[48]

Disallowed Losses

Related Taxpayers. Section 267 provides that realized losses from sales or exchanges of property, directly or indirectly, between certain related parties are

45. § 1014(e).
46. § 1014(b)(6).
47. § 2040(a).
48. § 1223(11).

not recognized. This loss disallowance provision applies to several types of related-party transactions. The most common involve (1) members of a family and (2) transactions between an individual and a corporation in which the individual owns, directly or indirectly, more than 50 percent in value of the corporation's outstanding stock. Section 707 provides a similar loss disallowance provision if the related parties are a partner and a partnership in which the partner owns, directly or indirectly, more than 50 percent of the capital interests or profits interests in the partnership. The rules governing the relationships covered by § 267 were discussed in Chapter 6. See Chapter 15 for the discussion of the special rules under § 1041 for property transfers between spouses or incident to divorce.

If income-producing or business property is transferred to a related taxpayer and a loss is disallowed, the basis of the property to the recipient is the property's cost to the transferee. However, if a subsequent sale or other disposition of the property results in a realized gain, the amount of gain is reduced by the loss that was previously disallowed.[49] This *right of offset* is not applicable if the original sale involved the sale of a personal use asset (e.g., the sale of a personal residence between related taxpayers). Likewise, this right of offset is available only to the original transferee (the related-party buyer).

EXAMPLE 33

F sells business property with an adjusted basis of $50,000 to his daughter, D, for its fair market value of $40,000.

- F's realized loss of $10,000 is not recognized.
- How much gain will D recognize if she sells the property for $52,000? D recognizes a $2,000 gain. Her realized gain is $12,000 ($52,000 less her basis of $40,000), but she can offset F's $10,000 loss against the gain.
- How much gain will D recognize if she sells the property for $48,000? D recognizes no gain or loss. Her realized gain is $8,000 ($48,000 less her basis of $40,000), but she can offset $8,000 of F's $10,000 loss against the gain. Note that F's loss can only offset D's gain. It cannot create a loss for D.
- How much loss will D recognize if she sells the property for $38,000? D recognizes a $2,000 loss, the same as her realized loss ($38,000 less $40,000 basis). F's loss does not increase D's loss. F's loss can be offset only against a gain. Since D has no realized gain, F's loss cannot be used and is never recognized. This example assumes that the property is business or income producing to D. If not, D's $2,000 loss is personal and is not recognized. ◆

The loss disallowance rules are designed to achieve two objectives. First, the rules prevent a taxpayer from directly transferring an unrealized loss to a related taxpayer in a higher tax bracket who could receive a greater tax benefit from the recognition of the loss. Second, the rules eliminate a substantial administrative burden on the Internal Revenue Service in terms of the appropriateness of the selling price (fair market value or not). The loss disallowance rules are applicable even where the selling price is equal to fair market value and can be validated (e.g., listed stocks).

The holding period of the buyer for the property is not affected by the holding period of the seller. That is, the buyer's holding period includes only the period of time he or she has held the property.[50]

Wash Sales. Section 1091 stipulates that in certain cases, a realized loss on the sale or exchange of stock or securities is not recognized. Specifically, if a taxpayer sells or exchanges stock or securities and within 30 days before *or* after the date of the sale or exchange acquires substantially identical stock or securities, any loss

49. § 267(d) and Reg. § 1.267(d)–1(a).

50. §§ 267(d) and 1223(2) and Reg. § 1.267(d)–1(c)(3).

realized from the sale or exchange is not recognized.[51] The term *acquire* means acquire by purchase or in a taxable exchange and includes an option to purchase substantially identical securities. *Substantially identical* means the same in all important particulars. Corporate bonds and preferred stock are normally not considered substantially identical to the corporation's common stock. However, if the bonds and preferred stock are convertible into common stock, they may be considered substantially identical under certain circumstances.[52] Attempts to avoid the application of the wash sales rules by having a related taxpayer repurchase the securities have been unsuccessful.[53] The wash sales provisions do *not* apply to gains.

Recognition of the loss is disallowed because the taxpayer is considered to be in substantially the same economic position after the sale and repurchase as before the sale and repurchase. This disallowance rule does not apply to taxpayers engaged in the business of buying and selling securities.[54] Investors, however, are not allowed to create losses through wash sales to offset income for tax purposes.

Realized loss that is not recognized is added to the basis of the substantially identical stock or securities whose acquisition resulted in the nonrecognition of loss.[55] In other words, the basis of the replacement stock or securities is increased by the amount of the unrecognized loss. If the loss were not added to the basis of the newly acquired stock or securities, the taxpayer would never recover the entire basis of the old stock or securities.

The basis of the new stock or securities includes the unrecovered portion of the basis of the formerly held stock or securities. Therefore, the holding period of the new stock or securities begins on the date of acquisition of the old stock or securities.[56]

EXAMPLE 34

T owns 100 shares of A Corporation stock (adjusted basis of $20,000), 50 shares of which she sells for $8,000. Ten days later, T purchases 50 shares of the same stock for $7,000. T's realized loss of $2,000 ($8,000 amount realized less $10,000 adjusted basis of 50 shares) is not recognized because it resulted from a wash sale. T's basis in the newly acquired stock is $9,000 ($7,000 purchase price plus $2,000 unrecognized loss from the wash sale). ◆

The taxpayer may acquire less than the number of shares sold in a wash sale. In this case, the loss from the sale is prorated between recognized and unrecognized loss on the basis of the ratio of the number of shares acquired to the number of shares sold.[57]

Tax Straddles. Before the enactment of § 1092, it was possible to use commodity tax straddles to shelter income by recognizing losses and deferring unrealized gains. With only a six-month holding period requirement at the time, the unrealized gain, when eventually realized, was likely to be taxed as favorable long-term capital gain.

Section 1092 was enacted to negate the beneficial results presented in the previous paragraph. However, in the interim period (1988–1990), subsequent legislation had repealed favorable tax treatment for long-term capital gains. Despite this, § 1092 was still needed to negate the beneficial straddle result of recognizing losses and deferring unrealized gains. With the partial reinstatement of favorable tax treatment for long-term capital gains in 1991, § 1092 once again serves both of the original purposes.

---

51. § 1091(a) and Reg. §§ 1.1091–1(a) and (f).

52. Rev.Rul. 56–406, 1956–2 C.B. 523.

53. *McWilliams v. Comm.*, 47–1 USTC ¶9289, 35 AFTR 1184, 67 S.Ct. 1477 (USSC, 1947).

54. Reg. § 1.1091–1(a).

55. § 1091(d) and Reg. § 1.1091–2(a).

56. § 1223(4) and Reg. § 1.1223–1(d).

57. § 1091(b) and Reg. § 1.1091–1(c).

A *straddle* is defined as offsetting positions with respect to personal property (e.g., buy and sell orders in the same commodity or a sell order with physical possession of the commodity).[58] Although a fluctuation in the market price may leave the taxpayer's economic position unchanged, an unrealized loss occurs on one position and an unrealized gain on the other. The liquidation of the loss position by the taxpayer would produce realized loss (probably a short-term capital loss). The unrealized gain would not be realized until a subsequent taxable year when the taxpayer closed that position (probably resulting in long-term capital gain).

As a general rule, the recognition of any loss with respect to one or more positions is limited in any taxable year by § 1092. The amount of the recognized loss that is permitted is equal to the excess of the realized loss over any unrealized gain on offsetting positions to the loss position. Nonrecognized losses under this provision are treated as having occurred in the following taxable year and are subject to the deferral rule for that taxable year.[59]

EXAMPLE 35

T purchases two gold futures contracts, one to buy and the other to sell, for $10,000 each in November 1992. T's position is a straddle because he has offsetting positions. When the market fluctuates, one position shows a gain and the other a loss. Before the end of 1992, T liquidates one position and realizes a $1,000 loss. At the same time, he has an unrealized gain of $1,000 on the offsetting position, which he does not liquidate. T's recognized loss is limited to the excess of the realized loss over the unrealized gain with respect to the offsetting position. In this example, T has no recognized loss (realized loss of $1,000 less unrealized gain of $1,000). ◆

The straddle limitations apply to certain positions in stock and most stock options. The limitations also apply to stock that is part of a straddle for which at least one of the offsetting positions is stock of a corporation formed or availed of for the purpose of taking offsetting positions to those taken by any shareholder.

Conversion of Property from Personal Use to Business or Income-Producing Use

As discussed previously, losses from the sale of personal use assets are not recognized for tax purposes, but losses from the sale of business and income-producing assets are deductible. Can a taxpayer convert a personal use asset that has declined in value to business (or income-producing) use and then sell the asset to recognize a business (or income-producing) loss? The tax law prevents this by specifying that the *original basis for loss* on personal use assets converted to business or income-producing use is the *lower* of the property's adjusted basis or fair market value on the date of conversion.[60] The *gain basis* for converted property is the property's adjusted basis on the date of conversion. The tax law is not concerned with gains on converted property because gains are recognized regardless of whether property is business, income producing, or personal use.

EXAMPLE 36

T's personal residence has an adjusted basis of $75,000 and a fair market value of $60,000. T converts the personal residence to rental property. His basis for loss is $60,000 (lower of $75,000 adjusted basis and fair market value of $60,000). The $15,000 decline in value is a personal loss and can never be recognized for tax purposes. T's basis for gain is $75,000. ◆

58. § 1092(c).
59. §§ 1092(a)(1)(A) and (B).
60. Reg. § 1.165–9(b)(2).

The basis for loss is also the *basis for depreciating* the converted property.[61] This is an exception to the general rule that provides that the basis for depreciation is the gain basis (e.g., property received by gift). This exception prevents the taxpayer from recovering a personal loss indirectly through depreciation of the higher original basis. After the property is converted, both its basis for loss and its basis for gain are adjusted for depreciation deductions from the date of conversion to the date of disposition. These rules apply only if a conversion from personal to business or income-producing use has actually occurred.

EXAMPLE 37

At a time when her personal residence (adjusted basis of $40,000) is worth $50,000, T converts one-half of it to rental use. The property is not MACRS recovery property. At this point, the estimated useful life of the residence is 20 years and there is no estimated salvage value. After renting the converted portion for five years, T sells the property for $44,000. All amounts relate only to the building; the land has been accounted for separately. T has a $2,000 realized gain from the sale of the personal use portion of the residence and a $7,000 realized gain from the sale of the rental portion. These gains are computed as follows:

	Personal Use	Rental
Original basis for gain and loss—adjusted basis on date of conversion (fair market value is greater than the adjusted basis)	$20,000	$20,000
Depreciation—five years	None	5,000
Adjusted basis—date of sale	$20,000	$15,000
Amount realized	22,000	22,000
Realized gain	$ 2,000	$ 7,000

◆

As discussed in Chapter 15, T may be able to defer recognition of part or all of the $2,000 gain from the sale of the personal use portion of the residence under § 1034. The $7,000 gain from the rental portion is recognized.

EXAMPLE 38

Assume the same facts as in the previous example, except that the fair market value on the date of conversion is $30,000 and the sales proceeds are $16,000. T has a $12,000 realized loss from the sale of the personal use portion of the residence and a $3,250 realized loss from the sale of the rental portion. These losses are computed as follows:

	Personal Use	Rental
Original basis for loss—fair market value on date of conversion (fair market value is less than the adjusted basis)	*	$15,000
Depreciation—five years	None	3,750
Adjusted basis—date of sale	$20,000	$11,250
Amount realized	8,000	8,000
Realized loss	$12,000	$ 3,250

*Not applicable.

The $12,000 loss from the sale of the personal use portion of the residence is not recognized. The $3,250 loss from the rental portion is recognized. ◆

61. Reg. § 1.167(g)–1.

Additional Complexities in Determining Realized Gain or Loss

Amount Realized. The calculation of the amount realized may appear to be one of the least complex areas associated with property transactions. However, because of the numerous positive and negative adjustments that may be required, the calculation of this amount can be complex and confusing. In addition, the determination of the fair market value of the items received by the taxpayer can be difficult. The following example provides insight into various items that can have an impact on the amount realized.

EXAMPLE 39

T sells an office building and the associated land on October 1, 1992. Under the terms of the sales contract, T is to receive $600,000 in cash. The purchaser is to assume T's mortgage of $300,000 on the property. To enable the purchaser to obtain adequate financing to pay the $600,000, T is to pay the $15,000 in points charged by the lender. The broker's commission on the sale is $45,000. The purchaser agrees to pay the property taxes for the entire year of $12,000. The amount realized by T is calculated as follows:

Selling price		
Cash	$600,000	
Mortgage assumed by purchaser	300,000	
Seller's property taxes paid by purchaser ($12,000 × 9/12)	9,000	$909,000
Less		
Broker's commission	$ 45,000	
Points paid by seller	15,000	60,000
Amount realized		$849,000

◆

Adjusted Basis. Three types of items tend to complicate the determination of adjusted basis. First, the applicable tax provisions for calculating the adjusted basis are dependent on how the property was acquired (e.g., purchase, taxable exchange, nontaxable exchange, gift, inheritance). Second, if the asset is subject to depreciation, cost recovery, amortization, or depletion, adjustments must be made to the basis during the time period the asset is held by the taxpayer. Upon disposition of the asset, the taxpayer's records for both of these items may be deficient. For example, the donee does not know the amount of the donor's basis or the amount of gift tax paid by the donor, or the taxpayer does not know how much depreciation he or she has deducted. Third, the complexity of the various positive and negative adjustments encountered in calculating the amount realized is also encountered in calculating the adjusted basis.

EXAMPLE 40

P purchased a personal residence in 1988. The purchase price and the related closing costs were as follows:

Purchase price	$125,000
Recording costs	140
Title fees and title insurance	815
Survey costs	115
Attorney's fees	750
Appraisal fee	60

Other relevant tax information for the house during the time it was owned by P is as follows:

- Constructed a swimming pool for medical reasons. The cost was $10,000, of which $3,000 was deducted as a medical expense.
- Added a solar heating system. The cost was $15,000.
- Deducted home office expenses of $6,000. Of this amount, $3,200 was for depreciation.
- None of the closing costs were deducted as moving expenses.

The adjusted basis for the house is calculated as follows:

Purchase price	$125,000
Recording costs	140
Title fees and title insurance	815
Survey costs	115
Attorney's fees	750
Appraisal fee	60
Swimming pool ($10,000 − $3,000)	7,000
Solar heating system	15,000
	$148,880
Less: Depreciation deducted on home office	(3,200)
Adjusted basis	$145,680

◆

Summary of Basis Adjustments

Some of the more common items that either increase or decrease the basis of an asset appear in Concept Summary 14–2.

In discussing the topic of basis, a number of specific techniques for determining basis have been presented. Although the various techniques are responsive to and mandated by transactions occurring in the marketplace, they do possess enough common characteristics to be categorized as follows:

- The basis of the asset may be determined by reference to the asset's cost.
- The basis of the asset may be determined by reference to the basis of another asset.
- The basis of the asset may be determined by reference to the asset's fair market value.
- The basis of the asset may be determined by reference to the basis of the asset to another taxpayer.

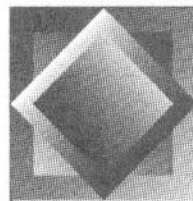

CONCEPT SUMMARY 14–2
ADJUSTMENTS TO BASIS

Item	Effect	Refer to Chapter	Explanation
Amortization of bond discount.	Increase	16	Amortization is mandatory for certain taxable bonds and elective for tax-exempt bonds.
Amortization of bond premium.	Decrease	14	Amortization is mandatory for tax-exempt bonds and elective for taxable bonds.
Amortization of covenant not to compete.	Decrease	16	Covenant must be for a definite and limited time period.

Item	Effect	Refer to Chapter	Explanation
Amortization of intangibles.	Decrease	9	Not all intangibles can be amortized (e.g., goodwill).
Assessment for local benefits.	Increase	11	To the extent not deductible as taxes (e.g., assessment for streets and sidewalks that increase the value of the property versus one for maintenance or repair or for meeting interest charges).
Bad debts.	Decrease	8	Only the specific charge-off method is permitted.
Capital additions.	Increase	14	Certain items, at the taxpayer's election, can be capitalized or deducted (e.g., selected indirect moving expenses and medical expenses).
Casualty.	Decrease	8	For a casualty loss, the amount of the adjustment is the summation of the deductible loss and the insurance proceeds received. For a casualty gain, the amount of the adjustment is the insurance proceeds received reduced by the recognized gain.
Condemnation.	Decrease	15	See casualty explanation.
Cost recovery.	Decrease	9	§ 168 is applicable to tangible assets placed in service after 1980 whose useful life is expressed in terms of years.
Depletion.	Decrease	9	Use the greater of cost or percentage depletion. Percentage depletion can still be deducted when the basis is zero.
Depreciation.	Decrease	9	§ 167 is applicable to tangible assets placed in service before 1981 and to tangible assets not depreciated in terms of years.
Easement.	Decrease		If the taxpayer does not retain any use of the land, all of the basis is allocable to the easement transaction. However, if only part of the land is affected by the easement, only part of the basis is allocable to the easement transaction.
Improvements by lessee to lessor's property.	Increase	5	Adjustment occurs only if the lessor is required to include the fair market value of the improvements in gross income under § 109.
Imputed interest.	Decrease	18	Amount deducted is not part of the cost of the asset.
Inventory: lower of cost or market.	Decrease	18	Not available if the LIFO method is used.
Investment tax credit.	Decrease	13	Amount is 50% (100% for transition property) of the investment tax credit. If the election to reduce the investment tax credit is made, no adjustment is required.
Investment tax credit recapture.	Increase	13	Amount is 50% (100% for transition property) of the investment tax credit recaptured. If the election to reduce the investment tax credit was made, no adjustment is required.
Limited expensing under § 179.	Decrease	9	Occurs only if the taxpayer elects § 179 treatment.
Medical capital expenditure permitted as a medical expense.	Decrease	11	Adjustment is the amount of the deduction (the effect on basis is to increase it by the amount of the capital expenditure net of the deduction).
Moving capital expenditure permitted as a moving expense.	Decrease	10	Adjustment is for the amount the taxpayer elects to deduct as an indirect moving expense (the effect on basis is to increase it by the amount of the capital expenditure net of the deduction).
Real estate taxes; apportionment between the buyer and seller.	Increase or Decrease	11	To the extent the buyer pays the seller's pro rata share, the buyer's basis is increased. To the extent the seller pays the buyer's pro rata share, the buyer's basis is decreased.
Rebate from manufacturer.	Decrease		Since the rebate is treated as an adjustment to the purchase price, it is not included in the buyer's gross income.
Stock dividend.	Decrease	5	Adjustment occurs only if the stock dividend is nontaxable. While the basis per share decreases, the total stock basis does not change.
Stock rights.	Decrease	14	Adjustment occurs only for nontaxable stock rights and only if the fair market value of the rights is at least 15% of the fair market value of the stock or, if less than 15%, the taxpayer elects to allocate the basis between the stock and the rights.
Theft.	Decrease	8	See casualty explanation.

Cost Identification and Documentation Considerations

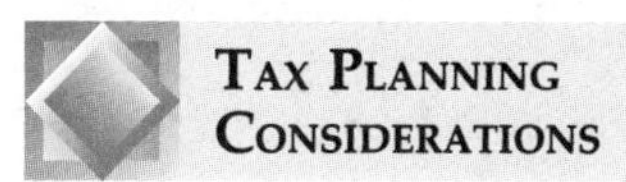

When multiple assets are acquired in a single transaction, the contract price must be allocated for several reasons. First, some of the assets may be depreciable while others are not. From the different viewpoints of the buyer and the seller, this may produce a tax conflict that needs to be resolved. That is, the seller prefers a high allocation for nondepreciable assets, whereas the purchaser prefers a high allocation for depreciable assets (see Chapters 16 and 17). Second, the seller needs to know the amount realized on the sale of the capital assets and the ordinary income assets so that the recognized gains and losses can be classified as capital or ordinary. For example, an allocation to goodwill or to a covenant not to compete (see Chapters 9, 16, and 17) produces different tax consequences to the seller. Third, the buyer needs the adjusted basis of each asset to calculate the realized gain or loss on the sale or other disposition of each asset.

Selection of Property for Making Gifts

A donor can achieve several tax advantages by making gifts of appreciated property. Income tax on the unrealized gain that would have occurred had the donor sold the property is avoided by the donor. A portion of this amount can be permanently avoided because the donee's adjusted basis is increased by part or all of any gift tax paid by the donor. Even without this increase in basis, the income tax liability on the sale of the property by the donee can be less than the income tax liability that would have resulted from the donor's sale of the property. This reduced income tax liability occurs if the donee is in a lower tax bracket than the donor. In addition, any subsequent appreciation during the time the property is held by the lower tax bracket donee results in a tax savings on the sale or other disposition of the property. Such gifts of appreciated property can be an effective tool in family tax planning.

Taxpayers should generally not make gifts of depreciated property (property that, if sold, would produce a realized loss) because the donor does not receive an income tax deduction for the unrealized loss element. In addition, the donee receives no benefit from this unrealized loss upon the subsequent sale of the property because of the loss basis rule. The loss basis rule provides that the donee's basis is the lower of the donor's basis or fair market value at the date of the gift. If the donor anticipates that the donee will sell the property upon receiving it, the donor should sell the property and take the loss deduction, assuming the loss is deductible. The donor can then give the proceeds from the sale to the donee.

Selection of Property for Making Bequests

A decedent's will should generally make bequests of appreciated property. Doing so enables both the decedent and the heir to avoid income tax on the unrealized gain because the recipient takes the fair market value as his or her basis.

Taxpayers generally should not make bequests of depreciated property (property that, if sold, would produce a realized loss) because the decedent does not receive an income tax deduction for the unrealized loss element. In addition, the heir will receive no benefit from this unrealized loss upon the subsequent sale of the property.

EXAMPLE 41

On the date of her death, W owned land held for investment purposes. The land had an adjusted basis of $600,000 and a fair market value of $100,000. If W had sold the property before her death, the recognized loss would have been $500,000. If H inherits the property and sells it for $60,000, the recognized loss will be $40,000 (the decline in value since W's death). In addition, regardless of the period of time the property is held by H, the holding period is long term (see Chapter 16). ◆

From an income tax perspective, it is preferable to transfer appreciated property as a bequest rather than as a gift. This results from the step-up in basis for inherited property, whereas for property received by gift, the donee has a carryover basis. However, in making this decision, the estate tax consequences of the bequest should also be weighed against the gift tax consequences of the gift.

Disallowed Losses

Section 267 Disallowed Losses. Taxpayers should be aware of the desirability of avoiding transactions that activate the loss disallowance provisions for related parties. This is so even in light of the provision that permits the related-party buyer to offset his or her realized gain by the related-party seller's disallowed loss. Even with this offset, several inequities exist. First, the tax benefit associated with the disallowed loss ultimately is realized by the wrong party (the related-party buyer rather than the related-party seller). Second, the tax benefit of this offset to the related-party buyer does not occur until the buyer disposes of the property. Therefore, the longer the time period between the purchase and disposition of the property by the related-party buyer, the less the economic benefit. Third, if the property does not appreciate to at least its adjusted basis to the related-party seller during the time period the related-party buyer holds it, part or all of the disallowed loss is permanently lost. Fourth, since the right of offset is available only to the original transferee (the related-party buyer), all of the disallowed loss is permanently lost if the original transferee subsequently transfers the property by gift or bequest.

EXAMPLE 42

T sells property with an adjusted basis of $35,000 to B, his brother, for $25,000, the fair market value of the property. The $10,000 realized loss to T is disallowed by § 267. If B subsequently sells the property to an unrelated party for $37,000, B has a recognized gain of $2,000 (realized gain of $12,000 reduced by disallowed loss of $10,000). Therefore, from the perspective of the family unit, the original $10,000 realized loss ultimately is recognized. However, if B sells the property for $29,000, he has a recognized gain of $0 (realized gain of $4,000 reduced by disallowed loss of $4,000 necessary to offset the realized gain). From the perspective of the family unit, $6,000 of the realized loss of $10,000 is permanently wasted ($10,000 realized loss minus $4,000 offset permitted). ◆

Wash Sales. The wash sales provisions can be avoided if the security is replaced within the statutory time period with a similar rather than a substantially identical security. For example, the sale of Bethlehem Steel common stock and a purchase of Inland Steel common stock is not treated as a wash sale. Such a procedure can enable the taxpayer to use an unrealized capital loss to offset a recognized capital gain. The taxpayer can sell the security before the end of the taxable year, offset the recognized capital loss against the capital gain, and invest the sales proceeds in a similar security.

Because the wash sales provisions do not apply to gains, it may be desirable to engage in a wash sale before the end of the taxable year. This recognized capital gain may be used to offset capital losses or capital loss carryovers from prior years. Since the basis of the replacement stock or securities will be the purchase price, the taxpayer in effect has exchanged a capital gain for an increased basis for the stock or securities.

Problem Materials

Discussion Questions

1. When will a property transaction result in a realized gain? A realized loss?
2. In addition to sales and exchanges, what are some other transactions that are treated as dispositions of property?
3. C and D each purchase 100 shares of stock of K, Inc., a publicly owned corporation, in July for $10,000 each. C sells his stock on December 31 for $14,000. Since K, Inc.'s stock is listed on a national exchange, D is able to ascertain that his shares are worth $14,000 on December 31. Does the tax law treat the appreciation in value of the stock differently for C and D? Explain.
4. What is included in the amount realized from a sale or other disposition of property?
5. If a taxpayer sells property for cash, the amount realized consists of the net proceeds from the sale. For each of the following, indicate the effect on the amount realized:
   - **a.** The property is sold on credit.
   - **b.** A mortgage on the property is assumed by the buyer.
   - **c.** The purchaser pays real property taxes that are treated as imposed on the seller.
6. If the buyer pays real property taxes that are treated as imposed on the seller, what are the effects on the seller's amount realized and the buyer's adjusted basis for the property? If the seller pays real property taxes that are treated as imposed on the buyer, what are the effects on the seller's amount realized and the buyer's adjusted basis for the property?
7. T is negotiating to buy some land. Under the first option, T will give S $70,000 and assume S's mortgage on the land for $30,000. Under the second option, T will give S $100,000, and S will immediately pay off the mortgage. T would like for his basis for the land to be as high as possible. Given this objective, which option should T select?
8. If the buyer of property assumes the seller's mortgage, why is the amount of the mortgage included in the amount realized by the seller? What effect does the mortgage assumption have on the seller's (a) adjusted basis for the mortgaged property and (b) realized gain or loss?
9. T purchases land from S. T gives S $40,000 in cash and agrees to pay S an additional $80,000 one year later plus interest at 12%.
   - **a.** What is T's adjusted basis for the land at the date purchased?
   - **b.** What is T's adjusted basis for the land one year later?
10. The taxpayer owns land and a building with an adjusted basis of $50,000 and a fair market value of $250,000. The property is subject to a mortgage of $400,000. Since the taxpayer is in arrears on the mortgage payments, the creditor is willing to accept the property in return for canceling the amount of the mortgage.
    - **a.** How can the adjusted basis of the property be less than the amount of the mortgage?
    - **b.** If the creditor's offer is accepted, what are the effects on the amount realized, the adjusted basis, and the realized gain or loss?
    - **c.** Does it matter in (b) if the mortgage is recourse or nonrecourse?
11. C and D each own an automobile that each uses exclusively in his respective trade or business. The adjusted basis of each automobile is $17,000, and the fair market value is $11,000. Both automobiles are destroyed in accidents. C's automobile is insured, and C receives insurance proceeds of $11,000. D's automobile is uninsured. Explain how the adjusted basis for each automobile is reduced to zero, even though one is insured and the other is uninsured.
12. T owns stock in X Corporation and Y Corporation. He receives a $1,000 distribution from both corporations. The instructions from X Corporation state that the $1,000 is

a dividend. The instructions from Y Corporation state that the $1,000 is not a dividend. What could cause the instructions to differ as to the tax consequences?

13. A taxpayer who acquires a taxable bond at a discount is required to amortize the discount, whereas a taxpayer who acquires a tax-exempt bond at a discount may elect to amortize the discount. What effect does the amortization have on the adjusted basis for the bonds? Why is the amortization mandatory for the taxable bond but elective for the tax-exempt bond?

14. A taxpayer who acquires a taxable bond at a premium may elect to amortize the premium, whereas a taxpayer who acquires a tax-exempt bond at a premium must amortize the premium. Why would a taxpayer make the amortization election for taxable bonds? What effect does the mandatory amortization of tax-exempt bonds have on taxable income?

15. J and K each own an automobile with an adjusted basis of $15,000. Each sells her automobile for $9,000. J is permitted to deduct a $6,000 loss on her tax return whereas K is not permitted to deduct any loss.

    a. Explain how this different tax treatment could occur.
    b. What would be the tax consequences if J and K each sold their automobiles for $18,000?

16. Discuss the relationship between the recovery of capital doctrine and the receipt of a dividend distribution.

17. E owns a life insurance policy that will pay $100,000 to R, his spouse, on his death. At the date of E's death, the total premiums E had paid on the policy were $65,000. In accordance with § 101(a)(1), R excludes the $100,000 of insurance proceeds. Discuss the relationship, if any, between the § 101 exclusion and the recovery of capital doctrine.

18. With respect to the recovery of capital doctrine, distinguish between a realized loss on which recognition is postponed and a realized loss that is never recognized.

19. Discuss the residual method as it applies to goodwill in the lump-sum purchase of a business. Why must this method be used for goodwill rather than the normal allocation method based on the fair market value of the individual assets acquired?

20. Discuss the differences in tax treatment for allocating basis to nontaxable stock dividends when the form of the dividend is a common stock dividend on common stock versus a preferred stock dividend on common stock.

21. Discuss the differences in tax treatment when stock rights are allocated a cost basis and when stock rights have no cost basis. When does each of these situations occur?

22. Why does the Code contain both a gain basis rule and a loss basis rule for gift property? Under what circumstances will these rules produce different basis amounts?

23. Discuss the different treatment of gift taxes paid with respect to the donee's basis for the property received for gifts before 1977 and gifts after 1976.

24. Discuss the differences in tax treatment between property sold before death and inherited property. Why is this important?

25. R makes a gift of an appreciated building to E. E dies three months later, and R inherits the building from E. During the period that E held the building, he deducted depreciation and made a capital expenditure. What effect might these items have on R's basis for the inherited building?

26. Immediately before his death in 1992, H sells securities (adjusted basis of $100,000) for their fair market value of $20,000. The sale was not to a related party. The securities were community property, and H is survived by his wife, W, who inherits all of his property.

    a. Did H act wisely? Why or why not?
    b. Suppose the figures are reversed (sale for $100,000 of property with an adjusted basis of $20,000). Would the sale be wise? Why or why not?

27. What is the holding period for property received by gift? What is the holding period for inherited property?

28. If a taxpayer sells income-producing or business property to a related party, any realized loss is disallowed by § 267.

a. How is the related-party purchaser's basis for the property determined?
b. If the related-party purchaser later sells the property for an amount greater than the related-party seller's adjusted basis for the property, have the related-party disallowance rules produced inequitable tax consequences?
c. If the initial sale produced a realized gain, what effect would § 267 have on recognition?

29. R owns 100 shares of stock in Z Corporation. Her adjusted basis for the stock is $5,000. On December 21, R sells the stock in the marketplace for $12,000. R purchases 100 shares of stock in Z Corporation in the marketplace on January 5 of the following year for $12,200.

a. What is R trying to achieve from a tax perspective?
b. Will she succeed?
c. Using the same data, except that R's adjusted basis for the stock is $15,000, respond to (a) and (b).

30. What is the basis for property converted from personal use to business or income-producing use when there is a loss? When there is a gain? Why is there a difference? How does conversion affect depreciation and why?

Problems

31. A sold her home for $350,000 in 1992. Selling expenses were $24,000. She had purchased it in 1986 for $190,000. During the period of ownership, A had:

- Deducted $57,500 office-in-home expenses which included $17,500 in depreciation. (Refer to Chapter 10.)
- Deducted a casualty loss to residential trees from a hurricane. The total loss was $14,000 (after the $100 floor and the 10% of adjusted gross income floor), and A's insurance company reimbursed A for $10,500. (Refer to Chapter 8.)
- Paid street paving assessment of $6,000 and added sidewalks for $8,000.
- Installed an elevator for medical reasons. The total cost was $20,000, and A deducted $11,000 as medical expenses. (Refer to Chapter 11.)
- Paid legal expenses of $2,000 in connection with the move to the home in 1986. A deducted these expenses as moving expenses. (Refer to Chapter 10.)
- Received $7,500 from a utility company for an easement to install underground utility lines across the property.

What is A's realized gain?

32. R bought a rental house at the beginning of 1987 for $80,000, of which $10,000 is allocated to the land and $70,000 to the building. Early in 1989, he had a tennis court built in the backyard at a cost of $5,000. R has deducted $32,200 for depreciation on the house and $1,300 for depreciation on the court. At the beginning of 1992, R sells the house and tennis court for $125,000 cash.

a. What is R's realized gain or loss?
b. If an original mortgage of $20,000 is still outstanding and the buyer assumes the mortgage in addition to the cash payment, what is R's realized gain or loss?
c. If the buyer takes the property subject to the mortgage, what is R's realized gain or loss?

33. T is negotiating the sale of a tract of his land to P. Use the following classification scheme to classify each of the items contained in the proposed sales contract:

Legend

DART	= Decreases amount realized by T.
IART	= Increases amount realized by T.
DABT	= Decreases adjusted basis to T.
IABT	= Increases adjusted basis to T.
DABP	= Decreases adjusted basis to P.
IABP	= Increases adjusted basis to P.

a. T is to receive cash of $50,000.
b. T is to receive P's note payable for $25,000, payable in three years.
c. P assumes T's mortgage of $5,000 on the land.
d. P agrees to pay the realtor's sales commission of $8,000.
e. P agrees to pay the property taxes on the land for the entire year. If each party paid his or her respective share, T's share would be $1,000, and P's share would be $3,000.
f. P pays legal fees of $500.
g. T pays legal fees of $750.

34. N's automobile, which is used exclusively in her business, is stolen. The adjusted basis is $18,000, and the fair market value is $23,000. N's adjusted gross income is $45,000.

    a. If N receives insurance proceeds of $22,500, what effect do the theft and the receipt of the insurance proceeds have on the adjusted basis of the automobile?
    b. If the automobile is not insured, what effect do the theft and the absence of insurance have on the adjusted basis of the automobile.

35. C and D each own 50% of the stock of a corporation. The earnings and profits of the corporation are $30,000. C's adjusted basis for the stock is $40,000. C and D each receive a cash distribution of $70,000 from the corporation.

    a. What effect does the distribution have on the adjusted basis of C's stock?
    b. What effect would the distribution have on the adjusted basis of C's stock if the earnings and profits of the corporation were $180,000?
    c. In (a) and (b), what is the effect on C's gross income?

36. B paid $270,000 for bonds with a face value of $250,000 at the beginning of 1988. The bonds mature in 10 years and pay 9% interest per year.

    a. If B sells the bonds for $255,000 at the beginning of 1992, is there a realized gain or loss? If so, how much?
    b. If B trades the bonds at the beginning of 1993 for stock worth $262,500, is there a realized gain or loss? If so, how much?

37. Which of the following would definitely result in a recognized gain or loss?

    a. K sells his lakeside cabin, which has an adjusted basis of $10,000, for $15,000.
    b. A sells his personal residence, which has an adjusted basis of $15,000, for $10,000.
    c. C's personal residence is on the site of a proposed airport and is condemned by the city. C receives $55,000 for the house, which has an adjusted basis of $65,000.
    d. Q's land is worth $40,000 at the end of the year. Q had purchased the land six months earlier for $25,000.
    e. J gives stock to his niece. J's adjusted basis is $8,000, and the fair market value is $5,000.

38. T's personal residence is condemned as part of an urban renewal project. Her adjusted basis for the residence is $130,000. She receives condemnation proceeds of $115,000 and invests the proceeds in stock.

    a. Calculate T's realized and recognized gain or loss.
    b. If the condemnation proceeds are $140,000, what are T's realized and recognized gain or loss?
    c. What are T's realized and recognized gain or loss in (a) if the house was rental property?

39. J owns 40% of the stock of LJ Corporation. He purchases undeveloped land from the corporation for $45,000. The fair market value of the land is $80,000.

    a. Calculate the amount of income, if any, that J must recognize.
    b. Calculate J's basis for the land.

40. R makes the following purchases and sales of stock:

Transaction	Date	No. of Shares	Company	Price per Share
Purchase	1–1–90	300	MDG	$ 75
Purchase	6–1–90	150	RU	300
Purchase	11–1–90	60	MDG	70
Sale	12–3–90	180	MDG	70
Purchase	3–1–91	120	RU	375
Sale	8–1–91	90	RU	330
Sale	1–1–92	150	MDG	90
Sale	2–1–92	75	RU	500

Assuming that R is unable to identify the particular lots that are sold with the original purchase, what is the realized gain or loss on each type of stock as of:

a. 7–1–90
b. 12–31–90
c. 12–31–91
d. 7–1–92

41. F purchases 100 shares of M Corporation stock on June 3, 1992, for $100,000. On August 25, 1992, F purchases an additional 50 shares of M Corporation stock for $40,000. According to market quotations, M Corporation stock is selling for $850 per share on December 31, 1992. F sells 60 shares of M Corporation stock on March 1, 1993, for $54,000.

a. What is the adjusted basis of F's M Corporation stock on December 31, 1992?
b. What is F's recognized gain or loss from the sale of M Corporation stock on March 1, 1993, assuming the shares sold are from the shares purchased on June 3, 1992?
c. What is F's recognized gain or loss from the sale of M Corporation stock on March 1, 1993, assuming F cannot adequately identify the shares sold?

42. P purchases the assets of a sole proprietorship from S. The adjusted basis of each of the assets on S's books and the fair market value of each asset as agreed to by P and S are as follows:

Asset	S's Adjusted Basis	FMV
Accounts receivable	$ –0–	$ 10,000
Notes receivable	15,000	20,000
Machinery and equipment	85,000	100,000
Building	100,000	300,000
Land	200,000	350,000

The purchase price is $900,000. Determine P's basis for each of the assets of the sole proprietorship.

43. K receives nontaxable stock rights with a fair market value of $1,900. The fair market value of the stock on which the rights were received is $12,000. The cost of the stock was $11,000.

a. What is the basis of the rights for purposes of exercise or sale?
b. What is the basis of the rights for purposes of exercise or sale if the fair market value of the rights is $1,500?

44. J owns 1,000 shares of Y Corporation stock with a basis of $10,000 and a fair market value of $14,000. She receives nontaxable stock rights to purchase additional shares. The rights have a fair market value of $2,000.

a. What is the basis of the stock and the basis of the stock rights?
b. What is the recognized gain or loss if the stock rights are sold for $2,000?
c. What is the recognized gain or loss if the stock rights are allowed to lapse?

45. T received various gifts over the years. He has decided to dispose of the following assets that he received as gifts:

a. In 1920, he received a Rolls Royce worth $22,000. The donor's adjusted basis for the auto was $16,000. T sells the auto for $45,000 in 1992.
b. In 1945, he received land worth $20,000. The donor's adjusted basis was $32,000. T sells the land for $87,000 in 1992.
c. In 1950, he received stock in G Company. The donor's adjusted basis was $1,000. The fair market value on the date of the gift was $3,000. T sells the stock for $3,500 in 1992.
d. In 1961, he received land worth $12,000. The donor's adjusted basis was $25,000. T sells the land for $9,000 in 1992.
e. In 1990, he received stock worth $30,000. The donor's adjusted basis was $40,000. T sells the stock in 1992 for $37,000.

What is the realized gain or loss from each of the preceding transactions? Assume in each of the gift transactions that no gift tax was paid.

46. A received a car from Z as a gift. Z paid $7,000 for the car. She had used it for business purposes and had deducted $2,000 for depreciation up to the time she gave the car to A. The fair market value of the car is $3,500.

a. Assuming A uses the car for business purposes, what is his basis for depreciation?
b. If the estimated useful life is two years (from the date of the gift), what is his depreciation deduction for each year? Use the straight-line method.
c. If A sells the car for $800 one year after receiving it, what is his gain or loss?
d. If A sells the car for $4,000 one year after receiving it, what is his gain or loss?

47. R receives a gift of property (after 1976) that has a fair market value of $100,000 on the date of gift. The donor's adjusted basis for the property was $40,000. Assume the donor paid gift tax of $15,000 on the gift.

a. What is R's basis for gain and loss and for depreciation?
b. If R had received the gift of property before 1977, what would his basis be for gain and loss and for depreciation?

48. L receives a gift of income-producing property that has an adjusted basis of $20,000 on the date of the gift. The fair market value of the property on the date of the gift is $15,000. Gift tax amounting to $500 was paid by the donor. L later sells the property for $16,500. Determine L's recognized gain or loss.

49. U is going to make a gift to N, his daughter, who is age 16. U is undecided as to whether he should give N $10,000 in cash or give her stock worth $10,000. The adjusted basis of the stock is $13,000. U anticipates that N will sell the stock.

a. Should U make a gift of the stock, or should he sell the stock and give the cash proceeds to N?
b. If the fair market value of the stock is $15,000, what factors should U consider in deciding whether he should make a gift of the stock or sell the stock and give the cash proceeds to N?
c. Assume the stock is family corporation stock and that N is not expected to sell it. The fair market value is $10,000. What are the tax consequences to U if he gives N $10,000 in cash and then sells the stock to N for $10,000?

50. T is planning to make a charitable contribution of stock worth $20,000 to the Boy Scouts. The stock T is considering contributing has an adjusted basis of $15,000. A friend has suggested that T sell the stock and contribute the $20,000 in proceeds rather than contribute the stock.

a. Should T follow the friend's advice? Why?
b. Assume the fair market value is only $13,000. In this case, should T follow the friend's advice? Why?
c. Rather than make a charitable contribution to the Boy Scouts, T is going to make a gift to N, his niece. Advise T regarding (a) and (b).

51. D inherits property from M, her mother. M's adjusted basis for the property is $100,000, and the fair market value is $725,000. Six months after M's death, the fair market value is $740,000. D is the sole beneficiary of M's estate.

    a. Can the executor of M's estate elect the alternate valuation date?
    b. What is D's basis for the property?

52. Q's estate includes the following assets available for distribution to R, one of Q's beneficiaries:

	Decedent's Adjusted Basis	FMV at Date of Death	FMV at Alternate Valuation Date
Cash	$10,000	$ 10,000	$ 10,000
Stock	40,000	125,000	60,000
Apartment building	60,000	300,000	325,000
Land	75,000	100,000	110,000

The fair market value of the stock six months after Q's death was $60,000. However, believing that the stock would continue to decline in value, the executor of the estate distributed the stock to R one month after Q's death. R immediately sold the stock for $85,000.

    a. Determine R's basis for the assets if the primary valuation date and amount apply.
    b. Determine R's basis for the assets if the executor elects the alternate valuation date and amount.

53. X inherits property from Z, her mother. Z's adjusted basis for the property is $450,000. At the date of Z's death, the fair market value of the property is $850,000. Six months later, the property is worth $830,000. The executor distributes the property to X seven months after Z's death when the property is worth $825,000.

    a. Can the executor of Z's estate elect the alternate valuation date? If so, what is X's basis for the property?
    b. If the executor uses the primary valuation date, what is X's basis for the property?

54. T makes a gift of 100 shares of appreciated stock to his uncle, G, on January 5, 1992. The basis of the stock is $3,150, and the fair market value is $5,250. G dies on October 8, 1992. During the period that G held the stock, he received a 5% nontaxable stock dividend. Under the provisions of G's will, T inherits 100 shares of the stock. The value of the stock for Federal estate tax purposes is $55 per share.

    a. What is the basis of the inherited stock to T?
    b. What is the basis of the inherited stock to T if T had given the stock to G on January 5, 1991?

55. H and W live in Louisiana, a community property state. They own land (community property) that has an adjusted basis to them of $100,000. At the date of W's death, the fair market value of the land is $140,000. Six months after W's death, the land is worth $150,000. What is H's basis for the land?

56. T owns undeveloped real estate with an adjusted basis of $80,000. T sells the real estate to her sister, N, for its fair market value of $65,000.

    a. Calculate T's realized and recognized gain or loss.
    b. If N later sells the real estate for $72,000, calculate N's realized and recognized gain or loss.
    c. Assume instead that T sold the real estate to N for its fair market value of $90,000. Calculate T's realized and recognized gain or loss.

57. T owns a 60% capital and profits interest in TS Partnership, which sells property to T for $75,000. The partnership's adjusted basis for the property is $90,000.

    a. Calculate the realized and recognized loss to the partnership.
    b. Calculate the basis of the property to T.

c. If T subsequently sells the property for $87,000, calculate T's realized and recognized gain or loss.
d. If T gives the property to his daughter, D, who subsequently sells it for $87,000, calculate D's realized and recognized gain or loss. Assume no gift tax is paid on the gift and the fair market value on the date of the gift is $80,000.
e. Determine the tax consequences in (a) through (d) if T is a shareholder and TS is a corporation.

58. M owns land with an adjusted basis of $30,000. M sells the land to her sister Q for the land's fair market value of $26,000. Q makes a gift of the land to her nephew N. Q pays gift tax of $1,000. At the date of the gift, the fair market value of the land is $29,000.

a. What is the realized and recognized gain or loss to N if he sells the land for $36,000?
b. What is the realized and recognized gain or loss to N if he sells the land for $23,000?
c. How would the results in (a) and (b) differ if N had inherited the property from Q?

59. On September 15, 1992, S decides to revise his stock holdings as follows:

Date	Company	No. of Shares	Trans-action	Price	Cost
9–10–92	Pan Am	100	Buy	$25/share	
9–15–92	Kodak	120	Sell	20/share	$25/share
9–15–92	Ford	70	Sell	25/share	20/share
9–15–92	IBM	95	Sell	5/share	10/share
9–15–92	Xerox	220	Sell	8/share	5/share
9–15–92	Pan Am	100	Sell	20/share	30/share
10–4–92	Ford	100	Buy	20/share	
10–8–92	ABC	120	Buy	7/share	
10–14–92	American	50	Buy	4/share	
10–25–92	Kodak	95	Buy	30/share	

a. What is the recognized gain or loss for each of the stocks sold on September 15?
b. Explain why the gain or loss is or is not recognized on each sale.

60. K purchased 100 shares of U Corporation common stock on June 6, 1991, for $20,000. He sold the stock on January 6, 1992, for $30,000. On January 28, 1992, he purchased another 100 shares of U Corporation common stock for $28,000.

a. What are K's realized and recognized gain or loss on January 6, 1992?
b. What is K's basis for the stock he purchased on January 28, 1992?
c. What would be your answer for (a) and (b) if K's cost of the stock on June 6, 1991, had been $35,000?

61. J purchases two wheat futures contracts, one to buy and one to sell, for $7,000 each in August 1992. In November 1992, J liquidates the position, showing a loss of $1,000. At the same time, the offsetting position is showing a gain of $975.

a. What is J's recognized loss?
b. Would liquidating the offsetting position in November 1992 affect the recognized loss?

62. A retires from a public accounting firm to enter private practice. He had bought a home two years earlier for $40,000. Upon beginning his business, he converts one-fourth of his home into an office. The fair market value of the home on the date of conversion (January 1, 1986) is $75,000. The adjusted basis is $56,000 (ignore land). A lives and works in the home for six years (after converting it to business use) and sells it at the end of the sixth year. A deducted $6,085 of cost recovery using the statutory percentage method.

a. How much gain or loss is recognized if A sells the property for $44,000?
b. If he sells the property for $70,000?

63. B's personal residence originally cost $150,000 (ignore land). After living in the house for five years, he converts it to rental property. At the date of conversion, the fair market value of the house is $130,000.

a. Calculate B's basis for loss for the rental property.
b. Calculate B's basis for depreciation for the rental property.
c. Calculate B's basis for gain for the rental property.

64. T, age 93, has accumulated substantial assets during his life. Among his many assets are the following, which he is considering giving to G, his grandson.

Assets	Adjusted Basis	Fair Market Value
X Corporation stock	$ 50,000	$700,000
Y Corporation stock	70,000	71,000
Z Corporation stock	200,000	50,000

T has been in ill health for the past five years. His physician has informed him that he probably will not live for more than six months. Advise T which of the stocks should be transferred as gifts and which as bequests.

CUMULATIVE PROBLEMS

65. Ada Johnson, age 28, is single and has no dependents. Her Social Security number is 444–11–3333, and she resides at 210 Avenue G, Kentwood, LA 70444. Her salary in 1992 was $25,000. She incurred unreimbursed expenses of $800 for travel and $500 for entertainment in connection with her job as an assistant personnel director. In addition, she had the following items of possible tax consequence in 1992:

a. Itemized deductions (not including any potential deductions mentioned previously), $5,800.
b. Proceeds from the October 8, 1992, sale of land inherited from her father on June 15, 1992 (fair market value on June 15 was $35,000; her father's adjusted basis was $15,000), $38,000.
c. Proceeds from the November 1, 1992, sale of 50 shares of X Corporation stock received as a gift from her father on October 5, 1976, when the fair market value of the stock was $6,000 (her father's adjusted basis in the stock was $5,500, and he paid gift tax of $800 on the transfer), $7,500.
d. Proceeds from the November 5, 1992, sale of her personal automobile, for which she had paid $4,500 in 1984, $3,100.
e. Proceeds from the December 3, 1992, sale of 10 shares of Y Corporation stock to her brother (she had paid $85 per share for the stock on February 7, 1992), $600.
f. Dividends received from a domestic corporation, $120.

Part 1—Tax Computation

Ada's employer withheld Federal income tax of $3,880. Compute Ada's net tax payable or refund due for 1992. Suggested software (if available): *TurboTax* or WFT tax planning software.

Part 2—Tax Planning

As of the beginning of 1993, Ada is promoted to the position of personnel director. The promotion will result in a salary increase. Her new position will result in an estimated increase in her expenses for travel from $800 to $3,000 and in her expenses for entertainment from $500 to $4,000. Her employer has offered her the following options.

a. Salary increase of $20,000.
b. Salary increase of $12,000 and reimbursement for all travel and entertainment expenses not in excess of $7,000.

Ada estimates that her itemized deductions (excluding any potential deductions for travel and entertainment) will remain at $5,800. She anticipates that no dividends will be received and no proceeds from asset sales will be received.

Calculate Ada's tax liability for 1993 under both option (a) and option (b) so she can decide which option to select. Suggested software (if available): WFT tax planning software.

66. Kenneth Cloud, age 67, is married and files a joint return with his wife, Sarah, age 65. Kenneth and Sarah are both retired. In 1991, they received Social Security benefits of $2,400. Kenneth's Social Security number is 366–55–1111, and Sarah's is 555–66–2222. They reside at 405 College Drive, Hammond, LA 70408.

Kenneth, who retired on January 1, 1991, receives benefits from a qualified pension plan of $600 a month for life. His total contributions to the plan were $18,000. Kenneth's life expectancy at the annuity starting date on January 1, 1991, was 18.4 years.

Sarah, who retired on December 31, 1990, started receiving benefits of $800 a month on January 1, 1991. Her life expectancy was 20 years from the annuity starting date, and her investment in the qualified pension plan was $57,600.

On September 27, 1991, Kenneth and Sarah received a 10% stock dividend on 50 shares of stock they owned. They had paid $11 a share for the stock on March 5, 1976. On December 16, 1991, they sold the 5 shares received as a stock dividend for $30 a share.

On January 10, 1991, Sarah sold the car she had used in commuting to and from work. She paid $5,000 for the car in 1984 and sold it for $3,500.

Kenneth and Sarah received a gift of 100 shares of stock from their son Thomas on July 14, 1978. Thomas's basis in the stock was $30 a share, and the fair market value at the date of gift was $20 a share. No gift tax was paid. Kenneth and Sarah sold the stock on October 8, 1991, for $15 a share.

Sarah's mother died on May 1, 1991. Sarah inherited her mother's personal residence, which had a fair market value of $112,000 on May 1. Her mother's adjusted basis was $80,000. At the end of 1991, Sarah was still listing the house with a realtor. The realtor estimated the house was worth $120,000 at December 31, 1991.

Kenneth and Sarah paid estimated Federal income tax of $200 and had itemized deductions of $6,800. If they have overpaid their Federal income tax, they want the amount refunded. Both Kenneth and Sarah wish to have $1 go to the Presidential Election Campaign Fund.

Compute their net tax payable or refund due for 1991. If you use tax forms for your computations, you will need Form 1040 and Schedules A, D, and R. Suggested software (if available): *TurboTax* or WFT tax planning software.

RESEARCH PROBLEMS

RESEARCH PROBLEM 1 On January 1, 1992, X, a major shareholder in H Corporation, purchases land from the company for $300,000. The fair market value of the land is $1,200,000, and the adjusted basis in the hands of the corporation is $400,000.

a. What are the possible tax consequences to X?

b. What is the basis of the land to X?

c. What is the tax consequence to H Corporation?

RESEARCH PROBLEM 2 T owns real estate with an adjusted basis of $600,000 and a fair market value of $1,100,000. The amount of the nonrecourse mortgage on the property is $2,500,000. Because of substantial past and projected future losses associated with the real estate development (occupancy rate of only 37% after three years), T deeds the property to the creditor.

a. What are the tax consequences to T?

b. Assume the data are the same, except the fair market value of the property is $2,525,000. Therefore, T also receives $25,000 from the creditor when he deeds the property to the creditor. What are the tax consequences to T?

Partial list of research aids:

Rev.Rul. 76–111, 1976–1 C.B. 214.
Crane v. Comm., 47 USTC ¶9217, 35 AFTR 776, 67 S.Ct. 1047 (USSC, 1947).

RESEARCH PROBLEM 3 O gives stock worth $400,000 to G. O's adjusted basis in the stock is $50,000. The gift taxes due are $118,400. As a condition for receiving the gift of stock, G agrees to pay the gift tax. The stock is transferred to G on February 5, 1992.

a. What are the income tax consequences to O?

b. What are the income tax consequences to O if the gift was made on February 5, 1981?

RESEARCH PROBLEM 4 W owns land that has an adjusted basis of $75,000 and a fair market value of $200,000. W has owned the land for five years. The land is subject to a mortgage of $100,000. W, an alumnus of State University, donates the land to State University. The university assumes W's mortgage on the land. What are the tax consequences to W?

Partial list of research aids:

Leo G. Ebben, 45 TCM 1283, T.C. Memo. 1983–200.

CHAPTER

PROPERTY TRANSACTIONS: NONTAXABLE EXCHANGES

OBJECTIVES

Discuss the rationale for nonrecognition (postponement) of gain in certain property transactions.

Identify the different types of nontaxable exchanges.

Explain the nonrecognition provisions and basis determination rules for like-kind exchanges.

Examine the nonrecognition provisions available on the involuntary conversion of property.

Describe the provisions for postponing recognition of gain on the sale and replacement of a personal residence.

Discuss the provisions for permanent exclusion of gain on the sale of a personal residence for taxpayers age 55 and older.

Identify tax planning opportunities related to the nonrecognition provisions discussed in the chapter.

OUTLINE

General Concept of a Nontaxable Exchange

A taxpayer who is going to replace a productive asset (e.g., machinery) used in a trade or business may structure the transactions as a sale of the old asset and the purchase of a new asset. Using this approach, any realized gain on the asset sale is recognized. The basis of the new asset is its cost. Conversely, the taxpayer may be able to trade the old asset for the new asset. This exchange of assets may qualify for nontaxable exchange treatment.

The tax law recognizes that nontaxable exchanges result in a change in the *form* but not in the *substance* of the taxpayer's relative economic position. The replacement property received in the exchange is viewed as substantially a continuation of the old investment.[1] Additional justification for nontaxable exchange treatment is that this type of transaction does not provide the taxpayer with the wherewithal to pay the tax on any realized gain. The nonrecognition provisions do not apply to realized losses from the sale or exchange of personal use assets. Such losses are not recognized because they are personal in nature and not because of any nonrecognition provision.

In a *nontaxable exchange*, realized gains or losses are not recognized. However, the nonrecognition is usually temporary. The recognition of gain or loss is *postponed* (deferred) until the property received in the nontaxable exchange is subsequently disposed of in a taxable transaction. This is accomplished by assigning a carryover basis to the replacement property.

Example 1

T exchanges property with an adjusted basis of $10,000 and a fair market value of $12,000 for property with a fair market value of $12,000. The transaction qualifies for nontaxable exchange treatment. T has a realized gain of $2,000 ($12,000 amount realized − $10,000 adjusted basis). His recognized gain is $0. His basis in the replacement property is a carryover basis of $10,000. Assume the replacement property is nondepreciable. If T subsequently sells the replacement property for $12,000, his realized and recognized gain will be the $2,000 gain that was postponed (deferred) in the nontaxable transaction. If the replacement property is depreciable, the carryover basis of $10,000 is used in calculating depreciation. ◆

In some nontaxable exchanges, only part of the property involved in the transaction qualifies for nonrecognition treatment. If the taxpayer receives cash or other nonqualifying property, part or all of the realized gain from the exchange is recognized. In these instances, gain is recognized because the taxpayer has changed or improved his or her relative economic position and has the wherewithal to pay income tax to the extent of cash or other property received.

It is important to distinguish between a nontaxable disposition, as the term is used in the statute, and a tax-free transaction. First, a direct exchange is not required in all circumstances (e.g., replacement of involuntarily converted property or sale and replacement of a personal residence). Second, as previously mentioned, the term *nontaxable* refers to postponement of recognition via a carryover basis. In a *tax-free* transaction, the nonrecognition is permanent (e.g., see the discussion later in the chapter of the § 121 election by a taxpayer age 55 or over to exclude gain on the sale of a residence). Therefore, the basis of any property acquired is not dependent on that of the property disposed of by the taxpayer.

1. Reg. § 1.1002–1(c).

Like-Kind Exchanges—§ 1031

◆

Section 1031 provides for nontaxable exchange treatment if the following requirements are satisfied:[2]

- The form of the transaction is an exchange.
- Both the property transferred and the property received are held either for productive use in a trade or business or for investment.
- The property is like-kind property.

Like-kind exchanges include business for business, business for investment, investment for business, or investment for investment property. Property held for personal use, inventory, and partnership interests (both limited and general) do not qualify under the like-kind exchange provisions. Securities, even though held for investment, do not qualify for like-kind exchange treatment.

The nonrecognition provision for like-kind exchanges is *mandatory* rather than elective. A taxpayer who wants to recognize a realized gain or loss will have to structure the transaction in a form that does not satisfy the statutory requirements for a like-kind exchange. This topic is discussed further under Tax Planning Considerations.

Like-Kind Property

"The words 'like-kind' refer to the nature or character of the property and not to its grade or quality. One kind or class of property may not . . . be exchanged for property of a different kind or class."[3]

Although the term *like-kind* is intended to be interpreted very broadly, three categories of exchanges are not included. First, livestock of different sexes do not qualify as like-kind property. Second, real estate can be exchanged only for other real estate, and personalty can be exchanged only for other personalty. For example, the exchange of a machine (personalty) for an office building (realty) is not a like-kind exchange. *Real estate* includes principally rental buildings, office and store buildings, manufacturing plants, warehouses, and land. It is immaterial whether real estate is improved or unimproved. Thus, unimproved land can be exchanged for an apartment house. *Personalty* includes principally machines, equipment, trucks, automobiles, furniture, and fixtures. Third, real property located in the United States exchanged for foreign real property (and vice versa) does not qualify as like-kind property.

Example 2

T made the following exchanges during the taxable year:

- **a.** Inventory for a machine used in business.
- **b.** Land held for investment for a building used in business.
- **c.** Stock held for investment for equipment used in business.
- **d.** A business truck for a business truck.
- **e.** An automobile used for personal transportation for an automobile used in business.
- **f.** Livestock for livestock of a different sex.
- **g.** Land held for investment in New York for land held for investment in London.

Exchanges (b), investment real property for business real property, and (d), business personalty for business personalty, qualify as exchanges of like-kind property.

---

2. § 1031(a) and Reg. § 1.1031(a)–1(a).

3. Reg. § 1.1031(a)–1(b).

Exchanges (a), inventory; (c), stock; (e), personal use automobile (not held for business or investment purposes); (f), livestock of different sexes; and (g), U.S. and foreign real estate do not qualify. ◆

A special provision applies if the taxpayers involved in the exchange are related parties under § 267(b). To qualify for like-kind exchange treatment, the taxpayer and the related party must not dispose of the like-kind property received in the exchange within the two-year period following the date of the exchange. If such an early disposition does occur, the postponed gain is recognized as of the date of the early disposition. Dispositions due to death, involuntary conversions, and certain non-tax avoidance transactions are not treated as early dispositions.

Regulations dealing with § 1031 like-kind exchange treatment were finalized in April 1991.[4] These Regulations provide that if the exchange transaction involves multiple assets of a business (e.g., a television station for another television station), the determination of whether the assets qualify as like-kind property will not be made at the business level. Instead, the underlying assets must be evaluated.

The Regulations also provide for greater specificity in determining whether depreciable tangible personal property is of a like kind or class. Such property held for productive use in a business is of a like class only if the exchanged property is within the same *general business asset class* (as specified by the IRS in Rev.Proc. 87–57 or as subsequently modified) or the same *product class* (as specified by the Department of Commerce). Property included in a general business asset class is evaluated under this system rather than under the product class system.

The following are examples of general business asset classes:

- Office furniture, fixtures, and equipment.
- Information systems (computers and peripheral equipment).
- Airplanes.
- Automobiles and taxis.
- Buses.
- Light general-purpose trucks.
- Heavy general-purpose trucks.

The new Regulations have the effect of making it more difficult to qualify for § 1031 like-kind exchange treatment for depreciable tangible personal property. For example, the exchange of office equipment for a computer does not qualify as the exchange of like-kind property. Even though both assets are depreciable tangible personal property, they are not like-kind property. The assets are in different general business asset classes.

Exchange Requirement

The transaction must actually involve a direct exchange of property to qualify as a like-kind exchange. The sale of old property and the purchase of new property, even though like-kind, is generally not an exchange. However, if the two transactions are mutually dependent, the IRS may treat them as a like-kind exchange. For example, if the taxpayer sells an old business machine to a dealer and purchases a new one from the same dealer, like-kind exchange treatment could result.[5]

The taxpayer may want to avoid nontaxable exchange treatment. Recognition of gain gives the taxpayer a higher basis for depreciation (see Example 32). To

4. Reg. §§ 1.1031(a)–2 and (j)–1.

5. Rev.Rul. 61–119, 1961–1 C.B. 395.

the extent that such gains would, if recognized, either receive favorable capital gain treatment or be passive activity income that could offset passive activity losses, it may be preferable to avoid the nonrecognition provisions through an indirect exchange transaction. For example, a taxpayer may sell property to one individual and follow the sale with a purchase of similar property from another individual. The taxpayer may also want to avoid nontaxable exchange treatment so that a realized loss can be recognized.

Boot

If the taxpayer in a like-kind exchange gives or receives some property that is not like-kind property, recognition may occur. Property that is not like-kind property, including cash, is referred to as *boot.* Although the term "boot" does not appear in the Code, tax practitioners commonly use it rather than using "property that is not like-kind property."

The *receipt* of boot will trigger recognition of gain if there is realized gain. The amount of the recognized gain is the *lesser* of the boot received or the realized gain (realized gain serves as the ceiling on recognition).

EXAMPLE 3

T and S exchange machinery, and the exchange qualifies as like-kind under § 1031. Since T's machinery (adjusted basis of $20,000) is worth $24,000 and S's machine has a fair market value of $19,000, S also gives T cash of $5,000. T's recognized gain is $4,000, the lesser of the realized gain ($24,000 amount realized − $20,000 adjusted basis = $4,000) or the fair market value of the boot received ($5,000). ◆

EXAMPLE 4

Assume the same facts as in the previous example, except that S's machine is worth $21,000 (not $19,000). Under these circumstances, S gives T cash of $3,000 to make up the difference. T's recognized gain is $3,000, the lesser of the realized gain ($24,000 amount realized − $20,000 adjusted basis = $4,000) or the fair market value of the boot received ($3,000). ◆

The receipt of boot does not result in recognition if there is realized loss.

EXAMPLE 5

Assume the same facts as in Example 3, except the adjusted basis of T's machine is $30,000. T's realized loss is $6,000 ($24,000 amount realized − $30,000 adjusted basis = $6,000 realized loss). The receipt of the boot of $5,000 does not trigger recognition. Therefore, the recognized loss is $0. ◆

The *giving* of boot usually does not trigger recognition. If the boot given is cash, any realized gain or loss is not recognized.

EXAMPLE 6

T and S exchange equipment in a like-kind exchange. T receives equipment with a fair market value of $25,000. T transfers equipment worth $21,000 (adjusted basis of $15,000) and cash of $4,000. T's realized gain is $6,000 ($25,000 amount realized − $15,000 adjusted basis − $4,000 cash). However, none of the realized gain is recognized. ◆

If, however, the boot given is appreciated or depreciated property, gain or loss is recognized to the extent of the differential between the adjusted basis and the fair market value of the boot. For this purpose, *appreciated or depreciated property* is defined as property whose adjusted basis is not equal to the fair market value.

EXAMPLE 7

Assume the same facts as in the previous example, except that T transfers equipment worth $10,000 (adjusted basis of $12,000) and boot worth $15,000 (adjusted basis of $9,000). T's realized gain appears to be $4,000 ($25,000 amount realized − $21,000 adjusted basis). Since realization previously has served as a ceiling on recognition, it appears that the recognized gain is $4,000 (lower of realized gain of $4,000 or amount of appreciation on boot of $6,000). However, the recognized gain actually is $6,000 (full amount of the appreciation on the boot). In effect, T must calculate the like-kind and boot parts of the transaction separately. That is, the realized loss of $2,000 on the like-kind property is not recognized ($10,000 fair market value − $12,000 adjusted basis), and the $6,000 realized gain on the boot is recognized ($15,000 fair market value − $9,000 adjusted basis). ◆

In one other similar circumstance, realization does not serve as a ceiling on recognition.

EXAMPLE 8

T and S exchange equipment in a like-kind exchange. T receives from S like-kind equipment with a fair market value of $25,000 and boot with a fair market value of $6,000. T gives up like-kind equipment with an adjusted basis of $12,000 and boot with an adjusted basis of $8,000. Although T's realized gain appears to be $11,000 ($25,000 + $6,000 − $12,000 − $8,000), T must report the like-kind and boot elements separately. It is therefore necessary to know the fair market value of the like-kind property and the boot transferred by T. Assume the fair market value of the like-kind equipment given up by T is $9,000 and that of the boot is $22,000. The realized loss of $3,000 on the like-kind property is not recognized ($9,000 fair market value − $12,000 adjusted basis), and the $14,000 realized gain on the boot is recognized ($22,000 fair market value − $8,000 adjusted basis). ◆

Basis and Holding Period of Property Received

If an exchange does not qualify as nontaxable under § 1031, gain or loss is recognized, and the basis of property received in the exchange is the property's fair market value. If the exchange qualifies for nonrecognition, the basis of property received must be adjusted to reflect any postponed (deferred) gain or loss. The *basis* of *like-kind property* received in the exchange is the property's fair market value less postponed gain or plus postponed loss. If the exchange partially qualifies for nonrecognition (if recognition is associated with boot), the basis of like-kind property received in the exchange is the property's fair market value less postponed gain or plus postponed loss. The *basis* of any *boot* received is the boot's fair market value.

If there is a postponed loss, nonrecognition creates a situation in which the taxpayer has recovered *less* than the cost or other basis of the property exchanged in an amount equal to the unrecognized loss. If there is a postponed gain, the taxpayer has recovered *more* than the cost or other basis of the property exchanged in an amount equal to the unrecognized gain.

EXAMPLE 9

T exchanges a building (used in his business) with an adjusted basis of $30,000 and fair market value of $38,000 for land with a fair market value of $38,000. The land is to be held as an investment. The exchange qualifies as like-kind (an exchange of business real property for investment real property). Thus, the basis of the land is $30,000 (the land's fair market value of $38,000 less the $8,000 postponed gain on the building). If the land is later sold for its fair market value of $38,000, the $8,000 postponed gain is recognized. ◆

EXAMPLE 10

Assume the same facts as in the previous example, except that the building has an adjusted basis of $48,000 and fair market value of only $38,000. The basis in the newly acquired land is $48,000 (fair market value of $38,000 plus the $10,000 postponed loss on the building). If the land is later sold for its fair market value of $38,000, the $10,000 postponed loss is recognized. ◆

The Code provides an alternative approach for determining the basis of like-kind property received:

Adjusted basis of like-kind property surrendered
+ Adjusted basis of boot given
+ Gain recognized
− Fair market value of boot received
− Loss recognized
= Basis of like-kind property received

This approach is logical in terms of the recovery of capital doctrine. That is, the unrecovered cost or other basis is increased by additional cost (boot given) or decreased by cost recovered (boot received). Any gain recognized is included in the basis of the new property. The taxpayer has been taxed on this amount and is now entitled to recover it tax-free. Any loss recognized is deducted from the basis of the new property. The taxpayer has received a tax benefit on that amount.

The *holding period* of the property surrendered in the exchange carries over and *tacks on* to the holding period of the like-kind property received.[6] The logic of this rule is derived from the basic concept of the new property as a continuation of the old investment. The boot received has a new holding period (from the date of exchange) rather than a carryover holding period.

Depreciation recapture potential carries over to the property received in a like-kind exchange.[7] See Chapter 17 for a discussion of this topic.

The following comprehensive example illustrates the like-kind exchange rules.

EXAMPLE 11

T exchanged the following old machines for new machines in five independent like-kind exchanges:

Exchange	Adjusted Basis of Old Machine	Fair Market Value of New Machine	Adjusted Basis of Boot Given	Fair Market Value of Boot Received
1	$4,000	$9,000	$ -0-	$ -0-
2	4,000	9,000	3,000	-0-
3	4,000	9,000	6,000	-0-
4	4,000	9,000	-0-	3,000
5	4,000	3,500	-0-	300

6. § 1223(1) and Reg. § 1.1223–1(a). For this carryover holding period rule to apply to like-kind exchanges after March 1, 1954, the like-kind property surrendered must have been either a capital asset or § 1231 property. See Chapters 16 and 17 for the discussion of capital assets and § 1231 property.

7. Reg. §§ 1.1245–2(a)(4) and 1.1250–2(d)(1).

T's realized and recognized gains and losses and the basis of each of the like-kind properties received are as follows:

Exchange	Realized Gain (Loss)	Recognized Gain (Loss)	New Basis Calculation: Old Adj. Basis	+	Boot Given	+	Gain Recognized	−	Boot Received	=	New Basis
1	$ 5,000	$ -0-	$4,000	+	$ -0-	+	$ -0-	−	$ -0-	=	$ 4,000*
2	2,000	-0-	4,000	+	3,000	+	-0-	−	-0-	=	7,000*
3	(1,000)	-(0)-	4,000	+	6,000	+	-0-	−	-0-	=	10,000**
4	8,000	3,000	4,000	+	-0-	+	3,000	−	3,000	=	4,000*
5	(200)	-(0)-	4,000	+	-0-	+	-0-	−	300	=	3,700**

*Basis may be determined in gain situations under the alternative method by subtracting the gain not recognized from the fair market value of the new property:
$9,000 − $5,000 = $4,000 for exchange 1.
$9,000 − $2,000 = $7,000 for exchange 2.
$9,000 − $5,000 = $4,000 for exchange 4.

**In loss situations, basis may be determined by adding the loss not recognized to the fair market value of the new property:
$9,000 + $1,000 = $10,000 for exchange 3.
$3,500 + $200 = $3,700 for exchange 5.

The basis of the boot received is the boot's fair market value. ◆

If the taxpayer either assumes a liability or takes property subject to a liability, the amount of the liability is treated as boot given. For the taxpayer whose liability is assumed or whose property is taken subject to the liability, the amount of the liability is treated as boot received. Example 12 illustrates the effect of such a liability. In addition, the example illustrates the tax consequences for both parties involved in the like-kind exchange.

EXAMPLE 12

X and Y exchange real estate investments. X gives up property with an adjusted basis of $250,000 (fair market value $400,000) that is subject to a mortgage of $75,000 (assumed by Y). In return for this property, X receives property with a fair market value of $300,000 (adjusted basis $200,000) and cash of $25,000.

- X's realized gain is $150,000. X gave up property with an adjusted basis of $250,000. X received $400,000 from the exchange ($300,000 fair market value of like-kind property plus $100,000 boot received). The boot received consists of the cash of $25,000 received from Y and X's mortgage of $75,000 that is assumed by Y.
- X's recognized gain is $100,000. The realized gain of $150,000 is recognized to the extent of boot received.
- X's basis in the real estate received from Y is $250,000. This basis can be computed by subtracting the postponed gain ($50,000) from the fair market value of the real estate received ($300,000). It can also be computed by adding the recognized gain ($100,000) to the adjusted basis of the real estate given up ($250,000) and subtracting the boot received ($100,000).
- Y's realized gain is $100,000. Y gave up property with an adjusted basis of $200,000 plus boot of $100,000 ($75,000 mortgage assumed plus $25,000 cash) or a total of $300,000. Y received $400,000 from the exchange (fair market value of like-kind property received).
- Y has no recognized gain because he did not receive any boot. The entire realized gain of $100,000 is postponed.
- Y's basis in the real estate received from X is $300,000. This basis can be computed by subtracting the postponed gain ($100,000) from the fair market value of the real estate received ($400,000). It can also be computed by adding

the boot given ($75,000 mortgage assumed by Y plus $25,000 cash) to the adjusted basis of the real estate given up ($200,000).[8] ◆

INVOLUNTARY CONVERSIONS—§ 1033
◆

General Scheme

Section 1033 provides that a taxpayer who suffers an involuntary conversion of property may postpone recognition of *gain* realized from the conversion. The objective of this provision is to provide relief to the taxpayer who has suffered hardship and does not have the wherewithal to pay the tax on any gain realized from the conversion. Postponement of realized gain is permitted to the extent that the taxpayer reinvests the amount realized from the conversion in replacement property. The rules for nonrecognition of gain are as follows:

- If the amount reinvested in replacement property *equals or exceeds* the amount realized, realized gain is *not recognized.*
- If the amount reinvested in replacement property is *less than* the amount realized, realized gain *is recognized* to the extent of the deficiency.

If a *loss* occurs on an involuntary conversion, § 1033 does not modify the normal rules for loss recognition. That is, if realized loss otherwise would be recognized, § 1033 does not change the result.

Involuntary Conversion Defined

An *involuntary conversion* results from the destruction (complete or partial), theft, seizure, requisition or condemnation, or the sale or exchange under threat or imminence of requisition or condemnation of the taxpayer's property.[9] To prove the existence of a threat or imminence of condemnation, the taxpayer must obtain confirmation that there has been a decision to acquire the property for public use. In addition, the taxpayer must have reasonable grounds to believe the property will be taken.[10] The property does not have to be sold to the authority threatening to condemn it to qualify for § 1033 postponement. If the taxpayer satisfies the confirmation and reasonable grounds requirements, he or she can sell the property to another party.[11] Likewise, the sale of property to a condemning authority by a taxpayer who acquired the property from its former owner with the knowledge that the property was under threat of condemnation also qualifies as an involuntary conversion under § 1033.[12]

Although most involuntary conversions are casualties or condemnations, the definition includes some special situations. Involuntary conversions, for example, include livestock destroyed by or on account of disease or exchanged or sold because of disease or solely on account of drought. A voluntary act, such as an act of arson by a taxpayer involving his or her own property, is not an involuntary conversion.[13]

8. Example (2) of Reg. § 1.1031(d)–2 illustrates a special situation where both the buyer and the seller transfer liabilities that are assumed or property is acquired subject to a liability by the other party.

9. § 1033(a) and Reg. §§ 1.1033(a)–1(a) and –2(a).

10. Rev.Rul. 63–221, 1963–2 C. B. 332, and *Joseph P. Balistrieri*, 38 TCM 526, T.C.Memo. 1979–115.

11. Rev.Rul. 81–180, 1981–2 C.B. 161.

12. Rev.Rul. 81–181, 1981–2 C.B. 162.

13. Rev.Rul. 82–74, 1982–1 C.B. 110.

Computing the Amount Realized

The amount realized from the condemnation of property usually includes only the amount received as compensation for the property.[14] Any amount received that is designated as severance damages by both the government and the taxpayer is not included in the amount realized. *Severance awards* usually occur when only a portion of the entire property is condemned (e.g., a strip of land is taken to build a highway). Severance damages are awarded because the value of the taxpayer's remaining property has declined as a result of the condemnation. Such damages reduce the basis of the property. However, if either of the following requirements is satisfied, the nonrecognition provision of § 1033 applies to the severance damages.

- Severance damages are used to restore the usability of the remaining property.
- The usefulness of the remaining property is destroyed by the condemnation, and the property is sold and replaced at a cost equal to or exceeding the sum of the condemnation award, severance damages, and sales proceeds.

EXAMPLE 13

The government condemns a portion of T's farmland to build part of an interstate highway. Because the highway denies T's cattle access to a pond and some grazing land, T receives severance damages in addition to the condemnation proceeds for the land taken. T must reduce the basis of the property by the amount of the severance damages. If the amount of the severance damages received exceeds the adjusted basis, T recognizes gain. ◆

EXAMPLE 14

Assume the same facts as in the previous example, except that T used the proceeds from the condemnation and the severance damages to build another pond and to clear woodland for grazing. Therefore, all the proceeds are eligible for § 1033 treatment. Thus, there is no possibility of gain recognition as the result of the amount of the severance damages received exceeding the adjusted basis. ◆

Replacement Property

The requirements for replacement property generally are more restrictive than those for like-kind property under § 1031. The basic requirement is that the replacement property be similar or related in service or use to the involuntarily converted property.[15]

Different interpretations of the phrase *similar or related in service or use* apply if the involuntarily converted property is held by an *owner-user* rather than an *owner-investor* (e.g., lessor). The taxpayer who uses the property in his or her trade or business is subject to a more restrictive test in terms of acquiring replacement property. For the owner-user, the *functional use test* applies, and for the owner-investor, the *taxpayer use test* applies.

Taxpayer Use Test. The taxpayer use test for owner-investors provides the taxpayer with more flexibility in terms of what qualifies as replacement property than does the functional use test for owner-users. Essentially, the properties

14. *Pioneer Real Estate Co.*, 47 B.T.A. 886 (1942), *acq.* 1943 C.B. 18.

15. § 1033(a) and Reg. § 1.1033(a)–1.

must be used by the taxpayer (the owner-investor) in similar endeavors. For example, rental property held by an owner-investor qualifies if replaced by other rental property, regardless of the type of rental property involved. The test is met when an investor replaces a manufacturing plant with a wholesale grocery warehouse if both properties are held for the production of rental income.[16] The replacement of a rental residence with a personal residence does not meet the test.[17]

Functional Use Test. Under this test, the taxpayer's use of the replacement property and of the involuntarily converted property must be the same. Replacing a manufacturing plant with a wholesale grocery warehouse, whether rented or not, does not meet this test. As indicated above, the IRS applies the taxpayer use test to owner-investors. However, the functional use test still applies to owner-users (e.g., a manufacturer whose manufacturing plant is destroyed by fire is required to replace the plant with another facility of similar functional use). Replacing a rental residence with a personal residence does not meet this test.

Special Rules. Under one set of circumstances, the broader replacement rules for like-kind exchanges are substituted for the narrow replacement rules normally used for involuntary conversions. This beneficial provision applies if business real property or investment real property is condemned. Therefore, the taxpayer has substantially more flexibility in selecting replacement property. For example, improved real property can be replaced with unimproved real property. Another special rule provides that proceeds from the involuntary conversion of livestock due to soil or other environmental contamination need be expended only for any property to be used for farming, including real property. Finally, another special rule permits an indirect replacement approach. Under this rule, the taxpayer can acquire a controlling interest (80 percent) in a corporation that owns property that qualifies as replacement property in lieu of purchasing the replacement property directly. However, the special rule that substitutes the broader replacement rules for like-kind exchanges cannot be used in conjunction with this indirect replacement approach.

The rules concerning the nature of replacement property are illustrated in Concept Summary 15–1.

Time Limitation on Replacement

The taxpayer normally has a two-year period after the close of the taxable year in which any gain is realized from the involuntary conversion to replace the property (*the latest date*).[18] This rule affords as much as three years from the date of realization of gain to replace the property if the realization of gain took place on the first day of the taxable year.[19] If the form of the involuntary conversion is the condemnation of real property used in a trade or business or held for investment, a three-year period is substituted for the normal two-year period. In this case, the taxpayer can actually have as much as four years from the date of realization of gain to replace the property.

16. *Loco Realty Co. v. Comm.*, 62–2 USTC ¶9657, 10 AFTR2d 5359, 306 F.2d 207 (CA–8, 1962).

17. Rev.Rul. 70–466, 1970–2 C.B. 165.

18. §§ 1033(a)(2)(B) and (g)(4) and Reg. § 1.1033(a)–2(c)(3).

19. The taxpayer can apply for an extension of this time period anytime before its expiration [Reg. § 1.1033(a)–2(c)(3)]. Also, the period for filing the application for extension can be extended if the taxpayer shows reasonable cause.

EXAMPLE 15

T's warehouse is destroyed by fire on December 16, 1991. The adjusted basis is $325,000. Proceeds of $400,000 are received from the insurance company on January 10, 1992. T is a calendar year taxpayer. The latest date for replacement is December 31, 1994 (the end of the taxable year in which realized gain occurred plus two years). The critical date is not the date the involuntary conversion occurred, but rather the date of gain realization. ◆

EXAMPLE 16

Assume the same facts as in the previous example, except T's warehouse is condemned. The latest date for replacement is December 31, 1995 (the end of the taxable year in which realized gain occurred plus three years). ◆

The *earliest date* for replacement typically is the date the involuntary conversion occurs. However, if the property is condemned, it is possible to replace the condemned property before this date. In this case, the earliest date is the date of the threat or imminence of requisition or condemnation of the property. The purpose of this provision is to enable the taxpayer to make an orderly replacement of the condemned property.

EXAMPLE 17

Assume the same facts as in Example 16. T can replace the warehouse before December 16, 1991 (the condemnation date). The earliest date for replacement is the date of the threat or imminence of requisition or condemnation of the warehouse. ◆

Nonrecognition of Gain

Nonrecognition of gain can be either mandatory or elective, depending upon whether the conversion is direct (into replacement property) or into money.

Direct Conversion. If the conversion is directly into replacement property rather than into money, nonrecognition of realized gain is *mandatory*. In this

CONCEPT SUMMARY 15–1
REPLACEMENT PROPERTY TESTS

Type of Property and User	Like-Kind Test	Taxpayer Use Test	Functional Use Test
Land used by a manufacturing company is condemned by a local government authority.	X		
Apartment and land held by an investor are sold due to the threat or imminence of condemnation.	X		
An investor's rented shopping mall is destroyed by fire; the mall may be replaced by other rental properties (e.g., an apartment building).		X	
A manufacturing plant is destroyed by fire; replacement property must consist of another manufacturing plant that is functionally the same as the property converted.			X
Personal residence of taxpayer is condemned by a local government authority; replacement property must consist of another personal residence.			X

case, the basis of the replacement property is the same as the adjusted basis of the converted property. Direct conversion is rare in practice and usually involves condemnations. The following example illustrates the application of the rules for direct conversions.

EXAMPLE 18

T's property with an adjusted basis of $20,000 is condemned by the state. T receives property with a fair market value of $50,000 as compensation for the property taken. Since the nonrecognition of realized gain is mandatory for direct conversions, T's realized gain of $30,000 is not recognized, and the basis of the replacement property is $20,000 (adjusted basis of the condemned property). ◆

Conversion into Money. If the conversion is into money, "at the election of the taxpayer the gain shall be recognized only to the extent that the amount realized upon such conversion . . . exceeds the cost of such other property or such stock."[20] This is the usual case, and nonrecognition (postponement) is *elective.*

The basis of the replacement property is the property's cost less postponed (deferred) gain.[21] If the election to postpone gain is made, the holding period of the replacement property includes the holding period of the converted property.

Section 1033 applies *only to gains* and *not to losses.* Losses from involuntary conversions are recognized if the property is held for business or income-producing purposes. Personal casualty losses are recognized, but condemnation losses related to personal use assets (e.g., a personal residence) are neither recognized nor postponed.

Examples 19 and 20 illustrate the application of the involuntary conversion rules.

EXAMPLE 19

T's building (used in his trade or business), with an adjusted basis of $50,000, is destroyed by fire in 1992. T is a calendar year taxpayer. In 1992, T receives an insurance reimbursement for the loss in the amount of $100,000. T invests $80,000 in a new building.

- T has until December 31, 1994, to make the new investment and qualify for the nonrecognition election.
- T's realized gain is $50,000 ($100,000 insurance proceeds received less $50,000 adjusted basis of old building).
- Assuming the replacement property qualifies as similar or related in service or use, T's recognized gain is $20,000. T reinvested $20,000 less than the insurance proceeds received ($100,000 proceeds minus $80,000 reinvested). Therefore, his realized gain is recognized to that extent.
- T's basis in the new building is $50,000. This is the building's cost of $80,000 less the postponed gain of $30,000 (realized gain of $50,000 less recognized gain of $20,000).
- The computation of realization, recognition, and basis would apply even if T was a real estate dealer and the building destroyed by fire was part of his inventory. Unlike § 1031, § 1033 generally does not exclude inventory. ◆

EXAMPLE 20

Assume the same facts as in the previous example, except that T receives only $45,000 (instead of $100,000) of insurance proceeds. T has a realized and recognized loss of $5,000. The basis of the new building is the building's cost of $80,000. If the destroyed

20. § 1033(a)(2)(A) and Reg. § 1.1033(a)–2(c)(1).

21. § 1033(b).

building was held for personal use, the recognized loss is subject to other limitations.[22] The loss of $5,000 is limited to the decline in fair market value of the property, and the amount of the loss is reduced first by $100 and then by 10% of adjusted gross income (refer to Chapter 8). ◆

Although the previous discussion describes an indirect conversion as a conversion into money, § 1033 refers to indirect conversions as conversions "into money or other property not similar or related in service or use to the converted property. . . . "[23] An indirect conversion into other than money would be rare, but it could occur and is treated the same as a conversion into money.

Involuntary Conversion of a Personal Residence

The tax consequences of the involuntary conversion of a personal residence depend upon whether the conversion is a casualty or condemnation and whether a realized loss or gain results.

Loss Situations. If the conversion is a condemnation, the realized loss is not recognized. Loss from the condemnation of a personal use asset is never recognized. If the conversion is a casualty (a loss from fire, storm, etc.), the loss is recognized subject to the personal casualty loss limitations.

Gain Situations. If the conversion is a condemnation, the gain may be postponed under either § 1033 or § 1034. That is, the taxpayer may elect to treat the condemnation as a sale under the deferral of gain rules relating to the sale of a personal residence under § 1034 (presented subsequently). If the conversion is a casualty, the gain is postponed only under the involuntary conversion provisions.

Reporting Considerations

An election to postpone gain normally is made on the return for the taxable year in which gain is realized. The taxpayer should attach to the return a statement that includes supportive details. If the property has not been replaced before filing the tax return, the taxpayer should also attach a supporting statement to the return for the taxable year in which the property is replaced.

If the property either is not replaced within the prescribed time period or is replaced at a cost less than anticipated, an amended return must be filed for the taxable year in which the election was made. A taxpayer who has elected § 1033 postponement and makes an appropriate replacement may not later revoke the election. In addition, once the taxpayer has designated qualifying property as replacement property, he or she cannot later change the designation.[24] If no election is made on the return for the taxable year in which gain is realized, an election may still be made within the prescribed time period by filing a claim for credit or refund.[25]

Involuntary conversions from casualty and theft are reported first on Form 4684, Casualties and Thefts. Casualty and theft losses on personal use property for the individual taxpayer are carried from Form 4684 to Schedule A of Form 1040. For other casualty and theft items, the Form 4684 amounts are generally

22. § 165(c)(3) and Reg. § 1.165–7.
23. § 1033(a)(2).
24. Rev.Rul. 83–39, 1983–1 C.B. 190.
25. Reg. § 1.1033(a)–2(c)(2).

reported on Form 4797, Sales of Business Property, unless Form 4797 is not required. In the latter case, the amounts are reported directly on the tax return involved.

Except for personal use property, recognized gains and losses from involuntary conversions other than by casualty and theft are reported on Form 4797. As stated previously, if the property involved in the involuntary conversion (other than by casualty and theft) is personal use property, any realized loss is not recognized. Any realized gain is treated as gain on a voluntary sale.

SALE OF A RESIDENCE—§ 1034

A realized loss from the sale of a personal residence is not recognized because the residence is personal use property. A realized gain is subject to taxation, however. The tax law includes two provisions under which all or part of the realized gain is either postponed or excluded from taxation. The first of these, § 1034, is discussed below. The second, § 121, is discussed later in the chapter.

Section 1034 provides for the *mandatory* nonrecognition of gain from the sale or exchange of a personal residence if the sales proceeds are reinvested in a replacement residence within a prescribed time period. Both the old and new residences must qualify as the taxpayer's principal residence. A houseboat or house trailer qualifies if it is used by the taxpayer as a principal residence.[26]

The reason for not recognizing gain when a residence is replaced by a new residence within the prescribed time period (discussed below) is that the new residence is viewed as a continuation of the investment. Also, if the proceeds from the sale are reinvested, the taxpayer does not have the wherewithal to pay tax on the realized gain. Beyond these fundamental concepts, Congress, in enacting § 1034, was concerned with the hardship of involuntary moves and the socially desirable objective of encouraging the mobility of labor.

Replacement Period

For the nonrecognition treatment to apply, the old residence must be replaced by a new residence within a period *beginning two years before* the sale of the old residence and *ending two years after* the sale. This four-year period applies regardless of whether the new residence is purchased or constructed. In addition to *acquiring* the residence during this period, the taxpayer must *occupy* and use the new residence as the principal residence during this same time period. The occupancy requirement has been strictly construed by both the IRS and the courts, and even circumstances beyond a taxpayer's control do not excuse noncompliance.[27]

EXAMPLE 21

T sells her personal residence from which she realizes a gain of $50,000. The construction of a new residence begins immediately after the sale. However, unstable soil conditions and a trade union strike cause unforeseen delays in construction. The new residence ultimately is completed and occupied by T 25 months after the sale of the old residence. Since the occupancy requirement has not been satisfied, § 1034 is inapplicable, and T must recognize a gain of $50,000 on the sale of the old residence. ◆

Taxpayers might be inclined to make liberal use of § 1034 as a means of speculating when the price of residential housing is rising. Without any time

26. Reg. § 1.1034–1(c)(3)(i).

27. *James A. Henry*, 44 TCM 844, T.C.Memo. 1982–469, and *William F. Peck*, 44 TCM 1030, T.C.Memo. 1982–506.

restriction on its use, § 1034 would permit deferral of gain on multiple sales of principal residences, each one of which would result in an economic profit. The Code curbs this approach by precluding the application of § 1034 to any sales occurring within two years of its last use.

EXAMPLE 22

After T sells his principal residence (the first residence) in March 1991 for $150,000 (realized gain of $60,000), he buys and sells the following (all of which qualify as principal residences):

	Date of Purchase	Date of Sale	Amount Involved
Second residence	April 1991		$160,000
Second residence		May 1992	180,000
Third residence	June 1992		200,000

Because multiple sales have occurred within a period of two years, § 1034 does not apply to the sale of the second residence. Thus, the realized gain of $20,000 [$180,000 (selling price) − $160,000 (purchase price)] must be recognized. ◆

The two-year rule precluding multiple use of § 1034 could create a hardship where a taxpayer is transferred by his or her employer and has little choice in the matter. For this reason, § 1034 was amended to provide an exception to the two-year rule when the sale results from a change in the location of employment. To qualify for the exception, a taxpayer must meet the distance and length-of-employment requirements specified for the deduction of moving expenses under § 217.[28]

EXAMPLE 23

Assume the same facts as in the previous example, except that in February 1992, T's employer transfers T to a job in another state. Consequently, the sale of the second residence and the purchase of the third residence were due to the relocation of employment. If T satisfies the distance and length-of-employment requirements of § 217, no gain is recognized on the sale of the first and second residences. ◆

The running of the time periods specified above (other than the two-year limit on multiple sales) is suspended during any time the taxpayer or spouse is on extended active duty (over 90 days or for an indefinite period) with the U.S. Armed Forces after the date the old residence is sold.[29] This suspension is limited to four years after the date the old residence is sold. A similar suspension is available to U.S. citizens who are employed outside the United States by nongovernmental employers (expatriates).[30]

EXAMPLE 24

T, an employee of F Corporation, sold his principal residence in Baltimore on July 5, 1992, because he had been transferred to the Berlin office on a one-year assignment. T returns to the United States on July 1, 1993, after completing the assignment. The latest date for a qualifying replacement is July 1, 1995 (i.e., two years after the end of the suspension period). ◆

28. Refer to Chapter 10 for the discussion of the rules governing the deduction for moving expenses.

29. § 1034(h)(1).

30. § 1034(k).

EXAMPLE 25

Assume the same facts as in the previous example, except that the assignment is for a three-year period. Therefore, T returns to the United States on July 1, 1995, after completing the assignment. Two years after the end of the suspension period is July 1, 1997. However, since the suspension period exception cannot result in extending the replacement time period beyond four years after the date the principal residence was sold, the latest date for a qualifying replacement is July 5, 1996. ◆

In one circumstance, the four-year limitation is extended for members of the U.S. Armed Forces. If they are stationed outside the United States or are required thereafter to reside in government quarters at a remote site, the four-year period is replaced with an eight-year period.[31]

Principal Residence

Both the old and new residences must qualify as the taxpayer's principal residence. Whether property is the taxpayer's principal residence depends ". . . upon all the facts and circumstances in each case."[32]

EXAMPLE 26

T sells his principal residence and moves to Norfolk, Virginia, where he is employed. He decides to rent an apartment in Norfolk because of its proximity to his place of employment. He purchases a beach house in Virginia Beach that he occupies most weekends. T does not intend to live in the beach house other than on weekends. The apartment in Norfolk is his principal place of residence. Therefore, the purchase of the beach house does not qualify as an appropriate replacement. ◆

If the old residence ceases to be the taxpayer's principal residence before its sale, the nonrecognition provision does not apply. For example, if the taxpayer abandons the old residence before its sale, the residence no longer qualifies as a principal residence.[33] If the old residence is converted to other than personal use (e.g., rental) before its sale, the nonrecognition provision does not apply. If the residence is only partially converted to business use, gain from the sale of the personal use portion still qualifies for nonrecognition. It is possible to convert part of a principal residence to business use and later to convert that part back to being part of the principal residence (e.g., a home office).[34]

Temporarily renting out the old residence before sale does not necessarily terminate its status as the taxpayer's principal residence,[35] nor does temporarily renting out the new residence before it is occupied by the taxpayer. An issue associated with temporarily renting out the old residence while attempting to sell it is whether a taxpayer is entitled to deduct expenses in excess of income relating to the rental of a residence before its sale. That is, is the old residence subject to the loss deduction rules for hobby loss activities? If it is, the deductions associated with the rental activity are limited to the rent income generated. The Tax Court concluded that since the property was considered to be the taxpayer's principal residence and as a result qualified for § 1034

31. § 1034(h)(2).

32. Reg. § 1.1034–1(c)(3).

33. *Richard T. Houlette*, 48 T.C. 350 (1967), and *Stolk v. Comm.*, 64–1 USTC ¶9228, 13 AFTR2d 535, 326 F.2d 760 (CA–2, 1964).

34. Rev.Rul. 82–26, 1982–1 C.B. 114.

35. *Robert W. Aagaard*, 56 T.C. 191 (1971), *acq.* 1971–2 C.B. 1; *Robert G. Clapham*, 63 T.C. 505 (1975); Rev.Rul. 59–72, 1959–1 C.B. 203; and Rev.Rul. 78–146, 1978–1 C.B. 260.

postponement of gain, the property was subject to the hobby loss limitations. The Court of Appeals reversed the Tax Court and held that the hobby loss provisions did not apply.[36]

Nonrecognition of Gain Requirements

Realized gain from the sale of the old residence is not recognized if the taxpayer reinvests an amount *at least equal* to the adjusted sales price of the old residence. Realized gain is recognized to the extent the taxpayer does not reinvest an amount at least equal to the adjusted sales price in a new residence. Therefore, the amount not reinvested is treated similarly to boot received in a like-kind exchange.

The *adjusted sales price* is the amount realized from the sale of the old residence less fixing-up expenses. The *amount realized* is calculated by reducing the selling price by the selling expenses. *Selling expenses* include items such as advertising the property for sale, real estate broker commissions, legal fees in connection with the sale, and loan placement fees paid by the taxpayer as a condition of the arrangement of financing for the buyer. To the extent that the selling expenses are deducted as moving expenses, they are not allowed as deductions in the computation of the amount realized (refer to Chapter 10).

Fixing-up expenses are personal in nature and are incurred by the taxpayer to assist in the sale of the old residence. Fixing-up expenses include such items as ordinary repairs, painting, and wallpapering. To qualify as a fixing-up expense, the expense must (1) be incurred for work performed during the 90-day period ending on the date of the contract of sale, (2) be paid within 30 days after the date of the sale, and (3) not be a capital expenditure.

Although selling expenses are deductible in calculating the amount realized, fixing-up expenses are not. Therefore, fixing-up expenses do not have an impact on the calculation of realized gain or loss. However, since fixing-up expenses are deductible in calculating the adjusted sales price, they do have the potential for producing tax benefit in that they reduce the amount of the reinvestment required to qualify for nonrecognition treatment. Conversely, if a replacement residence is not acquired, the fixing-up expenses produce no tax benefit.

Reducing the amount of the required reinvestment by the amount of fixing-up expenses is another application of the wherewithal to pay concept. To the extent that the taxpayer has expended part of the funds received from the sale in preparing the old residence for sale, he or she does not have the funds available to reinvest in the new residence.

As previously mentioned, fixing-up expenses are not considered in determining realized gain. They are considered only in determining how much realized gain is to be postponed. In addition, fixing-up expenses have no direct effect on the basis of the new residence. Indirectly, through their effect on postponed gain, they can bring about a lesser basis for the new residence. The effects of fixing-up expenses on the computation of gain realized and recognized and on basis are illustrated in Concept Summary 15–2 and in Example 27.

Capital Improvements

Capital improvements are added to the adjusted basis of a personal residence. The adjusted basis is used in computing gain or loss on a subsequent sale or

36. *Bolaris v. Comm.*, 85–2 USTC ¶9822, 56 AFTR2d 85–6472, 776 F.2d 1428 (CA–9, 1985).

other disposition of the property. In calculating the cost of a replacement residence (for determining the nonrecognition of gain under § 1034), only capital improvements made during a certain time period are counted. The time period begins two years before the date of sale of the old residence and ends two years after that date (the time period during which the old residence can be replaced).[37]

If the taxpayer receives a residence by gift or inheritance, the residence will not qualify as a replacement residence. However, if the taxpayer makes substantial capital expenditures (e.g., reconstruction or additions) to the property within the replacement time period, these expenditures do qualify.[38]

Basis and Holding Period of the New Residence

The *basis* of the new residence is the cost of the new residence less the realized gain not recognized (postponed gain). If there is any postponed gain, the *holding period* of the new residence includes the holding period of the old residence.

Concept Summary 15–2 summarizes the sale-of-residence concepts. Example 27 illustrates these concepts and the application of the nonrecognition provision.

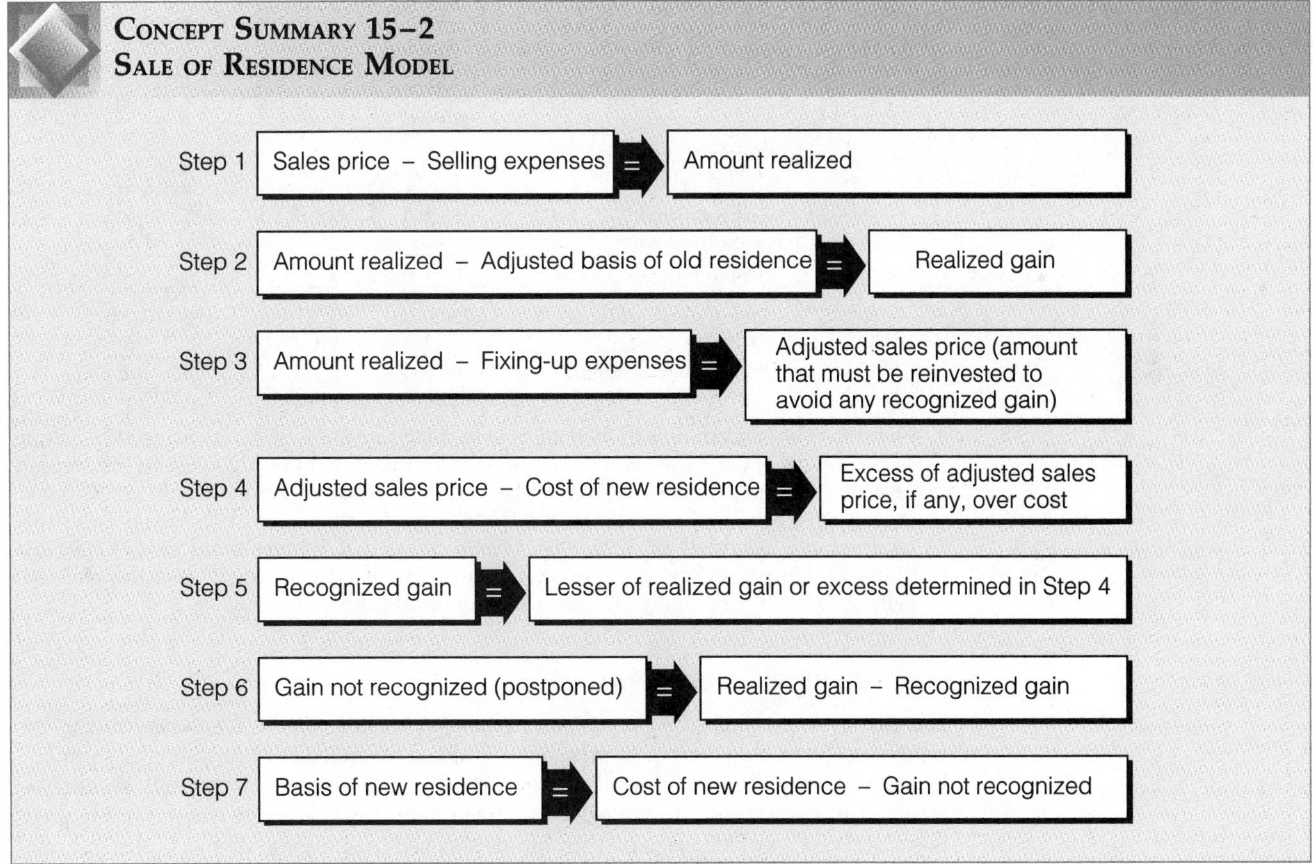

CONCEPT SUMMARY 15–2
SALE OF RESIDENCE MODEL
Step 1
Sales price − Selling expenses
=
Amount realized
Step 2
Amount realized − Adjusted basis of old residence
=
Realized gain
Step 3
Amount realized − Fixing-up expenses
=
Adjusted sales price (amount that must be reinvested to avoid any recognized gain)
Step 4
Adjusted sales price − Cost of new residence
=
Excess of adjusted sales price, if any, over cost
Step 5
Recognized gain
=
Lesser of realized gain or excess determined in Step 4
Step 6
Gain not recognized (postponed)
=
Realized gain − Recognized gain
Step 7
Basis of new residence
=
Cost of new residence − Gain not recognized

37. *Charles M. Shaw,* 69 T.C. 1034 (1978); Reg. § 1.1034–1(c)(4)(ii); and Rev.Rul. 78–147, 1978–1 C.B. 261.

38. Reg. §§ 1.1034–1(b)(7) and (9) and 1.1034–1(c)(4)(i).

EXAMPLE 27

T, age 47, sells her personal residence (adjusted basis of $136,000) for $244,000. She receives only $229,400 after paying a brokerage fee of $14,600. Ten days before the sale, T incurred and paid for qualified fixing-up expenses of $3,400. Two months later, T acquires a new residence. Determine the gain, if any, T must recognize and the basis of the new residence under each of the following circumstances:

1. The new residence costs $230,000.
2. The new residence costs $210,000.
3. The new residence costs $110,000.

		1	2	3
Step 1:	Sales price	$ 244,000	$ 244,000	$ 244,000
	– Selling expenses	(14,600)	(14,600)	(14,600)
	= Amount realized	$ 229,400	$ 229,400	$ 229,400
Step 2:	Amount realized	$ 229,400	$ 229,400	$ 229,400
	– Adjusted basis	(136,000)	(136,000)	(136,000)
	= Realized gain	$ 93,400	$ 93,400	$ 93,400
Step 3:	Amount realized	$ 229,400	$ 229,400	$ 229,400
	– Fixing-up expenses	(3,400)	(3,400)	(3,400)
	= Adjusted sales price	$ 226,000	$ 226,000	$ 226,000
Step 4:	Adjusted sales price	$ 226,000	$ 226,000	$ 226,000
	– Cost of new residence	(230,000)	(210,000)	(110,000)
	= Excess of ASP over cost	$ -0-	$ 16,000	$ 116,000
Step 5:	Recognized gain (lesser of Step 2 or Step 4)	$ -0-	$ 16,000	$ 93,400
Step 6:	Realized gain	$ 93,400	$ 93,400	$ 93,400
	– Recognized gain	(-0-)	(16,000)	(93,400)
	= Postponed gain	$ 93,400	$ 77,400	$ -0-
Step 7:	Cost of new residence	$ 230,000	$ 210,000	$ 110,000
	– Postponed gain	(93,400)	(77,400)	(-0-)
	= Basis of new residence	$ 136,600	$ 132,600	$ -0-

None of the realized gain of $93,400 is recognized in the first case because the actual reinvestment of $230,000 exceeds the required reinvestment of $226,000. In the second case, the recognized gain is $16,000 because the required reinvestment of $226,000 exceeds the actual reinvestment of $210,000 by this amount. In the third case, the required reinvestment of $226,000 exceeds the actual reinvestment of $110,000 by $116,000. Since this amount is greater than the realized gain of $93,400, the realized gain of $93,400 is recognized, and § 1034 deferral does not apply. ◆

Reporting Procedures

The taxpayer is required to report the details of the sale of the residence on the tax return for the taxable year in which gain is realized, even if all of the gain is postponed. If a new residence is acquired and occupied before filing, a statement should be attached to the return showing the purchase date, the cost, and date of occupancy. Form 2119, Sale or Exchange of Your Home, is used to show the details of the sale and replacement, and the taxpayer should retain a copy permanently as support for the basis of the new residence. If a replacement residence has not been purchased by the time the return is filed, the taxpayer should submit the details of the purchase on the return of the taxable year during which it occurs. If the old residence is not replaced within the prescribed time period, or if some recognized gain results, the taxpayer must file an amended return for the year in which the sale took place.

Sale of a Residence—§ 121

Taxpayers age 55 or older who sell or exchange their principal residence may *elect to exclude* up to $125,000 ($62,500 for married individuals filing separate returns) of realized gain from the sale or exchange.[39] The election can be made *only once.*[40] This provision differs from § 1034 where nonrecognition is mandatory and may occur many times during a taxpayer's lifetime. Section 121 also differs from § 1034 in that it does not require the taxpayer to purchase a new residence. The excluded gain is never recognized, whereas the realized gain not recognized under § 1034 is postponed by subtracting it from the cost of the new residence in calculating the adjusted basis.

This provision is the only case in the tax law where a realized gain from the disposition of property that is not recognized is excluded rather than merely postponed. The provision allows the taxpayer a permanent recovery of more than the cost or other basis of the residence tax-free.

Congress enacted § 121 simply to relieve older citizens of the large tax they might incur from the sale of a personal residence. The dollar and age limitations restrict the benefit of § 121 to taxpayers who presumably have a greater need for increased tax-free dollars.

Exclusion Requirements

The taxpayer must be at least age 55 before the date of the sale and have *owned* and *used* the residence as a principal residence for at least *three years* during the *five-year* period ending on the date of sale. The ownership and use periods do not have to be the same period of time. Short temporary absences (e.g., vacations) count as periods of use. If the residence is owned jointly by husband and wife, only one of the spouses is required to meet these requirements if a joint return is filed for the taxable year in which the sale took place.

In determining whether the ownership and use period requirements are satisfied, transactions affecting prior residences may be relevant. If a former residence is involuntarily converted and any gain is postponed under § 1033, the holding period of the former residence is added to the holding period of the replacement residence for § 121 purposes. However, if the realized gain is postponed under § 1034 (sale of residence provision), the holding period of the former residence is not added to the holding period of the replacement residence for § 121 purposes. In this instance, the holding period of the replacement residence begins with the acquisition date of the replacement residence.

Example 28

T has lived in his residence since 1984. The residence is involuntarily converted in July 1992. T purchases a replacement residence in August 1992. When the replacement residence is subequently sold, T includes the holding period of the involuntarily converted residence in determining whether he can satisfy the ownership and use requirements. ◆

Example 29

Assume the same facts as in the previous example, except that T's residence was not involuntarily converted. Instead, T sold it so that he could move into a larger house. When the replacement residence is subsequently sold, T is not permitted to include the holding period of the old residence in determining whether he can satisfy the ownership and use requirements. ◆

39. §§ 121(a), (b), and (c). For married taxpayers, each spouse must consent.

40. § 121(b)(2) and Reg. § 1.121–2(b). Only one election may be made by married individuals.

Relationship to Other Provisions

The taxpayer can treat an involuntary conversion of a principal residence as a sale for purposes of § 121. Any gain not excluded under § 121 is then subject to postponement under § 1033 or § 1034 (condemnation only), assuming the requirements of those provisions are met.

Any gain not excluded under § 121 from the sale of a residence is subject to postponement under § 1034, assuming the requirements of that provision are met. Examples 30 and 31 illustrate this relationship.

Making and Revoking the Election

The election not to recognize gain under § 121 may be made or revoked at any time before the statute of limitations expires. Therefore, the taxpayer generally has until the *later* of (1) three years from the due date of the return for the year the gain is realized or (2) two years from the date the tax is paid to make or revoke the election. The election is made by attaching a signed statement (showing all the details of the sale) to the return for the taxable year in which the sale took place. Form 2119 is used for this purpose. The election is revoked by filing a signed statement (showing the taxpayer's name, Social Security number, and taxable year for which the election was made) indicating the revocation.[41]

Computation Procedure

The following examples illustrate the application of both the § 121 and § 1034 provisions.

EXAMPLE 30

T sells his personal residence (adjusted basis of $32,000) for $205,000, of which he receives only $195,400 after the payment of selling expenses. Ten days before the sale, T incurred and paid for qualified fixing-up expenses of $6,400. T is age 55 and elects the exclusion of gain under § 121. He does not acquire a replacement residence. ◆

EXAMPLE 31

Assume the same facts as in the previous example, except that T acquires a new residence for $40,000 within the prescribed time period.

The solutions to Examples 30 and 31 are as follows:

	Example 30	Example 31
Amount realized ($205,000 − $9,600)	$ 195,400	$ 195,400
Adjusted basis	(32,000)	(32,000)
Realized gain	$ 163,400	$ 163,400
§ 121 exclusion	(125,000)	(125,000)
Realized gain after exclusion	$ 38,400	$ 38,400
Amount realized	$ 195,400	$ 195,400
Fixing-up expenses	(6,400)	(6,400)
Adjusted sales price	$ 189,000	$ 189,000
§ 121 exclusion	(125,000)	(125,000)
Adjusted sales price after exclusion	$ 64,000	$ 64,000
Cost of new residence	(–0–)	(40,000)
Excess of adjusted sales price after the exclusion over reinvestment	$ 64,000	$ 24,000

41. Reg. §§ 1.121–4(b) and (c).

	Example 30	Example 31
Recognized gain (lower of realized gain after exclusion or above excess)	$ 38,400	$ 24,000
Realized gain after exclusion	$ 38,400	$ 38,400
Recognized gain	(38,400)	(24,000)
Postponed gain	$ -0-	$ 14,400
Cost of new residence	$ -0-	$ 40,000
Postponed gain	(-0-)	(14,400)
Basis of new residence	$ -0-	$ 25,600

◆

Comparing the results of Examples 30 and 31 provides insight into the relationship between § 1034 and § 121. If T had not made the election to postpone gain under § 121 in Example 30, his recognized gain would have been $163,400 (the realized gain). Thus, the election resulted in the permanent exclusion of the $125,000 of realized gain by reducing the recognized gain to $38,400. Further documentation of the permanent nature of the § 121 exclusion is provided in the calculation of the basis of the new residence in Example 31. The $40,000 cost of the residence is reduced only by the postponed gain of $14,400. That is, it is not reduced by the amount of the § 121 exclusion. To postpone all of the $38,400 realized gain after the exclusion, T would have needed to reinvest $64,000 (the adjusted sales price after the exclusion). Also, note that the Example 30 results demonstrate that the realized gain after the exclusion is the ceiling on recognition.

OTHER NONRECOGNITION PROVISIONS

◆

The typical taxpayer experiences the sale of a residence or an involuntary conversion more frequently than the other types of nontaxable exchanges. Several additional nonrecognition provisions that are not as common are treated briefly in the remainder of this chapter.

Exchange of Stock for Property—§ 1032

Under § 1032, a corporation does not recognize gain or loss on the receipt of money or other property in exchange for its stock (including treasury stock). In other words, a corporation does not recognize gain or loss when it deals in its own stock. This provision is consistent with the accounting treatment of such transactions.

Certain Exchanges of Insurance Policies—§ 1035

Under this provision, no gain or loss is recognized from the exchange of certain insurance contracts or policies. The rules relating to exchanges not solely in kind and the basis of the property acquired are the same as under § 1031. Exchanges qualifying for nonrecognition include the following:

- The exchange of life insurance contracts.
- The exchange of a life insurance contract for an endowment or annuity contract.
- The exchange of an endowment contract for another endowment contract that provides for regular payments beginning at a date not later than the date payments would have begun under the contract exchanged.
- The exchange of an endowment contract for an annuity contract.
- The exchange of annuity contracts.

Exchange of Stock for Stock of the Same Corporation—§ 1036

A shareholder does not recognize gain or loss on the exchange of common stock solely for common stock in the same corporation or from the exchange of preferred stock for preferred stock in the same corporation. Exchanges between individual shareholders as well as between a shareholder and the corporation are included. The rules relating to exchanges not solely in kind and the basis of the property acquired are the same as under § 1031. For example, a nonrecognition exchange occurs when common stock with different rights, such as voting for nonvoting, is exchanged. A shareholder usually recognizes gain or loss from the exchange of common for preferred or preferred for common even though the stock exchanged is in the same corporation.

Certain Reacquisitions of Real Property—§ 1038

Under this provision, no loss is recognized from the repossession of real property sold on an installment basis. Gain is recognized to a limited extent.

Transfers of Property between Spouses or Incident to Divorce—§ 1041

Section 1041 provides that transfers of property *between spouses or former spouses incident to divorce* are nontaxable transactions. Therefore, the basis to the recipient is a carryover basis. To be treated as incident to the divorce, the transfer must be related to the cessation of marriage or occur within one year after the date on which the marriage ceases.

Section 1041 also provides for nontaxable exchange treatment on property transfers *between spouses during marriage.* The basis to the recipient spouse is a carryover basis.

Sale of Stock to Stock Ownership Plans or Certain Cooperatives—§ 1042

Section 1042 provides that the realized gain will be postponed if the taxpayer (or his or her executor) sells qualified securities to a qualified entity and, within a specified time period, purchases qualified replacement property. Qualified entities include an employee stock ownership plan (ESOP) and an eligible worker-owned cooperative. To qualify for this treatment, several statutory requirements must be satisfied.

Chapter 15 has covered certain situations in which realized gains or losses are not recognized (nontaxable exchanges). Chapters 16 and 17 are concerned with the *classification* of recognized gains and losses. That is, if a gain or loss is recognized, is it an ordinary or capital gain or loss? Chapter 16 discusses the tax consequences of capital gains and losses.

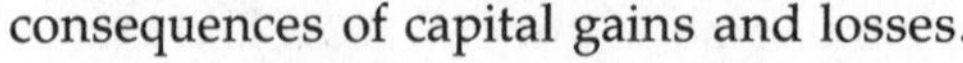

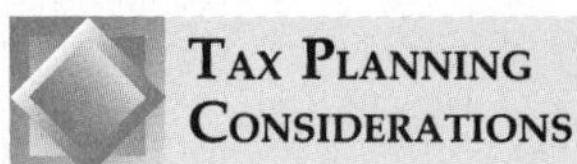

TAX PLANNING CONSIDERATIONS

Like-Kind Exchanges

Since application of the like-kind provisions is mandatory rather than elective, in certain instances it may be preferable to avoid qualifying for § 1031 nonrecognition. If the like-kind provisions do not apply, the end result may be the recognition of capital gain in exchange for a higher basis in the newly acquired asset. Also, the immediate recognition of gain may be preferable in certain situations. Examples where immediate recognition is beneficial include the following:

- Taxpayer has unused net operating loss carryovers.
- Taxpayer has unused general business credit carryovers.
- Taxpayer has suspended or current passive activity losses.
- Taxpayer expects his or her effective tax rate to increase in the future.

EXAMPLE 32

T disposes of a machine (used in his business) with an adjusted basis of $3,000 for $4,000. T also acquires a new business machine for $9,000. If § 1031 applies, the $1,000 realized gain is not recognized, and the basis of the new machine is reduced by $1,000 (from $9,000 to $8,000). If § 1031 does not apply, a $1,000 gain is recognized and may receive favorable capital gain treatment to the extent that the gain is not recognized as ordinary income due to the depreciation recapture provisions (see Chapter 17). In addition, the basis for depreciation on the new machine is $9,000 rather than $8,000 since there is no unrecognized gain. ◆

The application of § 1031 nonrecognition treatment should also be avoided when the adjusted basis of the property being disposed of exceeds the fair market value.

EXAMPLE 33

Assume the same facts as in the previous example, except the fair market value of the machine is $2,500. If § 1031 applies, the $500 realized loss is not recognized. To recognize the loss, T should sell the old machine and purchase the new one. The purchase and sale transactions should be with different taxpayers. ◆

On the other hand, the like-kind exchange procedure can be utilized to control the amount of recognized gain.

EXAMPLE 34

S has property with an adjusted basis of $40,000 and a fair market value of $100,000. P wants to buy S's property, but S wants to limit the amount of recognized gain on the proposed transaction. P acquires other like-kind property (from an outside party) for $80,000. P then exchanges this property and $20,000 cash for S's property. S has a realized gain of $60,000 ($100,000 amount realized − $40,000 adjusted basis). S's recognized gain is only $20,000, the lower of the boot received of $20,000 or the realized gain of $60,000. S's basis for the like-kind property is $40,000 ($40,000 adjusted basis + $20,000 gain recognized − $20,000 boot received). If S had sold the property to P for its fair market value of $100,000, the result would have been a $60,000 recognized gain ($100,000 amount realized − $40,000 adjusted basis) to S. It is permissible for S to identify the like-kind property that he wants P to purchase.[42] ◆

Involuntary Conversions

In certain cases, a taxpayer may prefer to recognize gain from an involuntary conversion. Keep in mind that § 1033, unlike § 1031 (dealing with like-kind exchanges), generally is an elective provision.

EXAMPLE 35

T has a $40,000 realized gain from the involuntary conversion of an office building. The entire proceeds of $450,000 are reinvested in a new office building. T, however, does not elect to postpone gain under § 1033 because of an expiring net operating loss carryover that is offset against the gain. Therefore, none of the realized gain of $40,000

42. *Franklin B. Biggs*, 69 T.C. 905 (1978); Rev.Rul. 57–244, 1957–1 C.B. 247; Rev.Rul. 73–476, 1973–2 C.B. 300; *Starker vs. U.S.*, 79–2 USTC ¶9541, 44 AFTR2d 79–5525, 602 F.2d 1341 (CA–9, 1979); and *Baird Publishing Co.*, 39 T.C. 608 (1962).

is postponed. By not electing § 1033 postponement, T's basis in the replacement property is the property's cost of $450,000 rather than $410,000 ($450,000 reduced by the $40,000 realized gain). ◆

Sale of a Personal Residence

Replacement Period Requirements. Several problems arise in avoiding the recognition of gain on the sale of a principal residence. Most of these problems can be resolved favorably through appropriate planning procedures. However, a few represent situations where the taxpayer has to accept the adverse tax consequences and possesses little, if any, planning flexibility. One pitfall concerns the failure to reinvest *all* of the proceeds from the sale of the residence in a new principal residence.

EXAMPLE 36

R sells her principal residence in January 1990 for $150,000 (adjusted basis of $40,000). Shortly thereafter, R purchases for $100,000 a 50-year-old house in a historical part of the community that she uses as her principal residence. R intends to significantly renovate the property over a period of time and make it more suitable to her living needs. In December 1992, R enters into a contract with a home improvement company to carry out the renovation at a cost of $60,000. It is clear that only $100,000 of the proceeds from the sale of the old residence has been reinvested in a new principal residence on a *timely* basis. Of the realized gain of $110,000, therefore, $50,000 ($150,000 adjusted sales price − $100,000 reinvested) must be recognized.[43] ◆

One problem that a taxpayer may not be in a position to do anything about is the acquisition of property *before* the beginning of the replacement period. Recall that the replacement period begins two years before the sale and ends two years after the sale.

EXAMPLE 37

T's employer transfers T to a different city in July 1990, at which time T lists his house for sale with a realtor. T purchases a principal residence in the city to which he is transferred in September 1990. Because of market conditions, T is unable to sell his original residence until December 1992. Since the sale does not occur within two years of the purchase, the residence T purchased in September 1990 is not a qualifying replacement residence. ◆

Principal Residence Requirement. Section 1034 will not apply unless the property involved is the taxpayer's principal residence. A potential hurdle arises in cases where the residence has been rented and therefore has not been occupied by the taxpayer for an extended period of time. Depending on the circumstances, the IRS may contend that the taxpayer has abandoned the property as his or her principal residence. The *key* to the abandonment issue is whether or not the taxpayer intended to reoccupy the property and use it as a principal residence upon returning to the locale. If the residence is, in fact, not reoccupied, the taxpayer should have a good reason to explain why it is not.

EXAMPLE 38

T is transferred by her employer to another office out of the state on a three-year assignment. It is the understanding of the parties that the assignment is temporary,

43. It has been assumed that § 121 did not apply.

and upon its completion, T will return to the original job site. During her absence, T rents her principal residence and lives in an apartment at the new location. T has every intention of reoccupying her residence. However, when she returns from the temporary assignment, she finds that the residence no longer suits her needs. Specifically, the public school located nearby where she had planned to send her children has been closed. As a consequence, T sells the residence and replaces it with one more conveniently located to a public school. Under these circumstances, it would appear that T is in an excellent position to show that she has not abandoned the property as her principal residence. She can satisfactorily explain why she did not reoccupy the residence before its sale.[44] ◆

The principal residence requirement can cause difficulty when a taxpayer works in two places and maintains more than one household. In such cases, the principal residence will be the location where the taxpayer lives most of the time.[45]

EXAMPLE 39

E is a vice president of Z Corporation and in this capacity spends about an equal amount of time in the company's New York City and Miami offices. E owns a house in each location and expects to retire in about five years. At that time, he plans to sell his New York home and use some of the proceeds to make improvements on the Miami property. Both homes have appreciated in value since their acquisition, and E expects the appreciation to continue. From a tax planning standpoint, E should be looking toward the use of §§ 121 and 1034 to shelter some or all of the gain he will realize on the future sale of the New York City home.[46] To do this, he should arrange his affairs so as to spend more than six months each year at that location. Upon its sale, therefore, the New York home will be his principal residence. ◆

Section 121 Considerations. Older individuals who may be contemplating a move from their home to an apartment should consider the following possibilities for minimizing or deferring taxes:

- Wait until age 55 to sell the residence and elect under § 121 to exclude up to $125,000 of the realized gain.
- Sell the personal residence under an installment contract to spread the gain over several years.[47]
- Sell the personal residence and purchase a condominium instead of renting an apartment, thereby permitting further deferral of the unrecognized gain.

The use of § 121 should be carefully considered. Although the use avoids the immediate recognition of gain, the election expends the full $125,000 allowed.

EXAMPLE 40

In 1992 T, age 55, sells his personal residence for an amount that yields a realized gain of $5,000. Presuming T does not plan to reinvest the sales proceeds in a new principal residence (take advantage of the deferral possibility of § 1034), should he avoid the recognition of this gain by utilizing § 121? Electing § 121 means that T will waste $120,000 of his lifetime exclusion. ◆

---

44. Rev.Rul. 78–146, 1978–1 C.B. 260. Compare *Rudolph M. Stucchi*, 35 TCM 1052, T.C.Memo. 1976–242.

45. Rev.Rul. 77–298, 1977–2 C.B. 308.

46. If E qualifies, § 121 would allow the first $125,000 of gain to be excluded. Further gain might be avoided under § 1034 to the extent the sales proceeds are applied toward improvements on the Miami home.

47. § 453(a). See the discussion of the installment method in Chapter 18.

In this connection, the use of § 121 by one spouse precludes the other spouse from later taking advantage of the exclusion.

EXAMPLE 41

Assume the same facts as in the previous example, except that T was married to W at the time of the sale. Later, T and W are divorced and W marries R. If T has used the § 121 exclusion, it is unavailable to W and R even though either one of them may otherwise qualify. This result occurs because when T made the election for the 1992 sale, it was necessary for W to join with him in making the election even if the residence was owned separately by T. For W and R to be able to make the § 121 election, W and T must revoke their prior election. Another planning approach is for R to sell his residence before marrying W and to elect the exclusion on that sale. ◆

A taxpayer who is eligible to elect § 121 exclusion treatment may choose not to do so in order to remain eligible to elect it in the future. In arriving at this decision, consideration must be given to the probability that the taxpayer will satisfy the three-out-of-five-year ownership and use period requirements associated with a residence sale in the future. As previously mentioned, the holding period for the occupancy and use requirements does carry over for a § 1033 involuntary conversion but does not carry over for a § 1034 sale.

Taxpayers should maintain records of both the purchase and sale of personal residences since the sale of one residence results in an adjustment of the basis of the new residence if the deferral provisions of § 1034 apply. Form 2119 should be filed with the tax return and a copy retained as support for the basis of the new residence. Detailed cost records should be retained for an indefinite period.

PROBLEM MATERIALS

DISCUSSION QUESTIONS

1. Distinguish between the following:
   a. A nontaxable exchange and a tax-free transaction.
   b. A nontaxable exchange and a taxable transaction.
2. Distinguish between a loss that is not recognized on a nontaxable exchange and a loss that is not recognized on the sale or exchange of a personal use asset.
3. Can the exchange of property held for productive use in a trade or business for investment property qualify for like-kind exchange treatment?
4. Why would a taxpayer want to avoid like-kind exchange treatment?
5. Which of the following qualify as like-kind exchanges under § 1031?
   a. Improved for unimproved real estate.
   b. Vending machine (used in business) for inventory.
   c. Rental house for truck (used in business).
   d. Business equipment for securities.
   e. Warehouse for office building (both used for business).
   f. Personal residence for apartment building (held for investment).
   g. Rental house for land (both held for investment).
   h. Ten shares of stock in X Corporation for 10 shares of stock in Y Corporation.
6. If a taxpayer exchanges his or her personal use car for another car to be held for personal use, any realized loss is not recognized. However, if realized gain occurs, the realized gain is recognized. Why?

7. What is boot, and how does it affect the recognition of gain or loss on a like-kind exchange when received by the taxpayer? How is the recognition of gain or loss affected when boot is given?
8. The receipt of boot in a like-kind exchange triggers the recognition of realized gain. If the boot received is greater than the realized gain, do the nontaxable exchange provisions produce a more favorable tax result than the taxable sale of one asset and the purchase of another asset?
9. Why does the receipt of boot in a like-kind exchange trigger the recognition of realized gain but does not trigger the recognition of realized loss?
10. The receipt of boot in a § 1031 exchange triggers the recognition of realized gain. The gain recognition will affect the basis of the property received by the taxpayer.

    a. Discuss the relationship between the realized gain and the boot received if the boot received is greater than the realized gain.
    b. Discuss the relationship between the realized gain and the boot received if the boot received is less than the realized gain.
    c. What effect does the recognition of gain have on the basis of the like-kind property received? Of the boot received?

11. Like-kind property received in a § 1031 exchange is assigned a carryover basis. Boot received in such an exchange is assigned a basis equal to fair market value.

    a. Discuss the equity of these different basis rules.
    b. Under what circumstances is the carryover basis for the like-kind property received equal to the fair market value of the property?

12. What is the holding period of like-kind property received in a like-kind exchange? For boot received? Why?
13. Mortgaged real estate may be received in a like-kind exchange. If the taxpayer assumes the mortgage, what effect does the mortgage have on the recognition of realized gain? On the basis of the real estate received?
14. A taxpayer's appreciated property is involuntarily converted. She receives insurance proceeds equal to the fair market value of the property. What is the minimum amount the taxpayer must reinvest in qualifying property to defer recognition of realized gain?
15. What are severance damages? How does the receipt of a severance award affect the basis of the remaining property?
16. A taxpayer's property is involved in an involuntary conversion. Are there any circumstances under which neither the functional use test nor the taxpayer use test is the appropriate test with respect to qualifying replacement property?
17. Taxpayer's warehouse is destroyed by fire. What are the different tax options available to the taxpayer (a) if he has a realized gain and (b) if he has a realized loss?
18. How long does a taxpayer have to replace involuntarily converted property and still qualify for nonrecognition of gain under § 1033?
19. Discuss the tax options available to the taxpayer when the form of the transaction is (a) a direct involuntary conversion and (b) an indirect involuntary conversion.
20. When does the holding period begin in an involuntary conversion for which the similar property rule is applicable? The like-kind property rule?
21. Z is notified by the city public housing authority on October 5, 1992, that his apartment building is going to be condemned as part of an urban renewal project. On October 12, 1992, S offers to buy the building from Z. Z sells the building to S on October 30, 1992. Condemnation occurs on February 1, 1993, and S receives the condemnation proceeds from the city. Assume both Z and S are calendar year taxpayers.

    a. What is the earliest date that Z can dispose of the building and qualify for § 1033 postponement treatment?
    b. Does the sale to S qualify as a § 1033 involuntary conversion?
    c. What is the latest date that S can acquire qualifying replacement property and qualify for postponement of the realized gain?
    d. What type of property will be qualifying replacement property?

22. How are corrections made for an involuntary conversion when a taxpayer elects to postpone gain and then does not reinvest within the time limits or does not reinvest a sufficient amount? How is postponement accomplished if reinvestment is made but postponement was not elected on the return for the taxable year in which gain was realized?
23. Discuss the justification for nonrecognition of gain on the sale or exchange of a principal residence. Discuss the justification for disallowance of loss.
24. Discuss all of the requirements for the replacement period of both purchased and constructed residences. Are there any exceptions?
25. T sells his principal residence on September 18, 1992. Although he does not replace it until August 19, 1996, the replacement qualifies for postponement treatment under § 1034. Discuss how this replacement could satisfy the residence replacement period requirement.
26. What is a principal residence? Can a taxpayer have more than one principal residence at one point in time?
27. J has owned and occupied a house as her principal residence for 10 years. She purchases a new residence in March 1992. She initially listed her old residence with a realtor in January 1992. Needing the cash flow, she rents the old residence to K for a six-month period beginning in March. She sells the old residence to P upon the expiration of the rental period in September. Does the sale of the old residence in September qualify as the sale of a principal residence?
28. Define each of the following associated with the sale of a residence:

    a. Amount realized.
    b. Adjusted sales price.
    c. Fixing-up expenses.

29. Explain how the following are determined on the sale or exchange of a residence:

    a. Realized gain.
    b. Recognized gain.
    c. Postponed gain.
    d. Basis of new residence.

30. Discuss the basis calculation formula as it applies to a new residence if:

    a. Realized gain is postponed.
    b. Realized loss is disallowed.
    c. Realized gain is recognized because the new residence is not acquired within the two-year time period from the sale of the old residence.

31. Can capital expenditures made to a house received by gift enable the taxpayer to qualify for postponement treatment under § 1034?
32. N sells his principal residence on September 7, 1992. In early December, his aunt gives him a house that he occupies immediately as his principal residence. Will this ownership and occupancy enable N to postpone the realized gain on the residence sale on September 7, 1992?
33. What does the § 121 exclusion cover? Is it elective? Does the old residence have to be replaced?
34. How many times can § 121 exclusion treatment be elected by a taxpayer? If the taxpayer is filing a joint return with his or her spouse, do both taxpayers have to meet the ownership and use requirements?
35. T converts her principal residence to rental property at the beginning of 1991 and sells the residence on the last day of 1992. Under what circumstances can T qualify for the § 121 exclusion?
36. A and B, both age 60, are sisters who live in the house they inherited from their parents 20 years ago. H and W, age 60, are married. They purchased their principal residence 7 years ago. Comment on any differences in the application of the § 121 exclusion to the sisters and the married couple.

Problems

37. C owns undeveloped land with an adjusted basis of $70,000. She exchanges it for other undeveloped land worth $145,000.

 a. What are C's realized and recognized gain or loss?
 b. What is C's basis in the undeveloped land she receives?

38. R owns an automobile that she uses exclusively in her business. The adjusted basis is $11,000, and the fair market value is $5,000. R exchanges the car for a light-duty truck that she will use exclusively in her business.

 a. What are R's realized and recognized gain or loss?
 b. What is her basis in the truck?
 c. What are the tax consequences to R in (a) and (b) if she will use the light-duty truck exclusively for personal purposes?

39. L owns a personal computer that he uses exclusively in his business. The adjusted basis is $3,000. L transfers the personal computer and cash of $2,000 to D for a laser printer worth $6,000 that he will use in his business.

 a. Calculate L's recognized gain or loss on the exchange.
 b. Calculate L's basis for the printer.

40. K exchanges an automobile used exclusively in his business for a light-duty truck that will be used in his business. The adjusted basis for the automobile is $8,000, and the fair market value of the truck is $7,000.

 a. Calculate K's recognized gain or loss on the exchange.
 b. Calculate K's basis for the truck.

41. T owns a car that she uses exclusively for personal purposes. Its original cost was $15,000, and the fair market value is $7,000. She exchanges the car and $18,000 cash for a new car.

 a. Calculate T's realized and recognized gain or loss.
 b. Calculate T's basis for the new car.

42. T owns land and building with an adjusted basis of $125,000 and a fair market value of $275,000. T exchanges the land and building for land with a fair market value of $175,000 that he will use as a parking lot. In addition, T receives stock worth $100,000.

 a. What is T's realized gain or loss?
 b. His recognized gain or loss?
 c. The basis of the land and the stock received?

43. D owns a machine that he uses in his business. The adjusted basis is $60,000, and the fair market value is $90,000. He exchanges it for another machine worth $50,000. D also receives cash of $40,000.

 a. Calculate D's realized and recognized gain or loss on the exchange.
 b. Calculate D's basis for the new machine.

44. T owns investment land with an adjusted basis of $35,000. P has offered to purchase the land from T for $175,000 for use in a real estate development. The amount offered by P is $10,000 in excess of what T perceives as the fair market value of the land. T would like to dispose of the land to P but does not want to incur the tax liability that would result. T identifies an office building with a fair market value of $175,000 that he would like to acquire. P purchases the office building and then exchanges the office building for T's land.

 a. Calculate T's realized and recognized gain on the exchange and T's basis for the office building.
 b. Calculate P's realized and recognized gain on the exchange and P's basis in the land.

45. What is the basis of the new property in each of the following exchanges?

a. Apartment building held for investment (adjusted basis $150,000) for lakefront property held for investment (fair market value $200,000).
b. Land and building used as a barber shop (adjusted basis $30,000) for land and building used as a grocery store (fair market value $350,000).
c. Office building (adjusted basis $30,000) for bulldozer (fair market value $42,000), both held for business use.
d. IBM common stock (adjusted basis $14,000) for Exxon common stock (fair market value $18,000).
e. Rental house (adjusted basis $90,000) for land held for investment (fair market value $115,000).

46. G owns Machine A, which he uses in his business. The adjusted basis of Machine A is $12,000, and the fair market value is $15,000. G sells Machine A for $15,000 to Q, who is a dealer. G then purchases Machine B, which would qualify as like-kind property, for $15,000 from J, who also is a dealer.

a. What are G's realized and recognized gain on the sale of Machine A?
b. What is G's basis for Machine B, which was acquired from J?
c. What factors would motivate G to sell Machine A and purchase the replacement Machine B rather than exchange one machine for the other?
d. Assume that the adjusted basis of Machine A is $15,000 and the fair market value of each machine is $12,000. Respond to (a) through (c).

47. G exchanges real estate held for investment plus stock for real estate to be held for investment. The stock transferred has an adjusted basis of $10,000 and a fair market value of $6,000. The real estate transferred has an adjusted basis of $15,000 and a fair market value of $22,000. The real estate acquired has a fair market value of $28,000.

a. What is G's realized gain or loss?
b. His recognized gain or loss?
c. The basis of the newly acquired real estate?

48. H exchanges a machine (adjusted basis of $30,000 and fair market value of $45,000) and undeveloped land held for investment (adjusted basis of $100,000 and fair market value of $305,000) for land worth $295,000 to be used in her business. The undeveloped land has a mortgage of $55,000 that the other party to the exchange assumes.

a. What is H's realized gain or loss?
b. Her recognized gain or loss?
c. The basis of the newly acquired real estate?

49. Determine the realized, recognized, and postponed gain or loss and the new basis for each of the following like-kind exchanges:

	Adjusted Basis of Old Asset	Boot Given	Fair Market Value of New Asset	Boot Received
a.	$ 7,000	$ -0-	$12,000	$4,000
b.	14,000	2,000	15,000	-0-
c.	3,000	7,000	8,000	500
d.	22,000	-0-	32,000	-0-
e.	10,000	-0-	11,000	1,000
f.	10,000	-0-	8,000	-0-

50. K owns an apartment house that has an adjusted basis of $900,000 but is subject to a mortgage of $300,000. She transfers the apartment house to D. K receives from D $125,000 in cash and an office building with a fair market value of $800,000 at the time of the exchange. D assumes the $300,000 mortgage on the apartment house.

a. What is K's realized gain or loss?
b. Her recognized gain or loss?
c. The basis of the newly acquired office building?

51. E converted her personal residence to rental property on January 1, 1991. At that time, the adjusted basis was $80,000, and the fair market value was $100,000. During the interim rental period, E deducted depreciation of $5,576. The rental property is condemned on December 31, 1992, in connection with an urban renewal project, and E receives condemnation proceeds of $60,000.

   a. What is the adjusted basis at the condemnation date?
   b. What is the recognized gain or loss on the condemnation?

52. For each of the following involuntary conversions, indicate whether the property acquired qualifies as replacement property:

   a. K owns a shopping mall that is destroyed by a tornado. The space in the mall was rented to various tenants. K uses the insurance proceeds to build a shopping mall in a neighboring community where no property has been damaged by tornadoes.
   b. L owns a warehouse that he uses in his business. The warehouse is destroyed by fire. Due to economic conditions in the area, L decides not to rebuild the warehouse. Instead, he uses the insurance proceeds to build a warehouse to be used in his business in another state.
   c. M's personal residence is condemned as part of a local government project to widen the highway from two lanes to four lanes. M uses the condemnation proceeds to purchase another personal residence.

53. Do the following qualify for involuntary conversion treatment?

   a. Purchase of a sporting goods store as a replacement for a bookstore (used in a business) that was destroyed by fire.
   b. Sale of a home because a neighbor converted his residence into a nightclub.
   c. Purchase of an airplane to replace a shrimp boat (used in a business) that was wrecked by a hurricane.
   d. Taxpayer's residence destroyed by a tornado and replaced with another residence.
   e. Investor's purchase of an apartment building to replace a rental house. The rental house was destroyed by a flood.

54. For each of the following, indicate the earliest and latest dates that qualifying replacement property can be acquired under § 1033:

   a. Business property that is stolen or destroyed.
   b. Personal use property that is stolen or destroyed.
   c. Business property that is condemned.
   d. Personal use property that is condemned.

55. R's office building, which is used in his business, is destroyed by a hurricane in September 1992. The adjusted basis is $225,000. R receives insurance proceeds of $350,000 in October 1992.

   a. Calculate R's realized gain or loss, recognized gain or loss, and basis for the replacement property if R acquires an office building for $390,000 in October 1992.
   b. Calculate R's realized gain or loss, recognized gain or loss, and basis for the replacement property if R acquires a warehouse for $330,000 in October 1992.
   c. Calculate R's realized gain or loss and recognized gain or loss if R does not acquire replacement property.

56. T's warehouse, which has an adjusted basis of $325,000 and a fair market value of $490,000, is condemned by an agency of the Federal government to make way for a highway interchange. The initial condemnation offer is $450,000. After substantial negotiations, the agency agrees to transfer to T a surplus warehouse that T believes is worth $490,000.

   a. What are the recognized gain or loss and the basis of the replacement warehouse if T's objective is to recognize as much gain as possible?
   b. What are the recognized gain or loss and the basis of the replacement warehouse if T's objective is to minimize gain recognition?

57. What are the *maximum* postponed gain or loss and the basis for the replacement property for the following involuntary conversions?

	Property	Type of Conversion	Amount Realized	Adjusted Basis	Amount Reinvested
a.	Drugstore (business)	Condemned	$160,000	$120,000	$100,000
b.	Apartments (investment)	Casualty	100,000	120,000	200,000
c.	Grocery store (business)	Casualty	400,000	300,000	350,000
d.	Residence (personal)	Casualty	16,000	18,000	17,000
e.	Vacant lot (investment)	Condemned	240,000	160,000	240,000
f.	Residence (personal)	Casualty	20,000	18,000	19,000
g.	Residence (personal)	Condemned	18,000	20,000	26,000
h.	Apartments (investment)	Condemned	150,000	100,000	200,000

58. A taxpayer realizes $200,000 from the involuntary conversion of a factory. The adjusted basis of the factory was $225,000, and in the same year taxpayer spends $190,000 for a new factory.

a. What is the realized gain or loss?
b. What is the recognized gain or loss?
c. What is the basis of the new factory?

59. Which of the following are selling expenses, fixing-up expenses, or neither?

a. New swimming pool.
b. Legal fees to clear title to residence.
c. Painting exterior of residence.
d. Repair of leaky plumbing.
e. New roof.
f. Advertising residence for sale.
g. Painting living and dining rooms.
h. Broker commissions.

60. T, age 42, has lived in her residence for three years. Her adjusted basis is $130,000. Knowing that she is going to move to another city, she lists her residence for sale in February 1990. When she moves in May 1990, she purchases another residence for $190,000. Due to market conditions, she does not sell her original residence until July 1992. The selling price is $225,000, selling expenses are $13,000, and fixing-up expenses are $4,000.

a. What is T's realized gain or loss?
b. The recognized gain or loss?
c. The basis of the new residence?

61. What are the realized, recognized, and postponed gain or loss, the new basis, and the adjusted sales price for each of the following? Assume that none of the taxpayers is 55 years of age or older.

a. R sells her residence for $90,000. The adjusted basis was $55,000. The selling expenses were $5,000. The fixing-up expenses were $3,000. She did not reinvest in a new residence.
b. D sells his residence for $170,000. The adjusted basis was $120,000. The selling expenses were $4,000. The fixing-up expenses were $6,000. D reinvested $160,000 in a new residence.
c. M sells her residence for $65,000. The adjusted basis was $35,000. The selling expenses were $1,000. The fixing-up expenses were $2,000. She reinvested $40,000.
d. B sells his residence for $70,000. The adjusted basis was $65,000. The selling expenses were $6,000. He reinvested $80,000.
e. C sells his residence for $100,000, and his mortgage is assumed by the buyer. The adjusted basis was $80,000; the mortgage, $50,000. The selling expenses were $4,000. The fixing-up expenses were $2,000. He reinvested $120,000.

62. T is a colonel in the U.S. Air Force who is stationed in Newport News, Virginia. He is being transferred to Turkey for a three-year tour of duty beginning on September 15, 1992. He sells his principal residence in Newport News on August 25, 1992, for $220,000. His adjusted basis is $120,000. The selling expenses are $12,000, and the fixing-up expenses are $3,000. He returns to the United States on September 15, 1995, and purchases a new residence for $210,000 in San Antonio, Texas, where he is now stationed.

    a. What is T's realized gain or loss?
    b. The recognized gain or loss?
    c. The basis of the residence?

63. On January 15, 1992, K, a 48-year-old widow, buys a new residence for $180,000. On March 1, 1992, she sells for an adjusted sales price of $197,000 her old residence, which had an adjusted basis of $110,000. No fixing-up expenses are incurred. Between April 1 and June 30, 1992, an addition to the house is constructed at a cost of $20,000.

    a. What is K's realized gain or loss?
    b. K's recognized gain or loss?
    c. K's basis for the new residence?

64. T, age 47, sells his residence in Richmond on May 5, 1992, for $115,000. He incurs realtor's commissions of $6,900 and qualified fixing-up expenses of $2,000. His adjusted basis is $70,000. T sells the house because his employer assigns him to a temporary job in another state. T moves back to Richmond in December 1993. However, he has decided that he enjoys being relieved of the responsibilities of home ownership. Therefore, he rents an apartment and does not purchase another residence by May 5, 1994.

    a. What should T have reported on his 1992 return with respect to the sale of his residence?
    b. What should T do in 1994 when he has not replaced the residence within the required two-year period?

65. H, age 60, and W, age 45, have been married for two years. H sells the personal residence in which H and W reside for $180,000. W has no ownership interest in the house. Legal fees and realtor's commissions are $15,000. Fixing-up expenses are $4,000. H's adjusted basis is $55,000. H has owned and occupied the house for the past 7 years and plans to elect the § 121 exclusion. H purchases a replacement residence 22 months after the sale for $135,000. Before her marriage to H, W was married to P. While married to W, P had sold his personal residence and elected § 121 treatment to exclude the realized gain. W joined P in making the election, even though she had no ownership interest in the house. P and W were divorced five years ago.

    a. Calculate H's realized gain, recognized gain, and basis for the replacement residence if H and W file a joint return.
    b. Calculate H's realized gain, recognized gain, and basis for the replacement residence if H and W file separate returns.
    c. Calculate H's realized gain, recognized gain, and basis for the replacement residence in (a) and (b) if P and W had filed separate returns during the taxable year that P elected § 121 treatment.
    d. Advise H on what action is necessary to maximize the § 121 exclusion.

66. Mr. T, age 57, is the sole owner of his principal residence. He has owned and occupied it for 10 years. Mrs. T, his spouse, refuses to join him in making the § 121 election.

    a. Can Mr. T elect the § 121 exclusion if he and Mrs. T file a joint return? If so, what is the available amount of the exclusion?
    b. Can Mr. T elect the § 121 exclusion if he files a separate return? If so, what is the available amount of the exclusion?
    c. If Mrs. T joins Mr. T in making the election, what is the available amount of the exclusion on a joint return? On a separate return?

67. L sold his residence, which he had owned and occupied for 20 years. The adjusted basis was $92,000, and the selling price was $275,000. The selling expenses were $16,000, and the fixing-up expenses were $5,000. He reinvested $90,000 in a new residence. L is 57 years old. What are the realized, recognized, and postponed gain or loss, the new basis, and the adjusted sales price if his objective is to minimize the recognized gain?

68. S, P, and K, who are sisters, sell their principal residence in which they have lived for the past 20 years. The youngest of the sisters is age 58. The selling price is $555,000, selling expenses and legal fees are $15,000, and the adjusted basis is $60,000 (the fair market value of the residence when inherited from their parents 20 years ago). Since the sisters are going to live in rental housing, they do not plan to acquire another residence.

   a. Can S, P, and K elect § 121 exclusion treatment?
   b. What are the realized and recognized gain?

69. Mr. T and Mrs. T are divorced on August 1, 1992. According to the terms of the divorce decree, Mr. T's ownership interest in the house is to be transferred to Mrs. T in exchange for the release from marital rights. Before the divorce, the house was jointly owned by Mr. T and Mrs. T. The adjusted basis and the fair market value at the date of the transfer are $130,000 and $270,000, respectively.

   a. Does the transfer of the house produce recognized gain to either Mr. T or Mrs. T?
   b. What is the basis of the house to Mrs. T?
   c. If the same transfer was made by Mr. T to Mrs. T for $135,000 and was not associated with a divorce, would either Mr. T or Mrs. T have recognized gain?

CUMULATIVE PROBLEMS

70. Tammy Walker, age 37, is a self-employed accountant. Tammy's Social Security number is 333–40–1111. Her address is 101 Glass Road, Richmond, VA 23236. Her income and expenses associated with her accounting practice for 1992 are as follows:

Revenues (cash receipts during 1992)	$115,000
Expenses	
Salaries	$ 32,000
Office supplies	1,100
Postage	500
Depreciation of equipment	22,000
Telephone	650
	$ 56,250

Since Tammy is a cash method taxpayer, she does not record her receivables as revenue until she receives cash payment. At the beginning of 1992, her accounts receivable were $12,000, and the balance had decreased to $8,000 by the end of the year. The balance on December 31, 1992, would have been $13,500, except that an account for $5,500 had become uncollectible in November.

Tammy used one room in her 10-room house as an office (400 square feet out of a total square footage of 4,000). She paid the following expenses related to the house during 1992:

Utilities	$3,000
Insurance	600
Property taxes	4,000
Repairs	1,400

Tammy had purchased the house on September 1, 1991 for $200,000. She sold her previous house on November 15, 1991, for $105,000. Her selling expenses had been

$9,000, and qualified fixing-up expenses were $1,100. Tammy and her former husband, Lou, had purchased the house in 1989 for $80,000. Tammy had received Lou's 50% ownership interest as part of their divorce settlement in August 1990. Tammy had not used any part of the former residence as a home office.

Tammy has one child, Thomas, age 17. Thomas lives with his father during the summer and with Tammy for the rest of the year. Tammy can document that she spent $8,000 during 1992 for the child's support. The father normally provides about $2,000 per year, but this year he gave the child a new car for Christmas. The cost of the car was $15,000. The divorce decree is silent regarding the dependency exemption for the child.

Under the terms of the divorce decree, Tammy is to receive alimony of $800 per month. The payments will terminate at Tammy's death or if Tammy should remarry.

Tammy provides part of the support of her mother, age 67. The total support for 1992 for her mother was as follows:

Social Security benefits	$4,800
From Tammy	1,900
From Bob, Tammy's brother	1,300
From Susan, Tammy's sister	2,000

Bob and Susan have both indicated their willingness to sign a multiple support waiver form if it will benefit Tammy.

Tammy's deductible itemized deductions during 1992, excluding any itemized deductions related to the house, were $7,000. She made estimated tax payments of $19,000.

Part 1 — Tax Computation

Compute Tammy's lowest net tax payable or refund due for 1992. Suggested software (if available): *TurboTax* for tax return or WFT tax planning software.

Part 2 — Tax Planning

Tammy and her former husband have been discussing the $800 alimony he pays her each month. Due to a health problem of his new wife, he does not feel that he can afford to continue to pay the $800 each month. He is in the 15% tax bracket. If Tammy will agree to decrease the amount by 25%, he will agree that the amount paid is not alimony for tax purposes. Assume that the other data used in calculating Tammy's taxable income for 1992 will apply for her 1993 tax return. Advise Tammy as to whether she should agree to her former husband's proposal. Suggested software (if available): WFT tax planning software.

71. Mary Gordon, age 41, is single and has no dependents. Mary's Social Security number is 999–00–1000. Mary resides at 9700 Linkmeadow, Sarasota, FL 33500. She is a self-employed operator of a sole proprietorship. During 1991, gross income from her business was $120,000, and business expenses were $65,000. In addition, she had the following property transactions related to her business (not reflected in the preceding income and expense figures):

a.	Cash received on February 26, 1991, on trade of a parcel of land on the outskirts of town (held for two years as a site for a new warehouse) for a lot near Mary's store. Mary intends to build a new warehouse on the lot. The old parcel had a fair market value of $28,000 and adjusted basis of $25,000. The fair market value of the new lot was $24,000.	$ 4,000
b.	Condemnation award received on July 11, 1991, from the state for an acre of unimproved land (used for parking delivery vans) adjacent to the store (adjusted basis of the land was $12,000). The land had been purchased on October 3, 1987.	30,000
c.	Cost of an acre of unimproved land (purchased on September 18, 1991) across the street from the store (the land is to be used for parking delivery vans).	25,000

Mary's personal transactions for 1991 were as follows:

d.	Cash received on January 16, 1991, on exchange of 50 shares of X Corporation stock (adjusted basis of $20 a share, fair market value of $50 a share) for 50 shares of Y Corporation stock (fair market value of $40 a share). X Corporation and Y Corporation are not related, and Mary had held the X Corporation stock for two years.	500
e.	Amount realized on November 14, 1991, on the sale of a condominium Mary used as her personal residence. The condominium, which was built in 1975, was acquired in 1983 as a replacement for the house in which she formerly resided. She paid $60,000 for the condominium, and the amount realized for the house she sold was $80,000 (no fixing-up expenses, and adjusted basis was $50,000). Mary is moving into an apartment and does not intend to replace the condominium.	65,000
f.	Loss of amount Mary loaned to a friend in 1988 (the friend declared bankruptcy in 1991).	3,000
g.	Mary's interest income on personal savings accounts.	500
h.	Itemized deductions in 1991.	4,500
i.	Estimated Federal income tax payments.	24,500

Compute Mary's lowest net tax payable or refund due for 1991, assuming Mary makes any available elections that will reduce the tax. If you use tax forms for your computations, you will need Forms 1040, 2119, and 4797 and Schedules A, B, C, D, and SE. [Any gain recognized from item (a), (b), or (c) is § 1231 gain (discussed in Chapter 17), is reported on Form 4797 and Schedule D, and is to be treated as long-term capital gain.] Suggested software (if available): *TurboTax* for tax return or WFT tax planning software.

RESEARCH PROBLEMS

RESEARCH PROBLEM 1 Ms. G had owned and used her house as her principal residence since 1946. However, 20% of the house had been used for business purposes as an office. On January 1, 1992, when Ms. G was over 55, she retired and moved to North Carolina. Ms. G rented her former residence for six months before its sale since no qualified buyer could be found. She purchased a new residence in North Carolina at a price that exceeded the adjusted sales price of the former residence.

a. What treatment should be given to the portion of the former residence used for business? Rental property?
b. May Ms. G make an election under § 121?
c. Are the nonrecognition of gain provisions of § 1034 available to Ms. G?

RESEARCH PROBLEM 2 S owned 3,000 acres of timberland in Oregon. CZ Corporation offered to purchase the property for $4.5 million. Since the adjusted basis for the land was only $400,000, S did not want to have the large recognized gain that would result. CZ Corporation offered to purchase the land on the installment method and thereby spread the recognized gain over the period of the installment payments. S rejected the proposal and countered with the following proposal.

- The land (fair market value of $4.5 million) would be transferred from S to CZ Corporation in exchange for a five-year contract under which S would have the right to identify real property that CZ Corporation would purchase and transfer to S.
- At the end of the five-year period, the remainder of the $4.5 million that had not been so expended would be transferred to S in cash.
- During the five-year period, the amount of the $4.5 million not expended by the end of each year was to be increased by a growth factor of 12% per year.

a. Does the exchange qualify as a like-kind exchange under § 1031?
b. What is the appropriate treatment of the growth factor?

Partial list of research aids:

Starker v. U.S., 75–1 USTC ¶9443, 35 AFTR2d 75–1550 (D.Ct. Ore., 1975).

RESEARCH PROBLEM 3 T owned property that had an adjusted basis of $125,000, of which $100,000 was allocated to the land and $25,000 to the building. The property was condemned by the state, and T received a $275,000 condemnation award. T spent $400,000 for new property, of which $100,000 was allocable to the land and $300,000 to the building. What is the basis of the replacement property, and how is it allocated to the land and the building?

Partial list of research aids:

Reg. § 1.1033(c)–1(a).
Rev.Rul. 73–18, 1973–1 C.B. 368.

RESEARCH PROBLEM 4 You are the general manager of the San Diego Padres, Inc. In order for the Padres to become a serious contender for the pennant, you believe player changes are necessary. Discussions are in progress with the general manager of the Toronto Blue Jays. He has offered to trade Tony Fernandez (an all-star shortstop) and $5 million to the Padres in exchange for Joe Carter (an all-star outfielder) and Roberto Alomar (an all-star second baseman). You have countered by expressing an interest in receiving Fernandez and Fred McGriff (an all-star first baseman) rather than the cash. You believe that if you are going to give up the power provided by Carter, you need to get a power hitter in return (i.e., McGriff). In addition, you vaguely remember from your MBA days that a player trade with no cash involved will provide better tax results. Before you finalize a trade, you need to know the tax consequences.

CHAPTER

PROPERTY TRANSACTIONS: CAPITAL GAINS AND LOSSES

OBJECTIVES

Discuss the rationale for separate reporting of capital asset transactions.

Define a capital asset and apply the definition.

Examine statutory expansions of the capital asset definition.

Discuss the rules relating to retirement of corporate obligations.

Discuss special rules for capital gain treatment: options, patents, franchises, and lease cancellation payments.

Discuss and apply the holding period rules for determining whether capital gain or loss is long term or short term.

Explain the tax treatment of capital gains and losses of noncorporate taxpayers.

Explain the differences in the tax treatment of capital gains and losses of corporate versus noncorporate taxpayers.

Discuss tax planning opportunities arising from the sale or exchange of capital assets.

OUTLINE

General Considerations

Rationale for Separate Reporting of Capital Gains and Losses

The tax law requires capital gains and losses to be separated from other types of gains and losses. There are two reasons for this treatment. First, long-term capital gains may be taxed at a lower rate than ordinary gains. An *alternative tax computation* is used to determine the tax when taxable income includes net long-term capital gain. Capital gains and losses must therefore be matched with one another to see if a net long-term capital gain exists. The alternative tax computation is discussed in the Tax Treatment of Capital Gains and Losses of Noncorporate Taxpayers portion of this chapter.

Why else does the Code require separate reporting of gains and losses and a determination of their tax character? The second reason is that a net capital loss is only deductible up to $3,000 per year. Excess loss over the annual limit carries over and may be deductible in a future tax year. Capital gains and losses must be matched with one another to see if a net capital loss exists.

For these reasons, capital gains and losses must be distinguished from other types of gains and losses. Most of this chapter and the next chapter describe the intricate rules for determining what type of gains and losses the taxpayer has.

As a result of the need to distinguish and separately match capital gains and losses, the individual tax forms include very extensive reporting requirements for capital gains and losses. This chapter will help you understand the principles underlying the forms. The forms are illustrated with examples at the end of the chapter.

General Scheme of Taxation

Recognized gains and losses must be properly classified. Proper classification depends upon three characteristics:

- The tax status of the property.
- The manner of the property's disposition.
- The holding period of the property.

The three possible tax statuses are capital asset, § 1231 asset, or ordinary asset. Property disposition may be by sale, exchange, casualty, theft, or condemnation. The two holding periods are one year or less (short term) and more than one year (long term).

The major focus of this chapter is capital gains and losses. Capital gains and losses usually result from the disposition of a capital asset. The most common disposition is a sale of the asset. Capital gains and losses can also result from the disposition of § 1231 assets, which is discussed in Chapter 17. Except in very limited circumstances, capital gains and losses cannot result from the disposition of ordinary assets.

Capital Assets

Definition of a Capital Asset

Personal use assets and investment assets are the most common capital assets owned by individual taxpayers. Personal use assets usually include items such as clothing, recreation equipment, a residence, and automobiles. Investment assets usually include corporate stocks and bonds, government bonds, and vacant land. Remember, however, that losses from the sale or exchange of personal use assets are not recognized. Therefore, the classification of such losses as capital losses can be ignored.

Due to the historical preferential treatment of capital gains, taxpayers have preferred that gains be capital gains rather than ordinary gains. As a result, a great many statutes, cases, and rulings have accumulated in the attempt to define what is and what is not a capital asset.

Capital assets are not directly defined in the Code. Instead, § 1221 defines what is *not* a capital asset. A capital asset is property held by the taxpayer (whether or not it is connected with the taxpayer's business) that is *not* any of the following:

- Inventory or property held primarily for sale to customers in the ordinary course of a business. The Supreme Court, in *Malat v. Riddell,* defined *primarily* as meaning *of first importance* or *principally.*[1]
- Accounts and notes receivable acquired from the sale of inventory or acquired for services rendered in the ordinary course of business.
- Depreciable property or real estate used in a business.
- Certain copyrights; literary, musical, or artistic compositions; or letters, memoranda, or similar property held by (1) a taxpayer whose efforts created the property; (2) in the case of a letter, memorandum, or similar property, a taxpayer for whom it was produced; or (3) a taxpayer in whose hands the basis of the property is determined, for purposes of determining gain from a sale or exchange, in whole or in part by reference to the basis of such property in the hands of a taxpayer described in (1) or (2).
- U.S. government publications that are (1) received by a taxpayer from the U.S. government other than by purchase at the price at which they are offered for sale to the public or (2) held by a taxpayer whose basis, for purposes of determining gain from a sale or exchange, is determined by reference to a taxpayer described in (1).

The Code defines what is not a capital asset. From the preceding list, it is apparent that inventory, accounts and notes receivable, and most fixed assets of a business are not capital assets. The following discussion provides further detail on each part of the capital asset definition.

Inventory. What constitutes inventory is determined by the taxpayer's business.

EXAMPLE 1

T Company buys and sells used cars. Its cars are inventory. Its gains from sale of the cars are ordinary income. ◆

EXAMPLE 2

S sells her personal use automobile at a $500 gain. The automobile is a personal use asset and, therefore, a capital asset. The gain is a capital gain. ◆

Accounts and Notes Receivable. Collection of an accrual basis account receivable usually does not result in a gain or loss because the amount collected equals the receivable's basis. However, the sale of an accrual basis receivable may result in a gain or loss because it will probably be sold for more or less than its basis. A cash basis account receivable has no basis. Sale of such a receivable will generate a gain. Collection of a cash basis receivable generates ordinary income rather than a gain. A gain usually requires a sale of the receivable. See the discussion of Sale or Exchange later in this chapter.

EXAMPLE 3

T Company has accounts receivable of $100,000. Because it needs working capital, it sells the receivables for $83,000 to a financial institution. If T Company is an accrual basis taxpayer, it has a $17,000 ordinary loss. Revenue of $100,000 would have been

1. 66–1 USTC ¶9317, 17 AFTR2d 604, 86 S.Ct. 1030 (USSC, 1966).

recorded and a $100,000 basis would have been established when the receivable was created. If T Company is a cash basis taxpayer, it has $83,000 of ordinary income because it would not have recorded any revenue earlier; thus, the receivable has no tax basis. ◆

Business Fixed Assets. Depreciable personal property and real estate (both depreciable and nondepreciable) used by a business are not capital assets. Thus, *business fixed assets* are generally not capital assets. The Code has a very complex set of rules pertaining to such property. One of these rules is discussed under Real Property Subdivided for Sale in this chapter. Chapter 17 discusses the potential capital gain treatment under § 1231 for business fixed assets.

Copyrights and Creative Works. Generally, the person whose efforts led to the copyright or creative work has an ordinary asset, not a capital asset. *Creative works* include the works of authors, composers, and artists. Also, the person for whom a letter, memorandum, or other similar property was created has an ordinary asset. Finally, a person receiving a copyright, creative work, letter, memorandum, or similar property by gift from the creator or the person for whom the work was created has an ordinary asset.

EXAMPLE 4

T is a part-time music composer. A music publisher purchases one of her songs for $5,000. T has a $5,000 ordinary gain from the sale of an ordinary asset. ◆

EXAMPLE 5

T received a letter from the President of the United States in 1962. In the current year, T sells the letter to a collector for $300. T has a $300 ordinary gain from the sale of an ordinary asset (because the letter was created for T). ◆

EXAMPLE 6

T gives a song she composed to her son. The son sells the song to a music publisher for $5,000. The son has a $5,000 ordinary gain from the sale of an ordinary asset. ◆

(Patents are subject to special statutory rules discussed later in the chapter.)

U.S. Government Publications. U.S. government publications received from the U.S. government (or its agencies) for a reduced price are not capital assets. This prevents a taxpayer from later donating the publications to charity and claiming a charitable contribution equal to the fair market value of the publications. A charitable contribution of a capital asset generally yields a deduction equal to the fair market value. A charitable contribution of an ordinary asset generally yields a deduction equal to less than the fair market value. If such property is received by gift from the original purchaser, the property is not a capital asset to the donee. (For a more comprehensive explanation of charitable contributions of property, refer to Chapter 11.)

Effect of Judicial Action

Court decisions play an important role in the definition of capital assets. Because the Code only lists categories of what are *not* capital assets, judicial interpretation is sometimes required to determine whether a specific item fits into one of those categories. The Supreme Court follows a literal interpretation of the categories. For instance, corporate stock is not mentioned in § 1221. Thus, corporate stock is *usually* a capital asset. However, what if corporate stock is purchased for resale to customers? Then it is *inventory* and not a capital asset because inventory is one of the categories in § 1221. (See the discussion of Dealers in Securities below.) A Supreme Court decision was required to make the distinction between capital asset and non-capital asset status when a taxpayer who did not normally acquire stock for resale to customers acquired stock with the intention of resale.[2] The Court decided that since the stock was not acquired primarily for sale to customers (the taxpayer did not sell the stock to its regular customers), the stock was a capital asset.

Often the crux of the capital asset determination hinges on whether the asset is held for investment purposes (capital asset) or business purposes (ordinary asset). The taxpayer's *use* of the property often provides objective evidence.

Example 7

T's business buys an expensive painting. If the painting is used to decorate T's office and is not of investment quality, the painting is depreciable and, therefore, not a capital asset. If T's business is buying and selling paintings, the painting is inventory and, therefore, an ordinary asset. If the painting is of investment quality and the business purchased it for investment, the painting is a capital asset, even though it serves a decorative purpose in T's office. *Investment quality* generally means that the painting is expected to appreciate in value. ◆

Because of the uncertainty associated with the capital asset definition, Congress has enacted several Code Sections to clarify the definition. These statutory expansions of the capital asset definition are discussed in the following section.

Statutory Expansions

Congress has often expanded the § 1221 general definition of a capital asset.

Dealers in Securities. As a general rule, securities (stocks, bonds, and other financial instruments) held by a dealer are considered to be inventory and are not, therefore, subject to capital gain or loss treatment. A *dealer in securities* is a merchant (e.g., a brokerage firm) that regularly engages in the purchase and resale of securities to customers. The dealer must identify any securities being held for investment. Generally, if a dealer clearly identifies certain securities as held for investment purposes by the close of business on the acquisition date, gain from the securities' sale will be capital gain. However, the gain will not be capital gain if the dealer ceases to hold the securities for investment prior to the sale. Losses are capital losses if at any time the securities have been clearly identified by the dealer as held for investment.[3]

Example 8

T is a securities dealer. She purchases 100 shares of XYZ stock. If T takes no further action, the stock is inventory and an ordinary asset. If she designates in her records that the stock is held for investment, the stock is a capital asset. T must designate the investment purpose by the close of business on the acquisition date. If T maintains her investment purpose and later sells the stock, the gain or loss is capital gain or loss. If T redesignates the stock as held for resale (inventory) and then sells it, any gain is ordinary, but any loss is capital loss. Stock designated as held for investment and then sold at a loss always yields a capital loss. ◆

---

2. *Arkansas Best v. Comm.*, 88–1 USTC ¶ 9210, 61 AFTR2d 88–655, 108 S.Ct. 971 (USSC, 1988).

3. §§ 1236(a) and (b) and Reg. § 1.1236–1(a). Section 107(b)(1) of the Deficit Reduction Act of 1984 authorizes the Treasury to impose earlier identification deadlines than the close of the business day. The Treasury could also provide by Regulations for a method of identification other than the taxpayer's records. At this writing, such Regulations have not been issued.

Real Property Subdivided for Sale. Substantial real property development activities may result in the owner being considered a dealer for tax purposes. Income from the sale of real estate property lots is treated as the sale of inventory (ordinary income) if the owner is considered to be a dealer. However, § 1237 allows real estate investors capital gain treatment if they engage in limited development activities. To be eligible for § 1237 treatment, the following requirements must be met:

- The taxpayer may not be a corporation.
- The taxpayer may not be a real estate dealer.
- No substantial improvements may be made to the lots sold. *Substantial* generally means more than a 10 percent increase in the value of a lot. Shopping centers and other commercial or residential buildings are considered substantial, while filling, draining, leveling, and clearing operations are not.
- The taxpayer must have held the lots sold for at least 5 years, except for inherited property. The substantial improvements test is less stringent if the property is held at least 10 years.

If the preceding requirements are met, all gain is capital gain until the tax year in which the sixth lot is sold. Sales of contiguous lots to a single buyer in the same transaction count as the sale of one lot. Beginning with the tax year the sixth lot is sold, some of the gain may be ordinary income. Five percent of the revenue from lot sales is potential ordinary income. That potential ordinary income is offset by any selling expenses from the lot sales. Practically, sales commissions often are at least 5 percent of the sales price, so none of the gain is treated as ordinary income.

If the requirements for § 1237 treatment are not met (e.g., the seller is a corporation), the gain still may not necessarily be ordinary income. The gain may be capital gain under § 1221 or § 1231 if the requirements of either of these sections are met.

Section 1237 does not apply to losses. A loss from the sale of subdivided real property is an ordinary loss unless the property qualifies as a capital asset under § 1221. The following example illustrates the application of § 1237.

EXAMPLE 9

T owns a large tract of land and subdivides it for sale. Assume T meets all the requirements of § 1237 and during the tax year sells the first 10 lots to 10 different buyers for $10,000 each. T's basis in each lot sold is $3,000, and T incurs total selling expenses of $4,000 on the sales. T's gain is computed as follows:

Selling price (10 × $10,000)		$100,000	
Basis (10 × $3,000)		(30,000)	
Excess over basis		$ 70,000	
Five percent of selling price	$ 5,000		
Selling expenses	(4,000)		
Amount of ordinary income			$ 1,000
Five percent of selling price	$ 5,000		
Excess of expenses over 5 percent of selling price	-0-	(5,000)	
Capital gain			65,000
Total gain ($70,000 − $4,000 selling expenses)			$66,000

◆

Lump-Sum Distributions. A *lump-sum distribution* is generally a distribution of an employee's entire qualified pension or profit sharing plan balance within one tax year. The distribution must result from the employee's (1) death, (2) reaching age 59½, or (3) separation from service with an employer. TRA of 1986 repealed a provision that allowed a portion of a lump-sum distribution to be treated as capital gain. However, partial capital gain treatment may still be available because transition rules allow certain taxpayers to continue using prior law. See Chapter 19 for a further discussion of lump-sum distributions.

Nonbusiness Bad Debts. A loan not made in the ordinary course of business is classified as a nonbusiness receivable. In the year the receivable becomes completely worthless, it is a *nonbusiness bad debt*, and the bad debt is treated as a short-term capital loss. Even if the receivable was outstanding for more than one year, the loss is still a short-term capital loss. This is an excellent example of the statutory expansion of capital gain and loss. It is not necessary to determine whether the asset was a capital asset or what the holding period was. The Code automatically provides that nonbusiness bad debts are short-term capital losses. Chapter 8 discusses nonbusiness bad debts more thoroughly.

Sale or Exchange

Recognition of capital gain or loss requires a sale or exchange of a capital asset. The Code uses the term *sale or exchange,* but does not define it. Generally, a sale involves the receipt of money and/or the assumption by the purchaser of liabilities for property. An exchange involves the transfer of property for other property. Thus, an involuntary conversion (casualty, theft, or condemnation) is not a sale or exchange. In several situations, the determination of whether a sale or exchange has taken place has been clarified by the enactment of Code Sections that specifically provide for sale or exchange treatment.

Recognized gains or losses from the cancellation, lapse, expiration, or any other termination of a right or obligation with respect to personal property (other than stock) that is or would be a capital asset in the hands of the taxpayer are capital gains or losses.[4] See the discussion under Options later in the chapter for more details.

Worthless Securities

Occasionally, securities such as stock and, especially, bonds may become worthless due to the insolvency of their issuer. If such a security is a capital asset, the loss is deemed to have occurred as the result of a sale or exchange on the *last day* of the tax year.[5] This last-day rule may have the effect of converting what otherwise would have been a short-term capital loss into a long-term capital loss. See Treatment of Capital Losses later in this chapter.

Section 1244 allows an ordinary deduction on disposition of stock at a loss. The stock must be that of a small business company, and the ordinary deduction is limited to $50,000 ($100,000 for married individuals filing jointly) per year. For a more detailed discussion, refer to Chapter 8.

Special Rule—Retirement of Corporate Obligations

A debt obligation (e.g., a bond or note payable) may have a tax basis in excess of or less than its redemption value because it may have been acquired at a

4. § 1234A.

5. § 165(g)(1).

premium or discount. Consequently, the collection of the redemption value may result in a loss or gain. Generally, the collection of a debt obligation is *not* a sale or exchange. Therefore, any loss or gain cannot be a capital loss or gain because no sale or exchange has taken place. However, if the debt obligation was issued by a corporation or certain government agencies, the collection of the redemption value is treated as a sale or exchange.[6]

EXAMPLE 10

T acquires $1,000 of XYZ Corporation bonds for $980 in the open market. If the bonds are held to maturity, the $20 difference between T's collection of the $1,000 maturity value and T's cost of $980 is treated as capital gain. If the obligation had been issued to T by an individual instead of by a corporation, T's $20 gain would be ordinary, since no sale or exchange of the debt by T occurred. ◆

Original Issue Discount. The benefit of the sale or exchange exception that allows a capital gain from the collection of certain obligations is reduced when the obligation has original issue discount. *Original issue discount (OID)* arises when the issue price of a debt obligation is less than the maturity value of the obligation. OID must generally be amortized over the life of the debt obligation. The OID amortization increases the basis of the bond. Most new publicly traded bond issues do not carry OID since the stated interest rate is set to make the market price on issue the same as the bond's face amount. In addition, even if the issue price is less than the face amount, the difference is not considered to be OID if the difference is less than one-fourth of 1 percent of the redemption price at maturity multiplied by the number of years to maturity.[7]

In the case where OID does exist, it may or may not have to be amortized, depending upon the date the obligation was issued. When OID is amortized, the amount of gain upon collection, sale, or exchange of the obligation is correspondingly reduced. The obligations covered by the OID amortization rules and the method of amortization are presented in §§ 1272–1275. Similar rules for other obligations can be found in §§ 1276–1288.

EXAMPLE 11

T purchases $10,000 of newly issued Y Corporation bonds for $6,000. The bonds have original issue discount of $4,000. T must amortize the discount over the life of the bonds. The OID amortization *increases* T's interest income. (The bonds were selling at a discount because the market rate of interest was greater than the bonds' interest rate.) After T has amortized $1,800 of OID, he sells the bonds for $8,000. T has a capital gain of $200 [$8,000 − ($6,000 cost + $1,800 OID amortization)]. The OID amortization rules prevent T from converting ordinary interest income into capital gain. Without the OID amortization, T would have capital gain of $2,000 ($8,000 − $6,000 cost). ◆

Options

Frequently, a potential buyer of property wants some time to make the purchase decision, but wants to control the sale and/or the sale price in the meantime. Options are used to achieve these objectives. The potential purchaser (grantee) pays the property owner (grantor) for an option on the property. The grantee then becomes the option holder. The option usually sets a price at which the grantee can buy the property and expires after a specified period of time.

6. § 1271.

7. § 1273(a)(3).

Sale of an Option. A grantee may sell or exchange the option rather than exercising it or letting it expire. Generally, the grantee's sale or exchange of the option results in capital gain or loss if the option property is (or would be) a capital asset to the grantee.[8]

Example 12

T wants to buy some vacant land for investment purposes. She cannot afford the full purchase price. Instead, she convinces the landowner (grantor) to sell her the right to purchase the land for $100,000 anytime in the next two years. T (grantee) pays $3,000 to obtain this option to buy the land. The option is a capital asset for T because if she actually purchased the land, the land would be a capital asset. Three months after purchasing the option, T sells it for $7,000. T has a $4,000 short-term capital gain on this sale since she held the option for one year or less. ◆

Failure to Exercise Options. If an option holder (grantee) fails to exercise the option, the lapse of the option is considered a sale or exchange on the option expiration date. Thus, the loss is a capital loss if the property subject to the option is (or would be) a capital asset in the hands of the grantee.

The grantor of an option on *stocks, securities, commodities, or commodity futures* receives short-term capital gain treatment upon the expiration of the option. Options on property other than stocks, securities, commodities, or commodity futures result in ordinary income to the grantor when the option expires. For example, an individual investor who owns certain stock (a capital asset) may sell a call option, entitling the buyer of the option to acquire the stock at a specified price higher than the value at the date the option is granted. The writer of the call receives a premium (e.g., 10 percent) for writing the option. If the price of the stock does not increase during the option period, the option will expire unexercised. Upon the expiration of the option, the grantor must recognize short-term capital gain. These provisions do not apply to options held for sale to customers (the inventory of a securities dealer).

Exercise of Options by Grantee. If the option is exercised, the amount paid for the option is added to the optioned property's selling price. This increases the gain (or reduces the loss) to the grantor resulting from the sale of the property. The grantor's gain or loss is capital or ordinary depending on the tax status of the property. The grantee adds the cost of the option to the basis of the property purchased.

Example 13

On September 1, 1987, X purchases 100 shares of Y Company stock for $5,000. On April 1, 1992, he writes a call option on the stock, giving the grantee the right to buy the stock for $6,000 during the following six-month period. X (the grantor) receives a call premium of $500 for writing the call.

- If the call is exercised by the grantee on August 1, 1992, X has $1,500 ($6,000 + $500 − $5,000) of long-term capital gain from the sale of the stock. The grantee has a $6,500 ($500 option premium + $6,000 purchase price) basis for the stock.
- Assume that X decides to sell his stock prior to exercise for $6,000 and enters into a closing transaction by purchasing a call on 100 shares of Y Company stock for $5,000. Since the Y stock is selling for $6,000, X must pay a call premium of $1,000. He recognizes a $500 short-term capital loss [$1,000 (call premium paid)

8. § 1234(a) and Reg. § 1.1234–1(a)(1). See the Glossary of Tax Terms in Appendix C for a definition of stock options. Stock options are discussed in Chapter 19.

– $500 (call premium received)] on the closing transaction. On the actual sale of the Y Company stock, X has a long-term capital gain of $1,000 [$6,000 (selling price) – $5,000 (cost)]. The grantee is not affected by X's closing transaction. The original option is still in existence, and the grantee's tax consequences will depend on what action the grantee takes—exercising the option, letting the option expire, or selling the option.

- Assume that the original option expired unexercised. X has a $500 short-term capital gain equal to the call premium received for writing the option. This gain is not recognized until the option expires. The grantee has a loss from expiration of the option. The nature of the loss will depend upon whether the option was a capital asset or an ordinary asset. ◆

Patents

Rationale for Capital Gain Treatment. The sale of a patent may result in long-term capital gain treatment whether the patent is a capital asset or not.[9] The encouragement of technological progress is the primary reason for this provision. Ironically, authors, composers, and artists are not eligible for capital gain treatment on their creations because such works are not capital assets. The Code allows special treatment for patents, but not for copyrights. Presumably, Congress chose not to use the tax law to encourage cultural endeavors. The following example illustrates the special treatment for patents.

EXAMPLE 14

T, a druggist, invents a pill-counting machine, which she patents. In consideration of a lump-sum payment of $200,000 plus $10 per machine sold, T assigns the patent to Drug Products, Inc. Assuming T has transferred all substantial rights, the question of whether the transfer is a sale or exchange of a capital asset is not relevant. T automatically has a long-term capital gain from both the lump-sum payment and the $10 per machine royalty to the extent these proceeds exceed her basis for the patent. ◆

CONCEPT SUMMARY 16–1
OPTIONS

Event	Effect on Grantor	Effect on Grantee
Option is granted.	Receives value and has a contract obligation (a liability).	Pays value and has a contract right (an asset).
Option expires.	Has a short-term capital gain if the option property is stocks, securities, commodities, or commodity futures. Otherwise, gain is ordinary income.	Has a loss (capital loss if option property would have been a capital asset for the grantee).
Option is exercised.	Amount received for option increases proceeds from sale of the option property.	Amount paid for option becomes part of the basis of the option property purchased.
Option is sold or exchanged by grantee.	Result depends upon whether option later expires or is exercised (see above).	Could have gain or loss (capital gain or loss if option property would have been a capital asset for the grantee).

9. § 1235.

Statutory Requirements. The key issues for the transfer of patent rights are as follows:

- Whether or not the patent is a capital asset.
- Whether the transfer is a sale or exchange.
- Whether or not all substantial rights to the patent (or an undivided interest in it) are transferred.

Section 1235 resolves whether the transfer is a sale or exchange of a capital asset. The statute provides that

> a transfer . . . of property consisting of all substantial rights to a patent, or an undivided interest therein which includes a part of all such rights, by any holder shall be considered the sale or exchange of a capital asset held for [the long-term holding period], regardless of whether or not payments in consideration of such transfer are (1) payable periodically over a period generally coterminous with the transferee's use of the patent, or (2) contingent on the productivity, use, or disposition of the property transferred.[10]

If the transfer meets the requirements, any gain or loss is *automatically* a long-term capital gain or loss regardless of whether the patent is a capital asset, whether the transfer is a sale or exchange, and how long the patent was held by the transferor.

Substantial Rights. To receive favorable capital gain treatment, all *substantial rights* to the patent (or an undivided interest in it) must be transferred. All substantial rights to a patent means all rights (whether or not then held by the grantor) that are valuable at the time the patent rights (or an undivided interest in the patent) are transferred. All substantial rights have not been transferred when the transfer is limited geographically within the issuing country or when the transfer is for a period less than the remaining life of the patent. The circumstances of the entire transaction, rather than merely the language used in the transfer instrument, are to be considered in deciding whether all substantial rights have been transferred.[11]

EXAMPLE 15

Assume T, the druggist in Example 14, only licensed Drug Products, Inc., to manufacture and sell the invention in Michigan. She retained the right to license the machine elsewhere in the United States. T has retained a substantial right and is not eligible for automatic long-term capital gain treatment. ◆

Holder Defined. The *holder* of a patent is usually the creator of the invention. A holder may also be a person who purchases the patent rights from the creator before the patented invention is reduced to practice. However, the creator's employer and certain parties related to the creator do not qualify as holders. Thus, in the common situation where an employer has all rights to an employee's inventions, the employer is not eligible for long-term capital gain treatment. More than likely, the employer will have an ordinary asset because the patent was developed as part of its business.

---

10. § 1235(a) and Reg. § 1.1235–1(a).

11. Reg. § 1.1235–2(b)(1).

Franchises, Trademarks, and Trade Names

A mode of operation, a widely recognized brand name (trade name), and a widely known business symbol (trademark) are all valuable assets. These assets may be licensed (commonly known as franchising) by their owner for use by other businesses. Many fast-food restaurants are franchises. The franchisee usually pays the owner (franchisor) an initial fee plus a contingent fee. The contingent fee is often based upon the franchisee's sales volume.

For Federal income tax purposes, a *franchise* is an agreement that gives the franchisee the right to distribute, sell, or provide goods, services, or facilities within a specified area.[12] A franchise transfer includes the grant of a franchise, transfers by one franchisee to another person, or the renewal of a franchise.

A franchise transfer is generally not a sale or exchange of a capital asset. Section 1253 provides that

> a transfer of a franchise, trademark, or trade name shall not be treated as a sale or exchange of a capital asset if the transferor retains any significant power, right, or continuing interest with respect to the subject matter of the [transfer].

Significant Power, Right, or Continuing Interest. *Significant powers, rights, or continuing interests* include control over assignment, quality of products and services, sale or advertising of other products or services, and the right to require that substantially all supplies and equipment be purchased from the transferor. Also included are the right to terminate the franchise at will and the right to substantial contingent payments. Most modern franchising operations involve some or all of these powers, rights, or continuing interests.

Noncontingent Payments. When the transferor retains a significant power, right, or continuing interest, the transferee's noncontingent payments to the transferor will be ordinary income to the transferor. The payments will be deductible by the transferee as ordinary deductions. However, the timing of the deduction will depend upon the form of the payment.

A noncontingent lump-sum payment of up to $100,000 is capitalized and may be amortized by the franchisee over the shorter of the franchise period or 10 years. Noncontingent lump-sum payments exceeding $100,000 must be capitalized and may be amortized over 25 years. Both types of amortization are subject to recapture as ordinary income under § 1245.[13]

In the unusual case where no significant power, right, or continuing interest is retained by the transferor, a sale or exchange may occur, and capital gain or loss treatment may be available. For capital gain or loss treatment to be available, the asset transferred must qualify as a capital asset.

EXAMPLE 16

S, a franchisee, sells the franchise to a third party. Payments to S are not contingent, and all significant powers, rights, and continuing interests are transferred. The gain (payments − adjusted basis) on the sale is a capital gain to S. ◆

Contingent Payments. Whether or not the tranferor retains a significant power, right, or continuing interest, contingent franchise payments are ordinary income for the franchisor and an ordinary deduction for the franchisee. For this purpose, a payment qualifies as a contingent payment only if the following requirements are met:

12. § 1253(b)(1).

13. See Chapter 17 for a discussion of the recapture provisions.

- The contingent amounts are part of a series of payments that are paid at least annually throughout the term of the transfer agreement.
- The payments are substantially equal in amount or are payable under a fixed formula.

Example 17

T, a spicy chicken franchisor, transfers a franchise to U for eight years. T retains a significant power, right, or continuing interest. U makes a noncontingent $50,000 payment to T and also agrees to pay T 15% of sales. The noncontingent payment is ordinary income to T and may be amortized over eight years by U. Eight years is the amortization period because the term of the franchise is less than 10 years. The contingent payments are ordinary income to T and business deductions for U as the payments are made. ◆

Sports Franchises. Professional sports franchises (e.g., the Detroit Tigers) are not covered by § 1253.[14] However, § 1056 restricts the allocation of sports franchise acquisition costs to player contracts. Player contracts are usually one of the major assets acquired with a sports franchise. These contracts last only for the time stated in the contract. Therefore, owners of sports franchises would like to allocate franchise acquisition costs disproportionately to the contracts so that the acquisition costs will be amortizable over the contracts' lives. Section 1056 prevents this by generally limiting the amount that can be allocated to player contracts to no more than 50 percent of the franchise acquisition cost. In addition, the seller of the sports franchise has ordinary income under § 1245 for the portion of the gain allocable to the disposition of player contracts.

Lease Cancellation Payments

The tax treatment of payments received for canceling a lease depends on whether the recipient is the lessor or the lessee and whether the lease is a capital asset or not.[15]

Lessee Treatment. Lease cancellation payments received by a lessee are treated as an exchange.[16] Thus, these payments may be capital gains if the lease is a capital asset. Generally, a lessee's lease is a capital asset if the property (either personalty or realty) is used for the lessee's personal use (e.g., his or her residence). A lessee's lease is an ordinary asset if the property is used in the lessee's trade or business.[17]

Example 18

T owns an apartment building that he is going to convert into an office building. S is one of the apartment tenants and receives $1,000 from T to cancel the lease. S has a capital gain of $1,000 (which will be long term or short term depending upon how long S has held the lease). T has an ordinary deduction of $1,000. ◆

Lessor Treatment. Payments received by a lessor for a lease cancellation are always ordinary income because they are considered to be in lieu of rental payments.[18]

14. § 1253(e).
15. See the Glossary of Tax Terms in Appendix C for definitions of the terms "lessor" and "lessee."
16. § 1241 and Reg. § 1.1241–1(a).
17. Reg. § 1.1221–1(b).
18. *Hort v. Comm.*, 41–1 USTC ¶9354, 25 AFTR 1207, 61 S.Ct. 757 (USSC, 1941).

EXAMPLE 19

M owns an apartment building near a university campus. P is one of the tenants. P is graduating early and offers M $800 to cancel P's lease. M accepts the offer. M has ordinary income of $800. P has a nondeductible payment since the apartment was personal use property. ◆

HOLDING PERIOD

Property must be held more than one year to qualify for long-term capital gain or loss treatment.[19] Property not held for the required long-term period will result in short-term capital gain or loss. To compute the holding period, start counting on the day after the property was acquired and include the day of disposition.

EXAMPLE 20

T purchases a capital asset on January 15, 1991, and sells it on January 16, 1992. T's holding period is more than one year. If T had sold the asset on January 15, 1992, the holding period would have been exactly one year, and the gain or loss would have been short term. ◆

To be held for more than one year, a capital asset acquired on the last day of any month must not be disposed of until on or after the first day of the thirteenth succeeding month.[20]

EXAMPLE 21

T purchases a capital asset on February 28, 1991. If T sells the asset on February 28, 1992, the holding period is one year, and T will have a short-term capital gain or loss. If T sells the asset on March 1, 1992, the holding period is more than one year, and T will have a long-term capital gain or loss. If T sells the asset on February 29, 1992, the holding period is short term because the asset was purchased on the last day of a month and was not disposed of on or after the first day of the thirteenth succeeding month. ◆

Review of Special Holding Period Rules

There are several special holding period rules.[21] The application of these rules depends on the type of asset and how it was acquired.

Nontaxable Exchanges. The holding period of property received in a like-kind exchange includes the holding period of the former asset if the property that has been exchanged is a capital asset or a § 1231 asset. In certain nontaxable transactions involving a substituted basis, the holding period of the former property is *tacked on* to the holding period of the newly acquired property.

EXAMPLE 22

X exchanges a business truck for another truck in a like-kind exchange. The holding period of the exchanged truck tacks on to the holding period of the new truck. ◆

EXAMPLE 23

T sells her personal residence and acquires a new residence. If the transaction qualifies for nonrecognition of gain on the sale of a residence, the holding period of the new residence includes the holding period of the former residence. ◆

19. § 1222.
20. Rev.Rul. 66–7, 1966–1 C.B. 188.
21. § 1223.

Certain Nontaxable Transactions Involving a Carryover of Another Taxpayer's Basis. The holding period of a former owner of property is tacked on to the present owner's holding period if the transaction is nontaxable and the basis of the property to the former owner carries over to the new owner.

EXAMPLE 24

T acquires 100 shares of A Corporation stock for $1,000 on December 31, 1988. The shares are transferred by gift to S on December 31, 1991, when the stock is worth $2,000. The donor's basis of $1,000 becomes the basis for determining gain or loss on a subsequent sale by S. S's holding period begins with the date the stock was acquired by T. ◆

EXAMPLE 25

Assume the same facts as in Example 24, except that the fair market value of the shares is only $800 on the date of the gift. The holding period begins on the date of the gift if S sells the stock for a loss. The value of the shares at the date of the gift is used in the determination of basis. If the shares are sold for $500 on April 1, 1992, S has a $300 recognized capital loss, and the holding period is from December 31, 1991, to April 1, 1992 (thus, the loss is short term). ◆

Certain Disallowed Loss Transactions. Under several Code provisions, realized losses are disallowed. When a loss is disallowed, there is no carryover of holding period. Losses can be disallowed under § 267 (sale or exchange between related taxpayers), § 707(b)(1) (sale or exchange involving controlled partnerships), and § 262 (sale or exchange of personal use assets) as well as other Code Sections. Taxpayers who acquire property in a disallowed loss transaction will have a new holding period begin and will have a basis equal to the purchase price.

EXAMPLE 26

J sells her personal residence at a loss. J may not deduct the loss because it arises from the sale of personal use property. J purchases a replacement residence for more than the selling price of her former residence. J has a basis equal to the cost of the replacement residence, and her holding period begins when she acquires the replacement residence. ◆

Inherited Property. The holding period for inherited property is treated as long term no matter how long the property is actually held by the heir. The holding period of the decedent or the decedent's estate is not relevant for the heir's holding period.

EXAMPLE 27

S inherits XYZ stock from her father. She receives the stock on April 1, 1992, and sells it on November 1, 1992. Even though the stock was not held more than one year, S receives long-term capital gain or loss treatment on the sale. ◆

Special Rules for Short Sales

The holding period of property sold short is determined under special rules provided in § 1233. A *short sale* occurs when a taxpayer sells borrowed property and repays the lender with substantially identical property either held on the date of the sale or purchased after the sale. Short sales usually involve corporate stock. The seller's objective is to make a profit in anticipation of a decline in the price of the stock. If the price declines, the seller in a short sale recognizes a profit equal to the difference between the sales price of the borrowed stock and the price paid for the replacement stock.

EXAMPLE 28

C does not own any shares of Z Corporation. However, C sells 30 shares of Z. The shares are borrowed from C's broker and must be replaced within 45 days. C has a short sale because he was short the shares he sold. C will *close* the short sale by purchasing Z shares and delivering them to his broker. If the original 30 shares were sold for $10,000 and C later purchases 30 shares for $8,000, he will have a gain of $2,000. C's hunch that the price of Z stock would decline was correct. C was able to profit from selling high and buying low. If C had to purchase Z shares for $13,000 to close the short sale, he would have a loss of $3,000. In this case, C has sold low and bought high—not the result he wanted! C also would be making a short sale (a *short sale against the box*) if he borrowed shares from his broker to sell and then closed the short sale by delivering other Z shares he owned at the time he made the short sale. ◆

A short sale gain or loss is a capital gain or loss to the extent that the short sale property constitutes a capital asset of the taxpayer. The gain or loss is not recognized until the short sale is closed. Generally, the holding period of the short sale property is determined by how long the property used to close the short sale was held. However, if *substantially identical property* (e.g., other shares of the same stock) is held by the taxpayer, the short-term or long-term character of the short sale gain or loss may be affected:

- If substantially identical property has *not* been held for the long-term holding period on the short sale date, the short sale *gain or loss* is short term.
- If substantially identical property has *been* held for the long-term holding period on the short sale date, the short sale *gain* is long term if the substantially identical property is used to close the short sale and short term if it is not used to close the short sale.
- If substantially identical property has *been* held for the long-term holding period on the short sale date, the short sale *loss* is long term whether or not the substantially identical property is used to close the short sale.
- If substantially identical property is acquired *after* the short sale date and on or before the closing date, the short sale *gain or loss* is short term.

Concept Summary 16–2 summarizes the short sale rules.

The short sale rules are intended to prevent the conversion of short-term capital gains into long-term capital gains and long-term capital losses into short-term capital losses. The following examples illustrate the application of the short sale rules.

EXAMPLE 29

On January 2, 1992, T purchases five shares of Y Corporation common stock for $100. On April 14, 1992, she engages in a short sale of five shares of the same stock for $150. On August 15, T closes the short sale by repaying the borrowed stock with the five shares purchased on January 2. T has a $50 short-term capital gain from the short sale because she had not held substantially identical shares for the long-term holding period on the short sale date. ◆

EXAMPLE 30

Assume the same facts as in the previous example, except that T closes the short sale on January 30, 1993, by repaying the borrowed stock with five shares purchased on January 29, 1993, for $200. The stock used to close the short sale was not the property purchased on January 2, 1992, but since T held short-term property at the April 14,

1992, short sale date, the gain or loss from closing the short sale is short term. T has a $50 short-term capital loss ($200 cost of stock purchased January 29, 1993, and a short sale selling price of $150). ◆

EXAMPLE 31

Assume the same facts as in Example 30. On January 31, 1993, T sells for $200 the stock purchased January 2, 1992. T's holding period for that stock begins January 30, 1993, because the holding period portion of the short sale rules applies to the substantially identical property in order of acquisition. T has a short-term capital gain of $100 ($100 cost of stock purchased January 2, 1992, and a selling price of $200). ◆

EXAMPLE 32

On January 2, 1992, T purchases five shares of X Corporation common stock for $100. She purchases five more shares of the same stock on April 14, 1992, for $200. On January 17, 1993, she sells short five shares of the same stock for $150. On September 30, 1993, she repays the borrowed stock with the five shares purchased on April 14,

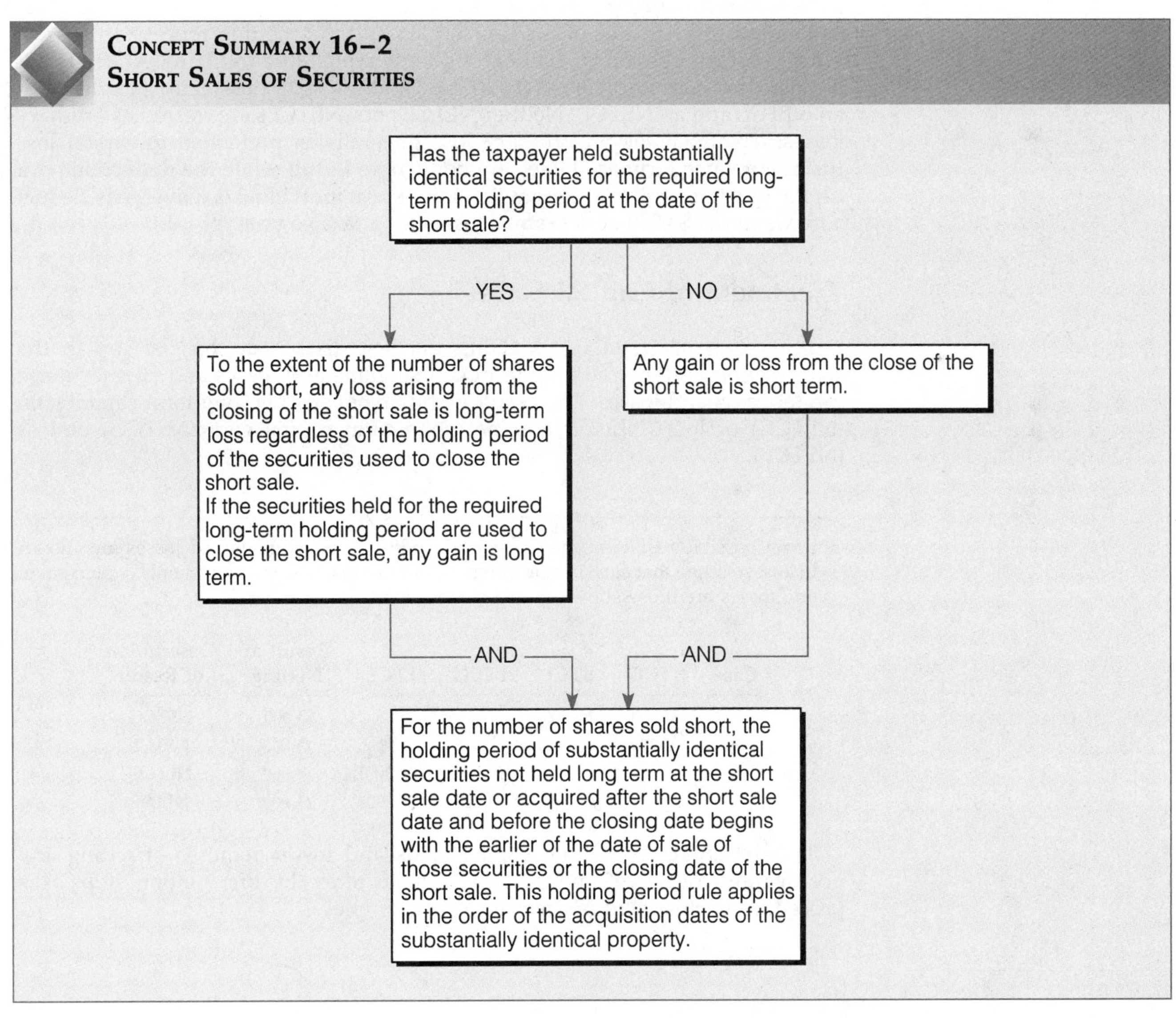
CONCEPT SUMMARY 16–2
SHORT SALES OF SECURITIES
Has the taxpayer held substantially identical securities for the required long-term holding period at the date of the short sale?
YES
NO
To the extent of the number of shares sold short, any loss arising from the closing of the short sale is long-term loss regardless of the holding period of the securities used to close the short sale.
If the securities held for the required long-term holding period are used to close the short sale, any gain is long term.
Any gain or loss from the close of the short sale is short term.
AND
AND
For the number of shares sold short, the holding period of substantially identical securities not held long term at the short sale date or acquired after the short sale date and before the closing date begins with the earlier of the date of sale of those securities or the closing date of the short sale. This holding period rule applies in the order of the acquisition dates of the substantially identical property.

1992, and sells the five shares purchased on January 2, 1992, for $200. T has a $50 long-term capital loss from the short sale because she held substantially identical shares for more than one year on the date of the short sale. T has a $100 long-term capital gain from the sale of the shares purchased on January 2, 1992.

Tax Treatment of Capital Gains and Losses of Noncorporate Taxpayers

All taxpayers net their capital gains and losses. Short-term gains and losses (if any) are netted against one another, and long-term gains and losses (if any) are netted against one another. The results will be net short-term gain or loss and net long-term gain or loss. If these two net positions are of opposite sign (one is a gain and one is a loss), they are netted against one another.

Six possibilities exist for the result after all possible netting has been completed. Three of these final results are gains, and three are losses. One possible result is a net long-term capital gain (NLTCG). Net long-term capital gains of noncorporate taxpayers are subject to beneficial treatment. A second possibility is a net short-term capital gain (NSTCG). Third, the netting may result in both NLTCG and NSTCG. The NLTCG portion of these net results is subject to a 28 percent maximum tax rate.

The last three results of the capital gain and loss netting process are losses. Thus, a fourth possibility is a net long-term capital loss (NLTCL). A fifth result is a net short-term capital loss (NSTCL). Finally, a sixth possibility includes both an NLTCL and an NSTCL. Neither NLTCLs nor NSTCLs are treated as ordinary losses. Treatment as an ordinary loss generally is preferable to capital loss treatment since ordinary losses are deductible in full while the deductibility of capital losses is subject to certain limitations. An individual taxpayer may deduct a maximum of $3,000 of net capital losses for a taxable year.[22]

Treatment of Capital Gains

Computation of Net Capital Gain. As just discussed, the *first step* in the computation is to net all long-term capital gains and losses and all short-term capital gains and losses. The result is the taxpayer's net long-term capital gain (NLTCG) or loss (NLTCL) and net short-term capital gain (NSTCG) or loss (NSTCL).

EXAMPLE 33

Some possible results of the first step in netting capital gains and losses are shown below. Assume that each case is independent (assume the taxpayer's only capital gains and losses are those shown in the given case).

Case	STCG	STCL	LTCG	LTCL	Result of Netting	Description of Result
A	$8,000	($5,000)			$3,000	NSTCG
B	2,000	(7,000)			(5,000)	NSTCL
C			$9,000	($1,000)	8,000	NLTCG
D			8,800	(9,800)	(1,000)	NLTCL

◆

The *second step* in netting capital gains and losses requires offsetting any positive and negative amounts that remain after the first netting step. This procedure is illustrated in the following examples.

22. § 1211(b).

EXAMPLE 34

Assume that T had all the capital gains and losses specified in Cases B and C in Example 33:

Case C ($9,000 LTCG − $1,000 LTCL)	$ 8,000	NLTCG
Case B ($2,000 STCG − $7,000 STCL)	(5,000)	NSTCL
Excess of NLTCG over NSTCL	$ 3,000	

◆

The excess of NLTCG over NSTCL is defined as *net capital gain (NCG)*. There is a $3,000 NCG in Example 34. There is an alternative tax computation when taxable income includes a NCG. The alternative tax computation taxes the NCG component of taxable income at a maximum tax rate of 28 percent. When taxable income including the NCG does not put the taxpayer into the 31 percent rate bracket, the alternative tax computation does not yield a tax benefit.

The *NCG alternative tax* is the summation of the following computations. It is illustrated in Example 35.

1. The tax computed using the regular rates on the greater of:

   a. Taxable income less the net capital gain, or
   b. The amount of taxable income taxed at a rate below 28 percent, plus

2. Twenty-eight percent of taxable income in excess of taxable income used in (1).

EXAMPLE 35

T, an unmarried taxpayer, has taxable income (TI) of $75,000. The taxable income includes NCG of $50,000. T's regular tax liability for 1992 is $18,905 [($21,450 × 15%) + 28%($51,900 − $21,450) + 31%($75,000 − $51,900)]. His alternative tax on net capital gains is calculated as follows:

1. Tax on greater of:	
a. TI less NCG ($75,000 − $50,000)	$ 4,212
b. TI taxed below 28% ($21,450), plus	
2. 28% of TI exceeding TI used in (1) [28% × ($75,000 − $25,000)]	14,000
Alternative tax on TI including NCG	$18,212

The NCG alternative tax saves T $693 ($18,905 − $18,212) in 1992. ◆

EXAMPLE 36

Assume that U had all the capital gains and losses specified in Cases A and D in Example 33:

Case A ($8,000 STCG − $5,000 STCL)	$ 3,000	NSTCG
Case D ($8,800 LTCG − $9,800 LTCL)	(1,000)	NLTCL
Excess of NSTCG over NLTCL	$ 2,000	

◆

There is no special name for the excess of NSTCG over NLTCL, nor is there any special tax treatment. The nature of the gain is short term, and the gain is treated the same as ordinary gain and is included in U's gross income.

Treatment of Capital Losses

Computation of Net Capital Loss. A *net capital loss (NCL)* results if capital losses exceed capital gains for the year. An NCL may be all long term, all short term, or part long and part short term.[23] The characterization of an NCL as long or short term is important in determining the capital loss deduction (discussed later in this chapter).

EXAMPLE 37

Three different individual taxpayers have the following capital gains and losses during the year:

Taxpayer	LTCG	LTCL	STCG	STCL	Result of Netting	Description of Result
R	$1,000	($2,800)	$1,000	($ 500)	($1,300)	NLTCL
S	1,000	(500)	1,000	(2,800)	(1,300)	NSTCL
T	400	(1,200)	500	(1,200)	(1,500)	NLTCL ($800)
						NSTCL ($700)

R's NCL of $1,300 is all long term. S's NCL of $1,300 is all short term. T's NCL is $1,500, $800 of which is long term and $700 of which is short term. ◆

Treatment of Net Capital Loss. An NCL is deductible from gross income to the extent of $3,000 per tax year.[24] Capital losses exceeding the loss deduction limits carry forward indefinitely. Thus, although there may or may not be beneficial treatment for capital gains, there is *unfavorable* treatment for capital losses in terms of the $3,000 annual limitation on deducting NCL against ordinary income. If the NCL includes both long-term and short-term capital loss, the short-term capital loss is counted first toward the $3,000 annual limitation.

EXAMPLE 38

T has an NCL of $5,000, of which $2,000 is STCL and $3,000 is LTCL. T has a capital loss deduction of $3,000 ($2,000 of STCL and $1,000 of LTCL) with an LTCL carryforward of $2,000. ◆

Carryovers. Taxpayers are allowed to carry over unused capital losses indefinitely. The STCL and LTCL carried over retain their character as STCL or LTCL.

EXAMPLE 39

In 1991, T incurred $1,000 of STCL and $11,000 of LTCL. In 1992, T has a $400 LTCG.

- T's NCL for 1991 is $12,000. T deducts $3,000 ($1,000 STCL and $2,000 LTCL). T has $9,000 of LTCL carried forward to 1992.
- T combines the $9,000 LTCL carryforward with the $400 LTCG for 1992. T has an $8,600 NLTCL for 1992. T deducts $3,000 of LTCL in 1992 and carries forward $5,600 of LTCL to 1993. ◆

23. § 1222(10) defines a net capital loss as the net loss after the capital loss deduction. However, that definition confuses the discussion of net capital loss. Therefore, net capital loss is used here to mean the result after netting capital gains and losses and before considering the capital loss deduction. The capital loss deduction is discussed under Treatment of Net Capital Loss in this chapter.

24. § 1211(b)(1). Married persons filing separate returns are limited to a $1,500 deduction per taxable year.

When a taxpayer has both a capital loss deduction and negative taxable income, a special computation of the capital loss carryover is required.[25] Specifically, the capital loss carryover is the NCL minus the lesser of:

- The capital loss deduction claimed on the return.
- The negative taxable income increased by the capital loss deduction claimed on the return and the personal and dependency exemption deduction.

Without this provision, some of the tax benefit of the capital loss deduction would be wasted when the deduction drives taxable income below zero.

EXAMPLE 40

In 1992, J has a $13,000 NCL (all long term), a $2,300 personal exemption deduction, and $4,000 negative taxable income. The negative taxable income includes a $3,000 capital loss deduction. The capital loss carryover to 1993 is $11,700 computed as follows:

- The $4,000 negative taxable income is treated as a negative number, but the capital loss deduction and personal exemption deduction are treated as positive numbers.
- $13,000 − the lesser of $3,000 (capital loss deduction) or $1,300 [− $4,000 (negative taxable income) + $3,000 (capital loss deduction) + $2,300 (personal exemption deduction)] = $13,000 − $1,300 = $11,700 carryover. ◆

CONCEPT SUMMARY 16–3
NONCORPORATE TAXPAYER'S TREATMENT OF NET CAPITAL GAIN OR LOSS

Net Capital Gain Treatment Summarized

1. All long-term capital gain	28% alternative tax is available, but is not always beneficial.
2. All short-term capital gain	Taxable as ordinary income.
3. Part long-term and part short-term capital gain	STCG portion taxable as ordinary income. 28% alternative tax is available for long-term capital gain portion, but is not always beneficial.

Net Capital Loss Treatment Summarized

4. All long-term capital loss	$1 of loss used to make $1 of deduction. Deduction is *for* AGI and limited to $3,000 per year. Portion of loss not used to make deduction carries forward indefinitely.
5. All short-term capital loss	$1 of loss used to make $1 of deduction. Deduction is *for* AGI and limited to $3,000 per year. Portion of loss not used to make deduction carries forward indefinitely.
6. Part long-term and part short-term capital loss	Short-term losses used first to make $3,000 deduction.

25. § 1212(b).

Reporting Procedures

The following discusses only 1991 tax forms because the 1992 tax forms were not available at the time of this writing.

Capital gains and losses are reported on Schedule D of the 1991 Form 1040 (reproduced on page 16–23). Part I of Schedule D is used to report short-term capital gains and losses. Part II of Schedule D is used to report long-term capital gains and losses. Part III summarizes the results of Parts I and II. Part IV contains the alternative tax computation for net long-term capital gains. Part V is used to compute the capital loss carryovers to 1992. Part VI is used to elect out of the installment method and to report a note at less than face value. Part VII is used to reconcile Form 1099–B information with the Schedule D information. (Parts V through VII are not reproduced here.) Parts I and II of the 1991 Schedule D–1 are used to report short- and long-term transactions, respectively. Schedule D–1 is used when there are more transactions than will fit in Part I or II of Schedule D. (Schedule D–1 is not reproduced here.)

EXAMPLE 41

During 1991, Erlyne Smith (Social Security number, 466–36–4596) had the following sales of capital assets (a 1991 example has been used, since a 1992 form was unavailable):

Description	Date Acquired	Date Sold	Selling Price	Cost Basis*
100 shares of W Corp. common stock	10/21/91	12/3/91	$11,000	$10,000
300 shares of X Corp. preferred stock	7/29/91	11/25/91	5,000	5,500
2,000 shares of Y Corp. common stock	1/31/81	2/12/91	8,000	7,000
40 shares of Z Corp. common stock	6/11/81	9/5/91	16,000	18,800

*Includes selling expenses (e.g., brokerage commissions).

Note that Erlyne's tax position is the same as that of R in Example 37. Thus, Erlyne has a NLTCL of $1,800 (Part II of Schedule D) and an NSTCG of $500 (Part I of Schedule D). These amounts are combined (see Part III of Schedule D) for a NLTCL of $1,300. All of the $1,300 is deductible *for* adjusted gross income as a capital loss deduction. There is no remaining capital loss to carry over to 1992. In completing a Schedule D for Erlyne Smith, it was assumed that she had no capital loss carryovers from prior years. Her total stock sales of $40,000 ($11,000 + $5,000 + $8,000 + $16,000) were reported to her by her broker on a Form 1099–B. ◆

SCHEDULE D (Form 1040)

Department of the Treasury
Internal Revenue Service

Capital Gains and Losses

(And Reconciliation of Forms 1099-B for Bartering Transactions)

▶ Attach to Form 1040. ▶ See Instructions for Schedule D (Form 1040).

▶ For more space to list transactions for lines 1a and 8a, get Schedule D-1 (Form 1040).

OMB No. 1545-0074

1991

Attachment Sequence No. **12A**

Name(s) shown on Form 1040: Erlyne Smith

Your social security number: 466 : 36 : 4596

Caution: *Add the following amounts reported to you for 1991 on Forms 1099-B and 1099-S (or on substitute statements):* ***(a)*** *proceeds from transactions involving stocks, bonds, and other securities, and* ***(b)*** *gross proceeds from real estate transactions not reported on another form or schedule. If this total does not equal the total of lines 1c and 8c, column (d), attach a statement explaining the difference.*

Part I Short-Term Capital Gains and Losses—Assets Held One Year or Less

(a) Description of property (Example, 100 shares 7% preferred of "Z" Co.)	(b) Date acquired (Mo., day, yr.)	(c) Date sold (Mo., day, yr.)	(d) Sales price (see instructions)	(e) Cost or other basis (see instructions)	(f) LOSS If (e) is more than (d), subtract (d) from (e)	(g) GAIN If (d) is more than (e), subtract (e) from (d)
1a Stocks, Bonds, Other Securities, and Real Estate. Include Form 1099-B and 1099-S Transactions. See instructions.						
100 Shares W Corp. Common Stock	10/21/91	12/ 3/91	11,000	10,000		1,000
300 Shares X Corp. Preferred Stock	7/29/91	11/25/91	5,000	5,500	500	
1b Amounts from Schedule D-1, line 1b (attach Schedule D-1)						
1c Total of All Sales Price Amounts. Add column (d) of lines 1a and 1b ▶ 1c			16,000			
1d Other Transactions (Do NOT include real estate transactions from Forms 1099-S on this line. Report them on line 1a.)						

		(f) LOSS	(g) GAIN
2	Short-term gain from sale or exchange of your home from Form 2119, line 10 or 14c		
3	Short-term gain from installment sales from Form 6252, line 22 or 30		
4	Net short-term gain or (loss) from partnerships, S corporations, and fiduciaries		
5	Short-term capital loss carryover from 1990 Schedule D, line 29		
6	Add lines 1a, 1b, 1d, and 2 through 5, in columns (f) and (g)	(500)	1,000
7	**Net short-term capital gain or (loss).** Combine columns (f) and (g) of line 6		500

Part II Long-Term Capital Gains and Losses—Assets Held More Than One Year

(a) Description of property	(b) Date acquired	(c) Date sold	(d) Sales price	(e) Cost or other basis	(f) LOSS	(g) GAIN
8a Stocks, Bonds, Other Securities, and Real Estate. Include Form 1099-B and 1099-S Transactions. See instructions.						
2,000 Shares Y Corp. Common Stock	1/31/81	2/12/91	8,000	7,000		1,000
40 Shares Z Corp. Common Stock	6/11/81	9/ 5/91	16,000	18,800	2,800	
8b Amounts from Schedule D-1, line 8b (attach Schedule D-1)						
8c Total of All Sales Price Amounts. Add column (d) of lines 8a and 8b ▶ 8c			24,000			
8d Other Transactions (Do NOT include real estate transactions from Forms 1099-S on this line. Report them on line 8a.)						

		(f) LOSS	(g) GAIN
9	Long-term gain from sale or exchange of your home from Form 2119, line 10 or 14c		
10	Long-term gain from installment sales from Form 6252, line 22 or 30		
11	Net long-term gain or (loss) from partnerships, S corporations, and fiduciaries		
12	Capital gain distributions		
13	Gain from Form 4797, line 7 or 9		
14	Long-term capital loss carryover from 1990 Schedule D, line 36		
15	Add lines 8a, 8b, 8d, and 9 through 14, in columns (f) and (g)	(2,800)	1,000
16	**Net long-term capital gain or (loss).** Combine columns (f) and (g) of line 16		(1,800)

For Paperwork Reduction Act Notice, see Form 1040 instructions. Cat. No. 11338H **Schedule D (Form 1040) 1991**

Schedule D (Form 1040) 1991 Attachment Sequence No. **12A** Page **2**

Name(s) shown on Form 1040. (Do not enter name and social security number if shown on other side.) | **Your social security number**

Part III Summary of Parts I and II

17	Combine lines 7 and 16 and enter the net gain or (loss) here. If the result is a gain, also enter the gain on Form 1040, line 13. (**Note:** *If both lines 16 and 17 are gains, see Part IV below.*)	(1,300)
18	If line 17 is a (loss), enter here and as a (loss) on Form 1040, line 13, the **smaller** of: **a** The (loss) on line 17; **or** **b** ($3,000) or, if married filing a separate return, ($1,500)	(1,300)

Note: *When figuring whether line 18a or 18b is* ***smaller,*** *treat both numbers as positive.*
Complete Part V if the loss on line 17 is more than the loss on line 18, OR if Form 1040, line 37, is zero.

Part IV **Tax Computation Using Maximum Capital Gains Rate**

USE THIS PART TO FIGURE YOUR TAX ONLY IF BOTH LINES 16 AND 17 ARE GAINS, AND:

You checked filing status box:	AND	Form 1040, line 37, is over:	You checked filing status box:	AND	Form 1040, line 37, is over:
1		$49,300	3		$41,075
2 or 5		$82,150	4		$70,450

19	Enter the amount from Form 1040, line 37	19	
20	Enter the **smaller** of line 16 or line 17.	20	
21	Subtract line 20 from line 19	21	
22	Enter: **a** $20,350 if you checked filing status box 1; **b** $34,000 if you checked filing status box 2 or 5; **c** $17,000 if you checked filing status box 3; or **d** $27,300 if you checked filing status box 4	22	
23	Enter the **greater** of line 21 or line 22.	23	
24	Subtract line 23 from line 19	24	
25	Figure the tax on the amount on line 23. Use the Tax Table or Tax Rate Schedules, whichever applies	25	
26	Multiply line 24 by 28% (.28)	26	
27	Add lines 25 and 26. Enter here and on Form 1040, line 38, and check the box for Schedule D	27	

TAX TREATMENT OF CAPITAL GAINS AND LOSSES OF CORPORATE TAXPAYERS

The treatment of a corporation's net capital gain or loss differs from the rules for individuals. Briefly, the differences are as follows:

- There is a NCG alternative tax rate of 34 percent. However, since the maximum corporate tax rate is 34 percent, the alternative tax is not beneficial.
- Capital losses offset only capital gains. No deduction of capital losses is permitted against ordinary taxable income (whereas a $3,000 deduction is allowed to individuals).[26]
- There is a three-year carryback and a five-year carryover period for net capital losses.[27] Corporate carryovers and carrybacks are always treated as short term, regardless of their original nature.

EXAMPLE 42

X Corporation has a $15,000 NLTCL for the current year and $57,000 of ordinary taxable income. X Corporation may not offset the $15,000 NLTCL against its ordinary income by taking a capital loss deduction. The $15,000 NLTCL becomes a $15,000 STCL for carryback and carryover purposes. This amount may be offset by capital gains in the three-year carryback period or, if not absorbed there, offset by capital gains in the five-year carryforward period. ◆

The rules applicable to corporations are discussed in greater detail in Chapter 20.

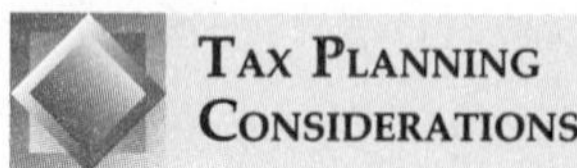

TAX PLANNING CONSIDERATIONS

Importance of Capital Asset Status

Why is capital asset status important when net long-term capital gain is subject to a maximum 28 percent tax rate? The 3 percent difference between the maximum 31 percent regular tax rate and the maximum 28 percent net long-term capital gain tax rate may generate significant tax savings for taxpayers in the highest regular tax bracket who can receive income in the form of long-term capital gains.

Capital asset status is also important because capital gains must be offset by capital losses. If a net capital loss results, the maximum deduction is $3,000 per year.

Consequently, capital gains and losses must be segregated from other types of gains and losses and must be reported separately on Schedule D of Form 1040.

26. § 1211(a).

27. § 1212(a)(1).

Planning for Capital Asset Status

It is important to keep in mind that capital asset status often is a question of objective evidence. Thus, property that is not a capital asset to one party may qualify as a capital asset to another party.

EXAMPLE 43

T, a real estate dealer, transfers by gift a tract of land to S, her son. The land was recorded as part of T's inventory (it was held for resale) and was therefore not a capital asset to T. S, however, treats the land as an investment. The land is a capital asset in S's hands, and any later taxable disposition of the property by S will yield a capital gain or loss. ◆

If proper planning is carried out, even a dealer may obtain long-term capital gain treatment on the sale of the type of property normally held for resale.

EXAMPLE 44

T, a real estate dealer, segregates tract A from the real estate he regularly holds for resale and designates the property as being held for investment purposes. The property is not advertised for sale and is disposed of several years later. The negotiations for the subsequent sale were initiated by the purchaser and not by T. Under these circumstances, it would appear that any gain or loss from the sale of tract A should be a capital gain or loss.[28] ◆

When a business is being sold, one of the major decisions usually concerns whether a portion of the sales price is goodwill. For the seller, goodwill generally represents the disposition of a capital asset. Goodwill has no basis and represents a residual portion of the selling price that cannot be allocated reasonably to the known assets. The amount of goodwill thus represents capital gain. The buyer purchasing goodwill has a capitalizable, nonamortizable asset—a very disadvantageous situation.

The buyer would prefer that the residual portion of the purchase price be allocated to a covenant not to compete (a promise that the seller will not compete against the buyer by conducting a business similar to the one that the buyer has purchased). Payments for a covenant not to compete are ordinary income to the seller, but are ordinary deductions for the buyer over the life of the covenant.

The case law requires a covenant not to compete to be clearly specified in the sales contract.[29] Otherwise, unallocated payments will be regarded as payments for goodwill.[30] The parties should therefore bargain for the nature of this portion of the sales price and clearly specify its nature in the sales contract.

EXAMPLE 45

M is buying J's dry cleaning proprietorship. An appraisal of the assets indicates that a reasonable purchase price would exceed the value of the known assets by $30,000. If the purchase contract does not specify the nature of the $30,000, the amount will be goodwill, and J will have a long-term capital gain of $30,000. M will have a nonamortizable $30,000 asset. If M is paying the extra $30,000 to prevent J from conducting another dry cleaning business in the area, J will have $30,000 of ordinary income. M will have a $30,000 deduction over the life of the covenant if the contract specifies the purpose for the payment. ◆

---

28. *Toledo, Peoria & Western Railroad Co.*, 35 TCM 1663, T.C. Memo. 1976–366.

29. See, for example, *James A. Patterson*, 49 TCM 670, T.C. Memo. 1985–53.

30. § 1060(a)(2).

Effect of Capital Asset Status in Other Than Sale Transactions

The nature of an asset (capital or ordinary) is important in determining the tax consequences that result when a sale or exchange occurs. It may, however, be just as significant in circumstances other than a taxable sale or exchange. When a capital asset is disposed of, the result is not always a capital gain or loss. Rather, in general, the disposition must be a sale or exchange. Collection of a debt instrument having a basis less than the face value results in an ordinary gain rather than a capital gain even though the debt instrument is a capital asset. The collection is not a sale or exchange. Sale of the debt shortly before the due date for collection will not produce a capital gain.[31] If selling the debt in such circumstances could produce a capital gain but collecting could not, the narrow interpretation of what constitutes a capital gain or loss would be frustrated. Another illustration of the sale or exchange principle involves a donation of certain appreciated property to a qualified charity. Recall that in certain circumstances, the measure of the charitable contribution is fair market value when the property, if sold, would have yielded a long-term capital gain [refer to Chapter 11 and the discussion of § 170(e)].

EXAMPLE 46

T wants to donate a tract of unimproved land (basis of $40,000 and fair market value of $200,000) held for the required long-term holding period to State University (a qualified charitable organization). However, T currently is under audit by the IRS for capital gains she reported on certain real estate transactions during an earlier tax year. Although T is not a licensed real estate broker, the IRS agent conducting the audit is contending that she has achieved dealer status by virtue of the number and frequency of the real estate transactions she has conducted. Under these circumstances, T would be well-advised to postpone the donation to State University until her status is clarified. If she has achieved dealer status, the unimproved land may be inventory (refer to Example 44 for another possible result), and T's charitable contribution deduction would be limited to $40,000. If not, and if the land is held as an investment, T's deduction is $200,000 (the fair market value of the property). ◆

Stock Sales

The following rules apply in determining the date of a stock sale:

- The date the sale is executed is the date of the sale. The execution date is the date the broker completes the transaction on the stock exchange.
- The settlement date is the date the cash or other property is paid to the seller of the stock. This date is *not* relevant in determining the date of sale.

EXAMPLE 47

T, a cash basis taxpayer, sells stock that results in a gain. The sale was executed on December 26, 1991. The settlement date is January 2, 1992. The date of sale is December 26, 1991 (the execution date). The holding period for the stock sold ends with the execution date. ◆

31. *Comm. v. Percy W. Phillips*, 60–1 USTC ¶9294, 5 AFTR2d 855, 275 F.2d 33 (CA–4, 1960).

Maximizing Benefits

Ordinary losses generally are preferable to capital losses because of the limitations imposed on the deductibility of net capital losses and the requirement that capital losses be used to offset capital gains. The taxpayer may be able to convert what would otherwise have been capital loss to ordinary loss. For example, business (but not nonbusiness) bad debts, losses from the sale or exchange of small business investment company stock, and losses from the sale or exchange of small business company stock all result in ordinary losses.[32]

Although capital losses can be carried over indefinitely, *indefinite* becomes definite when a taxpayer dies. Any loss carryovers not used by the taxpayer are permanently lost. That is, no tax benefit can be derived from the carryovers subsequent to death.[33] Therefore, the potential benefit of carrying over capital losses diminishes when dealing with older taxpayers.

It is usually beneficial to spread gains over more than one taxable year. In some cases, this can be accomplished through the installment sales method of accounting.

Year-End Planning

The following general rules can be applied for timing the recognition of capital gains and losses near the end of a taxable year:

- If the taxpayer already has recognized over $3,000 of capital loss, sell assets to generate capital gain equal to the excess of the capital loss over $3,000.

EXAMPLE 48

T has already incurred a $6,000 LTCL. T should generate $3,000 of capital gain. The gain will offset $3,000 of the loss. Thus, the remaining loss of $3,000 can be deducted against ordinary income. ◆

- If the taxpayer already has recognized capital gain, sell assets to generate capital loss equal to the capital gain. The gain will not be taxed, and the loss will be fully *deductible* against the gain.
- If the taxpayer's ordinary taxable income is already in the 28 percent bracket, it would make sense to recognize long-term capital gain rather than ordinary income where the taxpayer has a choice between the two. Such gain is taxed at the alternative rate of 28 percent whereas ordinary income may be taxed under the regular tax rates at 31 percent.

PROBLEM MATERIALS

DISCUSSION QUESTIONS

1. Why does the tax law require that capital gains and losses be separated from other types of gains and losses?
2. Proper classification of recognized gains and losses depends upon what three characteristics?

---

32. §§ 166(d), 1242, and 1244. Refer to the discussion in Chapter 8.

33. Rev.Rul. 74–175, 1974–1 C.B. 52.

3. Can the sale of personal use assets result in capital losses?
4. Does the tax law define "capital asset"?
5. T owns the following assets. Which of them are capital assets?
   a. Ten shares of Standard Motors common stock.
   b. A copyright on a song T wrote.
   c. A U.S. government savings bond.
   d. A note T received when he loaned $100 to a friend.
   e. A very rare copy of "Your Federal Income Tax" (a U.S. government publication that T purchased many years ago from the U.S. Government Printing Office).
   f. T's personal use automobile.
   g. A letter T received from a former U.S. President. T received the letter because he had complained to the President about the President's foreign policy.
6. Are business "fixed assets" capital assets?
7. Why do court decisions play an important role in the definition of capital assets?
8. Does the taxpayer's *use* of an asset determine whether the asset is a capital asset?
9. In what circumstances may real estate held for resale receive capital gain treatment?
10. A loan made by a taxpayer is a nonbusiness receivable. If the loan is not paid because the debtor defaults, what are the tax consequences?
11. A corporate bond is worthless due to a bankruptcy on May 10. At what date does the tax loss occur? (Assume the bond was held by an individual for investment purposes.)
12. R, a single individual, has a $25,000 loss from the sale of § 1244 small business company stock. How may R treat this loss?
13. Why does the Code require amortization of original issue discount? What is the effect of this amortization on the interest income of the taxpayer owning the bond? On the adjusted basis?
14. M, a real estate dealer, purchased for $25,000 a one-year option on 40 acres of farmland. If M is able to get the property rezoned for single-family residential development, she will exercise the option and purchase the land for $800,000. The rezoning effort is unsuccessful, and the option expires. How should the $25,000 be treated?
15. If a grantee of an option exercises the option, do the grantor's proceeds from the sale of the option property increase? Why?
16. When does the transfer of a patent result in long-term capital gain? Short-term capital gain? Ordinary income?
17. If an inventor's employer automatically has sole patent rights to the inventor's inventions, is the employer a holder of the patent?
18. What is a franchise? In practice, does the transfer of a franchise usually result in capital gain or loss treatment? Why or why not?
19. A transferor of a franchise receives a lump-sum noncontingent payment. Could the payment result in the recognition of long-term capital gain?
20. Why do you think § 1056 limits the amount of the cost of a sports franchise that can be allocated to player contracts? (*Hint:* Where would the player contracts appear on the books of the owner of the franchise?)
21. When are lease cancellation payments received by a lessee capital in nature? When are lease cancellation payments received by a lessor capital in nature?
22. Taxpayer is the lessee and the lease is on the taxpayer's residence. Taxpayer makes a payment to the lessor to cancel the lease. Why is the payment nondeductible?
23. What does it mean when a capital asset has been held "long term"?
24. In determining the long-term holding period, how is the day of acquisition counted? The day of disposition?
25. X owns A Corporation stock purchased on June 10, 1991, for $8,000 and B Corporation stock purchased on October 23, 1991, for $20,000. Both stocks are sold on April 23, 1992, for $30,000 each. What is X's adjusted gross income for 1992 if she also had wages of $80,000?

26. H exchanges a computer used in her business for another computer that she will use in her business. The transaction qualifies as a like-kind exchange. H had held the computer given up in the exchange for four years. The computers are § 1231 assets. What is the holding period of the computer received in the exchange on the day of its acquisition?
27. Define a short sale. Why does a seller enter into a short sale?
28. What is the general rule used to determine the holding period of property sold short? What is an exception to this rule, and why was the exception enacted?
29. Is there any reason a taxpayer would prefer to recognize a loss as a capital loss rather than as an ordinary loss?
30. Which type of gain would a taxpayer prefer to recognize in 1992: long-term capital gain, short-term capital gain, or ordinary income?
31. Which type of loss would a taxpayer prefer to incur in 1992: long-term capital loss, short-term capital loss, or ordinary loss?
32. Differentiate between the capital loss carryover rules for unused capital losses of individuals and corporations.

PROBLEMS

33. N had three property transactions during the year. She sold a vacation home used for personal purposes at a $21,000 gain. The home had been held for five years and had never been rented. N also sold an antique clock for $3,500 that she had inherited from her grandmother. The clock was valued in N's grandmother's estate at $5,000. N owned the clock for only four months. N sold these assets to finance her full-time occupation as a songwriter. Near the end of the year, N sold one of the songs she had written two years earlier. She received cash of $38,000 and a royalty interest in revenues derived from the merchandising of the song. N had no tax basis for the song. N had no other income and $18,000 in deductible songwriting expenses. Assuming the year is 1992, what is N's adjusted gross income?
34. F is the owner of a sole proprietorship. The business is on the cash basis of accounting and has $40,000 of accounts receivable. F is desperate for cash, so she sells the receivables to a collection agency for $23,000. How should F treat this sale of the receivables? How would the answer differ if F was on the accrual basis of accounting?
35. L is a dealer in securities. She purchased $10,000 of stock several years ago. She designated it as held for investment by the end of the day she acquired it. Two years later, she decided that she no longer wanted to hold the stock for investment and, therefore, redesignated it as held for sale in the ordinary course of her business. During the current year, she sold the stock for $35,000.

    a. What are the amount and nature of her gain from disposition of the stock?
    b. Assume the stock was sold for $8,000. What are the amount and nature of the loss from disposition of the stock?

36. A sells real estate lots, but meets all the conditions of § 1237. In 1992, she sells six lots, one lot each to B, C, D, and E and two adjacent lots to F. The sales price of each lot is $20,000. A's basis is $15,000 for each lot. Sales expenses are $500 per lot.

    a. What is the realized and recognized gain?
    b. Explain the nature of the gain (ordinary income or capital gain).
    c. Would your answers change if the two lots sold to F were not adjacent? If so, how?

37. M lends $5,000 to his close friend, B, on January 29, 1991. M is not in the business of making loans. On February 10, 1992, B is adjudicated bankrupt, and M receives only $1,000 as the first and only payment on the loan. What are the amount and nature of M's loss?
38. S purchases V common stock on December 7, 1991, for $3,678. She is notified in May 1992 that the stock is wholly worthless. What are the amount and nature of S's loss?
39. F purchases $100,000 of newly issued T Corporation bonds for $66,000. The bonds have original issue discount of $34,000. After F has held the bonds for two years and

has amortized $4,000 of the original issue discount, she sells the bonds for $88,000. What is F's adjusted basis for the bonds when she sells them, and what are the amount and nature of the gain from disposition of the bonds?

40. T is looking for vacant land to buy. She would hold the land as an investment. For $1,000, she is granted an 11-month option on January 1, 1992, to buy 10 acres of vacant land for $25,000. The owner (who is holding the land for investment) paid $10,000 for the land several years ago.

    a. Does the landowner have gross income when $1,000 is received for granting the option?
    b. Does T have an asset when the option is granted?
    c. If the option lapses, does the landowner have a recognized gain? If so, what type of gain? Does T have a recognized loss? If so, what type of loss?
    d. If the option is exercised and an additional $25,000 is paid for the land, how much recognized gain does the seller have? What type of gain? What is T's tax basis for the property?

41. In each of the following independent situations, determine whether the sale at a gain of all substantial rights in a patent qualifies for capital gain treatment:

    a. The creator sells the patent to a manufacturing company. The creator is not an employee of the manufacturing company.
    b. A manufacturing company owns a patent developed by one of its employees. It has been using the patent in its manufacturing process. The company sells the patent along with the assets of the manufacturing process.
    c. An investor buys a patent that has not been reduced to practice from the creator. After holding it for three months, she sells it to a retail company.

42. F, Inc., sells a franchise to R. The franchise contains many restrictions on how R may operate his store. For instance, R cannot use less than Grade 10 Idaho potatoes, must fry the potatoes at a constant 410 degrees, dress store personnel in F-approved uniforms, and have an F sign that meets detailed specifications on size, color, and construction. When the franchise contract is signed, R makes a noncontingent $40,000 payment to F. During the same year, R pays F $25,000 – 14% of R's sales. How does F treat each of these payments? How does R treat each of the payments?

43. E acquires 200 Z Corporation common shares at $10 per share on October 13, 1987. On August 10, 1991, E gives the shares to her son, B. At the time of the gift, the shares are worth $40 each. On May 11, 1992, B sells the shares for $45 each. What is B's gain? Is it short or long term?

44. J and S are brothers. J purchased a capital asset on January 10, 1992, for $10,000. On December 11, 1992, J sells the asset to S for $6,000, the property's fair market value. How do J and S treat this transaction?

45. T sells short 100 shares of A stock at $20 per share on January 15, 1992. He buys 200 shares of A stock on April 1, 1992, at $25 per share. On May 2, 1992, he closes the short sale by delivering 100 of the shares purchased on April 1.

    a. What are the amount and nature of T's loss upon closing the short sale?
    b. When does the holding period for the remaining 100 shares begin?
    c. If T sells (at $27 per share) the remaining 100 shares on January 20, 1993, what will be the nature of his gain or loss?

46. U (single with no dependents) has the following transactions in 1992:

Adjusted gross income (exclusive of capital gains and losses)	$80,000
Long-term capital gain	2,000
Long-term capital loss	(5,000)
Short-term capital gain	1,000
Short-term capital loss	(1,900)

What is U's net capital gain or loss?

47. In 1992, B (single with no dependents) had a recognized $18,000 LTCG from the sale of a personal residence. She also purchased from an inventor for $8,000 (and resold in two months for $7,000) a patent on a rubber bonding process. The patent had not yet been reduced to practice. B purchased the patent as an investment. Additionally, she had the following capital gains and losses from stock transactions:

Long-term capital loss	($3,000)
Long-term capital loss carryover from 1991	(12,000)
Short-term capital gain	21,000
Short-term capital loss	(6,000)

What is B's net capital gain or loss?

48. In 1992, W (single with no dependents) engaged in various stock transactions. W purchased R, Inc., common stock on January 10, for $8,000. The price began to plummet almost immediately. W sold the stock short on March 31, 1992, for $3,000. On June 11, 1992, W closed the short sale by delivering identical stock that she had purchased on June 10, 1992, for $10,000. On June 11, 1992, the price of the R stock was $12,000. A very favorable first-quarter earnings report (contrary to rumored large losses) accounted for the swings in the stock price. W also had the following stock transaction results: $500 STCG, $6,300 STCL, $700 LTCL, $43,500 LTCG. W has $210,000 of taxable income from sources other than those previously mentioned. The taxable income has already been adjusted the appropriate amount for the phase-out of the personal exemption deduction. What is W's net capital gain or loss? What is W's total tax liability?

49. For several years, K had rented an apartment for $3,000 per month. In 1992, a fire destroyed the apartment building. Under local law, the landlord was required to find comparable housing for K within five days. The landlord offered K $10,000 in lieu of suitable housing and in cancellation of the remaining two years of K's lease. K accepted. K's belongings were destroyed in the fire. All the belongings had been owned more than one year. K's insurance covered everything for replacement value. K received a check for $76,000. She prepared the following schedule to aid in your analysis:

Item	Adjusted Basis	FMV	Insurance Award	Action Taken	Amount Spent
Clothing	$25,000	$ 3,000	$25,000	Replaced	$40,000
Piano	8,000	12,000	10,000	Not replaced	—
Furniture	45,000	33,000	41,000	Replaced	38,000

K wishes to defer gains if possible. K's salary is $120,000. What is K's net capital gain or loss? K's adjusted gross income? K's basis for the replacement assets?

50. In 1992, V has a $4,800 net short-term capital loss and $4,030 of negative taxable income. He used the standard deduction and has one personal exemption. What is the amount of V's capital loss carryover to 1993?

51. For 1992, B completes the following stock transactions:

	Date Acquired	Cost	Date Sold	Selling Price
1,000 shares ABC	1/6/92	$4,000	8/2/92	$8,000
200 shares DEF	7/1/82	8,800	9/18/92	9,400
3,500 shares GHI	5/2/92	7,000	11/2/92	8,900
5,000 shares JKL	8/5/92	9,700	12/15/92	5,000

What is B's includible gain or deductible loss resulting from these stock sales?

52. X, an unmarried individual with no dependents, has the following 1992 transactions:

Adjusted gross income (exclusive of capital gains and losses)	$125,250
Long-term capital loss	(5,000)
Long-term capital gain	20,000
Short-term capital loss carryover	(2,000)

a. What is X's net capital gain or loss?
b. What is X's taxable income assuming he does not itemize and has one personal exemption?
c. What is X's tax on taxable income?

53. R Corporation has $16,800 of long-term capital loss for 1992 and $5,000 of other taxable income. What is its 1992 taxable income and the amount (if any) of its capital loss carryover?

CUMULATIVE PROBLEMS

54. Marvin and Sylvia Fryer (both 53) are married and file a joint return. Their address is 767 Clinton Street, Regon, Ohio 43763. Their Social Security numbers are 686–37–8757 and 687–45–2378, respectively. Marvin had a $32,000 salary as a copy machine repairman, and Sylvia had a $37,000 salary as a nurse. Sylvia inherited and then sold in two months 3,000 Exxon shares. The stock was valued in her mother's estate at $250,000 and was sold by Sylvia for $228,000. The Fryers had other stock sales resulting in a $5,000 short-term capital loss for the year. Marvin sold his baseball card collection for $5,500. He had owned the cards since he was eight years old. The cards were included in bubble gum packages he bought for $.05 each, and he sold 3,000 cards. Each package included three cards. The Fryers received $32,000 for a ramshackle cabin and 10 acres of land they had owned 11 years. The Fryers used the property for hunting and had paid $700 for it. The Fryers have $18,000 of itemized deductions, which include no medical expense, casualty loss, or investment interest expense deductions. The Fryers have no dependents. Marvin's employer withheld Federal income tax of $4,500, and Sylvia's employer withheld $4,900. They made no estimated tax payments. What is their 1992 taxable income and their net tax payable? Suggested software (if available): *TurboTax* for tax return or WFT tax planning software.

55. Tom Tenor, age 28, is an automobile mechanic. Tom lives at 518 Marigold Lane, Okemos, MI 48864. His Social Security number is 393–86–4502. He is single and has no dependents. In April 1992, while tinkering with his automobile, Tom devised a carburetor modification kit that increases gas mileage by 20%. He patented the invention and in June 1992 sold it to X Corporation for a lump-sum payment of $250,000 plus $5 per kit sold. Other information of potential tax consequence is as follows:

a. Cash received from X Corporation, which sold 20,000 kits in 1992, $100,000.
b. Wages earned as a mechanic from January 1 through June 17, $4,300.
c. Points paid on a $200,000 mortgage Tom incurred to buy a luxurious new home (he had previously lived in an apartment), $6,000.
d. State sales taxes paid on four new automobiles Tom acquired in 1992, $2,200.
e. Costs Tom incurred (including rent paid for a garage, materials, supplies, etc.) during the time he has continued his experimental activities and has worked on several potentially patentable automotive devices, $14,000.
f. Interest on home mortgage, $7,500.
g. Various miscellaneous itemized deductions (not including any potential deductions above), $9,400.
h. Interest income on savings account, $6,200.

Compute Tom's lowest legal tax liability, before prepayments or credits, for 1992. Suggested software (if available): *TurboTax* for tax return or WFT tax planning software.

56. Margaret Gill, age 33, is single with two dependents. Margaret is an insurance adjuster. She resides at 2510 Grace Avenue, Richmond, VA 23100. Her Social

Security number is 666–88–1000. The following information is for Margaret's 1991 tax year. She earned a $40,000 salary. Margaret received $35,000 of alimony and $40,000 of child support from her former husband. The children are Susan Gill (age 11, Social Security number 396–42–8909) and Jason Gill (age 9, Social Security number 396–43–9090). On March 1, 1982, she purchased 500 shares of People's Power Company for $10,000. She sold those shares on October 14, 1991, for $8,500 after receiving nontaxable dividends totaling $2,600 (including $700 in 1991). She also received $300 in taxable dividends in 1991 from People's Power Company. On November 7, 1983, Margaret purchased 1,000 shares of XYZ Corporation for $22,000. On February 12, 1991, she received an additional 100 shares in a nontaxable 10% stock dividend. On February 13, 1991, she sold those 100 shares for $2,500. During 1991, she paid $6,000 in deductible home mortgage interest, $1,200 in property taxes, $2,000 in state income taxes, $600 in sales tax, $2,300 in charitable contributions, and $1,500 in professional dues and subscriptions. Her employer withheld Federal income tax of $12,200. Compute Margaret's net tax payable or refund due for 1991. If you use tax forms for your computations, you will need Form 1040 and Schedules A, B, and D. Suggested software (if available): *TurboTax* for tax return or WFT tax planning software.

RESEARCH PROBLEMS

RESEARCH PROBLEM 1 The Banc Two Mortgage Company requires a fee of 1% of the remaining mortgage balance when a mortgage is paid off early. In the current year, Banc Two received $76,000 of such fees. What is the nature of the fee: ordinary income or capital gain?

Partial list of research aids:

The Prudential Insurance Co. of America, 89–2 USTC ¶9501, 64 AFTR2d 89–5225, 882 F.2d 832 (1989).
Azar Nut Co., 91–1 USTC ¶50,257, 67 AFTR2d 91–987, 931 F.2d 314 (affirming 94 T.C. 455).

RESEARCH PROBLEM 2 X Corporation runs a chain of dry cleaners. Borax is used heavily in X's dry cleaning process and has been in short supply several times in the past. X Corporation buys a controlling interest in Y Corporation—a borax mining concern. X's sole reason for purchasing the Y stock is to assure X of a continuous supply of borax if another shortage develops. Although borax must be refined before it is usable for dry cleaning purposes, a well-established commodities market exists for trading unrefined borax for refined borax. After owning the Y stock for several years, X sells the stock at a loss because Y is in difficult financial straits. X no longer needs to own Y because X has obtained an alternative source of borax. What is the nature of X's loss on the disposition of the Y Corporation stock?

RESEARCH PROBLEM 3 Treasury bills are short-term debt obligations issued by the U.S. government. As a result of a very old IRS Revenue Ruling, Treasury bills are *not* capital assets. Treasury bill futures are speculative investments that, in effect, "bet" on the direction Treasury bill interest rates will take. Are Treasury bill futures capital assets?

Partial list of research aids:

Rev.Rul. 51, 1953–1 C.B. 497.
Don D. Dial v. Comm., 58 TCM 1138, T.C. Memo. 1990–9.

CHAPTER

PROPERTY TRANSACTIONS: SECTION 1231 AND RECAPTURE PROVISIONS

OBJECTIVES

Explain the nature of § 1231 treatment of certain gains and losses.

Discuss the rationale for § 1231 treatment.

Define § 1231 assets.

Apply the special rules for certain § 1231 assets, including timber, coal, domestic iron ore, livestock, and unharvested crops.

Describe the procedure for computing § 1231 gains and losses.

Explain the rationale and procedures for §§ 1245 and 1250 recapture.

Discuss certain special recapture provisions.

Explain the treatment of gains and losses from dispositions of passive activity property.

Explain the tax form reporting of casualty losses and the gains and losses from the disposition of business property.

Develop tax planning ideas related to §§ 1231, 1245, and 1250.

OUTLINE

A long-term capital gain was defined in Chapter 16 as the recognized gain from the sale or exchange of a capital asset held for the required long-term holding period.[1] This chapter is concerned with § 1231, which applies to the sale or exchange of business properties and to certain involuntary conversions. The business properties are not capital assets because they are depreciable and/or are real property used in business or for the production of income. Section 1221(2) provides that such assets are not capital assets. Nonetheless, these business properties may be held for long periods of time and may be sold at a gain. Congress decided many years ago that such assets deserved *limited* capital gain–type treatment. Unfortunately, this limited capital gain–type treatment is very complex and difficult to understand.

Because the limited capital gain–type treatment sometimes gives too much tax advantage if assets are eligible for depreciation, certain recapture rules may remove the capital gain treatment when depreciation is taken. Thus, this chapter also covers the recapture provisions that tax as ordinary income certain gains that might otherwise qualify for long-term capital gain treatment.

The impact of the passive activity loss provisions (refer to Chapter 7) on the taxation of property gains and losses is also discussed briefly in this chapter.

SECTION 1231 ASSETS
◆

for AGI -(Losses)

Relationship to Capital Assets

Depreciable property and real property used in business are not capital assets.[2] Thus, the recognized gains from the disposition of such property (principally machinery, equipment, buildings, and land) would appear to be ordinary income rather than capital gain. Due to § 1231, however, *net gain* from the disposition of such property is sometimes *treated* as *long-term capital gain*. A long-term holding period requirement must be met; the disposition must generally be from a sale, exchange, or involuntary conversion; and certain recapture provisions must be satisfied for this result to occur. Section 1231 may also apply to involuntary conversions of capital assets. Since an involuntary conversion is not a sale or exchange, such a disposition would not normally result in a capital gain.

If the disposition of depreciable property and real property used in business results in a *net loss*, § 1231 *treats* the *loss* as an *ordinary loss* rather than as a capital loss. Ordinary losses are fully deductible *for* adjusted gross income (AGI). Capital losses are offset by capital gains, and, if any loss remains, the loss is deductible to the extent of $3,000 per year for individuals and is not deductible currently at all by regular corporations. It seems, therefore, that § 1231 provides the *best* of both potential results: net gain is treated as long-term capital gain, and net loss is treated as ordinary loss.

EXAMPLE 1

R sells business land and building at a $5,000 gain and business equipment at a $3,000 loss. Both properties were held for the long-term holding period. R's net gain is $2,000, and that net gain may (depending on various recapture rules discussed later in this chapter) be treated as a long-term capital gain under § 1231. ◆

EXAMPLE 2

S sells business equipment at a $10,000 loss and business land at a $2,000 gain. Both properties were held for the long-term holding period. S's net loss is $8,000, and that net loss is an ordinary loss. ◆

The rules regarding § 1231 treatment do *not* apply to *all* business property. Important in this regard are the holding period requirements and the fact that

1. The long-term holding period is more than one year.

2. § 1221(2).

the property must be either depreciable property or real estate used in business. Nor is § 1231 necessarily limited to business property. Transactions involving certain capital assets may fall into the § 1231 category. Thus, § 1231 singles out only some types of business property.

As discussed in Chapter 16, for 1991 and later years, there is a beneficial tax rate for long-term capital gains. Section 1231 requires netting of § 1231 gains and losses. If the result is a gain, the gain is treated as a long-term capital gain. The net gain is added to the "real" long-term capital gains (if any) and netted with capital losses (if any). Thus, the net § 1231 gain may eventually be taxed at the alternative long-term capital gain rate or help avoid the unfavorable net capital loss result. The § 1231 gain and loss netting may result in a loss. In this case, the loss is an ordinary loss and is deductible *for* AGI. Finally, § 1231 assets are treated the same as capital assets for purposes of the appreciated property charitable contribution provisions (refer to Chapter 11).

Justification for Favorable Tax Treatment

The favorable capital gain/ordinary loss treatment sanctioned by § 1231 can be explained by examining several historical developments. Before 1938, business property had been included in the definition of capital assets. Thus, if such property was sold for a loss (not an unlikely possibility during the depression years), a capital loss resulted. If, however, the property was depreciable and could be retained for its estimated useful life, much (if not all) of its costs could be recovered in the form of depreciation. Because the allowance for depreciation was fully deductible whereas capital losses were not, the tax law favored those who did not dispose of an asset. Congress recognized this inequity when it removed business property from the capital asset classification. During the period 1938–1942, therefore, all such gains and losses were ordinary gains and losses.

With the advent of World War II, two developments in particular forced Congress to reexamine the situation regarding business assets. First, the sale of business assets at a gain was discouraged because the gain would be ordinary income. Gains were common because the war effort had inflated prices. Second, taxpayers who did not want to sell their assets often were required to because of government acquisitions through condemnation. Often the condemnation awards resulted in large gains to taxpayers who were forced to part with their property and deprived them of the benefits of future depreciation deductions. Of course, the condemnations constituted involuntary conversions, the gain from which could be deferred through timely reinvestment in property that was "similar or related in service or use." But where was such property to be found in view of wartime restrictions and other governmental condemnations? The end product did not seem equitable: a large ordinary gain due to government action and no possibility of deferral due to government restrictions.

In recognition of these conditions, in 1942, Congress eased the tax bite on the disposition of some business property by allowing preferential capital gain treatment. Thus, the present scheme of § 1231 and the dichotomy of capital gain/ordinary loss treatment evolved from a combination of economic considerations existing in 1938 and 1942.

Property Included

Section 1231 property includes the following:

- Depreciable or real property used in business or for the production of income (principally machinery and equipment, buildings, and land).
- Timber, coal, or domestic iron ore to which § 631 applies.

- Livestock held for draft, breeding, dairy, or sporting purposes.
- Unharvested crops on land used in business.
- Certain nonpersonal use capital assets.

Property Excluded

Section 1231 property does *not* include the following:

- Property not held for the long-term holding period. Since the benefit of § 1231 is long-term capital gain treatment, the holding period must correspond to the more-than-one-year holding period that applies to capital assets. Livestock must be held at least 12 months (24 months in some cases). Unharvested crops do not have to be held for the required long-term holding period, but the land must be held for the long-term holding period.
- Property where casualty losses exceed casualty gains for the taxable year. If a taxpayer has a net casualty loss, the individual casualty gains and losses are treated as ordinary gains and losses.
- Inventory and property held primarily for sale to customers.
- Copyrights; literary, musical, or artistic compositions, etc.; and certain U.S. government publications.
- Intangible assets such as accounts receivable and notes receivable.

Notice that two of these items (inventory and copyrights, etc.) are also not capital assets (see the discussion in Chapter 16). Inventory and copyrights, etc., are ordinary assets.

Special Rules for Certain § 1231 Assets

A rather diverse group of assets is included under § 1231. The following discussion summarizes the special rules for some of those assets.

Timber. A taxpayer can *elect* to treat the cutting of timber held for sale or for use in business as a sale or exchange.[3] If the taxpayer makes this election, the transaction qualifies under § 1231. The taxpayer must have owned the timber or a contract to cut it on the first day of the year and for the long-term holding period before the date the cutting takes place. The recognized § 1231 gain or loss is determined at the time the timber is cut and is equal to the difference between the timber's fair market value as of the first day of the taxable year and the adjusted basis for depletion. If a taxpayer sells the timber for more or less than the fair market value as of the first day of the taxable year in which it is cut, the difference is ordinary income or loss.

This provision was enacted to provide preferential treatment relative to the natural growth value of timber, which takes a relatively long time to mature. Congress believed this favorable treatment would encourage reforestation of timber lands. If a taxpayer disposes of timber held for the long-term holding period, either by sale or under a royalty contract (where the taxpayer retains an economic interest in the property), the disposal is treated as a sale of the timber. Therefore, any gain or loss qualifies under § 1231.

Example 3

Several years ago, T purchased a tract of land with a substantial stand of trees on it. The land cost $40,000, and the timber cost $100,000. On the first day of 1992, the

3. § 631(a) and Reg. § 1.631–1.

timber was appraised at $250,000. In August 1992, T cut the timber and sold it for $265,000. T elects to treat the cutting as a sale or exchange under § 1231. T has a $150,000 § 1231 gain ($250,000 − $100,000) and a $15,000 ordinary gain ($265,000 − $250,000).

What if the timber had been sold for $235,000? T would still have a $150,000 § 1231 gain, but would also have a $15,000 ordinary loss. The price for computation of § 1231 gain is the price at the beginning of the year. Any difference between that price and the sales price is ordinary gain or loss. Here, since the price declined by $15,000, T has an ordinary loss in that amount. ◆

Coal or Domestic Iron Ore. If a taxpayer disposes of coal or domestic iron ore held for the long-term holding period, either by sale or under a royalty contract (where the taxpayer retains an economic interest in the property), the disposal is treated as a sale of the coal or domestic iron ore.[4] Therefore, any gain or loss qualifies under § 1231.

The provisions including coal and domestic iron ore royalties under § 1231 were enacted primarily to encourage the development and preservation of U.S. natural resources and to enable domestic producers to compete more favorably with foreign producers.

Livestock. Cattle and horses must be held 24 months or more and other livestock must be held 12 months or more to qualify under § 1231.[5] The primary reason for enacting this provision was the considerable amount of litigation over the character of livestock (whether livestock was held primarily for sale to customers [ordinary income] or for use in a trade or business [§ 1231 property]). Poultry is not livestock for purposes of § 1231.

Unharvested Crops. An unharvested crop on land used in business and held for the long-term holding period qualifies under § 1231 if the crop and land are disposed of at the same time to the same person. The cost of producing the crop must be capitalized (not expensed) for § 1231 to apply. This provision was enacted because taxpayers previously were able to recover the costs of producing crops through current deductions and were usually allowed long-term capital gain treatment on the disposition of the crop.

Certain Nonpersonal Use Capital Assets. *Nonpersonal use* property disposed of by casualty or theft may receive § 1231 treatment. Nonpersonal use property includes capital assets held for the production of income, such as an investment painting or investment land. Nonpersonal use property also includes business property. The casualty or theft *long-term* gains and losses from nonpersonal use property are combined (see Concept Summary 17–1). If the result is a gain, the gains and losses are treated as § 1231 transactions. If the result is a loss, § 1231 does not apply. Instead, the gains are treated as ordinary (even though some of them may initially be capital gains), the business losses are deductible *for* AGI, and the other losses (even though some of them may initially be capital losses) are deductible *from* AGI as miscellaneous losses subject to the 2 percent of AGI limitation. Thus, a nonpersonal use capital asset that is disposed of by casualty or theft may or may not be a § 1231 asset, depending on the result of the netting process. For simplicity, the rest of this chapter will use the term *casualty* to mean casualty *or* theft.

---

4. § 631(c) and Reg. § 1.631–3.

5. Note that the holding period is "12 months or more" and not "more than 12 months."

Personal use property casualty gains and losses are not subject to the § 1231 rules. If the result of netting these gains and losses is a gain, the net gain is a capital gain. If the netting results in a loss, the net loss is a deduction *from* AGI to the extent it exceeds 10 percent of AGI.

Casualties, thefts, and condemnations are *involuntary conversions.* Notice that condemnation gains and losses are not included in the netting processes discussed above. Long-term *recognized* condemnation gains and losses from the disposition of property held for business use and for the production of income are treated as § 1231 gains and losses. Involuntary conversion gains may be deferred if conversion proceeds are reinvested, but involuntary conversion losses are recognized (refer to Chapter 15) regardless of whether the conversion proceeds are reinvested.

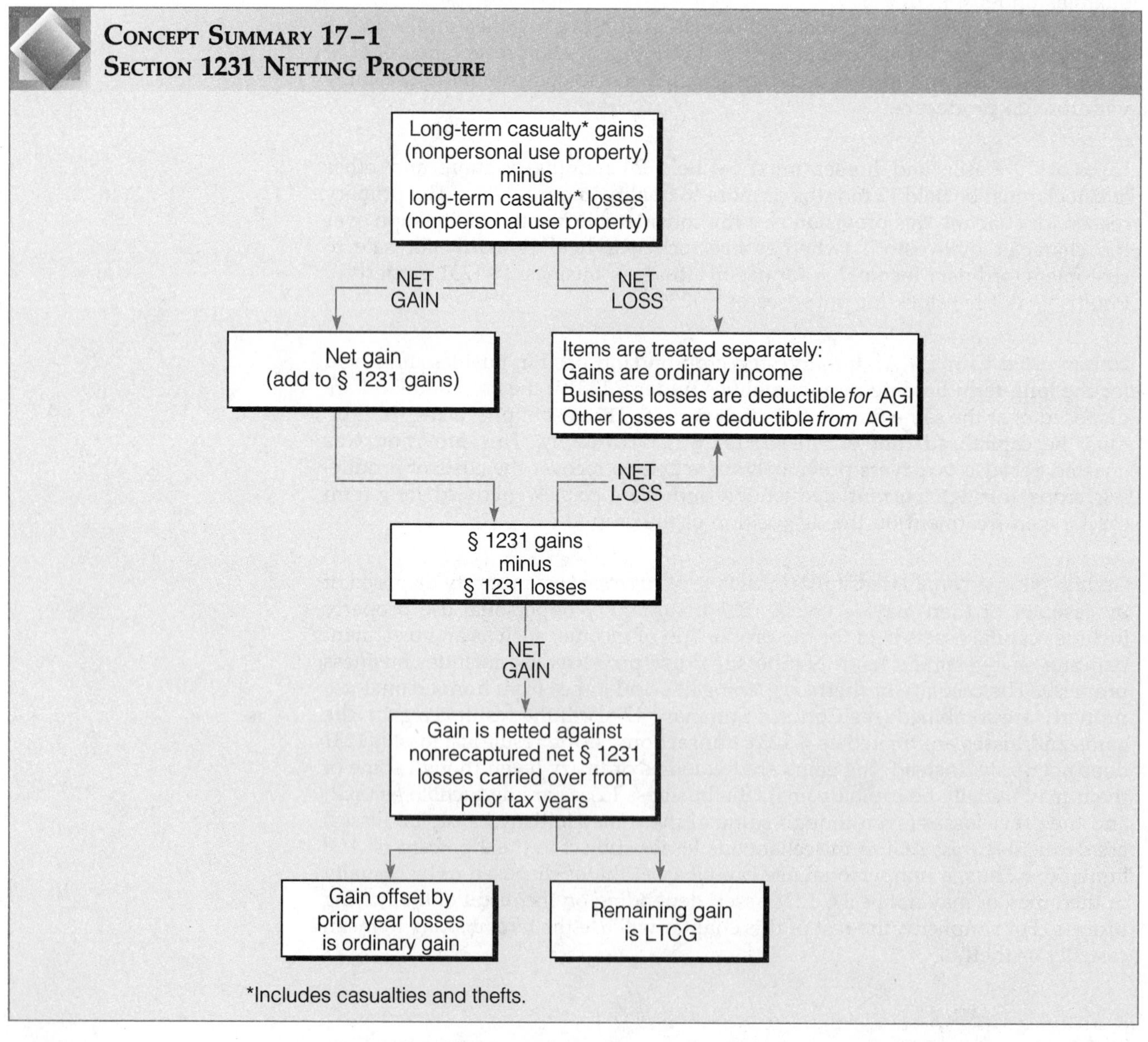

This variation in treatment between casualty and condemnation gains and losses sheds considerable light on what § 1231 is all about. Section 1231 has no effect on whether or not realized gain or loss is recognized. Instead, it merely dictates how such gain or loss might be *classified* (ordinary or capital) under certain conditions.

Personal use property condemnation gains and losses are not subject to the § 1231 rules. The gains are capital gains and the losses are nondeductible because they arise from the disposition of personal use property.

General Procedure for § 1231 Computation

The tax treatment of § 1231 gains and losses depends on the results of a rather complex *netting* procedure. The steps in this netting procedure are as follows.

Step 1: Casualty Netting. Net all long-term gains and losses from casualties of nonpersonal use property. Casualty gains result when insurance proceeds exceed the adjusted basis of the property.

a. If the casualty gains exceed the casualty losses, add the excess to the other § 1231 gains for the taxable year.
b. If the casualty losses exceed the casualty gains, exclude all losses and gains from further § 1231 computation. If this is the case, all casualty gains are ordinary income. Business casualty losses are deductible *for* AGI. Other casualty losses are deductible *from* AGI.

Step 2: § 1231 Netting. After adding any net casualty gain from Step 1a to the other § 1231 gains and losses (including recognized nonpersonal use property condemnation gains and losses), net all § 1231 gains and losses.

a. If the gains exceed the losses, the net gain is offset by the nonrecaptured § 1231 losses (see below) from prior tax years. To the extent of this offset, the net § 1231 gain is classified as ordinary gain. Any remaining gain is long-term capital gain.
b. If the losses exceed the gains, all gains are ordinary income. Business losses are deductible *for* AGI. Other casualty losses are deductible *from* AGI.

Step 3: § 1231 Lookback. The net § 1231 gain from Step 2a is offset by the nonrecaptured net § 1231 losses for the five preceding taxable years. For 1992, the lookback years are 1987, 1988, 1989, 1990, and 1991. To the extent of the nonrecaptured net § 1231 loss, the current year net § 1231 gain is ordinary income. The *nonrecaptured* net § 1231 losses are those that have not already been used to offset net § 1231 gains. Only the net § 1231 gain exceeding this net § 1231 loss carryforward is given long-term capital gain treatment. Concept Summary 17–1 summarizes the § 1231 computational procedure. Examples 6 and 7 illustrate the lookback procedure.

Examples 4 through 7 illustrate the application of the § 1231 computation procedure.

Example 4

During 1992, T had $125,000 of AGI before considering the following recognized gains and losses:

Capital Gains and Losses

Long-term capital gain	$3,000
Long-term capital loss	(400)
Short-term capital gain	1,000
Short-term capital loss	(200)

Casualties

Theft of diamond ring (owned four months)	$ (800)*
Fire damage to personal residence (owned 10 years)	(400)*
Gain from insurance recovery on accidental destruction of business truck (owned two years)	200

§ 1231 Gains and Losses from Depreciable Business Assets Held Long Term

Asset A	$ 300
Asset B	1,100
Asset C	(500)

Gains and Losses from Sale of Depreciable Business Assets Held Short Term

Asset D	$ 200
Asset E	(300)

*As adjusted for the $100 floor on personal casualty losses.

T had no net § 1231 losses in tax years before 1992.

Disregarding the recapture of depreciation and passive loss offset possibilities (discussed later in the chapter), T's gains and losses receive the following tax treatment:

- The diamond ring and the residence are personal use assets. Therefore, these casualties are not § 1231 transactions. The $800 (ring) plus $400 (residence) losses are potentially deductible *from* AGI. However, the total loss of $1,200 does not exceed 10% of AGI. Thus, only the business casualty remains. The $200 gain is added to the § 1231 gains.
- The gains from § 1231 transactions (Assets A, B, and C and the business casualty gain) exceed the losses by $1,100 ($1,600 less $500). This excess is a long-term capital gain and is added to T's other long-term capital gains.
- T's net long-term capital gain is $3,700 ($3,000 plus $1,100 from § 1231 transactions less the long-term capital loss of $400). T's net short-term capital gain is $800 ($1,000 less $200). The result is capital gain net income of $4,500. The $3,700 net long-term capital gain portion is eligible for the 28% alternative tax, and the $800 net short-term capital gain is subject to tax as ordinary income.[6]
- The gain and loss from Assets D and E (depreciable business assets held for less than the long-term holding period) are treated as ordinary gain and loss by T.

6. T's taxable income (unless the itemized deductions and the personal exemption and dependency deductions are extremely large) will put T in the 31% tax bracket. Thus, the 28% alternative tax computation will yield a lower tax. See Example 35 in Chapter 16.

Results of the Gains and Losses on T's Tax Computation

NLTCG	$ 3,700
NSTCG	800
Ordinary gain from sale of Asset D	200
Ordinary loss from sale of Asset E	(300)
AGI from other sources	125,000
AGI	$129,400

- T will have personal casualty losses of $800 (diamond ring) + $400 (personal residence). A personal casualty loss is deductible only to the extent it exceeds 10% of AGI. Thus, none of the $1,200 is deductible ($129,400 × 10% = $12,940). ◆

EXAMPLE 5

Assume the same facts as in Example 4, except the loss from Asset C was $1,700 instead of $500.

- The treatment of the casualty losses is the same as in Example 4.
- The losses from § 1231 transactions now exceed the gains by $100 ($1,700 less $1,600). As a result, the gains from Assets A and B and the business casualty gain are ordinary income, and the loss from Asset C is a deduction *for* AGI (a business loss). The same result can be achieved by simply treating the $100 net loss as a deduction *for* AGI.
- Capital gain net income is $3,400 ($2,600 long-term plus $800 short-term). The $2,600 net long-term capital gain portion is eligible for the 28% alternative tax, and the $800 net short-term capital gain is subject to tax as ordinary income.

Results of the Gains and Losses on T's Tax Computation

NLTCG	$ 2,600
NSTCG	800
Net ordinary loss on Assets A, B, and C and business casualty gain	(100)
Ordinary gain from sale of Asset D	200
Ordinary loss from sale of Asset E	(300)
AGI from other sources	125,000
AGI	$128,200

- None of the personal casualty losses will be deductible since $1,200 does not exceed 10% of $128,200. ◆

EXAMPLE 6

Assume the same facts as in Example 4, except that T has a $700 nonrecaptured net § 1231 loss from 1991.

- The treatment of the casualty losses is the same as in Example 4.
- The 1992 net § 1231 gain of $1,100 is treated as ordinary income to the extent of the 1991 nonrecaptured § 1231 loss of $700. The remaining $400 net § 1231 gain is a long-term capital gain and is added to T's other long-term capital gains.
- T's net long-term capital gain is $3,000 ($3,000 plus $400 from § 1231 transactions less the long-term capital loss of $400). T's net short-term capital gain is still $800 ($1,000 less $200). The result is capital gain net income of $3,800. The $3,000 net

long-term capital gain portion is eligible for the 28% alternative tax, and the $800 net short-term capital gain is subject to tax as ordinary income.

Results of the Gains and Losses on T's Tax Computation

NLTCG	$ 3,000
NSTCG	800
Ordinary gain from recapture of § 1231 losses	700
Ordinary gain from sale of Asset D	200
Ordinary loss from sale of Asset E	(300)
AGI from other sources	125,000
AGI	$129,400

- None of the personal casualty losses will be deductible since $1,200 does not exceed 10% of $129,400. ◆

EXAMPLE 7

Assume the same facts as in Example 4, except that in 1990 T had a net § 1231 loss of $2,700 and in 1991 a net § 1231 gain of $300.

- The treatment of the casualty losses is the same as in Example 4.
- The 1990 net § 1231 loss of $2,700 will have carried over to 1991 and been offset against the 1991 net § 1231 gain of $300. Thus, the $300 gain will have been ordinary income, and $2,400 of nonrecaptured 1990 net § 1231 loss will carry over to 1992. The 1992 net § 1231 gain of $1,100 will be offset against this loss, resulting in $1,100 of ordinary income. The nonrecaptured net § 1231 loss of $1,300 ($2,400 − $1,100) carries over to 1993.
- Capital gain net income is $3,400 ($2,600 net long-term capital gain plus $800 net short-term capital gain). The $2,600 net long-term capital gain portion is eligible for the 28% alternative tax, and the $800 net short-term capital gain is subject to tax as ordinary income.

Results of the Gains and Losses on T's Tax Computation

NLTCG	$ 2,600
NSTCG	800
Ordinary gain from recapture of § 1231 losses	1,100
Ordinary gain from sale of Asset D	200
Ordinary loss from sale of Asset E	(300)
AGI from other sources	125,000
AGI	$129,400

- None of the personal casualty losses will be deductible since $1,200 does not exceed 10% of $129,400. ◆

SECTION 1245 RECAPTURE

◆

Now that the basic rules of § 1231 have been introduced, it is time to add some complications. The Code contains two major *recapture* provisions—§§ 1245 and 1250. These provisions cause *gain* to be treated *initially* as ordinary gain. Thus, what may appear to be a § 1231 gain is ordinary gain instead. These recapture provisions may also cause a gain in a nonpersonal use casualty to be *initially* ordinary gain rather than casualty gain. Classifying gains (and losses) properly initially is important because improper initial classification may lead to incorrect mixing and matching of gains and losses. This section discusses the § 1245 recapture rules, and the next section discusses the § 1250 recapture rules.

Section 1245 prevents taxpayers from receiving the dual benefits of depreciation deductions that offset ordinary income plus § 1231 long-term capital gain treatment on the disposition of the depreciated property. Section 1245 applies primarily to non-real estate property such as machinery, trucks, and office furniture. Section 1245 requires recognized gain to be treated as ordinary income to the extent of depreciation taken on the property disposed of. Section 1245 does not apply if property is disposed of at a loss. Generally, the loss will be a § 1231 loss unless the form of the disposition is a casualty.

EXAMPLE 8

T purchased a $100,000 business machine and deducted $70,000 depreciation before selling it for $80,000. If it were not for § 1245, the $50,000 would be § 1231 gain ($80,000 amount realized less $30,000 adjusted basis). Section 1245 prevents this potentially favorable result by treating as ordinary income (not as § 1231 gain) any gain to the extent of depreciation taken. In this example, the entire $50,000 gain would be ordinary income. ◆

Section 1245 provides, in general, that the portion of recognized gain from the sale or other disposition of § 1245 property that represents depreciation (including § 167 depreciation, § 168 cost recovery, and § 179 immediate expensing) is *recaptured* as ordinary income. Thus, in Example 8, $50,000 of the $70,000 depreciation taken is recaptured as ordinary income when the business machine is sold. Only $50,000 is recaptured rather than $70,000 because T is only required to recognize § 1245 recapture ordinary gain equal to the lower of the depreciation taken or the gain recognized. In Example 8, the recognized gain is lower than the depreciation taken.

The method of depreciation (e.g., accelerated or straight-line) does not matter. All depreciation taken is potentially subject to recapture. Thus, § 1245 recapture is often referred to as *full recapture.* Any remaining gain after subtracting the amount recaptured as ordinary income will usually be § 1231 gain. The remaining gain would be casualty gain if it were disposed of in a casualty event. If the business machine in Example 8 had been disposed of by casualty and the $80,000 received had been an insurance recovery, T would still have a gain of $50,000, and the gain would still be recaptured by § 1245 as ordinary gain. The § 1245 recapture rules apply before there is any casualty gain. Since all the $50,000 gain is recaptured, no casualty gain arises from the casualty.

Although § 1245 applies primarily to non-real estate property, it does apply to certain real estate. Nonresidential real estate acquired after 1980 and before 1987 and for which accelerated depreciation (the statutory percentage method of the accelerated cost recovery system) is used is subject to the § 1245 recapture rules. Such property includes 15-year, 18-year, and 19-year nonresidential real estate.

The following examples illustrate the general application of § 1245.

EXAMPLE 9

On January 1, 1992, T sold for $13,000 a machine acquired several years ago for $12,000. She had taken $10,000 of depreciation on the machine.

- The recognized gain from the sale is $11,000. This is the amount realized of $13,000 less the adjusted basis of $2,000 ($12,000 cost less $10,000 depreciation taken).
- Depreciation taken is $10,000. Therefore, since § 1245 recapture gain is the lower of depreciation taken or gain recognized, $10,000 of the $11,000 recognized gain is ordinary income, and the remaining $1,000 gain is § 1231 gain.
- The § 1231 gain of $1,000 is also equal to the excess of the sales price over the original cost of the property ($13,000 − $12,000 = $1,000 § 1231 gain). ◆

EXAMPLE 10

Assume the same facts as in the previous example, except the asset is sold for $9,000 instead of $13,000.

- The recognized gain from the sale is $7,000. This is the amount realized of $9,000 less the adjusted basis of $2,000.
- Depreciation taken is $10,000. Therefore, since the $10,000 depreciation taken exceeds the recognized gain of $7,000, the entire $7,000 recognized gain is ordinary income.
- The § 1231 gain is zero. There is no § 1231 gain because the selling price ($9,000) does not exceed the original purchase price ($12,000). ◆

EXAMPLE 11

Assume the same facts as in Example 9, except the asset is sold for $1,500 instead of $13,000.

- The recognized loss from the sale is $500. This is the amount realized of $1,500 less the adjusted basis of $2,000.
- Since there is a loss, there is no depreciation recapture. All of the loss is § 1231 loss. ◆

The application of § 1245 recapture rules does not mean the depreciation deductions are lost. It means only that to the extent of depreciation taken, the gain does not qualify as casualty gain or for potential long-term capital gain treatment under § 1231. Thus, § 1245 deals only with the *classification* of the recognized gain and not with the *amount* of the recognized gain.

If § 1245 property is disposed of in a transaction other than a sale, exchange, or involuntary conversion, the maximum amount recaptured is the excess of the property's fair market value over its adjusted basis. See the discussion under Considerations Common to §§ 1245 and 1250 later in the chapter.

Section 1245 Property

Generally, § 1245 property includes all depreciable personal property (e.g., machinery and equipment), including livestock. Buildings and their structural components generally are not § 1245 property. The following property is *also* subject to § 1245 treatment:

- Amortizable personal property such as patents, copyrights, and leaseholds of § 1245 property. Professional baseball and football player contracts are § 1245 property.
- Amortization of reforestation expenditures and expensing of costs to remove architectural and transportation barriers to the handicapped and elderly.
- Section 179 immediate expensing of depreciable tangible personal property costs.
- Elevators and escalators acquired before January 1, 1987.
- Certain depreciable tangible real property (other than buildings and their structural components) employed as an integral part of certain activities such as manufacturing and production. For example, a natural gas storage tank where the gas is used in the manufacturing process is § 1245 property.
- Pollution control facilities, railroad grading and tunnel bores, on-the-job training, and child care facilities on which amortization is taken.
- Single-purpose agricultural and horticultural structures and petroleum storage facilities (e.g., a greenhouse or silo).
- As noted above, 15-year, 18-year, and 19-year nonresidential real estate for which accelerated cost recovery is used is subject to the § 1245 recapture

rules, although it is technically not § 1245 property. Such property would have been placed in service after 1980 and before 1987.

EXAMPLE 12

T acquired nonresidential real property on January 1, 1986, for $100,000. She used the statutory percentage method to compute the ACRS cost recovery. She sells the asset on January 15, 1992, for $120,000. The amount and nature of T's gain are computed as follows:

Amount realized			$120,000
Adjusted basis			
Cost		$100,000	
Less cost recovery:	1986	(8,800)	
	1987	(8,400)	
	1988	(7,600)	
	1989	(6,900)	
	1990	(6,300)	
	1991	(5,700)	
	1992	(217)	
January 15, 1992, adjusted basis			(56,083)
Gain realized and recognized			$ 63,917

The gain of $63,917 is treated as ordinary income to the extent of *all* depreciation taken because the property is 19-year nonresidential real estate for which accelerated depreciation was used. Thus, T reports ordinary income of $43,917 ($8,800 + $8,400 + $7,600 + $6,900 + $6,300 + $5,700 + $217) and § 1231 gain of $20,000 ($63,917 − $43,917). ◆

Observations on § 1245

- In most instances, the total depreciation taken will exceed the recognized gain. Therefore, the disposition of § 1245 property usually results in ordinary income rather than § 1231 gain. Thus, generally, no § 1231 gain will occur unless the § 1245 property is disposed of for more than its original cost. Refer to Examples 9 and 10.
- Recapture applies to the total amount of depreciation allowed or allowable regardless of the depreciation method used.
- Recapture applies regardless of the holding period of the property. Of course, the entire recognized gain would be ordinary income if the property were held for less than the long-term holding period because § 1231 would not apply.
- Section 1245 does not apply to losses, which receive § 1231 treatment.
- As discussed later in the chapter, gains from the disposition of § 1245 assets may also be treated as passive gains.

SECTION 1250 RECAPTURE
◆

Generally, *§ 1250 property* is depreciable real property (principally buildings and their structural components) that is not subject to § 1245.[7] Intangible real property, such as leaseholds of § 1250 property, is also included.

The recapture rules under § 1250 are substantially less punitive than the § 1245 recapture rules since only the amount of additional depreciation is subject

7. As previously discussed, in one limited circumstance, § 1245 does apply to nonresidential real estate. If the nonresidential real estate was placed in service after 1980 and before 1987 and accelerated depreciation was used, the § 1245 recapture rules rather than the § 1250 recapture rules apply.

to recapture. To have additional depreciation, accelerated depreciation must have been taken on the asset. Straight-line depreciation (except for property held one year or less) is not recaptured. Since real property placed in service after 1986 can only be depreciated using the straight-line method, there will be *no § 1250 depreciation recapture* on such property.

Section 1250 was enacted in 1964 for depreciable real property and has been revised many times. The provision prevents taxpayers from receiving the benefits of both *accelerated* depreciation (or cost recovery) deductions and subsequent long-term capital gain treatment upon the disposition of real property. If straight-line depreciation is taken on the property, § 1250 does not apply. Nor does § 1250 apply if the real property is sold at a loss. The loss will generally be a § 1231 loss unless the property is disposed of by casualty.

Section 1250 as originally enacted required recapture of a percentage of the additional depreciation deducted by the taxpayer. *Additional depreciation* is the excess of accelerated depreciation actually deducted over depreciation that would have been deductible if the straight-line method had been used. Since only the additional depreciation is subject to recapture, § 1250 recapture is often referred to as *partial recapture.*

Post-1969 additional depreciation on nonresidential real property is subject to 100 percent recapture (see Example 13). Post-1969 additional depreciation on residential property may be subject to less than 100 percent recapture (see Example 14).

If § 1250 property is disposed of in a transaction other than a sale, exchange, or involuntary conversion, the maximum amount recaptured is the excess of the property's fair market value over the adjusted basis. For example, if a corporation distributes property to its shareholders as a dividend, the property will have been disposed of at a gain if the fair market value is greater than the adjusted basis. The maximum amount of § 1250 recapture will be the amount of the gain.

The following discussion describes the computational steps prescribed in § 1250 and reflected on Form 4797 (Sales of Business Property).

Computing Recapture on Nonresidential Real Property

For § 1250 property other than residential rental property, the potential recapture is equal to the amount of additional depreciation taken since December 31, 1969. This nonresidential real property includes buildings such as offices, warehouses, factories, and stores. (The definition of and rules for residential rental housing are discussed later in the chapter.) The lower of the potential § 1250 recapture amount or the recognized gain is ordinary income. The following general rules apply:

- Post-1969 additional depreciation is depreciation taken in excess of straight-line after December 31, 1969.
- If the property is held for one year or less (usually not the case), all depreciation taken, even under the straight-line method, is additional depreciation.
- Special rules apply to dispositions of substantially improved § 1250 property. These rules are rather technical, and the reader should consult the examples in the Regulations for illustrations of their application.[8]

8. § 1250(f) and Reg. § 1.1250–5.

The following procedure is used to compute recapture on nonresidential real property under § 1250:

- Determine the recognized gain from the sale or other disposition of the property.
- Determine post-1969 additional depreciation.
- The lower of the recognized gain or the post-1969 additional depreciation is ordinary income.
- If any recognized gain remains (total recognized gain less recapture), it is § 1231 gain. However, it would be casualty gain if the disposition was by casualty.

The following example shows the application of the § 1250 computational procedure.

EXAMPLE 13

On January 3, 1980, T, an individual, acquired a new building at a cost of $200,000 for use in his business. The building had an estimated useful life of 50 years and no estimated salvage value. Depreciation has been taken under the 150% declining-balance method through December 31, 1991. Pertinent information with respect to depreciation taken follows:

Year	Undepreciated Balance (Beginning of the Year)	Current Depreciation Provision	Straight-Line Depreciation	Additional Depreciation
1980	$200,000	$ 6,000	$ 4,000	$ 2,000
1981	194,000	5,820	4,000	1,820
1982	188,180	5,645	4,000	1,645
1983	182,535	5,476	4,000	1,476
1984	177,059	5,312	4,000	1,312
1985	171,747	5,152	4,000	1,152
1986	166,595	4,998	4,000	998
1987	161,597	4,848	4,000	848
1988	156,749	4,702	4,000	702
1989	152,047	4,561	4,000	561
1990	147,486	4,425	4,000	425
1991	143,061	4,292	4,000	292
Total 1980–1991		$61,231	$48,000	$13,231

On January 2, 1992, the building was sold for $180,000. Compute the amount of § 1250 ordinary income and § 1231 gain.

- The recognized gain from the sale is $41,231. This is the difference between the $180,000 amount realized and the $138,769 adjusted basis ($200,000 cost less $61,231 depreciation taken).
- Post-1969 additional depreciation is $13,231.
- The amount of post-1969 ordinary income is $13,231. Since the post-1969 additional depreciation of $13,231 is less than the recognized gain of $41,231, the entire gain is not recaptured.
- The remaining $28,000 ($41,231 − $13,231) gain is § 1231 gain. ◆

Computing Recapture on Residential Rental Housing

Section 1250 recapture applies to the sale or other disposition of residential rental housing. Property qualifies as *residential rental housing* only if at least 80 percent of gross rent income is rent income from dwelling units.[9] The rules are the same as for other § 1250 property, except that only the post-1975 additional depreciation is recaptured in full. The post-1969 through 1975 recapture percentage is 100 percent less one percentage point for each full month the property is held over 100 months.[10] Therefore, the additional depreciation for periods after 1975 is initially applied against the recognized gain, and such amounts are recaptured in full as ordinary income. Any remaining recognized gain is then tested under the percentage rules applicable to the post-1969 through 1975 period. If any of the recognized gain is not absorbed by the recapture rules pertaining to the post-1969 period, the remaining gain is § 1231 gain.

EXAMPLE 14

Assume the same facts as in the previous example, except the building is residential rental housing.

- Post-1975 ordinary income is $13,231 (post-1975 additional depreciation of $13,231).
- Since the building was acquired in 1980, the post-1969 through 1975 recapture rules do not apply.[11]
- The remaining $28,000 ($41,231 − $13,231) gain is § 1231 gain. ◆

Under § 1250, when straight-line depreciation is used, there is no § 1250 recapture potential unless the property is disposed of in the first year of use. Before 1987, accelerated depreciation on real estate generally was available. For real property placed in service after 1986, however, only straight-line depreciation is allowed. Therefore, the § 1250 recapture rules will not apply to such property unless the property is disposed of in the first year of use.

EXAMPLE 15

T acquires a residential rental building on January 1, 1991, for $300,000. He receives an offer of $450,000 for the building in 1992 and sells it on December 23, 1992.

- T takes $20,909 [($300,000 × .03485) + ($300,000 × .03636 × 11.5/12) = $20,909] of total depreciation for 1991 and 1992, and the adjusted basis of the property is $279,091 ($300,000 − $20,909).
- T's recognized gain is $170,909 ($450,000 − $279,091).
- All of the gain is § 1231 gain. ◆

Section 1250 Recapture Situations

The § 1250 recapture rules apply to the following property for which accelerated depreciation was used:

- Residential real estate acquired before 1987.
- Nonresidential real estate acquired before 1981.
- Real property used predominantly outside the United States.
- Certain government-financed or low-income housing described in § 1250(a)(1)(B).

---

9. § 168(e)(2)(A) and Reg. § 1.167(j)–3(b)(1)(i).
10. §§ 1250(a)(1) and (2) and Reg. § 1.1250–1(d)(1)(i)(c).
11. If the building had been acquired on January 3, 1975, and sold on January 2, 1992, it would have been held 204 months. The recapture percentage for the 1975 additional depreciation would be 0% [100% less (204% less 100%)].

Concept Summary 17–2 compares and contrasts the § 1245 and § 1250 depreciation recapture rules.

Considerations Common to §§ 1245 and 1250

Exceptions

Recapture under §§ 1245 and 1250 does not apply to the following transactions.

Gifts. The recapture potential carries over to the donee.[12]

Example 16

T gives his daughter, D, § 1245 property with an adjusted basis of $1,000. The amount of recapture potential is $700. D uses the property in her business and claims further depreciation of $100 before selling it for $1,900. D's recognized gain is $1,000 (amount realized of $1,900 less $900 adjusted basis), of which $800 is recaptured as ordinary income ($100 depreciation taken by D plus $700 recapture potential carried over from T). The remaining gain of $200 is § 1231 gain. Even if D used the property for personal purposes, the $700 recapture potential would still be carried over. ◆

Death. Although not a very attractive tax planning approach, death eliminates all recapture potential.[13] In other words, any recapture potential does not carry over from a decedent to an estate or heir.

Concept Summary 17–2
Comparison of § 1245 and § 1250 Depreciation Recapture

	§ 1245	§ 1250
Property affected	All depreciable personal property, but also nonresidential real property acquired after December 31, 1980, and before January 1, 1987, for which accelerated cost recovery was used. Also includes miscellaneous items such as § 179 expense and amortization of patents and copyrights.	Residential real property acquired after December 31, 1980, and before January 1, 1987, on which accelerated cost recovery was taken. Residential real and nonresidential real property acquired after December 31, 1975, and before January 1, 1981, on which accelerated depreciation was taken.
Depreciation recaptured	Potentially all depreciation taken. If the selling price is greater than or equal to the original cost, all depreciation is recaptured. If the selling price is between the adjusted basis and the original cost, only some depreciation is recaptured.	Additional depreciation (the excess of accelerated cost recovery over straight-line cost recovery or the excess of accelerated depreciation over straight-line depreciation).
Limit on recapture	Lower of depreciation taken or gain recognized.	Lower of additional depreciation or gain recognized.
Treatment of gain exceeding recapture gain	Usually § 1231 gain.	Usually § 1231 gain.
Treatment of loss	No depreciation recapture; loss is usually § 1231 loss.	No depreciation recapture; loss is usually § 1231 loss.

12. §§ 1245(b)(1) and 1250(d)(1) and Reg. §§ 1.1245–4(a)(1) and 1.1250–3(a)(1).

13. §§ 1245(b)(2) and 1250(d)(2).

EXAMPLE 17

Assume the same facts as in Example 16, except T's daughter receives the property as a result of T's death. The $700 recapture potential from T is extinguished. D has a basis for the property equal to the property's fair market value (assume $1,700) at T's death. D will have a $300 gain when the property is sold because the selling price ($1,900) exceeds the property's adjusted basis ($1,700 original basis to D less $100 depreciation) by $300. Because of § 1245, $100 is ordinary income. The remaining gain of $200 is § 1231 gain. ◆

Charitable Transfers. The recapture potential reduces the amount of the charitable contribution deduction under § 170.[14]

EXAMPLE 18

T donates to his church § 1245 property with a fair market value of $10,000 and an adjusted basis of $7,000. Assume that the amount of recapture potential is $2,000 (the amount of recapture that would occur if the property were sold). T's charitable contribution deduction (subject to the limitations discussed in Chapter 11) is $8,000 ($10,000 fair market value less $2,000 recapture potential). ◆

Certain Nontaxable Transactions. These are transactions in which the transferor's adjusted basis of property carries over to the transferee.[15] The recapture potential also carries over to the transferee.[16] Included in this category are transfers of property pursuant to the following:

- Nontaxable incorporations under § 351.
- Certain liquidations of subsidiary companies under § 332.
- Nontaxable contributions to a partnership under § 721.
- Nontaxable reorganizations.

Gain may be recognized in these transactions if boot is received. If gain is recognized, it is treated as ordinary income to the extent of the recapture potential or recognized gain, whichever is lower.[17]

Like-Kind Exchanges (§ 1031) and Involuntary Conversions (§ 1033). Realized gain will be recognized to the extent of boot received under § 1031. Realized gain also will be recognized to the extent the proceeds from an involuntary conversion are not reinvested in similar property under § 1033. Such recognized gain is subject to recapture as ordinary income under §§ 1245 and 1250. The remaining recapture potential, if any, carries over to the property received in the exchange.

EXAMPLE 19

T exchanges § 1245 property with an adjusted basis of $300 for § 1245 property with a fair market value of $6,000. The exchange qualifies as a like-kind exchange under § 1031. T also receives $1,000 cash (boot). T's realized gain is $6,700 [amount realized of $7,000 less $300 (adjusted basis of property)]. Assuming the recapture potential is $7,500, § 1245 gain of $1,000 is recognized because boot of $1,000 is received. The remaining recapture potential of $6,500 carries over to the like-kind property received. ◆

---

14. § 170(e)(1)(A) and Reg. § 1.170A–4(b)(1). In certain circumstances, § 1231 gain also reduces the amount of the charitable contribution. See § 170(e)(1)(B).

15. §§ 1245(b)(3) and 1250(d)(3) and Reg. §§ 1.1245–4(c) and 1.1250–3(c).

16. Reg. §§ 1.1245–2(a)(4) and –2(c)(2) and 1.1250–2(d)(1) and (3) and –3(c)(3).

17. §§ 1245(b)(3) and 1250(d)(3) and Reg. §§ 1.1245–4(c) and 1.1250–3(c) . Some of these special corporate problems are discussed in Chapter 20. Partnership contributions are also discussed in Chapter 20.

Other Applications

Sections 1245 and 1250 apply notwithstanding any other provisions in the Code.[18] That is, the recapture rules under these Sections *override* all other Sections. Special applications include installment sales and property dividends.

Installment Sales. Recapture gain is recognized in the year of the sale.[19] All gain is ordinary income until the recapture potential is fully absorbed. Nonrecapture (§ 1231) gain is recognized under the installment method as cash is received.

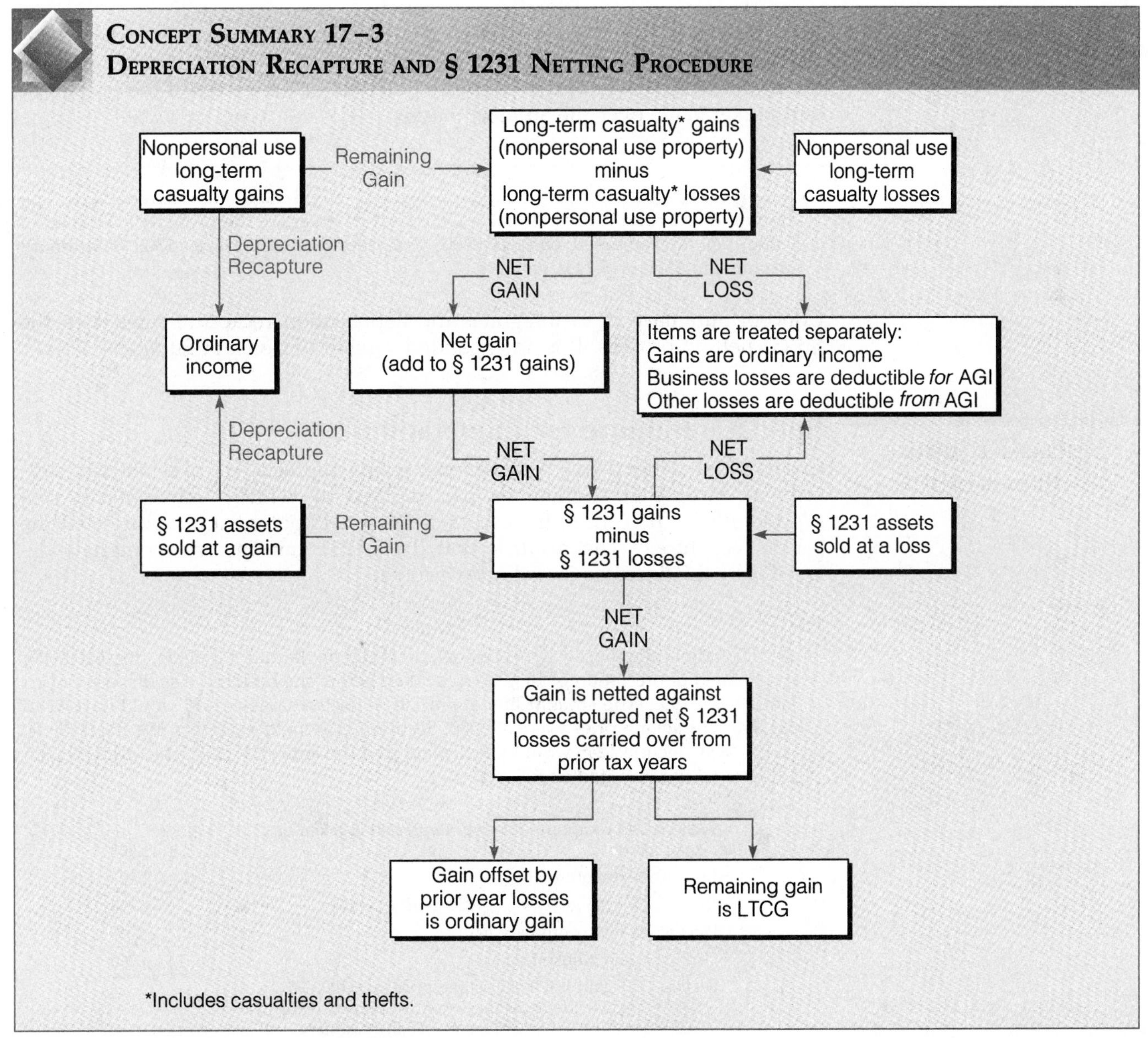

18. §§ 1245(d) and 1250(i).

19. § 453(i). The installment method of reporting gains on the sale of property is discussed in Chapter 18.

EXAMPLE 20

T sells § 1245 property for $20,000, to be paid in 10 annual installments of $2,000 each plus interest at 10%. T realizes a $6,000 gain from the sale, of which $4,000 is attributable to depreciation taken. If T uses the installment method, the entire $4,000 of recapture gain is recognized as ordinary income in the year of the sale. The $2,000 of nonrecapture (§ 1231) gain will be recognized at the rate of $200 per year for 10 years. ◆

Gain is also recognized on installment sales in the year of sale in an amount equal to the § 179 (immediate expensing) deductions taken with respect to the property sold.

Property Dividends. A corporation generally recognizes gain if it distributes appreciated property as a dividend. Recapture under §§ 1245 and 1250 applies to the extent of the lower of the recapture potential or the excess of the property's fair market value over the adjusted basis.[20]

EXAMPLE 21

X Corporation distributes § 1245 property as a dividend to its shareholders. The amount of the recapture potential is $300, and the excess of the property's fair market value over the adjusted basis is $800. X Corporation recognizes $300 of ordinary income and $500 of § 1231 gain. ◆

Concept Summary 17–3 integrates the depreciation recapture rules with the § 1231 netting process. It is an expanded version of Concept Summary 17–1.

SPECIAL RECAPTURE PROVISIONS

◆

Special Recapture for Corporations

Corporations (other than S corporations) selling depreciable real estate may have ordinary income in addition to that required by § 1250.[21] The *ordinary gain adjustment* is 20 percent of the excess of the § 1245 potential recapture over the § 1250 recapture.[22] The result is that the § 1231 gain is correspondingly decreased by this increase in ordinary income.

EXAMPLE 22

A corporation purchased a residential building on January 1, 1986, for $100,000. Accelerated depreciation of $43,900 was taken before the building was disposed of on January 15, 1992. The straight-line depreciation for the same period would have been $31,798. The selling price was $120,000. Section 1250 would recapture $12,102 ($43,900 − $31,798). Section 1245 would have recaptured the entire $43,900. The ordinary gain adjustment is computed as follows:

Section 1245 recapture (lower of depreciation taken or total gain)	$ 43,900
Less: Gain recaptured by § 1250	(12,102)
Excess of § 1245 gain over § 1250 gain	$ 31,798
Percentage that is ordinary gain	20%
Ordinary gain adjustment	$ 6,360
Section 1231 gain [$120,000 selling price − ($100,000 cost − $43,900 depreciation taken) = $63,900 gain; $63,900 − $12,102 § 1250 gain − $6,360 ordinary gain adjustment]	$ 45,438

◆

20. § 311(b) and Reg. §§ 1.1245–1(c) and –6(b) and 1.1250–1(a)(4), –1(b)(4), and –1(c)(2).

21. S corporations are discussed in Chapter 20.

22. § 291(a)(1).

Gain from Sale of Depreciable Property between Certain Related Parties

When the sale or exchange of property, which in the hands of the *transferee* is depreciable property (principally machinery, equipment, and buildings, but not land), is between certain related parties, any gain recognized is ordinary income.[23] This provision applies to both direct and indirect sales or exchanges. A *related party* is defined as an individual and his or her controlled corporation or partnership or a taxpayer and any trust in which the taxpayer (or the taxpayer's spouse) is a beneficiary.

EXAMPLE 23

T sells a personal use automobile (therefore nondepreciable) to her controlled corporation. The automobile, which was purchased two years ago, originally cost $5,000 and is sold for $7,000. The automobile is to be used in the corporation's business. If the related-party provision did not exist, T would realize a $2,000 long-term capital gain. The income tax consequences would be favorable because T's controlled corporation is entitled to depreciate the automobile based upon the purchase price of $7,000. Under the related-party provision, T's $2,000 gain is ordinary income. ◆

The related-party provision was enacted to prevent certain related parties from enjoying the dual benefits of long-term capital gain treatment (transferor) and a step-up in basis for depreciation (transferee). Recapture under §§ 1245 and 1250 applies first before recapture under the related-party provision.

Control means ownership of more than 50 percent in value of the corporation's outstanding stock or more than 50 percent of the capital interest or profits interest of a partnership. In determining the percentage of stock owned or partnership interest owned, the taxpayer must include the stock or partnership interest owned by related taxpayers as determined under the constructive ownership rules of § 267(c).

Section 267(a)(1) disallows a loss on the sale of property between certain related taxpayers. Therefore, a sale of property between certain related parties may result in ordinary income (if the property is depreciable in the hands of the transferee) or a nondeductible loss.

The related-party provision applies regardless of whether the transfer is from a shareholder or partner to the entity or from the entity to a shareholder or partner. Ordinary income treatment also applies to transfers between two corporations controlled by the same shareholder.

EXAMPLE 24

T, the sole shareholder of X Corporation, sells a building (adjusted basis of $40,000) for $100,000 to the corporation for use in its business. Since the building was depreciated by T using the straight-line method, none of the depreciation will be recaptured under § 1250. Nevertheless, the related-party provision applies to convert T's $60,000 § 1231 gain to ordinary income. The basis of the building to X Corporation is $100,000 (the building's cost). ◆

Rehabilitation Expenditures for Low-Income Rental Housing

Section 1250 recapture applies to the sale or other disposition of federally assisted housing projects and low-income housing for which rapid amortization of rehabilitation expenditures under § 167(k) has been taken. The rules are

23. § 1239.

generally the same as for residential rental housing except that post-1975 excess depreciation is not recaptured in full. That is, the post-1969 percentage rules continue to apply (the recapture percentage is 100 percent less one percentage point for each full month the property is held over 100 months).[24]

This preferential treatment stems from Congress's desire to stimulate the construction and reconstruction of low-income rental housing. The special rules for depreciating these properties are discussed in Chapter 9.

Intangible Drilling Costs and Depletion

Taxpayers may elect to either *expense or capitalize* intangible drilling and development costs for oil, gas, or geothermal properties.[25] *Intangible drilling and development costs* (*IDC*) include operator (one who holds a working or operating interest in any tract or parcel of land) expenditures for wages, fuel, repairs, hauling, and supplies. These expenditures must be incident to and necessary for the drilling of wells and preparation of wells for production. In most instances, taxpayers elect to expense IDC to maximize tax deductions during drilling.

Intangible drilling and development costs are subject to § 1254 recapture when the property is disposed of. The gain on the disposition of the property is subject to recapture as ordinary income as follows:

- For properties acquired before 1987, the IDC expensed after 1975 in excess of what cost depletion would have been had the IDC been capitalized.
- For properties acquired after 1986, the IDC expensed.

For properties acquired after 1986, depletion on oil, gas, geothermal, and other mineral properties is subject to recapture to the extent the depletion reduced the basis of the property. The combined IDC and depletion recapture may not exceed the recognized gain from disposition of the property. If the property is disposed of at a loss, no recapture occurs.

EXAMPLE 25

X acquired a working interest in certain oil and gas properties for $50,000 during 1991. He incurred $10,000 of IDC. X elected to expense these costs in 1991. In January 1992, the properties were sold for $60,000. Disregard any depreciation on tangible depreciable properties and assume that cost depletion would have amounted to $2,000 had the IDC been capitalized. Also, depletion of the working interest itself was $7,000. Thus, the basis of the working interest is $43,000 ($50,000 − $7,000). The gain realized and recognized is $17,000 ($60,000 − $43,000). The gain is recaptured as ordinary income to the extent of the expensed IDC ($10,000) and the depletion that reduced the property's basis ($7,000), which is equal to the recognized gain ($17,000). Therefore, $17,000 is recaptured. ◆

Special rules are provided for determining recapture upon the sale or other disposition of a portion or an undivided interest in oil, gas, geothermal, and other mineral properties.

PASSIVE ACTIVITY LOSSES

◆

Passive activity losses may result in current losses that are not deductible against nonpassive activity income.[26] If there is insufficient current passive income to absorb the passive losses, the losses are *suspended* until such time as

24. § 1250 (a)(1)(B)(iii). The Tax Reform Act of 1986 repealed the rapid amortization provision under § 167(k) effective for property acquired on or after January 1, 1987. See the Glossary of Tax Terms in Appendix C for a discussion of rehabilitation expenditures.
25. § 263(c).
26. § 469.

sufficient passive income is available to absorb them. (Passive activity losses are discussed in Chapter 7.) When a passive activity is disposed of, the suspended and current year losses of that activity are fully deductible. However, they also reduce the recognized gain, if any, from disposition of the activity. Any remaining gain is then available to allow other passive activity current and suspended losses to be currently deductible. The recognized gain still receives treatment under the normal property disposition rules discussed in Chapter 16 and in this chapter. If a passive activity is disposed of at a recognized loss, the loss is treated under the normal property disposition provisions. Thus, recognized *gains* from passive activity dispositions have a dual purpose: to allow deductibility of passive losses to the extent of the gain and to be treated under the normal property disposition rules. Recognized *losses* from passive activity dispositions do not have a dual purpose.

EXAMPLE 26

S disposes of a passive activity during 1992 at a $36,000 gain. The passive activity asset was a § 1231 asset, and the gain is a § 1231 gain. However, S has a current passive loss of $6,000 from this activity, no suspended losses from the activity, and $21,000 of current losses from another passive activity. The $36,000 gain allows the $6,000 and $21,000 passive losses to be fully deductible in 1992 as *for* AGI deductions. For purposes of computing S's net § 1231 gain, the full $36,000 of § 1231 gain is used. ◆

EXAMPLE 27

Assume the same facts as in the previous example, except that S has a $36,000 § 1231 loss rather than a gain. The § 1231 loss would be included in S's net § 1231 computation. The $6,000 current loss from the passive activity disposed of would be deductible in full as a deduction *for* AGI. The $21,000 loss from the other passive activity would not be deductible. ◆

REPORTING PROCEDURES

Noncapital gains and losses are reported on Form 4797, Sales of Business Property. Before filling out Form 4797, however, Form 4684, Casualties and Thefts, must be completed to determine whether or not any casualties will enter into the § 1231 computation procedure. Recall that gains from casualties may be recaptured by § 1245 or § 1250. These gains will not appear on Form 4684. Only long-term nonrecaptured nonpersonal use property casualty gains are netted against long-term nonpersonal use property casualty losses to determine whether there is a net gain to transfer to Part I of Form 4797.

The 1992 tax forms include a passive loss form (8582) for reporting the gains and losses from disposition of passive loss activities. Because the 1992 tax forms were unavailable at this writing, 1991 tax forms are used in the remainder of the discussion.

Form 4797 is divided into five parts, summarized as follows:

Part	Function
I	To report regular § 1231 gains and losses (including recognized gains and losses from certain involuntary conversions [condemnations]).
II	To report ordinary gains and losses.
III	To determine the portion of the gain that is subject to recapture (e.g., §§ 1245 and 1250 gain).
IV	To elect out of the installment method when reporting a note or other installment obligation at less than full face value.
V	Computation of recapture amounts under §§ 179 and 280F when business use of depreciable property drops to 50% or less.

Generally, the best approach to completing Form 4797 is to start with Part III. Once the recapture amount has been determined, it is transferred to Part II. The balance of any gain remaining after the recapture has been accounted for is transferred from Part III to Part I. Also transferred to Part I is any net gain from certain casualties and thefts as reported on Form 4684 (refer to above and Chapter 15). If the netting process in Part I results in a gain, such gain is reduced by the nonrecaptured net § 1231 losses from prior years (line 8 of Part I). Any remaining gain is shifted to Schedule D, Capital Gains and Losses, of Form 1040. If the netting process in Part I of Form 4797 results in a loss, it goes to Part II to be treated as an ordinary loss.

EXAMPLE 28

For 1991, Troy Williams (Social Security number 467–85–3036) had the following recognized gains and losses (a 1991 example has been used since 1992 forms were unavailable):

Sale of Depreciable Business Assets Held Long Term	
Asset A (Note 1)	$36,500
Asset B (Note 2)	19,411
Asset C (Note 3)	(880)

Sale of Depreciable Business Assets Held Short Term	
Asset D (Note 4)	$ (600)

Capital Assets	
Long-term gain (Note 5)	$ 3,000
Short-term loss (Note 6)	(200)

Note 1. Asset A was acquired on June 23, 1988, for $50,000. It was five-year MACRS property, and four years' cost recovery allowances totaled $38,480. The property was sold for $48,020 on August 31, 1991.

Note 2. Asset B was purchased on May 10, 1986, for $37,000. It was 19-year ACRS property. Using the statutory percentage method, cost recovery totaled $13,411. The property was sold for $43,000 on January 10, 1991. The building was residential rental property, and straight-line cost recovery for the period of ownership would have totaled $9,147.

Note 3. Asset C was purchased on December 9, 1988, for $16,000. It was five-year MACRS property, and four years' cost recovery totaled $12,314. The property was sold for $2,806 on December 30, 1991.

Note 4. Asset D was purchased for $7,000 on July 27, 1991. It was five-year MACRS property but proved unsuitable to Troy's business. Troy sold it for $6,400 on November 3, 1991.

Note 5. The LTCG resulted from the sale of 100 shares of X Corporation stock purchased for $10,000 on April 5, 1986. The shares were sold on October 21, 1991, for $13,223. Expenses of sale were $223.

Note 6. The STCL resulted from the sale of 50 shares of Y Corporation stock purchased for $350 on March 14, 1991. The shares were sold for $170 on August 20, 1991. Expenses of sale were $20.

The sale of assets A and B at a gain results in the recapture of cost recovery deductions. That recapture is shown in Part III of Form 4797. Some of the gain from the sale of asset B exceeds the recapture amount and is carried from line 32 to Part I, line 5, of Form 4797. On line 2, the loss from asset C appears. Part I is where the § 1231 netting process takes place. Assume Troy Williams has no nonrecaptured net § 1231 losses from prior years. The net gain on line 7 or 9 is transferred to Schedule D, line 13. In Part II of Form 4797, the ordinary gains are accumulated. On line 13, the recapture from line 31 (Part III) is shown. On line 10, the loss from asset D is shown. The net gain on line 18 is ordinary income and is transferred to Form 1040, line 15.

Schedule D, Part I, line 1a, reports the short-term capital loss from the Y Corporation stock. Part II of Schedule D has the net § 1231 gain transferred from Form 4797 on line 13 and the X Corporation gain on line 8a. The net capital gain is determined on line 17, Part III. The capital gain is then carried to line 13 of Form 1040.

Form 4797 and Schedule D (Parts I–III) for Troy Williams are reproduced on the following pages. ◆

Form **4797** Department of the Treasury Internal Revenue Service (T)

Sales of Business Property

(Also Involuntary Conversions and Recapture Amounts Under Sections 179 and 280F)

▶ Attach to your tax return. ▶ See separate instructions.

OMB No. 1545-0184 **1991** Attachment Sequence No. **27**

Name(s) shown on return: Troy Williams — Identifying number: 467-85-3036

Part I Sales or Exchanges of Property Used in a Trade or Business and Involuntary Conversions From Other Than Casualty or Theft—Property Held More Than 1 Year

1 Enter here the gross proceeds from the sale or exchange of real estate reported to you for 1991 on Form(s) 1099-S (or a substitute statement) that you will be including on line 2, 10, or 20 . . . . **1**

(a) Description of property	(b) Date acquired (mo., day, yr.)	(c) Date sold (mo., day, yr.)	(d) Gross sales price	(e) Depreciation allowed or allowable since acquisition	(f) Cost or other basis, plus improvements and expense of sale	(g) LOSS ((f) minus the sum of (d) and (e))	(h) GAIN ((d) plus (e) minus (f))
2							
ASSET C	12/9/88	12/30/91	2,806	12,314	16,000	880	

Line		(g)	(h)
3	Gain, if any, from Form 4684, Section B, line 21		
4	Section 1231 gain from installment sales from Form 6252, line 22 or 30		
5	Gain, if any, from line 32, from other than casualty or theft		15,147
6	Add lines 2 through 5 in columns (g) and (h)	(880)	15,147
7	Combine columns (g) and (h) of line 6. Enter gain or (loss) here, and on the appropriate line as follows:		14,267

Partnerships.—Enter the gain or (loss) on Form 1065, Schedule K, line 6. Skip lines 8, 9, 11, and 12 below.

S corporations.—Report the gain or (loss) following the instructions for Form 1120S, Schedule K, lines 5 and 6. Skip lines 8, 9, 11, and 12 below, unless line 7 is a gain and the S corporation is subject to the capital gains tax.

All others.—If line 7 is zero or a loss, enter the amount on line 11 below and skip lines 8 and 9. If line 7 is a gain and you did not have any prior year section 1231 losses, or they were recaptured in an earlier year, enter the gain as a long-term capital gain on Schedule D and skip lines 8, 9, and 12 below.

8 Nonrecaptured net section 1231 losses from prior years (see instructions) . . . .

9 Subtract line 8 from line 7. If zero or less, enter -0-. Also enter on the appropriate line as follows (see instructions):

S corporations.—Enter this amount (if more than zero) on Schedule D (Form 1120S), line 7, and skip lines 11 and 12 below.

All others.—If line 9 is zero, enter the amount from line 7 on line 12 below. If line 9 is more than zero, enter the amount from line 8 on line 12 below, and enter the amount from line 9 as a long-term capital gain on Schedule D.

Part II Ordinary Gains and Losses

10 Ordinary gains and losses not included on lines 11 through 16 (include property held 1 year or less):

(a)	(b)	(c)	(d)	(e)	(f)	(g)	(h)
ASSET D	7/27/91	11/3/91	6,400	0	7,000	600	

Line		(g)	(h)
11	Loss, if any, from line 7		
12	Gain, if any, from line 7, or amount from line 8 if applicable		
13	Gain, if any, from line 31		40,764
14	Net gain or (loss) from Form 4684, Section B, lines 13 and 20a		
15	Ordinary gain from installment sales from Form 6252, line 21 or 29		
16	Recapture of section 179 deduction for partners and S corporation shareholders from property dispositions by partnerships and S corporations (see instructions)		
17	Add lines 10 through 16 in columns (g) and (h)	(600)	40,764
18	Combine columns (g) and (h) of line 17. Enter gain or (loss) here, and on the appropriate line as follows:		40,164

a For all except individual returns: Enter the gain or (loss) from line 18 on the return being filed.

b For individual returns:

(1) If the loss on line 11 includes a loss from Form 4684, Section B, Part II, column (b)(ii), enter that part of the loss here and on line 20 of Schedule A (Form 1040). Identify as from "Form 4797, line 18b(1)." See instructions . . . 0

(2) Redetermine the gain or (loss) on line 18, excluding the loss, if any, on line 18b(1). Enter here and on Form 1040, line 15 . . . 40,164

For Paperwork Reduction Act Notice, see page 1 of separate instructions. Cat. No. 13086I Form **4797** (1991)

Form 4797 (1991) Page 2

Part III Gain From Disposition of Property Under Sections 1245, 1250, 1252, 1254, and 1255

19 Description of section 1245, 1250, 1252, 1254, or 1255 property:	Date acquired (mo., day, yr.)	Date sold (mo., day, yr.)
A ASSET A	6/23/88	8/31/91
B ASSET B	5/10/86	1/10/91
C		
D		

Relate lines 19A through 19D to these columns ▶	Property A	Property B	Property C	Property D
20 Gross sales price (**Note:** *See line 1 before completing.*)	48,020	43,000		
21 Cost or other basis plus expense of sale	50,000	37,000		
22 Depreciation (or depletion) allowed or allowable	38,480	13,411		
23 Adjusted basis. Subtract line 22 from line 21	11,520	23,589		
24 Total gain. Subtract line 23 from line 20	36,500	19,411		
25 **If section 1245 property:**				
a Depreciation allowed or allowable from line 22	38,480			
b Enter the **smaller** of line 24 or 25a	36,500			
26 **If section 1250 property:** If straight line depreciation was used, enter -0- on line 26g unless you are a corporation subject to section 291.				
a Additional depreciation after 1975 (see instructions)		4,264		
b Applicable percentage multiplied by the **smaller** of line 24 or line 26a (see instructions)		4,264		
c Subtract line 26a from line 24. If line 24 is not more than line 26a, skip lines 26d and 26e		15,147		
d Additional depreciation after 1969 and before 1976		0		
e Applicable percentage multiplied by the **smaller** of line 26c or 26d (see instructions)		0		
f Section 291 amount (corporations only)		0		
g Add lines 26b, 26e, and 26f		4,264		
27 **If section 1252 property:** Skip this section if you did not dispose of farmland or if you are a partnership.				
a Soil, water, and land clearing expenses				
b Line 27a multiplied by applicable percentage (see instructions)				
c Enter the **smaller** of line 24 or 27b				
28 **If section 1254 property:**				
a Intangible drilling and development costs, expenditures for development of mines and other natural deposits, and mining exploration costs (see instructions)				
b Enter the **smaller** of line 24 or 28a				
29 **If section 1255 property:**				
a Applicable percentage of payments excluded from income under section 126 (see instructions)				
b Enter the **smaller** of line 24 or 29a				

Summary of Part III Gains (Complete property columns A through D, through line 29b before going to line 30.)

30 Total gains for all properties. Add columns A through D, line 24	55,911
31 Add columns A through D, lines 25b, 26g, 27c, 28b, and 29b. Enter here and on line 13. (See the instructions for Part IV if this is an installment sale.)	40,764
32 Subtract line 31 from line 30. Enter the portion from casualty or theft on Form 4684, Section B, line 15. Enter the portion from other than casualty or theft on Form 4797, line 5	15,147

Part IV Election Not to Use the Installment Method (Complete this part only if you elect out of the installment method and report a note or other obligation at less than full face value.)

33 Check here if you elect out of the installment method ▶ ☐

34 Enter the face amount of the note or other obligation ▶ $ ______

35 Enter the percentage of valuation of the note or other obligation ▶ ______ %

Part V Recapture Amounts Under Sections 179 and 280F When Business Use Drops to 50% or Less (See instructions for Part V.)

	(a) Section 179	(b) Section 280F
36 Section 179 expense deduction or depreciation allowable in prior years		
37 Recomputed depreciation (see instructions)		
38 Recapture amount. Subtract line 37 from line 36. (See instructions for where to report.)		

SCHEDULE D (Form 1040)
Department of the Treasury Internal Revenue Service

Capital Gains and Losses

(And Reconciliation of Forms 1099-B for Bartering Transactions)

▶ Attach to Form 1040. ▶ See Instructions for Schedule D (Form 1040).
▶ For more space to list transactions for lines 1a and 8a, get Schedule D-1 (Form 1040).

OMB No. 1545-0074
1991
Attachment Sequence No. 12A

Name(s) shown on Form 1040: Troy Williams
Your social security number: 467 : 85 : 3036

Caution: *Add the following amounts reported to you for 1991 on Forms 1099-B and 1099-S (or on substitute statements):* **(a)** *proceeds from transactions involving stocks, bonds, and other securities, and* **(b)** *gross proceeds from real estate transactions not reported on another form or schedule. If this total does not equal the total of lines 1c and 8c, column (d), attach a statement explaining the difference.*

Part I Short-Term Capital Gains and Losses—Assets Held One Year or Less

(a) Description of property (Example, 100 shares 7% preferred of "Z" Co.)	(b) Date acquired (Mo., day, yr.)	(c) Date sold (Mo., day, yr.)	(d) Sales price (see instructions)	(e) Cost or other basis (see instructions)	(f) LOSS If (e) is more than (d), subtract (d) from (e)	(g) GAIN If (d) is more than (e), subtract (e) from (d)
1a Stocks, Bonds, Other Securities, and Real Estate. Include Form 1099-B and 1099-S Transactions. See instructions.						
Y Corp.						
50 shares	3/14/91	8/21/91	170	370	200	
1b Amounts from Schedule D-1, line 1b (attach Schedule D-1)						
1c Total of All Sales Price Amounts. Add column (d) of lines 1a and 1b . . ▶		1c	170			
1d Other Transactions (Do NOT include real estate transactions from Forms 1099-S on this line. Report them on line 1a.)						

Line	Description		(f) LOSS	(g) GAIN
2	Short-term gain from sale or exchange of your home from Form 2119, line 10 or 14c	2		
3	Short-term gain from installment sales from Form 6252, line 22 or 30	3		
4	Net short-term gain or (loss) from partnerships, S corporations, and fiduciaries .	4		
5	Short-term capital loss carryover from 1990 Schedule D, line 29	5		
6	Add lines 1a, 1b, 1d, and 2 through 5, in columns (f) and (g).	6	(200)	
7	**Net short-term capital gain or (loss).** Combine columns (f) and (g) of line 6	7		(200)

Part II Long-Term Capital Gains and Losses—Assets Held More Than One Year

(a) Description of property	(b) Date acquired	(c) Date sold	(d) Sales price	(e) Cost or other basis	(f) LOSS	(g) GAIN
8a Stocks, Bonds, Other Securities, and Real Estate. Include Form 1099-B and 1099-S Transactions. See instructions.						
X Corp.						
100 shares	4/ 5/86	10/21/91	13,223	10,223		3,000
8b Amounts from Schedule D-1, line 8b (attach Schedule D-1)						
8c Total of All Sales Price Amounts. Add column (d) of lines 8a and 8b . . ▶		8c	13,223			
8d Other Transactions (Do NOT include real estate transactions from Forms 1099-S on this line. Report them on line 8a.)						

Line	Description		(f) LOSS	(g) GAIN
9	Long-term gain from sale or exchange of your home from Form 2119, line 10 or 14c	9		
10	Long-term gain from installment sales from Form 6252, line 22 or 30	10		
11	Net long-term gain or (loss) from partnerships, S corporations, and fiduciaries .	11		
12	Capital gain distributions	12		
13	Gain from Form 4797, line 7 or 9	13		14,267
14	Long-term capital loss carryover from 1990 Schedule D, line 36.	14		
15	Add lines 8a, 8b, 8d, and 9 through 14, in columns (f) and (g)	15	( )	17,267
16	**Net long-term capital gain or (loss).** Combine columns (f) and (g) of line 15	16		17,267

For Paperwork Reduction Act Notice, see Form 1040 instructions. Cat. No. 11338H **Schedule D (Form 1040) 1991**

Schedule D (Form 1040) 1991 Attachment Sequence No. **12A** Page **2**

Name(s) shown on Form 1040. (Do not enter name and social security number if shown on other side.) | **Your social security number**

Part III **Summary of Parts I and II**

17	Combine lines 7 and 16 and enter the net gain or (loss) here. If the result is a gain, also enter the gain on Form 1040, line 13. (**Note:** *If both lines 16 and 17 are gains, see Part IV below.*)	17	17,067
18	If line 17 is a (loss), enter here and as a (loss) on Form 1040, line 13, the **smaller** of:		
a	The (loss) on line 17; **or**		
b	($3,000) or, if married filing a separate return, ($1,500)	18	( )

Note: *When figuring whether line 18a or 18b is* ***smaller,*** *treat both numbers as positive.*
Complete Part V if the loss on line 17 is more than the loss on line 18, OR if Form 1040, line 37, is zero.

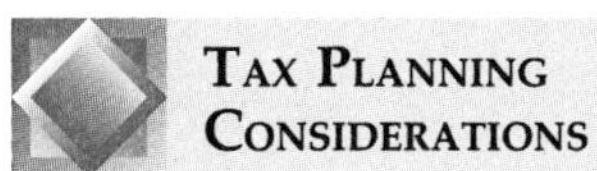

TAX PLANNING CONSIDERATIONS

Timing of § 1231 Gain

Although §§ 1245 and 1250 recapture much of the gain from the disposition of business property, sometimes § 1231 gain is still substantial. For instance, land held as a business asset will generate either § 1231 gain or § 1231 loss. If the taxpayer already has a capital loss for the year, the sale of land at a gain should be postponed so that the net § 1231 gain is not netted against the capital loss. The capital loss deduction will therefore be maximized for the current tax year, and the capital loss carryforward (if any) may be offset against the gain when the land is sold. If the taxpayer already has a § 1231 loss, § 1231 gains might be postponed to maximize the ordinary loss deduction this year. However, the carryforward of nonrecaptured § 1231 losses will make the § 1231 gain next year an ordinary gain.

EXAMPLE 29

T has a $2,000 net STCL for 1992. He could sell business land for a $3,000 § 1231 gain. He will have no other capital gains and losses or § 1231 gains and losses in 1992 or 1993. He has no nonrecaptured § 1231 losses from prior years. T is in the 28% tax bracket in 1992 and 1993. If he sells the land in 1992, he will have a $1,000 net LTCG ($3,000 § 1231 gain − $2,000 STCL) and will pay a tax of $280 ($1,000 × 28%). If T sells the land in 1993, he will have a 1992 tax savings of $560 ($2,000 capital loss deduction × 28% tax rate on ordinary income). In 1993, he will pay tax of $840 ($3,000 gain × 28%). By postponing the sale for a year, T will have the use of $840 ($560 + $280). ◆

EXAMPLE 30

S has a $15,000 § 1231 loss in 1992. He could sell business equipment for a $20,000 § 1231 gain and a $12,000 § 1245 gain. S is in the 28% tax bracket in 1992 and 1993. He has no nonrecaptured § 1231 losses from prior years. If he sells the equipment in 1992, he will have a $5,000 net § 1231 gain and $12,000 of ordinary gain. His tax would be $4,760 [($5,000 § 1231 gain × 28%) + ($12,000 ordinary gain × 28%)].

If S postpones the equipment sale until 1993, he would have a 1992 ordinary loss of $15,000 and tax savings of $4,200 ($15,000 × 28%). In 1993, he would have $5,000 of § 1231 gain (the 1992 § 1231 loss carries over and recaptures $15,000 of the 1993 § 1231 gain as ordinary income) and $27,000 of ordinary gain. His tax would be $8,960 [($5,000 § 1231 gain × 28%) + ($27,000 ordinary gain × 28%)]. By postponing the equipment sale, S has the use of $8,960 ($4,200 + $4,760). ◆

Timing of Recapture

Since recapture is usually not triggered until the property is sold or disposed of, it may be possible to plan for recapture in low-bracket or loss years. If a taxpayer has net operating loss carryovers that are about to expire, the recognition of ordinary income from recapture may be advisable to absorb the loss carryovers.

EXAMPLE 31

T has a $15,000 net operating loss carryover that will expire this year. He owns a machine that he plans to sell in the early part of next year. The expected gain of $17,000 from the sale of the machine will be recaptured as ordinary income under § 1245. T sells the machine before the end of this year and offsets $15,000 of the ordinary income against the net operating loss carryover. ◆

Postponing and Shifting Recapture

It is also possible to postpone recapture or to shift the burden of recapture to others. For example, recapture is avoided upon the disposition of a § 1231 asset if the taxpayer replaces the property by entering into a like-kind exchange. In this instance, recapture potential is merely carried over to the newly acquired property (refer to Example 19).

Recapture can be shifted to others through the gratuitous transfer of § 1245 or § 1250 property to family members. A subsequent sale of such property by the donee will trigger recapture to the donee rather than the donor (refer to Example 16). This procedure would be advisable only if the donee is in a lower income tax bracket than the donor.

Avoiding Recapture

The immediate expensing election (§ 179) is subject to § 1245 recapture. If the election is not made, the § 1245 recapture potential will accumulate more slowly (refer to Chapter 9). Since using the immediate expense deduction complicates depreciation and book accounting for the affected asset, not taking the deduction may make sense even though the time value of money might indicate it should be taken.

Disposing of Passive Activities

Taxpayers with suspended or current passive activity losses may wish to dispose of passive activities. The current and suspended losses of the activity disposed of will be fully deductible. If there is a recognized loss on the disposition, the loss will not be subject to the passive activity loss limitations. Rather, it will be classified and treated as a normal property disposition loss (refer to Example 27). If there is a recognized gain on the disposition, the gain will first absorb the current and suspended losses of the activity disposed of, and any remaining gain will absorb losses from other passive activities. The gain will also be treated under the normal property disposition rules (refer to Example 26).

Problem Materials

Discussion Questions

1. What types of transactions involving capital assets are included under § 1231? Why wouldn't they qualify for long-term capital gain treatment without § 1231?
2. Does § 1231 treatment apply to all business property?
3. The disposition of depreciable business property results in a net loss. How is the net loss treated for tax purposes?
4. What two major developments during World War II caused Congress to reexamine the tax treatment for disposition of business assets?
5. Name two types of assets that are neither § 1231 assets nor capital assets.

6. Is it possible to recognize both a gain and a loss on the sale of timber in one taxable year? How?
7. What circumstances must be met for an unharvested crop to receive preferential treatment under § 1231?
8. Do casualty losses from disposition of long-term nonpersonal use assets receive § 1231 treatment?
9. Do casualty gains from disposition of personal use assets receive § 1231 treatment?
10. Are recognized long-term business asset condemnation gains treated as § 1231 gains? (Ignore the possibility of depreciation recapture.)
11. If the result of the netting of § 1231 gains and losses is a net loss, how is the net loss treated?
12. How does the *lookback rule* change the character of a current year net § 1231 gain?
13. Fully depreciated business equipment purchased for $75,000 was stolen from V. It was not recovered, and the insurance reimbursement was $10,000. Is this $10,000 gain subject to depreciation recapture? Why?
14. What is recapture potential under § 1245? What factors limit it?
15. If a farmer buys a pig and uses MACRS, are the cost recovery deductions subject to § 1245 recapture if the pig is sold at a gain?
16. Differentiate between the types of property covered by §§ 1245 and 1250.
17. If depreciable real property is sold at a loss after being held long term, does § 1250 apply?
18. How does depreciation recapture under § 1245 differ from depreciation recapture under § 1250?
19. Why does § 1250 generally not apply to real estate acquired after 1986?
20. What is the definition of residential rental housing?
21. Do any of the recapture provisions apply to real property that is owned by a U.S. taxpayer, but used in Italy?
22. What happens to recapture potential when a gift is made?
23. A taxpayer disposes of property by casualty, but has recognized gain due to an insurance reimbursement that exceeded the amount of the casualty. The property was depreciable business property subject to § 1245 depreciation recapture. The insurance proceeds do not exceed the original cost of the property. How is the gain treated?
24. What happens to depreciation recapture potential under either § 1245 or § 1250 when a corporate taxpayer distributes depreciable equipment as a property dividend? Assume the equipment would have been sold at a gain if it were sold rather than distributed.
25. What special recapture provision applies only to regular corporations?
26. In general, how does the related-party ordinary income provision differ from §§ 1245 and 1250?
27. A taxpayer sells low-income rental housing acquired in 1985. The property had been held 80 months when it was sold. Rapid amortization of rehabilitation expenditures under § 167(k) had been taken. What is the recapture percentage?
28. X acquired a working interest in certain oil and gas properties for $100,000 in 1991. He incurred and paid $25,000 of intangible development and drilling costs that were expensed in 1991. In January 1992, he sold the properties for $110,000. Disregard any depreciation on tangible depreciable properties and assume that cost depletion would have amounted to $6,000. What are the nature and amount of the gain recognized?
29. If a taxpayer has a § 1231 gain from disposition of a passive activity, what may happen to the gain before it is treated under the normal § 1231 gain and loss netting process?
30. Are recognized losses from the disposition of a passive activity treated under the normal property disposition provisions?

31. Where in the tax forms is the §§ 1245 and 1250 depreciation recapture shown?
32. On what tax form and where on that form does the § 1231 netting process to determine whether there is a net § 1231 gain or loss take place?

PROBLEMS

33. Ms. S purchased a contract to cut timber on a 100-acre tract of land in South Dakota in March 1990 for $20,000. On January 1, 1991, the timber had a fair market value of $50,000. Because of careless cutting in November 1991, when the fair market value was $55,000, the wood was sold on January 30, 1992, for $49,000.

    a. What gain (loss) was realized in 1990, 1991, and 1992? What gain (loss) was recognized in 1990, 1991, and 1992?
    b. What was the nature of the gains (losses) in (a)? What assumption must be made?
    c. Does the answer change if the timber was sold in December of 1991? Why?
    d. If on January 1, 1991, the timber was worth only $18,000, was cut in November when worth $21,000, and was sold in December for $19,000, how would the answers to (a) and (b) change?

34. B owns a farming sole proprietorship. During the year, B sold a milk cow that he had owned for 13 months and a workhorse that he had owned for 56 months. The cow had an adjusted basis of $800 and was sold for $550. The horse had an adjusted basis of $350 and was sold for $1,000. B also has a $200 long-term capital loss from the sale of corporate stock. B has $55,000 of other AGI (not associated with the items above) for the year. B has no net § 1231 losses from previous years. What is the nature of the gains or losses from the disposition of the farm animals, and what is B's AGI for the year?
35. V has the following net § 1231 results for each of the years shown. What would be the nature of the net gains in 1991 and 1992?

Tax Year	Net § 1231 Loss	Net § 1231 Gain
1987	$ 5,000	
1988	7,000	
1989	35,000	
1990		$10,000
1991		30,000
1992		15,000

36. T, who owns and operates a farm business, had the following transactions during 1992:

    - Damage from the wreck of a business machine held more than one year due to hurricane ($15,000 loss).
    - Sale of a mechanical rake bought on April 1 and sold on September 1 ($600 gain). (Disregard recapture.)
    - Sale of farmland with unharvested crops, held four years ($12,000 gain).
    - Recovery on theft of a family brooch owned for 10 years ($10,000 gain).
    - Fire in silo on December 6, purchased May 8 ($1,000 loss).
    - Sale of grist mill owned 11 years ($3,000 loss).
    - Sale of 15 shares of Q Corporation stock held four months ($1,800 gain).

    a. How is each transaction treated?
    b. What is T's 1992 AGI?

37. R owned a number of parking lots throughout the city. In 1992, R sold two parcels of unimproved real estate that he had used since 1978 in his parking lot business. The sale of parcel A resulted in a $6,000 recognized loss, and the sale of parcel B generated a $10,000 recognized gain. R also had a long-term capital loss of $7,000 from a sale of stock he had held for investment. R's AGI was $50,000 before taking the previous transactions into consideration. Compute R's 1992 AGI after including the described transactions.

38. S Corporation sold machines A and B during the current year. The machines had been purchased for $180,000 and $240,000, respectively. The machines were purchased eight years ago and were depreciated to zero. Machine A was sold for $40,000, and machine B for $260,000. What amount of gain is recognized by S, and what is the nature of the gain?

39. On March 1, 1988, N buys and places in service a new seven-year machine for $25,000. On April 1, 1992, N sells the machine for $2,000. Cost recovery deductions to date have been $17,841.

    a. What is N's realized and recognized loss?
    b. What is the nature of the loss?

40. R Manufacturing purchases a $3,000,000 propane storage tank and places it on a permanent framework outside R's plant. The propane is drawn from the tank through a hose and valve system into the burners underneath R's chemical vats. After $1,800,000 of depreciation has been taken on the tank, it is sold for $2,300,000. What is the nature and amount of R's gain or loss from the disposition of the tank?

41. On June 1, 1989, T acquired a retail store for $400,000. The store was 31.5-year real property, and the straight-line cost recovery method was used. The store was sold on June 21, 1992, for $390,000. Depreciation taken totaled $38,000. What are the amount and nature of T's gain or loss from disposition of the store?

42. On January 1, 1982, T acquired a $600,000 residential building for use in his rental activity. T took $450,000 of cost recovery on the building before disposing of it for $800,000 on January 1, 1992. For the period T held the building, straight-line cost recovery would have been $400,000. What is amount and nature of T's gain from disposition of the property?

43. D is the sole proprietor of a trampoline shop. During 1992, the following transactions occurred:

    - Unimproved land adjacent to the store was condemned by the city on February 1. The condemnation proceeds were $25,000. The land, acquired in 1982, had an allocable basis of $15,000. D has additional parking across the street and plans to use the condemnation proceeds to build his inventory.
    - A truck used to deliver trampolines was sold on January 2 for $3,500. The truck was purchased on January 2, 1988, for $6,000. On the date of sale, the adjusted basis was $2,509.
    - D sold an antique rowing machine at an auction. Net proceeds were $3,900. The rowing machine was purchased as used equipment 17 years ago for $5,200 and is fully depreciated.
    - D sold an apartment building for $200,000 on September 1. The rental property was purchased on September 1, 1989, for $150,000 and was being depreciated over a 27.5-year life using the straight-line method. At the date of sale, the adjusted basis was $124,783. This is D's only passive activity, and D has no current or suspended losses from this activity.
    - D's personal yacht was stolen September 5. The yacht had been purchased in August at a cost of $25,000. The fair market value immediately preceding the theft was $20,000. D was insured for 50% of the original cost, and he received $12,500 on December 1.
    - D sold a Buick on May 1 for $9,600. The vehicle had been used exclusively for personal purposes. It was purchased on September 1, 1987, for $10,800.
    - An adding machine used by D's bookkeeper was sold on June 1. Net proceeds of the sale were $135. The machine was purchased on June 2, 1988, for $350. It was being depreciated over a five-year life employing the straight-line method. The adjusted basis on the date of sale was $95.
    - D's trampoline stretching machine (owned two years) was stolen on May 5, but the business's insurance company will not pay any of the machine's value because D failed to pay the insurance premium. The machine had a fair market value of $8,000 and an adjusted basis of $6,000 at the time of theft.
    - D had AGI of $4,000 from sources other than those described above.

a. For each transaction, what are the amount and nature of recognized gain or loss?
b. What is D's 1992 AGI?

44. R purchased a building in April 1991 for $200,000. He sold the building on December 23, 1992, for $235,000. What would be the nature and amount of R's gain assuming the following:

a. The building is residential rental real estate, and total cost recovery of $12,121 was taken.
b. The building is a retail store and was sold for $150,000, and total cost recovery of $10,583 was taken.

45. On February 10, 1992, S sold land A ($55,000 cost; $50,000 sales price), land B ($35,000 cost; $75,000 sales price), and building B ($40,000 cost; $45,000 sales price). Land A was vacant land that S had purchased for investment in 1986. Land B had building B on it, and both assets had been purchased in January 1991. The building was used in S's business, and $1,375 of depreciation had been taken on it. S has $1,490 nonrecaptured § 1231 losses from prior years. What are the amount and nature of each gain or loss, and what is S's AGI for 1992?

46. Refer to the facts of Problem 45. Rework the problem assuming S was a corporation.

47. P owned a § 1245 asset with an adjusted basis of $5,000. The amount of depreciation deducted by P was $6,000 ($5,000 adjusted basis + $6,000 depreciation = $11,000 original cost). On May 1, 1990, P made a gift of the asset to his child, C, when the fair market value was $22,500. C used the asset for two years (deducting an additional $2,000 of depreciation) in her business. On November 7, 1992, C sold the asset for $36,000.

a. What is C's basis for the asset on November 7, 1992?
b. What are the amount and character of C's recognized gain?
c. How would your answers in (a) and (b) differ if C had received the asset as a result of P's death?

48. T transferred forklifts used in his factory with recapture potential of $6,500 to a dealer in exchange for new forklifts worth $8,000 and $1,500 of marketable securities. The transaction qualified as a § 1031 like-kind exchange. T had an adjusted basis in the equipment of $6,000.

a. What is T's realized and recognized gain or loss?
b. What is the nature of the recognized gain or loss?
c. How would the answer to (a) or (b) change if no marketable securities were involved?

49. E organizes a corporation of which she is the sole shareholder. She sells to the corporation for $25,500 business land that cost $18,000 and has a fair market value of $25,500. Several years later, the corporation sells the land for $12,000. What are the tax ramifications of this transfer?

50. J sold an apartment building she had owned for three years for $35,000 in 1992. The building had an adjusted basis of $40,000 and was sold to J's brother at its FMV. The furniture in the building was sold to an unrelated party, and a $28,000 § 1245 gain resulted. J sold the land to her brother for a loss of $20,000. J had other income of $78,000 and $75,000 of expenses deductible for AGI. What is J's 1992 AGI? Assume the real estate was not a passive activity and J had no nonrecaptured § 1231 losses.

51. X acquired a working interest in an oil property for $60,000 on February 10, 1991. She incurred $15,000 of intangible drilling and development costs and elected to expense them. On April 20, 1992, the property was sold for $150,000. Cost depletion on the IDC would have been $3,000 if those costs had been capitalized. Also, depletion of the working interest itself was $6,000. What are the amount and nature of the gain from disposing of the property?

52. In 1992, M disposes of passive activity A for a $15,000 § 1245 gain and a $30,000 § 1231 gain. M has no suspended losses from this activity but has a current operating loss of $3,000. M also has a current operating loss of $8,700 from passive activity B, but has no suspended losses from that activity. M has no other property transactions during 1992 and has no nonrecaptured § 1231 losses. What is the treatment of the gains from the disposition of activity A?

53. Refer to the facts of Problem 52. Assume that M has a $45,000 § 1231 loss rather than a gain from the disposition of the passive activity. What is the treatment of the loss from the disposition of activity A?

54. Refer to the sample 1991 Form 4797 and Form 1040 Schedule D in the text. Taxpayer E has the following items on these forms:

Item	Form 4797		Schedule D	
Property A (§ 1245 property)	Line 22	$86,000		
	Line 24	96,000		
Property B (§ 1250 property)	Line 24	34,000		
	Line 26a	32,000		
Property C			Line 8a	($3,000)

E has no nonrecaptured § 1231 losses from prior years. What is E's entry on line 17 of Schedule D?

CUMULATIVE PROBLEMS

55. Glen and Diane Okumura are married, file a joint return, and live at 39 Kaloa Street, Honolulu, Hawaii 56790. Glen's Social Security number is 777–88–2000 and Diane's is 888–77–1000. The Okumuras have two dependent children, Amy (age 15) and John (age 9). Glen works for the Hawaii Public Works Department, and Diane owns a retail dress shop. The Okumuras had the following transactions during 1992:

   a. Glen earned $57,000 in wages and had Federal income tax withholding of $14,000.
   b. Diane had net income of $98,000 from the dress shop and made Federal income tax estimated payments of $24,000.
   c. The Okumuras sold a small apartment building for $165,000 on November 15, 1992. The building was acquired in October 1986 for $300,000, accelerated cost recovery of $132,900 was taken, and $108,549 of straight-line cost recovery would have been taken for the same time period. The apartment building was a passive activity, with a $2,000 1992 operating loss, and $4,500 of prior-year suspended passive activity losses.
   d. Diane sold a delivery truck used in her business. The truck cost $35,000, $21,700 of cost recovery had been taken, and it was sold for $18,000.
   e. The Okumuras received $13,000 in dividends on various domestic corporation stock that they own.
   f. The Okumuras sold stock for a $15,000 long-term capital gain and other stock at a $6,000 short-term capital loss.
   g. The Okumuras had the following itemized deductions: $1,000 unreimbursed medical expenses; $10,500 personal use property taxes; $7,000 qualified residence interest; $3,000 consumer interest; $1,500 of Glen's unreimbursed employee business expenses; $535 of investment-related expenses; and $6,300 of state income taxes paid.

   Compute the Okumuras' 1992 net tax payable or refund due. (Ignore self-employment tax.) Suggested software (if available): *TurboTax* for tax return or WFT tax planning software.

56. Linda Franklin is an attorney. She is single and lives at 1619 Merry Lane, Cantone, TN 16703. Her Social Security number is 345–67–8900. Linda receives a salary of $45,000. During 1991, she had the following property transactions:

a. Sales of stock held for investment:

Stock	Selling Price	Basis	Date Sold	Date Acquired
Acme Corporation	$2,000	$ 1,400	6/30/1991	12/31/1990
Bareham Corporation	8,000	10,500	12/31/1991	7/15/1991
Cronin, Inc.	9,400	5,400	7/26/1991	5/2/1981
Davis Corporation	1,800	2,900	10/18/1991	10/17/1984

b. Complete destruction of a personal use travel trailer in a wreck on August 1 (basis, $6,500; fair market value, $5,000; reimbursement for loss by insurance company, $3,000). Linda had bought the trailer on June 12, 1987.

c. Sale of photocopying machine used in business for $2,800 on November 6. Linda had acquired the machine on April 29, 1989, for $4,000 and had taken $2,163 of depreciation on it.

d. Sale of typewriter used in business on January 15 for $500. The typewriter was acquired on May 8, 1989, at a cost of $1,000; depreciation of $395 had been deducted.

e. Cash dividends of $5,000 (all from Bareham stock).

Compute Linda Franklin's AGI from these transactions. If you use tax forms in your computations, you will need Forms 1040, 4684, and 4797 and Schedule D. Suggested software (if available): *TurboTax* for tax return or WFT tax planning software.

RESEARCH PROBLEMS

RESEARCH PROBLEM 1 S owns a professional football franchise. He has received an offer of $80 million for the franchise, all the football equipment, the rights to concession receipts, the rights to a stadium lease, and the rights to all the player contracts owned by S. Most of the players have been with the team for quite a long time and have contracts that were signed several years ago. The contracts have been substantially depreciated. S is concerned about potential § 1245 recapture when the contracts are sold. He has heard about "previously unrecaptured depreciation with respect to initial contracts" and would like to know more about it. Find a definition for that phrase and write an explanation of it.

Partial list of research aids:

§ 1245(a)(4).

RESEARCH PROBLEM 2 On May 10, 1985, D purchased a $160,000 building (but not the land) that was 60 feet wide, 80 feet deep, and two stories high. The front 60 feet of the 80-foot first-floor depth was rented as a retail store. The remaining 20 feet of the first floor and all of the second floor were rented for residential use. D used the ACRS statutory percentages and sold the building for $140,000 in 1992. D is unsure whether all the depreciation is subject to recapture by § 1245, some of it is subject to recapture by § 1250, or none of it is subject to recapture.
Does § 1245 or § 1250 recapture apply in this situation?

RESEARCH PROBLEM 3 Wellco, Inc., owns numerous working interests in oil and gas properties. Wellco has expensed intangible drilling and development costs on all the properties. Wellco transfers overriding nonworking royalty interests in some of its properties to a trust for the benefit of its shareholders. Must Wellco recapture the intangible drilling and development costs when this transfer is made?

Partial list of research aids:

§ 1254.
Houston Oil and Minerals Corporation v. Comm., 91–1 USTC ¶50,067, 67 AFTR2d 91–492, 922, F.2d 283 (*aff'g.* 92 T.C. 1331).

RESEARCH PROBLEM 4 During 1992, Honest John's Auto Sales, a dealer in new and used cars, sold some new cars, some used cars, some company cars (used in the business to run errands, etc.), and some demonstrators. Since Honest John's is a dealer, can any of these sales be considered sales of § 1231 assets?

Partial list of research aids:

§ 1231(b).
Latimer-Looney Chevrolet, Inc., 19 T. C. 120 (1952), *acq.*

PART

ACCOUNTING PERIODS, ACCOUNTING METHODS, AND DEFERRED COMPENSATION

Part VI provides a more comprehensive examination of the accounting periods and accounting methods that were introduced in Part II. A discussion of special accounting methods is also included. Part VI concludes with an analysis of the tax consequences of deferred compensation transactions.

CHAPTER

CHAPTER

ACCOUNTING PERIODS AND METHODS

OBJECTIVES

Explain the tax year provisions and the requirements for adopting and changing the tax year.

Describe the rules of income and expense recognition for the cash and accrual methods of tax accounting.

Analyze the procedures for changing accounting methods.

Explain and illustrate the installment method of accounting.

Analyze the imputed interest rules applicable to installment sales.

Explain the alternative methods of accounting for long-term contracts.

Summarize inventory accounting requirements and explain LIFO procedures.

Identify tax planning opportunities related to accounting periods and accounting methods.

OUTLINE

Earlier chapters discussed the types of income subject to tax (gross income and exclusions) and allowable deductions.[1] This chapter focuses on the related issue of the periods in which income and deductions are reported. Generally, a taxpayer's income and deductions must be assigned to particular 12-month periods—calendar years or fiscal years.

Income and deductions are placed within particular years through the use of tax accounting methods. The basic accounting methods are the cash method, accrual method, and hybrid method. Other special purpose methods are available for specific circumstances or types of transactions such as the installment method and the methods used for long-term construction contracts.

An entire subchapter of the Code, Subchapter E, is devoted to accounting periods and accounting methods. Over the long run, the accounting period used by a taxpayer will not affect the aggregate amount of reported taxable income. However, taxable income for any particular year may vary significantly due to the use of a particular reporting period. Also, through the choice of accounting methods or accounting periods, it is possible to postpone the recognition of taxable income and to enjoy the benefits from deferring the related tax. This chapter discusses the taxpayer's alternatives for accounting periods and accounting methods.

Accounting Periods

In General

A taxpayer who keeps adequate books and records may be permitted to elect a *fiscal year,* a 12-month period ending on the last day of a month other than December. Otherwise, a *calendar year* must be used.[2] Frequently, corporations can satisfy the recordkeeping requirements and elect to use a fiscal year.[3] Often the fiscal year conforms to a natural business year (e.g., a summer resort's fiscal year may end on September 30, after the close of the season). Individuals seldom use a fiscal year because they do not maintain the necessary books and records and because complications can arise as a result of changes in the tax law (e.g., often the transition rules and effective dates differ for fiscal year taxpayers).

Generally, a taxable year may not exceed 12 calendar months. However, if certain requirements are met, a taxpayer may elect to use an annual period that varies from 52 to 53 weeks.[4] In that case, the year-end must be on the same day of the week (e.g., the Tuesday falling closest to October 31 or the last Tuesday in October). The day of the week selected for ending the year will depend upon business considerations. For example, a retail business that is not open on Sundays may end its tax year on a Sunday so that it can take an inventory without interrupting business operations.

Example 1

T is in the business of selling farm supplies. His natural business year terminates at the end of October with the completion of harvesting. At the end of the fiscal year, T must take an inventory, which is most easily accomplished on a Tuesday. Therefore, T could adopt a 52–53 week tax year ending on the Tuesday closest to October 31. If T selects this method, the year-end date may fall in the following month if that Tuesday is closer to October 31. The tax year ending in 1992 will contain 53 weeks beginning on Wednesday, October 30, 1991, and ending on Tuesday, November 3, 1992. The tax year

1. See Chapters 4, 5, and 6.
2. § 441(c) and Reg. § 1.441–1(b)(1)(ii).
3. Reg. § 1.441–1(e)(2).
4. § 441(f).

ending in 1993 will have 52 weeks beginning on Wednesday, November 4, 1992, and ending on Tuesday, November 2, 1993. ◆

Partnerships and S Corporations. When a partner's tax year and the partnership's tax year differ, the partner will enjoy a deferral of income. This results because the partner reports his or her share of the partnership's income and deductions for the partnership's tax year ending within or with the partner's tax year.[5] For example, if the tax year of the partnership ends on January 31, a calendar year partner will not report partnership profits for the first 11 months of the partnership tax year until the following year. Therefore, partnerships are subject to special tax year requirements.

In general, the partnership tax year must be the same as the tax year of the majority interest partners. The *majority interest partners* are the partners who own a greater than 50 percent interest in the partnership capital and profits. If the majority owners do not have the same tax year, the partnership must adopt the same tax year as its principal partners. A *principal partner* is a partner with a 5 percent or more interest in the partnership capital or profits.[6]

EXAMPLE 2

The XYZ Partnership is owned equally by X Corporation, Y Corporation, and individual Z. The partners have the following tax years.

	Partner's Tax Year Ending
X	June 30
Y	June 30
Z	December 31

The partnership's tax year must end on June 30. If Y as well as Z's year ended on December 31, the partnership would be required to adopt a calendar year. ◆

If the principal partners do not all have the same tax year and no majority of partners have the same tax year, the partnership must use a year that results in the *least aggregate deferral* of income.[7] Under the least aggregate deferral method, the different tax years of the principal partners are tested to determine which produces the least aggregate deferral. This is calculated by first multiplying the combined percentages of the principal partners with the same tax year by the months of deferral for the test year. Once this is done for each set of principal partners with the same tax year, the resulting products are summed to produce the aggregate deferral. After calculating the aggregate deferral for each of the test years, the test year with the smallest summation (the least aggregate deferral) is the tax year for the partnership.

EXAMPLE 3

The DE Partnership is owned equally by D and E. D's fiscal year ends on March 31, and E's fiscal year ends on August 31. The partnership must use the partner's fiscal year that will result in the least aggregate deferral of income. Therefore, the fiscal years ending March 31 and August 31 must both be tested.

5. Reg. § 1.706–1(a).
6. §§ 706(b)(1)(B) and 706(b)(3).
7. Temp.Reg. § 1.706–1T(a)(2).

Test for Fiscal Year Ending March 31

Partner	Year Ends	Profit %	Months of Deferral	Product
D	3–31	50	0	0
E	8–31	50	5	2.5
Aggregate deferral months				2.5

Thus, with a year ending March 31, E would be able to defer his half of the income for five months. That is, E's share of the partnership income for the fiscal year ending March 31, 1993, would not be included in his income until August 31, 1993.

Test for Fiscal Year Ending August 31

Partner	Year Ends	Profit %	Months of Deferral	Product
D	3–31	50	7	3.5
E	8–31	50	0	0
Aggregate deferral months				3.5

Thus, with a year ending August 31, D would be able to defer her half of the income for seven months. That is, D's share of the partnership income for the fiscal year ending August 31, 1993, would not be included in her income until March 31, 1994.

The year ending March 31 must be used because it results in the least aggregate deferral of income. ◆

Generally, S corporations must adopt a calendar year.[8] However, partnerships and S corporations may *elect* an otherwise *impermissible year* under any of the following conditions:

- A business purpose for the year can be demonstrated.[9]
- The partnership's or S corporation's year results in a deferral of not more than three months' income, and the entity agrees to make required tax payments.[10]
- The entity retains the same year as was used for the fiscal year ending in 1987, provided the entity agrees to make required tax payments.

Business Purpose. The only business purpose for a fiscal year that the IRS has acknowledged is the need to conform the tax year to the natural business year of a business.[11] Generally, only seasonal businesses have a natural business year. For example, the natural business year for a department store may end on January 31, after Christmas returns have been processed and clearance sales have been completed.

Required Tax Payments. Under this system, tax payments are due from the partnership or S corporation by April 15 of each tax year.[12] The amount due is computed by applying the highest individual tax rate plus 1 percent to an estimate of the deferral period income. The deferral period runs from the close of the fiscal year to the end of the calendar year. Estimated income for this period

8. §§ 1378(a) and (b).
9. §§ 706(b)(1)(C) and 1378(b)(2).
10. § 444.
11. Rev.Rul. 87–57, 1987–2 C.B. 117.
12. §§ 444(c) and 7519.

is based on the average monthly earnings for the previous fiscal year. The amount due is reduced by the amount of required tax payments for the previous year.[13]

EXAMPLE 4

S, Inc., an S corporation, elected a fiscal year ending September 30. R is the only shareholder. For the fiscal year ending September 30, 1992, S, Inc., earned $100,000. The required tax payment for the previous year was $5,000. The corporation must pay $3,000 by April 15, 1993, calculated as follows:

$$(\$100{,}000 \times 3/12 \times 32\%^*) - \$5{,}000 = \$3{,}000$$

*Maximum § 1 rate of 31% + 1%. ◆

Personal Service Corporations (PSCs). A PSC is a corporation whose shareholder-employees provide personal services (e.g., medical, dental, legal, accounting, engineering, actuarial, consulting, or performing arts). Generally, a PSC must use a calendar year.[14] However, a PSC can *elect* a fiscal year under any of the following conditions:

- A business purpose for the year can be demonstrated.
- The PSC year results in a deferral of not more than three months' income, the corporation pays the shareholder-employee's salary during the portion of the calendar year after the close of the fiscal year, and the salary for that period is at least proportionate to the shareholder-employee's salary received for the fiscal year.[15]
- The PSC retains the same year it used for the fiscal year ending in 1987, provided it satisfies the latter two requirements in the preceding option.

EXAMPLE 5

Y's corporation paid Y a salary of $120,000 during its fiscal year ending September 30, 1992. The corporation cannot satisfy the business purpose test for a fiscal year. The corporation can continue to use its fiscal year without any negative tax effects, provided Y receives at least $30,000 (3 months/12 months × $120,000) as salary during the period October 1 through December 31, 1992. ◆

If the salary test is not satisfied, the PSC can retain the fiscal year, but the corporation's deduction for salary for the fiscal year is limited to the following:

$$A + A(F/N)$$

Where A = Amount paid after the close of the fiscal year
F = Number of months in fiscal year minus number of months from the end of the fiscal year to the end of the ongoing calendar year
N = Number of months from the end of the fiscal year to the end of the ongoing calendar year

EXAMPLE 6

Assume the corporation in the previous example paid Y $10,000 of salary during the period October 1 through December 31, 1992. The deduction for Y's salary for the

13. § 7519(b).
14. § 441(i).
15. §§ 444 and 280H.

corporation's fiscal year ending September 30, 1993, is thus limited to $40,000 calculated as follows:

$$\$10{,}000 + \left[\$10{,}000\left(\frac{12-3}{3}\right)\right] = \$10{,}000 + \$30{,}000 = \$40{,}000$$ ◆

Making the Election

A taxpayer elects to use a calendar or fiscal year by the timely filing of his or her initial tax return. For all subsequent years, the taxpayer must use this same period unless approval for change is obtained from the IRS.[16]

Changes in the Accounting Period

A taxpayer must obtain consent from the IRS before changing the tax year.[17] This power to approve or not to approve a change is significant in that it permits the IRS to issue authoritative administrative guidelines that must be met by taxpayers who wish to change their accounting period. An application for permission to change tax years must be made on Form 1128, Application for Change in Accounting Period, and must be filed on or before the fifteenth day of the second calendar month following the close of the short period that results from the change in accounting period.[18]

EXAMPLE 7

Beginning in 1992, T Corporation, a calendar year taxpayer, would like to switch to a fiscal year ending March 31. The corporation must file Form 1128 by May 15, 1992. ◆

IRS Requirements. The IRS will not grant permission for the change unless the taxpayer can establish a substantial business purpose for the request. One substantial business purpose is to change to a tax year that coincides with the *natural business year* (the completion of an annual business cycle). The IRS applies an objective gross receipts test to determine if the entity has a natural business year. At least 25 percent of the entity's gross receipts for the 12-month period must be realized in the final 2 months of the 12-month period for three consecutive years.[19]

EXAMPLE 8

A Virginia Beach motel had gross receipts as follows:

	1990	1991	1992
July–August receipts	$ 300,000	$250,000	$ 325,000
September 1–August 31 receipts	1,000,000	900,000	1,250,000
Receipts for 2 months divided by receipts for 12 months	30.0%	27.8%	26.0%

16. Reg. §§ 1.441–1(b)(3) and 1.441–1(b)(4).

17. § 442. Under certain conditions, corporations are allowed to change tax years without obtaining IRS approval. See Reg. § 1.442–1(c)(1).

18. Reg. § 1.442–1(b)(1). In Example 7, the first period after the change in accounting period (January 1, 1992, through March 31, 1992) is less than a 12-month period and is referred to as a *short period*.

19. Rev.Proc. 87–32, 1987–1 C.B. 131, and Rev.Rul. 87–57, 1987–2 C.B. 117.

Since it satisfies the natural business year test, the motel will be allowed to use a fiscal year ending August 31. ◆

The IRS usually establishes certain conditions that the taxpayer must accept if the approval for change is to be granted. In particular, if the taxpayer has a net operating loss for the short period, the IRS may require that the loss be carried forward and allocated equally over the 6 following years.[20] As you may recall (refer to Chapter 8), net operating losses are ordinarily carried back for 3 years and forward for 15 years.

EXAMPLE 9

X Corporation changed from a calendar year to a fiscal year ending September 30. The short period return for the nine months ending September 30, 1992, reflected a $60,000 net operating loss. The corporation had taxable income for 1989, 1990, and 1991. As a condition for granting approval, the IRS requires X to allocate the $60,000 loss over the next six years, rather than carrying the loss back to the three preceding years (the usual order for applying a net operating loss). Thus, X Corporation will reduce its taxable income by $10,000 each year ending September 30, 1993, through September 30, 1998. ◆

Taxable Periods of Less Than One Year

A *short year* (or short period) is a period of less than 12 calendar months. A taxpayer may have a short year for (1) the first income tax return, (2) the final income tax return, or (3) a change in the tax year. If the short period results from a change in the taxpayer's annual accounting period, the taxable income for the period must be annualized. Due to the progressive tax rate structure, taxpayers could reap benefits from a short-period return if some adjustments were not required. Thus, the taxpayer is required to do the following:

1. Annualize the short-period income.

$$\text{Annualized income} = \text{Short-period income} \times \frac{12}{\text{Number of months in the short period}}$$

2. Compute the tax on the annualized income.
3. Convert the tax on the annualized income to a short-period tax.

$$\text{Short-period tax} = \text{Tax on annualized income} \times \frac{\text{Number of months in the short period}}{12}$$

EXAMPLE 10

B Corporation obtained permission to change from a calendar year to a fiscal year ending September 30, beginning in 1992. For the short period January 1 through September 30, 1992, the corporation's taxable income was $48,000. The relevant tax rates and the resultant short-period tax are as follows:

20. Rev.Proc. 85–16, 1985–1 C.B. 517.

Amount of Taxable Income	Tax Calculation
\$1–\$50,000	15% of taxable income
\$50,001–\$75,000	\$7,500 plus 25% of taxable income in excess of \$50,000

Annalized income
($48,000 × 12/9) = $64,000
Tax on annualized income
$7,500 + .25 ($64,000 − $50,000) =
$7,500 + $3,500 = $11,000
Short-period tax = ($11,000 × 9/12) = $8,250
Annualizing the income increased the tax by $1,050:

Tax with annualizing	\$8,250
Tax without annualizing (.15 × \$48,000)	7,200
	\$1,050

◆

Rather than annualize the short-period income, the taxpayer can elect to calculate the tax for a 12-month period beginning on the first day of the sh[illegible] period and (2) convert the tax in (1) to a short-period tax as follows:[21]

$$\frac{\text{Taxable income for short period}}{\text{Taxable income for the 12-month period}} \times \text{Tax on the 12 months of income}$$

EXAMPLE 11

Assume B Corporation's taxable income for the calendar year 1992 was $60,000. The tax on the full 12 months of income would have been $10,000 [$7,500 + .25 ($60,000 − $50,000)]. The short-period tax would be $8,000 ($48,000/$60,000 × $10,000). Thus, if the corporation utilized this option, the tax for the short period would be $8,000 (rather than $8,250, as calculated in Example 10). ◆

For individuals, annualizing requires some special adjustments:[22]

- Deductions must be itemized for the short period (the standard deduction is not allowed).
- Personal and dependency exemptions must be prorated.

Fortunately, individuals rarely change tax years.

Mitigation of the Annual Accounting Period Concept

Several provisions in the Code are designed to give the taxpayer relief from the seemingly harsh results that may be produced by the combined effects of an arbitrary accounting period and a progressive rate structure. For example, under the net operating loss carryback and carryover rules, a loss in one year can be carried back and offset against taxable income for the preceding 3 years. Unused net operating losses are then carried over for 15 years.[23] In addition, the Code provides special relief provisions for casualty losses pursuant to a disaster and for the reporting of insurance proceeds from destruction of crops.[24]

21. § 443(b)(1).
22. § 443(b)(2) and Reg. § 1.443–1(a)(2).
23. § 172. Refer to Chapter 8.
24. §§ 165(i) and 451(d). Refer to Chapter 8.

Restoration of Amounts Received under a Claim of Right. The court-made *claim of right doctrine* applies when the taxpayer receives property as income and treats it as his or her own but a dispute arises over the taxpayer's rights to the income.[25] According to the doctrine, the taxpayer must include the amount as income in the year of receipt. The rationale for the doctrine is that the Federal government cannot await the resolution of all disputes before exacting a tax. As a corollary to the doctrine, if the taxpayer is later required to repay the funds, generally a deduction is allowed in the year of repayment.[26]

EXAMPLE 12

In 1992, T received a $5,000 bonus computed as a percentage of profits. In 1993, T's employer determined that the 1992 profits had been incorrectly computed, and T had to refund the $5,000 in 1993. T was required to include the $5,000 in his 1992 income, but he can claim a $5,000 deduction in 1993. ◆

In Example 12 the transactions were a wash; that is, the income and deduction were the same ($5,000). Suppose, however, T was in the 31 percent tax bracket in 1992 but in the 15 percent bracket in 1993. Without some relief provision, the mistake would be costly to T. T paid $1,550 tax in 1992 (.31 × $5,000), but the deduction reduced his tax liability in 1993 by only $750 (.15 × $5,000). The Code does provide the needed relief in such cases. Under § 1341, when income that has been taxed under the claim of right doctrine must later be repaid, in effect, the taxpayer gets to apply to the deduction the tax rate of the year that will produce the greatest tax benefit. Thus, in Example 12, the repayment in 1993 would reduce T's 1993 tax liability by the greater 1992 rate (.31) applied to the $5,000. However, relief is provided only in cases where the tax is significantly different; that is, when the deduction for the amount previously included in income exceeds $3,000.

ACCOUNTING METHODS

◆

Permissible Methods

Section 446 requires the taxpayer to compute taxable income using the method of accounting regularly employed in keeping his or her books, provided the method clearly reflects income. The Code recognizes the following as generally permissible methods:

- The cash receipts and disbursements method.
- The accrual method.
- A hybrid method (a combination of cash and accrual).

The Regulations refer to these alternatives as *overall methods* and add that the term *method of accounting* includes not only the overall method of accounting of the taxpayer but also the accounting treatment of any item.[27]

Generally, any of the three methods of accounting may be used if the method is consistently employed and clearly reflects income. However, the taxpayer is required to use the accrual method for sales and costs of goods sold if inventories are an income-producing factor to the business.[28] Other situations in

25. *North American Consolidated Oil Co. v. Burnet*, 3 USTC ¶943, 11 AFTR 16, 52 S.Ct. 613 (USSC, 1932). See the Glossary of Tax Terms in Appendix C for a discussion of the term "claim of right doctrine."

26. *U.S. v. Lewis*, 51–1 USTC ¶9211, 40 AFTR 258, 71 S.Ct. 522 (USSC, 1951).

27. Reg. § 1.446–1(a)(1).

28. Reg. § 1.446–1(a)(4)(i).

which the accrual method is required are discussed later. Special methods are also permitted for installment sales, long-term construction contracts, and farmers.

A taxpayer who has more than one trade or business may use a different method of accounting for each trade or business activity.[29] Furthermore, a different method of accounting may be used to determine income from a trade or business than is used to compute nonbusiness items of income and deductions.[30]

EXAMPLE 13

T operates a grocery store and owns stock and bonds. The sales and cost of goods sold from the grocery store must be computed by the accrual method because inventories are material. However, T can report his dividends and interest under the cash method. ◆

The Code grants the IRS broad powers to determine whether the taxpayer's accounting method *clearly reflects income.* Thus, if the method employed does not clearly reflect income, the IRS has the power to prescribe the method to be used by the taxpayer.[31]

Cash Receipts and Disbursements Method—Cash Basis

Most individuals and many businesses use the cash basis to report income and deductions. The popularity of this method can largely be attributed to its simplicity and flexibility.

Under the cash method, income is not recognized until the taxpayer actually receives, or constructively receives, cash or its equivalent. Cash is constructively received if it is available to the taxpayer.[32] Deductions are generally permitted in the year of payment. Thus, year-end accounts receivable, accounts payable, and accrued income and deductions are not included in the determination of taxable income.

In many cases, a taxpayer using the cash method can choose the year in which a deduction is claimed simply by postponing or accelerating the payment of expenses. For fixed assets, however, the cash basis taxpayer claims deductions through depreciation or amortization, the same as an accrual basis taxpayer does. In addition, prepaid expenses must be capitalized and amortized if the life of the asset extends substantially beyond the end of the tax year.[33] Most courts have applied the one-year rule to determine whether capitalization and amortization are required. According to this rule, capitalization is required only if the asset has a life that extends beyond the tax year following the year of payment.[34]

Restrictions on Use of the Cash Method. Using the cash method to measure income from a merchandising or manufacturing operation would often yield a distorted picture of the results of operations. Income for the period would largely be a function of when payments were made for goods or materials. Thus, the Regulations prohibit the use of the cash method (and require the accrual method) to measure sales and cost of goods sold if inventories are material to the business.[35]

The prohibition on the use of the cash method if inventories are material and the rules regarding prepaid expenses (discussed above) are intended to assure

29. § 446(d).
30. Reg. § 1.446–1(c)(1)(iv)(b).
31. § 446(b).
32. Reg. § 1.451–1(a). Refer to Chapter 4 for a discussion of constructive receipt.
33. Reg. § 1.461–1(a)(1).
34. *Zaninovich v. Comm.*, 80–1 USTC ¶9342, 45 AFTR2d 80–1442, 616 F.2d 429 (CA–9, 1980), *rev'g* 69 T.C. 605 (1978). Refer to Chapter 6 for further discussion of the one-year rule.
35. Reg. § 1.446–1(a)(4)(i).

that annual income is clearly reflected. However, certain taxpayers may not use the cash method of accounting for Federal income tax purposes regardless of whether inventories are material. The accrual basis must be used to report the income earned by (1) a corporation (other than an S corporation), (2) a partnership with a corporate partner, and (3) a tax shelter.[36] This accrual basis requirement has three exceptions:[37]

- A farming business.
- A qualified personal service corporation (e.g., a corporation performing services in health, law, engineering, architecture, accounting, actuarial science, performing arts, or consulting).
- An entity that is not a tax shelter whose average annual gross receipts for the most recent three-year period are $5,000,000 or less.

Farming. Although inventories are material to farming operations, the IRS long ago created an exception to the general rule and allows farmers to use the cash method of accounting.[38] The purpose of the exception is to relieve the small farmer from the bookkeeping burden of accrual accounting. However, tax shelter promoters recognized, for example, that by deducting the costs of a crop in one tax year and harvesting the crop in a later year, income could be deferred from tax. Thus, §§ 447 and 464 were enacted to prevent the use of the cash method by certain farming corporations and limited partnerships (farming syndicates).[39]

Farmers who are allowed to use the cash method of accounting must nevertheless capitalize their costs of raising trees when the preproduction period is greater than two years.[40] Thus, a cash basis apple farmer must capitalize the cost of raising trees until the trees produce in merchantable quantities. Cash basis farmers can elect not to capitalize these costs, but if the election is made, the alternative depreciation system (refer to Chapter 9) must be used for all farming property.

Generally, the cost of purchasing an animal must be capitalized. However, the cash basis farmer's cost of raising the animal can be expensed.[41]

Accrual Method

All Events Test for Income. Under the accrual method, an item is generally included in gross income for the year in which it is earned, regardless of when the income is collected. An item of income is earned when (1) all the events have occurred to fix the taxpayer's right to receive the income and (2) the amount of income (the amount the taxpayer has a right to receive) can be determined with reasonable accuracy.[42]

Example 14

A, a calendar year taxpayer who uses the accrual basis of accounting, was to receive a bonus equal to 6% of B Corporation's net income for its fiscal year ending each June 30. For the fiscal year ending June 30, 1992, B Corporation had net income of $240,000,

36. § 448(a). For this purpose, the hybrid method of accounting is considered the same as the cash method.
37. § 448(b).
38. Reg. § 1.471–6(a).
39. Section 447(c) contains counter-exceptions that allow certain closely held corporations to use the cash method. See also § 464(c).
40. § 263A(d).
41. Reg. § 1.162–12(a).
42. Reg. § 1.451–1(a). Refer to Chapter 4 for further discussion of the accrual basis.

and for the six months ending December 31, 1992, the corporation's net income was $150,000. A will report $14,400 (.06 × $240,000) for 1992 because her rights to the amount became fixed when B Corporation's year closed. However, A would not accrue income based on the corporation's profits for the last six months of 1992 since her right to the income does not accrue until the close of the corporation's tax year. ◆

In a situation where the accrual basis taxpayer's right to income is being contested and the income has not yet been collected, generally no income is recognized until the dispute has been settled.[43] Before the settlement, "all of the events have not occurred that fix the right to receive the income."

All Events and Economic Performance Tests for Deductions. An all events test applies to accrual basis deductions. A deduction cannot be claimed until (1) all the events have occurred to create the taxpayer's liability and (2) the amount of the liability can be determined with reasonable accuracy.[44] Once these requirements are satisfied, the deduction will be permitted only if economic performance has occurred.[45]

The economic performance test addresses situations in which the taxpayer has either of the following obligations:

1. To pay for services or property to be provided in the future.
2. To provide services or property (other than money) in the future.

When services or property are to be provided to the taxpayer in the future (situation 1), economic performance occurs when the property or services are actually provided by the other party.

EXAMPLE 15

An accrual basis calendar year taxpayer, PS, Inc., promoted a boxing match held in the company's arena on December 31, 1992. AM, Inc., had contracted to clean the arena for $5,000, but did not actually perform the work until January 1, 1993. PS, Inc., did not pay the $5,000 until 1994. Although financial accounting would require PS, Inc., to accrue the $5,000 cleaning expense in 1992 to match the revenues from the fight, the economic performance test was not satisfied until 1993, when AM, Inc., performed the service. Thus, PS, Inc., must deduct the expense in 1993. ◆

If the taxpayer is obligated to provide property or services (situation 2), economic performance occurs (and thus the deduction is allowed) in the year the taxpayer provides the property or services.

EXAMPLE 16

T Corporation, an accrual basis taxpayer, is in the strip mining business. According to the contract with the landowner, the company must reclaim the land. The estimated cost of reclaiming land mined in 1992 was $500,000, but the land was not actually reclaimed until 1994. The all events test was satisfied in 1992. The obligation existed, and the amount of the liability could be determined with reasonable accuracy. However, the economic performance test was not satisfied until 1994. Therefore, the deduction is not allowed until 1994.[46] ◆

The economic performance test is waived, and thus year-end accruals can be deducted, if all the following conditions (*recurring item exception*) are met:

---

43. *Burnet v. Sanford & Brooks Co.*, 2 USTC ¶636, 9 AFTR 603, 51 S.Ct. 150 (USSC, 1931).
44. § 461(h)(4).
45. § 461(h).
46. See § 468 for an elective method for reporting reclamation costs.

- The obligation exists and the amount of the liability can be reasonably estimated.
- Economic performance occurs within a reasonable period (but not later than 8½ months after the close of the taxable year).
- The item is recurring in nature and is treated consistently by the taxpayer.
- Either the accrued item is not material, or accruing it results in a better matching of revenues and expenses.

Example 17

M Corporation often sells goods that are on hand but cannot be shipped for another week. Thus, the sales account usually includes revenues for some items that have not been shipped at year-end. M Corporation is obligated to pay shipping costs. Although the company's obligation for shipping costs can be determined with reasonable accuracy, economic performance is not satisfied until M Corporation (or its agent) actually delivers the goods. However, accruing shipping costs on sold items will better match expenses with revenues for the period. Therefore, the company should be allowed to accrue the shipping costs on items sold but not shipped at year-end. ◆

The economic performance test as set forth in the Code does not address all possible accrued expenses. That is, in some cases, the taxpayer incurs cost even though no property or services were received. In these instances, according to proposed Regulations, economic performance generally is not satisfied until the liability is paid. The following liabilities are cases in which payment is generally the only means of satisfying economic performance:[47]

1. Worker's compensation.
2. Torts.
3. Breach of contract.
4. Violation of law.
5. Rebates and refunds.
6. Awards, prizes, and jackpots.
7. Insurance, warranty, and service contracts.[48]
8. Taxes.

Example 18

M Corporation sold defective merchandise that injured a customer. M admitted liability in 1992, but did not pay the claim until January 1993. The customer's tort claim cannot be deducted until it is paid. ◆

However, items (5) through (8) above are eligible for the aforementioned recurring item exception.

Example 19

Q Corporation filed its 1992 state income tax return in March 1993. At the time the return was filed, Q was required to pay an additional $5,000. The state taxes are eligible for the recurring item exception. Thus, the $5,000 of state income taxes can be deducted on the corporation's 1992 Federal tax return. The deduction is allowed because all the events had occurred to fix the liability as of the end of 1992, the payment was made within 8½ months after the end of the tax year, the item is recurring in nature, and allowing the deduction in 1992 produces a good matching of revenues and expenses. ◆

---

47. Prop.Reg. §§ 1.461–4(g)(2)–(6) and 1.461–5(c).
48. This item applies to contracts the taxpayer enters into for his or her own protection, rather than the taxpayer's liability as insurer, warrantor, or service provider.

Reserves. Generally, the all events and economic performance tests will prevent the use of reserves (e.g., for product warranty expense) frequently used in financial accounting to match expenses with revenues. However, small banks are allowed to use a bad debt reserve.[49] Furthermore, an accrual basis taxpayer in a service business is permitted to not accrue revenue that appears uncollectible based on experience. In effect, this approach indirectly allows a reserve.[50]

Hybrid Method

A *hybrid method* of accounting involves the use of more than one method. For example, a taxpayer who uses the accrual basis to report sales and cost of goods sold but uses the cash basis to report other items of income and expense is employing a hybrid method. The Code permits the use of a hybrid method provided the taxpayer's income is clearly reflected.[51] A taxpayer who uses the accrual method for business expenses must also use the accrual method for business income (a cash method may not be used for income items if the taxpayer's expenses are accounted for under the accrual method).

It may be preferable for a business that is required to report sales and cost of goods sold on the accrual method to report other items of income and expense under the cash method. The cash method permits greater flexibility in the timing of income and expense recognition.

Change of Method

The taxpayer, in effect, makes an election to use a particular accounting method when an initial tax return is filed using that method. If a subsequent change in method is desired, the taxpayer must obtain the permission of the IRS. The request for change is made on Form 3115, Application for Change in Accounting Method. Generally, the form must be filed within the first 180 days of the taxable year of the desired change.[52]

As previously mentioned, the term *accounting method* encompasses not only the overall accounting method used by the taxpayer (the cash or accrual method) but also the treatment of any material item of income or deduction.[53] Thus, a change in the method of deducting property taxes from a cash basis to an accrual basis that results in a deduction for taxes in a different year constitutes a change in an accounting method. Another example of accounting method change is a change involving the method or basis used in the valuation of inventories. However, a change in treatment resulting from a change in underlying facts does not constitute a change in the taxpayer's method of accounting.[54] For example, a change in employment contracts so that an employee accrues one day of vacation pay for each month of service rather than 12 days of vacation pay for a full year of service is a change in the underlying facts and is not, therefore, an accounting method change.

Correction of an Error. A change in accounting method should be distinguished from the *correction of an error.* An error can be corrected (by filing amended returns) by the taxpayer without permission, and the IRS can simply

49. § 585.
50. § 448(d)(5).
51. § 446(c).
52. Reg. § 1.446–1(e)(3). The deadline may be extended to within the first nine months of the year of the change if the taxpayer can show good cause for the delay in filing the request.
53. Reg. § 1.446–1(a)(1). See the Glossary of Tax Terms in Appendix C for a discussion of the term "accounting method."
54. Reg. § 1.446–1(e)(2)(ii)(b).

adjust the taxpayer's liability if an error is discovered on audit of the return. Some examples of errors are incorrect postings, errors in the calculation of tax liability or tax credits, deductions of business expense items that are actually personal, and omissions of income and deductions.[55] Unless the taxpayer or the IRS corrects the error within the statute of limitations, the taxpayer's total lifetime taxable income will be overstated or understated by the amount of the error.

Change from an Incorrect Method. An *incorrect accounting method* is the consistent (year-after-year) use of an incorrect rule to report an item of income or expense. The incorrect accounting method generally will not affect the taxpayer's total lifetime income (unlike the error). That is, an incorrect method has a self-balancing mechanism. For example, deducting freight on inventory in the year the goods are purchased, rather than when the inventory is sold, is an incorrect accounting method. The total cost of goods sold over the life of the business is not affected, but the year-to-year income is incorrect.[56]

If a taxpayer is employing an incorrect method of accounting, permission must be obtained from the IRS to change to a correct method. An incorrect method is not treated as a mechanical error that can be corrected by merely filing an amended tax return.

The tax return preparer as well as the taxpayer will be subject to penalties if the tax return is prepared using an incorrect method of accounting and permission for a change to a correct method has not been requested.[57]

Net Adjustments Due to Change in Accounting Method. In the year of a change in accounting method, some items of income and expense may have to be adjusted to prevent the change from distorting taxable income.

EXAMPLE 20

In 1992, Z Corporation, with consent from the IRS, switched from the cash to the accrual basis for reporting sales and cost of goods sold. The corporation's accrual basis gross profit for the year was computed as follows:

Sales		$100,000
Beginning inventory	$ 15,000	
Purchases	60,000	
Less: Ending inventory	(10,000)	
Cost of goods sold		(65,000)
Gross profit		$ 35,000

At the end of the previous year, Z Corporation had accounts receivable of $25,000 and accounts payable for merchandise of $34,000. The accounts receivable from the previous year in the amount of $25,000 were never included in gross income since Z was on the cash basis and did not recognize the uncollected receivables. In the current year, the $25,000 was not included in the accrual basis sales since the sales were made in a prior year. Therefore, a $25,000 adjustment to income is required to prevent the receivables from being omitted from income.

The corollary of failure to recognize a prior year's receivables is the failure to recognize a prior year's accounts payable. The beginning of the year's accounts payable were not included in the current or prior year's purchases. Thus, a deduction

55. Reg. § 1.446–1(e)(2)(ii)(b).

56. But see *Korn Industries v. U.S.*, 76–1 USTC ¶9354, 37 AFTR2d 76–1228, 532 F.2d 1352 (Ct.Cls., 1976).

57. § 446(f). See *West's Federal Taxation: Corporations, Partnerships, Estates, and Trusts*, Chapter 16.

for the $34,000 was not taken in either year and is therefore included as an adjustment to income for the period of change.

An adjustment is also required to reflect the $15,000 beginning inventory that Z deducted (due to the use of a cash method of accounting) in the previous year. In this instance, the cost of goods sold during the year of change was increased by the beginning inventory and resulted in a double deduction.

The net adjustment due to the change in accounting method is computed as follows:

Beginning inventory (deducted in prior and current year)	$ 15,000
Beginning accounts receivable (omitted from income)	25,000
Beginning accounts payable (omitted from deductions)	(34,000)
Net increase in taxable income	$ 6,000

◆

Disposition of the Net Adjustment. Generally, if the IRS *requires* the taxpayer to change an accounting method, the net adjustment is added to or subtracted from the income for the year of the change. In cases of positive (an increase in income) adjustments in excess of $3,000, the taxpayer is allowed to calculate the tax by spreading the adjustment over one or more previous years.[58]

To encourage taxpayers to *voluntarily* change from incorrect methods and to facilitate changes from one correct method to another, the IRS generally allows the taxpayer to spread the adjustment into future years. Assuming the taxpayer files a timely request for change (Form 3115), the allocation periods in Concept Summary 18–1 generally apply.[59]

EXAMPLE 21

Z Corporation in Example 20 voluntarily changed from an incorrect method (the cash basis was incorrect because inventories were material to the business) to a correct method. The company must add $2,000 (1/3 × $6,000 positive adjustment) to its 1992, 1993, and 1994 income. ◆

SPECIAL ACCOUNTING METHODS

Generally, accrual basis taxpayers recognize income when goods are sold and shipped to the customer. Cash basis taxpayers generally recognize income from a sale on the collection of cash from the customer. The tax law provides special accounting methods for certain installment sales and long-term contracts. These special methods were enacted, in part, to assure that the tax will be due when the taxpayer is best able to pay the tax.

Installment Method

Under the general rule for computing the gain or loss from the sale of property, the taxpayer recognizes the entire amount of gain or loss upon the sale or other disposition of the property.

EXAMPLE 22

A sells property to B for $10,000 cash plus B's note (fair market value and face amount of $90,000). A's basis in the property was $15,000. Gain or loss is computed under either the cash or accrual basis as follows:

58. § 481(b).

59. Rev.Proc. 84–74, 1984–2 C.B. 736, modifying Rev.Proc. 80–51, 1980–2 C.B. 818.

Amount realized	
Cash down payment	$ 10,000
Note receivable	90,000
	$100,000
Basis in the property	(15,000)
Realized gain	$ 85,000

◆

In Example 22, the general rule for recognizing gain or loss requires A to pay a substantial amount of tax on the gain in the year of sale even though only $10,000 cash was received. Congress enacted the installment sales provisions to prevent this sort of hardship by allowing the taxpayer to spread the gain from installment sales over the collection period. The installment method is a very important planning tool because of the tax deferral possibilities. The relevant Code provisions are summarized as follows:

Section	Subject
453	General rules governing the installment method (e.g., when applicable), related-party transfers, and special situations (e.g., certain corporate liquidations).
453A	Special rules for nondealers of real property.
453B	Gain or loss recognition upon the disposition of installment obligations.
1038	Rules governing the repossession of real estate sold under the installment method.
483, 1272, 1274	Calculation and amortization of imputed interest.

Eligibility and Calculations. The installment method applies to *gains* (but not losses) from the sale of property where the seller will receive at least one payment *after* the year of sale. For many years, practically all gains from the sale of property were eligible for the installment method. However, in recent years, the Code has been amended to *deny* the use of the installment method for the following:[60]

CONCEPT SUMMARY 18–1
ADJUSTMENT PERIODS

Change	Type of Adjustment	Allocation Period
Incorrect to correct method	Positive	Three years—year of change and the two succeeding years
Incorrect to correct method	Negative	Year of change
Correct to correct	Positive	Six years—year of change and the five succeeding years
Correct to correct	Negative	Six years—year of change and the five succeeding years

60. §§ 453(b), (i), and (l).

- Gains on property held for sale in the ordinary course of business.
- Depreciation recapture under § 1245 or § 1250.
- Gains on stocks or securities traded on an established market.

As an exception to the first item, the installment method may be used to report gains from sales of the following:[61]

- Timeshares units (e.g., the right to use real property for two weeks each year).
- Residential lots (if the seller is not to make any improvements).
- Any property used or produced in the trade or business of farming.

The Nonelective Aspect. Regardless of the taxpayer's method of accounting, as a general rule, eligible sales *must* be reported by the installment method.[62] A special election is required to report the gain by any other method of accounting (see the discussion in a subsequent section of this chapter).

Computing the Gain for the Period. The gain reported on each sale is computed by the following formula:

$$\frac{\text{Total gain}}{\text{Contract price}} \times \text{Payments received} = \text{Recognized gain}$$

The taxpayer must compute each variable as follows:

1. *Total gain* is the selling price reduced by selling expenses and the adjusted basis of the property. The selling price is the total consideration received by the seller, including notes receivable from the buyer and the seller's liabilities assumed by the buyer.
2. *Contract price* is the selling price less the seller's liabilities that are assumed by the buyer. Generally, the contract price is the amount, other than interest, the seller will receive from the purchaser.
3. *Payments received* are the collections on the contract price received in the tax year. This generally is equal to the cash received less the interest income collected for the period. If the buyer pays any of the seller's expenses, the seller regards the amount paid as a payment received.

EXAMPLE 23

The seller is not a dealer, and the facts are as follows:

Sales price		
Cash down payment	$ 1,000	
Seller's mortgage assumed	3,000	
Notes payable to the seller	13,000	$ 17,000
Selling expenses		(500)
Seller's basis		(10,000)
Total gain		$ 6,500

The contract price is $14,000 ($17,000 − $3,000). Assuming the $1,000 is the only payment in the year of sale, the gain in that year is computed as follows:

61. § 453(l)(2).

62. § 453(a).

$$\frac{\$6{,}500 \text{ (total gain)}}{\$14{,}000 \text{ (contract price)}} \times \$1{,}000 = \$464 \begin{array}{l}\text{(gain recognized}\\ \text{in year of sale)}\end{array}$$ ◆

If the sum of the seller's basis and selling expenses is less than the liabilities assumed by the buyer, the difference must be added to the contract price and to the payments (treated as *deemed payments*) received in the year of sale.[63] This adjustment to the contract price is required so that the ratio of total gain to contract price will not be greater than one. The adjustment also accelerates the reporting of income from the deemed payments.

EXAMPLE 24

Assume the same facts as in Example 23, except that the seller's basis in the property is only $2,000. The total gain, therefore, is $14,500 [$17,000 − ($2,000 + $500)]. Payments in the year of sale are $1,500 and are calculated as follows:

Down payment	$1,000
Excess of mortgage assumed over seller's basis and expenses ($3,000 − $2,000 − $500)	500
	$1,500

The contract price is $14,500 [$17,000 (selling price) − $3,000 (seller's mortgage assumed) + $500 (excess of mortgage assumed over seller's basis and selling expenses)]. The gain recognized in the year of sale is computed as follows:

$$\frac{\$14{,}500 \text{ (total gain)}}{\$14{,}500 \text{ (contract price)}} \times \$1{,}500 = \$1{,}500$$

In subsequent years, all amounts the seller collects on the note principal ($13,000) will be recognized gain ($13,000 × 100%). ◆

As previously discussed, gain attributable to ordinary income recapture under §§ 1245 and 1250 is *ineligible* for installment reporting. Therefore, the § 1245 or § 1250 gain realized must be recognized in the year of sale, and the installment sale gain is the remaining gain.

EXAMPLE 25

T sold an apartment building for $50,000 cash and a $75,000 note due in two years. T's basis in the property was $25,000, and $40,000 ordinary income was recaptured under § 1250.

T's realized gain is $100,000 ($125,000 − $25,000), and the $40,000 recapture must be recognized in the year of sale. Of the $60,000 remaining § 1231 gain, $24,000 must be recognized in the year of sale:

$$\frac{\text{§ 1231 gain}}{\text{Contract price}} \times \text{Payments received}$$

$$= \frac{\$125{,}000 - \$25{,}000 - \$40{,}000}{\$125{,}000} \times \$50{,}000$$

$$= \frac{\$60{,}000}{\$125{,}000} \times \$50{,}000 = \$24{,}000$$

The remaining realized gain of $36,000 ($60,000 − $24,000) will be recognized as the $75,000 note is collected. ◆

63. Temp.Reg. § 15a.453–1(b)(2)(iii).

Other Amounts Considered as Payments Received. Congress and the IRS have added the following items to be considered as payments received in the year of sale:[64]

- Purchaser's evidence of indebtedness payable on demand and certain other readily tradable obligations (e.g., bonds traded on a stock exchange).
- Purchaser's evidence of indebtedness secured by cash or its equivalent.

In the absence of the first adjustment, the seller will have control over the year the gain is reported—whenever he or she demands payment or sells the tradable obligations. The seller receiving the obligations secured by cash can often post them as collateral for a loan and have the cash from the sale. Thus, there would be no justification for deferring the tax.

Imputed Interest. Sections 483 and 1274 provide that if a deferred payment contract for the sale of property with a selling price greater than $3,000 does not contain a reasonable interest rate, a reasonable rate is imputed. The imputing of interest effectively restates the selling price of the property to equal the sum of the payments at the date of the sale and the discounted present value of the future payments. The difference between the present value of a future payment and the payment's face amount is taxed as interest income, as discussed in the following paragraphs. Thus, the imputed interest rules prevent sellers of capital assets from increasing the selling price to reflect the equivalent of unstated interest on deferred payments and thereby converting ordinary (interest) income into long-term capital gains. In addition, the imputed interest rules are important because they affect the timing of income recognition.

Generally, if the contract does not charge at least the Federal rate, interest will be imputed at the Federal rate. The Federal rate is the interest rate the Federal government pays on new borrowing and is published monthly by the IRS.[65]

As a general rule, the buyer and seller must account for interest on the accrual basis with semiannual compounding.[66] Requiring the use of the accrual basis assures that the seller's interest income and the buyer's interest expense are reported in the same tax year. Under pre-1984 law, the cash basis seller did not report interest income until it was actually collected, but an accrual basis buyer could deduct the interest as it accrued. The following example illustrates the calculation and amortization of imputed interest.

EXAMPLE 26

T, a cash basis taxpayer, sold land on January 1, 1992, for $100,000 cash and $3,000,000 due on December 31, 1993, with 5% interest payable December 31, 1992, and December 31, 1993. At the time of the sale, the Federal rate was 8% (compounded semiannually). Because T did not charge at least the Federal rate, interest will be imputed at 8% (compounded semiannually).

Date	Payment	Present Value (at 8%) on 1/1/1992	Imputed Interest
12/31/1992	$ 150,000	$ 138,750	$ 11,250
12/31/1993	3,150,000	2,693,250	456,750
	$3,300,000	$2,832,000	$468,000

64. § 453(f)(4) and Temp.Reg. § 15a.453–1(e).

65. § 1274(d)(1). There are three Federal rates: short-term (not over three years), mid-term (over three years but not over nine years), and long-term (over nine years).

66. §§ 1274(a), 1273(a), and 1272(a).

Thus, the selling price will be restated to $2,932,000 ($100,000 + $2,832,000) rather than $3,100,000 ($100,000 + $3,000,000), and T will recognize interest income in accordance with the following amortization schedule:

	Beginning Balance	Interest Income (at 8%)*	Received	Ending Balance
1992	$2,832,000	$231,091	$ 150,000	$2,913,091
1993	2,913,091	236,909	3,150,000	-0-

*Compounded semiannually.

◆

Congress has created several exceptions regarding the rate at which interest is imputed and the method of accounting for the interest income and expense. The general rules and exceptions are summarized in Concept Summary 18–2.

CONCEPT SUMMARY 18–2
INTEREST ON INSTALLMENT SALES

	Imputed Interest Rate
General rule	Federal rate
Exceptions	
■ Principal amount not over $2.8 million.[1]	Lesser of Federal rate or 9%
■ Sale of land (with a calendar year ceiling of $500,000) between family members (the seller's spouse, brothers, sisters, ancestors, or lineal descendants).[2]	Lesser of Federal rate or 6%

	Method of Accounting for Interest	
	Seller's Interest Income	Buyer's Interest Expense
General rule[3]	Accrual	Accrual
Exceptions		
■ Total payments under the contract are $250,000 or less.[4]	Taxpayer's overall method	Taxpayer's overall method
■ Sale of a farm (sales price of $1 million or less).[5]	Taxpayer's overall method	Taxpayer's overall method
■ Sale of a principal residence.[6]	Taxpayer's overall method	Taxpayer's overall method
■ Sale for a note with a principal amount of not over $2 million, the seller is on the cash basis, the property sold is not inventory, and the buyer agrees to report expense by the cash method.[7]	Cash	Cash

1. § 1274A. This amount is adjusted annually for inflation. For 1992, the amount is $3,234,900.
2. §§ 1274(c)(3)(F) and 483(e).
3. §§ 1274(a) and 1272(a)(3).
4. §§ 1274(c)(3)(C) and 483.
5. §§ 1274(c)(3)(A) and 483.
6. §§ 1274(c)(3)(B) and 483.
7. § 1274A(c). This amount is adjusted annually for inflation. For 1992, the amount is $2,310,600.

Related-Party Sales of Nondepreciable Property. Because of favorable judicial authority, it was possible (with proper planning) to use the installment sales approach beneficially in sales between related parties. A subsequent cash sale by the related-party purchaser to a third party could result in little or no recognized gain.

EXAMPLE 27

F and D (father and daughter) each own substantial investment properties. F would like to sell a capital asset that has a basis of $20,000 and a fair market value of $100,000. He could easily sell the property for cash, but that would result in a taxable gain for the year. To defer the tax while enjoying the proceeds of the sale, F and D could structure transactions as follows:

First Disposition. F sells the asset to D for $100,000 and receives $10,000 cash and a $90,000 interest-bearing long-term note. In the year of the sale, he reports a gain of $8,000, computed as follows:

$$\frac{\$100{,}000 - \$20{,}000}{\$100{,}000} \times \$10{,}000 = \$8{,}000$$

F has a $72,000 deferred gain.

Second Disposition. D has a basis in the asset of $100,000 (cost). Soon after purchasing the asset from F, D sells it on the open market for $100,000. D has no recognized gain because the selling price is equal to the basis. The net result of the two transactions is that the family unit (F and D) has $100,000 cash and a deferred tax liability that will not come due until the future, when D pays F the principal on the note. The interest payments will be a wash within the family—F's income will be offset by D's deduction. ◆

Although transactions depicted in Example 27 had to be carefully planned, before 1980 they could succeed.[67] Obviously, this scheme was too good to survive. Thus, Congress added a provision to the Code to close this loophole.[68] Basically, the related-party installment sales rules assume that the proceeds of the second sale are used to pay the note owed to the first seller. Thus, the deferred gain from the first disposition is accelerated to the date of the second disposition.

EXAMPLE 28

Assume the same facts as in Example 27, except D sold the asset for $110,000. D realized and must recognize a $10,000 gain, and F must recognize his previously deferred $72,000 gain, even though D did not retire the note payable to F. ◆

However, even with this modification of the rules, Congress did not eliminate the benefits of all related-party installment sales.

- Related parties include the first seller's brothers, sisters, ancestors, lineal descendants, controlled corporations, and partnerships, trusts, and estates in which the seller has an interest.[69]
- There is no acceleration if the second disposition occurs more than two years after the first sale.[70]

---

67. For a taxpayer success in this area, see *Rushing v. Comm.*, 71–1 USTC ¶9339, 27 AFTR2d 71–1139, 441 F.2d 593 (CA–5, 1971), *aff'g* 52 T.C. 888 (1969). For examples of where the plan was unsuccessful, see *Paul G. Lustgarten*, 71 T.C. 303 (1978), and *Phillip W. Wrenn*, 67 T.C. 576 (1976).

68. § 453(e).

69. § 453(f)(1), cross-referencing §§ 267(b) and 318(a). Although spouses are related parties, the exemption of gain between spouses (§ 1041) makes the second disposition rules inapplicable when the first sale was between spouses.

70. § 453(e)(2). But see § 453(e)(2)(B) for extensions of the two-year period.

Thus, if the taxpayer can sell the property to an unrelated party (not a related party) or patient family member, the intrafamily installment sale is still a powerful tax planning tool. Other exceptions also can be applied in some circumstances.[71]

Related-Party Sales of Depreciable Property. The installment method cannot be used to report a gain on the sale of depreciable property to a controlled entity. The purpose of this rule is to prevent the seller from deferring gain (until collections are received) while the related purchaser is enjoying a stepped-up basis for depreciation purposes.[72]

The prohibition on the use of the installment method applies to sales between the taxpayer and a partnership or corporation in which the taxpayer holds a more-than-50 percent interest. Constructive ownership rules are used in applying the ownership test (e.g., the taxpayer is considered to own stock owned by a spouse and certain other family members).[73] However, if the taxpayer can establish that tax avoidance was not a principal purpose of the transaction, the installment method can be used to report the gain.

EXAMPLE 29

P purchased an apartment building from his controlled corporation, S Corporation. P was short of cash at the time of the purchase (December 1992), but was to collect a large cash payment in January 1993. The agreement required P to pay the entire arm's length price in January 1993. P had good business reasons for acquiring the building. S Corporation should be able to convince the IRS that tax avoidance was not a principal purpose for the installment sale because the tax benefits are not overwhelming. The corporation will report all of the gain in the year following the year of sale, and the building must be expensed over 27.5 years (the cost recovery period). ◆

Disposition of Installment Obligations

The law prevents taxpayers from avoiding the recognition of deferred gross profit on installment obligations through various means (e.g., the sale of installment notes or the distribution of such notes to shareholders). The taxpayer must pay the tax on the portion of gross profits that was previously deferred as follows:[74]

> If an installment obligation is satisfied at other than its face value or distributed, transmitted, sold, or otherwise disposed of, gain or loss shall result to the extent of the difference between the basis of the obligation and either of the following:

- The amount realized, in the case of satisfaction at other than face value or in a sale or exchange.
- The fair market value of the obligation at the time of distribution, transmission, or disposition, in the case of the distribution, transmission, or disposition other than by sale or exchange.

The gift of an installment note will be treated as a taxable disposition by the donor. The amount realized from the cancellation is the face amount of the note if the parties (obligor and obligee) are related to each other.[75]

71. See §§ 453(e)(6) and (7).
72. § 453(g).
73. §§ 1239(b) and (c).
74. § 453B(a).
75. § 453B(f)(2).

EXAMPLE 30

F cancels a note issued by D (F's daughter) that arose in connection with the sale of property. At the time of the cancellation, the note had a basis to F of $10,000, a face amount of $25,000, and a fair market value of $20,000. Presuming the initial sale by F qualified as an installment sale, the cancellation would result in gain of $15,000 ($25,000 − $10,000) to F. ◆

Certain exceptions to the recognition of gain provisions are provided for transfers of installment obligations pursuant to tax-free incorporations under § 351, contributions of capital to a partnership, certain corporate liquidations, transfers due to the taxpayer's death, and transfers between spouses or incident to divorce.[76] In such instances, the deferred profit is merely shifted to the transferee, who is responsible for the payment of tax on the subsequent collections of the installment obligations.

Pledging Installment Obligations

Borrowing and using installment obligations as security for the loan may be a means of receiving the cash from installment obligations without recognizing income. However, the Code specifically requires that a seller of property (other than farming property) must treat amounts borrowed as collections on the contract, where the installment obligations serve as security for the debt.[77] This acceleration of gain applies to an amount borrowed when all of the following characteristics are present:

- The indebtedness is secured by an installment obligation arising from the sale of property (realty and personalty).
- The selling price is greater than $150,000.
- The property was either used in the taxpayer's trade or business or was held for the production of rental income.

EXAMPLE 31

In 1992, T sold land used in his business for $500,000 (basis of $150,000). T received $200,000 cash and an interest-bearing note for $300,000 due in 1995. In 1993, T borrowed $250,000 using the note as security. The receipt of the loan proceeds will cause T to recognize gain of $175,000 [($500,000 − $150,000)/ $500,000 × $250,000]. When T collects the note in 1995, he must recognize the balance of the realized gain of $35,000 (.70 × $50,000). ◆

Interest on Deferred Taxes

With the installment method, the seller earns interest on the receivable. The receivable includes the deferred gain. Thus, one could argue that the seller is earning interest on the deferred taxes. Some commentators reason that the government is, in effect, making interest-free loans to taxpayers who report gains by the installment method. Following the argument that the amount of the deferred taxes is a loan, the taxpayer is required to pay interest on the deferred taxes in some situations.[78]

The taxpayer is required to pay interest on the deferred taxes only if both of the following requirements are met:

76. §§ 453B(c), (d), and (g). See Chapter 20 for a discussion of some of these subjects.

77. §§ 453A(b) and (d).

78. § 453A.

- The installment obligation arises from the sale of property (other than farming property) for more than $150,000.
- Such installment obligations outstanding at the close of the tax year exceed $5 million.

Interest on the deferred taxes is payable only for the portion of the taxes that relates to the installment obligations in *excess* of $5 million. The interest is calculated using the underpayment rate in § 6621.

Repossessions of Property

Generally, the repossession of property is a taxable event. Thus, the taxpayer must recognize gain or loss equal to the fair market value of the property received (reduced by repossession expenses) less the unrecovered basis.[79]

Example 32

T sold the stock in his closely held corporation to B for $125,000 (a down payment of $30,000 and an installment note for $95,000). T's basis for the stock was $50,000. B defaulted on the note after paying $10,000 on the principal. T foreclosed and received the stock when it had a fair market value of $60,000.

T had recognized gain of $24,000 under the installment method as follows:

$$\frac{\$125{,}000 - \$50{,}000}{\$125{,}000} \times (\$30{,}000 + \$10{,}000) = \$24{,}000$$

Therefore, at the time of repossession, T's unrecovered basis in the note is $34,000 ($50,000 original basis − $16,000 amount of collections treated as a recovery of capital). T must recognize a $26,000 ($60,000 − $34,000) gain from the repossession. ◆

Repossession of Real Property. A special provision prohibits the recognition of loss and limits the gain recognized from a repossession of real property.[80] Generally, the gain recognized from the repossession cannot exceed the total cash collected (other than interest) by the seller less the gain previously recognized from collections.[81] In other words, the total gain from the repossessed property cannot exceed the cash receipts.

Example 33

S sold land for $100,000, but collected only $30,000 before the purchaser defaulted. S's basis in the land was $20,000, repossession expenses are $5,000, and the fair market value of the land at the time of repossession is $110,000. The recognized gain from repossession of $6,000 is calculated as follows:

Cash collected	$ 30,000
Less: Gain previously recognized (80% × $30,000)	(24,000)
Gain on repossession	$ 6,000

◆

As a further limitation, the gain from repossession cannot exceed the seller's original gain less the sum of the previously recognized gain and the expenses of repossession [in Example 33, $80,000 − ($24,000 + $5,000) = $51,000].[82] Thus,

79. Reg. § 1.453–2(d).
80. § 1038.
81. If the seller receives property other than the repossessed property, its fair market value is added to the cash proceeds.
82. Reg. §§ 1.1038–1(c) and (h).

the seller is not taxed on any appreciation in the value of the property from the date of sale to the date of repossession.

The seller's basis for the repossessed property is calculated as follows:[83]

Seller's unrecovered basis for the note
+ Recognized gain on the repossession
+ Repossession expenses

In Example 33, S's basis for the repossessed land would be $25,000 [($70,000 × 20%) + $6,000 + $5,000].

Electing Out of the Installment Method

A taxpayer can *elect not to use* the installment method. The election is made by reporting on a timely filed return the gain computed by the taxpayer's usual method of accounting (cash or accrual).[84] However, the Regulations provide that the amount realized by a cash basis taxpayer cannot be less than the value of the property sold. This rule differs from the usual cash basis accounting rules (discussed earlier),[85] which measure the amount realized in terms of the fair market value of the property received. The net effect of the Regulations is to allow the cash basis taxpayer to report his or her gain as an accrual basis taxpayer. The election is frequently applied to year-end sales by taxpayers who expect to be in a higher tax bracket in the following year.

EXAMPLE 34

On December 31, 1992, T sold land to B for $20,000 (fair market value). The cash was to be paid on January 4, 1993. T is a cash basis taxpayer, and his basis in the land is $8,000. T has a large casualty loss and very little other income in 1992. Thus, his marginal tax rate in 1992 is 15%. He expects his rate to increase to 31% in 1993.

The transaction constitutes an installment sale because a payment will be received in a tax year after the tax year of disposition. B's promise to pay T is an installment obligation, and under the Regulations, the value of the installment obligation is equal to the value of the property sold ($20,000). If T elects out of the installment method, he would shift $12,000 of gain ($20,000 − $8,000) from the expected 31% rate in 1993 to the 15% rate in 1992. The expected tax savings of $1,920 [(.31 − .15)($12,000)] may exceed the benefit of the tax deferral available with the installment method. ◆

Revocation of the Election. Permission of the IRS is required to revoke an election not to use the installment method.[86] The stickiness of the election is an added peril.

Long-Term Contracts

A *long-term contract* is a building, installation, construction, or manufacturing contract that is entered into but not completed within the same tax year. However, a manufacturing contract is long term *only* if the contract is to manufacture (1) a unique item not normally carried in finished goods inventory or (2) items that normally require more than 12 calendar months to complete.[87] An item is *unique* if it is designed to meet the customer's particular needs and is not suitable for use by others. A contract to perform services (e.g., auditing or

83. Reg. § 1.1038–1(g)(1).
84. § 453(d) and Temp.Reg. § 15a.453–1(d). See also Rev.Rul. 82–227, 1982–2 C.B. 89.
85. Refer to Chapter 4, Example 9.
86. § 453(d)(3) and Temp.Reg. § 15a.453–1(d)(4).
87. § 460(f) and Reg. § 1.451–3(b).

legal services) is not considered a contract for this purpose and thus cannot qualify as a long-term contract.

EXAMPLE 35

T, a calendar year taxpayer, entered into two contracts during the year. One contract was to construct a building foundation. Work was to begin in October 1991 and was to be completed by June 1992. The contract is long term because it will not be entered into and completed in the same tax year. The fact that the contract requires less than 12 calendar months to complete is not relevant because the contract is not for manufacturing. The second contract was for architectural services to be performed over two years. These services will not qualify for long-term contract treatment because the taxpayer will not build, install, construct, or manufacture a product. ◆

Generally, the taxpayer must accumulate all of the direct and indirect costs incurred under a contract. This means the production costs must be accumulated and allocated to individual contracts. Furthermore, mixed services costs, costs that benefit contracts as well as the general administrative operations of the business, must be allocated to production. Concept Summary 18–3 lists the types of costs that must be accumulated and allocated to contracts. The taxpayer must develop reasonable bases for cost allocations.[88]

EXAMPLE 36

C, Inc., uses detailed cost accumulation records to assign labor and materials to its contracts in progress. The total cost of fringe benefits is allocated to a contract on the following basis:

$$\frac{\text{Labor on the contract}}{\text{Total salaries and labor}} \times \text{Total cost of fringe benefits}$$

Similarly, storage and handling costs for materials are allocated to contracts on the following basis:

$$\frac{\text{Contract materials}}{\text{Materials purchases}} \times \text{Storage and handling costs}$$

The cost of the personnel operations, a mixed services cost, is allocated between production and general administration based on the number of employees in each function. The personnel cost allocated to production is allocated to individual contracts on the basis of the formula used to allocate fringe benefits. ◆

The accumulated costs are deducted when the revenue from the contract is recognized. Generally, two methods of accounting are used in varying circumstances to determine when the revenue from a contract is recognized:[89]

- The completed contract method.
- The percentage of completion method.

The completed contract method may be used for (1) home construction contracts (contracts in which at least 80 percent of the estimated costs are for dwelling units in buildings with four or fewer units) and (2) certain other real estate construction contracts. Other real estate contracts can qualify for the completed contract method if the following requirements are satisfied:

---

88. Temp.Reg. § 1.263A–1T(b)(3)(iii)(A)(1).

89. § 460.

- The contract is expected to be completed within the two-year period beginning on the commencement date of the contract.
- The contract is performed by a taxpayer whose average annual gross receipts for the three taxable years preceding the taxable year in which the contract is entered into do not exceed $10 million.

All other contractors must use the percentage of completion method.

CONCEPT SUMMARY 18–3
CONTRACT COSTS, MIXED SERVICES COSTS, AND CURRENT EXPENSE ITEMS FOR CONTRACTS

	Contracts Eligible for the Completed Contract Method	Other Contracts
Contract costs:		
Direct materials (a part of the finished product).	Capital	Capital
Indirect materials (consumed in production but not in the finished product, e.g., grease and oil for equipment).	Capital	Capital
Storage, handling, and insurance on materials.	Expense	Capital
Direct labor (worked on the product).	Capital	Capital
Indirect labor (worked in the production process but not directly on the product, e.g., a construction supervisor).	Capital	Capital
Fringe benefits for direct and indirect labor (e.g., vacation, sick pay, unemployment, and other insurance).	Capital	Capital
Pension costs for direct and indirect labor:		
■ Current cost.	Expense	Capital
■ Past service costs.	Expense	Capital
Depreciation on production facilities:		
■ For financial statements.	Capital	Capital
■ Tax depreciation in excess of financial statements.	Expense	Capital
Depreciation on idle facilities.	Expense	Expense
Property taxes, insurance, rent, and maintenance on production facilities.	Capital	Capital
Bidding expenses—successful.	Expense	Capital
Bidding expenses—unsuccessful.	Expense	Expense
Interest to finance real estate construction.	Capital	Capital
Interest to finance personal property:		
■ Construction period of one year or less.	Expense	Expense
■ Construction period exceeds one year and costs exceed $1,000,000.	Capital	Capital
■ Construction period exceeds two years.	Capital	Capital
Mixed services costs:		
Personnel operations.	Expense	Allocate
Data processing.	Expense	Allocate
Purchasing.	Expense	Allocate
Selling, general, and administrative expenses (including an allocated share of mixed services)	Expense	Expense
Losses	Expense	Expense

Completed Contract Method. Under the *completed contract method*, no revenue from the contract is recognized until the contract is completed and accepted. However, a taxpayer may not delay completion of a contract for the principal purpose of deferring tax.[90]

In some instances, the original contract price may be disputed, or the buyer may want additional work to be done on a long-term contract. If the disputed amount is substantial (it is not possible to determine whether a profit or loss will ultimately be realized on the contract), the Regulations provide that no amount of income or loss is recognized until the dispute is resolved. In all other cases, the profit or loss (reduced by the amount in dispute) is recognized in the current period on completion of the contract. However, additional work may need to be performed with respect to the disputed contract. In this case, the difference between the amount in dispute and the actual cost of the additional work will be recognized in the year the work is completed rather than in the year in which the dispute is resolved.[91]

EXAMPLE 37

B, a calendar year taxpayer utilizing the completed contract method of accounting, constructed a building for C under a long-term contract. The gross contract price was $500,000. B finished construction in 1992 at a cost of $475,000. When C examined the building, he insisted that the building be repainted or the contract price be reduced. The estimated cost of repainting is $10,000. Since under the terms of the contract, B is assured of a profit of at least $15,000 ($500,000 − $475,000 − $10,000) even if the dispute is ultimately resolved in favor of C, B must include $490,000 ($500,000 − $10,000) in gross income and is allowed deductions of $475,000 for 1992.

In 1993, B and C resolve the dispute, and B repaints certain portions of the building at a cost of $6,000. B must include $10,000 in 1993 gross income and may deduct the $6,000 expense in that year. ◆

EXAMPLE 38

Assume the same facts as in the previous example, except the estimated cost of repainting the building is $50,000. Since the resolution of the dispute completely in C's favor would mean a net loss on the contract for B ($500,000 − $475,000 − $50,000 = $25,000 loss), B does not recognize any income or loss until the year the dispute is resolved. ◆

Frequently, a contractor receives payment at various stages of completion. For example, when the contract is 50 percent complete, the contractor may receive 50 percent of the contract price less a retainage. The taxation of these payments is generally governed by Regulation § 1.451–5 "advance payments for goods and long-term contracts" (discussed in Chapter 4). Generally, contractors are permitted to defer the advance payments until the payments are recognized as income under the taxpayer's method of accounting.

Percentage of Completion Method. In 1986, Congress began limiting the circumstances under which the completed contract method could be used. However, rather than totally disallowing the use of the completed contract method, Congress created the *percentage of completion–capitalized cost method*. Under this method, 40 percent of the items produced under a contract were accounted for by the percentage of completion method, and the remaining 60 percent could be accounted for under the completed contract method. Subsequent legislation increased the 40 percent, initially to 70 percent and finally to 90

90. Reg. § 1.451–3(b)(2).

91. Reg. § 1.451–3(d)(2)(ii)–(vii), Example (2).

percent. The Revenue Reconciliation Act of 1989 effectively *repealed* the percentage of completion–capitalized cost method. Therefore, only the percentage of completion method can be used to account for long-term contracts unless the taxpayer qualifies for one of the two exceptions that permit the completed contract method to be used (home construction contracts and certain other real estate construction contracts).[92]

Under the *percentage of completion method,* a portion of the gross contract price is included in income during each period as the work progresses. The revenue accrued each period is computed as follows:[93]

$$\frac{C}{T} \times P$$

Where C = Contract costs incurred during the period
T = Estimated total cost of the contract
P = Contract price

All of the costs allocated to the contract during the period are deductible from the accrued revenue.[94] Because T in this formula is an estimate that frequently differs from total actual costs, which are not known until the contract has been completed, the profit on a contract for a particular period may be overstated or understated.

EXAMPLE 39

B, Inc., entered into a contract that was to take two years to complete, with estimated total costs of $225,000. The contract price was $300,000. Costs of the contract for 1992, the first year, totaled $135,000. The gross profit reported by the percentage of completion method for 1992 was $45,000 [($135,000/$225,000 × $300,000) − $135,000]. The contract was completed at the end of 1993 at a total cost of $270,000. In retrospect, 1992 profit should have been $15,000 [($135,000/$270,000 × $300,000) − $135,000]. Thus, taxes were overpaid in 1992. ◆

A *de minimis* rule enables the contractor to delay the recognition of income for a particular contract under the percentage of completion method. If less than 10 percent of the estimated contract costs have been incurred by the end of the taxable year, the taxpayer can elect to defer the recognition of income and the related costs until the taxable year in which cumulative contract costs are at least 10 percent of the estimated contract costs.[95]

Lookback Provisions. In the year a contract is completed, a *lookback* provision requires the recalculation of annual profits reported on the contract under the percentage of completion method. Interest is paid to the taxpayer if taxes were overpaid, and interest is payable by the taxpayer if there was an underpayment.[96]

EXAMPLE 40

Assume B, Inc., in Example 39, was in the 34% tax bracket in both years and the relevant interest rate was 10%. For 1992, the company paid excess taxes of $10,200

92. Certain residential construction contracts that do not qualify to use the completed contract method may still use the percentage of completion–capitalized cost method, using the 70 percent factor. See § 460(b)(5).

93. § 460(b)(1)(A).

94. Reg. § 1.451–3(c)(3).

95. § 460(b)(5).

96. § 460(b)(2).

[($45,000 − $15,000) × .34]. When the contract is completed at the end of 1993, B, Inc., should receive interest of $1,020 for one year on the tax overpayment ($10,200 × .10). ◆

INVENTORIES

Generally, tax accounting and financial accounting for inventories are much the same:

- The use of inventories is necessary to clearly reflect the income of any business engaged in the production and sale or purchase and sale of goods.[97]
- The inventories should include all finished goods, goods in process, and raw materials and supplies that will become part of the product (including containers).
- Inventory rules must give effect to the *best* accounting practice of a particular trade or business, and the taxpayer's method should be consistently followed from year to year.
- All items included in inventory should be valued at either (1) cost or (2) the lower of cost or market value.

The following are *not* acceptable methods or practices in valuing inventories:

- A deduction for a reserve for anticipated price changes.
- The use of a constant price or nominal value for a so-called normal quantity of materials or goods in stock (e.g., the base stock method).
- The inclusion in inventory of stock in transit to which title is not vested in the taxpayer.
- The direct costing approach (excluding fixed indirect production costs from inventory).
- The prime costing approach (excluding all indirect production costs from inventory).

The reason for the similarities between tax and financial accounting for inventories is that § 471 sets forth what appears to be a two-prong test. Under this provision "inventories shall be taken . . . on such basis . . . as conforming as nearly as may be to the *best accounting practice* in the trade or business and as most *clearly reflecting the income.*" The best accounting practice is synonymous with generally accepted accounting principles (hereafter referred to as GAAP). However, the IRS determines whether an inventory method clearly reflects income.

In *Thor Power Tool Co. v. Comm.*, there was a conflict between the two tests.[98] The taxpayer's method of valuing obsolete parts was in conformity with GAAP. The IRS, however, successfully argued that the clear reflection of income test was not satisfied because the taxpayer's procedures for valuing its inventories were contrary to the Regulations. Under the taxpayer's method, inventories for parts in excess of estimated future sales were written off (expensed), although the parts were kept on hand and their asking prices were not reduced. [Under Regulation § 1.471–4(b), inventories cannot be written down unless the selling prices also are reduced.] The taxpayer contended that conformity to GAAP creates a presumption that the method clearly reflects income. The Supreme Court disagreed, concluding that the clear reflection of income test was *paramount*. Moreover, it is the opinion of the IRS that controls in determining

97. § 471(a) and Reg. §§ 1.471–1 and –2.

98. 79–1 USTC ¶9139, 43 AFTR2d 79–362, 99 S.Ct. 773 (USSC, 1979).

whether the method of inventory clearly reflects income. Thus, the best accounting practice test was rendered practically meaningless. It follows that the taxpayer's method of inventory must strictly conform to the Regulations regardless of what GAAP may require.

Determining Inventory Cost

For merchandise purchased, cost is the invoice price less trade discounts plus freight and other handling charges.[99] Cash discounts approximating a fair interest rate can be deducted or capitalized at the taxpayer's option, providing the method used is consistently applied.

Uniform Capitalization. In 1986, Congress added § 263A, which significantly affects the inventory rules, to the Code. Section 263A provides that for inventory and property produced by the taxpayer, ". . . (A) the direct cost of such property, and (B) such property's share of those indirect costs (including taxes) part or all of which are allocable to such property" must be capitalized. The Committee Reports observe that Congress is attempting to achieve a set of capitalization rules that will apply to all types of businesses: contractors, manufacturers, farmers, wholesalers, and retailers.[100] Congress has labeled the system *uniform capitalization rules,* and practitioners refer to the rules as a *super-full absorption costing system.*

According to the Committee Reports, the cost of goods produced or manufactured by the taxpayer must be determined by using the rules developed for long-term contracts as outlined in Concept Summary 18–3 (see the "Other Contracts" column). In general, these rules result in capitalization (as inventory) of all costs except selling and general and administrative expenses that are not related to production (e.g., general accounting).

Wholesalers and retailers are required to capitalize the costs of acquiring and storing goods as well as the purchase price of the goods and any related taxes. The Conference Committee Report lists the following indirect costs that must be capitalized:

- All storage costs for wholesalers.
- Offsite storage costs for retailers.
- Purchasing costs (e.g., buyers' wages or salaries).
- Handling, processing, assembly, and repackaging.
- The portion of general and administrative costs allocable to these functions.

Mixed services costs must be allocated to offsite storage, purchasing, and packaging on the basis of direct labor costs of these departments as a percentage of total payroll. Thus, the storage, purchasing, and packaging costs allocated to ending inventory include some general and administrative expense.

The uniform capitalization rules may result in some costs being capitalized for tax purposes but not for financial accounting purposes. For example, a wholesaler's or a manufacturer's storage costs are generally expensed for financial reporting purposes, but are capitalized for tax purposes. Also, the taxpayer may capitalize straight-line depreciation of production equipment for financial accounting purposes, but the total tax depreciation must be capitalized under uniform capitalization.

99. Reg. § 1.471–3(b).

100. H. Rep. 99–841, 99th Cong., 2nd Sess., 1986, pp. 302–309. See also Temp. Reg. § 1.263A–1T.

Lower of Cost or Market. Except for those taxpayers who use the LIFO method, inventories may be valued at the lower of cost or replacement cost (*market*).[101] Taxpayers using LIFO must value inventory at cost. However, the write-down of damaged or shopworn merchandise and goods that are otherwise unsalable at normal prices is not considered to be an application of the lower of cost or market method. Such items should be valued at bona fide selling price less direct cost of disposal.[102]

In the case of excess inventories (as in *Thor Power Tool Co.*, discussed above), the goods can be written down only to the taxpayer's offering price. If the offering price on the goods is not reduced, the goods must be valued at cost.

EXAMPLE 41

The Z Publishing Company invested $50,000 in printing 10,000 copies of a book. Although only 7,000 copies were sold in the first 3 years and none in the next 5 years, management is convinced that the book will become a classic in 20 years. Z Company leaves the price the same as it was when the book was first distributed ($15 per copy). The remaining 3,000 books must be valued at cost ($15,000). Note that the tax law provides an incentive for the taxpayer to destroy or abandon its excess inventory and obtain an immediate deduction rather than wait for the event of future sales. ◆

In applying the lower of cost or market method, *each* item included in the inventory must be valued at the lower of its cost or market value.[103]

EXAMPLE 42

The taxpayer's ending inventory is valued as follows:

Item	Cost	Market	Lower of Cost or Market
A	$5,000	$ 4,000	$4,000
B	3,000	2,000	2,000
C	1,500	6,000	1,500
	$9,500	$12,000	$7,500

Under the lower of cost or market method, the taxpayer's inventory would be valued at $7,500 rather than $9,500. ◆

Determining Cost—Specific Identification, FIFO, and LIFO. In some cases, it is feasible to determine the cost of the particular item sold. For example, an automobile dealer can easily determine the specific cost of each automobile that has been sold. However, in most businesses it is necessary to resort to a flow of goods assumption such as *first in, first out* (FIFO), *last in, first out* (LIFO), or an *average cost* method. A taxpayer may use any of these methods, provided the method selected is consistently applied from year to year.

During a period of rising prices, LIFO will generally produce a lower ending inventory valuation and will result in a greater cost of goods sold than would be obtained under the FIFO method. The following example illustrates how LIFO and FIFO affect the computation of the cost of goods sold.

EXAMPLE 43

On January 1, 1992, the taxpayer opened a retail store to sell refrigerators. At least 10 refrigerators must be carried in inventory to satisfy customer demands. The initial

101. Reg. § 1.472–4.
102. Reg. § 1.471–2(c).
103. Reg. § 1.471–4(c).

investment in the 10 refrigerators is $5,000. During the year, 10 refrigerators were sold at $750 each and were replaced at a cost of $6,000 ($600 each). Gross profit under the LIFO and FIFO methods is computed as follows:

		FIFO		LIFO
Sales (10 × $750)		$ 7,500		$ 7,500
Beginning inventory	$ 5,000		$ 5,000	
Purchases	6,000		6,000	
	$11,000		$11,000	
Ending inventory				
10 × $600	(6,000)			
10 × $500			(5,000)	
Cost of goods sold		(5,000)		(6,000)
Gross profit		$ 2,500		$ 1,500

◆

The LIFO Election

A taxpayer may adopt LIFO by merely using the method in the tax return for the year of the change and by attaching Form 970 (Application to Use LIFO Inventory Method) to the tax return. Thus, a taxpayer does not have to request approval for changes within the first 180 days of the tax year. Once the election is made, it cannot be revoked. However, a prospective change from LIFO to any other inventory method can be made if the consent of the IRS is obtained.[104]

The beginning inventory valuation for the first year LIFO is used is computed by the costing method employed in the preceding year. Thus, the beginning LIFO inventory is generally the same as the closing inventory for the preceding year. However, since lower of cost or market cannot be used in conjunction with LIFO, previous write-downs to market for items included in the beginning inventory must be restored to income. The amount the inventories are written up is an adjustment due to a change in accounting method.[105] However, the usual rules for disposition of the adjustments under Revenue Procedure 84–74 are not applicable.[106] The taxpayer is allowed to spread the adjustment ratably over the year of the change and the two succeeding years.

EXAMPLE 44

In 1991, T used the lower of cost or market FIFO inventory method. The FIFO cost of his ending inventory was $30,000, and the market value of the inventory was $24,000. Therefore, the ending inventory for 1991 was $24,000. T switched to LIFO in 1992 and was required to write up the beginning inventory to $30,000. T must add $2,000 ($6,000 ÷ 3) to his income for each of the years 1992, 1993, and 1994. ◆

Congress added this provision to the Code to overrule the previous IRS policy of requiring the taxpayer to include the entire adjustment in income for the year preceding the change to LIFO.[107]

Once the LIFO election is made for tax purposes, the taxpayer's financial reports to owners and creditors must also be prepared on the basis of LIFO.[108] The *conformity* of financial reports to tax reporting is specifically required by the

104. Reg. §§ 1.472–3(a) and 1.472–5 and Rev.Proc. 84–74, 1984–2 C.B. 736 at 742.

105. Reg. § 1.472–2(c). In Rev.Rul. 76–282, 1976–2 C.B. 137, the IRS required the restoration of write-downs for damaged and shopworn goods when the taxpayer switched to LIFO.

106. 1984–2 C.B. 736.

107. § 472(d), overruling the IRS position cited in Footnote 105.

108. § 472(c).

Code and is strictly enforced by the IRS. However, the Regulations permit the taxpayer to make a footnote disclosure of the net income computed by another method of inventory valuation (e.g., FIFO).[109]

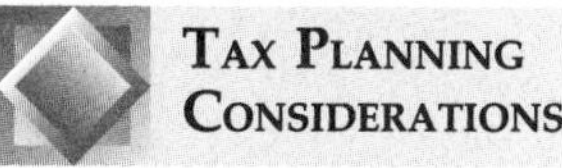

TAX PLANNING CONSIDERATIONS

Taxable Year

Under the general rules for tax years, partnerships and S corporations frequently will be required to use a calendar year. However, if the partnership or S corporation can demonstrate a business purpose for a fiscal year, the IRS will allow the entity to use the requested year. The advantage to the fiscal year is that the calendar year partners and S corporation shareholders may be able to defer from tax the income earned from the close of the fiscal year until the end of the calendar year. Tax advisers for these entities should apply the IRS's gross receipts test described in Revenue Procedure 87–32 to determine if permission for the fiscal year will be granted.

Cash Method of Accounting

The cash method of accounting gives the taxpayer considerable control over the recognition of expenses and some control over the recognition of income. This method can be used by proprietorships, partnerships, and small corporations (gross receipts of $5 million or less) that provide services (inventories are not material to the service business). Farmers (except certain farming corporations) can also use the cash method.

Installment Method

Unlike the accrual and cash methods, the installment method results in an interest-free loan (of deferred taxes) from the government. Thus, the installment method is a powerful tax planning tool and should be considered when a sale of eligible property is being planned. Note, however, that the provision that requires interest to be paid on the deferred taxes on certain installment obligations reduces this benefit.

Related Parties. Intrafamily installment sales can still be a useful family tax planning tool. If the related party holds the property more than two years, a subsequent sale will not accelerate the gain from the first disposition. Patience and forethought are rewarded.

The 6 percent limitation on imputed interest on sales of land between family members enables the seller to convert ordinary income into capital gain or make what is, in effect, a nontaxable gift. If the selling price is raised to adjust for the low interest rate charges on an installment sale, the seller has more capital gain but less ordinary income than would be realized from a sale to an unrelated party. If the selling price is not raised and the specified interest of 6 percent is charged, the seller enables the relative to have the use of the property without having to pay for its full market value. As an additional benefit, the bargain sale is not a taxable gift.

Disposition of Installment Obligations. A disposition of an installment obligation is also a serious matter. Gifts of the obligations will accelerate income to the seller. The list of taxable and nontaxable dispositions of installment obligations should not be trusted to memory. In each instance where transfers of

---

109. Reg. § 1.472–2(e).

installment obligations are contemplated, the practitioner should conduct research to be sure he or she knows the consequences.

LIFO

During periods of inflation, LIFO results in the deferral of tax. The only major disadvantage to LIFO is the financial-tax conformity requirement. However, this disadvantage can be overcome through footnote disclosure of earnings as computed under FIFO.

PROBLEM MATERIALS

DISCUSSION QUESTIONS

1. X recently began conducting an office supply business as a corporation. Z began conducting his law practice through a corporation. Neither corporation has made an S election. What tax year alternatives are available to the X business that are not available to the Z business?
2. Why would a C corporation want to use a tax year other than a calendar year?
3. What do you think of a proposed change in the tax law to allow S corporations and partnerships to select a tax year independent of the tax years of the shareholders and partners? The change is supposedly justified on the basis that tax accountants should be allowed to spread their work more evenly throughout the year.
4. How does a partnership establish a business purpose for a tax year that differs from its partners' tax years?
5. D is an orthopedic surgeon who practices in a ski area. He recently incorporated his practice and elected S corporation treatment. D's brother has recommended that the corporation elect a year ending April 30th, right after the close of the ski season. What is your advice to D?
6. In which of the following situations must a taxpayer annualize income?
   - **a.** The first tax year.
   - **b.** The year an individual marries.
   - **c.** The final return.
   - **d.** A year of a change in the tax year.
7. T is an accrual basis taxpayer. In 1992, T sold property to a customer and collected the purchase price of $1,000. Later in 1992, the customer claimed the property was defective and asked for a refund. The dispute was settled in 1993 when T gave the customer a $250 refund. T was in the 31% tax bracket in 1992 and is in the 15% tax bracket in 1993. Is any special relief available for T?
8. T is the sole shareholder of an accrual basis S corporation, X, Inc. If T forms another S corporation, Z, Inc., does the fact that X, Inc., uses the accrual method mean that Z, Inc., is required to use the accrual method?
9. X Corporation is a retailer, and its annual gross receipts have never exceeded $5,000,000. Y Corporation is a retailer whose gross receipts have never been less than $5,000,000 for a tax year. X and Y are C corporations and have been in existence for more than four years. What accounting method options are available to each corporation for the following types of income and deductions?
   - **a.** Inventories.
   - **b.** Accrued payroll taxes.
   - **c.** Sales of merchandise.
   - **d.** Income from repair services.

10. T buys and sells produce. His annual gross receipts are less than $5,000,000. Approximately 30% of his sales are on account. T sells all of his inventory each day. Thus, he has no beginning or ending inventory each year. Is T required to use the accrual method of accounting?

11. B, a certified public accountant, recently obtained a new client. The client is a retail grocery store that has used the cash method to report its income since it began doing business. Will B incur any liability if he prepares the tax return in accordance with the cash method and does not advise the client of the necessity of seeking the IRS's permission to change to the accrual method?

12. In December 1992, a cash basis taxpayer paid January through June 1993 management fees in connection with his rental properties. The fees were $4,000 per month. Compute the 1992 expense under the following assumptions:

    a. The fees were paid by an individual who derived substantially all of his income from the properties.
    b. The fees were paid by a tax-shelter partnership.

13. T Corporation, an accrual basis taxpayer, had taxable income for 1992. However, T's accountant was ill, and the taxable income for 1992 was not computed until July 1993. The state income tax return for 1992 was filed in August 1993, and $3,000 in state income taxes were paid at that time. Can the 1992 state income taxes be deducted in calculating the corporation's 1992 Federal taxable income?

14. Compare the cash basis and accrual basis of accounting as applied to the following:

    a. Fixed assets.
    b. Prepaid rental income.
    c. Prepaid interest expense.
    d. A note received for services performed if the market value and face amount of the note differ.

15. When are reserves for estimated expenses allowed for tax purposes? What is the role of the matching concept in tax accounting?

16. What difference does it make whether the taxpayer or the IRS initiates the change in accounting method?

17. What is the procedure for obtaining consent to change a method of accounting?

18. Which of the following require the permission of the IRS?

    a. A change from the cash to the accrual basis for deducting property tax expenses.
    b. The correction of a prior year's return when the double-declining balance method was incorrectly used to compute the amortization of a patent.
    c. A change from direct costing to the full absorption method of valuing inventories.
    d. A change from the FIFO to the LIFO inventory method.
    e. A change from cost to the lower of cost or market method of valuing inventories.
    f. A write-down of damaged merchandise to net realizable value when the taxpayer has consistently used cost to value the inventories.
    g. The use of the lower of cost or market method in conjunction with the LIFO inventory method.
    h. A change from the LIFO to the FIFO inventory method.

19. What difference does it make whether the taxpayer is deemed to have used an incorrect accounting method versus having committed an error?

20. X has made Y an offer on the purchase of a capital asset. X will pay (1) $200,000 cash or (2) $50,000 cash and a 12% installment note for $150,000 guaranteed by City Bank of New York. If Y sells for $200,000 cash, he will invest the after-tax proceeds in certificates of deposit yielding 12% interest. Y's cost of the asset is $25,000. Why would Y prefer the installment sale?

21. Which of the following are eligible for installment reporting? Assume some payments are received after the year of sale and the sales are for gains.

a. Fully depreciated equipment sold for $50,000. The original cost of the equipment was $75,000.
b. Sale of a tractor by a farm equipment dealer.
c. Sale of stock in a family-controlled corporation.
d. Sale of residential lots.

22. In 1992, the taxpayer sold some real estate and received an installment note. The sale met all of the requirements for using the installment method, but the taxpayer did not know that the installment method could be used. Thus, the entire gain was reported in the year of sale. In 1993, the taxpayer learns that she could have used the installment method. Is there anything she can do? Explain.

23. T, a cash basis taxpayer, sold land in December 1992. At the time of the sale, T received $10,000 cash and a note for $90,000 due in 90 days. T expects to be in a much higher tax bracket in 1993. Can T report the entire gain in 1992?

24. How does the buyer's assumption of the seller's liabilities in an installment sale affect the following?

a. Selling price.
b. Contract price.
c. Buyer's payments in the year of sale.

25. In 1992 S, a cash basis taxpayer, sold land to P, an accrual basis taxpayer. The principal and interest were due in two years, and the interest was equal to the Federal rate. Neither the buyer nor the seller is a dealer in real estate. Indicate when the buyer and seller will report their interest expense and income in each of the following cases:

a. The selling price is $2.5 million.
b. The selling price is $200,000.
c. The selling price is $600,000.

26. On June 1, 1990, Father sold land to Son for $100,000. Father reported the gain by the installment method, with the gain to be spread over five years. In May 1992, Son received an offer of $150,000 for the land, to be paid over three years. What would be the tax consequences of Son's sale?

27. In 1991, T sold a building to his 100% controlled corporation. The entire purchase price is to be paid in 1992. When should T report the gain on the sale of the building?

28. What is the tax effect of a gift of an installment obligation?

29. T sold stock in a closely held corporation for $7 million. T received a $1 million down payment and was to receive the balance of the sales price over the next 10 years. Should T elect not to use the installment method so that she can avoid having to pay interest on the deferred taxes?

30. T sold real estate on the installment method. The selling price was $400,000, and the realized gain was $300,000. After T collected $150,000, the buyer missed two monthly payments. This gave T the right to foreclose on the property. The fair market value of the property had declined to $250,000. How does the tax law discourage T from foreclosing on the property?

31. What are the advantages of using the completed contract method to report income from a long-term contract?

32. Explain how inventory Regulations provide an incentive for a corporation to dispose of its obsolete excess inventories.

33. Contrast the procedures for changing to the LIFO inventory method with the general requirements for making a change in an accounting method.

34. Discuss the problems that could result from footnote disclosures of net income computed by the FIFO method when the taxpayer uses the LIFO method to report its taxable income.

PROBLEMS

35. L, M, and N are unrelated corporations engaged in real estate development. The three corporations formed a joint venture (treated as a partnership) to develop a

tract of land. Assuming the venture does not have a natural business year, what tax year must the joint venture adopt under the following circumstances?

		Tax Year Ending	Interest in Joint Venture
a.	L	Sept. 30	60%
	M	June 30	20%
	N	March 31	20%
b.	L	Sept. 30	30%
	M	June 30	40%
	N	January 31	30%

36. What tax years should be used in the following cases?

    a. A department store operated by an S corporation.
    b. A public accounting practice operated by a professional corporation.
    c. A farm operated by a partnership whose partners are calendar year individuals.

37. Z conducted his professional practice through Z, Inc. The corporation uses a fiscal year ending September 30 even though the business purpose test for a fiscal year cannot be satisfied. For the year ending September 30, 1992, the corporation paid Z a salary of $150,000, and during the period January through September 1992, the corporation paid Z a salary of $120,000.

    a. How much salary should Z receive during the period October 1 through December 31, 1992?
    b. Assume Z received only $30,000 salary during the period October 1 through December 31, 1992. What would be the consequences to Z, Inc.?

38. P Corporation is in the business of sales and home deliveries of fuel oil and currently uses a calendar year for reporting its taxable income. However, P's natural business year ends April 30. For the short period, January 1, 1992, through April 30, 1992, the corporation earned $32,000. Assume the corporate tax rates are as follows: 15% on taxable income of $50,000 or less, 25% on taxable income over $50,000 but not over $75,000, and 34% on taxable income over $75,000.

    a. What must P Corporation do to change its taxable year?
    b. Compute P Corporation's tax for the short period.

39. L, a cash basis taxpayer, owned a building that he leased to T. In 1992, T prepaid the 1993 rent. During 1993, the building was destroyed by fire. Under the lease agreement, L was required to refund $6,000 to T. Also, in June 1992, L paid the insurance premium on the property for the next 12 months. After the building was destroyed in 1993, L got a $600 refund on the insurance premium. L was in the 31% marginal tax bracket in 1992 and in the 15% marginal tax bracket in 1993. What are the effects of the refunds on L's 1993 tax liability?

40. Compute the taxpayer's income or deductions for 1992 using (1) the cash basis and (2) the accrual basis for each of the following:

    a. In 1992, the taxpayer purchased new equipment for $100,000. The taxpayer paid $25,000 in cash and gave a $75,000 interest-bearing note for the balance. The equipment has a MACRS life of five years, the mid-year convention applies, and the § 179 election was not made.
    b. In December 1992, the taxpayer collected $10,000 for January rents. In January 1993, the taxpayer collected $2,000 for December 1992 rents.
    c. In December 1992, the taxpayer paid office equipment insurance premiums for January–June 1993 of $30,000.

41. Which of the following businesses must use the accrual method of accounting?

    a. A corporation with annual gross receipts of $12 million from equipment rentals.
    b. A partnership (not a tax shelter) engaged in farming and with annual gross receipts of $8 million.

c. A corporation that acts as an insurance agent, with annual gross receipts of $1 million.
d. A manufacturer with annual gross receipts of $600,000.
e. A retailer with annual gross receipts of $250,000.

42. Z Company calculated its accrual basis income for its first year of operations. Net income before tax was $30,000. For tax purposes, the company would like to elect the method that will minimize its taxable income for the year. Compute Z's minimum taxable income, given the following information at the end of the first year:

Inventory	$12,000
Accounts receivable	25,000
Office supplies	1,800
Prepaid insurance (6 months)	1,200
Accounts payable (merchandise)	3,000

43. T receives appliances from the manufacturer on consignment and collects a 5% commission on any sales made during the year. T is an accrual basis taxpayer and made total sales during the year of $750,000. However, the manufacturer is usually a few weeks behind in recording T's sales and at the end of the year recorded only $600,000 in sales. T argues that he should report income for the year of only $30,000 (5% × $600,000), since that was all he had a right to receive for the year. T had no right to the commissions on the other $150,000 sales until the manufacturer reported them in the following year. What is T's correct taxable income for the year? Explain.

44. Determine when T, an accrual basis taxpayer, should record the expenses in each of the following cases:

a. A customer returned defective merchandise to T in December 1992. The customer claimed the goods did not meet specifications and threatened to sue T for breach of contract. T admitted liability in 1992, but did not pay the damages until January 1993.
b. A customer slipped and fell on the business premises in 1992. T admitted liability, and a settlement was reached late in the year. Under the terms of the settlement, T was to pay the customer's medical expenses. By the end of 1992, the total medical expenses associated with the injury were determined. However, some of the expenses were for doctor visits that were to be spread over an 18-month period, and payments would not be made until the time of the visits.
c. In March 1993, the company filed its 1992 state income tax return and paid the balance due on 1992 state income taxes.

45. In 1992, the taxpayer was required to switch from the cash to the accrual basis of accounting for sales and cost of goods sold. Taxable income for 1992 computed under the cash basis was $40,000. Relevant account balances were as follows:

	Beginning of the Year	End of the Year
Accounts receivable	$24,000	$30,000
Accounts payable	9,000	8,000
Inventory	7,000	4,000

Compute the following:

a. The adjustment due to the change in accounting method.
b. The accrual basis taxable income for 1992.

46. H Finance Company experiences bad debts of about 4% of its outstanding loans. At the end of the year, the company had outstanding receivables of $18 million. This balance included $3 million of accrued interest receivable. The company's loan loss reserve for the year was computed as follows:

Balance, January 1, 1992	$650,000
Accounts written off as uncollectible	
Loans made in 1992	(10,000)
Loans made in prior years	(35,000)
Collections on loans previously written off	9,000
Adjustment to required balance	106,000
Balance, December 31, 1992	$720,000

a. Determine the effects of the above on the company's taxable income for 1992.
b. Assume that H Finance Company has used the reserve method to compute its taxable income for the 10 years the company has been in existence. In 1992, you begin preparing the company's tax return. What should be done with regard to the reserve?

47. In 1992, the taxpayer changed from the cash to the accrual basis of accounting for sales, cost of goods sold, and accrued expenses. Taxable income for 1992 computed under the cash method was $45,000. Relevant account balances are as follows:

	Beginning of the Year	End of the Year
Accounts receivable	$ 3,000	$12,000
Accounts payable	-0-	-0-
Accrued expenses	2,000	1,000
Inventory	10,000	16,000

a. Compute the accrual basis taxable income for 1992 and the adjustment due to the change in accounting method.
b. Assuming the change was voluntary, how will the adjustment due to the change be treated?

48. T, a cash basis taxpayer, has agreed to sell land to Z, Inc., a well-established and highly profitable company. Z is willing to (1) pay $100,000 cash or (2) pay $25,000 cash and the balance ($75,000) plus interest at 10% (the Federal rate) in two years. T is in the 35% marginal tax bracket (combined Federal and state) for all years and believes he can reinvest the sales proceeds and earn a 14% before-tax rate of return.

a. Should T accept the deferred payments option if his basis in the land is $10,000?
b. Do you think your results would change if T's basis in the land is $90,000?

49. S, who is not a dealer, sold an apartment house to P during the current year (1992). The closing statement for the sale is as follows:

Total selling price		$100,000
Add: P's share of property taxes (6 months) paid by S		2,500
Less: S's 11% mortgage assumed by P	$55,000	
P's refundable binder ("earnest money") paid in 1991	1,000	
P's 11% installment note given to S	30,000	
S's real estate commissions and attorney's fees	7,500	(93,500)
Cash paid to S at closing		$ 9,000
Cash due from P = $9,000 + $7,500 expenses		$ 16,500

During 1992, S collected $4,000 in principal on the installment note and $2,000 interest. S's basis in the property was $70,000 [$85,000 − $15,000 (depreciation)], and there was $9,000 in potential depreciation recapture under § 1250. The Federal rate is 9%.

a. Compute the following:
   1. Total gain.
   2. Contract price.

3. Payments received in the year of sale.
4. Recognized gain in the year of sale and the character of such gain.

(*Hint:* Think carefully about the manner in which the property taxes are handled before you begin your computations.)

b. Same as (a)(2) and (3), except S's basis in the property was $45,000.

50. On June 30, 1992, T sold property for $250,000 cash on the date of sale and a $750,000 note due on September 30, 1993. No interest was stated in the contract. The present value of the note (using 13.2%, which was the Federal rate) was $640,000. T's basis in the property was $400,000, and $40,000 of the gain was depreciation recapture under § 1245. Expenses of the sale totaled $10,000, and T was not a dealer in the property sold.

a. Compute T's gain to be reported in 1992.
b. Compute T's interest income for 1993.

51. On July 1, 1991, a cash basis taxpayer sold land for $400,000 due on the date of the sale and $3,000,000 principal and $370,800 interest (6%) due on June 30, 1993. The seller's basis in the land was $500,000. The Federal short-term rate was 8%, compounded semiannually.

a. Compute the seller's interest income and gain in 1991, 1992, and 1993.
b. Same as (a), except that the amount due in two years was $1,000,000 principal and $254,400 interest and the purchaser will use the cash method to account for interest.

52. M made an installment sale of land and a building to N. There was no ordinary income recapture on the building. At the time of the sale, the Federal rate was 8%, and the market rate on similar contracts was 15%. Under the contract, N would make payments as follows:

Cash at closing, July 1, 1992	$ 50,000
Interest at 10%, due June 30, 1993*	30,750
Interest at 10%, due June 30, 1994*	30,750
Principal due June 30, 1994	300,000

*Interest is compounded semiannually.

a. Will interest be imputed on the contract?
b. Assuming M is a cash basis taxpayer, what is her interest income for 1992 under the contract?
c. Assuming N is an accrual basis taxpayer, what is her interest expense for 1992 under the contract?

53. On December 30, 1992, Father sold land to Son for $10,000 cash and a 7% installment note with a face amount of $190,000. In 1993, after paying $30,000 on the principal of the note, Son sold the land. In 1994, Son paid Father $25,000 on the note principal. Father's basis in the land was $50,000. Assuming Son sold the land for $250,000, compute Father's taxable gain in 1993.

54. X sold land to an unrelated party in 1991. X's basis in the land was $40,000, and the selling price was $100,000—$25,000 payable at closing and $25,000 (plus 10% interest) due January 1, 1992, 1993, and 1994. What would be the tax consequences of the following? [Treat each part independently and assume (1) X did not elect out of the installment method and (2) the installment obligations have values equal to their face amounts.]

a. In 1992, X gave to his daughter the right to collect all future payments on the installment obligations.
b. In 1992, after collecting the payment due on January 1, X transferred the installment obligation to his 100% controlled corporation in exchange for additional shares of stock.

c. On December 31, 1992, X received the payment due on January 1, 1993. On December 15, 1993, X died, and the remaining installment obligation was transferred to X's estate. The estate collected the amount due on January 1, 1994.

55. T, who is not a dealer in real estate, sold rental real estate for $75,000 cash and $225,000 due in three years, plus interest equal to the Federal rate. T's cost of the real estate was $90,000, and there was no depreciation recapture. T did not elect out of the installment method. Determine the tax consequences of the following:

a. When the $225,000 note came due, the purchaser defaulted and T repossessed the property. The property's value was $300,000.
b. One year before maturity, T borrowed $100,000 and used the installment obligation as collateral for the loan.

56. The R Construction Company reports its income by the completed contract method. At the end of 1992, the company completed a contract to construct a building at a total cost of $980,000. The contract price was $1,200,000. However, the customer refused to accept the work and would not pay anything on the contract because he claimed the roof did not meet specifications. R's engineers estimated it would cost $140,000 to bring the roof up to the customer's standards. In 1993, the dispute was settled in the customer's favor; the roof was improved at a cost of $170,000, and the customer accepted the building and paid the $1,200,000.

a. What would be the effects of the above on R's taxable income for 1992 and 1993?
b. Same as (a), except R had $1,100,000 accumulated cost under the contract at the end of 1992.

57. X Company is a real estate construction company with average annual gross receipts of $3 million. X uses the completed contract method, and the contracts require 18 months to complete. Which of the following costs would be allocated to construction in progress by X?

a. The payroll taxes on direct labor.
b. The current services pension costs for employees whose wages are included in direct labor.
c. Accelerated depreciation on equipment used on contracts.
d. Sales tax on materials assigned to contracts.
e. The past service costs for employees whose wages are included in direct labor.
f. Bidding expenses for contracts awarded.

58. Indicate the accounting method that should be used to compute the income from the following contracts:

a. A contract to build six jet aircraft.
b. A contract to build a new home. The contractor's average annual gross receipts are $15 million.
c. A contract to manufacture 3,000 pairs of boots for a large retail chain. The manufacturer has several contracts to produce the same boot for other retailers.
d. A contract to pave a parking lot. The contractor's average annual gross receipts are $2 million.

59. T Company makes gasoline storage tanks. Everything produced is under contract (that is, the company does not produce until it gets a contract for a product). The company makes three basic models. However, the tanks must be adapted to each individual customer's location and needs (e.g., the location of the valves, the quality of the materials and insulation). Discuss the following issues relative to the company's operations:

a. An examining IRS agent contends that each of the company's contracts is to produce a "unique product." What difference does it make whether the product is unique rather than a "shelf item"?
b. Producing one of the tanks takes over one year from start to completion, and the total cost is in excess of $1 million. What costs must be capitalized for this contract that are not subject to capitalization for a contract with a shorter duration and lower cost?

c. What must the taxpayer do with the costs of bidding on contracts?
d. The company frequently makes several cost estimates for a contract, using various estimates of materials costs. These costs fluctuate almost daily. Assuming the taxpayer must use the percentage of completion method to report the income from the contract, what will be the consequence if the taxpayer uses the highest estimate of a contract's cost and the actual cost is closer to the lowest estimated cost?

60. The A Construction Company reports its income by the percentage of completion method. In 1992, the company entered into a contract to build a warehouse for $1,500,000. A estimated that the total cost of the contract would be $900,000. At the end of 1992, the company had $750,000 of accumulated costs for the contract, and the architect estimated that it would cost an additional $210,000 to complete the contract. In 1993, the contract was completed at a total cost of $1,050,000.

a. Determine A's profit on the contract that should be reported for 1992.
b. Determine A's profit on the contract that should be reported for 1993.
c. Under the lookback provisions, what are the consequences to A of having incorrectly estimated the costs of the contract?

61. How would interest provisions in the tax law impact upon the following events?

a. The taxpayer reports income by the percentage of completion method. In 1993, the taxpayer completed a real estate construction contract that yielded a total profit of $750,000. One-half of the costs of the contract were incurred in 1992, and the taxpayer reported $400,000 as percentage of completion profit that year. The disproportionate profit reported in 1992 was due to an overestimation of the total profit on the contract.
b. The contractor in (a) received progress payments from the customer, but generally the total cost accumulated on the contract was $100,000 greater than the progress payments. The contractor financed the balance of the cost with a bank loan. The customer financed the payments made with a construction loan.
c. The contractor in (a) completed the contract at the end of 1993. At that time, the customer owed the contractor $100,000. Also, in 1993, the customer went bankrupt, and the contractor was unable to collect the $100,000.

62. Determine whether the following costs must be added to inventory:

a. The taxpayer bottles wine as part of his wholesale business and must incur $150,000 in warehousing to store the wine for six months before the wine is offered for sale. The taxpayer owns the warehouse.
b. Interest allocable to the wine in storage [in (a)] is $30,000.
c. A real estate developer incurred $50,000 interest during construction.
d. A chain of retail stores operates a warehouse. The total cost of operating the warehouse (e.g., depreciation, wages) for the year was $2 million, of which $500,000 is attributable to (allocated on the basis of costs) storing goods still on hand at year-end.

63. T Company produces small machinery. The company also produces parts used to repair the machinery. The parts may be sold for several years after the company has discontinued the product. The company has on hands parts with an original cost of $600,000. The total offering price on these goods is $960,000. However, the company expects to sell only 80% of the parts on hand. The excess parts are kept in case the estimates are incorrect.

a. Can the company deduct the excess inventory under the lower of cost or market rule?
b. Assume that T Company deducted the cost of the excess parts on hand. While the parts were still on hand, the company elected LIFO. What are the implications of the change in inventory method?

64. In 1992, T changed from the use of the lower of cost or market FIFO method to the LIFO method. The ending inventory for 1991 was computed as follows:

Item	FIFO Cost	Replacement Cost	Lower of Cost or Market
A	$10,000	$18,000	$10,000
B	25,000	20,000	20,000
			$30,000

a. What is the correct beginning inventory in 1992 under the LIFO method?
b. What immediate tax consequences (if any) would result from the switch to LIFO?

RESEARCH PROBLEMS

RESEARCH PROBLEM 1 R Company is a wholesaler with a fiscal year ending October 31, after it has shipped all of its Christmas goods. Management of R is considering changing its terms of sale for some of its goods so that the goods are on consignment until November 30, and title does not pass to the retailer until that date. Under present terms, title to the goods passes at the time of shipment. Management would like to know the tax consequences of the change in terms.

Partial list of research aids:

Hallmark Cards, Inc. & Subsidiaries, 90 T.C. 26 (1988).

RESEARCH PROBLEM 2 R Company discovered certain equipment used in its repair operations had been accounted for as inventory rather than as fixed assets. This incorrect treatment applied to all years in which the equipment had been used, and all of those years are open under the statute of limitations. The taxpayer filed amended returns for all years affected by the incorrect treatment to obtain a refund of overpayments of taxes for the years affected. The IRS refused to accept the amended returns. The IRS reasoned that the taxpayer was actually changing accounting methods and this can only be accomplished through a request for change in methods. In addition, the IRS concluded that an adjustment due to a voluntary change in accounting method must be taken into income for the year of the change. Is the IRS correct?

RESEARCH PROBLEM 3 In November 1992, A agreed to purchase stock from B for $1 million. The transaction was to be closed on December 28, 1992. In early December 1992, B became concerned about the taxes due on the sale in 1992. B suggested that the transaction be deferred until January 1993, but A insisted that the stock be transferred on December 28, 1992. A and B agreed that the cash paid by A on December 28, 1992, would be held by the First Bank as A's escrow agent, and the funds would be dispersed to B on January 4, 1993. The IRS agent insists that the escrow amount was constructively received by B in 1992 and that B therefore cannot defer his gain until 1993 under the installment sales rules. Is the agent correct?

Partial list of research aids:

Reed v. Comm., 83–2 USTC ¶9728, 53 AFTR2d 84–335 (CA–1, 1983).

RESEARCH PROBLEM 4 The controlling shareholder transferred real estate to his controlled corporation in a transaction originally characterized as an installment sale. Now the shareholder is considering canceling the corporation's indebtedness to him. The shareholder has asked you to explain to him the tax consequences of canceling the debt.

RESEARCH PROBLEM 5 You recently contracted to perform tax services for a new funeral home. In preparing the initial tax return, you must decide whether the funeral home can use the cash method of accounting. When discussing this issue with the manager, the manager points out that the company is actually a service business and that the only materials involved are caskets, which average only 15% of the price of a funeral. Is the funeral home required to use the accrual method of accounting?

CHAPTER

DEFERRED COMPENSATION

OBJECTIVES

Distinguish between qualified and nonqualified compensation arrangements.

Distinguish between qualified defined contribution and qualified defined benefit plans.

Discuss the tax advantages of an employee stock ownership plan.

Determine the various qualification requirements and tax consequences of qualified plans.

Calculate the limitations on contributions to and benefits from qualified plans.

Discuss the benefits of a cash or deferred arrangement plan [§ 401(k) plan].

Discuss the qualified plan (Keogh plan) available to a self-employed person.

Compare a simplified employee pension (SEP) plan with a Keogh plan.

Discuss the Individual Retirement Account (IRA) and compare it with the § 401(k) plan.

Explain the value of nonqualified deferred compensation plans and nonqualified stock options.

Compare restricted property plans with incentive stock options.

Identify tax planning opportunities related to deferred compensation.

OUTLINE

This chapter discusses the various types of deferred compensation arrangements available to employees and self-employed individuals. *Deferred compensation* refers to an arrangement under which an employee receives compensation for services after the period when the services were performed.[1] The tax law encourages employers to offer deferred compensation plans to their employees to supplement the Federal Social Security retirement system. Contributions to a qualified pension, profit sharing, or stock bonus plan are immediately deductible by the employer. Employees are generally not taxed until the funds are made available to them. In addition, the income earned on the contributions to the plan is not subject to tax until the funds are made available to the employees.

A variety of deferred compensation arrangements are being offered to employees, including the following:

- Qualified profit sharing plans.
- Qualified pension plans.
- Employee stock ownership plans.
- Cash or deferred arrangement plans.
- Tax-deferred annuities.
- Incentive stock option plans.
- Nonqualified deferred compensation plans.
- Restricted property plans.
- Cafeteria benefit plans.

In addition to the various types of deferred compensation, employees may receive other valuable fringe benefits. Examples of such benefits include group term life insurance, medical reimbursement plans, company-supplied automobiles, education expense reimbursement plans, and group legal services.[2]

The Code, in certain circumstances, prohibits a deduction for certain types of fringe benefits such as a golden parachute payment. Refer to the subsequent discussion under Nonqualified Deferred Compensation Plans.

QUALIFIED PENSION, PROFIT SHARING, AND STOCK BONUS PLANS

◆

The Federal government has encouraged private pension and profit sharing plans to keep retired people from becoming dependent on the government. Therefore, the Federal tax law provides substantial tax benefits for plans that meet certain requirements. The major requirement for qualification is that a plan not discriminate in favor of highly compensated employees.

Types of Plans

There are three types of qualified plans: pension, profit sharing, and stock bonus plans.

Pension Plans. A *pension plan* is a deferred compensation arrangement that provides for systematic payments of definitely determinable retirement benefits to employees who meet the requirements set forth in the plan. Benefits are generally measured by and based on such factors as years of service and employee compensation. Employer contributions under a qualified pension plan must *not* depend on profits. In addition, they must be sufficient to provide

1. For a more comprehensive definition of deferred compensation, see the Glossary of Tax Terms in Appendix C.

2. Refer to the discussions in Chapters 4 and 5.

definitely determinable benefits on some actuarial basis (except for a defined contribution pension plan).

There are basically two types of qualified pension plans: defined benefit plans and defined contribution plans.

A *defined benefit plan* includes a formula that defines the benefits employees are to receive.[3] Under such a plan, an employer must make annual contributions based upon actuarial computations that will be sufficient to pay the vested retirement benefits. If a plan document permits, employees may make contributions to the pension fund. Separate accounts are not maintained for each participant. A defined benefit plan provides some sense of security for employees since the benefits may be expressed in fixed dollar amounts.

Under a *defined contribution pension plan* (or money purchase plan), a separate account must be maintained for each participant. Benefits are based solely on (1) the amount contributed and (2) income from the fund that accrues to the participant's account.[4] In essence, the plan defines the amount the employer is required to contribute (e.g., a flat dollar amount, an amount based on a special formula, or an amount equal to a certain percentage of compensation). Consequently, actuarial calculations are not required to determine the employer's annual contribution. Upon retirement, an employee's pension depends on the value of his or her account. Although it is not mandatory, a plan may require or permit employee contributions to the pension fund.

Example 1

The qualified pension plan of X Company calls for both the employer and employee to contribute annually to the pension trust an amount equal to 5% of the employee's compensation. Since the employer's rate of contribution is fixed, this pension plan is a defined contribution plan. If the plan called for contributions sufficient to provide retirement benefits equal to 30% of the employee's average salary for the last five years, it would be a defined benefit plan. ◆

Concept Summary 19–1 compares and contrasts a defined benefit plan and a defined contribution plan.

Profit Sharing Plans. A *profit sharing plan* is a deferred compensation arrangement established and maintained by an employer to provide for employee participation in the company's profits. Contributions are paid from the employer's current or accumulated profits to a trustee and are commingled in a single trust fund. Thus, an employer does not have to have a profit for the current year to make a contribution (the contribution can be from accumulated profits).

In a profit sharing plan, separate accounts are maintained for each participant. The plan must provide a definite, predetermined formula for allocating the contributions (made to the trustee) among the participants. Likewise, it must include a definite, predetermined formula for distributing the accumulated funds after a fixed number of years, on the attainment of a stated age, or on the occurrence of certain events such as illness, layoff, or retirement. A company is not required to contribute a definite, predetermined amount to the plan, although substantial and recurring contributions must be made to meet the permanency requirement. Forfeitures arising under this plan do not have to be used to reduce the employer's contribution. Instead, forfeitures may be used to increase the individual accounts of the remaining participants as long as these

3. § 414(j).

4. § 414(i).

increases do not result in prohibited discrimination.[5] Since a profit sharing plan does not necessarily emphasize retirement income, benefits to employees may normally be distributed through lump-sum payouts.

Stock Bonus Plans. A *stock bonus plan* is another form of deferred compensation. In this case, an employer establishes and maintains the plan in order to contribute shares of its stock. The contributions need not be dependent on the employer's profits. A stock bonus plan is subject to the same requirements as a profit sharing plan for purposes of allocating and distributing the stock among the employees.[6] Any benefits of the plan are distributable in the form of stock of the employer company, except that distributable fractional shares may be paid in cash.

Employee Stock Ownership Plans. An *employee stock ownership plan (ESOP)* is a stock bonus trust that qualifies as a tax-exempt employee trust under § 401(a). Technically, an ESOP is a defined contribution plan that is either a qualified stock bonus plan or a stock bonus and a money purchase plan, each of which is qualified under § 401(a). An ESOP must invest primarily in qualifying employer securities.[7]

CONCEPT SUMMARY 19–1
DEFINED BENEFIT PLAN AND DEFINED CONTRIBUTION PLAN COMPARED

Defined Benefit Plan	Defined Contribution Plan
Includes a pension plan.	Includes profit sharing, stock bonus, money purchase, target benefit, qualified cash or deferred compensation, and employee stock ownership plans.
Determinable benefits based upon years of service and average compensation. Benefits calculated by a formula.	An account for each participant. Ultimate benefits depend upon contributions and investment performance.
Maximum annual *benefits* payable may not exceed the smaller of (1) $112,221 (in 1992)* or (2) 100% of the participant's average earnings in the three highest years of employment.	Maximum annual *contribution* to an account may not exceed the smaller of (1) $30,000** or (2) 25% of the participant's compensation.
Forfeitures must reduce subsequent funding costs and cannot increase the benefits any participant can receive under the plan.	Forfeitures may be allocated to the accounts of remaining participants.
Subject to minimum funding requirement in order to avoid penalties.	Exempt from funding requirements.
Greater administrative and actuarial costs and greater reporting requirements.	Costs and reporting requirements less burdensome.
Subject to plan termination insurance.	Not subject to plan termination insurance.
More favorable to employees who are older when plan is adopted since it is possible to fund higher benefits over a shorter period.	More favorable to younger employees since, over a longer period, higher benefits may result.

*This amount is indexed annually.
**The $30,000 amount becomes subject to indexing when the dollar limitation for a defined benefit plan exceeds $120,000.

5. Reg. §§ 1.401–1(b) and 1.401–4(a)(1)(iii).
6. Reg. § 1.401–1(b)(1)(iii).
7. § 4975(e)(7).

Since the corporation can contribute stock rather than cash, there is no cash-flow drain. If stock is contributed, no cash outlay is required, and the corporation receives a tax deduction equal to the fair market value of the stock. Under § 1032, the employer-corporation does not recognize a gain or loss on the contributed stock. The corporation may deduct dividends paid in cash (or dividends used to repay certain ESOP loans) on shares held by an ESOP. One-half of the interest earned by an institutional lender or mutual fund on a loan to an ESOP may be excluded from gross income where the proceeds are used to buy employer securities. However, the Revenue Reconciliation Act of 1989 limits this interest exclusion. For loans made after November 17, 1989, the exclusion is available only if the ESOP owns more than 50 percent of the employer's stock. The tax savings accruing under the plan may have a favorable impact on the company's working capital. An ESOP also provides flexibility, since contributions may vary from year to year and, in fact, may be omitted in any one year.[8]

A company can fund the ESOP by acquiring outstanding shares of stock from its shareholders, who receive capital gain treatment upon the sale of their stock. Owners of small closely held corporations may elect nonrecognition treatment for any gain realized on the sale of securities to an ESOP where qualified replacement property [defined in § 1042(c)(4)] is purchased during a 15-month period. This 15-month period begins 3 months before the date of the sale and ends 12 months after that date.[9] For sales after July 10, 1989, however, nonrecognition treatment is permitted only if the seller has held the securities for at least three years prior to the sale to the ESOP.

Employees are not subject to tax until they receive a distribution of stock or cash from the trust. Whenever a distribution of employer securities is treated as a lump-sum distribution, recognition of the net unrealized appreciation in such securities in the year of distribution can be postponed. Unless a taxpayer elects otherwise, such net unrealized appreciation is not included in the basis of the securities and is recognized in a subsequent taxable transaction.[10] Distributions to employees may be made entirely in cash or partly in cash and partly in employer securities. A participant must have the right to demand the entire distribution in the form of employer securities.[11]

EXAMPLE 2

T Company establishes an ESOP for its employees and contributes unissued stock to the ESOP trust. The company receives a deduction for the contribution, and there is no cash-flow drain. The employees are not subject to tax until a subsequent stock or cash distribution from the trust. ◆

EXAMPLE 3

The ESOP of T Company borrows $100,000 from City Bank in January 1992. The loan is secured by the stock interest and is guaranteed by the company. The ESOP buys stock for the trust from a shareholder of T Company for $100,000. The shareholder has owned the stock for four years. The shares are then allocated among the employees' retirement accounts. The shareholder obtains capital gain treatment on the sale or can elect nonrecognition treatment if qualified replacement securities are purchased during a 15-month period. T Company makes deductible contributions to the ESOP, which, in turn, pays off the loan. If the ESOP owns more than 50% of T Company's stock, the bank can exclude from gross income 50% of any interest earned on the loan to T Company's ESOP. ◆

8. Reg. § 1.401–1(b)(2).

9. Refer to the discussion in Chapter 15.

10. §§ 402(e)(4)(D)(ii) and (J).

11. § 409(h)(1).

Qualification Requirements

A number of qualification requirements must be satisfied in order for a plan to receive favorable tax treatment. To be *qualified,* a plan must meet the following requirements:

- Exclusive benefit requirement.
- Nondiscrimination requirements.
- Participation and coverage requirements.
- Vesting requirements.
- Distribution requirements.

These qualification rules are highly technical and numerous. Thus, an employer should submit a retirement plan to the IRS for a determination letter regarding the qualified status of the plan and trust. A favorable determination letter may be expected within 6 to 12 months, indicating that the plan meets the qualification requirements and that the trust is tax-exempt. However, the continued qualification of the plan depends upon its actual operations. Therefore, the operations of the plan should be reviewed periodically.

Exclusive Benefit Requirement. A pension, profit sharing, or stock bonus trust must be created by an employer for the exclusive benefit of employees or their beneficiaries. Under a prudent person concept, the IRS specifies four investment conditions for meeting the *exclusive benefit* requirement:[12]

- The cost of the investment must not exceed the fair market value at the time of purchase.
- A fair return commensurate with prevailing rates must be provided.
- Sufficient liquidity must be maintained to permit distributions in accordance with the terms of the qualified plan.
- The safeguards and diversity that a prudent investor would adhere to must be present.

Nondiscrimination Requirements. The contributions and benefits under a plan must *not discriminate* in favor of highly compensated employees. A plan is not considered discriminatory merely because the contributions and benefits on behalf of the employees are uniformly related to their compensation.[13] For example, a pension plan that provides for the allocation of employer contributions based upon a flat 3 percent of each employee's compensation would not be discriminatory despite the fact that highly paid employees receive greater benefits.

Qualified plans may be integrated with Social Security (employer FICA contributions for covered employees may be taken into account) in order to avoid giving lower-level employees proportionately greater benefits or contributions. Integrated plans may not reduce a participant's benefits or contributions to less than one-half of what they would have been without integration.

Participation and Coverage Requirements. A qualified plan must provide, at a minimum, that all employees in the covered group who are 21 years of age are eligible to participate after completing one year of service. A year of service is generally defined as the completion of 1,000 hours of service within a measuring

12. § 401(a); Rev.Rul. 65–178, 1965–2 C.B. 94, and Rev.Rul. 73–380, 1973–2 C.B. 124.

13. §§ 401(a)(4) and (5).

period of 12 consecutive months. As an alternative, where the plan provides that 100 percent of an employee's accrued benefits will be vested upon entering the plan, the employee's participation may be postponed until the later of age 21 or two years from the date of employment.[14] Once the age and service requirements are met, an employee must begin participating no later than the *earlier* of the following:

- The first day of the first plan year beginning after the date upon which the requirements were satisfied.
- Six months after the date on which the requirements were satisfied.[15]

Example 4

X Corporation has a calendar year retirement plan covering its employees. The corporation adopts the most restrictive eligibility rules permitted. Employee A, age 21, is hired on January 31, 1991, and meets the service requirement over the next 12 months (completes at least 1,000 hours by January 31, 1992). A must be included in this plan no later than July 31, 1992, because the 6-month limitation would be applicable. If the company had adopted the two-year participation rule, A must be included in the plan no later than July 31, 1993. ◆

Since a qualified plan must be primarily for the benefit of employees and be nondiscriminatory, the plan has to cover a reasonable percentage of the company employees. A plan will be qualified only if it satisfies one of the following tests:[16]

- The plan benefits at least 70 percent of all non-highly compensated employees (the *percentage test*).
- The plan benefits a percentage of non-highly compensated employees equal to at least 70 percent of the percentage of highly compensated employees benefiting under the plan (the *ratio test*).
- The plan meets the *average benefits test.*

If a company has no highly compensated employees, the retirement plan will automatically satisfy the coverage rules.

To satisfy the *average benefits test,* the plan must benefit any employees who qualify under a classification set up by the employer and found by the Secretary of the Treasury not to be discriminatory in favor of highly compensated employees (the classification test). In addition, the average benefit percentage for non-highly compensated employees must be at least 70 percent of the average benefit percentage for highly compensated employees. The *average benefit percentage* means, with respect to any group of employees, the average of the benefit percentages calculated separately for each employee in the group. The term *benefit percentage* means the employer-provided contributions (including forfeitures) or benefits of an employee under all qualified plans of the employer, expressed as a percentage of that employee's compensation.

An employee is *highly compensated* if, at any time during the year or the preceding year, the employee satisfies *any* of the following:[17]

- Was a 5 percent owner of the company.
- Received more than $93,518 (in 1992) in annual compensation from the employer.

14. §§ 410(a)(1)(A) and (B).

15. § 410(a)(4).

16. § 410(b).

17. §§ 401(a)(4) and 414(q).

- Received more than $62,345 (in 1992) in annual compensation from the employer *and* was a member of the top-paid group of the employer.
- Was an officer of the company and received compensation greater than 150 percent of the maximum statutory dollar amount of the annual addition to a defined contribution plan ($30,000 × 150% = $45,000).

An employee who is among the top 20 percent of the employees on the basis of compensation paid during the year is a member of the top-paid group. The $62,345 and $93,518 amounts are indexed annually.[18]

An additional *minimum participation* test must also be met. A plan must cover at least 40 percent of all employees or, if fewer, at least 50 employees on one representative day of the plan year. In determining all employees, nonresident aliens, certain union members, and employees not fulfilling the minimum age or years-of-service requirement of the plan may be excluded.[19]

EXAMPLE 5

M Corporation's retirement plan meets the 70% test (the percentage test) because 70% of all non-highly compensated employees are benefited. The company has 100 employees, but only 38 of these employees are covered by the plan. Therefore, this retirement plan does not meet the minimum participation requirement. ◆

Vesting Requirements. An employee's right to accrued benefits derived from his or her own contributions must be nonforfeitable from the date of contribution. The accrued benefits derived from employer contributions must be nonforfeitable in accordance with one of two alternative minimum vesting schedules. The purpose of the *vesting requirements* is to protect an employee who has worked a reasonable period of time for an employer from losing employer contributions because of being fired or changing jobs.

A plan will not be a qualified plan unless a participant's employer-provided benefits vest at least as rapidly as under one of *two alternative minimum vesting schedules.* To satisfy the *first alternative,* a participant must have a nonforfeitable right to 100 percent of his or her accrued benefits derived from employer contributions upon completion of five years of service (five-year or cliff vesting). The *second alternative* is satisfied if a participant has a nonforfeitable right at least equal to a percentage of the accrued benefits derived from employer contributions as depicted in Figure 19–1 (graded vesting). Of the two alternatives, cliff vesting minimizes administration expenses for a company and provides more vesting for a long-term employee. Neither vesting schedule applies to top-heavy plans.

EXAMPLE 6

M has six years of service completed as of February 2, 1992, his employment anniversary date. If his defined benefit plan has a five-year (cliff) vesting schedule,

FIGURE 19–1
Three-to-Seven-Year Vesting

Years of Service	Nonforfeitable Percentage
3	20%
4	40%
5	60%
6	80%
7 or more	100%

18. The indexed amounts for 1992 are provided.

19. §§ 401(a)(26) and 410(b)(3) and (4).

100% of M's accrued benefits are vested. If, however, the plan uses the graded vesting rule, M's nonforfeitable percentage is 80%. ◆

Distribution Requirements. Uniform *minimum distribution rules* exist for all qualified defined benefit and defined contribution plans, Individual Retirement Accounts (IRAs) and annuities, unfunded deferred compensation plans of state and local governments and tax-exempt employers, and tax-sheltered custodial accounts and annuities. Distributions must begin no later than April 1 of the calendar year following the calendar year in which the participant attains age 70½. This commencement date is not affected by the actual date of retirement or termination.[20]

Once age 70½ is reached, minimum annual distributions must be made over the life of the participant or the lives of the participant and a designated individual beneficiary. The amount of the required minimum distribution for a particular year is determined by dividing the account balance as of December 31 of the prior year by the applicable life expectancy. The life expectancy of the owner and his or her beneficiary is based upon the expected return multiples in the Regulations, using ages attained within the calendar year the participant reaches age 70½.[21]

EXAMPLE 7

B reaches age 70½ in 1992, and he will also be age 71 in 1992. His retirement account (an IRA) has a balance of $120,000 on December 31, 1991. B must withdraw $7,843 for the 1992 calendar year, assuming his multiple is 15.3 ($120,000 ÷ 15.3). This distribution need not be made until April 1, 1993, but a second distribution must be made by December 31, 1993. ◆

Failure to make a minimum required distribution to a particular participant results in a 50 percent nondeductible excise tax on the excess in any taxable year of the amount that should have been distributed over the amount that actually was distributed. The tax is imposed on the individual required to take the distribution (the payee).[22] The Secretary of the Treasury is authorized to waive the tax for a given taxpayer year if the taxpayer is able to establish that the shortfall is due to reasonable error and that reasonable steps are being taken to remedy the shortfall.

If a taxpayer receives an *early distribution* from a qualified retirement plan, a 10 percent additional tax is levied on the full amount of any distribution includible in gross income.[23] For this purpose, the term qualified retirement plan includes a qualified defined benefit plan or defined contribution plan, a tax-sheltered annuity or custodial account, or an IRA. Certain distributions, however, are *not* treated as early distributions:

- Made on or after the date the employee attains age 59½.
- Made to a beneficiary (or the estate of an employee) on or after the death of the employee.
- Attributable to the employee's being disabled.
- Made as part of a scheduled series of substantially equal periodic payments (made not less frequently than annually) for the life of the participant (or the joint lives of the participant and the participant's beneficiary).

20. § 401(a)(9).
21. Reg. § 1.72–9. Refer to Chapter 4.
22. § 4974(a).
23. § 72(t). See Lt.Rul. 8837071.

- Made to an employee after separation from service because of early retirement under the plan after attaining age 55. This exception to early distribution treatment does not apply to an IRA.
- Used to pay medical expenses to the extent that the expenses are deductible under § 213 (determined regardless of whether or not the taxpayer itemizes deductions). This exception to early distribution treatment does not apply to an IRA.

A 15 percent excise tax is imposed on excess distributions from qualified plans.[24] The tax is levied on the individual with respect to whom the excess distribution is made and is reduced by the amount of the tax imposed on early distributions (to the extent attributable to the excess distribution). An *excess distribution* is the aggregate amount of the retirement distributions during the taxable year for an individual to the extent that amount exceeds the greater of $150,000 or $112,500 (1992 indexed amount is $140,276). Thus, for 1992 the annual limitation is $150,000. Once the indexed $112,500 amount exceeds the $150,000, the indexed amount will become the annual limit. The following distributions are *not* subject to this limitation:

- Any retirement distribution made after the death of the individual.
- Any retirement distribution payable to an alternate payee in conformance with a qualified domestic relations order.
- Any retirement distribution attributable to the employee's investment in the contract (after-tax contributions).
- Any retirement distribution not included in gross income by reason of a rollover contribution.

If the taxpayer elects lump-sum distribution treatment,[25] the $150,000 limit is applied separately to the lump-sum distribution and is increased to five times the generally applicable limit with respect to that distribution (to $750,000).

EXAMPLE 8

E, age 65, has accumulated $960,000 in a defined contribution plan, $105,000 of which represents her own after-tax contributions. Receiving a lump-sum distribution would result in an excise tax of $15,750.

Account balance	$ 960,000
Less after-tax contributions	(105,000)
Less lump-sum limitation	(750,000)
Amount subject to tax	$ 105,000
15% excise tax	×.15
Excise tax due	$ 15,750

If E receives the distribution in the form of an annuity over her expected lifetime of 20 years, her yearly distributions of $48,000 *plus* related interest would probably be less than the $150,000 annual distribution limit. ◆

A grandfather provision exists with respect to accrued benefits as of August 1, 1986.[26]

24. § 4981A.
25. Refer to Chapter 16 for the definition of a lump-sum distribution.
26. § 4981A(c)(5).

Tax Consequences to the Employee and Employer

In General. Although employer contributions to qualified plans are generally deductible immediately (subject to contribution and deductibility rules), these amounts are not subject to taxation until distributed to employees.[27] If benefits are paid with respect to an employee (to a creditor of the employee, a child of the employee, etc.), the benefits paid are treated as if paid to the employee. When benefits are distributed to employees, or paid with respect to an employee, the employer does not receive another deduction.

The tax benefit to the employee amounts to a substantial tax deferral and may be viewed as an interest-free loan from the government to the trust fund. Another advantage of a qualified plan is that any income earned by the trust is not taxable to the trust.[28] Employees, in effect, are taxed on such earnings when they receive the retirement benefits.

The taxation of amounts received by employees in periodic or installment payments is generally subject to the annuity rules in § 72 (refer to Chapter 4). Employee contributions have previously been subject to tax and are therefore included in the employee's *investment in the contract.* Two other alternative options are available for benefit distributions. A taxpayer may roll over the benefits into an IRA or another qualified employer retirement plan.[29] A taxpayer also may receive the distribution in a lump-sum payment.

Lump-Sum Distributions from Qualified Plans. The annuity rules do not apply to a lump-sum distribution. All such payments are taxed in one year. Since lump-sum payments have been accumulated over a number of years, bunching retirement benefits into one taxable year may impose a high tax burden because of progressive rates. To overcome this bunching effect, for many years the tax law has provided favorable treatment for certain lump-sum distributions. Major changes were made in the lump-sum distribution rules by TRA of 1986. Transitional provisions allow a participant who reached age 50 before January 1, 1986 (born before 1936) to elect the pre-1987 rules on a limited basis.

Under the pre-1987 rules, the taxable amount is allocated between a capital gain portion and an ordinary income portion (which may be subject to a special 10-year averaging treatment).[30] That portion attributable to the employee's service before 1974 qualifies for capital gain treatment. That portion attributable to the employee's service after 1973 is included as ordinary income when received and may be taxed under the 10-year averaging provision. An employee must be a plan participant for at least five years to take advantage of the 10-year averaging option. It is possible to defer tax on some or all of the distribution, provided that the employee elects to roll over the distribution by transferring the proceeds to an IRA or another qualified employer retirement plan.[31]

An employee may *elect* to treat all of the distribution as ordinary income subject to the 10-year forward averaging provision.[32] In some instances, ordinary income treatment is preferable to long-term capital gain treatment because of the favorable averaging technique.

Special preferential averaging treatment of qualified lump-sum distributions can be used only once during a recipient's lifetime. In the case of a small lump-sum distribution, a recipient may prefer to pay ordinary income tax on the

---

27. § 402(a)(1).

28. § 501(a).

29. Refer to the subsequent discussion in this chapter under Individual Retirement Accounts (IRAs).

30. § 402(e)(1)(C) of the IRC of 1954.

31. § 402(a)(5).

32. § 402(e)(4)(L).

amount and save the averaging election for a larger lump-sum distribution in the future.

To determine the tax on a lump-sum distribution, it is necessary to compute the taxable portion of the distribution by subtracting employee contributions and the net unrealized appreciation in the value of any distributed securities of the employer corporation.[33] The taxable amount is then reduced by a minimum distribution allowance to arrive at the amount that is eligible for the 10-year income averaging provisions.[34] The portion of the lump-sum distribution that is treated as a long-term capital gain is equal to the following:

$$\text{Taxable amount} \times \frac{\text{Years of service before 1974}}{\text{Total years of service}}$$

(computed without being reduced by the minimum distribution allowance)

The applicable capital gain rate is 20 percent.

After 1986, subject to the transition rule for recipients born before 1936 mentioned earlier, the 10-year forward averaging rule for lump-sum distributions is replaced by a 5-year forward averaging rule.[35] Only one lump-sum distribution received after age 59½ is eligible for the averaging treatment. Furthermore, capital gain treatment for lump-sum distributions (associated with participation before 1974) is repealed. However, for a lump-sum distribution after December 31, 1986, and before January 1, 1992, an employee may elect capital gain treatment for a percentage of the amount that would have qualified for capital gain treatment before TRA of 1986 (see Figure 19–2).

EXAMPLE 9

T, age 65 and married, retires at the end of 1992 and receives a lump-sum distribution of $100,000 from his company's profit sharing plan. This plan includes $5,000 of his own contributions and $10,000 of unrealized appreciation on his employer's common stock. The distributee has been a participant in the plan for 20 years. Since T had attained age 50 before January 1, 1986, he is eligible to elect the pre-1987 10-year forward averaging technique (using 1986 rates and the zero bracket amount).[36] Refer to the computation model in Concept Summary 19–2.

FIGURE 19–2
Phase-Out of Capital Gain Percentage for Lump-Sum Distributions

Distributions during Calendar Year	Available Percentage
1987	100%
1988	95%
1989	75%
1990	50%
1991	25%
1992 and thereafter	0%

33. § 402(e)(4)(J) provides that before any distribution a taxpayer may elect not to have this subtraction associated with employer securities apply.

34. § 402(e)(1)(D) defines the *minimum distribution allowance* as the smaller of $10,000 or one-half of the total taxable amount of the lump-sum distribution, reduced by 20% of the amount, if any, by which such total taxable amount exceeds $20,000. Thus, for lump-sum distributions of $70,000 or more, there will be no minimum distribution allowance.

35. § 402(e)(1).

36. See the Glossary of Tax Terms in Appendix C for a definition of the zero bracket amount.

Taxable portion of the lump-sum distribution [$100,000 − $5,000 (employee contribution) − $10,000 (unrealized appreciation of employer securities)]		$85,000
Less: Minimum distribution allowance ½ of the taxable amount up to $20,000	$ 10,000	
Less: 20% of the taxable amount in excess of $20,000: 20% × ($85,000 − $20,000)	(13,000)	
Minimum distribution allowance		-0-
Taxable amount		$85,000
Computation of tax under 10-year averaging:		
Long-term capital gain portion:		
$\$85{,}000 \times \frac{1 \text{ (service before 1974)}}{20 \text{ (total service years)}} = \$4{,}250 \times .20 =$		$ 850
Ordinary income portion: 10 times the tax on $10,555[37] [1/10($85,000 − $4,250) + $2,480]		11,225
Tax on lump-sum distribution		$12,075

Thus, T's capital gain on the distribution is $4,250 and is subject to a 20% capital gain rate. Here T may wish to elect to treat the entire distribution as ordinary income using the 10-year forward averaging approach rather than taxing the capital gain portion at the 20% capital gain rate. The tax liability of $11,905 would be less than the previously calculated tax liability of $12,075. The capital gain on the unrealized appreciation in the employer's common stock is not taxable until T sells the stock. In essence, the cost basis of the securities to the trust becomes the tax basis to the employee.[38] If T keeps the securities until he dies, there may be some income tax savings on this gain to the extent the estate or the heirs obtain a step-up in basis. ◆

CONCEPT SUMMARY 19–2
MODEL FOR LUMP-SUM DISTRIBUTION COMPUTATION

1. Start with the total lump-sum distribution and deduct any employee contributions and unrealized appreciation in employer securities.
2. Divide the result into the capital gain portion and the ordinary income portion.*
3. Multiply the capital gain portion by the capital gain rate of 20 percent.
4. Reduce the ordinary income portion by the minimum distribution allowance.
5. Divide the ordinary income portion into 5 or 10 equal portions, whichever is appropriate.
6. Compute the tax on the result in step 5 using the 1986 or current rate schedules (whichever is appropriate) for single taxpayers.
7. Multiply the resulting tax by 5 or 10, whichever is appropriate.
8. Add the results in steps 3 and 7.

*In certain circumstances, none of the taxable amount of the distribution will be eligible for capital gain treatment. In other circumstances, the taxpayer may choose to treat none of the taxable amount as capital gain even though part could qualify.

---

37. In making this tax computation, it is necessary to use the 1986 Tax Rate Schedule for single taxpayers and to add $2,480 (the zero bracket amount) to the taxable income. Thus, the tax was computed on $10,555, which is $8,075 (1/10 of $80,750) plus $2,480. Note that the tax rates provided in the instructions for Form 4972 (Tax on Lump-Sum Distributions) have already been adjusted for the zero bracket amount (i.e., it is not necessary to add the zero bracket amount in making the calculation).

38. § 402(e)(4)(J).

If T (in Example 9) uses the 5-year forward averaging provision instead, the following results are produced:

Taxable amount	$85,000
Computation of tax under 5-year averaging:	
Long-term capital gain portion:	
$\$85{,}000 \times \dfrac{1 \text{ (service before 1974)}}{20 \text{ (total service years)}} = \$4{,}250 \times .20 =$	$ 850
Ordinary income portion:	
5 times the tax on $16,150[39]	
⅕($85,000 − $4,250)	12,112
Tax on lump-sum distribution	$12,962

Thus, T's capital gain on the distribution is $4,250 (the same as in the 10-year averaging calculation). The capital gain is subject to a 20 percent capital gain rate.[40] Once again the taxpayer may wish to elect to treat the entire distribution as ordinary income using the 5-year forward averaging approach rather than taxing the capital gain portion at the 20 percent capital gain rate. The tax liability of $12,750 would be less than the previously calculated tax liability of $12,962. Since the ordinary income tax under 10-year forward averaging is less than the ordinary income tax under 5-year forward averaging, it appears that T's best alternative is to use the 10-year forward averaging provision and treat the capital gain as ordinary income.

Limitations on Contributions to and Benefits from Qualified Plans

In General. The limitations on contributions to and benefits from qualified plans appearing in § 415 must be written into a qualified plan. The plan terminates if these limits are exceeded. Section 404 sets the limits on deductibility applicable to the employer. The limit on the amount deductible under § 404 may have an impact on the amount the employer is willing to contribute, however. In fact, under § 404(j), a defined benefit plan or defined contribution plan is not allowed a deduction for the amount that exceeds the § 415 limitations.

Defined Contribution Plans. Under a *defined contribution plan* (money purchase pension, profit sharing, or stock bonus plan), the annual addition to an employee's account cannot exceed the smaller of $30,000 or 25 percent of the employee's compensation.[41] The $30,000 amount is to be indexed once the statutory ceiling for defined benefit plans (discussed next) reaches $120,000.

Defined Benefit Plans. Under a *defined benefit plan,* the annual benefit payable to an employee is limited to the smaller of $112,221 (in 1992)[42] or 100 percent of the employee's average compensation for the highest three years of employ-

39. In making this tax computation, it is necessary to use the 1992 Tax Rate Schedule for single taxpayers.

40. Note that since T qualifies under the transition rules (attained age 50 before January 1, 1986), he is eligible to elect capital gain treatment (without any percentage reduction) in conjunction with 5-year forward averaging.

41. § 415(c).

42. This amount is indexed annually.

ment. This benefit limit is subject to a $10,000 *de minimis* floor. The $112,221 limitation is reduced actuarially if the benefits begin before the Social Security normal retirement age (currently age 65). The $112,221 amount is increased actuarially if the benefits begin after the Social Security normal retirement age. The dollar limit on annual benefits ($112,221) is reduced by one-tenth for each year of *participation* under 10 years by the employee. Furthermore, the 100 percent of compensation limitation and the $10,000 *de minimis* floor are reduced proportionately for a participant who has less than 10 years of *service* with the employer.[43]

EXAMPLE 10

Employee A's average compensation for the highest three years of employment is $87,000. Although the § 415(b)(1) limitation does not limit the deduction, the defined benefit plan would not qualify if the plan provides for benefits in excess of the smaller of (1) $87,000 or (2) $112,221 for Employee A in 1992 (assuming retirement age of 65). ◆

EXAMPLE 11

P has participated for four years in a defined benefit plan and has six years of service with her employer. Her average compensation for the three highest years is $50,000. Her four years of participation reduce her dollar limitation to $44,888 ($112,221 × 4/10). Her six years of service reduce her 100% of compensation limitation to 60%. Therefore, her limit on annual benefits is $30,000 ($50,000 × 60%). ◆

For collectively bargained plans with at least 100 participants, the annual dollar limitation is the greater of $68,212 or one-half of the $112,221 monetary limit.

The amount of compensation that may be taken into account under any plan is limited to $228,860 (in 1992).[44] Thus, the benefits highly compensated individuals receive may be smaller as a percentage of their pay than those received by non-highly compensated employees.

EXAMPLE 12

M Corporation has a defined contribution plan with a 10% contribution formula. An employee earning less than $228,860 in 1992 would not be affected by this includible compensation limitation. However, an employee earning $300,000 in 1992 would have only 7.63% of compensation allocated to his or her account because of the $228,860 limit on includible compensation. ◆

Two methods can be used to determine the maximum deduction a corporation is permitted for contributions to pension plans. First, an aggregate cost method allows an actuarially determined deduction based on a level amount, or a level percentage, of compensation over the remaining future service of covered participants. Second, the employer is permitted to deduct the so-called normal cost plus no more than 10 percent of the past service costs.

The employer's contribution is deductible in the tax year such amounts are paid to the pension trust. However, both cash and accrual basis employers may defer the payment of contributions with respect to any tax year until the date fixed for filing the taxpayer's Federal income tax return for that year (including extensions).[45] In effect, the corporation is allowed a deduction to the extent it is compelled to make such contributions to satisfy the funding requirement. If an

43. § 415(b).

44. §§ 401(a)(17) and 404(l).

45. §§ 404(a)(1) and (6).

amount in excess of the allowable amount is contributed in any tax year, the excess may be carried forward and deducted in succeeding tax years (to the extent the carryover plus the succeeding year's contribution does not exceed the deductible limitation for that year).[46]

EXAMPLE 13

During 1992, Y Corporation contributes $17,500 to its qualified pension plan. Normal cost for this year is $7,200, and the amount necessary to pay retirement benefits on behalf of employee services before 1992 is $82,000 (past service costs). The corporation's maximum deduction would be $15,400. This amount consists of the $7,200 normal cost plus 10% ($8,200) of the past service costs. The corporation would have a $2,100 [$17,500 (contribution) − $15,400 (deduction)] contribution carryover. ◆

EXAMPLE 14

Assume in the previous example that Y Corporation has normal cost in 1993 of $7,200 and contributes $10,000 to the pension trust. The corporation's maximum deduction would be $15,400. Y Corporation may deduct $12,100, composed of this year's contribution ($10,000) plus the $2,100 contribution carryover. ◆

A 10 percent excise tax is imposed on nondeductible contributions. The tax is levied on the employer making the contribution. The tax applies to nondeductible contributions for the current year and any nondeductible contributions for the preceding year that have not been eliminated by the end of the current year (as a carryover or by being returned to the employer in the current year).[47]

Profit Sharing and Stock Bonus Plan Limitations. The maximum deduction permitted to an employer each year for contributions to profit sharing and stock bonus plans is 15 percent of the compensation paid or accrued with respect to plan participants. Any nondeductible excess, a so-called contribution carryover, may be carried forward indefinitely and deducted in subsequent years. The maximum deduction in any succeeding year is 15 percent of all compensation paid or accrued during that taxable year. An employer can circumvent the 15 percent limitation by establishing a money purchase pension plan as a supplement to the profit sharing or stock bonus plan. When there are two or more plans, a maximum deduction of 25 percent of the compensation paid is allowable.[48]

Top-Heavy Plans

A special set of rules is imposed upon so-called top-heavy plans to discourage retirement plans from conferring disproportionate benefits upon key employees. Top-heaviness is determined on an annual basis.

In general, a *top-heavy plan* allocates more than 60 percent of the cumulative benefits to key employees, or the plan is part of a top-heavy plan. *Key employees* are defined as follows:

- Officers. However, for purposes of this definition, only the smaller of (1) 50 officers or (2) three employees or 10 percent of all employees (whichever is greater) may be considered officers.
- The 10 employees owning the largest interest in the employer (using the constructive ownership rules of § 318).

46. § 404(a)(1)(D).
47. § 4972.
48. §§ 404(a)(3)(A) and (a)(7).

- A greater-than-5 percent owner of the employer.
- A greater-than-1 percent owner of the employer with annual compensation in excess of $150,000.[49]

An employee need fall within only one of these categories to be classified as a key employee. However, a key employee does not include officers paid $45,000 or less a year. In addition, for purposes of the 10-employees provision, a key employee does not include an employee whose annual compensation from the employer is $30,000 or less. Employees receiving no compensation for five years are disregarded in testing for top-heavy status.

Top-heavy plans have the following additional requirements:

- The plan must provide for greater portability for participants who are non-key employees. An employee's right to the accrued benefits derived from employer contributions must become nonforfeitable under either of two vesting schedules. Under the first schedule, an employee who has at least three years of service with the employer must have a nonforfeitable right to 100 percent of his or her accrued benefits derived from employer contributions. Under the second schedule, a six-year graded vesting schedule must be met (see Figure 19–3).[50]
- Minimum nonintegrated contributions or benefits must be provided for plan participants who are non-key employees. In a *defined benefit plan*, these employees must be provided with a minimum nonintegrated normal retirement benefit of 2 percent of their average compensation (for their five highest years) per year of service. However, this minimum benefit does not have to provide more than 20 percent of their average compensation for the five highest years. In a *defined contribution plan*, non-key employees must receive a minimum nonintegrated contribution of the smaller of 3 percent of pay per year or the largest percentage at which contributions are made on behalf of a key employee for the year.[51]
- The aggregate limit on contributions and benefits must be reduced for certain key employees. The aggregate limit for a key employee is the smaller of 1.0 (with respect to the dollar limit) or 1.4 (as applied to the percentage limitation). However, the aggregate limit may be increased to the smaller of 1.25 or 1.4, respectively, if certain conditions are met.[52]
- A 10 percent penalty tax is imposed upon distributions before age 59½ to the extent that the amounts distributed are attributable to years in which

FIGURE 19–3
Top-Heavy Graded Vesting

Years of Service	Vested Percentage
2	20%
3	40%
4	60%
5	80%
6 or more	100%

49. § 416(i)(1).
50. § 416(b).
51. §§ 416(c) and (e).
52. § 415(e).

the person was a 5 percent owner of the company (whether or not the plan was top-heavy in those years).[53]

To prevent an employer from avoiding the top-heavy rules by establishing a one-person corporate shell, § 269A allows the IRS to allocate any income or deductions between the personal service corporation and its employee-owner. An employee-owner is any employee who owns more than 10 percent of the outstanding stock of the personal service corporation on any day during the tax year.

Cash or Deferred Arrangement Plans

A *cash or deferred arrangement plan,* hereafter referred to as a *§ 401(k) plan,* allows participants to elect either to receive up to $8,728 (in 1992)[54] in cash or to have a contribution made on their behalf to a profit sharing or stock bonus plan. The plan may also be in the form of a salary reduction agreement between an eligible participant and an employer under which a contribution will be made only if the participant elects to reduce his or her compensation or to forgo an increase in compensation.

Any pretax amount elected by the employee as a plan contribution is not includible in gross income and is 100 percent vested. Any employer contributions are tax deferred, as are earnings on contributions in the plan.

EXAMPLE 15

X participates in a § 401(k) plan of his employer. The plan permits the participants to choose between a full salary or a reduced salary where the reduction becomes a before-tax contribution to a retirement plan. X elects to contribute 10% of his annual compensation of $30,000 to the plan. Income taxes are paid on only $27,000. No income taxes are paid on the $3,000—or on any earnings—until it is distributed from the plan to X. The main benefit of a § 401(k) plan is that X can shift a portion of his income to a later taxable year. ◆

The maximum employee annual elective contribution to a § 401(k) plan is $8,728 (in 1992), but such amount is reduced dollar for dollar by other salary-reduction contributions to tax-sheltered annuities and simplified employee pension plans. Elective contributions in excess of the maximum limitation are taxable in the year of deferral. These amounts may be distributed from the plan tax-free before April 15 of the following year. Excess amounts not timely distributed will be taxable in the year of distribution, even though they were included in income in the year of deferral.

A 10 percent excise tax is imposed on the employer for excess contributions not withdrawn from the plan within 2½ months after the close of the plan year. The plan will lose its qualified status if these excess contributions (and any related income) are not withdrawn by the end of the plan year following the plan year in which the excess contributions were made.[55]

EXAMPLE 16

T, an employee of a manufacturing corporation, defers $10,728 in a § 401(k) plan in 1992. The $2,000 excess deferral, along with the appropriate earnings, must be

53. § 401(a)(9).
54. This amount is indexed annually.
55. § 4979(a).

returned to the employee by April 15, 1993. This $2,000 excess amount plus related income is taxable to the employee in 1992 and will be taxed again upon distribution (if made after April 15, 1993). There will be a 10% tax on the employer on any excess contributions not returned within 2½ months after the close of the plan year. ◆

Complicated antidiscrimination provisions apply to § 401(k) plans.

RETIREMENT PLANS FOR SELF-EMPLOYED INDIVIDUALS

Since 1962, self-employed individuals and their employees have been eligible to receive qualified retirement benefits under what are known as *H.R. 10 (Keogh) plans*. Because of contribution limitations and other restrictions, self-employed plans previously were less attractive than corporate plans. Contributions and benefits of a self-employed person now are subject to the general corporate provisions. Basically, self-employed persons are now on a parity with corporate employees. Consequently, Keogh plans can now provide a self-employed person with an adequate retirement base.

A variety of funding vehicles can be used for Keogh investments, such as mutual funds, annuities, real estate shares, certificates of deposit, debt instruments, commodities, securities, and personal properties. Investment in most collectibles is not allowed in a self-directed plan. When an individual decides to make all investment decisions, a self-directed retirement plan is established. Otherwise the individual may prefer to invest the funds with a financial institution such as a broker, a bank, or a savings and loan institution.

Coverage Requirements

Generally, the corporate coverage rules apply to Keogh plans. Thus, the percentage, ratio, and average benefits tests previously discussed also apply to self-employed plans. In addition, the more restrictive top-heavy plan rules apply to Keogh plans.[56] An individual covered under a qualified corporate plan as an employee may also establish a Keogh plan for earnings from self-employment.

Contribution Limitations

A self-employed individual may annually contribute the smaller of $30,000 or 25 percent of earned income to a *defined contribution* Keogh plan.[57] However, if the defined contribution plan is a profit sharing plan, a 15 percent deduction limit applies. Under a *defined benefit* Keogh plan, the annual benefit payable to an employee is limited to the smaller of $112,221 (in 1992) or 100 percent of the employee's average compensation for the three highest years of employment.[58] An employee includes a self-employed person. More restrictive rules apply to a top-heavy plan.

Earned income refers to net earnings from self-employment as defined in § 1402(a).[59] Net earnings from self-employment means the gross income derived by an individual from any trade or business carried on by such individual, less appropriate deductions, plus the distributive share of income or loss from a partnership.[60] Earned income is reduced by contributions to a Keogh plan on such an individual's behalf.[61]

---

56. § 401(d).
57. § 415(c)(1).
58. § 415(b)(1). This amount is indexed annually.
59. § 401(c)(2).
60. § 1402(a).
61. § 401(c)(2)(A)(v).

P, a partner, has earned income in 1992 (before any Keogh contribution) of $130,000. The maximum contribution to a defined contribution plan is $26,000, calculated from the following formula: $130,000 − .25X = X, where X is earned income reduced by P's Keogh contribution. Solving this equation, X = $104,000; thus, the contribution limit is .25 × $104,000 = $26,000. To achieve the maximum contribution of $30,000, P would have to earn at least $150,000. In essence, a self-employed individual can contribute 20% of *gross* earned income. (The partner could contribute only 13.043% of self-employment gross earned income if this were a profit sharing plan.) ◆

Many Keogh plans will be considered top-heavy plans (refer to the previous discussion). For nondiscrimination purposes, the 25 percent limitation on the employee contribution is computed on the first $228,860 (in 1992) of earned income.

EXAMPLE 18

T, a self-employed accountant, has a money purchase plan with a contribution rate of 5% of compensation. T's earned income before the retirement contribution is $230,000. T's contribution would be limited to $10,898 ($228,860 − .05X = X), since X = $217,962 and .05 × $217,962 = $10,898. ◆

Although a Keogh plan must be established before the end of the year in question, contributions may be made up to the normal filing date for such year.

INDIVIDUAL RETIREMENT ACCOUNTS (IRAs)

◆

General Rules

Employees not covered by another qualified plan can establish their own tax-deductible IRAs. The contribution ceiling is the smaller of $2,000 (or $2,250 for spousal IRAs) or 100 percent of compensation.[62] If the taxpayer or spouse is an active participant in another qualified plan, the IRA deduction limitation is phased out *proportionately* between certain adjusted gross income (AGI) ranges, as shown in Figure 19–4.[63]

AGI is calculated taking into account any § 469 passive losses and § 86 taxable Social Security benefits and ignoring any § 911 foreign income exclusion, § 135 savings bonds interest exclusion, and the IRA deduction. There is a $200 floor on the IRA deduction limitation for individuals whose AGI is not above the phase-out range.

EXAMPLE 19

In 1992, Mr. and Mrs. Q had compensation income of $27,000 and $20,000, respectively. Their AGI for 1992 was $47,000. Mr. Q was an active participant in his

FIGURE 19–4
Phase-Out of IRA Deduction

AGI Filing Status	Phase-Out Begins	Phase-Out Ends
Single and head of household	$25,000	$35,000
Married, filing joint return	40,000	50,000
Married, filing separate return	–0–	10,000

62. §§ 219(b)(1) and (c)(2).

63. § 219(g). However, a special rule in § 219(g)(4) allows a married person filing a separate return to avoid the phase-out rules even though the spouse is an active participant. The individual must live apart from the spouse at all times during the taxable year and must not be an active participant in another qualified plan.

employer's qualified retirement plan. Mr. and Mrs. Q may *each* contribute $600 to an IRA. The deductible amount for each is reduced from $2,000 by $1,400 because of the phase-out mechanism:

$$\frac{\$7,000}{\$10,000} \times \$2,000 = \$1,400 \text{ reduction}$$ ◆

EXAMPLE 20

An unmarried individual is an active participant in his employer's qualified retirement plan. With AGI of $34,500, he would normally have an IRA deduction limit of $100 {$2,000 − [($34,500 − $25,000)/$10,000 × $2,000]}. However, because of the special floor provision, a $200 IRA deduction is allowable. ◆

To the extent that an individual is ineligible to make a deductible contribution to an IRA, *nondeductible contributions* can be made to separate accounts.[64] The nondeductible contribution will be subject to the same dollar limits for deductible contributions of $2,000 of earned income ($2,250 for a spousal IRA). Income in the account accumulates tax-free until distributed. Only the account earnings will be taxed upon distribution. A taxpayer may elect to treat deductible IRA contributions as nondeductible. If an individual has no taxable income for the year after taking into account other deductions, the election would be beneficial. The election is made on the individual's tax return for the taxable year to which the designation relates.

Simplified Employee Pension Plans. An employer may contribute to an IRA covering an employee an amount equal to the lesser of $30,000 or 15 percent of the employee's earned income.[65] In such a plan, the corporation must make contributions for *each* employee who has reached age 21, has performed service for the employer during the calendar year and at least three of the five preceding calendar years, and has received at least $374 (in 1992) in compensation from the employer for the year.[66] Known as *simplified employee pension (SEP) plans*, these plans are subject to many of the same restrictions applicable to qualified plans (e.g., age and period-of-service requirements, top-heavy rules, and nondiscrimination limitations). Concept Summary 19–3 compares a SEP with a Keogh plan.

Employees who participate in salary reduction SEPs may elect to have contributions made to the SEP or to receive contributions in cash.[67] If an employee elects to have contributions made on his or her behalf to the SEP, the contribution is not treated as having been distributed or made available to the employee (i.e., no constructive receipt). The election to have amounts contributed to a SEP or received in cash is available only if at least 50 percent of the employees eligible to participate elect to have amounts contributed to the SEP. This exception to the constructive receipt principle is available only in a taxable year in which the employer maintaining the SEP has 25 or fewer employees eligible to participate at all times during the preceding year. In addition, the deferral percentage for each highly compensated employee cannot exceed 125 percent of the average deferral percentage for all other eligible employees.

The amounts contributed to a SEP by an employer on behalf of an employee and the elective deferrals under a SEP are excludible from gross income. Elective deferrals under a SEP are subject to a statutory ceiling of $8,728 (in 1992). Only $228,860 (in 1992) in compensation may be taken into account in making the SEP

64. § 408(o).
65. § 408(j).
66. § 408(k)(2). This amount is indexed annually.
67. § 408(k)(6).

computation. An employer is permitted to elect to use its taxable year rather than the calendar year for purposes of determining contributions to a SEP.[68]

Spousal IRA. If both spouses work, each can individually establish an IRA. When only one spouse is employed, an IRA can be established for the nonemployed spouse if the employed spouse is eligible to establish an IRA. The maximum deduction for the individual and spouse is the lesser of 100 percent of the compensation income of the working spouse or $2,250. One spouse is permitted to elect to be treated, for this purpose, as having no earned income, thus allowing the contributing spouse to make the additional $250 contribution to an IRA. The contribution may be allocated to either spouse in any amount up to $2,000, and a joint return must be filed. The spousal IRA deduction is also proportionately reduced for active participants whose AGI exceeds the above target ranges.

EXAMPLE 21

X, who is married, is eligible to establish an IRA. He received $30,000 in compensation in 1992. He can contribute a total of $2,250 to a spousal IRA, to be divided in any manner between the two spouses, except that no more than $2,000 can be allocated to either spouse. ◆

EXAMPLE 22

Assume the same facts as in the previous example, except that X's spouse has earned income of $100. Absent the election to treat the spouse's earned income as zero, the maximum IRA contribution is $2,100 ($2,000 for X and $100 for X's spouse). With the election, $2,250 can be contributed under the spousal IRA provision. ◆

CONCEPT SUMMARY 19–3
KEOGH PLAN AND SEP COMPARED

	Keogh	SEP
Form	Trust.	IRA.
Establishment	By end of year.	By extension due date of employer.
Type of plan	Qualified.	Qualified.
Contributions to plan	By extension due date.	By extension due date of employer.
Vesting rules	Qualified plan rules.	100% immediately.
Participants' rules	Flexible.	Stricter.
Lump-sum distributions	Yes, favorable 5-year or 10-year forward averaging.	No, ordinary income.
$5,000 death benefit exclusion	Yes.	No.
Deduction limitation	Varies.*	Smaller of $30,000 or 15% of earned income.
Self as trustee	Yes.	No.

*For a defined contribution pension plan, the limit is the smaller of $30,000 or 20% of self-employment income. A defined contribution profit sharing plan has a 13.043% deduction limit. A defined benefit Keogh plan's limit is the smaller of $112,221 (in 1992) or 100% of the employee's average compensation for the highest three years of employment.

68. § 404(h)(1)(A). The $8,728 and $228,860 amounts are indexed annually.

Alimony is considered to be earned income for purposes of IRA contributions. Thus, a person whose only income is alimony can contribute to an IRA.[69]

Timing of Contributions. Contributions (both deductible and nondeductible) can be made to an IRA anytime before the due date of the individual's tax return.[70] For example, an individual can establish and contribute to an IRA through April 15, 1993 (the return due date), and deduct this amount on his or her tax return for 1992. IRA contributions that are made during a tax return extension period do not satisfy the requirement of being made by the return due date. An employer can make contributions up until the time of the due date for filing the return (including extensions) and treat those amounts as a deduction for the prior year.[71] As noted earlier, a similar rule applies to Keogh plans. However, the Keogh plan must be established before the end of the tax year. Contributions to the Keogh plan may then be made anytime before the due date of the individual's tax return.

Penalty Taxes for Excess Contributions

A cumulative, nondeductible 6 percent excise penalty tax is imposed on the smaller of (1) any excess contributions or (2) the market value of the plan assets determined as of the close of the tax year. *Excess contributions* are any contributions that exceed the maximum limitation and contributions that are made during or after the tax year in which the individual reaches age 70½.[72] A taxpayer is not allowed a deduction for excess contributions. If the excess is corrected by contributing less than the deductible amount for a later year, a deduction then is allowable in the later year as a *makeup* deduction.

An excess contribution is taxable annually until returned to the taxpayer or reduced by the underutilization of the maximum contribution limitation in a subsequent year. The 6 percent penalty tax can be avoided if the excess amounts are returned.[73]

EXAMPLE 23

T, age 55, creates an IRA in 1992 and contributes $2,300 in cash to the plan. T has earned income of $22,000. T is allowed a $2,000 deduction *for* AGI for 1992. Assuming the market value of the plan assets is at least $300, there is a nondeductible 6% excise penalty tax of $18 ($300 × 6%). The $300 may be subject to an additional penalty tax in future years if it is not returned to T or reduced by underutilization of the $2,000 maximum contribution limitation. ◆

Taxation of Benefits

A participant has a zero basis in the deductible contributions to an IRA because such contributions are not taxed currently.[74] Once retirement payments are received, they are ordinary income and are not subject to the 5-year or 10-year averaging allowed for lump-sum distributions. Payments made to a participant from deductible IRAs before age 59½ are subject to a nondeductible 10 percent penalty tax on such actual, or constructive, payments.[75]

69. § 219(f)(1).
70. § 219(f)(3).
71. § 404(h)(1)(B).
72. §§ 4973(a)(1) and (b).
73. §§ 408(d)(4) and 4973(b)(2).
74. § 408(d)(1).
75. § 72(t).

All IRAs of an individual are treated as one contract, and all distributions during a taxable year are treated as one distribution. If an individual withdraws an amount from an IRA during a taxable year and the individual previously has made both deductible and nondeductible IRA contributions, the excludible amount must be calculated. The amount excludible from gross income for the taxable year is calculated by multiplying the amount withdrawn by a percentage. The percentage is calculated by dividing the individual's aggregate nondeductible IRA contributions by the aggregate balance of all his or her IRAs (including rollover IRAs and SEPs).[76]

EXAMPLE 24

P, age 59, has a $12,000 deductible IRA and a $2,000 nondeductible IRA (without any earnings). P withdraws $1,000 from the nondeductible IRA in 1992. The excludible portion is $143 ($2,000/$14,000 × $1,000), and the includible portion is $857 ($12,000/$14,000 × $1,000). P must pay a 10% penalty tax on a prorated portion considered withdrawn from the deductible IRA and earnings in either type of IRA. Thus, the 10% penalty tax is $85.70 (10% × $857). ◆

An IRA may be the recipient of a rollover from another qualified plan (including another IRA). Such a tax-free rollover for distributions from qualified plans is an alternative to the taxable 5-year or 10-year forward averaging techniques.[77] A partial rollover of at least 50 percent of the balance from an IRA also is subject to tax-free treatment. A distribution from a qualified plan is not included in gross income if it is transferred within 60 days of distribution to an IRA or another qualified plan. Further, any rollover amount in an IRA can later be rolled over into another qualified plan if the IRA consists of only the amounts from the original plan.

NONQUALIFIED DEFERRED COMPENSATION PLANS

Underlying Rationale for Tax Treatment

Nonqualified deferred compensation (NQDC) plans provide a flexible way for an executive to defer income taxes on income payments until a possible lower tax bracket year. Where the deferred compensation is credited with annual earnings until payment, the entire deferred compensation, not the after-tax amount, is generating investment income. Also, most deferred compensation plans do not have to meet the discrimination, funding, coverage, and other requirements of qualified plans. In addition to these advantages for the employee, the employer may not have a current cash outflow.

The doctrine of constructive receipt is an important concept relating to the taxability of nonqualified deferred compensation.[78] In essence, if a taxpayer irrevocably earns income but may elect to receive it now or at a later date, the income is constructively received and is immediately taxed. Income is not constructively received, however, if the taxpayer's control over the amounts earned is subject to substantial limitations or restrictions.

Another important concept is the economic benefit theory. Although a taxpayer does not have a present right to income, the income will be taxable if a right in the form of a negotiable promissory note exists. Notes and other evidences of indebtedness received in payment for services constitute income to the extent of their fair market value at the time of the transfer.[79]

76. § 408(d)(2).
77. §§ 402(a)(5) and 408(d)(3).
78. § 451(a) and Reg. § 1.451–2.
79. Reg. § 1.61–2(d)(4).

Example 25

R Corporation and B, a cash basis employee, enter into an employment agreement that provides an annual salary of $120,000 to B. Of this amount, $100,000 is to be paid in current monthly installments, and $20,000 is to be paid in 10 annual installments beginning at B's retirement or death. Although R Corporation maintains a separate account for B, that account is not funded (the employee is merely an unsecured creditor of the corporation). The $20,000 is not considered constructively received and is deferred. Compensation of $100,000 is currently taxable to B and deductible to R Corporation. The other $20,000 will be taxable and deductible when paid in future years. ◆

Tax Treatment to the Employer and Employee

The tax treatment of an NQDC plan depends on whether it is *funded* or *unfunded* and whether it is *forfeitable* or *nonforfeitable*. In an unfunded NQDC plan, the employee relies upon the company's mere promise to make the compensation payment in the future. An unfunded, unsecured promise to pay, not represented by a negotiable note, effectively defers the recognition of income. Thus, the employee is taxed later when the compensation is actually paid or made available.[80] Similarly, the employer is allowed a deduction when the employee recognizes income.[81]

An escrow account can be set up by the employer to accumulate deferred payments on behalf of the employee. These funds may be invested by the escrow agent for the benefit of the employee.[82] By avoiding income recognition until the benefits from the escrow custodial account are received, the employee postpones the tax. It is usually desirable not to transfer securities to the escrow agent because the IRS might attempt to treat such transfers as property transferred in connection with the performance of services under § 83. With such treatment, the transaction would be required to have a substantial risk of forfeiture and nontransferability (otherwise the compensation income would be taxable immediately). An escrow arrangement can be appropriate for a professional athlete or entertainer whose income is earned in a few peak years.

Example 26

H, a professional athlete, is to receive a bonus for signing an employment contract. An NQDC plan is established to defer the income beyond H's peak income years. The bonus is transferred by the employer to an escrow agent who invests the funds in securities, etc., which may act as a hedge against inflation. The bonus is deferred for 10 years and becomes payable gradually in years 11 through 15. The bonus is taxable to H and deductible by the employer when H receives the payments in years 11 through 15. ◆

It is also possible to provide for NQDC through an internally funded revocable trust or through an externally funded nonexempt trust.[83] The detailed requirements relative to such arrangements are beyond the scope of this text. Generally, however, funded NQDC plans must be forfeitable to keep the compensation payments from being taxable immediately. In most instances, employees prefer to have some assurance that they will ultimately receive benefits from the nonqualified deferred compensation (that the plan provides for nonforfeitable benefits). In such instances, the plan will have to be unfunded to prevent immediate taxation to the employee. Note that most funded NQDC plans are subject to many of the provisions that apply to qualified plans.

80. Rev.Rul. 60–31, 1960–1 C.B. 174; Reg. § 1.451–2(a); *U.S. v. Basye*, 73–1 USTC ¶9250, 31 AFTR2d 73–802, 93 S.Ct. 1080 (USSC, 1973).

81. §§ 404(a) and (d).

82. Rev.Rul. 55–525, 1955–2 C.B. 543.

83. Rev.Rul. 67–289, 1967–2 C.B. 163; Reg. § 1.83–1(a).

When to Use an NQDC Arrangement. As a general rule, NQDC plans are more appropriate for executives in a financially secure company. Because of the need for currently disposable income, such plans are usually not appropriate for young employees.

An NQDC plan can reduce an employee's overall tax payments by deferring the taxation of income to later years (possibly when the employee is in a lower tax bracket). In effect, these plans may produce a form of income averaging. Further, NQDC plans may discriminate in favor of shareholders, officers, specific highly compensated key employees, or a single individual.

Certain disadvantages should be noted. Nonqualified plans are usually required to be unfunded, which means that an employee is not assured that funds ultimately will be available to pay the benefits. Also, the employer's tax deduction is postponed until the employee is taxed on those payments.

Golden Parachute Arrangements. Certain excessive severance payments to employees may be penalized. The Code denies a deduction to an employer who makes a payment of cash or property to an employee or independent contractor that satisfies both of the following conditions:

- The payment is contingent on a change of ownership of a corporation through a stock or asset acquisition.
- The aggregate present value of the payment equals or exceeds three times the employee's (or independent contractor's) average annual compensation.[84]

The law recognizes that a corporation may provide monetary benefits to key employees if those employees lose their jobs as a result of a change in ownership of the corporation. These payments may be unreasonable or not really for services rendered. Such payments are referred to in the Code as *golden parachute payments,* a term that, in essence, means *excess severance pay.* The disallowed amount is the excess of the payment over a statutory base amount (a five-year average of compensation if the taxpayer was an employee for the entire five-year period). Further, a 20 percent excise tax is imposed on the recipient on the receipt of these parachute payments, to be withheld at the time of payment.[85]

EXAMPLE 27

P, an executive, receives a golden parachute payment of $380,000 from his employer. His average annual compensation for the most recent five tax years is $120,000. The corporation will be denied a deduction for $260,000 ($380,000 payment − $120,000 base amount). P's excise tax is $52,000 ($260,000 × 20%). ◆

Golden parachute payments do not include payments to or from qualified pension, profit sharing, stock bonus, annuity, or simplified employee pension plans. Also excluded is the amount of the payment that, in fact, represents reasonable compensation for personal services actually rendered or to be rendered. S corporations are not subject to the golden parachute rules. Generally, corporations that do not have stock that is readily tradable on an established securities market or elsewhere are also exempt. Such excluded payments are not taken into account when determining whether the threshold (the aggregate present value calculation) is exceeded.

84. § 280G.

85. § 4999.

General Provisions

A *restricted property plan* is an arrangement whereby an employer transfers property (e.g., stock of the employer-corporation) to a provider of services at no cost or at a bargain price. The purpose of a restricted stock plan is to retain the services of key employees who might otherwise leave. The employer hopes that such compensation arrangements will encourage company growth and attainment of performance objectives. Section 83 was enacted in 1969 to provide rules for the taxation of incentive compensation arrangements, which previously were governed by judicial and administrative interpretations. Although the following discussion refers to an employee as the provider of the services, the services need not be performed by an employee (§ 83 also applies to independent contractors).

Restricted Property Plans

As a general rule, if an employee performs services and receives property (e.g., stock), the fair market value of that property in excess of any amount paid by the employee is includible in his or her gross income. The time for inclusion is the earlier of (1) the time the property is no longer subject to a substantial risk of forfeiture or (2) the time the property is transferable by the employee. The fair market value of the property is determined without regard to any restriction, except a restriction that by its terms will never lapse.[86] Since the amount of the compensation is determined at the date that the restrictions lapse or when the property is transferable, the opportunity to generate capital gain treatment on the property is denied during a period when the ordinary income element is being deferred.

Example 28

On October 1, 1988, W Corporation sold to J, an employee, 100 shares of W Corporation stock for $10 per share. At the time of the sale, the fair market value of the stock was $100 per share. Under the terms of the sale, each share of stock was nontransferable and subject to a substantial risk of forfeiture (which was not to lapse until October 1, 1992). Evidence of these restrictions was stamped on the face of the stock certificates. On October 1, 1992, the fair market value of the stock was $250 per share. Since the stock was nontransferable and was subject to a substantial risk of forfeiture, J did not include any compensation in gross income during 1988 (assuming no special election was made). Instead, J was required to include $24,000 of compensation in gross income [100 shares × ($250 less $10 per share)] during 1992. If for some reason the substantial risk of forfeiture had occurred (e.g., the plan required J to surrender the stock to the corporation if he voluntarily terminated his employment with the company before October 1, 1992) and J never received the stock certificates, he would have been allowed a capital loss of $1,000 (the extent of his investment). ◆

Substantial Risk of Forfeiture

A *substantial risk of forfeiture* exists if a person's rights to full enjoyment of property are conditioned upon the future performance, or the refraining from the performance, of substantial services by that individual.[87] For example, if an employee must return the property (receiving only his or her original cost, if any) should there be a failure to complete a substantial period of service (for any reason), the property is subject to a substantial risk of forfeiture. Another such situation exists when an employer can compel an employee to return the property due to a breach of a substantial covenant not to compete. Any

86. § 83(a)(1); *Miriam Sakol*, 67 T.C. 986 (1977); *T. M. Horwith*, 71 T.C. 932 (1979).

87. § 83(c); Regulation § 1.83–3(c)(2) includes several examples of restricted property arrangements.

substantial risk of forfeiture should be stated on the face of the stock certificates. Assuming that a substantial risk of forfeiture does not exist, the property received is valued at its fair market value, ignoring any restrictions, except for one instance dealing with closely held stock.

Special Election Available

An employee may elect within 30 days after the receipt of restricted property to recognize immediately as ordinary income the fair market value in excess of the amount paid for the property. Any appreciation in the value of the property after receipt is classified as capital gain instead of ordinary income. No deduction is allowed to the employee for taxes paid on the original amount included in income if the property is subsequently forfeited.[88] The employee is permitted to take a capital loss for any amounts that were actually paid for the property. Furthermore, in such a case, the employer must repay taxes saved by any compensation deduction taken in the earlier year.[89]

Any increase in value between the time the property is received and the time it becomes either nonforfeitable or transferable is taxed as ordinary income if no special election is made by the employee. However, if the employee elects to be taxed immediately on the difference between the cost and fair market value on the date of issue, any future appreciation is treated as capital gain. In determining whether the gain is long term or short term, the holding period starts when the employee is taxed on the ordinary income.[90]

EXAMPLE 29

On July 1, 1982, F Company sold 100 shares of its preferred stock, worth $15 per share, to D (an employee) for $5 per share. The sale was subject to D's agreement to resell the preferred shares to the company for $5 per share if D terminated employment during the following 10 years. Assume that the stock had a value of $25 per share on July 1, 1992, and D sold the stock for $30 per share on October 10, 1992. D made the special election to include the original spread (between the value in 1982 of $15 and the amount paid of $5) in income for 1982. D was required to recognize $1,000 of compensation income in 1982 ($15 − $5 = $10 × 100 shares), at which time his holding period in his stock began. D's tax basis in the stock was $1,500 ($1,000 + $500). When the preferred stock was sold in 1992, D recognized a $1,500 long-term capital gain ($30 × 100 shares − $1,500). ◆

EXAMPLE 30

Assume the same facts as in Example 29, except that D sells the stock in 1993 (rather than 1992). No gain would be recognized by D in 1992 when the substantial risk of forfeiture lapses. Instead, D would recognize the $1,500 long-term capital gain in 1993. ◆

This special provision is usually not elected since it results in an immediate recognition of income and adverse tax consequences result from a subsequent forfeiture. However, the special election may be attractive in the following situations:

- The bargain element is relatively small.
- Substantial appreciation is expected in the future.
- A high probability exists that the restrictions will be met.

88. § 83(b).
89. Reg. §§ 1.83–6(c) and 2(a).
90. § 1223(6).

Employer Deductions

At the time the employee is required to include the compensation in income, the employer is allowed a tax deduction for the same amount. The employer must withhold on this amount in accordance with § 3402. In the no-election situation, the deduction is limited to the fair market value of the restricted property (without regard to the restrictions) at the time the restrictions lapse, reduced by the amount originally paid for the property by the employee.[91] When the employee elects to be taxed immediately, the corporate deduction also is accelerated and deductible in like amount. In cases of deferred income recognition, the employer can receive a very sizable deduction if the property has appreciated.

EXAMPLE 31

On March 14, 1990, F Corporation sold to G, an employee, 10 shares of F common stock for $100 per share. The employer corporation and the employee were calendar year taxpayers. The common stock was subject to a substantial risk of forfeiture and was nontransferable; both conditions were to lapse on March 14, 1992. At the time of the sale, the fair market value of the common stock (without considering the restrictions) was $1,000 per share. On March 14, 1992, the restrictions lapsed when the fair market value of the stock was $2,000 per share. No special election was made by the employee. In 1992, G realized ordinary income of $19,000 (10 shares at $2,000 per share less the $100 per share paid by G). Likewise, F Corporation was allowed a $19,000 compensation deduction in 1992. ◆

EXAMPLE 32

In the previous example, assume that the employee had made the special election. Since the employee was taxed on $9,000 in 1990, the corporation was allowed to deduct a like amount in 1990. No deduction would be available in 1992. ◆

STOCK OPTIONS

In General

Various equity types of stock option programs are available for an employee's compensation package. Some authorities believe that some form of *equity kicker* is needed to attract new management, convert key officers into *partners* by giving them a share of the business, and retain the services of executives who might otherwise leave. Encouraging the management of a business to have a proprietary interest in its successful operation should provide executives with a key motive to expand the company and improve its profits.

An *option* gives an individual the right to purchase a stated number of shares of stock from a corporation at a certain price within a specified period of time. The optionee must be under no obligation to purchase the stock, and the option may be revocable by the corporation. The option must be in writing, and its terms must be clearly expressed.[92]

Incentive Stock Options

An equity type of stock option called an *incentive stock options (ISO)* is available for options granted after 1975 and exercised after 1980.[93] An ISO arrangement

91. Reg. § 1.83–6(a).

92. Reg. §§ 1.421–1(a)(1) and –7(a)(1).

93. Qualified stock options were available under § 422 (prior to repeal by the Revenue Reconciliation Act of 1990) for certain qualified options granted before May 21, 1976. These qualified stock options had many of the statutory requirements of ISOs, but ISOs have a more favorable tax treatment.

receives much the same tax treatment previously accorded to restricted and qualified stock option plans. There are no tax consequences when the option is granted, but the *spread* (the excess of the fair market value of the share at the date of exercise over the option price[94]) is a tax preference item for purposes of the alternative minimum tax. The determination of fair market value is made without regard to any lapse restrictions (a restriction that will expire after a period of time). After the option is exercised and when the stock is sold, any gain therefrom is taxed as a long-term capital gain if certain holding period requirements are met. To qualify as a long-term capital gain, the employee must not dispose of the stock within two years after the option is granted or within one year after acquiring the stock.[95] If the employee meets the holding period requirements, none of these transactions generate any business deduction for the employer.[96]

Since some beneficial treatment for long-term capital gains for the individual has been restored beginning in 1991, ISOs have regained some of their tax appeal on the gain side. In addition, an employee who has capital losses would prefer capital gain treatment.

EXAMPLE 33

E Corporation granted an ISO for 100 shares of its stock to R, an employee, on March 18, 1989. The option price was $100, and the fair market value was $100 on the date of grant. R exercised the option on April 1, 1991, when the market value of the stock was $200 per share. He sold the stock on April 6, 1992, for $300 per share. R did not recognize any ordinary income on the date of the grant or the exercise date since the option qualified as an ISO. E Corporation received no compensation deduction. R would have a $10,000 tax preference item on the exercise date. He would have a long-term capital gain upon the sale of the stock in 1992 of $20,000 [($300 − $100) × 100], since the one-year and two-year holding periods and other requirements would have been met. ◆

As a further requirement for ISO treatment, the option holder must be an employee of the issuing corporation from the date the option is granted until 3 months (12 months if disabled) before the date of exercise. Exceptions are made for parent and subsidiary situations, corporate reorganizations, and liquidations. The holding period and the employee-status rules just described (the one-year, two-year, and three-month requirements) are waived in the case of the death of an employee. Also, in certain situations involving an insolvent employee, the holding period rules are modified.[97]

EXAMPLE 34

Assume the same facts as in the previous example, except that R was not employed by E Corporation for six months before the date he exercised the options. R must recognize ordinary income to the extent of the spread, assuming there was no substantial risk of forfeiture. Thus, R would recognize $10,000 [($200 − $100) × 100] of ordinary income on the exercise date, since R was not an employee of E Corporation at all times during the period beginning on the grant date and ending three months before the exercise date. E Corporation is allowed a deduction at the same time that R reports the ordinary income. ◆

If the holding period requirements are not satisfied but all other conditions are met, the tax is still deferred to the point of the sale. However, the difference

94. §§ 422(a), 421(a)(1), and 57(a)(3).
95. § 422(a)(1).
96. § 421(a)(2).
97. §§ 422(a)(2) and (c)(3).

between the option price and the value of the stock at the date the option was exercised will be treated as ordinary income. The difference between the amount realized for the stock and the value of the stock at the date of exercise will be short-term or long-term capital gain, depending on the holding period of the stock itself. The employer will be allowed a deduction equal to the amount recognized by the employee as ordinary income.

EXAMPLE 35

Assume the same facts as in Example 33, except that R sold the stock on March 22, 1992, for $290 per share. Since R did not hold the stock itself for at least one year, $10,000 of the gain would be treated as ordinary income in 1992, and E Corporation would be allowed a $10,000 compensation deduction in 1992. The remaining $9,000 would be a short-term capital gain ($29,000 − $20,000). ◆

Qualification Requirements for Incentive Stock Option Plans. An *incentive stock option* is an option granted to an individual, for any reason connected with his or her employment, to purchase stock of a corporation.[98] The option is granted by the employer-corporation or by a parent or subsidiary corporation of the employer-corporation. An employee can use company stock to pay for the stock when exercising an option without disqualifying the ISO plan.

For an option to qualify as an ISO, the terms of the option itself must meet the following conditions:

- The option must be granted under a plan specifying the number of shares of stock to be issued and the employees or class of employees eligible to receive the options. The plan must be approved by the shareholders of the corporation within 12 months before or after the plan is adopted.
- The option must be granted within 10 years of the date the plan is adopted or of the date the plan is approved by the shareholders, whichever date is earlier.
- The option must by its terms be exercisable only within 10 years of the date it is granted.
- The option price must equal or exceed the fair market value of the stock at the time the option is granted. This requirement is deemed satisfied if there has been a good faith attempt to value the stock accurately, even if the option price is less than the stock value.
- The option by its terms must be nontransferable other than at death and must be exercisable during the employee's lifetime only by the employee.
- The employee must not, immediately before the option is granted, own stock representing more than 10 percent of the voting power or value of all classes of stock in the employer corporation or its parent or subsidiary. (Here, the attribution rules of § 267 are applied in modified form.) However, the stock ownership limitation will be waived if the option price is at least 110 percent of the fair market value (at the time the option is granted) of the stock subject to the option and the option by its terms is not exercisable more than five years from the date it is granted.[99]

An overall limitation is imposed on the amount of ISOs that can be exercised in one year. This limit is set at $100,000 per year (based on the value of the stock determined at the time the option is granted) per employee.

98. § 422(b).

99. § 422(c)(5).

Nonqualified Stock Options

A *nonqualified stock option (NQSO)* does not satisfy the statutory requirements for ISOs. In addition, a stock option that otherwise would qualify as an ISO will be treated as a nonqualified stock option if the terms of the stock option provide that it is not an ISO. If the NQSO has a readily ascertainable fair market value (e.g., the option is traded on an established exchange), the value of the option must be included in the employee's income at the date of grant. Thereafter, capital gain or loss is recognized only upon the disposal of the optioned stock. The employee's basis is the amount paid for the stock plus any amount reported as ordinary income. The employer obtains a corresponding tax deduction at the same time and to the extent that ordinary income is recognized by the employee.[100]

EXAMPLE 36

On February 1, 1991, J is granted an NQSO to purchase 100 shares of stock from the employer at $10 per share. On this date, the option is selling for $2 on an established exchange. J exercised the option on March 30, 1992, when the stock was worth $20 per share. On June 5, 1992, J sold the optioned stock for $22 per share.

- J must report ordinary income of $200 ($2 × 100 shares) on the date of grant (February 1, 1991), since the option has a readily ascertainable fair market value.
- Upon the sale of the stock (June 5, 1992), J must report a long-term capital gain of $1,000 [($22 − $12) × 100 shares].
- At the date of grant (February 1, 1991), the employer will receive a tax deduction of $200, the amount of income reported by J. ◆

If an NQSO does not have a readily ascertainable fair market value, an employee does not recognize income at the grant date. However, as a general rule, ordinary income must be reported in the year of exercise (the difference between the fair market value of the stock at the exercise date and the option price).[101] The amount paid by the employee for the stock plus the amount reported as ordinary income becomes the basis. Any appreciation above that basis is taxed as a long-term capital gain upon disposition (assuming the stock is held for the required long-term holding period after exercise). The corporation receives a corresponding tax deduction at the same time and to the extent that ordinary income is recognized by the employee.

EXAMPLE 37

On February 3, 1990, S was granted an NQSO for 100 shares of common stock at $10 per share. On the date of the grant, there was no readily ascertainable fair market value for the option. S exercised the options on January 3, 1991, when the stock was selling for $15 per share. S sold one-half of the shares on April 15, 1991, and the other half on September 17, 1992. The sale price on both dates was $21 per share. S would recognize no income on the grant date (February 3, 1990) but would recognize $500 ($1,500 − $1,000) of ordinary income on the exercise date (January 3, 1991). S would recognize a short-term capital gain of $300 on the sale of the first half in 1991 and a $300 long-term capital gain on the sale of the second batch of stock in 1992 [½($2,100 − $1,500)]. ◆

The major *advantages* of NQSOs can be summarized as follows:

- A tax deduction is available to the corporation without a cash outlay.
- The employee receives capital gain treatment on any appreciation in the stock starting either at the exercise date or at the date of grant if the option has a readily ascertainable fair market value.

100. Reg. §§ 1.421–6(c), (d), (e), and (f); Reg. § 1.83–7.

101. Reg. § 1.83–7(a); Reg. § 1.421–6(d).

- Options can be issued at more flexible terms than under ISO plans (e.g., longer exercise period and discount on exercise price).

A major *disadvantage* is that the employee must recognize ordinary income on the exercise of the option or at the date of grant if the option has a readily ascertainable market value, without receiving cash to pay the tax.

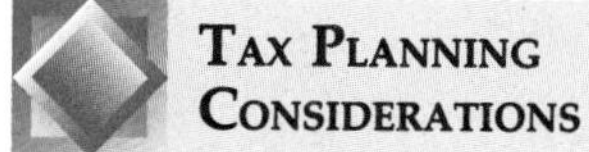

TAX PLANNING CONSIDERATIONS

Deferred Compensation

The dramatic lowering of individual tax rates to 28 percent (33 percent for certain individuals due to the phase-out of the 15 percent rate and personal exemptions) and the elimination of favorable capital gain treatment by the Tax Reform Act of 1986 have had an impact on the attractiveness of deferral techniques. While the direct and indirect increases in the individual tax rates and the restoration of a beneficial alternative tax for net capital gains by the Revenue Reconciliation Act of 1990 may partially restore the attractiveness of deferred compensation, the aforementioned factors are still having a negative impact. Further, with individual rates generally lower than corporate tax rates, current deductibility to the employer is more advantageous. The tightening of the antidiscrimination rules may increase the costs to the employer of providing deferred compensation. Finally, restrictions upon the deductibility of interest expense make it more costly for an employee to borrow money as part of a compensation program. Payment of compensation in cash in 1992 still may be quite beneficial, however, especially if tax rates increase in future years.

Qualified Plans

Qualified plans provide maximum tax benefits for employers, since the employer receives an immediate tax deduction for contributions to such plans and the income that is earned on the contributions is not taxable to the employer. The employer contributions and the trust earnings are not taxed to the employees until those funds are made available to them.

Qualified plans are most appropriate where it is desirable to provide benefits for a cross section of employees. In some closely held corporations, the primary objective is to provide benefits for the officer-shareholder group and other highly paid personnel. The nondiscrimination requirements that must be met in a qualified plan may prevent such companies from attaining these objectives. Thus, a nonqualified arrangement may be needed as a supplement to, or used in lieu of, the qualified plan.

Self-Employed Retirement Plans

A Keogh or IRA participant may make a deductible contribution for a tax year up to the time prescribed for filing the individual's tax return. A Keogh plan must have been established by the end of the tax year (December 31) to obtain a current deduction for the contribution made in the subsequent year. An individual can establish an IRA after the end of the tax year and still receive a current deduction for the contribution made in the subsequent year. However, since the deductibility of contributions to IRAs has been restricted for many middle-income and upper-income taxpayers, Keogh plans are likely to become more important.

Individual Retirement Accounts

Fewer taxpayers are now allowed to make deductible contributions to IRAs. A working taxpayer not covered by another qualified plan may still deduct IRA contributions up to the smaller of $2,000 or 100 percent of earned income. If both spouses work, each may individually establish an IRA. Where only one spouse has earned income, an IRA may be established for the nonworking spouse. A total of $2,250 may then be contributed to the two IRAs. If the nonworking spouse has a small amount of income (e.g., jury duty), an election may be made to ignore such income for spousal IRA purposes.

A married couple may put $4,000 into an IRA when one spouse works for the other spouse. This requires paying the *employee spouse* $2,000 in salary and having him or her make an independent contribution to an IRA. This extra $2,000, however, is subject to FICA.

A single working taxpayer covered by another retirement plan may deduct a $2,000 IRA contribution only if adjusted gross income (AGI) is less than $25,000 a year. For married couples filing jointly, the ceiling is $40,000. The IRA deduction is reduced proportionately as AGI increases within a $10,000 phase-out range above the $25,000 and $40,000 ceilings.

IRA and Keogh participants can self-direct their investments into a wide variety of assets. The participant self-directs the investments into various assets even though the assets are under the control of a trustee or custodian. The acquisition by an IRA or self-directed Keogh or corporate plan of collectibles (e.g., art, gems, metals) is treated as a distribution (taxed). For an IRA or Keogh participant under age 59½, there would also be a 10 percent premature distribution penalty. However, state-issued coins and gold and silver eagle coins issued by the United States may be placed in IRAs.

Comparison of § 401(k) Plan with IRA

Most employees will find a § 401(k) plan more attractive than an IRA. Probably the biggest limitation of an IRA is the $2,000 maximum shelter. Under § 401(k), employees are permitted to shelter compensation up to $8,728 (in 1992).[102] The new restrictions on deducting contributions to IRAs for many middle-income and upper-income taxpayers may cause many employees to utilize § 401(k) plans more frequently.

Another difference between § 401(k) plans and IRAs is the manner in which the money is treated. Money placed in an IRA may be tax deductible, whereas dollars placed in a § 401(k) plan are considered to be deferred compensation. Thus, a § 401(k) reduction may reduce profit sharing payments, group life insurance, and Social Security benefits. Concept Summary 19–4 compares a § 401(k) plan with an IRA.

Nonqualified Deferred Compensation (NQDC) Plans

Nonqualified deferred compensation arrangements such as restricted property plans can be useful to attract executive talent or to provide substantial retirement benefits for executives. A restricted property plan may be used to retain a key employee of a closely held company when management continuity problems are anticipated. Without such employees, the untimely death or disability of one of the owners might cause a disruption of the business with an attendant loss in value for his or her heirs. Such plans may discriminate in favor of officers and other highly paid employees. The employer, however, does not receive a tax deduction until the employee is required to include the deferred compensation in income (upon the lapse of the restrictions).

---

102. This amount is indexed annually.

The principal advantage of NQDC plans is that the employee can defer the recognition of income to future periods when his or her income tax bracket may be lower (e.g., during retirement years). The time value benefits from the deferral of income should also be considered. However, with such low individual tax rates in 1992, an executive with a deferred compensation arrangement entered into in a prior year may wish to accelerate the income into 1992 since individual tax rates in future years may be higher.

The principal disadvantage of NQDC plans could be the bunching effect that takes place on the expiration of the period of deferral. In some cases, planning can alleviate this result.

EXAMPLE 38

During 1992, executive A enters into an agreement to postpone a portion of her payment for current services until retirement. The deferred amount is not segregated from the company's general assets and is subject to normal business risk. The entire payment, not the after-tax amount, is invested in securities and variable annuity contracts. A is not taxed on the payment in 1992, and the company receives no deduction in 1992. If A receives the deferred payment in a lump sum when she retires, the tax rates may be higher and more progressive than in 1992. Thus, A may wish to arrange for a number of payments over a number of years to be made to her or a designated beneficiary. ◆

Stock Options

Rather than paying compensation in the form of corporate stock, an alternative approach is to issue options to an employee to purchase stock at a specific price. Stock option plans are used more frequently by publicly traded companies than by closely held companies. This difference is due to the problems of determining the value of the stock of a company that is not publicly held.

CONCEPT SUMMARY 19–4
SECTION 401(K) PLAN AND IRA COMPARED

	§ 401(k) Plan	IRA
Deduction limitation	Smaller of $8,728 (in 1992) or approximately 25% of total earnings. Limited by antidiscrimination requirements of § 401(k)(3).	$2,000 or 100% of compensation.
Distributions	Early withdrawal possible if for early retirement (55 or over) or to pay medical expenses.	10% penalty for early withdrawals.
Effect on gross earnings	Gross salary reduction, which may reduce profit sharing contributions, Social Security benefits, and group life insurance.	No effect.
Employer involvement	Must keep records; monitor for compliance with antidiscrimination test.	Minimal.
Lump-sum distributions	Favorable 5-year or 10-year forward averaging.	Ordinary income.
Timing of contribution	Within 30 days of plan year-end or due date of employer's return.*	Grace period up to due date of tax return.
Loans from plan	Yes.	No.

*Elective contributions must be made to the plan no later than 30 days after the end of the plan year, and nonelective contributions no later than the due date of the tax return (including extensions).

Concept Summary 19–5
Incentive Stock Options and Nonqualified Stock Options Compared

	ISO	NQSO
Granted at any price	No	Yes
May have any duration	No	Yes
Governing Code Section	§ 422	§ 83
Spread subject to alternative minimum tax	Yes	No
Deduction to employer for spread	No	Yes
Type of gain/loss on disposal	Capital	Capital
Statutory amount ($100,000) limitation	Yes	No

Nonqualified stock options (NQSOs) are more flexible and less restrictive than incentive stock options (ISOs). For example, the holding period for an NQSO is not as long as that for an ISO. Further, the option price of an NQSO may be less than the fair market value of the stock at the time the option is granted. An NQSO creates an employer deduction that lowers the cost of the NQSO to the employer. The employer may pass along this tax savings to the employee in the form of a cash payment. Both the employer and the employee may be better off by combining NQSOs with additional cash payments rather than using ISOs. See Concept Summary 19–5.

Flexible Benefit Plans

Employees may be permitted to choose from a package of employer-provided fringe benefits.[103] In these so-called *cafeteria benefit plans,* some of the benefits chosen by an employee may be taxable, and some may be statutory nontaxable benefits (e.g., health and accident insurance and group term life insurance).

Employer contributions made to a flexible plan are included in an employee's gross income only to the extent that the employee actually elects the taxable benefits. Certain nondiscrimination standards with respect to coverage, eligibility for participation, contributions, and benefits must be met. Thus, such a plan must cover a fair cross section of employees. Also, a flexible plan cannot include an election to defer compensation, and a key employee is not exempt from taxation on the taxable benefits made available where more than 25 percent of the statutory nontaxable benefits are provided to key employees.

Problem Materials

Discussion Questions

1. Compare and contrast defined contribution and defined benefit pension plans.
2. Compare and contrast qualified pension and profit sharing plans.

---

103. § 125.

3. Determine whether each of the following independent statements best applies to a defined contribution plan (DCP), defined benefit plan (DBP), both (B), or neither (N):

   a. Includes an employee stock ownership plan (ESOP).
   b. Forfeitures can be allocated to the remaining participants' accounts.
   c. Requires greater reporting requirements and more actuarial and administrative costs.
   d. Forfeitures can revert to the employer.
   e. More favorable to employees who are older at the time of the adoption of the plan.
   f. Employee forfeitures can be used to reduce future contributions by the employer.
   g. May exclude employees who begin employment within five years of normal retirement age.
   h. Annual addition to each employee's account may not exceed the smaller of $30,000 or 25% of the employee's salary.
   i. The final benefit to a participant depends upon investment performance.
   j. To avoid penalties, the amount of annual contributions must meet minimum funding requirements.

4. Indicate whether the following statements apply to a pension plan (P), a profit sharing plan (PS), both (B), or neither (N):

   a. Forfeited amounts can be used to reduce future contributions by the employer.
   b. Allocation of forfeitures may discriminate in favor of the prohibited group (highly compensated employees).
   c. Forfeitures can revert to the employer.
   d. Forfeitures can increase plan benefits by allocating the forfeitures to participants.
   e. An annual benefit of $60,000 could be payable on behalf of a participant.
   f. More favorable to employees who are older at the time of the adoption of the qualified plan.

5. When will the $30,000 maximum annual contribution to a defined contribution plan be indexed?
6. What are the tax and financial advantages accruing to a company that adopts an employee stock ownership plan (ESOP) for employees?
7. List the qualification requirements that must be satisfied in order for a qualified plan to receive favorable tax treatment.
8. Is it possible to provide greater vested benefits for highly paid employees and still meet the nondiscrimination requirements under a qualified pension plan? Explain.
9. Once the age and service requirements are met, when must an employee begin participating in a qualified plan?
10. What is vesting, and how will vesting requirements help employees who do not remain with one employer during their working years?
11. What are the minimum coverage requirements for qualified pension or profit sharing plans?
12. Discuss the tax consequences to employee, employer, and the trust of a qualified pension or profit sharing plan.
13. What three alternative options are available for distributions of benefits from a qualified retirement plan?
14. How are lump-sum distributions from qualified plans taxed to the recipients (capital gain or ordinary income)? Is income averaging available to an employee who receives a lump-sum distribution?
15. Which of the following would be considered a tax benefit or advantage of a qualified retirement plan?

   a. Certain lump-sum distributions may be subject to capital gain treatment.
   b. Employer contributions are currently deductible.
   c. Employee contributions are currently deductible.

d. The qualified trust is tax-exempt as to all income (other than unrelated business income).
e. In a lump-sum distribution, any capital gain tax on the portion attributable to any unrealized appreciation in the stock of the employer at the time of distribution is deferred until the time the employee disposes of such stock in a taxable transaction.
f. Election may be made to allow a lump-sum distribution to be subject to a 5-year or 10-year forward averaging technique.

16. What ceiling limitations have been placed on employer contributions (relative to individual employees) to defined contribution and defined benefit plans?
17. What is a top-heavy plan?
18. List the additional qualification requirements for top-heavy retirement plans.
19. Determine the 1992 indexed amounts for the following items:
    a. Maximum annual contribution to a defined contribution plan.
    b. Maximum annual benefits payable by a defined benefit plan.
    c. The $150,000 or $112,500 amounts for calculating the 15 percent excise tax imposed on excess distributions.
    d. The maximum amount of the annual contribution to a cash or deferred arrangement plan.
20. Discuss the differences between a Keogh plan and an Individual Retirement Account (IRA).
21. What tax-free alternative is available for the 5-year or 10-year forward averaging techniques for lump-sum distributions?
22. A nonqualified deferred compensation plan is taxable under the constructive receipt doctrine for which of the following situations:
    a. The contract is funded, and there is no substantial risk of forfeiture.
    b. Same as (a), except the employee must work for three years.
    c. An agreement to defer payment is entered into after compensation is earned.
    d. The agreement is entered into before services are rendered.
    e. In (a), the contract is not funded.
23. What is the major disadvantage of a nonqualified deferred compensation plan?
24. What is a golden parachute payment?
25. Explain the difference in the tax treatment of an employer and employee (or other provider of services) with respect to the general rule (no election) and the special election under § 83(b) when dealing with a restricted property plan. Explain the risk aspect of this tax provision.
26. What is a substantial risk of forfeiture? Why is it necessary to impose this restriction on the transfer of restricted property?
27. Determine which of the following conditions would cause options to fall *outside* the qualification requirements for incentive stock options:
    a. The employee disposes of his stock within 15 months from the date of the granting of the options.
    b. The employee is allowed to exercise the options up to 12 years from the date the options are granted.
    c. The employee is transferred to the parent of the corporation six months before he exercises the options.
    d. The option price is 112% of the fair market value of the stock on the grant date, and the shareholder owns 15% of the stock.
    e. The option may be exercised by the employee's spouse in the event of the employee's death.
28. Would a 30-year-old executive of T Corporation earning $100,000 prefer an extra $20,000 bonus or the option to purchase $20,000 worth of securities for $5,000 from the employer under a nonqualified stock option plan in 1992?
29. Compare and contrast an IRA and a § 401(k) plan.

30. Explain what is meant by a cafeteria benefit plan.
31. Indicate whether each of the following items is considered a nonqualified compensation plan (N), a qualified compensation plan (Q), or both (B):

    a. Individual Retirement Account.
    b. Incentive stock option.
    c. Group term life insurance.
    d. Cafeteria plan.
    e. Pension plan.
    f. Employee stock ownership plan.
    g. Nonqualified stock option.
    h. Keogh plan.
    i. Simplified employee pension plan.

PROBLEMS

32. N Corporation has a total of 1,000 employees, of whom 700 are non-highly compensated. The retirement plan covers 300 non-highly compensated employees and 200 highly compensated employees. Does this plan satisfy the minimum coverage test for 1992?
33. F Corporation's pension plan benefits 620 of its 1,000 highly compensated employees during 1992. How many of its 620 non-highly compensated employees must benefit to meet the ratio test for the minimum coverage requirement?
34. A retirement plan covers 72% of the non-highly compensated individuals. The plan benefits 49 of the 131 employees. Determine if the participation requirement is met for 1992.
35. An employee of P, Inc., has completed five years of employment and is 50% vested in her retirement plan. Does this plan meet the minimum vesting standards required for 1992?
36. M, age 46, is the sole remaining participant of a money purchase pension plan. The plan is terminated, and a $150,000 taxable distribution is made to M. Calculate the amount of any early distribution penalty tax.
37. In 1992, T receives a $170,000 distribution from his qualified retirement plan. If this amount is not a lump-sum distribution, calculate the amount of any excess distribution penalty tax. T made no after-tax contributions to the plan.
38. Participant T received a distribution from a qualified plan that was entitled to capital gain treatment under § 402(a)(2). The 100 shares of the employer company stock received have a tax basis of $20 per share and a fair market value of $85 per share. T sold this stock five months after the distribution for $110 per share. Calculate the amount and character of any gain to T.
39. When K retires in 1992, he receives a lump-sum distribution of $50,000 from a noncontributory qualified pension plan. His active period of participation was from January 1, 1971, through December 31, 1978. Assume that K attained age 50 before January 1, 1986. If K files a joint return with his wife in 1992 and elects to use the 10-year forward averaging provision, calculate (a) his separate tax on this distribution and (b) the capital gain portion.
40. E receives a $150,000 lump-sum distribution in 1992 from a contributory pension plan, which includes employer common stock with net unrealized appreciation of $20,000. E contributed $20,000 to the qualified plan while he was an active participant from February 10, 1973, to February 10, 1978. Assume that E attained age 50 before January 1, 1986.

    a. Calculate the total taxable amount.
    b. Calculate the separate tax assuming E elects to use the 5-year or 10-year forward averaging provision.
    c. Calculate the capital gain portion. (Treat part of a calendar month as one month.)

41. R has been an active participant in a defined benefit plan for 17 years. During her last 5 years of employment, R earned $20,000, $30,000, $45,000, $50,000, and $60,000, respectively (representing R's highest income years).

a. Calculate R's maximum allowable benefits from this qualified plan (assume there are fewer than 100 participants) in 1992.
b. Assume that R's average compensation for her three high years is $80,000. Calculate R's maximum allowable benefits.

42. The compensation paid by M Corporation to the plan participants of a profit sharing plan in 1992 was $33,300. During 1992, M Corporation contributed $10,000 to the plan.

a. Calculate M Corporation's deductible amount for 1992.
b. Calculate the amount of the contribution carryover from 1992.

43. Determine the maximum contributions to a qualified plan in the following independent situations:

a. M is covered by a money purchase pension plan and has an annual salary of $160,000 in 1992.
b. N is a participant in a profit sharing plan and has an annual salary of $110,000 in 1992.
c. P is a participant in a money purchase pension plan and has an annual salary of $220,000 in 1992. The plan has a 10% contribution formula.

44. Determine the maximum annual benefits payable to an employee from a defined benefit plan in the following independent situations:

a. Q, age 65, has been a participant for 12 years, and his highest average compensation for 3 years is $85,000.
b. M, age 66, has been a participant for 8 years (11 years of service), and her highest average compensation for 3 years is $86,000.
c. P, age 67, has been a participant for 11 years in a collectively bargained plan with 238 participants. His highest average compensation for 3 years is $70,300.

45. During 1992, N is a key employee of a top-heavy pension plan. His salary is $240,000. Calculate N's maximum contribution to such a defined benefit plan.

46. Determine the minimum nonintegrated contributions or benefits for a plan participant who is a non-key employee in a top-heavy plan for the following independent situations:

a. X is a participant in P Company's defined contribution plan. His high five-year average compensation is $26,000, and his current year compensation is $32,000.
b. Assume the same data as in (a), except that the largest percentage contribution on behalf of a key employee is 2%.
c. Y is an 11-year participant in D Company's defined benefit plan. His high 5-year average compensation is $30,000, and his current year compensation is $34,000. His company has contributed $5,600 to his plan during the past 10 years.

47. N has 5 years of service completed as of March 2, 1992, her employment anniversary date. Her plan uses the graded vesting rule.

a. How much is N's nonforfeitable percentage if the plan is not top-heavy?
b. Assume the plan is top-heavy in 1992. How much is N's nonforfeitable percentage?
c. Assume the plan is top-heavy in 1992 and the company uses cliff vesting. How much is N's nonforfeitable percentage?

48. Q, a single individual, participates in a § 401(k) plan of his employer. The plan permits participants to choose between a full salary or a reduced salary where the reduction becomes a before-tax contribution to a retirement plan. Q elects to contribute 10% of his annual compensation of $82,000 to the plan. On what amount of his salary are income taxes paid in 1992?

49. F earns $220,000 of self-employment net income in 1992 in a sole proprietorship.

a. Calculate the maximum amount that F can deduct for contributions to a defined contribution Keogh plan.

b. Suppose F contributes more than the allowable amount to the Keogh plan. What are the consequences to F?
c. Can F retire and begin receiving Keogh payments at age 55?

50. X, a married individual filing a joint return, is a member of a Keogh pension plan. For 1992, his adjusted gross income is $42,000, and X would like to contribute as much as is allowed to an IRA. Calculate the amount that X can contribute and the amount he can deduct.

51. Answer the following independent questions with respect to IRA contributions:

a. During 1992, A earns a salary of $25,000 and is not an active participant in any other qualified plan. His wife has no earned income. What is the maximum total deductible contribution to their IRAs? A wishes to contribute as much as possible to his own IRA.
b. B has earned income during 1992 of $23,000, and her husband has earned income of $1,900. They are not active participants in any other qualified plan. What is the maximum contribution to their IRAs?
c. X's employer makes a contribution of $3,500 to X's simplified employee pension plan. If X's earned income is $27,000 and AGI is $24,000 during 1992, what amount, if any, can X also contribute to an IRA?

52. G Company pays bonuses each year to its key executives. The specific employees to receive bonuses and the amount of bonus for each recipient are determined on December 1 of each year. Each employee eligible for a bonus may decide on or before November 15 of each year to postpone the receipt of the bonus until retirement or death. An employee electing to postpone receipt of a bonus is allowed to designate, at any time before retirement, the time and manner of the postretirement payments and to designate the persons to receive any amount payable after death. Since most employees elect to defer their bonuses, separate accounts are *not* maintained for each employee. When would these bonuses be taxed to the executives and be deductible by G Company?

53. N is a disqualifying individual, as defined under § 280G, who receives a possible golden parachute payment of $520,000 from her employer. Her base amount (average annual compensation for the most recent five tax years) is $200,000.

a. Calculate the amount deductible by N's employer and any excise tax payable by N.
b. Assume that N's base amount is $110,000 and N receives $310,000. Calculate the employer's deduction and N's excise tax.

54. Executive R receives a $600,000 payment under a golden parachute agreement entered into on January 14, 1992. R's base amount from C Corporation is $140,000.

a. What amount is not deductible to C Corporation under § 280G?
b. What total tax must R pay, assuming a 31% tax rate?
c. Answer (a) and (b) assuming the payment is $400,000.

55. On February 20, 1992, G (an executive of R Corporation) purchased 100 shares of R stock (selling at $20 a share) for $10. A condition of the transaction was that G must resell the stock to R at cost if he leaves his employer voluntarily within five years of receiving the stock (assume this represents a substantial risk of forfeiture).

a. Assuming that no special election is made under § 83(b), what amount, if any, is taxable to G in 1992?
b. Five years later when the stock is selling for $40 a share, G is still employed by the same firm. What amount of ordinary income, if any, is taxable to G?
c. What amount, if any, is deductible by R as compensation expense five years later?
d. Assuming G made the § 83(b) special election in 1992, what amount would be taxable in 1992?
e. In (d), what amount would be deductible by R Corporation five years later?
f. Under (d), assume G sold all the stock six years later for $65 per share. How much capital gain is included in G's gross income?

g. In (d), what loss is available to G if he voluntarily resigns before the five-year period and does not sell the stock back to the corporation?
h. In (g), in the year G resigns, what amount, if any, would be taxable to R Corporation?

56. On July 2, 1988, P Corporation sold 1,000 of its common shares (worth $14 per share) to its employee C for $5 per share. The sale was subject to C's agreement to resell the shares to the corporation for $5 per share if his employment is terminated within the following four years. The shares had a value of $24 per share on July 2, 1992. C sold the shares for $31 per share on September 16, 1992. No special election under § 83(b) is made.

a. What amount, if any, will be taxed to C on July 2, 1988?
b. On July 2, 1992?
c. On September 16, 1992?
d. What deduction, if any, will P Corporation obtain?
e. Assume the same facts but that C makes the election under § 83(b). What amount, if any, will be taxed to C on July 2, 1988?
f. Will the assumption made in (e) have any effect on any deduction P Corporation will receive? Explain.

57. R exercises incentive stock options for 100 shares of X Corporation stock on May 21, 1992, at the option price of $100 per share when the fair market value is $120 per share. She sells the 100 shares of common stock three and one-half years later for $140.

a. Calculate the total long-term capital gain on this sale.
b. Assume R holds the stock seven months and sells the shares for $140 per share. Calculate any ordinary income on the sale.
c. In (b), what amount can X Corporation deduct?
d. Suppose R holds the stock for two years and sells the shares for $115 per share. Calculate any capital gain on this transaction.
e. In (a), assume the options are nonqualified options with a nonascertainable fair market value on the date of the grant. Calculate total long-term capital gain, if any, in the year of sale.
f. In (e), assume that each option has an ascertainable fair market value of $10 on the date of the grant and no substantial risk of forfeiture exists. Calculate total long-term capital gain, if any, on the date of the sale.

58. On November 19, 1990, J is granted a nonqualified stock option to purchase 100 shares of S Company (on that date the stock is selling for $8 per share and the option price is $9 per share). J exercises the option on August 21, 1991, when the stock is selling for $10 per share. Five months later, J sells the shares for $11.50 per share.

a. What amount is taxable to J in 1990?
b. What amount is taxable to J in 1991?
c. What amount and type of gain is taxable to J in 1992?
d. What amount, if any, is deductible by S Company in 1991?
e. What amount, if any, is recognized in 1992 if the stock is sold for $9.50 per share?

RESEARCH PROBLEMS

RESEARCH PROBLEM 1 A taxpayer and his sister owned and operated a mail-order business in corporate form. The corporation used the homes of the taxpayer and sister for corporate mail-order activities (assembling, storing inventory, etc.). The corporation paid the taxpayer and sister rent for the use of the homes. Such payments were deducted as rent and reported by the two parties on their tax returns. The IRS disallowed most of the deduction, contending that the rent was excessive. Is the excessive rent deductible as compensation?

Partial list of research aids:

Multnomah Operating Co., 57–2 USTC ¶9979, 52 AFTR 672, 248 F.2d 661 (CA–9, 1957).

RESEARCH PROBLEM 2 F had been a participant in the pension plan of Post, Inc., since 1974. In 1989, he terminated employment with Post, Inc., and became an employee of Daily, Inc. In 1973, the IRS issued a letter that the pension plan was qualified under § 401(a) and that the pension trust was therefore exempt from tax under § 501(a). In 1992, the Commissioner examined the pension plan and determined that the plan discriminated among salaried employees. The Commissioner revoked the plan's qualified status and the trust's exempt status retroactively to January 1, 1989. When F changed jobs in 1989, he rolled over his distribution from the pension plan to an IRA under § 402(a)(5). Discuss F's tax situation.

RESEARCH PROBLEM 3 H and W were married, but H died on February 25, 1992. During 1992, H earned $5,226 in wages, but W had no earned income. Neither had contributed any money to an IRA during 1992. What amount, if any, can be contributed to H's IRA and/or W's spousal IRA?

RESEARCH PROBLEM 4 What is a phantom stock plan? Outline the tax aspects.

RESEARCH PROBLEM 5 What are stock appreciation rights? Determine their tax treatment.

PART

CORPORATIONS AND PARTNERSHIPS

The primary orientation of this text is toward basic tax concepts and the individual taxpayer. Although many of these tax concepts also apply to corporations and partnerships, numerous tax concepts apply specifically to corporations or partnerships. An overview of these provisions is presented in Part VII. Comprehensive coverage of these topics appears in *West's Federal Taxation: Corporations, Partnerships, Estates, and Trusts.*

CHAPTER

CORPORATIONS AND PARTNERSHIPS

OBJECTIVES

Compare the income tax treatment of corporations with that applicable to individuals.

Introduce the rules governing the formation, operation, and liquidation of a corporation.

Discuss the utility of an S election and the tax consequences that result.

Summarize the tax rules that apply to the formation and operation of a partnership.

Evaluate the advantages and disadvantages of the various forms of conducting a business.

Illustrate how to use various entities to reduce the overall income tax burden of the family unit.

OUTLINE

Until now the text has concentrated on the Federal income taxation of individual taxpayers. However, some awareness of the tax implications of other business forms is necessary in order to make even the most basic business decisions.

EXAMPLE 1

U and T are contemplating entering into a new business venture that will require additional capital investment by other parties. As the venture will involve financial risk, both U and T are concerned about personal liability. Further, they would prefer to avoid any income taxes at the entity level. Both U and T would like to take advantage of any losses the venture might generate during its formative period. ◆

In choosing the form for carrying out the venture, U and T will have to consider using a corporation. The corporate form limits a shareholder's liability to the amount invested in the stock. Regular corporations, however, are subject to the corporate income tax. Furthermore, losses incurred by corporations do not pass through to the shareholders. Perhaps the ideal solution would be to use the corporate form and elect to be taxed as an S corporation. The election would avoid the corporate income tax and permit the pass-through of losses while providing limited liability for the shareholders.

Although the resolution of the problem posed by Example 1 seems simple enough, it did not consider the possible use of a partnership. More important, the decision required *some* knowledge of corporations and the S corporation election. This chapter is intended to provide such knowledge by briefly reviewing the tax consequences of the various forms of business organization.

WHAT IS A CORPORATION?

Compliance with State Law

A company must comply with the specific requirements for corporate status under state law. For example, it is necessary to draft and file articles of incorporation with the state regulatory agency, be granted a charter, and issue stock to shareholders.

Compliance with state law, although important, is not the only requirement that must be met to qualify for corporate *tax* status. For example, a corporation qualifying under state law may be disregarded as a taxable entity if it is a mere sham lacking in economic substance. The key consideration is the degree of business activity conducted at the corporate level.

EXAMPLE 2

C and D are joint owners of a tract of unimproved real estate that they wish to protect from future creditors. C and D form R Corporation, to which they transfer the land in return for all of the corporation's stock. The corporation merely holds title to the land and conducts no other activities. In all respects, R Corporation meets the legal requirements of a corporation under applicable state law. Nevertheless, R Corporation probably would not be recognized as a separate entity for corporate tax purposes under these facts.[1] ◆

EXAMPLE 3

Assume the same facts as in Example 2. In addition to holding title to the land, R Corporation leases the property, collects rents, and pays the property taxes. R

1. See *Paymer v. Comm.*, 45–2 USTC ¶9353, 33 AFTR 1536, 150 F.2d 334 (CA–2, 1945).

Corporation probably would be treated as a corporation for Federal income tax purposes because of the scope of its activities. ◆

In some instances, the IRS has attempted to disregard (or collapse) a corporation in order to make the income taxable directly to the shareholders.[2] In other cases, the IRS has asserted that the corporation is a separate taxable entity so as to assess tax at the corporate level and to tax corporate distributions to shareholders as dividend income (double taxation).[3]

The Association Approach

An organization not qualifying as a regular corporation under state law may nevertheless be taxed as a corporation under the association approach. The designation given to an entity under the state law is not controlling. For example, a partnership of physicians has been treated as an association even though state law prohibited the practice of medicine in the corporate form. The partnership thus was subject to the Federal income tax rules applicable to corporations.[4] Another sensitive area involves limited partnerships where the only general partner is a corporation. Unless certain prescribed guidelines are carefully followed, the IRS will treat the partnership as an association.[5]

Whether or not an entity will be considered an association for Federal income tax purposes depends upon the number of corporate characteristics it possesses. According to court decisions and the Regulations, corporate characteristics include the following:[6]

1. Associates.
2. An objective to carry on a business and divide the gains therefrom.
3. Continuity of life.
4. Centralized management.
5. Limited liability.
6. Free transferability of interests.

The Regulations state that an unincorporated organization shall not be classified as an association unless it possesses *more* corporate than noncorporate characteristics. In making this determination, the characteristics common to both corporate and noncorporate business organizations are to be disregarded. Both corporations and partnerships generally have associates (shareholders and partners) and an objective to carry on a business and divide the gains. Therefore, only if a partnership has at least three of attributes 3 through 6 will it be treated as an association (taxable as a corporation).

EXAMPLE 4

The XYZ Partnership agreement provides for the following: the partnership terminates with the withdrawal of a partner; all of the partners have authority to participate in the management of the partnership; all of the partners are individually liable for the debts of the partnership; and a partner may not freely transfer his or her interest in the partnership to another. None of the corporate attributes 3 through 6 are present. Since the majority requirement of the Regulations is not satisfied, XYZ is not taxable as an association. ◆

2. *Floyd Patterson*, 25 TCM 1230, T.C. Memo. 1966–239, *aff'd.* in 68–2 USTC ¶9471, 22 AFTR2d 5810 (CA–2, 1968).
3. *Raffety Farms Inc. v. U.S.*, 75–1 USTC ¶9271, 35 AFTR2d 75–811, 511 F.2d 1234 (CA–8, 1975).
4. *U.S. v. Kintner*, 54–2 USTC ¶9626, 46 AFTR 995, 216 F.2d 418 (CA–5, 1954).
5. Rev.Proc. 89–12, 1989–1 C.B. 798.
6. Reg. § 301.7701–2(a).

Income Tax Considerations

◆

General Tax Consequences of Different Forms of Business Entities

Business operations may be conducted as a sole proprietorship, as a partnership, or in corporate form.

- Sole proprietorships are not separate taxable entities. The owner of the business reports all business transactions on his or her individual income tax return.
- Partnerships are not subject to the income tax. Under the *conduit* concept, the various tax attributes of the partnership's operations flow through to the individual partners to be reported on their personal income tax returns.
- The regular corporate form of doing business carries with it the imposition of the corporate income tax. The corporation is recognized as a separate taxpaying entity. Income is taxed to the corporation as earned and taxed again to the shareholders as dividends when distributed.
- A regular corporation may elect to be taxed as an S corporation. This special treatment is similar (although not identical) to the partnership rules. Income tax is generally avoided at the corporate level, and shareholders are taxed currently on the taxable income of the S corporation.

Individuals and Corporations Compared—An Overview

Similarities between Corporate and Individual Tax Rules. The gross income of a corporation is determined in much the same manner as for individuals. Both individuals and corporations are entitled to exclusions from gross income, such as interest on municipal bonds. The tax rules for gains and losses from property transactions are also treated similarly. For example, whether a gain or loss is capital or ordinary depends on the nature and use of the asset rather than the type of taxpayer. Upon the sale or other taxable disposition of depreciable personalty, the recapture rules of § 1245 make no distinction between corporate and noncorporate taxpayers. In the case of the recapture of depreciation on real property (§ 1250), however, corporate taxpayers are treated more severely in terms of tax consequences. Under § 291, corporations must recognize as additional ordinary income 20 percent of the excess of the amount that would be recaptured under § 1245 over the amount recaptured under § 1250 (refer to Example 22, Chapter 17).

The business deductions of corporations parallel those available to individuals. Corporate deductions are allowed for all ordinary and necessary expenses paid or incurred in carrying on a trade or business under the general rule of § 162(a). Corporations may also deduct interest (§ 163), certain taxes (§ 164), losses (§ 165), bad debts (§ 166), depreciation (§ 167), cost recovery (§ 168), charitable contributions subject to corporate limitation rules (§ 170), net operating losses (§ 172), research and experimental expenditures (§ 174), and other less common deductions.

Many of the tax credits available to individuals, such as the foreign tax credit (§ 27), can be claimed by corporations. Not available to corporations are certain credits that are personal in nature. Examples of credits not available to corporations include the child and dependent care expenses credit (§ 21), the credit for the elderly or disabled (§ 22), and the earned income credit (§ 32).

Corporations usually have the same choices of accounting periods as do individuals. Like an individual, a corporation may choose a calendar year or a fiscal year for reporting purposes. Corporations do enjoy greater flexibility in the election of a tax year. For example, corporations usually can have different tax years from those of their shareholders. Also, a newly formed corporation generally has a free choice of any approved accounting period without having to obtain the consent of the IRS. As noted in Chapter 18, however, personal service corporations are subject to severe restrictions on the use of a fiscal year.

The use of the cash method of accounting is denied to large corporations (those with average annual gross receipts in excess of $5 million). Smaller corporations as well as qualified personal service corporations and other corporations engaged in the trade or business of farming have a choice between the cash or accrual method of accounting for tax purposes. Both individuals and corporations that maintain inventory for sale to customers are required to use the accrual method of accounting for determining sales and cost of goods sold.

Dissimilarities. Both noncorporate and corporate taxpayers are subject to three income tax rates. For individuals, the three rates are 15, 28, and 31 percent. For corporations, the rates are 15, 25, and 34 percent. Corporate taxpayers lose the benefits of the lower brackets (using a phase-out approach) once taxable income reaches a certain level. Noncorporate taxpayers, however, continue to enjoy the benefits of the lower brackets even though they have reached the higher taxable income levels.

Both corporate and noncorporate taxpayers are subject to the alternative minimum tax (AMT). For AMT purposes, many adjustments and tax preference items are the same for both, but other adjustments and tax preferences apply only to corporations or only to individuals. Corporate tax rates are discussed later in the chapter. The AMT is discussed at length in Chapter 12. See also the coverage in *West's Federal Taxation: Corporations, Partnerships, Estates, and Trusts.*

All allowable corporate deductions are treated as business expenses. The determination of adjusted gross income, so essential for individuals, has no relevance to corporations. Corporations need not be concerned with classifying deductions into *deduction for* and *deduction from* categories. The standard deduction, itemized deductions, and personal and dependency exemptions are not available to corporations.

Specific Provisions Compared

Corporate and individual tax rules also differ in the following areas:

- Capital gains and losses.
- Charitable contributions.
- Net operating losses.
- Special deductions for corporations.

Capital Gains and Losses. Both corporate and noncorporate taxpayers are required to aggregate gains and losses from the taxable sale or exchange of capital assets. (Refer to Chapter 16 for a description of the netting process that takes place after the aggregation has been completed.) For net long-term capital gains, individual taxpayers enjoy a minimal advantage (the alternative tax). In no event will the gains be taxed at a rate in excess of 28 percent. In the case of corporations, all capital gains are treated as ordinary income. Therefore, the net long-term capital gains of a corporation could be taxed at a rate of 34 percent (the highest bracket applicable to corporations).

Significant differences exist in the treatment of capital losses for income tax purposes. Individuals, for example, can annually deduct up to $3,000 of net capital losses against ordinary income. Corporations are not permitted to use net capital losses to offset ordinary income. Net capital losses can be used only to offset past or future capital gains.[7] Unlike individuals, corporations are not allowed an unlimited carryover period for capital losses. Instead, they may carry back excess capital losses to the three preceding years, applying them initially to the earliest year. If not exhausted by the carryback, remaining unused capital losses may be carried over for a period of five years from the year of the loss.[8]

When carried back or over, *both* short-term capital losses and long-term capital losses are treated as short-term capital losses by corporate taxpayers. For noncorporate taxpayers, a capital loss does not lose its identity. Thus, long-term capital losses of noncorporate taxpayers are carried forward as long-term capital losses, and short-term capital losses are carried forward as short-term capital losses.

EXAMPLE 5

T Corporation, a calendar year taxpayer, incurs a long-term net capital loss of $5,000 for 1992. None of the capital loss may be deducted in 1992. T Corporation may, however, carry the loss back to years 1989, 1990, and 1991 (in this order) and offset any capital gains recognized in these years. If the carryback does not exhaust the loss, the loss may be carried over to 1993, 1994, 1995, 1996, and 1997 (in this order). Such capital loss carrybacks or carryovers are treated as short-term capital losses. ◆

Charitable Contributions. Generally, a charitable contribution deduction is allowed only for the tax year in which the payment is made. However, an important exception is made for accrual basis corporations. The deduction may be claimed in the tax year *preceding* payment if the following conditions are satisfied:

- The contribution is authorized by the board of directors by the end of that tax year *and*
- The contribution is paid on or before the fifteenth day of the third month of the next tax year.[9]

EXAMPLE 6

On December 28, 1992, the board of directors of XYZ Corporation, a calendar year accrual basis taxpayer, authorizes a $5,000 donation to a qualified charity. The donation is paid on March 14, 1993. XYZ Corporation may claim the $5,000 donation as a deduction for 1992. As an alternative, XYZ Corporation may claim the deduction in 1993 (the year of payment). ◆

Like individuals, corporations are not permitted an unlimited charitable contribution deduction. In any one year, a corporate taxpayer is limited to 10 percent of taxable income. For this purpose, taxable income is computed without regard to the charitable contribution deduction, any net operating loss carryback or capital loss carryback, or the dividends received deduction.[10] Any contributions in excess of the 10 percent limitation are carried over to the five succeeding tax years. Any carryover must be added to subsequent contributions and is subject to the 10 percent limitation. In applying the limitation, the most recent contributions must be deducted first.[11]

---

7. §§ 1211(a) and (b).
8. § 1212(a).
9. § 170(a)(2).
10. § 170(b)(2).
11. § 170(d)(2).

EXAMPLE 7

During 1992, T Corporation (a calendar year taxpayer) had the following income and expenses:

Income from operations	$140,000
Expenses from operations	110,000
Dividends received	10,000
Charitable contributions made in 1992	5,000

For the purposes of the 10% limitation only, T Corporation's taxable income is $40,000 ($140,000 − $110,000 + $10,000). Consequently, the allowable charitable contribution deduction for 1992 is $4,000 (10% × $40,000). The $1,000 unused portion of the contribution is carried over to 1993, 1994, 1995, 1996, and 1997 (in that order) until exhausted. ◆

EXAMPLE 8

Assume the same facts as in Example 7. In 1993, T Corporation has taxable income (after adjustments) of $50,000 and makes a charitable contribution of $4,800. The maximum deduction allowed for 1993 is $5,000 (10% × $50,000). The first $4,800 of the allowed deduction must be allocated to the 1993 contributions, and the $200 excess is carried over from 1992. The remaining $800 of the 1992 contribution is carried over to 1994, etc. ◆

As noted in Chapter 11, the deduction for charitable contributions of ordinary income property is limited to the lesser of the fair market value or the adjusted basis of the property. A special rule permits a corporation to contribute inventory (ordinary income property) to certain charitable organizations and receive a deduction equal to the adjusted basis plus one-half of the difference between the fair market value and the adjusted basis of the property.[12] In no event, however, may the deduction exceed twice the adjusted basis of the property. To qualify for this exception, the inventory must be used by the charity in its exempt purpose for the care of *children*, the *ill*, or the *needy.*

EXAMPLE 9

In the current year, W Company (a retail clothier) donates sweaters and overcoats to Sheltering Arms (a qualified charity caring for the homeless). The clothing is inventory and has a basis of $10,000 and a fair market value of $14,000. If W Company is a corporation, the charitable contribution that results is $12,000 [$10,000 (basis) + $2,000 (50% of the appreciation of $4,000)]. In contrast, if W Company is not a corporation, the charitable contribution is limited to $10,000 (basis). ◆

Net Operating Losses. The computation of a net operating loss for individuals was discussed in Chapter 8. Corporations are not subject to the complex adjustments required for individuals (e.g., a corporation has no adjustments for nonbusiness deductions or capital gains and losses). Corporations are subject to fewer adjustments than individuals are because a corporation's loss more clearly approximates a true economic loss. Artificial deductions (e.g., personal and dependency exemptions) that merely generate paper losses are not permitted for corporations.

In computing the net operating loss of a corporation, the dividends received deduction (discussed below) can be claimed in determining the amount of the loss.[13] Corporate net operating losses may be carried back 3 years and forward

12. § 170(e)(3).

13. § 172(d).

15 years (or taxpayers may elect to forgo the carryback period) to offset taxable income for those years.

EXAMPLE 10

In 1992, XYZ Corporation has gross income of $200,000 and deductions of $300,000, excluding the dividends received deduction. XYZ Corporation received taxable dividends of $100,000 from Exxon stock. XYZ Corporation has a net operating loss of $170,000, computed as follows:

Gross income (including Exxon dividends)		$200,000
Less: Business deductions	$300,000	
Dividends received deduction (70% × $100,000)	70,000	370,000
Taxable income (loss)		($170,000)

◆

EXAMPLE 11

Assume the same facts as in Example 10 and that XYZ Corporation had taxable income of $40,000 in 1989. The net operating loss of $170,000 is carried back to 1989 (unless XYZ elects not to carry back the loss to that year). The carryover to 1990 is $130,000, computed as follows:

Taxable income for 1989	$ 40,000
Less: Net operating loss carryback from 1992	170,000
Carryover of unabsorbed 1992 loss	($130,000)

◆

In Example 11, the carryback to 1989 might have been ill-advised if XYZ Corporation had little, if any, taxable income in 1990 and 1991 and if it anticipated large amounts of taxable income in the immediate future. In that case, the *election to forgo* the carryback might generate greater tax savings. In this regard, three points should be considered. First, the time value of the tax refund that is lost by not using the carryback procedure must be considered. Second, the election to forgo a net operating loss carryback is irrevocable. Thus, it cannot be changed later if the future high profits do not materialize. Third, future increases or decreases in corporate income tax rates that can reasonably be anticipated should be considered.

Deductions Available Only to Corporations

Dividends Received Deduction. The purpose of the dividends received deduction is to prevent triple taxation. Without the deduction, income paid to a corporation in the form of a dividend would be subject to taxation for a second time (once to the distributing corporation) with no corresponding deduction to the distributing corporation. A third level of tax would be assessed on the shareholders when the recipient corporation distributed the income to its shareholders. Since the dividends received deduction may be less than 100 percent, the law provides only partial relief.

The amount of the dividends received deduction depends upon the percentage of ownership the recipient corporate shareholder holds in the corporation making the dividend distribution.[14] For dividends received or accrued, the *deduction percentage* is summarized as follows:

14. § 243(a).

Percentage of Ownership by Corporate Shareholder	Deduction Percentage
Less than 20%	70%
20% or more (but less than 80%)	80%
80% or more	100%

The dividends received deduction may be limited to a percentage of the taxable income of a corporation computed without regard to the net operating loss deduction, the dividends received deduction, or any capital loss carryback to the current tax year. The percentage of taxable income limitation corresponds to the deduction percentage. Thus, if a corporate shareholder owns less than 20 percent of the stock in the distributing corporation, the dividends received deduction is limited to 70 percent of taxable income (as previously defined). However, this limitation does not apply if the corporation has a net operating loss for the current taxable year.[15]

In working with these myriad rules, the following steps need to be taken:

1. Multiply the dividends received by the deduction percentage.
2. Multiply the taxable income (as previously defined) by the deduction percentage.
3. The deduction is limited to the lesser of Step 1 or Step 2, unless subtracting the amount derived from Step 1 from taxable income (as previously defined) generates a negative number. If so, the amount derived in Step 1 should be used.

EXAMPLE 12

P, R, and T Corporations are three unrelated calendar year corporations and have the following transactions for 1992:

	P Corporation	R Corporation	T Corporation
Gross income from operations	$ 400,000	$ 320,000	$ 260,000
Expenses from operations	(340,000)	(340,000)	(340,000)
Dividends received from domestic corporations (less than 20% ownership)	200,000	200,000	200,000
Taxable income before the dividends received deduction	$ 260,000	$ 180,000	$ 120,000

In determining the dividends received deduction, use the step procedure just described:

	P Corporation	R Corporation	T Corporation
Step 1 (70% × $200,000)	$140,000	$140,000	$140,000
Step 2			
70% × $260,000 (taxable income)	$182,000		
70% × $180,000 (taxable income)		$126,000	
70% × $120,000 (taxable income)			$ 84,000

15. § 246(b).

	P Corporation	R Corporation	T Corporation
Step 3			
Lesser of Step 1 or Step 2	$140,000	$126,000	
Generates a net operating loss			$140,000

◆

R Corporation is subject to the 70 percent of taxable income limitation. It does not qualify for the loss rule treatment, since subtracting $140,000 (Step 1) from $180,000 does not yield a loss. T Corporation qualifies for the loss rule treatment because subtracting $140,000 (Step 1) from $120,000 does yield a loss. In summary, each corporation has the following dividends received deduction for 1992: $140,000 for P Corporation, $126,000 for R Corporation, and $140,000 for T Corporation. If a corporation already has a net operating loss before any dividends received deduction is claimed, the full dividends received deduction (as calculated in Step 1) is allowed.

Deduction of Organizational Expenditures. Under § 248, a corporation may elect to amortize organizational expenses over a period of 60 months or more. If the election is not made on a timely basis, the expenditures cannot be deducted until the corporation ceases to conduct business and liquidates. The election is made in a statement attached to the corporation's return for its first taxable year.

Organizational expenditures include the following:

- Legal services incident to organization (e.g., drafting the corporate charter, bylaws, minutes of organizational meetings, terms of original stock certificates).
- Necessary accounting services.
- Expenses of temporary directors and of organizational meetings of directors and shareholders.
- Fees paid to the state of incorporation.

Expenditures that do not qualify include those connected with issuing or selling shares of stock or other securities (e.g., commissions, professional fees, and printing costs) or with the transfer of assets to a corporation. These expenditures are generally added to the capital account and are not subject to amortization.

Determination of Corporate Tax Liability

Income Tax Rates. Current rates applicable to corporations are as follows:

Taxable Income	Tax Rate
$50,000 or less	15%
Over $50,000 but not over $75,000	25%
Over $75,000	34%

For a corporation that has taxable income in excess of $100,000 for any taxable year, the amount of the tax is increased by the lesser of (1) 5 percent of the excess or (2) $11,750. In effect, the additional tax means a 39 percent rate for every dollar of taxable income from $100,000 to $335,000.[16] Thus, the benefits of the lower rates on the first $75,000 of taxable income completely phase out at $335,000.

Example 13

X Corporation, a calendar year taxpayer, has taxable income of $90,000 for 1992. The income tax liability will be $18,850 determined as follows: $7,500 (15% × $50,000) + $6,250 (25% × $25,000) + $5,100 (34% × $15,000). ◆

Example 14

Y Corporation, a calendar year taxpayer, has taxable income of $335,000 for 1992. The income tax liability will be $113,900 determined as follows: $7,500 (15% × $50,000) + $6,250 (25% × $25,000) + $88,400 (34% × $260,000) + $11,750 (5% × $235,000). Note that the tax liability of $113,900 is 34% of $335,000. ◆

Qualified personal service corporations are taxed at a flat 34 percent rate on all taxable income. They do not enjoy the tax savings of the 15 percent (on the first $50,000) and 25 percent (on the next $25,000) lower brackets. For this purpose, a *qualified personal service corporation* is one that is substantially employee owned and engages in one of the following activities: health, law, engineering, architecture, accounting, actuarial science, performing arts, or consulting.

Alternative Minimum Tax. Corporations are subject to an alternative minimum tax (AMT) that is structured in the same manner as that applicable to individuals. The AMT for corporations, as for individuals, defines a more expansive tax base than for the regular tax. Like individuals, corporations are required to apply a minimum tax rate to the expanded base and pay the difference between the tentative AMT liability and the regular tax. Many of the adjustments and tax preference items necessary to arrive at alternative minimum taxable income (AMTI) are the same for individuals and corporations. Although the objective of the AMT is the same for individuals and for corporations, the rate and exemptions are different. Computation of the AMT is discussed in Chapter 12. See also the coverage in *West's Federal Taxation: Corporations, Partnerships, Estates, and Trusts.*

Corporate Filing Requirements

A corporation must file a return whether it has taxable income or not.[17] A corporation that was not in existence throughout an entire annual accounting period is required to file a return for the fraction of the year during which it was in existence. In addition, the corporation must file a return even though it has ceased to do business if it has valuable claims for which it will bring suit. It is relieved of filing returns once it ceases business and dissolves.

The corporate return is filed on Form 1120 unless the corporation is a small corporation entitled to file the shorter Form 1120–A. A corporation may file Form 1120–A if it meets *all* of the following requirements:

- Gross receipts or sales are under $500,000.
- Total income (gross profit plus other income including gains on sales of property) is under $500,000.
- Total assets are under $500,000.

16. § 11(b).

17. § 6012(a)(2).

- The corporation is not involved in a dissolution or liquidation.
- The corporation is not a member of a controlled group or a personal holding company.
- The corporation does not file a consolidated return.
- The corporation does not have ownership in a foreign corporation.
- The corporation does not have foreign shareholders who directly or indirectly own 50 percent or more of its stock.

Corporations making the S corporation election (discussed later in the chapter) file on Form 1120S.

The return must be filed on or before the fifteenth day of the third month following the close of the corporation's tax year. Corporations can receive an automatic extension of six months for filing the corporate return by filing Form 7004 by the due date of the return. However, the IRS may terminate an extension by mailing a 10-day notice to the taxpayer corporation.[18]

A corporation must make payments of estimated tax unless its tax liability can reasonably be expected to be less than $500.[19] For 1992, the payments must be at least 93 percent of the corporation's final tax. These payments may be made in four installments due on or before the fifteenth day of the fourth, sixth, ninth, and twelfth months of the corporate taxable year. The full amount of the unpaid tax is due on the date of the return. Failure to make the required estimated tax prepayments will result in a nondeductible penalty being imposed on the corporation. The penalty can be avoided, however, if any of the various exceptions apply.[20]

Reconciliation of Corporate Taxable Income and Accounting Income

Taxable income and accounting net income are seldom the same amount. For example, a difference may arise if the corporation uses accelerated depreciation for tax purposes and straight-line depreciation for accounting purposes.

Many items of income for accounting purposes, such as proceeds from a life insurance policy on the death of a corporate officer and interest on municipal bonds, may not be includible in calculating taxable income. Some expense items for accounting purposes, such as expenses to produce tax-exempt income, estimated warranty reserves, a net capital loss, and Federal income taxes, are not deductible for tax purposes.

Schedule M–1 on the last page of Form 1120 is used to reconcile accounting net income (net income after Federal income taxes) with taxable income (as computed on the corporate tax return before the deduction for a net operating loss and the dividends received deduction). In the left-hand column of Schedule M–1, net income per books is added to the following: the Federal income tax liability for the year, the excess of capital losses over capital gains (which cannot be deducted in the current year), income for tax purposes that is not income in the current year for accounting purposes, and expenses recorded on the books that are not deductible on the tax return. In the right-hand column, income recorded on the books that is not currently taxable or is tax-exempt and deductions for tax purposes that are not expenses for accounting purposes are totaled and subtracted from the left-hand column total to arrive at taxable income (before the net operating loss or dividends received deductions).

18. § 6081.

19. § 6655(f).

20. See § 6655 for the penalty involved and the various exceptions.

EXAMPLE 15

During 1992, T Corporation had the following transactions:

Net income per books (after tax)	$92,400
Taxable income	50,000
Federal income tax liability (15% × $50,000)	7,500
Interest income from tax-exempt bonds	5,000
Interest paid on loan, the proceeds of which were used to purchase the tax-exempt bonds	500
Life insurance proceeds received as a result of the death of a key employee	50,000
Premiums paid on key employee life insurance policy	2,600
Excess of capital losses over capital gains	2,000

For book and tax purposes, T Corporation determines depreciation under the straight-line method. T Corporation's Schedule M–1 for the current year follows.

Schedule M-1 Reconciliation of Income per Books With Income per Return *(This schedule does not have to be completed if the total assets on line 15, column (d), of Schedule L are less than $25,000.)*

1 Net income per books	92,400	7 Income recorded on books this year not included on this return (itemize): a Tax-exempt interest $ 5,000 Life insurance proceeds on key employee $50,000	55,000
2 Federal income tax	7,500		
3 Excess of capital losses over capital gains	2,000		
4 Income subject to tax not recorded on books this year (itemize):		8 Deductions on this return not charged against book income this year (itemize):	
5 Expenses recorded on books this year not deducted on this return (itemize):		a Depreciation $	
a Depreciation $		b Contributions carryover $	
b Contributions carryover $			
c Travel and entertainment $ Int. on tax-exempt bonds $500, Prem. on key employee ins. $2,600	3,100	9 Add lines 7 and 8	55,000
6 Add lines 1 through 5	105,000	10 Income (line 28, page 1)—line 6 less line 9	50,000

◆

Schedule M–2 reconciles unappropriated retained earnings at the beginning of the year with unappropriated retained earnings at year-end. Beginning balance plus net income per books, as entered on line 1 of Schedule M–1, less dividend distributions during the year equals ending retained earnings. Other sources of increases or decreases in retained earnings are also listed on Schedule M–2.

EXAMPLE 16

Assume the same facts as in Example 15. T Corporation's beginning balance in unappropriated retained earnings is $125,000, and T distributed a cash dividend of $30,000 to its shareholders during the year. Based on these further assumptions, T Corporation has the following Schedule M–2 for the current year.

Schedule M-2 Analysis of Unappropriated Retained Earnings per Books (Line 25, Schedule L) *(This schedule does not have to be completed if the total assets on line 15, column (d), of Schedule L are less than $25,000.)*

1 Balance at beginning of year	125,000	5 Distributions: a Cash	30,000
2 Net income per books	92,400	b Stock	
3 Other increases (itemize):		c Property	
		6 Other decreases (itemize):	
		7 Add lines 5 and 6	30,000
4 Add lines 1, 2, and 3	217,400	8 Balance at end of year (line 4 less line 7)	187,400

◆

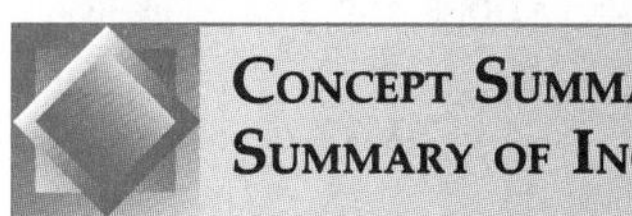

Concept Summary 20–1
Summary of Income Tax Consequences

	Individuals	Corporations
Computation of gross income	§ 61.	§ 61.
Computation of taxable income	§§ 62, 63(b) through (h).	§ 63(a). Concept of AGI has no relevance.
Deductions	Trade or business (§ 162); nonbusiness (§ 212); some personal and employee expenses (generally deductible as itemized deductions).	Trade or business (§ 162).
Charitable contributions	Limited in any tax year to 50% of AGI; 30% for long-term capital gain property unless election is made to reduce fair market value of gift; 20% for long-term capital gain property contributed to private nonoperating foundations.	Limited in any tax year to 10% of taxable income computed without regard to the charitable contribution deduction, net operating loss or capital loss carryback, and dividends received deduction.
	Time of deduction—year in which payment is made.	Time of deduction—year in which payment is made unless accrual basis taxpayer. Accrual basis corporation may take deduction in year preceding payment if contribution was authorized by board of directors by end of that year and contribution is paid by fifteenth day of third month of following year.
Casualty losses	$100 floor on nonbusiness casualty and theft losses; nonbusiness casualty and theft losses deductible only to extent losses exceed 10% of AGI.	Deductible in full.
Depreciation recapture for § 1250 property	Recaptured to extent accelerated depreciation exceeds straight-line.	20% of excess of amount that would be recaptured under § 1245 over amount recaptured under § 1250 is additional ordinary income under § 291.
Net operating loss	Adjusted for nonbusiness deductions over nonbusiness income and for personal and dependency exemptions.	Generally no adjustments.
Dividend exclusion or deduction	None.	Generally 70% of dividends received.
Long-term capital gains	Taxed at a rate no higher than 28%.	Taxed using regular corporate rates.
Capital losses	Only $3,000 of capital loss can offset ordinary income; loss is carried forward indefinitely to offset capital gains or ordinary income up to $3,000; carryovers remain long term or short term (as the case may be).	Can offset only capital gains; carried back three years and forward five years; carrybacks and carryovers are treated as short-term losses.
Passive activity losses	Generally deductible only against income from passive activities.	For regular corporations, no limitation on deductibility. Personal service corporations and certain closely held corporations, however, are subject to same limitations as imposed on individuals. A closely held corporation is one where 5 or fewer individuals own more than 50% of the stock either directly or indirectly.
Tax rates	Mildly progressive with three rates (15%, 28%, and 31%).	Mildly progressive with three rates (15%, 25%, and 34%); lower brackets phased out between $100,000 and $335,000 of taxable income.

	Individuals	Corporations
Alternative minimum tax	Applied at a 24% rate to AMT base (taxable income as modified by certain adjustments plus preference items minus exemption amount); exemption allowed depending on filing status (e.g., $40,000 for married filing jointly); exemption phase-out begins when AMTI reaches a certain amount (e.g., $150,000 for married filing jointly).	Applied at a 20% rate to AMT base (taxable income as modified by certain adjustments plus preference items minus exemption amount); $40,000 exemption allowed but phase-out begins once AMTI reaches $150,000; adjustments and tax preference items similar to those applicable to individuals but also include 75% of adjusted current earnings (ACE) over AMTI.

Capital Contributions

FORMING THE CORPORATION
◆

The receipt of money or property in exchange for capital stock produces neither recognized gain nor loss to the recipient corporation.[21] Gross income of a corporation does not include shareholders' contributions of money or property to the capital of the corporation.[22] Contributions by nonshareholders are also excluded from the gross income of a corporation.[23] The basis of the property (capital transfers by nonshareholders) to the corporation is zero.

EXAMPLE 17

A city donates land worth $200,000 to X Corporation as an inducement for X to locate in the city. The receipt of the land does not represent gross income. The land's basis to the corporation is zero. ◆

Thin Capitalization. The advantages of capitalizing a corporation with debt may be substantial. Interest on debt is deductible by the corporation, while dividend payments are not. Further, the shareholders are not taxed on loan repayments unless the payments exceed basis. If a company is capitalized solely with common stock, subsequent repayments of such capital contributions are likely to be treated as dividends to the shareholders.

In certain instances, the IRS will contend that debt is really an equity interest and will deny the shareholders the tax advantages of debt financing. If the debt instrument has too many features of stock, it may be treated as a form of stock, and principal and interest payments are treated as dividends.[24]

The form of the instrument will not assure debt treatment, but failure to observe certain formalities in creating the debt may lead to an assumption that the purported debt is a form of stock. The debt should be in proper legal form, bear a legitimate rate of interest, have a definite maturity date, and be repaid on a timely basis. Payments should not be contingent upon earnings. Further, the debt should not be subordinated to other liabilities, and proportionate holdings of stock and debt should be avoided or minimized.

21. § 1032.
22. § 118.
23. *Edwards v. Cuba Railroad Co.*, 1 USTC ¶139, 5 AFTR 5398, 45 S.Ct. 614 (USSC, 1925).
24. Section 385 lists several factors that might be used to determine whether a debtor-creditor relationship or a shareholder-corporation relationship exists.

Transfers to Controlled Corporations

Without special provisions in the Code, a transfer of property to a corporation in exchange for its stock would be a sale or exchange of property and would constitute a taxable transaction to the transferor shareholder. Section 351 provides for the nonrecognition of gain or loss upon such transfers of property if the transferors are in control of the corporation immediately after the transfer. Gain or loss is merely postponed in a manner similar to a like-kind exchange.[25] The following requirements must be met to qualify under § 351:

- The transferors must be in control of the corporation immediately after the exchange. *Control* is defined as ownership of at least 80 percent of the total combined voting power of all classes of stock entitled to vote and at least 80 percent of the total number of shares of all other classes of stock.[26]
- Realized gain (but not loss) is recognized to the extent that the transferors receive property other than stock. Such nonqualifying property is commonly referred to as boot.[27]

If the requirements of § 351 are satisfied and no boot is involved, nonrecognition of gain or loss is *mandatory.*

Basis Considerations and Computation of Gain. The nonrecognition of gain or loss is accompanied by a carryover of basis. The basis of stock received in a § 351 transfer is determined as follows:

- Start with the adjusted basis of the property transferred by the shareholder.
- Add any gain recognized by the shareholder as a result of the transfer.
- Subtract the fair market value of any boot received by the shareholder from the corporation.[28]

The basis of properties received by the corporation is the basis in the hands of the transferor increased by the amount of any gain recognized to the transferor shareholder.[29]

EXAMPLE 18

A and B, individuals, form X Corporation. A transfers property with an adjusted basis of $30,000 and a fair market value of $60,000 for 50% of the stock. B transfers property with an adjusted basis of $40,000 and a fair market value of $60,000 for the remaining 50% of the stock. The realized gain ($30,000 for A and $20,000 for B) is not recognized on the transfer because the transfer qualifies under § 351. The basis of the stock to A is $30,000, and the basis of the stock to B is $40,000. X Corporation has a basis of $30,000 in the property transferred by A and a basis of $40,000 in the property transferred by B. ◆

EXAMPLE 19

C and D form Y Corporation with the following investments: C transfers property (adjusted basis of $30,000 and fair market value of $70,000), and D transfers cash of $60,000. Each receives 50 shares of the Y Corporation stock, but C also receives $10,000

25. Refer to the discussion in Chapter 15.
26. § 368(c).
27. For transfers before October 3, 1989, certain long-term debt (i.e., securities) of the corporation received by the shareholder was not treated as boot.
28. § 358(a).
29. § 362(a).

in cash. Assume each share of the Y Corporation stock is worth $1,200. C's realized gain is $40,000, determined as follows:

Value of the Y Corporation stock received [50 (shares) × $1,200 (value per share)]	$ 60,000
Cash received	10,000
Amount realized	$ 70,000
Less basis of property transferred	(30,000)
Realized gain	$ 40,000

C's recognized gain is $10,000, the lesser of the realized gain ($40,000) or the fair market value of the boot received ($10,000). C's basis in the Y Corporation stock is $30,000, computed as follows:

Basis in the property transferred	$ 30,000
Plus recognized gain	10,000
	$ 40,000
Less boot received	(10,000)
Basis to C of the Y Corporation stock	$ 30,000

Y Corporation's basis in the property transferred by C is $40,000 [$30,000 (basis of the property to C) + $10,000 (gain recognized by C)]. D neither realizes nor recognizes gain or loss and will have a basis in the Y Corporation stock of $60,000. ◆

Shareholders who receive noncash boot have a basis in the property equal to the fair market value. The receipt of stock for the performance of *services* always results in ordinary income to the transferor shareholder. An example might be an attorney who does not charge a fee for incorporating a business but instead receives the value equivalent in stock of the newly formed corporation.

OPERATING THE CORPORATION
◆

Dividend Distributions

Corporate distributions of cash or property to shareholders are treated as ordinary dividend income to the extent the corporation has accumulated *or* current earnings and profits (E & P).[30] In determining the source of the distribution, a dividend is deemed to have been made initially from current E & P.

EXAMPLE 20

As of January 1, 1992, Y Corporation has a deficit in accumulated E & P of $30,000. For tax year 1992, it has current E & P of $10,000. In 1992, the corporation distributes $5,000 to its shareholders. The $5,000 distribution is treated as a taxable dividend, since it is deemed to have been made from current E & P. This is the case even though Y Corporation still has a deficit in its accumulated E & P at the end of 1992. ◆

If a corporate distribution is not covered by E & P (either current or past), it is treated as a return of capital (refer to the discussion of the recovery of capital doctrine in Chapter 4). This treatment allows the shareholder to apply the amount of the distribution against the basis of the stock investment and therefore represents a nontaxable return of capital. Any amount received in

30. § 316.

excess of the stock basis is classified as a capital gain (if the stock is a capital asset in the hands of the shareholder).

Example 21

When X Corporation has no E & P (either current or accumulated), it distributes cash of $30,000 to its sole shareholder, Ms. T. The basis of Ms. T's stock investment is $20,000. Based on these facts, the $30,000 distribution Ms. T receives is accounted for as follows:

Return of capital (nontaxable)	$20,000
Capital gain	10,000
Total amount of distribution	$30,000

After the distribution, Ms. T has a basis of zero in her stock investment. ◆

Concept of Earnings and Profits. The term *earnings and profits* is not defined in the Code, although § 312 does include certain transactions that affect E & P. Although E & P and the accounting concept of retained earnings have certain similarities, they differ in numerous respects. For example, although a nontaxable stock dividend is treated as a capitalization of retained earnings for accounting purposes, it does not decrease E & P for tax purposes. Taxable dividends do reduce E & P but cannot yield a deficit. Referring to Example 21, after the distribution, X Corporation's E & P remains zero rather than being a negative amount.

Generally, *current E & P* for a taxable year is taxable income plus or minus certain adjustments (e.g., an addition is made for tax-exempt income). Federal income taxes are subtracted from taxable income in arriving at current E & P. *Accumulated E & P* is the sum of the corporation's past current E & P. A detailed discussion of the concept of E & P is beyond the scope of this chapter.

Property Dividends. A distribution of property to a shareholder is measured by the fair market value of the property on the date of distribution. The shareholder's basis in the property received is also the fair market value.[31]

Example 22

P Corporation has E & P of $60,000. It distributes land with a fair market value of $50,000 (adjusted basis of $30,000) to its sole shareholder, T (an individual). T has a taxable dividend of $50,000 and a basis in the land of $50,000. ◆

A corporation that distributes appreciated property to its shareholders as a dividend must recognize the amount of the appreciation as gain.

Example 23

Assume the same facts as in Example 22. P Corporation must recognize a gain of $20,000 on the distribution it made to T. ◆

However, if the property distributed has a basis in excess of its fair market value, the distributing corporation cannot recognize any loss.

Constructive Dividends. Many taxpayers mistakenly assume that dividend consequences do not take place unless the distribution carries the formalities of

31. § 301.

a dividend (declaration date, record date, payment date). They further assume that dividends must be paid out to all shareholders on a pro rata basis. This may not be the case when closely held corporations are involved. Here, the key to dividend treatment depends upon whether the shareholders derive a benefit from the corporation that cannot be otherwise classified (e.g., reasonable salary). The following are examples of *constructive dividends*:

- Salaries paid to shareholder-employees that are not reasonable (refer to Example 5 in Chapter 6).
- Interest on debt owed by the corporation to shareholders that is reclassified as equity because the corporation is thinly capitalized (refer to the earlier discussion in this chapter).
- Excessive rent paid by a corporation for the use of shareholder property. Whether the rent is excessive is to be tested by use of the arm's length standard (refer to Example 24 in Chapter 1).
- Advances to shareholders that are not bona fide loans.
- Interest-free (or below-market) loans to shareholders. In this situation, the dividend component is the difference between the interest provided for, if any, and that calculated using the market rate.
- Shareholder use of corporate property for less than an arm's length rate.
- Absorption by the corporation of a shareholder's personal expenses.
- Bargain purchase of corporate property by shareholders.

Like regular dividends, constructive dividends must be covered by E & P to carry dividend income consequences to the shareholders. As noted above, however, constructive dividends need not be available to all shareholders on a pro rata basis.

Although dividends reduce the E & P of a corporation, they are not deductible for income tax purposes. In this regard, certain constructive dividends could have subtle tax consequences for all parties concerned.

Example 24

Z Corporation makes a loan to one of its shareholders, T. No interest is provided for, but application of the market rate would produce $20,000 of interest for the term of the loan. Presuming the loan is bona fide, the following results occur:

- T has dividend income of $20,000.
- Z Corporation has interest income of $20,000.
- T might obtain an interest deduction of $20,000.

Not only does Z Corporation have to recognize income of $20,000, but it also obtains no income tax deduction for the $20,000 constructive dividend. ◆

Example 25

Assume the same facts as in Example 24, except that the loan to T was not bona fide. In this event, the full amount of the loan is regarded as a dividend to T. Therefore, the interest element is not a factor, since no bona fide loan ever existed. ◆

Stock Redemptions

If a corporation redeems a shareholder's stock, one of two possible outcomes occurs:

- The redemption may qualify as a sale or exchange under § 302 or § 303. In that case, capital gain or loss treatment usually applies to the qualifying shareholders.

- The redemption will be treated as a dividend under § 301, provided the distributing corporation has E & P.

EXAMPLE 26

T owns 300 shares of X Corporation stock as an investment. The shares have a basis to T of $100 each, for a total of $30,000. When the fair market value of a share is $200, X Corporation redeems 200 of T's shares. If the redemption qualifies for sale or exchange treatment, the result is a capital gain to T of $20,000 [$40,000 (redemption price) − $20,000 (basis in 200 shares)]. T's basis in the remaining 100 shares is $10,000 [$30,000 (basis in the original shares) − $20,000 (basis in the shares redeemed)]. ◆

EXAMPLE 27

Assume the same facts as in Example 26, except that the redemption does not qualify for sale or exchange treatment. Presuming adequate E & P, the redemption results in $40,000 dividend income. T's basis in the remaining 100 shares now becomes $30,000, or $300 per share. ◆

A stock redemption qualifies as a sale or exchange if it meets any of the safe harbors of § 302 or § 303. For a discussion of these provisions, see *West's Federal Taxation: Corporations, Partnerships, Estates, and Trusts*.

LIQUIDATING THE CORPORATION

◆

Unlike dividend distributions or stock redemptions, where the distributing corporation continues its operations, *liquidating distributions* occur during the termination of the business. All debts are paid, and any remaining corporate assets are distributed pro rata to the shareholders in exchange for their stock. Once these distributions are completed, the corporation undergoing liquidation will cease to be a separate tax entity.

General Rule of § 331

Under the general rule, the shareholders recognize gain or loss in a corporate liquidation. The amount of recognized gain or loss is measured by the difference between the fair market value of the assets received from the corporation and the adjusted basis of the stock surrendered. The shareholders recognize capital gain or loss if the stock is a capital asset.[32]

EXAMPLE 28

Pursuant to a complete liquidation, X Corporation distributes $100,000 in cash to T, one of its shareholders. If T's basis in the stock surrendered is $40,000, T must recognize a gain of $60,000. If T held the stock as an investment, the $60,000 gain will be capital gain—either short term or long term (depending on the holding period). ◆

Exception to the General Rule

Section 332 is an exception to the general rule that the shareholder recognizes gain or loss on a corporate liquidation. If a parent corporation liquidates a subsidiary corporation in which it owns at least 80 percent of the voting power and value of the stock, no gain or loss is recognized by the parent company. The subsidiary must distribute all of its property in complete liquidation of all of its

32. If the stock is held as an investment, which is usually the case, gain or loss will be capital. Stock owned by a broker probably will be inventory and therefore will not constitute a capital asset. Thus, the gain or loss on this type of stock is ordinary and not capital.

stock within the taxable year or within three years from the close of the tax year in which the first distribution occurred.

Basis Determination—§§ 334 and 338

General Rule. Where gain or loss is recognized upon the complete liquidation of a corporation, the basis of the property received by the shareholders is the property's fair market value.[33]

Subsidiary Liquidation Basis Rules. The general rule is that the property received by the parent corporation in a complete liquidation of its subsidiary under § 332 has the same basis it had in the hands of the subsidiary (a carryover basis).[34] The parent's basis in the stock of the liquidated subsidiary disappears.

EXAMPLE 29

P, the parent corporation, has a basis of $20,000 in the stock of S Corporation, a subsidiary in which it owns 85% of all classes of stock. P Corporation purchased the stock of S Corporation 10 years ago. In the current year, P Corporation liquidates S Corporation and receives assets worth $50,000 with a tax basis to S Corporation of $40,000. P Corporation would have a basis of $40,000 in the assets, with a potential gain upon sale of $10,000. P Corporation's original $20,000 basis in the S Corporation stock disappears. ◆

An exception to the carryover of basis rule is provided in § 338. Under this exception, the parent company may elect to receive a basis for the assets equal to the adjusted basis of the stock of the subsidiary. In effect, the initial acquisition of the subsidiary is treated as if the parent company had acquired the assets (rather than the stock) of the subsidiary.

The following requirements must be met:

- The parent must *purchase* at least 80 percent of the total combined voting power of all classes of stock and at least 80 percent of all other classes of stock (except nonvoting preferred) within a 12-month period.
- By the fifteenth day of the ninth month beginning after the month in which the 80 percent control requirement noted above is met, the parent corporation *elects* to have § 338 apply.

EXAMPLE 30

P Corporation acquires 100% of the stock of S Corporation for $1,000,000 cash in a taxable purchase transaction on January 1, 1992. On February 1, 1992, S Corporation is liquidated into P under § 338. The adjusted basis of S Corporation's net assets is $800,000. Since P acquired at least 80% of the stock in a taxable purchase transaction and made a timely election under § 338, P Corporation's basis in the net assets of S is $1,000,000 (the amount paid for the S stock). The transaction is treated as if P acquired the S Corporation assets for $1,000,000 instead of acquiring S's stock for $1,000,000. ◆

Effect of the Liquidation on the Corporation

Having examined what happens to the shareholder upon the liquidation of a corporation, what happens at the corporate level? Here, § 336 applies to dictate the tax consequences to the corporation being liquidated.

33. § 334(a).

34. § 334(b)(1).

Under § 336, the distributing corporation recognizes gain or loss upon complete liquidation. In this regard, it does not matter whether the corporation distributes the property in-kind (*as is*) to the shareholders or first sells the property and then distributes the proceeds.

EXAMPLE 31

Pursuant to a complete liquidation, R Corporation distributes the following assets to its shareholders: undeveloped land held as an investment (basis of $150,000 and fair market value of $140,000) and marketable securities (basis of $160,000 and fair market value of $200,000). Since R Corporation is treated as if it had sold the property, a gain of $40,000 results from the securities, and a loss of $10,000 results from the land. ◆

The deductibility of losses may be restricted by the related-party rules of § 267 (refer to Chapter 6) if certain conditions exist (e.g., the distributions are not pro rata).[35]

A wholly owned subsidiary corporation does not recognize gain or loss when the parent corporation uses the basis option of § 334(b)(1). The reason for the special treatment is that under § 334(b)(1), the subsidiary's basis (and all other tax attributes) in the assets carries over to the parent corporation.

THE S ELECTION

Justification for the Election

Numerous nontax reasons exist for operating a business in the corporate form (e.g., limited liability). Consequently, the existence of income tax disadvantages (e.g., double taxation of corporate income and shareholder dividends) should not deter business people from using the corporate form. To prevent tax considerations from interfering with the exercise of sound business judgment, Congress enacted Subchapter S of the Code.

To qualify for S status, the corporation must be a *small business corporation*.[36] This includes any corporation that has the following characteristics:

- Is a domestic corporation.
- Is not a member of an affiliated group.
- Has no more than 35 shareholders.
- Has as its shareholders only individuals, estates, and certain trusts.
- Does not have a nonresident alien as a shareholder.
- Has only one class of stock outstanding.

These characteristics must continue to exist if an electing S corporation is to maintain S status.

Making the Election. The election is made by filing Form 2553, and *all* shareholders must consent. Special rules apply to husbands and wives where stock is jointly held and to minors.

To be effective for the current year, the election must be filed anytime during the preceding taxable year or on or before the fifteenth day of the third month of the current year.[37]

EXAMPLE 32

T, a calendar year taxpayer, is a regular corporation that wishes to elect S status for 1992. If the election is filed anytime from January 1, 1991, through March 15, 1992, it will be effective for 1992. ◆

35. § 336(d).
36. § 1361(b).
37. § 1362.

Loss of the Election. Termination of the S election may occur *voluntarily* (a majority of the shareholders file to revoke the election) or *involuntarily.* The termination may occur involuntarily in *any* of the following ways:

- The corporation ceases to qualify as a small business corporation (e.g., the number of shareholders exceeds 35, or a partnership becomes a shareholder).
- The corporation has passive investment income (e.g., interest, dividends) in excess of 25 percent of gross receipts for a period of three consecutive years. This possibility applies only if the corporation was previously a regular corporation and has earnings and profits from that period.

If the holders of a *majority* of the shares consent to a voluntary revocation of S status, the election to revoke must be made on or before the fifteenth day of the third month of the tax year to be effective for that year.

EXAMPLE 33

The shareholders of T Corporation, a calendar year S corporation, elect to revoke the election on January 4, 1992. Assuming the election is duly executed and timely filed, T Corporation will become a regular corporation for calendar year 1992. If the election to revoke is not made until June 1992, T Corporation will not become a regular corporation until calendar year 1993. ◆

Suppose the shareholders in Example 33 file the election to revoke on January 4, 1992, but do not want the revocation to take place until 1993. If the election so specifies, T Corporation will cease to have S status as of January 1, 1993.

In the case where S status is lost because of a disqualifying act (involuntarily), the loss of the election takes effect as of the date on which the event occurs.

EXAMPLE 34

T Corporation has been a calendar year S corporation for several years. On August 13, 1992, one of its shareholders sells her stock to Y Corporation. Since T Corporation no longer satisfies the definition of a small business corporation (it has another corporation as a shareholder), the election has been involuntarily terminated. For calendar year 1992, therefore, T Corporation will be an S corporation through August 12 and a regular corporation from August 13 through December 31, 1992. ◆

In the event the election is lost through a violation of the passive investment income limitation, the loss of S status starts at the beginning of the next tax year.

Barring certain exceptions, the loss of the election places the corporation in a five-year holding period before S status can be reelected.

Operational Rules

The S corporation is primarily a tax-reporting rather than a taxpaying entity. In this respect, the entity is taxed much like a partnership.[38] Under the conduit concept, the taxable income and losses of an S corporation flow through to the shareholders who report them on their personal income tax returns.

To ascertain the annual tax consequences to each shareholder, it is necessary to carry out two steps at the S corporation level. First, all corporate transactions

38. This is not to imply that an S corporation is always free from the income tax. For example, a tax may be imposed on certain built-in gains or certain excessive passive investment income.

that will flow through to the shareholders on an *as is* basis under the conduit approach must be set aside. Second, what remains is aggregated as the taxable income of the S corporation and is allocated to each shareholder on a per-share and per-day of stock ownership basis.[39]

Separately Stated Items. The following are some of the items that do not lose their identity as they pass through the S corporation and are therefore picked up by each shareholder on an *as is* basis:

- Tax-exempt income.
- Long-term and short-term capital gains and losses.
- Section 1231 gains and losses.
- Charitable contributions.
- Foreign tax credits.
- Depletion.
- Nonbusiness income or loss under § 212.
- Intangible drilling costs.
- Investment interest, income, and expenses covered under § 163(d).
- Certain portfolio income.
- Passive activity gains, losses, and credits under § 469.
- AMT adjustments and tax preference items.

The reason these items are separately stated is that each may lead to a different tax result when combined with a particular shareholder's other transactions.

EXAMPLE 35

X and Y are equal shareholders in P Corporation (an S corporation). For calendar year 1992, each must account for one-half of a corporate short-term capital gain of $6,000. X has no other capital asset transactions, and Y has a short-term capital loss of $3,000 from the sale of stock in ABC Corporation. In terms of overall effect, the difference between the two taxpayers is significant. Although both must report the short-term capital gain pass-through, Y will neutralize its inclusion in gross income by offsetting it with the $3,000 short-term capital loss from the sale of the stock in ABC Corporation. To X, the short-term capital gain pass-through results in additional ordinary income of $3,000. ◆

Taxable Income. After the separately stated items have been removed, the balance represents the taxable income of the S corporation. In arriving at taxable income, the dividends received deduction (§ 243) and the net operating loss deduction (§ 172) are not allowed. An S corporation does come under the regular corporate rules, however, for purposes of amortization of organizational expenditures (§ 248).

Once taxable income has been determined, it passes through to each shareholder as of the last day of the S corporation's tax year.

EXAMPLE 36

X Corporation, a calendar year S corporation, had the following transactions during the current year:

39. § 1366.

Sales		$ 40,000
Cost of goods sold		(23,000)
Other income		
*Tax-exempt interest	$ 300	
*Long-term capital gain	500	800
Other expenses		
*Charitable contributions	$ 400	
Advertising expense	1,500	
Other operating expenses	2,000	
*Short-term capital loss	150	(4,050)
Net income per books		$ 13,750

When the items that are to be separately stated (those preceded by an asterisk [*]) and shown *as is* by each shareholder are withdrawn, X Corporation has the following taxable income:

Sales		$ 40,000
Cost of goods sold		(23,000)
Other expenses		
Advertising expense	$1,500	
Other operating expenses	2,000	(3,500)
Taxable income		$ 13,500

◆

EXAMPLE 37

If T owned 10% of the stock in X Corporation (refer to Example 36) during all of the current year, he must account for the following:

Separately stated items	
Tax-exempt interest	$ 30
Long-term capital gain	50
Charitable contributions	40
Short-term capital loss	15
Taxable income (10% of $13,500)	1,350

Some of the separately stated items need not be reported on T's individual income tax return (e.g., the tax-exempt interest). Others must be reported but may not lead to tax consequences. T's share of X Corporation's taxable income ($1,350) is picked up by T as ordinary income. ◆

Treatment of Losses. As previously noted, separately stated loss items (e.g., capital losses, § 1231 losses) flow through to the shareholders on an *as is* basis. Their treatment by a shareholder depends on the shareholder's individual income tax position. If the S corporation's taxable income determination results in an operating loss, it also passes through to the shareholders. As is the case with separately stated items, the amount of the loss each shareholder receives depends on the stock ownership during the year.

EXAMPLE 38

In 1992, Y Corporation (a calendar year S corporation) incurred an operating loss of $36,600. During 1992, T's ownership in Y Corporation was as follows: 20% for 200 days and 30% for 166 days. T's share of the loss is determined as follows:

($36,600 × 200/366) × 20%	=	$4,000
($36,600 × 166/366) × 30%	=	4,980
Total loss		$8,980

Presuming the basis limitation does not come into play (see the following discussion), T deducts $8,980 in arriving at adjusted gross income. ◆

Basis Determination. A shareholder's *basis* in the stock of an S corporation, like that of a regular corporation, is the original investment plus additional capital contributions less return of capital distributions. At this point, however, the symmetry disappears. Generally, basis is increased by the pass-through of income items (including those separately stated) and decreased by the loss items (including those separately stated).[40]

EXAMPLE 39

In 1992, M Corporation is formed with an investment of $100,000, of which T contributed $20,000 for a 20% stock interest. A timely S election is made, and for 1992, M Corporation earns taxable income of $15,000. T's basis in her stock investment now becomes $23,000 [$20,000 (original capital contribution) + $3,000 (the 20% share of the corporation's taxable income assigned to T)]. ◆

Distributions by an S corporation reduce the basis of a shareholder's stock investment. However, if the amount of the distribution exceeds basis, the excess normally receives capital gain treatment.

As previously noted, operating losses of an S corporation pass through to the shareholders and reduce the basis in their stock investment. Because the basis of the stock cannot fall below zero, an excess loss is then applied against the basis of any loans the shareholder may have made to the corporation.

EXAMPLE 40

Z Corporation, a calendar year S corporation, has an operating loss of $60,000 for 1992. T, a 50% shareholder, has an adjusted basis in his stock investment of $25,000 and has made loans to the corporation of $5,000. Based on these facts, T may take full advantage of the $30,000 loss (50% of $60,000) on his 1992 individual income tax return. T's basis in the stock and the loans must be reduced accordingly, and both will be zero after the pass-through. ◆

In the event the basis limitation precludes an operating loss from being absorbed, the loss can be carried forward and deducted when and if it is covered by basis.

EXAMPLE 41

Assume the same facts as in Example 40, except that T had not made any loans to Z Corporation. Further assume that Z Corporation has taxable income of $15,000 in the following year (1993). T's tax situation for 1992 and 1993 is summarized as follows:

Ordinary loss for 1992	$25,000
Restoration of stock basis in 1993 (50% of $15,000)	7,500
Income to be reported in 1993	7,500
Loss allowed for 1993 ($30,000 − $25,000)	5,000
Basis in stock account after 1993 ($7,500 − $5,000)	2,500

40. § 1367.

Thus, T's unabsorbed loss of $5,000 from 1992 carries over to 1993 and is applied against the $7,500 of ordinary income for that year. ◆

Nature of Partnership Taxation

Unlike corporations, partnerships are not considered separate taxable entities. Each member of a partnership is subject to income tax on his or her distributive share of the partnership's income, even if an actual distribution is not made. The tax return (Form 1065) required of a partnership serves only to provide information necessary in determining the character and amount of each partner's distributive share of the partnership's income and expense. Because a partnership acts as a conduit, items that pass through to the partners do not lose their identity. For example, tax-exempt income earned by a partnership is picked up by the partners as tax-exempt income. In this regard, partnerships function in much the same fashion as S corporations, which also serve as conduits.

A partnership is considered a separate taxable entity for purposes of making various elections and selecting its taxable year, method of depreciation, and accounting method. A partnership is also treated as a separate legal entity under civil law with the right to own property in its own name and to transact business free from the personal debts of its partners.

Partnership Formation

Recognition of Gain or Loss. Section 721 contains the general rule that no gain or loss is recognized by a partnership or any of its partners on the contribution of property in exchange for a capital interest in the partnership. The general rule also applies to all subsequent contributions of property.

There are certain exceptions to the nonrecognition of gain or loss rule including the following:

- If the transfer of property by a partner to the partnership results in the receipt of money or other consideration by the partner, the transaction will be treated as a sale or exchange rather than as a contribution of capital.
- If a partnership interest is received in exchange for services rendered or to be rendered by the partner to the partnership, the fair market value of the transferred capital interest is regarded as compensation for services rendered. In such cases, the recipient of the capital interest must recognize the amount as ordinary income in the year actually or constructively received.
- If property that is subject to a liability in excess of its basis is contributed to a partnership, the contributing partner may recognize gain.

Basis of a Partnership Interest. The contributing *partner's basis* in the partnership interest received is the sum of money contributed plus the adjusted basis of any other property transferred to the partnership.

EXAMPLE 42

In return for the contribution of property (with a basis of $50,000 and a fair market value of $80,000) and cash of $10,000 to the KLM Partnership, T receives a 10% capital interest worth $90,000. Although T has a realized gain of $30,000 ($90,000 − $60,000) on the transfer, none of the gain is recognized. The basis of T's interest in the KLM Partnership is $60,000 [$50,000 (basis of property contributed) + $10,000 (cash contribution)]. ◆

A partner's basis in the partnership interest is determined without regard to any amount reflected on the partnership's books as capital, equity, or a similar account.

EXAMPLE 43

U and V form an equal partnership with a cash contribution of $30,000 from U and a property contribution (adjusted basis of $18,000 and fair market value of $30,000) from V. Although the books of the UV Partnership may reflect a credit of $30,000 to each partner's capital account, only U has a tax basis of $30,000 in his partnership interest. V's tax basis in his partnership interest is $18,000, the amount of his tax basis in the property contributed to the partnership. ◆

After its initial determination, the basis of a partnership interest is subject to continuous fluctuations. A partner's basis is increased by additional contributions and the sum of his or her current and prior years' distributive share of the following:

- Taxable income of the partnership, including capital gains.
- Tax-exempt income of the partnership.
- The excess of the deductions for depletion over the basis of the partnership's property subject to depletion.[41]

Similarly, the basis of a partner's interest is decreased, but not below zero, by distributions of partnership property and by the sum of the current and prior years' distributive share of the following:

- Partnership losses, including capital losses.
- Partnership expenditures that are not deductible in computing taxable income or loss and that are not capital expenditures.

Changes in the liabilities (including trade accounts payable, bank loans, etc.) of a partnership also affect the basis of a partnership interest. A partner's basis is increased by his or her assumption of partnership liabilities and by his or her pro rata share of liabilities incurred by the partnership. Likewise, the partner's basis is decreased by the amount of any personal liabilities assumed by the partnership and by the pro rata share of any decreases in the liabilities of the partnership.

EXAMPLE 44

X, Y, and Z form the XYZ Partnership with the following contributions: cash of $50,000 from X for a 50% interest in capital and profits, cash of $25,000 from Y for a 25% interest, and property valued at $33,000 from Z for a 25% interest. The property contributed by Z has an adjusted basis of $15,000 and is subject to a mortgage of $8,000, which is assumed by the partnership. Z's basis in his interest in the XYZ Partnership is $9,000, determined as follows:

Adjusted basis of Z's contributed property	$15,000
Less portion of mortgage assumed by X and Y and treated as a distribution of money to Z (75% of $8,000)	(6,000)
Basis of Z's interest in XYZ Partnership	$ 9,000

◆

41. § 705(a).

EXAMPLE 45

Assuming the same facts as in Example 44, X and Y have a basis in their partnership interests of $54,000 and $27,000, respectively.

	X	Y
Cash contribution	$50,000	$25,000
Plus portion of mortgage assumed and treated as an additional cash contribution:		
(50% of $8,000)	4,000	
(25% of $8,000)		2,000
Basis of interest in XYZ Partnership	$54,000	$27,000

◆

Partnership's Basis in Contributed Property. Section 723 states that the *basis of property* contributed to a partnership by a partner is the adjusted basis of the property to the contributing partner at the time of the contribution. Additionally, the holding period of the property for the partnership includes the period during which the property was held by the contributing partner. This is logical, since the partnership's basis in the property is the same basis the property had in the hands of the partner.[42]

EXAMPLE 46

In 1992, R contributed equipment with an adjusted basis of $10,000 and fair market value of $30,000 to the RST Partnership in exchange for a one-third interest in the partnership. No gain or loss is recognized by R. The basis in the equipment is $10,000 to the RST Partnership. If R had acquired the equipment in 1986, the holding period for the RST Partnership would include the period from 1986 through 1992. ◆

Partnership Operation

Measuring and Reporting Partnership Income. Although a partnership is not subject to Federal income taxation, it is required to determine its taxable income and file an income tax return for information purposes.[43] The tax return, Form 1065, is due on the fifteenth day of the fourth month following the close of the taxable year of the partnership.

In measuring and reporting partnership income, certain transactions must be segregated and reported separately on the partnership return. Items such as charitable contributions, capital gains and losses, and foreign taxes are excluded from partnership taxable income and are allocated separately to the partners.[44] These items must be segregated and allocated separately because they affect the computation of various exclusions, deductions, and credits at the individual partner level. For example, one of the partners may have made personal charitable contributions in excess of the ceiling limitations on his or her individual tax return. Therefore, partnership charitable contributions are excluded from partnership taxable income and are reported separately on the partnership return.

A second step in the measurement and reporting process is the computation of the partnership's ordinary income or loss. The taxable income of a partnership is computed in the same manner as the taxable income of an individual taxpayer. However, a partnership is not allowed the following deductions:[45]

---

42. § 1223(2).
43. § 6031.
44. § 702(a).
45. § 703(a).

- The deduction for personal and dependency exemptions.
- The deduction for taxes paid to foreign countries or possessions of the United States.
- The deduction for charitable contributions.
- The deduction for net operating losses.
- The additional itemized deductions allowed individuals in §§ 211 through 219.

The partnership's ordinary income or loss and each of the items requiring separate treatment are reported in the partnership's information return and allocated to the partners in accordance with their distributive shares.

Limitation on Partner's Share of Losses. A partner's deduction of the distributive share of partnership losses (including capital losses) could be limited. The limitation is the adjusted basis of the partnership interest at the end of the partnership year in which the losses were incurred.

The limitation for partnership loss deductions is similar to that applicable on losses of S corporations. Like S corporation losses, partnership losses may be carried forward by the partner and utilized against future increases in the basis of the partnership interest. Such increases might result from additional capital contributions to the partnership, from additional partnership liabilities, or from future partnership income.

EXAMPLE 47

C and D do business as the CD Partnership, sharing profits and losses equally. All parties use the calendar year for tax purposes. As of January 1, 1992, C's basis in his partnership interest is $25,000. The partnership sustained an operating loss of $80,000 in 1992 and earned a profit of $70,000 in 1993. For the calendar year 1992, C may claim only $25,000 of his $40,000 distributive share of the partnership loss (one-half of the $80,000 loss). As a result, the basis in his partnership interest is reduced to zero as of January 1, 1993, and he must carry forward the remaining $15,000 of partnership losses. ◆

EXAMPLE 48

Assuming the same facts as in Example 47, what are the income tax consequences for C in 1993? Since the partnership earned a profit of $70,000 for the calendar year 1993, C reports income from the partnership of $20,000 ($35,000 distributive share of income for 1993 less the $15,000 loss not allowed for 1992). The adjusted basis of his partnership interest now becomes $20,000. ◆

Transactions between Partner and Partnership. A partner engaging in a transaction with the partnership is generally regarded as a nonpartner or outsider. However, the Code includes certain exceptions to prevent unwarranted tax avoidance. For instance, under § 707(b)(1), losses from the sale or exchange of property are disallowed if they arise in either of the following cases:

- Between a partnership and a person whose direct or indirect interest in the capital or profits of the partnership is more than 50 percent.
- Between two partnerships in which the same persons own more than a 50 percent interest in the capital or profits.

If one of the purchasers later sells the property, any gain realized will be recognized only to the extent that it exceeds the loss previously disallowed.

EXAMPLE 49

R owns a 60% interest in the capital and profits of the RST Partnership. In the current year, R sells property with an adjusted basis of $50,000 to the partnership for its fair market value of $35,000. The $15,000 loss is not deductible since R's ownership interest is more than 50%. If the RST Partnership later sells the property for $40,000, none of the $5,000 (sale price of $40,000 less adjusted basis to partnership of $35,000) gain will be recognized since it is offset by $5,000 of the previously disallowed loss of $15,000. The unused loss of $10,000, however, is of no tax benefit either to the partnership or to R. ◆

Payments made by a partnership to one of its partners for services rendered or for the use of capital, to the extent they are determined without regard to the income of the partnership, are treated by the partnership in the same manner as payments made to a person who is not a partner. Referred to as *guaranteed payments* under § 707(c), these payments are generally deductible by the partnership as a business expense. The payments must be reported as ordinary income by the receiving partner. Their deductibility distinguishes guaranteed payments from a partner's distributive share of income that is not deductible by the partnership.

EXAMPLE 50

Under the terms of the LMN Partnership agreement, N is entitled to a fixed annual salary of $18,000 without regard to the income of the partnership. He is also to share in the profits and losses of the partnership as an equal partner. After deducting the guaranteed payment, the partnership has $36,000 of ordinary income. N must include $30,000 as ordinary income on his income tax return for his tax year with or within which the partnership tax year ends ($18,000 guaranteed payment plus his one-third distributive share of partnership income of $12,000). ◆

Other Partnership Considerations. Complex tax provisions involving liquidating and nonliquidating distributions and the sale of a partnership interest are beyond the scope of this text and are discussed in depth in *West's Federal Taxation: Corporations, Partnerships, Estates, and Trusts*.

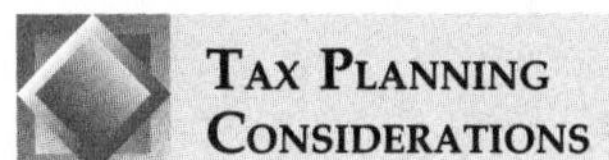
TAX PLANNING CONSIDERATIONS

Corporate versus Noncorporate Forms of Business Organization

The decision to use the corporate form in conducting a trade or business must be weighed carefully. Besides the nontax aspects of the corporate form (limited liability, continuity of life, free transferability of interest, centralized management), tax ramifications play an important role in any such decision. Close attention should be paid to the following:

1. The corporate form means the imposition of the corporate income tax. Corporate-source income will be taxed twice—once as earned by the corporation and again when distributed to the shareholders. Since dividends are not deductible, a strong incentive exists in a closely held corporation to structure corporate distributions in a deductible form. Profits may be bailed out by the shareholders in the form of salaries, interest, or rents. These procedures lead to a multitude of problems, one of which, the reclassification of debt as equity, has been discussed. The problems of unreasonable salaries and rents were discussed in Chapter 6.
2. Assuming the current tax rates remain in effect, the top rates definitely favor the noncorporate taxpayer over the corporate taxpayer. For example,

the top rate for individuals is 31 percent for 1992. For corporations, the top rate is 34 percent. The differential is not so pronounced, however, if one presumes a shareholder with a top rate of 31 percent and a corporation that limits its taxable income to $100,000. This approach avoids the phase-out of the 15 percent and 25 percent lower brackets. Here, the time value of the taxes saved (by not distributing dividends and postponing the effect of the double tax) could make operating a business in the corporate form advantageous.

3. Corporate-source income loses its identity as it passes through the corporation to the shareholders. Thus, items possessing preferential tax treatment (e.g., interest on municipal bonds) are not taxed as such to the shareholders.
4. As noted earlier, it may be difficult for shareholders to recover some or all of their investment in the corporation without an ordinary income result. Recall that most corporate distributions are treated as dividends to the extent of the corporation's earnings and profits. Structuring the capital of the corporation to include debt is a partial solution to this problem. Thus, the shareholder-creditor could recoup part of his or her investment through the tax-free payment of principal. Too much debt, however, may lead to the debt being reclassified as equity.
5. Corporate losses cannot be passed through to the shareholders.
6. The liquidation of a corporation may generate tax consequences to both the corporation and its shareholders.
7. The corporate form provides the shareholders with the opportunity to be treated as employees for tax purposes if they render services to the corporation. This status makes a number of attractive tax-sheltered fringe benefits available (e.g., group term life insurance). These benefits are not available to partners and sole proprietors.

Regular Corporation versus S Status

Due to the pass-through concept, the use of S status generally avoids the income tax at the corporate level, bringing the individual income tax into play. As noted in item 2 in the previous section, the differential between the maximum rates applicable to noncorporate and corporate taxpayers generally makes the former more advantageous from a tax standpoint. The S election enables a business to operate in the corporate form, avoid the corporate income tax, and take advantage of the lower rates usually applicable to individuals. Also, losses incurred at the corporate level pass through to the shareholders, who will utilize them on their individual returns (compare with item 5).

Several problems exist with corporations electing S status. First, the election is available only to small business corporations. Consequently, many corporations will not qualify for the election. Second, S corporations are subject to the rules governing regular corporations unless otherwise specified in the Code. For example, if an S corporation carries out a stock redemption or is liquidated, the rules covering regular corporations apply. Third, some states do not recognize S status for purposes of state and local taxation. Therefore, an S corporation might be subject to a state franchise tax (refer to Chapter 1) or a state or local income tax.

Use of an Entity to Reduce the Family Income Tax Burden

One objective of tax planning is to keep the income from a business within the family unit but to disperse the income in such a manner as to minimize the overall tax burden. To the extent feasible, therefore, income should be shifted from higher bracket to lower bracket family members.

Unfortunately, the income from property (a business) cannot be shifted to another without also transferring an interest in the property. If, for example, a father wants to assign income from his sole proprietorship to his children, he must form a partnership or incorporate the business.[46] In either case, the transfer of the interest may be subject to the Federal gift tax. But any potential gift tax can be eliminated or controlled through judicious use of the annual exclusion, the election to split gifts (for married donors), and the unified tax credit (refer to the discussion of the Federal gift tax in Chapter 1).

Consequently, the first problem to be resolved becomes which form of business organization will best fit the objective of income shifting. For the partnership form, one major obstacle arises. The family partnership rules of § 704(e) preclude the assignment of income to a family member unless capital is a material income-producing factor. If not, the family member must contribute substantial or vital services. Ordinarily, capital is not a material income-producing factor if the income of the business consists principally of compensation for personal services performed by members or employees of the partnership. Conversely, capital is a material income-producing factor if the operation of the business entails a substantial investment in physical assets (e.g., inventory, plant, machinery, or equipment).

Income shifting through the use of a partnership, therefore, may be ineffectual if a personal service business is involved. In fact, it could be hopeless if the assignees are minors. The use of the corporate form usually involves no such impediment. Regardless of the nature of the business, a gift of stock carries with it the attributes of ownership. Thus, dividends paid on stock are taxed to the owner of the stock.

But what if the corporate form is utilized and the S election is made? A new hurdle arises under the Code. Section 1366(e) authorizes the IRS to make adjustments in situations where shareholders are not being adequately compensated for the value of their services or capital provided to an S corporation in a family setting.

EXAMPLE 51

The stock of an S corporation is held equally by T and his three minor children (ages 14, 15, and 16). Without help from his children, T runs the business for which he pays himself an annual salary of $20,000. If $50,000 is a reasonable amount for the value of these services, the IRS may allocate $30,000 of the corporation's taxable income from the children to T. ◆

Thus, an S corporation suffers from the same vulnerability that exists with family partnerships.

A further factor that favors the corporate form (either a regular or an S corporation) as a device for income splitting is the ease with which it can be carried out. Presuming the entity already exists, the transfer of stock merely requires an entry in the corporation's stock ledger account. In contrast, a gift of a partnership interest probably requires an amendment to the articles of copartnership. If minors are to be the assignees (donees), a state's Uniform Gifts to Minors Act provides a useful and flexible means of holding a stock interest

46. Income shifting will not work, however, if the minor is under 14 years of age. In such cases, net unearned income (refer to the discussion in Chapter 3) of the child is taxed at the parents' tax rate. § 1(g).

until the assignees become adults.[47] In the case of a partnership interest, however, a guardianship may have to be set up to achieve the same flexibility. In summary, the transfer of stock is more convenient and, since it usually avoids legal problems, can be less expensive.

Regardless of the form of organization used for the business, income shifting will not take place unless the transfer is complete.[48] If the donor continues to exercise control over the interest transferred and does not recognize and protect the ownership rights of the donee, the IRS may argue that the transfer is ineffective for tax purposes. In that case, the income from the transferred interest continues to be taxed to the donor.

Problem Materials

Discussion Questions

1. What is the role of state law in determining whether or not an entity will be classified as a corporation for Federal income tax purposes?
2. Why would the IRS assert in some instances that an entity should be taxed as a corporation rather than as a noncorporate entity?
3. When will an entity be classified as a corporation under the association approach?
4. When contrasted with the partnership, the corporate form of doing business results in another layer of Federal income tax. Explain.
5. Section 1250 may compel the recapture of depreciation as ordinary income upon the sale or other taxable disposition of depreciable real estate. In the application of § 1250, are corporate and noncorporate taxpayers treated the same way? Explain.
6. In what respects do the income tax rates applicable to corporations differ from those applicable to individuals?
7. Are the net long-term capital gains of individual taxpayers taxed in the same manner as those of corporate taxpayers? Explain.
8. Contrast the corporate tax rules for deducting net capital losses with the rules for individuals. Are the corporate capital loss rules *more* or *less* favorable than the capital loss provisions for individuals? Why?
9. What requirements must be met to properly accrue a charitable contribution that is paid in the year following the year of the deduction?
10. How are corporate charitable contributions treated when they exceed the maximum limitations?
11. Is it possible for a corporation to donate inventory to a charitable organization and claim some of the appreciation as a deduction? Explain.
12. Why are the corporate net operating loss adjustments substantially different from the NOL adjustments for individual taxpayers?
13. Why would a corporation elect not to carry back an NOL to a particular year?
14. What is the rationale for the dividends received deduction for corporate shareholders?
15. The amount of the dividends received deduction may depend on the percentage of ownership held by the corporate shareholder. Explain.

---

47. The Uniform Gifts to Minors Act is explained in the discussion following Example 61 in Chapter 4.

48. *Ginsberg v. Comm.*, 74–2 USTC ¶9660, 34 AFTR2d 74–5760, 502 F.2d 965 (CA–6, 1974), and *Michael F. Beirne*, 61 T.C. 268 (1973).

16. Distinguish between expenditures that qualify as organizational expenditures and those that do not qualify.
17. The 5% additional corporate income tax is not appropriate when taxable income reaches $335,000. Why?
18. Qualified personal service corporations need not be concerned about keeping taxable income at $100,000 or less. Please comment.
19. Under what circumstances may a corporation file a Form 1120–A (rather than Form 1120)?
20. What purpose does the Schedule M–1 reconciliation of Form 1120 serve for the taxpayer? For the IRS?
21. In order to convince a corporation to open a manufacturing facility in its community, a city donates land to the corporation. Does the donation generate income to the corporation? What basis will the corporation have in the land?
22. Why is it usually advantageous to capitalize a corporation by using debt? Is it possible that the debt will be reclassified as equity? Why?
23. If § 351 applies, no realized gain or loss is ever recognized. Comment on the validity of this statement.
24. If appreciated property is transferred to a corporation in a nontaxable exchange under § 351, does the corporation recognize gain if it sells the property immediately at its fair market value? Why?
25. In a § 351 transfer to a controlled corporation, what is the shareholder's basis for the stock received from the corporation?
26. C, D, E, F, and G form T Corporation. Each receives 20% of the stock of the corporation. Except for G, all parties transfer property in return for the stock. G, an attorney, receives his stock for the legal services he provides in forming T Corporation. Discuss the tax consequences to C, D, E, F, and G.
27. How do the following transactions affect the earnings and profits of a corporation?

    a. A nontaxable stock dividend issued to the shareholders.
    b. Receipt of interest on municipal bonds.
    c. Federal corporate income tax liability.

28. When is a distribution by a corporation to its shareholders treated by the shareholders as a return of capital? When can a shareholder have a capital gain on a distribution received from a corporation?
29. A corporation distributes a property dividend to its shareholders.

    a. Is any gain or loss recognized by the distributing corporation?
    b. What basis will the shareholders have in the property?

30. T, the sole shareholder of R Corporation, sells property to the corporation for $10,000 more than its fair market value. Discuss the tax ramifications of this transaction.
31. On March 19, 1992, the holders of 80% of the shares of X Corporation, a calendar year taxpayer, elect to terminate S status. For what year will X Corporation first become a regular corporation?
32. What are some examples of separately stated items that pass through "as is" to an S corporation's shareholders? Why is this procedure required?
33. If an S corporation incurs an operating loss, how is the loss apportioned to the shareholders?
34. Compare the nonrecognition of gain or loss on contributions to a partnership with the similar provision found in corporate formation (§ 351). What are the major differences and similarities?
35. Under what circumstances does the receipt of a partnership interest result in the recognition of ordinary income? What is the effect of this on the partnership and the other partners?
36. How is a contributing partner's basis in a partnership interest determined?

37. What transactions or events will cause a partner's basis in his or her partnership interest to fluctuate continuously?
38. Describe the two-step approach used in determining partnership income. Why is the computation necessary?
39. To what extent can a partner deduct his or her distributive share of partnership losses? What happens to any unused losses?
40. What are guaranteed payments? When might such payments be used?

PROBLEMS

41. Q Corporation has net short-term capital gains of $30,000 and net long-term capital losses of $80,000 during 1992. Taxable income from other sources is $500,000. Prior years' transactions included the following:

1988	Net short-term capital gains	$50,000
1989	Net long-term capital gains	30,000
1990	Net short-term capital gains	20,000
1991	Net long-term capital gains	10,000

   a. How are the capital gains and losses treated on the 1992 tax return?
   b. Compute the capital loss carryback to the carryback years.
   c. Compute the amount of capital loss carryover, if any, and designate the years to which the loss may be carried.

42. During 1992, T Corporation, a calendar year taxpayer, had the following income and expenses:

Income from operations	$225,000
Expenses from operations	165,000
Dividends from domestic corporations	15,000
NOL carryover from 1991	4,500

On May 1, 1992, T Corporation made a contribution to a qualified charitable organization of $10,500 in cash (not included in any of the items listed above).

   a. Determine T Corporation's deduction for charitable contributions for 1992.
   b. What happens to any portion of the contribution not deductible in 1992?

43. V Company is a wholesale grocery business. During 1992, it donated canned and dried food (held as inventory) to the local Salvation Army. The basis of the food is $15,000, and it has a fair market value of $18,000. Based on the following assumptions, what amount qualifies as a charitable contribution?
   a. V Company is a sole proprietorship.
   b. V Company is a regular corporation.

44. During 1992, Z Corporation had net income from operations of $200,000. In addition, Z Corporation received dividends in the following amounts: $30,000 from R Corporation and $20,000 from T Corporation. Z Corporation owns 15% of the stock of R Corporation and 30% of the stock of T Corporation. Determine Z Corporation's dividends received deduction for 1992.

45. In each of the following independent situations, determine the dividends received deduction. Assume that none of the corporate shareholders owns 20% or more of the stock in the corporations paying the dividends.

	X Corporation	Y Corporation	Z Corporation
Income from operations	$ 350,000	$ 400,000	$ 350,000
Expenses from operations	(300,000)	(450,000)	(370,000)
Qualifying dividends	50,000	100,000	100,000

46. In each of the following independent situations, determine the corporation's income tax liability. Assume that all corporations use a calendar year for tax purposes and that the tax year involved is 1992.

	Taxable Income
C Corporation	$ 40,000
D Corporation	110,000
E Corporation	350,000
F Corporation	90,000

47. Using the following legend, classify each statement accordingly:

Legend

I = Applies to the income taxation of individuals.
C = Applies to the income taxation of regular corporations.
B = Applies to the income taxation of both individuals and regular corporations.
N = Applies to the income taxation of neither individuals nor regular corporations.

- **a.** Net capital losses cannot be carried back.
- **b.** Net capital losses can be carried over indefinitely.
- **c.** Net capital losses cannot offset other income.
- **d.** Net long-term capital gains cannot be taxed at a rate in excess of 28%.
- **e.** An accrual basis taxpayer cannot deduct charitable contributions until the year of payment.
- **f.** A dividends received deduction may be available.
- **g.** The application of § 1250 (the recapture of depreciation claimed on certain real property) may yield more ordinary income.
- **h.** The concept of adjusted gross income (AGI) has no relevance.
- **i.** Percentage limitations may restrict the amount of charitable deductions that can be claimed in any one tax year.
- **j.** Casualty losses are deductible in full.
- **k.** Tax rates are only mildly progressive.
- **l.** More adjustments are necessary to arrive at a net operating loss deduction.

48. E and F form P Corporation with the following investments: E transfers cash of $300,000, and F transfers land worth $320,000. The land has an adjusted basis to F of $290,000. Each of the transferors receives 50% of the stock of P Corporation. In addition to stock, F receives $20,000 cash from P Corporation. All of P Corporation's stock has a fair market value of $600,000.

- **a.** Do the transfers qualify under § 351?
- **b.** What is F's realized gain (or loss)? Recognized gain (or loss)?
- **c.** What is F's basis in the P Corporation stock?
- **d.** What is P Corporation's basis in the land?

49. C and D form T Corporation with the following investments: C transfers cash of $200,000 while D transfers land worth $230,000 (adjusted basis of $250,000). In return, each receives 50% of T Corporation's stock. In addition to stock, D receives $30,000 cash from T Corporation. All of T Corporation's stock has a fair market value of $400,000.

- **a.** What is D's realized gain (or loss)? Recognized gain (or loss)?
- **b.** What is D's basis in the T Corporation stock?
- **c.** What is T Corporation's basis in the land?

50. T, the sole shareholder of R Corporation, has a basis in her stock investment of $12,500. At a time when R Corporation has earnings and profits of $15,000, it distributes cash of $30,000 to T. What are the tax consequences to T of the $30,000 distribution?

51. The stock of Q Corporation is held equally by T (an individual) and R Corporation. At a time when Q Corporation has earnings and profits of $400,000, it distributes the following property dividends to T and to R Corporation:

	Asset Distributed	Adjusted Basis to Q Corporation	Fair Market Value
To T	Land (Parcel A)	$ 20,000	$100,000
To R Corp.	Land (Parcel B)	120,000	100,000

a. What are the income tax consequences to T?
b. What are the income tax consequences to R Corporation?
c. What are the income tax consequences to Q Corporation?

52. At a time when O Corporation has ample earnings and profits, it redeems 500 of T's 1,500 shares for their fair market value of $500,000 ($1,000 for each share). All of T's shares were acquired 10 years ago as an investment and have an adjusted basis of $150,000 ($100 for each share).

a. Describe the tax effect of the redemption if it qualifies for sale or exchange treatment.
b. Describe the tax effect of the redemption if it does not qualify for sale or exchange treatment.

53. In the current year, X Corporation is liquidated under the general rules of § 331. The company distributes its only asset (land with a fair market value of $100,000 and adjusted basis of $20,000) to T, an individual who holds all of the X Corporation stock as an investment. T's basis in the stock of X Corporation is $60,000. X Corporation has earnings and profits of $10,000.

a. What are the amount and character of the gain or loss recognized by T upon the receipt of the land in exchange for the stock?
b. What is T's basis in the land?
c. Is there any tax effect to X Corporation? Explain.

54. Ten years ago, P Corporation purchased all of the stock of X Corporation for $100,000. In the current year, X Corporation has a basis in its assets of $300,000 and a fair market value of $400,000. P Corporation liquidates X Corporation and receives all of its assets.

a. Does P Corporation recognize any gain as a result of the liquidation?
b. What is P Corporation's basis for the assets it receives from X Corporation?

55. During 1992, Z Corporation (a calendar year accrual basis S corporation) had the following transactions:

Sales	$400,000
Cost of goods sold	200,000
Interest on municipal bonds	2,000
Long-term capital gain	3,000
Short-term capital loss	4,000
Advertising expense	3,000
Cash dividends on Exxon stock	3,500
Charitable contributions	1,000
Salaries and wages	40,000
Amortization of organizational expenditures	300

a. Determine Z Corporation's separately stated items for 1992.
b. Determine Z Corporation's taxable income for 1992.

56. X Corporation, a calendar year taxpayer, was formed in January 1991. For tax year 1991, it had taxable income of $25,000. For tax year 1992, a net operating loss of

$25,000 resulted. X anticipates taxable income of $100,000 for tax year 1993. Discuss the disposition of the 1992 net operating loss under each of the following assumptions:

a. X Corporation is an S corporation.
b. X Corporation is not an S corporation.

57. In 1992, Z Corporation (a calendar year S corporation) had a net operating loss of $73,200. R, a calendar year individual, held stock in Z Corporation as follows: 40% for 200 days and 60% for 166 days. Based on these facts, what is R's loss pass-through for 1992?

58. A, B, and C form the ABC Partnership on January 1, 1992. In exchange for a 30% capital interest, A transfers property (basis of $14,000, fair market value of $25,000) subject to a liability of $10,000. The liability is assumed by the partnership. B transfers property (basis of $24,000, fair market value of $15,000) for a 30% capital interest, and C transfers cash of $20,000 for the remaining 40% capital interest.

a. How much gain must A recognize on the transfer?
b. What is A's basis in her partnership interest?
c. How much loss may B recognize on the transfer?
d. What is B's basis in her partnership interest?
e. What is C's basis in her partnership interest?
f. What basis will the ABC Partnership have in the property transferred by A? The property transferred by B?
g. What would be the tax consequences to A if the basis of the property she contributed is only $9,000?

59. As of January 1, 1991, D had a basis of $26,000 in his 25% capital interest in the DEF Partnership. He and the partnership use the calendar year for tax purposes. The partnership incurred an operating loss of $120,000 for 1991 and a profit of $80,000 for 1992.

a. How much, if any, loss may D recognize for 1991?
b. How much income must D recognize for 1992?
c. What basis will D have in his partnership interest as of January 1, 1992?
d. What basis will D have in his partnership interest as of January 1, 1993?
e. What year-end tax planning would you suggest to ensure that a partner could deduct all of his or her share of any partnership losses?

60. T owns a 51% interest in the capital and profits of the TUV Partnership. In 1991, T sells property (adjusted basis of $120,000) to the partnership for the property's fair market value of $109,000. In 1992, TUV Partnership sells the same property to an outsider for $112,000.

a. What are T's tax consequences on the 1991 sale?
b. What are TUV Partnership's tax consequences on the 1992 sale?

RESEARCH PROBLEMS

RESEARCH PROBLEM 1 R and T are brothers and equal shareholders in Z Corporation, a calendar year taxpayer. In 1992, as employees, they incurred certain travel and entertainment expenditures on behalf of Z Corporation. Because Z Corporation was in a precarious financial condition, R and T decided not to seek reimbursement for these expenditures. Instead, on his own individual return (Form 1040), each brother deducted what he had spent. Upon audit of the returns filed by R and T for 1992, the IRS disallowed these expenditures. Do you agree? Why or why not?

Partial list of research aids:

Roy L. Harding, 29 TCM 789, T.C.Memo. 1970–179.

RESEARCH PROBLEM 2 T incorporates her retail clothing business. She transfers all her business assets (total basis of $100,000 and fair market value of $95,000) along with business liabilities of $10,000 and a personal note in the amount of $15,000 to the corporation for 100% of its stock. The note is for money borrowed from the bank six months before incorporation to finance improvements on her home. What are the tax consequences of the transfer?

Research Problem 3 During the latter part of 1992, the three shareholders of an S corporation terminate the election but do not inform the IRS. Is the entity still an S corporation?

Research Problem 4 T and a number of her friends want to diversify their investment portfolios. With this in mind, they form a partnership to which they transfer appreciated securities. Each transferor receives an interest in the new partnership proportionate to the value of the securities transferred. Will the creation of the partnership be tax-free? Why or why not?

APPENDIX

TAX RATE SCHEDULES AND TABLES

1991 Tax Rate Schedules

Schedule X—Use if your filing status is **Single**

If taxable income is: Over—	But not over—	The tax is:	of the amount over—
$0	$20,350	.... **15%**	**$0**
20,350	49,300	**$3,052.50 + 28%**	**20,350**
49,300	....	**11,158.50 + 31%**	**49,300**

Schedule Z—Use if your filing status is **Head of household**

If taxable income is: Over—	But not over—	The tax is:	of the amount over—
$0	$27,300	.... **15%**	**$0**
27,300	70,450	**$4,095.00 + 28%**	**27,300**
70,450	....	**16,177.00 + 31%**	**70,450**

Schedule Y-1—Use if your filing status is **Married filing jointly or Qualifying widow(er)**

If taxable income is: Over—	But not over—	The tax is:	of the amount over—
$0	$34,000	.... **15%**	**$0**
34,000	82,150	**$5,100.00 + 28%**	**34,000**
82,150	....	**18,582.00 + 31%**	**82,150**

Schedule Y-2—Use if your filing status is **Married filing separately**

If taxable income is: Over—	But not over—	The tax is:	of the amount over—
$0	$17,000	.... **15%**	**$0**
17,000	41,075	**$2,550.00 + 28%**	**17,000**
41,075	....	**9,291.00 + 31%**	**41,075**

1991 Tax Table

Use if your taxable income is less than $50,000. If $50,000 or more, use the Tax Rate Schedules.

Example: *Mr. and Mrs. Brown are filing a joint return. Their taxable income on line 37 of Form 1040 is $25,300. First, they find the $25,300–25,350 income line. Next, they find the column for married filing jointly and read down the column. The amount shown where the income line and filing status column meet is $3,799. This is the tax amount they must write on line 38 of their return.*

Sample Table

At least	But less than	Single	Married filing jointly *	Married filing separately	Head of a household
		Your tax is—			
25,200	**25,250**	4,418	3,784	4,853	3,784
25,250	**25,300**	4,432	3,791	4,867	3,791
25,300	**25,350**	4,446	(3,799)	4,881	3,799
25,350	**25,400**	4,460	3,806	4,895	3,806

If line 37 (taxable income) is— At least	But less than	And you are— Single	Married filing jointly *	Married filing separately	Head of a household
		Your tax is—			
$0	**$5**	$0	$0	$0	$0
5	**15**	2	2	2	2
15	**25**	3	3	3	3
25	**50**	6	6	6	6
50	**75**	9	9	9	9
75	**100**	13	13	13	13
100	**125**	17	17	17	17
125	**150**	21	21	21	21
150	**175**	24	24	24	24
175	**200**	28	28	28	28
200	**225**	32	32	32	32
225	**250**	36	36	36	36
250	**275**	39	39	39	39
275	**300**	43	43	43	43
300	**325**	47	47	47	47
325	**350**	51	51	51	51
350	**375**	54	54	54	54
375	**400**	58	58	58	58
400	**425**	62	62	62	62
425	**450**	66	66	66	66
450	**475**	69	69	69	69
475	**500**	73	73	73	73
500	**525**	77	77	77	77
525	**550**	81	81	81	81
550	**575**	84	84	84	84
575	**600**	88	88	88	88
600	**625**	92	92	92	92
625	**650**	96	96	96	96
650	**675**	99	99	99	99
675	**700**	103	103	103	103
700	**725**	107	107	107	107
725	**750**	111	111	111	111
750	**775**	114	114	114	114
775	**800**	118	118	118	118
800	**825**	122	122	122	122
825	**850**	126	126	126	126
850	**875**	129	129	129	129
875	**900**	133	133	133	133
900	**925**	137	137	137	137
925	**950**	141	141	141	141
950	**975**	144	144	144	144
975	**1,000**	148	148	148	148
1,000					
1,000	**1,025**	152	152	152	152
1,025	**1,050**	156	156	156	156
1,050	**1,075**	159	159	159	159
1,075	**1,100**	163	163	163	163
1,100	**1,125**	167	167	167	167
1,125	**1,150**	171	171	171	171
1,150	**1,175**	174	174	174	174
1,175	**1,200**	178	178	178	178
1,200	**1,225**	182	182	182	182
1,225	**1,250**	186	186	186	186
1,250	**1,275**	189	189	189	189
1,275	**1,300**	193	193	193	193

If line 37 (taxable income) is— At least	But less than	And you are— Single	Married filing jointly *	Married filing separately	Head of a household
		Your tax is—			
1,300	**1,325**	197	197	197	197
1,325	**1,350**	201	201	201	201
1,350	**1,375**	204	204	204	204
1,375	**1,400**	208	208	208	208
1,400	**1,425**	212	212	212	212
1,425	**1,450**	216	216	216	216
1,450	**1,475**	219	219	219	219
1,475	**1,500**	223	223	223	223
1,500	**1,525**	227	227	227	227
1,525	**1,550**	231	231	231	231
1,550	**1,575**	234	234	234	234
1,575	**1,600**	238	238	238	238
1,600	**1,625**	242	242	242	242
1,625	**1,650**	246	246	246	246
1,650	**1,675**	249	249	249	249
1,675	**1,700**	253	253	253	253
1,700	**1,725**	257	257	257	257
1,725	**1,750**	261	261	261	261
1,750	**1,775**	264	264	264	264
1,775	**1,800**	268	268	268	268
1,800	**1,825**	272	272	272	272
1,825	**1,850**	276	276	276	276
1,850	**1,875**	279	279	279	279
1,875	**1,900**	283	283	283	283
1,900	**1,925**	287	287	287	287
1,925	**1,950**	291	291	291	291
1,950	**1,975**	294	294	294	294
1,975	**2,000**	298	298	298	298
2,000					
2,000	**2,025**	302	302	302	302
2,025	**2,050**	306	306	306	306
2,050	**2,075**	309	309	309	309
2,075	**2,100**	313	313	313	313
2,100	**2,125**	317	317	317	317
2,125	**2,150**	321	321	321	321
2,150	**2,175**	324	324	324	324
2,175	**2,200**	328	328	328	328
2,200	**2,225**	332	332	332	332
2,225	**2,250**	336	336	336	336
2,250	**2,275**	339	339	339	339
2,275	**2,300**	343	343	343	343
2,300	**2,325**	347	347	347	347
2,325	**2,350**	351	351	351	351
2,350	**2,375**	354	354	354	354
2,375	**2,400**	358	358	358	358
2,400	**2,425**	362	362	362	362
2,425	**2,450**	366	366	366	366
2,450	**2,475**	369	369	369	369
2,475	**2,500**	373	373	373	373
2,500	**2,525**	377	377	377	377
2,525	**2,550**	381	381	381	381
2,550	**2,575**	384	384	384	384
2,575	**2,600**	388	388	388	388
2,600	**2,625**	392	392	392	392
2,625	**2,650**	396	396	396	396
2,650	**2,675**	399	399	399	399
2,675	**2,700**	403	403	403	403

If line 37 (taxable income) is— At least	But less than	And you are— Single	Married filing jointly *	Married filing separately	Head of a household
		Your tax is—			
2,700	**2,725**	407	407	407	407
2,725	**2,750**	411	411	411	411
2,750	**2,775**	414	414	414	414
2,775	**2,800**	418	418	418	418
2,800	**2,825**	422	422	422	422
2,825	**2,850**	426	426	426	426
2,850	**2,875**	429	429	429	429
2,875	**2,900**	433	433	433	433
2,900	**2,925**	437	437	437	437
2,925	**2,950**	441	441	441	441
2,950	**2,975**	444	444	444	444
2,975	**3,000**	448	448	448	448
3,000					
3,000	**3,050**	454	454	454	454
3,050	**3,100**	461	461	461	461
3,100	**3,150**	469	469	469	469
3,150	**3,200**	476	476	476	476
3,200	**3,250**	484	484	484	484
3,250	**3,300**	491	491	491	491
3,300	**3,350**	499	499	499	499
3,350	**3,400**	506	506	506	506
3,400	**3,450**	514	514	514	514
3,450	**3,500**	521	521	521	521
3,500	**3,550**	529	529	529	529
3,550	**3,600**	536	536	536	536
3,600	**3,650**	544	544	544	544
3,650	**3,700**	551	551	551	551
3,700	**3,750**	559	559	559	559
3,750	**3,800**	566	566	566	566
3,800	**3,850**	574	574	574	574
3,850	**3,900**	581	581	581	581
3,900	**3,950**	589	589	589	589
3,950	**4,000**	596	596	596	596
4,000					
4,000	**4,050**	604	604	604	604
4,050	**4,100**	611	611	611	611
4,100	**4,150**	619	619	619	619
4,150	**4,200**	626	626	626	626
4,200	**4,250**	634	634	634	634
4,250	**4,300**	641	641	641	641
4,300	**4,350**	649	649	649	649
4,350	**4,400**	656	656	656	656
4,400	**4,450**	664	664	664	664
4,450	**4,500**	671	671	671	671
4,500	**4,550**	679	679	679	679
4,550	**4,600**	686	686	686	686
4,600	**4,650**	694	694	694	694
4,650	**4,700**	701	701	701	701
4,700	**4,750**	709	709	709	709
4,750	**4,800**	716	716	716	716
4,800	**4,850**	724	724	724	724
4,850	**4,900**	731	731	731	731
4,900	**4,950**	739	739	739	739
4,950	**5,000**	746	746	746	746

Continued on next page

* This column must also be used by a qualifying widow(er).

1991 Tax Table—*Continued*

If line 37 (taxable income) is—		And you are—			
At least	But less than	Single	Married filing jointly *	Married filing separately	Head of a household
		Your tax is—			
5,000					
5,000	5,050	754	754	754	754
5,050	5,100	761	761	761	761
5,100	5,150	769	769	769	769
5,150	5,200	776	776	776	776
5,200	5,250	784	784	784	784
5,250	5,300	791	791	791	791
5,300	5,350	799	799	799	799
5,350	5,400	806	806	806	806
5,400	5,450	814	814	814	814
5,450	5,500	821	821	821	821
5,500	5,550	829	829	829	829
5,550	5,600	836	836	836	836
5,600	5,650	844	844	844	844
5,650	5,700	851	851	851	851
5,700	5,750	859	859	859	859
5,750	5,800	866	866	866	866
5,800	5,850	874	874	874	874
5,850	5,900	881	881	881	881
5,900	5,950	889	889	889	889
5,950	6,000	896	896	896	896
6,000					
6,000	6,050	904	904	904	904
6,050	6,100	911	911	911	911
6,100	6,150	919	919	919	919
6,150	6,200	926	926	926	926
6,200	6,250	934	934	934	934
6,250	6,300	941	941	941	941
6,300	6,350	949	949	949	949
6,350	6,400	956	956	956	956
6,400	6,450	964	964	964	964
6,450	6,500	971	971	971	971
6,500	6,550	979	979	979	979
6,550	6,600	986	986	986	986
6,600	6,650	994	994	994	994
6,650	6,700	1,001	1,001	1,001	1,001
6,700	6,750	1,009	1,009	1,009	1,009
6,750	6,800	1,016	1,016	1,016	1,016
6,800	6,850	1,024	1,024	1,024	1,024
6,850	6,900	1,031	1,031	1,031	1,031
6,900	6,950	1,039	1,039	1,039	1,039
6,950	7,000	1,046	1,046	1,046	1,046
7,000					
7,000	7,050	1,054	1,054	1,054	1,054
7,050	7,100	1,061	1,061	1,061	1,061
7,100	7,150	1,069	1,069	1,069	1,069
7,150	7,200	1,076	1,076	1,076	1,076
7,200	7,250	1,084	1,084	1,084	1,084
7,250	7,300	1,091	1,091	1,091	1,091
7,300	7,350	1,099	1,099	1,099	1,099
7,350	7,400	1,106	1,106	1,106	1,106
7,400	7,450	1,114	1,114	1,114	1,114
7,450	7,500	1,121	1,121	1,121	1,121
7,500	7,550	1,129	1,129	1,129	1,129
7,550	7,600	1,136	1,136	1,136	1,136
7,600	7,650	1,144	1,144	1,144	1,144
7,650	7,700	1,151	1,151	1,151	1,151
7,700	7,750	1,159	1,159	1,159	1,159
7,750	7,800	1,166	1,166	1,166	1,166
7,800	7,850	1,174	1,174	1,174	1,174
7,850	7,900	1,181	1,181	1,181	1,181
7,900	7,950	1,189	1,189	1,189	1,189
7,950	8,000	1,196	1,196	1,196	1,196

If line 37 (taxable income) is—		And you are—			
At least	But less than	Single	Married filing jointly *	Married filing separately	Head of a household
		Your tax is—			
8,000					
8,000	8,050	1,204	1,204	1,204	1,204
8,050	8,100	1,211	1,211	1,211	1,211
8,100	8,150	1,219	1,219	1,219	1,219
8,150	8,200	1,226	1,226	1,226	1,226
8,200	8,250	1,234	1,234	1,234	1,234
8,250	8,300	1,241	1,241	1,241	1,241
8,300	8,350	1,249	1,249	1,249	1,249
8,350	8,400	1,256	1,256	1,256	1,256
8,400	8,450	1,264	1,264	1,264	1,264
8,450	8,500	1,271	1,271	1,271	1,271
8,500	8,550	1,279	1,279	1,279	1,279
8,550	8,600	1,286	1,286	1,286	1,286
8,600	8,650	1,294	1,294	1,294	1,294
8,650	8,700	1,301	1,301	1,301	1,301
8,700	8,750	1,309	1,309	1,309	1,309
8,750	8,800	1,316	1,316	1,316	1,316
8,800	8,850	1,324	1,324	1,324	1,324
8,850	8,900	1,331	1,331	1,331	1,331
8,900	8,950	1,339	1,339	1,339	1,339
8,950	9,000	1,346	1,346	1,346	1,346
9,000					
9,000	9,050	1,354	1,354	1,354	1,354
9,050	9,100	1,361	1,361	1,361	1,361
9,100	9,150	1,369	1,369	1,369	1,369
9,150	9,200	1,376	1,376	1,376	1,376
9,200	9,250	1,384	1,384	1,384	1,384
9,250	9,300	1,391	1,391	1,391	1,391
9,300	9,350	1,399	1,399	1,399	1,399
9,350	9,400	1,406	1,406	1,406	1,406
9,400	9,450	1,414	1,414	1,414	1,414
9,450	9,500	1,421	1,421	1,421	1,421
9,500	9,550	1,429	1,429	1,429	1,429
9,550	9,600	1,436	1,436	1,436	1,436
9,600	9,650	1,444	1,444	1,444	1,444
9,650	9,700	1,451	1,451	1,451	1,451
9,700	9,750	1,459	1,459	1,459	1,459
9,750	9,800	1,466	1,466	1,466	1,466
9,800	9,850	1,474	1,474	1,474	1,474
9,850	9,900	1,481	1,481	1,481	1,481
9,900	9,950	1,489	1,489	1,489	1,489
9,950	10,000	1,496	1,496	1,496	1,496
10,000					
10,000	10,050	1,504	1,504	1,504	1,504
10,050	10,100	1,511	1,511	1,511	1,511
10,100	10,150	1,519	1,519	1,519	1,519
10,150	10,200	1,526	1,526	1,526	1,526
10,200	10,250	1,534	1,534	1,534	1,534
10,250	10,300	1,541	1,541	1,541	1,541
10,300	10,350	1,549	1,549	1,549	1,549
10,350	10,400	1,556	1,556	1,556	1,556
10,400	10,450	1,564	1,564	1,564	1,564
10,450	10,500	1,571	1,571	1,571	1,571
10,500	10,550	1,579	1,579	1,579	1,579
10,550	10,600	1,586	1,586	1,586	1,586
10,600	10,650	1,594	1,594	1,594	1,594
10,650	10,700	1,601	1,601	1,601	1,601
10,700	10,750	1,609	1,609	1,609	1,609
10,750	10,800	1,616	1,616	1,616	1,616
10,800	10,850	1,624	1,624	1,624	1,624
10,850	10,900	1,631	1,631	1,631	1,631
10,900	10,950	1,639	1,639	1,639	1,639
10,950	11,000	1,646	1,646	1,646	1,646

If line 37 (taxable income) is—		And you are—			
At least	But less than	Single	Married filing jointly *	Married filing separately	Head of a household
		Your tax is—			
11,000					
11,000	11,050	1,654	1,654	1,654	1,654
11,050	11,100	1,661	1,661	1,661	1,661
11,100	11,150	1,669	1,669	1,669	1,669
11,150	11,200	1,676	1,676	1,676	1,676
11,200	11,250	1,684	1,684	1,684	1,684
11,250	11,300	1,691	1,691	1,691	1,691
11,300	11,350	1,699	1,699	1,699	1,699
11,350	11,400	1,706	1,706	1,706	1,706
11,400	11,450	1,714	1,714	1,714	1,714
11,450	11,500	1,721	1,721	1,721	1,721
11,500	11,550	1,729	1,729	1,729	1,729
11,550	11,600	1,736	1,736	1,736	1,736
11,600	11,650	1,744	1,744	1,744	1,744
11,650	11,700	1,751	1,751	1,751	1,751
11,700	11,750	1,759	1,759	1,759	1,759
11,750	11,800	1,766	1,766	1,766	1,766
11,800	11,850	1,774	1,774	1,774	1,774
11,850	11,900	1,781	1,781	1,781	1,781
11,900	11,950	1,789	1,789	1,789	1,789
11,950	12,000	1,796	1,796	1,796	1,796
12,000					
12,000	12,050	1,804	1,804	1,804	1,804
12,050	12,100	1,811	1,811	1,811	1,811
12,100	12,150	1,819	1,819	1,819	1,819
12,150	12,200	1,826	1,826	1,826	1,826
12,200	12,250	1,834	1,834	1,834	1,834
12,250	12,300	1,841	1,841	1,841	1,841
12,300	12,350	1,849	1,849	1,849	1,849
12,350	12,400	1,856	1,856	1,856	1,856
12,400	12,450	1,864	1,864	1,864	1,864
12,450	12,500	1,871	1,871	1,871	1,871
12,500	12,550	1,879	1,879	1,879	1,879
12,550	12,600	1,886	1,886	1,886	1,886
12,600	12,650	1,894	1,894	1,894	1,894
12,650	12,700	1,901	1,901	1,901	1,901
12,700	12,750	1,909	1,909	1,909	1,909
12,750	12,800	1,916	1,916	1,916	1,916
12,800	12,850	1,924	1,924	1,924	1,924
12,850	12,900	1,931	1,931	1,931	1,931
12,900	12,950	1,939	1,939	1,939	1,939
12,950	13,000	1,946	1,946	1,946	1,946
13,000					
13,000	13,050	1,954	1,954	1,954	1,954
13,050	13,100	1,961	1,961	1,961	1,961
13,100	13,150	1,969	1,969	1,969	1,969
13,150	13,200	1,976	1,976	1,976	1,976
13,200	13,250	1,984	1,984	1,984	1,984
13,250	13,300	1,991	1,991	1,991	1,991
13,300	13,350	1,999	1,999	1,999	1,999
13,350	13,400	2,006	2,006	2,006	2,006
13,400	13,450	2,014	2,014	2,014	2,014
13,450	13,500	2,021	2,021	2,021	2,021
13,500	13,550	2,029	2,029	2,029	2,029
13,550	13,600	2,036	2,036	2,036	2,036
13,600	13,650	2,044	2,044	2,044	2,044
13,650	13,700	2,051	2,051	2,051	2,051
13,700	13,750	2,059	2,059	2,059	2,059
13,750	13,800	2,066	2,066	2,066	2,066
13,800	13,850	2,074	2,074	2,074	2,074
13,850	13,900	2,081	2,081	2,081	2,081
13,900	13,950	2,089	2,089	2,089	2,089
13,950	14,000	2,096	2,096	2,096	2,096

* This column must also be used by a qualifying widow(er).

Continued on next page

1991 Tax Table—*Continued*

If line 37 (taxable income) is— At least	But less than	And you are— Single	Married filing jointly *	Married filing separately	Head of a household
		Your tax is—			
14,000					
14,000	14,050	2,104	2,104	2,104	2,104
14,050	14,100	2,111	2,111	2,111	2,111
14,100	14,150	2,119	2,119	2,119	2,119
14,150	14,200	2,126	2,126	2,126	2,126
14,200	14,250	2,134	2,134	2,134	2,134
14,250	14,300	2,141	2,141	2,141	2,141
14,300	14,350	2,149	2,149	2,149	2,149
14,350	14,400	2,156	2,156	2,156	2,156
14,400	14,450	2,164	2,164	2,164	2,164
14,450	14,500	2,171	2,171	2,171	2,171
14,500	14,550	2,179	2,179	2,179	2,179
14,550	14,600	2,186	2,186	2,186	2,186
14,600	14,650	2,194	2,194	2,194	2,194
14,650	14,700	2,201	2,201	2,201	2,201
14,700	14,750	2,209	2,209	2,209	2,209
14,750	14,800	2,216	2,216	2,216	2,216
14,800	14,850	2,224	2,224	2,224	2,224
14,850	14,900	2,231	2,231	2,231	2,231
14,900	14,950	2,239	2,239	2,239	2,239
14,950	15,000	2,246	2,246	2,246	2,246
15,000					
15,000	15,050	2,254	2,254	2,254	2,254
15,050	15,100	2,261	2,261	2,261	2,261
15,100	15,150	2,269	2,269	2,269	2,269
15,150	15,200	2,276	2,276	2,276	2,276
15,200	15,250	2,284	2,284	2,284	2,284
15,250	15,300	2,291	2,291	2,291	2,291
15,300	15,350	2,299	2,299	2,299	2,299
15,350	15,400	2,306	2,306	2,306	2,306
15,400	15,450	2,314	2,314	2,314	2,314
15,450	15,500	2,321	2,321	2,321	2,321
15,500	15,550	2,329	2,329	2,329	2,329
15,550	15,600	2,336	2,336	2,336	2,336
15,600	15,650	2,344	2,344	2,344	2,344
15,650	15,700	2,351	2,351	2,351	2,351
15,700	15,750	2,359	2,359	2,359	2,359
15,750	15,800	2,366	2,366	2,366	2,366
15,800	15,850	2,374	2,374	2,374	2,374
15,850	15,900	2,381	2,381	2,381	2,381
15,900	15,950	2,389	2,389	2,389	2,389
15,950	16,000	2,396	2,396	2,396	2,396
16,000					
16,000	16,050	2,404	2,404	2,404	2,404
16,050	16,100	2,411	2,411	2,411	2,411
16,100	16,150	2,419	2,419	2,419	2,419
16,150	16,200	2,426	2,426	2,426	2,426
16,200	16,250	2,434	2,434	2,434	2,434
16,250	16,300	2,441	2,441	2,441	2,441
16,300	16,350	2,449	2,449	2,449	2,449
16,350	16,400	2,456	2,456	2,456	2,456
16,400	16,450	2,464	2,464	2,464	2,464
16,450	16,500	2,471	2,471	2,471	2,471
16,500	16,550	2,479	2,479	2,479	2,479
16,550	16,600	2,486	2,486	2,486	2,486
16,600	16,650	2,494	2,494	2,494	2,494
16,650	16,700	2,501	2,501	2,501	2,501
16,700	16,750	2,509	2,509	2,509	2,509
16,750	16,800	2,516	2,516	2,516	2,516
16,800	16,850	2,524	2,524	2,524	2,524
16,850	16,900	2,531	2,531	2,531	2,531
16,900	16,950	2,539	2,539	2,539	2,539
16,950	17,000	2,546	2,546	2,546	2,546
17,000					
17,000	17,050	2,554	2,554	2,557	2,554
17,050	17,100	2,561	2,561	2,571	2,561
17,100	17,150	2,569	2,569	2,585	2,569
17,150	17,200	2,576	2,576	2,599	2,576
17,200	17,250	2,584	2,584	2,613	2,584
17,250	17,300	2,591	2,591	2,627	2,591
17,300	17,350	2,599	2,599	2,641	2,599
17,350	17,400	2,606	2,606	2,655	2,606
17,400	17,450	2,614	2,614	2,669	2,614
17,450	17,500	2,621	2,621	2,683	2,621
17,500	17,550	2,629	2,629	2,697	2,629
17,550	17,600	2,636	2,636	2,711	2,636
17,600	17,650	2,644	2,644	2,725	2,644
17,650	17,700	2,651	2,651	2,739	2,651
17,700	17,750	2,659	2,659	2,753	2,659
17,750	17,800	2,666	2,666	2,767	2,666
17,800	17,850	2,674	2,674	2,781	2,674
17,850	17,900	2,681	2,681	2,795	2,681
17,900	17,950	2,689	2,689	2,809	2,689
17,950	18,000	2,696	2,696	2,823	2,696
18,000					
18,000	18,050	2,704	2,704	2,837	2,704
18,050	18,100	2,711	2,711	2,851	2,711
18,100	18,150	2,719	2,719	2,865	2,719
18,150	18,200	2,726	2,726	2,879	2,726
18,200	18,250	2,734	2,734	2,893	2,734
18,250	18,300	2,741	2,741	2,907	2,741
18,300	18,350	2,749	2,749	2,921	2,749
18,350	18,400	2,756	2,756	2,935	2,756
18,400	18,450	2,764	2,764	2,949	2,764
18,450	18,500	2,771	2,771	2,963	2,771
18,500	18,550	2,779	2,779	2,977	2,779
18,550	18,600	2,786	2,786	2,991	2,786
18,600	18,650	2,794	2,794	3,005	2,794
18,650	18,700	2,801	2,801	3,019	2,801
18,700	18,750	2,809	2,809	3,033	2,809
18,750	18,800	2,816	2,816	3,047	2,816
18,800	18,850	2,824	2,824	3,061	2,824
18,850	18,900	2,831	2,831	3,075	2,831
18,900	18,950	2,839	2,839	3,089	2,839
18,950	19,000	2,846	2,846	3,103	2,846
19,000					
19,000	19,050	2,854	2,854	3,117	2,854
19,050	19,100	2,861	2,861	3,131	2,861
19,100	19,150	2,869	2,869	3,145	2,869
19,150	19,200	2,876	2,876	3,159	2,876
19,200	19,250	2,884	2,884	3,173	2,884
19,250	19,300	2,891	2,891	3,187	2,891
19,300	19,350	2,899	2,899	3,201	2,899
19,350	19,400	2,906	2,906	3,215	2,906
19,400	19,450	2,914	2,914	3,229	2,914
19,450	19,500	2,921	2,921	3,243	2,921
19,500	19,550	2,929	2,929	3,257	2,929
19,550	19,600	2,936	2,936	3,271	2,936
19,600	19,650	2,944	2,944	3,285	2,944
19,650	19,700	2,951	2,951	3,299	2,951
19,700	19,750	2,959	2,959	3,313	2,959
19,750	19,800	2,966	2,966	3,327	2,966
19,800	19,850	2,974	2,974	3,341	2,974
19,850	19,900	2,981	2,981	3,355	2,981
19,900	19,950	2,989	2,989	3,369	2,989
19,950	20,000	2,996	2,996	3,383	2,996
20,000					
20,000	20,050	3,004	3,004	3,397	3,004
20,050	20,100	3,011	3,011	3,411	3,011
20,100	20,150	3,019	3,019	3,425	3,019
20,150	20,200	3,026	3,026	3,439	3,026
20,200	20,250	3,034	3,034	3,453	3,034
20,250	20,300	3,041	3,041	3,467	3,041
20,300	20,350	3,049	3,049	3,481	3,049
20,350	20,400	3,060	3,056	3,495	3,056
20,400	20,450	3,074	3,064	3,509	3,064
20,450	20,500	3,088	3,071	3,523	3,071
20,500	20,550	3,102	3,079	3,537	3,079
20,550	20,600	3,116	3,086	3,551	3,086
20,600	20,650	3,130	3,094	3,565	3,094
20,650	20,700	3,144	3,101	3,579	3,101
20,700	20,750	3,158	3,109	3,593	3,109
20,750	20,800	3,172	3,116	3,607	3,116
20,800	20,850	3,186	3,124	3,621	3,124
20,850	20,900	3,200	3,131	3,635	3,131
20,900	20,950	3,214	3,139	3,649	3,139
20,950	21,000	3,228	3,146	3,663	3,146
21,000					
21,000	21,050	3,242	3,154	3,677	3,154
21,050	21,100	3,256	3,161	3,691	3,161
21,100	21,150	3,270	3,169	3,705	3,169
21,150	21,200	3,284	3,176	3,719	3,176
21,200	21,250	3,298	3,184	3,733	3,184
21,250	21,300	3,312	3,191	3,747	3,191
21,300	21,350	3,326	3,199	3,761	3,199
21,350	21,400	3,340	3,206	3,775	3,206
21,400	21,450	3,354	3,214	3,789	3,214
21,450	21,500	3,368	3,221	3,803	3,221
21,500	21,550	3,382	3,229	3,817	3,229
21,550	21,600	3,396	3,236	3,831	3,236
21,600	21,650	3,410	3,244	3,845	3,244
21,650	21,700	3,424	3,251	3,859	3,251
21,700	21,750	3,438	3,259	3,873	3,259
21,750	21,800	3,452	3,266	3,887	3,266
21,800	21,850	3,466	3,274	3,901	3,274
21,850	21,900	3,480	3,281	3,915	3,281
21,900	21,950	3,494	3,289	3,929	3,289
21,950	22,000	3,508	3,296	3,943	3,296
22,000					
22,000	22,050	3,522	3,304	3,957	3,304
22,050	22,100	3,536	3,311	3,971	3,311
22,100	22,150	3,550	3,319	3,985	3,319
22,150	22,200	3,564	3,326	3,999	3,326
22,200	22,250	3,578	3,334	4,013	3,334
22,250	22,300	3,592	3,341	4,027	3,341
22,300	22,350	3,606	3,349	4,041	3,349
22,350	22,400	3,620	3,356	4,055	3,356
22,400	22,450	3,634	3,364	4,069	3,364
22,450	22,500	3,648	3,371	4,083	3,371
22,500	22,550	3,662	3,379	4,097	3,379
22,550	22,600	3,676	3,386	4,111	3,386
22,600	22,650	3,690	3,394	4,125	3,394
22,650	22,700	3,704	3,401	4,139	3,401
22,700	22,750	3,718	3,409	4,153	3,409
22,750	22,800	3,732	3,416	4,167	3,416
22,800	22,850	3,746	3,424	4,181	3,424
22,850	22,900	3,760	3,431	4,195	3,431
22,900	22,950	3,774	3,439	4,209	3,439
22,950	23,000	3,788	3,446	4,223	3,446

* This column must also be used by a qualifying widow(er).

Continued on next page

1991 Tax Table—*Continued*

If line 37 (taxable income) is—		And you are—			
At least	But less than	Single	Married filing jointly *	Married filing sepa-rately	Head of a house-hold
		Your tax is—			
23,000					
23,000	23,050	3,802	3,454	4,237	3,454
23,050	23,100	3,816	3,461	4,251	3,461
23,100	23,150	3,830	3,469	4,265	3,469
23,150	23,200	3,844	3,476	4,279	3,476
23,200	23,250	3,858	3,484	4,293	3,484
23,250	23,300	3,872	3,491	4,307	3,491
23,300	23,350	3,886	3,499	4,321	3,499
23,350	23,400	3,900	3,506	4,335	3,506
23,400	23,450	3,914	3,514	4,349	3,514
23,450	23,500	3,928	3,521	4,363	3,521
23,500	23,550	3,942	3,529	4,377	3,529
23,550	23,600	3,956	3,536	4,391	3,536
23,600	23,650	3,970	3,544	4,405	3,544
23,650	23,700	3,984	3,551	4,419	3,551
23,700	23,750	3,998	3,559	4,433	3,559
23,750	23,800	4,012	3,566	4,447	3,566
23,800	23,850	4,026	3,574	4,461	3,574
23,850	23,900	4,040	3,581	4,475	3,581
23,900	23,950	4,054	3,589	4,489	3,589
23,950	24,000	4,068	3,596	4,503	3,596
24,000					
24,000	24,050	4,082	3,604	4,517	3,604
24,050	24,100	4,096	3,611	4,531	3,611
24,100	24,150	4,110	3,619	4,545	3,619
24,150	24,200	4,124	3,626	4,559	3,626
24,200	24,250	4,138	3,634	4,573	3,634
24,250	24,300	4,152	3,641	4,587	3,641
24,300	24,350	4,166	3,649	4,601	3,649
24,350	24,400	4,180	3,656	4,615	3,656
24,400	24,450	4,194	3,664	4,629	3,664
24,450	24,500	4,208	3,671	4,643	3,671
24,500	24,550	4,222	3,679	4,657	3,679
24,550	24,600	4,236	3,686	4,671	3,686
24,600	24,650	4,250	3,694	4,685	3,694
24,650	24,700	4,264	3,701	4,699	3,701
24,700	24,750	4,278	3,709	4,713	3,709
24,750	24,800	4,292	3,716	4,727	3,716
24,800	24,850	4,306	3,724	4,741	3,724
24,850	24,900	4,320	3,731	4,755	3,731
24,900	24,950	4,334	3,739	4,769	3,739
24,950	25,000	4,348	3,746	4,783	3,746
25,000					
25,000	25,050	4,362	3,754	4,797	3,754
25,050	25,100	4,376	3,761	4,811	3,761
25,100	25,150	4,390	3,769	4,825	3,769
25,150	25,200	4,404	3,776	4,839	3,776
25,200	25,250	4,418	3,784	4,853	3,784
25,250	25,300	4,432	3,791	4,867	3,791
25,300	25,350	4,446	3,799	4,881	3,799
25,350	25,400	4,460	3,806	4,895	3,806
25,400	25,450	4,474	3,814	4,909	3,814
25,450	25,500	4,488	3,821	4,923	3,821
25,500	25,550	4,502	3,829	4,937	3,829
25,550	25,600	4,516	3,836	4,951	3,836
25,600	25,650	4,530	3,844	4,965	3,844
25,650	25,700	4,544	3,851	4,979	3,851
25,700	25,750	4,558	3,859	4,993	3,859
25,750	25,800	4,572	3,866	5,007	3,866
25,800	25,850	4,586	3,874	5,021	3,874
25,850	25,900	4,600	3,881	5,035	3,881
25,900	25,950	4,614	3,889	5,049	3,889
25,950	26,000	4,628	3,896	5,063	3,896

If line 37 (taxable income) is—		And you are—			
At least	But less than	Single	Married filing jointly *	Married filing sepa-rately	Head of a house-hold
		Your tax is—			
26,000					
26,000	26,050	4,642	3,904	5,077	3,904
26,050	26,100	4,656	3,911	5,091	3,911
26,100	26,150	4,670	3,919	5,105	3,919
26,150	26,200	4,684	3,926	5,119	3,926
26,200	26,250	4,698	3,934	5,133	3,934
26,250	26,300	4,712	3,941	5,147	3,941
26,300	26,350	4,726	3,949	5,161	3,949
26,350	26,400	4,740	3,956	5,175	3,956
26,400	26,450	4,754	3,964	5,189	3,964
26,450	26,500	4,768	3,971	5,203	3,971
26,500	26,550	4,782	3,979	5,217	3,979
26,550	26,600	4,796	3,986	5,231	3,986
26,600	26,650	4,810	3,994	5,245	3,994
26,650	26,700	4,824	4,001	5,259	4,001
26,700	26,750	4,838	4,009	5,273	4,009
26,750	26,800	4,852	4,016	5,287	4,016
26,800	26,850	4,866	4,024	5,301	4,024
26,850	26,900	4,880	4,031	5,315	4,031
26,900	26,950	4,894	4,039	5,329	4,039
26,950	27,000	4,908	4,046	5,343	4,046
27,000					
27,000	27,050	4,922	4,054	5,357	4,054
27,050	27,100	4,936	4,061	5,371	4,061
27,100	27,150	4,950	4,069	5,385	4,069
27,150	27,200	4,964	4,076	5,399	4,076
27,200	27,250	4,978	4,084	5,413	4,084
27,250	27,300	4,992	4,091	5,427	4,091
27,300	27,350	5,006	4,099	5,441	4,102
27,350	27,400	5,020	4,106	5,455	4,116
27,400	27,450	5,034	4,114	5,469	4,130
27,450	27,500	5,048	4,121	5,483	4,144
27,500	27,550	5,062	4,129	5,497	4,158
27,550	27,600	5,076	4,136	5,511	4,172
27,600	27,650	5,090	4,144	5,525	4,186
27,650	27,700	5,104	4,151	5,539	4,200
27,700	27,750	5,118	4,159	5,553	4,214
27,750	27,800	5,132	4,166	5,567	4,228
27,800	27,850	5,146	4,174	5,581	4,242
27,850	27,900	5,160	4,181	5,595	4,256
27,900	27,950	5,174	4,189	5,609	4,270
27,950	28,000	5,188	4,196	5,623	4,284
28,000					
28,000	28,050	5,202	4,204	5,637	4,298
28,050	28,100	5,216	4,211	5,651	4,312
28,100	28,150	5,230	4,219	5,665	4,326
28,150	28,200	5,244	4,226	5,679	4,340
28,200	28,250	5,258	4,234	5,693	4,354
28,250	28,300	5,272	4,241	5,707	4,368
28,300	28,350	5,286	4,249	5,721	4,382
28,350	28,400	5,300	4,256	5,735	4,396
28,400	28,450	5,314	4,264	5,749	4,410
28,450	28,500	5,328	4,271	5,763	4,424
28,500	28,550	5,342	4,279	5,777	4,438
28,550	28,600	5,356	4,286	5,791	4,452
28,600	28,650	5,370	4,294	5,805	4,466
28,650	28,700	5,384	4,301	5,819	4,480
28,700	28,750	5,398	4,309	5,833	4,494
28,750	28,800	5,412	4,316	5,847	4,508
28,800	28,850	5,426	4,324	5,861	4,522
28,850	28,900	5,440	4,331	5,875	4,536
28,900	28,950	5,454	4,339	5,889	4,550
28,950	29,000	5,468	4,346	5,903	4,564

If line 37 (taxable income) is—		And you are—			
At least	But less than	Single	Married filing jointly *	Married filing sepa-rately	Head of a house-hold
		Your tax is—			
29,000					
29,000	29,050	5,482	4,354	5,917	4,578
29,050	29,100	5,496	4,361	5,931	4,592
29,100	29,150	5,510	4,369	5,945	4,606
29,150	29,200	5,524	4,376	5,959	4,620
29,200	29,250	5,538	4,384	5,973	4,634
29,250	29,300	5,552	4,391	5,987	4,648
29,300	29,350	5,566	4,399	6,001	4,662
29,350	29,400	5,580	4,406	6,015	4,676
29,400	29,450	5,594	4,414	6,029	4,690
29,450	29,500	5,608	4,421	6,043	4,704
29,500	29,550	5,622	4,429	6,057	4,718
29,550	29,600	5,636	4,436	6,071	4,732
29,600	29,650	5,650	4,444	6,085	4,746
29,650	29,700	5,664	4,451	6,099	4,760
29,700	29,750	5,678	4,459	6,113	4,774
29,750	29,800	5,692	4,466	6,127	4,788
29,800	29,850	5,706	4,474	6,141	4,802
29,850	29,900	5,720	4,481	6,155	4,816
29,900	29,950	5,734	4,489	6,169	4,830
29,950	30,000	5,748	4,496	6,183	4,844
30,000					
30,000	30,050	5,762	4,504	6,197	4,858
30,050	30,100	5,776	4,511	6,211	4,872
30,100	30,150	5,790	4,519	6,225	4,886
30,150	30,200	5,804	4,526	6,239	4,900
30,200	30,250	5,818	4,534	6,253	4,914
30,250	30,300	5,832	4,541	6,267	4,928
30,300	30,350	5,846	4,549	6,281	4,942
30,350	30,400	5,860	4,556	6,295	4,956
30,400	30,450	5,874	4,564	6,309	4,970
30,450	30,500	5,888	4,571	6,323	4,984
30,500	30,550	5,902	4,579	6,337	4,998
30,550	30,600	5,916	4,586	6,351	5,012
30,600	30,650	5,930	4,594	6,365	5,026
30,650	30,700	5,944	4,601	6,379	5,040
30,700	30,750	5,958	4,609	6,393	5,054
30,750	30,800	5,972	4,616	6,407	5,068
30,800	30,850	5,986	4,624	6,421	5,082
30,850	30,900	6,000	4,631	6,435	5,096
30,900	30,950	6,014	4,639	6,449	5,110
30,950	31,000	6,028	4,646	6,463	5,124
31,000					
31,000	31,050	6,042	4,654	6,477	5,138
31,050	31,100	6,056	4,661	6,491	5,152
31,100	31,150	6,070	4,669	6,505	5,166
31,150	31,200	6,084	4,676	6,519	5,180
31,200	31,250	6,098	4,684	6,533	5,194
31,250	31,300	6,112	4,691	6,547	5,208
31,300	31,350	6,126	4,699	6,561	5,222
31,350	31,400	6,140	4,706	6,575	5,236
31,400	31,450	6,154	4,714	6,589	5,250
31,450	31,500	6,168	4,721	6,603	5,264
31,500	31,550	6,182	4,729	6,617	5,278
31,550	31,600	6,196	4,736	6,631	5,292
31,600	31,650	6,210	4,744	6,645	5,306
31,650	31,700	6,224	4,751	6,659	5,320
31,700	31,750	6,238	4,759	6,673	5,334
31,750	31,800	6,252	4,766	6,687	5,348
31,800	31,850	6,266	4,774	6,701	5,362
31,850	31,900	6,280	4,781	6,715	5,376
31,900	31,950	6,294	4,789	6,729	5,390
31,950	32,000	6,308	4,796	6,743	5,404

* This column must also be used by a qualifying widow(er).

Continued on next page

1991 Tax Table—*Continued*

If line 37 (taxable income) is—		And you are—			
At least	But less than	Single	Married filing jointly *	Married filing separately	Head of a household
		Your tax is—			
32,000					
32,000	**32,050**	6,322	4,804	6,757	5,418
32,050	**32,100**	6,336	4,811	6,771	5,432
32,100	**32,150**	6,350	4,819	6,785	5,446
32,150	**32,200**	6,364	4,826	6,799	5,460
32,200	**32,250**	6,378	4,834	6,813	5,474
32,250	**32,300**	6,392	4,841	6,827	5,488
32,300	**32,350**	6,406	4,849	6,841	5,502
32,350	**32,400**	6,420	4,856	6,855	5,516
32,400	**32,450**	6,434	4,864	6,869	5,530
32,450	**32,500**	6,448	4,871	6,883	5,544
32,500	**32,550**	6,462	4,879	6,897	5,558
32,550	**32,600**	6,476	4,886	6,911	5,572
32,600	**32,650**	6,490	4,894	6,925	5,586
32,650	**32,700**	6,504	4,901	6,939	5,600
32,700	**32,750**	6,518	4,909	6,953	5,614
32,750	**32,800**	6,532	4,916	6,967	5,628
32,800	**32,850**	6,546	4,924	6,981	5,642
32,850	**32,900**	6,560	4,931	6,995	5,656
32,900	**32,950**	6,574	4,939	7,009	5,670
32,950	**33,000**	6,588	4,946	7,023	5,684
33,000					
33,000	**33,050**	6,602	4,954	7,037	5,698
33,050	**33,100**	6,616	4,961	7,051	5,712
33,100	**33,150**	6,630	4,969	7,065	5,726
33,150	**33,200**	6,644	4,976	7,079	5,740
33,200	**33,250**	6,658	4,984	7,093	5,754
33,250	**33,300**	6,672	4,991	7,107	5,768
33,300	**33,350**	6,686	4,999	7,121	5,782
33,350	**33,400**	6,700	5,006	7,135	5,796
33,400	**33,450**	6,714	5,014	7,149	5,810
33,450	**33,500**	6,728	5,021	7,163	5,824
33,500	**33,550**	6,742	5,029	7,177	5,838
33,550	**33,600**	6,756	5,036	7,191	5,852
33,600	**33,650**	6,770	5,044	7,205	5,866
33,650	**33,700**	6,784	5,051	7,219	5,880
33,700	**33,750**	6,798	5,059	7,233	5,894
33,750	**33,800**	6,812	5,066	7,247	5,908
33,800	**33,850**	6,826	5,074	7,261	5,922
33,850	**33,900**	6,840	5,081	7,275	5,936
33,900	**33,950**	6,854	5,089	7,289	5,950
33,950	**34,000**	6,868	5,096	7,303	5,964
34,000					
34,000	**34,050**	6,882	5,107	7,317	5,978
34,050	**34,100**	6,896	5,121	7,331	5,992
34,100	**34,150**	6,910	5,135	7,345	6,006
34,150	**34,200**	6,924	5,149	7,359	6,020
34,200	**34,250**	6,938	5,163	7,373	6,034
34,250	**34,300**	6,952	5,177	7,387	6,048
34,300	**34,350**	6,966	5,191	7,401	6,062
34,350	**34,400**	6,980	5,205	7,415	6,076
34,400	**34,450**	6,994	5,219	7,429	6,090
34,450	**34,500**	7,008	5,233	7,443	6,104
34,500	**34,550**	7,022	5,247	7,457	6,118
34,550	**34,600**	7,036	5,261	7,471	6,132
34,600	**34,650**	7,050	5,275	7,485	6,146
34,650	**34,700**	7,064	5,289	7,499	6,160
34,700	**34,750**	7,078	5,303	7,513	6,174
34,750	**34,800**	7,092	5,317	7,527	6,188
34,800	**34,850**	7,106	5,331	7,541	6,202
34,850	**34,900**	7,120	5,345	7,555	6,216
34,900	**34,950**	7,134	5,359	7,569	6,230
34,950	**35,000**	7,148	5,373	7,583	6,244

If line 37 (taxable income) is—		And you are—			
At least	But less than	Single	Married filing jointly *	Married filing separately	Head of a household
		Your tax is—			
35,000					
35,000	**35,050**	7,162	5,387	7,597	6,258
35,050	**35,100**	7,176	5,401	7,611	6,272
35,100	**35,150**	7,190	5,415	7,625	6,286
35,150	**35,200**	7,204	5,429	7,639	6,300
35,200	**35,250**	7,218	5,443	7,653	6,314
35,250	**35,300**	7,232	5,457	7,667	6,328
35,300	**35,350**	7,246	5,471	7,681	6,342
35,350	**35,400**	7,260	5,485	7,695	6,356
35,400	**35,450**	7,274	5,499	7,709	6,370
35,450	**35,500**	7,288	5,513	7,723	6,384
35,500	**35,550**	7,302	5,527	7,737	6,398
35,550	**35,600**	7,316	5,541	7,751	6,412
35,600	**35,650**	7,330	5,555	7,765	6,426
35,650	**35,700**	7,344	5,569	7,779	6,440
35,700	**35,750**	7,358	5,583	7,793	6,454
35,750	**35,800**	7,372	5,597	7,807	6,468
35,800	**35,850**	7,386	5,611	7,821	6,482
35,850	**35,900**	7,400	5,625	7,835	6,496
35,900	**35,950**	7,414	5,639	7,849	6,510
35,950	**36,000**	7,428	5,653	7,863	6,524
36,000					
36,000	**36,050**	7,442	5,667	7,877	6,538
36,050	**36,100**	7,456	5,681	7,891	6,552
36,100	**36,150**	7,470	5,695	7,905	6,566
36,150	**36,200**	7,484	5,709	7,919	6,580
36,200	**36,250**	7,498	5,723	7,933	6,594
36,250	**36,300**	7,512	5,737	7,947	6,608
36,300	**36,350**	7,526	5,751	7,961	6,622
36,350	**36,400**	7,540	5,765	7,975	6,636
36,400	**36,450**	7,554	5,779	7,989	6,650
36,450	**36,500**	7,568	5,793	8,003	6,664
36,500	**36,550**	7,582	5,807	8,017	6,678
36,550	**36,600**	7,596	5,821	8,031	6,692
36,600	**36,650**	7,610	5,835	8,045	6,706
36,650	**36,700**	7,624	5,849	8,059	6,720
36,700	**36,750**	7,638	5,863	8,073	6,734
36,750	**36,800**	7,652	5,877	8,087	6,748
36,800	**36,850**	7,666	5,891	8,101	6,762
36,850	**36,900**	7,680	5,905	8,115	6,776
36,900	**36,950**	7,694	5,919	8,129	6,790
36,950	**37,000**	7,708	5,933	8,143	6,804
37,000					
37,000	**37,050**	7,722	5,947	8,157	6,818
37,050	**37,100**	7,736	5,961	8,171	6,832
37,100	**37,150**	7,750	5,975	8,185	6,846
37,150	**37,200**	7,764	5,989	8,199	6,860
37,200	**37,250**	7,778	6,003	8,213	6,874
37,250	**37,300**	7,792	6,017	8,227	6,888
37,300	**37,350**	7,806	6,031	8,241	6,902
37,350	**37,400**	7,820	6,045	8,255	6,916
37,400	**37,450**	7,834	6,059	8,269	6,930
37,450	**37,500**	7,848	6,073	8,283	6,944
37,500	**37,550**	7,862	6,087	8,297	6,958
37,550	**37,600**	7,876	6,101	8,311	6,972
37,600	**37,650**	7,890	6,115	8,325	6,986
37,650	**37,700**	7,904	6,129	8,339	7,000
37,700	**37,750**	7,918	6,143	8,353	7,014
37,750	**37,800**	7,932	6,157	8,367	7,028
37,800	**37,850**	7,946	6,171	8,381	7,042
37,850	**37,900**	7,960	6,185	8,395	7,056
37,900	**37,950**	7,974	6,199	8,409	7,070
37,950	**38,000**	7,988	6,213	8,423	7,084

If line 37 (taxable income) is—		And you are—			
At least	But less than	Single	Married filing jointly *	Married filing separately	Head of a household
		Your tax is—			
38,000					
38,000	**38,050**	8,002	6,227	8,437	7,098
38,050	**38,100**	8,016	6,241	8,451	7,112
38,100	**38,150**	8,030	6,255	8,465	7,126
38,150	**38,200**	8,044	6,269	8,479	7,140
38,200	**38,250**	8,058	6,283	8,493	7,154
38,250	**38,300**	8,072	6,297	8,507	7,168
38,300	**38,350**	8,086	6,311	8,521	7,182
38,350	**38,400**	8,100	6,325	8,535	7,196
38,400	**38,450**	8,114	6,339	8,549	7,210
38,450	**38,500**	8,128	6,353	8,563	7,224
38,500	**38,550**	8,142	6,367	8,577	7,238
38,550	**38,600**	8,156	6,381	8,591	7,252
38,600	**38,650**	8,170	6,395	8,605	7,266
38,650	**38,700**	8,184	6,409	8,619	7,280
38,700	**38,750**	8,198	6,423	8,633	7,294
38,750	**38,800**	8,212	6,437	8,647	7,308
38,800	**38,850**	8,226	6,451	8,661	7,322
38,850	**38,900**	8,240	6,465	8,675	7,336
38,900	**38,950**	8,254	6,479	8,689	7,350
38,950	**39,000**	8,268	6,493	8,703	7,364
39,000					
39,000	**39,050**	8,282	6,507	8,717	7,378
39,050	**39,100**	8,296	6,521	8,731	7,392
39,100	**39,150**	8,310	6,535	8,745	7,406
39,150	**39,200**	8,324	6,549	8,759	7,420
39,200	**39,250**	8,338	6,563	8,773	7,434
39,250	**39,300**	8,352	6,577	8,787	7,448
39,300	**39,350**	8,366	6,591	8,801	7,462
39,350	**39,400**	8,380	6,605	8,815	7,476
39,400	**39,450**	8,394	6,619	8,829	7,490
39,450	**39,500**	8,408	6,633	8,843	7,504
39,500	**39,550**	8,422	6,647	8,857	7,518
39,550	**39,600**	8,436	6,661	8,871	7,532
39,600	**39,650**	8,450	6,675	8,885	7,546
39,650	**39,700**	8,464	6,689	8,899	7,560
39,700	**39,750**	8,478	6,703	8,913	7,574
39,750	**39,800**	8,492	6,717	8,927	7,588
39,800	**39,850**	8,506	6,731	8,941	7,602
39,850	**39,900**	8,520	6,745	8,955	7,616
39,900	**39,950**	8,534	6,759	8,969	7,630
39,950	**40,000**	8,548	6,773	8,983	7,644
40,000					
40,000	**40,050**	8,562	6,787	8,997	7,658
40,050	**40,100**	8,576	6,801	9,011	7,672
40,100	**40,150**	8,590	6,815	9,025	7,686
40,150	**40,200**	8,604	6,829	9,039	7,700
40,200	**40,250**	8,618	6,843	9,053	7,714
40,250	**40,300**	8,632	6,857	9,067	7,728
40,300	**40,350**	8,646	6,871	9,081	7,742
40,350	**40,400**	8,660	6,885	9,095	7,756
40,400	**40,450**	8,674	6,899	9,109	7,770
40,450	**40,500**	8,688	6,913	9,123	7,784
40,500	**40,550**	8,702	6,927	9,137	7,798
40,550	**40,600**	8,716	6,941	9,151	7,812
40,600	**40,650**	8,730	6,955	9,165	7,826
40,650	**40,700**	8,744	6,969	9,179	7,840
40,700	**40,750**	8,758	6,983	9,193	7,854
40,750	**40,800**	8,772	6,997	9,207	7,868
40,800	**40,850**	8,786	7,011	9,221	7,882
40,850	**40,900**	8,800	7,025	9,235	7,896
40,900	**40,950**	8,814	7,039	9,249	7,910
40,950	**41,000**	8,828	7,053	9,263	7,924

* This column must also be used by a qualifying widow(er).

Continued on next page

1991 Tax Table—*Continued*

If line 37 (taxable income) is— At least	But less than	And you are— Single	Married filing jointly *	Married filing sepa-rately	Head of a house-hold
		Your tax is—			
41,000					
41,000	41,050	8,842	7,067	9,277	7,938
41,050	41,100	8,856	7,081	9,291	7,952
41,100	41,150	8,870	7,095	9,307	7,966
41,150	41,200	8,884	7,109	9,322	7,980
41,200	41,250	8,898	7,123	9,338	7,994
41,250	41,300	8,912	7,137	9,353	8,008
41,300	41,350	8,926	7,151	9,369	8,022
41,350	41,400	8,940	7,165	9,384	8,036
41,400	41,450	8,954	7,179	9,400	8,050
41,450	41,500	8,968	7,193	9,415	8,064
41,500	41,550	8,982	7,207	9,431	8,078
41,550	41,600	8,996	7,221	9,446	8,092
41,600	41,650	9,010	7,235	9,462	8,106
41,650	41,700	9,024	7,249	9,477	8,120
41,700	41,750	9,038	7,263	9,493	8,134
41,750	41,800	9,052	7,277	9,508	8,148
41,800	41,850	9,066	7,291	9,524	8,162
41,850	41,900	9,080	7,305	9,539	8,176
41,900	41,950	9,094	7,319	9,555	8,190
41,950	42,000	9,108	7,333	9,570	8,204
42,000					
42,000	42,050	9,122	7,347	9,586	8,218
42,050	42,100	9,136	7,361	9,601	8,232
42,100	42,150	9,150	7,375	9,617	8,246
42,150	42,200	9,164	7,389	9,632	8,260
42,200	42,250	9,178	7,403	9,648	8,274
42,250	42,300	9,192	7,417	9,663	8,288
42,300	42,350	9,206	7,431	9,679	8,302
42,350	42,400	9,220	7,445	9,694	8,316
42,400	42,450	9,234	7,459	9,710	8,330
42,450	42,500	9,248	7,473	9,725	8,344
42,500	42,550	9,262	7,487	9,741	8,358
42,550	42,600	9,276	7,501	9,756	8,372
42,600	42,650	9,290	7,515	9,772	8,386
42,650	42,700	9,304	7,529	9,787	8,400
42,700	42,750	9,318	7,543	9,803	8,414
42,750	42,800	9,332	7,557	9,818	8,428
42,800	42,850	9,346	7,571	9,834	8,442
42,850	42,900	9,360	7,585	9,849	8,456
42,900	42,950	9,374	7,599	9,865	8,470
42,950	43,000	9,388	7,613	9,880	8,484
43,000					
43,000	43,050	9,402	7,627	9,896	8,498
43,050	43,100	9,416	7,641	9,911	8,512
43,100	43,150	9,430	7,655	9,927	8,526
43,150	43,200	9,444	7,669	9,942	8,540
43,200	43,250	9,458	7,683	9,958	8,554
43,250	43,300	9,472	7,697	9,973	8,568
43,300	43,350	9,486	7,711	9,989	8,582
43,350	43,400	9,500	7,725	10,004	8,596
43,400	43,450	9,514	7,739	10,020	8,610
43,450	43,500	9,528	7,753	10,035	8,624
43,500	43,550	9,542	7,767	10,051	8,638
43,550	43,600	9,556	7,781	10,066	8,652
43,600	43,650	9,570	7,795	10,082	8,666
43,650	43,700	9,584	7,809	10,097	8,680
43,700	43,750	9,598	7,823	10,113	8,694
43,750	43,800	9,612	7,837	10,128	8,708
43,800	43,850	9,626	7,851	10,144	8,722
43,850	43,900	9,640	7,865	10,159	8,736
43,900	43,950	9,654	7,879	10,175	8,750
43,950	44,000	9,668	7,893	10,190	8,764
44,000					
44,000	44,050	9,682	7,907	10,206	8,778
44,050	44,100	9,696	7,921	10,221	8,792
44,100	44,150	9,710	7,935	10,237	8,806
44,150	44,200	9,724	7,949	10,252	8,820
44,200	44,250	9,738	7,963	10,268	8,834
44,250	44,300	9,752	7,977	10,283	8,848
44,300	44,350	9,766	7,991	10,299	8,862
44,350	44,400	9,780	8,005	10,314	8,876
44,400	44,450	9,794	8,019	10,330	8,890
44,450	44,500	9,808	8,033	10,345	8,904
44,500	44,550	9,822	8,047	10,361	8,918
44,550	44,600	9,836	8,061	10,376	8,932
44,600	44,650	9,850	8,075	10,392	8,946
44,650	44,700	9,864	8,089	10,407	8,960
44,700	44,750	9,878	8,103	10,423	8,974
44,750	44,800	9,892	8,117	10,438	8,988
44,800	44,850	9,906	8,131	10,454	9,002
44,850	44,900	9,920	8,145	10,469	9,016
44,900	44,950	9,934	8,159	10,485	9,030
44,950	45,000	9,948	8,173	10,500	9,044
45,000					
45,000	45,050	9,962	8,187	10,516	9,058
45,050	45,100	9,976	8,201	10,531	9,072
45,100	45,150	9,990	8,215	10,547	9,086
45,150	45,200	10,004	8,229	10,562	9,100
45,200	45,250	10,018	8,243	10,578	9,114
45,250	45,300	10,032	8,257	10,593	9,128
45,300	45,350	10,046	8,271	10,609	9,142
45,350	45,400	10,060	8,285	10,624	9,156
45,400	45,450	10,074	8,299	10,640	9,170
45,450	45,500	10,088	8,313	10,655	9,184
45,500	45,550	10,102	8,327	10,671	9,198
45,550	45,600	10,116	8,341	10,686	9,212
45,600	45,650	10,130	8,355	10,702	9,226
45,650	45,700	10,144	8,369	10,717	9,240
45,700	45,750	10,158	8,383	10,733	9,254
45,750	45,800	10,172	8,397	10,748	9,268
45,800	45,850	10,186	8,411	10,764	9,282
45,850	45,900	10,200	8,425	10,779	9,296
45,900	45,950	10,214	8,439	10,795	9,310
45,950	46,000	10,228	8,453	10,810	9,324
46,000					
46,000	46,050	10,242	8,467	10,826	9,338
46,050	46,100	10,256	8,481	10,841	9,352
46,100	46,150	10,270	8,495	10,857	9,366
46,150	46,200	10,284	8,509	10,872	9,380
46,200	46,250	10,298	8,523	10,888	9,394
46,250	46,300	10,312	8,537	10,903	9,408
46,300	46,350	10,326	8,551	10,919	9,422
46,350	46,400	10,340	8,565	10,934	9,436
46,400	46,450	10,354	8,579	10,950	9,450
46,450	46,500	10,368	8,593	10,965	9,464
46,500	46,550	10,382	8,607	10,981	9,478
46,550	46,600	10,396	8,621	10,996	9,492
46,600	46,650	10,410	8,635	11,012	9,506
46,650	46,700	10,424	8,649	11,027	9,520
46,700	46,750	10,438	8,663	11,043	9,534
46,750	46,800	10,452	8,677	11,058	9,548
46,800	46,850	10,466	8,691	11,074	9,562
46,850	46,900	10,480	8,705	11,089	9,576
46,900	46,950	10,494	8,719	11,105	9,590
46,950	47,000	10,508	8,733	11,120	9,604
47,000					
47,000	47,050	10,522	8,747	11,136	9,618
47,050	47,100	10,536	8,761	11,151	9,632
47,100	47,150	10,550	8,775	11,167	9,646
47,150	47,200	10,564	8,789	11,182	9,660
47,200	47,250	10,578	8,803	11,198	9,674
47,250	47,300	10,592	8,817	11,213	9,688
47,300	47,350	10,606	8,831	11,229	9,702
47,350	47,400	10,620	8,845	11,244	9,716
47,400	47,450	10,634	8,859	11,260	9,730
47,450	47,500	10,648	8,873	11,275	9,744
47,500	47,550	10,662	8,887	11,291	9,758
47,550	47,600	10,676	8,901	11,306	9,772
47,600	47,650	10,690	8,915	11,322	9,786
47,650	47,700	10,704	8,929	11,337	9,800
47,700	47,750	10,718	8,943	11,353	9,814
47,750	47,800	10,732	8,957	11,368	9,828
47,800	47,850	10,746	8,971	11,384	9,842
47,850	47,900	10,760	8,985	11,399	9,856
47,900	47,950	10,774	8,999	11,415	9,870
47,950	48,000	10,788	9,013	11,430	9,884
48,000					
48,000	48,050	10,802	9,027	11,446	9,898
48,050	48,100	10,816	9,041	11,461	9,912
48,100	48,150	10,830	9,055	11,477	9,926
48,150	48,200	10,844	9,069	11,492	9,940
48,200	48,250	10,858	9,083	11,508	9,954
48,250	48,300	10,872	9,097	11,523	9,968
48,300	48,350	10,886	9,111	11,539	9,982
48,350	48,400	10,900	9,125	11,554	9,996
48,400	48,450	10,914	9,139	11,570	10,010
48,450	48,500	10,928	9,153	11,585	10,024
48,500	48,550	10,942	9,167	11,601	10,038
48,550	48,600	10,956	9,181	11,616	10,052
48,600	48,650	10,970	9,195	11,632	10,066
48,650	48,700	10,984	9,209	11,647	10,080
48,700	48,750	10,998	9,223	11,663	10,094
48,750	48,800	11,012	9,237	11,678	10,108
48,800	48,850	11,026	9,251	11,694	10,122
48,850	48,900	11,040	9,265	11,709	10,136
48,900	48,950	11,054	9,279	11,725	10,150
48,950	49,000	11,068	9,293	11,740	10,164
49,000					
49,000	49,050	11,082	9,307	11,756	10,178
49,050	49,100	11,096	9,321	11,771	10,192
49,100	49,150	11,110	9,335	11,787	10,206
49,150	49,200	11,124	9,349	11,802	10,220
49,200	49,250	11,138	9,363	11,818	10,234
49,250	49,300	11,152	9,377	11,833	10,248
49,300	49,350	11,166	9,391	11,849	10,262
49,350	49,400	11,182	9,405	11,864	10,276
49,400	49,450	11,197	9,419	11,880	10,290
49,450	49,500	11,213	9,433	11,895	10,304
49,500	49,550	11,228	9,447	11,911	10,318
49,550	49,600	11,244	9,461	11,926	10,332
49,600	49,650	11,259	9,475	11,942	10,346
49,650	49,700	11,275	9,489	11,957	10,360
49,700	49,750	11,290	9,503	11,973	10,374
49,750	49,800	11,306	9,517	11,988	10,388
49,800	49,850	11,321	9,531	12,004	10,402
49,850	49,900	11,337	9,545	12,019	10,416
49,900	49,950	11,352	9,559	12,035	10,430
49,950	50,000	11,368	9,573	12,050	10,444

* This column must also be used by a qualifying widow(er).

50,000 or over — use tax rate schedules

1992 Tax Rate Schedules

Single—Schedule X

If taxable income is: Over—	But not over—	The tax is:	of the amount over—
$0	$21,450	..........15%	**$0**
21,450	51,900	**$3,217.50 + 28%**	**21,450**
51,900	....	**11,743.50 + 31%**	**51,900**

Head of household—Schedule Z

If taxable income is: Over—	But not over—	The tax is:	of the amount over—
$0	$28,750	..........15%	**$0**
28,750	74,150	**$4,312.50 + 28%**	**28,750**
74,150	....	**17,024.50 + 31%**	**74,150**

Married filing jointly or Qualifying widow(er)—Schedule Y-1

If taxable income is: Over—	But not over—	The tax is:	of the amount over—
$0	$35,800	..........15%	**$0**
35,800	86,500	**$5,370.00 + 28%**	**35,800**
86,500	....	**19,566.00 + 31%**	**86,500**

Married filing separately—Schedule Y-2

If taxable income is: Over—	But not over—	The tax is:	of the amount over—
$0	$17,900	..........15%	**$0**
17,900	43,250	**$2,685.00 + 28%**	**17,900**
43,250	....	**9,783.00 + 31%**	**43,250**

APPENDIX

TAX FORMS

Form **1040EZ**

Department of the Treasury—Internal Revenue Service

Income Tax Return for Single Filers With No Dependents (T) **1991**

OMB No. 1545-0675

Name & address

Use the IRS label (see page 10). If you don't have one, please print.

LABEL HERE

Print your name (first, initial, last)

Home address (number and street). (If you have a P.O. box, see page 11.) | Apt. no.

City, town or post office, state, and ZIP code. (If you have a foreign address, see page 11.)

Please print your numbers like this: 9876543210

Your social security number

Please see instructions on the back. Also, see the Form 1040EZ booklet.

Presidential Election Campaign (see page 11) Do you want $1 to go to this fund? **Note:** *Checking "Yes" will not change your tax or reduce your refund.* ▶ Yes No

Dollars Cents

Report your income

Attach Copy B of Form(s) W-2 here. Attach tax payment on top of Form(s) W-2.

1 Total wages, salaries, and tips. This should be shown in Box 10 of your W-2 form(s). (Attach your W-2 form(s).) 1

2 Taxable interest income of $400 or less. If the total is more than $400, you cannot use Form 1040EZ. 2

3 Add line 1 and line 2. This is your **adjusted gross income.** 3

Note: *You **must** check Yes or No.*

4 Can your parents (or someone else) claim you on their return?
- ☐ **Yes.** Do worksheet on back; enter amount from line E here.
- ☐ **No.** Enter 5,550.00. This is the total of your standard deduction and personal exemption. 4

5 Subtract line 4 from line 3. If line 4 is larger than line 3, enter 0. This is your **taxable income.** 5

Figure your tax

6 Enter your Federal income tax withheld from Box 9 of your W-2 form(s). 6

7 **Tax.** Use the amount on **line 5** to find your tax in the tax table on pages 16-18 of the booklet. Enter the tax from the table on this line. 7

Refund or amount you owe

8 If line 6 is larger than line 7, subtract line 7 from line 6. This is your **refund.** 8

9 If line 7 is larger than line 6, subtract line 6 from line 7. This is the **amount you owe.** Attach your payment for full amount payable to the "Internal Revenue Service." Write your name, address, social security number, daytime phone number, and "1991 Form 1040EZ" on it. 9

Sign your return

Keep a copy of this form for your records.

I have read this return. Under penalties of perjury, I declare that to the best of my knowledge and belief, the return is true, correct, and complete.

Your signature X | Date | Your occupation

For IRS Use Only — Please do not write in boxes below.

For Privacy Act and Paperwork Reduction Act Notice, see page 4 in the booklet. Cat. No. 11329W Form 1040EZ (1991)

1991 Instructions for Form 1040EZ

Use this form if

- Your filing status is single.
- You were under 65 and not blind at the end of 1991.
- You do not claim any dependents.
- Your taxable income (line 5) is less than $50,000.
- You had **only** wages, salaries, tips, and taxable scholarship or fellowship grants, and your taxable interest income was $400 or less. **Caution:** *If you earned tips (including allocated tips) that are not included in Box 13 and Box 14 of your W-2, you may not be able to use Form 1040EZ. See page 12 in the booklet.*
- You did not receive any advance earned income credit payments.

If you are not sure about your filing status, see page 6 in the booklet. If you have questions about dependents, see Tele-Tax (topic no. 155) on page 25 in the booklet.

If you can't use this form, see Tele-Tax (topic no. 152) on page 25 in the booklet.

Completing your return

Please print your numbers inside the boxes. Do not type your numbers. Do not use dollar signs.

Most people can fill out the form by following the instructions on the front. But you will have to use the booklet if you received a scholarship or fellowship grant or tax-exempt interest income (such as on municipal bonds). Also use the booklet if you received a 1099-INT showing income tax withheld (backup withholding) or if you had two or more employers and your total wages were more than $53,400.

Remember, you must report your wages, salaries, and tips even if you don't get a W-2 form from your employer. You must also report all your taxable interest income, including interest from savings accounts at banks, savings and loans, credit unions, etc., even if you don't get a Form 1099-INT.

If you paid someone to prepare your return, that person must also sign it and show other information. See page 15 in the booklet.

Standard deduction worksheet for dependents who checked "Yes" on line 4

Fill in this worksheet to figure the amount to enter on line 4 if someone can claim you as a dependent (even if that person chooses not to claim you).

A. Enter the amount from line 1 on front.	**A.**	
B. Minimum amount.	**B.**	550.00
C. Compare the amounts on lines A and B above. Enter the LARGER of the two amounts here.	**C.**	
D. Maximum amount.	**D.**	3,400.00
E. Compare the amounts on lines C and D above. Enter the SMALLER of the two amounts here and on line 4 on front.	**E.**	

If you checked "No" because no one can claim you as a dependent, enter 5,550.00 on line 4. This is the total of your standard deduction (3,400.00) and personal exemption (2,150.00).

Avoid common mistakes

This checklist is to help you make sure that your form is filled out correctly.

1. Are your name, address, and social security number on the label correct? If not, did you correct the label?
2. If you didn't get a label, did you enter your name, address (including ZIP code), and social security number in the spaces provided on page 1 of Form 1040EZ?
3. Did you check the "Yes" box on line 4 if your parents (or someone else) can claim you as a dependent on their 1991 return (even if they choose not to claim you)? If no one can claim you as a dependent, did you check the "No" box?
4. Did you enter an amount on line 4? If you checked the "Yes" box on line 4, did you fill out the worksheet above to figure the amount to enter? If you checked the "No" box, did you enter 5,550.00?
5. Did you check your computations (additions, subtractions, etc.) especially when figuring your taxable income, Federal income tax withheld, and your refund or amount you owe?
6. Did you use the amount from **line 5** to find your tax in the tax table? Did you enter the correct tax on line 7?
7. Did you attach your W-2 form(s) to the left margin of your return? And, did you sign and date Form 1040EZ and enter your occupation?

Mailing your return

Mail your return by **April 15, 1992**. Use the envelope that came with your booklet. If you don't have that envelope, see page 19 in the booklet for the address to use.

Form **1040A** Department of the Treasury—Internal Revenue Service

U.S. Individual Income Tax Return (T) **1991** OMB No. 1545-0085

Step 1
Label
(See page 16.)

Use the IRS label. Otherwise, please print or type.

LABEL HERE

Your first name and initial	Last name	
If a joint return, spouse's first name and initial	Last name	
Home address (number and street). (If you have a P.O. box, see page 16.)		Apt. no.
City, town or post office, state, and ZIP code. (If you have a foreign address, see page 16.)		

Your social security no.

Spouse's social security no.

For Privacy Act and Paperwork Reduction Act Notice, see page 3.

Presidential Election Campaign Fund (see page 17)
Do you want $1 to go to this fund? . . . . ☐ Yes ☐ No
If joint return, does your spouse want $1 to go to this fund? ☐ Yes ☐ No

Note: *Checking "Yes" will not change your tax or reduce your refund.*

Step 2
Check your filing status
(Check only one.)

1 ☐ Single
2 ☐ Married filing joint return (even if only one had income)
3 ☐ Married filing separate return. Enter spouse's social security number above and spouse's full name here ▶ ______
4 ☐ Head of household (with qualifying person). (See page 18.) If the qualifying person is a child but not your dependent, enter this child's name here ▶ ______
5 ☐ Qualifying widow(er) with dependent child (year spouse died ▶ 19 ____). (See page 19.)

Step 3
Figure your exemptions
(See page 20.)

If more than seven dependents, see page 23.

6a ☐ **Yourself.** If your parent (or someone else) can claim you as a dependent on his or her tax return, do not check box 6a. But be sure to check the box on line 18b on page 2.
b ☐ **Spouse**

No. of boxes checked on 6a and 6b ____

c **Dependents:**

(1) Name (first, initial, and last name)	(2) Check if under age 1	(3) If age 1 or older, dependent's social security number	(4) Dependent's relationship to you	(5) No. of months lived in your home in 1991

No. of your children on 6c who:
• lived with you ____
• didn't live with you due to divorce or separation (see page 23) ____
No. of other dependents listed on 6c ____
Add numbers entered on lines above ☐

d If your child didn't live with you but is claimed as your dependent under a pre-1985 agreement, check here . . . ▶ ☐
e Total number of exemptions claimed.

Step 4
Figure your total income

Attach Copy B of your Forms W-2 and 1099-R here.

Attach check or money order on top of any Forms W-2 or 1099-R.

7 Wages, salaries, tips, etc. This should be shown in Box 10 of your W-2 form(s). (Attach Form(s) W-2.) 7
8a **Taxable** interest income (see page 26). (If over $400, also complete and attach Schedule 1, Part I.) 8a
b **Tax-exempt** interest. (DO NOT include on line 8a.) 8b
9 Dividends. (If over $400, also complete and attach Schedule 1, Part II.) 9
10a Total IRA distributions. 10a — 10b Taxable amount (see page 27). 10b
11a Total pensions and annuities. 11a — 11b Taxable amount (see page 27). 11b
12 Unemployment compensation (insurance) from Form(s) 1099-G. 12
13a Social security benefits. 13a — 13b Taxable amount (see page 31). 13b
14 Add lines 7 through 13b (far right column). This is your **total income.** ▶ 14

Step 5
Figure your adjusted gross income

15a Your IRA deduction from applicable worksheet. 15a
b Spouse's IRA deduction from applicable worksheet. **Note:** *Rules for IRAs begin on page 33.* 15b
c Add lines 15a and 15b. These are your **total adjustments.** 15c
16 Subtract line 15c from line 14. This is your **adjusted gross income.** (If less than $21,250, see "Earned income credit" on page 41.) ▶ 16

Cat. No. 11327A

1991 Form 1040A Page 2

Step 6

17 Enter the amount from line 16. 17

18a Check if: ☐ **You** were 65 or older ☐ Blind / ☐ **Spouse** was 65 or older ☐ Blind } **Enter number of boxes checked** ▶ 18a ☐

b If your parent (or someone else) can claim you as a dependent, check here . . . . ▶ 18b ☐

c If you are married filing separately and your spouse files Form 1040 and itemizes deductions, see page 37 and check here . ▶ 18c ☐

Figure your standard deduction,

19 Enter the **standard deduction** shown below for your filing status. **But if you checked any box on line 18a or b,** go to page 37 to find your standard deduction. **If you checked box 18c,** enter -0-.

- Single—$3,400 • Head of household—$5,000
- Married filing jointly or Qualifying widow(er)—$5,700
- Married filing separately—$2,850 19

20 Subtract line 19 from line 17. (If line 19 is more than line 17, enter -0-.) 20

exemption amount, and taxable income

21 Multiply $2,150 by the total number of exemptions claimed on line 6e. 21

22 Subtract line 21 from line 20. (If line 21 is more than line 20, enter -0-.) This is your **taxable income.** ▶ 22

Step 7

Figure your tax, credits, and payments

If you want the IRS to figure your tax, see the instructions for line 22 on page 38.

23 Find the tax on the amount on line 22. Check if from: ☐ Tax Table (pages 44–49) or ☐ Form 8615 (see page 39) 23

24a Credit for child and dependent care expenses. Complete and attach Schedule 2. 24a

b Credit for the elderly or the disabled. Complete and attach Schedule 3. 24b

c Add lines 24a and 24b. These are your **total credits.** 24c

25 Subtract line 24c from line 23. (If line 24c is more than line 23, enter -0-.) 25

26 Advance earned income credit payments from Form W-2. 26

27 Add lines 25 and 26. This is your **total tax.** ▶ 27

28a Total Federal income tax withheld. (If any tax is from Form(s) 1099, check here ▶ ☐ .) 28a

b 1991 estimated tax payments and amount applied from 1990 return. 28b

c **Earned income credit.** Complete and attach Schedule EIC. 28c

d Add lines 28a, 28b, and 28c. These are your **total payments.** ▶ 28d

Step 8

Figure your refund or amount you owe

29 If line 28d is more than line 27, subtract line 27 from line 28d. This is the amount you **overpaid.** 29

30 Amount of line 29 you want **refunded to you.** 30

31 Amount of line 29 you want **applied to your 1992 estimated tax.** 31

Attach check or money order on top of Form(s) W-2, etc., on page 1.

32 If line 27 is more than line 28d, subtract line 28d from line 27. This is the **amount you owe.** Attach check or money order for full amount payable to the "Internal Revenue Service." Write your name, address, social security number, daytime phone number, and "1991 Form 1040A" on it. 32

33 Estimated tax penalty (see page 43). 33

Step 9

Sign your return

Keep a copy of this return for your records.

Under penalties of perjury, I declare that I have examined this return and accompanying schedules and statements, and to the best of my knowledge and belief, they are true, correct, and complete. Declaration of preparer (other than the taxpayer) is based on all information of which the preparer has any knowledge.

▶ Your signature	Date	Your occupation
▶ Spouse's signature (if joint return, BOTH must sign)	Date	Spouse's occupation

Paid preparer's use only

Preparer's signature ▶	Date	Check if self-employed ☐	Preparer's social security no.
Firm's name (or yours if self-employed) and address ▶		E.I. No.	
		ZIP code	

Schedule 1 (Form 1040A) — Department of the Treasury—Internal Revenue Service

Interest and Dividend Income for Form 1040A Filers (T)

1991 — OMB No. 1545-0085

Name(s) shown on Form 1040A | **Your social security number**

Part I — Interest income

(See pages 26 and 50.)

Complete this part and attach Schedule 1 to Form 1040A if:

- You have over $400 in taxable interest, or
- You are claiming the exclusion of interest from series EE U.S. savings bonds issued after 1989.

If you are claiming the exclusion or you received, as a nominee, interest that actually belongs to another person, see page 50.

Note: *If you received a Form 1099–INT, Form 1099–OID, or substitute statement, from a brokerage firm, enter the firm's name and the total interest shown on that form.*

			Amount
1	List name of payer	1	
2	Add the amounts on line 1.	2	
3	Enter the excludable savings bond interest, if any, from Form 8815, line 14. Attach Form 8815 to Form 1040A.	3	
4	Subtract line 3 from line 2. Enter the result here and on Form 1040A, line 8a.	4	

Part II — Dividend income

(See pages 26 and 51.)

Complete this part and attach Schedule 1 to Form 1040A if you received over $400 in dividends.

If you received, as a nominee, dividends that actually belong to another person, see page 51.

Note: *If you received a Form 1099–DIV, or substitute statement, from a brokerage firm, enter the firm's name and the total dividends shown on that form.*

			Amount
5	List name of payer	5	
6	Add the amounts on line 5. Enter the total here and on Form 1040A, line 9.	6	

Form **1040** Department of the Treasury—Internal Revenue Service
U.S. Individual Income Tax Return 1991

For the year Jan.–Dec. 31, 1991, or other tax year beginning , 1991, ending , 19 | OMB No. 1545-0074

Label

(See instructions on page 11.)

Use the IRS label. Otherwise, please print or type.

LABEL HERE

Your first name and initial	Last name	Your social security number
If a joint return, spouse's first name and initial	Last name	Spouse's social security number
Home address (number and street). (If you have a P.O. box, see page 11.)	Apt. no.	**For Privacy Act and Paperwork Reduction Act Notice, see instructions.**
City, town or post office, state, and ZIP code. (If you have a foreign address, see page 11.)		

Presidential Election Campaign (See page 11.)

Do you want $1 to go to this fund?	Yes	No	**Note:** *Checking "Yes" will not change your tax or reduce your refund.*
If joint return, does your spouse want $1 to go to this fund?	Yes	No	

Filing Status

Check only one box.

1 ☐ Single
2 ☐ Married filing joint return (even if only one had income)
3 ☐ Married filing separate return. Enter spouse's social security no. above and full name here. ▶
4 ☐ Head of household (with qualifying person). (See page 12.) If the qualifying person is a child but not your dependent, enter this child's name here. ▶
5 ☐ Qualifying widow(er) with dependent child (year spouse died ▶ 19). (See page 12.)

Exemptions

(See page 12.)

6a ☐ **Yourself.** If your parent (or someone else) can claim you as a dependent on his or her tax return, do not check box 6a. But be sure to check the box on line 33b on page 2 .

b ☐ **Spouse**

No. of boxes checked on 6a and 6b ____

c **Dependents:**

If more than six dependents, see page 13.

(1) Name (first, initial, and last name)	(2) Check if under age 1	(3) If age 1 or older, dependent's social security number	(4) Dependent's relationship to you	(5) No. of months lived in your home in 1991

No. of your children on 6c who:
- lived with you ____
- didn't live with you due to divorce or separation (see page 14) ____

No. of other dependents on 6c ____

d If your child didn't live with you but is claimed as your dependent under a pre-1985 agreement, check here ▶ ☐

e Total number of exemptions claimed

Add numbers entered on lines above ▶ ☐

Income

Attach Copy B of your Forms W-2, W-2G, and 1099-R here.

If you did not get a W-2, see page 10.

Attach check or money order on top of any Forms W-2, W-2G, or 1099-R.

7	Wages, salaries, tips, etc. *(attach Form(s) W-2)*	7	
8a	**Taxable** interest income *(also attach Schedule B if over $400)*	8a	
b	**Tax-exempt** interest income (see page 16). DON'T include on line 8a **8b**		
9	Dividend income *(also attach Schedule B if over $400)*	9	
10	Taxable refunds of state and local income taxes, if any, from worksheet on page 16	10	
11	Alimony received	11	
12	Business income or (loss) *(attach Schedule C)*	12	
13	Capital gain or (loss) *(attach Schedule D)*	13	
14	Capital gain distributions not reported on line 13 (see page 17)	14	
15	Other gains or (losses) *(attach Form 4797)*	15	
16a	Total IRA distributions **16a**	**16b** Taxable amount (see page 17)	16b	
17a	Total pensions and annuities **17a**	**17b** Taxable amount (see page 17)	17b	
18	Rents, royalties, partnerships, estates, trusts, etc. *(attach Schedule E)*	18	
19	Farm income or (loss) *(attach Schedule F)*	19	
20	Unemployment compensation (insurance) (see page 18)	20	
21a	Social security benefits. **21a**	**21b** Taxable amount (see page 18)	21b	
22	Other income (list type and amount—see page 19)	22	
23	Add the amounts shown in the far right column for lines 7 through 22. This is your **total income** ▶	23	

Adjustments to Income

(See page 19.)

24a	Your IRA deduction, from applicable worksheet on page 20 or 21	24a	
b	Spouse's IRA deduction, from applicable worksheet on page 20 or 21	24b	
25	One-half of self-employment tax (see page 21)	25	
26	Self-employed health insurance deduction, from worksheet on page 22	26	
27	Keogh retirement plan and self-employed SEP deduction	27	
28	Penalty on early withdrawal of savings	28	
29	Alimony paid. Recipient's SSN ▶	29	
30	Add lines 24a through 29. These are your **total adjustments** ▶	30	

Adjusted Gross Income

31	Subtract line 30 from line 23. This is your **adjusted gross income.** *If this amount is less than $21,250 and a child lived with you, see page 45 to find out if you can claim the "Earned Income Credit" on line 56.* ▶	31	

Cat. No. 11320B

Form 1040 (1991) Page 2

Tax Computation

If you want the IRS to figure your tax, see page 24.

32 Amount from line 31 (adjusted gross income) . . . **32**

33a Check if: ☐ **You** were 65 or older, ☐ Blind; ☐ **Spouse** was 65 or older, ☐ Blind.
Add the number of boxes checked above and enter the total here . . . ▶ **33a**

b If your parent (or someone else) can claim you as a dependent, check here ▶ **33b** ☐

c If you are married filing a separate return and your spouse itemizes deductions, or you are a dual-status alien, see page 23 and check here . . . ▶ **33c** ☐

34 Enter the **larger** of your:
- **Itemized deductions** (from Schedule A, line 26), **OR**
- **Standard deduction** (shown below for your filing status). **Caution:** *If you checked **any** box on line 33a or b, go to page 23 to find your standard deduction. If you checked box 33c, your standard deduction is zero.*
  - Single—$3,400
  - Head of household—$5,000
  - Married filing jointly or Qualifying widow(er)—$5,700
  - Married filing separately—$2,850

34

35 Subtract line 34 from line 32 . . . **35**

36 If line 32 is $75,000 or less, multiply $2,150 by the total number of exemptions claimed on line 6e. If line 32 is over $75,000, see page 24 for the amount to enter . . . **36**

37 **Taxable income.** Subtract line 36 from line 35. (If line 36 is more than line 35, enter -0-.) . **37**

38 Enter tax. Check if from **a** ☐ Tax Table, **b** ☐ Tax Rate Schedules, **c** ☐ Schedule D, or **d** ☐ Form 8615 (see page 24). (Amount, if any, from Form(s) 8814 ▶ **e** ______ .) **38**

39 Additional taxes (see page 24). Check if from **a** ☐ Form 4970 **b** ☐ Form 4972 . . . **39**

40 Add lines 38 and 39 . . . ▶ **40**

Credits

(See page 25.)

41 Credit for child and dependent care expenses *(attach Form 2441)* **41**

42 Credit for the elderly or the disabled *(attach Schedule R)* . . **42**

43 Foreign tax credit *(attach Form 1116)* . . . **43**

44 Other credits (see page 25). Check if from **a** ☐ Form 3800 **b** ☐ Form 8396 **c** ☐ Form 8801 **d** ☐ Form (specify) ______ **44**

45 Add lines 41 through 44 . . . **45**

46 Subtract line 45 from line 40. (If line 45 is more than line 40, enter -0-.) . . . ▶ **46**

Other Taxes

47 Self-employment tax *(attach Schedule SE)* . . . **47**

48 Alternative minimum tax *(attach Form 6251)* . . . **48**

49 Recapture taxes (see page 26). Check if from **a** ☐ Form 4255 **b** ☐ Form 8611 **c** ☐ Form 8828 . **49**

50 Social security and Medicare tax on tip income not reported to employer *(attach Form 4137)* . **50**

51 Tax on an IRA or a qualified retirement plan *(attach Form 5329)* . . . **51**

52 Advance earned income credit payments from Form W-2 . . . **52**

53 Add lines 46 through 52. This is your **total tax** . . . ▶ **53**

Payments

Attach Forms W-2, W-2G, and 1099-R to front.

54 Federal income tax withheld (if any is from Form(s) 1099, check ▶ ☐) **54**

55 1991 estimated tax payments and amount applied from 1990 return . **55**

56 **Earned income credit** *(attach Schedule EIC)* . . . **56**

57 Amount paid with Form 4868 (extension request) . . . **57**

58 Excess social security, Medicare, and RRTA tax withheld (see page 27) . **58**

59 Other payments (see page 27). Check if from **a** ☐ Form 2439 **b** ☐ Form 4136 . . . **59**

60 Add lines 54 through 59. These are your **total payments** . . . ▶ **60**

Refund or Amount You Owe

61 If line 60 is more than line 53, subtract line 53 from line 60. This is the amount you **OVERPAID** . . ▶ **61**

62 Amount of line 61 to be **REFUNDED TO YOU** . . . ▶ **62**

63 Amount of line 61 to be **APPLIED TO YOUR 1992 ESTIMATED TAX** ▶ **63**

64 If line 53 is more than line 60, subtract line 60 from line 53. This is the **AMOUNT YOU OWE**. Attach check or money order for full amount payable to "Internal Revenue Service." Write your name, address, social security number, daytime phone number, and "1991 Form 1040" on it. . **64**

65 Estimated tax penalty (see page 28). Also include on line 64. **65**

Sign Here

Keep a copy of this return for your records.

Under penalties of perjury, I declare that I have examined this return and accompanying schedules and statements, and to the best of my knowledge and belief, they are true, correct, and complete. Declaration of preparer (other than taxpayer) is based on all information of which preparer has any knowledge.

Your signature	Date	Your occupation
Spouse's signature (if joint return, BOTH must sign)	Date	Spouse's occupation

Paid Preparer's Use Only

Preparer's signature	Date	Check if self-employed ☐	Preparer's social security no.
Firm's name (or yours if self-employed) and address		E.I. No.	
		ZIP code	

SCHEDULES A&B (Form 1040)

Department of the Treasury Internal Revenue Service (T)

Schedule A—Itemized Deductions

(Schedule B is on back)

▶ Attach to Form 1040. ▶ See Instructions for Schedules A and B (Form 1040).

OMB No. 1545-0074

1991

Attachment Sequence No. **07**

Name(s) shown on Form 1040 | Your social security number

Medical and Dental Expenses		**Caution:** *Do not include expenses reimbursed or paid by others.*		
	1	Medical and dental expenses. (See page 38.)	1	
	2	Enter amount from Form 1040, line 32 [2]		
	3	Multiply line 2 above by 7.5% (.075)	3	
	4	Subtract line 3 from line 1. Enter the result. If less than zero, enter -0- ▶		4
Taxes You Paid (See page 38.)	5	State and local income taxes	5	
	6	Real estate taxes	6	
	7	Other taxes. (List—include personal property taxes.) ▶	7	
	8	Add lines 5 through 7. Enter the total ▶		8
Interest You Paid (See page 39.)	9a	Home mortgage interest and points reported to you on Form 1098	9a	
	b	Home mortgage interest not reported to you on Form 1098. (If paid to an individual, show that person's name and address.) ▶	9b	
Note: Personal interest is no longer deductible.	10	Points not reported to you on Form 1098. (See instructions for special rules.)	10	
	11	Investment interest (attach Form 4952 if required). (See page 40.)	11	
	12	Add lines 9a through 11. Enter the total ▶		12
Gifts to Charity (See page 40.)		**Caution:** *If you made a charitable contribution and received a benefit in return, see page 40.*		
	13	Contributions by cash or check	13	
	14	Other than cash or check. (You **MUST** attach Form 8283 if over $500.)	14	
	15	Carryover from prior year	15	
	16	Add lines 13 through 15. Enter the total ▶		16
Casualty and Theft Losses	17	Casualty or theft loss(es) (attach Form 4684). (See page 40.) ▶		17
Moving Expenses	18	Moving expenses (attach Form 3903 or 3903F). (See page 41.) ▶		18
Job Expenses and Most Other Miscellaneous Deductions	19	Unreimbursed employee expenses—job travel, union dues, job education, etc. (You **MUST** attach Form 2106 if required. See instructions.) ▶	19	
(See page 41 for expenses to deduct here.)	20	Other expenses (investment, tax preparation, safe deposit box, etc.). List type and amount ▶	20	
	21	Add lines 19 and 20	21	
	22	Enter amount from Form 1040, line 32 [22]		
	23	Multiply line 22 above by 2% (.02)	23	
	24	Subtract line 23 from line 21. Enter the result. If less than zero, enter -0- ▶		24
Other Miscellaneous Deductions	25	Other (from list on page 41 of instructions). List type and amount ▶		25
Total Itemized Deductions	26	• If the amount on Form 1040, line 32, is $100,000 or less ($50,000 or less if married filing separately), add lines 4, 8, 12, 16, 17, 18, 24, and 25. Enter the total here. • If the amount on Form 1040, line 32, is more than $100,000 (more than $50,000 if married filing separately), see page 42 for the amount to enter. ▶		26
		Caution: *Be sure to enter on Form 1040, line 34, the* ***LARGER*** *of the amount on line 26 above or your standard deduction.*		

Schedules A&B (Form 1040) 1991 — OMB No. 1545-0074 — Page 2

Name(s) shown on Form 1040. (Do not enter name and social security number if shown on other side.) | Your social security number

Schedule B—Interest and Dividend Income

Attachment Sequence No. 08

Part I Interest Income

(See pages 15 and 43.)

If you received more than $400 in taxable interest income, or you are claiming the exclusion of interest from series EE U.S. savings bonds issued after 1989 (see page 43), you must complete Part I. List ALL interest received in Part I. If you received more than $400 in taxable interest income, you must also complete Part III. If you received, as a nominee, interest that actually belongs to another person, or you received or paid accrued interest on securities transferred between interest payment dates, see page 43.

Note: If you received a Form 1099-INT, Form 1099-OID, or substitute statement, from a brokerage firm, list the firm's name as the payer and enter the total interest shown on that form.

	Interest Income		Amount
1	Interest income. (List name of payer—if any interest income is from seller-financed mortgages, see instructions and list this interest first.) ▶	1	
2	Add the amounts on line 1	2	
3	Enter the excludable savings bond interest, if any, from Form 8815, line 14. Attach Form 8815 to Form 1040	3	
4	Subtract line 3 from line 2. Enter the result here and on Form 1040, line 8a ▶	4	

Part II Dividend Income

(See pages 16 and 43.)

If you received more than $400 in gross dividends and/or other distributions on stock, you must complete Parts II and III. If you received, as a nominee, dividends that actually belong to another person, see page 43.

Note: If you received a Form 1099-DIV, or substitute statement, from a brokerage firm, list the firm's name as the payer and enter the total dividends shown on that form.

	Dividend Income		Amount
5	Dividend income. (List name of payer—include on this line capital gain distributions, nontaxable distributions, etc.) ▶	5	
6	Add the amounts on line 5	6	
7	Capital gain distributions. Enter here and on Schedule D* — 7		
8	Nontaxable distributions. (See the inst. for Form 1040, line 9.) — 8		
9	Add lines 7 and 8	9	
10	Subtract line 9 from line 6. Enter the result here and on Form 1040, line 9 ▶	10	

**If you received capital gain distributions but do not need Schedule D to report any other gains or losses, see the instructions for Form 1040, lines 13 and 14.*

Part III Foreign Accounts and Foreign Trusts

(See page 43.)

	If you received more than $400 of interest or dividends, OR if you had a foreign account or were a grantor of, or a transferor to, a foreign trust, you must answer both questions in Part III.	Yes	No
11a	At any time during 1991, did you have an interest in or a signature or other authority over a financial account in a foreign country (such as a bank account, securities account, or other financial account)? (See page 43 for exceptions and filing requirements for Form TD F 90-22.1.)		
b	If "Yes," enter the name of the foreign country ▶		
12	Were you the grantor of, or transferor to, a foreign trust that existed during 1991, whether or not you have any beneficial interest in it? If "Yes," you may have to file Form 3520, 3520-A, or 926		

For Paperwork Reduction Act Notice, see Form 1040 instructions. — Schedule B (Form 1040) 1991

SCHEDULE C (Form 1040)

Department of the Treasury Internal Revenue Service (T)

Profit or Loss From Business

(Sole Proprietorship)

▶ **Partnerships, joint ventures, etc., must file Form 1065.**

▶ **Attach to Form 1040 or Form 1041.** ▶ **See Instructions for Schedule C (Form 1040).**

OMB No. 1545-0074

1991

Attachment Sequence No. **09**

Name of proprietor | **Social security number (SSN)**

A Principal business or profession, including product or service (see instructions) | **B** Enter principal business code (from page 2) ▶

C Business name | **D Employer ID number (Not SSN)**

E Business address (including suite or room no.) ▶
City, town or post office, state, and ZIP code

F Accounting method: **(1)** ☐ Cash **(2)** ☐ Accrual **(3)** ☐ Other (specify) ▶

G Method(s) used to value closing inventory: **(1)** ☐ Cost **(2)** ☐ Lower of cost or market **(3)** ☐ Other (attach explanation) **(4)** ☐ Does not apply (if checked, skip line H)

		Yes	No
H	Was there any change in determining quantities, costs, or valuations between opening and closing inventory? (If "Yes," attach explanation.)		
I	Did you "materially participate" in the operation of this business during 1991? (If "No," see instructions for limitations on losses.)		

J If this is the first Schedule C filed for this business, check here ▶ ☐

Part I Income

1	Gross receipts or sales. **Caution:** *If this income was reported to you on Form W-2 and the "Statutory employee" box on that form was checked, see the instructions and check here* ▶ ☐	1	
2	Returns and allowances	2	
3	Subtract line 2 from line 1	3	
4	Cost of goods sold (from line 40 on page 2)	4	
5	Subtract line 4 from line 3 and enter the **gross profit** here	5	
6	Other income, including Federal and state gasoline or fuel tax credit or refund (see instructions)	6	
7	Add lines 5 and 6. This is your **gross income** ▶	7	

Part II Expenses (*Caution: Enter expenses for business use of your home on line 30.*)

8	Advertising	8		21	Repairs and maintenance	21	
9	Bad debts from sales or services (see instructions)	9		22	Supplies (not included in Part III)	22	
10	Car and truck expenses (see instructions—also attach **Form 4562**)	10		23	Taxes and licenses	23	
11	Commissions and fees	11		24	Travel, meals, and entertainment:		
12	Depletion	12		a	Travel	24a	
13	Depreciation and section 179 expense deduction (not included in Part III) (see instructions)	13		b	Meals and entertainment		
14	Employee benefit programs (other than on line 19)	14		c	Enter 20% of line 24b subject to limitations (see instructions)		
15	Insurance (other than health)	15		d	Subtract line 24c from line 24b	24d	
16	Interest:			25	Utilities	25	
a	Mortgage (paid to banks, etc.)	16a		26	Wages (less jobs credit)	26	
b	Other	16b		27a	Other expenses (**list type and amount**):		
17	Legal and professional services	17					
18	Office expense	18					
19	Pension and profit-sharing plans	19					
20	Rent or lease (see instructions):						
a	Vehicles, machinery, and equipment	20a					
b	Other business property	20b		27b	Total other expenses	27b	

28	Add amounts in columns for lines 8 through 27b. These are your **total expenses** before expenses for business use of your home ▶	28	
29	Tentative profit (loss). Subtract line 28 from line 7	29	
30	Expenses for business use of your home (attach **Form 8829**)	30	
31	**Net profit or (loss).** Subtract line 30 from line 29. If a profit, enter here and on Form 1040, line 12. Also enter the net profit on Schedule SE, line 2 (statutory employees, see instructions). If a loss, you MUST go on to line 32 (fiduciaries, see instructions)	31	

32 If you have a loss, you MUST check the box that describes your investment in this activity (see instructions)
If you checked 32a, enter the loss on Form 1040, line 12, and Schedule SE, line 2 (statutory employees, see instructions). If you checked 32b, you MUST attach **Form 6198.**

32a ☐ All investment is at risk.
32b ☐ Some investment is not at risk.

Schedule C (Form 1040) 1991 Page **2**

Part III Cost of Goods Sold *(See instructions.)*

33	Inventory at beginning of year. (If different from last year's closing inventory, attach explanation.)	33		
34	Purchases less cost of items withdrawn for personal use	34		
35	Cost of labor. (Do not include salary paid to yourself.)	35		
36	Materials and supplies	36		
37	Other costs	37		
38	Add lines 33 through 37	38		
39	Inventory at end of year	39		
40	**Cost of goods sold.** Subtract line 39 from line 38. Enter the result here and on page 1, line 4	40		

Part IV Principal Business or Professional Activity Codes

Locate the major category that best describes your activity. Within the major category, select the activity code that most closely identifies the business or profession that is the principal source of your sales or receipts. **Enter this 4-digit code on page 1, line B.** *For example, real estate agent is under the major category of* ***"Real Estate,"*** *and the code is "5520."* (**Note:** *If your principal source of income is from farming activities, you should file* ***Schedule F*** *(Form 1040), Profit or Loss From Farming.)*

Agricultural Services, Forestry, Fishing

Code

1990 Animal services, other than breeding
1933 Crop services
2113 Farm labor & management services
2246 Fishing, commercial
2238 Forestry, except logging
2212 Horticulture & landscaping
2469 Hunting & trapping
1974 Livestock breeding
0836 Logging
1958 Veterinary services, including pets

Construction

0018 Operative builders (for own account)

Building Trade Contractors, Including Repairs

0414 Carpentering & flooring
0455 Concrete work
0273 Electrical work
0299 Masonry, dry wall, stone, & tile
0257 Painting & paper hanging
0232 Plumbing, heating, & air conditioning
0430 Roofing, siding & sheet metal
0885 Other building trade contractors (excavation, glazing, etc.)

General Contractors

0075 Highway & street construction
0059 Nonresidential building
0034 Residential building
3889 Other heavy construction (pipe laying, bridge construction, etc.)

Finance, Insurance, & Related Services

6064 Brokers & dealers of securities
6080 Commodity contracts brokers & dealers; security & commodity exchanges
6148 Credit institutions & mortgage bankers
5702 Insurance agents or brokers
5744 Insurance services (appraisal, consulting, inspection, etc.)
6130 Investment advisors & services
5777 Other financial services

Manufacturing, Including Printing & Publishing

0679 Apparel & other textile products
1115 Electric & electronic equipment
1073 Fabricated metal products
0638 Food products & beverages
0810 Furniture & fixtures
0695 Leather footwear, handbags, etc.
0836 Lumber & other wood products
1099 Machinery & machine shops
0877 Paper & allied products
1057 Primary metal industries
0851 Printing & publishing
1032 Stone, clay, & glass products
0653 Textile mill products
1883 Other manufacturing industries

Mining & Mineral Extraction

1537 Coal mining
1511 Metal mining
1552 Oil & gas
1719 Quarrying & nonmetallic mining

Real Estate

5538 Operators & lessors of buildings, including residential
5553 Operators & lessors of other real property
5520 Real estate agents & brokers
5579 Real estate property managers
5710 Subdividers & developers, except cemeteries
6155 Title abstract offices

Services: Personal, Professional, & Business Services

Amusement & Recreational Services

9670 Bowling centers
9688 Motion picture & tape distribution & allied services
9597 Motion picture & video production
9639 Motion picture theaters
8557 Physical fitness facilities
9696 Professional sports & racing, including promoters & managers
9811 Theatrical performers, musicians, agents, producers & related services
9613 Video tape rental
9837 Other amusement & recreational services

Automotive Services

8813 Automotive rental or leasing, without driver
8953 Automotive repairs, general & specialized
8839 Parking, except valet
8896 Other automotive services (wash, towing, etc.)

Business & Personal Services

7658 Accounting & bookkeeping
7716 Advertising, except direct mail
7682 Architectural services
8318 Barber shop (or barber)
8110 Beauty shop (or beautician)
8714 Child day care
6676 Communication services
7872 Computer programming, processing, data preparation & related services
7922 Computer repair, maintenance, & leasing
7286 Consulting services
7799 Consumer credit reporting & collection services
8755 Counseling (except health practitioners)
6395 Courier or package delivery
7732 Employment agencies & personnel supply
7518 Engineering services
7773 Equipment rental & leasing (except computer or automotive)
8532 Funeral services & crematories
7633 Income tax preparation
7914 Investigative & protective services
7617 Legal services (or lawyer)
7856 Mailing, reproduction, commercial art, photography, & stenographic services
7245 Management services
8771 Ministers & chaplains
8334 Photographic studios
7260 Public relations
6536 Public warehousing
7708 Surveying services
8730 Teaching or tutoring
6510 Trash collection without own dump
6692 Utilities (dumps, snowplowing, road cleaning, etc.)
7880 Other business services
6882 Other personal services

Hotels & Other Lodging Places

7237 Camps & camping parks
7096 Hotels, motels, & tourist homes
7211 Rooming & boarding houses

Laundry & Cleaning Services

7450 Carpet & upholstery cleaning
7419 Coin-operated laundries & dry cleaning
7435 Full-service laundry, dry cleaning, & garment service
7476 Janitorial & related services (building, house, & window cleaning)

Medical & Health Services

9274 Chiropractors
9233 Dentist's office or clinic
9217 Doctor's (M.D.) office or clinic
9456 Medical & dental laboratories
9472 Nursing & personal care facilities
9290 Optometrists
9258 Osteopathic physicians & surgeons
9241 Podiatrists
9415 Registered & practical nurses
9431 Offices & clinics of other health practitioners (dieticians, midwives, speech pathologists, etc.)
9886 Other health services

Miscellaneous Repair, Except Computers

9019 Audio equipment & TV repair
9035 Electrical & electronic equipment repair, except audio & TV
9050 Furniture repair & reupholstery
2881 Other equipment repair

Trade, Retail—Selling Goods to Individuals & Households

3038 Catalog or mail order
3012 Selling door to door, by telephone or party plan, or from mobile unit
3053 Vending machine selling

Selling From Showroom, Store, or Other Fixed Location

Apparel & Accessories

3921 Accessory & specialty stores & furriers for women
3939 Clothing, family
3772 Clothing, men's & boys'
3913 Clothing, women's
3756 Shoe stores
3954 Other apparel & accessory stores

Automotive & Service Stations

3558 Gasoline service stations
3319 New car dealers (franchised)
3533 Tires, accessories, & parts
3335 Used car dealers
3517 Other automotive dealers (motorcycles, recreational vehicles, etc.)

Building, Hardware, & Garden Supply

4416 Building materials dealers
4457 Hardware stores
4473 Nurseries & garden supply stores
4432 Paint, glass, & wallpaper stores

Food & Beverages

0612 Bakeries selling at retail
3086 Catering services
3095 Drinking places (bars, taverns, pubs, saloons, etc.)
3079 Eating places, meals & snacks
3210 Grocery stores (general line)
3251 Liquor stores
3236 Specialized food stores (meat, produce, candy, health food, etc.)

Furniture & General Merchandise

3988 Computer & software stores
3970 Furniture stores
4317 Home furnishings stores (china, floor coverings, drapes)
4119 Household appliance stores
4333 Music & record stores
3996 TV, audio & electronic stores
3715 Variety stores
3731 Other general merchandise stores

Miscellaneous Retail Stores

4812 Boat dealers
5017 Book stores, excluding newsstands
4853 Camera & photo supply stores
3277 Drug stores
5058 Fabric & needlework stores
4655 Florists
5090 Fuel dealers (except gasoline)
4630 Gift, novelty & souvenir shops
4838 Hobby, toy, & game shops
4671 Jewelry stores
4895 Luggage & leather goods stores
5074 Mobile home dealers
4879 Optical goods stores
4697 Sporting goods & bicycle shops
5033 Stationery stores
4614 Used merchandise & antique stores (except motor vehicle parts)
5884 Other retail stores

Trade, Wholesale—Selling Goods to Other Businesses, etc.

Durable Goods, Including Machinery Equipment, Wood, Metals, etc.

2634 Agent or broker for other firms—more than 50% of gross sales on commission
2618 Selling for your own account

Nondurable Goods, Including Food, Fiber, Chemicals, etc.

2675 Agent or broker for other firms—more than 50% of gross sales on commission
2659 Selling for your own account

Transportation Services

6619 Air transportation
6312 Bus & limousine transportation
6361 Highway passenger transportation (except chartered service)
6114 Taxicabs
6635 Travel agents & tour operators
6338 Trucking (except trash collection)
6551 Water transportation
6650 Other transportation services

8888 **Unable to classify**

SCHEDULE D (Form 1040)

Department of the Treasury
Internal Revenue Service

Capital Gains and Losses

(And Reconciliation of Forms 1099-B for Bartering Transactions)

▶ Attach to Form 1040. ▶ See Instructions for Schedule D (Form 1040).

▶ For more space to list transactions for lines 1a and 8a, get Schedule D-1 (Form 1040).

OMB No. 1545-0074

1991

Attachment Sequence No. **12A**

Name(s) shown on Form 1040 | **Your social security number**

Caution: *Add the following amounts reported to you for 1991 on Forms 1099-B and 1099-S (or on substitute statements):* ***(a)*** *proceeds from transactions involving stocks, bonds, and other securities, and* ***(b)*** *gross proceeds from real estate transactions not reported on another form or schedule. If this total does not equal the total of lines 1c and 8c, column (d), attach a statement explaining the difference.*

Part I Short-Term Capital Gains and Losses—Assets Held One Year or Less

(a) Description of property (Example, 100 shares 7% preferred of "Z" Co.)	(b) Date acquired (Mo., day, yr.)	(c) Date sold (Mo., day, yr.)	(d) Sales price (see instructions)	(e) Cost or other basis (see instructions)	(f) LOSS If (e) is more than (d), subtract (d) from (e)	(g) GAIN If (d) is more than (e), subtract (e) from (d)
1a Stocks, Bonds, Other Securities, and Real Estate. Include Form 1099-B and 1099-S Transactions. See instructions.						
1b Amounts from Schedule D-1, line 1b (attach Schedule D-1)						
1c Total of All Sales Price Amounts. Add column (d) of lines 1a and 1b . . ▶		1c				
1d Other Transactions (Do NOT include real estate transactions from Forms 1099-S on this line. Report them on line 1a.)						

			(f)	(g)
2	Short-term gain from sale or exchange of your home from Form 2119, line 10 or 14c	2		
3	Short-term gain from installment sales from Form 6252, line 22 or 30	3		
4	Net short-term gain or (loss) from partnerships, S corporations, and fiduciaries .	4		
5	Short-term capital loss carryover from 1990 Schedule D, line 29	5		
6	Add lines 1a, 1b, 1d, and 2 through 5, in columns (f) and (g).	6	( )	
7	**Net short-term capital gain or (loss).** Combine columns (f) and (g) of line 6		7	

Part II Long-Term Capital Gains and Losses—Assets Held More Than One Year

(a)	(b)	(c)	(d)	(e)	(f)	(g)
8a Stocks, Bonds, Other Securities, and Real Estate. Include Form 1099-B and 1099-S Transactions. See instructions.						
8b Amounts from Schedule D-1, line 8b (attach Schedule D-1)						
8c Total of All Sales Price Amounts. Add column (d) of lines 8a and 8b . . ▶		8c				
8d Other Transactions (Do NOT include real estate transactions from Forms 1099-S on this line. Report them on line 8a.)						

			(f)	(g)
9	Long-term gain from sale or exchange of your home from Form 2119, line 10 or 14c	9		
10	Long-term gain from installment sales from Form 6252, line 22 or 30	10		
11	Net long-term gain or (loss) from partnerships, S corporations, and fiduciaries .	11		
12	Capital gain distributions	12		
13	Gain from Form 4797, line 7 or 9	13		
14	Long-term capital loss carryover from 1990 Schedule D, line 36.	14		
15	Add lines 8a, 8b, 8d, and 9 through 14, in columns (f) and (g)	15	( )	
16	**Net long-term capital gain or (loss).** Combine columns (f) and (g) of line 15		16	

For Paperwork Reduction Act Notice, see Form 1040 instructions. Cat. No. 11338H **Schedule D (Form 1040) 1991**

Schedule D (Form 1040) 1991 — Attachment Sequence No. 12A — Page 2

Name(s) shown on Form 1040. (Do not enter name and social security number if shown on other side.) | Your social security number

Part III Summary of Parts I and II

17	Combine lines 7 and 16 and enter the net gain or (loss) here. If the result is a gain, also enter the gain on Form 1040, line 13. (**Note:** *If both lines 16 and 17 are gains, see Part IV below.*)	17	
18	If line 17 is a (loss), enter here and as a (loss) on Form 1040, line 13, the **smaller** of:		
a	The (loss) on line 17; **or**		
b	($3,000) or, if married filing a separate return, ($1,500)	18	( )

Note: *When figuring whether line 18a or 18b is* **smaller,** *treat both numbers as positive.*
Complete Part V if the loss on line 17 is more than the loss on line 18, OR if Form 1040, line 37, is zero.

Part IV Tax Computation Using Maximum Capital Gains Rate

USE THIS PART TO FIGURE YOUR TAX ONLY IF BOTH LINES 16 AND 17 ARE GAINS, AND:

You checked filing status box:	AND	Form 1040, line 37, is over:	You checked filing status box:	AND	Form 1040, line 37, is over:
1		$49,300	3		$41,075
2 or 5		$82,150	4		$70,450

19	Enter the amount from Form 1040, line 37	19	
20	Enter the **smaller** of line 16 or line 17.	20	
21	Subtract line 20 from line 19	21	
22	Enter: **a** $20,350 if you checked filing status box 1; **b** $34,000 if you checked filing status box 2 or 5; **c** $17,000 if you checked filing status box 3; or **d** $27,300 if you checked filing status box 4	22	
23	Enter the **greater** of line 21 or line 22.	23	
24	Subtract line 23 from line 19	24	
25	Figure the tax on the amount on line 23. Use the Tax Table or Tax Rate Schedules, whichever applies	25	
26	Multiply line 24 by 28% (.28)	26	
27	Add lines 25 and 26. Enter here and on Form 1040, line 38, and check the box for Schedule D	27	

Part V Capital Loss Carryovers from 1991 to 1992

Section A.—Carryover Limit

28	Enter the amount from Form 1040, line 35. If a loss, enclose the amount in parentheses	28	
29	Enter the loss from line 18 as a positive amount	29	
30	Combine lines 28 and 29. If zero or less, enter -0-.	30	
31	Enter the **smaller** of line 29 or line 30	31	

Section B.—Short-Term Capital Loss Carryover to 1992 (Complete this section only if there is a loss on both lines 7 and 18.)

32	Enter the loss from line 7 as a positive amount			32	
33	Enter the gain, if any, from line 16.	33			
34	Enter the amount from line 31	34			
35	Add lines 33 and 34			35	
36	**Short-term capital loss carryover to 1992.** Subtract line 35 from line 32. If zero or less, enter -0-			36	

Section C.—Long-Term Capital Loss Carryover to 1992 (Complete this section only if there is a loss on both lines 16 and 18.)

37	Enter the loss from line 16 as a positive amount					37	
38	Enter the gain, if any, from line 7			38			
39	Enter the amount from line 31	39					
40	Enter the amount, if any, from line 32.	40					
41	Subtract line 40 from line 39. If zero or less, enter -0-			41			
42	Add lines 38 and 41					42	
43	**Long-term capital loss carryover to 1992.** Subtract line 42 from line 37. If zero or less, enter -0-					43	

Part VI Election Not To Use the Installment Method (Complete this part only if you elect out of the installment method and report a note or other obligation at less than full face value.)

44	Check here if you elect out of the installment method	▶ ☐
45	Enter the face amount of the note or other obligation	▶
46	Enter the percentage of valuation of the note or other obligation	▶ %

Part VII Reconciliation of Forms 1099-B for Bartering Transactions (Complete this part if you received one or more Forms 1099-B or substitute statements reporting bartering income.)

			Amount of bartering income from Form 1099-B or substitute statement reported on form or schedule
47	Form 1040, line 22	47	
48	Schedule C, D, E, or F (Form 1040) (specify) ▶	48	
49	Other form or schedule (identify) (if nontaxable, indicate reason—attach additional sheets if necessary):	49	
50	**Total.** Add lines 47 through 49. This amount should be the same as the total bartering income on all Forms 1099-B and substitute statements received for bartering transactions	50	

SCHEDULE E (Form 1040)

Department of the Treasury
Internal Revenue Service (T)

Supplemental Income and Loss

(From rents, royalties, partnerships, estates, trusts, REMICs, etc.)

▶ Attach to Form 1040 or Form 1041.

▶ See Instructions for Schedule E (Form 1040).

OMB No. 1545-0074

1991

Attachment Sequence No. **13**

Name(s) shown on return | **Your social security number**

Part I Income or Loss From Rentals and Royalties **Note:** *Report farm rental income or loss from* ***Form 4835*** *on page 2, line 39.*

1	Show the kind and location of each **rental property:**
A	
B	
C	

2 For each rental property listed on line 1, did you or your family use it for personal purposes for more than the greater of 14 days or 10% of the total days rented at fair rental value during the tax year? (See instructions.)

	Yes	No
A		
B		
C		

Rental and Royalty Income:		Properties A	Properties B	Properties C	Totals (Add columns A, B, and C.)
3 Rents received	3				3
4 Royalties received	4				4
Rental and Royalty Expenses:					
5 Advertising	5				
6 Auto and travel	6				
7 Cleaning and maintenance	7				
8 Commissions	8				
9 Insurance	9				
10 Legal and other professional fees	10				
11 Mortgage interest paid to banks, etc. (see instructions)	11				11
12 Other interest	12				
13 Repairs	13				
14 Supplies	14				
15 Taxes	15				
16 Utilities	16				
17 Wages and salaries	17				
18 Other (list) ▶	18				
19 Add lines 5 through 18	19				19
20 Depreciation expense or depletion (see instructions)	20				20
21 Total expenses. Add lines 19 and 20	21				
22 Income or (loss) from rental or royalty properties. Subtract line 21 from line 3 (rents) or line 4 (royalties). If the result is a (loss), see instructions to find out if you must file **Form 6198**	22				
23 Deductible rental loss. **Caution:** *Your rental loss on line 22 may be limited. See instructions to find out if you must file* ***Form 8582***	23	( )	( )	( )	

24 **Income.** Add rental and royalty income from line 22. Enter the total income here	24	
25 **Losses.** Add royalty losses from line 22 and rental losses from line 23. Enter the total losses here	25	( )
26 Total rental and royalty income or (loss). Combine lines 24 and 25. Enter the result here. If Parts II, III, IV, and line 39 on page 2 do not apply to you, enter the amount from line 26 on Form 1040, line 18. Otherwise, include the amount from line 26 in the total on line 40 on page 2	26	

Schedule E (Form 1040) 1991 Attachment Sequence No. 13 Page 2

Name(s) shown on return. (Do not enter name and social security number if shown on other side.)	Your social security number

Note: *If you report amounts from farming or fishing on Schedule E, you must enter your gross income from those activities on line 41 below.*

Part II Income or Loss From Partnerships and S Corporations

If you report a loss from an at-risk activity, you MUST check either column **(e)** or **(f)** of line 27 to describe your investment in the activity. See instructions. If you check column **(f)**, you must attach **Form 6198**.

27	(a) Name	(b) Enter **P** for partnership; **S** for S corporation	(c) Check if foreign partnership	(d) Employer identification number	Investment At Risk? (e) All is at risk	(f) Some is not at risk
A						
B						
C						
D						
E						

	Passive Income and Loss		Nonpassive Income and Loss		
	(g) Passive loss allowed (attach **Form 8582** if required)	(h) Passive income from **Schedule K–1**	(i) Nonpassive loss from **Schedule K–1**	(j) Section 179 expense deduction from **Form 4562**	(k) Nonpassive income from **Schedule K–1**
A					
B					
C					
D					
E					
28a Totals					
b Totals					

29 Add columns (h) and (k) of line 28a. Enter the total income here	29	
30 Add columns (g), (i), and (j) of line 28b. Enter the total here	30	( )
31 Total partnership and S corporation income or (loss). Combine lines 29 and 30. Enter the result here and include in the total on line 40 below	31	

Part III Income or Loss From Estates and Trusts

32	(a) Name	(b) Employer identification number
A		
B		
C		

	Passive Income and Loss		Nonpassive Income and Loss	
	(c) Passive deduction or loss allowed (attach **Form 8582** if required)	(d) Passive income from **Schedule K–1**	(e) Deduction or loss from **Schedule K–1**	(f) Other income from **Schedule K–1**
A				
B				
C				
33a Totals				
b Totals				

34 Add columns (d) and (f) of line 33a. Enter the total income here	34	
35 Add columns (c) and (e) of line 33b. Enter the total here	35	( )
36 Total estate and trust income or (loss). Combine lines 34 and 35. Enter the result here and include in the total on line 40 below	36	

Part IV Income or Loss From Real Estate Mortgage Investment Conduits (REMICs)—Residual Holder

37 (a) Name	(b) Employer identification number	(c) Excess inclusion from **Schedules Q,** line 2c (see instructions)	(d) Taxable income (net loss) from **Schedules Q,** line 1b	(e) Income from **Schedules Q,** line 3b

38 Combine columns (d) and (e) only. Enter the result here and include in the total on line 40 below	38	

Part V Summary

39 Net farm rental income or (loss) from **Form 4835**. (Also complete line 41 below.)	39	
40 TOTAL income or (loss). Combine lines 26, 31, 36, 38, and 39. Enter the result here and on Form 1040, line 18 ▶	40	
41 **Reconciliation of Farming and Fishing Income:** Enter your **gross** farming and fishing income reported in Parts II and III and on line 39 (see instructions)	41	

SCHEDULE EIC (Form 1040A or 1040)

Department of the Treasury Internal Revenue Service (T)

Earned Income Credit

▶ Attach to Form 1040A or 1040. ▶ See Instructions for Schedule EIC.

TIP: **Why not let the IRS figure the credit for you? Give us only the information asked for on this page and we'll do the rest.**

OMB No. 1545-0074

1991

Attachment Sequence No. **43**

Name(s) shown on return

Your social security number

Part I General Information

To take this credit

- You MUST have worked and earned **LESS** than $21,250, **AND**
- Your adjusted gross income (Form 1040A, line 16, or Form 1040, line 31) MUST be LESS than $21,250, **AND**
- Your filing status can be any status **except** married filing a separate return, **AND**
- You MUST have at least one qualifying child (see boxes below), **AND**
- You cannot be a qualifying child yourself.

A **qualifying child** is a child who:

is your:		was (at the end of 1991):		who (in 1991):
son daughter adopted child grandchild stepchild or foster child	**AND**	under age 19 or under age 24 and a full-time student or any age and permanently and totally disabled	**AND**	lived with you in the U.S. for more than 6 months* (or all year if a foster child)*

*If the child didn't live with you for the required time (for example, was born in 1991), see the **Exception** on page 57 of 1040A booklet (or page 45 of 1040 booklet).

If you don't have any qualifying children, **STOP** **here. You cannot take this credit.**

If you have at least one qualifying child, go to Part II. (But if the child was married or is also a qualifying child of another person, see page 57 of 1040A booklet (or page 46 of 1040 booklet).)

Part II Information About Your Two Youngest Qualifying Children

If more than two qualifying children, see page 58 of 1040A booklet (or page 46 of 1040 booklet). **1(a)** Child's name (first, initial, and last name)	**(b)** Child's year of birth	For a child born **BEFORE 1973,** check if child was— **(c)** a student **under age 24** at end of 1991	**(d)** disabled (see booklet)	**(e)** If child was born **BEFORE 1991,** enter the child's social security number	**(f)** Child's relationship to you (for example, son, grandchild, etc.)	**(g)** Number of months child lived with you in the U.S. in 1991
	19					
	19					

Caution: *If a child you listed above was born in 1991* ***AND*** *you chose to claim the credit for child care expenses for this child on* ***Schedule 2*** *(Form 1040A) or* ***Form 2441*** *(Form 1040), check here* . . . . ▶ ☐

Do you want the IRS to figure the credit for you?

- **Yes** ▶ Fill in **Part III** below — **AND** ▶ Enter the amount from Form 1040A, line 16, or Form 1040, line 31, here ▶ ....
- **No** ▶ Go to **Part IV** on the back now

Part III Other Information

2 If you received any **nontaxable earned income** (see page 58 of 1040A booklet or page 46 of 1040 booklet) such as combat pay and military housing and subsistence, enter the total of that income on line 2. Also list type and amount here ▶	2	
3 If you paid for health insurance that covered at least one qualifying child: **a** First, enter the name of your insurance company here ▶ .... **b** Then, enter the total amount you paid in 1991 for health insurance that covered at least one qualifying child. (See page 59 of 1040A booklet or page 46 of 1040 booklet.)	3b	

If you want the IRS to figure the credit for you, **STOP** **here!**

Attach this schedule to your return. If filing Form 1040A, print "EIC" on the line next to line 28c.
If filing Form 1040, print "EIC" on the dotted line next to line 56.

For Paperwork Reduction Act Notice, see Form 1040A or 1040 instructions. Cat. No. 13339M **Schedule EIC (Form 1040A or 1040) 1991**

Schedule EIC (Form 1040A or 1040) 1991 Page **2**

Part IV Figure Your Earned Income Credit—You can take ALL THREE parts of the credit if you qualify

BASIC CREDIT

4 Enter the amount from line 7 of Form 1040A or Form 1040 (wages, salaries, tips, etc.). If you received a taxable scholarship or fellowship grant, see page 60 of 1040A booklet (or page 47 of 1040 booklet) for the amount to enter 4

5 If you received any **nontaxable earned income** (see page 58 of 1040A booklet or page 46 of 1040 booklet) such as combat pay and military housing and subsistence, enter the total of that income on line 5. Also list type and amount here ▶ 5

6 **Form 1040 Filers Only:** If you were self-employed or reported income and expenses on Schedule C as a statutory employee, enter the amount from line 4 of the worksheet on page 48 of 1040 booklet 6

7 Add lines 4, 5, and 6. This is your **earned income** . . . . ▶ 7

Caution: ***If line 7 above is $21,250 or more,*** **STOP** *HERE. Enter "NO" on Form 1040A, line 28c (or on Form 1040, line 56). You* ***cannot*** *take the earned income credit.*

8 Use the amount on **line 7** above to look up your credit in **TABLE A** on pages **61–62** of 1040A booklet (or pages **49–50** of 1040 booklet). Then, enter the credit here. 8

9 Enter your **adjusted gross income** (from Form 1040A, line 16, or Form 1040, line 31). . . ▶ 9

10 **Is line 9 $11,250 or more?**

- **YES.** Use the amount on **line 9** to look up your credit in **TABLE A** on pages **61–62** of 1040A booklet (or pages **49–50** of 1040 booklet). Then, enter the credit here 10
- **NO.** Enter the amount from line 8 on line 11.

11 Look at lines 8 and 10. Enter the **smaller** of the two amounts here. This is your **basic credit** . 11

NEXT: *To take the health insurance credit, fill in lines 12a–16. To take the extra credit for a child born in 1991, fill in lines 17–19. Otherwise, go to line 20 now.*

HEALTH INSURANCE CREDIT—Take this credit **ONLY** if you paid for health insurance that covered at least one qualifying child.

12a Enter the name of your health insurance company here ▶ ....

b Enter the total amount you paid in 1991 for health insurance that covered at least one qualifying child. (See page 60 of 1040A booklet or page 47 of 1040 booklet.) 12b

13 Look at the amount on **line 7** above. Use that amount to look up your credit in **TABLE B** on page **63** of 1040A booklet (or page **51** of 1040 booklet). Then, enter the credit here 13

14 Look at lines 12b and 13. Enter the **smaller** of the two amounts here 14

15 Look at the amount on **line 9** above. **Is line 9 $11,250 or more?**

- **YES.** Use the amount on **line 9** to look up your credit in **TABLE B** on page **63** of 1040A booklet (or page **51** of 1040 booklet). Then, enter the credit here 15
- **NO.** Enter the amount from line 14 on line 16.

16 Look at lines 14 and 15. Enter the **smaller** of the two amounts here. This is your **health insurance credit** 16

EXTRA CREDIT FOR CHILD BORN IN 1991—Take this credit **ONLY** if:

- You listed in Part II a child born in 1991, **AND**
- You did not take the credit for child care expenses on **Schedule 2** or **Form 2441** for the same child.

TIP: You can take **both** the **basic credit** and the **extra credit** for your child born in 1991.

17 Look at the amount on **line 7** above. Use that amount to look up your credit in **TABLE C** on page **64** of 1040A booklet (or page **52** of 1040 booklet). Then, enter the credit here 17

18 Look at the amount on **line 9** above. **Is line 9 $11,250 or more?**

- **YES.** Use the amount on **line 9** to look up your credit in **TABLE C** on page **64** of 1040A booklet (or page **52** of 1040 booklet). Then, enter the credit here 18
- **NO.** Enter the amount from line 17 on line 19.

19 Look at lines 17 and 18. Enter the **smaller** of the two amounts here. This is your **extra credit for a child born in 1991** 19

TOTAL EARNED INCOME CREDIT

20 Add lines 11, 16, and 19. Enter the total here and on Form 1040A, line 28c (or on Form 1040, line 56). This is your **total earned income credit** . . . . ▶ 20

Schedule R
(Form 1040)

Department of the Treasury
Internal Revenue Service (T)

Credit for the Elderly or the Disabled

▶ Attach to Form 1040. ▶ See separate instructions for Schedule R.

OMB No. 1545-0074

1991

Attachment Sequence No. **16**

Name(s) shown on Form 1040 | **Your social security number**

You may be able to use Schedule R to reduce your tax if by the end of 1991:

- You were age 65 or older, **OR** • You were under age 65, you retired on **permanent and total** disability, and you received taxable disability income.

But you must also meet other tests. See the separate instructions for Schedule R.
Note: *In most cases, the IRS can figure the credit for you. See page 24 of the Form 1040 instructions.*

Part I Check the Box for Your Filing Status and Age

If your filing status is:	And by the end of 1991:	Check only one box:
Single, Head of household, or Qualifying widow(er) with dependent child	1 You were 65 or older	1 ☐
	2 You were under 65 and you retired on permanent and total disability . . .	2 ☐
Married filing a joint return	3 Both spouses were 65 or older	3 ☐
	4 Both spouses were under 65, but only one spouse retired on permanent and total disability	4 ☐
	5 Both spouses were under 65, and both retired on permanent and total disability	5 ☐
	6 One spouse was 65 or older, and the other spouse was under 65 and retired on permanent and total disability	6 ☐
	7 One spouse was 65 or older, and the other spouse was under 65 and **NOT** retired on permanent and total disability	7 ☐
Married filing a separate return	8 You were 65 or older and you did not live with your spouse at any time in 1991	8 ☐
	9 You were under 65, you retired on permanent and total disability, and you did not live with your spouse at any time in 1991	9 ☐

If you checked Box 1, 3, 7, or 8, skip Part II and complete Part III on the back. All others, complete Parts II and III.

Part II Statement of Permanent and Total Disability (Complete only if you checked Box 2, 4, 5, 6, or 9 above.)

IF: 1 You filed a physician's statement for this disability for 1983 or an earlier year, or you filed a statement for tax years after 1983 and your physician signed line B on the statement, **AND**

2 Due to your continued disabled condition, you were unable to engage in any substantial gainful activity in 1991, check this box . . . . ▶ ☐

- If you checked this box, you do not have to file another statement for 1991.
- If you did **not** check this box, have your physician complete the following statement.

Physician's Statement (See instructions at bottom of page 2.)

I certify that ______________________________
Name of disabled person

was permanently and totally disabled on January 1, 1976, or January 1, 1977, **OR** was permanently and totally disabled on the date he or she retired. If retired after December 31, 1976, enter the date retired. ▶ ____________

Physician: Sign your name on **either** line A or B below.

A The disability has lasted, or can be expected to last, continuously for at least a year . . . . . ______________________
Physician's signature Date

B There is no reasonable probability that the disabled condition will ever improve . . . . ______________________
Physician's signature Date

Physician's name | Physician's address

Part III Figure Your Credit

10 **If you checked (in Part I):** **Enter:**
Box 1, 2, 4, or 7 . . . . $5,000
Box 3, 5, or 6 . . . . $7,500
Box 8 or 9 . . . . $3,750 } **10**

Caution: *If you checked Box 2, 4, 5, 6, or 9 in Part I, you **MUST** complete line 11 below. Otherwise, skip line 11 and enter the amount from line 10 on line 12.*

11 If you checked Box 6 in Part I, enter on line 11 the taxable disability income of the spouse who was under age 65 **PLUS** $5,000. Otherwise, enter on line 11 your taxable disability income (and also your spouse's if you checked Box 5 in Part I) that you reported on Form 1040. (For more details on what to include, see the instructions.) **11**

12 If you completed line 11 above, compare lines 10 and 11, and enter the **smaller** of the two amounts here. Otherwise, enter the amount from line 10 . . . . **12**

13 Enter the following pensions, annuities, or disability income that you (and your spouse if you file a joint return) received in 1991 (see instructions):

a Nontaxable part of social security benefits, and Nontaxable part of railroad retirement benefits treated as social security. } . . . **13a**

b Nontaxable veterans' pensions, and Any other pension, annuity, or disability benefit that is excluded from income under any other provision of law. } . . . **13b**

c Add lines 13a and 13b. (Even though these income items are not taxable, they **must** be included here to figure your credit.) If you did not receive any of the types of nontaxable income listed on line 13a or 13b, enter -0- on line 13c **13c**

14 Enter the amount from Form 1040, line 32 **14**

15 **If you checked (in Part I):** **Enter:**
Box 1 or 2 . . . . . . $7,500
Box 3, 4, 5, 6, or 7 . . . $10,000
Box 8 or 9 . . . . . . $5,000 } **15**

16 Subtract line 15 from line 14. If line 15 is more than line 14, enter -0- **16**

17 Divide line 16 above by 2 . . . . **17**

18 Add lines 13c and 17 . . . . **18**

19 Subtract line 18 from line 12. If the result is zero or less, stop here; you **cannot** take the credit. Otherwise, go to line 21 . . . . **19**

20 Decimal amount used to figure the credit . . . . **20** ×**.15**

21 Multiply line 19 above by the decimal amount (.15) on line 20. Enter the result here and on Form 1040, line 42. **Caution:** *If you file Schedule C, D, E, or F (Form 1040), your credit may be limited. See the instructions for line 21 for the amount of credit you can claim* **21**

Instructions for Physician's Statement

Taxpayer

If you retired after December 31, 1976, enter the date you retired in the space provided in Part II.

Physician

A person is permanently and totally disabled if **both** of the following apply:

1. He or she cannot engage in any substantial gainful activity because of a physical or mental condition, and

2. A physician determines that the disability has lasted, or can be expected to last, continuously for at least a year, or can lead to death.

SCHEDULE SE (Form 1040)

Department of the Treasury
Internal Revenue Service (T)

Self-Employment Tax

▶ **See Instructions for Schedule SE (Form 1040).**

▶ **Attach to Form 1040.**

OMB No. 1545-0074

1991

Attachment Sequence No. **17**

Name of person with **self-employment** income (as shown on Form 1040)	Social security number of person with **self-employment** income ▶	

Who Must File Schedule SE

You must file Schedule SE if:

- Your *net earnings from self-employment from other than church employee income* (line 4 of Short Schedule SE or line 4c of Long Schedule SE) were $400 or more; **OR**
- You had church employee income (as defined in the instructions) of $108.28 or more;

AND

- Your wages (and tips) subject to social security AND Medicare tax (or railroad retirement tax) were less than $125,000.

Exception: If your only self-employment income was from earnings as a minister, member of a religious order, or Christian Science practitioner, AND you filed **Form 4361** and received IRS approval not to be taxed on those earnings, DO NOT file Schedule SE. Instead, write "Exempt–Form 4361" on Form 1040, line 47.

Note: *Most people can use Short Schedule SE on this page. But you may have to use Long Schedule SE on the back.*

Who MUST Use Long Schedule SE (Section B)

You must use Long Schedule SE if ANY of the following apply:

- You received wages or tips **and** the total of all of your wages (and tips) subject to social security, Medicare, or railroad retirement tax plus your net earnings from self-employment is more than $53,400;
- You use either "optional method" to figure your net earnings from self-employment (see Section B, Part II, and the instructions);
- You are a minister, member of a religious order, or Christian Science practitioner and you received IRS approval (by filing Form 4361) not to be taxed on your earnings from these sources, but you owe self-employment tax on other earnings;
- You had church employee income of $108.28 or more that was reported to you on Form W-2; **OR**
- You received tips subject to social security, Medicare, or railroad retirement tax, but you did not report those tips to your employer.

Section A—Short Schedule SE (Read above to see if you must use Long Schedule SE on the back (Section B).)

1	Net farm profit or (loss) from Schedule F (Form 1040), line 37, and farm partnerships, Schedule K-1 (Form 1065), line 15a	**1**		
2	Net profit or (loss) from Schedule C (Form 1040), line 31, and Schedule K-1 (Form 1065), line 15a (other than farming). See instructions for other income to report	**2**		
3	Combine lines 1 and 2	**3**		
4	**Net earnings from self-employment.** Multiply line 3 by .9235. If less than $400, **do not** file this schedule; you **do not** owe self-employment tax. **Caution:** *If you received wages or tips, and the total of your wages (and tips) subject to social security, Medicare, or railroad retirement tax plus the amount on line 4 is more than $53,400, you cannot use Short Schedule SE. Instead, use Long Schedule SE on the back* . . . . ▶	**4**		
5	**Self-employment tax.** If the amount on line 4 is: • $53,400 or less, multiply line 4 by 15.3% (.153) and enter the result. • More than $53,400, but less than $125,000, multiply the amount in excess of $53,400 by 2.9% (.029). Add $8,170.20 to the result and enter the total. • $125,000 or more, enter $10,246.60. Also enter this amount on Form 1040, line 47	**5**		

Note: *Also enter one-half of the amount from line 5 on* ***Form 1040, line 25.***

For Paperwork Reduction Act Notice, see Form 1040 instructions. Cat. No. 11358Z **Schedule SE (Form 1040) 1991**

Schedule SE (Form 1040) 1991 — Attachment Sequence No. 17 — Page 2

Name of person with **self-employment** income (as shown on Form 1040)	Social security number of person with **self-employment** income ▶	

Section B—Long Schedule SE (Before completing, see if you can use Short Schedule SE on the other side (Section A).)

A If you are a minister, member of a religious order, or Christian Science practitioner, AND you filed **Form 4361,** but you had $400 or more of **other** net earnings from self-employment, check here and continue with Part I . . . . . . ▶ ☐

B If your only income subject to self-employment tax is church employee income and you are **not** a minister or a member of a religious order, skip lines 1 through 4b. Enter -0- on line 4c and go to line 5a.

Part I Self-Employment Tax

1	Net farm profit or (loss) from Schedule F (Form 1040), line 37, and farm partnerships, Schedule K-1 (Form 1065), line 15a. (**Note:** *Skip this line if you use the farm optional method. See requirements in Part II below and in the instructions.)*			1		
2	Net profit or (loss) from Schedule C (Form 1040), line 31, and Schedule K-1 (Form 1065), line 15a (other than farming). See instructions for other income to report. (**Note:** *Skip this line if you use the nonfarm optional method. See requirements in Part II below and in the instructions.)*			2		
3	Combine lines 1 and 2			3		
4a	If line 3 is more than zero, multiply line 3 by .9235. Otherwise, enter the amount from line 3 here			4a		
b	If you elected one or both of the optional methods, enter the total of lines 17 and 19 here			4b		
c	Combine lines 4a and 4b. If less than $400, **do not** file this schedule; you **do not** owe self-employment tax. (**Exception:** *If less than $400 and you had church employee income, enter -0- and continue.)* ▶			4c		
5a	Enter your church employee income from Form W-2. **Caution:** *See the instructions for definition of church employee income*	5a				
b	Multiply line 5a by .9235. (If less than $100, enter -0-.)	5b				
6	**Net earnings from self-employment.** Add lines 4c and 5b			6		
7	Maximum amount of combined wages and self-employment earnings subject to social security tax or the 6.2% portion of the 7.65% railroad retirement (tier 1) tax for 1991			7	$53,400	00
8a	Total social security wages and tips (from Form(s) W-2) and railroad retirement (tier 1) compensation	8a				
b	Unreported tips subject to social security tax (from Form 4137, line 9) or railroad retirement (tier 1) tax	8b				
c	Add lines 8a and 8b			8c		
9	Subtract line 8c from line 7. If zero or less, enter -0- here and on line 10 and go to line 12a ▶			9		
10	Multiply the **smaller** of line 6 or line 9 by 12.4% (.124)			10		
11	Maximum amount of combined wages and self-employment earnings subject to Medicare tax or the 1.45% portion of the 7.65% railroad retirement (tier 1) tax for 1991			11	$125,000	00
12a	Total Medicare wages and tips (from Form(s) W-2) and railroad retirement (tier 1) compensation	12a				
b	Unreported tips subject to Medicare tax (from Form 4137, line 14) or railroad retirement (tier 1) tax	12b				
c	Add lines 12a and 12b			12c		
13	Subtract line 12c from line 11. If zero or less, enter -0- here and on line 14 and go to line 15			13		
14	Multiply the **smaller** of line 6 or line 13 by 2.9% (.029)			14		
15	**Self-employment tax.** Add lines 10 and 14. Enter the result here and on Form 1040, line 47. **Note:** *Also enter one-half of the amount from line 15 on* ***Form 1040, line 25.***			15		

Part II Optional Methods To Figure Net Earnings (See "Who Can File Schedule SE" and "Optional Methods" in the instructions.)

Farm Optional Method. You may use the farm optional method **only** if **(a)** Your gross farm income[1] was not more than $2,400 **or (b)** Your gross farm income[1] was more than $2,400 and your net farm profits[2] were less than $1,733.

16	Maximum income for optional methods	16	$1,600	00
17	Enter the **smaller** of: two-thirds (⅔) of gross farm income[1] **or** $1,600. Also include this amount on line 4b above	17		

Nonfarm Optional Method. You may use the nonfarm optional method **only** if **(a)** Your net nonfarm profits[3] were less than $1,733 and also less than 72.189% of your gross nonfarm income[4] **and (b)** You had net SE earnings of at least $400 in 2 of the prior 3 years. **Caution:** *You may use the nonfarm optional method no more than five times.*

18	Subtract the amount on line 17, if any, from line 16 and enter the result	18		
19	Enter the **smaller** of: two-thirds (⅔) of gross nonfarm income[4] **or** the amount on line 18. Also include this amount on line 4b above	19		

[1] From Schedule F (Form 1040), line 11, and Schedule K-1 (Form 1065), line 15b.
[2] From Schedule F (Form 1040), line 37, and Schedule K-1 (Form 1065), line 15a.
[3] From Schedule C (Form 1040), line 31, and Schedule K-1 (Form 1065), line 15a.
[4] From Schedule C (Form 1040), line 7, and Schedule K-1 (Form 1065), line 15c.

Form **1040-ES**

Department of the Treasury
Internal Revenue Service

Estimated Tax for Individuals

This package is primarily for first-time filers of estimated tax.

OMB No. 1545-0087

1992

Paperwork Reduction Act Notice

We ask for the information on the payment–vouchers to carry out the Internal Revenue laws of the United States. You are required to give us the information. We need it to ensure that you are complying with these laws and to allow us to figure and collect the right amount of tax.

The time needed to complete the worksheets and prepare and file the payment–vouchers will vary depending on individual circumstances. The estimated average time is: Recordkeeping, 1 hr., 19 min.; Learning about the law, 20 min.; Preparing the worksheets and payment–vouchers, 49 min.; Copying, assembling, and sending the payment–voucher to the IRS, 10 min. If you have comments concerning the accuracy of these time estimates or suggestions for making this package easier, we would be happy to hear from you. You can write to both the Internal Revenue Service, Washington, DC 20224, Attention: IRS Reports Clearance Officer, T:FP; and the Office of Management and Budget, Paperwork Reduction Project (1545-0087), Washington, DC 20503. DO NOT send the payment–vouchers to either of these offices. Instead, see Where To File Your Payment-Voucher on page 5.

Purpose of This Package

Use this package to figure and pay your estimated tax. Estimated tax is the method used to pay tax on income that is not subject to withholding; for example: earnings from self-employment, interest, dividends, rents, alimony, etc.

This package is primarily for first-time filers who are or may be subject to paying estimated tax. This package can also be used if you did not receive or have lost your preprinted 1040-ES package. The estimated tax worksheet on page 3 will help you figure the correct amount to pay. The vouchers in this package are for crediting your estimated tax payments to your account correctly. Use the Record of Estimated Tax Payments on page 5 to keep track of the payments you have made and the number and amount of your remaining payments.

After we receive your first payment–voucher from this package, we will mail you a preprinted 1040-ES package with your name, address, and social security number on each payment–voucher. Use the preprinted vouchers when you receive them to make your **remaining** estimated tax payments for the year. This will speed processing, reduce processing costs, and reduce the chance of errors.

Do not use the vouchers in this package to notify the IRS of a **change of address.** If you have a new address, get **Form 8822,** Change of Address, by calling 1-800-829-3676. Send the completed form to the Internal Revenue Service Center where you filed your last tax return.

Who Must Make Estimated Tax Payments

In most cases, you must make estimated tax payments if you expect to owe, after subtracting your withholding and credits, at least $500 in tax for 1992, and you expect your withholding and credits to be less than the **smaller** of:

- 90% of the tax shown on your 1992 tax return, or
- 100% of the tax shown on your 1991 tax return (the return must cover all 12 months).

Caution: If 100% of your 1991 tax is the **smaller** of the two amounts, see **Limit on Use of Prior Year's Tax** on this page for special rules that may apply to you.

Generally, you do not have to pay estimated tax if you were a U.S. citizen or resident alien for all of 1991 and you had no tax liability for the full 12-month 1991 tax year.

The estimated tax rules apply to:

- U.S. citizens and residents,
- Residents of Puerto Rico, the Virgin Islands, Guam, the Commonwealth of the Northern Mariana Islands, and American Samoa, and
- Nonresident aliens (use Form 1040-ES(NR)).

If you also receive salaries and wages, you can avoid having to make estimated tax payments by asking your employer to take more tax out of your earnings. To do this, file a new **Form W-4,** Employee's Withholding Allowance Certificate, with your employer.

Caution: You may not make joint estimated tax payments if you or your spouse is a nonresident alien, you are separated under a decree of divorce or separate maintenance, or you and your spouse have different tax years.

Additional Information You May Need

Most of the information you will need can be found in:

Pub. 505, Tax Withholding and Estimated Tax

Other available information:

Pub. 553, Highlights of 1991 Tax Changes

Instructions for the 1991 Forms 1040 or 1040A

For forms and publications, call 1-800-829-3676

For assistance, call 1-800-829-1040

Tax Law Changes Effective for 1992

Use your 1991 tax return as a guide for figuring your estimated tax, but be sure to consider the changes noted in this section. For other changes that may affect your 1992 estimated tax, see Pub. 553.

Expiring Tax Provisions. At the time this package went to print, several tax provisions, including the self-employed health insurance deduction, were scheduled to expire 12/31/91. See Pub. 553 to find out if these provisions were extended.

Limit on Use of Prior Year's Tax. Some individuals (other than farmers and fishermen) with income over a certain amount must make a special computation to figure their estimated tax payments. Although these individuals may use 100% of their 1991 tax to figure the amount of their first payment, they may not be able to use that amount to figure their remaining payments. To see if this special computation applies to you, first fill in the 1992 Estimated Tax Worksheet (on page 3) through line 14b. Then, answer the questions below. But if you answer NO to any question, stop and read the instructions below question 3.

1. Did you make any estimated tax payments for 1991, 1990, or 1989, **OR** were you charged an estimated tax penalty for any of those years? (If either applies, answer "Yes.") . . . . ☐ Yes ☐ No

2. Is your 1992 adjusted gross income (AGI) on line 1 of the worksheet more than $75,000 ($37,500 if married filing separately)? . . . . ☐ Yes ☐ No

3. Do you expect your 1992 modified AGI (defined on page 2) to exceed your 1991 actual AGI by more than $40,000 ($20,000 if married filing separately)? . . . . . . ☐ Yes ☐ No

If you answered NO to any of the questions above, you don't have to make the special computation. Instead, fill in the rest of the worksheet on page 3.

If you answered YES to all three of the questions above, you must make the special computation. Do not fill in the rest of the worksheet on page 3. Instead, use the **1992 Estimated Tax Worksheet Limiting Use of Prior Year's Tax** in Pub. 505 to figure all your estimated tax payments. That worksheet uses 100% of your 1991 tax to figure your first payment.

Cat. No. 11340T

(Continued on page 2)

Modified AGI for this purpose means AGI figured without including any gain from the sale or exchange of your main home or gain from a casualty, theft, condemnation, or other involuntary conversion required to be shown on your 1992 return. Partners and shareholders in an S corporation must include their income, gains and losses (other than from the disposition of their interests in a partnership or S corporation), and deductions for 1991 from the partnership or S corporation instead of the amounts for 1992. But this rule does not apply to general partners, partners who owned at least a 10% capital or profit interest in the partnership, or shareholders who owned at least 10% of the stock (vote or value) of the S corporation.

Standard Deduction for 1992. If you do not itemize your deductions, you may take the 1992 standard deduction listed below:

Filing Status	Standard Deduction
Married filing jointly or Qualifying widow(er)	$6,000
Head of household	$5,250
Single	$3,600
Married filing separately	$3,000

Caution: If you can be claimed as a dependent on another person's 1992 return, your standard deduction is the greater of $600 or your earned income, up to the standard deduction amount.

An additional amount is added to the standard deduction if:

1. You are an unmarried individual (single or head of household) and are:

65 or older or blind	$900
65 or older and blind	$1,800

2. You are a married individual (filing jointly or separately) or a qualifying widow(er) and are:

65 or older or blind	$700
65 or older and blind	$1,400
Both spouses 65 or older	$1,400*
Both spouses 65 or older and blind	$2,800*

* If married filing separately, these amounts apply only if you can claim an exemption for your spouse.

To Figure Your Estimated Tax Use

- The 1992 Estimated Tax Worksheet on page 3
- The instructions below for the worksheet on page 3
- The 1992 Tax Rate Schedules on this page
- Your 1991 tax return as a guide

See the 1991 Instructions for Form 1040 or 1040A for information on figuring your income, deductions, and credits, including the taxable amount of social security benefits.

To amend or correct your estimated tax, see Amending Estimated Tax Payments on page 4.

Instructions for Worksheet on Page 3

Line 7—Additional Taxes. Enter the additional taxes from **Form 4970,** Tax on Accumulation Distribution of Trusts, or **Form 4972,** Tax on Lump-Sum Distributions.

Line 9—Credits. See the 1991 Form 1040, lines 41 through 45, or Form 1040A, lines 24a and 24b, and the related instructions.

Line 11—Self-Employment Tax. If you and your spouse make joint estimated tax payments and you both have self-employment income, figure the self-employment tax separately. Enter the total on line 11. When figuring your estimate of 1992 net earnings from self-employment, be sure to use only 92.35% of your total net profit from self-employment.

If your estimate of 1992 net earnings from self-employment is more than $55,500 but less than $130,200, multiply the amount in excess of $55,500 by .029. Add $8,491.50 to the result and enter the total on line 11. If your estimate of 1992 net earnings from self-employment is $130,200 or more, enter $10,657.80 on line 11.

Line 12—Other Taxes. Enter any other taxes, such as tax on early distributions (Form 5329, Part II, only), and alternative minimum tax. Do not include any recapture of Federal mortgage subsidy. For details, see page 26 of the 1991 Instructions for Form 1040. You do not have to include social security and Medicare tax on tip income not reported to your employer or uncollected employee social security and Medicare or RRTA tax on tips or group-term life insurance.

1992 Tax Rate Schedules

Caution: *Do not use these Tax Rate Schedules to figure your 1991 taxes. Use only to figure your 1992 estimated taxes.*

Single—Schedule X

If line 5 is: Over—	But not over—	The tax is:	of the amount over—
$0	$21,450	.........15%	**$0**
21,450	51,900	**$3,217.50 + 28%**	**21,450**
51,900	....	**11,743.50 + 31%**	**51,900**

Head of household—Schedule Z

If line 5 is: Over—	But not over—	The tax is:	of the amount over—
$0	$28,750	.........15%	**$0**
28,750	74,150	**$4,312.50 + 28%**	**28,750**
74,150	....	**17,024.50 + 31%**	**74,150**

Married filing jointly or Qualifying widow(er)—Schedule Y-1

If line 5 is: Over—	But not over—	The tax is:	of the amount over—
$0	$35,800	.........15%	**$0**
35,800	86,500	**$5,370.00 + 28%**	**35,800**
86,500	....	**19,566.00 + 31%**	**86,500**

Married filing separately—Schedule Y-2

If line 5 is: Over—	But not over—	The tax is:	of the amount over—
$0	$17,900	.........15%	**$0**
17,900	43,250	**$2,685.00 + 28%**	**17,900**
43,250	....	**9,783.00 + 31%**	**43,250**

1992 Estimated Tax Worksheet (keep for your records)

1	Enter amount of adjusted gross income you expect in 1992	1	
2	• If you plan to itemize deductions, enter the estimated total of your itemized deductions. **Caution:** If line 1 above is over $105,250 ($52,625 if married filing separately), your deduction may be reduced. See Pub. 505 for details. • If you do not plan to itemize deductions, see **Standard Deduction for 1992** on page 2, and enter your standard deduction here.	2	
3	Subtract line 2 from line 1	3	
4	Exemptions. Multiply $2,300 by the number of personal exemptions. If you can be claimed as a dependent on another person's 1992 return, your personal exemption is not allowed. **Caution:** If line 1 above is over $157,900 ($131,550 if head of household; $105,250 if single; $78,950 if married filing separately), get Pub. 505 to figure the amount to enter	4	
5	Subtract line 4 from line 3	5	
6	**Tax.** Figure your tax on the amount on line 5 by using the 1992 Tax Rate Schedules on page 2. DO NOT use the Tax Table or the Tax Rate Schedules in the 1991 Form 1040 or Form 1040A instructions. **Caution:** If you have a net capital gain and line 5 is over $86,500 ($74,150 if head of household; $51,900 if single; $43,250 if married filing separately), get Pub. 505 to figure the tax	6	
7	Additional taxes (see line 7 instructions)	7	
8	Add lines 6 and 7	8	
9	Credits (see line 9 instructions). Do not include any income tax withholding on this line	9	
10	Subtract line 9 from line 8. Enter the result, but not less than zero	10	
11	Self-employment tax. Estimate of 1992 net earnings from self-employment $..................; if **$55,500 or less,** multiply the amount by .153; if **more than $55,500,** see line 11 instructions for the amount to enter. **Caution:** If you also have wages subject to social security or Medicare tax, get Pub. 505 to figure the amount to enter	11	
12	Other taxes (see line 12 instructions)	12	
13a	Add lines 10 through 12	13a	
b	Earned income credit and credit from **Form 4136**	13b	
c	Subtract line 13b from line 13a. Enter the result, but not less than zero. **THIS IS YOUR TOTAL 1992 ESTIMATED TAX** ▶	13c	
14a	Multiply line 13c by 90% (66⅔% for farmers and fishermen) — 14a		
b	Enter 100% of the tax shown on your 1991 tax return — 14b **Caution:** If 14b is **smaller** than 14a **and** line 1 above is over $75,000 ($37,500 if married filing separately), stop here and see **Limit on Use of Prior Year's Tax** on page 1 before continuing.		
c	Enter the **smaller** of line 14a or 14b. **THIS IS YOUR REQUIRED ANNUAL PAYMENT** ▶ **Caution:** Generally, if you do not prepay at least the amount on line 14c, you may owe a penalty for not paying enough estimated tax. To avoid a penalty, make sure your estimate on line 13c is as accurate as possible. If you prefer, you may pay 100% of your 1992 estimated tax (line 13c). For more details, get Pub. 505.	14c	
15	Income tax withheld and estimated to be withheld during 1992 (including income tax withholding on pensions, annuities, certain deferred income, etc.)	15	
16	Subtract line 15 from line 14c. (**Note:** *If line 13c minus line 15 is less than $500, you do not have to make estimated tax payments.*) If you are applying an overpayment from 1991 to 1992 estimated tax, see **How To Complete and Use the Payment–Voucher** on page 4	16	
17	If the first payment you are required to make is due April 15, 1992, enter ¼ of line 16 (minus any 1991 overpayment that you are applying to this installment) here and on your payment-voucher(s)	17	

Payment Due Dates

Use one of the following charts to determine your payment due dates. Payments are due by the dates indicated whether or not you are outside the United States and Puerto Rico.

You may have a large change in income, deductions, additional taxes, or credits during the year that may require you to make estimated tax payments. If you meet the requirement to make estimated tax payments after March 31, use Chart B. Otherwise, use Chart A to determine the payment due dates.

Whether you have steady or unexpected income, you do not have to make the payment due January 15, 1993, if you:

- File your 1992 Form 1040 or 1040A by February 1, 1993, and
- Pay the entire balance due with the return.

Chart A—Individuals With Steady Income. You may pay all of your estimated tax by April 15, 1992, or in four equal amounts by the dates below.

Estimated payments due by:

1st Payment	April 15, 1992
2nd Payment	June 15, 1992
3rd Payment	Sept. 15, 1992
4th Payment	Jan. 15, 1993

Chart B—Individuals With Unexpected Income. Use the amount on line 16 of the estimated tax worksheet, minus any 1991 overpayment that was applied to 1992, for the estimated tax due.

If the requirement to pay estimated tax is met after:	Payment date is:	Of the estimated tax due, pay:
Mar. 31 and before June 1	June 15, 1992	1/2
May 31 and before Sept. 1	Sept. 15, 1992	3/4
Aug. 31	Jan. 15, 1993	all

Farmers and Fishermen. If at least two-thirds of your gross income for 1991 or 1992 is from farming or fishing, you may do one of the following:

- Pay all of your estimated tax by January 15, 1993, or
- File your 1992 Form 1040 by March 1, 1993, and pay the total tax due. In this case, 1992 estimated payments are not required.

Fiscal Year Filers. You are on a fiscal year if your 12-month tax period ends on any day except December 31. Due dates for fiscal year filers are the 15th day of the 4th, 6th, and 9th months and the 1st month of the following fiscal year. If any payment date falls on a Saturday, Sunday, or legal holiday, use the next working day.

Amending Estimated Tax Payments

To change or amend your estimated payments, first refigure your estimated tax using the worksheet on page 3. From your new estimated tax, subtract any amount of 1991 tax overpayment credited to 1992 and any estimated payments made to date. Make your remaining payments using the instructions for Payment Due Dates on this page.

When a Penalty is Applied

In some cases, you may owe a penalty when you file your return. The penalty is imposed on each underpayment for the number of days it remains unpaid. A penalty may be applied if you did not pay enough estimated tax, or you did not make the payments on time or in the required amount. A penalty may apply even if you have an overpayment on your tax return.

The penalty may be waived under certain conditions. See Pub. 505 for details.

How To Complete and Use the Payment-Voucher

There is a separate voucher for each due date. Please be sure you use the voucher with the correct due date shown in the upper right corner. Complete and send in the voucher only if a payment is due. To complete your voucher:

- Type or print your name, address, and social security number in the space provided on the voucher. If filing a joint voucher, also enter your spouse's name and social security number.
- Enter the amount you are sending in on the payment line of the voucher. You may apply all or part of your 1991 overpayment to any voucher.
- Enclose your payment, making the check or money order payable to: "Internal Revenue Service" (Not "IRS").
- Do not staple or attach your payment to the voucher.
- Write your social security number and "1992 Form 1040-ES" on your check or money order.
- Mail your payment-voucher to the address shown on page 5 for the place where you live.
- Fill in the Record of Estimated Tax Payments on page 5 for your files.

If you changed your name and made estimated tax payments using your old name, attach a statement to the front of your 1992 Form 1040 or 1040A. List all of the estimated tax payments you and your spouse made for 1992, the address where you made the payments, and the name(s) and social security number(s) under which you made the payments.

Record of Estimated Tax Payments (see page 4 for correct payment due dates)

Payment number	(a) Date	(b) Amount paid		(c) 1991 overpayment credit applied		(d) Total amount paid and credited (add (b) and (c))	
1							
2							
3							
4							
Total . . . . ▶							

Where To File Your Payment-Voucher

Mail your payment-voucher to the Internal Revenue Service at the address shown below for the place where you live. **Do not** mail your tax return to this address. Also do not mail your estimated tax payments to the address shown in the Form 1040 or 1040A instructions.

Note: *For proper delivery of your estimated tax payment, you must include the P.O. box number, if any, in the address.*

If you live in:	Use this address:
New Jersey, New York (New York City and counties of Nassau, Rockland, Suffolk, and Westchester)	P.O. Box 162 Newark, NJ 07101-0162
New York (all other counties), Connecticut, Maine, Massachusetts, New Hampshire, Rhode Island, Vermont	P.O. Box 371999 Pittsburgh, PA 15250-7999
Delaware, District of Columbia, Maryland, Pennsylvania, Virginia	P.O. Box 8318 Philadelphia, PA 19162-0825
Florida, Georgia, South Carolina	P.O. Box 62001 Philadelphia, PA 19162-0300
Indiana, Kentucky, Michigan, Ohio, West Virginia	P.O. Box 7422 Chicago, IL 60680-7422
Alabama, Arkansas, Louisiana, Mississippi, North Carolina, Tennessee	P.O. Box 371300M Pittsburgh, PA 15250-7300
Illinois, Iowa, Minnesota, Missouri, Wisconsin	P.O. Box 6413 Chicago, IL 60680-6413
Kansas, New Mexico, Oklahoma, Texas	P.O. Box 970001 St. Louis, MO 63197-0001
Alaska, Arizona, California (counties of Alpine, Amador, Butte, Calaveras, Colusa, Contra Costa, Del Norte, El Dorado, Glenn, Humboldt, Lake, Lassen, Marin, Mendocino, Modoc, Napa, Nevada, Placer, Plumas, Sacramento, San Joaquin, Shasta, Sierra, Siskiyou, Solano, Sonoma, Sutter, Tehama, Trinity, Yolo, and Yuba), Colorado, Idaho, Montana, Nebraska, Nevada, North Dakota, Oregon, South Dakota, Utah, Washington, Wyoming	P.O. Box 510000 San Francisco, CA 94151-5100
California (all other counties), Hawaii	P.O. Box 54030 Los Angeles, CA 90054-0030
American Samoa	P.O. Box 8318 Philadelphia, PA 19162-0825
Guam	Commissioner of Revenue and Taxation 855 West Marine Drive Agana, GU 96910
The Commonwealth of the Northern Mariana Islands	P.O. Box 8318 Philadelphia, PA 19162-0825
Puerto Rico (or if excluding income under section 933)	P.O. Box 8318 Philadelphia, PA 19162-0825
Virgin Islands: Nonpermanent residents	P.O. Box 8318 Philadelphia, PA 19162-0825
Permanent residents*	V.I. Bureau of Internal Revenue Lockharts Garden No. 1A Charlotte Amalie St. Thomas, VI 00802
All A.P.O. and F.P.O. addresses	P.O. Box 8318 Philadelphia, PA 19162-0825
Foreign country: U.S. citizens and those filing Form 2555 or Form 4563	P.O. Box 8318 Philadelphia, PA 19162-0825

* You must prepare separate vouchers for estimated income tax and self-employment tax payments. Send the income tax vouchers to the V.I. address and the self-employment tax vouchers to the address for V.I. nonpermanent residents shown above.

Tear off here

Form **1040-ES** Department of the Treasury Internal Revenue Service | **1992 Payment-Voucher 4** | OMB No. 1545-0087

Calendar year—Due Jan. 15, 1993

Return this voucher with check or money order payable to the **"Internal Revenue Service."** Please write your social security number and "1992 Form 1040-ES" on your check or money order. Please do not send cash. Enclose, but do not staple or attach, your payment with this voucher. File only if you are making a payment of estimated tax.

Amount of payment	Please type or print			
		Your first name and initial	Your last name	Your social security number
		If joint payment, complete for spouse		
		Spouse's first name and initial	Spouse's last name	Spouse's social security number
		Address (number, street, and apt. no.)		
$........		City, state, and ZIP code		

For Paperwork Reduction Act Notice, see instructions on page 1.

Form **1040-ES** Department of the Treasury Internal Revenue Service

1992 Payment-Voucher 3

OMB No. 1545-0087

Calendar year—Due Sept. 15, 1992

Return this voucher with check or money order payable to the **"Internal Revenue Service."** Please write your social security number and "1992 Form 1040-ES" on your check or money order. Please do not send cash. Enclose, but do not staple or attach, your payment with this voucher. File only if you are making a payment of estimated tax.

Amount of payment	Please type or print			
		Your first name and initial	Your last name	Your social security number
		If joint payment, complete for spouse		
		Spouse's first name and initial	Spouse's last name	Spouse's social security number
		Address (number, street, and apt. no.)		
$........		City, state, and ZIP code		

For Paperwork Reduction Act Notice, see instructions on page 1.

Tear off here

Form **1040-ES** Department of the Treasury Internal Revenue Service

1992 Payment-Voucher 2

OMB No. 1545-0087

Calendar year—Due June 15, 1992

Return this voucher with check or money order payable to the **"Internal Revenue Service."** Please write your social security number and "1992 Form 1040-ES" on your check or money order. Please do not send cash. Enclose, but do not staple or attach, your payment with this voucher. File only if you are making a payment of estimated tax.

Amount of payment	Please type or print			
		Your first name and initial	Your last name	Your social security number
		If joint payment, complete for spouse		
		Spouse's first name and initial	Spouse's last name	Spouse's social security number
		Address (number, street, and apt. no.)		
$........		City, state, and ZIP code		

For Paperwork Reduction Act Notice, see instructions on page 1.

Tear off here

Form **1040-ES** Department of the Treasury Internal Revenue Service

1992 Payment-Voucher 1

OMB No. 1545-0087

Calendar year—Due April 15, 1992

Return this voucher with check or money order payable to the **"Internal Revenue Service."** Please write your social security number and "1992 Form 1040-ES" on your check or money order. Please do not send cash. Enclose, but do not staple or attach, your payment with this voucher. File only if you are making a payment of estimated tax.

Amount of payment	Please type or print			
		Your first name and initial	Your last name	Your social security number
		If joint payment, complete for spouse		
		Spouse's first name and initial	Spouse's last name	Spouse's social security number
		Address (number, street, and apt. no.)		
$........		City, state, and ZIP code		

For Paperwork Reduction Act Notice, see instructions on page 1.

Form **2106** | **Employee Business Expenses** | OMB No. 1545-0139

▶ See separate instructions.

▶ Attach to Form 1040.

Department of the Treasury (T)
Internal Revenue Service

1991
Attachment Sequence No. **54**

Your name	Social security number	Occupation in which expenses were incurred

Part I **Employee Business Expenses and Reimbursements**

STEP 1 Enter Your Expenses		Column A Other Than Meals and Entertainment	Column B Meals and Entertainment
1 Vehicle expense from line 22 or line 29	1		
2 Parking fees, tolls, and local transportation, including train, bus, etc.	2	125	
3 Travel expense while away from home overnight, including lodging, airplane, car rental, etc. **Do not** include meals and entertainment	3		
4 Business expenses not included on lines 1 through 3. **Do not** include meals and entertainment	4		
5 Meals and entertainment expenses. (See instructions.)	5		615
6 **Total expenses.** In Column A, add lines 1 through 4 and enter the result. In Column B, enter the amount from line 5.	6	125	615

Note: *If you were not reimbursed for any expenses in Step 1, skip line 7 and enter the amount from line 6 on line 8.*

STEP 2 Enter Amounts Your Employer Gave You for Expenses Listed in STEP 1

7 Enter amounts your employer gave you that were **not** reported to you in Box 10 of Form W-2. Include any amount reported under code "L" in Box 17 of your Form W-2. (See instructions.)	7	Ø	Ø

STEP 3 Figure Expenses To Deduct on Schedule A (Form 1040)

8 Subtract line 7 from line 6	8	125	615
Note: *If **both columns** of line 8 are zero, **stop here.** If Column A is less than zero, report the amount as income and enter -0- on line 10, Column A. See the instructions for how to report.*			
9 Enter 20% (.20) of line 8, Column B	9		123
10 Subtract line 9 from line 8	10	125	492
11 Add the amounts on line 10 of both columns and enter the total here. **Also enter the total on Schedule A (Form 1040), line 19.** (Qualified performing artists and individuals with disabilities, see the instructions for special rules on where to enter the total.) ▶	11		617

For Paperwork Reduction Act Notice, see instructions. Cat. No. 11700N Form **2106** (1991)

615
x .20
123.0

615
123
492

2,200
x .2
440.0

2,200
440
1,760

Part II Vehicle Expenses (See instructions to find out which sections to complete.)

Section A.—General Information		(a) Vehicle 1	(b) Vehicle 2
12 Enter the date vehicle was placed in service	12	/ /	/ /
13 Total mileage vehicle was used during 1991	13	miles	miles
14 Miles included on line 13 that vehicle was used for business	14	miles	miles
15 Percent of business use (divide line 14 by line 13)	15	%	%
16 Average daily round trip commuting distance	16	miles	miles
17 Miles included on line 13 that vehicle was used for commuting	17	miles	miles
18 Other personal mileage (add lines 14 and 17 and subtract the total from line 13)	18	miles	miles

19 Do you (or your spouse) have another vehicle available for personal purposes? ☐ Yes ☐ No

20 If your employer provided you with a vehicle, is personal use during off duty hours permitted? ☐ Yes ☐ No ☐ Not applicable

21a Do you have evidence to support your deduction? ☐ Yes ☐ No **21b** If "Yes," is the evidence written? ☐ Yes ☐ No

Section B.—Standard Mileage Rate (Use this section only if you own the vehicle.)

22 Multiply line 14 by 27.5¢ (.275). Enter the result here and on line 1. (Rural mail carriers, see instructions.)	22	

Section C.—Actual Expenses		(a) Vehicle 1		(b) Vehicle 2	
23 Gasoline, oil, repairs, vehicle insurance, etc.	23				
24a Vehicle rentals	24a				
b Inclusion amount	24b				
c Subtract line 24b from line 24a	24c				
25 Value of employer-provided vehicle (applies only if 100% of annual lease value was included on Form W-2. See instructions.)	25				
26 Add lines 23, 24c, and 25	26				
27 Multiply line 26 by the percentage on line 15	27				
28 Enter amount from line 38 below	28				
29 Add lines 27 and 28. Enter total here and on line 1	29				

Section D.—Depreciation of Vehicles (Use this section only if you own the vehicle.)

		(a) Vehicle 1		(b) Vehicle 2	
30 Enter cost or other basis. (See instructions.)	30				
31 Enter amount of section 179 deduction. (See instructions.)	31				
32 Multiply line 30 by line 15. (See instructions if you elected the section 179 deduction.)	32				
33 Enter depreciation method and percentage. (See instructions.)	33				
34 Multiply line 32 by the percentage on line 33. (See instructions.)	34				
35 Add lines 31 and 34	35				
36 Enter the limitation amount from the table in the line 36 instructions	36				
37 Multiply line 36 by the percentage on line 15	37				
38 Enter the **smaller** of line 35 or line 37. Also enter the amount on line 28 above	38				

Form **2119**

Department of the Treasury
Internal Revenue Service

Sale of Your Home

▶ Attach to Form 1040 for year of sale.

▶ See separate instructions. ▶ Please print or type.

OMB No. 1545-0072

1991

Attachment Sequence No. **20**

Your first name and initial. (If joint return, also give spouse's name and initial.)	Last name	Your social security number
Fill in Your Address Only If You Are Filing This Form by Itself and Not With Your Tax Return	Present address (no., street, and apt. no., rural route, or P.O. box no. if mail is not delivered to street address)	Spouse's social security number
	City, town or post office, state, and ZIP code	

Caution: *If the home sold was financed (in whole or part) from a mortgage credit certificate or the proceeds of a tax-exempt qualified mortgage bond, you may owe additional tax. Get* **Form 8828,** *Recapture of Federal Mortgage Subsidy, for details.*

Part I General Information

1a	Date your former main home was sold (month, day, year) . . . . ▶	**1a**	/ /
b	Face amount of any mortgage, note (e.g., second trust), or other financial instrument on which you will get periodic payments of principal or interest from this sale (see instructions) . . .	**1b**	
2	Have you bought or built a new main home?		☐ Yes ☐ No
3	Is or was any part of either main home rented out or used for business? (If "Yes," see instructions.) . .		☐ Yes ☐ No

Part II Gain on Sale (Do not include amounts you deduct as moving expenses.)

4	Selling price of home. (Do not include personal property items that you sold with your home.)	**4**	
5	Expense of sale. (Include sales commissions, advertising, legal, etc.)	**5**	
6	Amount realized. Subtract line 5 from line 4	**6**	
7	Basis of home sold (see instructions)	**7**	
8a	**Gain on sale.** Subtract line 7 from line 6	**8a**	

- If line 8a is zero or less, stop here and attach this form to your return.
- If line 2 is "Yes," you **must** go to Part III or Part IV, whichever applies. Otherwise, go to line 8b.

b If you haven't replaced your home, do you plan to do so within the replacement period (see instructions)? ☐ Yes ☐ No

- If "Yes," stop here, attach this form to your return, and see **Additional Filing Requirements** in the instructions.
- If "No," you **must** go to Part III or Part IV, whichever applies.

Part III One-Time Exclusion of Gain for People Age 55 or Older (If you are not taking the exclusion, go to Part IV now.)

9a	Who was age 55 or older on date of sale?		☐ You ☐ Your spouse ☐ Both of you
b	Did the person who was age 55 or older own and use the property as his or her main home for a total of at least 3 years (except for short absences) of the 5-year period before the sale? (If "No," go to Part IV now.)		☐ Yes ☐ No
c	**If line 9b is "Yes," do you elect to take the one-time exclusion?** (If "No," go to Part IV now.) . . .		☐ Yes ☐ No
d	At time of sale, who owned the home?		☐ You ☐ Your spouse ☐ Both of you
e	Social security number of spouse at time of sale if you had a different spouse from the one above at time of sale. (If you were not married at time of sale, enter "None.") . . . . . ▶	**9e**	
f	**Exclusion.** Enter the **smaller** of line 8a or $125,000 ($62,500, if married filing separate return)	**9f**	

Part IV Adjusted Sales Price, Taxable Gain, and Adjusted Basis of New Home

10	Subtract line 9f from line 8a	**10**	

- If line 10 is zero, stop here and attach this form to your return.
- If line 2 is "Yes," go to line 11 now.
- If you are reporting this sale on the installment method, stop here and see the line 1b instructions.
- All others, stop here and **enter the amount from line 10 on Schedule D, line 2 or line 9.**

11	Fixing-up expenses (see instructions for time limits)	**11**	
12	**Adjusted sales price.** Subtract line 11 from line 6	**12**	
13a	Date you moved into new home (month, day, year) ▶ / / **b** Cost of new home	**13b**	
14a	Add line 9f and line 13b	**14a**	
b	Subtract line 14a from line 12. If the result is zero or less, enter -0-	**14b**	
c	**Taxable gain.** Enter the **smaller** of line 10 or line 14b	**14c**	

- If line 14c is zero, go to line 15 and attach this form to your return.
- If you are reporting this sale on the installment method, see the line 1b instructions and go to line 15.
- All others, **enter the amount from line 14c on Schedule D, line 2 or line 9,** and go to line 15.

15	Postponed gain. Subtract line 14c from line 10	**15**	
16	**Adjusted basis of new home.** Subtract line 15 from line 13b	**16**	

Sign Here Only If You Are Filing This Form by Itself and Not With Your Tax Return

Under penalties of perjury, I declare that I have examined this form, including attachments, and to the best of my knowledge and belief, it is true, correct, and complete.

Your signature	Date	Spouse's signature	Date
▶ (If a joint return, both must sign.)		▶	

For Paperwork Reduction Act Notice, see separate instructions. Cat. No. 11710J Form **2119** (1991)

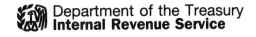

1991 Department of the Treasury Internal Revenue Service

Instructions for Form 2119

Sale of Your Home

Paperwork Reduction Act Notice.—We ask for the information on this form to carry out the Internal Revenue laws of the United States. You are required to give us the information. We need it to ensure that you are complying with these laws and to allow us to figure and collect the right amount of tax.

The time needed to complete and file this form will vary depending on individual circumstances. The estimated average time is:

Recordkeeping	46 min.
Learning about the law or the form	13 min.
Preparing the form	44 min.
Copying, assembling, and sending the form to the IRS	20 min.

If you have comments concerning the accuracy of these time estimates or suggestions for making this form more simple, we would be happy to hear from you. You can write to both the **Internal Revenue Service,** Washington, DC 20224, Attention: IRS Reports Clearance Officer, T:FP; and the **Office of Management and Budget,** Paperwork Reduction Project (1545-0072), Washington, DC 20503. **Do not** send this form to either of these offices. Instead, see **When and Where To File** on this page.

General Instructions

Purpose of Form

Use Form 2119 to report the sale of your main home. If you replaced your main home, use Form 2119 to postpone all or part of the gain. Form 2119 is also used by people who were age 55 or older on the date of sale to elect a one-time exclusion of the gain on the sale.

Caution. *If the home you sold was financed (in whole or in part) from a mortgage credit certificate or the proceeds of a tax-exempt qualified mortgage bond, you may owe additional tax. Get* **Form 8828,** *Recapture of Federal Mortgage Subsidy, for details.*

Main Home.—Your main home is the one you live in most of the time. It can be a house, houseboat, housetrailer, cooperative apartment, condominium, etc.

Additional Information

You may want to get **Pub. 523,** Tax Information on Selling Your Home, for more details.

Who Must File

You must file Form 1040 with Form 2119 for the year in which you sell your main home, even if the sale resulted in a loss or you are electing the one-time exclusion for people age 55 or older. There may be additional filing requirements as well. See **When and Where To File** below.

If part of your home was rented out or used for business in the year of sale, report that part of the sale on **Form 4797,** Sales of Business Property. See the instructions for line 3.

If you sold your home on the installment method, complete Form 2119 and **Form 6252,** Installment Sale Income.

If your home was damaged by fire, storm, or other casualty, see **Form 4684,** Casualties and Thefts, and its separate instructions, and **Pub. 547,** Nonbusiness Disasters, Casualties, and Thefts.

If your home was condemned for public use, you can choose to postpone gain under the rules for a condemnation, or you can choose to treat the transaction as a sale of your home. For details, see Pub. 523.

If your home was sold in connection with a divorce or separation, see Pub. 523. Also, get **Pub. 504,** Tax Information for Divorced or Separated Individuals.

Which Parts To Complete

Parts I and II.—You must complete Parts I and II.

Part III.—Complete this part only if you qualify for the **One-Time Exclusion for People Age 55 or Older** (explained later), and you want to make the election for this sale.

Part IV.—Complete line 10 even if you did not take the exclusion in Part III. Complete lines 11 through 16 only if line 10 is more than zero and you answered "Yes" on line 2.

When and Where To File

File Form 2119 with your tax return for the year of sale.

Additional Filing Requirements.—If you have not replaced your home, but plan to do so within the replacement period (defined on page 2), you will also have to complete a second Form 2119.

- You must file the second Form 2119 by itself if:

1. You planned to replace your home within the replacement period, **and**

2. You later replaced your home within the replacement period, **and**

3. Your taxable gain (line 14c on the second Form 2119) is zero.

If your taxable gain is zero, no tax is due, but you must still file the second form to show that you replaced your home within the replacement period. Enter your name and address, and sign and date the second form. If a joint return was filed for the year of sale, both you and your spouse must sign the second Form 2119. Send the form to the place where you would file your next tax return based on the address where you now live.

- You must file **Form 1040X,** Amended U.S. Individual Income Tax Return, for the year of sale with the second Form 2119 attached if:

1. You planned to replace your home when you filed your tax return, you later replaced your home within the replacement period, **and** you had a taxable gain on line 14c of the second Form 2119; **or**

2. You planned to replace your home when you filed your tax return, but did **not** do so within the replacement period; **or**

3. You did **not** plan to replace your home when you filed your tax return and included the gain in income, but later you did replace your home within the replacement period.

Report the correct amount of gain from Form 2119 on Schedule D (Form 1040) and attach both forms to Form 1040X. Interest will be charged on any additional tax due. If tax is to be refunded to you, interest will be included with the refund.

One-Time Exclusion for People Age 55 or Older

Generally, you can elect to exclude from your income up to $125,000 ($62,500 if married filing a separate return) of the gain from one sale of any main home you choose. However, for sales after July 26, 1978, the exclusion is available only once. To make the election for this sale, complete Part III and answer "Yes" on line 9c. You qualify to make the election if you meet **ALL** of the following tests:

1. You or your spouse were age 55 or older on the date of sale,

2. Neither you nor your spouse have ever excluded gain on the sale of a home after July 26, 1978, and

3. The person who was age 55 or older owned and lived in the home for periods adding up to at least 3 years within the 5-year period ending on the date of sale.

For purposes of test 3, if you were physically or mentally unable to care for yourself, count as time living in your main home any time during the 5-year period that you lived in a facility such as a nursing home. The facility must be licensed by a state (or political subdivision) to care for people in your condition. For this rule to apply, you must have owned and used your residence as your main home for a total of at least 1 year during the 5-year period. See Pub. 523 for more details.

The gain excluded is never taxed. But, if the gain is more than the amount excluded, complete Part IV to figure whether the excess gain is included in your income or postponed. If the gain is less than $125,000 ($62,500 if married filing a separate return), the difference **cannot** be excluded on a future sale of another main home. Generally, you can make or revoke the election within 3 years from the due date of your return (including extensions) for the year of sale. To make or revoke the election, file Form 1040X with Form 2119 attached.

Married Taxpayers.—If you and your spouse owned the property jointly and file a joint return, only one of you must meet the age, ownership, and use tests to be able to make the election. If you did not own the property jointly, the spouse who owned the property must meet these tests.

If you were married at the time of sale, both you and your spouse must agree to exclude the gain. If you do not file a joint return with that spouse, your spouse must agree to exclude the gain by signing a statement saying, "I agree to the Part III election." The statement and signature may be made on a separate piece of paper or in the bottom margin of Form 2119.

If you sell a home while you are married, and one spouse already made the election prior to the marriage, neither of you can exclude gain on the sale.

The election to exclude gain does not apply separately to you and your spouse. If you elect to exclude gain during marriage and later divorce, neither of you can make the election again.

Postponing Gain

If you buy or build another main home and move into it within the replacement period (defined below), you must postpone all or part of the gain in most cases. The amount of gain postponed is shown on line 15.

If one spouse dies after the old home is sold and before the new home is bought, the gain from the sale of the old home is postponed if the above requirements are met, the spouses were married on the date of death, and the surviving spouse uses the new home as his or her main home. This rule applies regardless of whether the title of the old home is in one spouse's name or is held jointly. For more details, see Pub. 523.

If you bought more than one main home during the replacement period, only the last one you bought qualifies as your new main home for postponing gain. If you sold more than one main home during the replacement period, any sale after the first one does not qualify for postponing gain. However, these rules do not apply if you sold your home because of a job change that qualifies for a moving expense deduction. If this is the case, file a Form 2119 for each sale, for the year of the sale, and attach an explanation for each sale (except the first) to Form 2119. For more details on qualifications for moving expenses, get **Pub. 521,** Moving Expenses.

Replacement Period.—Generally, the replacement period starts 2 years before and ends 2 years after the date you sell your former main home. The replacement period may be longer if you are on active duty in the U.S. Armed Forces for more than 90 days, or if you live and work outside the U.S. For more details, see Pub. 523.

Applying Separate Gain to Basis of New Home.—If you are married and the old home was owned by only one spouse, but you and your spouse own the new home jointly, you and your spouse may elect to divide the gain and the adjusted basis. If you owned the old home jointly, and you now own new homes separately, you may elect to divide the gain to be postponed. In either situation, you both must:

1. Use the old and new homes as your main homes, and

2. Sign a statement that says, "We agree to reduce the basis of the new home(s) by the gain from selling the old home." This statement can be made in the bottom margin of Form 2119 or on an attached sheet.

If you both do not meet these two requirements, you must report the gain in the regular way without allocation.

Line Instructions

You may not take double benefits. For example, you cannot use the moving expenses that are part of your moving expense deduction on **Form 3903,** Moving Expenses, to lower the amount of gain on the sale of your old home or to add to the cost of your new home.

Line 1b.—If you report the gain from the sale of your home on Form 6252 using the installment method, complete Form 2119 first. When completing Form 6252, be sure to enter the total of lines 9f and 15 of Form 2119 on line 11 of Form 6252. Do not enter the gain from Form 2119 on Schedule D (Form 1040).

Note: *Report interest you receive on a note (or other financial instrument) as interest income for the tax year in which you receive it.*

Line 3.—If any part of either home was rented out or used for business for which a deduction is allowed, check "Yes."

• If part of your former main home was rented out or used for business in the year of sale, treat the sale as two separate sales. Report the part of the sale that applies to the rental or business use on Form 4797. Report only the part of the sale that represents your main home on Form 2119. You must allocate the sales price, expense of sale, and the basis of the property sold between Forms 2119 and 4797.

Note: *Only the part of the fixing-up expenses that applies to your main home may be included on line 11. These amounts are not allowed on Form 4797.*

Attach a statement showing the total selling price of the property and the method used to allocate the amounts between Forms 2119 and 4797. You cannot postpone or take the one-time exclusion on the part of the gain that is reported on Form 4797.

• If part of your new main home is rented out or used for business, enter on line 13b only the part of the total cost of the property that is allocable to your new main home. Attach a statement showing the total cost of the property and the allocation between the part that is your new main home and the part that is rented out or used for business.

Line 4—Selling Price of Home.—Enter the gross sales price of your old home. Generally, this includes the amount of money you received, plus all notes, mortgages, or other debts that are part of the sale, and the fair market value of any other property you received.

Line 5—Expense of Sale.—Enter your expense of sale, such as commissions, advertising expenses, and attorney and legal fees, that you paid in selling your old home. Loan charges, such as points charged to the seller, are also selling expenses. Do not include fixing-up expenses on this line, but see the instructions for line 11.

Line 7—Basis of Home Sold.—Include the cost of any capital improvements, and subtract any depreciation, casualty losses, or energy credits you reported on your tax return(s) that were related to your old home.

If you filed a Form 2119 when you originally bought your old home (to postpone gain on a previous sale of a home), use the adjusted basis of the new home from the last line of that Form 2119 as the starting point to figure the basis of your old home. If you did not file a Form 2119 to postpone gain when you originally bought your old home, use the cost of the home including any expenses incurred to buy the home as the starting point.

For more details or if you acquired your home other than by purchase, such as by gift, inheritance, or trade, see Pub. 523 and **Pub. 551,** Basis of Assets.

Line 11—Fixing-up Expenses.—Enter the amount paid for work performed on your old home in order to help sell it. Do not include amounts that are otherwise deductible, or selling expenses included on line 5. The expenses must be for work performed within 90 days before the contract to sell the home was signed and paid within 30 days after the sale. Do not include expenses for permanent improvements or replacements, which should be added to the basis of the property sold.

Line 13b—Cost of New Home.—The cost of your new home includes one or more of the following:

1. Cash payments,

2. The amount of any mortgage or other debt on the new home,

3. Commissions and other purchase expenses you paid that were not deducted as moving expenses, and

4. Any capital expenses incurred within 2 years before or 2 years after the sale of your old home.

If you build your new home, include all construction costs incurred within 2 years before and 2 years after the sale of the old home. Do not include the value of your own labor.

Form **2120**
(Rev. May 1991)
Department of the Treasury
Internal Revenue Service

Multiple Support Declaration

► **Attach to Form 1040 or Form 1040A.**

OMB No. 1545-0071
Expires 5-31-94

Attachment
Sequence No. **50**

Name of taxpayer claiming person as a dependent	**Social security number**
	: :

During the calendar year 19 __________ , I paid over 10% of the support of

____
(Name of person)

I could have claimed this person as a dependent except that I did not pay over 50% of his or her support. I understand that this person is being claimed as a dependent on the income tax return of

____
(Name)

____
(Address)

I agree not to claim this person as a dependent on my Federal income tax return for any tax year that began in this calendar year.

______________________________________ (Your signature) ______________ (Your social security number)

______________ (Date) ______________________________________ (Address)

Instructions

Paperwork Reduction Act Notice

We ask for the information on this form to carry out the Internal Revenue laws of the United States. You are required to give us the information. We need it to ensure that you are complying with these laws and to allow us to figure and collect the right amount of tax.

The time needed to complete and file this form will vary depending on individual circumstances. The estimated average time is: **Recordkeeping,** 7 minutes; **Learning about the law or the form,** 2 minutes; **Preparing the form,** 7 minutes; **Copying, assembling, and sending the form to the IRS,** 10 minutes.

If you have comments concerning the accuracy of these time estimates or suggestions for making this form more simple, we would be happy to hear from you. You can write to both the IRS and the Office of Management and Budget at the addresses listed in the instructions of the tax return with which this form is filed.

Purpose

When two or more individuals together pay over 50% of another person's support, Form 2120 is used to allow one of them to claim the person as a dependent for tax purposes.

General Information

To claim someone as a dependent, you must pay over 50% of that person's living expenses (support). However, sometimes no one individual pays over 50%; but two or more together provide over 50% of the support. If each individual could have claimed the person as a dependent except for the 50% support rule, then one individual, but only one, can still claim the dependent.

All of those who paid over 10% of the support should decide who will claim the person as a dependent. If you are chosen, you can claim the dependent only if

- You paid over 10% of the support, AND
- All others who paid over 10% agree not to claim the person as a dependent.

How To File

The individuals who agree not to claim the person as a dependent do so by each signing a Form 2120. They give the signed forms to the one who does claim the person as a dependent.

If you are the one who claims the person as a dependent, you must attach all Forms 2120 from the others to YOUR return. Be sure to enter your name and social security number at the top of each Form 2120. In addition, you must meet all of the other rules for claiming dependents. See **Pub. 501,** Exemptions, Standard Deduction, and Filing Information.

Form **2210**

Department of the Treasury
Internal Revenue Service

Underpayment of Estimated Tax by Individuals and Fiduciaries

▶ See separate instructions.
▶ Attach to Form 1040, Form 1040A, Form 1040NR, or Form 1041.

OMB No. 1545-0140
1991
Attachment Sequence No. **06**

Name(s) shown on tax return | **Identifying number**

Note: *In most cases, you do not need to file Form 2210. The IRS will figure any penalty you owe and send you a bill. See Part I to find out if you should file Form 2210. If you do not need to file Form 2210, you still may use it to figure your penalty. Enter the amount from line 20 or line 34 on the penalty line of your return, but do not attach Form 2210.*

Part I Reasons For Filing—If 1a, b, or c below applies to you, you may be able to lower or eliminate your penalty. But you MUST check the boxes that apply and file Form 2210 with your tax return. If 1d below applies to you, check that box and file Form 2210 with your tax return.

1 Check whichever boxes apply (if none of the boxes apply, **do not** file Form 2210):

a ☐ You request a **waiver.** (In certain circumstances, the IRS will waive all or part of the penalty. See the instructions for **Waiver of Penalty.**)

b ☐ You use the **annualized income installment method.** (If your income varied during the year, this method may reduce the amount of one or more required installments. See **Instructions for Annualized Income Installment Worksheet**).

c ☐ You had Federal income tax withheld from wages and you treat it as paid for estimated tax purposes when it was **actually withheld** instead of evenly on the payment due dates. (See the instructions for line 22.)

d ☐ Your required annual payment (line 13 below) is based on your 1990 tax and you filed or are filing a joint return for either 1990 or 1991 but not for both years.

Part II Required Annual Payment—All filers must complete this part.

2	Enter your 1991 tax after credits (see instructions)			2	
3	Other taxes (see instructions)			3	
4	Add lines 2 and 3			4	
5	Earned income credit	5			
6	Credit for Federal tax on fuels	6			
7	Add lines 5 and 6			7	
8	Current year tax. Subtract line 7 from line 4			8	
9	Multiply line 8 by 90% (.90)	9			
10	Withholding taxes. **Do not** include any estimated tax payments on this line (see instructions)			10	
11	Subtract line 10 from line 8. If less than $500, stop here; **do not** complete or file this form. You do not owe the penalty			11	
12	Prior year (1990) tax. (**Caution:** *See instructions.*)			12	
13	**Required annual payment.** Enter the **smaller** of line 9 or line 12 (see instructions)			13	

Note: *If line 10 is equal to or more than line 13, stop here; you do not owe the penalty. Do not file Form 2210 unless you checked box 1d above.*

Part III Short Method (Caution: *Read the instructions to see if you can use the short method. If you checked box **1b** or **c** in Part I, skip this part and go to Part IV.*)

14	Enter the amount, if any, from line 10 above	14			
15	Enter the total amount, if any, of estimated tax payments you made	15			
16	Add lines 14 and 15			16	
17	**Total underpayment for year.** Subtract line 16 from line 13. (If zero or less, stop here; you do not owe the penalty. Do not file Form 2210 unless you checked box 1d above.)			17	
18	Multiply line 17 by .06391			18	
19	• If the amount on line 17 was paid **on or after** 4/15/92, enter -0-. • If the amount on line 17 was paid **before** 4/15/92, make the following computation to find the amount to enter on line 19. Amount on line 17 × Number of days paid before 4/15/92 × .00025			19	
20	**PENALTY.** Subtract line 19 from line 18. Enter the result here and on Form 1040, line 65; Form 1040A, line 33; Form 1040NR, line 65; or Form 1041, line 26 ▶			20	

For Paperwork Reduction Act Notice, see page 1 of separate instructions. Cat. No. 11744P Form **2210** (1991)

Part IV Regular Method (See the instructions if you are filing Form 1040NR.)

Section A—Figure Your Underpayment		Payment Due Dates (a) 4/15/91	(b) 6/15/91	(c) 9/15/91	(d) 1/15/92
21 Required installment. Divide line 13 by 4 and enter the result in each column. **Exception:** If you use the Annualized Income Installment Worksheet, see the instructions on page 4. Be sure you checked the box on line 1b in Part I	21				
22 Estimated tax paid and tax withheld. (See instructions.) For column (a) only, also enter the amount from line 22 on line 26. (If line 22 is equal to or more than line 21 for all payment periods, stop here; you do not owe the penalty. Do not file Form 2210 unless you checked a box in Part I.)	22				
Complete lines 23 through 29 of one column before going to the next column. **23** Enter amount, if any, from line 29 of previous column	23				
24 Add lines 22 and 23	24				
25 Add amounts on lines 27 and 28 of the previous column	25				
26 Subtract line 25 from line 24. If zero or less, enter -0-. For column (a) only, enter the amount from line 22 .	26				
27 If the amount on line 26 is zero, subtract line 24 from line 25. Otherwise, enter -0-	27				
28 Underpayment. If line 21 is equal to or more than line 26, subtract line 26 from line 21. Then go to line 23 of next column. Otherwise, go to line 29 . . ▶	28				
29 Overpayment. If line 26 is more than line 21, subtract line 21 from line 26. Then go to line 23 of next column	29				

Section B—Figure the Penalty (Complete lines 30 through 33 of one column before going to the next column.)

Rate Period 1		4/15/91	6/15/91	9/15/91	
April 16, 1991—December 31, 1991 **30** Number of days FROM the date shown above line 30 TO the date the amount on line 28 was paid **or** 12/31/91, whichever is earlier	30	Days:	Days:	Days:	
31 Underpayment on line 28 (see instructions) × Number of days on line 30 / 365 × .10 ▶	31	$	$	$	

Rate Period 2		12/31/91	12/31/91	12/31/91	1/15/92
January 1, 1992—April 15, 1992 **32** Number of days FROM the date shown above line 32 TO the date the amount on line 28 was paid **or** 4/15/92, whichever is earlier	32	Days:	Days:	Days:	Days:
33 Underpayment on line 28 (see instructions) × Number of days on line 32 / 366 × .09 ▶	33	$	$	$	$

34 PENALTY. Add all amounts on lines 31 and 33 in all columns. Enter the total here and on Form 1040, line 65; Form 1040A, line 33; Form 1040NR, line 65; or Form 1041, line 26. . . . . . . ▶ | 34 | $

Form **2441**

Department of the Treasury
Internal Revenue Service (T)

Child and Dependent Care Expenses

▶ Attach to Form 1040.

▶ See separate instructions.

OMB No. 1545-0068

1991

Attachment Sequence No. 21

Name(s) shown on Form 1040 | Your social security number

- If you are claiming the child and dependent care credit, complete Parts I and II below. But if you received employer-provided dependent care benefits, first complete Part III on the back.
- If you are not claiming the credit but you received employer-provided dependent care benefits, only complete Part I below and Part III on the back.

Caution: *If you have a child who was born in 1991 and the amount on Form 1040, line 32, is less than $21,250, see page 1 of the instructions before completing this form.*

Part I **Persons or Organizations Who Provided the Care—You must complete this part.** (See the instructions. If you need more space, use the bottom of page 2.)

1 (a) Name	(b) Address (number, street, apt. no., city, state, and ZIP code)	(c) Identifying number (SSN or EIN)	(d) Amount paid (see instructions)

2 Add the amounts in column (d) of line 1 . . . . **2**

Note: *If you paid cash wages of $50 or more in a calendar quarter to an individual for services performed in your home, you must file an employment tax return. Get* **Form 942** *for details.*

Part II **Credit for Child and Dependent Care Expenses**

3 Enter the number of qualifying persons cared for in 1991. (See the instructions for the definition of a qualifying person.) **Caution:** *To qualify, the person(s)* **must** *have shared the same home with you in 1991* . . . . ▶

4 Enter the amount of **qualified** expenses you incurred and actually paid in 1991. See the instructions to find out which expenses qualify. **Caution:** *If you completed Part III on page 2, do* **not** *include on this line any excluded benefits shown on line 25* **4**

5 Enter $2,400 ($4,800 if you paid for the care of two or more qualifying persons). **5**

6 If you completed Part III on page 2, enter the **excluded benefits,** if any, from line 25 . . . . **6**

7 Subtract line 6 from line 5. (If the result is zero or less, skip lines 8 through 13. Enter -0- on line 14, and go to line 15.) **7**

8 Compare the amounts on lines 4 and 7. Enter the **smaller** of the two amounts here . . . **8**

9 You **must** enter your **earned income**. (See the instructions for the definition of earned income.) **9**

Note: *If you are not filing a joint return, skip line 10 and go to line 11.*

10 If you are married filing a joint return, you **must** enter your spouse's earned income. (If your spouse was a full-time student or disabled, see the instructions for the amount to enter.) . . **10**

11
- If you are married filing a joint return, compare the amounts on lines 8, 9, and 10. Enter the **smallest** of the three amounts here.
- All others, compare the amounts on lines 8 and 9. Enter the **smaller** of the two amounts here.

. . . . **11**

12 Enter the amount from Form 1040, line 32 . . . . **12**

13 Enter the decimal amount from the table below that applies to the amount on line 12 . . . **13** ×

If line 12 is: Over—	But not over—	Decimal amount is:	If line 12 is: Over—	But not over—	Decimal amount is:
$0	10,000	.30	$20,000	22,000	.24
10,000	12,000	.29	22,000	24,000	.23
12,000	14,000	.28	24,000	26,000	.22
14,000	16,000	.27	26,000	28,000	.21
16,000	18,000	.26	28,000	No limit	.20
18,000	20,000	.25			

14 Multiply line 11 above by the decimal amount on line 13 . . . . **14**

15 Multiply any qualified expenses for 1990 that you paid in 1991 by the decimal amount that applies to the amount on your 1990 Form 1040, line 32, or Form 1040A, line 17. (You must complete Part I and attach a statement. See the instructions.) **15**

16 Add lines 14 and 15. See the instructions for the amount of credit you can claim. **16**

For Paperwork Reduction Act Notice, see separate instructions. Cat. No. 11862M Form **2441** (1991)

Form 2441 (1991) Page **2**

Part III **Employer-Provided Dependent Care Benefits**—Complete this part only if you received employer-provided dependent care benefits. Also, be sure to complete Part I.

17	Enter the total amount of employer-provided dependent care benefits you received for 1991. (This amount should be shown in Box 22 of your W-2 form(s).) Do **not** include amounts that were reported to you as wages in Box 10 of Form(s) W-2	17	
18	Enter the amount forfeited, if any. **Caution:** *See the instructions*	18	
19	Subtract line 18 from line 17	19	
20	Enter the total amount of **qualified** expenses incurred in 1991 for the care of a qualifying person. (See the instructions.)	20	
21	Compare the amounts on lines 19 and 20. Enter the **smaller** of the two amounts here	21	
22	You **must** enter your **earned income**. (See the instructions for lines 9 and 10 for the definition of earned income.)	22	
23	If you were married at the end of 1991, you **must** enter your spouse's earned income. (If your spouse was a full-time student or disabled, see the instructions for lines 9 and 10 for the amount to enter.)	23	
24	• If you were married at the end of 1991, compare the amounts on lines 22 and 23. Enter the **smaller** of the two amounts here. • If you were unmarried, enter the amount from line 22 here.	24	
25	**Excluded benefits.** Enter here the **smallest** of the following: • The amount from line 21, or • The amount from line 24, or • $5,000 ($2,500 if married filing a separate return).	25	
26	**Taxable benefits.** Subtract line 25 from line 19. Enter the result, but not less than zero. Also, include this amount in the total on Form 1040, line 7. On the dotted line next to line 7, write "DCB"	26	

Note: *If you are also claiming the child and dependent care credit, fill in Form 1040 through line 40. Then complete Part II of this form.*

Form **3800**

Department of the Treasury
Internal Revenue Service

General Business Credit

▶ Attach to your tax return.

▶ See separate instructions.

OMB No. 1545–0895

1991

Attachment Sequence No. **22**

Name(s) as shown on return | **Identifying number**

Part I Tentative Credit

1a	Current year investment credit (Form 3468, Part I)	**1a**	
b	Current year jobs credit (Form 5884, Part I)	**1b**	
c	Current year credit for alcohol used as fuel (Form 6478)	**1c**	
d	Current year credit for increasing research activities (Form 6765, Part III)	**1d**	
e	Current year low-income housing credit (Form 8586, Part I)	**1e**	
f	Current year enhanced oil recovery credit (Form 8830, Part I)	**1f**	
g	Current year disabled access credit (Form 8826, Part I)	**1g**	
h	**Current year general business credit.** Add lines 1a through 1g	**1h**	
2	Passive activity credits included on lines 1a through 1g (see instructions)	**2**	
3	Subtract line 2 from line 1h	**3**	
4	Passive activity credits allowed in 1991 (see instructions)	**4**	
5	Carryforward of general business credit, WIN credit, or ESOP credit to 1991 (see instructions)	**5**	
6	Carryback of general business credit to 1991 (see instructions)	**6**	
7	**Tentative general business credit**. Add lines 3 through 6	**7**	

Part II General Business Credit Limitation Based on Amount of Tax

8a	Individuals. Enter amount from Form 1040, line 40				
b	Corporations. Enter amount from Form 1120, Schedule J, line 3 (or Form 1120-A, Part I, line 1)			**8**	
c	Other filers. Enter regular tax before credits from your return				
9	Credits that reduce regular tax before the general business credit—				
a	Credit for child and dependent care expense (Form 2441)	**9a**			
b	Credit for the elderly or the disabled (Schedule R (Form 1040))	**9b**			
c	Foreign tax credit (Form 1116 or Form 1118)	**9c**			
d	Possessions tax credit (Form 5735)	**9d**			
e	Mortgage interest credit (Form 8396)	**9e**			
f	Credit for fuel from a nonconventional source	**9f**			
g	Orphan drug credit (Form 6765)	**9g**			
h	Add lines 9a through 9g			**9h**	
10	Net regular tax. Subtract line 9h from line 8			**10**	
11	Tentative minimum tax (see instructions):				
a	Individuals. Enter amount from Form 6251, line 20				
b	Corporations. Enter amount from Form 4626, line 14			**11**	
c	Estates and trusts. Enter amount from Form 8656, line 37				
12	Net income tax:				
a	Individuals. Add line 10 above and line 22 of Form 6251				
b	Corporations. Add line 10 above and line 16 of Form 4626			**12**	
c	Other filers. See instructions				
13	If line 10 is more than $25,000, enter 25% (.25) of the excess			**13**	
14	Subtract line 11 or line 13, whichever is greater, from line 12. If less than zero, enter -0-			**14**	
15	**General business credit allowed for current year.** Enter the **smaller** of line 7 or line 14. Also enter this amount on Form 1040, line 44; Form 1120, Schedule J, line 4e; Form 1120-A, Part I, line 2a; or on the appropriate line of your return. (Individuals, estates, and trusts, see instructions if the credit for increasing research activities is claimed. C corporations, see instructions for Schedule A if any regular investment credit carryforward is claimed or if the corporation has undergone a post-1986 "ownership change.")			**15**	

For Paperwork Reduction Act Notice, see page 1 of the separate instructions to this form. Cat. No. 12392F Form **3800** (1991)

Form **3903**

Department of the Treasury
Internal Revenue Service

Moving Expenses

▶ Attach to Form 1040.

▶ See separate instructions.

OMB No. 1545-0062

1991

Attachment Sequence No. **62**

Name(s) shown on Form 1040	Your social security number

1	Enter the number of miles from your **old** home to your **new** workplace	1	
2	Enter the number of miles from your **old** home to your **old** workplace	2	
3	Subtract line **2** from line **1**. Enter the result (but not less than zero) ▶	3	

If line **3** is 35 or more miles, complete the rest of this form. If line 3 is less than 35 miles, you may not deduct your moving expenses. This rule does not apply to members of the armed forces.

Part I Moving Expenses

Note: *Any payments your employer made for any part of your move (including the value of any services furnished in kind) should be included on your Form W-2. Report that amount on* ***Form 1040, line 7.*** *See* ***Reimbursements*** *in the instructions.*

Section A.—Transportation of Household Goods						
4	Transportation and storage for household goods and personal effects				4	
Section B.—Expenses of Moving From Old To New Home						
5	Travel and lodging **not** including meals		5			
6	Total meals	6				
7	Multiply line 6 by 80% (.80)		7			
8	Add lines 5 and 7				8	
Section C.—Pre-move Househunting Expenses and Temporary Quarters (for any 30 days in a row after getting your job)						
9	Pre-move travel and lodging **not** including meals		9			
10	Temporary quarters expenses **not** including meals		10			
11	Total meal expenses for both pre-move househunting and temporary quarters	11				
12	Multiply line 11 by 80% (.80)		12			
13	Add lines 9, 10, and 12		13			
Section D.—Qualified Real Estate Expenses						
14	Expenses of (check one): **a** ☐ selling or exchanging your old home, or **b** ☐ if renting, settling an unexpired lease.		14			
15	Expenses of (check one): **a** ☐ buying your new home, or **b** ☐ if renting, getting a new lease.		15			

Part II Dollar Limits

16	Enter the **smaller** of: • The amount on line 13, or • $1,500 ($750 if married filing a separate return, and at the end of 1991 you lived with your spouse who also started work in 1991).	16			
17	Add lines 14, 15, and 16	17			
18	Enter the **smaller** of: • The amount on line 17, or • $3,000 ($1,500 if married filing a separate return, and at the end of 1991 you lived with your spouse who also started work in 1991).			18	
19	Add lines 4, 8, and 18. This is your moving expense deduction. **Enter here and on Schedule A (Form 1040), line 18** ▶			19	

For Paperwork Reduction Act Notice, see separate instructions. Cat. No. 12490K Form **3903** (1991)

Form **4255** (Rev. April 1991) Department of the Treasury Internal Revenue Service

Recapture of Investment Credit

(Including Energy Investment Credit)

▶ Attach to your income tax return.

OMB No. 1545-0166 Expires 4-30-94

Attachment Sequence No. **65**

Name(s) as shown on return	**Taxpayer Identifying number**

Properties	Kind of property—State whether recovery or nonrecovery (see the Instructions for Form 3468 for definitions). If energy property, show type. Also indicate if rehabilitation expenditure property.
A	
B	
C	
D	

Original Investment Credit

Computation Steps: (see Specific Instructions)	**Properties** A	B	C	D
1 Original rate of credit				
2 Date property was placed in service				
3 Cost or other basis				
4 Original estimated useful life or class of property				
5 Applicable percentage				
6 Original qualified investment (Multiply line 3 by the percentage on line 5.)				
7 Original credit (Multiply line 6 by the percentage on line 1.)				
8 Date property ceased to be qualified investment credit property				
9 Number of full years between the date on line 2 and the date on line 8				

Computation of Recapture Tax

	A	B	C	D
10 Recapture percentage (from instructions)				
11 Tentative recapture tax (Multiply line 7 by the percentage on line 10.)				

12 Add line 11, columns A through D

13 Enter tax from property ceasing to be at risk, or for which there was an increase in nonqualified nonrecourse financing (attach separate computation).

14 Total—Add lines 12 and 13

15 Portion of original credit (line 7) not used to offset tax in any year, plus any carryback and carryforward of credits you can now apply to the original credit year because you have freed up tax liability in the amount of the tax recaptured (Do not enter more than line 14—see instructions)

16 Total increase in tax—Subtract line 15 from line 14. Enter here and on the appropriate line of your tax return

General Instructions

(Section references are to the Internal Revenue Code before amendment by the Revenue Reconciliation Act of 1990 (the Act), unless otherwise noted.)

Paperwork Reduction Act Notice.—We ask for the information on this form to carry out the Internal Revenue laws of the United States. You are required to give us the information. We need it to ensure that you are complying with these laws and to allow us to figure and collect the right amount of tax.

The time needed to complete and file this form will vary depending on individual circumstances. The estimated average time is:

Recordkeeping	7 hr., 53 min.
Learning about the law or the form	2 hr., 23 min.
Preparing and sending the form to IRS	2 hr., 37 min.

If you have comments concerning the accuracy of these time estimates or suggestions for making this form more simple, we would be happy to hear from you. You can write to both the IRS and the Office of Management and Budget at the addresses listed in the instructions of the tax return with which this form is filed.

Purpose of Form.—Use Form 4255 to figure the increase in tax for the recapture of investment credit for regular and energy property.

You must refigure the credit if you took it in an earlier year, but disposed of the property before the end of the recapture period or the useful life you used to figure the original credit. You must also refigure the credit if you returned leased property (on which you had taken a credit) to the lessor before the end of the recapture period or useful life.

You must refigure the credit if you changed the use of property so that it no longer qualifies as regular or energy investment credit property. For example, you must refigure the credit if you change the use of property from business use to personal use, or if there is any decrease in the percentage of business use of investment credit property. See sections 50(a)(2) (as amended by the Act), 47(a)(3), 47(a)(5)(C), and 49(e)(2) for information on recapture for progress expenditure property. Also see the instructions for line 13 regarding recapture if property ceases to be at risk, or if there is an increase in nonqualified, nonrecourse financing related to certain at-risk property placed in service after July 18, 1984.

If certain "listed property" (i.e., automobiles, certain other vehicles, computers, and property used for entertainment, recreation, or amusement) placed in service after June 18, 1984, ceases to be used more than 50% for business, you may have to recapture investment credit taken on the property. See section 280F for details.

An election to be treated as an S corporation does not automatically trigger recapture of investment credit taken before the election was effective. However, the S corporation is liable for any recapture of investment credit taken before the election.

If property on which you took both regular and energy investment credit ceases to be energy credit property, but still qualifies as regular investment credit property, you need only refigure the energy investment credit. However, if you took both credits, and you dispose of the property, or the property ceases to be both energy and regular investment credit property, you must refigure both credits.

If you are an S corporation, a partnership, or an estate or trust that allocated any or all of the investment credit to your shareholders, partners, or beneficiaries, you must give them the information they need to refigure the credit. See Regulations sections 1.47-4, 1.47-5 and 1.47-6.

Partners, shareholders and beneficiaries.—If your Schedule K-1 shows that you must recapture investment credit taken in an earlier year, you will need your retained copy of the original Form 3468 to complete lines 1 through 9 of this Form 4255.

Special Rules.—If you took a credit on the following kinds of property, see the sections listed below before you complete Form 4255:

Property	Section
Motion picture films and video tapes	47(a)(8)
Ships	46(g)(4)
Commuter highway vehicles	47(a)(4)

If you took any nonconventional source fuel credit, see section 29(b)(4).

If, before the end of the recapture period, you dispose of recovery property placed in service after 1982 (or the business use percentage decreases), increase the basis of this property by 50% of the recapture amount unless you originally made the section 48(q)(4) election to take a reduced credit instead of reducing the basis of the property.

Note: *The Act changed these rules for property eligible for the rehabilitation credit under section 47, as amended by the Act. Increase the basis of this property by 100% of the recapture amount instead of 50%. For details, see sections 50(c)(2) and 50(c)(3), as amended by the Act.*

Specific Instructions

Note: *Do not figure the recapture tax on lines 1 through 12 for property ceasing to be at risk, or if there is an increase in nonqualified, nonrecourse financing related to certain at-risk property placed in service after July 18, 1984. Figure the recapture tax for these properties on separate schedules and enter the recapture tax on line 13. Include any unused credit for these properties on line 15.*

Lines A through D.—Describe the property for which you must refigure the credit.

Complete lines 1 through 11 for each property on which you are refiguring the credit. Use a separate column for each item. If you must recapture both the energy investment credit and the regular investment credit for the same item, use a separate column for each credit. If you need more columns, use additional Forms 4255, or other schedules with all the information shown on Form 4255. Enter the total from the separate sheets on line 12.

Line 1.—Enter the rate you used to figure the original credit from the tables below:

Regular Investment Property

Qualifying property acquired or constructed and placed in service	10%

If at the time the credit was taken the regular 10% credit above was subject to all or part of the 35% reduction under section 49(c), reduce the 10% accordingly.

For example, if a 10% regular credit was used in calendar year 1987 when it was reduced by 17.5% under section 49(c), enter 8.25% on line 1 (10% minus 17.5% of 10%). If parts of the credit were used in different tax years (for example, part in 1986 when the full 10% was allowed, part in 1987 when the 10% credit was reduced under 49(c) by a portion of 35%, and part in 1988 when the credit was reduced by 35%), use a weighted average based on the portion of the credit used in each year.

Be sure to include any ESOP credit, or other credits listed under the special rules above.

See section 46(b)(4) for the rates for qualified rehabilitation expenditures made after 1981.

Energy Investment Property

See the table in section 46(b)(2)(A) for a listing of the energy percentages. For property eligible under section 48(a), as amended by the Act, the percentage is 10%.

Reforestation Credit Property

The reforestation percentage is 10% for property eligible under section 48(b), as amended by the Act.

Line 2.—For both recovery and nonrecovery property, enter the first day of the first month, and the year, that the property was available for service.

Line 3.—Enter the cost or other basis that you used to figure the original credit.

Line 4.—Enter the estimated useful life that you used to figure the original credit for nonrecovery property. Enter the class of property for recovery property.

Line 5.—Enter the applicable percentage that you used to figure the original qualified investment from the tables below:

Nonrecovery Property

Original estimated useful life	Applicable percentage
3 or more but less than 5 years	33⅓%
5 or more but less than 7 years	66⅔%
7 or more years	100%

Recovery Property

Class of property	Applicable percentage
Other	100%

Section 48(q) Election Recovery Property

(Placed in service after 12/31/82 and before 1/1/86)

Class of property	Applicable percentage
Other	80%

Generally, the applicable percentage will be 100% for property eligible for the investment credit under section 46, as amended by the Act.

Line 8.—Generally, this will be the date you disposed of the property. See Regulations section 1.47-1(c) for more information.

Line 9.—Do not enter partial years. If the property was held less than 12 months, enter zero.

Line 10.—Enter the recapture percentage from the following tables:

Nonrecovery Property

If number of full years on line 9 of Form 4255 is:	The recapture percentage for property with an original useful life of: 3 or more but less than 5 years is:	5 or more but less than 7 years is:	7 or more years is:
0	100	100	100
1	100	100	100
2	100	100	100
3	0	50	66.6
4	0	50	66.6
5	0	0	33.3
6	0	0	33.3

Recovery Property

If number of full years on line 9 of Form 4255 is:	The recapture percentage for: Other than 3-year property is:
0	100
1	80
2	60
3	40
4	20

For property eligible for the investment credit under section 46, as amended by the Act, the recapture percentage is the same as the recapture percentage in the above table for Recovery Property.

Decrease in Business Use.—If you take investment credit for property and the percentage of business use in a later year falls below the percentage for the year placed in service, you are treated as having disposed of part of the property and may have to recapture part of the investment credit.

Line 12.—If you have used more than one Form 4255, or separate sheets to list additional items on which you figured an increase in tax, write on the dotted line "Tax from attached, $ ...." Include the amount in the total for line 12.

Line 13.—For certain taxpayers, the basis or cost of property placed in service after February 18, 1981, is limited to the amount the taxpayer is at risk for the property at year-end. For property placed in service after July 18, 1984, the basis or cost must be reduced by the amount of any "nonqualified, nonrecourse financing" related to the property at year-end. If property ceases to be at risk in a later year, or if there is an increase in nonqualified, nonrecourse financing, recapture may be required. See section 49(b), as amended by the Act, for details. Attach a separate computation schedule to figure the recapture tax and enter the total tax on line 13.

Line 15.—If you did not use all the credit you originally figured, either in the year you figured it or in a carryback or carryforward year, you do not have to recapture the amount of the credit you did not use. In refiguring the credit for the original credit year, be sure to take into account any carryforwards from previous years, plus any carrybacks arising within the 3 taxable years after the original credit year that are now allowed because the recapture and recomputation of the original credit made available some additional tax liability in that year. See Regulations section 1.47-1(d) and Revenue Ruling 72-221 for more information.

Note: *You must also take into account any applicable 35% reduction in credit under section 49(c)(2) when computing the amount to enter on line 15.*

Figure the unused portion on a separate sheet and enter it on this line. Do not enter more than the recapture tax on line 14.

Reminder: Be sure to adjust your current unused credit to reflect any unused portion of the original credit that was entered on line 15 of this form.

Form **4562**

Department of the Treasury Internal Revenue Service (T)

Depreciation and Amortization
(Including Information on Listed Property)

▶ See separate instructions. ▶ Attach this form to your return.

OMB No. 1545-0172

1991

Attachment Sequence No. 67

Name(s) shown on return | Identifying number

Business or activity to which this form relates

Part I **Election To Expense Certain Tangible Property (Section 179) (Note:** *If you have any "Listed Property," complete Part V.)*

1	Maximum dollar limitation (see instructions)	1	$10,000
2	Total cost of section 179 property placed in service during the tax year (see instructions)	2	
3	Threshold cost of section 179 property before reduction in limitation	3	$200,000
4	Reduction in limitation—Subtract line 3 from line 2, but do not enter less than -0-	4	
5	Dollar limitation for tax year—Subtract line 4 from line 1, but do not enter less than -0-	5	

	(a) Description of property	(b) Cost	(c) Elected cost
6			
7	Listed property—Enter amount from line 26	7	

8	Total elected cost of section 179 property—Add amounts in column (c), lines 6 and 7	8	
9	Tentative deduction—Enter the lesser of line 5 or line 8	9	
10	Carryover of disallowed deduction from 1990 (see instructions)	10	
11	Taxable income limitation—Enter the lesser of taxable income or line 5 (see instructions)	11	
12	Section 179 expense deduction—Add lines 9 and 10, but do not enter more than line 11	12	
13	Carryover of disallowed deduction to 1992—Add lines 9 and 10, less line 12 ▶ 13		

Note: *Do not use Part II or Part III below for automobiles, certain other vehicles, cellular telephones, computers, or property used for entertainment, recreation, or amusement (listed property). Instead, use Part V for listed property.*

Part II **MACRS Depreciation For Assets Placed in Service ONLY During Your 1991 Tax Year (Do Not Include Listed Property)**

	(a) Classification of property	(b) Mo. and yr. placed in service	(c) Basis for depreciation (Business/investment use only—see instructions)	(d) Recovery period	(e) Convention	(f) Method	(g) Depreciation deduction
14	General Depreciation System (GDS) (see instructions):						
a	3-year property						
b	5-year property						
c	7-year property						
d	10-year property						
e	15-year property						
f	20-year property						
g	Residential rental property			27.5 yrs.	MM	S/L	
				27.5 yrs.	MM	S/L	
h	Nonresidential real property			31.5 yrs.	MM	S/L	
				31.5 yrs.	MM	S/L	
15	Alternative Depreciation System (ADS) (see instructions):						
a	Class life					S/L	
b	12-year			12 yrs.		S/L	
c	40-year			40 yrs.	MM	S/L	

Part III **Other Depreciation (Do Not Include Listed Property)**

16	GDS and ADS deductions for assets placed in service in tax years beginning before 1991 (see instructions)	16	
17	Property subject to section 168(f)(1) election (see instructions)	17	
18	ACRS and other depreciation (see instructions)	18	

Part IV **Summary**

19	Listed property—Enter amount from line 25	19	
20	Total—Add deductions on line 12, lines 14 and 15 in column (g), and lines 16 through 19. Enter here and on the appropriate lines of your return. (Partnerships and S corporations—see instructions)	20	
21	For assets shown above and placed in service during the current year, enter the portion of the basis attributable to section 263A costs (see instructions) 21		

For Paperwork Reduction Act Notice, see page 1 of the separate instructions. Cat. No. 12906N Form **4562** (1991)

Part V **Listed Property.—Automobiles, Certain Other Vehicles, Cellular Telephones, Computers, and Property Used for Entertainment, Recreation, or Amusement**

If you are using the standard mileage rate or deducting vehicle lease expense, complete columns (a) through (c) of Section A, all of Section B, and Section C if applicable.

Section A.—Depreciation (Caution: *See instructions for limitations for automobiles.)*

22a Do you have evidence to support the business/investment use claimed? ☐ **Yes** ☐ **No** **22b** If "Yes," is the evidence written? ☐ **Yes** ☐ **No**

(a) Type of property (list vehicles first)	(b) Date placed in service	(c) Business/investment use percentage	(d) Cost or other basis	(e) Basis for depreciation (business/investment use only)	(f) Recovery period	(g) Method/Convention	(h) Depreciation deduction	(i) Elected section 179 cost
23 *Property used more than 50% in a qualified business use (see instructions):*								
		%						
		%						
		%						
24 *Property used 50% or less in a qualified business use (see instructions):*								
		%				S/L –		
		%				S/L –		
		%				S/L –		

25 Add amounts in column (h). Enter the total here and on line 19, page 1 . . . . **25**

26 Add amounts in column (i). Enter the total here and on line 7, page 1 . . . . **26**

Section B.—Information Regarding Use of Vehicles—*If you deduct expenses for vehicles:*

- *Always complete this section for vehicles used by a sole proprietor, partner, or other "more than 5% owner," or related person.*
- *If you provided vehicles to your employees, first answer the questions in Section C to see if you meet an exception to completing this section for those vehicles.*

	(a) Vehicle 1		(b) Vehicle 2		(c) Vehicle 3		(d) Vehicle 4		(e) Vehicle 5		(f) Vehicle 6	
27 Total business/investment miles driven during the year (DO NOT include commuting miles).												
28 Total commuting miles driven during the year												
29 Total other personal (noncommuting) miles driven												
30 Total miles driven during the year—Add lines 27 through 29												
	Yes	No	Yes	No	Yes	No	Yes	No	Yes	No	Yes	No
31 Was the vehicle available for personal use during off-duty hours?												
32 Was the vehicle used primarily by a more than 5% owner or related person? . .												
33 Is another vehicle available for personal use?												

Section C.—Questions for Employers Who Provide Vehicles for Use by Their Employees
(Answer these questions to determine if you meet an exception to completing Section B. **Note:** *Section B must always be completed for vehicles used by sole proprietors, partners, or other more than 5% owners or related persons.)*

	Yes	No
34 Do you maintain a written policy statement that prohibits all personal use of vehicles, including commuting, by your employees?		
35 Do you maintain a written policy statement that prohibits personal use of vehicles, except commuting, by your employees? (See instructions for vehicles used by corporate officers, directors, or 1% or more owners.) .		
36 Do you treat all use of vehicles by employees as personal use?		
37 Do you provide more than five vehicles to your employees and retain the information received from your employees concerning the use of the vehicles?		
38 Do you meet the requirements concerning qualified automobile demonstration use (see instructions)? . .		

Note: *If your answer to 34, 35, 36, 37, or 38 is "Yes," you need not complete Section B for the covered vehicles.*

Part VI **Amortization**

(a) Description of costs	(b) Date amortization begins	(c) Amortizable amount	(d) Code section	(e) Amortization period or percentage	(f) Amortization for this year
39 Amortization of costs that begins during your 1991 tax year:					

40 Amortization of costs that began before 1991 . . . . **40**

41 Total. Enter here and on "Other Deductions" or "Other Expenses" line of your return **41**

Form **4684**

Department of the Treasury
Internal Revenue Service

Casualties and Thefts

▶ See separate instructions.
▶ Attach to your tax return.
▶ Use a separate Form 4684 for each different casualty or theft.

OMB No. 1545-0177

1991

Attachment Sequence No. **26**

Name(s) shown on tax return | Identifying number

Note: *Use Section A for casualties and thefts of personal use property and Section B for business and income-producing property.*

SECTION A.—Personal Use Property *(Casualties and thefts of property* ***not*** *used in a trade or business or for income-producing purposes)*

1 Description of properties (show kind, location, and date acquired for each):
Property **A** ....
Property **B** ....
Property **C** ....
Property **D** ....

		Properties (use a separate column for each property lost or damaged from one casualty or theft)			
		A	B	C	D
2 Cost or other basis of each property	2				
3 Insurance or other reimbursement (whether or not you submitted a claim). See instructions	3				
Note: *If line 2 is* ***more*** *than line 3, skip line 4.*					
4 Gain from casualty or theft. If line 3 is **more than** line 2, enter the difference here and skip lines 5 through 9 for that column. (If line 3 includes an amount that you did not receive, see instructions.)	4				
5 Fair market value **before** casualty or theft	5				
6 Fair market value **after** casualty or theft	6				
7 Subtract line 6 from line 5	7				
8 Enter the **smaller** of line 2 or line 7	8				
9 Subtract line 3 from line 8 (If zero or less, enter -0-.)	9				

10 Casualty or theft loss. Add the amounts on line 9. Enter the total	10	
11 Enter the amount from line 10 or $100, whichever is **smaller**	11	
12 Subtract line 11 from line 10	12	
Caution: *Use only one Form 4684 for lines 13 through 18.*		
13 Add the amounts on line 12 of all Forms 4684, Section A	13	
14 Combine the amounts from line 4 of all Forms 4684, Section A	14	
15 • If line 14 is **more than** line 13, enter the difference here and on Schedule D. Do not complete the rest of this section (see instructions). • If line 14 is **less than** line 13, enter -0- here and continue with the form. • If line 14 is **equal to** line 13, enter -0- here. Do not complete the rest of this section.	15	
16 If line 14 is **less than** line 13, enter the difference	16	
17 Enter 10% of your adjusted gross income (Form 1040, line 32). Estates and trusts, see instructions	17	
18 Subtract line 17 from line 16. If zero or less, enter -0-. Also enter result on Schedule A (Form 1040), line 17. Estates and trusts, enter on the "Other deductions" line of your tax return	18	

Form 4684 (1991) Attachment Sequence No. 26 Page 2

Name(s) shown on tax return. (Do not enter name and identifying number if shown on other side.) | Identifying number

SECTION B.—Business and Income-Producing Property *(Casualties and thefts of property used in a trade or business or for income-producing purposes)*

Part I Casualty or Theft Gain or Loss (Use a separate Part I for each casualty or theft)

1 Description of properties (show kind, location, and date acquired for each):

Property **A** ....

Property **B** ....

Property **C** ....

Property **D** ....

		Properties (use a separate column for each property lost or damaged from one casualty or theft)			
		A	B	C	D
2 Cost or adjusted basis of each property	2				
3 Insurance or other reimbursement (whether or not you submitted a claim). See the instructions for Section A, line 3	3				
Note: *If line 2 is **more** than line 3, skip line 4.* 4 Gain from casualty or theft. If line 3 is **more than** line 2, enter the difference here and on line 11 or line 16, column (**c**), except as provided in the instructions for line 15. Also, skip lines 5 through 9 for that column. (If line 3 includes an amount that you did not receive, see the instructions for Section A, line 4.)	4				
5 Fair market value **before** casualty or theft	5				
6 Fair market value **after** casualty or theft	6				
7 Subtract line 6 from line 5	7				
8 Enter the **smaller** of line 2 or line 7	8				
Note: *If the property was totally destroyed by casualty, or lost from theft, enter on line 8 the amount from line 2.* 9 Subtract line 3 from line 8 (If zero or less, enter -0-.)	9				

10 Casualty or theft loss. Add the amounts on line 9. Enter the total here and on line 11 **or** line 16 (see instructions). | 10 |

Part II Summary of Gains and Losses (from separate Parts I)

	(a) Identify casualty or theft		(b) Losses from casualties or thefts		(c) Gains from casualties or thefts includible in income
			(i) Trade, business, rental or royalty property	(ii) Income-producing property	
	Casualty or Theft of Property Held One Year or Less				
11			( )	( )	
			( )	( )	
12	Totals. Add the amounts on line 11	12	( )	( )	
13	Combine line 12, columns (b)(i) and (c). Enter the net gain or (loss) here and on Form 4797, Part II, line 14. (If Form 4797 is not otherwise required, see instructions.)			13	
14	Enter the amount from line 12, column (b)(ii) here and on Schedule A (Form 1040), line 20. Partnerships, S corporations, estates and trusts, see instructions			14	
	Casualty or Theft of Property Held More Than One Year				
15	Casualty or theft gains from Form 4797, Part III, line 32			15	
16			( )	( )	
			( )	( )	
17	Total losses. Add amounts on line 16, columns (b)(i) and (b)(ii)	17	( )	( )	
18	Total gains. Add lines 15 and 16, column (c)			18	
19	Add amounts on line 17, columns (b)(i) and (b)(ii)			19	
20	If the loss on line 19 is **more than** the gain on line 18:				
a	Combine line 17, column (b)(i) and line 18, and enter the net gain or (loss) here. Partnerships and S corporations see the note below. All others enter this amount on Form 4797, Part II, line 14. (If Form 4797 is not otherwise required, see instructions.)			20a	
b	Enter the amount from line 17, column (b)(ii) here. Partnerships and S corporations see the note below. Individuals enter this amount on Schedule A (Form 1040), line 20. Estates and trusts, enter on the "Other deductions" line of your tax return			20b	
21	If the loss on line 19 is **equal to** or **less than** the gain on line 18, combine these lines and enter here. Partnerships see the note below. All others enter this amount on Form 4797, Part I, line 3			21	

Note: *Partnerships, enter the amount from line 20a, 20b, or line 21 on Form 1065, Schedule K, line 7. S corporations, enter the amount from line 20a or 20b on Form 1120S, Schedule K, line 6.*

Form **4797**

Department of the Treasury
Internal Revenue Service (T)

Sales of Business Property

(Also Involuntary Conversions and Recapture Amounts Under Sections 179 and 280F)

▶ Attach to your tax return. ▶ See separate instructions.

OMB No. 1545-0184

1991

Attachment Sequence No. **27**

Name(s) shown on return | **Identifying number**

Part I Sales or Exchanges of Property Used in a Trade or Business and Involuntary Conversions From Other Than Casualty or Theft—Property Held More Than 1 Year

1 Enter here the gross proceeds from the sale or exchange of real estate reported to you for 1991 on Form(s) 1099-S (or a substitute statement) that you will be including on line 2, 10, or 20 . . . . **1**

(a) Description of property	(b) Date acquired (mo., day, yr.)	(c) Date sold (mo., day, yr.)	(d) Gross sales price	(e) Depreciation allowed or allowable since acquisition	(f) Cost or other basis, plus improvements and expense of sale	(g) LOSS ((f) minus the sum of (d) and (e))	(h) GAIN ((d) plus (e) minus (f))
2							

3 Gain, if any, from Form 4684, Section B, line 21 . . . .

4 Section 1231 gain from installment sales from Form 6252, line 22 or 30 . . . .

5 Gain, if any, from line 32, from other than casualty or theft . . . .

6 Add lines 2 through 5 in columns (g) and (h) . . . . ( )

7 Combine columns (g) and (h) of line 6. Enter gain or (loss) here, and on the appropriate line as follows: . . . .

Partnerships.—Enter the gain or (loss) on Form 1065, Schedule K, line 6. Skip lines 8, 9, 11, and 12 below.

S corporations.—Report the gain or (loss) following the instructions for Form 1120S, Schedule K, lines 5 and 6. Skip lines 8, 9, 11, and 12 below, unless line 7 is a gain and the S corporation is subject to the capital gains tax.

All others.—If line 7 is zero or a loss, enter the amount on line 11 below and skip lines 8 and 9. If line 7 is a gain and you did not have any prior year section 1231 losses, or they were recaptured in an earlier year, enter the gain as a long-term capital gain on Schedule D and skip lines 8, 9, and 12 below.

8 Nonrecaptured net section 1231 losses from prior years (see instructions) . . . .

9 Subtract line 8 from line 7. If zero or less, enter -0-. Also enter on the appropriate line as follows (see instructions): .

S corporations.—Enter this amount (if more than zero) on Schedule D (Form 1120S), line 7, and skip lines 11 and 12 below.

All others.—If line 9 is zero, enter the amount from line 7 on line 12 below. If line 9 is more than zero, enter the amount from line 8 on line 12 below, and enter the amount from line 9 as a long-term capital gain on Schedule D.

Part II Ordinary Gains and Losses

10 Ordinary gains and losses not included on lines 11 through 16 (include property held 1 year or less):

11 Loss, if any, from line 7 . . . .

12 Gain, if any, from line 7, or amount from line 8 if applicable . . . .

13 Gain, if any, from line 31 . . . .

14 Net gain or (loss) from Form 4684, Section B, lines 13 and 20a . . . .

15 Ordinary gain from installment sales from Form 6252, line 21 or 29 . . . .

16 Recapture of section 179 deduction for partners and S corporation shareholders from property dispositions by partnerships and S corporations (see instructions) . . . .

17 Add lines 10 through 16 in columns (g) and (h) . . . . ( )

18 Combine columns (g) and (h) of line 17. Enter gain or (loss) here, and on the appropriate line as follows: . . . .

a For all except individual returns: Enter the gain or (loss) from line 18 on the return being filed.

b For individual returns:

(1) If the loss on line 11 includes a loss from Form 4684, Section B, Part II, column (b)(ii), enter that part of the loss here and on line 20 of Schedule A (Form 1040). Identify as from "Form 4797, line 18b(1)." See instructions . . .

(2) Redetermine the gain or (loss) on line 18, excluding the loss, if any, on line 18b(1). Enter here and on Form 1040, line 15 . . .

For Paperwork Reduction Act Notice, see page 1 of separate instructions. Cat. No. 13086I Form **4797** (1991)

Form 4797 (1991) Page **2**

Part III Gain From Disposition of Property Under Sections 1245, 1250, 1252, 1254, and 1255

19 Description of section 1245, 1250, 1252, 1254, or 1255 property:	Date acquired (mo., day, yr.)	Date sold (mo., day, yr.)
A		
B		
C		
D		

Relate lines 19A through 19D to these columns ▶	Property A	Property B	Property C	Property D
20 Gross sales price (**Note:** *See line 1 before completing.*)				
21 Cost or other basis plus expense of sale				
22 Depreciation (or depletion) allowed or allowable				
23 Adjusted basis. Subtract line 22 from line 21				
24 Total gain. Subtract line 23 from line 20				
25 **If section 1245 property:**				
a Depreciation allowed or allowable from line 22				
b Enter the **smaller** of line 24 or 25a				
26 **If section 1250 property:** If straight line depreciation was used, enter -0- on line 26g unless you are a corporation subject to section 291.				
a Additional depreciation after 1975 (see instructions)				
b Applicable percentage multiplied by the **smaller** of line 24 or line 26a (see instructions)				
c Subtract line 26a from line 24. If line 24 is not more than line 26a, skip lines 26d and 26e				
d Additional depreciation after 1969 and before 1976				
e Applicable percentage multiplied by the **smaller** of line 26c or 26d (see instructions)				
f Section 291 amount (corporations only)				
g Add lines 26b, 26e, and 26f				
27 **If section 1252 property:** Skip this section if you did not dispose of farmland or if you are a partnership.				
a Soil, water, and land clearing expenses				
b Line 27a multiplied by applicable percentage (see instructions)				
c Enter the **smaller** of line 24 or 27b				
28 **If section 1254 property:**				
a Intangible drilling and development costs, expenditures for development of mines and other natural deposits, and mining exploration costs (see instructions)				
b Enter the **smaller** of line 24 or 28a				
29 **If section 1255 property:**				
a Applicable percentage of payments excluded from income under section 126 (see instructions)				
b Enter the **smaller** of line 24 or 29a				

Summary of Part III Gains (Complete property columns A through D, through line 29b before going to line 30.)

30 Total gains for all properties. Add columns A through D, line 24	
31 Add columns A through D, lines 25b, 26g, 27c, 28b, and 29b. Enter here and on line 13. (See the instructions for Part IV if this is an installment sale.)	
32 Subtract line 31 from line 30. Enter the portion from casualty or theft on Form 4684, Section B, line 15. Enter the portion from other than casualty or theft on Form 4797, line 5	

Part IV Election Not to Use the Installment Method (Complete this part only if you elect out of the installment method and report a note or other obligation at less than full face value.)

33 Check here if you elect out of the installment method . . . ▶ ☐

34 Enter the face amount of the note or other obligation . . . ▶ $ ______

35 Enter the percentage of valuation of the note or other obligation . . . ▶ ______ %

Part V Recapture Amounts Under Sections 179 and 280F When Business Use Drops to 50% or Less (See instructions for Part V.)

	(a) Section 179	(b) Section 280F
36 Section 179 expense deduction or depreciation allowable in prior years		
37 Recomputed depreciation (see instructions)		
38 Recapture amount. Subtract line 37 from line 36. (See instructions for where to report.)		

Form **4868** Department of the Treasury Internal Revenue Service

Application for Automatic Extension of Time To File U.S. Individual Income Tax Return

OMB No. 1545-0188

1991

Please Type or Print

Your first name and initial	Last name	Your social security number
If a joint return, spouse's first name and initial	Last name	Spouse's social security number
Present home address (number, street, and apt. no. or rural route). (If you have a P.O. box, see the instructions.)		
City, town or post office, state, and ZIP code		

Note: *File this form with the Internal Revenue Service Center where you are required to file your income tax return, and pay any amount(s) you owe.* ***This is not an extension of time to pay your tax.***

I request an automatic 4-month extension of time to August 17, 1992, to file Form 1040A or Form 1040 for the calendar year 1991 (or if a fiscal year Form 1040 to ...., 19 ...., for the tax year ending........................, 19 ....).

1 Total tax liability for 1991. This is the amount you expect to enter on line 27 of Form 1040A, or line 53 of Form 1040. If you do not expect to owe tax, enter -0- **1**

Caution: *You* ***MUST*** *enter an amount on line 1 or your extension will be denied. You can estimate this amount, but be as exact as you can with the information you have. If we later find that your estimate was not reasonable, the extension will be null and void.*

2 Federal income tax withheld **2**

3 1991 estimated tax payments (include 1990 overpayment allowed as a credit) . . **3**

4 Other payments and credits you expect to show on Form 1040A or Form 1040 . . **4**

5 Add lines 2, 3, and 4 . . . . **5**

6 **BALANCE DUE** (subtract line 5 from line 1). ***To get this extension, you MUST pay in full the balance due with this form.*** (If line 5 is more than line 1, enter -0-.) . . . . ▶ **6**

If you expect to owe gift or generation-skipping transfer (GST) tax, complete line 7 (and 8a or 8b if applicable). Do not include income tax on these lines. (See the instructions.)

7 If you or your spouse plan to file a gift tax return (Form 709 or 709-A) for 1991, generally due by April 15, 1992, see the instructions and check here . . } **Yourself** ▶ ☐ **Spouse** ▶ ☐

8a Enter the amount of gift or GST tax that **you** are paying with this form **8a**

b Enter the amount of gift or GST tax that **your spouse** is paying with this form **8b**

Signature and Verification

Under penalties of perjury, I declare that I have examined this form, including accompanying schedules and statements, and to the best of my knowledge and belief, it is true, correct, and complete; and, if prepared by someone other than the taxpayer, that I am authorized to prepare this form.

Signature of taxpayer ▶ ______________________ Date ▶ ______________

Signature of spouse ▶ ______________________ Date ▶ ______________

(If filing jointly, BOTH must sign even if only one had income)

Signature of preparer other than taxpayer ▶ Date ▶

If correspondence regarding this extension is to be sent to you at an address other than that shown above, or to an agent acting for you, please enter the name of the agent and/or the address where it should be sent.

Please Type or Print

Name
Number and street (or P.O. box number if mail is not delivered to street address)
City, town or post office, state, and ZIP code

General Instructions

Paperwork Reduction Act Notice.—We ask for the information on this form to carry out the Internal Revenue laws of the United States. You are required to give us the information. We need it to ensure that you are complying with these laws and to allow us to figure and collect the right amount of tax.

The time needed to complete and file this form will vary depending on individual circumstances. The estimated average time is: **Recordkeeping,** 26 min.; **Learning about the law or the form,** 11 min.; **Preparing the form,** 20 min.; and **Copying, assembling, and sending the form to the IRS,** 20 min.

If you have comments concerning the accuracy of these time estimates or suggestions for making this form more simple, we would be happy to hear from you. You can write to both the **Internal Revenue Service,** Washington, DC 20224, Attention: IRS Reports Clearance Officer, T:FP; and the **Office of Management and Budget,** Paperwork Reduction Project (1545-0188), Washington, DC 20503. Do not send this form to either of these offices. Instead, see **Where To File.**

Purpose

Use Form 4868 to ask for 4 more months to file **Form 1040A** or **Form 1040**. You do not have to explain why you are asking for the extension. We will contact you only if your request is denied.

To get the extra time you **MUST:**

1. Fill in Form 4868 correctly, **AND**

2. File it by the due date of your return, **AND**

3. Pay ALL of the amount shown on line 6.

If you already had 2 extra months to file because you were "out of the country" (explained later) when your return was due, then use this form to ask for an additional 2 months to file.

Do not file Form 4868 if you want the IRS to figure your tax, or are under a court order to file your return by the regular due date. **Note:** *An extension of time to file your 1991* ***calendar*** *year income tax return also extends the time to file a gift tax return* ***(Form 709*** *or* ***709-A)*** *for 1991.*

If the automatic extension does not give you enough time, you can later ask for additional time. But you'll have to give a good reason, and it must be approved by the IRS. To ask for the additional time, you must do **either** of the following:

1. File **Form 2688**, Application for Additional Extension of Time To File U.S. Individual Income Tax Return.

2. Explain your reason in a letter. Mail it to the address under **Where To File.**

File Form 4868 ***before*** you file Form 2688 or write a letter asking for more time. Only in cases of undue hardship will we approve your request for more time without first receiving Form 4868. If you need this extra time, ask for it early so that you can still file your return on time if your request is not approved.

When To File Form 4868

File Form 4868 by April 15, 1992. If you are filing a fiscal year Form 1040, file Form 4868 by the regular due date of your return.

If you had 2 extra months to file your return because you were out of the country, file Form 4868 by June 15, 1992, for a 1991 calendar year return.

Where To File

Mail this form to the **Internal Revenue Service Center** for the place where you live.

If you live in:	Use this address:
Florida, Georgia, South Carolina	Atlanta, GA 39901
New Jersey, New York (New York City and counties of Nassau, Rockland, Suffolk, and Westchester)	Holtsville, NY 00501
New York (all other counties), Connecticut, Maine, Massachusetts, New Hampshire, Rhode Island, Vermont	Andover, MA 05501
Illinois, Iowa, Minnesota, Missouri, Wisconsin	Kansas City, MO 64999
Delaware, District of Columbia, Maryland, Pennsylvania, Virginia	Philadelphia, PA 19255
Indiana, Kentucky, Michigan, Ohio, West Virginia	Cincinnati, OH 45999
Kansas, New Mexico, Oklahoma, Texas	Austin, TX 73301
Alaska, Arizona, California (counties of Alpine, Amador, Butte, Calaveras, Colusa, Contra Costa, Del Norte, El Dorado, Glenn, Humboldt, Lake, Lassen, Marin, Mendocino, Modoc, Napa, Nevada, Placer, Plumas, Sacramento, San Joaquin, Shasta, Sierra, Siskiyou, Solano, Sonoma, Sutter, Tehama, Trinity, Yolo, and Yuba), Colorado, Idaho, Montana, Nebraska, Nevada, North Dakota, Oregon, South Dakota, Utah, Washington, Wyoming	Ogden, UT 84201
California (all other counties), Hawaii	Fresno, CA 93888
Alabama, Arkansas, Louisiana, Mississippi, North Carolina, Tennessee	Memphis, TN 37501
American Samoa	Philadelphia, PA 19255
Guam	Commissioner of Revenue and Taxation 855 West Marine Drive Agana, GU 96910
Puerto Rico (or if excluding income under section 933) Virgin Islands: Nonpermanent residents	Philadelphia, PA 19255
Virgin Islands: Permanent residents	V.I. Bureau of Internal Revenue Lockharts Garden No. 1A Charlotte Amalie, St. Thomas, VI 00802
Foreign country: U.S. citizens and those filing Form 2555 or Form 4563	Philadelphia, PA 19255
All A.P.O. and F.P.O. addresses	Philadelphia, PA 19255

Filing Your Tax Return

You may file Form 1040A or Form 1040 any time before the extension of time is up. But remember, Form 4868 does not extend the time to pay taxes. If you do not pay the amount due by the regular due date, you will owe interest. You may also be charged penalties.

Interest.—You will owe interest on any tax not paid by the regular due date of your return. The interest runs until you pay the tax. Even if you had a good reason for not paying on time, you will still owe interest.

Late payment penalty.—Generally, the penalty is ½ of 1% of any tax (other than estimated tax) not paid by the regular due date. It is charged for each month or part of a month that the tax is unpaid. The maximum penalty is 25%. You might not owe this penalty if you have a good reason for not paying on time. Attach a statement to your return explaining the reason.

Late filing penalty.—A penalty is usually charged if your return is filed after the due date (including extensions). It is usually 5% of the tax not paid by the regular due date for each month or part of a month that your return is late. Generally, the maximum penalty is 25%. If your return is more than 60 days late, the minimum penalty will be $100 or the balance of tax due on your return, whichever is smaller. You might not owe the penalty if you have a good reason for filing late. Attach a full explanation to your return if you file late.

How to claim credit for payment made with this form.—When you file your return, show the amount of any payment (line 6) sent with Form 4868. Form 1040A filers should include the payment on line 28d and write "Form 4868" and the amount paid in the space to the left. Form 1040 filers should enter it on line 57.

If you and your spouse each filed a separate Form 4868, but later file a joint return for 1991, enter the total paid with the two Forms 4868 on the correct line of your joint return.

If you and your spouse jointly filed Form 4868, but later file separate returns for 1991, you may enter the total amount paid with Form 4868 on either of your separate returns. Or, you and your spouse may divide the payment in any agreed amounts. Be sure each separate return has the social security numbers of both spouses.

Specific Instructions

Name, address, and social security number.—Enter your name, address, and social security number. If you are married filing a joint return, also enter your spouse's name and social security number. If your post office does not bring mail to your street address and you have a P.O. box, enter your box number instead.

Note: *If you changed your mailing address after you filed your last return, you should use* ***Form 8822****, Change of Address, to notify the IRS of the change. (A new address shown on Form 4868 will not update your record.) To order Form 8822, call 1-800-TAX-FORM (1-800-829-3676).*

Fiscal year filers.—Below your address, enter the date your 4-month extension will end and the date your tax year ends.

Out of the country.—If you already had 2 extra months to file because you were a U.S. citizen or resident and were out of the country on the due date of your return, write **"Taxpayer Abroad"** across the top of this form. For this purpose, "out of the country" means either (1) you live outside the United States and Puerto Rico, AND your main place of work is outside the United States and Puerto Rico, **or** (2) you are in military or naval service outside the United States and Puerto Rico.

Line 7.—If you or your spouse are also using the extra 4 months to file a 1991 gift tax return, check whichever box applies on line 7. However, if your spouse files a separate Form 4868, do not check the box for your spouse.

Lines 8a and 8b.—Enter the amount you (or your spouse) expect to owe on these lines. If your spouse files a separate Form 4868, enter on your form only the total gift tax and GST tax you expect to owe. Pay in full with this form to avoid interest and penalties. If paying gift and GST taxes on time would cause you undue hardship (not just inconvenience), attach an explanation to this form.

Your signature.—This form must be signed. If you plan to file a joint return, both of you should sign. If there is a good reason why one of you cannot, then the other spouse may sign for both. Attach an explanation why the other spouse cannot sign.

Others who can sign for you.—Anyone with a power of attorney can sign. But the following can sign for you without a power of attorney:

- Attorneys, CPAs, and enrolled agents.
- A person in close personal or business relationship to you who is signing because you cannot. There must be a good reason why you cannot sign (such as illness or absence). Attach an explanation to the form.

Form **4952**

Department of the Treasury
Internal Revenue Service

Investment Interest Expense Deduction

▶ **Attach to your tax return.**

OMB No. 1545-0191

1991

Attachment Sequence No. **72**

Name(s) shown on return | **Identifying number**

1	Investment interest expense paid or accrued in 1991. See instructions	1	
2	Disallowed investment interest expense from 1990 Form 4952, line 23	2	
3	Total investment interest expense. Add lines 1 and 2	3	
4	**Net investment income.** See instructions	4	
5	**Disallowed investment interest expense to be carried forward to 1992.** Subtract line 4 from line 3. If zero or less, enter -0-	5	
6	**Investment interest expense deduction.** Enter the smaller of line 3 or line 4. See instructions	6	

General Instructions

Paperwork Reduction Act Notice

We ask for the information on this form to carry out the Internal Revenue laws of the United States. You are required to give us the information. We need it to ensure that you are complying with these laws and to allow us to figure and collect the right amount of tax.

The time needed to complete and file this form will vary depending on individual circumstances. The estimated average time is:

Recordkeeping . . . . 13 min.
Learning about the law or the form . . . . . . 14 min.
Preparing the form . . . . . . 11 min.
Copying, assembling, and sending the form to the IRS . . 10 min.

If you have comments concerning the accuracy of these time estimates or suggestions for making this form more simple, we would be happy to hear from you. You can write to both the IRS and the Office of Management and Budget at the addresses listed in the instructions for the tax return with which this form is filed.

Purpose of Form

Interest expense paid by an individual, estate, or a trust on a loan that is allocable to property held for investment (defined on page 2), may not be fully deductible in the current year. Form 4952 is used to figure the amount of investment interest expense deductible for the current year and the amount, if any, to carry forward to future years.

For more details, get **Pub. 550,** Investment Income and Expenses.

Who Must File

If you are an individual, estate, or a trust, and you claim a deduction for investment interest expense, you must complete and attach Form 4952 to your tax return, unless **all** of the following apply:

- Your only investment income was from interest or dividends,
- You have no other deductible expenses connected with the production of interest or dividends,
- Your investment interest expense is not more than your investment income, and
- You have no carryovers of investment interest expense from 1990.

Allocation of Interest Expense Under Temporary Regulations Section 1.163-8T

If you paid or accrued interest on a loan and you used the proceeds of the loan for more than one purpose, you may have to allocate the interest paid. This is necessary because of the different rules that apply to investment interest, personal interest, trade or business interest, home mortgage interest, and passive activity interest. See Pub. 550.

Specific Instructions

Line 1—Investment Interest Expense

Enter the investment interest paid or accrued during the tax year, regardless of when the indebtedness was incurred. Include interest paid or accrued on a loan (or part of a loan) that is allocable to property held for investment.

Be sure to include investment interest expense reported to you on Schedule K-1 from a partnership or an S corporation. Include amortization of bond premium on taxable bonds purchased after October 22, 1986, but before January 1, 1988, unless you elected to offset amortizable bond premium against the interest payments on the bond. A taxable bond is a bond on which the interest is includible in gross income.

Investment interest expense does not include the following:

- Home mortgage interest;
- Interest expense that is properly allocable to a passive activity (see **Passive Activities** below);
- Any interest expense that is capitalized, such as construction interest subject to section 263A; or
- Interest expense related to tax-exempt interest income under section 265.

Passive Activities

Investment interest expense does not include any interest expense that is taken into account in determining your income or loss from a passive activity. However, interest expense that is properly allocable to portfolio income is investment interest expense and is not taken into account when determining your income or loss from a passive activity. Portfolio income includes income (not derived in the ordinary course of a trade or business) from interest, dividends, annuities, royalties, and net gain from the disposition of property held for investment. See the instructions for Schedule E (Form 1040) for the definition of passive activity.

Line 4—Net Investment Income

Net investment income is the excess, if any, of investment income over investment expenses (see page 2). Include investment income and expenses reported to you on Schedule K-1 from a partnership or an S corporation. Also include net investment income from an estate or a trust.

Investment Income

Investment income includes income (not derived in the ordinary course of a trade or business) from interest, dividends, annuities, royalties, and net gain from the disposition of property held for investment (including capital gain distributions from mutual funds). Net income from the following passive activities is also treated as investment income:

- Rental of substantially nondepreciable property;
- Equity-financed lending activities; and
- Acquisition of certain interests in a pass-through entity licensing intangible property.

See Temporary Regulations section 1.469-2T(f)(10) for details.

In addition to the activities listed above, net passive income from a passive activity of a publicly traded partnership (as defined in section 469(k)(2)) is also included in investment income. See Notice 88-75, 1988-2 C.B. 386, for details.

Investment income does not include Alaska Permanent Fund Dividends. See Rev. Rul. 90-56, 1990-2 C.B. 102.

Property Held for Investment

Property held for investment includes property that produces investment income. However, it does not include an interest in a passive activity. See **Passive Activities,** on page 1, for more details.

Property held for investment also includes an interest in an activity of conducting a trade or business in which you did not materially participate and that is not a passive activity. For example, a working interest in an oil or gas property that is not a passive activity is property held for investment if you did not materially participate in the activity.

Investment Expenses

Investment expenses are your allowed deductions, other than interest expense, directly connected with the production of investment income. For example, depreciation or depletion allowed on assets that produce investment income is an investment expense.

Investment expenses do not include any deductions taken into account in determining your income or loss from a passive activity.

If you have investment expenses that are included as a miscellaneous itemized deduction on line 20 of Schedule A (Form 1040), you may not have to use all of the amount for purposes of line 4 of Form 4952. The 2% adjusted gross income limitation on Schedule A may reduce the amount.

To figure the amount to use, compare the amount of the investment expenses included on line 20 of Schedule A with the total miscellaneous expenses on line 24 of Schedule A. The smaller of the investment expenses included on line 20 or the total of line 24 is the amount to use to figure the investment expense for line 4.

Example. Assume line 20 of Schedule A includes investment expenses of $3,000, and line 24 is $1,300 after the 2% adjusted gross income limitation. Investment expenses of $1,300 are used to figure the amount of investment expense for line 4. If investment expenses of $800 were included on line 20 and line 24 was $1,300, investment expenses of $800 would be used.

If you have investment expenses reported on a form or schedule other than Schedule A, include those expenses when figuring investment expenses for line 4.

Line 6—Investment Interest Expense Deduction

This is the amount you may deduct as investment interest expense.

Individuals

Enter the amount from line 6 on line 11 of Schedule A (Form 1040), even if all or part of it is attributable to a partnership or an S corporation. However, if any portion of this amount is attributable to royalties, enter that portion of the interest expense on Schedule E (Form 1040).

Estates and Trusts

Enter the amount from line 6 on line 10 of Form 1041.

Form 6198

If any portion of the deductible investment interest expense is attributable to an activity for which you are not at risk, you must also use **Form 6198,** At-Risk Limitations, to figure your deductible investment interest expense. Enter the portion attributable to the at-risk activity on line 4 of Form 6198. Reduce line 6 of Form 4952 by the amount entered on Form 6198. See Form 6198 and its instructions for more details, especially the instructions for line 4 of that form.

Alternative Minimum Tax

Deductible interest expense is an adjustment for alternative minimum tax purposes. Get **Form 6251,** Alternative Minimum Tax—Individuals, or **Form 8656,** Alternative Minimum Tax—Fiduciaries.

Form **4972**

Department of the Treasury
Internal Revenue Service

Tax on Lump-Sum Distributions

(Use This Form Only for Lump-Sum Distributions From Qualified Retirement Plans)

▶ **Attach to Form 1040 or Form 1041.** ▶ **See separate instructions.**

OMB No. 1545-0193

1991

Attachment Sequence No. **28**

Name of recipient of distribution | **Identifying number**

Part I Complete this part to see if you qualify to use Form 4972.

			Yes	No
1	Did you roll over any part of the distribution? If "Yes," do not complete the rest of this form.	1		
2	Was the retirement plan participant born before 1936 (and, if deceased, was the participant at least 50 years old at the date of death)? If "No," do not complete the rest of this form	2		
3	Was this a lump-sum distribution from a qualified pension, profit-sharing, or stock bonus plan? (See **Distributions That Qualify for the 20% Capital Gain Election or for 5- or 10-Year Averaging** in the instructions.)	3		
	If "No," do not complete the rest of this form.			
4	Was the participant in the plan for at least 5 years before the year of the distribution?	4		
5	Was this distribution paid to you as a beneficiary of a plan participant who died?	5		
	If you answered "No" to 4 **and** 5, do not complete the rest of this form.			
6	Was the plan participant:			
a	An employee who received the distribution because he or she quit, retired, was laid off or fired? . . .	6a		
b	Self-employed or an owner-employee who became permanently and totally disabled before the distribution?	6b		
c	Age 59½ or older at the time of the distribution?	6c		
	If you answered "No" to question 5 and **all** parts of question 6, do not complete the rest of this form.			
7	Did you use Form 4972 in a prior year for any distribution received after 1986 from a plan for the same plan participant, including you, for whom the 1991 distribution was made? If "Yes," do not complete the rest of this form	7		

If you qualify to use this form, you may choose to use Part II, Part III, or Part IV; **or** Part II and Part III; **or** Part II and Part IV.

Part II Complete this part to choose the 20% capital gain election. (See instructions.)

1	Capital gain part from Box 3 of Form 1099-R. (See instructions.)	1	
2	Multiply line 1 by 20% (.20) and enter here. If you do not elect to use Part III or Part IV, also enter the amount on Form 1040, line 39, or Form 1041, Schedule G, line 1b	2	

Part III Complete this part to choose the 5-year averaging method. (See instructions.)

1	Ordinary income from Form 1099-R, Box 2a minus Box 3. If you did not make the Schedule D election or complete Part II, enter the taxable amount from Box 2a of Form 1099-R. (See instructions.) . .				1	
2	Death benefit exclusion. (See instructions.)				2	
3	Total taxable amount—Subtract line 2 from line 1				3	
4	Current actuarial value of annuity, if applicable (from Form 1099-R, Box 8)				4	
5	Adjusted total taxable amount—Add lines 3 and 4. If this amount is $70,000 or more, skip lines 6 through 9, and enter this amount on line 10				5	
6	Multiply line 5 by 50% (.50), but **do not** enter more than $10,000 . .			6		
7	Subtract $20,000 from line 5. If line 5 is $20,000 or less, enter -0-	7				
8	Multiply line 7 by 20% (.20)			8		
9	Minimum distribution allowance—Subtract line 8 from line 6				9	
10	Subtract line 9 from line 5				10	
11	Federal estate tax attributable to lump-sum distribution. Do not deduct on Form 1040 or Form 1041 the amount attributable to the ordinary income entered on line 1. (See instructions.) . .				11	
12	Subtract line 11 from line 10				12	
13	Multiply line 12 by 20% (.20)				13	
14	Tax on amount on line 13. See instructions for Tax Rate Schedule				14	
15	Multiply line 14 by five (5). If no entry on line 4, skip lines 16 through 21. Enter the amount on line 22				15	
16	Divide line 4 by line 5 and enter the result as a decimal. (See instructions.)				16	
17	Multiply line 9 by the decimal amount on line 16				17	
18	Subtract line 17 from line 4				18	
19	Multiply line 18 by 20% (.20)				19	
20	Tax on amount on line 19. See instructions for Tax Rate Schedule				20	
21	Multiply line 20 by five (5)				21	
22	Subtract line 21 from line 15. (Multiple recipients, see instructions.)				22	
23	Tax on lump-sum distribution—Add Part II, line 2, and Part III, line 22. Enter on Form 1040, line 39, or Form 1041, Schedule G, line 1b. . . . . ▶				23	

For Paperwork Reduction Act Notice, see separate instructions. Cat. No. 13187U Form **4972** (1991)

Part IV **Complete this part to choose the 10-year averaging method.** (See instructions.)

1	Ordinary income part from Form 1099-R, Box 2a minus Box 3. If you did not make the Schedule D election or complete Part II, enter the taxable amount from Box 2a of Form 1099-R. (See instructions.)	1	
2	Death benefit exclusion. (See instructions.)	2	
3	Total taxable amount—Subtract line 2 from line 1	3	
4	Current actuarial value of annuity, if applicable (from Form 1099-R, Box 8)	4	
5	Adjusted total taxable amount—Add lines 3 and 4. If this amount is $70,000 or more, skip lines 6 through 9, and enter this amount on line 10	5	
6	Multiply line 5 by 50% (.50), but **do not** enter more than $10,000 — 6		
7	Subtract $20,000 from line 5. If line 5 is $20,000 or less, enter -0- — 7		
8	Multiply line 7 by 20% (.20) — 8		
9	Minimum distribution allowance—Subtract line 8 from line 6	9	
10	Subtract line 9 from line 5	10	
11	Federal estate tax attributable to lump-sum distribution. Do not deduct on Form 1040 or Form 1041 the amount attributable to the ordinary income entered on line 1. (See instructions.)	11	
12	Subtract line 11 from line 10	12	
13	Multiply line 12 by 10% (.10)	13	
14	Tax on amount on line 13. See instructions for Tax Rate Schedule	14	
15	Multiply line 14 by ten (10). If no entry on line 4, skip lines 16 through 21. Enter this amount on line 22	15	
16	Divide line 4 by line 5 and enter the result as a decimal. (See instructions.)	16	
17	Multiply line 9 by the decimal amount on line 16	17	
18	Subtract line 17 from line 4	18	
19	Multiply line 18 by 10% (.10)	19	
20	Tax on amount on line 19. See instructions for Tax Rate Schedule	20	
21	Multiply line 20 by ten (10)	21	
22	Subtract line 21 from line 15. (Multiple recipients, see instructions.)	22	
23	Tax on lump-sum distribution—Add Part II, line 2, and Part IV, line 22. Enter on Form 1040, line 39, or Form 1041, Schedule G, line 1b ▶	23	

Form **6251**

Department of the Treasury
Internal Revenue Service

Alternative Minimum Tax—Individuals

▶ See separate instructions.

▶ Attach to Form 1040 or Form 1040NR. Estates and trusts, use Form 8656.

OMB No. 1545-0227

1991

Attachment Sequence No. **32**

Name(s) shown on Form 1040 | **Your social security number**

1	Enter the amount from Form 1040, line 35. (If Form 1040, line 35 is less than zero, enter as a negative amount.)			1	
2	Net operating loss deduction, if any, from Form 1040, line 22. (Enter as a positive amount.)			2	
3	Overall itemized deductions limitation (see instructions)			3	( )
4	Combine lines 1, 2, and 3			4	
5	**Adjustments:** (See instructions before completing.)				
a	Standard deduction, if any, from Form 1040, line 34	5a			
b	Medical and dental expenses. (Enter the smaller of the amount from Schedule A (Form 1040), line 4 or 2½% of Form 1040, line 32.)	5b			
c	Miscellaneous itemized deductions from Schedule A (Form 1040), line 24	5c			
d	Taxes from Schedule A (Form 1040), line 8	5d			
e	Refund of taxes	5e	( )		
f	Certain home mortgage interest	5f			
g	Investment interest expense	5g			
h	Depreciation of tangible property placed in service after 1986	5h			
i	Circulation and research and experimental expenditures paid or incurred after 1986	5i			
j	Mining exploration and development costs paid or incurred after 1986	5j			
k	Long-term contracts entered into after 2/28/86	5k			
l	Pollution control facilities placed in service after 1986	5l			
m	Installment sales of certain property	5m			
n	Adjusted gain or loss and incentive stock options	5n			
o	Certain loss limitations	5o			
p	Tax shelter farm loss	5p			
q	Passive activity loss	5q			
r	Beneficiaries of estates and trusts	5r			
s	Combine lines 5a through 5r			5s	
6	**Tax preference items:** (See instructions before completing.)				
a	Appreciated property charitable deduction	6a			
b	Tax-exempt interest from private activity bonds issued after 8/7/86	6b			
c	Depletion	6c			
d	Accelerated depreciation of real property placed in service before 1987	6d			
e	Accelerated depreciation of leased personal property placed in service before 1987	6e			
f	Amortization of certified pollution control facilities placed in service before 1987	6f			
g	Intangible drilling costs	6g			
h	Add lines 6a through 6g			6h	
7	Combine lines 4, 5s, and 6h			7	
8	Energy preference adjustment for certain taxpayers. (Do not enter more than 40% of line 7.) See instructions			8	
9	Subtract line 8 from line 7			9	
10	Alternative tax net operating loss deduction. See instructions for limitations			10	
11	**Alternative minimum taxable income.** Subtract line 10 from line 9. If married filing separately, see instructions			11	
12	Enter: $40,000 ($20,000 if married filing separately; $30,000 if single or head of household)			12	
13	Enter: $150,000 ($75,000 if married filing separately; $112,500 if single or head of household).			13	
14	Subtract line 13 from line 11. If zero or less, enter -0- here and on line 15 and go to line 16			14	
15	Multiply line 14 by 25% (.25)			15	
16	**Exemption.** Subtract line 15 from line 12. If zero or less, enter -0-. If completing this form for a child under age 14, see instructions for amount to enter			16	
17	Subtract line 16 from line 11. If zero or less, enter -0- here and on line 22 and skip lines 18 through 21.			17	
18	Multiply line 17 by 24% (.24)			18	
19	Alternative minimum tax foreign tax credit. See instructions			19	
20	Tentative minimum tax. Subtract line 19 from line 18			20	
21	Enter your tax from Form 1040, line 38, minus any foreign tax credit on Form 1040, line 43. If an amount is entered on line 39 of Form 1040, see instructions			21	
22	**Alternative minimum tax.** Subtract line 21 from line 20. If zero or less, enter -0-. Enter this amount on Form 1040, line 48. If completing this form for a child under age 14, see instructions for amount to enter			22	

For Paperwork Reduction Act Notice, see separate instructions. Cat. No. 13600G Form **6251** (1991)

Form **6252**

Department of the Treasury
Internal Revenue Service

Installment Sale Income

▶ See separate instructions. ▶ Attach to your tax return.
Use a separate form for each sale or other disposition of property on the installment method.

OMB No. 1545-0228
1991
Attachment Sequence No. **79**

Name(s) shown on return | **Identifying number**

A Description of property ▶ ....

B Date acquired (month, day, and year) ▶ / / **C** Date sold (month, day, and year) ▶ / /

D Was the property sold to a related party after May 14, 1980? See instructions . . . ☐ Yes ☐ No

E If the answer to D is "Yes," was the property a marketable security? If "Yes," complete Part III. If "No," complete Part III for the year of sale and for 2 years after the year of sale . . . ☐ Yes ☐ No

Part I Gross Profit and Contract Price *(Complete this part for the year of sale only.)*

1	Selling price including mortgages and other debts. Do not include interest whether stated or unstated		1
2	Mortgages and other debts the buyer assumed or took the property subject to, but not new mortgages the buyer got from a bank or other source.	2	
3	Subtract line 2 from line 1	3	
4	Cost or other basis of property sold	4	
5	Depreciation allowed or allowable	5	
6	Adjusted basis. Subtract line 5 from line 4	6	
7	Commissions and other expenses of sale	7	
8	Income recapture from Form 4797, Part III. See instructions	8	
9	Add lines 6, 7, and 8		9
10	Subtract line 9 from line 1. If zero or less, do not complete the rest of this form		10
11	If the property described in question A above was your main home, enter the total of lines 9f and 15 from Form 2119. Otherwise, enter -0-		11
12	**Gross profit.** Subtract line 11 from line 10		12
13	Subtract line 9 from line 2. If zero or less, enter -0-		13
14	**Contract price.** Add line 3 and line 13		14

Part II Installment Sale Income *(Complete this part for the year of sale and any year you receive a payment or have certain debts you must treat as a payment on installment obligations.)*

15	Gross profit percentage. Divide line 12 by line 14. For years after the year of sale, see instructions		15
16	**For year of sale only**—Enter amount from line 13 above; otherwise, enter -0-		16
17	Payments received during year. See instructions. Do not include interest whether stated or unstated		17
18	Add lines 16 and 17		18
19	Payments received in prior years. See instructions. Do not include interest whether stated or unstated	19	
20	**Installment sale income.** Multiply line 18 by line 15		20
21	Part of line 20 that is ordinary income under recapture rules. See instructions		21
22	Subtract line 21 from line 20. Enter here and on Schedule D or Form 4797		22

Part III Related Party Installment Sale Income *(Do not complete if you received the final payment this tax year.)*

F Name, address, and taxpayer identifying number of related party ....

G Did the related party, during this tax year, resell or dispose of the property ("second disposition")? . . . ☐ Yes ☐ No

H **If the answer to question G is "Yes," complete lines 23 through 30 below unless one of the following conditions is met (check only the box that applies).**

- ☐ The second disposition was more than 2 years after the first disposition (other than dispositions of marketable securities). If this box is checked, enter the date of disposition (month, day, year). ▶ / /
- ☐ The first disposition was a sale or exchange of stock to the issuing corporation.
- ☐ The second disposition was an involuntary conversion where the threat of conversion occurred after the first disposition.
- ☐ The second disposition occurred after the death of the original seller or buyer.
- ☐ It can be established to the satisfaction of the Internal Revenue Service that tax avoidance was not a principal purpose for either of the dispositions. If this box is checked, attach an explanation. See instructions.

23	Selling price of property sold by related party	23
24	Enter contract price from line 14 for year of first sale	24
25	Enter the **smaller** of line 23 or line 24	25
26	Total payments received by the end of your 1991 tax year. Add lines 18 and 19	26
27	Subtract line 26 from line 25. If zero or less, enter -0-	27
28	Multiply line 27 by the gross profit percentage on line 15 for year of first sale	28
29	Part of line 28 that is ordinary income under recapture rules. See instructions	29
30	Subtract line 29 from line 28. Enter here and on Schedule D or Form 4797	30

For Paperwork Reduction Act Notice, see separate instructions. Cat. No. 13601R Form **6252** (1991)

Form **8283** (Rev. March 1990)

Department of the Treasury Internal Revenue Service

Noncash Charitable Contributions

▶ **Attach to your tax return if the total claimed deduction for all property contributed exceeds $500.**

▶ **See separate Instructions.**

OMB No. 1545-0908 Expires 2-28-93

Attachment Sequence No. **55**

Name(s) shown on your income tax return | **Identification number**

Note: *Compute the amount of your contribution deduction before completing Form 8283. (See your tax return instructions.)*

Section A Include in Section A **only** items (or groups of similar items) for which you claimed a deduction of $5,000 or less per item or group, and certain publicly traded securities (see Instructions).

Part I Information on Donated Property

1	**(a)** Name and address of the donee organization	**(b)** Description of donated property (attach a separate sheet if more space is needed)
A		
B		
C		
D		
E		

Note: *If the amount you claimed as a deduction for the item is $500 or less, you do not have to complete columns (d), (e), and (f).*

	(c) Date of the contribution	**(d)** Date acquired by donor (mo., yr.)	**(e)** How acquired by donor	**(f)** Donor's cost or adjusted basis	**(g)** Fair market value	**(h)** Method used to determine the fair market value
A						
B						
C						
D						
E						

Part II Other Information—If you gave less than an entire interest in property listed in Part I, complete lines 2a–2e. If restrictions were attached to a contribution listed in Part I, complete lines 3a–3c.

2 If less than the entire interest in the property is contributed during the year, complete the following:

a Enter letter from Part I that identifies the property ________. (If Part II applies to more than one property, attach a separate statement.)

b Total amount claimed as a deduction for the property listed in Part I for this tax year ________________; for any prior tax year(s) ________________

c Name and address of each organization to which any such contribution was made in a prior year (complete only if different than the donee organization above).

Name of charitable organization (donee)

Address (number and street)

City or town, state, and ZIP code

d The place where any tangible property is located or kept ________________

e Name of any person, other than the donee organization, having actual possession of the property ________________

3 If conditions were attached to any contribution listed in Part I, answer the following questions and attach the required statement (see Instructions):

		Yes	No
a	Is there a restriction, either temporary or permanent, on the donee's right to use or dispose of the donated property? . .		
b	Did you give to anyone (other than the donee organization or another organization participating with the donee organization in cooperative fundraising) the right to the income from the donated property or to the possession of the property, including the right to vote donated securities, to acquire the property by purchase or otherwise, or to designate the person having such income, possession, or right to acquire?		
c	Is there a restriction limiting the donated property for a particular use?		

For Paperwork Reduction Act Notice, see separate Instructions. Form **8283** (Rev. 3-90)

Form 8283 (Rev. 3-90) Page 2

Name(s) shown on your income tax return	Identification number

Section B **Appraisal Summary**—Include in Section B only items (or groups of similar items) for which you claimed a deduction of more than $5,000 per item or group. *(Report contributions of certain publicly traded securities only in Section A.)*

If you donated art, you may have to attach the complete appraisal. See the **Note** in Part I below.

Part I Information on Donated Property *(To be completed by the taxpayer and/or appraiser.)*

1 Check type of property:

☐ Art* (contribution of $20,000 or more) ☐ Real Estate ☐ Gems/Jewelry ☐ Stamp Collections
☐ Art* (contribution of less than $20,000) ☐ Coin Collections ☐ Books ☐ Other

*Art includes paintings, sculptures, watercolors, prints, drawings, ceramics, antique furniture, decorative arts, textiles, carpets, silver, rare manuscripts, historical memorabilia, and other similar objects. **Note:** *If you donated art after December 31, 1987, and your total art contribution deduction was $20,000 or more, you must attach a complete copy of the signed appraisal. See Instructions.*

2	(a) Description of donated property (attach a separate sheet if more space is needed)	(b) If tangible property was donated, give a brief summary of the overall physical condition at the time of the gift	(c) Appraised fair market value
A			
B			
C			
D			

	(d) Date acquired by donor (mo., yr.)	(e) How acquired by donor	(f) Donor's cost or adjusted basis	(g) For bargain sales after 6/6/88, enter amount received	See Instructions: (h) Amount claimed as a deduction	See Instructions: (i) Average trading price of securities
A						
B						
C						
D						

Part II Taxpayer (Donor) Statement—List any item(s) included in Part I above that is (are) separately identified in the appraisal as having a value of $500 or less. See Instructions.

I declare that the following item(s) included in Part I above has (have) to the best of my knowledge and belief an appraised value of not more than $500 (per item). *(Enter identifying letter from Part I and describe the specific item)*: ______

Signature of taxpayer (donor) ▶ Date ▶

Part III Certification of Appraiser *(To be completed by the appraiser of the above donated property.)*

I declare that I am not the donor, the donee, a party to the transaction in which the donor acquired the property, employed by, married to, or related to any of the foregoing persons, or an appraiser regularly used by any of the foregoing persons and who does not perform a majority of appraisals during the taxable year for other persons.

Also, I declare that I hold myself out to the public as an appraiser or perform appraisals on a regular basis; and that because of my qualifications as described in the appraisal, I am qualified to make appraisals of the type of property being valued. I certify that the appraisal fees were not based upon a percentage of the appraised property value. Furthermore, I understand that a false or fraudulent overstatement of the property value as described in the qualified appraisal or this appraisal summary may subject me to the civil penalty under section 6701(a) (aiding and abetting the understatement of tax liability). I affirm that I have not been barred from presenting evidence or testimony by the Director of Practice.

Please Sign Here Signature ▶ Title ▶ Date of appraisal ▶

Business address	Identification number

City or town, state, and ZIP code

Part IV Donee Acknowledgment *(To be completed by the charitable organization.)*

This charitable organization acknowledges that it is a qualified organization under section 170(c) and that it received the donated property as described in Part I on ______ (Date).

Furthermore, this organization affirms that in the event it sells, exchanges, or otherwise disposes of the property (or any portion thereof) within 2 years after the date of receipt, it will file an information return (**Form 8282,** Donee Information Return) with the IRS and furnish the donor a copy of that return. This acknowledgment does not represent concurrence in the claimed fair market value.

Name of charitable organization (donee)	Employer identification number	
Address (number and street)	City or town, state, and ZIP code	
Authorized signature	Title	Date

*U.S. GPO:1991-518-933/20355

Form **8332**
(Rev. September 1990)
Department of the Treasury
Internal Revenue Service

Release of Claim to Exemption for Child of Divorced or Separated Parents

► **Attach to Tax Return of Parent Claiming Exemption.**

OMB No. 1545-0915
Expires 6-30-93
Attachment Sequence No. **51**

Name(s) of parent claiming exemption | **Social security number**

Part I Release of Claim to Exemption for Current Year

I agree not to claim an exemption for ______________________
Name(s) of child (or children)

for the tax year 19 _____ .

______________________ ______________________ ______________________
Signature of parent releasing claim to exemption | Social security number | Date

If you choose not to claim an exemption for this child (or children) for future tax years, complete Part II, as explained in the instructions below.

Part II Release of Claim to Exemption for Future Years

I agree not to claim an exemption for ______________________
Name(s) of child (or children)

for tax year(s) ______________________
(Specify. See instructions.)

______________________ ______________________ ______________________
Signature of parent releasing claim to exemption | Social security number | Date

Paperwork Reduction Act Notice.— We ask for the information on this form to carry out the Internal Revenue laws of the United States. You are required to give us this information. We need it to ensure that you are complying with these laws and to allow us to figure and collect the right amount of tax.

The time needed to complete and file this form will vary depending on individual circumstances. The estimated average time is:

Recordkeeping . . . . 7 min.
Learning about the law or the form . . . . 5 min.
Preparing the form . . . . . . 7 min.
Copying, assembling, and sending the form to IRS . . . . 14 min.

If you have comments concerning the accuracy of these time estimates or suggestions for making this form more simple, we would be happy to hear from you. You can write to both the IRS and the Office of Management and Budget at the addresses listed in the instructions for the return with which this form is filed.

Purpose of Form.—This form may be used by a **custodial parent** to release his or her claim to a child's exemption. This form is completed by the custodial parent and is given to the **noncustodial parent** who will claim the exemption. The noncustodial parent who will claim the child's exemption must attach this form or a similar statement to his or her tax return.

The **custodial parent** is the parent who had custody of the child for most of the year. The **noncustodial parent** is the parent who had custody for the shorter period or who did not have custody at all.

Instead of using this form, a similar statement may be used. The similar statement must contain the same information that is required by this form.

Children of Divorced or Separated Parents.—Special rules apply to determine if the support test is met for children of parents who are divorced or legally separated under a decree of divorce or separate maintenance or separated under a written separation agreement. The rules also apply to children of parents who did not live together at any time during the last 6 months of the year, even if they do not have a separation agreement.

The general rule is that the custodial parent is treated as having provided over half of the child's support if **both 1** and **2** below apply. This means that the custodial parent can claim the child's exemption if the other four dependency tests in the Instructions for Form 1040 or Form 1040A are also met.

1. The child receives over half of his or her total support from both of the parents; **AND**

2. The child was in the custody of one or both of his or her parents for more than half of the year.

Note: *Public assistance payments, such as Aid to Families with Dependent Children, are not support provided by the parents.*

Exception.—The general rule does not apply if **any** of the following applies:

- The custodial parent agrees not to claim the child's exemption by signing this form or similar statement, and the noncustodial parent attaches the form or similar statement to his or her tax return for the tax year. (See **Instructions for Custodial Parent,** later.)
- The child is treated as having received over half of his or her total support from a person under a multiple support agreement (**Form 2120,** Multiple Support Declaration).
- A qualified divorce decree or written agreement went into effect before 1985 and it states that the noncustodial parent can claim the child as a dependent. But the noncustodial parent must have given at least $600 for the child's support during the year. (The noncustodial parent must also check the box on line 6d of Form 1040 or Form 1040A.) This rule does not apply if the decree or agreement was changed after 1984 to say that the noncustodial parent cannot claim the child as a dependent.

Additional Information.—For more information, get **Pub. 504,** Tax Information for Divorced or Separated Individuals.

Instructions for Custodial Parent.—You may agree to release your claim to the child's exemption for the current tax year or for future years, or both.

Part I should be completed if you agree to release your claim to the child's exemption for the current tax year.

Part II should be completed if you agree to release your claim to the child's exemption for a specified number of future years, or for all future years. If you are releasing claim for all future years, write "all future years" in the space provided in Part II.

Instructions for Noncustodial Parent. —Attach Form 8332 or a similar statement to your tax return for the tax year in which you claim the child's exemption. If the custodial parent completed Part II, you must attach a copy of this form to your tax return for each succeeding year in which you claim the exemption.

You may claim the exemption **only** if the other four dependency tests in the Form 1040 or 1040A Instructions are met.

Form **8582**

Department of the Treasury
Internal Revenue Service

Passive Activity Loss Limitations

▶ See separate instructions.
▶ Attach to Form 1040 or Form 1041.

OMB No. 1545-1008
1991
Attachment Sequence No. 88

Name(s) shown on return	Identifying number

Part I 1991 Passive Activity Loss

Caution: *See the instructions for Worksheets 1 and 2 on pages 7 and 8 before completing Part I.*

Rental Real Estate Activities With Active Participation (For the definition of active participation see **Active Participation in a Rental Real Estate Activity** in the instructions.)				
1a Activities with net income (from Worksheet 1, column (a)) . . .	1a			
b Activities with net loss (from Worksheet 1, column (b))	1b	( )		
c Prior year unallowed losses (from Worksheet 1, column (c)) . .	1c	( )		
d Combine lines 1a, 1b, and 1c			1d	
All Other Passive Activities				
2a Activities with net income (from Worksheet 2, column (a)) . . .	2a			
b Activities with net loss (from Worksheet 2, column (b))	2b	( )		
c Prior year unallowed losses (from Worksheet 2, column (c)) . .	2c	( )		
d Combine lines 2a, 2b, and 2c			2d	
3 Combine lines 1d and 2d. If the result is net income or -0-, see the instructions for line 3. If this line and line 1d are losses, go to line 4. Otherwise, enter -0- on line 9 and go to line 10. . .			3	

Part II Special Allowance for Rental Real Estate With Active Participation

Note: *Treat all numbers entered in Part II as positive amounts. (See instructions on page 8 for examples.)*

4 Enter the **smaller** of the loss on line 1d or the loss on line 3			4	
5 Enter $150,000. If married filing separately, see the instructions .	5			
6 Enter modified adjusted gross income, but not less than -0- (see instructions)	6			
Note: *If line 6 is equal to or greater than line 5, skip lines 7 and 8, enter -0- on line 9, and then go to line 10. Otherwise, go to line 7.*				
7 Subtract line 6 from line 5.	7			
8 Multiply line 7 by 50% (.5). **Do not** enter more than $25,000. If married filing separately, see instructions			8	
9 Enter the **smaller** of line 4 or line 8			9	

Part III Total Losses Allowed

10 Add the income, if any, on lines 1a and 2a and enter the total	10	
11 **Total losses allowed from all passive activities for 1991.** Add lines 9 and 10. See the instructions to find out how to report the losses on your tax return	11	

For Paperwork Reduction Act Notice, see separate instructions. Cat. No. 63704F Form **8582** (1991)

Form **8606**

Department of the Treasury
Internal Revenue Service

Nondeductible IRA Contributions, IRA Basis, and Nontaxable IRA Distributions

▶ Please see Recordkeeping Requirements on page 2.
▶ Attach to Form 1040, Form 1040A, or Form 1040NR.

OMB No. 1545-1007
1991
Attachment Sequence No. 47

Name. (If married, file a separate Form 8606 for each spouse. See instructions.) | Your social security number

Fill in Your Address Only If You Are Filing This Form by Itself and Not With Your Tax Return ▷ Home address (number and street, or P.O. box if mail is not delivered to your home) | Apt. no.
City, town or post office, state, and ZIP code

1	Enter the total value of **ALL** your IRAs as of 12/31/91. (See instructions.)	1	
2	Enter your IRA contributions for 1991 that you choose to be nondeductible. Include those made during 1/1/92–4/15/92 that were for 1991. (See instructions.)		2
3	Enter your total IRA basis for 1990 and prior years. (See instructions.)		3
4	Add lines 2 and 3. If you did not receive any IRA distributions (withdrawals) in 1991, skip lines 5 through 13 and enter this amount on line 14		4
5	Enter only those contributions included on line 2 that were made during 1/1/92–4/15/92. (This amount will be the same as line 2 if all of your nondeductible contributions for 1991 were made in 1992 by 4/15/92.) (See instructions.)		5
6	Subtract line 5 from line 4		6
7	Enter the amount from line 1 plus any outstanding rollovers. (See instructions.)	7	
8	Enter the total IRA distributions received during 1991. Do not include amounts rolled over before 1/1/92. (See instructions.)	8	
9	Add lines 7 and 8	9	
10	Divide line 6 by line 9 and enter the result as a decimal (to at least two places). Do not enter more than "1.00"	10 .	
11	Multiply line 8 by line 10. This is the amount of your **nontaxable distributions for 1991.** (See instructions.) ▶		11
12	Subtract line 11 from line 6. This is the **basis in your IRA(s) as of 12/31/91**		12
13	Enter the amount, if any, from line 5		13
14	Add lines 12 and 13. This is your **total IRA basis for 1991 and prior years** ▶		14

Sign Here Only If You Are Filing This Form by Itself and Not With Your Tax Return — Under penalties of perjury, I declare that I have examined this form, including accompanying attachments, and to the best of my knowledge and belief, it is true, correct, and complete.

▶ Your signature ▶ Date

Paperwork Reduction Act Notice.—We ask for the information on this form to carry out the Internal Revenue laws of the United States. You are required to give us the information. We need it to ensure that you are complying with these laws and to allow us to figure and collect the right amount of tax.

The time needed to complete and file this form will vary depending on individual circumstances. The estimated average time is: **Recordkeeping,** 26 minutes; **Learning about the law or the form,** 7 minutes; **Preparing the form,** 22 minutes; and **Copying, assembling, and sending the form to the IRS,** 20 minutes.

If you have comments concerning the accuracy of these time estimates or suggestions for making this form more simple, we would be happy to hear from you. You can write to both the **Internal Revenue Service,** Washington, DC 20224, Attention: IRS Reports Clearance Officer, T:FP; and the **Office of Management and Budget,** Paperwork Reduction Project (1545-1007), Washington, DC 20503. **DO NOT** send this form to either of these offices. Instead, see **When and Where To File** on this page.

General Instructions

Purpose of Form.—You must use Form 8606 to report your IRA contributions that you choose to be nondeductible. You may wish to make nondeductible contributions, for example, if all or part of your contributions are not deductible because of the income limitations for IRAs. First, figure your deductible contributions using the instructions for Form 1040 or Form 1040A, whichever apply to you. Report the deductible contributions on Form 1040, Form 1040A, or Form 1040NR. Then, enter on line 2 of Form 8606 the amount you choose to be nondeductible.

The part of any distributions you receive attributable to nondeductible contributions will not be taxable. If you have at any time made nondeductible contributions, also use Form 8606 to figure the nontaxable part of any IRA distributions you received in 1991. Line 11 will show the amount that is not taxable.

Who Must File.—You must file Form 8606 for 1991 if **either** of the following applies:

- You made nondeductible contributions to your IRA for 1991, or
- You received IRA distributions in 1991 **and** you have at any time made nondeductible contributions to any of your IRAs.

When and Where To File.—Attach Form 8606 to your 1991 Form 1040, Form 1040A, or Form 1040NR.

If you are required to file Form 8606, but do not have to file an income tax return because you do not meet the requirements for filing a return, you still have to file a Form 8606 with the Internal Revenue Service at the time and place you would be required to file Form 1040, Form 1040A, or Form 1040NR.

Penalty for Not Filing Form 8606.—The law provides for a penalty if you make nondeductible IRA contributions and do not file Form 8606. You will have to pay a $50 penalty for each failure to file Form 8606, unless you can show that the failure to file was due to reasonable cause.

Penalty for Overstatement.—If you overstate your nondeductible contributions on this form for any tax year, you must pay a penalty of $100 for each overstatement, unless it was due to reasonable cause.

Recordkeeping Requirements.—To verify the nontaxable part of distributions from your IRA, keep a copy of this form together with copies of the following forms and records until all distributions are made from your IRA(s):

- Forms 1040 (or Forms 1040A or Forms 1040NR) filed for each year you make a nondeductible contribution,
- Forms 5498 or similar statements received each year showing contributions you made,
- Forms 5498 or similar statements you received showing the value of your IRA(s) for each year you received a distribution, and
- Forms 1099-R and W-2P received for each year you received a distribution.

Additional Information.—For more information on nondeductible contributions, IRA basis, and distributions, get **Pub. 590,** Individual Retirement Arrangements (IRAs).

Amending Form 8606.—After you file your return, you may change, if you wish, a nondeductible contribution made on a prior year's return to a deductible contribution or vice versa. To do this, fill out a new Form 8606 showing the revised information and attach it to **Form 1040X,** Amended U.S. Individual Income Tax Return. Send both of these forms to the Internal Revenue Service Center shown in the Form 1040X instructions for your area.

Specific Instructions

Note: *If you made nondeductible contributions for 1991 and you also received an IRA distribution in 1991, you may have to make a special computation before filling out this form. See Pub. 590 for details. If you have to make the special computation, Pub. 590 will tell you the lines on Form 8606 that you must fill out.*

Name and Social Security Number.—Enter your name and social security number. If you file a joint return on Form 1040 or Form 1040A, show the name and social security number of the spouse whose IRA information is shown.

Line 1.—Enter the total value of **ALL** your IRAs as of 12/31/91. You should receive a statement by 1/31/92 for each IRA account showing the value on 12/31/91.

Line 2.—If you used IRA Worksheet 2 in the instructions for Form 1040 or Form 1040A, enter on line 2 of Form 8606 any nondeductible contributions shown on line 10 of that worksheet in the Form 1040 instructions or line 8 of that worksheet in the Form 1040A instructions. If any nondeductible contributions were made to an IRA for your nonworking spouse, complete a separate Form 8606 for your spouse. Enter on line 2 of your spouse's Form 8606 any nondeductible contributions for your nonworking spouse from the appropriate lines of IRA Worksheet 2.

You may also choose to treat any part of deductible contributions as nondeductible. To do this, include on line 2 of Form 8606 any deductible contributions that you are treating as nondeductible.

Note: *You cannot take a deduction for the amount on line 2.*

If none of your contributions are deductible, you may still choose to make a nondeductible contribution up to a maximum of $2,000 (but not more than your earned income). Enter your contributions that you are treating as nondeductible on line 2 of Form 8606.

If contributions were also made to an IRA for your nonworking spouse and none of the contributions are deductible, you may still make nondeductible contributions up to a maximum of $2,250 (but not more than your earned income). Enter on line 2 of your Form 8606 the total nondeductible contributions that you are making to your IRA. Enter the balance on line 2 of your nonworking spouse's Form 8606. You cannot contribute more than $2,000 to either your IRA or your spouse's IRA. Also, the total of the two amounts cannot be more than $2,250 and not more than your earned income.

If you used IRA Worksheet 1 in the instructions for Form 1040 or Form 1040A, the amount shown on line 3 of that worksheet is the amount of your contributions that you may deduct. However, you may choose to make all or part of that amount nondeductible. Enter on line 2 of your Form 8606 the difference between the amount you are deducting and the amount shown on line 3 of IRA Worksheet 1.

If contributions were made to an IRA for your nonworking spouse, the amount shown on line 8 of IRA Worksheet 1 is the amount of the allowable deduction for your nonworking spouse's IRA. However, you can treat all or part of that amount as nondeductible. Enter on line 2 of your nonworking spouse's Form 8606 the difference between the amount that is deducted for your nonworking spouse and the amount on line 8 of IRA Worksheet 1.

Line 3.—Your total IRA basis for 1990 and prior years is the total of all your nondeductible IRA contributions for 1987 through 1990 minus the total of any nontaxable IRA distributions received in those years. If this is the first year you are required to file Form 8606, enter zero. If you filed a **1990** or **1989** Form 8606, enter the amount from line 14 of the **last** Form 8606 you filed. Otherwise, enter the total of the amounts from lines 7 and 16 of your **1988** Form 8606. Or, if you didn't file a 1988 Form 8606, enter the total of the amounts from lines 4 and 13 of your **1987** Form 8606.

Line 5.—If you made contributions both in 1991 and 1992 that are for 1991, you may choose to apply the contributions made in 1991 first to nondeductible contributions and then to deductible contributions, or vice versa. However, the amount on line 2 minus the amount on line 5 cannot be more than the IRA contributions you actually made in 1991.

Example. You made contributions of $1,000 in 1991, and $1,000 in 1992. $1,500 of your contributions are deductible and $500 are nondeductible. You choose $500 of your contribution in 1991 to be nondeductible. In this case, the $500 would be entered on line 2, but not on line 5, and would become part of your basis for 1991.

Line 6.—Although the 1991 IRA contributions you made during 1/1/92–4/15/92 (line 5) can be treated as nondeductible for purposes of line 2, they are not included in your basis for purposes of figuring the nontaxable part of any distributions you received in 1991. This is the reason you subtract line 5 from line 4.

Line 7.—Enter the amount from line 1 plus any outstanding rollovers. A **rollover** is a tax-free distribution from one IRA that is then contributed to another IRA. The rollover contribution must be made within 60 days of receiving the distribution from the first IRA. An **outstanding rollover** is any amount distributed to you from one IRA within 60 days of the end of 1991 (between November 2 and December 31) that you did not roll over to another IRA by 12/31/91, but that you roll over to another IRA in 1992 within the normal 60-day rollover period.

If you do not have any outstanding rollovers, line 7 will be the same as line 1.

Line 8.—Do not include on line 8 any distributions that were (1) received in 1991 and rolled over to another IRA by 12/31/91, (2) outstanding rollovers included on line 7, (3) contributions under Internal Revenue Code section 408(d)(4) that were returned to you on or before the due date of the return, or (4) excess contributions under Internal Revenue Code section 408(d)(5) that were returned to you after the due date of the return.

Line 11.—This is the amount of your nontaxable IRA distributions for 1991. Subtract this amount from your total distributions shown on line 8. The difference is your taxable distributions to be reported on Form 1040, line 16b, or Form 1040A, line 10b, whichever applies.

Line 12.—The basis in your IRA as of 12/31/91 is the total of your nondeductible IRA contributions made in 1991 and prior years minus the total of any nontaxable IRA distributions received in those years. If you have basis in your IRA(s), part of each subsequent IRA distribution will be nontaxable until your basis is reduced to zero.

Line 14.—Your total IRA basis for 1991 and prior years includes your IRA basis as of 12/31/91 and any nondeductible IRA contributions for 1991 that you made in 1992 by 4/15/92. This amount will be used on Form 8606 in future years if you make nondeductible IRA contributions or receive distributions.

Form **8615**

Department of the Treasury
Internal Revenue Service

Tax for Children Under Age 14 Who Have Investment Income of More Than $1,100

▶ **See instructions below and on back.**

▶ **Attach ONLY to the Child's Form 1040, Form 1040A, or Form 1040NR.**

OMB No. 1545-0998

1991

Attachment Sequence No. **33**

General Instructions

Purpose of Form. For children under age 14, investment income (such as taxable interest and dividends) over $1,100 is taxed at the parent's rate if the parent's rate is higher than the child's rate. If the child's investment income is more than $1,100, use this form to see if any of the child's investment income is taxed at the parent's rate and, if so, to figure the child's tax.

Investment Income. As used on this form, "investment income" includes all taxable income other than earned income as defined on page 2. It includes income such as taxable interest, dividends, capital gains, rents, royalties, etc. It also includes pension and annuity income and income (other than earned income) received as the beneficiary of a trust.

Who Must File. Generally, Form 8615 must be filed for any child who was under age 14 on January 1, 1992, and who had more than $1,100 of investment income. If neither parent was alive on December 31, 1991, do not use Form 8615. Instead, figure the child's tax in the normal manner.

Note: *The parent may be able to elect to report the child's interest and dividends on his or her return. If the parent makes this election, the child will not have to file a return or Form 8615. For more details, see the instructions for Form 1040 or Form 1040A, or get* ***Form 8814,*** *Parent's Election To Report Child's Interest and Dividends.*

Additional Information. For more details, get **Pub. 929,** Tax Rules for Children and Dependents.

Incomplete Information for Parent. If a child's parent or guardian cannot obtain the information needed to complete Form 8615 before the due date of the child's return, reasonable estimates of the parent's taxable income or filing status and the net investment income of the parent's other children may be made. The appropriate line of Form 8615 must be marked "Estimated." For more details, see Pub. 929.

(Instructions continue on back.)

Child's name shown on return	**Child's social security number**
A Parent's name (first, initial, and last). (**Caution:** See instructions on back before completing.)	**B Parent's social security number**

C Parent's filing status (check one):
☐ Single, ☐ Married filing jointly, ☐ Married filing separately, ☐ Head of household, or ☐ Qualifying widow(er)

Step 1 Figure child's net investment income

1	Enter child's investment income, such as taxable interest and dividend income (see the instructions). (If this amount is $1,100 or less, stop here; do not file this form.)	1	
2	If the child DID NOT itemize deductions on Schedule A (Form 1040 or Form 1040NR), enter $1,100. If the child ITEMIZED deductions, see the instructions	2	
3	Subtract line 2 from line 1. (If the result is zero or less, stop here; do not complete the rest of this form but ATTACH it to the child's return.)	3	
4	Enter child's **taxable** income (from Form 1040, line 37; Form 1040A, line 22; or Form 1040NR, line 35)	4	
5	Compare the amounts on lines 3 and 4. Enter the **smaller** of the two amounts here ▶	5	

Step 2 Figure tentative tax based on the tax rate of the parent listed on line A

6	Enter parent's **taxable** income (from Form 1040, line 37; Form 1040A, line 22; Form 1040EZ, line 5; or Form 1040NR, line 35). If the parent transferred property to a trust, see instructions	6	
7	Enter the total, if any, of the net investment income from Forms 8615, line 5, of ALL OTHER children of the parent. (Do not include the amount from line 5 above.)	7	
8	Add lines 5, 6, and 7	8	
9	Tax on line 8 based on the **parent's** filing status (see instructions). If from Schedule D, enter amount from line 20 of that Schedule D here ▶ ______	9	
10	Enter parent's tax (from Form 1040, line 38; Form 1040A, line 23; Form 1040EZ, line 7; or Form 1040NR, line 36). If from Schedule D, enter amount from line 20 of that Schedule D here ▶ ______	10	
11	Subtract line 10 from line 9. (If line 7 is blank, enter on line 13 the amount from line 11; skip lines 12a and 12b.)	11	
12a	Add lines 5 and 7 | 12a | ______		
b	Divide line 5 by line 12a. Enter the result as a decimal (rounded to two places)	12b	× .
13	Multiply line 11 by line 12b ▶	13	

Step 3 Figure child's tax

	Note: *If lines 4 and 5 above are the same, go to line 16.*		
14	Subtract line 5 from line 4 | 14 | ______		
15	Tax on line 14 based on the **child's** filing status (see instructions). If from Schedule D, enter amount from line 20 of that Schedule D here ▶ ______	15	
16	Add lines 13 and 15	16	
17	Tax on line 4 based on the **child's** filing status (see instructions). If from Schedule D, check here ▶ ☐	17	
18	Enter the **larger** of line 16 or 17 here and on Form 1040, line 38; Form 1040A, line 23; or Form 1040NR, line 36. Be sure to check the box for "Form 8615" even if line 17 is more than line 16 ▶	18	

For Paperwork Reduction Act Notice, see back of form. Cat No. 64113U Form **8615** (1991)

Paperwork Reduction Act Notice. We ask for the information on this form to carry out the Internal Revenue laws of the United States. You are required to give us the information. We need it to ensure that you are complying with these laws and to allow us to figure and collect the right amount of tax.

The time needed to complete and file this form will vary depending on individual circumstances. The estimated average time is: **Recordkeeping**, 13 min.; **Learning about the law or the form**, 12 min.; **Preparing the form**, 44 min.; and **Copying, assembling, and sending the form to the IRS**, 17 min.

If you have comments concerning the accuracy of these time estimates or suggestions for making this form more simple, we would be happy to hear from you. You can write to both the IRS and the Office of Management and Budget at the addresses listed in the instructions of the tax return with which this form is filed.

Line Instructions

(Section references are to the Internal Revenue Code.)

Lines A and B. If the child's parents were married to each other and filed a joint return, enter the name and social security number (SSN) of the parent who is listed first on the joint return. For example, if the father's name is listed first on the return and his SSN is entered in the block labeled "Your social security number," enter his name on line A and his SSN on line B.

If the parents were married but filed separate returns, enter the name and SSN of the parent who had the **higher** taxable income. If you do not know which parent had the higher taxable income, see Pub. 929.

If the parents were unmarried, treated as unmarried for Federal income tax purposes, or separated either by a divorce or separate maintenance decree, enter the name and SSN of the parent who had custody of the child for most of the year (the custodial parent).

Exception. If the custodial parent remarried and filed a joint return with his or her spouse, enter the name and SSN of the person listed first on the joint return, even if that person is not the child's parent. If the custodial parent and his or her spouse filed separate returns, enter the name and SSN of the person with the **higher** taxable income, even if that person is not the child's parent.

Note: *If the parents were unmarried but lived together during the year with the child, enter the name and SSN of the parent who had the **higher** taxable income.*

Line 1. If the child had no earned income (defined later), enter the child's adjusted gross income (from Form 1040, line 32; Form 1040A, line 17; or Form 1040NR, line 31).

If the child had earned income, use the following worksheet to figure the amount to enter on line 1. But, if the child files **Form 2555,** Foreign Earned Income, has a net loss from self-employment, or claims a net operating loss deduction, **do not** use the worksheet below. Instead, use the worksheet in Pub. 929 to figure the amount to enter on line 1.

Worksheet (keep for your records)

1. Enter the amount from the child's Form 1040, line 23; Form 1040A, line 14; or Form 1040NR, line 23, whichever applies . . . ______
2. Enter the child's **earned income** (defined below) plus any deduction the child claims on Form 1040, line 28, or Form 1040NR, line 27, whichever applies ______
3. Subtract line 2 from line 1. Enter the result here and on Form 8615, line 1 . . ______

Earned income includes wages, tips, and other payments received for personal services performed. Generally, earned income is the total of the amounts reported on Form 1040, lines 7, 12, and 19; Form 1040A, line 7; or Form 1040NR, lines 8, 13, and 20.

Line 2. If the child itemized deductions, enter on line 2 the **greater** of:

- $550 plus the portion of the amount on Schedule A (Form 1040), line 26 (or Schedule A (Form 1040NR), line 10), that is directly connected with the production of the investment income on Form 8615, line 1; OR
- $1,100.

Line 6. Enter the taxable income shown on the parent's tax return. If the parent's taxable income is less than zero, enter zero on line 6. If the parent filed a joint return, enter the taxable income shown on that return even if the parent's spouse is not the child's parent. If the parent transferred property to a trust which sold or exchanged the property during the year at a gain, include any gain that was taxed to the trust under section 644 in the amount entered on line 6. Write "Section 644" and the amount on the dotted line next to line 6. Also, see the instructions for line 10.

Line 7. If the individual identified as the parent on this Form 8615 is also identified as the parent on any other Form 8615, add the amounts, if any, from line 5 on each of the other Forms 8615 and enter the total on line 7.

Line 9. Figure the tax using the Tax Table, Tax Rate Schedules, or **Schedule D** (Form 1040), Capital Gains and Losses, whichever applies. If any net capital gain is included on lines 5, 6, and/or 7, the tax on the amount on line 8 may be less if Part IV of Schedule D can be used to figure the tax. See Pub. 929 for details on how to figure the net capital gain included on line 8 and how to complete Schedule D. Schedule D should be used to figure the tax if:

the parent's filing status is	AND	the amount on Form 8615, line 8, is over:
• Single		$49,300
• Married filing jointly or Qualifying widow(er)		$82,150
• Married filing separately		$41,075
• Head of household		$70,450

If Schedule D is used to figure the tax, enter on Form 8615, line 9, the amount from line 27 of that Schedule D. Also, enter the amount from line 20 of that Schedule D in the space next to line 9.

Line 10. Enter the tax shown on the parent's tax return. If the parent filed a joint return, enter the tax shown on that return even if the parent's spouse is not the child's parent.

If line 6 includes any gain taxed to a trust under section 644, add the tax imposed under section 644(a)(2)(A) to the tax shown on the parent's return. Enter the total on line 10 instead of entering the tax from the parent's return. Write "Section 644" on the dotted line next to line 10.

Line 15. Figure the tax using the Tax Table, Tax Rate Schedule X, or Schedule D, whichever applies. If line 14 is more than $49,300 and includes any net capital gain, the tax may be less if Schedule D is used to figure the tax. See Pub. 929 for details on how to figure the net capital gain included on line 14 and how to complete Part IV of Schedule D.

Line 17. Figure the tax as if these rules did not apply. For example, if the child files Schedule D and can use Part IV to figure his or her tax, complete Part IV on the child's actual Schedule D.

Amended Return. If after the child's return is filed, the parent's taxable income is changed or the net investment income of any of the parent's other children is changed, the child's tax must be refigured using the adjusted amounts. If the child's tax is changed as a result of the adjustment(s), file **Form 1040X,** Amended U.S. Individual Income Tax Return, to correct the child's tax.

Alternative Minimum Tax. A child whose tax is figured on Form 8615 may be subject to the alternative minimum tax. For details, get **Form 6251,** Alternative Minimum Tax—Individuals, and its instructions.

Form **8829**

Department of the Treasury
Internal Revenue Service

Expenses for Business Use of Your Home

▶ File with Schedule C (Form 1040).

▶ See instructions on back.

OMB No. 1545-1256

1991

Attachment Sequence No. **66**

Name of proprietor | Your social security number

Part I Part of Your Home Used for Business

1	Area used exclusively for business (see instructions). Include area used for inventory storage or as a day-care facility that does not meet exclusive use test	1	
2	Total area of home	2	
3	Divide line 1 by line 2. Enter the result as a percentage	3	%

- **For day-care facilities not used exclusively for business, also complete lines 4–6.**
- **All others, skip lines 4–6 and enter the amount from line 3 on line 7.**

4	Total hours facility used for day care during the year. Multiply days used by number of hours used per day	4	hr.
5	Total hours available for use during the year (365 days x 24 hours) (see instructions).	5	8,760 hr.
6	Divide line 4 by line 5. Enter the result as a decimal amount	6	.
7	Business percentage. For day-care facilities not used exclusively for business, multiply line 6 by line 3 (enter the result as a percentage). All others, enter the amount from line 3 ▶	7	%

Part II Figure Your Allowable Deduction

			(a) Direct expenses	(b) Indirect expenses		
8	Enter the amount from Schedule C, line 29. (If more than one place of business, see instructions.)				8	
9	Casualty losses	9				
10	Deductible mortgage interest	10				
11	Real estate taxes	11				
12	Add lines 9, 10, and 11	12				
13	Multiply line 12, column (b) by line 7		13			
14	Add line 12, column (a) and line 13				14	
15	Subtract line 14 from line 8. If zero or less, enter -0-				15	
16	Excess mortgage interest (see instructions)	16				
17	Insurance	17				
18	Repairs and maintenance	18				
19	Utilities	19				
20	Other expenses	20				
21	Add lines 16 through 20	21				
22	Multiply line 21, column (b) by line 7		22			
23	Carryover of operating expenses from 1990		23			
24	Add line 21 in column (a), line 22, and line 23				24	
25	Allowable operating expenses. Enter the **smaller** of line 15 or line 24				25	
26	Limit on excess casualty losses and depreciation. Subtract line 25 from line 15				26	
27	Excess casualty losses (see instructions)		27			
28	Depreciation of your home from Part III below		28			
29	Carryover of excess casualty losses and depreciation from 1990		29			
30	Add lines 27 through 29				30	
31	Allowable excess casualty losses and depreciation. Enter the **smaller** of line 26 or line 30				31	
32	Add lines 14, 25, and 31				32	
33	Casualty losses included on lines 14 and 31. (Carry this amount to **Form 4684,** Section B.)				33	
34	Allowable expenses for business use of your home. Subtract line 33 from line 32. Enter here and on Schedule C, line 30 ▶				34	

Part III Depreciation of Your Home

35	Enter the **smaller** of your home's adjusted basis or its fair market value (see instructions)	35	
36	Value of land included on line 35	36	
37	Basis of building. Subtract line 36 from line 35	37	
38	Business basis of building. Multiply line 37 by line 7	38	
39	Depreciation percentage (see instructions)	39	%
40	Depreciation allowable. Multiply line 38 by the percentage on line 39. Enter here and on line 28 above	40	

Part IV Carryover of Unallowed Expenses to 1992

41	Operating expenses. Subtract line 25 from line 24. If less than zero, enter -0-	41	
42	Excess casualty losses and depreciation. Subtract line 31 from line 30. If less than zero, enter -0-	42	

For Paperwork Reduction Act Notice, see back of form. Cat. No. 13232M Form **8829** (1991)

General Instructions

Paperwork Reduction Act Notice.—We ask for the information on this form to carry out the Internal Revenue laws of the United States. You are required to give us the information. We need it to ensure that you are complying with these laws and to allow us to figure and collect the right amount of tax.

The time needed to complete and file this form will vary depending on individual circumstances. The estimated average time is: **Recordkeeping,** 52 min.; **Learning about the law or the form,** 7 min.; **Preparing the form,** 1 hr., 13 min.; and **Copying, assembling, and sending the form to the IRS,** 20 min.

If you have comments concerning the accuracy of these time estimates or suggestions for making this form more simple, we would be happy to hear from you. You can write to both the IRS and the Office of Management and Budget at the addresses listed in the instructions for Form 1040.

Purpose of Form

Use Form 8829 to figure the allowable expenses for business use of your home on **Schedule C** (Form 1040) and any carryover to 1992 of amounts not deductible in 1991.

You must meet specific requirements to deduct expenses for the business use of your home. Even if you meet these requirements, your deductible expenses are limited. For details, get **Pub. 587,** Business Use of Your Home.

Who May Deduct Expenses for Business Use of a Home

General rule.—You may deduct business expenses that apply to a part of your home **only** if that part is exclusively used on a regular basis:

- As your principal place of business for any of your trades or businesses; or
- As a place of business used by your patients, clients, or customers to meet or deal with you in the normal course of your trade or business; or
- In connection with your trade or business if it is a separate structure that is not attached to your home.

Exception for storage of inventory.—You may also deduct expenses that apply to space within your home if it is the **only** fixed location of your trade or business. The space must be used on a regular basis to store inventory from your trade or business of selling products at retail or wholesale.

Exception for day-care facilities.—If you use space in your home on a regular basis in your trade or business of providing day care, you may be able to deduct the business expenses even though you use the same space for nonbusiness purposes.

Specific Instructions

Part I

Lines 1 and 2.—You may use square feet to determine the area on lines 1 and 2. If the rooms in your home are about the same size, you may figure area using the number of rooms instead of square feet. You may use any other reasonable method if it accurately figures your business percentage on line 7.

Line 4.—Enter the total number of hours the facility was used for day care during the year.

Example. Your home is used Monday through Friday for 12 hours per day for 250 days during the year. It is also used on 50 Saturdays for 8 hours per day. Enter 3,400 hours on line 4 (3,000 hours for weekdays plus 400 hours for Saturdays).

Line 5.—If you started or stopped using your home for day care in 1991, you must prorate the number of hours based on the number of days the home was available for day care. Cross out the preprinted entry on line 5. Multiply 24 hours by the number of days available and enter the result.

Part II

Enter as direct or indirect expenses only expenses for the business use of your home (i.e., expenses allowable only because your home is used for business). Other expenses, such as salaries, supplies, and business telephone expenses, which are deductible elsewhere on Schedule C, should not be entered on Form 8829.

Direct expenses benefit only the business part of your home. They include painting or repairs made to the specific area or room used for business. Enter 100% of your direct expenses on the appropriate expense line in column (a).

Indirect expenses are for keeping up and running your entire home. They benefit both the business and personal parts of your home. Generally, enter 100% of your indirect expenses on the appropriate expense line in column (b). **Exception:** If the business percentage of an indirect expense is different from the percentage on line 7, enter only the business part of the expense on the appropriate line in column (a), and leave that line in column (b) blank. For example, your electric bill is $800 for lighting, cooking, laundry, and television. If you reasonably estimate $300 of your electric bill is for lighting and you use 10% of your home for business, enter $30 on line 19 in column (a) and leave line 19 in column (b) blank.

Line 8.—If all of the gross income from your trade or business is from the business use of your home, enter on line 8 the amount from Schedule C, line 29.

If part of the income is from a place of business other than your home, you must first determine the part of your gross income (Schedule C, line 7) from the business use of your home. In making this determination, consider the amount of time you spend at each location as well as other facts. After determining the part of your gross income from the business use of your home, subtract from that amount the total from Schedule C, line 28. Enter the result on line 8 of Form 8829.

Lines 9, 10, and 11.—Enter only the amounts that would be deductible whether or not you used your home for business (i.e., amounts allowable as itemized deductions on **Schedule A** (Form 1040)).

Treat **casualty losses** as personal expenses for this step. Figure the amount to enter on line 9 by completing Form 4684, Section A. When figuring line 17 of Section A, enter 10% of your adjusted gross income excluding the gross income from business use of your home and the deductions attributable to that income. Include on line 9 of Form 8829 the amount from Form 4684, Section A, line 18. See line 27 to deduct part of the casualty losses not allowed because of the limits on Form 4684, Section A.

Do not file or use that Form 4684 to figure the amount of casualty losses to deduct on Schedule A. Instead, complete a separate Form 4684 to deduct the personal portion of your casualty losses.

On line 10, include only **mortgage interest** that would be deductible on Schedule A and that qualifies as a direct or indirect expense. Do not include interest on a mortgage loan that did not benefit your home (e.g., a home equity loan used to pay off credit card bills, to buy a car, or to pay tuition costs).

Line 16.—If the amount of home mortgage interest you deduct on Schedule A is limited, enter the part of the excess mortgage interest that qualifies as a direct or indirect expense. Do not include mortgage interest on a loan that did not benefit your home (explained above).

Line 20.—If you rent rather than own your home, include the rent you paid on line 20, column (b).

Line 23.—If you were unable to deduct all of your 1990 operating expenses due to the limit on the deductible amount, enter on line 23 the amount of operating expenses you are carrying forward to 1991.

Line 27.—Multiply your casualty losses in excess of the amount on line 9 by the business percentage of those losses and enter the result.

Line 29.—If you were unable to deduct all of your 1990 excess casualty losses and depreciation due to the limit on the deductible amount, enter the amount of excess depreciation and casualty losses you are carrying forward to 1991.

Part III

Lines 35 through 37.—Enter on line 35 the cost or other basis of your home, or if less, the fair market value of your home on the date you first used the home for business. **Do not** adjust this amount for depreciation claimed or changes in fair market value after the year you first used your home for business. Allocate this amount between land and building values on lines 36 and 37.

Show on an attached schedule the cost or other basis of additions and improvements placed in service after you began to use your home for business. Do not include any amounts on lines 35 through 38 for these expenditures. Instead, see the instructions for line 40.

Line 39.—If you first used your home for business in 1991, enter the percentage for the month you first used it for business.

Jan.	3.042%	**July**	1.455%
Feb.	2.778%	**Aug.**	1.190%
March	2.513%	**Sept.**	0.926%
April	2.249%	**Oct.**	0.661%
May	1.984%	**Nov.**	0.397%
June	1.720%	**Dec.**	0.132%

If you first used your home for business before 1991 and after 1986, enter 3.175%. If the business use began before 1987 or you stopped using your home for business before the end of the year, see **Pub. 534,** Depreciation, for the percentage to enter.

Line 40.—Include on line 40 depreciation on additions and improvements placed in service after you began using your home for business. See Pub. 534 to figure the amount of depreciation allowed on these expenditures. Attach a schedule showing how you figured depreciation on any additions or improvements. Write "See attached" below the entry space.

Complete and attach **Form 4562,** Depreciation and Amortization, if you first used your home for business in 1991 or you are depreciating additions or improvements placed in service in 1991. If you first used your home for business in 1991, enter on Form 4562, in column (c) of line 14h, the amount from line 38 of Form 8829. Then enter on Form 4562, in column (g) of line 14h, the amount from line 40 of Form 8829.

APPENDIX

GLOSSARY OF TAX TERMS

The words and phrases in this glossary have been defined to reflect their conventional use in the field of taxation. The definitions may therefore be incomplete for other purposes.

A

Accelerated cost recovery system (ACRS). A method in which the cost of tangible property is recovered over a prescribed period of time. Enacted by the Economic Recovery Tax Act (ERTA) of 1981 and substantially modified by the Tax Reform Act (TRA) of 1986 (the modified system is referred to as MACRS), the approach disregards salvage value, imposes a period of cost recovery that depends upon the classification of the asset into one of various recovery periods, and prescribes the applicable percentage of cost that can be deducted each year. § 168.

Accelerated depreciation. Various methods of depreciation that yield larger deductions in the earlier years of the life of an asset than the straight-line method. Examples include the double declining-balance and the sum-of-the-years' digits methods of depreciation. § 167.

Accident and health benefits. Employee fringe benefits provided by employers through the payment of health and accident insurance premiums or the establishment of employer-funded medical reimbursement plans. Employers generally are entitled to a deduction for such payments, whereas employees generally exclude the fringe benefits from gross income. §§ 105 and 106.

Accounting income. The accountant's concept of income is generally based upon the realization principle. Financial accounting income may differ from taxable income (e.g., accelerated depreciation might be used for Federal income tax and straight-line depreciation for financial accounting purposes). Differences are included in a reconciliation of taxable and accounting income on Schedule M–1 of Form 1120 for corporations. Seventy-five percent of the excess of adjusted current earnings over alternative minimum taxable income is an adjustment for alternative minimum tax purposes for a corporation in 1992. See *alternative minimum tax.*

Accounting method. The method under which income and expenses are determined for tax purposes. Major accounting methods are the cash basis and the accrual basis. Special methods are available for the reporting of gain on installment sales, recognition of income on construction projects (the completed contract and percentage of completion methods), and the valuation of inventories (last-in, first-out and first-in, first-out). §§ 446–474. See also *accrual method, cash method, completed contract method, percentage of completion method,* etc.

Accounting period. The period of time, usually a year, used by a taxpayer for the determination of tax liability. Unless a fiscal year is chosen, taxpayers must determine and pay their income tax liability by using the calendar year (January 1 through December 31) as the period of measurement. An example of a fiscal year is July 1 through June 30. A change in accounting periods (e.g., from a calendar year to a fiscal year) generally requires the consent of the IRS. A new taxpayer, such as a newly formed corporation or an estate created upon the death of an individual taxpayer, is free to select either a calendar or a fiscal year without the consent of the IRS. Limitations exist on the accounting period that may be selected by a partnership, an S corporation, and a personal service corporation. §§ 441–444.

Accrual method. A method of accounting that reflects expenses incurred and income earned for any one tax year. In contrast to the cash basis of accounting, expenses do not have to be paid to be deductible nor does income have to be received to be taxable. Unearned income (e.g., prepaid interest and rent) generally is taxed in the year of receipt regardless of the method of accounting used by the taxpayer. § 446(c)(2). See also *accounting method, cash method,* and *unearned income.*

Accumulated earnings tax. A special tax imposed on corporations that accumulate (rather than distribute) their earnings beyond the reasonable needs of the business. The tax is imposed on accumulated taxable income and is imposed in addition to the corporate income tax. §§ 531–537.

ACE adjustment. See *business untaxed reported profits.*

Acquiescence. In agreement with the result reached. The IRS follows a policy of either acquiescing (*A, Acq.*) or nonacquiescing (*NA, Non-Acq.*) in the results reached in the Regular decisions of the U.S. Tax Court.

ACRS. See *accelerated cost recovery system.*

Additional depreciation. The excess of the amount of depreciation actually deducted over the amount that would have been deducted had the straight-line method been used. § 1250(b). See also *Section 1250 recapture.*

Adjusted basis. The cost or other basis of property reduced by depreciation (cost recovery) allowed or allowable and increased by capital improvements. See also *basis* and *realized gain or loss.*

Adjusted gross income. A determination peculiar to individual taxpayers. Generally, it represents gross income less business expenses, expenses attributable to the production of rent or royalty income, the allowed capital loss deduction, and certain personal expenses (deductions *for* adjusted gross income). See also *gross income.* § 62.

Ad valorem tax. A tax imposed on the value of property. The most familiar ad valorem tax is that imposed by states, counties, and cities on real estate. Ad valorem taxes can, however, be imposed upon personal property (e.g., a motor vehicle tax based on the value of an automobile). §§ 164(a)(1) and (2).

Advance payments. In general, prepayments for services or goods are includible in gross income upon receipt of the advance payments (for both accrual and cash basis taxpayers). However, Rev.Proc. 71–21 (1971–2 C.B. 549) provides guidelines for the deferral of tax on certain advance payments providing specific conditions are met.

AFTR. Published by Prentice-Hall, *American Federal Tax Reports* contains all of the Federal tax decisions issued by the U.S. District Courts, U.S. Claims Court, U.S. Courts of Appeals, and U.S. Supreme Court.

AFTR2d. The second series of the *American Federal Tax Reports.*

Alimony payments. Alimony and separate maintenance payments are includible in the gross income of the recipient and are deductible by the payor. The payments must be made in discharge of a legal obligation arising from a marital or family relationship. Child support and voluntary payments are not treated as alimony. Alimony is deductible *for* AGI. §§ 62(10), 71, and 215. See also *child support payments.*

Alimony recapture. The amount of alimony that previously has been included in the gross income of the recipient and deducted by the payor that now is deducted by the recipient and included in the gross income of the payor as the result of front-loading. § 71(f).

All events test. For accrual method taxpayers, income is earned when (1) all the events have occurred that fix the right to receive the income and (2) the amount can be determined with reasonable accuracy. Accrual of income cannot be postponed simply because a portion of the income may have to be returned in a subsequent period. The all events test also is utilized to determine when expenses can be deducted by an accrual basis taxpayer. The application of the test could cause a variation between the treatment of an item for accounting and for tax purposes. For example, a reserve for warranty expense may be properly accruable under generally accepted accounting principles but not be deductible under the Federal income tax law. Because of the application of the all events test, the deduction becomes available in the year the warranty obligation becomes fixed and the amount is determinable with reasonable certainty. Reg. §§ 1.446–1(c)(1)(ii) and 1.461–1(a)(2).

Alternate valuation date. Property passing from a person by reason of death may be valued for death tax purposes as of the date of death or the alternate valuation date. The alternate valuation date is six months from the date of death or the date the property is disposed of by the estate, whichever comes first. To use the alternate valuation date, the executor or administrator of the estate must make an affirmative election. The election of the alternate valuation date is not available unless it decreases both the amount of the gross estate *and* the estate tax liability. §§ 1014(a) and 2032.

Alternative depreciation system. A cost recovery system that produces a smaller deduction than would be calculated under ACRS. The alternative system must be used in certain instances and can be elected in other instances. § 168(g). See also *cost recovery allowance.*

Alternative minimum tax (AMT). The alternative minimum tax is imposed only to the extent it exceeds the regular income tax (in effect, the tax liability is the greater of the tax liability calculated using the AMT rules and that calculated using the regular income tax rules). The AMT rate (24 percent for the individual taxpayer and 20 percent for the corporate taxpayer) is applied to the AMT base. The AMT base is calculated by modifying taxable income for the following: (1) add tax preferences, (2) add certain adjustments, (3) deduct certain adjustments, and (4) deduct the exemption amount. §§ 55–59. See also *business untaxed reported profits.*

Alternative tax. An option that is allowed in computing the tax on net capital gain. The rate is 34 percent of net capital gain for corporations and 28 percent for noncorporate taxpayers. For 1988 through 1990, the alternative tax did not produce a beneficial result. For 1991 and thereafter, the alternative tax can produce beneficial results for the noncorporate taxpayer because the regular tax rates can be as high as 31 percent. §§ 1(h) and 1201. See also *net capital gain.*

Amortization. The allocation (and charge to expense) of the cost or other basis of an intangible asset over the asset's estimated useful life. Intangible assets that have an indefinite life (e.g., goodwill) are not amortizable. Examples of amortizable intangibles include patents, copyrights, and leasehold interests. See also *estimated useful life* and *goodwill.*

Amount realized. The amount received by a taxpayer on the sale or other disposition of property. The measure of the amount realized is the sum of the cash and the fair market value of any property or services received, plus any related debt assumed by the buyer. Determining the amount realized is the starting point for arriving at realized gain or loss. The amount realized is defined in § 1001(b) and the related Regulations. See also *realized gain or loss* and *recognized gain or loss.*

Annuity. A fixed sum payable to a person at specified intervals for a specific period of time or for life. Payments represent a partial return of capital and a return (interest) on the capital investment. Therefore, an exclusion ratio must be used to compute the amount of nontaxable income. The exclusion ratio is used until the annuitant has recovered his or her investment in the annuity contract. Thereafter, all of the annuity payments received are included in gross income. § 72. See also *qualified pension or profit sharing plan.*

Appellate court. For Federal tax purposes, appellate courts include the Courts of Appeals and the Supreme Court. If the party losing in the trial (or lower) court is dissatisfied with the result, the dispute may be carried to the appropriate appellate court. See also *Court of Appeals* and *trial court.*

Arm's length transaction. The standard under which unrelated parties would determine an exchange price for a transaction. Suppose, for example, X Corporation sells property to its sole shareholder for $10,000. In testing whether the $10,000 is an "arm's length" price, one would ascertain the price that would have been negotiated between the corporation and an unrelated party in a bargained exchange.

Asset Depreciation Range system. A system of estimated useful lives for categories of tangible assets prescribed by the IRS. The system provides a range for each category that extends from 20 percent above to 20 percent below the guideline class lives prescribed by the IRS.

Assignment of income. A procedure whereby a taxpayer attempts to avoid the recognition of income by assigning the property that generates the income to another. Such a procedure will not avoid the recognition of income by the taxpayer making the assignment if it can be said that the income was earned at the point of the transfer. In this case, usually referred to as an anticipatory assignment of income, the income will be taxed to the person who earns it.

Association. An organization treated as a corporation for Federal tax purposes even though it may not qualify as such under applicable state law. An entity designated as a trust or a partnership, for example, may be classified as an association if it clearly possesses corporate attributes. Corporate attributes include centralized management, continuity of life, free transferability of interests, and limited liability. § 7701(a)(3).

Attribution. Under certain circumstances, the tax law applies attribution rules to assign to one taxpayer the ownership interest of another taxpayer. If, for example, the stock of X Corporation is held 60 percent by M and 40 percent by S, M may be deemed to own 100 percent of X Corporation if M and S are mother and son. In that case, the stock owned by S is attributed to M. See, for example, §§ 267 and 318.

Audit. Inspection and verification of a taxpayer's return or other transactions possessing tax consequences. See also *correspondence audit, field audit,* and *office audit.*

Automatic mileage method. See *automobile expenses.*

Automobile expenses. Automobile expenses are generally deductible only to the extent the automobile is used in business or for the production of income. Personal commuting expenses are not deductible. The taxpayer may deduct actual expenses (including depreciation and insurance) or the standard (automatic) mileage rate may be used (27.5 cents per mile for 1991 and 28 cents per mile for 1992) during any one year. Automobile expenses incurred for medical purposes or in connection with job-related moving expenses are deductible to the extent of actual out-of-pocket expenses or at the rate of 9 cents per mile (12 cents for charitable activities). See also *transportation expenses.*

B

Bad debts. A deduction is permitted if a business account receivable subsequently becomes partially or completely worthless, providing the income arising from the debt previously was included in income. Available methods are the specific charge-off method and the reserve method. However, except for certain financial institutions, TRA of 1986 repealed the use of the reserve method for 1987 and thereafter. If the reserve method is used, partially or totally worthless accounts are charged to the reserve. A nonbusiness bad debt deduction is allowed as a short-term capital loss if the loan did not arise in connection with the creditor's trade or business activities. Loans between related parties (family members) generally are classified as nonbusiness. § 166. See also *nonbusiness bad debts.*

Basis. The acquisition cost assigned to an asset for income tax purposes. For assets acquired by purchase, the basis is the cost (§ 1012). Special rules govern the basis of property received by virtue of another's death (§ 1014) or by gift (§ 1015), the basis of stock received on a transfer of property to a controlled corporation (§ 358), the basis of the property transferred to the corporation (§ 362), and the basis of property received upon the liquidation of a corporation (§§ 334 and 338). See also *adjusted basis.*

Bonus depreciation. See *Section 179 expensing.*

Book value. The net amount of an asset after reduction by a related reserve. The book value of accounts receivable, for example, is the face amount of the receivables less the reserve for bad debts. The book value of a building is the cost less the accumulated depreciation.

Boot. Cash or property of a type not included in the definition of a nontaxable exchange. The receipt of boot will cause an otherwise nontaxable transfer to become taxable to the extent of the lesser of the fair market value of such boot or the realized gain on the transfer. Examples of nontaxable exchanges that could be partially or completely taxable due to the receipt of boot include transfers to controlled corporations [§ 351(b)] and like-kind exchanges [§ 1031(b)]. See also *realized gain or loss* and *recognized gain or loss.*

Bribes and illegal payments. Section 162 denies a deduction for bribes or kickbacks, fines and penalties paid to a government official or employee for violation of law, and two-thirds of the treble damage payments made to claimants for violation of the antitrust law. Denial of a deduction for bribes and illegal payments is based upon the judicially established principle that allowing such payments would be contrary to public policy.

B.T.A. The Board of Tax Appeals was a trial court that considered Federal tax matters. This court is now the U.S. Tax Court.

Burden of proof. The requirement in a lawsuit to show the weight of evidence and thereby gain a favorable decision. Except in cases of tax fraud, the burden of proof in a tax case generally will be on the taxpayer.

Business energy tax credit. See *energy tax credit—business property.*

Business expenses. See *trade or business expenses.*

Business gifts. Business gifts are deductible only to the extent that each gift does not exceed $25 per person per year. Exceptions are made for gifts costing $4 or less and for certain employee awards. § 274(b).

Business untaxed reported profits. Such profits are a positive adjustment for purposes of the corporate alternative minimum tax. For taxable years beginning after 1989, the amount is 75 percent of the excess of adjusted current earnings over the alternative minimum taxable income (AMTI). §§ 56(c)(1) and (g). See also *alternative minimum tax.*

C

Canons of taxation. Criteria used in the selection of a tax base that were originally discussed by Adam Smith in *The Wealth of Nations.* Canons of taxation include equality, convenience, certainty, and economy.

Capital asset. Broadly speaking, all assets are capital except those specifically excluded by the Code. Major categories of noncapital assets include property held for resale in the normal course of business (inventory), trade accounts and notes receivable, and depreciable property and real estate used in a trade or business (§ 1231 assets). § 1221. See also *capital gain* and *capital loss.*

Capital contributions. Various means by which a shareholder makes additional funds available to the corporation (placed at the risk of the business) without the receipt of additional stock. Such contributions are added to the basis of the shareholder's existing stock investment and do not generate income to the corporation. § 118.

Capital expenditure. An expenditure that should be added to the basis of the property improved. For income tax purposes, this generally precludes a full deduction for the expenditure in the year paid or incurred. Any capital recovery in the form of a tax deduction must come in the form of depreciation. § 263.

Capital gain. The gain from the sale or exchange of a capital asset. See also *capital asset* and *net capital gain.*

Capital gain net income. If the total capital gains for the tax year exceed the total capital losses, the result is capital gain net income. Note that the term does not distinguish between the long-term and short-term gains. § 1222(9). See also *net capital gain.*

Capital gain or loss holding period. The period of time that a capital asset is held by the taxpayer. To qualify for long-term treatment, the asset must be held for more than one year. See also *holding period.*

Capital loss. The loss from the sale or exchange of a capital asset. See also *capital asset.*

Cash basis. See *accounting method* and *cash method.*

Cash equivalent doctrine. Generally, a cash basis taxpayer does not report income until cash is constructively or actually received. Under the cash equivalent doctrine, cash basis taxpayers are required to report income if they receive the equivalent of cash (e.g., property is received) in a taxable transaction.

Cash method. A method of accounting under which the taxpayer generally reports income when cash is collected and reports expenses when cash payments are made. However, for fixed assets, the cash basis taxpayer claims deductions through depreciation or amortization in the same manner as an accrual basis taxpayer. Prepaid expenses must be capitalized and amortized if the life of the asset extends "substantially beyond" the end of the tax year. See also *constructive receipt.*

Casualty loss. A casualty is defined as "the complete or partial destruction of property resulting from an identifiable event of a sudden, unexpected or unusual nature" (e.g., floods, storms, fires, auto accidents). Individuals may deduct a casualty loss only if the loss is incurred in a trade or business or in a transaction entered into for profit or arises from fire, storm, shipwreck, or other casualty or from theft. Individuals usually deduct personal casualty losses as itemized deductions subject to a $100 nondeductible amount and to an annual floor equal to 10 percent of adjusted gross income that applies after the $100 per casualty floor has been applied. Special rules are provided for the netting of certain casualty gains and losses. See also *disaster loss* and *Section 1231 gains and losses.*

C corporation. A corporation that has not elected conduit treatment under § 1361. See also *S corporation status.*

Cert. den. By denying the Writ of Certiorari, the U.S. Supreme Court refuses to accept an appeal from a U.S. Court of Appeals. The denial of certiorari does not, however, mean that the U.S. Supreme Court agrees with the result reached by the lower court.

Certiorari. Appeal from a U.S. Court of Appeals to the U.S. Supreme Court is by Writ of Certiorari. The Supreme Court does not have to accept the appeal and usually does not (*cert. den.*) unless there is a conflict among the lower courts that needs to be resolved or a constitutional issue is involved.

Change in accounting method. A change in the taxpayer's method of accounting (e.g., from FIFO to LIFO) generally requires prior approval from the IRS. Generally, a request must be filed within 180 days after the beginning of the taxable year of the desired change. In some instances, the permission for change will not be granted unless the taxpayer agrees to certain adjustments prescribed by the IRS.

Change in accounting period. A taxpayer must obtain the consent of the IRS before changing his or her tax year. Income for the short period created by the change must be annualized.

Charitable contributions. Contributions are deductible (subject to various restrictions and ceiling limitations) if made to qualified nonprofit charitable organizations. A cash basis taxpayer is entitled to a deduction solely in the year of payment. Accrual basis corporations may accrue contributions at year-end if payment is properly authorized before the end of the year and payment is made within two and one-half months after the end of the year. § 170.

Child and dependent care credit. A tax credit ranging from 20 percent to 30 percent of employment-related expenses (child and dependent care expenses) for amounts of up to $4,800 is available to individuals who are employed (or deemed to be employed) and maintain a household for a dependent child under age 13, disabled spouse, or disabled dependent. § 21.

Child support payments. Payments for child support do not constitute alimony and are therefore not includible in gross income by the recipient or deductible as alimony by the payor. Generally, none of the amounts paid are regarded as child support unless the divorce decree or separation agreement specifically calls for child support payments. However, if the amount of the payment to the former spouse would be reduced upon the happening of a contingency related to a child (e.g., the child attains age 21 or dies), the amount of the future reduction in the payment will be deemed child support for post-1984 agreements and decrees. § 71(c). See also *alimony payments.*

Claim of right doctrine. A judicially imposed doctrine applicable to both cash and accrual basis taxpayers that holds that an amount is includible in income upon actual or constructive receipt if the taxpayer has an unrestricted claim to the payment. For the tax treatment of amounts repaid when previously included in income under the claim of right doctrine, see § 1341.

Claims Court. One of three Federal trial courts that consider Federal tax controversy. Appeal from the U.S. Claims Court (formerly to the U.S. Supreme Court) now goes to the Court of Appeals for the Federal Circuit. See also *trial court.*

Clear reflection of income. The IRS has the authority to redetermine a taxpayer's income using a method that clearly reflects income if the taxpayer's method does not do so. § 446(b).

In addition, the IRS may apportion or allocate income among various related businesses if income is not "clearly reflected." § 482.

Closely held corporation. A corporation where the stock ownership is not widely dispersed. Instead, a few shareholders are in control of corporate policy and are in a position to benefit personally from that policy.

Community property. Louisiana, Texas, New Mexico, Arizona, California, Washington, Idaho, Nevada, and Wisconsin have community property systems. The rest of the states are classified as common law jurisdictions. The difference between common law and community property systems centers around the property rights possessed by married persons. In a common law system, each spouse owns whatever he or she earns. Under a community property system, one-half of the earnings of each spouse is considered owned by the other spouse. Assume, for example, H and W are husband and wife and their only income is the $50,000 annual salary H receives. If they live in New York (a common law state), the $50,000 salary belongs to H. If, however, they live in Texas (a community property state), the $50,000 salary is divided equally, in terms of ownership, between H and W. See also *separate property*.

Completed contract method. A method of reporting gain or loss on certain long-term contracts. Under this method of accounting, gross income and expenses are recognized in the tax year in which the contract is completed. Reg. § 1.451–3. Limitations exist on a taxpayer's ability to use the completed contract method. § 460. See also *percentage of completion method*.

Component depreciation. The process of dividing an asset (e.g., a building) into separate components or parts for the purpose of calculating depreciation. The advantage of dividing an asset into components is to use shorter depreciation lives for selected components under § 167. Generally, the same cost recovery period must be used for all the components of an asset under § 168.

Condemnation. The taking of property by a public authority. The property is condemned as the result of legal action, and the owner is compensated by the public authority. The power to condemn property is known as the right of eminent domain.

Conduit concept. An approach assumed by the tax law in the treatment of certain entities and their owners. Specific tax characteristics pass through the entity without losing their identity. For example, items of income and expense, capital gains and losses, tax credits, etc., realized by a partnership pass through the partnership (a conduit) and are subject to taxation at the partner level. Also, in an S corporation, certain items pass through and are reported on the returns of the shareholders.

Constructive ownership. See *attribution*.

Constructive receipt. If income is unqualifiedly available, it will be subject to the income tax even though it is not physically in the taxpayer's possession. An example is accrued interest on a savings account. Under the constructive receipt of income concept, the interest will be taxed to a depositor in the year it is available rather than the year actually withdrawn. The fact that the depositor uses the cash basis of accounting for tax purposes is irrelevant. See Reg. § 1.451–2.

Consumer interest. Interest expense of the taxpayer of a personal nature (not trade or business interest, investment interest, qualified residence interest, or passive activity interest). TRA of 1986 provided that no deduction is permitted for consumer interest. However, the provision was not fully effective until 1991. § 163(h). See also *qualified residence interest*.

Contributions to the capital of a corporation. See *capital contributions*.

Convention expenses. Travel expenses incurred in attending a convention are deductible if the meetings are related to a taxpayer's trade or business or job-related activities. If, however, the convention trip is primarily for pleasure, no deduction is permitted for transportation expenses. Likewise, if the expenses are for attending a convention related to the production of income (§ 212), no deduction is permitted. Specific limitations are provided for foreign convention expenses. See § 274(n) for the limitations on the deductions for meals. § 274(h).

Correspondence audit. An audit conducted by the IRS by mail. Typically, the IRS writes to the taxpayer requesting the verification of a particular deduction, exemption, or credit. The completion of a special form or the remittance of copies of records or other support is all that is requested of the taxpayer. To be distinguished from a *field audit* or an *office audit*.

Cost recovery allowance. The portion of the cost of an asset written off under ACRS (or MACRS), which replaced the depreciation system as a method for writing off the cost of an asset for most assets placed in service after 1980 (after 1986 for MACRS). § 168. See also *alternative depreciation system*.

Cost recovery period. A period specified in the Code for writing off the cost of an asset under ACRS or MACRS.

Court of Appeals. Any of 13 Federal courts that consider tax matters appealed from the U.S. Tax Court, U.S. Claims Court, or a U.S. District Court. Appeal from a U.S. Court of Appeals is to the U.S. Supreme Court by Writ of Certiorari. See also *appellate court*.

D

Death benefit. A payment made by an employer to the beneficiary or beneficiaries of a deceased employee on account of the death of the employee. Under certain conditions, the first $5,000 of the payment is exempt from the income tax. § 101(b)(1).

Death tax. See *estate tax*.

Declaration of estimated tax. A procedure whereby individuals and corporations are required to make quarterly installment payments of estimated tax. Individuals are required to make the declaration and file quarterly payments of the estimated tax if certain requirements are met. In 1992, a declaration is not required for an individual whose estimated tax is reasonably expected to be less than $500.

Deductions for adjusted gross income. See *adjusted gross income*.

Deductions from adjusted gross income. See *itemized deductions*.

Deferred compensation. Compensation that will be taxed when received or upon the removal of certain restrictions on receipt and not when earned. Contributions by an employer to a qualified pension or profit sharing plan on behalf of an employee are an example. The contributions will not be taxed to the employee until the funds are made available or distributed to the employee (e.g., upon retirement). See also *qualified pension or profit sharing plan*.

Deficiency. Additional tax liability owed by a taxpayer and assessed by the IRS. See also *statutory notice of deficiency*.

Dependency deduction. See *personal and dependency exemptions*.

Depletion. The process by which the cost or other basis of a natural resource (e.g., an oil or gas interest) is recovered upon extraction and sale of the resource. The two ways to determine the depletion allowance are the cost and percentage (or statutory) methods. Under the cost method, each unit of production sold is assigned a portion of the cost or other basis of the interest. This is determined by dividing the cost or other basis by the total units expected to be recovered. Under the percentage (or statutory) method, the tax law provides a special percentage factor for different types of minerals and other natural resources. This percentage is multiplied by the gross income from the interest to arrive at the depletion allowance. §§ 613 and 613A.

Depreciation. The deduction of the cost or other basis of a tangible asset over the asset's estimated useful life. § 167. For intangible assets, see *amortization*. For natural resources, see *depletion*. Also see *estimated useful life*. The depreciation system was replaced by ACRS for most assets placed in service after 1980 but still applies for assets placed in service before 1981. See also *recapture of depreciation*.

Determination letter. Upon the request of a taxpayer, a District Director will comment on the tax status of a completed transaction. Determination letters are most frequently used to clarify employee versus self-employed status, to determine whether a pension or profit sharing plan qualifies under the Code, and to determine the tax-exempt status of certain nonprofit organizations.

Direct charge-off method. See *specific charge-off method*.

Disabled access credit. A tax credit whose purpose is to encourage small businesses to make their businesses more accessible to disabled individuals. The credit is equal to 50 percent of the eligible expenditures that exceed $250 but do not exceed $10,250. Thus, the maximum amount for the credit is $5,000. The adjusted basis for depreciation is reduced by the amount of the credit. § 44. See also *general business credit*.

Disaster loss. A casualty sustained in an area designated as a disaster area by the President of the United States. In such an event, the disaster loss may be treated as having occurred in the taxable year immediately preceding the year in which the disaster actually occurred. Thus, immediate tax benefits are provided to victims of a disaster. § 165(i). See also *casualty loss*.

Dissent. To disagree with the majority. If, for example, Judge B disagrees with the result reached by Judges C and D (all of whom are members of the same court), Judge B could issue a dissenting opinion.

District Court. A Federal District Court is a trial court for purposes of litigating (among others) Federal tax matters. It is the only trial court where a jury trial can be obtained. See also *trial court*.

Dividends received deduction. A deduction allowed a corporate shareholder for dividends received from a domestic corporation. The percentage applied in calculating the dividends received deduction varies according to the percentage of stock ownership. If the stock ownership percentage is less than 20 percent, the percentage is 70 percent of the dividends received. If the stock ownership percentage is at least 20 percent but less than 80 percent, the percentage is 80 percent. If the stock ownership percentage is at least 80 percent, the percentage is 100 percent. §§ 243–246A.

E

Earned income. Income from personal services as distinguished from income generated by property. See §§ 32 and 911 and the related Regulations.

Earned income credit. A tax credit whose purpose is to provide assistance to certain low-income individuals who have a qualifying child. This refundable credit consists of three components: basic earned income credit, supplemental young child credit, and supplemental health insurance credit. For each component, the earned income (subject to a statutory ceiling of $7,520 for 1992) is multiplied by a statutory rate (which varies depending on whether the taxpayer has only one qualifying child or more than one qualifying child). For 1992, once the earned income exceeds $11,840, the credit is phased out using a phase-out rate that is also dependent on the number of qualifying children. § 32.

Earnings and profits. A tax concept peculiar to corporate taxpayers that measures economic capacity to make a distribution to shareholders that is not a return of capital. Such a distribution will result in dividend income to the shareholders to the extent of the corporation's current and accumulated earnings and profits.

Education expenses. Employees may deduct education expenses if such items are incurred either (1) to maintain or improve existing job-related skills or (2) to meet the express requirements of the employer or the requirements imposed by law to retain employment status. The expenses are not deductible if the education is required to meet the minimum educational standards for the taxpayer's job or if the education qualifies the individual for a new trade or business. Reg. § 1.162–5.

Employee expenses. The deductions *for* adjusted gross income include reimbursed expenses and certain expenses of performing artists. All other employee expenses are deductible *from* adjusted gross income. § 62. See also *trade or business expenses*.

Energy tax credit—business property. A 10 percent tax credit is available to businesses that invest in certain energy property. The purpose of the credit is to create incentives for conservation and to penalize the increased use of oil and gas. The business energy tax credit applies to equipment with an estimated useful life of at least three years that uses fuel or feedstock other than oil or natural gas (e.g., solar, wind). §§ 46(2) and 48(a). See also *estimated useful life* and *investment tax credit*.

Entertainment expenses. These expenses are deductible only if they are directly related to or associated with a trade or business. Various restrictions and documentation requirements have been imposed upon the deductibility of entertainment expenses to prevent abuses by taxpayers. See, for example, the provision contained in § 274(n) that disallows 20 percent of entertainment expenses. § 274.

Estate tax. A tax imposed on the right to transfer property by reason of death. Thus, an estate tax is levied on the decedent's estate and not on the heir receiving the property. §§ 2001 and 2002.

Estimated useful life. The period over which an asset will be used by a particular taxpayer. Although the period cannot be longer than the estimated physical life of an asset, it could be shorter if the taxpayer does not intend to keep the asset until it wears out. Assets such as goodwill do not have an estimated useful life. The estimated useful life of an asset is essential to measuring the annual tax deduction for depreciation and amortization. An asset subject to ACRS or MACRS is written off over a specified cost recovery period rather than over its estimated useful life.

Excise tax. A tax on the manufacture, sale, or use of goods or on the carrying on of an occupation or activity. Also a tax on the transfer of property. Thus, the Federal estate and gift taxes are, theoretically, excise taxes.

F

Fair market value. The amount at which property would change hands between a willing buyer and a willing seller, neither being under any compulsion to buy or sell and both having reasonable knowledge of the relevant facts. Reg. § 20.2031–1(b).

F.2d. An abbreviation for the Second Series of the *Federal Reporter*, the official series where decisions of the U.S. Claims Court (before October 1982) and the U.S. Courts of Appeals are published.

F.Supp. The abbreviation for the *Federal Supplement*, the official series where the reported decisions of the U.S. District Courts are published.

Field audit. An audit by the IRS conducted on the business premises of the taxpayer or in the office of the tax practitioner representing the taxpayer. To be distinguished from a *correspondence audit* or an *office audit*.

First-in, first-out (FIFO). An accounting method for determining the cost of inventories. Under this method, the inventory on hand is deemed to be the sum of the cost of the most recently acquired units. See also *last-in, first-out (LIFO)*.

Foreign earned income exclusion. The foreign earned income exclusion is a relief provision that applies to U.S. citizens working in a foreign country. To qualify for the exclusion, the taxpayer must be either a bona fide resident of the foreign country or present in the country for 330 days during any 12 consecutive months. The exclusion is limited to $70,000. § 911.

Foreign tax credit or deduction. Both individual taxpayers and corporations may claim a foreign tax credit on income earned and subject to tax in a foreign country or U.S. possession. As an alternative to the credit, a deduction may be taken for the foreign taxes paid. §§ 27, 164, and 901–905.

Franchise. An agreement that gives the transferee the right to distribute, sell, or provide goods, services, or facilities within a specified area. The cost of obtaining a franchise may be amortized over the life of the agreement. In general, a franchise is a capital asset and results in capital gain or loss if all significant powers, rights, or continuing interests are transferred pursuant to the sale of a franchise. § 1253.

Fringe benefits. Compensation or other benefits received by an employee that are not in the form of cash. Some fringe benefits (e.g., accident and health plans, group term life insurance) may be excluded from the employee's gross income and therefore are not subject to the Federal income tax.

Fruit and the tree doctrine. The courts have held that an individual who earns income from property or services cannot assign that income to another. For example, a father cannot assign his earnings from commissions to his child and escape income tax on those amounts.

G

General business credit. The summation of the following nonrefundable business credits: investment tax credit, jobs credit, alchohol fuels credit, research activities credit, low-income housing credit, and disabled access credit. The amount of general business credit that can be used to reduce the tax liability is limited to the taxpayer's net income tax reduced by the greater of (1) the tentative minimum tax or (2) 25 percent of the net regular tax liability that exceeds $25,000. Unused general business credits can be carried back 3 years and forward 15 years. § 38.

Gift. A transfer of property for less than adequate consideration. Gifts usually occur in a personal setting (such as between members of the same family). Gifts are excluded from the income tax but may be subject to the *gift tax*.

Gift tax. A tax imposed on the transfer of property by gift. The tax is imposed upon the donor of a gift and is based upon the fair market value of the property on the date of the gift. §§ 2501–2524.

Goodwill. The ability of a business to generate income in excess of a normal rate on assets due to superior managerial skills, market position, new product technology, etc. In the purchase of a business, goodwill represents the difference between the purchase price and the value of the net assets acquired. Goodwill is an intangible asset that possesses an indefinite life and therefore cannot be amortized for Federal income tax purposes. Reg. § 1.167(a)–3. See also *amortization*.

Government bonds issued at a discount. Certain U.S. government bonds (Series E and EE) are issued at a discount and do not pay interest during the life of the bonds. Instead, the bonds are redeemable at increasing fixed amounts. Thus, the difference between the purchase price and the amount received upon redemption represents interest income to the holder. A cash basis taxpayer may defer recognition of gross income until the bonds are redeemed. For Series EE savings bonds issued after 1989, the interest otherwise taxable at redemption can be excluded if the bonds are qualified educational savings bonds. As an alternative to deferring recognition of gross income until the bonds are redeemed, the taxpayer may elect to include in gross income on an annual basis the annual increase in the value of the bonds. § 454.

Gross income. Income subject to the Federal income tax. Gross income does not include income for which the Code permits exclusion treatment (e.g., interest on municipal bonds). For a manufacturing or merchandising business, gross income means gross profit (gross sales or gross receipts less cost of goods sold). § 61 and Reg. § 1.61–3(a).

Group term life insurance. Life insurance coverage permitted by an employer for a group of employees. Such insurance is renewable on a year-to-year basis and does not accumulate in value (i.e., no cash surrender value is built up). The premiums paid by the employer on the insurance are not taxed to an employee on coverage of up to $50,000 per person. § 79 and Reg. § 1.79–1(a).

H

Head of household. An unmarried individual who maintains a household for another and satisfies certain conditions set forth in § 2(b). Such status enables the taxpayer to use a set of income tax rates [see § 1(b)] that are lower than those applicable to other unmarried individuals [§ 1(c)] but higher than those applicable to surviving spouses and married persons filing a joint return [§ 1(a)]. See also *tax rate schedules.*

Hobby loss. A nondeductible loss arising from a personal hobby as contrasted with an activity engaged in for profit. Generally, the law provides a rebuttable presumption that an activity is engaged in for profit if profits are earned during any three or more years during a five-year period. § 183. See also *vacation home.*

Holding period. The period of time property has been held for income tax purposes. The holding period is crucial in determining whether gain or loss from the sale or exchange of a capital asset is long term or short term. See also *capital gain or loss holding period.* § 1223.

Home office expenses. See *office-in-the-home expenses.*

H.R. 10 plan. See *self-employment retirement plan.*

I

Imputed interest. For certain long-term sales of property, the IRS can convert some of the gain from the sale into interest income if the contract does not provide for a minimum rate of interest to be paid by the purchaser. The application of this procedure has the effect of forcing the seller to recognize less long-term capital gain and more ordinary income (interest income). §§ 483 and 1274 and the Regulations thereunder. In addition, interest income and interest expense are imputed (deemed to exist) on interest-free or below-market rate loans between certain related parties. See also *interest-free loans.* § 7872.

Individual retirement account (IRA). Individuals with earned income who are not active participants in qualified retirement plans are permitted to set aside up to 100 percent of their salary per year (generally not to exceed $2,000 or $2,250 for a spousal IRA) for a retirement account. The amount set aside can be deducted by the taxpayer and will be subject to income tax only upon withdrawal. Specific requirements are established for the withdrawal of such funds, and penalties are provided for failure to comply. If the employee is an active participant in a qualified retirement plan, the IRA deduction is phased out once adjusted gross income exceeds certain amounts. Even if the IRA deduction has been completely phased out, the taxpayer can still make a nondeductible contribution. § 219. See also *simplified employee pensions.*

Installment method. A method of accounting enabling a taxpayer to spread the recognition of gain on the sale of property over the payout period. Under this procedure, the seller computes the gross profit percentage from the sale (the gain divided by the contract price) and applies it to each payment received to arrive at the gain to be recognized. §§ 453 and 453A.

Intangible drilling and development costs. Taxpayers may elect to expense or capitalize (subject to amortization) intangible drilling and development costs. However, ordinary income recapture provisions apply to oil and gas properties on a sale or other disposition if the expense method is elected. §§ 263(c) and 1254(a).

Interest-free loans. Bona fide loans that carry no interest (or a below-market rate). If made in a nonbusiness setting, the imputed interest element is treated as a gift from the lender to the borrower. If made by a corporation to a shareholder, a constructive dividend could result. In either event, the lender may have interest income to recognize, and the borrower may be able to deduct interest expense. § 7872.

Investigation of a new business. Expenditures by taxpayers who are not engaged in a trade or business incurred in the evaluation of prospective business activities (acquiring an existing business or entering into a new trade or business). If the expenditures are general, it is the position of the IRS that no deduction is permitted even if the investigation is abandoned because the taxpayer is not engaged in a trade or business. The courts, however, have permitted a loss deduction providing the expenditures were specific.

Investment indebtedness. If funds are borrowed by noncorporate taxpayers for the purpose of purchasing or continuing to hold investment property, some portion of the interest expense deduction may be disallowed. The interest deduction is generally limited to net investment income. Amounts that are disallowed may be carried forward and treated as investment interest of the succeeding year. Prior to 1991, the net investment income ceiling was increased by a statutory dollar amount that was being phased out (i.e., the phase-out was complete in 1991). § 163(d).

Investment tax credit. A tax credit that usually was equal to 10 percent (unless a reduced credit was elected) of the qualified investment in tangible personalty used in a trade or business. If the tangible personalty had a recovery period of five years or more, the full cost of the property qualified for the credit. Only 60 percent of cost qualified for property with a recovery period of three years. However, the regular investment tax credit was repealed by TRA of 1986 for property placed in service after December 31, 1985. §§ 46–48. See also *recapture of investment tax credit, general business credit,* and *Section 38 property.*

Involuntary conversion. The loss or destruction of property through theft, casualty, or condemnation. Any gain realized on an involuntary conversion can, at the taxpayer's election, be postponed (deferred) for Federal income tax purposes if the owner reinvests the proceeds within a prescribed period of time in property that is similar or related in service or use. § 1033.

IRA. See *individual retirement account.*

Itemized deductions. Certain personal expenditures allowed by the Code as deductions *from* adjusted gross income. Examples include certain medical expenses, interest on home mortgages, and charitable contributions. Itemized deductions are reported on Schedule A of Form 1040. Certain miscellaneous itemized deductions are reduced by 2 percent of the taxpayer's adjusted gross income. In addition, a taxpayer whose adjusted gross income exceeds $100,000 ($50,000 for married filing separately) must reduce the itemized deductions by 3 percent of the excess of adjusted gross income over $100,000. For 1992, the indexed amount for the $100,000 is $105,250 and the indexed amount for the $50,000 is $52,625. Medical, casualty and theft, and investment interest deductions are not subject to the 3 percent reduction. The 3 percent reduction may not reduce itemized deductions that are subject to the reduction to below 20 percent of their initial amount. §§ 63(d), 67, and 68.

J

Jobs credit. Employers are allowed a tax credit equal to 40 percent of the first $6,000 of wages (per eligible employee) for the first year of employment. Eligible employees include certain hard-to-employ individuals (e.g., youths from low-income families, handicapped persons). The employer's deduction for wages is reduced by the amount of the credit taken. For qualified summer youth employees, the 40 percent rate is applied to the first $3,000 of qualified wages. §§ 51 and 52.

K

Keogh plan. See *self-employment retirement plan.*

L

Last-in, first-out (LIFO). An accounting method for valuing inventories for tax purposes. Under this method, it is assumed that the inventory on hand is valued at the cost of the earliest acquired units. § 472 and the related Regulations. See also *first-in, first-out (FIFO).*

Lessee. One who rents property from another. In the case of real estate, the lessee is also known as the tenant.

Lessor. One who rents property to another. In the case of real estate, the lessor is also known as the landlord.

Life insurance proceeds. Generally, life insurance proceeds paid to a beneficiary upon the death of the insured are exempt from Federal income tax. An exception is provided when a life insurance contract has been transferred for valuable consideration to another individual who assumes ownership rights. In that case, the proceeds are income to the assignee to the extent that the proceeds exceed the amount paid for the policy plus any subsequent premiums paid. Insurance proceeds may be subject to the Federal estate tax if the decedent retained any incidents of ownership in the policy before death or if the proceeds are payable to the decedent's estate. §§ 101 and 2042.

Like-kind exchange. An exchange of property held for productive use in a trade or business or for investment (except inventory, stocks and bonds, and partnership interests) for other investment or trade or business property. Unless non-like-kind property is received (boot), the exchange will be nontaxable. § 1031. See also *boot.*

Limited expensing. See *Section 179 expensing.*

Liquidation of a corporation. In a complete or partial liquidation of a corporation, amounts received by the shareholders in exchange for their stock are usually treated as a sale or exchange of the stock resulting in capital gain or loss treatment. § 331. Special rules apply to the liquidation of a subsidiary under § 332. Generally, a liquidation is a taxable event to the corporation. § 336. Special rules apply to a parent corporation that is liquidating a subsidiary. § 337.

Low-income housing. Low-income housing is rental housing that is a dwelling unit for low- or moderate-income individuals or families. Beneficial tax treatment is in the form of the *low-income housing credit.* § 42. See also *accelerated cost recovery system.*

Low-income housing credit. Beneficial treatment to owners of low-income housing is provided in the form of a tax credit. The calculated credit is claimed in the year the building is placed in service and in the following nine years. § 42. See also *general business credit.*

Lump-sum distribution. Payment of the entire amount due at one time rather than in installments. Such distributions often occur from qualified pension or profit sharing plans upon the retirement or death of a covered employee. The recipient of a lump-sum distribution may recognize both long-term capital gain and ordinary income upon the receipt of the distribution. The ordinary income portion may be subject to a special five-year or ten-year income averaging provision. § 402(e).

M

MACRS. See *accelerated cost recovery system (ACRS).*

Majority interest partners. Partners who have more than a 50 percent interest in partnership profits and capital, counting only those partners who have the same taxable year, are referred to as majority interest partners. The term is of significance in determining the appropriate taxable year of a partnership. § 706(b). See also *accounting period* and *principal partner.*

Marital deduction. A deduction allowed upon the transfer of property from one spouse to another. The deduction is allowed under the Federal gift tax for lifetime (inter vivos) transfers or under the Federal estate tax for death (testamentary) transfers. §§ 2056 and 2523.

Medical expenses. Medical expenses of an individual, spouse, and dependents are allowed as an itemized deduction to the extent that such amounts (less insurance reimbursements) exceed 7.5 percent of adjusted gross income. § 213.

Mitigation of the annual accounting period concept. Various tax provisions that provide relief from the effect of the finality of the annual accounting period concept. For example, the *net operating loss* provisions provide relief to a taxpayer whose business profits and losses for different taxable years fluctuate. See also *accounting period.*

Moving expenses. A deduction *from* AGI is permitted to employees and self-employed individuals provided certain tests are met. The taxpayer's new job must be at least 35 miles farther from the old residence than the old residence was from the former place of work. In addition, an employee must be employed on a full-time basis at the new location for 39 weeks in the 12-month period following the move. Ceiling limitations are placed on indirect expenses (e.g., house-hunting trips and temporary living expenses), but no ceiling exists for direct moving expenses (e.g., expenses of moving personal belongings and traveling). § 217.

N

Necessary. Appropriate and helpful in furthering the taxpayer's business or income-producing activity. §§ 162(a) and 212. See also *ordinary.*

Net capital gain. The excess of the net long-term capital gain for the tax year over the net short-term capital loss. § 1222(11). See also *alternative tax.*

Net operating loss. To mitigate the effect of the annual accounting period concept, § 172 allows taxpayers to use an excess loss of one year as a deduction for certain past or future years. In this regard, a carryback period of 3 years and a carryforward period of 15 years are allowed. See also *mitigation of the annual accounting period concept.*

Net worth method. An approach used by the IRS to reconstruct the income of a taxpayer who fails to maintain adequate records. Under this approach, the gross income for the year is the increase in net worth of the taxpayer (assets in excess of liabilities) with appropriate adjustment for nontaxable receipts and nondeductible expenditures. The net worth method often is used when tax fraud is suspected.

Ninety-day letter. See *statutory notice of deficiency.*

Nonbusiness bad debts. A bad debt loss not incurred in connection with a creditor's trade or business. The loss is deductible as a short-term capital loss and will be allowed only in the year the debt becomes entirely worthless. In addition to family loans, many investor losses fall into the classification of nonbusiness bad debts. § 166(d). See also *bad debts.*

Nonqualified deferred compensation plans. Compensation arrangements that are frequently offered to executives. Such plans may include stock options, restricted stock, etc. Often, an executive may defer the recognition of taxable income. The employer, however, does not receive a tax deduction until the employee is required to include the compensation in income. See also *restricted property.*

Nonrecourse debt. An obligation on which the endorser is not personally liable. An example of a nonrecourse debt is a mortgage on real estate acquired by a partnership without the assumption of any liability on the mortgage by the partnership or any of the partners. The acquired property generally is pledged as collateral for the loan.

O

Office audit. An audit by the IRS of a taxpayer's return that is conducted in the agent's office. To be distinguished from a *correspondence audit* or a *field audit.*

Office-in-the-home expenses. Employment and business-related expenses attributable to the use of a residence (e.g., den or office) are allowed only if the portion of the residence is exclusively used on a regular basis as a principal place of business of the taxpayer or as a place of business that is used by patients, clients, or customers. If the expenses are incurred by an employee, the use must be for the convenience of the employer as opposed to being merely appropriate and helpful. § 280A.

Open transaction. A judicially imposed doctrine that allows the taxpayer to defer all gain until he or she has collected an amount equal to the adjusted basis of assets transferred pursuant to an exchange transaction. This doctrine has been applied where the property received in an exchange has no ascertainable fair market value due to the existence of contingencies. The method is permitted only in very limited circumstances. See also *recovery of capital doctrine.*

Options. The sale or exchange of an option to buy or sell property results in capital gain or loss if the property is a capital asset. Generally, the closing of an option transaction results in short-term capital gain or loss to the writer of the call and the purchaser of the call option. § 1234.

Ordinary. Common and accepted in the general industry or type of activity in which the taxpayer is engaged. It comprises one of the tests for the deductibility of expenses incurred or paid in connection with a trade or business; for the production or collection of income; for the management, conservation, or maintenance of property held for the production of income; or in connection with the determination, collection, or refund of any tax. §§ 162(a) and 212. See also *necessary.*

Organizational expenses. A corporation may elect to amortize organizational expenses over a period of 60 months or more. Certain expenses of organizing a company do not qualify for amortization (e.g., expenditures connected with issuing or selling stock or other securities). § 248.

Outside salesperson. An outside salesperson solicits business away from the employer's place of business on a full-time basis. The employment-related expenses of an outside salesperson are itemized deductions unless reimbursed by the employer. If reimbursed, such expenses are deductible *for* AGI.

P

Partnerships. A partnership is treated as a conduit and is not subject to taxation. Various items of partnership income, expenses, gains, and losses flow through to the individual partners and are reported on the partners' personal income tax returns.

Passive activity. A trade or business activity in which the taxpayer does not materially participate is subject to limitations on the deduction of losses and credits. Rental activities and limited partnership interests are inherently passive. However, relief from passive activity limitation treatment is provided for certain rental real estate if the taxpayer actively participates in the activity. The annual ceiling on the relief is $25,000. § 469. See also *portfolio income.*

Passive investment income. As defined in § 1362(d)(3)(D), passive investment income means gross receipts from royalties, certain rents, dividends, interest, annuities, and gains from the sale or exchange of stock and securities. Revocation of the S corporation election may occur in certain cases when the S corporation has passive investment income in excess of 25 percent of gross receipts for a period of three consecutive years.

Passive loss. Any loss from (1) activities in which the taxpayer does not materially participate, (2) rental activities, or (3) tax shelter activities. Net passive losses cannot be used to offset income from nonpassive sources. Rather, they are suspended until the taxpayer either generates net passive income (and a deduction of the losses is allowed) or disposes of the underlying property (at which time the loss deductions are allowed in full). Landlords who actively participate in the rental activities can deduct up to $25,000 of passive losses annually. However, this amount is phased out when the landlord's AGI exceeds $100,000. Passive loss limitations were phased in beginning in 1987 and were not fully effective until 1991. See also *portfolio income.*

Patent. A patent is an intangible asset that may be amortized over the asset's remaining life. The sale of a patent usually results in favorable long-term capital gain treatment. § 1235.

Percentage of completion method. A method of reporting gain or loss on certain long-term contracts. Under this method of accounting, the gross contract price is included in income as the contract is being completed. § 460 and Reg. § 1.451–3. See also *completed contract method.*

Personal and dependency exemptions. The tax law provides an exemption for each individual taxpayer and an additional exemption for the taxpayer's spouse if a joint return is filed. An individual may also claim a dependency exemption for each dependent, provided certain tests are met. The amount of the personal and dependency exemptions is $2,150 in 1991 and $2,300 in 1992. The $2,150 ($2,300) amount is indexed for inflation. The exemption is subject to phase-out once adjusted gross income exceeds certain statutory threshold amounts. § 151.

Personal expenses. Expenses of an individual for personal reasons that are not deductible unless specifically provided for under the tax law. § 262.

Personal property. Generally, all property other than real estate. It is sometimes referred to as personalty when real estate is termed realty. Personal property also can refer to property that is not used in a taxpayer's trade or business or held for the production or collection of income. When used in this sense, personal property can include both realty (e.g., a personal residence) and personalty (e.g., personal effects such as clothing and furniture).

Personal residence. The sale of a personal residence generally results in the recognition of capital gain (but not loss). However, the gain may be deferred if the adjusted sales price of the old residence is reinvested in the purchase of a new residence within certain prescribed time periods. Also, taxpayers age 55 or older may exclude $125,000 of the gain from tax, provided certain requirements are met. §§ 1034 and 121.

Personalty. All property other than realty (real estate). Personalty usually is categorized as tangible or intangible property. Tangible personalty includes such assets as machinery and equipment, automobiles and trucks, and office equipment. Intangible personalty includes stocks and bonds, goodwill, patents, trademarks, and copyrights.

Points. Loan origination fees that may be deductible as interest by a buyer of property. A seller of property who pays points is required to reduce the selling price and therefore does not receive an interest deduction. See *prepaid interest* for the timing of the interest deduction.

Pollution control facilities. A certified pollution control facility, the cost of which may be amortized over a 60-month period if the taxpayer elects. § 169.

Portfolio income. The term is relevant in applying the limitation on passive activity losses and credits. Although normally considered passive in nature, for this purpose portfolio income is treated as nonpassive. Therefore, net passive losses and credits cannot be offset against portfolio income. Examples of portfolio income are interest, dividends, annuities, and certain royalties. § 469. See also *passive activity.*

Prepaid expenses. Cash basis as well as accrual basis taxpayers usually are required to capitalize prepayments for rent, insurance, etc., that cover more than one year. Deductions are taken during the period the benefits are received.

Prepaid interest. In effect, the Code places cash basis taxpayers on an accrual basis for purposes of recognizing a deduction for prepaid interest. Thus, interest paid in advance is deductible as an interest expense only as it accrues. The one exception to this rule involves the interest element when a cash basis taxpayer pays points to obtain financing for the purchase of a principal residence (or to make improvements thereto) if the payment of points is an established business practice in the area in which the indebtedness is incurred and the amount involved is not excessive. § 461(g). See also *points.*

Principal partner. A partner with a 5 percent or greater interest in partnership capital or profits. § 706(b)(3). See also *majority interest partners.*

Prizes and awards. The fair market value of a prize or award generally is includible in gross income. However, exclusion is permitted if the prize or award is made in recognition of religious, charitable, scientific, educational, artistic, literary, or civic achievement, and the recipient transfers the award to a qualified governmental unit or a nonprofit organization. In that case, the recipient must be selected without any action on his or her part to enter a contest or proceeding, and the recipient must not be required to render substantial future services as a condition of receiving the prize or award. § 74.

Public policy limitation. See *bribes and illegal payments.*

Q

Qualified pension or profit sharing plan. An employer-sponsored plan that meets the requirements of § 401. If these requirements are met, none of the employer's contributions to the plan will be taxed to the employee until distributed to him or her (§ 402). The employer will be allowed a deduction in the year the contributions are made (§ 404). See also *annuity* and *deferred compensation.*

Qualified residence interest. A term relevant in determining the amount of interest expense the individual taxpayer may deduct as an itemized deduction for what otherwise would be disallowed as a component of personal interest (consumer interest). Qualified residence interest consists of interest paid on qualified residences (principal residence and one other residence) of the taxpayer. Debt that qualifies as qualified residence interest is limited to $1 million of debt to acquire, construct, or substantially improve qualified residences (acquisition indebtedness) plus $100,000 of other debt secured by qualified residences (home equity indebtedness). The home equity indebtedness may not exceed the fair market value of a qualified residence reduced by the acquisition indebtedness for that residence. § 163(h)(3). See also *consumer interest.*

R

RAR. A revenue agent's report, which reflects any adjustments made by the agent as a result of an audit of the taxpayer. The RAR is mailed to the taxpayer along with the 30-day letter, which outlines the appellate procedures available to the taxpayer.

Realized gain or loss. The difference between the amount realized upon the sale or other disposition of property and the adjusted basis of the property. § 1001. See also *adjusted basis* and *recognized gain or loss.*

Realty. All real estate, including land and buildings. Permanent improvements to a building (fixtures) become realty if their removal would cause significant damage to the property. An example of a fixture is the installation of a central air conditioning or heating system to a building. Thus, personalty can become realty through the fixture reclassification.

Reasonable needs of the business. See *accumulated earnings tax.*

Recapture. To recover the tax benefit of a deduction or a credit previously taken.

Recapture of depreciation. Upon the disposition of depreciable property used in a trade or business, gain or loss is determined measured by the difference between the consideration received (the amount realized) and the adjusted basis of the property. Before the enactment of the recapture of depreciation provisions of the Code, any such gain recognized could be § 1231 gain and usually qualified for long-term capital gain treatment. The recapture provisions of the Code (e.g., §§ 1245 and 1250) may operate to convert some or all of the previous § 1231 gain into ordinary income. The justification for recapture of depreciation is that it prevents a taxpayer from deducting depreciation at ordinary income rates and having the related gain on disposition taxed at capital gain rates. The recapture of depreciation rules do not apply when the property is disposed of at a loss. See also *residential rental property, Section 1231 gains and losses, Section 1245 recapture,* and *Section 1250 recapture.*

Recapture of investment tax credit. When investment tax credit property is disposed of or ceases to be used in the trade or business of the taxpayer, some or all of the investment tax credit claimed on the property may be recaptured as additional tax liability. The amount of the recapture is the difference between the amount of the credit originally claimed and what should have been claimed in light of the length of time the property was actually held or used for qualifying purposes. § 50. See also *investment tax credit.*

Recapture potential. Reference is to property that, if disposed of in a taxable transaction, would result in the recapture of depreciation (§§ 1245 or 1250) and/or of the investment tax credit (§ 50).

Recognized gain or loss. The portion of realized gain or loss that is considered in computing taxable income. See also *realized gain or loss.*

Recovery of capital doctrine. When a taxable sale or exchange occurs, the seller may be permitted to recover his or her investment (or other adjusted basis) in the property before gain or loss is recognized. See also *open transaction.*

Regulations. Treasury Department Regulations represent the position of the IRS as to how the Internal Revenue Code is to be interpreted. Their purpose is to provide taxpayers and IRS personnel with rules of general and specific application to the various provisions of the tax law. Regulations are published in the *Federal Register* and in all tax services.

Related-party transactions. The tax law places restrictions upon the recognition of gains and losses between related parties because of the potential for abuse. For example, restrictions are placed on the deduction of losses from the sale or exchange of property between related parties. A related party includes a corporation controlled by the taxpayer. § 267.

Research activities credit. A tax credit whose purpose is to encourage research and development. It consists of two components: the incremental research activities credit and the basic research credit. The incremental research activities credit is equal to 20 percent of the excess of qualified research expenditures over the base amount. The basic research credit is equal to 20 percent of the excess of basic research payments over the base amount. § 41. See also *general business credit.*

Research and experimentation expenditures. The Code provides three alternatives for the tax treatment of research and experimentation expenditures. They may be expensed in the year paid or incurred, deferred subject to amortization, or capitalized. If the taxpayer does not elect to expense such costs or to defer them subject to amortization (over 60 months), the expenditures must be capitalized. § 174. Two types of research activities credits are available: the basic research credit and the incremental research activities credit. The rate for each type is 20 percent. § 41.

Reserve for bad debts. A method of accounting whereby an allowance is permitted for estimated uncollectible accounts. Actual write-offs are charged to the reserve, and recoveries of amounts previously written off are credited to the reserve. The Code permits only certain financial institutions to use the reserve method. § 166. See also *specific charge-off method.*

Reserves for estimated expenses. Except in the limited case for bad debts, reserves for estimated expenses (e.g., warranty service costs) are not permitted for tax purposes even though such reserves are appropriate for financial accounting purposes. See also *all events test.*

Residential rental property. Buildings for which at least 80 percent of the gross rents are from dwelling units (e.g., an apartment building). This type of building is distinguished from nonresidential (commercial or industrial) buildings in applying the recapture of depreciation provisions. The term also is relevant in distinguishing between buildings that are eligible for a 27.5-year life versus a 31.5-year life for MACRS purposes. Generally, residential buildings receive preferential treatment. §§ 168(e)(2) and 1250. See also *recapture of depreciation.*

Restricted property. An arrangement whereby an employer transfers property (usually stock) to an employee at a bargain price (for less than the fair market value). If the transfer is accompanied by a substantial risk of forfeiture and the property is not transferable, no compensation results to the employee until the restrictions disappear. An example of a substantial risk of forfeiture would be a requirement that the employee return the property if his or her employment is terminated within a specified period of time. § 83. See also *nonqualified deferred compensation plans.*

Retirement of corporate obligations. The retirement of corporate and certain government obligations is considered to be a sale or exchange. Gain or loss, upon the retirement of a corporate obligation, therefore, is treated as capital gain or loss rather than as ordinary income or loss. §§ 1271–1275.

Return of capital doctrine. See *recovery of capital doctrine.*

Revenue Procedure. A matter of procedural importance to both taxpayers and the IRS concerning the administration of the tax law is issued by the National Office of the IRS as a Revenue Procedure (abbreviated Rev.Proc.). A Revenue Procedure is first published in an *Internal Revenue Bulletin* (I.R.B.) and later transferred to the appropriate *Cumulative Bulletin* (C.B.). Both the *Internal Revenue Bulletin* and the *Cumulative Bulletin* are published by the U.S. Government Printing Office.

Revenue Ruling. A Revenue Ruling (abbreviated Rev.Rul.) is issued by the National Office of the IRS to express an official interpretation of the tax law as applied to specific transactions. It is more limited in application than a Regulation. A Revenue Ruling is first published in an *Internal Revenue Bulletin* (I.R.B.) and later transferred to the appropriate *Cumulative Bulletin* (C.B.). Both the *Internal Revenue Bulletin* and the *Cumulative Bulletin* are published by the U.S. Government Printing Office.

S

Salvage value. The estimated amount a taxpayer will receive upon the disposition of an asset used in the taxpayer's trade or business. Salvage value is relevant in calculating depreciation under § 167, but is not relevant in calculating cost recovery under § 168.

Scholarships. Scholarships are generally excluded from the gross income of the recipient unless the payments are a disguised form of compensation for services rendered. However, the Code imposes restrictions on the exclusion. The recipient must be a degree candidate. The excluded amount is limited to amounts used for tuition, fees, books, supplies, and equipment required for courses of instruction. Amounts received for room and board are not eligible for the exclusion. § 117.

S corporation status. An elective provision permitting certain small business corporations (§ 1361) and their shareholders to elect (§ 1362) to be treated for income tax purposes in accordance with the operating rules of §§ 1363–1379. Of major significance are the facts that S status avoids the corporate income tax and corporate losses can be claimed by the shareholders. See also *C corporation.*

Section 38 property. Property that qualified for the investment tax credit. Generally, this included all tangible property (other than real estate) used in a trade or business. § 48 prior to repeal by the Revenue Reconciliation Act of 1990. See also *investment tax credit.*

Section 179 expensing. The ability to deduct a capital expenditure in the year an asset is placed in service rather than over the asset's useful life or cost recovery period. The annual ceiling on the deduction is $10,000. However, the deduction is reduced dollar for dollar when § 179 property placed in service during the taxable year exceeds $200,000. In addition, the amount expensed under § 179 cannot exceed the aggregate amount of taxable income derived from the conduct of any trade or business by the taxpayer.

Section 1231 assets. Depreciable assets and real estate used in a trade or business and held for the required long-term holding period. Under certain circumstances, the classification also includes timber, coal, domestic iron ore, livestock (held for draft, breeding, dairy, or sporting purposes), and unharvested crops. § 1231(b).

Section 1231 gains and losses. If the net result of the combined gains and losses from the taxable dispositions of § 1231 assets plus the net gain from the involuntary conversion of nonpersonal use assets is a gain, the gains and losses from § 1231 assets are treated as long-term capital gains and losses. In arriving at § 1231 gains, however, the depreciation recapture provisions (e.g., §§ 1245 and 1250) are first applied to produce ordinary income. If the net result of the combination is a loss, the gains and losses from § 1231 assets are treated as ordinary gains and losses. § 1231(a). See also *recapture of depreciation.*

Section 1244 stock. Stock issued under § 1244 by qualifying small business corporations. If § 1244 stock is disposed of at a loss or becomes worthless, the shareholders may claim an ordinary loss rather than the usual capital loss. The annual ceiling on the ordinary loss treatment is $50,000 ($100,000 for married individuals filing jointly). See also *worthless securities.*

Section 1245 property. Property that is subject to the recapture of depreciation under § 1245. For a definition of § 1245 property, see § 1245(a)(3). See also *Section 1245 recapture.*

Section 1245 recapture. Upon a taxable disposition of § 1245 property, all depreciation claimed on the property after 1961 will be recaptured as ordinary income (but not to exceed the recognized gain from the disposition). See also *recapture of depreciation.*

Section 1250 property. Real estate that is subject to the recapture of depreciation under § 1250. For a definition of § 1250 property, see § 1250(c). See also *Section 1250 recapture.*

Section 1250 recapture. Upon a taxable disposition of § 1250 property, some or all of the additional depreciation claimed on the property may be recaptured as ordinary income. Various recapture rules apply depending upon the type of property (residential or nonresidential real estate) and the date acquired. Generally, the additional depreciation is recaptured in full to the extent of the gain recognized. See also *additional depreciation* and *recapture of depreciation.*

Self-employment retirement plan. A designation for retirement plans available to self-employed taxpayers. Also referred to as H.R. 10 and Keogh plans. Under such plans, a taxpayer may deduct each year up to either 20 percent of net earnings from self-employment or $30,000, whichever is less. If the plan is a profit sharing plan, the percentage is 13.043 percent.

Self-employment tax. In 1992, a tax of 12.4 percent is levied on individuals with net earnings from self-employment (up to $55,500) to provide Social Security benefits (i.e., the old age, survivors, and disability insurance portion) for such individuals. In addition, in 1992, a tax of 2.9 percent is levied on individuals with net earnings from self-employment (up to $130,200) to provide Medicare benefits (i.e., the hospital insurance portion) for such individuals. If a self-employed individual also receives wages from an employer that are subject to FICA, the self-employment tax will be reduced if total income subject to Social Security and Medicare is more than $55,500 (associated with the Social Security portion) and $130,200 (associated with the Medicare portion). A partial deduction is allowed in calculating the self-employment tax.

Separate property. In a community property jurisdiction, separate property is the property that belongs entirely to one of the spouses. Generally, it is property acquired before marriage or acquired after marriage by gift or inheritance. See also *community property.*

Short sales. A short sale occurs when a taxpayer sells borrowed property (usually stock) and repays the lender with substantially identical property either held on the date of the short sale or purchased after the sale. No gain or loss is recognized until the short sale is closed, and such gain or loss is generally short term. § 1233.

Simplified employee pensions. An employer may make contributions to an employee's IRA in amounts not exceeding the lesser of 15 percent of compensation or $30,000 per individual. These employer-sponsored simplified employee pensions are permitted only if the contributions are nondiscriminatory and are made on behalf of all employees who have attained age 21 and have worked for the employer during at least three of the five preceding calendar years. § 219(b). See also *individual retirement account.*

Small business corporation. A corporation that satisfies the definition of § 1361(b), § 1244(c)(3), or both. Satisfaction of § 1361(b) permits an S corporation election, and satisfaction of § 1244 enables the shareholders of the corporation to claim an ordinary loss. See also *S corporation status* and *Section 1244 stock.*

Specific charge-off method. A method of accounting for bad debts in which a deduction is permitted only when an account becomes partially or completely worthless. See also *reserve for bad debts.*

Standard deduction. The individual taxpayer can either itemize deductions or take the standard deduction. The amount of the standard deduction depends on the taxpayer's filing status (single, head of household, married filing jointly, surviving spouse, or married filing separately). For 1992, the amount of the standard deduction ranges from $3,000 to $6,000. Additional standard deductions of either $700 (for married taxpayers) or $900 (for single taxpayers) are available if the taxpayer is either blind or age 65 or over. Limitations exist on the amount of the standard deduction of a taxpayer who is another taxpayer's dependent. Beginning in 1989, the standard deduction amounts were adjusted for inflation. § 63(c). See also *zero bracket amount.*

Statute of limitations. Provisions of the law that specify the maximum period of time in which action may be taken on a past event. Code §§ 6501–6504 contain the limitation periods applicable to the IRS for additional assessments, and §§ 6511–6515 relate to refund claims by taxpayers.

Statutory notice of deficiency. Commonly referred to as the 90-day letter, this notice is sent to a taxpayer upon request, upon the expiration of the 30-day letter, or upon exhaustion by the taxpayer of his or her administrative remedies before the IRS. The notice gives the taxpayer 90 days in which to file a petition with the U.S. Tax Court. If a petition is not filed, the IRS will issue a demand for payment of the assessed deficiency. §§ 6211–6216. See also *thirty-day letter.*

Stock option. The right to purchase a stated number of shares of stock from a corporation at a certain price within a specified period of time.

Stock redemptions. The redemption of the stock of a shareholder by the issuing corporation will be treated as a sale or exchange of the stock if the redemption is not a dividend. §§ 301 and 302.

T

Targeted jobs tax credit. See *jobs credit.*

Tax avoidance. The minimization of one's tax liability by taking advantage of legally available tax planning opportunities. Tax avoidance can be contrasted with tax evasion, which entails the reduction of tax liability by illegal means.

Tax benefit rule. A rule that limits the recognition of income from the recovery of an expense or loss properly deducted in a prior tax year to the amount of the deduction that generated a tax benefit. § 111.

Tax Court. The U.S. Tax Court is one of three trial courts of original jurisdiction that decide litigation involving Federal income, estate, or gift taxes. It is the only trial court where the taxpayer need not first pay the deficiency assessed by the IRS. The Tax Court will not have jurisdiction over a case unless the statutory notice of deficiency (90-day letter) has been issued by the IRS and the taxpayer files the petition for hearing within the time prescribed.

Tax credit for elderly or disabled. An elderly (age 65 and over) or disabled taxpayer may receive a tax credit amounting to 15 percent of $5,000 ($7,500 for qualified married individuals filing jointly). This amount is reduced by Social Security benefits, excluded pension benefits, and one-half of the taxpayer's adjusted gross income in excess of $7,500 ($10,000 for married taxpayers filing jointly). § 22.

Tax-free exchange. Transfers of property specifically exempted from Federal income tax consequences. Examples are a transfer of property to a controlled corporation under § 351(a) and a like-kind exchange under § 1031(a). The recognition of gain or loss is postponed, rather than being permanently excluded, through the assignment of a carryover basis to the replacement property.

Tax home. Since travel expenses of an employee are deductible only if the taxpayer is away from home, the deductibility of such expenses rests upon the definition of tax home. The IRS position is that tax home is the business location, post, or station of the taxpayer. If an employee is temporarily reassigned to a new post for a period of one year or less, the taxpayer's home should be his or her personal residence and the travel expenses should be deductible. If the assignment is for more than two years, the IRS position is that it is indefinite or permanent and the taxpayer is therefore not in travel status. If the assignment is for between one and two years, the IRS position is that the location of the tax home will be determined on the basis of the facts and circumstances. The courts are in conflict regarding what constitutes a person's home for tax purposes. See also *travel expenses.*

Tax preference items. Those items set forth in § 57 that may result in the imposition of the alternative minimum tax. See also *alternative minimum tax.*

Tax rate schedules. Rate schedules appearing in Appendix A that are used by upper-income taxpayers and those not permitted to use the tax table. Separate rate schedules are provided for married individuals filing jointly, head of household, single taxpayers, estates and trusts, and married individuals filing separate returns. § 1.

Tax table. A tax table appearing in Appendix A that is provided for taxpayers with less than $50,000 of taxable income. Separate columns are provided for single taxpayers, married taxpayers filing jointly, head of household, and married taxpayers filing separately. § 3.

Thin corporation. When debt owed by a corporation to its shareholders is large relative to its capital structure (stock and shareholder equity), the IRS may contend that the corporation is thinly capitalized. In effect, this means that some or all of the debt will be reclassified as equity. The immediate result is to disallow any interest deduction to the corporation on the reclassified debt. To the extent of the corporation's earnings and profits, interest payments and loan repayments are treated as dividends to the shareholders. § 385.

Thirty-day letter. A letter that accompanies a revenue agent's report (RAR) issued as a result of an IRS audit of a taxpayer (or the rejection of a taxpayer's claim for refund). The letter outlines the taxpayer's appeal procedure before the IRS. If the taxpayer does not request any such procedures within the 30-day period, the IRS will issue a *statutory notice of deficiency* (the 90-day letter).

Timber. Special rules apply to the recognition of gain from the sale of timber. A taxpayer may elect to treat the cutting of timber that is held for sale or use in a trade or business as a sale or exchange. If the holding period requirements are met, the gain is recognized as § 1231 gain and may therefore receive long-term capital gain treatment. § 631.

Trade or business expenses. Deductions *for* AGI that are attributable to a taxpayer's business or profession. Some employee expenses may also be treated as trade or business expenses. See also *employee expenses.*

Transportation expenses. Transportation expenses for an employee include only the cost of transportation (taxi fares, automobile expenses, etc.) in the course of employment when the employee is not away from home in travel status. Commuting expenses are not deductible. See also *automobile expenses.*

Travel expenses. Travel expenses include meals and lodging and transportation expenses while away from home in the pursuit of a trade or business (including that of an employee). See also *tax home.*

Trial court. The court of original jurisdiction; the first court to consider litigation. In Federal tax controversies, trial courts include U.S. District Courts, the U.S. Tax Court, and the U.S. Claims Court. See also *appellate court.*

U

Unearned (prepaid) income. For tax purposes, prepaid income (e.g., rent) is taxable in the year of receipt. In certain cases involving advance payments for goods and services, income may be deferred. See Rev.Proc. 71–21 (1971–2 C.B. 549) and Reg. § 1.451–5. See also *accrual method.*

Unreasonable compensation. Under § 162(a)(1), a deduction is allowed for "reasonable" salaries or other compensation for personal services actually rendered. To the extent compensation is excessive ("unreasonable"), no deduction will be allowed. The problem of unreasonable compensation usually is limited to closely held corporations where the motivation is to pay out profits in some form deductible to the corporation. Deductible compensation, therefore, becomes an attractive substitute for nondeductible dividends when the shareholders are also employees of the corporation.

USTC. Published by Commerce Clearing House, *U.S. Tax Cases* contain all of the Federal tax decisions issued by the U.S. District Courts, U.S. Claims Court, U.S. Courts of Appeals, and the U.S. Supreme Court.

V

Vacation home. The Code places restrictions upon taxpayers who rent their residences or vacation homes for part of the tax year. The restrictions may result in a scaling down of expense deductions for the taxpayers. § 280A. See also *hobby loss.*

W

Wash sale. A loss from the sale of stock or securities that is disallowed because the taxpayer has within 30 days before or after the sale acquired stock or securities that are substantially identical to those sold. § 1091.

Worthless securities. A loss (usually capital) is allowed for a security that becomes worthless during the year. The loss is deemed to have occurred on the last day of the year. Special rules apply to securities of affiliated companies and small business stock. § 165. See also *Section 1244 stock.*

Writ of certiorari. See *certiorari.*

Z

Zero bracket amount. A deduction that was generally available to all individual taxpayers in arriving at taxable income. It represented the equivalent of the standard deduction for taxable years before 1987. The taxpayer did not take a deduction for the zero bracket amount because it was built into the tax tables and tax rate schedules. Because the amount was built-in, if the taxpayer itemized deductions, only the excess itemized deductions (amount of the itemized deductions in excess of the zero bracket amount) were deductible. TRA of 1986 repealed the zero bracket amount and replaced it with the standard deduction for 1987 and thereafter. The zero bracket amount for 1986 is presently used in the 10-year forward averaging calculation for lump-sum distributions. § 63(c). See also *standard deduction.*

APPENDIX

TABLE OF CODE SECTIONS CITED

[See Title 26 U.S.C.A.]

I.R.C. Sec.	This Work Page
410(b)	19–7
410(b)(3)	19–8
410(b)(4)	19–8
414(i)	19–3
414(j)	19–3
414(q)	19–7
415	19–14
415(b)	19–15
415(b)(1)	19–15, 19–19
415(c)	19–14
415(c)(1)	19–19
415(e)	19–17
416(b)	19–17
416(c)	19–17
416(e)	19–17
416(i)(1)	19–17
421	4–21
421(a)	12–11
421(a)(1)	19–30
421(a)(2)	19–30
422	4–22, 19–29, 19–36
422(a)	19–30
422(a)(1)	19–30
422(a)(2)	19–30
422(b)	19–31
422(c)(3)	19–30
422(c)(5)	19–31
422(e)	4–23
441(a)	4–6
441(c)	18–2
444(d)	4–6
441(f)	18–2
441(i)	18–5
442	2–9, 18–6
443(b)(1)	18–8
443(b)(2)	18–8
444	18–4, 18–5
444(c)	18–4
446	2–9, 18–9
446(a)	6–7
446(b)	4–7, 4–12, 6–8, 18–10
446(c)	18–14
446(d)	18–10
446(e)	4–7, 6–8
446(f)	18–15
447	18–11
447(c)	18–11
448	6–9
448(a)	18–11
448(b)	18–11
448(d)	7–7
448(d)(5)	18–14
451(a)	19–24
451(d)	18–8
453	2–30, 18–17
453(a)	4–7, 15–27, 18–18
453(b)	4–7
453(b)(i)(l)	18–17
453(d)	18–26
453(d)(3)	18–26
453(e)	18–22
453(e)(2)	18–22
453(e)(2)(B)	18–22
453(e)(6)	18–23
453(e)(7)	18–23
453(f)(1)	18–22
453(f)(4)	18–20
453(g)	18–23
453(i)	17–19
453(l)(2)	18–18
453A	4–7, 18–17, 18–24
453A(b)	18–24
453A(d)	18–24
453B	18–17
453B(a)	18–23
453B(c)	18–24
453B(d)	18–24
453B(f)(2)	18–23
453B(g)	18–24
460	18–27
460(b)(1)(A)	18–30
460(b)(2)	18–30
460(b)(5)	18–30
460(f)	18–26
461(g)(1)	11–16
461(g)(2)	11–15, 11–39
461(h)	18–12
461(h)(1)	6–9
461(h)(2)(A)	6–9
461(h)(2)(B)	6–9
461(h)(3)(A)	6–9
461(h)(4)	18–12
464	18–11
464(c)	18–11
465(b)(1)	7–3
465(e)	7–4
468	18–12
469	7–6, 7–9, 7–14, 7–15, 17–22, 19–20, 20–24
469(a)	7–6, 12–9
469(b)	7–24
469(c)(2)	7–15
469(d)(1)	7–18
469(d)(2)	7–25
469(f)	7–31
469(g)(2)	7–30
469(g)(3)	7–30
469(i)	7–27
469(i)(3)(B)	13–10
469(i)(3)(C)	13–17
469(i)(6)	7–27
469(j)(2)	7–7
469(j)(5)	7–27
469(j)(6)	7–30
469(j)(8)	7–15
471	18–31
471(a)	18–31
472(c)	12–25, 18–34
472(d)	18–34
481(b)	18–16
483	18–17, 18–20, 18–21
483(e)	18–21
501	11–19
501(a)	19–11, 19–43
585	18–14
611(a)	9–29
612	9–28
613	9–31
613(a)	9–29
613(e)	12–16
613A	9–29

APPENDIX

TABLE OF REGULATIONS CITED

Temporary Treasury Regulations

Proposed Treasury Regulations

Treasury Regulations

Treasury Regulations

Treasury Regulations

Appendix

Table of Revenue Procedures and Revenue Rulings Cited

Revenue Procedure

Rev.Proc.	This Work Page
71–21	4–13, 4–14, 4–36
72–10	9–7
80–51	18–16
83–35	9–7, 9–8
83–78	2–38
84–74	18–16, 18–34
85–16	18–7
85–49	11–5
87–1	2–25
87–32	18–6, 18–35
87–56	2–32, 9–10, 9–25, 9–51, 12–7
87–57	9–39, 9–45, 9–46, 15–4
89–12	20–3
91–67	10–13
92–3	2–9
92–17	10–8

Revenue Rulings

Rev.Rul.	This Work Page
51	16–33
54–567	2–27
55–261	11–4
55–273	4–52
55–525	19–25
56–60	14–14
56–406	14–17
57–244	15–25
57–344	3–10
57–345	11–9
57–418	6–13
58–419	3–10
59–72	15–17
59–86	14–13
60–31	4–10, 19–25
61	4–2
61–119	15–4
62–102	5–6
63–221	15–9
63–232	8–8
65–34	2–27
65–178	19–6
65–235	2–32
66–7	16–14
67–289	19–25
67–297	11–15
68–212	11–4
68–579	5–39
68–662	6–11
69–185	2–38
69–292	10–23
70–466	15–11
70–622	11–9
71–190	11–11
71–425	5–3
72–312	4–15
72–545	6–20
72–592	8–8
73–18	15–39
73–136	11–12
73–380	19–6
73–476	15–25
73–529	10–15
74–78	10–23
74–175	16–27
74–187	11–12

APPENDIX

CITATOR EXAMPLE

ILLUSTRATION OF THE USE OF THE CITATOR[1]

Background

The *Federal Tax Citator* is a separate multivolume service with monthly supplements. Cases reported by the *Citator* are divided into the various issues involved. Since the researcher may be interested in only one or two issues, only those cases involving the particular issue need to be checked.

The *Federal Tax Citator* includes the following volumes, each of which covers particular period of time:

- Volume 1 (1863–1941)
- Volume 2 (1942–1948)
- Volume 3 (1948–1954)
- Volume 1, Second Series (1954–1977)
- Volume 2, Second Series (1978–1989)
- Annual cumulative supplements (1990 and 1991)
- Monthly cumulative supplements (paperback)

Through the use of symbols, the *Citator* indicates whether a decision has been followed, explained, criticized, questioned, or overruled by a later court decision. These symbols are reproduced in Figure E–1.

Example

Determine the background and validity of *Adda v. Comm.*, 37 AFTR 654, 171 F.2d 457 (CA–4, 1948).

1. Features in the *Federal Tax Citator* that do not appear in the CCH *Citator* include the following: (1) distinguishes between the various issues in the case, (2) lists all court decisions that cite the court decision being researched, (3) indicates the relationship (e.g., explained, criticized, followed, or overruled) between the court decision being researched and subsequent decisions, and (4) pinpoints the exact page on which one court decision is cited by another court decision. Prior to the acquisition of Prentice-Hall Information Services, the *Federal Tax Citator* was published by Prentice-Hall. The *Federal Tax Citator* is now published by Research Institute of America.

Solution

Turning directly to the case itself (reproduced as Figure E–2), note the two issues involved (issues 1 and 2). For purposes of emphasis, these issues have been bracketed and identified by a marginal notation in the figure. The reason for the division of the issues becomes apparent when the case is traced through the *Citator.*

Refer to Volume 3 of the First Series (covering the period from October 7, 1948, through July 29, 1954) of the *Federal Tax Citator.* The case reference is located on page 5505, which is reproduced in Figure E–3.

FIGURE E–1

Citator Symbols*

COURT DECISIONS

Judicial History of the Case

a	affirmed (by decision of a higher court)
d	dismissed (appeal to a higher court dismissed)
m	modified (decision modified by a higher court, or on rehearing)
r	reversed (by a decision of a higher court)
s	same case (e.g., on rehearing)
rc	related case (companion cases and other cases arising out of the same subject matter are so designated)
x	certiorari denied (by the Supreme Court of the United States)
(C or G)	The Commissioner or Solicitor General has made the appeal
(T)	Taxpayer has made the appeal
(A)	Tax Court's decision acquiesced in by Commissioner
(NA)	Tax Court's decision nonacquiesced in by Commissioner
sa	same case affirmed (by the cited case)
sd	same case dismissed (by the cited case)
sm	same case modified (by the cited case)
sr	same case reversed (by the cited case)
sx	same case—certiorari denied

Syllabus of the Cited Case

iv	four (on all fours with the cited case)
f	followed (the cited case followed)
e	explained (comment generally favorable, but not to a degree that indicates the cited case is followed)
k	reconciled (the cited case reconciled)
n	dissenting opinion (cited in a dissenting opinion)
g	distinguished (the cited case distinguished either in law or on the facts)
l	limited (the cited case limited to its facts. Used when an appellate court so limits a prior decision, or a lower court states that in its opinion the cited case should be so limited)
c	criticized (adverse comment on the cited case)
q	questioned (the cited case not only criticized, but its correctness questioned)
o	overruled

*Reproduced from the *Federal Tax 2nd Citator* with the permission of the publisher, Research Institute of America, Englewood Cliffs, NJ 07632.

FIGURE E–2

ADDA v. COMMISSIONER OF INTERNAL REVENUE.

No. 5796.

United States Court of Appeals
Fourth Circuit.

Dec. 3, 1948.

ISSUE 1

1. Internal revenue ⚷792

Where nonresident alien's brother residing in United States traded for alien's benefit on commodity exchanges in United States at authorization of alien, who vested full discretion in brother with regard thereto, and many transactions were effected through different brokers, several accounts were maintained, and substantial gains and losses realized, transactions constituted a "trade or business," profits of which were "capital gains" taxable as income to the alien. 26 U.S.C.A. § 211(b).

See Words and Phrases, Permanent Edition, for other judicial constructions and definitions of "Capital Gains" and "Trade or Business".

ISSUE 2

2. Internal revenue ⚷792

The exemption of a nonresident alien's commodity transactions in the United States provided for by the Internal Revenue Code does not apply where alien has agent in United States using his own discretion in effecting transactions for alien's account. 26 U.S.C.A. § 211(b).

On Petition to Review the Decision of The Tax Court of the United States.

Petition by Fernand C. A. Adda to review a decision of the Tax Court redetermining a deficiency in income tax imposed by the Commissioner of Internal Revenue.

Decision affirmed.

Rollin Browne and Mitchell B. Carroll, both of New York City, for petitioner.

Irving I. Axelrad, Sp. Asst. to Atty. Gen. (Theron Lamar Caudle, Asst. Atty. Gen., and Ellis N. Slack and A. F. Prescott, Sp. Assts. to Atty. Gen., on the brief), for respondent.

Before PARKER, Chief Judge, and SOPER and DOBIE, Circuit Judges.

PER CURIAM.

[1, 2] This is a petition by a non-resident alien to review a decision of the Tax Court. Petitioner is a national of Egypt, who in the year 1941 was residing in France. He had a brother who at that time was residing in the United States and who traded for petitioner's benefit on commodity exchanges in the United States in cotton, wool, grains, silk, hides and copper. This trading was authorized by petitioner who vested full discretion in his brother with regard thereto, and it resulted in profits in the sum of $193,857.14. The Tax Court said: "While the number of transactions or the total amount of money involved in them has not been stated, it is apparent that many transactions were effected through different brokers, several accounts were maintained, and gains and losses in substantial amounts were realized. This evidence shows that the trading was extensive enough to amount to a trade or business, and the petitioner does not contend, nor has he shown, that the transactions were so infrequent or inconsequential as not to amount to a trade or business." We agree with the Tax Court that, for reasons adequately set forth in its opinion, this income was subject to taxation, and that the exemption of a non-resident alien's commodity transactions in the United States, provided by section 211(b) of the Internal Revenue Code, 26 U.S.C.A. § 211(b), does not apply to a case where the alien has an agent in the United States using his own discretion in effecting the transactions for the alien's account. As said by the Tax Court, "Through such transactions the alien is engaging in trade or business within the United States, and the profits on these transactions are capital gains taxable to him." Nothing need be added to the reasoning of the Tax Court in this connection, and the decision will be affirmed on its opinion.

Affirmed.

FIGURE E–3

ADAMSON, JAMES H. & MARION C. v U. S., — F Supp —, 36 AFTR 1529, 1946 P.-H. ¶ 72,418 (DC Calif) (See Adamson v U. S.)

ADAMSON, R. R., MRS., — BTA —, 1934 (P.-H.) BTA Memo. Dec. ¶ 34,370

ADAMSON v U. S., 26 AFTR 1188 (DC Calif, Sept 8, 1939)
iv—Coggan, Linus C., 1939 (P.-H.) BTA Memo. Dec. page 39—806

ADAMSON; U. S. v, 161 F(2d) 942, 35 AFTR 1404 (CCA 9)
1—Lazier v U. S., 170 F(2d) 524, 37 AFTR 545, 1948 P.-H. page 73,174 (CCA 8)
1—Grace Bros., Inc. v Comm., 173 F(2d) 178, 37 AFTR 1014, 1949 P.-H. page 72,433 (CCA 9)
1—Briggs; Hofferbert v, 178 F(2d) 744, 38 AFTR 1219, 1950 P.-H. page 72,267 (CCA 4)
1—Rogers v Comm., 180 F(2d) 722, 39 AFTR 115, 1950 P.-H. page 72,531 (CCA 3)
1—Lamar v Granger, 99 F Supp 41, 40 AFTR 270, 1951 P.-H. page 72,945 (DC Pa)
1—Herbert v Riddell, 103 F Supp 383, 41 AFTR 975, 1952 P.-H. page 72,383 (DC Calif)
1—Hudson, Galvin, 20 TC 737, 20-1953 P.-H. TC 418

ADAMSON v U. S., — F Supp —, 36 AFTR 1529, 1946 P.-H. ¶ 72,418 (DC Calif, Jan 28, 1946)

ADAMS-ROTH BAKING CO., 8 BTA 458
1—Gunderson Bros. Engineering Corp., 16 TC 129, 16-1951 P.-H. TC 72

ADAMSTON FLAT GLASS CO. v COMM., 162 F(2d) 875, 35 AFTR 1579 (CCA 6)
4—Forrest Hotel Corp. v. Fly, 112 F Supp 789, 43 AFTR 1080, 1953 P.-H. page 72,856 (DC Miss)

ADDA v COMM., 171 F(2d) 457, 37 AFTR 654, 1948 P.-H. ¶ 72,655 (CCA 4, Dec 3, 1948)
Cert. filed, March 1, 1949 (T)
No cert. (G) 1949 P-H ¶ 71,050
x—Adda v Comm., 336 US 952, 69 S Ct 883, 93 L Ed 1107, April 18, 1949 (T)
sa—Adda, Fernand C. A., 10 TC 273 (No. 33), ¶ 10.33 P.-H. TC 1948
iv—Milner Hotels, Inc., N. Y., 173 F (2d) 567, 37 AFTR 1170, 1949 P.-H. page 72,528 (CCA 6)
1—Nubar; Comm. v, 185 F(2d) 588, 39 AFTR 1315, 1950 P.-H. page 73,423 (CCA 4)
g-1—Scottish Amer. Invest. Co., Ltd., The, 12 TC 59, 12-1949 P.-H. TC 32
g-1—Nubar, Zareh, 13 TC 579, 13-1949 P.-H. TC 318

ADDA, FERNAND C. A., 10 TC 273 (No. 33), ¶ 10.33 P.-H. TC 1948 (A) 1948-2 CB 1
a—Adda v Comm., 171 F(2d) 457, 37 AFTR 654, 1948 P.-H. ¶ 72,655 (CCA 4)
1—Nubar; Comm. v, 185 F(2d) 588, 39 AFTR 1315, 1950 P.-H. page 73,423 (CCA 4)
g-1—Scottish Amer. Invest. Co., Ltd., The, 12 TC 59, 12-1949 P.-H. TC 32
g-1—Nubar, Zareh, 13 TC 579, 13-1949 P.-H. TC 318

ADDA, FERNAND C. A., 10 TC 1291 (No. 168), ¶ 10.168 P.-H. TC 1948 (A) 1953-1 CB 3, 1953 P.-H. ¶ 76,453 (NA) 1948-2 CB 5, 1948 P.-H. ¶ 76,434 withdrawn
1—Scottish Amer. Invest. Co., Ltd., The, 12 TC 59, 12-1949 P.-H. TC 32

ADDA INC., 9 TC 199 (A) 1949-1 CB 1, 1949 P.-H. ¶ 76,260 (NA) 1947-2 CB 6 withdrawn
a—Adda, Inc.; Comm. v, 171 F(2d) 367, 37 AFTR 641, 1948 P.-H. ¶ 72,654 (CCA 2)
a—Adda, Inc.; Comm. v, 171 F(2d) 367, 37 AFTR 641, 1949 P.-H. ¶ 72,303 (CCA 2)
e-1—G.C.M. 26069, 1949-2 CB 38, 1949 P.-H. page 76,226
3—Koshland, Execx.; U.S. v, 208 F(2d) 640, — AFTR —, 1953 P.-H. page 73,597 (CCA 9)
4—Kent, Otis Beall, 1954 (P. H.) TC Memo. Dec. page 54—17

ADDA, INC.; COMM. v, 171 F(2d) 367, 37 AFTR 641, 1948 P.-H. ¶ 72,654 (CCA 2, Dec 6, 1948)
sa—Adda, Inc., 9 TC 199
s—Adda, Inc.; Comm. v, 171 F(2d) 367, 37 AFTR 641, 1949 P.-H. ¶ 72,303 (CCA 2) reh. den.
e-1—G.C.M. 26069, 1949-2 CB 39, 1949 P.-H. page 76,227
e-2—G.C.M. 26069, 1949-2 CB 39, 1949 P.-H. page 76,227

ADDA, INC.; COMM. v, 171 F(2d) 367, 37 AFTR 641, 1949 P.-H. ¶ 72,303 (CCA 2, Dec 6, 1948) reh. den.
sa—Adda, Inc., 9 TC 199
s—Adda, Inc.; Comm. v, 171 F(2d) 367, 37 AFTR 641, 1948 P.-H. ¶ 72,654 (CCA 2)

ADDISON-CHEVROLET SALES, INC. v CHAMBERLAIN, L. A. & NAT. BANK OF WASH., THE, — F Supp —, — AFTR —, 1954 P.-H. ¶ 72,550 (DC DC) (See Campbell v Chamberlain)

ADDISON v COMM., 177 F(2d) 521, 38 AFTR 821, 1949 P.-H. ¶ 72,637 (CCA 8, Nov 3, 1949)
sa—Addison, Irene D., — TC —, 1948 (P.-H.) TC Memo. Dec. ¶ 48,177
1—Roberts, Supt. v U. S., 115 Ct Cl 439, 87 F Supp 937, 38 AFTR 1314, 1950 P.-H. page 72,292
1—Cold Metal Process Co., The, 17 TC 934, 17-1951 P.-H. TC 512
1—Berger, Samuel & Lillian, 1954 (P.-H.) TC Memo. Dec. page 54—232
2—Urquhart, George Gordon & Mary F., 20 TC 948, 20-1953 P.-H. TC 536

ADDISON, IRENE D., — TC —, 1948 (P.-H.) TC Memo. Dec. ¶ 48,177
App (T) Jan 14, 1949 (CCA 8)
a—Addison v Comm., 177 F(2d) 521, 38 AFTR 821, 1949 P.-H. ¶ 72,637 (CCA 8)
1—Urquhart, George Gordon & Mary F., 20 TC 948, 20-1953 P.-H. TC 536

ADDITON, HARRY L. & ANNIE S., 3 TC 427
1—Lum, Ralph E., 12 TC 379, 12-1949 P.-H. TC 204
1—Christie, John A. & Elizabeth H., — TC —, 1949 (P.-H.) TC Memo. Dec. page 49—795

ADDRESSOGRAPH - MULTIGRAPH CORP., 1945 (P.-H.) TC Memo. Dec. ¶ 45,058
f-10—Rev. Rul. 54-71, 1954 P.-H. page 76,453

ADDRESSOGRAPH-MULTIGRAPH CORP. v U. S., 112 Ct Cl 201, 78 F Supp 111, 37 AFTR 53, 1948 P.-H. ¶ 72,504 (June 1, 1948)
No cert (G) 1949 P.-H. ¶ 71,041
1—New Oakmont Corp., The v U. S., 114 Ct Cl 686, 86 F Supp 901, 38 AFTR 924, 1949 P.-H. page 73,181

ADELAIDE PARK LAND, 25 BTA 211
g—Amer. Security & Fidelity Corp., — BTA —, 1940 (P.-H.) BTA Memo. Dec. page 40—571

ADELPHI PAINT & COLOR WORKS, INC., 18 BTA 436
1—Neracher, William A., — BTA —, 1939 (P.-H.) BTA Memo. Dec. page 39—69
1—Lyman-Hawkins Lumber Co., — BTA —, 1939 (P.-H.) BTA Memo. Dec. page 39—350

ADEMAN v U. S., 174 F(2d) 283, 37 AFTR 1406 (CCA 9, April 25, 1949)

ADICONIS, NOELLA L. (PATNAUDE), 1953 (P.-H.) TC Memo. Dec. ¶ 53,305

ADJUSTMENT BUREAU OF ST. LOUIS ASSN., OF CREDIT MEN, 21 BTA 232
1—Cook County Loss Adjustment Bureau, — BTA —, 1940 (P.-H.) BTA Memo. Dec. page 40—331

ADKINS, CHARLES I., — BTA —, 1933 (P.-H.) BTA Memo. Dec. ¶ 33,457

ADLER v COMM., 77 F(2d) 733, 16 AFTR 162 (CCA 5)
g-2—McEuen v Comm., 196 F(2d) 130, 41 AFTR 1172, 1952 P.-H. page 72,604 (CCA 5)

Reproduced from the *Federal Tax 2nd Citator* with the permission of the publisher, Research Institute of America, Englewood Cliffs, NJ 07632.

Correlating the symbols in Figure E–1 with the shaded portion of Figure E–3 reveals the following information about *Adda v. Comm.:*

- Application for certiorari (appeal to the U.S. Supreme Court) filed by the taxpayer (T) on March 1, 1949.
- Certiorari was denied (x) by the U.S. Supreme Court on April 18, 1949.
- The trial court decision is reported in 10 T.C. 273 and was affirmed on appeal (sa) to the Fourth Court of Appeals.
- During the time frame of Volume 3 of the *Citator* (October 7, 1948, through July 29, 1954), one decision (*Milner Hotels, Inc.*) has agreed "on all fours with the cited case" (iv). One decision (*Comm. v. Nubar*) has limited the cited case to its facts (l) and two decisions (*The Scottish American Investment Co., Ltd.* and *Zareh Nubar*) have distinguished the cited case on issue number one (g-1).

Reference to Volume 1 of the *Citator* Second Series (covering the period from 1954 through 1977) shows *Adda v. Comm.* on page 25, which is reproduced in Figure E–4.

Correlating the symbols in Figure E–1 with the shaded portion of Figure E–4 reveals the following additional information about *Adda v. Comm.:*

- The case was cited without comment in two rulings and two cases: *Rev.Rul. 56–145, Rev.Rul. 56–392, Balanovski,* and *Liang.*
- It was followed in *Asthmanefrin Co.* (f-1).
- It was distinguished in *de Vegvar* and *Purvis* (g-1).
- It was reconciled in *deKrause* (k-1).

Reference to the "Court Decisions" section of Volume 2, Second Series of the *Citator* (covering the period from 1978 through 1989) shows that *Adda v. Comm.* was cited in *Judith C. Connelly* and *Robert E. Cleveland,* with each case limited to its facts (l). This page (22) is reproduced in Figure E–5.

The *Citator* includes an annual cumulative supplement (i.e., 1990 and 1991), and a cumulative monthly supplement is published each month. Be sure to refer to these supplements, or very recent citations might be overlooked. No citations appear in the supplements for *Adda v. Comm.*

Except as otherwise noted, it appears that *Adda v. Comm.* has withstood the test of time.

FIGURE E–4

ADASKAVICH, STEPHEN A. v U.S., 39 AFTR2d 77-517, 422 F Supp 276 (DC Mont) (See Wiegand, Charles J., Jr. v U.S.)
AD. AURIEMA, INC., 1943 P-H TC Memo ¶ 43,422
e-1—Miller v U.S., 13 AFTR2d 1515, 166 Ct Cl 257, 331 F2d 859
ADAY v SUPERIOR CT. OF ALAMEDA COUNTY, 8 AFTR2d 5367, 13 Cal Reptr 415, 362 P2d 47 (Calif, 5-11-61)
ADCO SERVICE, INC., ASSIGNEE v CYBERMATICS, INC., 36 AFTR2d 75-6342 (NJ) (See Adco Service, Inc., Assignee v Graphic Color Plate)
ADCO SERVICE, INC., ASSIGNEE v GRAPHIC COLOR PLATE, 36 AFTR2d 75-6342 (NJ, Supr Ct, 11-10-75)
ADCO SERVICE, INC., ASSIGNEE v GRAPHIC COLOR PLATE, INC., 36 AFTR2d 75-6342 (NJ) (See Adco Service, Inc., Assignee v Graphic Color Plate)
ADDA v COMM., 171 F2d 457, 37 AFTR 654 (USCA 4)
Rev. Rul. 56-145, 1956-1 CB 613
1—Balanovski; U.S. v, 236 F2d 304, 49 AFTR 2013 (USCA 2)
1—Liang, Chang Hsiao, 23 TC 1045, 23-1955 P-H TC 624
f-1—Asthmanefrin Co., Inc., 25 TC 1141, 25-1956 P-H TC 639
g-1—de Vegvar, Edward A. Neuman, 28 TC 1061, 28-1957 P-H TC 599
g-1—Purvis, Ralph E. & Patricia Lee, 1974 P-H TC Memo 74-669
k-1—deKrause, Piedad Alvarado, 1974 P-H TC Memo 74-1291
1—Rev. Rul. 56-392, 1956-2 CB 971
ADDA, FERNAND C.A., 10 TC 273, ¶ 10,133 P-H TC 1948
1—Balanovski; U.S. v, 236 F2d 303, 49 AFTR 2012 (USCA 2)
1—Liang, Chang Hsiao, 23 TC 1045, 23-1955 P-H TC 624
g-1—de Vegvar, Edward A. Neuman, 28 TC 1061, 28-1957 P-H TC 599
g-1—Purvis, Ralph E. & Patricia Lee, 1974 P-H TC Memo 74-669
k-1—deKrause, Piedad Alvarado, 1974 P-H TC Memo 74-1291
ADDA, INC., 9 TC 199
Pardee, Marvin L., Est. of, 49 TC 152, 49 P-H TC 107 [See 9 TC 206-208]
f-1—Asthmanefrin Co., Inc., 25 TC 1141, 25-1956 P-H TC 639
1—Keil Properties, Inc. (Dela), 24 TC 1117, 24-1955 P-H TC 615
1—Saffan, Samuel, 1957 P-H TC Memo 57—701
1—Rev. Rul. 56-145, 1956-1 CB 613
1—Rev. Rul. 56-392, 1956-2 CB 971
4— Midler Court Realty, Inc., 61 TC 597, 61 P-H TC 368
ADDA, INC.; COMM. v, 171 F2d 367, 37 AFTR 641 (USCA 2)
1—Pardee, Marvin L., Est. of, 49 TC 152, 49 P-H TC 107
1—Saffan, Samuel, 1957 P-H TC Memo 57-701
2—Midler Court Realty, Inc., 61 TC 597, 61 P-H TC 368
ADDELSTON, ALBERT A. & SARAH M., 1965 P-H TC Memo ¶ 65,215
ADDISON v COMM., 177 F2d 521, 38 AFTR 821 (USCA 8)
g-1—Industrial Aggregate Co. v U.S., 6 AFTR2d 5963, 284 F2d 645 (USCA 8)
1—Sturgeon v McMahon, 155 F Supp 630, 52 AFTR 789 (DC NY)
1—Gilmore v U.S., 16 AFTR2d 5211, 5213, 245 F Supp 384, 386 (DC Calif)
1—Waldheim & Co., Inc., 25 TC 599, 25-1955 P-H TC 332
g-1—Galewitz, Samuel & Marian, 50 TC 113, 50 P-H TC 79
1—Buder, G. A., Est. of, 1963 P-H TC Memo 63-345
e-1—Rhodes, Lynn E. & Martha E., 1963 P-H TC Memo 63-1374
2—Shipp v Comm., 217 F2d 402, 46 AFTR 1170 (USCA 9)

ADDISON—Contd.
g-2—Industrial Aggregate Co. v U.S., 6 AFTR2d 5964, 284 F2d 645 (USCA 8)
e-2—Buder, Est. of v Comm., 13 AFTR2d 1238, 330 F2d 443 (USCA 8)
2—Iowa Southern Utilities Co. v Comm., 14 AFTR2d 5063, 333 F2d 385 (USCA 8)
2—Kelly, Daniel, S.W., 23 TC 687, 23-1955 P-H TC 422
f-2—Morgan, Joseph P., Est. of, 37 TC 36, 37, 37-1961 P-H TC 26, 27
n-2—Woodward, Fred W. & Elsie M., 49 TC 385, 49 P-H TC 270
ADDISON, IRENE D., 1948 P-H TC Memo ¶ 48,177
1—Waldheim & Co., Inc., 25 TC 599, 25-1955 P-H TC 332
f-1—Morgan, Joseph P., Est. of, 37 TC 36, 37, 37-1961 P-H TC 26, 27
1—Buder, G. A., Est. of, 1963 P-H TC Memo 63-345
e-1—Rhodes, Lynn E. & Martha E., 1963 P-H TC Memo 63-1374
ADDISON, JOHN MILTON, BKPT; U.S. v, 20 AFTR2d 5630, 384 F2d 748 (USCA 5) (See Rochelle Jr., Trtee; U.S. v)
ADDRESSOGRAPH - MULTIGRAPH CORP., 1945 P-H TC Memo ¶ 45,058
Conn. L. & P. Co., The v U.S., 9 AFTR2d 679, 156 Ct Cl 312, 314, 299 F2d 264
Copperhead Coal Co., Inc., 1958 P-H TC Memo 58-33
1—Seas Shipping Co., Inc. v Comm., 19 AFTR2d 596, 371 F2d 529 (USCA 2)
e-1—Hitchcock, E. R., Co., The v U.S., 35 AFTR2d 75-1207, 514 F2d 487 (USCA 2)
f-2—Vulcan Materials Co. v U.S., 25 AFTR2d 70-446, 308 F Supp 57 (DC Ala)
f-3—Marlo Coil Co. v U.S., 1969 P-H 58,133 (Ct Cl Comr Rep)
4—United Gas Improvement Co. v Comm., 240 F2d 318, 50 AFTR 1354 (USCA 3)
10—St. Louis Co. (Del) (in Dissolution) v U.S., 237 F2d 156, 50 AFTR 257 (USCA 3)
ADDRESSOGRAPH - MULTIGRAPH CORP. v U.S., 112 Ct Cl 201, 78 F Supp 111, 37 AFTR 53
f-1—St. Joseph Lead Co. v U.S., 9 AFTR2d 712, 299 F2d 350 (USCA 2)
e-1—Central & South West Corp. v U.S., 1968 P-H 58,175 (Ct Cl Comr Rep)
1—Smale & Robinson, Inc. v U.S., 123 F Supp 469, 46 AFTR 375 (DC Calif)
1—St. Joseph Lead Co. v U.S., 7 AFTR2d 401, 190 F Supp 640 (DC NY)
1—Eisenstadt Mfg. Co., 28 TC 230, 28-1957 P-H TC 132
f-2—St. Joseph Lead Co. v U.S., 9 AFTR2d 712, 299 F2d 350 (USCA 2)
f-3—Consol. Coppermines Corp. v U.S., 8 AFTR2d 5873, 155 Ct Cl 736, 296 F2d 745
ADELAIDE PARK LAND, 25 BTA 211
g—Custom Component Switches, Inc. v U.S., 19 AFTR2d 560 (DC Calif) [See 25 BTA 215]
O'Connor, John C., 1957 P-H TC Memo 57-190
ADELBERG, MARVIN & HELEN, 1971 P-H TC Memo ¶ 71,015
ADELMAN v U.S., 27 AFTR2d 71-1464, 440 F2d 991 (USCA 9, 5-3-71)
sa—Adelman v U.S., 24 AFTR2d 69-5769, 304 F Supp 599 (DC Calif)
ADELMAN v U.S., 24 AFTR2d 69-5769, 304 F Supp 599 (DC Calif, 9-30-69)
a—Adelman v U.S., 27 AFTR2d 71-1464, 440 F2d 991 (USCA 9)
ADELSON, SAMUEL; U.S. v, 52 AFTR 1798 (DC RI) (See Sullivan Co., Inc.; U.S. v)
ADELSON v U.S., 15 AFTR2d 246, 342 F2d 332 (USCA 9, 1-13-65)
sa—Adelson v U.S., 12 AFTR2d 5010, 221 F Supp 31 (DC Calif)
g-1—Greenlee, L. C. & Gladys M., 1966 P-H TC Memo 66-985
f-1—Cochran, Carol J., 1973 P-H TC Memo 73-459
f-1—Marchionni, Siro L., 1976 P-H TC Memo 76-1321
f-2—Krist, Edwin F. v Comm., 32 AFTR2d 73-5663, 483 F2d 1351 (USCA 2)
f-2—Fugate v U.S., 18 AFTR2d 5607, 259 F Supp 401 (DC Tex) [See 15 AFTR2d 249, 342 F2d 335]

FIGURE E–5

22 **ADAMSON—ADELSON**

ADAMSON, LEE A., 1981 PH TC Memo ¶ 81,285 (See Petty, R. M. & Allene A.)
ADAMSON, RAY P., 1981 PH TC Memo ¶ 81,285 (See Petty, R. M. & Allene A.)
ADAMSON, ROY & CATHERINE, 1986 PH TC Memo ¶ 86,489
f-1—Dew, James Edward, 91 TC 626, 91 PH TC 310
e-1—Telfeyan, Louis & Lynn, 1988 PH TC Memo 88-2146
e-1—Bullock, Kenneth & Gail, 1988 PH TC Memo 88-2706
ADAMSON, SANDRA L., 1981 PH TC Memo ¶ 81,285 (See Petty, R. M. & Allene A.)
ADAMSON; U.S. v, 161 F2d 942, 35 AFTR 1404 (USCA 9)
e-1—Inco Electroenergy Corp., 1987 PH TC Memo 87-2295
ADAMUCCI, RICHARD, 1987 PH TC Memo ¶ 87,378 (See Batastini, Paul J. & Amelia)
ADCOCK, HOMER & DOROTHY, 1982 PH TC Memo ¶ 82,206
e-1—Kauffman, Wilma G., 1982 PH TC Memo 82-2193
e-1—Scallen, Stephen B. & Chacke Y., 1987 PH TC Memo 87-2134
ADDA v COMM., 171 F2d 457, 37 AFTR 654 (USCA 4)
1—Connelly, Judith C., 1982 PH TC Memo 82-2866
1—Cleveland, Robert E., 1983 PH TC Memo 83-1223
ADDA, FERNAND C.A., 10 TC 273, ¶ 10.133 PH TC 1948
1—Connelly, Judith C., 1982 PH TC Memo 82-2866
1—Cleveland, Robert E., 1983 PH TC Memo 83-1223
ADDA, INC., 9 TC 199
e—Hodges, Irene McLaughlin & Thomas Lyman, 1985 PH TC Memo 85-2062 [See 9 TC 210-211]
1—Security Bancorp, Inc. v U.S., 48 AFTR2d 81-5514 (DC Mich)
4—Watson Land Co., 1983 PH TC Memo 83-744
ADDA, INC.; COMM. v, 171 F2d 367, 37 AFTR 641 (USCA 2)
Security Bancorp, Inc. v U.S., 48 AFTR2d 81-5514 (DC Mich)
Watson Land Co., 1983 PH TC Memo 83-744
e—Hodges, Irene McLaughlin & Thomas Lyman, 1985 PH TC Memo 85-2062
ADDEO, ARTHUR J., Jr. & MARY, 1984 PH TC Memo ¶ 84,493
e-1—Brown, Stewart L., 1986 PH TC Memo 86-1153
ADDINGTON, DOUGLAS F., 1986 PH TC Memo ¶ 86,358 (See Hoak, Roderick C. & Cornelia)
ADDINGTON, WILLIAM H. & DONNA L., 1980 PH TC Memo ¶ 80,046
a—Court Order, 10-20-81, 663 F2d 104 (USCA 5)
d—1981 PH 61,000 (USCA 10)
ADDISON, ALBERT I., 1979 PH TC Memo ¶ 79,317
e-1—Ridenour, Harry P., Jr. v U.S., 52 AFTR2d 83-5589, 3 Cl Ct 134
e-1—Reinhardt, Jules & Marilyn D., 85 TC 526, 85 PH TC 299
ADDISON INTERNAT., INC., 90 TC 1207, ¶ 90.78 PH TC
a—Addison Internat., Inc. v Comm., 64 AFTR2d 89-5747, 887 F2d 660 (USCA 6)
rc—Rocky Mountain Associates Internat., Inc., 90 TC 1241, 1242, 90 PH TC 637, 638
g-1—Butka, David J. & Sabine I., 91 TC 130, 91 PH TC 66
ADDISON INTERNAT., INC. v COMM., 64 AFTR2d 89-5747, 887 F2d 660 (USCA 6, 10-10-89)
sa—Addison Internat., Inc., 90 TC 1207, ¶ 90.78 PH TC
ADDRESSOGRAPH-MULTIGRAPH CORP., 1945 PH TC Memo ¶ 45,058
1—Buffalo Wire Works Co., Inc., 74 TC 938, 74 PH TC 509
g-1—Maier Brewing Co., 1987 PH TC Memo 87-1978
ADEE, ALLEN R., TRUST NO. 1 v U.S., 52 AFTR2d 83-6437 (DC Kan, 7-19-83)
ADEE, DONALD P., TRUSTEE v U.S., 52 AFTR2d 83-6437 (DC Kan) (See Adee, Allen R., Trust No. 1 v U.S.)
ADEE, JACK R., TRUSTEE v U.S., 52 AFTR2d 83-6437 (DC Kan) (See Adee, Allen R., Trust No. 1 v U.S.)
ADELBERG, MARVIN & HELEN M., 1985 PH TC Memo ¶ 85,597
a—Court Order, 1-21-87, 811 F2d 1507 (USCA 9)
e-1—Chao, Wen Y. & Ching J., 92 TC 1144, 92 PH TC 577
e-1—Nicklo, Joseph J., 1988 PH TC Memo 88-1199
ADELEKE, JOEL & CATHERINE A., 1980 PH TC Memo ¶ 80,479
e-1—Pike-Biegunski, Maciej Jan & Denise Nadine, 1984 PH TC Memo 84-1123
ADELMAN v U.S., 27 AFTR2d 71-1464, 440 F2d 991 (USCA 9)
e-1—Barbados #7 Ltd., 92 TC 813, 92 PH TC 409
ADELMAN v U.S., 24 AFTR2d 69-5769, 304 F Supp 599 (DC Calif)
e-2—Barbados #7 Ltd., 92 TC 813, 92 PH TC 409
ADELSON, SHELDON G. v U.S., 54 AFTR2d 84-5428, 737 F2d 1569 (USCA Fed, 6-28-84)
remg—Adelson, Sheldon G. v U.S., 52 AFTR2d 83-5211 (Cl Ct)
s—Adelson, Sheldon G. v U.S., 51 AFTR2d 83-574 (Cl Ct) 535 F Supp 1082
s—Adelson, Sheldon G. v U.S., 54 AFTR2d 84-5959, 6 Cl Ct 102
rc—Adelson, Sheldon G. v U.S., 57 AFTR2d 86-736, 782 F2d 1010 (USCA Fed)
rc—Adelson, Sheldon G. v U.S., 59 AFTR2d 87-993, 12 Cl Ct 231
e-1—Larson, Roger Roy, In re, 62 AFTR2d 88-5801, 862 F2d 117 (USCA 7)
e-1—Raab, George S. v I.R.S., 57 AFTR2d 86-715, 86-716 (DC Pa)
ADELSON, SHELDON G. v U.S., 57 AFTR2d 86-736, 782 F2d 1010 (USCA Fed, 1-29-86)
remg—Adelson, Sheldon G. v U.S., 54 AFTR2d 84-5959, 6 Cl Ct 102
rc—Adelson, Sheldon G. v U.S., 54 AFTR2d 84-5428, 737 F2d 1569 (USCA Fed)
rc—Adelson, Sheldon G. v U.S., 52 AFTR2d 83-5211, 2 Cl Ct 591
rc—Adelson, Sheldon G. v U.S., 51 AFTR2d 83-574, 1 Cl Ct 61, 553 F Supp 1082
rc—Adelson, Sheldon G. v U.S., 59 AFTR2d 87-993, 12 Cl Ct 231
ADELSON, SHELDON G. v U.S., 51 AFTR2d 83-574, 1 Cl Ct 61, 553 F Supp 1082 (12-27-82)
s—Adelson, Sheldon G. v U.S., 54 AFTR2d 84-5428, 737 F2d 1569 (USCA Fed)
s—Adelson, Sheldon G. v U.S., 52 AFTR2d 83-5211, 2 Cl Ct 591
rc—Adelson, Sheldon G. v U.S., 57 AFTR2d 86-736, 782 F2d 1010 (USCA Fed)
rc—Adelson, Sheldon G. v U.S., 54 AFTR2d 84-5959, 6 Cl Ct 102
rc—Adelson, Sheldon G. v U.S., 59 AFTR2d 87-993, 12 Cl Ct 231
e-1—Mann, Guy L. Est. of, 53 AFTR2d 84-1304, 731 F2d 273 (USCA 5)
ADELSON, SHELDON G. v U.S., 52 AFTR2d 83-5211, 2 Cl Ct 591 (6-14-83)
remd—Adelson, Sheldon G. v U.S., 54 AFTR2d 84-5428, 737 F2d 1569 (USCA Fed)
s—Adelson, Sheldon G. v U.S., 51 AFTR2d 83-574 (Cl Ct) 553 F Supp 1082
rc—Adelson, Sheldon G. v U.S., 57 AFTR2d 86-736, 782 F2d 1010 (USCA Fed)
rc—Adelson, Sheldon G. v U.S., 54 AFTR2d 84-5959, 6 Cl Ct 102
rc—Adelson, Sheldon G. v U.S., 59 AFTR2d 87-993, 12 Cl Ct 231
ADELSON, SHELDON G. v U.S., 54 AFTR2d 84-5959, 6 Cl Ct 102 (9-12-84)
remd—Adelson, Sheldon G. v U.S., 57 AFTR2d 86-736, 782 F2d 1010 (USCA Fed)
s—Adelson, Sheldon G. v U.S., 54 AFTR2d 84-5428, 737 F2d 1569 (USCA Fed)
rc—Adelson, Sheldon G. v U.S., 51 AFTR2d 83-574, 1 Cl Ct 61, 553 F Supp 1082
rc—Adelson, Sheldon G. v U.S., 52 AFTR2d 83-5211, 2 Cl Ct 591
rc—Adelson, Sheldon G. v U.S., 59 AFTR2d 87-993, 12 Cl Ct 231

APPENDIX

COMPREHENSIVE TAX RETURN PROBLEMS

Problem 1

1. Ronald M. and Susan J. Bradford, both age 45, are married and file a joint income tax return. Ronald is employed as an engineer, and Susan is a self-employed attorney. They have three dependent children: John, age 12; Paul, age 14; and George, age 17. Since June 15, 1990, Susan's nephew, Eric Jones, has lived with them. Eric, whose parents were killed in an automobile accident, is 19 years old and is a full-time student at Purdue University. Eric works part-time and earned $2,400 during the year. Ronald and Susan provided over half of Eric's support for the year. The Bradfords live at 1864 Southern Avenue, Lafayette, IN 47902. Ronald's Social Security number is 233–45–6789, and Susan's is 345–67–8910. Other relevant Social Security numbers are as follows: Eric, 265–33–1982; John, 459–86–8554; Paul, 431–96–8134; and George, 455–94–6765.
2. From January 1 to May 20, Ronald earned $30,000 from Research Corporation, Mobile, Alabama. Research Corporation withheld Federal income tax of $5,183.16, state income tax of $900, and $2,295 of Social Security and Medicare tax. Ronald received a better offer from Hi-Tech Corporation of Lafayette, Indiana, and began working for Hi-Tech on June 1, earning $49,000 in his new job. Hi-Tech withheld Federal income tax of $9,543, state income tax of $1,470, and $3,748.50 of Social Security and Medicare tax. On December 20, Ronald received a year-end bonus of $1,000 from Hi-Tech. Social Security and Medicare tax withheld amounted to $76.50. This amount was included on his W–2 Form, which also reported his salary of $49,000 and moving expense reimbursement of $3,000 (see item 10), for a total of $53,000.
3. Susan was employed until May 31, 1991 as a staff attorney by Brown and Company, a law firm in Mobile, Alabama. During that time she earned $25,000. Her employer withheld $4,745 of Federal income tax, $750 of state income tax, and $1,912.50 of Social Security and Medicare tax.
4. Ronald and Susan received the following interest income during 1991:

First National Bank	$ 350
Second National Bank	1,300
Lafayette Savings & Loan	865

5. The Bradfords received the following dividend income during 1991:

Abner Corporation	$780
Bailey Corporation	430
Crown Corporation	600

On December 10, they gave 100 shares of Edwards Corporation stock to their oldest son, George. The stock's basis was $5,000, and its fair market value was $8,000. On December 15, Edwards Corporation declared a dividend of $10 per share. The dividend was payable December 30 to shareholders of record as of December 20.

6. Upon moving to Lafayette, Susan was unable to find suitable employment with a law firm. As a result, she established her own practice, beginning July 1, 1991. Her office is located at 234 Lahr Street, Lafayette, IN 47902, and she practices under the name of "S. J. Bradford, Attorney." Her employer identification number is 12–3456789. She elected to use the cash basis of accounting. The following items relate to her practice during 1991:

Gross receipts from clients	$65,000
Expenses	
Advertising	1,200
Bank service charges	68
Dues and publications	550
Insurance	4,500
Interest	1,370
Legal and professional services	900
Office rent	7,300
Office supplies	925
Utilities and phone	820
Secretary's wages	6,400
Payroll taxes	660
Contributions to employee pension plans	960
Miscellaneous expenses	375

Susan used her personal automobile for business purposes, accumulating a total of 5,000 business miles from July 1 to December 31. She acquired the following equipment for use in her business (with all assets being placed in service on July 1):

Office furniture	$8,000
Microcomputer	4,200
Printer	1,500

Susan elected to expense the maximum allowable portion of the cost of the office furniture under the provisions of § 179. She elected to compute her cost recovery allowance on all of the assets using the MACRS percentage method.

On November 15, a client who owed Susan $1,000 for services rendered was declared bankrupt. Susan feels there is no chance to collect any of the account.

7. The Bradfords were involved in several property transactions during the year:

a. On March 5, they acquired 100 shares of Simpson Corporation common stock for $162 a share. The company experienced financial difficulties and did not pay the regular semiannual dividend in June. As a result, Ronald and Susan decided to sell the stock before matters got worse. On November 23, they sold the stock for $50 a share.

b. On May 6, 1968, Susan inherited a vacation home in Florida from her Uncle Marvin. Marvin's adjusted basis for the property was $38,000. The fair market value at the date of Marvin's death was $52,000 (the value elected by the executor of Marvin's estate). Because the Bradfords felt they would not be able to return to Florida frequently enough to justify keeping the home, they sold it on August 12 for $157,000.

c. When they decided to move from Mobile to Lafayette, they sold their Alabama residence. The selling price of the home was $200,000, and the broker charged a 5% sales commission. The Bradfords incurred fixing-up expenses of $2,000 on the residence, which they had owned since October 4, 1975. Their basis in the residence was $110,000. In Lafayette, they acquired a new residence for $166,000. The closing date on the sale of their Mobile residence was May 30. They moved into the new Lafayette residence on June 1.

d. On November 29, Susan sold a one-acre lot in Mobile to her sister Sarah. Susan's basis in the lot was $15,000. She sold the lot for $10,000. Susan had purchased the lot on April 17, 1978.

8. The Bradfords own a rental house located at 512 Walker Street, Huntsville, AL 35899. The rental unit was occupied during the entire year, producing rent income of $14,000. Since they were unable to manage the property personally, the Bradfords paid a commission, of $1,400 to a property management company. The only other expenditures related to the property were $2,000 for real property taxes and $800 for real estate insurance on the property. The property was acquired on March 2, 1983, at a cost of $100,000, of which $10,000 was allocated to the lot. The rental house is being depreciated over a 15-year period using the statutory ACRS percentage rate.
9. On January 2, 1988 Ronald loaned $3,000 to his friend, David Smith, who signed a note agreeing to repay the loan on June 30, 1990. David declared bankruptcy in October, 1991, and Ronald was unable to collect on the loan.
10. The Bradford family incurred the following expenses in moving from Mobile to Lafayette:

Cost of moving household goods	$3,600
Travel, meals ($200), and lodging	600
House-hunting expenses (including meals of $100)	1,100
Temporary living expenses including meals of $200 (5 days)	800
Cost of fitting drapes in new house	900

Hi-Tech Corporation reimbursed Ronald for $3,000 of the moving expenses. The reimbursement was included on Ronald's W–2 Form (refer to item 2).

11. Ronald attended an engineering convention in Boston in October, incurring the following unreimbursed expenses:

Airfare	$560
Taxi fares	35
Lodging	300
Meals	75

12. Susan contributed $4,000 to her Keogh plan. The contribution was made in December 1991.
13. The Bradfords had the following expenditures during the year:

Prescription medicines and drugs	$ 980
Medical insurance premiums	1,540
Doctor and hospital bills	2,450
Real estate taxes on residence	6,540
Home mortgage interest	8,630
Credit card interest on consumer purchases	948
Cash contributions	
Community church	2,200
United Way	1,500
Professional dues and subscriptions	1,300
Tax return preparation fee	500

14. On August 1, the Bradfords acquired a rundown garage apartment for $15,000 (not including land). They planned to restore the apartment to good condition and hold it as rental property. On October 5, the electrician they had hired to rewire the

apartment accidentally left his soldering iron on while he was away for lunch. When he returned, fire had destroyed the apartment. Unfortunately, the Bradfords had not insured the building. Between August 1 and October 5, they had spent $1,700 on repairs on the apartment.

15. The Bradfords paid $500 each month for household and child care expenses. They filed the appropriate employment tax returns. Their employer identification number is 22–3344556. Relevant information regarding the providers of child care are as follows: Mary Tyler, 111 Main St., Mobile, AL 35761; Social Security number 461–66–5201; $2,500 (amount paid). Ann Weaver, 407 Elm Avenue, Lafayette, IN 47902; Social Security number 359–46–3211; $3,500 (amount paid).
16. The Bradfords made timely estimated Federal income tax payments of $34,000 during the year.
17. Ronald and Susan both desire that $1 be directed to the Presidential Election Campaign Fund.

Requirements
Complete the Bradfords' Federal income tax return for 1991. If they have a refund due, they would like to receive the entire amount and not have it credited against tax for next year.

Problem 2

Roy C. Long (age 50) and Reba A. Long (age 48) have been married for 25 years and currently reside in a condominium located at 685 Palomar Drive, Decatur, IL 62525. They have two daughters, both grown and self-supporting. However, Reba's widowed mother (Lucille Armbrust, age 68) lives with them.

Approximately 15 years ago, Roy established his first liquor retail outlet. Over the years, the operation has been increasingly profitable and has grown to four stores, one of which has become particularly well known for its assortment of fine wines. Shortly after the start of the business, Roy requested and obtained approval from the IRS to change from the cash to the accrual method of accounting. Roy continued to use the cash method for nonbusiness income and expenses. Roy decided to stay with the calendar year for reporting purposes as it ideally suited the nature of his business.

An unadjusted and partial income statement for "Roy's Emporium of Wines and Spirits" for 1991 contains the following information:

Sales		$1,877,150
Cost of goods sold—		
Beginning inventory	$ 305,000	
Purchases	1,300,000	
Less final inventory (based on year-end physical count)	(308,000)	1,297,000
Gross profit		$ 580,150
Other income—		
Proceeds from the condemnation of land and building	$ 185,000	
Refund from the cancellation of a casualty insurance policy	3,200	
Proceeds from the sale of scanner register	8,000	
Proceeds from the sale of two manual typewriters and one calculator	100	196,300
Total income		$ 776,450
Other expenses—		
Depreciation	$?	
Bad debts	7,000	
Advertising	42,000	

Wages	$287,000	
Taxes	51,115	
Insurance	18,000	
Rent	68,400	
Repairs	5,600	
Charitable contributions	500	
Chamber of Commerce dues	100	
Credit reports	860	
Telephone	8,200	
Utilities	19,600	
Armored car pickup service	2,400	
Delivery expense	5,300	
Office supplies	3,800	
Fine for selling to underage customer	500	
Attorney's fee	2,233	
Employer contributions to H.R. 10 (Keogh) plan	43,050	
Leasehold improvements	32,000	597,658
Net income before depreciation and income taxes		$ 178,792

Further explanation concerning some of these items appears below:

1. Inventory is valued at the lower of cost or market. Losses due to spoilage and breakage are minimal and are not accounted for separately. The suppliers replace any merchandise pilfered or damaged during shipping. The purchases account, however, has not been adjusted to reflect the burglary to Store No. 1 on the night of March 13, 1991. On this occasion, merchandise (mainly vintage wines) purchased in 1991 with a cost of $9,800 (retail value of $20,200) was stolen. Roy filed a claim with Security Insurance Co. for $16,160 for the loss. The carrier denied the claim on the grounds that the negligence of Roy's employees led to the loss. Roy promptly instituted court proceedings against Security Insurance Co., although his attorney advised him that under the terms of the policies, the results of the litigation could go either way.
2. Roy was so upset by the claims performance of Security Insurance Co. that on July 1, 1991, he canceled the coverage on his business. The three-year policy had been taken out on July 1, 1989, at a cost of $15,000, and the refund of $3,200 was the amount of the premium returnable under the terms of the contract for the remaining coverage of one year. On July 1, 1991, Roy replaced the coverage with a policy issued by the Safeguard Insurance Company. The policy cost $18,000 and provides protection from casualties for a three-year period.
3. Ordinarily, Roy's sales are on a cash-carry basis. With better customers, however, credit sales are permitted. Bad debts are reported under the specific charge-off method. During 1991, Roy wrote off 12 accounts, totaling $8,200, as being worthless. He did, however, recover $1,200 from an account written off and deducted for tax year 1990. The sales figure reflects credit sales for 1991 and includes amounts not yet collected.
4. In 1990, the city of Decatur instituted condemnation proceedings against the property where Store No. 1 was located; the city intended to use the property for a bus storage and repair facility. After considerable negotiations, an out-of-court settlement was reached on April 1, 1991, whereby Roy transferred title to the property for a price of $185,000 (its agreed-to fair market value). Information concerning the property is as follows:

Date of acquisition	December 18, 1986
Cost of acquisition	$100,000
Method of depreciation	Statutory percentage

For both the cost of the property and the condemnation award, assume 10% is attributable to the land and 90% to the building.

On January 20, 1992, Roy reinvested $195,000 ($185,000 condemnation award plus $10,000) in a new warehouse. The warehouse will be used to store the extra inventory needed for Roy's liquor stores.

5. Being an innovative person who is interested in labor-saving devices, Roy decided to experiment with an automated checkout system. On August 1, 1989, he purchased a new scanner cash register for $22,000. The equipment was immediately installed in Store No. 3 and continued to operate until it was removed and sold to a supermarket on May 1, 1991.

   Roy decided to abandon the experiment for several reasons. For one, much of the merchandise (particularly imported goods) stocked in his store did not contain the universal product code. More importantly, many of Roy's customers objected to the absence of price labels on each product. The scanner had an estimated useful life of 10 years.

   Bonus depreciation under § 179 was claimed for tax year 1989.

6. The manual typewriters and the calculator were acquired in 1979 at a total cost of $850 and, based on an estimated useful life of 10 years (no salvage value), were fully depreciated through tax year 1990. In computing the depreciation deducted, the straight-line method was used. They were sold on July 15, 1991.

7. Of the $42,000 spent on advertising, $4,000 was for full-page ads in newspapers trying to influence the general public against a bill pending in the state legislature that would impose stricter gun controls. Roy, an avid hunter, is a member of the National Rifle Association and a firm believer in the right of citizens to possess arms.

8. Roy prides himself on full compliance with the state and local liquor control laws. In spite of this attitude, one of his employees became careless and was caught selling liquor to minors. Quite distraught over the possible effect of a conviction and fine on his reputation, Roy hired the best attorney in town to contest the proceeding. The effort proved fruitless and Roy was fined $500. The attorney was paid $2,233 for services rendered. These amounts are included in Roy's unadjusted income statement.

9. The charitable contribution of $500 on the income statement represents a cash gift to the United Fund in the name of the business.

10. The charge for armored car service provides for daily pickups of cash from all four retail outlets.

11. Taxes of $51,115 include the employer's share of the FICA tax, FUTA, ad valorem state and local taxes on business property, and various license fees.

12. Roy is not known for paying generous salaries to his employees, but he does provide coverage, at the rate of 15% under an H.R. 10 (Keogh) plan instituted several years ago. The amount of $43,050 contributed to this plan in 1991 does not include coverage for Roy. Also, the $287,000 figure for wages does not include any sums Roy may have withdrawn from the business.

13. Anticipating the loss of the building through condemnation by the city of Decatur [see item (4) above], Roy located and rented another facility for Store No. 1. Although the location was ideal and the rent was reasonable, the condition of the building was not. Because Store No. 1 is Roy's greatest revenue producer (largely due to its selection of fine wines) and his pride and joy (the business started here), he felt compelled to improve the facility. The location was renovated at a cost of $32,000, with the improvements being completed and the premises occupied by April 1, 1991. Under the terms of the lease, Roy has the right to occupancy for 10 years with the option to renew for another 10 years. Roy estimates that the useful life of the improvements is 12 years. He is not certain whether the option to renew the lease will be exercised.

14. With the exception of the leasehold improvements to Store No. 1, Roy is not a believer in a heavy investment in capital for the business. In three of his stores, for example, all improvements (such as counters and shelves) were furnished by the lessors of the buildings and are reflected in the rents Roy pays. Depreciation information on the remaining assets is summarized as follows:

Asset	Date Acquired	Cost
Delivery truck #1	2/1/90	$10,500
Delivery truck #2	5/2/91	11,200
Refrigeration equipment	8/30/89	18,700
Office equipment	11/1/81	4,600

15. The delivery expense of $5,300 consists of the operating costs (e.g., gasoline, oil, tires) involved in the use of the two delivery trucks. It does not, however, include any depreciation [see item (14)].
16. Repairs to the leased buildings Roy uses in the business are his responsibility as a tenant. One item for $2,500 (included in the $5,600 total) was for the replacement of an air conditioning unit at Store No. 2. Although it was not his obligation, Roy had the work done because the landlord was out of town and customers were complaining about the lack of temperature control. Roy was reimbursed for this expense by the landlord in early 1992.

Roy and Reba had the following nonbusiness transactions for 1991:

17. Interest income of $18,465 on City of Decatur general revenue bonds.
18. Accrued (but undistributed) interest income of $18,500 on Roy's H.R. 10 (Keogh) plan.
19. Dividend income of $12,800 from Decatur Lumber Company, a locally owned corporation of which Roy owns 1% of the stock.
20. Payment of $3,200 for medical insurance premiums on a policy covering Roy and his family. Similar coverage is provided for Roy's employees, and these premiums are included as part of the wages amount of $287,000.
21. On March 10, 1991, the Longs sold their home of 15 years for $280,000. Details concerning the sale and the property are summarized below:

Sales commissions	$16,800
Qualified fixing-up expenses	3,800
Original cost	50,000
Capital improvements (e.g., swimming pool, landscaping, central air conditioning)	20,000

Ad valorem real estate taxes on the property for 1991 amounted to $3,695, all of which was paid on December 10, 1991, by the purchaser.

On February 14, 1992, for a price of $162,000, the Longs acquired title to a new condominium that they occupied shortly thereafter.

The sale of the house and the purchase of the condominium were due to the favorable real estate market and the Longs' desire for a smaller and less demanding place to live. The condominium is closer to Roy's businesses and requires less upkeep.

22. During 1991, Roy paid income taxes to Illinois as follows:

Prepayments for tax year 1991	$4,000
Amount due on April 15, 1991, for tax year 1990	500

Roy estimates that he will owe additional state income taxes of $400 for tax year 1991.

23. On March 20, 1992, Roy mailed a check for $7,500 to the trustee of the H.R. 10 plan. This represented Roy's contribution on his own behalf for tax year 1991.
24. During 1991, the Longs made the following additional expenditures:

Interest on bank loans [the proceeds of which were used to purchase some of the City of Decatur bonds—see item (17) above]	$4,400
Interest on amounts borrowed against life insurance policies [the proceeds of which were used to help purchase some of the Decatur Lumber Company stock—see item (19)]	2,200

Premiums on life insurance policies (Roy is the owner and insured, and Reba is the beneficiary)	$3,600
Ad valorem real estate taxes on the condominium (from the date of purchase through December 31, 1991)	2,800
Check mailed on May 1, 1991, to a local CPA for the preparation of the 1990 Federal and state income tax returns	1,200

25. On June 1, 1991, Roy transferred 200 shares of Decatur Lumber Company to St. Mary's Catholic Church (Decatur) in satisfaction of the Longs' church pledge of $4,000 for years 1991–1992 ($2,000 each year). The stock, acquired in June 1985, had a basis of $10 per share and a fair market value of $20 per share on the date of the transfer.
26. As noted earlier, Reba's mother (Lucille) lives with the Longs who furnish all of her support. During 1991, Lucille's only source of income was Social Security payments in the amount of $2,850 and interest income from a savings account of $983. The interest income was not withdrawn, and the Social Security payments were deposited in Reba's savings account.
27. During 1991, the Longs made four timely payments of $7,000 each to the IRS. These prepayments of 1991 income taxes were based on the Federal income tax liability they incurred and paid for tax year 1990.

Requirements

Based on the following assumptions, prepare a joint income tax return for the Longs for tax year 1991. The return should be in good form and should include all necessary supporting schedules.

Assumptions

a. Although the return is being prepared as of its due date (April 15, 1992), you are aware that Roy has reinvested the condemnation proceeds [item (4)] in a new warehouse in early 1992.

b. Medical and drug expenses for 1991 do not exceed the 7.5% limitation.

c. Other relevant information concerning the Longs is summarized below:

- "Roy's Emporium of Wines and Spirits" has an employer identification number of 37–4811838.
- Roy's Social Security number is 540–44–6957, Reba's is 542–02–3701, and Lucille's is 101–62–1776.
- As a business address, Roy uses the location for Store No. 3: 1340 Grizzly Drive, Decatur, IL 62525.

APPENDIX

TABLE OF CASES CITED

E

F

G

H

I

J

K

L

M

N

O

P

R

S

T

U

V

W

Y

Z

Subject Index

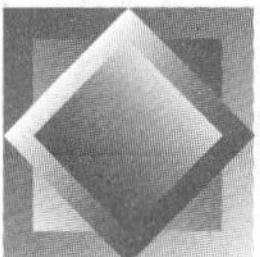

A

D

E

F

J

K

L

M

N

Q

R

S

T

U